R

P9-BJR-859

# Contemporary
# Literary Criticism

# Guide to Gale Literary Criticism Series

| For criticism on | Consult these Gale series |
|---|---|
| Authors now living or who died after December 31, 1959 | *CONTEMPORARY LITERARY CRITICISM (CLC)* |
| Authors who died between 1900 and 1959 | *TWENTIETH-CENTURY LITERARY CRITICISM (TCLC)* |
| Authors who died between 1800 and 1899 | *NINETEENTH-CENTURY LITERATURE CRITICISM (NCLC)* |
| Authors who died between 1400 and 1799 | *LITERATURE CRITICISM FROM 1400 TO 1800 (LC)*<br><br>*SHAKESPEAREAN CRITICISM (SC)* |
| Authors who died before 1400 | *CLASSICAL AND MEDIEVAL LITERATURE CRITICISM (CMLC)* |
| Black writers of the past two hundred years | *BLACK LITERATURE CRITICISM (BLC)* |
| Authors of books for children and young adults | *CHILDREN'S LITERATURE REVIEW (CLR)* |
| Dramatists | *DRAMA CRITICISM (DC)* |
| Hispanic writers of the late nineteenth and twentieth centuries | *HISPANIC LITERATURE CRITICISM (HLC)* |
| Native North American writers and orators of the eighteenth, nineteenth, and twentieth centuries | *NATIVE NORTH AMERICAN LITERATURE (NNAL)* |
| Poets | *POETRY CRITICISM (PC)* |
| Short story writers | *SHORT STORY CRITICISM (SSC)* |
| Major authors from the Renaissance to the present | *WORLD LITERATURE CRITICISM, 1500 TO THE PRESENT (WLC)* |

ISSN 0091-3421

Volume 101

# Contemporary Literary Criticism

Excerpts from Criticism of the Works
of Today's Novelists, Poets, Playwrights,
Short Story Writers, Scriptwriters, and
Other Creative Writers

**Deborah A. Stanley**
EDITOR

**Tim Akers**
**Pamela S. Dear**
**Jeff Hunter**
**Daniel Jones**
**John D. Jorgenson**
**Jerry Moore**
**Polly A. Vedder**
**Tim White**
**Thomas Wiloch**
**Kathleen Wilson**
ASSOCIATE EDITORS

GALE

DETROIT • NEW YORK • TORONTO • LONDON

Library of Congress Catalog Card Number 76-46132
ISBN 0-7876-1191-3
ISSN 0091-3421

Printed in the United States of America
10 9 8 7 6 5 4 3 2 1

# Contents

Preface  vii

Acknowledgments  xi

# Preface

## A Comprehensive Information Source
## on Contemporary Literature

Named "one of the twenty-five most distinguished reference titles published during the past twenty-five years" by *Reference Quarterly,* the *Contemporary Literary Criticism (CLC)* series provides readers with critical commentary and general information on more than 2,000 authors now living or who died after December 31, 1959. Previous to the publication of the first volume of *CLC* in 1973, there was no ongoing digest monitoring scholarly and popular sources of critical opinion and explication of modern literature. *CLC,* therefore, has fulfilled an essential need, particularly since the complexity and variety of contemporary literature makes the function of criticism especially important to today's reader.

## Scope of the Series

*CLC* presents significant passages from published criticism of works by creative writers. Since many of the authors covered by *CLC* inspire continual critical commentary, writers are often represented in more than one volume. There is, of course, no duplication of reprinted criticism.

Authors are selected for inclusion for a variety of reasons, among them the publication or dramatic production of a critically acclaimed new work, the reception of a major literary award, revival of interest in past writings, or the adaptation of a literary work to film or television.

Attention is also given to several other groups of writers-authors of considerable public interest—about whose work criticism is often difficult to locate. These include mystery and science fiction writers, literary and social critics, foreign writers, and authors who represent particular ethnic groups within the United States.

## Format of the Book

Each *CLC* volume contains about 500 individual excerpts taken from hundreds of book review periodicals, general magazines, scholarly journals, monographs, and books. Entries include critical evaluations spanning from the beginning of an author's career to the most current commentary. Interviews, feature articles, and other published writings that offer insight into the author's works are also presented. Students, teachers, librarians, and researchers will find that the generous excerpts and supplementary material in *CLC* provide them with vital information required to write a term paper, analyze a poem, or lead a book discussion group. In addition, complete bibliographical citations note the original source and all of the information necessary for a term paper footnote or bibliography.

## Features

A *CLC* author entry consists of the following elements:

■ The **Author Heading** cites the author's name in the form under which the author has most commonly published, followed by birth date, and death date when applicable. Uncertainty as to a birth or death date is indicated by a question mark.

■ A **Portrait** of the author is included when available.

■ A brief **Biographical and Critical Introduction** to the author and his or her work precedes the excerpted criticism. The first line of the introduction provides the author's full name, pseudonyms (if applicable), nationality, and a listing of genres in which the author has written. To provide users with easier access to information, the biographical and critical essay included in each author entry is divided into four categories: "Introduction," "Biographical Information," "Major Works," and "Critical Reception." The introductions to single-work entries—entries that focus on well known and frequently studied books, short stories, and poems—are similarly organized to quickly provide readers with information on the plot and major characters of the work being discussed, its major themes, and its critical reception. Previous volumes of *CLC* in which the author has been featured are also listed in the introduction.

■ A list of **Principal Works** notes the most important writings by the author. When foreign-language works have been translated into English, the English-language version of the title follows in brackets.

■ The **Excerpted Criticism** represents various kinds of critical writing, ranging in form from the brief review to the scholarly exegesis. Essays are selected by the editors to reflect the spectrum of opinion about a specific work or about an author's literary career in general. The excerpts are presented chronologically, adding a useful perspective to the entry. All titles by the author featured in the entry are printed in boldface type, which enables the reader to easily identify the works being discussed. Publication information (such as publisher names and book prices) and parenthetical numerical references (such as footnotes or page and line references to specific editions of a work) have been deleted at the editor's discretion to provide smoother reading of the text.

■ Critical essays are prefaced by **Explanatory Notes** as an additional aid to readers. These notes may provide several types of valuable information, including: the reputation of the critic, the importance of the work of criticism, the commentator's approach to the author's work, the purpose of the criticism, and changes in critical trends regarding the author.

■ A complete **Bibliographical Citation** designed to help the user find the original essay or book precedes each excerpt.

■ Whenever possible, a recent, previously unpublished **Author Interview** accompanies each entry.

■ A concise **Further Reading** section appears at the end of entries on authors for whom a significant amount of criticism exists in addition to the pieces reprinted in *CLC*. Each citation in this section is accompanied by a descriptive annotation describing the content of that article. Materials included in this section are grouped under various headings (e.g., Biography, Bibliography, Criticism, and Interviews) to aid users in their search for additional information. Cross-references to other useful sources published by Gale Research in which the author has appeared are also included: *Authors in the News, Black Writers, Children's Literature Review, Contemporary Authors, Dictionary of Literary Biography, DISCovering Authors, Drama Criticism, Hispanic Literature Criticism, Hispanic Writers, Native North American Literature, Poetry Criticism, Something about the Author, Short Story Criticism, Contemporary Authors Autobiography Series,* and *Something about the Author Autobiography Series.*

## Other Features

*CLC* also includes the following features:

- An **Acknowledgments** section lists the copyright holders who have granted permission to reprint material in this volume of *CLC*. It does not, however, list every book or periodical reprinted or consulted during the preparation of the volume.

- Each new volume of *CLC* includes a **Cumulative Topic Index,** which lists all literary topics treated in *CLC, NCLC, TCLC,* and *LC 1400-1800.*

- A **Cumulative Author Index** lists all the authors who have appeared in the various literary criticism series published by Gale Research, with cross-references to Gale's biographical and autobiographical series. A full listing of the series referenced there appears on the first page of the indexes of this volume. Readers will welcome this cumulated author index as a useful tool for locating an author within the various series. The index, which lists birth and death dates when available, will be particularly valuable for those authors who are identified with a certain period but whose death dates cause them to be placed in another, or for those authors whose careers span two periods. For example, Ernest Hemingway is found in *CLC,* yet F. Scott Fitzgerald, a writer often associated with him, is found in *Twentieth-Century Literary Criticism.*

- A **Cumulative Nationality Index** alphabetically lists all authors featured in *CLC* by nationality, followed by numbers corresponding to the volumes in which the authors appear.

- An alphabetical **Title Index** accompanies each volume of *CLC.* Listings are followed by the author's name and the corresponding page numbers where the titles are discussed. English translations of foreign titles and variations of titles are cross-referenced to the title under which a work was originally published. Titles of novels, novellas, dramas, films, record albums, and poetry, short story, and essay collections are printed in italics, while all individual poems, short stories, essays, and songs are printed in roman type within quotation marks; when published separately (e.g., T. S. Eliot's poem *The Waste Land),* the titles of long poems are printed in italics.

- In response to numerous suggestions from librarians, Gale has also produced a **Special Paperbound Edition** of the *CLC* title index. This annual cumulation, which alphabetically lists all titles reviewed in the series, is available to all customers and is typically published with every fifth volume of *CLC.* Additional copies of the index are available upon request. Librarians and patrons will welcome this separate index: it saves shelf space, is easy to use, and is recyclable upon receipt of the next edition.

## Citing *Contemporary Literary Criticism*

When writing papers, students who quote directly from any volume in the Literary Criticism Series may use the following general forms to footnote reprinted criticism. The first example pertains to material drawn from periodicals, the second to material reprinted in books:

[1]Alfred Cismaru, "Making the Best of It," *The New Republic,* 207, No. 24, (December 7, 1992), 30, 32; excerpted and reprinted in *Contemporary Literary Criticism,* Vol. 85, ed. Christopher Giroux (Detroit: Gale Research, 1995), pp. 73-4.

[2]Yvor Winters, *The Post-Symbolist Methods* (Allen Swallow, 1967); excerpted and reprinted in *Contemporary Literary Criticism,* Vol. 85, ed. Christopher Giroux (Detroit: Gale Research, 1995), pp. 223-26.

# Suggestions Are Welcome

The editors hope that readers will find *CLC* a useful reference tool and welcome comments about the work. Send comments and suggestions to: Editors, *Contemporary Literary Criticism,* Gale Research, Penobscot Building, Detroit, MI 48226-4094.

# Acknowledgments

The editors wish to thank the copyright holders of the excerpted criticism included in this volume and the permissions managers of many book and magazine publishing companies for assisting us in securing reproduction rights. We are also grateful to the staffs of the Detroit Public Library, the Library of Congress, the University of Detroit Mercy Library, Wayne State University Purdy/Kresge Library Complex, and the University of Michigan Libraries for making their resources available to us. Following is a list of the copyright holders who have granted us permission to reproduce material in this volume of *CLC*. Every effort has been made to trace copyright, but if omissions have been made, please let us know.

**COPYRIGHTED EXCERPTS IN *CLC*, VOLUME 101, WERE REPRODUCED FROM THE FOLLOWING PERIODICALS:**

*America,* v. 150, April 28, 1984 for a review of "The Island of Crimea". Copyright © 1984. All rights reserved. Reproduced with permission of America Press, Inc., 106 West 56th Street, New York, NY 10019 and the author.—*The Antioch Review,* v. 52, Fall, 1994. Copyright © 1994 by the Antioch Review Inc. Reproduced by permission of the Editors.— *Book World--The Washington Post,* v. XXIV, June 6, 1994. © 1994, Washington Post Book World Service/Washington Post Writers Group. Reproduced with permission.— *Books Abroad,* v. 48, Summer, 1974. Copyright 1974 by the University of Oklahoma Press. Reproduced by permission of the publisher.— *Canadian Literature,* v. 122-23, Autumn-Winter, 1989 for a review of "Albertine in Five Times" by Jerry Wasserman. Reproduced by permission of the author.— *Chicago Tribune,* June 26, 1994 for "The Land of the Wounded Men" by Bruce Allen. © copyrighted 1994, Chicago Tribune Company. All rights reserved. Reproduced by permission of the author.—*The Christian Science Monitor,* May 17, 1995 for "The Information--An Unpleasant, Familiar-Sounding Book" by Merle Rubin. Copyright © 1995 by The Christian Science Publishing Society. All rights reserved. Reproduced by permission of the author.—*Cineaste,* v. XIX, January, 1980. Copyright © 1980 by Cineaste Publishers, Inc. Reproduced by permission.—*Commonweal,* v. CXVIII, April 19, 1991; v. 119, September 25, 1992; November 4, 1994. Copyright © 1991, 1992 and 1994 by the Commonweal Publishing Co., Inc. All reproduced by permission of Commonweal Foundation.—*Concerning Poetry,* v, 12, Spring, 1979. Copyright © 1979, Western Washington University. Reproduced by permission.— *Criticism,* v. VIII, Fall, 1966. Copyright, 1966, Wayne State University Press. Reprinted by permission of the publisher.— *English,* v. 42, Summer, 1993 for "Problems When Time Moves Backwards: Martin Amis's Time Arrow" by Maya Slater. Copyright © 1973 by The English Association. Reproduced by permission of the publisher and the author.—*Film Quarterly,* v. XVII, Winter, 1973-74 for "Truffaut's Georgeous Killers" by Marsha Kinder and Beverle Houston. Copyright © 1973 by The Regents of the University of California. Reproduced by permission of The Regents and the authors.—*The French Review,* v. 63, February, 1990. Copyright 1990 by the American Association of Teachers of French. Reproduced by permission.—*Journal of Modern Literature,* v. 16, No. 4, Spring, 1990. © Temple University 1990. Reproduced by permission.—*Literature/Film Quarterly,* v. 1, July, 1973; v. 18, 1990; v. 22, 1994. Copyright © 1973, 1990, 1994 by Salisbury State College. All reproduced by permission.—*London Review of Books,* v. 17, May 11, 1995 for "Satisfaction" by Julian Loose. Appears here by permission of the *London Review of Books* and the author.— *Los Angeles Times Book Review,* June 9, 1985;

# Vassily Aksyonov

## 1932-

(Full name Vassily Pavlovich Aksyonov; also transliterated as Vassily Aksenov) Russian novelist, dramatist, short story writer, scriptwriter, and children's author.

The following entry provides an overview of Aksyonov's career through 1995. For further information of his life and career, see *CLC*, Volumes 22 and 37.

## INTRODUCTION

Widely known for his association with the "youth prose" movement in Russian literature, Vassily Aksyonov has established himself as a satirist whose topics include political corruption, the Soviet regime, alienation, adolescent angst, and cultural differences between the East and West. His surrealistic techniques coupled with his use of jargon and slang are trademark characteristics of Aksyonov's fiction. The blending of real historical events into his novels has also distinguished Aksyonov's work. Novels such as *Ozhog* (1980; *The Burn*) and *Ostrov Krym* (1981; *The Island of Crimea*) address a variety of issues such as political imprisonment, exile, corruption, and isolation.

### Biographical Information

Born on August 20, 1932, in Kazan, U.S.S.R., Vassily Pavlovich Aksyonov has gained increasing recognition as a writer of satirical, surrealistic fiction. His mother, Eugenia Semenovna Ginzburg, was a history instructor at Kazan University. Her prison-camp memoir *Journey into the Whirlwind* (1962) established her as a well-known writer and heavily influenced Vassily's most ambitious and successful novel, *The Burn*. His father, Pavel Vasilievich Aksyonov, was a professional Communist Party member. Both of Aksyonov's parents were impprisoned in 1937, and in 1948 he joined his mother in Magadan, where she was living in exile, and completed his elementary education in 1950. In 1956 he graduated from the First Leningrad Medical Institute as a medical doctor. Aksyonov served as staff physician in a tuberculosis clinic until 1958 and as a specialist in adolescent tuberculosis until 1960. After the publication of his novel *Kollegi* (1961; *Colleagues*) in 1960 in two issues of *Yunost'* (*Youth*) magazine, Aksyonov left medicine to pursue writing full time. During the 1960s Aksyonov's novels enjoyed a period of popularity when Soviet restraints on literature were less rigid. In the 1970s, censorship and increasing conflict with Soviet officials prompted him to leave his

homeland. Called the Russian J. D. Salinger by many critics for his treatment of youth, alienation, and the search for meaning, Aksyonov has been praised for the wide scope of his novels, his social satire, and his historical scholarship. His works continue to be translated into English, and currently Aksyonov is again being recognized as a prominent voice in literature.

### Major Works

Aksyonov's first two novels, *Colleagues* and *Zvezdnyi bilet* (1961; *A Ticket to the Stars*), received widespread attention in the Soviet Union. *A Ticket to the Stars* focuses on rebellious teenagers in Moscow and was popular for its depiction of rowdy, flippant youth. Critiqued heavily for its experimental nature and its use of jargon and slang, the novel offended many Soviet officials. The novel's irreverent attitude and the author's subsequent writings prompted a public scolding from Premier Nikita Khrushchev in 1963 and a forced apology from Aksyonov. *Pora, moi drug, pora* (1964; *It's Time, My Friend, It's Time*) examines the themes of alienation and the search for meaning. The surrealistic novel *The Burn* has many autobiographical elements and traces the development of five alternate versions of Tolya Von Steinbock's persona. Divided into three sections, *The Burn* focuses on three different periods in Tolya's life. In *The Island of Crimea,* set on the Crimean peninsula, Aksyonov imagines that Crimea is an autonomous society separated from the Soviet Union. The novel is another social satire reliant on a stretch of the imagination, but it is deemed less surrealistic and far-fetched than Aksyonov's previous works. *Skazi izjum!* (1985; *Say Cheese!*) presents an account of Aksyonov's emigration to America and provides an insightful look into Soviet culture and regime. *Pokolenie zimy* (1993; *Generations of Winter*) is a sweeping epic that begins during the 1920s and ends with the conclusion of World War II. The novel has been compared to the works of Leo Tolstoy and Aleksandr Solzhenitsyn.

**Critical Reception**

Throughout his career Aksyonov has presented satires of both Eastern and Western society. His work has frequently been criticized for its use of dated slang, jargon, surrealistic techniques, inside jokes, and farcical situations. Critic Priscilla Meyer asserts that *A Ticket to the Stars* and *Colleagues* both attempt "to show that while contemporary youth may look and talk like *stiliagi* ("beatniks"), they nonetheless shared the ideals of the previous generation." Examining themes of alienation and adolescent rebellion, *A Ticket to the Stars* offended the "Old Guard," but was very popular with the Russian youth, according to Meyer. Aksyonov's critique of the Russian regime continued in *The Burn,* and the author was forced to leave his homeland upon the novel's publication in 1980. In his review of *The Burn,* Czech novelist Josef Skvorecky calls Aksyonov "an epoch-making writer" whose "stunning inferno" of Stalinism reminded him of the paintings of Hieronymus Bosch. Critics such as Fernanda Eberstadt fault the novel for its "authorial self-indulgence," and "stale literary fashions," but most critics regard it highly. Meyer states: "By recapitulating his own biography, Aksyonov writes a literary-historical confession that traces the effects of Stalinism on the author's generation from the 1940s to the mid-1970s." *Say Cheese!* likewise is lauded for its insightful look at life during the Soviet regime. Eva Hoffman describes the book as a "disturbing and persuasive probe into the inner mechanisms of the Soviet machine on the eve of potential disintegration—or glasnost." Critic Jay Parini calls *Generations of Winter* "a masterly, rather self-consciously Tolstoyan epic that opens in the late 1920s and ends, hauntingly, amid the ruins of World War II." According to Adam Hochschild review of the novel, Aksyonov's blending of fact and fiction, his frequent quoting of great Russian poets, and his excellent grasp of history allow the author to present an "absorbing," all-encompassing epic in which "everything rings true."

## PRINCIPAL WORKS

*Kollegi* [*Colleagues*] (novel) 1961
*Zvezdnyi bilet* [*A Ticket to the Stars*] (novel) 1961
*Apel'siny iz Marokko* [*Oranges from Morocco*] (novel) 1962
*Pora, moi drug, pora* [*It's Time, My Friend, It's Time*] (novel) 1964
*The Destruction of Pompei and Other Stories* (short stories) 1965
*Zatovarennaia bochkotara* [*The Tare of Barrels*] (novel) 1968
*Randevu* [*Rendezvous*] (novella) 1971
*Liubov'k elektrichestvu* [*Love for Electricity*] (novel) 1971
*Ozhog* [*The Burn*] (novel) 1980
*Ostrov Krym* [*The Island of Crimea*] (novel) 1981
*Skazi izjum!* [*Say Cheese!*] (novel) 1985
*V poiskakh grustnogo bebi: Kniga ob Amerike* [*In Search of Melancholy Baby*] (nonfiction) 1987
*\*Pokolenie zimy* [*Generations of Winter*] (novel) 1993
*\*Voina i tiur'ma* [*War and Prison*] (novel) 1993
*\*Tiur'ma i mir* [*Prison and Peace*] (novel) 1994

\* These works comprise a trilogy, *Moskovskaia saga* [*Moscow Saga*].

## CRITICISM

### Deming Brown (essay date Spring 1965)

SOURCE: "Vasili Aksenov at 33," in *Tri-Quarterly*, No. 2, Spring, 1965, pp. 75-83.

[*In the following essay, Brown examines a variety of Aksyonov's works and provides an overview of the author's career.*]

Kirpichenko, a roughneck tractor driver in the Soviet Far East, begins his vacation with a three-day binge, then boards a jet for Moscow. On the plane he is fatally dazzled by the beautiful stewardess Tanya. Tamed and bemused, he spends the rest of his vacation, and all his money, flying back and forth on the Moscow-Khabarovsk run, hoping for another glimpse of Tanya. When he finally sees her again in the airport, it is too late; the broken giant retains his fair vision, but he must go back to work.

Uncle Mitya, a taxi-driver in Yalta who is plagued by speeding tickets, tries to immunize himself by marrying off his daughter, a sister-in-law, and sundry other in-laws to the local traffic cops. The marriages succeed, but the project backfires: Uncle Mitya finds himself hemmed in by his new relatives—staunch enforcers of the law who are first of all anxious to demonstrate their impartiality by pinching him as often as possible.

Georgi Abramashvili is an eighteen-year-old lifeguard at Sukhumi who is awaiting his draft call. He spends his sunny days impressing the girls on the beach with spectacular handstands. At night he courts trouble with the Komsomol by evading service in the local *druzhina*. One fine evening this Tarzan is introduced to sex (and cigarettes!) by the vacationing Alina. Next day Alina's husband arrives, there is a fight, and Abramashvili is publicly denounced for hooliganism. The army, he decides, will be fine. He might even get to be a cosmonaut!

Kirpichenko, Uncle Mitya, and Georgi Abramashvili would seem to have little in common. In the context of contemporary Soviet literature, however, there is much that unites them. All three are ordinary, stumbling, bewildered guys, trying to get along in the world without too much discomfort, largely unconcerned with the fate of society at large. They are only minimally aware, if at all, of participating in the building of communism. All three, in fact, would be vulnerable to the accusation that their horizons are narrow, that they lack any sense of the lofty purpose of life, and that they are ideologically too passive to play a conscious role in shaping the world about them. It is just as true, however, that these three fictional characters, conceived by their author in a spirit of irony, sympathy and humor, are interesting, colorful and believable. They are typical of the best characters in the Soviet literature of the nineteen sixties precisely because of their authenticity and lack of schematic adulteration.

The creator of these characters, from three separate short stories, is Vasili Aksenov, a 33-year-old Muscovite who five years ago abandoned his profession as a physician to take up a career in literature. Since his first appearance in print in 1959, Aksenov has published three novels, one novella and roughly a dozen short stories. He has also done scenarios of two of his novels and one or two independent scenarios. Together with Evgeny Evtushenko and a few other prominent writers, he is an editor of the outstandingly successful monthly magazine *Yunost'* (Youth). Aksenov is one of the half-dozen most promising young writers in the U.S.S.R. today, and he is certainly one of the busiest.

Aksenov is also controversial. His second novel, *A Starry Ticket,* which appeared in the summer of 1961, featured an engagingly irreverent and rebellious group of Soviet teenagers, rock-and-rolling runaways from the discipline of both parents and society, whose pungent, flip language was loaded with foreignisms (especially Americanisms) and whose sceptical, wry view of the Soviet middle-class success pattern earned their creator, for a time, the title of the Russian

Salinger. Aksenov's "starry boys," as hostile critics have come to call them, met with bitter disapproval from the watchdogs of orthodoxy, who not only resented their hip lingo (a mixture of foreign borrowings, pure invention, Soviet underworld argot, and jargon from the concentration camps), but, even more seriously, were shocked by their open though adolescent mockery of Soviet sacred cows. Because of this novel and subsequent literary sins in the same vein, Aksenov got a parental scolding from Khrushchev in the spring of 1963 and was forced to make a public apology. Since then his published works appear to have been free of literary heresy, although they have retained in large measure the saucy flavor that has always irritated his critics. At the same time his writing continues to be experimental. It has its ups and downs. His most recent novel, *It's Time, My Friend, It's Time,* published last summer, was in many respects an artistic failure. On the other hand, his three most recently published short stories display the strength and charm of the best of Aksenov. Even more important, both the novel and the stories give evidence of a literary mind that has not lost its restlessness.

One of Aksenov's great strengths is his sense of fun—a fascination for the grotesque that suggests a combination of [Nikolai] Gogol and a somewhat milder Joseph Heller. He purposely lets things get out of hand. Kirpichenko, in his search for Tanya, covers the 4,000 air miles between Moscow and Khabarovsk not once, but ceaselessly, back and forth, back and forth. The boys in *A Starry Ticket,* picking up odd jobs for eating money on their runaway to Estonia, are hired to repaint the hull of a black fishing trawler. They find some red paint and decorate the hull with it.

> But then we started to wonder whether it wouldn't be even nicer if we painted the whole ship red. Shouldn't we turn everything red that had been black until then? Go over the whole thing with bucket and brush and, before anyone knew what had happened, the entire thing would be red.

When the boss discovers his tomato-colored ship the next morning, he, too, crimsons. At times Aksenov's taste for the extravagant and the improbable get him involved in huge, farcical situations that can best be described as a kind of rollicking panic. A ship from Morocco, laden with oranges, arrives in the dead of winter at a remote port on the island of Sakhalin. The locals, many of whom have never seen an orange, rush in from every outlying village and work-site, clogging the roads and plowing through the snow on tractors, dump trucks, motorcycles, road graders, bulldozers, cars and buses. Nanaian tribesmen on dogsleds join the crush. A steamy bacchanal ensues as the entire populace, punctuating its revelry with fistfights, gorges on oranges. What happens is plausible, but it is somehow heightened, larger than life, and juicier.

Like many young Soviet poets and writers, Aksenov is fascinated with the jet age and awed by speed. The world of his novels and stories is full of cars, helicopters and airplanes. But he is not a naive worshiper of technology, and, unlike many of his more chauvinistic compatriots, he seems to have reacted to Soviet achievements in space with equanimity. There is evidence in his writing of a healthy respect for the ominousness of violent motion. A major development in *A Starry Ticket* turns on a catastrophic plane crash. And the most poignant character in *It's Time, My Friend, It's Time,* the ungainly young misfit and dreamer Kyanukuk (who, among other things, has made up the story that he is about to be selected as an exchange student at the University of Michigan), dies as his motorcycle crashes at top speed into a piece of highway construction equipment.

Aksenov likes to describe movement, both of people and of things. His characters love sports and play them well. (Wilt the Stilt Chamberlain is the idol of one of them.) They are handy with their fists and quick to resort to them. They are intrigued by rhythms, and collect jazz tapes and dance steps. Dimka, one of the boys in *A Starry Ticket,* gets a job as a bricklayer's helper and, relishing the sarcasm, describes his work:

> Talk of a complicated occupation: you put a couple of bricks on top of the belt and when they're gone, you put a couple more on . . . And so I took two bricks and put them on the belt, too. And to think it was a human being who invented a damned contraption like the conveyor belt! It never stops moving, that belt, and you keep putting bricks on it two by two and your pile grows smaller while the wall gets taller and taller. . . .

Motion—even when it is absurd and purposeless—holds a special charm for Aksenov and seems important to him in and for itself. One of his most recent stories concerns the nostalgic visit of an old man (now rehabilitated and pensioned after eighteen years' imprisonment and exile under Stalin) to the village of his birth. There he finds a boyhood acquaintance whose nickname is Dikoi (The Strange One). Fifty years before, the narrator, with a group of other boys, had smashed a weird, Rube Goldberg machine which Dikoi was building in a deserted bathhouse. They talk of their lives and, as the visitor is about to leave, his host takes him to a locked shed in back of his hut.

> I saw the same intricate machine which we had broken in the bathhouse. It was built along the same lines, only more complicated, more majestic. The machine was moving, wheels rotated, big and small, the spokes and levers moved silently, the belt-drive slid quietly over the pulleys, and there was the weak click of a little board, a little board, a little board . . .

"Remember?" Dikoi whispered.

"I remember," I also whispered.

The little board clicked, as if ticking off the years of our lives to the end, and even beyond the end, back and forth, and we didn't even know where these noises were rolling to . . .

I felt sick.

"An amusing gadget," I said in a sarcastic voice, to give myself courage. "What's it for? Eh, Dikoi?"

"Simply, Pavlusha, for motion," he answered again in a whisper, still looking at the wheels.

"And when did you start it up?" I again asked sarcastically.

"When? I don't know, don't remember. Long ago, very long. You see, it doesn't stop."

"What is it—perpetual motion?"

He turned to me and his eyes gleamed madly, not from the electric light but from the light of the early moon.

"It seems, yes," he whispered with a sickly smile, "but perhaps not. So . . . let's take another look . . ."

Motion in this story is more than just a thing in itself, for it has a distinctly symbolic function as well. We are concerned at the moment, however, not so much with Aksenov's ideas as with his writer's temperament—the way he uses words to convey the shape and texture of life. His style of writing is truly arresting (much more so, unfortunately, in Russian than in English translation). It is based, first of all, on a very heavy use of dialogue—brisk, racy, ironical, quarrelsome, tart. Most of his abundant humor, and a great deal of his narrative development, is located in the dialogue. Since Aksenov is also particularly fond of first-person narrative, his dialogue is, more often than not, *reported* dialogue, in which the narrator himself (not the author) has been closely involved, either as a participant or as an interested observer. This method lends an intimacy and warmth, as well as an especially opinionated flavor to the writing. Furthermore, since the narrator is as candid in reporting his own feelings as he is in recounting the utterances of others, there shines through his joking, mocking, sceptical, off-beat language a startling emotional authenticity. Aksenov and his generation have grown up under the genial influence of the matchless Soviet satirists Ilf and Petrov. His own language and attitudes, as well as those of his characters, bears heavily the imprint of these wisely crazy humorists, who were always alert to the phony and ridiculous in Soviet life. At the same time, Aksenov is more serious than Ilf and Petrov; whereas they attempted to get at the truth through wild indirection, Aksenov tries more often to name things for what they are. As a consequence, he has cultivated, in both his first-person and his third-person narrative, a vein of terse, laconic description and exposition based largely on verbs and nouns. It is not surprising that one of his few acknowledged mentors is Ernest Hemingway.

Aksenov's style, however, is more than just a mixture of colorful dialogue and telegraphic authorial statement, for it is full of all kinds of tricks and surprises. Some of these, such as his occasional bizarre experiments with typography, are merely amusing. More interesting and meaningful is the allusiveness of his prose, which is so crammed with topical references that his works constitute a small, though slanted, encyclopedia of contemporary Soviet life. (There are Soviet critics who would deny him this value by arguing that he portrays only a narrow, special, and negligible segment of the Russian scene, but his very popularity among the generation whose life he describes testifies to his relevance.) He cites snatches of songs, current slogans and catchwords, the names of sports greats and movie stars. He parodies the clichés of newspapers and classroom, the cozy advice of parents, and the smug admonitions of the collective. Much of his language is figurative, and it is particularly rich in bold and sprightly metaphors. Interjections and wry rhetorical questions abound. The sentences themselves are short and choppy, enabling the writer to draw attention to the individual word. This is particularly important, for ultimately the most distinctive thing about Aksenov is his vocabulary.

> **One of the reasons why Aksenov's characters talk as they do is that they are profoundly dissatisfied with the stale, hypocritical, hollow vocabulary that was foisted on the Soviet people during a quarter-century of Stalinism.**
>
> **—*Deming Brown***

There have been many complaints, even from critics who are benevolently disposed toward him, about Aksenov's stock of words. A couple of years ago the humor magazine *Crocodile,* only half in jest, printed a sample glossary of Aksenov for the guidance of readers who were stumped by his outlandish vocabulary. Everyone agrees that the salty, swinging language of his characters can actually be heard on Moscow streets and Siberian construction sites. The trouble is, as the venerable writer and language authority Kornei Chukovski has remarked, such slang *should* not be heard

anywhere: it is a threat to the purity of Russian! Others who object to Aksenov's esoteric jargon see it as an ugly symptom of incipient disrespectfulness and cynicism among Soviet young people and view his writing as a pernicious influence on youth. Such critics, bigoted and hidebound though they may be, have a point. One of the reasons why Aksenov's characters talk as they do is that they are profoundly dissatisfied with the stale, hypocritical, hollow vocabulary that was foisted on the Soviet people during a quarter-century of Stalinism and, despite some reforms, continues to plague Soviet public life.

Although they are dissatisfied with many things, Aksenov's characters are really not cynical at all. And although some of them do resemble in some respects the *stilyagi*—approximate Soviet equivalents of England's "mods"—Aksenov takes pains to distinguish them from truly anti-social parasites. They are wary of emotional and intellectual commitments, but underneath their scepticism and occasional surface callousness there is an idealism of a rather pristine type. With few exceptions, Aksenov's characters observe a clear, if unspoken moral code that emphasizes simple honor and decency, faithfulness in love and in friendship, the dignity of conscientious effort, and efficiency and trustworthiness in one's work. Despite their attempts to cultivate the flippant sneer and a certain premature, world-weary acidity, they are ultimately warm and engaging.

It is important to distinguish, however, between various types of characters in Aksenov. First of all, he does not write exclusively about young people. Middle-aged persons crop up even in his earliest stories and, if his most recent publications are an indication, he is also interested in the elderly. Furthermore, although teenagers continue to fascinate him, he has recently tended to concentrate on characters in their twenties or early thirties. These, of course, are his own contemporaries. Whereas he portrays his teenagers with an amused, ironical, older-brotherly affection, he depicts his contemporaries with a deep, involved sympathy.

The problems which this latter group faces are universal ones—finding and keeping a mate, discovering the fact of inevitable death and somehow digesting it, selecting one's life work and qualifying for it, and reconciling one's ideals with an imperfect world. Since Aksenov's characters, by and large, are never more than mildly neurotic, they approach these problems with a minimum of self-deception, with energy and with courage. This is not to say that they do not flounder, waste time and talent, or engage in aggressive or self-destructive behavior. Love in his stories is very frequently a source of mutual torture or agonizing loneliness. And although Aksenov, like all contemporary Soviet writers, spares the reader the lurid details of sex, he quite freely shows its uglier implications as well as its charm. Nevertheless, he avoids the extremes of human behavior; his people bloody each other's noses but they do not murder; they get the blues but they do not remain permanently on dead center; they gripe about working conditions but they stay on the job; they run away but they come home. Aksenov believes that the human situation is good and that its maladjustments are curable.

Aksenov has had to overcome, however, a tendency toward superficial sunniness. His first novel, *Colleagues,* often reads like a study in socialist realism. It is the story of how three friends, just out of medical school, pass the initial tests of their ability, moral fibre and stamina. While two of them are marking time in the port of Leningrad, awaiting assignment as ship's doctors, their Komsomol vigilance helps to break up a ring of embezzlers. The third, assigned to a rural dispensary in Karelia, becomes a kind of Dr. Kildare of the wilderness and proves his mettle in a series of rugged adventures. The novel climaxes in a suspenseful midnight surgical operation. The young rural doctor, knifed while thwarting a burglary, is saved by his two medical-school pals, who have appeared on the scene in the nick of time. This novel was filmed, and one is tempted to conclude that Aksenov had the scenario in mind when he plotted it.

*Colleagues* is by no means devoid of serious social commentary or moral probing. A number of references to problems of Soviet public life and institutions indicate that Aksenov is seriously and intelligently concerned with telling the truth about the society in which he lives. There are alcoholics, common criminals, and other flotsam and jetsam in the novel; the poverty of collective farms is mentioned; there is reference to bureaucratic corruption and official stuffed-shirtism and hypocrisy. One of his young doctors complains, in a remark that has frequently been re-quoted:

> If you only knew, I'm fed up to the teeth with it, all this drumming in of propaganda, all these high-falutin' words. I know there's a host of fine idealists like yourself who're always mouthing them, but there are also thousands of scoundrels who just parrot them. I don't doubt Beria too used the same language while he was deceiving the Party. Now that such a lot of things have become clear to us, such language rings very false. So for Heaven's sake let's manage without claptrap. I love my country, I love its system, and I wouldn't give a thought about giving an arm or a leg or my life for it. But all I'm responsible to is my own conscience, not any fetishes of words. All they do is make it more difficult to see the realities of life. See what I mean?

Aksenov has in fact endowed this particular character with a formidable *Weltschmerz.* In his person the author poses a question which few Soviet writers in recent times have dared to dwell on:

> We spin philosophies, we battle for progressive ideas, we babble about the usefulness of working for the community, we build up theories, but in the last resort we all break down into a number of chemical elements, just like plants and animals which don't dabble in theories. It's all a tragicomedy and nothing more. People are wont to say: we all come to it at the end. All of us. Both the leaders of productivity and the idlers, both the decent ones and the rogues. But where is this *it* where we're all going to be, eh? There isn't anywhere. Just darkness. What do I really care about anything in the world if I always have that awareness that the time will come when I shall vanish forever?

Having raised this question, however, Aksenov in effect dismisses it by bathing it in a mist of communist affirmation. He prescribes comradeship and socially constructive activity—scarcely an exhaustive answer.

After his sojourn with teenagers in *A Starry Ticket,* Aksenov returned to the concerns of persons his own age. *Oranges from Morocco, It's Time, My Friend, It's Time* and several of his recent short stories have centered on the problems of emotional and social adjustment that face young Soviet adults. There is generally less pink-cheeked enthusiasm among them than among the heroes of *Colleagues.* They brood, drift from job to job, disappoint and sometimes insult one another. They wander about the country puzzled, frustrated and dissatisfied, and often they behave more like victims of a social order than builders of one. Their ability to see the funny side of things and to ridicule themselves does prevent them from seeming simply sour and lugubrious. And as a rule they experience some sort of saving revelation, or at least there are indications that their problems are beginning to straighten out. All the same, Aksenov endows these characters with dignity and genuine pathos, and in determining their fates he avoids doctrinaire optimism and pat solutions.

*Oranges from Morocco* is a series of character portraits strung together by a couple of love intrigues and the dominating episode of the oranges. Its main figures are Victor Koltyga, who works on an oil prospecting rig in what he sarcastically describes as "this stupendous, enchanting, stinking valley" and dreams of quitting the Soviet Far East forever; Nikolai Kalchanov, a Pechorinesque engineer who is bitterly and hopelessly in love with another man's wife; German Kovalev, a sailor who writes atrocious poetry; Liudmilla Kravchenko, a prim, model Komsomokla who dutifully reads Gorky and finds it shocking that other girls are unwilling to show their diaries; and Valentin Kostyukovski, an undisciplined knockabout whose father, a distinguished professor, sat for sixteen years in a concentration camp and left him, in effect, a homeless orphan. The oranges, and the spontaneous celebration which they occasion, bring welcome extra color into their lives and produce confrontations that set each one of them off in a new direction. This story has been attacked by Soviet critics on the grounds that all of the characters tend to use the same vulgar jargon and for this reason are not sufficiently differentiated, and that the changes in their lives and their relationships that come about as a result of this one event are insufficiently motivated. Such criticism is warranted. Nearly all of the characters do speak in the same tone, and the dimensions of the story are indeed too small to encompass and justify so many fundamental changes in private individual destinies. Some critics have argued further, however, that the characters themselves are deficient in moral and intellectual stature, and that their problems are essentially trivial. Similar charges, as a matter of fact, have been directed at most of Aksenov's writing, and his ultimate reputation will depend, to a great extent, on whether or not such charges are valid. For this reason it is important to try to determine just how relevant and profound Aksenov's images of young adults really are.

It would be difficult to argue that such characters as Kirpichenko, Georgi Abramashvili and the persons in *Oranges from Morocco* have an impressive intellectual and moral stature. Aside from the fact that they are healthy and working and that they get along passably well with their fellow men, there is little to recommend them as exemplars of constructive thought and demeanor in any society. But this does not mean that as images in literature they are superficial. One of Aksenov's best stories—perhaps his finest—concerns a sports-loving young lathe operator who is taking care of his six-year-old daughter on a Sunday afternoon because his wife, who is well on her way to a doctor's degree, is presumably studying somewhere. Father and daughter stroll to a park, where he has a beer with some old soccer-playing buddies. Suddenly he realizes that his wife, who has surpassed him in life, is not studying but is having a rendezvous. The discovery that part of his world is about to cave in produces a momentary panic. As he looks at his little daughter, however, he feels a new sense of responsibility and purpose in life: taking care of her is ample reason for living. There are other threads in the story—and some symbolism—that lend it profundity. Nevertheless the story depends mainly on this central situation—the ordinary, private circumstances of a simple, decent man who is experiencing a major disappointment in life.

In another, more recent story of Aksenov, the naive example of a three-year-old boy gives his father courage to make an important (but unspecified) phone call over which he has been fearfully procrastinating for days. Ostensibly this episode, too, is a slight one; like the story just mentioned, it has practically nothing to do with society and absolutely nothing to do with the building of communism. On the other hand, both stories, in the tenderness and delicacy with which they

report on mundane but vital human problems, have ultimately more to say about contemporary Soviet society than the most earnest socialist-realist tract. However, a number of Soviet critics (those of a conservative or crypto-Stalinist inclination—and there are still a great many of them) are infuriated at any displacement of the civic element in Soviet literature by the personal element. The notion that there are human problems that do not lend themselves to the therapy of the collective, or for which ideological solutions are irrelevant, is anathema to these critics. It is such persons, in the main, who accuse Aksenov of being superficial. If for this reason Aksenov is in fact superficial, so then are a vast number of other prominent young writers who are attempting to produce similarly modest, Chekhovian slices of Soviet life.

Another reason for the accusation that Aksenov's characters lack stature is their reticence—their preference for silence or at best a cryptic response to challenges that are supposed to produce ringing communist answers. One of their major traits is their passion for seeing things simply and clearly, without the encumbrance of ideological preconceptions. They abhor lofty words, not because they are incapable of understanding them, but because in a Soviet context these words have become the labels of planned lives in a planned society. Aksenov's young people are seeking independent answers to the questions they ask of life, since they are weary of prefabricated solutions. Hence the irony with which they refer to practically everything that is orthodox and established, the relish with which they pronounce new words, and the eagerness with which they embrace things that are foreign or off-beat. Aksenov's characters, I would submit, are not superficial. They are simply engaged in the serious, dangerous, and infinitely trying task of sloughing off the ideological excrescence of forty years of Party misrule. As the thaw continues, they will find more positive, committed ways of expressing that which is already in their hearts.

## Priscilla Meyer (essay date Fall 1973)

SOURCE: "Aksenov and Soviet Literature of the 1960s," in *Russian Literature Triquarterly*, No. 6, Fall, 1973, pp. 446-60.

[*In the following essay, Meyer discusses several of Aksyonov's works and comments on the author's place in the "Young Prose" movement in Russian literature.*]

After Stalin's death Soviet literature had no rich indigenous tradition to proceed from directly, but there was a wide variety of elements, both Russian and Western, from which a new synthesis could be drawn. The first change that took place after 1953 broadened the range of permissible subject matter, and the first Thaw produced a rash of stories attacking bureaucratization. Subsequently, translations of contemporary Western literature (the journal *Foreign Literature* began publishing in 1955) and later the republication of Russian literature of the first third of this century (Blok in 1963, Olesha, Tsvetaeva, and Pasternak in 1965, Bely in 1966, Balmont in 1969) provided material for stylistic innovation. Psychologically, Khrushchev's "Secret Speech" at the 22nd Party Congress in 1956 had an enormous effect on the generation from which the new readers and writers of the 1960s were to emerge: the opening up of possibilities produced a general sense of exhilaration, a sense that if you were honest, talented and even innovative, you could become successful. This drew a large number of people into literature, especially from the generation born in the late 1920s and early 1930s. The burst of new literary productions appeared in a raft of new literary journals: *Iunost'*, *Neva*, and *Druzhba narodov* were founded in 1955, *Molodaia gvardiia* in 1956, *Don* and *Voprosy literatury* in 1957, *Pod'em*, *Moskva* and *Russkaia literatura* in 1958.

Soviet prose of the 1960s published within the USSR falls into three main groups: "war prose" (e.g., Baklanov, Bondarev, Astafiev), "village prose" (e.g., Abramov, Tendriakov, Soloukhin, Belov), and "young prose" (e.g., Aksenov, Gladilin, Bitov, Vladimov, Voinovich). Only Young Prose will be discussed here, because of the three groups, it most clearly reflected the changes in Soviet society that had taken place since World War II and triggered a great deal of controversy in which some central issues were raised.

The main subject of Young Prose, the "youth theme," is the adolescent's struggle to find his place in society. His problems are partly caused by his rejection of the values of his parents' generation, as epitomized by the work ethic. The maturational process is treated, as both Soviet and Western critics have remarked, in very personal terms. The explanation for this choice of theme and its treatment may be primarily sociological.

The Young Prose constituency came from the first Soviet generation that had never fought a war and had grown up during a period of increasing prosperity. In contrast to the Stakhanovite shock work mentality of the 1930s and 1940s, the years in which this generation attained awareness were characterized by a more relaxed rate of economic growth, the transformation of the country from an agrarian to an urban society, the spread of mass literacy, mass media and higher education, and increased leisure time. One of the consequences of all this was the creation of a new expanded urban intelligentsia, and it is this class which produced the authors of Young Prose. Their experience directly mirrored their middle class, small nuclear family origins: on finishing high school they were not forced to go to war or do hard labor, but rather had a wide range of possibilities open to

them. The main force acting on them was the pressure to individual achievement typically produced by nuclear families. Growing up under circumstances analogous to those of youth in the United States, they had similar problems choosing professions and life styles, and therefore took longer to mature than did their parents. This naturally had important implications for literature: while Socialist Realism was designed to motivate the unsophisticated masses to shock labor and therefore had to be simple, the problem of motivation in Young Prose was vastly more complex. To convince a hip Moscow teenager who spends his time listening to American jazz on his tape recorder of the rewards of becoming a useful member of society, literature had to appeal to him as an individual, not as a representative of a class; to spend years in educational institutions in order to become an engineer or a doctor, one had to be motivated internally, not externally by the demands of society. Accordingly, the focus in literature shifted from the social to the personal and Socialist Realism, which remained the dominant mode in the first half of the sixties, was modernized to accommodate social change. Once literature was freed from the necessity of making clear value judgements for the benefit of the lowest-common-denominator reader, stylistic experimentation began to creep in. Ambiguity, the obscuring of objective reality, the explicit exploration of the unconscious, and verbal play became increasingly important in the second half of the sixties, and this may be correlated with the shift in traditions influencing Young Prose: in the earlier period [William] Faulkner's multiple narrators, [John] Dos Passos' inclusion of documents into the text, and Salinger's adolescent hero who attacks Establishment phonies in a slangy first person became favorite devices, but with the maturation of the authors and the new input of the more sophisticated pre-1932 Russian tradition, Young Prose outgrew much of this and began to "reflect Soviet reality" less literally. The first influence was superficial; the American devices were mostly inserted into the Russian context intact. Young Prose also showed the general effects of Hemingway's terseness and Salinger's directness, while the overlap with Dos Passos' theme of generational conflict was probably the cause of his popularity rather than the result of his influence. The second set of influences will eventually prove more interesting to examine, but the reassimilation of early Soviet literature is only just beginning—a good example would be Olesha's influence on Bitov.

The center of Young Prose activity was the journal *Youth*, founded by Valentin Kataev and co-edited by, among others, his proteges Aksenov and Gladilin. It was the publication of Gladilin's "Chronicle of the Times of Viktor Podgursky" in 1956 that first called attention to the journal and that initiated Young Prose. The story elicited no response from the press, but caused great excitement among youth of Gladilin's age (he was then twenty) because it reflected their own experience honestly and directly, without the traditional "varnishing." It is important to realize that it was this desire to "write about my friends in the language they themselves spoke, and not to create some romantic directive ideal which nauseated me" that motivated the authors of Young Prose, the desire to establish their own identities, and not any specifically political considerations: "I was then still very naive and didn't pose any of the larger questions." Aksenov's oft-quoted pronouncement that "a writer must have the same blood-type as his contemporaries" in order to be understood displays a similar attitude. Aksenov developed the "youth theme" most fully and interestingly of all the young writers, and caused the most critical furor. His growth as a writer parallels the evolution of the "New" literature of the sixties as a whole, so a survey of his work provides a good sense of the period.

Aksenov's writing may be divided into two main periods, of which the first (1958-1964) is largely autobiographical. Born in 1932 of parents who were intellectuals and leading members of the Communist Party, Aksenov graduated from the Leningrad Medical Institute in 1956, whereupon he went to work as a seaport quarantine doctor, and then as a general practitioner in the Far North. During the last two years of his medical practice, he specialized in tuberculosis and began to write, publishing his first story in *Youth* in 1959. With the success of his novella (*povest'*) *Colleagues,* published in *Youth* in 1960, Aksenov left medicine to become a professional writer.

In the earliest group of stories written between 1958-1960 the medical profession is used to examine the work ethic. The traditional ideals of heroes wholly dedicated to the medical needs of provincial villages are juxtaposed to the desire for self-fulfillment which is connected to the cultural and educational attractions of the city. In *Colleagues,* the hero converts his cynical friends into idealistic doctors; in **"A Medical Unit and a Half"** the heroine refuses the temptation of a job in the city because of her sense of duty to her patients; and in **"From Dawn 'til Dusk"** a young lab worker comes to appreciate the value of his work when he discovers that his girlfriend's father has lung cancer. While stylistically and thematically these stories are still very close to Socialist Realism, the right of the individual to personal development is given serious weight, and the conflict is only resolved (rather than suppressed) in one story, **"Samson and Samsonella,"** and then by rearranging the elements so that professional concerns are located in the city and personal pleasures in the village: the young doctor abandons a burgeoning romance in the village to become a medical researcher in Leningrad.

Aksenov's second novella, *A Ticket to the Stars* (1961), also endorses the work ethic, and yet it provoked a barrage of criticism. The story about four Moscow teenagers who run away to Estonia rather than enter the university offended the

Old Guard: the "star boys" had received all the educational and material advantages only to throw them away for a frivolous existence. Furthermore, they spoke a slangy lingo studded with Westernisms. Aksenov's polemic was lost on the very people he was addressing. As in *Colleagues,* Aksenov wanted to show that while contemporary youth may look and talk like *stiliagi* ("beatniks"), they nonetheless shared the ideals of the previous generation. Seventeen-year-old Dimka joins a fishing cooperative and gains maturity through his exhilarating experience of collective labor, but at the same time he shares Holden Caulfield's hatred of phonies and rhetoric, and the fresh directness of tone plus the jazzy portraits of contemporary teenagers made *A Ticket to the Stars* enormously successful among Soviet youth.

To examine the problem of maturation, Aksenov retraced his steps to the point of high school graduation, and *A Ticket to the Stars* demonstrates why one shouldn't be expected to decide one's future at this early stage, but the question "a ticket to what?" remains unanswered. Aksenov's later heroes are older but no more able to answer this than Dimka, and delayed adolescence is the dominant theme of several stories written between 1960-1962. In **"Surprises"** (1960) Mitia returns to Moscow after three years' absence to find his friends married and with children, while he at twenty-six is still stuck in adolescent patterns; in **"A Change of Life Style"** (1961) Genia at thirty-one hides behind his work to avoid marrying the woman he loves out of fear of abandoning his student way of life.

Kirpichenko, the hero of **"Halfway to the Moon"** (1962), is psychologically akin to Mitia and Genia, but the story was probably selected for translation into English because of its metaphoric level. Kirpichenko spends his vacation flying back and forth between Moscow and Khabarovsk trying to find a stewardess he's fallen in love with on sight. His epic quest ends when he finally glimpses Tania in the Moscow airport as he is returning to Khabarovsk for good. He makes no attempt to approach her, only imagining how he will preserve her in memory. Kirpichenko, a belligerent worker who avoids sentiment in his routine sexual encounters, is transformed by his exposure to Tania, "a woman of the kind that doesn't really exist, the kind that's as far away from you as the moon." He starts reading Chekhov, he learns to think, to cry, and begins to understand "everything he hadn't understood in his . . . youth—the Siberian hillocks standing out in the pink light of dawn, and melting snow, and tiredness after work . . . —all these things were Tania." Tania is a Russian proletarian's Muse, Kirpichenko's Lolita. A metaphoric synthesis of Love and Art, she can only be possessed mentally. While this interpretation is the most interesting (speculations about Kirpichenko's salary notwithstanding), the hero's passion for an inaccessible woman should also be noted, as it allies him with Aksenov's stunted men who are unable to establish happy love relationships.

Aksenov had first proposed the work ethic, and then self-fulfillment through love, as means of outgrowing adolescence. When both solutions fail, he moves on to the next stage of life—parenthood. Sergei of **"Papa, What Does It Spell?"** (1962)—this and **"Halfway to the Moon"** are Aksenov's best early stories—is thirty-two, married, and has a six-year-old, he lives in an artificially preserved past with his former teammates. In the course of the story he moves from resenting Olia for requiring adulthood of him to finding the whole meaning of his life in her existence. During the summer Sunday they spend walking around Moscow, Sergei's growing awareness of his arrested development is nicely brought out by little incidents which occur against the background roar of the radio broadcast of the soccer game Olia's presence has kept him from attending: they pass a mirror which is hung too high to reflect Olia; they meet a factory colleague at the carousel who irritates Sergei by acting the proud father—the model Sergei knows he should emulate; they see a tall schoolboy who recalls Sergei's youth. Sergei is not fulfilled either at work or in his marriage. His sudden decision to live for his daughter represents an escape, a reversion to a still earlier stage of childhood through identification with his child, and not a solution. This interpretation is confirmed by a later story, **"Little Whale, Varnisher of Reality"** (1964) in which the father avoids the stresses of his own reality by joining his three-year-old son in the child's rosy world of fantasy.

---

**Almost all Aksenov's stories written before 1965 reflect the problems of his contemporaries in a style that differs from Socialist Realism mainly in its racy diction. In his later stories, Aksenov waxes increasingly literary; as he loses interest in problem-solving, he becomes more involved in fantasy and stylistic play.**

—*Priscilla Meyer*

---

Aksenov's third novella *Oranges from Morocco* (1962), a free-for-all occasioned by the arrival of a shipload of oranges at a Far Eastern seaport, abandons the problems of maturation to play (rather unsuccessfully) with a variety of first person narrators *a la* Faulkner, and his next long work, *It's Time, My Love, It's Time* (1963), along with "Little Whale," is the last treatment of the youth theme. At twenty-five Valia Marvich also suffers from delayed adolescence. He can't commit himself to a career or live happily with his wife, a dazzling movie actress (the adoring young man spurned and tormented by a glamorous dominating woman is an uncommonly prominent feature of Young Prose).

Marvich, like Dimka, allegedly solves his problems by joining a construction collective, but his enthusiasm for simple laborers (he is an *intelligent* and would-be writer) really stands the work ethic on its head: the conditions of collective labor allow the *intelligent* (Russian word meaning a member of the intelligentsia) to avoid the problems posed by individual interaction. Work becomes a means of therapy for Marvich rather than the object of his dedication. It is difficult not to internalize a dominant social myth, the literary expression of which will call forth its own parody as the myth loses its viability, and Marvich's idealization of labor betrays literary origins. It is only the intellectual who can long for the life of the noble savage. Village life is similarly romanticized in stories written by the urban intelligentsia. The contrast with the depiction of the decaying provinces prevalent before the revolution suggests that, like Young Prose as a whole, this kind of idealization should be examined in the context of urbanization.

Almost all Aksenov's stories written before 1965 reflect the problems of his contemporaries in a style that differs from Socialist Realism mainly in its racy diction. In his later stories, Aksenov waxes increasingly literary; as he loses interest in problem-solving, he becomes more involved in fantasy and stylistic play. Many of these stories are little more than entertaining anecdotes, like **"The Beautiful Comrade Furazhkin"** (1964) in which an Odessa cab driver and smuggler marries his daughter to a cop to avoid arrest (despite its humor, the story was greeted by an indignant letter in *Pravda* from some real Odessa hackies). But Aksenov uses the humorous stories to experiment with narrative devices. In **"Where the Rhododendrons Grow"** (1967) the anecdote (two lexicographers—Ozhegov and Ushakov—are chased up a tree by a wild boar during their vacation in the Caucasus) is only an excuse to play with the authorial persona:

> It would have long ago been time for me to throw this story into the bottom of the basket or stick it in the pillow-case, for what can be the purpose of telling about the absurd vacation of two completely absurd (although personally likeable) people . . .

And to parody Gogol:

> Such is the Russian man. He has only to pull out of his usual circle when he will immediately begin to grieve over this circle, and he will throw himself at any member of "his" group with verbal outpourings, with an open, responsive, throbbing soul. This becomes particularly acute in a foreign country. I remember in one . . . little town in the wilds of Central Europe I met a man from Moscow, whom I knew very little, and not even a very pleasant man, actually disgusting, vile. Well, we embraced, and got

drunk, and talked, and in Moscow later only bowed to each other from a distance.

Aksenov's latest story of this genre, **"Rendezvous"** (1971), is a satiric allegory with a grotesque finale in which the hero, an hyperbolic embodiment of popular success modeled, rumor has it, on Evtushenko, is confronted by his whorish Muse on a construction site at the outskirts of Moscow. Here the Gogolian influence, as well as its Bulgakovian variant, is more profound. The grotesque is not merely verbal, but inheres in the vision of society.

The anecdotal stories develop a device that is important for the more substantial works, the injection of pure fantasy into an ostensibly realistic (if absurd) narrative. Pale-blue fauns and green-braided maidens flit by Ushakov and Ozhegov, the first-person narrator of **"Furazhkin"** continues to report events he can't be witnessing, and in **"Rendezvous"** a school chum suddenly ascends thirty meters into the air, as does a dream Hitler in the reminiscence **"On the Square and Across the River"** (1967).

Objective reality is destroyed in the serious stories initially in more traditional ways. First it is fragmented by shifting narrative times. Both **"Lunches of 1943"** (1962) and **"Oddball"** (1964) begin with the hero's memories of childhood which are interspliced with the narrative present in a way designed to maximize the shock of transition. However, there is no confusion of past and present, and the flashbacks are basically expository. The stories remain fully realistic, although **"Oddball"** has a fantastic element. An old Bolshevik returns to his native village after an active life to find that his oddball childhood classmate has built an elaborated version of a machine he first invented as a boy. The machine, a metaphor for the waste of potential, is utterly functionless, it merely runs.

> "What is it, a perpetual motion machine or what?"
>
> He turned to me, and his eyes sparked terrifyingly not now in the electric light, but in the light of the early moon.
>
> "Seems to be," he whispered, "seems to be."

The story is only about motion, and then about motion through time, inasmuch as motion underscores the waste of human talent in backwaters. Jets keep flying over the village; technology, an ambiguous symbol of progress, defines Oddball's backwardness.

In the next step away from representing objective reality, the categories of past and present in the hero's interior monologue are replaced by those of the unconscious and the con-

scious, and in **"The Victory"** (1965) subjective reality acquires primacy for the first time. Although the early works deal with underlying psychological truths, these are conveyed only through externals (e.g., Sergei's encounters in **"Papa!"**), not through a stream of associations as in **"The Victory"** where the chessgame becomes a Rorschach onto which the grandmaster projects his fantasies. The levels of fantasy and reality merge; the narrative makes no distinction between the grandmaster's thoughts and actions:

> Standing up from behind the terrace for a second, he saw that G. O. had taken his rook.

It is no longer possible to tell, as it was in **"Lunches"** and **"Oddball,"** whether the hero's thoughts represent fantasies or memories of real events, nor is it important. The primary level of reality is the grandmaster's psychology, the symbolic significance of which is underscored by the fantastic ending. The shy, insecure grandmaster, so passive that he "can't avoid at least two games," is unable to counter aggression. He protects himself by withdrawing into fantasy, priding himself on never having committed any "really treacherous acts." The irony of the story is that there is no irony to G. O.'s victory: on the psychological level the grandmaster does lose the game by "running" from conflict with G. O. The same paradigm is followed by Marvich in **"It's Time."** He also prides himself on never having committed any treacheries, realizes that "myths of youth will not suffice," and fails to defend himself against a bully. The larger significance of the story lies in the meaning that the game, a metaphor of life, holds for each of the characters. For the grandmaster, chess is literary: it evokes associations, thoughts of love, life, death, creativity, and he finds an aesthetic "magic" in mating his opponent. For G. O. (Makarov suggests the initials stand for *Glavnaia Opasnost'*—the Main Danger) the game is an expression of hostility, a means of waging war ("Khas-Bulat the brave . . .") The grandmaster, a "runt" (the Russian *khiliak* carries the overtone of "Jew" as well, which casts some light on the exchange about Jewish chessplayers), prepares a supply of gold medals because he, the intellectual and aesthete, will always lose to the practical man of action, and the best he can do is buy off the aggressor.

In *The Shop-worn Tare of Barrels (Zatovarennaia bochkotara,* 1968) Aksenov synthesizes elements from all types of his earlier stories. The premise is taken from an autobiographical incident . . . , and fantasy, humor, parody and narrative play are integrated into an allegory. Even the early didacticism is present, but in general abstract moral terms rather than special prescriptive ones. The story of a trip to Koriazhsk becomes a Pilgrim's Progress toward the goodness in the characters, each of whom finds he is having the same collective dream of the Good Man. In the course of their journey, the *bochkotara,* a collection of empty barrels which is to be delivered to the railway station in a pick-up truck, becomes a symbol of the communality of mankind, and as such unites the disparate passengers. Grampa, Mochenkin, an old pisser who writes daily denunciations, the naive schoolteacher Irina, Vadim Afanasievich, the tweedy intellectual and others, mellowed by their common love for the bochkotara, are equally outraged when they turn it in at the station only to have it refused, and are condemned to journey onward together towards the Good Man forever. The chance assortment of representative types *a la Dead Souls* (Aksenov likes the grand hotel device and used it the same way in *Oranges from Morocco*) provides material for satire and parody. The Intellectual knows every detail down to the nicknames of all the animals of "Khali-Gali", a South American country no one has ever heard of, and Volodia the worker recounts his adventures in a style parodying proletarian speech and Soviet official jargon at once:

> . . . in short me and Edik dropped in to the division of labor and hiring and there one mug six by six shoots us to the general committee of the roadworkers' union and with us was that I don't remember now Ovanesian-Petrosian-Oganesian a blond we played with as forwards on "Vodnik" in Krasnovodsk well someone leaned on the counter boo-hoo he says I'll send you to a work colony well who needs that lucky I knew the guy from the farm brigade you he says Volodia listen to me and apply your forces to writing an application moved by emotion well of course rev rev rev and Edik and me were chasing rafts down the Amur let's go he says to the Komsomol lake we dug it ourselves we'll boat on it ourselves . . .

*Bochkotara* contains wildly eclectic ingredients; the folk element, including a triadic structure and a regular refrain, mixes with the ads, slogans and songs of pop culture. The central metaphor is based on the current custom of redeeming beer bottles in order to buy more beer with the deposit money, so Soviets immediately associate the symbol of brotherhood with the drinking bout. Literary influences also contribute to the borshch. The characters' personalities are revealed through their dreams and letters which are recorded under headings ("Irina's Second Dream," "Volodia's letter to Sima," etc.) in the Dos Passos (via Gladilin?) manner. One interview with a pilot

> "Do you see God, Comrade Kulachenko?"

> "I don't see God!"

> "Hurray! There is no God! Our prognoses have been confirmed!"

> "And do you see angels?"

> "I just saw one."

recalls Kataev's play with Communist ideology in *The Embezzlers:*

> We are flying . . . higher, higher. Perhaps further on we'll find angels and God? But no, they're not there either . . . But where are the angels? Where then is God? It's all just an ignorant lie of the priests . . .

In *Bochkotara* Aksenov finally achieves what he was attempting in *Oranges,* a novel critics justifiably faulted for not differentiating the speech of the multiple narrators. In the later novel, social classes are vividly differentiated by their dialogue as well as their world views, and the adventure is more than a mere pretext to assemble comic figures. Furthermore, the language of *Bochkotara* is rich, zany and largely untranslatable, as illustrated by the epigraph "from the newspapers," a nonsensical sentence composed of slang and made-up words which are chosen chiefly for their alliterative value:

> Zatovarilas' bochkotara, zatsvela zhltym tvetkom, zatarilas', zatiurilas', i s mesta tronulas'.

Although Aksenov is most interested in pursuing this self-consciously literary tack, his latest work is a documentary biography of Lev Krasin which was commissioned for the series "Flaming Revolutionaries," a series which includes Gladilin's *Robespierre.* Basically an historical dramatization of the 1905-1908 period, *Love of Electricity* nonetheless incorporates many of Aksenov's favorite themes and devices. His fascination with technology is a propos, since Krasin was simultaneously a Bolshevik and a respectable electrical engineer, and the title contains the central metaphor of the book, revolution as electricity. One review complained that Aksenov chose Krasin not for his historical significance but for artistic purposes, and that the fictional Viktor Gorizontov is given as much attention as Krasin. The novel's seriousness is in fact undercut by Gorizontov, a comic *bogatyr* dedicated to revolution, whose improbable adventures betray Aksenov's love of the fantastic, the incongruous and the absurd. In addition, the scraggly image of the bee-keeper, a symbol of the Little Man, recurs throughout the novel undermining its realism. The bee-keeper keeps appearing like Hitchcock from behind the newspapers of various European countries to ask the meaning of the world turmoil he's reading about, which makes one question the larger meaning of the events described. Aksenov very competently sustains a multi-centered narrative, challenging the reader to assemble a variety of subplots which ultimately merge into an impressionistic but comprehensive picture of the 1905 revolution. **"The Victory,"** *Bochkotara* and *Love of Electricity* indicate that Aksenov is now ready for work on a bigger scale and in greater depth.

Aksenov moved from being strictly realistic to focussing on unconscious reality, and most recently has used allegory and metaphor to destroy objective reality altogether. It's significant that this same line of development has been followed by others as well, notably by Andrei Bitov, whose recent story *The Wheel. Notes of a Novice* uses the extended metaphor more subtly.

Over the last ten years Soviet fiction has grown less preoccupied with narrowly local problems and become enriched partly through greater awareness of other literatures. Socialist Realism was a significant influence on the fiction of the early sixties, and it is important to appreciate that tradition for its value as social myth before attempting to understand the nature of the transition that Young Prose effected. The study of recent Soviet literature has been weakened by its lack of a theoretical basis. The assumption that Soviet and Western fictions fulfill the same functions in their respective societies has contributed to the trivialization of the texts. Young Prose has produced a literature that fulfills Western criteria better than did Socialist Realism, but the implications of that statement are complex and have not yet been explored.

The literature of the 1960s is immature, but it presents an excellent opportunity for studying problems of literary evolution. The period is short, and there is a small core of central authors, all of whom have grown up under Soviet rule. Most important, one can follow the tradition of Young Prose from its inception and ascertain with unusual precision what influences have been introduced. This closed system with its finite and easily traced inputs may prove too simple a test case to provide useful insights into instances where the interaction of literary traditions is more complex, but the literature of the 1960s cannot be understood without such an approach.

## John J. Johnson Jr. (essay date 1979)

SOURCE: "Introduction: The Life and Works of Aksyonov," in *The Steel Bird and Other Stories,* by Vassily Aksyonov, Ardis, 1979, pp. ix-xxvii.

[*In the following essay, Johnson discusses several of Aksyonov's novels and short stories and provides a comprehensive look at the author's career.*]

Vasily Pavlovich Aksenov was born on August 20, 1932 in Kazan. His mother, Eugenia Semenovna Ginzburg, was a history instructor at Kazan University who later became a well-known writer for her prison-camp memoir *Journey into the Whirlwind* (1962). His father, Pavel Vasilievich Aksenov,

was a leading member of the Tartar Regional Committee of the Party, a professional Party man and revolutionary.

Previous to the Stalinist incarceration of his parents in 1937 Aksenov lived in a happy home that in addition to his parents consisted of his older brother, Alyosha, who died in the blockade of Leningrad, an older sister, Mayka, presently a Russian language teacher at Moscow University, a nurse, Fima, and his paternal grandmother, who was glowingly described by Ginzburg in her memoirs. Although the memoirs mention young Vasily as a two-year-old, he was actually four years old when his mother was arrested in February 1937, and almost five when his father was arrested later that year. Eugenia Ginzburg spent two years in Yaroslavl, followed by sixteen years in the Far East region of the Kolyma River, first at Magadan, then Elgen (the Yakut word for "dead"), then back in Magadan, "farther from Moscow than California," Aksenov once said, with an average temperature of -4 degrees Centigrade. His father ended up on the Pechora River in Siberia, 10,000 kilometers from his wife.

In 1948, at the end of his eighth year in school (on a ten-year system), Aksenov joined his mother, who was by then out of the camp and living as an exile in Magadan. (His father had not yet been released.) In 1950, still in Magadan, he completed his elementary education. He then returned from the Far East to Leningrad where in 1956 he graduated as a doctor from the First Leningrad Medical Institute named after I. L. Pavlov.

From August 1956 until October 1957, Aksenov worked in the quarantine service of the Leningrad seaport and then in a hospital for water transportation workers located in the village of Voznesenye on Lake Onega, which is still in the Leningrad administrative district. In 1957 Aksenov met his future wife, Kira, in Leningrad, at a dance. He once recalled how he used to love to "rock to Bill Haley at university parties." Kira was from Moscow, and he followed her there after their marriage at the end of 1957.

From December 1957 until June 1958 he was a staff physician in the TB clinic located in the village of Grebneva in the Moscow area. Then until September 1960 he was a specialist in adolescent tuberculosis in a Moscow TB clinic. In July of 1959 *Youth* (*Yunost'*) magazine published two stories, **"Our Vera Ivanovna"** and **"Paved Roads,"** which announced him as a new and interesting writer. Then in June and July of 1960 his novel *The Colleagues* was presented in two issues of the same magazine. Controversy immediately pushed him into the foreground, and he left medicine to write full time. In the same year his only child, Alyosha, was born.

Much of Aksenov's early work is autobiographical or heavily drawn from a familiar environment. **"Our Vera Ivanovna"** is set in a hospital much like the one he knew in Voznesenye.

A government minister from Moscow finds himself hampered by a possible heart condition and a doctor who treats him as she would a regular patient. A flash flood forces him to help evacuate the hospital and then help look for the doctor, whom they so badly need. In admiration he now invites her to Moscow to have a plush job. Typical of Aksenov's early stories, the moral is meant to be obvious, and so she refuses because the people need her more.

**"Paved Roads"** is much more significant because it is an early example of the "youth story" genre on which Aksenov's controversial name was built. As a twenty-six-year-old writer he felt close ties to the young and to their highly colloquial speech. He chose to portray the generation that he saw and heard as they really were, not as the political theoreticians had hoped they would be. In this story twenty-five-year-old Gleb Pomorin returns from the army and tries to make a smooth transition back into civilian society. He runs into an old friend, Gerka, who seems to be living quite well: smoking foreign cigarettes and driving his own car. Slowly the new immorality of his old friend unwinds. "Work! That's a laugh! People go to work, save their money, dream of the future, but I want it all now: a dacha, a car, a good suit, women. That's happiness!" Further revelations show that Gerka is a *fartsovshchik* (black market operator), and because of his relative wealth he has managed to coax Gleb's former girl-friend into a living arrangement with him. At the end, as Gerka runs from formerly fleeced road-pavers, the morally indignant Gleb notes: "He won't get far: the earth will burn under his feet. Our roads aren't for the likes of him." Clearly, here and in later works the moral message of Aksenov is to show that all young people are not alike, that they cannot be condemned as a generation. Yet his insistence on revealing the problem side of the young generation bore a mixed blessing—popularity with some, infamy with others. While the first group was large and representative of the reading public as a whole, the latter group was in power.

Aksenov's attitude toward young people is more thoroughly developed in *The Colleagues*. Here three young people, recent graduates of medical school, Maximov, Karpov and Zelenin, are faced with their mandatory postgraduate assignments. Maximov and Karpov accept work as shipboard doctors because of the promised travel and excitement. Zelenin opts for more dedicated work in a village.

One scene in the novel highlights Aksenov's main argument in this period. The three young men, out for a walk, encounter an invalid from the war who sizes them up by their clothing and hair-length and then proceeds to verbally abuse them as "hippies." The argument against the older generation's prejudice is immediately evident by the fact that these are doctors about to serve society in positions of responsibility. In their work they cross all kinds of realities, mostly unheard of in Soviet literature but well-known in real life.

Karpov's girl friend marries a local laboratory researcher to avoid an unattractive post-graduate work assignment. The ship doctors find bribery and corruption in the port service. Zelenin finds alcoholism, violence and inhuman living conditions in his remote village location. But morality wins again, i.e., the girl is forever miserable, the doctors expose the corruption and Zelenin joins the dedicated local authorities in building a new order.

The controversy that sprung up following this novel posed questions far beyond the scope of the book or the writings of Aksenov as a whole. Writers and critics paired off into camps either attacking or approving of the new presentation of reality, of the new image of youth which was referred to as the "youth-theme" genre.

Because of the success of *The Colleagues* Aksenov left medicine at the end of 1960 and dedicated his life to writing. In an article which might be interpreted as an announcement of his intentions, he attacks the anti-youth attitude of the critics and the older generation as a whole. "We're talking about people who don't believe in youth, who consider them a generation of 'hippies' and pretty bourgeois. Not to believe in youth is to not believe in our future." His intention was to write about youth as he saw them, as he felt they really were. While his intention seems to have been logical and worthy of pursuit, it clashed in principle with the make-believe world of socialist realism and inflexible Soviet rhetoric.

The problems of youth and their solutions are even more sharply drawn in Aksenov's most famous work *A Ticket to the Stars* (1961). "The heroes of this work seek answers to the questions: how should I live and for what purpose? They do not want ready answers, relieving them of their responsibilities. They seek their own solutions." Aksenov, in fact, has caught the most characteristic psychological feature of young people in those years—striving for their own, personal answer in their relationship to life. The key difference in *A Ticket to the Stars* is that he delivers his message from the view-point of seventeen-year-old high school students just when they are graduating and learning to cope with the world. When the older generation attacks them they can not yet claim to be doctors and responsible citizens. Where Aksenov showed the attacks in *The Colleagues* to be purely an *argumentum ad hominem* and not logically directed to the philosophical beliefs of the young, he now strips his heroes of that defense. The basic story is that upon graduation four young people decide not to go on with school right away, nor to go off to work, but instead to head for the Baltic Sea beaches and enjoy life. When their money runs out they take jobs in a fishing collective, and in the end they are better people for it. However, this moral improvement did not prevent violent attacks on the novel by critics who were fearful of the example of freedom of action that it set for young people.

During 1961 a stage version of *The Colleagues* was produced in numerous theaters throughout the Soviet Union. In August 1962 it was performed by Moscow's Maly Theater Company at an international festival in the Paris Theater of Nations. 1962 was a year of travel not only for Aksenov's works but for Aksenov himself. The mandatory first trip to socialist nations sent him to Poland; he then joined a delegation to Japan and relaxed in India on his return home. Meanwhile his first movie *My Younger Brother* (1962) based on *A Ticket to the Stars* was finally on the screens at home, having been held up nearly a year for ideological reasons.

> **In 1962 Aksenov was already thirty years old and an internationally known writer for two years. Naturally he found it difficult to continue to identify with teenagers and young street types, and as his circle of friends and life-style changed, so did his stories.**
>
> —*John J. Johnson Jr.*

Following his success with longer works Aksenov composed a number of short stories most of which were published for the first time much later in collections. **"The Ejection Seat"** (1961) shows certain narrow-minded types, here military airmen, who have little respect for other people until they establish a strange and artificial liaison (a "granfalloon" in [Kurt] Vonnegut's terminology) that bonds them together—here the bond is having been catapulted from an ejection seat. **"Changing a Way of Life"** (1961), which is translated here, is about a hard working businessman who takes some time off at the beach for a change in his life-style. The real change comes when he reevaluates his relationship with his girl friend and the reader is left to believe that he may finally marry her. "The Lunches of '43" (1962), also found here, may be thought of as one of Aksenov's early experimental works. The story takes place on a train with the hero certain that he has recognized a traveling companion as a friend from his childhood. Through the use of erratic time changes and flashbacks he tells the full story of their relationship, concentrating on the school lunches that he was forced by the bully to hand over in 1943.

The experimental nature of the time sequence in **"The Lunches of '43"** was new to Aksenov but used not long before by Valentin Kataev, one of Aksenov's early mentors. Kataev was editor of *Youth* magazine in the period that Aksenov began to submit manuscripts and is known to have reworked the entire first part of *The Colleagues*. What is especially interesting in **"The Lunches of '43"** is the psychological portrayal of the hero. Aksenov seems to portray

this character in a very personal and internal world somewhat reminiscent of [Fyodor] Dostoevsky's humiliated men. For political reasons the hero is not as humiliated nor as pessimistic as with Dostoevsky's heroes, but the literary connection, if not the intention, is there.

In 1962 Aksenov was already thirty years old and an internationally known writer for two years. Naturally he found it difficult to continue to identify with teenagers and young street types, and as his circle of friends and life-style changed, so did his stories.

Highly representative of this maturing yet still young hero is thirty-two year old Sergei, the chief character of the significantly successful short story **"Papa, What Does it Spell?"** (1962). Sergei is a former soccer player who never made it to the big leagues as he dreamed and now feels the emptiness of his present life. We slowly learn that the things which he holds in esteem—his work, his sports, his family and his friends—are all eroding in value under the banality of everyday life.

Sergei's wife, Alla, must attend a conference at her institute, so he must watch Olga, his daughter, on a day when he had planned to meet his friends and take in a soccer game. What appears to be a mild conflict at the outset soon develops into a serious disruption of his various relationships: his friends see him for the first time as a family man; Olga has no interest in going to the game and insists upon going to a park instead; his daughter, surprisingly seems to know one of his friends very well, explained by frequent, hitherto unknown, meetings with Alla, meetings which imply an adulterous relationship. A phone call to the institute reveals that there is no conference that day and Alla is nowhere to be found.

Sergei is therefore forced to review his life and relationships, portrayed with obvious sympathy from the author. Almost instant maturity is accompanied by a growing concern and feeling of responsibility for his daughter.

> "... he thought about how his daughter would grow up, how she would be eight, fourteen and then sixteen, seventeen, twenty ... how she would go away to pioneer camp and come back, how he would teach her to swim, what a fashionable little lady she would become and how she would neck in the stairway with some hippie or other, how they would sometime or other go off somewhere, maybe to the sea."

Aksenov ends the story on this thought, a bond of unity with his daughter against all else in the world.

**"Half-way to the Moon"** (1962) is probably Aksenov's most internationally known short work. He was inspired in this effort by a real-life character who got on an airplane with him in Khabarovsk. When this worker, straight from the taiga, took off his outer coat, the stewardess offered to take it from him and hang it up. "He was so stunned by this" Aksenov later explained in an interview "that he gasped dumbfoundedly: 'Do you believe that? She took my coat for me! . . . '." The effect of this kindness on the worker can apparently be compared to the effect of art or music on the savage beast. The story derived from this event is described by one critic as a "variation on the theory of moral self-perfection." What this critic describes is a "Jack London device: 'a wild' worker meets a heavenly creature—a girl of 'the highest order' . . . and his soul, dedicated to beauty, finally sees the light!"

The story which is included in this collection received much praise for its aspects of contemporaneousness: it is a jet-age search for love covering half the distance to the moon. However, if moral awakening is accomplished then the import of the story should be seen instead in the internal distance traveled by the hero. Clearly a new emphasis and a more mature hero were evident in Aksenov's work by 1962.

In general 1962 had been a year of literary hope and advancement. [Aleksandr] Solzhenitsyn had been published by order of Khrushchev. In November Aksenov was made an editor of *Youth* along with Evtushenko and Rozov. "The hopes of 1962 were perhaps best expressed by the poet Alexander Tvardovsky: 'In art and literature, as in love, one can lie only for a while; sooner or later comes the time to tell the truth.'" But in this hope and openness, in this very push for the truth were to be found the roots of the oncoming reaction. "The mood of the artistic and literary intelligentsia in 1962 can perhaps best be gauged from [Leonid] Ilichev's complaint that 'in certain intellectual milieux it is considered unseemly and unfashionable to defend correct Party positions.'" The mood of the neo-Stalinists, then, was to put an end to the literary liberalism.

In December Khrushchev drew the attention of the world by attacking an art exhibit at the Manael Riding Stables. His personal attack on Boris Birger, Ernst Neizvestny and others was thought to be a warning to the proponents of the new creativity in all arts. The attack, however specific and personal in form, was indeed a declaration of war by the old-school realists (i.e., socialist idealists) on the representatives of alternative art forms (i.e., emancipatory realists, modernists, abstractionists, etc.).

But by 1962 Aksenov was not writing the offending "youth stories," at least not exclusively. He no longer felt close to younger people. He felt that a generation change had taken place and that the characteristics of his early heroes, so heatedly denied by official party critics, were no longer to be found in young people. His new novel of January 1963, *Oranges from Morocco,* which had been released at the begin-

ning of the attack, was instead about workers in the Far East. Aksenov explained that as a writer he did not feel himself limited to youth problems. However, not everyone was pleased with the descriptions of these workers in *Oranges*.

The story is simply an event and various people's reactions to that event. The event is the arrival of a ship loaded with oranges from Morocco. The reactions are not complimentary, however honest they might be. An American reader could be easily confused by what truly seems to be an exaggerated portrayal. Life practically stops for hundreds of miles around while all available personnel and means of transportation are directed toward the port. The fallacy here is in comparing two remotely different cultures, for although an orange brings very little attention in America and is available throughout the year, everywhere, the same humble orange was then rarely seen in the Soviet Union in winter except in large cities and in the southern climates. At the time that the story was written oranges commonly sold on the black market for more than a dollar apiece. It is then consistent with known realities about the supply system and the attitude of Soviet citizens toward the arrival of such goods to assume that the apparent exaggeration is, in fact, responsibly close to the mark.

Perhaps because of this disparity in cultural reactions to oranges the novel has never been well received abroad. Its scope compared to the "youth themes" may be justly considered excessively provincial. Regardless of Aksenov's movement away from the polemical stories which instigated the attack on his ideological correctness, the unfriendly description of greedy and coarse workers riding their tractors into town for oranges and not off into a socialist sunset led to further attacks.

The journals in February and March were filled with attacks on the "young" writers, Aksenov often being singled out, like Socrates, as an example of a corrupter of youth. On March 8, 1963, a meeting of intellectuals was called in the Kremlin. Khrushchev and Ilichev elaborated the correct party position and called for renouncements of former ideological errors. The first to do so were Simonov and Shostakovich. They were soon followed by Neizvestny, Rozhdestvensky, Voznesensky and others. Another meeting was called by the Writers' Union to escalate the attack. A writer named Vladimir Firsev delivered the following message:

> What compliments were not showered upon Evtushenko, Akhmadulina, Aksenov! . . . But have we re-educated comrades Aksenov, Evtushenko, Voznesensky by continuously letting them go on foreign trips, by putting them on editorial boards, and by publishing their works in enormous editions? It is they who have been 'educating' readers during that time, and often they have educated them in such

a way that it will take us a lot of work to liquidate the consequences of their educational efforts.

The threat of this official speech, then, was clear—they were subject to losing their travel abroad, their positions on journals and their normal publication rights. Evtushenko recanted on March 29. Aksenov who had been conveniently out of town during the writers' meeting returned and, like Galileo, recanted.

April 3, 1963, in *Pravda,* he said that under the threat of imperialism Soviet writers must recognize their responsibility. They must be prepared to answer for every line which could be misinterpreted in the West. "I, like any writer," he added "am trying to create my own, unique, positive hero who would be at the same time a true son of his times—a man with strong bones and a normal circulatory system, a decent, open soul, with a concept in mind concentrating into one thought all the magnitude, optimism and complexity of our communist era."

His promise here to create a positive hero "of his times" in a normal human being was in a sense, a reworked description of his heroes as they might be described in communist propaganda. By this interpretation one could suggest that he actually meant real-life people who live in this contemporary world with all its problems and who reflect not the weak official optimism which he always rejected by the "complexity of our communist era" which is what he always wrote about.

As Thomas Whitney has pointed out [in *The New Writing in Russia,* University of Michigan Press, 1964], world influence and opinion had an effect on the events of 1963 in the Soviet Union. China had played up the ideological controversy that year and the Stalinists found themselves in a more important battle than controlling the "young writers." The western communists had, moreover, taken a stand against the new literary policies outlined above. Even Soviet bloc nations such as Poland had reacted critically to the literary repression. The result was a letup in the clampdown of early 1963.

1963 also saw the release of a film, **When the Bridges Go Up,** written by Aksenov in 1962 and identified in the press as "based on the short story" although no such story ever existed. The same year his earlier film **The Colleagues** was shown at Mar-del-Plata, Argentina at a film festival which he also attended as a member of the delegation.

A travel article, **"Japanese Jottings"** (1963), which is translated in this book, was written in a form that seems to repeat itself often whenever Aksenov wishes to relate his various impressions of a foreign land. It is an enigmatic rendering of witty statements and allusions intended to give an overall

view by its juxtaposed dashes of color. On canvas it would be called impressionism. Amazingly its experimental form has never drawn criticism from the old-school Socialist realists.

Previously, form took less of a role in Aksenov's work than content. "I think about form" he said once, "when I'm not writing. When I write, I don't think about it." However, progress in literature for Aksenov often meant the ability to go off in any and all directions. As the force of his "youth themes" genre was slowed by time and by criticism, he began more and more to experiment in form.

In 1964 a novel written by Aksenov in 1963 was serialized in the journal, *The Young Guard.* **It's Time, My Friend, It's Time** (1964) was an attempt to supply the positive hero which he had promised in his recantation. This positive hero is Valya Marvich, a driver attached to a movie crew which is shooting a film in Estonia. In the manner of Aksenov's earlier "youth stories," and this may be chronologically the last example of that genre, Marvich questions his life and the direction it is going. Since Marvich is no longer young, this mature hero is given an appropriate adult complication to his search—he is additionally confused about the renewal of feelings from his former marriage. Another new feature found here that becomes typical for the mature hero in Aksenov is that he is always a loner: always aloof, an individual in the collective. The strength of the novel lies in Marvich's internal psychological conflict between his ideals and his failure to realize them within his circle of friends and loved ones. Marvich is a very real, atypical for Soviet literature, positive hero, who searches for truth and his ideals in a real world filled with negative activities and people. The credibility of both the positive hero and of the author is maintained.

From 1964 to 1966 Aksenov wrote a number of short stories that were to appear in collections of 1966 and 1969 as well as in literary journals individually. These stories are significant in so far as they reveal both a new interest and a new emphasis in his creations, completing the break with "youth themes" begun in 1962. His works of this period involve the growing importance for Aksenov of fantasy and imagination. They emphasize exaggeration and irony in style, deviance and ill-adjustment in characterization.

One of the best of these stories and a good example of his new style and characterization is **"The Odd-Ball"** (1964). Far from a "youth" story, it is about two old men, one of whom, Zbaikov, is an old bolshevik revolutionary and victim of Stalinism, as was Aksenov's own father. The other, the "odd-ball" from Zbaikov's childhood, has never left his village except to shop in a neighboring village. As the old friends meet and talk, the reader is struck by the tremendous differences in the fates of these two men. "Odd-ball" complains that they would not take him in the Red Army and was even passed up in the Stalinist excesses of the 1930s. "'Ye-ah' drawled Odd-ball, 'I didn't even get to go to prison.'" There is a tacit agreement that Zbaikov, even with his horrible experiences of war and prison, has lived a better life than a man whose life has apparently been no better than a farm animal's.

Then in the closing pages the irony sets in. "Odd-ball" ends up to be an engineering genius who has built himself a radio by means of which he is in constant touch with cities from London to Honolulu. He then decides to show his old friend his secret machine. His machine is a *perpetuum mobile* which has been running for many, many years. "'What is it then, a perpetual motion machine, or what?' 'Seems to be,' he whispered. 'Seems to be.'"

Another classic example of the deviant in Aksenov's works is Uncle Mitya from **"Comrade Smart-hat"** (1964). Uncle Mitya is a taxi driver and perhaps more basically a capitalist "hustler" in a communist society. In this story his illegal activities are in jeopardy because of police surveillance in general and because of the special attention of officer Ivan Yermakov, whom he calls "Comrade Smart-hat." Uncle Mitya plots to encourage Yermakov's interest in his daughter assuming that once they are married he will have *carte blanche* in his business. However, the irony is that after the marriage the local police redouble their efforts to keep Uncle Mitya, their new relative, in line.

In this same period a "youth" story of sorts does crop up, but with some interesting experimentation. **"Local Trouble-maker Abramashvili"** (1964) is the story of a life-guard at the Gagra beach area in Soviet Georgia. The impression presented at first corresponds to the Soviet stereotype for such a situation. The reader is prepared to learn how the local "hot-blooded" native boys seduce the "fair-skinned" Russian girls on vacation. Ironically, it is eighteen year old Gogi Abramashvili, who is seduced by the northern Alina in her hotel room. "'Well, you've had a pretty good day' she said tenderly, 'your first cigarette, your first woman'." Gogi falls in love.

The following night he tries to talk to her at a dance and learns that her husband, who Gogi did not know existed, has unexpectedly arrived, as a result of which she does not want anything more to do with him. Gogi reacts angrily and is led out by the *druzhinniki,* the voluntary, civilian patrol. Several days later the town bulletin board, maintained by the *druzhinniki,* bears a picture of Gogi and the message that girls are forbidden to dance with the "local troublemaker Abramashvili."

What is unusually experimental in this story is not at first clear to the western reader. Sex in the West is a normal part of literature even to the point where critics refer to the "man-

datory sex scenes" of a best seller. On the other hand sex is at best considered underground literature in both the Russian tradition and the Soviet present. While there are no sexually explicit scenes in the story, there are numerous implications and references to the contemporary sexual norms of Soviet youth. Soviet sociologists are only now, fifteen years later, dealing with the reality described in circumlocution by Aksenov in this story.

A basis in autobiographical fact which was found in Aksenov's earlier works is also found in **"Little Whale, Varnisher of Reality"** (1964). "Little Whale" is in fact Aksenov's son, Alyosha whom he actually nicknamed "Whale" and who was born in 1960 making him the same age as the young hero of the story. The story which is included here is, in essence, a study of what is reality and what is imagination—a subject that Aksenov was to explore in many of his future works. Stories from this period that are also included in this volume are, **"It's a Pity You Weren't With Us," "The Victory"** and **"Ginger From Next Door." "It's a Pity You Weren't With Us,"** a short story written in 1964 is also the name of a collection of stories published in 1969. The story is an unusual, thought-provoking assessment of the lives of some very unusual people. **"The Victory"** (1965) is one of Aksenov's most successful stories. Outwardly it is the story of a grand master at chess playing a game on a train with a chance passenger. The ironic ending is one of the best in Aksenov's works.

**"Ginger From Next Door"** (1966) is, like **"The Lunches of '43,"** a chronologically disconnected remembrance of childhood. This time it is more clearly Aksenov's own remembrance, as he refers to his one-time home in the former residence of industrial engineer Zherebtsov, in Kazan. The chief difference is that his fantasies change in this period from mental exercises to actual occurrences, in a fictional form, of course. Aksenov, by this period, already refused to make a clear distinction between "acceptable" descriptive fiction and his creative fantasies in prose. At a much later time he clarified his stance, somewhat:

> The imagination of an artist is, after all, also reality. Fantasy is perhaps no less real than the rustle of leaves . . . I sometimes think that real events which surround us, such as sunsets, river currents, stones, birds and sand are not any less mysterious than fantasy is . . . The artist only gives a name to the yet unknown, he penetrates into another dimension and gives a name to previously unseen bodies, gives them form, color and sound. He substitutes them for life in the opinion of some people. I suggest that subjects of art do not substitute for life but that they become new states within it, that is, they refurbish life and expand its horizons.

Therefore there are no clear lines as to where the reality of the traditional, practical sort blends into the emancipatory reality of the Aksenov philosophic idealism.

Another story that returns to his life in the former residence of industrial engineer Zherebtsov, in Kazan, is **"On the Square and Beyond the River"** (1966). On the surface it is a memory of the last day of World War II. But then there is the addition of a Gogolian or Hoffmannesque fantasy tale which is given at an ambiguous moment that allows it to be interpreted as a dream, or as one critic called it, a nightmare. When the message comes over the radio declaring victory over Hitler's Germany, the square becomes filled with jubilant people including a circus troop, which because it is real yet somehow imaginary, sets up the dream sequence which is imaginary yet somehow real. The dream sequence begins with the appearance of an unknown man seeking refuge. The young hero senses an evil creature and begins a chase onto the square and beyond the river. The creature flies off making sounds like a metallic bird and plunges into a lake. It is the symbolic death of Hitler.

Strange symbolic birds making metallic sounds were not new to Aksenov. In 1965 Aksenov had already written one of his most successful fantasy tales with these same characteristics, called **The Steel Bird** (1965). For over a decade he attempted to get the text published in the Soviet Union, but to no avail. A short excerpt called **"The House on Lamplight Alley"** (1966) was published in *The Literary Gazette* but since it only concerned one of the minor characters of the story, it was irrelevant to the main plot. The Russian text was published by Ardis last year in the inaugural issue of a new Russian-language literary almanac and the first English translation is available in this volume.

Anatoli Gladilin, a close friend of Aksenov and a writer who is mentioned in passing in the text of **The Steel Bird,** has written in the Western press about the first reading of the short novel. In those days a group of short story writers would meet regularly in the Central Club of the Writers' Union in Moscow to preview and critique the members' newest works. The reading of **The Steel Bird** attracted a "standing room only" audience and instead of reading only the thirty or forty pages scheduled, Aksenov was encouraged to read the entire work of over a hundred pages which required several hours and set a new time record for such readings. "Everyone was absolutely certain," wrote Gladilin, "that the story would, naturally, be published, the disagreements arose only concerning the literary journal: where to send it—to *New World (Novyi mir)* or to *Youth?*" However neither journal, nor any Soviet journal for that matter, dared to take that step.

The editors felt, perhaps justifiably, that the allegory was dangerous, that the satire on Soviet society was too clear. Aksenov felt that the satire was not on any specific society but on mankind as a whole and more specifically on the nature of man in a totalitarian society. He challenged the decision against printing the work on the grounds that to see Soviet society implied was to take the position that Soviet society was totalitarian and oppressive. Aksenov and Gladilin both have expressed the attitude that the work should be considered "pro-Soviet," that it points out the pitfalls of the improper path to communism, the cult of personality, and is not critical of a properly run Soviet government. The editors apparently saw something in their society that Aksenov hoped was not there and in rejecting the work gave support to that impropriety by refusing to expose it.

The story itself was inspired by poetic lines which are repeated in the book as the theme of a cornet-a-pistons: "reason gave us steel wing-like arms / and instead of a heart, a flaming motor." The name, *The Steel Bird,* came later from the text of a 1930s aviation song that included the following stanza (in my translation):

> There, where the infantry can not pass
> Where there are no rushing armored-trains
> No heavy tank crawls through the grass
> That is where the steel bird reigns.

The book opens in Moscow in Lamplight Alley in the spring of 1948 with the appearance of the ultimate of Aksenov's deviants, Veniamin Fedoseevich Popenkov. Popenkov is bearing two sacks from which something dark continues to drip. Because he understands the metallic language of the cornet-a-pistons which the housing manager plays, he is able to convince the manager to let him move into the elevator of the house at number 14 Lamplight Alley. At first he only occupies the elevator after all the residents are in bed, hiding in dark corners during the daytime. Significantly, all the residents get used to his presence and they begin to accept him. As the book progresses, there are constantly hints that he can fly, that he is not really human, that he speaks a strange metallic language and that he is changing from a weak "street rat" to a strong commanding "man of steel." One night Popenkov goes into convulsions in the elevator. As he is nursed back to health, the residents vote to shut down the elevator for his comfort. Gradually he takes over the entrance way and the staircase is blocked off. The residents accept this and get used to using the emergency stairwell to the rear. Popenkov gains more and more power until he has a number of the residents working for him, making counterfeit French tapestries. The wife of a Vice Minister who lived at number 14 leaves her husband for Popenkov and brings her apartment full of antiques to his vestibule residence. By this point his power becomes seemingly immense.

The doctors now decide that he is not a human, not exactly an airplane, nor a bird but a combination: a steel bird. Then in 1953, when Stalin dies, Popenkov somehow is among the close, privileged mourners. However his private plans for the house at number 14 Lamplight Alley are to get everyone involved in work, to forget their sadness by labor. His new wife does not approve of his using Tsvetkova, her former husband's mistress, for such productive work.

"Ha-ha-ha, you need Tsvetkova do you?" patronized Popenkov with laughter. "Take her, baby."

"Thank you," mysteriously smiled Zinochka.

"What do you want to do with her? Fuchi elazi kompfor trandiratziyu?" asked Popenkov.

"Fuchi emazi kir madagor" said Zinochka.

"Kekl fedekl?" laughed Popenkov.

"Chlok buritano," giggled Zinochka.

"Kukubu!" exclaimed Popenkov.

His wife who now spoke his language learned that there were steel birds all over the world but that he was the head of all of them. In the night he flies off to digest the metal statues of the world, from the Bronze Horseman to Abraham Lincoln. He is symbolically now in control of history: "There will not be a past, there will not be a future and I've already eaten the present," he announces. The weight of his body increases (caused by his midnight snacking) and the house at number 14 begins to tilt. When the walls begin to crack, the residents finally revolt, eventually conquering the steel bird. At this point the housing manager returns like the cavalry on a white steed to announce that the residents have been given a new apartment building. It should be noted that it is not the infantry, nor an armored-train, nor a heavy tank that penetrates the realm of the steel bird but a horseman. The new building that he promises will be almost entirely glass and plastic, with light-blue bathtubs, garbage disposals, swimming pools for everyone. So the residents leave. A few moments later the house at number 14 collapses, leaving only the elevator shaft upon which sits the steel bird. Months later he alights from his perch and flies over Moscow. Behind him stretch two dark trails, like the earlier droppings from his sacks, which are then scattered in the wind.

Clearly Aksenov means to say that human beings must avoid accepting and getting used to their oppression. He clearly is saying that such criticism is not only of Soviet society but of all totalitarian societies. There are steel birds everywhere, perhaps the image of Hitler in **"On the Square and Beyond the River"** is one of them. For the present time it seems that the Soviet one is the chief one. Popenkov is not Stalin, as some would guess, but in the tradition of Stalin. Popenkov mourns the death of Stalin but goes on to oppress his people

and to establish his own cult of personality. Technology has helped him to bolt down the fates of men. Stalin once called the true Soviet man a screw in the machine of society. Man's emotions and his spiritual side have in this way, and by this type, been neglected, while reason and technology have turned his arms into steel wings, his heart into a flaming motor. He has judged his progress by trips to the moon and steel birds in the sky, leaving human beings to be dominated by computers and mechanical men. A computer language is, perhaps, no more intelligible to the soul than the ravings of the steel bird. Aksenov has every right to be disgusted that such a work can not be printed in all countries, for it is written for the sake of all human beings in all political systems.

> **Clearly Aksenov means to say [in *The Steel Bird*] that human beings must avoid accepting and getting used to their oppression. He clearly is saying that such criticism is not only of Soviet society but of all totalitarian societies.**
>
> —*John J. Johnson Jr.*

Ironically one of the several things that Aksenov had published in those years included **"The Dotted Line of Progress"** (1966) which is a short statement praising the progress of man when the Soviet apparatus *lunakhod* was landed on the moon.

Less ironically and more tragically Aksenov was among the protesters arrested in 1966 on Red Square. The group had been against the unveiling of a bust of Stalin which now marks his grave-site behind Lenin's mausoleum. Many of those who suffered needlessly due to the cult of personality, as Aksenov's family did, felt that the raising of any monument to Stalin was a symbolic gesture, beginning an attitude of acceptance of his crimes.

There were also some good events in those years such as the release of *The Journey* (1966), a film based on three short stories by Aksenov: **"Papa, What Does It Spell?,"** **"The Lunches of '43"** and **"Half-way to the Moon."** He also traveled a great deal: Rome, to a writers' conference, and Yugoslavia in 1965; Japan, Austria, Switzerland and Munich in 1966; Bulgaria and London in 1967. This last trip would prove to be his last chance to travel to the West for eight years. Another good event was the award of first prize in a literary contest sponsored by *Trud* newspaper. The story that won was called **"The Light-blue Sea Cannons"** (1967). It is a story told from the point of view of a young boy concerning his uncle's ironical service during World War II.

In the same period as these stories Aksenov wrote three plays which he labeled as "satirical fantasies." Although they remain unpublished one of them, *Always For Sale* (1965), ran for a long time at the Contemporary Theater in Moscow. The play was very controversial and has been called a number of things from "Philistine fantasy" to "the study of Man." Speaking of this play, a critic said: "The question of his 'grown-up' generation has become for Aksenov the question of *man*. His heroes now live not only in a defined slice of history but in the history of mankind as a whole."

One light, humorous story of this period concerned one of Aksenov's sporting passions: boxing. **"A Poem of Ecstasy"** (1968) tells the story of a young boxer who becomes convinced by the example of Muhammad Ali's poetry that the fine arts, especially music and poetry, are the key to modern boxing success. In the amateur championships he is victorious thanks to his construction in the ring of a "symphonic poem of ecstasy."

A much longer story, **"The Overloaded Packing-barrels"** (1968) is, according to the subtitle, a "tale with exaggerations and dreams." In many respects it is the logical culmination of Aksenov's fantasy stories. It is an example of the Russian literary tradition of viewing the normal in a fresh, new, but inevitably strange way (*ostranenie*). Consistent with this appraisal the tale has been compared to the work of Bulgakov, Olesha and Gogol. The unconventionality of his point of view caused much misunderstanding, confusion and even anger.

The external plot of the story begins with the need to move a load of barrels from the village general store to the regional center. Various people who do not know each other, yet need to go to the regional center, end up on the truck as fellow passengers. There is a scholar from Moscow who is the world's foremost expert on the country of Haligaliya (cf. Eng. Hully-gully, a dance which in Russian is called hali-gali) to which he is unable to get a visa. The old timer, Mochenkin, specializes in complaints, recommendations, requests and other official forms. The teacher, Irina Valentinovna, who is going on vacation, is a beautiful young lady with no admirers except a fourteen-year-old schoolboy. The sailor, Gleb, is returning to his Black Sea assignment. The driver is Vladimir Teleskopov who is the boy-friend of Sima the woman in charge of the barrels. Sima does not travel with them but continues, nevertheless, to be a character throughout the tale. Along the way other people are added and subtracted from their group.

As these people travel with the packing-barrels, several unusual things happen. The sailor and the teacher become romantically involved. All of them, even the driver, fall asleep and their dreams are presented. At first they are all individual dreams, unified only by the appearance for each of them of the "Good Man" approaching in the morning dew. The sleep of the driver ends in a minor accident which is followed by an airplane crash caused somehow, it is implied, by the eyes of the teacher in her new powerful role of blossoming woman. They arrive in a village to learn that they are not on course and spend the first night there. The scholar learns that Teleskopov, the driver, has been by accident to Haligaliya and they are united by a love for the same girl who lives in this distant fairy-tale land. In the second round of dreams the new-found friends become characters in each other's dreams. Among the several days they spend completing this short trip, one is spent in a town where Teleskopov is thrown in jail by a former suitor of Sima's. His sentence is reduced to a fine for the sake of the packing-barrels. The fine is then cancelled by a kiss from Irina Valentinovna. The most important development is that they all become bonded together by mutual love and respect for the barrels. When the depot refuses the barrels for being overloaded, they all reboard the truck and drive off together. In the final, mutual dream, the barrels float off to sea, singing gaily on their endless journey. Somewhere on an island, the "Good Man" waits for them, forever.

What all this means is a subjective decision similar to the interpretation of a symbolic poem. There are some factual observations that deserve note, however. The "Good Man" represents an ideal, a noble goal for each and every one of them. But just as people in general use indefinable abstract words to communicate concepts such as "God," "freedom" and "truth," these people use the "Good Man" as a variable concept: for each one of them the goal is as individual and different as they are one from the other. They all are dreamers, a fact which extends their "truths" to emotional and spiritual concepts beyond the realm of the material and the physically possible. Aksenov's concept of reality, as has been shown above, is liberating and stretches beyond the borders of Soviet reality and of all human reality in free-flying thought waves. Lastly, the barrels begin in a normal, though overloaded, form and become first metaphorically humanized, then literally on their own, loved and respected by the people around them. "We," one of the characters says, speaking for the group, "are simply people of different views and different professions, voluntarily united on the basis of love and respect for our packing-barrels."

Perhaps, in speculation, these people are then symbolic of the people of the world and the barrels are the "teeming" overloaded populations of humanity as a whole. Humanity to the individual is sometimes animate, sometimes remote and seemingly inanimate. The more people strive for the ideal, the "Good Man" as each individual interprets him, the more love and respect each has for humanity, whether that humanity in its overloaded, overpopulated mass is acceptable to others or not. The planet Earth bearing humanity, like an uncontrollable truck, goes on its way wherever it wants to, whenever it wants. "I don't know when we'll see each other again," Teleskopov writes to Sima, "because we are going where our dear packing-barrels want to, not where we want to. Do you understand?" (p. 58) Its goal in its random course is not always in conjunction with the ideal, and so people must unite and help each other bring it there. If this is impossible, then they, with the wisdom of the philosophies of the East, must accept their fate and ride along.

Also in speculation note that there are corrupt officials in this story who use their power to jail the innocent (Teleskopov). However the corrupt are here eventually softened by *philos,* love for humanity (the barrels) and set straight by *eros,* love for an individual (Irina Valentinovna). Note also that the pilot who spreads manure on the earth (a propagandist of any political view) is brought down by *eros* and *philos* together. In his dream sequence there is a hint that even *agape,* love for God (the angel), may be involved as well. Remember he never rides with the people (he is towed behind in his plane) and so he is never more than remotely connected with the people and with humanity. In time, without having learned from humanity, he returns to the skies to fertilize the earth with his manure.

Another excellent story and one of Aksenov's favorites is **"The Rendezvous"** (1969) published in 1971. It is the story of a most popular and talented individual: a poet, hockey star, mathematician, a Soviet Renaissance man and jet-setter. Feeling unloved, he goes off on a mysterious rendezvous that puts an end to his search but only at the price of his life.

During the next several years Aksenov experimented with various types of prose. He also wrote a number of humorous feuilletons for *The Literary Gazette* which included several stories about a character called Memozov. Memozov is a playful character device Aksenov likes to refer to as his antiauthor.

One type of genre which he tried was the "chronicle novel" which was a popular form of writing in the early 1970s. For a series on famous revolutionaries he was asked to provide a book on Leonid Krasin, an electrical engineer and bolshevik revolutionary. The novel, *Love For Electricity* (1971), uses actual documents from the period intertwined with fictional embellishment. Even though it is basically about the tragedy of the revolution for the intellectuals who started it, that fact is generally misunderstood and so it is currently on the list of recommended books for school children.

A less serious experiment was an adventure novel, *Gene Green-The Untouchable,* which he participated in with two other authors. The book is the story of CIA agent No. 014 (twice what 007 was!). The pseudonym given as author, Grivady Gorpozhaks, actually represents a combination of

the names of the three authors together who are identified only as translators of individual chapters. Of the thirty-two chapters, Aksenov wrote eight and collaborated on another four.

Another type of prose which he attempted is the children's book. *My Granddad the Monument* (1972) and its continuation, *The Box in Which Something Rattles* (1976), are highly adventurous tales based around the Leningrad Pioneer (like a Boy Scout) Gennady Stratofontov.

In 1975 Aksenov came to America as a Regent Lecturer for the University of California. After a long series of lectures at UCLA he made a short lecture tour to Stanford and Berkeley, and then visited the University of Michigan and Indiana University on his return to New York City. On his way back to Moscow he also spent time in London, Venice and Milano. From this prolonged stay abroad came the shorter works **"The Asphalt Orangery"** (1976) and **"About That Similarity"** (1977) and a long work about his impressions of America called *'Round the Clock Non-Stop* (1976). This last work which includes the anti-author Memozov is an important work in that it sums up and explains many of his previous writings.

Meanwhile in 1976 one of his older stories was dug from the files and printed. **"Swanny Lake"** (1968) is an autobiographical piece with little "Whale" and his father joining "Whale's" grandfather, obviously based on Aksenov's real-life father, for a day at the lake. The internal thoughts of the three generations are artistically interwound to provide a charming yet meaningful message.

Two other short stories of that year **"Out of Season"** (1976) and **"The Sea and Tricks"** (1976) are actually parts of a longer work, *In Search of a Genre,* which was published in full in January of 1978.

Recently Aksenov has traveled a great deal in Europe, to Germany, Paris, Corsica and Bordeaux. He presently lives in Moscow with his wife Kira, his son Alyosha, who is no longer "little Whale" but an eighteen-year-old art student, and his dog Ralph Emerson Klychin. He recently began filming *A Center From the Skies,* a filmscript he wrote about a basketball player. Currently he is translating E. L. Doctorow's *Ragtime* into Russian.

## Ivan Gold (review date 11 December 1983)

SOURCE: "Exit, Pursued by a Bear," in *The New York Times Book Review,* December 11, 1983, p. 11.

[*In the following review, Gold lauds* The Island of Crimea, *praising Aksyonov's skill as a novelist.*]

I remember my relief as a young man to discover that the apparently monstrous mass of Greenland in the atlas is a necessary map maker's illusion, that while it is "the largest island in the world," Greenland is not, in fact, the approximate size of four Australias or capable of entirely covering the North American continent, which it abuts. But so far as I know, no one has yet blown the whistle on Rand McNally for its Soviet Union, which lumbers into the picture from the west (with all of Asia clinging to its underbelly) like an obese dragon, snaps hungrily at Alaska and, after the comparatively small interval of Canada and the North Atlantic, shambles off stage right dragging the rest of Europe behind it like so many tin cans at its tail. No one, that is, has explained away the Soviet Union's bulk as a cartographic aberration, and with Moscow's tendency to secure its borders by the threat and use of military force, it is no great wonder that Soviet paranoia should give rise to paranoia in a good portion of the rest of the world.

These thoughts follow a reading of Vassily Aksyonov's remarkable novel *The Island of Crimea*. Mr. Aksyonov's fictional Soviet Union is only slightly less substantial than the one on the map and no less ominous. Through a series of flukes, the island of Crimea (a peninsula, actually, but joined to the mainland by an isthmus more tenuous than most) has become an independent nation in the aftermath of the Russian Revolution of 1917, when the White Russians escaped there and a British lieutenant in his cups had his gunners blow up the frozen straits across which the Red Army was pursuing them. Over the next 50-odd years, for various reasons, it remained in the interests of the Soviet Union more or less to ignore the tiny, bustling Western-style democracy that sprang up right off its shores. And yet the island itself, amid the political and nationalistic ferment characteristic of a free state, harbors people who would like to see a reunion with the mainland.

Prominent among them is 46-year-old Andrei Arsenievich Luchnikov (or Looch, as he is familiarly known in international circles), the editor and publisher of *The Russian Courier*. We first encounter him in his lavish offices atop a skyscraper in downtown Simferopol, the Crimean capital, lying on a rug "in the asana of perfect repose." But there is too much happening in the world for him to meditate properly, and before long Luchnikov (a semiprofessional racing car driver in his younger days) is tooling in his turbo along Simferopol's "state-of-the-art freeways," answering a summons from his father, Arseny. Luchnikov senior, one of the original "provacuees" (provisional evacuees, as they came to be called), is a millionaire horse breeder, a Slavophile with many American and European friends, and a history professor. He is considered by some to be a candidate for President of Crimea.

At his father's estate, Looch is surprised to find his own 19-year-old son, Anton, whom he has lost touch with for a year after divorcing the boy's mother. Something of a hippie, Anton has been globe-trotting and is presently attended by two beautiful American women a few years older than he is, whom Looch first sees as they rise nude from the swimming pool. Three generations of Luchnikovs, then, are presented in the first 20 pages, and Looch himself will be a grandfather before the end.

His father has summoned him to inform him of a right-wing plot against Looch's life. Luchnikov is not at first inclined to take this very seriously: "There isn't a day that goes by at the *Courier* without a call from one or another of them; 'Commie bastard, Kremlin whore, Yid yes man.'" But after a visit from, and a quick tumble with, one of his son's American friends, who calls him "Mr. Marlboro," Looch escapes on an adventure that takes him to Paris, to jail, to the arms of a former mistress and to a steam bath with Moscow's mighty, where he is reminded of something: "No, not Roman senators. Why, of course! The Mafia! That's it. Chicago, the roaring twenties, a Hollywood B-movie, the *nouveau riche* combination of ferocity and flab, the sense of power usurped."

The movies figure large. In Paris, an attempt is made on Luchnikov's life, and a passerby says, "I've never seen anything like it in my life! Just like in the *films noirs!*" An American film maker beseeches Luchnikov to do the screenplay for "a blockbuster. A good old-fashioned sweeping epic about the reunification of Crimea and Russia. Tragic, lyric, ironic, dramatic, realistic, surrealistic—a sure winner. The totalitarian colossus devours the carefree bunny rabbit at the latter's request."

That, in fact, is how the book ends, with Crimean television covering virtually every public and private act. Having finally acceded to Crimea's request to become another of its republics, the Soviet Union cannot let this occur peacefully but must invade the island, with the cover story that it is merely conducting war games in the area.

Luchnikov does not merely gad about. His struggles with the idea of a God could slip easily into a 19th-century Russian novel, and a long essay he writes about Stalinism and the possibility of Russia's long-term recovery from its horrors might impress even Aleksandr Solzhenitsyn.

*The Island of Crimea* is a stunning performance, reading for much of its length like a bizarre yet joyous collaboration between Dostoyevsky and Thomas Pynchon. It is a profoundly political and contemporary statement but with none of the shrillness and compromise with literary quality we have almost come to expect from books of its kind. Mr. Aksyonov is brilliantly served by his translator, Michael Henry Heim, who leaves us with the startling image of a "helicopter-speckled sky."

Mr. Aksyonov, who is now 51, lives in Washington. Soviet authorities are busy expunging his name and work from the literary record in Russia. His father was a Communist Party official and his mother, the historian Eugenia Ginzburg, became famous for her memoirs about her two decades in Stalin's labor camps. Mr. Aksyonov began writing novels shortly after he graduated from medical school, and by 1961 his first works had earned him an international reputation as a leader of a new generation of Soviet writers. By 1979 he was leading the group of Moscow writers who tried to set up an uncensored periodical, *Metropol,* and the next year, when his novel *The Burn* was published in Italy, he was forced to emigrate from the Soviet Union. *The Burn* is due to be published in English next year. Readers of *The Island of Crimea* have much to look forward to.

### Jerome Donnelly (review date 28 April 1984)

SOURCE: "The Island of Crimea," in *America,* Vol. 150, No. 16, April 28, 1984, pp. 322-23.

[*In the following brief review, Aksyonov's use of satire in* The Island of Crimea *is compared to the satirical elements found in Jonathan Swift's* Gulliver's Travels.]

A classic joke current among Russian dissidents runs, "What is the difference between Communism and capitalism? Answer: Capitalism is the exploitation of some individuals by other individuals. Communism is just the opposite." Vassily Aksyonov's new novel, *The Island of Crimea,* draws a sharp cultural distinction between the two "isms" by creating a geographic fantasy in which the Crimean peninsula is no longer part of the Soviet Union but is instead an island, distinct from the Soviet mainland and economic system, reminiscent of Hong Kong's relation to mainland China.

Although this is the first of his novels to be translated and published in the United States, Aksyonov is a well-known and widely read if officially unpopular Russian writer. More fortunate than his parents, who suffered persecution and exile (Aksyonov's mother, Eugenia Ginsburg, has written a justly celebrated account of the family ordeal), Aksyonov managed to leave Moscow for the United States five years ago after battling Soviet censors and physical intimidation.

*The Island of Crimea* provides an interesting example of fiction that has gained popularity among the Russian reading public in proportion to how much it has offended the government. The central character, for example, is far too freewheeling to fit the Soviet mold; Crimean-raised Andrei Arsenievich Luchnikov is a television personality and race car driver with an Oxford education, wealth, expertise in karate and celebrity status as a writer, and he mingles just as easily with high-living Parisians or his son's hippy friends as he does with Russian generals.

Luchnikov has become involved with the Common Fate League, whose goal is Russian revitalization through reunification of Crimea with Russia. The Soviet Government, though committed to a policy of swallowing the island, nervously balks at the unforeseen consequences of this Crimean tonic. Personal policy struggles dominate Luchnikov's own affairs as with one hand he attempts to separate the woman he loves from her mainland husband while with the other he tries to restore generational equilibrium with his disaffected son and with his White Russian father, one of a group of restless, permanent exiles on Crimea. Keeping in motion all of these involvements plus dealing with an assortment of international characters sometimes strains Aksyonov's talents. Perhaps he most succeeds in presenting a fascinating variety of cultural views, a sense of the varied texture of Russian cultural attitudes ranging from immobilized military bureaucrats whose minds are locked into a revolutionary past to the utterly detached free spirits who definitely rejoice in crisscrossing borders for sport.

The basis for these tensions derives from Aksyonov's fantasy Crimea, which operates much as Swift's islands do in contriving opportunities for satiric juxtaposition. And like Swift's, Aksyonov's satire cuts both ways. Even if at first it seems to, the bleakness of Soviet culture does not make a utopia of Crimea and the West. To idealize Western values would involve a mechanical response and would be to ignore the way in which the seeming perfection of a sharply contrasting freedom and dazzling material prosperity too often result in an obsession with consumption—just as the glittering exquisiteness of Lilliputian scale gradually yields to a vision of the tiny islanders' pettiness and pride. Yet, the freedom of the West, which includes the freedom to appreciate the present in light of a cultural past not limited to 1917, offers spiritual possibilities that Luchnikov senses even in such a simple act as walking in old sections of Paris and "enjoying the feel of the priceless medieval cobblestones through his shoes."

Despite flaws in character and momentum (and dialogue, where once or twice characters sound uncomfortably close to those "wild and crazy guys" formerly of Saturday evening television), Aksyonov succeeds in structuring layers of conflict and resolution. What the novel lacks in humor, it makes up for in brilliant, hallucinatory passages sometimes recalling that Russian master of hallucinatory comic fiction, Mikhail Bulgakov. Yet if Aksyonov's fiction does not accept a mechanical operation of the spirit, neither does it invite a prostration of spirit before comic absurdity. Instead, in depicting both public and private realms, his novel holds to the possibilities of hope and reconciliation in an affirmation of spirit.

## Ronald E. Peterson (review date Fall 1984)

SOURCE: A review of *The Island of Crimea,* in *Slavic and East European Journal,* Vol. 28, No. 3, Fall, 1984, pp. 410-11.

[*In the following review of* The Island of Crimea, *Peterson points out the variations in different translations of the novel and builds a case for the merits of Heim's translation.*]

**The Island of Crimea,** a translation of Vasilij Aksenov's **Ostrov Krym** (1981), is the first of his novels printed abroad to appear in English. Two others, which were in fact published earlier, *Ozhog* and *Zolotaja naša zhelezka* (both 1980), have also been translated and will be brought out in the near future: **The Burn,** in Michael Glenny's rendition, by Random House, and **Our Golden Ironburg,** translated by this reviewer for Ardis. Since **The Island of Crimea** has the most appeal for a Western reader, its appearance first is appropriate, and the responses in the media have been largely favorable, though in some cases reviewers have mistakenly assumed that it is his *first* novel to appear in English, overlooking his work of the early 1960's.

Aksenov's intentions, as stated in his 1983 Preface to the English version, center on an investigation, in fictional form, of the question "What if Crimea had developed as a Russian, yet Western, democracy alongside the totalitarian mainland?" But *The Island of Crimea* is more than a response to a "what if" scenario and more than a fanciful refutation of the "Soviet authorities' . . . firm and realistic view of geography . . . that the world rests on three whales and two elephants." Though one can agree with the reviewer for *Newsweek* (21 November 1983) that it helps to be familiar with the background Aksenov relies upon, still the motives for wanting to reunite with the rest of the USSR seem quite clear: "Because Russia needs Russians" to help it (185). True, Aksenov is harsh on Stalin, Stalinism, the KGB, official lack of tolerance, and other aspects of current life in his native land, but he also displays a belief in Russia's role as a messianic nation and in the necessity of allowing the liberal elements of the Russian intelligentsia to play a part in shaping a more positive future for the country.

Fortunately for the author and his readers here, the translation is quite good. Professor Heim, certainly one of the better translators in our field, has come up with an English version that is true to the spirit of the original yet avoids the pitfall of a too literal, word-by-word rendering. Aksenov himself advocates a free approach in this area, and he dislikes footnotes and other such aids in his fiction, so Professor Heim's accomplishment is doubly impressive, especially since Aksenov's style and fondness for paronomasia make this task rather difficult. One central example of Aksenov's tendency to use puns, for instance, calling the island "OK" or "Okay," is not amenable to an exact rendering, thus Heim explains unobtrusively: "OK being the initials for its Russian name, Ostrov Krym." He is also adept at inventing suitable phrasing when appropriate: for example, the original *ibu* and *ebu* tribes becomes the "Kikuyus and the Wiskruyus," a *podljanocka* reappears as an "off-white lie," and Walter Gesundheit, a TV host whose name appears only in the translation, is a punning combination wholly appropriate to Aksenov's style of writing. Occasionally, however, some of the choices are less understandable: Hollywood for Beverly Hills, a "new Mercedes" for a Japanese Datsun, and "he ran up to twenty-one meters" for "jadro letelo stabil'no za dvadcat' odin metr." And there is one significant misstep, which substantially alters the sense at the end of the fifth chapter: Luchnikov's interlude with the French sex kittens does not signal the "dawn of civilization," but rather the "twilight" (in the original—*zakat civilizacii*).

But where Professor Heim's efforts truly shine are his renderings of the original's fairly numerous English phrases into the urbane, witty, hip, colloquial, idiomatic English these cosmopolitan characters should command. "He's blotto" ([325], instead of the original "He is a heavy drunk"), "As you wish" ([155], for "Up to you"), and "Barfsville' (20) are just a few examples. Because of these and other felicities, the English version of this "Russian, yet Western" novel (based in part on impressions gained when Aksenov visited UCLA in 1975) at times works better than the original. And it is a pleasure to recommend it to scholars, students, and general readers alike.

## Josef Skvorecký (essay date 31 December 1984)

SOURCE: "The Mess of Mother Russia," in *The New Republic,* Vol. 191, No. 27, December 31, 1984, pp. 30, 32-3.

[*Skvorecký is a noted Czech-Canadian political novelist. In the following review, he praises* The Burn *and calls Aksyonov an "epochmaking writer."*]

Much of the effect of literary art depends on a kind of inside knowledge, on the reverberations of personal association. We miss a lot even in the thoroughly explicated plays of Shakespeare; and even such relatively simple works as *Babbitt* certainly appear richer to a Midwestern contemporary of [Sinclair] Lewis than to a high school girl studying American literature in Peking. Still, more than enough remains in a great book like *The Canterbury Tales,* for instance, to make it a best-seller in Prague in the early 1950s—although that book's appeal for the Czechs lay, admittedly, not just in the work's intrinsic value, but also in its side delights. "The Miller's Tale," unexpurgated because it was a classic, was a rare, juicy morsel for readers starving on a diet of novels in which, if a newlywed Stakhanovite wanted to indicate to her husband that he had brought her into an interesting condition, she had to lead him under a blossoming cherry tree, point out a nestful of newly hatched birds, and blush.

At the beginning of Aksyonov's immensely rich novel, a sexy Muscovite—the females of that cynical city blush only on the pages of prizewinning Soviet novels; in Aksyonov's book they fuck like mad—brings the scientist Aristarkh Apollinarievich Kunitser a glass container swarming with drosophila flies. I wonder how much is lost here on a young American reader who never studied Soviet history. For me the entire stunning inferno of *The Burn* is embodied in this tiny fruit fly. In the opening pages of the book, it functions like [Marcel] Proust's madeleine. I remember well the article in the Charles University student newspaper in which the author skillfully built up the tension toward his final horror, which came when the door opened to the Laboratory of Genetics where the obscurantist-non-Marxist Professor of Biology Sekla kept his—drosophilae! In Soviet demonology of the late '40s, the drosophila occupied a place second only to Trotsky. To high school students it was the creation of an American Jew, Thomas Hunt Morgan, and Gregory Mendel, a Czech Catholic monk straight out of Matthew Gregory Lewis. After Academician Lysenko's celebrated victory on the biological front, Mendel's statue was duly removed from its pedestal in the Moravian capital of Brno. When, in the '60s, an International Biological Conference was held in that city, it required a long search before the stone likeness of Mendel was found, covered by dust and debris, in somebody's wine cellar. In the minds of the Young Pioneers, the monk merged with the other kike, Morgan, into a bogeyman called Mendelmorgan, ideally suited to put the fear of the party into little boys and untenured professors. That is what Aksyonov's madeleine means for me. But not, I'm afraid, for many Americans. (An American editor removed a drosophila story from the fifth chapter of my own novel *Miss Silver's Past;* he said it was irrelevant and digressive.)

And many such madeleines are strewn over the surreal and, alas, so real, landscape of this story of five Russian men who share the patronym Apollinarievich, and are really embodiments of the same Aksyonov. Like Apollinaire's celebrated poem, this novel, with its five sons of the poet who "did not respect any fame," is a veritable *Zone,* very hard to sum up. It is an Old Man River full of rafts, Jims, creaky steamers with dead Paps inside, and lynching parties; a "sweet" Thames bearing empty bottles, sandwich papers, silk handkerchiefs, cardboard boxes, cigarette ends. Toward the end, Kunitser-Sabler-Malkolmov-Kvastishchev-Pantelei-Aksyonov, in one of his/their nightmarish dream-realities, swim in a ghostly stream, "pushing aside old tin cans ... used condoms, lumps of matted hair, eggshells, countless

nail clippings . . . rotten vegetables, used toilet paper. . . ." The river, that symbol of life in schoolroom essays, has changed here into a symbol of the Soviet homeland.

Quite often the book resembles a surrealist comedy—minus the irreverence. Apparently one cannot be irreverent in Russia, the graveyard of so many millions of victims of perpetual misrule. Even "hilarious" scenes—like the one featuring the sculptor Kvastishchev and his "model"(a sexually interconnected circle of bodies consisting of himself and two K.G.B. hookers)—are played out against ominous backgrounds. (In this case, a purring Chaika limousine arrives, bearing the dangerous customer Lygher, once a powerful officer in the town of Magadan, the heart of the sinister Kolyma region.) It is a surrealistically complex novel, a book of "many oddities," as the author himself describes it. Those who still think that Soviet writers may have a great subject, but that their methods of shaping it are outdated, should read *The Burn* at once.

It oscillates continually between reality and fantasy; its point of view migrates through several minds, the minds mingle, then the minds separate—in short, it is a fireworks of modernistic techniques. Both rough and tender, like the blues, it is full of hate and in the next moment brimming with love. And love is pornographically physical, yet a bliss of the soul. I don't remember many love scenes in literature that can match the final lovemaking of the Victim (all the main characters merge together in the last section of the novel) and the dream/real girl Alisa, the wife of a prominent member of the New Class, but also a poor Polish prisoner-girl who once tries to commit suicide by biting off the neck of a cologne bottle.

All this "deliberate confusion," however, does not betray the author, free at last from both political and aesthetic censorship, who wants to show off his mastery of the tools now at his disposal. A survivor of Stalin's and Brezhnev's deliberate confusion is trying here—and trying with success—to tell the truth about his terrible life. He brings to mind the quintessential evocations of the medieval sense of hell, the works of Hieronymus Bosch, whose paintings, with their amazing proto-surrealism, use a very similar technique.

In the heart of the confusion is a simple, archetypical Soviet story. It is the story of Tolya Bokov, the half-Jewish son of a "Trotskyite man and a Bukharinite woman" who, at the age of 5, after the arrest of both parents, is sent to an orphanage for "children of enemies of the people." Ten years later the boy's mother is released, but ordered to stay in Magadan in "internal exile." The boy is permitted to join her, only to witness her rearrest a short time later, when Stalin commands that all who have served their sentences, and are now relatively "free" as internal exiles, be sent back to the camps on the same charges for which they were incarcerated years ago.

In the purgatory of Magadan the boy sees many other examples of Marxist re-education. One sticks in his mind forever. Bringing food for his imprisoned mother, he accidentally sees an event straight out of Auschwitz. The interrogator, Captain Cheptsov, asks a tortured prisoner "kindly": "Have they been beating you, Sanya?" "Yes, they have, citizen Captain," whispers the young man in pain. "And did they beat you like this?" asks Cheptsov and jabs his elbow into the prisoner's right eye. Sanya's eyeball is instantaneously suffused with blood. At that moment the boy is spotted and, with a mighty kick, Cheptsov sends him flying, so that the precious bottle of milk in the boy's bundle, destined for his mother, breaks into smithereens.

The boy grows up to become the five incarnations of Aksyonov—I believe this is essentially an autobiographical story. Captain Cheptsov ages into a mean old-age pensioner who supplements his income by working as an informer/cloakroom attendant in a hard-currency bar. At this point the two meet again. Cheptsov has caught his daughter typing up leaflets for a dissident organization. He beats her up and, his erotic/sadistic passions aroused, he rapes her. Then he departs for the K.G.B. headquarters to "do his duty," i.e., to rat on the girl. Unfortunately (that is, fortunately), he meets two drunkards, and under the impact of their sarcasm, but also under the load of his gnawing memories, he attempts suicide by ramming his head against a radiator. In the emergency room he is saved by Tolya Bokov—in his incarnation as the famous surgeon Malkolmov—who injects into his veins the mysterious substance Lymph-D, distilled from the "lacerated souls" of his Russian patients. Cheptsov comes to life, to appear in another surreal scene on the TV screens in Tolya's native village, from which he admonishes the collective farmers: "Repent of violence, cruelty, cowardice and lies! Repent, you cohorts of steel and you sportsmen heroes of the Munich Olymp—" whereupon he flows "arms and legs spread-eagled like a sky diver into the depths of the television set." Thus the simple, archetypal backbone of a complex story, set in the black cosmos of the Soviet Marxist state.

The story meanders among visions, evocations, vignettes, nightmares—among all those madeleines. Closest to my heart, naturally, is the saxophone which belongs to Samson Apollinarievitch Sabler, a Soviet jazzman. "You'll have affairs, little Samsik," says a lovely promiscuous lady of real virtue after she frees Samson of the burden of male virginity, "only don't give up your sax!" The beloved instrument, a source of joy and truth, eventually becomes a weapon. With it Samsik cuts open the forehead of the leader of the Komsomol vigilantes who raided a concert of his band. He is then beaten up by the SA-like thugs. After he comes to, he searches desperately for his horn. He finds it. His sax is "lying alongside him, with a little drop of the enemy's blood still stuck to its bell. Proud sax, golden weapon!"

However, the Komsomol *Sturm-Abteilung Führer* is not the only enemy whose head is smitten with this particular madeleine. Another is a fascistoid mercenary in Africa whose armored carrier has been showering machine-gun bullets on a jungle hospital. The two identical uses of the saxophone thus introduce the inevitable question about the identical nature, and therefore identical accompanying phenomena, of totalitarian regimes, right and left—if, indeed, the old distinction from the days of the National Assembly in Paris still applies to modern dictatorships.

The identity is suggested mostly by images—for instance, of a brutal store manageress, a typical product of a society where all authority is firmly vested in those firmly vested in authority, who reminds the hero of ". . . the cloak-room attendant in the bar . . . [of] Theodore the mercenary in Katanga"; the "cloakroom attendant," of course, is the sadist interrogator Cheptsov. A few times the hint is direct: " . . . our brothers in class, the German Nazis." But such outspokenness is rare and marginal. After having been made witness to the spectral march of women convicts through the permafrost landscape of Siberia, to the vision of the camp bosses entertained by prisoner-actors doing endless time in hopeless Madagan, or to the lot of the "lucky" twenty-fivers in the uranium mines on the Chukchi Peninsula, where one year counts as five but the prisoners' life expectancy is six months—after such and similar scenes from hell, the thoughtful reader will inevitably find himself, without the help of straightforward comparisons, facing Nathanael West's question: "The problem as to why against Fascism and why not against Communism disturbs my sleep." I wish it would disturb the sleep of many in North America.

Can anyone dare to expect a graduate of the world of Magadan to embrace revolution? "Evolution, revolution, pollution" goes the stream of consciousness in Kvastishchev's head, and thinking about his "pal Patrick Thunderjet," an American in Moscow, he cannot remember whether Thunderjet is "professor of Kremlinology . . . or criminology." He decides that there is really no difference. Elsewhere, meditating on Lenin's famous slogan "Communism equals Soviet power plus the electrification of the whole country," the writer Pantelei says to himself: "In that case, what's missing? Surely we have long since electrified the whole country, haven't we?" And in another scene, discussing the West with the Kremlicriminologist, he observes: "A few years back the only people I took seriously were those scatty flower children, but now even they have degenerated into revolutionaries; in other words, they've become an organized gang."

But are lackluster attitudes toward the revolution and the revolutionaries in the Soviet Union limited to the degenerate sons of Trotskyite fathers and Bukharinite mothers who were admittedly rehabilitated but (observe the totalitarian logic) "the fruit never falls far from the tree"? Hardly. When the American Kremlicriminologist, in need of cash after a drunken bout, sells his shoes to a man standing in line for a shipment of shoes that is rumored to be due for delivery at the GUM department store opposite the Kremlin, this is what happens:

> . . . the line disintegrated, turned into a mob, and surrounded the two extraterrestrial visitors with footwear to sell. . . . The mob waved its arms, shouted something, like at some spontaneous meeting in the days of the First Russian Revolution.

In the context of contemporary Russian literature, Vassily Aksyonov is not just an important writer; he is an epochmaking writer. We who were there, and some American scholars, know what he is talking about when, in an imaginary conversation with Hemingway, the hero of **The Burn** tells Papa: "Ernest! 'Your Cat in the Rain' changed my whole life. Thank you for the overkill." That confrontation with the American virtuoso of the literary dialogue led to Aksyonov's first novel, **A Ticket to the Stars,** with its rich evocations of the speech of Moscow's "guys and dolls" of the early '60s, the time of hope. These youngsters who rediscovered jazz and modern Russian poetry, who courageously spoke up in defense of democracy and demonstrated for freedom—these instinctive swallows of the Russian Spring were truly "Aksyonov's generation."

But all that is gone now.

> In the damp winter of 1966, Moscow put two . . . lads from one of *our* houses on trial. Then four more. Then more, singly, in pairs, in whole batches. They demoted *our* professors, fired *our* theater directors, closed *our* cafés. . . . The epoch of Lenin's centennial began. The Neanderthal features of that old *Pravda* hawk Yurii Zhukov dominated the television screen . . . the disintegration began.

Afterward came the "fraternal help for the Czech enemies" and "everybody stopped blabbering. . . . Today's young people," muses Pantelei, "would regard . . . demonstrations as impossible. Some of them imagined that such things had only happened before the Revolution."

Paradise of bourgeois democracy lost. The hopeful Moscow of the '60s has changed into "a sullen, tight-lipped city, equipped with the last word in word filters and jamming devices." A major tragedy for Russia. A dangerous tragedy for the world.

## Priscilla Meyer (essay date Winter 1986)

SOURCE: "Aksenov and Stalinism: Political, Moral and

Literary Power," in *Slavic and East European Journal,* Vol. 30, No. 4, Winter, 1986, pp. 509-25.

[*In the following review, Meyer discusses the influences that* Bulgakov's Master and Margarita *and* Journey Into the Whirlwind, *the prison camp memoirs of Aksyonov's mother, had on* The Burn.]

Stalinism has necessarily been a central subject of serious Russian literature since the 1930s. The grotesque nature of Stalinist society has generated memoirs more fantastic than fiction and novels especially rooted in history. Survivors of the experience are unavoidably concerned with the moral problems of resisting and responding to evil, torn between a desire for revenge and the ideal of forgiveness. Aksenov's **The Burn** (*Ozhog*) must be read in the context of this history and the texts it produced. The burn of the title refers both to Stalinism and to the burn of creativity. By recapitulating his own biography, Aksenov writes a literary-historical confession that traces the effects of Stalinism on the author's generation from the 1940s to the mid-1970s. In attempting to reconcile his love of Russian culture with his hatred of Russian barbarity, Aksenov sets the novel in dialogue with two authoritative texts: his mother's memoir of her years in Stalin's camps provides the focus of the moral dimension of **The Burn,** while Bulgakov's *Master and Margarita,* probably the single greatest work of art produced in response to Stalinism, is **The Burn**'s stylistic parent. An analysis of that dialogue is the focus of this paper.

> **In the context of contemporary Russian literature, Vassily Aksyonov is not just an important writer; he is an epochmaking writer.**
>
> **—Josef Skvorecký**

In defining his personal relationship to the history and literature of his time, Aksenov also incorporates his own development as a writer. In **The Burn** he refers explicitly to **A Ticket to the Stars** (*Zvezdnyj bilet*), **Surplussed Barrelware** (*Zatovarennaja bochkotara*), **"The Steel Bird"** (**"Stal'naja ptica"**), and **"The Heron"** (**"Caplja"**), and indirectly to at least **"Wish You Were Here"** (**"Zhal', chto vas ne bylo s nami"**), **"The Victory"** (**"Pobeda"**), and **"Rendezvous"** (**"Randevu"**). A brief review of Aksenov's biography and of the themes, motifs, and structures that recur in **The Burn** will therefore be useful.

1. History: Aksenov's Biography. Aksenov was born 20 August 1932 in Kaza . His mother, Evgenija Ginzburg, taught history at Kaza University; his father, Pavel Aksenov, was

an important Communist Party official. His parents were arrested in 1937, when he was four years old. His mother served a ten-year sentence and then settled in exile in Magadan, Siberia, with her second husband, Anton Val'ter, a prisoner who worked as a doctor. There Aksenov rejoined his mother when he was seventeen, finished high school in 1950, and, because his parents said "it's easier for doctors in the camps" . . . , enrolled in the First Leningrad Medical Institute, from which he graduated in 1956. He worked briefly as a quarantine doctor in the port of Leningrad, and then was sent as a general practitioner to a village on Lake Onega. There he began to write, publishing two stories in 1959. With the success of his first novella, *Colleagues* (*Kollegi,* 1960), Aksenov and his first wife moved to Moscow, where he soon left work in tuberculosis clinics to become a professional writer (Johnson; Meyer, "Aksenov and Soviet Literature of the 1960s").

Aksenov's first works described the personal world of his contemporaries, written in the language they spoke. The thaw of the Xruščev period allowed his "new" voice to be popular—his rejection of official clichés came at the right moment. But when the thaw ended, he was attacked by conservatives, and on 8 March 1963 he was made to recant publicly at a writers' meeting by Xruščev himself. This personal humiliation and the end of liberalization were a turning point for Aksenov. His first "happy" period was over . . . , and his style became increasingly grotesque, outgrowing the limits of the permissible.

In 1965 he wrote **"The Steel Bird,"** an allegory of the rebirth of Stalinism and of the possibility of popular resistance to it; it was rejected by Soviet publishers and only appeared in the United States in 1977. After the trial of Sinjavskij and Daniel' (1966) and the invasion of Czechoslovakia (1968), it became clear that many of the gains the intelligentsia had made under Xruščev had been lost. **"Wish You Were Here"** (1969) was the last collection of stories Aksenov published in the USSR. That year he began writing *The Burn* in anger and desperation; he completed it in 1975. In the same year he was a visiting lecturer at the University of California, Los Angeles; he managed to publish an account of his California experiences, **"Round the Clock Nonstop"** (**"Kruglie sutki non-stop"**), in *Novyj mir* in 1976. But his participation in promoting the unofficial almanac *Metropol',* which appeared in the United States in 1979 after being rejected by Soviet publishers, in addition to the publication of *The Steel Bird* and *The Burn* in the West, resulted in his forced emigration in 1980 (the story is told in *Say Cheese!* [*Skazhi izjum!*]). Since settling in Washington, D.C., Aksenov has published collections of plays and stories, including the recent **"Svijazhsk"** (1981), which summarizes the themes of his early stories and reveals their hidden religious basis. . . . Three novels have also appeared: *The Burn* (1980), *The Island of Crimea* (*Ostrov Krym,* 1981), and *Say Cheese!* (1985).

2. Literature: Aksenov's Literary Development. Aksenov's early works include four novellas and over a dozen stories. His first two stories and *Colleagues* concern young doctors like himself. Aksenov says he "armored" (*broniroval*) *Colleagues* from the start with the intention of publishing it . . . , but the novella nonetheless reflects his own ideas. Certainly the conflict between cynicism and optimism is resolved firmly in favor of the latter in a self-consciously socialist-realistic way, but the theme of tension between the desire to belong to the collective and the need for personal fulfillment is constant in Aksenov's work. In *Colleagues* this theme involves choosing a career as a writer in Moscow over self-sacrifice as a village doctor. After all, Aksenov greatly admired his stepfather, who selflessly cared for prisoners and their jailers in Siberia, as made clear in *The Burn*. Besides making his stories officially acceptable, Aksenov's endorsement of the values of social service fulfills one set of his ideals by proxy, while allowing him to pursue the rewards of professional writing. This early model illuminates the degree to which *The Burn* is an expiatory novel that affirms a love for Mother Russia even while accepting the necessity of leaving her for the West.

The second novella, *A Ticket to the Stars* (1962), describes four teenagers who run off to Estonia to find themselves. The stars in the title are emblematic of an ideal—Dimka's quest for meaning in life is a process of learning to distinguish between the ersatz painted stars on the ceiling of a barroom and his true star. This pattern is found in all of Aksenov's work: in the romantic tradition, a spiritual ideal is represented by the stars, the moon, an art, a science, even by sport, and is contrasted to its desecration (Meyer, "Basketball").

In Aksenov's third novella, *Oranges from Morocco* (*Apel'siny iz Marokko,* 1963), the ideal is represented by mundane bright spheres that carry associations of distant freedom. The quest for the exotic oranges is set in Siberia. The bleak Siberian landscape of volcanic hills, which in *The Burn* are associated with Stalin's camps, is transformed into a happy realm of play. Aksenov exercises his own freedom stylistically, scrambling chronology and a variety of first-person narratives that explicitly reject official language.

*It's Time, My Friend, It's Time* (*Pora, moi drug, pora,* 1964) is close to *The Burn* in structure. A moral quest in three parts, the novella describes the ambivalence of twenty-five-year-old Valja Marvich. Like all of Aksenov's semi-autobiographical characters, he alternates between comfortable, passive conformity and the more demanding active role that challenges that conformity. Valja insists on his identity with the worker Serega in order to justify becoming a writer-*intelligent*. The ideal dimension of this role is represented by Puškin (joined in *The Burn* by Gogol', Mandel'štam, and Bulgakov); its pitfalls are parodied in the figure of a slick professional writer. The novella's title, taken from Puškin's poem, emphasizes the ideal of freedom represented in *It's Time* by a fantastic character from Estonia who dies racing off on a motorcycle for champagne (compare Sanja Gurchenko and his Fiat in Rome of *The Burn*). Freedom is always associated with foreignness. The novella's villain is a bully, who beats up Valja and humiliates him in an explicitly sexual way, hitting him "in a place that's not talked about" (the Chepcov role in *The Burn*). Valja deliberates about the morality of his response to Oleg: "I swore to myself I'd forget about that magnificent feeling called hate, biological hate, holy hate" (65-66). This question becomes the central moral problem of *The Burn*. In both works, the solution is suspended at the end in a series of disembodied dialogues with characters living and dead. In *The Burn* all these elements are considered in socio-historical terms in relation to political powerlessness; in the early novellas they are treated psychologically, but the pattern of validating literary creation as a way to resolve conflict recurs, as we will see below.

While the novellas are sociologically oriented, Aksenov's stories were conceived as a continuation of the tradition of Russian prose interrupted in the 1920s. The stories combine realism with the avant-garde, seen by Aksenov as a continuation of Gogol's fantastic tales. . . . This accounts for the greater sophistication of stories written as early as 1961 (e.g., **"Halfway to the Moon"**), whose thematics persist throughout Aksenov's work. The ideal realm, here represented by a "beautiful lady," is at odds with Soviet *pošlost'*; the hero mistakes a "Neznakomka" for his muse-beloved, as in Gogol's "Nevskij Prospekt," but disillusionment brings about the hero's metamorphosis. The worker falls in love with a stylish Moscow stewardess, which opens him to spiritual existence.

After 1963, the stories became less realistic, increasingly emphasizing the degradation of Russian culture. **"The Victory"** was able to appear in *Junost'* (1965) because it presents the intelligentsia's struggle metaphorically and apparently ambiguously. A passive, shy grandmaster of chess is incapable of refusing to play with a thuggish stranger, and "loses" though he has put his opponent in checkmate. The grandmaster wears simple ties that bear the hidden label "House of Dior"; to him "this small secret had always been a source of comfort and warmth" (Eng. trans., 191). The ineffectuality of this "secret" in securing the grandmaster's victory suggests the irrelevance of European tastes and ideals, as well as the grandmaster's cowardice in hiding them. His cultural and spiritual life may be superior to the aggressiveness of G.O. (the initials may stand for *Glavnaja opasnost'*—the main danger), but the grandmaster knows he will lose the game; his values are impotent on the plane of reality, a recurring dilemma in Aksenov's work. At the end the story shifts to the fantastic as the grandmaster engraves one of a store of gold medals prepared for such inevitable occasions

in order to commemorate G.O.'s victory; his defeat is made acceptable from the distance of the artistic dimension.

In *Surplussed Barrelware* (1968), as in *Oranges,* an array of social types journey toward an ideal, here explicitly identified as the Good Man. Two characters dream independently of him, an idea used almost allegorically, as in *The Burn.* But while *Oranges* was optimistic, here bureaucrats reject the sublimated religious love for the barrelware that unites the questers. . . . In *The Burn* the questers themselves conspire with the bureaucrats in degrading their ideals.

*The Burn* was begun with no idea of publication in the Soviet Union, but Aksenov used its central ideas in the novella *Rendezvous* (1971). In Ljova Malaxitov, the scholar, poet, sportsman, film producer, and jazz musician, Aksenov paints a satirical portrait of the Moscow intelligentsia, removing the thematics of Stalinism in order to produce a publishable variant of material from *The Burn.*

3. Synthesis: *The Burn.* Book 1, "The Men's Club," describes the debauched state of the intelligentsia in the late 1960s. Malaxitov's professions are distributed to five characters, who represent the cream of the arts and sciences: the research biologist Aristarx Kunicer, the saxophonist Samson Sabler, the doctor Gennadij Mal'kochmov, the sculptor Radius Xvastiš ev, the writer Pantelej Pantelej. They share a patronymic—Apollinarievi —and a common past, represented by the character Tolja fon Štejnbok. The story of Tolja's life with his mother in Magadan in the late 1940s, which closely resembles Aksenov's, is told in fragments embedded in book 2, "Five in Solitary." Here too we discover the origins of the recurring character Chepcov in the KGB officer who rearrests Tolja's mother. Book 3, "The Victim's Last Adventure," dissolves into a phantasmagoria that merges historical periods and transfers the conflict between the oppressors and the intelligentsia to the imaginative plane, where it is left in suspension. The members of the intelligentsia, although cast as victims, are shown to be as depraved as their oppressors, and hence unwittingly in collusion with them.

Aksenov represents the intelligentsia's problem as a failure to attend to and protect its muse. The literal basis of this central metaphor is established in a Magadan scene: Tolja is unable to rescue a Polish girl, Alisa, from a convoy of prisoners. The pathos of her situation is underscored by the prospect of her rape by prison guards. By the 1960s Alisa reappears as a loose society woman; in book 3 she is also a KGB spy. That is, having stood by while she was raped, the intelligentsia then takes advantage of her, and she finally betrays them: political sticks and material carrots have reduced them to a state of lazy provincialism and impotent passivity.

The heroes have lost their memory. Throughout book 1 they

keep trying to remember their collective past, the tragedy of fon Štejnbok. They have trouble recalling Mandel'štam's poem, "Sleeplessness, Homer," and even the poet's name. Their muse is in such a state that she has trouble reminding them of their literary and historical heritage. One of the guises of the heroes' muse is Arina Beljakova, the first woman Samsik Sabler makes love to:

> Her mission was very important, though somewhat ridiculous for a European girl. For six months since the showing of the movie [*The Witch*] in the Soviet Union, she had been walking the wet, uneasy streets of this city, where she had once run away from the School for Noble Young Ladies, and would unexpectedly . . . accost the local Samsiks, the pathetic little offspring of the Stalinist era, lead them away to the crumbling houses of the Silver Age, and teach them to love, appearing to them as an unforgettable image of freedom.

To provide an image of freedom, the muse must inspire them with the culture of the Silver Age and of Europe. The beautiful French movie actress Marina Vlady, who starred in the French film *The Witch,* played that role in reality for Aksenov's generation, since she was married to Vysockij. The character Arina Beljakova suggests Aksenov's own muse, combining love, medicine, and literature. Her sexual education of Samsik is linked to Tolja's first sexual experience: in Beljakova's Silver Age apartment building all the cables and pipes are overheated and shine through the walls; Tolja loses his innocence in "the Crimea," a manhole full of underground steam pipes where the ex-zeks of Magadan live while waiting for transportation out of Siberia. Both scenes of initiation are followed by KGB raids: becoming a man involves recognizing and remembering the reality of political oppression.

Contemporary images of freedom are to be found in Western films showing a world in which the sense of ambivalence and inadequacy plaguing Aksenov's generation has no basis. In the late 1940s in Magadan, Tolja sees *Stagecoach* seven times. The Ringo Kid, who eliminates two Apaches at a gallop, is the perfect teen-age image of bravery against all odds. But Tolja's identification with him is useless in real life—he can only fantasize rescuing Alisa from the convoy or his friend Sanja from Chepcov's brutal interrogation. The latter fantasy is imagined in English, because it is unthinkable within the Russian context. The Magadan cinema highlights Tolja's confusion: since he wants to be a normal Soviet schoolboy, he is ashamed of his parents, who are "enemies of the people," but he reveres his mother and Martin, a Volga German and a practicing Catholic. *Stagecoach* provides an escape to a mythical America. In the 1960s it is replaced by European films with "Brigitte and Claudia

Cardinale and Sophia Loren and that fat Anita and Monica the intellectual and Julia-keep-your-hands-off."

Aksenov conveys the spirit of the 1960s, when Russia opened up to the West, by studding the text with Marlboro cigarettes, Danish beer, names associated with American jazz (Thelonius Monk, Willis Conover), Greenwich Village, Soviet copies of American baseball shoes, a "shabby little jacket from Liberty's," even Yul Brynner's bald head. The names of Western cities appear throughout—Paris, London, Rome, San Diego, Pisa, Oxford—to collapse the imaginative distance, while highlighting the political one, between them and Moscow:

> No friends the truth is dearer to us
> What's more the door we long for is so near
> To walk along Picadilly for a few bars
> to turn onto the Nevskij through the Arc de Triomphe
> swim across the wall and jump over the Spree
> then to the Nikitskij Gate through Rockefeller Center.

But the meaning of the West for them is lost, as its objects become empty status symbols and mere luxuries. The writer Pantelej walks off with the liquor from a party at the Brazilian embassy, where he finds:

> Gordon's Gin and Cinzano Dry and Queen Anne and Armagnac and Mumm and Campari and Remy Martin and Ballantine's and Smirnoff and Benedictine surrounded by a guard of Schweppes and Coca-Cola.

That this sense of freedom is an illusion becomes clear when Pantelej is summoned to the chief censor (the "High Priest"): the latter surreptitiously smokes a Kent, while, like the grandmaster in **"Victory,"** Pantelej wears his Oxford tie and a California button that says "Fuck Censorship!" pinned to the *lining* of his jacket. The Western objects lead to the novel's central problem—the intelligentsia's failure to resist repression.

4. Aksenov's dialogue with Ginzburg's memoirs: Responses to Stalinism. The history of the confrontation between the generation of the 1960s and Stalinism in **The Burn** begins with Tolja's first encounter with Chepcov. The scene is based on Aksenov's own experience, as recounted by his mother in part 2 of her memoirs. The connection is emphasized by the closeness of the name Chepcov to that of Chencov of the memoir. . . . Just as the novel's social analysis depends on our knowledge of Russian history, the power of Aksenov's concretization of the traumatic burn in Tolja's experience relies on our ability to fill in the details, to relate the character to Aksenov himself. **The Burn,** then, is written in dialogue with his mother. Both writers try to understand the

tragedies of their personal lives in the context of Russian history, and consider how to respond: should one, can one, forgive? Mother and son respond differently both stylistically and ethically.

A. Style. The problem of the relationship of reality to fiction is addressed by the use of the motif of the fairy tale. Ginzburg contrasts the surreal horror of the real world of Stalin's camps to the purity of children's fantasy. When working at the Magadan kindergarten, she staged "Puss in Boots" and "The Seven Little Kids." The script for the first was confiscated at the time of her arrest as potentially subversive material. The broadcast of the second cost her her job—an ex-zek cannot be given public prominence. The tragic irony of the confusion between the two disparate worlds shows her real life to be more fantastic than fairy tales, while the private, innocent domain of children's stories is fraught with political perils. Ginzburg was one of the first to recognize Stalin (whom she calls "the Georgian dragon") in Kornej Chukovskij's children's tale "The Cockroach" ("Tarakanišče"); as a result of mentioning this at home, she was denounced, fired from her job, and threatened with a third arrest. . . .

Ginzburg, like Tolja, goes to the Magadan cinema, but with opposite emotions. Fresh from prison camp, she is taken to "a quite incomprehensible film about spies.". . . After ten years in camp with all sorts of alleged "spies," the film about fictional spies seems simply silly. A real spy later denounces her. Awaiting arrest, she goes to the cinema—"It's perfect peace of mind for at least two hours.". . . The fantasy world of the film can distract from all-too-dramatic reality, but there can be no confusion between which is which.

Ginzburg's husband Anton, the model for Martin in *The Burn,* was a practicing Catholic. The night before he is to report for rearrest, they go to an Italian film in which a Catholic mass is shown. Anton calls Ginzburg a Hottentot because she has never attended mass, while behind them someone says "Fancy that! How they used to worship God! Just as if he were Stalin!". . . The inversion of God and Stalin and the word *Hottentot* in the context of the dragon imagery of *Whirlwind* casts the camp nightmare as a twenty-year-long pagan blood sacrifice. The Italian film provides the perspective from which to view it, but the film is only a substitution for reality, a reminder of moral values already held. For Ginzburg the freedom presented in the Western film is the possibility of practicing Catholicism. It contrasts strongly with Aksenov's stylistic use of film for carnival effects under the more general rubric of freedom.

After decades of exposure to distorting, abstract language, Ginzburg values the direct relationship of word to object as a means to truth. While she uses fairy tales specifically to tell her own tragic Cinderella tale, Aksenov is allegorical. Parallel to her "Georgian dragon" and "Tarakanišče" is

Xvastišchev's sculpture of a dinosaur named "Smirenie" (humility, submissiveness). Its victims are the Muse and the young Tolja, betrayed by his older brothers, the creative intelligentsia. Chepcov is a kind of eternal Kaščej Bessmertnyj, who rises from near death, and there is a magical helper, Sanja. Aksenov replaces Ginzburg's particular, realistic method with a general, schematic one. Right after a reference to Bulgakov's *Master and Margarita,* Aksenov quotes the song of the Stalin period, "We were born to turn fairy tales into reality" . . . ; he has turned reality into a modernist allegory, juxtaposing Bulgakov's, Stalin's, Ginzburg's, and his own "fairy tales" to the history they share.

B. Moral Response. The moral problem of *The Burn*—revenge or acceptance—is focused on Chepcov, and here particularly Aksenov struggles with his mother's resolution of the issue. Her acceptance of Christian ideals is clear in her treatment of Chencov, as it is of all the evil she describes: forgive them, for they know not what they do. She shows compassion for all and looks for the best in people. Though she mocks Chencov, calling him a knight errant, she is grateful to him when he comforts Vasja:

> "It's not for long. . . . It's not like '37. You'll be seeing in the new year together."

> Taught by all those years of lies, I had not believed him at the time. In retrospect I am grateful to Chencov for his humane attempt to give us some assurance, and glad for him that his heart had stirred at the sight of my parting from Vasja.

In *The Burn,* Aksenov describes her "hatred" for Chencov. In her memoirs, Ginzburg chooses not to harbor her hatred; perhaps this is a deliberate distortion of historical truth, but it is made in the name of what she considers to be a higher moral truth. For Aksenov, Chepcov personifies the banality of evil. He appears in various disguises—a spy-cloakroom attendant at Kunicer's institute; at the Hotel National; as Theodorus, a mercenary soldier in Africa; as a nurse in a sobering-up station; in book 3 as a face on a television screen; finally as a "cheerful, friendly old janitor" in a "Chinese museum" on the moon, no longer a man but a "philosophical construct." His epithet is his "two hot greedy and mocking eyes like ripe cherries," or other little berries—cranberries, black cherries—by association with Jagoda, the chairman of the NKVD until he was shot in 1937, and Berija (note Sergeant Berija Jagodovich Gribochujev of the cloakroom guard at Pantelej's recantation . . .).

The focus of Aksenov's characterization of Chepcov is his sadomasochistic sexuality, which is linked to the emasculation of his victims. When Chepcov comes to arrest Tolja's mother, he sexually humiliates Tolja, kicking aside the screen that hides his bed to expose his masturbatory activity. Tolja imagines Chepcov undressed: "A huge figure of a man with resilient buttocks, a hairy, protruding stomach, a heavy pendulous penis like that of a dominant male in a herd of seals, a wrinkled old killer." The description is repeated in a flashback of this scene, thereby explicitly connecting sexual and political impotence: "Weakness, the fear of helplessness . . . you're in the hands of the *apparat,* in the huge, inhuman, subterranean grip of the state!" As Chepcov leaves with Tolja's mother, Tolja thinks "at any second he may go for you, this bull, and will start to maul you and push you around as though you were a woman!" The oppressors are all marked as sexually perverse: when the High Priest interviews Pantelej, they show each other their tattoos. The High Priest reveals the same "little pendant of wrinkled skin" as Chepcov, and he ends his striptease panting. Chepcov's Magadan superior enjoys whipping his daughter's buttocks; twenty years later in Moscow Chepcov rapes his stepdaughter in fury, when he realizes she's typing dissident literature given her by her lover: sexual sadism and ideological persecution are linked. Interrogating prisoners (pincers to the testicles) brings Chepcov to the verge of orgasm, and he enjoys his own pain while wrestling with a fellow spy-cloakroom attendant.

The perversion of normal instincts by the oppressors and their victims motivates the abundantly described sexual debauchery with which Aksenov enjoys characterizing the intelligentsia. Their humiliation is shown as a loss of manhood and of innocence, from which they escape into alcohol and promiscuous sex. Their debauchery is continuous with that of their jailers. At the beginning of *The Burn* Kunicer makes sexual use of a seventeen-year-old (like the Polish Alisa) lab assistant, Inna. The name of the stepdaughter Chepcov rapes is Nina. Aksenov connects the two acts: "Inna! he wanted to shout after her. Nina, Marina, or whatever your name is." Afterwards Kunicer is irritated by Inna's nakedness, just as Nina is disgusted by her stepfather's. But Inna is in league with Chepcov in his incarnation as cloakroom attendant at Kunicer's institute; she reports to him after leaving Kunicer's office. The victims and their jailers are intertwined; in Inna they coexist. The compassion of Ginzburg's memoirs extends to her jailers; the revulsion in Aksenov's novel extends to the jailed.

Outside the amphisbaena of victims and victimizers, Aksenov posits an alternative, a "third model," as it is called by its inventor, Sanja Gurchenko. In the course of *The Burn* Sanja evolves from Tolja's Magadan adventure-hero into a more universal ideal figure. The moral counterpart to the aesthetic muses, Sanja represents the Judeo-Christian tradition alluded to throughout the novel. As a teenager, Tolja had admired Sanja as a real-life Ringo Kid, daring and independent, and had therefore been surprised that Sanja accepted Martin's Catholicism, since Tolja thought the two realms mutually contradictory. Pantelej meets Sanja twenty years later in Rome, where Sanja is a Jesuit priest, combining in adult form

the same duality. For Aksenov, he represents both the ideals Aksenov and his mother learned from Anton Val'ter and the sportsman Aksenov continues to associate with the "healthy" Soviet life:

> He looked more like a professional ice-hockey player than a priest. Under his black cassock, topped by a clerical collar, one could sense a lean, trained, athletic body. . . . What was extraordinary was the fact that there was an elusive something in his looks that was definitely Soviet.

"He could have played a part in a cowboy movie, that priest," says Pantelej of him. Pantelej and Gurchenko drink together and cruise around Rome in the priest's Fiat. All the elements of Aksenov's ideal world are combined: the *La Dolce Vita* aspect of Italy is reconciled with both the Vatican spiritual and ancient Roman physical aspects. Pantelej says, "That night was a very special night in my life, a night like a beacon. After such a night you could go into the wastes of Siberia, you could even go to prison." The strong religious sense that enabled Martin to survive the camps and maintain his extraordinary generosity even toward his own jailers was difficult for Tolja to accept as a teenager; it seemed weak, passive, shameful from the "healthy" Soviet perspective. Here Aksenov has his cake and eats it too: *La Dolce Vita* and macho pride plus purity of spirit. Aksenov suggests that this is not only a personal ideal, but a model for his generation. Pantelej tells a secretary of the Writers' Union about meeting Sanja, and the secretary turns out to have had almost the same experience. "Perhaps, old man, you and I both dreamed this?" Like the characters in *Barrelware,* the two men dream independently of the Good Man, thereby confirming his objective existence.

In response to Pantelej's questions about God, Gurchenko presents the idea of a third model, which he defines as follows:

> Sometimes man comes close to it in moments of creativity—in music, in poetry, in mathematics—but he only just comes close, he only senses its presence. . . . It is impossible to understand. . . . The inexplicable—that is the third model. . . . The higher emotions . . . are inexplicable, fantastic, and it is with them that the precepts of Christianity are concerned. Christianity is like a breakthrough into space, that most courageous and far-reaching spurt toward the third model. Christianity, being itself fantastic, relies on fantastic emotions and proves the existence of the fantastic.

Applying this view to life, Gurchenko concludes:

> It is not so much our *actions* that are important and meaningful—since no matter what we may do, such

actions are neither small nor great—as the spiritual meaning of our actions; in other words, the quality that belongs to the realm of the fantastic, that is what is capable of breaking through toward the "third model," into the truly real world.

Aksenov applies Gurchenko's third model within *The Burn* to determine how to respond to Stalin's crimes, how to forgive oneself for failing to protect one's loved ones, how to accept one's own impotence. Martin, preaching forgiveness, reads Tolja the Passion according to Saint Matthew. Tolja is torn between "the avenging Ringo Kid and the all-forgiving Christ." He cannot accept the ideal of forgiveness: projecting his sense of sexual humiliation onto Christ, he imagines Christ on the cross without a loincloth, mocked for his nakedness. The same drama is enacted in a previous scene at the Yalta sobering-up station by Dr. Mal'kol'mov, who feels rage at "this Stalinist cannibal" Chepcov and prays for forgiveness: "You must know, oh Lord, that I don't have the strength to show pity for a man like this!" Later Dr. Mal'kol'mov treats Chepcov, who is on the verge of death. First he thinks, "Your two hands are saving the life of a sadist; they're resuscitating a criminal. . . ." But Mal'kol'mov is a doctor, and so he answers himself, "Your hands are incapable of exacting revenge." Kunicer, the dissident scientist, acts similarly. When Nina asks if he is going to kill Chepcov for raping her, he replies, "I am a Christian."

The contradiction between the morality of forgiveness and avenging the innocent is resolved by means of the "Third Model." Fiction itself is the realm of the inexplicable, the fantastic; beyond action, it is a means of breaking through toward the "truly real world." In the novel Aksenov does wreak revenge on Chepcov. Just as the KGB officer revealed Tolja's embarrassing private sexual world behind the screens, Aksenov shows Chepcov in all his depravity, panting with pleasure as he tortures and rapes. At the same time, Mal'kol'mov, the doctor (Martin is a doctor, Aksenov was a doctor), can resuscitate Chepcov with his brilliant discovery, "Lymph-D," a kind of elixir of life and spiritual fluid, the antipode of the shameful semen that flows so conspicuously through *The Burn*. That is, the creative intelligentsia, as forgiving Christ, can be a life-giver even unto the evildoer: Aksenov mercilessly exposes the evil, but forgives and restores the life of the evil human being. Before doing so, he torments Chepcov a little by having him recognize his own "crimes." Agonized by the conflict between his duty to turn in his stepdaughter for typing *samizdat* manuscripts and his love for her, Chepcov renounces the actions of his lifetime and rams his head repeatedly against a radiator. It is not for one man to judge another; Aksenov has Chepcov pass judgment on himself. In this way Aksenov entertains the whole range of variations of hate, contempt, revenge, and Christian forgiveness, all of which he sees as a fitting response to Stalin's evil. In this imaginative process, he expiates his guilt

at being unable to take action in daily life, while taking action here according to Gurchenko's philosophy.

5. Bulgakov and *The Burn*. In opposing political power through spiritual authority, Aksenov follows the Russian romantic literary tradition from Puškin to Solzhenicyn, in which literary artists are the earthly representatives of Christian values. Aksenov's faith that literature can affect political life is supported by the section "The Evolution of a Type Discovered by Zoščenko." Zhdanov is the next evolutionary stage of the type described by Zoščenko's boors and bureaucrats and Bulgakov's dog-turned-man Sharik (*Heart of a Dog*). Aksenov identifies the chief conflict of his time as "Zoščenko vs. Zhdanov." The evolution of his generation away from believing in Zhdanov he attributes to the effects of the author's "sole defensive weapon—Awareness":

> It took several years to comprehend the true force of that weapon. Then we admitted that it was this world, the world of calm little loners, the world of poets, that was the true world, and that the other one . . . was false, ephemeral, and already reeking of decay.

Zhepcov evolves out of Zoščenko's bathhouse attendant; Bulgakov's vision inspires *The Burn* at a deeper level. The importance of *The Master and Margarita* for Aksenov's generation as a whole and for *The Burn* has been recognized . . . , and its stylistic presence noted: "the evaluative ironic suffixes and particles in the speech of the neutral narrator . . . , the free handling of time and space, the system of doubles, the active inclusion of the fantastic in the weave of events.". . .

In fact, the very structure of *The Burn* is based on Bulgakov's novel, both the comic, fantastic dimension and the religious, eternal one. The former is signalled in the text: the fivesome, temporarily represented by a narrational "I," flies to the Crimea with two friends and participates in a series of festive adventures, which culminate in Yalta with a masked ball in the Café Oreanda. Through these scenes float pink tenruble notes, "like the money that cascaded onto the theater audience in Bulgakov's novel *Master and Margarita*" (as the translator renders "takaja pošla bulgakovščina" of the original). The Yalta scenes deliberately evoke *Master and Margarita*: the barmaid calls the KGB to report the bizarre barefoot trio, but "Alas, the vigilant lady was unable to finish her report." But where Bulgakov would have this culminate in the retribution exacted by Azazello and company, in *The Burn* the trio is co-opted: the barmaid decides they are KGB agents too and feeds them Intourist goodies. The episodes culminate in a ball scene that parodies universal brotherhood: flower-children win over a major general, who faints at the "damned hallucination" of floating rubles. Everyone ends up at the police station, the scene of a happening more bizarre than anything you might see in a foreign film. . . . The duty room was invaded by an incredible rabble of people, . . . two men in masks, . . . and a dubious-looking character of clearly foreign origin even though he had a Komsomol badge pinned directly onto the skin of his bare chest.

The dubious foreigner is Patrick Thunderjet, a professor from Oxford. Introduced at the beginning of the book as a friend of the five heroes, he is contrasted to Bulgakov's Satan, who appears suddenly in Stalin's Moscow. But Thunderjet has none of the metaphysical powers of the "foreign professor." There is no identifiable agent of the floating rubles in Yalta; though Thunderjet and friends "remind everyone present of the proximity of frightening infernal forces," his name refers only to his jet-setting, and no cosmic clap of thunder ever occurs. In *Master and Margarita* evil deeds are discrete, identifiable, however various in magnitude; in *The Burn* the boundaries between good and evil are diffuse: Gogolian *pošlost'* reigns with little hope of apocalypse. Bulgakov's heroes are redeemed through love and compassion; in *The Burn* the redemptive forces are memory (of fon Shtejnbok and Russian literature), which has been lost, and faith (in a Catholic Christ), which has emigrated.

The Yalta scenes are based on actual events that Aksenov describes in a review of G. S. Smith's *Songs to Seven Strings:*

> Once upon a time there was a unique area in the Eastern Crimea near the ancient volcano of Kara Dag, a land of easy-going, unrestrained humor and a certain degree of frivolity, a Mecca for young Soviet intellectuals of the 1960s. During the summer seasons of 1967-68, in the tiny coves and inlets, accessible only to the initiated, the "Kara Dag Free Republic" was established. On a night of shooting stars, August 21, 1968, this first multi-party Russian institution since the Civil War was destroyed by the joint forces of the local militia, Komsomol vigilantes and a unit of border guards. This event remained unnoticed by the civilized world because of a similar operation in Prague.

Like the merriment in Bulgakov's Variety Theater during Stalin's purges, the Yalta scenes are a feast during the plague, set against the background of the invasion of Czechoslovakia. Like the Kara Dag intellectuals, the revelers at the Café Oreanda end up in the sobering-up station, where Chepcov wields his sadistic power over the forces of love and brotherhood. The Crimean setting bears the closest resemblance to an image of freedom that Aksenov can locate within the USSR, from **"Wish You Were Here"** to *The Island of Crimea.* But like the freedom of "Crimean Island," which ends in a Soviet invasion, the carnival free-for-alls of both

the Yalta episodes and the Magadan "Crimea" are cut short by Chepcov's group arrests.

*Master and Margarita* and *The Burn* depict their authors' contemporary Moscow as fantastic in contrast to a realistically described historical past. Bulgakov's documentary scenes are based on the Gospel according to Saint Matthew, and are interspersed among the fantastic events of Stalin's Moscow in the 1930s. In *The Burn* scenes in "documentary black and white," as Mal'cev put it . . . , are set in Stalin's Magadan of the 1940s, where Martin reads the Gospel according to Saint Matthew to Tolja, and a similar passion is acted out, the crucifixion of Tolja fon Štejnbok (Christ as man) cum Sanja Gurchenko (Christ as spirit). These scenes are interlarded among fantastic events set in Moscow of the 1960s. Bulgakov's cast is made up of comic caricatures; only the Master and Margarita are depicted realistically. In *The Burn* the only characters with psychological depth are Tolja and his mother. The mysterious figure of Sanja provides them, through Martin, with the connection to the ideal of the third model; he is the Holy Ghost, Martin is Father, and Tolja, the Son. In the role of Pilate, Chepcov does the authorities' political dirty work; like Bulgakov's Pilate, he suffers the torments of conscience and is forgiven, consigned to an extraterrestrial space by the author. Like the Master, Tolja is resurrected by a divinely inspired Gospel writer, the author himself, whose autobiography is the point of departure for the novel—both authors, like their heroes, are politically persecuted for their art, and are mirrored within the novels by parodies of Soviet writers, Ivan the Homeless and Pantelej Pantelej.

But who plays the role of Margarita? Bulgakov's heroine functions within the plot line as the Master's faithful lover and the preserver of his manuscript. On the metaphysical level, Bulgakov characterizes his muse by her bravery, constancy, selflessness, and, above all, compassion. These qualities enable her to redeem Frieda, and to resurrect the Master's manuscript, which underscores the theme of the religious dimension of art. The same role is played in *The Burn* invisibly by Aksenov's mother, Evgenija Ginzburg.

Like Bulgakov, Aksenov explores the problem of evil, and the role of the Word, religious and literary, in combatting it. Bulgakov's novel does so from an eternal perspective lent him by his approaching death. Aksenov's novel, written inside the madhouse, carries the present torment of memory and continuing schizophrenia, almost as if seen through the eyes of Ivan the Homeless. Spirit may win out in God's concept of time, but it suffers in the short term which humans experience. Sanja combines the pure, ideal aspects of religion, sport, and a free-wheeling Western style of life, but he has also been rendered impotent by forced labor in the uranium mines. As Aksenov once said, "Manuscripts don't burn, but they sure rot well" (**"Beseda"**). Aksenov's art has been burned by the Chepcovs of this world, who always get the oranges, the stars, the basketballs, the gold medals, and, in *The Burn,* a place on the moon, if only as a philosophical construct.

### Richard Eder (review date 28 June 1987)

SOURCE: A review of *In Search of Melancholy Baby,* in *Los Angeles Times Book Review,* June 28, 1987, pp. 3, 7.

[*In the following review, Eder discusses the shortcomings of Aksyonov's book* In Search of Melancholy Baby.]

Vassily Aksyonov, whose novel, *The Burn,* is one of the masterpieces of dissident Soviet literature, has been living in this country for the last half-dozen years. He is not really qualified to write about the United States. He is marvelously well qualified to write about himself in the United States.

*In Search of Melancholy Baby* does too much of the first and too little of the second. It takes a long time for an emigre to arrive; particularly, an emigre writer. The flowers are different, Josef Brodsky once pointed out; and more important, the words for the flowers are different.

Aksyonov is getting here, as we can see from the mordant and singularly voiced passages that sprout here and there in these American reflections. He is not here yet, as we see from the rather familiar generalities, sometimes whimsical and sometimes solemn, that threaten to turn his book into a Visitor's Book.

Or, if you like, he has arrived and unpacked everything but himself. He has still to make himself the metaphor for his America; the kind of thing that Vladimir Nabokov did with his fictional selves in *Lolita* and *Pnin.*

Aksyonov left the Soviet Union in 1980 after the failure of a Russian gamble. (Russian gambles are to gambles as Russian roulette is to roulette.) Along with other leading writers, Lev Kopelev among them, he attempted to challenge the long icing-over of the 1960s thaw by opening the desk-drawers in which Soviet writers were depositing their work and publishing a selection of them under the title of "Metropol"—not secretly but publicly. It was like planting strawberries in January.

Exiled, he crisscrossed the United States, speaking and occupying writer's residencies at universities all around the country. Finally he settled in Washington as a fellow of the Kennan Institute, and a teacher at Goucher College and Johns Hopkins University in Baltimore.

Aksyonov says fairly predictable things about the fresh and uninscribed minds he finds at Goucher, predominately a college for women. He is taken aback by the students' ignorance of world history and literature; and moved by their eagerness to be taught. A note of sharpness—one of his literary strengths and used too little in this book—comes when he compares the place to the Smolny Institute for Daughters of the Nobility in Czarist Russia.

Another sharpness, rich in possibilities, is his comment on the institution of the university writer-in-residence. "The writer is as common on American campuses as the cocker spaniel is in American homes," he writes. A comfortable kind of writer, he implies; and a comfortable kind of dog; lacking in literary and canine bite, respectively.

There are other sharpnesses, here and there. He goes into a left book store in Washington and examines the posters of Stalin, Brezhnev, Mao Tse-tung and Ho Chi Minh. Which, he asks the puzzled proprietor, does he find most attractive "in terms of male beauty?"

That is the astringent Aksyonov of *The Burn.* But much of the book is taken up by the polite Aksyonov of the refugee visa. At one point, in fact, a passing remark places the book's airiness in a sober context. The writer, who finally gained resident status after much pain and anxiety, lets us know that he is not totally past feeling that being offensive could lead to deportation.

There is not a great deal that is either offensive or particularly stimulating in the author's observations about motels, supermarkets, landscapes, junk mail, banks, food, the gay rights movement, or cocktail parties. In Washington, he remarks, the weather is humid and people talk about politics all the time.

Although not above noticing that there are rats in his neighborhood's back alleys, and that it can take forever to get anything fixed, he can be startlingly Pollyannaish. Living in a $1,200-a-month apartment, he speculates that American energies have nowhere to go "now that Capitalism has brought luxury to the millions."

He calls Bronxville—one of the most expensive New York suburbs—"the real America of neat little towns." He tells us that taking money from the rich will not remedy economic and social inequality; and that the ideal situation is inequality above an assumed threshold. That assumed threshold consists of everyone having a place to live, food to eat and clothes to wear. It is a lot to assume, even for a recent emigre.

Aksyonov is out of sympathy with the rhetoric and assumptions of the peace movement—understandably, as an exile from a country where the peace movement exists only to protest *American* missiles. Here too, he is polite, commenting that the United States' virtue is to allow foolishness as well as sense.

But politeness is not Aksyonov. There is a feeling of discomfort about the book, heightened by an English that is commendable but treacherous. "What has he got against America, that big wig German?" he asks of a critical European intellectual.

He is, as I say, not really here yet. A series of interleaved notes for a future novel about America promises that the author will have something more idiosyncratic to offer. Unfortunately, the notes are jumbled and unclear; a low-energy phase of Aksyonov's surreal current.

Some of the best passages, in fact, go back to the Soviet Union. A Soviet officer on the Chinese border laments that if war comes, the Chinese will invade and confiscate his new motorcycle. Isn't he afraid of the Americans as well? Aksyonov asks. No, the major replies, because the United States "respects private property."

He recalls the Hemingway passion that swept the Russian intelligentsia in the '50s and '60s. There was the emphasis on the solitary hero, of course; there was also the drinking. Russian culture, Aksyonov reflects, has a periodic need for some new romantic justification of alcohol. "Now Russians could drink with Hemingway in a new American cosmopolitan fashion."

And he writes of what American jazz meant to his generation: an escape from regimentation and the leaden cult of the socially commendable. One of the friends of his youth, now a general in the Soviet Strategic Air Command, is an impassioned jazz fanatic.

When Aksyonov tells him he is emigrating to the United States and will be able to hear their heroes perform live, the general replies:

"It's not the same. I don't go to their concerts when they come. You see, I don't want them to turn into living people, people like me. It would destroy my world. I need them to be inaccessible. I need their music to come from east of the sun and west of the moon."

The phrase blazes up in the fissures both of our world and of ourselves. Aksyonov, who once listened to a pirated version of "Melancholy Baby" stamped upon an old X-ray plate, has an artist's courage, not a general's. He has not found Melancholy Baby yet; he has taken the risk of never finding it. If he does, it will be in himself, wherever he is, and maybe even in Washington.

## Richard Lingeman (review date 19 July 1987)

SOURCE: "He Likes It Here, Mostly," in *The New York Times Book Review,* July 19, 1987, p. 5.

[*In the following review, Lingeman comments on Aksyonov's* In Search of Melancholy Baby, *noting that the book, an account of Aksyonov's life in America after his expulsion from the Soviet Union, provides many witty and satirical insights into life in both countries.*]

In 1980, after his novel of life among the Moscow culturati, *The Burn,* was published in Italy, Vassily Aksyonov was expelled from the Soviet Union. Now he is an outspoken skeptic about glasnost in the Russian literary diaspora. *The Burn* is written in a brilliantly subversive style, stuffed with satire, surrealism, anarchic Henry Milleresque bawdiness, and thrown in the face of Soviet realism.

His latest book, *In Search of Melancholy Baby,* an account of his new life in America, will earn its author no rehabilitative points with the Ministry of Culture. Actually, before his expulsion, Mr. Aksyonov published another book on the United States describing a visit he made here in 1975. But then he was a writer in good standing, with a car and a dacha in the suburbs; also, detente was briefly in the air. Now, he is a prominent dissident, stripped of his citizenship, and his reflections are as unwelcome in the Soviet Union as are Aleksandr Solzhenitsyn's.

He might be said to have been drawn tropistically to America at an early age. Even Siberia, where he lived in exile with his mother, the historian Eugenia Ginzburg, was a place "farther from Moscow than from California." He vividly recalls his first naïve contacts with those Stone Age Soviet beatniks known as *stilyagi,* who introduced him to bootlegged songs by Bing Crosby, Nat King Cole, Peggy Lee and Louis Armstrong, surreptitiously recorded on X-ray plates. He reminds us that there is a sturdy pro-American strain in Soviet culture that survived the icy blasts of anti-American propaganda at the height of the cold war.

If Mr. Aksyonov brought to America more affinities than most Russian emigrants, he did not leave behind that sense of irony that is the hallmark of Russian literature. He notes, for example, that he came to America to write a novel about a Russian entangled in the Laocoönish coils of the Soviet bureaucracy and himself became bogged down in the paper swamp of the United States Immigration and Naturalization Service, some of whose minions he finds as boorish as their Soviet counterparts. He describes a frustrating encounter with one civil servant in particular, a black woman who reacted angrily to his suggestion that the information on a certain form he neglected to fill out could be found in his computerized file: "Are you trying to teach me my job? . . . You have no rights in this country! You're a refugee!"

Mr. Aksyonov sensed a reverse racism in her outburst, but a Polish friend who had lived here longer than he offered some tempering observations about the complexity of interracial encounters in America, compelling Mr. Aksyonov to recognize that he was not as free of racist sentiments as he imagined. Welcome to America, where the rituals of race can be as intricate and subtle as court etiquette in medieval Japan—and as historically determined.

Mr. Aksyonov demonstrates that he has made considerable progress in penetrating to the reality behind the appearances of American life. He understands that the Watergate fuss was an exercise in the "*consolidation* of American democracy," rather than an orgy of irresponsible, destructive criticism, as many of his fellow émigrés saw it; and he grasps the elemental truth that "as patriotic as the great majority of Americans are, they do not identify their country with its government"—unlike you know where. He has considerable to say about provincialism and the complacent ignorance of many Americans about the rest of the world, rationalized by asserting that anything they don't know about isn't *worth* knowing about. He decries the commercialization of American literature, comparing the brand-name best-seller writers the system breeds with the *nomenklatura*—the elite—of the Soviet bureaucracy. He hates Los Angeles (in Hollywood "everyone's eyes seemed glazed over with dollar signs") and likes Washington, where he now lives contentedly with his wife, Maya. He finds the architectural hodgepodge of our cities baffling and decides that it reflects an indigenous esthetic, "American pop," which only someone born here can appreciate.

Outweighing these negative reactions, he inhales optimism in the American air, an energizing hope of finding something better, materially speaking. He attributes this tonic atmosphere to something he calls "beneficent inequality"—the opportunity for all to aspire to at least a middle-class level of material comfort. America's consumer society "offers a new kind of equality, an equality based on the marketplace rather than on Marxism or other social theories." Here the rich man has his Rolls-Royce, but the poor man can buy a Honda. Well, a Hyundai is more like it at today's prices, and how about the numerous poor women who are heads of households and hard pressed to afford public transportation? But Mr. Aksyonov hasn't regressed to Social Darwinism: he stipulates that the poverty line "must allow for a basic level of human dignity . . . a place to live, food to eat, clothes to wear."

Not that Mr. Aksyonov is uncritical of American capitalism. Noting the rat-infested alley behind his Washington apartment, he wonders about the efficiency of the four privately owned sanitation companies that are supposed to take away the trash but don't. In Russia similar conditions would cause a citizen to cry, "How is this possible under socialism?" No one in the United States, however, says, "How is that possible under capitalism!" He fears that the latter is "undergoing a Socialist warp of apathy, poor service, and hackwork," though I doubt that socialism has much to do with it.

Still, Mr. Aksyonov scores some satirical points in his observations of his adopted homeland; these are neatly captured in the translation by Michael Henry Heim and Antonina W. Bouis. He can be quite witty, as when he writes about his misadventures with American landlords and Texans who can't place the language he is speaking with his wife. What one misses in this account is a sense of the texture and quiddities of ordinary American life, and, at the opposite end of the spectrum, something about the nonmaterial values. The author bounces from Soviet émigré colonies in Soho and Brighton Beach to the tower above the Smithsonian Institution, where he had a fellowship at the Kennan Institute for Advanced Russian Studies, to the campuses of some 50 universities where he has been a writer in residence, with stopovers at innumerable HoJos and Holiday Inns en route. His peregrinations are understandable in terms of the need to earn a living, but they have given him a somewhat skewed perspective and make his book a kind of mini-Watts Tower of bright, fragmentary vignettes—*objets trouvés*. It's a rhinestone-cowboy-movie-Pop-upscale America. What is lacking is a sense of land and sky and what Lyndon Johnson used to call, "P-e-e-p-u-l folks!"

In *The Burn*, a character laments her lost "homeland—unhomeland, distant and sweet, stormy." Perhaps that is ever the fate of the exile, caught between the homeland unhomeland he left behind and the one to which he fled; uprooted from one, and not yet planted in the other.

## Stanislaw Baranczak (review date 7 September 1987)

SOURCE: "The New Alrightniks," in *The New Republic*, Vol. 197, No. 10, September 7, 1987, pp. 36-38.

[*In the following review, Baranczak discusses Aksyonov's* In Search of Melancholy Baby, *pointing out that the account* "illustrates two sides of the émigré's problem at once."]

Every Nabokov fan remembers the scene in *Pnin* in which the hero, an émigré Russian scholar who has lived for years on an American college campus, attempts to purchase some sports equipment:

Pnin entered a sport shop in Waindell's Main Street

and asked for a football. The request was unseason-able but he was offered one.

"No, no," said Pnin, "I do not wish an egg or, for example, a torpedo. I want a simple football ball. Round!"

And with wrists and palms he outlined a portable world. It was the same gesture he used in class when speaking of the "harmonical wholeness" of Pushkin.

The salesman lifted a finger and silently fetched a soccer ball.

"Yes, this I will buy," said Pnin with dignified sat-isfaction.

This captures perfectly the Eastern European's experience in this country. We come here with our portable worlds sharply outlined. The years of living *there,* the cultural ste-reotypes we have inherited, the semantic distinctions that our native tongues imply—all have created in each of us a repertory of mental mannerisms that we, in our naïveté, take for a reflection of reality. One has only to pass through the now-symbolic Ellis Island for this illusion to burst with a bang. It's not only that the New World turns out to be actu-ally new and surprising at every step. What throws an East-ern European émigré off balance even more is that his semantic system itself seems not to correspond to American reality. A word that in his system of thinking referred to a nicely rounded object denotes here something like "an egg or, for example, a torpedo."

There are two ways of dealing with this problem. One is Pninification: the émigré sticks to his old mental habits and semantic categories, and gradually encloses himself in the cocoon of his Old World personality. (And he is at liberty to do so: this is, after all, a free country.) The other is the method adopted by the hero of Paul Mazursky's *Moscow on the Hudson,* who insists on playing his tenor saxophone like Lester Young and Coleman Hawkins. He may be different, but he wants to join in, which is the only way (not always satisfactory, to be sure) of understanding the nature of the difference.

Vassily Aksyonov has chosen to join in. Written for an American audience, **In Search of Melancholy Baby** is a book-length autobiographical essay (whose chapters are in-terspersed with "Sketches for a Novel to Be") on a Soviet émigré's perception of America. (Aksyonov has lived in the United States since 1980.) The book illustrates two sides of the émigré's problem at once. In the spirit of a rich literary tradition dating back to Montesquieu's *Persian Letters,* it tries to reveal some truths about a country that only a visitor from a different part of the world can discern. At the same time, the encounter with America serves as a way of reveal-ing truths about the Soviet mentality, and the Soviet reality of which it is a product. It's as if Montesquieu's device were used to say as much about Persia as about France.

Both of Aksyonov's inquiries spring from the overwhelm-ing sensation of cultural difference that is the lot of every newcomer from behind the Iron Curtain. From smells to in-tellectual discoveries, from food and cars to natural land-scapes and urban planning (or the lack thereof), from taxes and finances to interracial relations and sexual mores, from sports and cocktail parties to the literary scene and the po-litical system: everything is new. Some of the oppositions of the émigré's experience are almost distressingly symmetri-cal; but founded as they are on the author's empirical obser-vation of both worlds, they serve to convince us that the American and Soviet ways of life indeed differ in every es-sential aspect:

> America's prosperity becomes apparent the moment you leave her large cities. In Russia the opposite is the case. What remains after the military has drained off most of the resources goes toward maintaining a minimal level of decency in the cities; the country-side and villages are left to rot. . . .

> Among the even more striking differences is the dif-ference in the way people learn about what goes on in the economy. The citizen of a society with a "planned economy" has no way of assessing his country's coffers (*Pravda*'s daily hip-hip-hoorays to economic growth and prosperity notwithstanding); the citizen of a free market society has a never-end-ing stream of hard figures to go by. The Soviet feels he is astride a gigantic inert mass; the American en-joys the sensation of rising and falling; of pulsating activity; it may look chaotic but it is very much alive.

From such observations a highly favorable image of America arises—the image of a society based on what Aksyonov calls "beneficent inequality" or "economic inequality in a frame-work of human dignity," a society "freer of xenophobia than any other nation," a society that sincerely sets itself the task of resolving all its inner conflicts. Aksyonov places himself unabashedly among the "Soviet Americanophiles," and he goes to such extremes in his enthusiasm for the USA that he begins to sound decidedly conservative by American stan-dards. Though he declares his support for "liberalism," he means only (with a characteristically Eastern European twist) that in the age-long strife between the principle of liberty and the principle of equality he is on the side of liberty. His Soviet experience has taught him to distrust "the utopias of equality," which never work out anyway, and to place the highest value on freedom, in spite of the social and economic strings attached to it.

The political orientation of Aksyonov's readers will, I think, largely determine the way his portrayal of America is received. Liberals (this time in the American sense) will probably excoriate him for having painted too rosy a picture. The charge is false. From his vantage point Aksyonov can see the South Bronx as well as Beverly Hills. His account devotes a great deal of attention not only to "American fascinations" but also to "American frustrations." Aksyonov's greatest surprise, among these frustrations, was not the existence of enclaves of destitution or racial tension (he found the reality itself much less shocking than its inflated image in Soviet propaganda), but what he calls "American provinciality":

> In the Soviet Union we pictured Americans as "citizens of the world," cosmopolitans; here we find them to be detached, withdrawn, sequestered in their American planet. . . . In a closed society like the Soviet Union, public interest . . . is directed outward, while in open, democratic America it is almost wholly inner directed. The outside world interests Americans much less. . . . Despite the Iron Curtain the Soviet Union is in many ways closer to Europe than Europe's closest political and economic partner, America.

Provinciality and isolation also mark contemporary American literature, he claims. Both these features, along with the pressures of the commercial market, have caused it to "simply take its place in the ranks of Western literature as a whole. Now the aura of the hazardous undertaking belongs to the oppositional literatures of Eastern Europe and the Soviet Union."

Now and again, amid the oppositions, Aksyonov points out disquieting analogies—the paperscape produced by both countries' bureaucracies, for instance, and the fact that "while the U.S.S.R. inches toward capitalism, capitalism [in the United States] is undergoing a Socialist warp of apathy, poor service, and hackwork." Still, the most revealing parts of the book are those in which Aksyonov portrays not America, but popular Soviet misconceptions about America. These come in many shapes and sizes, from propaganda's outright lies (according to which America is a land of universal misery, oppression, and injustice) to the illusions of the "Soviet Americanophiles":

> Soviet propaganda has piled up so many lies in its lifetime that it now gives reverse results: a certain brand of "critically thinking" Soviet citizen—and most of the new émigrés fall into the pattern—no longer believes a word of it; the critically thinking Soviet rejects both lies of propaganda and the scraps of truth the propaganda machine needs to make the lies appear true.

But beyond the fabrications of propaganda and the fantasies of the pro-Western intelligentsia, we find yet another Soviet vision of America. This is the body of genuine beliefs shared by party apparatchiks and their hired intellectuals, most especially the so-called National Bolsheviks. Aksyonov meticulously analyzes their writings on America. Theirs is a vision marked by utter "disdain for the strength of America and the West in general" and "contempt for America's lack of unity," which in the Soviet strongmen's minds can only be identified with decadence and degeneration.

Aksyonov argues exactly the opposite. For him, "If America was unified along Soviet or Iranian lines, it would no longer be America. It must therefore instill in its population a passionate desire to defend its multiplicity, its ferment, its intellectual and aesthetic waverings." He doesn't mince words in his conclusion:

> Let me call a spade a spade: the anti-Americans of this world—Gabriel García Márquez included—are enemies of freedom and friends of a global concentration camp. The paradox of it all is that to remain what it is America must defend even its own anti-Americans.

Another "paradox of it all" (I would add) is that the first of the sentences quoted above has a rather right-wingish ring to it, while the second would probably be criticized as too liberal, if not leftist, by a good half of Aksyonov's fellow Eastern European exiles. Aksyonov's book should be compared with Solzhenitsyn's famous Harvard speech, or with Zinoviev's *Homo Sovieticus*. Their differences aside, Solzhenitsyn and Zinoviev share the notion that the very premises of democracy are the cause of its ultimate weakness, its ineffectuality in the struggle against totalitarianism. Aksyonov, by contrast, represents a position far more akin to Western values, far more supportive of them.

Which comes as no surprise, if you consider his background. His youthful cult of America in the Moscow of the '50s—when, as he notes, jazz was America's secret weapon, and the pro-Western stateniks emerged as the first Soviet dissidents—seems to lead directly into his present situation as a Russian writer who makes his home in Washington, D.C. To return to *Pnin,* there is a scene in which the hero says in his funny accent: "In two-three years I will also be taken for an American," and every American present roars with laughter. When Aksyonov declares in his final chapter: "Now I am . . . almost an American myself," we are compelled to take his words, accent or no accent, at face value—and, at the same time, to hope that he will never give up that "almost," which, for both the writer and his readers, makes all the difference.

## Michael Wood (review date 24 January 1988)

SOURCE: "Patriots and Other Suspects," in *The New York Times Book Review*, January 24, 1988, pp. 9-10.

[*In the following review, Wood discusses several plays included in Aksyonov's collection* Quest for an Island.]

The cold war appears to have ended not in a thaw but in a world of thin ice. Détente itself is perhaps inseparable from suspicion, and in an uncertain world dissidents are almost impossible to hold in any sort of steady focus. Heroes abroad, rebels at home, scapegoats, martyrs, traitors, criminals, they qualify for a whole range of prominent roles. The one role they can't have, sadly, is the one they most seek: that of the person who refuses all the overwritten scripts on offer. What if a dissident were to become a hero at home, for example, as Vassily Aksyonov imagines in one of his earlier novels, *The Island of Crimea*? "Who was the true hero of today's Russia, who was braver—the cosmonaut or the dissident? A childish question, perhaps, but worthy of serious consideration." The dissident as *patriot:* even in a state of détente such a picture is not intelligible to pursuers of un-Russian or un-American activities.

"We Russians are known for our imagination," a character ironically says in the same novel. He means that much party propaganda is just fantasy, but also that Russians are capable of imagining what reality makes little promise of. Mr. Aksyonov himself is a dramatic case in point. He was born in 1932, the son of the writer and dissident Eugenia Ginzburg, with whom he lived for some time in internal exile in Siberia. He became a doctor, a novelist and playwright, worked for the publication of hitherto banned writings (by himself and others) in an anthology called "Metropol," and was expelled from the Soviet Union in 1980. His other novels include *The Burn* and *In Search of Melancholy Baby*.

The four stories and two plays in *Quest for an Island* are carefully dated, and the dates themselves tell a story of disappointment and loss. A story called **"Looking for Climatic Asylum"** is marked January 1980, Moscow, and complains playfully about Russian weather. "The climate of our capital city is poor. I hope I'm not giving away a state secret by saying that Moscow's climate is none too good." An American visitor says he doesn't understand how people live there, and the narrator "naturally," as he says, takes this as "a political jape." It isn't. Asked if the climate really is any better in Copenhagen, the American says he doesn't see how people can live there either. Where can people live? California, where else? The narrator thinks of going abroad. "To capitalist foreign countries?" his wife asks warily. "Well," he mumbles, "warm foreign countries." In a dream he arrives in California and is made welcome by a policeman:

"'You're seeking political asylum, I take it.'

"'No sir, climatic.'

"'From Copenhagen, eh?'

"'No, but you're close. Moscow.'

"'Okay, go to the right.' He pointed, explaining 'Political asylum to the left, climatic to the right.'"

Awake again, and off to work, the narrator feels his Moscow world change; children play, moods lighten, memory colors the drab city.

"Suddenly I understood what it was. On that day, in the midst of winter, the scent of spring had broken through. . . . No, I simply couldn't live without the expectation of spring. There lies the sole, yet powerful charm of our wretched climate: expectation."

The last sentence is barbed, but the touch is light, and we shouldn't read this story as a heavy political jape after all. But perhaps the lightness itself is political, or what certain politics won't permit. The next story in this volume is dated May 1981, Santa Monica.

The other works in this collection are earlier (1967, 1977-78, and two from 1979), and reflect European travels as well as returns to Russia. **"The Destruction of Pompeii"** mischievously confuses the Roman and Russian empires, and projects a decaying world which is visited and renewed by the attentions of a scorching volcano, a second Pompeii. *Quest for an Island* is a sort of comic retake of Thomas Mann's "Death in Venice": Leopold Bar, "the most important essayist alive in Europe today," holidays in Corsica, "an island of little brave men and big cowardly dogs." Bar is the enemy of irony and smiles ("irony charts a path to capitulation"), and thus a reverse image of Mr. Aksyonov himself, who sees in irony whatever salvation there is.

Of the two plays, **"The Four Temperaments"** is a mock-Expressionist romp in which the angel of death is conducting an experiment in human progress, hampered by a shabby eagle with likable, unprogressive qualities, and by the fact that the script has the set falling down around him all the time, because there aren't enough hooks and nails and clamps to hold it up.

The other play, **"The Heron,"** is (among other things) a parody of Chekhov, in which three sisters, two reformed intellectuals, a diplomat, an athlete, an informer, a manager and a couple of peasants grope for the lost meaning of life. They are situated near the Polish border, and some of them long for Warsaw as the Prozorov sisters long for Moscow.

All are tormented by the cry of a heron, who is also a Polish seamstress (no timid naturalism here). The heron, and the diffuse aspiration she comes to represent, redeem the characters and transfigure them, but since the set includes a rifle, and since Chekhov says a rifle hanging on the wall in the first act must go off in the last, the heron is shot. A dramatic rule becomes a brilliant metaphor not for destiny but for a spineless submission to rules. The heron bequeaths an egg, however, which both tempts and parodies our optimism, our need for uplifting endings. The last question (and the last line of the play) is, "Is there anything really left?" The date here is 1979, Peredelkino.

It is obviously impossible to judge Aksyonov's tone in translation, but from this collection, the work of several translators, we can guess at its sprightly irreverence; the cosmopolitan allusions and the shape of many of the jokes and similes must have traveled pretty directly from the Russian. Figures of speech keep becoming literal, for instance, as they constantly do with the Marx Brothers. A man is said to have lost touch with his native soil, and his son, a champion high jumper, says he has lost touch with the soil too: "two-and-a-half meters." Leopold Bar looks up at the empty night sky and thinks there is no God, then realizes that there is something there. Not God, as it happens, but "a dark gray, nearly black dirigible . . . hanging there before the dawn . . . asking no questions, giving no answers."

Mr. Aksyonov's irony is at its trickiest and most characteristic in his description of two "suspicious" characters in **"The Heron."** One is suspicious because he has jeans and long hair and a monocle, the other because his performance as a "crystal-pure" Soviet worker is so impeccable. Both are former intellectuals trying to live down their disorderly, scribbling past, their interest in jazz and poetry and the West and the like; and the grace and pathos in the gag comes from the shift in the meaning of "suspicious." The first character looks suspicious to official opinion (and maybe to others too, for other reasons: is he an informer?); the second is suspicious because his very acceptability to official opinion argues a life of self-suppression and distortion. A dissident is someone who protests all subjection to such antics, against the institutions that trade on our fear and fatigue and greed.

The most affecting piece in this book is the latest, the one written in Santa Monica. **"The Hollow Herring"** recounts with all the breezy allusive wit Aksyonov commands ("Can you think of a profession that is farther from faith than that of a Soviet basketball trainer?") the religious awakening of a basketball coach. Secretly christened as a child, he feels the old faith return to him, and in a scene which recalls, say, Philip Roth's story *The Conversion of the Jews,* crosses himself live on Russian television, and so do the team members, the team doctor, the second trainer and the masseur. Mr. Aksyonov relishes and underscores the reversals: Marxism-Leninism has become a religion in Russia, and so old or alien religions are now a form of atheism. But they are an atheism of the heart, Mr. Aksyonov seems to suggest; they respect the tenacity of the past and the plurality of the present.

Here as elsewhere, Vassily Aksyonov mourns the loss of what he calls "enchantment": "It must be that it's impossible to live without being enchanted by life," one of his protagonists says. If this is true, it's equally true in California and Copenhagen and Moscow. The sadder truth is that the unenchanted life, if not worth living, is nevertheless lived all over the place. What ought to be impossible is the imagination's acceptance of that fact.

## Eva Hoffman (review date 26 July 1989)

SOURCE: "On Soviet Dissidence as Both Sides Falter," in *The New York Times,* July 26, 1989, p. C21.

[*In the following review, Hoffman faults* Say Cheese! *for its tendency to utilize jokes and satire only humorous to Russian readers, but asserts that the book provides an insightful look into Russia and its political regime.*]

Among Soviet writers, moral dissidence has a long and honorable tradition. Vassily Aksyonov is one of the few, however, who have managed to match their oppositional message with an equally liberated style. In the Soviet Union, Mr. Aksyonov was celebrated as one of the most provocative voices—free-wheeling, satirical, formally daring—of the postwar generation. In 1980, he was forced to emigrate, after he instigated a bold effort to create the first uncensored magazine, *Metropol,* and after his novel *The Burn* was published in the West. In the United States, where he now lives, *The Burn* met with wide critical acclaim; and since then Mr. Aksyonov has published several books, including a highly polished collection of stories, *Quest for an Island,* and *In Search of Melancholy Baby,* an émigré's account of his fantasied and real encounters with his adopted country.

Although *Say Cheese!* is being published for the first time now, it was written between 1980 and 1983, right after Mr. Aksyonov was exiled; and while it has all the scope, ambition and toughness of his other writing, it is in many ways a novel caught in a classical émigré dilemma, between audiences, historical periods and worlds.

Loosely, *Say Cheese!* can be seen as a sequel to *The Burn,* or at least the next chapter in the saga of Soviet rebellion, dissidence and the doings of Moscow's bohemia. Whereas the action of *The Burn* unrolled during the 1960's and its mood alternated between the exhilaration of the first, fresh thaw and the leaden oppressiveness of the subsequent clampdown, *Say Cheese!* takes place in the murkier atmosphere of the late 1970's, when the air has begun to fizzle out of the ideological balloon and the war between apostasy and official religion has become more tired and pointless, though it is still ugly, brutish and long.

The beleaguered good guys this time are a group of feckless, innovative and politically problematic photographers who run afoul of the authorities when they decide to publish a small edition of *Say Cheese!*, the first uncensored photo collection in the Soviet Union. To their own enormous surprise, this seemingly insignificant gesture brings down on them the entire apparatus of K.G.B. surveillance, and the increasingly discomfiting attentions of the State Photographic Directorate of Ideological Control.

The story of the confrontation between the Cheesers and the collected forces of the Evil Empire gives Mr. Aksyonov a chance to compile a virtual guide to Moscow's underground life, activities and illicit etiquette. There are the lurking tails, and the practically uncloseted plainclothes agents; there are car chases, diversionary tactics for opening exhibitions and counterdiversionary punctured tires. There are also carousing parties, flowing vodka and camaraderie, soirees at embassies and lots of very vigorous and very anesthetic sex.

The action of *Say Cheese!* is episodic, and it jump-cuts between a large cast of characters on both sides of the great Soviet divide. But the novel has a protagonist in Maxim Ogorodnikov, or Ogo, a talented artist, daredevil and womanizer who philosophizes about the "astral" implications of photography and eludes his state pursuers with considerable élan. In an ingenious twist on the escape gambit, he manages to slip across those supposedly iron borders and go on a picaresque tour of émigré landscapes—from a social conference in West Berlin, where he shocks comrades from both East and West with his "anti-Soviet" views, to Paris, where multinational decadence lives and thrives, to New York, where, among his exiled Moscow buddies he finds squabbles, influence mongering and sheer intercontinental treachery.

All of this is material for black comedy or detective derring-do, and there are elements of both in *Say Cheese!* But the story Mr. Aksyonov ends up telling is much sadder and bitterer than that. "What do they want from us?!" Ogo shouts at one point, and the question echoes several times within the novel. There is, of course, no answer. The games of hide-and-seek that Mr. Aksyonov depicts have no rationale or goal, but they turn quite deadly nevertheless. His party apparatchiks are no longer the true believers of the Stalinist or even the Brezhnev era; they are bumbling opportunists who dispiritedly spout approved jargon, anxiously vie for position and power, and secretly admire the sophistication of their artistic victims.

Nor are their methods what they used to be. No one in the novel is sent to Siberia or given mind-addling drugs. But still, the expense of spirit exacted by the watchdogs' ubiquitous presence is enormous. Ogo, caught in the quagmire of stupidity, lies and perpetual shadowboxing, begins to suffer attacks of nausea and emptiness that bring him close to a sort of existential self-annihilation. His literal annihilation may or may not be an accident.

This is a bleak and complicated picture, and Mr. Aksyonov's tone, as he paints it, sometimes oscillates uneasily between acid mockery and more somber hues. In part, this is undoubtedly because of his theme's ambiguities, and its gradual darkening. But if his ironies are sometimes forced or his satiric thrust less than sure, it may be because Mr. Aksyonov, in this transitional novel, sometimes seems uncertain of the audience he is aiming for. What to a Russian reader may be an obvious laugh is often, to an American, a baffling inside joke; and Mr. Aksyonov sometimes seems to compensate for this double context by a harsh exaggeration of emotion, or by rather strained, jocularly explicatory authorial intrusions.

Still, for all the difficulties of cross-cultural translation, *Say Cheese!* is a disturbing and persuasive probe into the inner mechanisms of the Soviet machine on the eve of potential disintegration—or glasnost. The novel ends on a surreal and benignly whimsical vision that may be read as a premonition of a better era; in any case, one hopes Mr. Aksyonov's diagnosis is no longer accurate or in imminent need of non-fictional revival.

## Zinovy Zinik (review date 13 August 1989)

SOURCE: "The Soviet Union Is No Joke," in *Los Angeles Times Book Review*, August 13, 1989, pp. 2, 10.

[*In the following review, Zinik, a novelist, points out the autobiographical aspects of* Say Cheese! *and faults the novel for its use of 1960s Russian jargon.*]

Vassily Aksyonov tells his story of Moscow life of the 1970s as an adventure yarn about a group of dissident photographers who, in spite of KGB schemings, produce an "underground" photography album, *Say Cheese!* and, having failed to publish it officially, smuggle it to the West. In flashbacks between the actions we learn life stories of all the participants of this enterprise, spearheaded by the ringleader of the group, Maxim Ogorodnikov, who walks recklessly through life on a tightrope between his seven ex-wives, his numerous lovers and colleagues, some of whom are KGB informers. His mother's apartment on Gorky Street is full of old Bolshevik memorabilia. His stepbrother, a Soviet journalist stationed mainly abroad, is also a KGB general assigned to the propaganda department.

The hero's physical strength and sexual prowess, his reckless determination and the sheer energy he always exudes make him a natural leader among his friends who, brave and honest as they are, cannot match Ogorodnikov's ability to tackle with the same panache as he does any dangerous confrontation with the authorities. In the course of expanding the official norms of artistic freedom, he makes his way from the basement studios of Moscow's "underground" to a loft party in New York's SoHo. As a result of his James-Bondian behavior, he is eventually deprived of all privileges associated with the Soviet elite. That incenses him so much that he braces himself for a head-on collision (in both the symbolic, and the literary sense) with the KGB. Crippled in a car crash masterminded by KGB operators at the end of his life journey, the hero does not lose his sense of moral superiority.

This tragic finale is a logical consequence of the profusion of cars that crops up from every corner of Aksyonov's book. Each and everyone of them, be it a KGB surveillance vehicle or a friend's banger, is described by the author with feverish obsessiveness and a loving attention to detail regardless of the appropriateness of the occasion. The same absurdly inappropriate attention is given, say, to the hero's clothes, especially to those with a foreign trade mark. The scarcity of goods on the shop shelves means that the opportunity to dress decently or to drive a decent car is the only proof that one belongs to that exclusive class of people who have access to the system of distribution of goods that others in the Soviet Union would not get for any amount of money in the world. Such access is granted to those who are either loyal to the party and system, or related to and affiliated with those who have already passed the exams and received the certificate of being ideologically kosher. Thus, the material aspects of Soviet existence, having acquired an ideological dimension, become part of the spiritual life of the country. Aksyonov's characters with material goods is meant to demonstrate that this corruption of spirit has encompassed the entire country. Nobody's immune. Everyone is either a scoundrel or an outright murderer and informer. Those who survive are changed beyond recognition. Ogorodnikov's life story is the epitome of such change.

In one blurb Aksyonov is quoted as saying that the character of Ogorodnikov in *Say Cheese!* is a "composite" of various persons he has known, but acknowledges that he "does look like me, just a little." Intentionally or not, Aksyonov's protagonist emerges from the novel as a rather unpleasant individual. Having read about Ogorodnikov, the reader might expect that once outside the Soviet Union, in the West, away from the accursed Soviet system, without its *apparatchiks* and lackeys to blame for his own mistakes, the hero would realize his own personal inadequacies. But no, not yet. With an amazing, motherly loyalty to his creation, Aksyonov is always at hand to provide him with emotional assistance to extricate himself from compromising situations.

The world outside turns out to be no better than the Soviet prison. Paris *émigré* life is run by the Cold-Warmongers who exploit every remark accidentally uttered by Ogorodnikov to whip up anti-Soviet hysteria. New York swarms with shady publishers and greedy gallery owners anxious to make easy money by capitalizing on the suffering of the Russian intelligentsia. This ignorant mob is manipulated by a sinister Alik Konsky. "Everything in his hands. He's a universally recognized authority on Russian photography. Didn't you know that in Moscow? Just imagine, he's started this snob idea in New York that Russian photography requires translation into Western languages. . . . And if you dare say anywhere that it's all bull, you immediately become an Eastern Barbarian and are sent off to the second rank."

If the figure of Ogorodnikov "just a little" resembles Aksyonov, the portrait of Konsky is undeniably that of the poet Josef Brodsky. In principle, there is nothing wrong in such direct borrowings from life—and Brodsky's life story is already a part of Russian history, open for everyone to borrow, free of charge—but Aksyonov's assault would have been understandable and expedient had he meant to debunk this westernized Nobel Prize laureate. Regrettably, though, Aksyonov uses a distorted version of someone else's life story to exonerate his own hero of existential crises that are not dissimilar to those suffered by the author. For that purpose, for example, Aksyonov makes his hero a victim of a conspiracy, orchestrated by Konsky and "his groupies" and not without KGB help, aimed to discredit Ogorodnikov artistically and to provoke him into an act of defection.

There is a lot of wishful thinking here. I wouldn't have touched upon the subject had the autobiographical and semi-documentary nature of this novel not been openly publicized in the blurb: "In 1979 Vassily Aksyonov spearheaded the effort to create *Metropol,* the first uncensored album of Soviet literature. He was forced to emigrate the following year when his satirical novel, **The Burn,** was published in the West."

In real life, Aksyonov was accused by some of his comrades-in-arms of using "Metropol" as a publicity springboard—to jump over the Iron Curtain and land safely in the West. In *Say Cheese!* his photographic double is flying abroad, not to defect but to show the world that he is smart enough to outdo even the KGB operators. Disillusioned with the West, he returns to Moscow to face the music. It is his brother, a corrupt Soviet journalist and KGB man who defects to the West, while our hero is doomed to remain crippled in his motherland—again an allusion to a life story of a Russian novelist Andrej Bitov and his journalist brother Oleg.

In order to liberate his novelistic spirit and imagination, Aksyonov employs a number of devices, the main one of which is to present Soviet literature and the life of the Moscow literati, thinly disguised as that of the photography world. It works perfectly well as a witty metaphor at the beginning but slowly the parable becomes repetitive and over-strained. When Ogorodnikov arrives in New York, he discovers that, under the influence of the gifted manipulator, Konsky, in all major publishing houses "our negatives are treated with this idiotic translating developer, a mixture of potash and chili sauce."

Ironically, that remark about "idiotic translating developer" becomes a self-parody when applied to Aksyonov's novel itself. Every portrait in this action-packed "photo-album" is treated with "a mixture of potash and chili sauce," to blur the resemblance to a living prototype. Even Moscow geography and the names of the streets are slightly distorted to fit the style of an allegory, to distance the reader from the genre of memoirs into which the author is constantly slipping. Fortunately or not, these aspects of the novel will be lost on the American reader, who will also be relieved of the task of coping with the horribly outdated jargon, a brat-pack lingo of 1960s Moscow, spluttered out on every page with the generosity of a child with a bottle of ketchup (or chili sauce?). What remains is Aksyonov's nostalgia for the sense of camaraderie, with much boozing and swearing, being adored by aging girlfriends and hated by the Party mob.

The hero's pseudo-populist, folksy, bad guy's artificial manner of speech was employed in the 1960s by Aksyonov and his mates with the aim of distancing themselves from the vulgar crowd as well as from the newspeak of officialdom— of which, in fact, they were the most privileged part. That is, probably, the real tragedy behind Aksyonov's attempt here to extricate himself from the rest of the Soviet literary Establishment and to set the record straight. The "Metropol" enterprise was, in fact, not "the first uncensored album of Soviet literature," as described in the blurb, but indeed the first abortive mission to reform the literary Establishment from the inside, by official means. It is the intimacy of the inside information about the establishment that makes Aksyonov's account so remarkable. It is an emotional description of a bureaucratic mechanism in which Aksyonov was a prominent cog. The heroic deeds that Ogorodnikov and his lads commit on the pages of the novel say more about the harshness and stupidity of the Soviet officialdom (thoroughly exposed many times before) than about the tragic character of their predicament. Their tragedy is that they think they've become martyrs of the spiritual liberation of the nation, while in fact they've simply lost the privileges associated with their social position.

## Irving Howe (review date 18 and 25 September 1989)

SOURCE: "Correlation of Farces," in *The New Republic*, Vol. 201, No. 3896/3897, September 18 and 25, 1989, pp. 52-53.

[*In the following review, Howe lauds the farcical aspects of* Say Cheese! *but faults the novel's attempts at seriousness in the latter half of the book.*]

There's a lot of pleasure to be had from the first half of this novel, a satiric farce about the life of culture in Brezhnev's Russia. Vassily Aksyonov, an émigré Russian now living in the United States, writes with the happy abandon of a true farceur. He commands a taste for the ridiculous, cares little for cautions of verisimilitude, and has a ready supply of puns, jokes, and saucy footnotes. His episodic narrative might almost be taken for a picaresque tale, were its hero not deprived of the picaro's traditional freedom to roam and to poke about.

*Say Cheese!* draws upon Aksyonov's own experiences. In 1979 he was a central figure within a group of "intellectual gangsters," that is, serious Russian writers who wanted to issue *Metropol*, the first uncensored anthology of Soviet literature. The results proved to be most unpleasant, Aksyonov resigning from the Writers Union because it expelled two of his colleagues and a year later emigrating from the Soviet Union. In *Say Cheese!,* Russian writers are neatly transformed into Russian photographers, but the cultural bureaucrats harassing them in the name of the Party and History remain pretty much the same. The basic situation is ambiguous, one of neither total unfreedom or total freedom.

They are a lively bunch, these photographers. They carouse, achieve enviable results with women, snap fine pictures; but some nub of memory or imagination troubles them. They aspire, as they would put it, to the manliness that is a sign of creative independence. So they plan a picture album that won't be submitted to the censors: a seemingly innocent, even innocuous venture, but it sets off a flurry of intrigues and counter-moves among the cultural overseers.

The struggle that breaks out between the "New Wave" photographers and "the glands" (a nickname for "the organs" of State Security) is a curious mixture of the ominous and the farcical. Ominous, because the non-terrorist repressions of the Brezhnev regime are brutal enough. Farcical, because neither side, bureaucrats or artists, is prepared for a complete showdown. The situation has a certain resemblance to those silent-film comedies in which a multitude of violent motions settles into calm—yet with the crucial difference that "the glands" are still there, very real, very powerful.

Aksyonov's depiction of his photographers contains a motif

of male bonding, rather innocent despite the virtuoso sex. They are quite serious artists, but also behave like rambunctious adolescents—and somehow Aksyonov makes it all very appealing. Allergic to political cant, the photographers are intuitively anarchist in spirit and style—which seems exactly right for farce, since in its disdain for official proprieties and big questions, farce is a genre with affinities to anarchism. It's also a spirit—anarchism—appropriate for the sclerotic Brezhnev regime.

Leading the New Wave is Max Ogordnikov, who combines genius with irreverence, and who is also a veteran skirt-chaser now into his seventh marriage. (During a visit to New York, Ogo rises, after an initial Stendhalian embarrassment with his publisher's secretary, to seven powerful orgasms in rapid succession. Talk of lucky numbers!) Ogo despises the cultural bureaucrats not so much because he is committed heart and soul to democracy, but because they evoke in him an irritable boredom: it's tiresome to have to submit your work to a dimwit like Fotii Feklovich, "First Secretary" of photography, a character who last inhabited Gogol's *The Inspector General."*

"I'm tired," explains Ogo, "of only playing their games, I'd like to play just once to my own taste, as if they didn't exist, after all it's not against them, just without them . . ." This strikes me as one of Aksyonov's cleverest strokes: to show how *boredom* with bureaucracy can lead to artistic defiance.

The resourceful Ogo manages, by tricking his bosses, to have an unsanctioned trip to Germany and the United States, with an eye toward getting the New Wave album published. In Germany he has a very funny encounter with an enraged ultraleftist bedecked in rags, who turns out to be (of course) the son-in-law of a billionaire. In New York, Ogo meets Alex Konsky, the émigré photographer who now "dictates [cultural] fashion." Reports another émigré: "In New York it's hard to work seriously in Russian art unless you kiss Alex Konsky's ass. . . . He's started this snob idea that Russian photography requires translation into Western language." This "unbribable genius of pure form" has become a virtuoso in the American art of making it, and it figures that he will stick out his foot to trip up Ogo's project.

But about halfway, alas, *Say Cheese!* succumbs to seriousness. There's a sound logic behind this: Aksyonov is being faithful to the social reality that constitutes his setting; and by the last third of the book, the conflict between New Wave and "glands" has turned quite deadly. While plausible as rendered history, the literary result is unfortunate. It's a case of historical conscience triumphing over a gift of farce; of reality over art.

Farce, as the masters of silent film understood, is a short-breathed form. It is a kick in the pants, a slide on the banana

peel, and then do it again. And again. In farce, development yields to repetition, or more accurately, repetition *is* development—but it can't go on for 404 pages. Had Aksyonov cut his book by a third, mostly in the last third, he'd have had a marvelous piece of work. As it is, much of it offers acute pleasure.

I suspect, but of course I cannot prove, that there is another reason for the novel's decline into seriousness. With rare exceptions like the early Waugh and the early Amis, writers of farce seem to feel uneasy at the thought of staying with the mode they have begun with, as if it's a violation of man and nature. They want also to show that they are serious and thoughtful people, able to don the double-breasted suits of respectability. It never works.

## William Phillips (review date Winter 1991)

SOURCE: "Dissidents Abroad," in *Partisan Review,* Vol. LVIII, No. 1, Winter, 1991, pp. 149-50.

[*In the following brief review, Aksyonov's novel* Say Cheese! *is lauded as a "well-made, surprisingly fluid" book.*]

Conformists are all alike; dissidents are all different—and more original. Andrei Sinyavsky's and Vassily Aksyonov's new novels are striking examples of this literary rule. *Say Cheese!* by Aksyonov is a very amusing and skillfull work, as it charts the waters of the dissident imagination. *Goodnight* by Sinyavsky (writing as Abram Tertz) is a strange, haunting mixture of narrative, commentary, and rumination. Both writers live in exile, Sinyavsky in Paris, Aksyonov in Washington, D.C. Sinyavsky spent seven years in a labor camp for having a premature criticism of socialist realism smuggled to the West, using the pseudonym of Abram Tertz. Aksyonov was forced to leave the Soviet Union for "treasonable" writings. Sinyavsky strikes one as the most profound and resourceful Russian writer today; Aksyonov as one of the most intelligent.

*Say Cheese!* tells the rambling story of Russian people caught in the Kafkaesque web of Soviet bureaucratic constrictions, evading the fatalities of the life dictated from above through irony, doubletalk, and cunning. (One is reminded of Joyce's "silence, exile, and cunning.") In a sense there is no story, only a series of comic incidents as everyone tries to escape from his or her prescribed existence. It is a well-made novel, surprisingly fluid in the agile twists and turns of the narrative and its utter disregard of earlier Soviet literary conventions. It has the free flow of an American-style novel, but it is not a blockbuster. It is a contemporary, not a modern, novel.

The prevailing spirit of *Say Cheese!* is irreverence, which I suppose is the basic substance of dissidence. In this respect, *Say Cheese!* reminds one of the eighteenth-century British picaresque novel, set, however, in Stalinized Russia. It turns around the escapades of a group of underground photographers, called Cheesers, who defy the government with unsocialist photography. The main character, an antihero, Max "Ogo" Ogorodnikov, is a sexual and political adventurer who moves from woman to woman, place to place, caper to caper, thumbing his nose at authority, and ending up at a swish party in New York. It is most entertaining, but it raises the question of topically dissident writing. For Gorbachev, in taking Russia at least partly out of its past, has lifted it to a new level of problematic freedoms that tends to make earlier pictures of Russia seem somewhat out of date.

However, the novel does recreate a sense of what appears to be the life of the country, even now in the Gorbachev era. One gets the impression of an interweaving of identities, a whirlpool of spying, infiltrating, snitching, defying the regime, whoring, drinking, evading the secret police. The KGB penetrates every bit of life, sometimes comically, sometimes brutally. The whole is Russia. Everyone is playing cat-and-mouse with everyone else. And it is all drenched in suffering, opportunism, soul-seeking. Looking for sexual recognition, Max has had seven wives and countless women. There are fifty characters moving in and out of the pages of the novel, all making their way through the ambiguities of Soviet existence, puffing themselves up, mocking themselves and each other. And everyone plays his role, somewhere between belonging to and subverting the regime. Aksyonov tells it all with a sharp sardonic eye and ear, as he satirically catches the pieties of the official language. In fact, the novel is a verbal *tour de force,* chatty, and sprawling verbally over a landscape that seems so unreal to us, and is made both more and less real by Aksyonov's merging of reality with farce.

## Jay Parini (review date 17 July 1994)

SOURCE: "Counterrevolutionary Families Are All the Same," in *New York Times Book Review,* July 17, 1994, p. 6.

[*In the review of* Generations of Winter *below, Parini, an educator, poet, and novelist, compares Aksyonov to Leo Tolstoy and Aleksandr Solzhenitsyn, lauding Aksyonov's "deft historical scholarship."*]

Vassily Aksyonov is the most widely admired Russian novelist of his generation. A physician by training, he enraged the Soviet literary establishment with his jazzy second novel, *Ticket to the Stars* (1961), which featured the urbanized, Western-influenced youth of the day. Defying censorship at every turn, he produced a blistering sequence of novels and

plays during the next two decades; in 1979, he was among the group that published a dissident anthology, *Metropol,* in a symbolic edition of one. The next year, with the appearance of his novel *The Burn*—a brilliant, surreal fantasia on Soviet life—he was forced to emigrate.

In exile in the United States, Mr. Aksyonov wrote several remarkable novels, including *The Island of Crimea* and *Say Cheese!* The post-modern, almost Pynchonesque feel of this recent work may have left readers unprepared for his latest novel, *Generations of Winter,* a masterly, rather self-consciously Tolstoyan epic that opens in the late 1920's and ends, hauntingly, amid the ruins of World War II.

Mr. Aksyonov's personal history has certainly prepared him for the task of writing this book. His mother was Eugenia Ginzburg, author of *Journey Into the Whirlwind* and *Within the Whirlwind,* memoirs of the years she spent in the Stalinist camps at Kolyma and in exile in Siberia. A devout Marxist, she was arrested in 1937, when Mr. Aksyonov was not yet 5 years old, and "purged." She spent the next 18 years in prisons, labor camps and forced exile and did not see her son again until he was 16. Although he has written about this experience before, most notably in *The Burn,* Mr. Aksyonov takes full possession of his past in this rich work of memory and invention.

*Generations of Winter* operates on that tantalizing border between fact and fiction. Real figures—generals, politicians, artists—mingle with imaginary ones; even Stalin himself puts in several appearances, as do other major players in his murderous regime. The focus of the novel, however, is the fictional Gradov family, over whom Dr. Boris Nikitovich Gradov presides as a benign patriarch. Dr. Gradov is "one of the best surgeons in Moscow. Even 'makers of history' had to reckon with specialists of his caliber." As a result, he and his family enjoy Silver Forest, a lovely dacha outside Moscow that seems far from the madding Kremlin crowd; until the late 1930's, they continue to live as their bourgeois counterparts might have before the Bolsheviks seized power.

As in *War and Peace,* a handful of fictional characters engage our sympathy early in the novel, and we follow closely as they descend into the Soviet labyrinth, some never to return. In particular, we track the careers of Kirill, Nikita and Nina Gradov, the children of the great doctor and his long-suffering wife, Mary. Kirill is a keen Marxist who marries an equally ardent ideologue, Cecilia Rosenbloom; as party activists, they are the True Believers in the family. Nikita is devoid of political idealism; a military man to the bones, he rises quickly to become a leading officer in the Red Army. Nina is a cynical poet, a bohemian of sorts, and thus a threat to the family; one fully expects her to suffer at the hands of the secret police.

Alas, nothing makes sense in Stalin's world. It is Government policy to strike randomly, keeping the entire population in a state of perpetual apprehension. The military, the intelligentsia and the general populace are powerless as state terrorism spirals inward, crushing its own people: "Nothing special is happening," observes Nikita, in the eerily ironic tone that pervades the narrative. "The only thing that's happening is a silent conspiracy of millions upon millions of people who have reached a tacit agreement that nothing is happening." But something dreadful *is* happening.

It would be unfair to readers to say who gets swept into concentration camps and who doesn't; it is enough to suggest that the unpredictability of the plot keeps one perpetually frightened. *Generations of Winter* captures the anxiety, the Kafkaesque pointlessness of state cruelty, with ferocious artistry. The portraits of camp life and the torture chambers of the N.K.V.D. are harrowing. Indeed, we feel something like relief that World War II begins: at least in the context of global conflict, the ghastly panorama of human suffering described by Mr. Aksyonov seems vaguely comprehensible.

Through the character of Nina, the author derides the pretensions of the Soviet literary scene. "The literature of socialist realism was in full flower," he writes, witheringly. "Formalism had already been completely rooted out. Soviet poets, playwrights and novelists had been gathered up in a single union and were vigorously turning out the works the people needed." *Generations of Winter* is seeded with quotations from the great Russian poets, whom the novelist obviously reveres. (Indeed, one of the most moving scenes in his mother's memoir occurs when she and her son are reunited and recognize their deep connection to each other through a common interest in Russian poetry.) It is, however, unfortunate that the allusive resonance of this novel is, perhaps necessarily, lost in translation.

Mr. Aksyonov has never been easy to translate, in part because he relishes slang and likes hearing various levels of diction clash. But the translators of *Generations of Winter,* John Glad and Christopher Morris, seem at a loss to find the appropriate registers. A man who propositions Nina Gradov, for example, says to her, "Just look at me. I'm suffering because you won't put out!" A few lines later, brushing him off, she responds: "Yes, I'm married, you swindling nincompoop." In another chapter, we read of one character that a "thought flashed through Styopka's noggin." Elsewhere, a young man asks his friend. "Shall we hop on up to the Party Committee hall?" Similar oddities occur throughout the novel, but the sweep of the narrative is such that one soon overlooks them.

Again like Tolstoy, whom he invokes directly and indirectly throughout the book, Mr. Aksyonov pauses at several key places to reflect on the laws of history, attempting to bring

his endlessly tragic story into perspective. That he does not succeed was perhaps inevitable; the enormity of Stalin's crimes against humanity will take centuries to absorb. But *Generations of Winter* is unquestionably a triumph for Vassily Aksyonov: an act of remembrance, a piece of deft historical scholarship and a substantial work of fiction that will sit comfortably in years to come on the shelf beside Aleksandr Solzhenitsyn's *One Day in the Life of Ivan Denisovich* and the *Kolyma Tales* of Varlam Shalamov.

## Adam Hochschild (review date 7 August 1994)

SOURCE: "War and Peace, Part II," in *Los Angeles Times Book Review,* August 7, 1994, pp. 1, 11.

[*Hochschild is a nonfiction writer whose works include* The Unquiet Ghost: Russians Remember Stalin. *In the review below, he asserts that the model for Aksyonov's* Generations of Winter *is Tolstoy's* War and Peace *and praises Aksyonov's realistic descriptions, calling the novel "absorbing" and claiming that "everything rings true."*]

Near the end of her memoirs of Stalin's gulag, the writer Eugenia Ginzburg describes an extraordinary scene. She had just finished many years' imprisonment in Kolyma—the harshest, coldest, most feared region of the vast labor camp system, in the far northeast corner of Siberia, not far from Alaska. Like most newly released prisoners, Ginzburg had to remain in internal exile for some years more. Her husband also had vanished into the gulag, and, while she was in prison, one of her two sons had died in the siege of Leningrad. But the authorities permitted her surviving son to join her in exile. In 1948, he made the long trip to Kolyma, a 16-year-old with a knapsack on his back. She had not seen him for 11 years and greatly feared that they would have nothing in common. But "I found myself catching my breath with joyful astonishment when that very first night he started to recite from memory the very poems that had been my constant companions during my fight for survival in the camps."

To Russian readers the scene is even more moving, because they know that this tall, thin teenager with his knapsack grew up to become Vassily Aksyonov, one of the best-loved dissident writers of the 1960s and '70s.

Aksyonov stayed on in Kolyma with his mother for several years. There has been surprisingly little about the world of the gulag in his books so far, even though he left the reach of Soviet censors when he moved to the United States 14 years ago. He used a little of his Kolyma experience in his surreal 1980 novel *The Burn,* but there and in other books, his characteristic voice has been one of satire, fantasy and the grotesque, bold stylistic experimentation and comic use of slang. Some call Aksyonov a Russian J. D. Salinger.

*Generations of Winter* is a startling departure from all this. Except for occasional flourishes, its form is that of classic late 19th-Century realism, something as unexpected from Aksyonov as it would be from Salinger or Pynchon. As in what is clearly its model, *War and Peace,* the narrator is omniscient, and historical characters—Stalin, Molotov, Beria and others—stroll through the pages along with home-grown ones. Although Aksyonov's characters are not as memorable as Tolstoy's (whose are?), this is as absorbing as any novel I have come across in the last few years. I read it past bedtime at night and before getting to work in the morning, and found my mind wandering off to it during the day.

One reason people write traditional realist novels these days is that modern readers are jaded. Film, radio, first-person journalism, prying biographers and, above all, TV, have saturated us with reality. And so who are you, impudent novelist, to make up details about a prisoner's interrogation, or about what food was served at a Kremlin reception, or about what passed through Stalin's mind as he greeted his guests?

Aksyonov, however, has the authority to tell all this, and much more. His father was a high party official and member of the Central Executive Committee of the U.S.S.R. Both his parents spent many years in the gulag. Aksyonov himself grew up among exiles, the bereaved and survivors. Yet even if we did not know all this about him, we would hear no false notes in this novel. Everything rings true. Take this passing description of well-to-do players on a Moscow tennis court in 1930: "All three were representatives of the 'famous lawyer' type, a class that had survived the Revolution, returned fully to life, and now would take any case except one involving the defense of an accused man."

*Generations of Winter* pans across a quarter century of Soviet history, from 1921 to 1945. At center stage is the Gradov family, and their children, friends and relatives, all members of that caste which in Russia has always thought of itself as a race apart, the intelligentsia. Boris Gradov is a distinguished surgeon; his wife Mary is a pianist. Under the steadily darkening sky of those years, their *dacha* on the outskirts of Moscow is an oasis of music, books, poetry, good food and spirited talk.

The times sweep several of the Gradovs into prison, or into World War II, or, in one case, both. Army general Nikita Gradov, the eldest son, is arrested in Stalin's Great Purge of the late 1930s. After four years as a slave laborer in the gold mines of Kolyma, emaciated and barely alive, he is plucked from the gulag and given a high army command. A story most improbable—except that such things happened. Some of the officers who led the Red Army to victory, such as

Gen. (later Marshal) Konstantin Rokossovsky and Gen. Alexander Gorbatov, had been half-starved prisoners a few months before. Russian history has always been stranger than fiction.

One thing that gives that history its aura of tragedy is that there seem so many turning points when it could have taken a different course. What if the Bolsheviks had not established their all-powerful secret police in 1917? What if they had not dissolved the Constituent Assembly of 1918, chosen in the first real free elections Russia had ever known? What if they had not suppressed the Kronstadt revolt of 1921?

Kronstadt was perhaps the last of the great "what if's." After it was over, the Soviet Union's course was fixed inevitably toward an absolutism more terrible than that of the czars. Thousands of radical sailors on the Baltic fortress island of Kronstadt mutinied against the government. They demanded such things as elections by secret ballot, free trade unions and the freeing of political prisoners. Trotsky and Lenin sent troops across the ice to crush the rebellion, with heavy loss of life on both sides.

In *Generations of Winter,* the young officer Nikita Gradov follows orders to help suppress the revolt. Sick at heart, he knows that he is betraying what he had hoped the Russian Revolution would be. For the rest of his life memories of Kronstadt haunt him. They come pouring out even when he is beaten into a state of delirium by secret police interrogators 16 years later.

For Nikita's father, the surgeon, the key act of betrayal comes in 1925. Officials ask him to give his medical opinion that army commander Mikhail Frunze needs an operation. (At the time, apparently, several doctors were pressured into doing this. Frunze, potentially a strong rival to Stalin, then died mysteriously during the surgery.) When Dr. Gradov at first balks, secret policemen make veiled threats against his daughter, and he gives in.

These two early betrayals set the pattern for more. The political betrayals are echoed by sexual betrayals. As with Dr. Gradov and his son, sometimes even these are almost life-and-death choices: Thrown into the gulag, Nikita Gradov's wife, a great beauty, becomes the mistress of a camp commandant to gain herself enough food to survive. When she and her husband are released and reunited, he sees her well-fed body and realizes what has happened. He cannot forgive her. The virus of betrayal then travels down through the generations to their teen-age son. He runs away from home to join the Red Army, only to find himself behind the lines fighting not the Germans, but the Soviet Union's nominal ally, the Poles.

Few of the characters in this novel are untarnished, and that is part of its emotional accuracy. The toll taken in any tyranny is not measured only in physical suffering, but also in complicity. The prisoner who has almost starved can recover; the friend whose denunciation sent him or her to prison never can. And even without denunciations, tens of millions of Soviets had to make countless other betrayals to keep their jobs or their lives: teachers taught history they knew was false; scientists embraced Lysenko's wishful-thinking biology; writers hailed Stalin as the greatest genius of all time.

With a hand never too heavy, Aksyonov shows us what it was like to live through such times. Moreover, he gives us men and women who are painfully aware of their complicity, but who must go on living nonetheless. And go on they do: At the end of *Generation of Winter*'s 600 pages some cycles of action are uncompleted, others are newly begun and key characters are still in moral transit. One senses a sequel to come. I await it eagerly.

### Christopher Lehmann-Haupt (review date 8 August 1994)

SOURCE: "A Russian Family Copes with Stalinism's Evils," in *The New York Times,* August 8, 1994, p. C16.

[*In the review below, Lehmann-Haupt faults* Generations of Winter *for its use of archaic jargon and slang but nevertheless calls the book "monumental" and finds the language less distracting as the novel progresses.*]

There are a few hurdles to overcome before you can get caught up in the powerful sweep of Vassily Aksyonov's *Generations of Winter,* a Tolstoyan historical novel that is a departure from the author's previous, less traditional fiction (*The Island of Crimea, Say Cheese!, The Burn*) and traces the roller-coaster fortunes of one Russian family from 1925, the year of Stalin's ascent to power, to 1945, the end of World War II.

"'So you're not afraid?'" asks an American journalist in Moscow on page 10 "with the directness of a quarterback shotgunning the ball across midfield into his opponent's territory." The metaphor seems as anachronistic as some of the slang the characters employ, with their references to women as broads, food as grub and the head as a noggin.

"'All right, let's go chow down!'" one character says "delightedly, even though at one time, he found this sort of Moscow Communist slang repulsive." "Chow down" is Moscow Communist slang? This will come as surprising news to veterans of the United States Army. In short, those who translated *Generations* from the Russian seem at times to be groping wildly.

Yet the deeper you get into Mr. Aksyonov's story, the more trivial the lapses in dialogue seem. What first catches your interest is the scene in which Boris Nikitovich Gradov, a fictional Moscow surgeon, is called away from a party at his home to attend to the Commissar for Defense, Mikhail Frunze, an actual historical figure, who has collapsed from a hemorrhaging ulcer. Frunze whispers desperately to Gradov that he doesn't require surgery. Gradov agrees. But a team of Kremlin physicians decides to operate anyway, and when Gradov objects, he is told to wait in an adjoining room. Of course Frunze dies, and Gradov begins to experience what will shortly become an epidemic of bad consciences.

This scene will later be mirrored when Gradov is called to the Kremlin to look after Stalin himself, who has gone into convulsions from being constipated. In the interval, both of Gradov's sons have been arrested and sent to the gulag—the older one, Gen. Nikita Borisovich, on the trumped-up charge of conspiring against the revolution with his immediate superior, Marshal Vasily Blücher; the younger one, Kirill, for being Nikita's brother.

When Gradov relieves Stalin's agony with an enema, the tyrant is wordlessly grateful. As the passage reads: "The human face surfaced and trembled nearby. Ask for anything, Professor, and it's yours. Ask me for your sons, and they'll be with you in two days. Ask me now, Professor, while I want to thank you; later on it will be too late." But Gradov cannot bring himself to ask a favor of a patient. Later, when he meets Stalin at a Kremlin gathering, they shake hands. "They looked each other in the eye for several seconds. If he asks me about his sons now, I'll destroy him, thought Stalin."

The Gradov family is endlessly appealing, from Boris's Georgian wife, Mary Vakhtangovna, who comforts the family by playing Chopin on the piano, to their daughter Nina, a tempestuously romantic poet who worships Osip Mandelstam. But the real protagonist is the novel's narrator, who modulates his voice limitlessly. He steps up close to describe the most intimate of love scenes and the most brutal incidents of torture in the basement of the infamous Lubyanka. He backs far away to report the great battles that turned away the invading Nazis in the winter of 1941 and the sickening massacre of Ukrainian Jews in a ravine near Chernigov in the summer of 1943.

This narrator waxes chatty when parsing Tolstoy's theory of history in *War and Peace.* He turns satiric in describing Lenin's return to earth as a large male squirrel. And he disappears from the page in Dos Passos-like intermissions that sum up history according to stories in the press.

That this voice is endlessly mutable is just as well, because some of the scenes it describes are so extreme in their cruelty or treachery that no appropriate comment is left to be made.

Irina, Nina Gradov's editor at *Working Woman,* a newspaper, remarks of an article Nina has written that it contains "traces of your habitual irony." She adds: "The time for irony is over, Nina. It is our fate to live in heroic times." To which Nina responds, "Without irony, Irka, it's simply impossible to get through these heroic times." Without irony, it's impossible to get through the events of Mr. Aksyonov's novel.

The narrator does convey movingly why good people continued to fight and die for the Soviet Union. After Nikita Gradov is rehabilitated and given command of a special strike force to attack the invading Germans, he is decorated by Stalin. At the ceremony, he wonders what would happen if he ordered his bodyguards "to wipe out this whole group." A moment later: "A wave of genuine, unfeigned enthusiasm suddenly washed over him, having its origins in his total attachment to everything that at that moment embodied his country, even to this collection of faces, to them especially and particularly, a group that just a few minutes before, he had imagined as the targets of his loyal machine gunners."

At the end of this monumental story you learn that Nikita's brother, Kirill, is still alive in the gulag. He has discovered Jesus Christ. For an instant you think that here is Mr. Aksyonov's message: the only rational response to Russian history is religious faith. But then you remember that up until this point Kirill Gradov has been the most rigidly doctrinaire of Marxists. All the narrator is saying is that Kirill has switched religions.

Or is that really all the narrator is saying? Maybe faith is his message after all.

## John Banville (review date 3 November 1994)

SOURCE: "War without Peace," in *New York Review of Books,* Vol. XLI, No. 18, November 3, 1994, pp. 4-6.

[*In the review below, Banville lauds* Generations of Winter *as a "major document of our times, and one with lasting power."*]

In *Generations of Winter* Vassily Aksyonov has set out bravely, one might even say brazenly, to write a twentieth-century *War and Peace,* mingling fictional and historical characters in a great sprawling saga tracing the history of the Soviet Union. This first volume runs from 1925 to 1945; a second volume brings the story into the post-war era. The surprise is that he has succeeded to a remarkable degree. To predict at this point that his novel will prove as enduring as

Tolstoy's classic is, of course, impossible. There is a certain coarseness in Aksyonov's literary manner which can be apt, certainly, for the task at hand—has there ever been a coarser place than Stalin's Russia?—but the book's sturdy, carpentered quality at times seems too clumsy to bear comparison with Tolstoy's exquisitely balanced artistic effects. All the same, Aksyonov's energy, inventiveness, and insouciance have resulted in what is surely a major document of our times, and one with lasting power.

> [In *Generations of Winter,*] Aksyonov's energy, inventiveness, and insouciance have resulted in what is surely a major document of our times, and one with lasting power.
>
> —*John Banville*

Obviously any Russian author attempting to write a work on such a scale would find himself stumbling in Tolstoy's shadow. Aksyonov's solution to the problem is to turn on his heel and grin defiantly in his great predecessor's face. He has not so much struck the father dead as given him a playful pat on the cheek. The text abounds in references to *War and Peace* whether in an epigraph, in offhand allusions to Tolstoy's characters, or in passages such as this, from the preface to the second part of the book, which is called "War and Jail":

> Not long ago, we were reading *War and Peace*—for the first time since childhood, we must admit, and not at all in connection with the beginning of *War and Jail* but for pure reading pleasure—and came upon a number of Tolstoy's thoughts on the riddles of history, which sometimes touch us joyfully by their similarities with our own thoughts but which at other times lead into a blind alley.

The plural pronoun suggests arch humor rather than even a small degree of modesty. Elsewhere Aksyonov plays a game with old-fashioned styles of narration, as in this passage from early in the book where we are first introduced to the heroine—or one of the heroines—of the book, Nina Gradov, who is destined to become a renowned poet, a sort of cross between Akhmatova and Tsvetayeva:

> The front doors banged then, quick steps sounded, and Nina burst into the dining room. Her dark chestnut hair was disheveled, her bright blue eyes were shining, the collar of her overcoat was turned up, and she was carrying a briefcase under her arm, as well as a knapsack full of books.

"Hello, family!" she yelped. She rushed over to Veronika, kissed her on the lips and once on the stomach [Veronika is pregnant], then flopped down for a moment onto Nikita's lap, shook the hand of Kirill the Party worker, and said with tragic seriousness: "All that we have is yours, comrades tough as stone!" Like an English lady, she extended her hand to be kissed by Leonid Valentinovich Pulkovo and then bestowed a kiss on everyone else.

Passages such as this, which could have come from any second-rate nineteenth-century Russian novel—or novelette—make the reader's heart sink, but Aksyonov is fully conscious of the effect he is creating, and this portrait of the typical Russian heroine—the chestnut hair, the bright blue eyes—is weighted heavily with irony, as the reader will presently discover. The vicissitudes that await Nina, as well as her brothers Nikita and Kirill and sister-in-law Veronika, will very soon wipe off entirely any trace of an indulgent smile that the early pages of the novel may appear to wear. The horrors of Stalinism were far greater than those of the Napoleonic invasion.

Vassily Aksyonov was born in Kazan in 1933. His mother was the historian Eugenia Ginzburg (the book is dedicated to her memory and to that of his father, Pavel Aksyonov), and he spent much of his childhood with her in exile in Siberia. Memories of those years no doubt helped him to write the gulag sections of *Generations of Winter* with such immediacy. In the 1960s he was an energetic and, insofar as the times and the censors would allow, successful writer of novels, literary criticism, and screenplays. In 1980 he traveled to the United States, and settled in Washington to work on a novel at the Wilson Center. In January of the following year the Soviet government stripped him of his citizenship. Throughout the 1980s he lived in the US and produced novels, the best known of which is *The Burn,* and a cheerful and charming memoir, *In Search of Melancholy Baby,* of the splendors and miseries (very few of the latter) of the first years of his life in America.

In his work up to now Aksyonov has been exuberant, cocksure, and faintly "experimental," in a relaxed, late-Modernist way. With *Generations of Winter,* however, he has put together something more formidable, and what a tank of a book it is. It grinds its way with unstoppable force across the vast territory of the former Soviet Union, from Moscow to Siberia, from Georgia to the Western front during the Hitler war. So vast is the scale of the work, so palpable the passing of the years, that at the end of the book the reader feels he has completed an immense journey through space and time; looking back to the opening pages is like flicking through the earliest photographs in a family album.

The family in question is the Gradovs, headed by Boris Gradov, an eminent surgeon, and therefore a person of consequence, since the Party hierarchy likes to look after its own health. When the book opens it is 1925, the Revolution is still young, and the country, and especially its capital city, is feverish with a sense of the possibilities of the future. Already, of course, the forces of totalitarianism and repression are at work, as Stalin and his henchmen position themselves to destroy or neutralize their opponents. Aksyonov very cunningly implicates the Gradovs in the destiny of the country by making Boris a leading member of the medical team assigned to treat Stalin's opponent, the Commissar for Defense Mikhail Frunze, for stomach ulcers; Boris is an excellent doctor, and knows that Frunze does not need the operation that others in the medical team, and the political puppeteers controlling them, insist is necessary. During a crucial Politburo meeting Frunze suffers a hemorrhage and collapses. Stalin seizes his chance.

> "We must bring in the best doctors," announced Stalin. "Burdenko, Rozanov, Gradov . . . the Party cannot allow such a son to be lost."
>
> Trotsky was right, thought Zinoviev. This man will say whatever raises him higher than anyone else, even if only an inch.
>
> Stalin walked over to the table and sat down. His seat, though one of many, suddenly appeared to be the center of the oval. Perhaps, in accordance with the rules of drama, attention was fixed on him because he had appeared at a decisive moment, or perhaps it was something else; whatever the reason, it was indeed Stalin whom the dazed members of the Politburo and the government were looking at. It was obvious that, all the different interpretations of the meaning of Frunze's illness notwithstanding, a motif of fate and gloom had been introduced beneath the arches of the Kremlin, as though a flight of Valkyries had winged past.
>
> Stalin looked out the window for a minute or two at the indifferent clouds passing in the October sky, then intoned: ". . . but eternally green is the tree of life . . ."
>
> The Party men, who had long experiences in emigration behind them, remembered that the great man himself, Lenin, had loved to repeat this line from Faust.
>
> "Let's continue." With a benign gesture, Stalin proposed that they return to the order of business.

This passage illustrates very well Aksyonov's method. He is undaunted by the usual problem faced by the historical novelist, that of finding ways to neutralize the chilling effect of famous names ("I say, Mozart, isn't that young Beethoven over there?"). He mingles historical and fictional characters with such skill that only a reader with a detailed knowledge of Soviet history will be able to distinguish all of the real from all of the invented. He is not afraid to write of the top Soviet leaders and feels no need to introduce them with tiresome physical descriptions ("Trotsky was right, thought Zinoviev"). Also characteristic are the brief nod in the direction of postmodernism ("in accordance with the rules of drama") and the Wagnerian swish of those Valkyries' wings. What is most impressive in this scene, however, is the subtlety and economy of the portrait of Stalin, the self-serving monster posing as devoted Party man yet at the same time demonstrating that he is the true successor to Lenin. With that "benign gesture" Frunze's fate is sealed.

The document directing that the Commissar be operated upon is drawn up, and Boris, after an icy interview with a pair of Kafkaesque NKVD men, puts his name to it. Although he is allowed to remain outside the operating theater while the murder is being committed by the rest of the medical team, he knows very well that he has done something that will haunt him for the rest of his days. He retreats at once to the family dacha in Silver Forest, where his wife, Mary Vakhtangovna, will try to soothe his conscience with the Chopin études she plays at times of family crisis. Mary, a Georgian, is a figure straight out of Thomas Mann: passionate, artistic, loving, and a little silly; Aksyonov uses her to introduce the theme of the warm south, the land of blue skies and "ripe pears that resembled the breasts of young Greek girls," which is also, ironically, the birthplace of Iosif Vissarionovich himself, the Man of Steel who will wreak terrible damage upon the Gradov family and the millions of other families over whom he comes to exercise absolute power.

Aksyonov leaves no doubt whatever that the tragedy of the Soviet Union from the 1930s onward was largely the work of one man. The portrait of Stalin here seems broadly drawn but it also has many subtle touches. It catches his intelligence as well as his vulgarity, his genius for manipulating people as well as his stupidity as a commander, his slippery charm as well as his absolute wickedness. *Generations of Winter* is genuinely frightening in showing the tragedy of a vast country when put into the hands of the worst possible people. In this version of *Animal Farm* it is the stoats and the weasels who are in charge.

The narrative is a long descent from light into darkness. The early sections give a vivid sense of what it must have been like to live in a time of genuine social transformation, when considerable numbers of people, especially among the intelligentsia, felt the discomforts and privations of the post-revolutionary period could be cheerfully borne since sacrifices would be justified with the imminent arrival of the Future. Here is the book's opening paragraph:

> Just think—in 1925, the eighth year of the Revolution, a traffic jam in Moscow! All Nikolskaya Street, which runs from the Lubyanka prison through the heart of Kitai-gorod down to Red Square, is filled with streetcars, wagons, and automobiles. Next to the open-air market, they're unloading crates of fresh fish from heavy carts. Beneath the arch on Tretyakovsky Street one can hear the neighing of horses, the tooting of truck drivers' horns, and the swearing of a cart driver. The police will hurry to the scene, blowing their whistles ingenuously, as if not yet entirely convinced of the reality of their exclusively local, nonpolitical—that is, perfectly normal—role. Everything has the appearance of an amateur production, even the people's fury seems put on. The most important thing, though, is that everyone's happy to play along. The traffic jam on Nikolskaya Street is, in fact, a cause for rejoicing, like a glass of hot milk for someone who has been shivering with fever: life is coming back, along with dreams of prosperity.

For many people Russia probably did look this way at a time of hope. Everything had been turned on its head and the new prospects opened up seemed dizzying. Aksyonov is good at finding the telling detail, such as the arrival in the Twenties of the Charleston: "the *dernier cry* of the season delighted the 'old fogeys' of the bourgeoisie but outraged the 'progressive' young people." Amid all the bustle many ignored the lowering shadow cast by the Lubyanka.

Very soon, by the beginning of the 1930s, the prison shadow reaches as far as the Gradov sanctuary at Silver Forest. Despite Boris's eminence, first his son Nikita, a brilliant military strategist, is arrested by the secret police, then Nikita's brother Kirill, a fiercely dogmatic member of the Party, is also seized. Both disappear into the wastes of the Siberian labor camps, although Nikita returns at the most desperate stage of the war to lead Stalin's armies in the campaign against the Nazi invasion. The descriptions of Nikita's time in the Kolyma camp are perhaps the finest and certainly the most terrifying passages in the book. Here again Aksyonov picks out details with accuracy and wit:

> On the one hand, it was a horrifying thought that the police were purging the country of its best people, but on the other, it was the basis for a certain pride— you were sharing the fate of good men, not those from the gutter.

Despite the book's humor and narrative verve, I confess there were passages in it so painful that it was difficult for me to go on reading them, whether the descriptions of Gradov's parents' grief as their sons are taken from them, or the scenes of violence and misery during the collectivization period, or the account of the Nazi massacres of Jews, or of the "22 methods of active investigation," i.e., torture, used in KGB interrogations. Perhaps the most convincing villain in a book rich in villains—from Stalin himself through his fellow Georgian Lavrenti Beria down to the countless Party fixers and military opportunists—is the fictitious Semyon Stroilo, whom we first meet as the youthful lover of Nina Gradov. Stroilo is the archetypal cog in the totalitarian machine. A secret police spy, he plays the part of the Trotskyite proletarian for Nina's benefit and then, during a security police raid on a Trotskyite demonstration, points her out among others as an opponent of the increasingly powerful Stalinist faction in the regime. Later in the book he turns up as an NKVD colonel in charge of interrogations. Here he is seen losing control during the torture of an elderly Jewess:

> Something suddenly snapped in Colonel Stroilo . . . his ardent heart was acting up, and his hands at that point were relatively unstained. He rushed forward, pushed aside his comrades surrounding the criminal, threw the old woman onto the couch, yanked her skirt off, bared the bitch's rear end, took off his solid, heavy belt with a star on the buckle, and went to work with it on her flaccid, decrepit buttocks. He kept at it until the bitch stopped howling and until he went into convulsions, convulsions of fountain-like ejaculations, as had sometimes happened in the days of his youth, many years before, with the professor's daughter [Nina]; he felt very awkward then in front of his comrades.

The word "ardent" in that passage is a masterful touch, as is the torturer's awkwardness before his bestial fellows.

Aksyonov admirably stays in control of his authorial emotions. He never allows his indignation or his compassion to gain the upper hand. There are none of the "big scenes" that a lesser novelist might have permitted himself in the course of an immense historical narrative. He keeps a skeptic's eye both on his characters and on himself as a narrator. Veronika, Nikita's beautiful and dissatisfied wife, is, in the old phrase, no better than she should be: she wants money and men and the world's admiration, and is determined to have them, whether as Marshal Gradov's wife in the upper strata of Moscow society, or in the wastes of the labor camp where she survives by prostituting herself to the camp commander.

> The terrible vicissitudes of life, all the ups and downs and ups again have changed Veronika a great deal, thought Mary. Her entire life right now is a sort of challenge—to everyone around her, to impoverished Moscow, to the past. She goes around in chic out-

fits, wearing furs, earrings, all of which are daring, if not to say impudent.

These thoughts occur to the aging Mary Gradov, Veronika's mother-in-law, as she walks through the streets of wartime Moscow meditating on the fate of her family. Where we might have expected a misty-eyed version of the Eternal Mother, Aksyonov's sharp glance sees through a decent, self-deluding, snobbish woman:

> Mary pretended not to notice the curious, delighted stares, not to hear the murmurs: "Marshal Gradov's mother in a streetcar, just think! Marshal Gradov's mother, what a lady, what modesty—no, can that really be Marshal Gradov's mother here in a trolley with us?" The news passed endlessly from people getting off the car to those getting on, while Mary Vakhtangovna sat bursting with pride, but not giving any indication that these discussions had anything to do with her, an upright, stern, humble Russian intellectual, the mother of Marshal Gradov, defender of the Motherland. "Look out there citizens, don't push like that—the marshal's mother is on board!"

The broader political argument that underlies the narrative—that the Revolution was started by bad men and hijacked by worse, who proceeded virtually to destroy Russia and its satellites—seems all too accurate and familiar, especially when considered from the perspective of the 1990s. Recently in these pages David Remnick provided an apposite quotation from Solzhenitsyn: "It is thanks to ideology that it fell to the twentieth century to experience villainy on a scale of millions." What allows Stalin, Beria, and Stroilo—no less than Hitler, Himmler, and Eichmann—to act as they do is the knowledge that the worst of crimes, enormities beyond the world's imaginings, could be justified in the name of an idea. Yet at the heart of the book also there is the sense that somehow Russia is a country cursed by fate and doomed to suffer endlessly. One of the more sympathetic characters in the book, the doctor Savva Kitaigorodsky, Nina's husband, puts this view as follows:

> All of modern Russian history looks like a series of breakers—waves of retribution. The February Revolution was retribution for our ruling aristocracy's arrogance and narrow-minded immovability in relation to the people. The October Revolution and the Civil War were retribution against the bourgeoisie and the intelligentsia for their obsessive summons to revolution, for the stirring up of the masses. Collectivization and the campaign against the kulaks were retribution against the peasants for their cruelty in the Civil War, for beating up the clergymen, for the bloodthirsty anarchism. The current purges

are retribution against the revolutionaries for the violence they wreaked upon the peasants. . . . As for the future, it's impossible to predict, but logically we can suppose that there will be even more waves, until this whole cycle of false aspirations comes to an end . . .

One should not presume to suggest that one character's words express the author's own opinions, but this bleak yet exalted view of destiny is consistent with the unexpectedly inspirational ending of the book, when Kirill Gradov, still a prisoner in the icy wastes of Kolyma labor camp, discovers religion in a scene of great intensity. The reigning spirit in these pages is not Tolstoy but Dostoyevsky.

> I am prepared to believe that *Generations of Winter* will live for a very long time, and be seen as one of the more significant historical and literary achievements of a terrible century.
>
> —*John Banville*

As I earlier remarked, one can only give a preliminary report on a work of such vastness, intricacy, and ambition which is still only half-published; yet I am prepared to believe that *Generations of Winter* will live for a very long time, and be seen as one of the more significant historical and literary achievements of a terrible century.

## Philippe D. Radley (review date Spring 1995)

SOURCE: A review of *Moscow Saga*, in *World Literature Today*, Vol. 69, No. 2, Spring, 1995, pp. 387-88.

[*In the following favorable review, Radley provides brief synopses of* Generations of Winter, War and Prison, *and* Prison and Peace, *which make up the three-volume set entitled* Moscow Saga. *Radley includes a brief discussion of three major techniques Aksyonov uses in the novels.*]

Beginning in 1925 with a conversation between an American newspaperman and a politically intriguing Russian political scientist and ending with the final years of the book's central character, Dr. Boris Nikolaevich Gradov, Vassily Aksyonov's major fictional chronicle of the bitter Stalin years evokes all the grandeur of Tolstoy and all the inhuman psychology of Dostoevsky. Aksyonov, arguably the finest novelist now writing in Russian, has abandoned the allusiveness of much of his earlier work to write directly of Russian history and current events.

There are two sets of protagonists, real and fictional, in the three-volume *Moskovskaia saga* (*Moscow Saga*). The fictional ones revolve around the Gradovs, a family pictured in several generations, commencing with Dr. Gradov, a dedicated physician and author whose aim is to cure wherever possible. Twice he is given the possibility of helping Stalin: early in volume 1, *Pokolenie zimy* (*Generations of Winter*), he relieves the brute's crippling constipation, prompting the latter's exhortation to ask for whatever he wants. Gradov refuses, even though his two sons have been arrested and his daughter is in hiding. One son has become enamored of communist theory, though this does not save him from exile to Siberia, where, at the end of volume 2, *Voina i tiur'ma* (*War and Prison*), he has become a religious convert. The other son is eventually rehabilitated so as to serve as a general during the Great War, and then, on the point of arrest again, he is killed. The daughter is a poet reminiscent of Akhmatova, with whom she shares the terror of writing on threat of death.

On the eve of Stalin's death, Gradov is again summoned to the Kremlin, this time to confirm (or deny) a diagnosis Stalin does not wish to hear. This painful scene is a metaphor of the entire trilogy: our dedicated and moral, much-suffering hero must face his past—i.e., Stalin—and help it. He is professional enough to tell Stalin in volume 3, *Tiur'ma i mir* (*Prison and Peace*), that he "would recommend . . . a complete change in [his] way of life . . . [and that he] no longer work." As Gradov speaks, the reader goes back over all the horrors depicted in the earlier pages and contemplates what this means now to Russian history, and would have meant, if it had come true earlier. Would none of these all too familiar horrors have come to pass? We have been through the arrests, the beatings—a particularly brutal one of a Jewish woman that makes its disgusting leader, Stroilo, a Soviet bureaucratic horror, come to a sexual climax is a metaphor for them all—the camps, the war (Gorni [Babi] Yar is evoked in terrifying detail). Why not kill Stalin, the reader wonders?

Aksyonov's point is that where the real characters are concerned, the events must be those of historical truth. And that historical truth is everywhere. Major (Stalin and Beria in particular) and minor (Bazarov, a minor communist theoretician; Ordzhonokidze, a Georgian communist whom Stalin destroyed) characters are thrown into the novelistic mix. In every case where one interacts with a fictional character, the events are either true or believable. Thus Beria's befriending of a Gradov friend and taking him to Moscow with him to do his dirty work serves the historical novel's purpose: to make the reader aware that the Gradovs themselves are swimming, against their will, in this filth, all the while giving us the goods on the real perpetrators.

So much has been written, both fact and fiction, on this period, that it would have been unwise for Aksyonov to attempt to write investigative history. He does not try. He is giving us instead a re-created Russia and what some for the most part sympathetic folk did to survive it. Dr. Gradov is present from beginning to end, as a kind of unwilling patriarch who manages to live up to his own doctor's credo. His story, Aksyonov makes clear, is *not* unique. Indeed, it would have been completely lost had not the "packet" which contained it been "sold in 1991 for 300 dollars to an American tourist on the Arbat." The reader, however, will not learn history: he will, rather, learn of those possibilities ignored by history which now reside as fiction.

Aksyonov would not be Aksyonov without authorial tricks. I list three kinds below; the reader should note that there are many others. 1) The author intervenes on numerous occasions to inform the reader of what he is about to see, and appears as a weary but wise guide: at the beginning of part 3 he tells us of Stalin the "God," not "God, Creator of all Things" but rather the "usurper of the revolution's bright ideas" who, amazingly, owned five different cars in which he rode through Moscow. It is up to the writer to investigate this phenomenon: "And so, we have come to this moment where we begin our third volume, toward the end of the forties, when the country, having displayed miracles of courage, was burdened by the stunning fear of Stalin's five cars." This is where the fictionist outshines the historian: he can investigate the five cars and attempt an explanation, and in so doing he can possibly explain an age and an era.

2) The author/narrator invades the personal life of the Kremlin and its leaders, particularly its sexuality and its biological functions. The book is full of references to Stalin's constipation and Beria's "shit" and evokes, in particularly vulgar vocabulary, the vicious sexuality of the communist leaders. This coarseness is a calculated effect: it is Aksyonov's statement on the events. When Dr. Gradov cures Stalin's constipation, Aksyonov slyly stresses that this in no way meant that there was no shit left in Stalin. 3) At several points in the book, in classic Dos Passos style, Aksyonov provides actual contemporaneous press-clipping excerpts from Russian and Western books, magazines, and newspapers. This is always followed by a prose poem which serves as a perspective through time on the events: Aksyonov moves back to the eighteenth century only to jump forward to the 1980s.

*Moskovskaia saga* is a major work and a major achievement. A review of this length cannot begin to do it justice. Suffice it to say that anyone who cares about Russian literature today must read it.

---

# FURTHER READING

**Criticism**

Bayley, John. "Kitsch and the Novel." *New York Review of Books* XXXI, No. 18 (22 November 1984): 28-32.
    A review of *The Island of Crimea, The Burn,* and works by several other Russian authors.

Brown, Deming. Review of *The Island of Crimea,* by Vassily Aksyonov. *Slavic Review* 42, No. 2 (Summer 1983): 336-37.
    Brief plot synopsis of and introduction to *The Island of Crimea.*

Eberstadt, Fernanda. A review of *The Burn,* by Vassily Aksyonov. *Commentary* 80, No. 1 (July 1985): 39-41.
    Discusses the mixture of attitudes Aksyonov takes in *The Burn.*

Hosking, Geoffrey. "The Ascent out of Inhumanity." *Times Literary Supplement* 4095 (25 September 1981): 1087.
    Discusses Aksyonov's two novels, *The Burn* and *The Island of Crimea,* and Aksyonov's place as a novelist of the 1960s.

Matich, Olga. "Vasilii Aksyonov and the Literature of Convergence: Ostrov Krym as Self-Criticism." *Slavic Review* 47, No. 4 (Winter, 1988): 642-51.
    Focuses on the literary style and "antiutopian" quality of *The Island of Crimea.*

Muchnic, Helen. "From Russia with Candor." *The New York Times Book Review* (27 February 1983): 1, 32-33.
    A review of *Metropol,* a literary almanac co-edited by Aksyonov and others, published in 1979.

Robinson, Harlow. "From Moscow: fiction, poems, and more." *Christian Science Monitor* (12 August 1983): B3.
    A review of *Metropol.*

---

**Additional coverage of Aksyonov's life and career is contained in *Contemporary Authors,* Vols. 53-56, and *Contemporary Authors New Revision Series,* Vols. 12 and 48.**

# Martin Amis
## 1949-

(Born Martin Louis Amis) English novelist, critic, short story writer, editor, scriptwriter, and nonfiction writer.

The following entry provides an overview of Amis's career through 1996. For further information on his life and works, see *CLC,* Volumes 4, 9, 38, and 62.

## INTRODUCTION

Regarded as a groundbreaking novelist, Amis satirizes the scabrous excesses of youth and contemporary society with an irreverent and incisive wit similar to that of his father, author Kingsley Amis. Employing fast-paced prose infused with contemporary slang and profanity, Amis portrays characters who are obsessed with sex, drugs, violence, and materialistic pursuits. Amis—who is commonly known as Britain's *enfant terrible*—has been the subject of strong debate for the past two decades. He has been lauded as an insightful satirist, but he has been dismissed by many critics as "gratuitously malevolent," according to Susan Morrison. Like such satirists as Jonathan Swift and Angus Wilson, with whom he has been compared, Amis is widely regarded as a moralist whose novels admonish the vices of his age. Jerome Charyn commented: "Amis is so horrified by the world he sees in the process of formation that he feels compelled to warn us all about it."

### Biographical Information

Born in Oxford, England, Martin Amis is the son of well-known British author Kingsley Amis and Hilary Bardwell Amis. He attended more than thirteen schools while he was growing up in Britain, Spain, and the United States, and underwent a variety of experiences in his formative years. After attending several "crammers"—special tutorials designed to help students prepare for university entrance examinations—Amis accomplished no small feat by attaining a formal first in English at Exeter College, Oxford. He later became a member of the editorial staff at the *London Times Literary Supplement.* At the age of twenty-four, Amis won the Somerset Maugham Award for his first novel, *The Rachel Papers* (1974). He became the literary editor of *The New Statesman,* wrote numerous articles, and produced two more novels: *Dead Babies* in 1975 and *Success* in 1978. He followed these achievements with *Other People* (1981), *Money* (1984), *London Fields* (1989), *Time's Arrow* (1991), and *The Information* (1995). A collection of essays and a collection of short stories followed while Amis was a staff writer and reviewer for the *London Observer.* Amis's extensive travels

and rich personal experience of metropolitan London life have impacted the major themes in his works: greed, money, sex, alienation, and the human condition.

### Major Works

Amis's first novel, *The Rachel Papers,* is about a young man's passage from adolescence into adulthood. Charles Highway, the protagonist, is an egocentric English youth who relates his misadventures in graphic and humorous detail on the eve of his twentieth birthday. *Dead Babies* is a black comedy about a group of deviant youths who gather at a country home for a weekend of sex, drugs, verbal abuse, and physical violence. *Success* focuses on the relationship between two cohabiting foster brothers, one aristocratic and one working-class, and their comparative degrees of social, economic, and sexual success. The theme of rivalry between two protagonists reemerges in one of Amis's later novels, *The Information. Money* has been praised as one of Amis's best works. This ambitious novel explores such topics as greed, excess, self-destruction, cultural deprivation, sex, and love—all elements that have become standards in Amis's later work. *London Fields,* set in 1999 against a backdrop of impending environmental, economic, and military disaster, enlarges upon themes examined in *Money* and *Success.* *Time's Arrow* is about Tod Friendly, an American doctor who becomes progressively younger in Amis's reverse-time narrative. He ends up running a Nazi concentration camp, where he discovers himself to be "death doctor" Odilo Unverdorben. *Visiting Mrs. Nabokov* (1993) is a collection of sketches and essays detailing Amis's visits with various personalities, including Saul Bellow, John Updike, and Roman Polanski. *The Information,* Amis's most recent work, employs many of the themes and devices used in earlier works. The two central characters, Richard Tull and Gwynn Barry, compete for literary fame and glory in a rivalry much like the rivalries employed in *London Fields* and *Success.* Strongly autobiographical, *The Information* is a satire of London literary life. It serves as Amis's comment on the tenacious and competitive nature of the literary world.

**Critical Reception**

Most critics have found Amis's first three novels—*The Rachel Papers, Dead Babies,* and *Success*—remarkably similar. As Neil Powell noted, "each is a social and sexual satire in which an unlikely hero emerges as a precarious survivor while the beautiful and damned all around him go to pieces." According to Charles Michener, *The Rachel Papers* is largely autobiographical, and Amis revealed to the critic that the novel is about the year he spent in "crammers" before attending Oxford. Powell contends that Amis made *Dead Babies* lewd and obscene in an effort to numb readers and that the author's "attempts at ironic or satirical detachment, employing updated Swiftian or Fieldingesque devices, are uneasy." He faults Amis for relying on the bombastic and sensational to sell his readers, and questions whether the author will ever outgrow his penchant for depicting the gratuitous and obscene. *Time's Arrow* has been faulted for both its confusing time structure and its controversial subject matter involving the Holocaust. Many critics focused on Amis's reversal of cause and effect in the narration of the tale, and took issue with his fictionalization of the historical record of Nazi Germany. Nevertheless, commentators typically acknowledged that the satirical elements of the plot work effectively, and that the magnitude of telling a story in reverse presented Amis with special challenges. John Updike wrote: "Amis's ambitious concerns with inhumanity, time, and the unthinkable converge in *Time's Arrow,* a work of impressive intensity and virtuosity, albeit bristling with problematical aspects." According to Maya Slater, who found the narrative hard to follow: "Amis, by reversing the order of events, has deprived us of our ease of reading." *Visiting Mrs. Nabokov* is a collection of short essays and sketches written on assignment for various British and American magazines. Francine Prose noted: "[The essays] . . . move quickly; they don't ask much of us, or offend." Yet Chris

Savage King found Amis's personal sketches to be tedious and pretentious. King wrote, "I used to find Amis an entertaining writer. I found this collection pretty miserable." *The Information,* which examines the subject of literary envy, has had a favorable reception. Calling the novel ". . . a study of envy and egomania that happens to play itself out in the world of publishing," Julian Loose has claimed that "the primary pleasure of reading *The Information* is that of being regularly swept up in . . . epic, frothy, digressions." Others agree that *The Information* is full of literary allusions and is noteworthy for its examination of life in the publishing industry. "*The Information.* . . . comes to us under a storm of attendant publicity about its roots in real life," wrote Ed Morales. Many laud the novel as a culmination of Amis's strengths. Adam Mars-Jones holds: "[*The Information*] . . . has everything in common with *Money* and *London Fields* in terms of tone and territory." Pulling together several of the themes and motifs of his earlier works, *The Information* has been praised as a synthesis of Amis's work, but it has also been observed that the novel is a rehashing of his often used literary devices. Merle Rubin contends: "It may . . . strike many readers as perhaps a little too familiar-sounding if they've read Mr. Amis's earlier books."

---

## PRINCIPAL WORKS

*The Rachel Papers* (novel) 1974
*Dead Babies* (novel) 1975
*Success* (novel) 1978
*Other People: A Mystery Story* (novel) 1981
*Money: A Suicide Note* (novel) 1984
*The Moronic Inferno and Other Visits to America* (essays) 1986
*Einstein's Monsters* (essays and short stories) 1987
*London Fields* (novel) 1989
*Time's Arrow, or The Nature of the Offense* (novel) 1991
*Visiting Mrs. Nabokov and Other Excursions* (essays) 1993
*The Information* (novel) 1995

---

## CRITICISM

**Neil Powell (essay date 1981)**

SOURCE: "What Life Is: The Novels of Martin Amis," in *PN Review,* Vol. 7, No. 6, 1981, p. 42-45.

[*In the following essay, Powell provides overviews and analyses of three of Amis's early novels,* The Rachel Papers, Dead Babies, *and* Success.]

*Success* is a funny thing. In literature (as K.W. Gransden

observed in an amiable poem on *Poetry Now* recently), there are those notable popular successes which turn up, still in their paper jackets but a little tatty, cluttering the shelves of second-hand bookshops a couple of decades later, their authors either forgotten or remembered merely as instances of the fickleness of reputations. Then there are the successes which enjoy a quite different kind of life, even though their 'literary' reputations may stand hardly higher than those of the first sort: books which are distinctively of their time and which, though by no means great works of art, succeed through accuracy of detail and of tone—as, for instance, *Saturday Night and Sunday Morning* does. And finally, there are the successes which endure, which are never to be found gathering dust on bookshop shelves, and of which the paperback spines, after a decent interval, change colour from orange to the dignified grey of the Penguin Modern Classics.

Martin Amis's three novels belong at present to the second category of success: but, such is the league-table logic of this particular game, they may be promoted or relegated, depending on the whims of fashion and that old common arbitrator, Time. Amis has certainly been the most praised and the most publicised new writer of full-length fiction in England in the past decade (the qualification 'full-length' is made necessary by the stories of Ian McEwan), and not without reason. Reviewing his third novel—called, of course, *Success*—Tom Paulin commented: 'His exploration isn't merely personal and neurotic—it is deeply sensitive to the mood of the late 1970s, and anyone who belongs to Amis's generation must recognise his understanding of where we are now.' Paulin is right; but his comment is as ambiguous, and in precisely the same way, as the novels themselves. In *Success,* which one would guess to be the culmination of this particular vein in Amis's work, the very title embodies a self-negating reflexive loop: if the novel is about the valuelessness of success in London in the late 1970s, then the success of the novel in London in the late 1970s is valueless.

The three novels—*The Rachel Papers, Dead Babies* and *Success*—have a great deal in common: each is a social and sexual satire in which an unlikely hero emerges as a precarious survivor while the beautiful and damned all around him go to pieces. Amis's preoccupation is with deception in all its forms, but especially self-deception: his extravagantly attractive and 'successful' characters (Quentin in *Dead Babies,* Gregory in *Success*) are destroyed—self-destroyed—with extraordinary completeness and extraordinary relish. Yet the novels are not simply fables about superficiality: the endings of *Dead Babies* and *Success* are, despite their apparent resolutions, ambivalent and pessimistic.

*The Rachel Papers* is the slightest of the three. Several charges may be brought against it: that it is unscrupulous, a piece of expedient hackwork; that it relies overwhelmingly on stereotypes and easy allusions; that it received attention and commendation mainly as the first novel by the son of an established writer whose own first novel had caused a stir, thus offering irresistible comparisons for reviewers between the relative irreverence of two generations. All these charges—and there are doubtless others—have some truth in them, but they do not invalidate the novel's two clear qualities: the vitality (though it sometimes turns into twitchiness) of the writing; and the exactness with which Amis catches a certain manner of speech and, since this is a first-person narrative, thought—a style which is not naturally demotic but which is rather the style of people who unconsciously ape the media's versions of actual speech, at once spontaneous and stereotyped. Orwell once complained of sentences in which phrases are 'tacked together like the sections of a prefabricated hen-house': most of Amis's characters speak and think like that; and so, sometimes, does their author.

Charles Highway, the narrator of *The Rachel Papers,* is the prototype Amis hero: clever, articulate, self-conscious (he knows when he's speaking 'in idiomatic lower-middle'), determined to overcome what he sees as his personal deficiencies. These, typically, are the first things we learn about him:

> I wear glasses for a start, have done since I was nine. And my medium-length, arseless, waistless figure, corrugated ribcage and bandy legs gang up to dispel any hint of aplomb. . . . I remember I used to have to fold the bands of my trousers almost double, and bulk out the seats with shirts intended for grown men. I dress more thoughtfully now, though not so much with taste as with insight.

That passage sets the tone of the book, both in its preoccupation with physical surface details and in its closing juxtaposition: *The Rachel Papers* certainly achieves insight at the expense of taste. Between seven p.m. and midnight on the evening before his twentieth birthday, Charles shuffles and reshuffles the experiences of the preceding months, in which two goals—Rachel and Oxford—are interwoven and achieved. He is vulnerable and absurd, given to translating his problems into an 'Anxiety Top Ten', complete with the patter of a disc-jockey and 'Last week's positions in brackets'. Sub-cultural shorthand is his characteristic mode: 'to be against the Beatles (late-middle period),' he reflects, 'is to be against life.'

But this intellectual level—though it serves well enough for his seduction of Rachel, and the discoveries and disappointments which follow from that—seems both feeble in a supposedly brilliant Oxford candidate and tedious in the narrative figure of a novel. When Charles tries to *think,* the results are discouraging:

Don't I ever do anything but take soulful walks down the Bayswater Road, I thought, as I walked soulfully down the Bayswater Road.

Very well: demonically mechanical cars; potent solid living trees; unreal distant-seeming buildings; blotchy extra-terrestrial wayfarers; Intense Consciousness of Being; pathetic fallacy plus omnipresent *déjà vu,* cosmic angst, metaphysical fear, a feeling both claustrophobic and agoraphobic, the teenager's religion. The Rev. Northrop Frye fetchingly terms it 'queasy apocalyptic foreboding'. An Angus Wilson character terms it 'adolescent egotism', thereby driving me almost to suicide last Christmas. Is *that* all it fucking is, I thought.

Or:

I experienced thrilling self-pity. 'What will that mind of yours get up to next?' I said, recognising the self-congratulation behind this thought and the self-congratulation behind that recognition on the self-congratulation behind recognizing that recognition.

Steady on. What's so great about going mad?

But even that was pretty arresting. Even that, come on now, was a pretty arresting thing for a nineteen-year-old boy to have thought.

This style, though (like everything else in the novel) it testifies to Amis's understanding of the late-adolescent mind, does rather soon become wearisome. Near the end of the book, however, Amis artfully tries to distance himself from his narrator. Charles arrives for his Oxford interview, is directed to Dr Charles Knowd's room, and there discovers 'a pair of hippies'.

One of them presumably the doctor, waved his hand at me and said without looking up:

'The room across the corridor. Five minutes.'

There was a further hippie in the room across the corridor.

This further hippie, plainly a proto-Appleseeder from *Dead Babies* ('"What's your name?" "Highway." What's yours? Manson?'), informs Charles that Dr Knowd is 'About the coolest guy in Oxford' and goes on to discomfort him by dropping names like Berryman, Snodgrass, Sexton, Duncan, Hecht. Charles wonders: 'Who *were* these people? I had studied neither the Extremists nor the Liverpudlians.' But Knowd, despite his appearance, turns out to be the necessary correc-

tive to the prevailing narrative viewpoint. He begins, 'Mr. Highway . . . do you like literature?' and goes on to analyse, concisely and ruthlessly, the faults of Charles's essays—which are, naturally, the faults of his first-person narrative. He concludes with a remark which must also be Amis's wry, concealed acknowledgement of what *he's* up to in the novel:

'I won't go on . . . Literature has a kind of life of its own, you know. You can't just use it . . . ruthlessly, for your own ends. I'm sorry, am I being unfair?'

In *Dead Babies,* 'we have gone on ahead a small distance in time'—about a decade, in fact, represented in an entirely arbitrary way by retrospective references to a 'battered '78 Chevrolet' or '1979 Moet & Chandon' and by such props as an 'I-type Jaguar' or a 'DC70'. The novel concerns the appalling inhabitants of Appleseed Rectory and their three American weekend visitors: the shift forward in time allows Amis considerable licence in constructing his frightful vision. The book is full of literary and other allusions: a novel of Iris Murdoch's is mentioned, reminding us that this enclosed country-house plot is a development or a perversion of a typically Murdochian world; Quentin's magazine *Yes* has 'won outspoken praise from William Burroughs, Gore Vidal, Angus Wilson—writers evidently among Amis's influences and his targets. On a different level, the idea of flower-power gone to seed is plainly suggested by 'Appleseed' (Apple was of course The Beatles' company) while it is no coincidence that the diabolical drug-mixer, Marvell Buzhardt, shares a name with the author of 'The Garden'.

The Appleseeders are a grotesque bunch. The sanest of them is probably Diana Parry, who 'spends a lot of time wondering what the hell she's doing in Appleseed Rectory' and who, before the final catastrophe asks: 'Don't you think we must have made a mistake a long time ago to end up like this. That something went wrong and that's why we're all so dead now . . . Baby?' Her boyfriend, Andy Adorno, is a pastiche of trendy machismo: keen on drinking, fighting and swearing, but sexually disappointing and the only character to respond in a conventionally 'sentimental' way to the bizarre death of The Mandarin, Celia's cat, which goes berserk after Marvell has drugged its food:

Andy returned for the last time to The Mandarin's body. 'I loved that cat,' he said unsteadily. 'I did.'

'It just checked out, man,' said Marvell.

'Yeah,' said Andy, breathing in. 'But Jesus I hate this no-good motherfucking chickenshit weekend.'

That provides a marginal degree of redemption for Andy. Celia is the least vividly realised of the Appleseeders, largely because her main function is to be married to the 'super-man' Quentin Villiers ('The versatility of the fellow!') who is the presiding or at any rate the manipulating genius behind Appleseed Rectory and who

> can talk all day to a butcher about the longevity of imported meats, to an air-hostess about safety regulations in the de Gaulle hangars, to an insurance salesman about post-dated transferable policies, to a poet about non-typographical means of distinguishing six-syllable three-lined stanzas and nine-syllable two-line ones, to an economist about pre-war counter-inflationary theory, to a zoologist about the compensatory eye movements of the iguana. Just so, he can address a barrow-boy in rhyming slang, a tourist in yokel French, a Sunderlander in Geordie, a Newmarket tout in genteel Cambridgeshire, a gypsy in Romany.

He is, then, a kind of Everyman. But we are warned:

> Watch Quentin closely. Everyone else does. Stunned by his good looks, proportionately taken aback by his friendliness and accessibility, flattered by his interest, struck by the intimacy of his manner and lulled by the hypnotic sonority of his voice—it is impossible to meet Quentin without falling a little bit in love.

The two remaining residents are Giles Coldstream—perhaps the one real comic creation in the novel, endearingly neurotic and gin-sodden, obsessed with dentistry—and Keith Whitehead. Little Keith is the Court Dwarf, revoltingly obese, distinguished from the others by a background which might be called 'ordinarily' dreadful rather than modishly, affluently dreadful. He suffers and (therefore?) survives.

Even more grotesque are the three Americans—Marvell Buzhardt, Skip Marshall and Roxeanne Smith—who seem to be the forces of destruction, who frighten even Diana and Andy, and who more than frighten Keith. But they are merely catalysts: the real danger, and the source of the novel's thriller-aspect, lies elsewhere.

The hurtling, obsessive obscenity of *Dead Babies*—which I shall not try to illustrate here—is in the end, as it is intended to be, numbing: that, after all, is part of the satirist's moral. Yet, like all Amis's novels, the book has a soft side and strikes unexpected notes of wry gentleness: when the assembled company is 'a-wheeze with boredom' after watching 'unspeakable acts' (catalogued nonetheless) performed on film and Marvell promises something 'new' and 'different', the treat turns out to be a scene enacted with vintage Hollywood decorum. The point, of course, is that it is infinitely more erotic than the hard-core pornography. The watchers, attuned

to a more brutalised world, are confused and astonished. But by now it is too late for redemption—as we have been told, in a passage of sudden dazzling eloquence, a few pages before:

> Yes, it was seven o'clock and a pall of thunder hung over the Rectory rose-gardens. The formerly active air was now so weighed down that it seeped like heavy water over the roof. Darkness flowed in the distance, and the dusk raked like a black searchlight across the hills and towards them.

> But pity the dead babies. Now, before it starts. They couldn't know what was behind them, nor what was to come. The past? They had none. Like children after a long day's journey, their lives arranged themselves in a patchwork of vanished mornings, lost afternoons and probable yesterdays.

Those two beautifully balanced paragraphs show Amis's writing at its best: in their context—they occur abruptly in the harshest section of the book—they are stunningly effective. However, that awkward 'Yes . . .' hints at a narrative weakness: the problem of tone is no more resolved here than it was in *The Rachel Papers*, and Amis's attempts at ironic or satirical detachment, employing updated Swiftian or Fieldingesque devices, are uneasy.

*Dead Babies* has an epigraph from Menippus: '. . . and so even when (the satirist) presents a vision of the future, his business is not prophecy, just as his subject is not tomorrow . . . it is today.' *Success* brings us back to today. It is a logical development: one novel implies the other. If the future is *Dead Babies*, then *Success* is the present which predetermines it.

*Success* consists of twelve chapters, each corresponding to a month of the year; and in each chapter the two alternating narrators, who share a flat in Bayswater, give their versions of the month's events—first Terence Service (short, unattractive, 'unsuccessful', but ambitious, a slightly less grotesque version of Little Keith), then his foster-brother Gregory Riding (tall, attractive, apparently successful, a self-confessed manipulator, a variation on the theme of Quentin). Most of Amis's characters have horrifying backgrounds but Terry's, like Keith's is explicitly working-class: it is this which seems to provide them both with their improbable resilience. Terry, though, is adopted at the age of nine by the philanthropic Mr Riding after his seven-year-old sister has been murdered by his father:

> I don't know whether my father killed my mother; but I bloody know he killed my sister, because I was there at the time and watched him as he did so. (Suck on that. It's easy enough to see what it was that

fucked me up. I go on about all this a lot. I make no apologies. It's just too bad, I'm allowed to go on about it, on account of it fucking me up.)

Gregory, by contrast, at first seems prosperous and secure, with his numerous girlfriends and boyfriends, his expensive car, his prestigious art gallery job. But *Success* is a see-saw, and it gradually becomes clear that Gregory's opulent world is a fabrication: 'It was a lie. I tell lies. I'm a liar. I always have been. I'm sorry.' And with Gregory's recognition of his own deceptions and self-deceptions comes his parallel recognition of Terry's increasing success:

> And Terry. What is this with him now? No, *don't* tell me. Don't tell me he's becoming a success. No, don't tell me that. . . .

> But the yobs are winning. And Terry, of course, is 'doing well'. He is *doing well*. Of course. He has shown that he will perform what is necessary to succeed. He has shown that he is prepared to trade his days. He is doing well.

The contest, then, is between a liar and a yob: there's little to choose between them. Success is style, and style is everything. So, towards the end of the novel, Terry's 'chippy' aggressive manner gives way to something approaching Gregory's urbanity, which meanwhile collapses. Finally, Gregory's father dies; the foster-brothers revisit the 'rotting and near-worthless' Riding home; and Terry, not Gregory, returns at once 'down the unravelling track, on the look-out for London. I sip my drink. I'm going to be all right.' Gregory, on the other hand, is left to his childhood landscape and to a belated truthful confrontation with childish terrors:

> I stand behind the row of birches. I'm cold—I want to shiver and sob. I look up. Something's coming. Oh, go *away*. Against the hell of sunset the branches bend and break. The wind will never cease to craze the frightening leaves.

The novel's closing pages are ambiguous: though superficially pessimistic, they look to me (this may be a wilfully bucolic misreading) to point in favour of Gregory's derelict state, to suggest that the terrors and the comforts of the rural world may be bleak but at least they have depth and reality. Here, at least, the future of *Dead Babies* seems avoidable.

Amis's novels pose a number of general problems. The first, rather slippery one involves the distinction between pornography and literature: it seems to me that in all three novels—but most noticeably in *Dead Babies*—there are passages where the ironist's or satirist's distancing fails entirely. This is an aspect of the uncertainty of tone which so often weakens Amis's writing. Pornography fulfils a simple and per-

haps necessary purpose; whereas literature is altogether more complicated. We need to distinguish between them not for censorious reasons but because the two things demand different kinds of intention and response. A work of literature may be endangered where the simpler level of intention and response gets in the way of the more subtle and complex one: such a confusion happens too often in Amis's novels and provokes those familiar comments ('Extravagantly sexual . . . highly enjoyable') which are quoted on the paperback editions of his books and in which reviewers, understandably enough, attempt to have it both ways. Among a novelist's desperate remedies, the gratuitous, knowing obscenity—like the one-line joke—is a stand-by to be used sparingly.

The second problem is related to the first. Because Amis's characters live in an echoing present ('The past? They had none.'), their allusions and their vocabulary belong to a world of crazily foreshortened historical perspectives. A central passage in *The Rachel Papers* presupposes a detailed knowledge of *Sergeant Pepper's Lonely Hearts Club Band*; Andy, in *Dead Babies*, habitually adds a redundant 'is all' to the ends of his sentences; Terry, in *Success*, obsessively uses the word '*tonto*', in italics, an extreme example of localised slang which seems to mean mad'. These are random instances of an overstrained contemporaneity: the cumulative effect of such things is drastically to restrict the potential range of the novels.

---

**Stifled by its insistence on the present, by its pop and media allusiveness, and by its introverted slang, Amis's language becomes *only* of its time and lacks even the ambition of timelessness.**

**—*Neil Powell***

---

But what about the potential range of *the novel*? What effect is Amis's success, or *Success*, likely to have upon the language of fiction? In Arnold Bennett's *The Old Wives' Tale*, the final section is called 'What Life Is'. That too is a second-division novel, though a remarkably good one, and in its intention of providing a detailed record of two contrasting sisters' lives it has something in common with *Success*. Amis is in many ways the more polished and skilful of the two writers, but it is Bennett's 'life' which moves and convinces. Why? Not, I think, because life has changed (though obviously it has) but because, whereas in Bennett language is enriching, in Amis it is deadening, reductive. One has, in *The Old Wives' Tale*, a deep sense of both change and continuity in historical time, sustained by Bennett's allusions to real events of some importance and to alterations in the texture of life. In Amis, the resonance has gone and the language of fiction has become as formulaic and as ephemeral as last year's pop music. Stifled by its insistence on the present, by its pop and media allusiveness, and by its introverted slang, Amis's language becomes *only* of its time and lacks even the ambition of timelessness.

Except, that is, for those moments—the occasional patches of brilliance in *Dead Babies,* the end of *Success*—when Amis seems to reach out towards a larger fictional world: then one can see what a fine writer he could be if he were to allow himself a greater historical range, a deeper commitment to the enduring realities of time and place. I hope that his future novels will show a decisive break with (to borrow a line from Thom Gunn) 'the limitations where he found success' and will find him using his talent more positively, less defensively. But success is a funny thing, and it may take time to grow out of it.

## Susan Morrison (interview date 17 May 1990)

SOURCE: "The Wit and Fury of Martin Amis," in *Rolling Stone,* No. 578, May 17, 1990, pp. 95-99, 101-02.

[*In the following interview, Amis discusses his work, literary influences, and techniques, and his reputation as a misogynist, among other topics.*]

"Look, we're not running this."

That's what Martin Amis said to his London publishers when they showed him a proposed advertisement for his new novel, *London Fields.* Over a picture of a rancid meat pie crawling with maggots, the ad read: "Today, in London, the average man will think about sex 20 times. One man in three will masturbate. One person will be murdered within three days. A woman will be sexually assaulted every three hours. And five children will die from parental abuse within the week. *London Fields* . . . [is] a novel about ordinary, everyday life."

Amis wanted to lose the meat pie.

Long hailed—and heckled—as the *enfant terrible* of English fiction, Martin Amis is no longer an *enfant* (he's forty) and less *terrible* than ever (he changes diapers—"but only the damp ones"). Nonetheless, his sixth and most ambitious novel is a whopping nightmare of spiritual and planetary decay. What many critics have failed to point out, though, is that far from being a daunting or depressing nightmare of spiritual and planetary decay, *London Fields* is enormously fun. And funny.

Set on the eve of the millennium in Amis's own neighbor-

hood of West London, the novel follows a frighteningly intelligent *femme fatale* named Nicola Six and the trio of clueless lunks that she has cast as accomplices in her own exquisitely art-directed murder: Keith Talent, the lowlife hustler who fills his days with lifeless sex and a viscous liqueur called *porno*; Guy Clinch, the ardent upper-class wimp so out of touch with his own drives that he hauls his Nicola-induced erection around third-world London like an unfamiliar crutch; and Samson Young, the terminally ill and terminally pretentious American narrator, who thinks he's stumbled across the perfect real-life murder to novelize. Along with Nicola and Sam (as in Uncle), the planet is dying, too, and Amis draws on his dazzling arsenal of sometimes soaring, sometimes lurching, always merciless prose to describe its last pathetic chugs and sputters.

The literary community has been split down the middle about Martin Amis for the better part of two decades, ever since the publication of his first novel, *The Rachel Papers,* a scatological swoon of wise-guy adolescent horniness. Saul Bellow, a mentor, has compared him to Flaubert and Joyce, and to his many lay fans he is nothing short of a cult hero. But other readers and critics, particularly among his countrymen, find him and his work gratuitously malevolent; the judges of Britain's Booker Prize last year snubbed *London Fields,* presumably for what some perceived as the novelist's bad attitude toward his female characters. Though he enjoys a close relationship with his father, Kingsley, the author of *Lucky Jim,* Amis is hardly a literary lion at home: The father rarely finishes the son's novels, complaining of their "compulsive vividness"; and Antonia, Martin's American wife of six years—"not by any means a fanatical fan of mine"—will only read the books he's written since meeting her.

At the time of this interview, Amis had been talking to the press about *London Fields* for six months, and though clearly ambivalent about the novelist's obligation to be a human Cliffs Notes, he was gracious, gentler than advertised and disarmingly polite. We met at his office—actually a paper-strewn converted bachelor pad draped with Indian print bedspreads—on the second floor of a tumbling-down Victorian house a mile from where he conducts his family-man life with his wife and their two young sons. Compact and well proportioned, and capped with what looked like a hastily self-inflicted haircut, he could have passed for a hard-living American college boy, in his tennis sneakers, hemmed jeans and white button-down shirt. He folds himself up tightly as he talks, and he says the word *yeah* often, drawing it out for maximum American street-smart effect.

Amis has done time as a reporter, and in an article about meeting Saul Bellow, he confessed that "as a journalist, you hope for lunacy, spite, deplorable indiscretions, a full-scale nervous breakdown in mid-interview." I had no such luck with Amis, but I did discover some things just as shocking, given his reputation as a sneering little tough guy: He cries at movies; he likes Lite beer; he drives to his daily tennis game in the family station wagon wearing a Fauntleroyish get-up of linen blazer, white shirt and shorts; and, most endearing, every now and then he lisps a little. Which isn't to say he's not acerbic, incisive, quick with a derisive laugh and fully capable of writing words that send the squeamish running for their Barbara Pym. And he says he has terrible tennis manners.

[*Morrison*]: *In* **London Fields,** *the narrator makes the point that people would rather read about misfortune than happiness. Why?*

[Amis]: As the narrator says, who else but Tolstoy could make happiness swing on the page? It's dreadfully difficult to write about happiness in a way that makes you smile. When everything's just fine in a novel or in life, we're usually thinking, "Yeah, yeah, yeah.." It's like the letter home from the holidays: "Having a nice time" isn't what you want to read really, is it? What I am interested in is heavy comedy, rather than light comedy. It's a wincing laughter, or a sort of funky laughter, rather than tee-hee-hee. Sort of a hung-over laughter, where it hurts.

*Reviewers often call your books mean spirited or misanthropic, ignoring the fact that they're also incredibly funny.*

The comedy is the main thing, and I feel best as a writer when comic invention is flowing. There's a bit in **London Fields** where one of the characters, Keith, is sitting around with all these sachets of perfume that he's bought, and they turn out to be water; then he sells the water and gets counterfeit notes for that; and then he buys vodka with the counterfeit notes, but then the vodka turns out to be the perfume. And when I'm doing that, I think, "God, this is just great stuff. Where did it come from?" It just sort of flows. You're in a bit of trouble if you're trying to think up snappy one-liners. Humor can't just be a foam on top of things. It has to be an undercurrent and emerge naturally from the situation.

But you're dead right in that that is how I would like reviews to begin and end—with talk of this. If you start off with the premise of me being a comic writer, you are taking an interesting line because there are clearly things in my novels that shouldn't really be in comic novels. And there are people who don't like that, who just want the comedy. But I think that comedy never works when all it is, is comedy. Then it's just Fran Lebowitz.

*What do you find funny?*

Conversations with friends. I find my children quite funny. Children are, of course, very funny. I was very amused by this little piece about me in one paper that began, "Martin Amis is a vile little fuck who loves his children."
*Do you laugh a lot?*

Yeah, quite a lot. It's my theory that when you're about thirty-eight, your laugh divides—you have the big laugh, which is really you, and then you have this other laugh, the one you've developed for social occasions. And to my horror, I sometimes hear this second kind of chortle come out of me. But whenever you hear someone *really* laugh, then you're seeing them the way they truly are, the way you don't often see them. I like to think that I make myself laugh like that quite a lot. Laughter takes place in there [*gesturing to his office*]. But it isn't a polite chortle.

*Are the writers who influenced your comic sensibility different from those who had the most impact on your writing style?*

One and the same, really. The sort of haughty tone is definitely Vladimir Nabokov, who has a glacially haughty tone about everything. But only in a few novels is it allowed to lead the pack, and they're my favorites: *Lolita, Despair, Laughter in the Dark.* The Philip Roth of *Portnoy's Complaint*, Joseph Heller certainly—those sentences turning around on themselves that he did so wonderfully in *Something Happened.* Dickens has had a very deep influence on me—the Mandarin rhythms of his sentences. Even Wodehouse, Waugh.

*Last fall Tom Wolfe caused quite a stir with an essay in* Harper's *magazine in which he chastised America's fiction writers for writing tiny and anemic novels of private experience rather than big realistic novels based on the kind of exhaustive reporting that he does. Do you agree?*

I thought Wolfe's essay was one of those pieces where the writer is saying, "Everyone should be more like me." I'm sure lots of writers wish they *were* more like Tom Wolfe. But what is his ratio—that a novel should be sixty-five-percent research, thirty-five-percent inspiration? With me, it's now ten-percent research and ninety-percent inspiration, which I think is harder work, really. I keep meaning to research things, to go to prisons and child-abuse centers, but in the end I just make it up. You take a bit of experience and pass it through your psyche.

But Wolfe's emphases are right, society is your subject. Salman Rushdie wrote a piece in praise of George Orwell called "Inside the Whale," in which he says that writers can't live inside the whale; they've got to be out in the big sea. And Salman pointed out: "There is no whale. You are in the sea, whether you like it or not."

*You have said that the thing that prevents your father from finishing your books is your love of a kind of postmodern literary prankishness—having a character called Martin Amis in* **Money,** *giving characters your initials in* **London Fields,** *and that sort of thing. How would you defend it?*

Well, it all comes under the main heading of "Fucking Around With the Reader." My father thinks that there's an orderly contract between writer and reader, which has very much to do with his generation, and he's incensed by any breach of those rules. I would justify it very simply and pragmatically by saying that once a lot of writers have become interested in something, then it's useless to say to them, "Snap out of it; you're just annoying." Because it's clearly an evolutionary development, and this is what writers need to do. And this doesn't come naturally to my father. He's in the position of someone in fifteenth-century Venice or Florence saying: "You know, I don't like this perspective stuff. Get back to when we didn't know about perspective. Stop fucking around and get back to what we know." On the other hand, perspective was such an obvious gain for painting, whereas this kind of literary innovation is, even to me, not such an obvious gain. But it has happened, and it will last for a certain time before writers move on to something else.

It's funny that I have always done it up to a point, even in my first novel. I'm all for this intense relationship with the reader. I really want the reader in there. I don't know who the reader is, but I really want him close. In *The Rachel Papers* the narrator-protagonist says coyly at one point, *Here come the sexy bits, Are you sitting comfortably?* And suddenly the reader is not just reading but is individualized. My narrators have always been shadowy figures. I've always been a kind of shadowy figure hanging around my novels. Then eventually, in **Money,** I myself come in as a bit part. Actually, I think in my case, and perhaps this is part of the reason why all this happened, I feel a sort of guilt about creating characters, guilt about making them suffer.

*So it is important for you to show that you're the puppet master, so that readers won't think that your characters are real?*

I learned very early on that no matter how much you do to forestall it, the reader will believe in the characters and feel concern for them. That's an unstoppable thing. The reader is doing a huge job of assigning life to characters, imagining what they look like. Nabokov used to say that what the reader *shouldn't* do is identify with the character. What the reader should do is identify with the writer. You try and see what the writer is up to, what the writer is arranging and what the writer's point is. Identify with the art, not the people.

*Do you start with characters? Theme? Plot?*

I start with characters, really. Situations. I like to let my char-

acters get up a head of steam and have a bit of life of their own. I like to let the characters lead me a bit. When I start, I know quite a lot about the beginning and quite a lot about the end and usually quite a lot about some key bit in the middle. And that's it. I do a lot of piecemeal doodling in longhand for a long time, for years. I do this scene. I try that. Bits from the end might be written quite early on. I write on the left-hand side of these big notebooks. The right-hand side is blank, and there I just jot down thoughts, good observations. Some are labeled "Beauties"—things I've got to get in, scenes that have to be fitted in at some time, things that may not have much to do with what's on the left-hand side. Then it's a huge job of transferring the longhand onto a typescript. By which time, there are still great holes in it. Then for a year I just do the last draft, adding a lot of new stuff and organizing it.

*What are you working on next?*

It sounds ridiculous in summary, but it's a novella about a Nazi doctor. The ridiculous thing about it—although I'm pretty sure that I have got something to say with it—is that it's done backwards in time. And I mean literally backwards. The whole physical universe is backwards. People walk backwards, wake up in the evening and then go through the day and then go to bed in the morning. What you're always looking for is a way to see the world differently. So you do it through the eyes of a drunk [as in **Money**] or an amnesiac [as in **Other People**]. With this one, the point is that moral acts are reversed if you reverse time. For instance, the giving of a gift is in fact the taking of a gift. Thus, by the time you get to Auschwitz, there's a miracle of beneficence. And the narrating voice of course doesn't see that it's all over, that he's going backwards.

After this is over, I'm going to write what feels at the moment like a light novel about literary envy. This will be a way of getting at the humorous end of self-conscious postmodern fiction. It's going to be about two writers who sort of love-hate each other and their varying fortunes. It's about (*a*) the writer's ego, which I'm afraid is a shamingly vast subject, and (*b*) middle age. My novels are really about what it's like to be a certain age—the midthirties in **London Fields,** the early thirties in **Money,** et cetera.

This literary-envy novel is going to be an awful lot about the subsidiaries of writing, rather than writing itself. These are giving interviews, being photographed, talking to TV crews, everything that gets in the way of writing. Of which there has never been as much as there is now. At no point in history has the writer spent so much time telling everyone what he's saying. I don't really think this can be terribly good for a writer, if only because it signifies a loss of innocence. Also, it tips the reader. It makes the reader concentrate too much on your so-called ideas. I don't have Idea 1 when I'm writing a book. I have a situation, and I have a preoccupation. But I don't have an idea about the end of the planet, nuclear weapons, any of that stuff. That's the stuff you talk about in interviews. It's a bit of lit crit from the author. But there's been so much of that, that by the time the reader—and this would include the reviewer—gets going, he thinks that what you're doing is trying to flesh out ideas with fiction. And it's not even the other way round. The ideas are just in your head. They're not part of an agenda or a program. They've nothing to do with what you're trying to say. You're not trying to say anything. What you're trying to say is *the novel*, that 470 pages of work. People say, "What did you mean by it?" I meant *that* [*points to book*]. I didn't mean something you could put on a badge. It's starting to screw up the emphasis of reading.

*Why did the satirical British magazine* Private Eye *used to call you "Smarty Anus"?*

Just because it sounds quite like Martin Amis, I suppose [*laughs*]. And, well because of the dirty stuff in the books. Here in England success is regarded with narrow-eyed suspicion rather than wide eyes. They had me as this guy with a word processor who was rattling out stories to get big advances. It seems to me a despairing view of the world. I think that's the depths of despair, to think that everyone is in everything for the money.

*In* Money *and* London Fields, *there is a sense of real anxiety about money, the force of money replacing the class system. Do you think there's something comforting in the order of the class system that is slipping?*

I have nothing but hatred and contempt for the class system. But it does have a redeeming feature, in that it directs you towards cultivation. When Magic Johnson or some other American sports star has got his ranch house and his three cars and all that, he is not going to feel that he is missing out on anything, because he lives in a money society, a pleasure society. But when one of our sports stars has got the house and the tennis court, and he may even dress up on weekends and ride a horse and chase a weasel or a rabbit, he still knows that there's an awful lot of ground to go. And this has to do with reading and not being ignorant, not having this terror of ignorance—the chasm where you have nothing to grip on to. So the class system is always directing you there.

*Various critics have described this book as your most X rated, but in fact it's a long, long tease, and sex is conspicuously absent.*

There isn't that much sex in my stuff. There's a lot of talk about it, but not a great deal of bump and grind. There used to be more. I would defend my interest in it, though. My father, for instance, says that sex is a dead end in fiction. But

I think that just as you find out something about someone when they laugh—when they really laugh—you find out a lot by seeing them in a sexual situation. Almost the first thing I ask about a character that I am about to get going on is "What are they like in the sack?" Not "Are they good in the sack?" but "How in touch with themselves are they in the sack?" That dimension is always there. At the age of seventy, I can't see myself going on about it quite so much. I do expect there to be a natural evolution away from it.

> My father, for instance, says that sex is a dead end in fiction. But I think that just as you find out something about someone when they laugh—when they really laugh—you find out a lot by seeing them in a sexual situation.
>
> —*Martin Amis*

*So you think the fact that there's no real sex in* London Fields *is a function of your own—you used the term first—middle age?*

Well, there's still too much of it in there to be . . . [*Laughs*] There's life in the old boy yet—from that point of view. Come on, I now find myself in the position of saying there actually is quite a lot of sex in the book. There is a lot of fantasy, a lot of necking and petting. Even if there were 470 pages of gross pornography, it still wouldn't be the real thing. It would still be all an act, an artifice.

*When you do write about sex, it's always described as terribly self-conscious, solipsistic and even unpleasurable. During a sex scene in* The Rachel Papers, *the character Charles Highway says he wishes he could stop for "a cup of tea and a think." Your characters seem uneasy and preoccupied during sex, and they're mocked if they hope for any kind of transcendence. Is your view of sex so bleak?*

It's part of a genuine idea about modern life—that it's so mediated that authentic experience is much harder to find. Authentic everything is much harder to find. In all sorts of areas of our behavior, even in the sack, we're thinking, "How does this measure up? How will this look?" We've all got this idea of what it should be like—from movies, from pornography. I'm interested in two extremes. The first is the idea that the earth moves, this great union is found, and the self is lost. That comes from D. H. Lawrence and Romantic poetry and is what we all devoutly hope for. The other extreme is sort of athletic—the hot lay, where the self is in fact not lost in the moment but is masterful and dominant. And that comes at us from another direction—from advertising and pornography and trash fiction.

*You think that's the more prevalent view?*

I think it is. Although I do think romantic love is the self's most urgent quest. Young Charles in **The Rachel Papers** is looking for love. Certainly, when I was that age, love was the quest. Of course, there was a slight suspicion that maybe you were really interested in love because you heard that you got better sex that way.

*Again and again you've had to fend off the charge of misogyny in your work. How does it make you feel personally when people say that you hate women?*

If it's a woman saying it, and she really means it, then I'm sad. I'm disappointed. But I wouldn't change a word of anything I've written or I am going to write. I would say that my first three books are not antifeminist but prefeminist. Gloria Steinem's book *Outrageous Acts and Everyday Rebellions* slightly changed the way I thought about feminism. Just her simple technique of switching the sex roles, saying imagine if a man could have a period, he'd brag about how long and how heavy it was, et cetera. All that is great, and I just assented to that. You've got to get past the idea that there are all sorts of risky, alarm issues in my books—rape, masturbation, pornography—and see what's really going on. Then the woman reader has got to look into herself and say, "Is there an undertow here of this guy despising women?" I think the opposite is true.

I consider **Money** my feminist book. The hero does start to see the light, and being the kind of person he is, he fails to move into the light. In **London Fields** another kind of novelist wouldn't have had two extremes like Keith and Guy. He would have had one character, half of whom wants to sexually enjoy and even abuse Nicola and half of whom wants to overvalue her and adore her. These are two warring instincts in every man. Even in the best love you've got in you, there is a defiling element.

*In your earlier work there don't seem to be any sacred cows, but in* **London Fields** *you are newly politicized about the environment, about nuclear issues and about child abuse. Perhaps feminist readers are thinking, "Well, he's got some issues now. Why not feminism?"*

The reason I write about nuclear weapons and about the environment in **London Fields** has nothing to do with an ameliorist attitude towards them. It's just that they excite my imagination. Feminism doesn't excite me in that way—although I am profeminist. The trouble is, it doesn't swing on the page. You know the old saw about "What is a feminist's sexual fantasy"? It's not that she's sitting in the

desert when a sheik rides past and swings her onto the back of his horse, takes her off to some sumptuous cave and sleeps with her forty times in twenty-four hours. The feminist's sexual fantasy is that while she's having a cup of coffee in a cafe, she strikes up a conversation with a man who runs a kindergarten in Hampstead, they go to a couple of Bulgarian films, and then, when the time is right, they begin to have very caring sex. It doesn't really swing, does it, as a sexual fantasy? Give me the sheik with his glistening voice.

*There is an implication in* **London Fields** *that the world isn't inherently screwed up but that we've screwed it up and that perhaps we have the power to fix it.*

We've screwed it up. The earth is four and a half billion years old. Imagine it as a forty-five-year-old person. Nothing is known about the first sixteen years of his life. Last week apelike creatures evolved into man. Agriculture began at the weekend. In the last sixty seconds, industrialization began, and in that one minute we turned paradise into a toilet. Certainly it's man who's done it. But it may be that it's idle to do anything but witness this process. It may just be deeply and essentially human to self-destruct. It's our nature. But I would say also that that's a counsel of despair, and I don't see how anyone with children can believe it. You've got to love those who will come after.

*What would be your prescription for fixing up the world?*

As an experiment, I rather like this Vaclav Havel idea—rule by artists. I think that, particularly in America, the career politician is now such an atrocious figure that, as Gore Vidal said, anyone who is prepared to run for president should be disqualified from doing so. So I'd change the whole ballgame.

*There's Havel in Czechoslovakia, and Vargas Llosa now in Peru. Who would be your philosopher-kings in England and America?*

Not Norman Mailer. What a thought! You'd have gladiatorial games probably—a sort of Caligulan rule by men. No, it would have to be someone who's prepared to do it. And you don't want someone with too much vision. I wouldn't want to do it. I'd hate it. I wouldn't let my dad do it. Someone like [British novelist] David Lodge would be a perfectly good prime minister. Pragmatic. Good at administration. And for America, maybe David Mamet.

*Though he's a Thatcherite now, your father was an Angry Young Man in the Fifties. Do you ever worry that as you get older, you'll become conservative, too?*

I really do doubt it. He was a Communist, which I never have been; he was a member of the party. But the key thing about him and his contemporaries—these former Angry

Young Men, all of whom tend to be rightwing now—is that while they weren't born into poverty, they didn't have much money. Then they made some money, and they wanted to hang on to it. And they lived through a time when the left was very aggressive and when union power made life unpleasant. There are many aspects of the left that I find unappealing, but what I am never going to be is right-wing in my heart. Before I was even the slightest bit politicized, it was always the poor I looked at. That seemed to be the basic fact about society—that there are poor people, the plagued, the unadvantaged. And that is somewhere near the root of what I write about.

I really do believe that people are nice, one at a time. Even Germans. I am surprised by it. The bigger the unit, the worse it gets. Small may not be beautiful, but big is crazy. I fear for loss of individuality. In any kind of socialist utopia, one that worked, writing would become a very dull business. Because writers thrive on disparity. The reason that this preposterous notion of communism had such a long run is because it's deep in the human heart to want equality, to want everyone to be happy. It's a disaster as a political system, but the desire will always be there. But human nature wasn't made for that. Human nature was destined for disparity.

*Who intimidates you?*

Philosophers do. Their style of mind is different from mine, and I admire it, although I don't understand it. My wife does philosophy. It amazes me, the sort of things she's dealing with. My wife's first husband was a prominent linguistic philosopher, so she has lots of philosopher friends who have become my friends. And anyone who knows more than I do about anything intimidates me. My wife's area is the philosophy of art. Those who know about fine art, who really feel and understand it, intimidate me.

*You've written two books about the United States—**Money** and **The Moronic Inferno**—and you seem to have a kind of passionate ambivalence about the country.*

I love America. I think it's great. Even Ronald Reagan is great—personally. On the other hand, it's quite right to say that for years he got away with this image that he never told a lie, that all he did was tell a blooper. No, they *were* lies, and he is a liar. But he's got charm, and I am not resistant to it, the sort of amazing American serendipity in it.

The bit of America I've come to know best is the little-town America of Cape Cod and Wellfleet [Massachusetts]. My wife's father has a turkey camp there, which we take for a few weeks a year. It's full of the sort of couples that might be on the target list for a thrusting new magazine: "He is a child psychiatrist; she illustrates children's books." But there's an awful lot of general, everyday "I'm okay, you're

okay" small-time American good humor. I love the exotic names on the mailboxes, these names that are all *s*'s and *j*'s and *w*'s and *k*'s.

*Did your fascination with America begin during the year you spent in Princeton when your father was teaching there?*

Oh, definitely. It was 1958 or 1957; I was eight. On Christmas Day, I looked at the presents I got, and I just thought, "This is an incredible country." My parents gave parties for the faculty crowd, and I'd get three dollars for being a drinks waiter. I had a crew cut. I had fat whitewalls on my bike. It was a great time. Also, I didn't spend my time watching junk TV. There were cartoons, but not the sort of stuff that kids watch now. Not *Teenage Mutant Ninja Turtles,* not *Transformers.*

*Why do you live in London?*

I don't want my children to be American children. One of the things I don't like about America is this ten-minute-childhood idea—that childhood lasts for ten minutes and then what you've got is a wised-up little monster who is six years old and no longer a child. I saw *Batman* with my wife, and we loved it. But she turned to me and said, "It would make me sick to think of a child of mine seeing this." And I know American five-year-olds who have seen *Batman* eight times. No, the hell with that. I want my children to have more innocence than America seems to allow.

*You were an infamous bachelor. How has marriage and fatherhood changed you?*

It changes things so completely that you lose your point of comparison. It's relaxing for the ego somewhat, to have something that you'd so gladly die for. You get out of the self a bit. The real reason that one does it is because it's just the next thing. Like leaving home—it might be very nice at home, but you have to leave and go on to the next thing. If you're going to do a job of being a human being, then you just do these things. And in my case, by the time you're thirty-something, you're ready, you're desperate, really. You've had enough of those middle years. What's so great about having children is that it's the ordinary miracle; it's the miracle that happens to everyone. Two of you go into that room, and three come out.

Of course, being married and having children does cut into your dating.

*Has it been a burden to have been so precocious, to have been a boy wonder?*

I hope to Christ I'm not an aging boy wonder. I *am* forty now. It slightly alarms me when people call me "the bad boy of English fiction." I'm not a boy. I don't mind the "bad" really. It's the "boy" that is embarrassing. And I feel that this "bad boy" stuff denies me readers. I think there are a lot of people who think that my work is just a stew of used condoms. I'm a bit more interested now in feeling that I am a middle-aged writer with a body of work. I still feel the same, though. I believe that we don't really change much. Time moves past you, but you're still the same.

### D. J. Taylor (review date 27 September 1991)

SOURCE: "Backward Steps," in *New Statesman and Society,* Vol. 4, No. 170, September 27, 1991, p. 55.

[*In the following negative review, Taylor discusses the time structure of* Time's Arrow, *calling the novel "an entertaining conceit wound out to extravagant length."*]

The "time's arrow" metaphor has obviously been knocking around in Martin Amis' consciousness for a year or two. Nearly used as the title of what became **London Fields,** it now surfaces at the masthead of this ingeniously bulked out novella—one of those short books that have been artfully got up to resemble a medium-sized book, with a price to match.

The arrow in question points backwards: a man's life viewed in reverse by an observant but understandably baffled intelligence, defined as "the soul he should have had, who came at the wrong time, after it was too late".

The note of dislocation, whether actual or spiritual, is a constant. Our acquaintance with septuagenarian Tod Friendly begins on his deathbed (a hospital stake-out attended by levées of doctors) subsequently taking in a back-to-front recapitulation of his career.

As a conceit, it is meticulously done, each gesture and inflection fitting perfectly into the reverse tape loop, so that the general effect resembles a video on the rewind: the puzzling cars with their five reverse gears, the server's arbitrary pocketing of the ball that concludes a point in tennis, the bewildering ritual of eating out ("Rounding it off with a cocktail, we finish our meal and sit there doggedly describing it to the waiter, with the menu there to jog our memory").

Nervously joky at first, the narrative soon reveals a great deal of potentially disturbing baggage: the capering demons of Tod's dreams, the hint of a heavily camouflaged past, or rather future. And sure enough, having sped through Tod's time as a none too scrupulous American medic and his burdensome love life, the path stretches back, by means of aliases and subterfuge, to the unpromising chaos of central Europe—

where, as a functionary at Auschwitz and Treblinka, "Odilo Unverdorben" assists in the destruction of the Jews.

Here the tape loop works its most chilling trick. The gas-chambers, naturally enough, have the effect of *creating* life. Enlightenment is urged on the alter-ego, "on the day I saw the old Jew float to the surface of the deep latrine, how he splashed and struggled into life . . ." The book ends somewhere in the wastes of early 1920s childhood, Odilo and his "soul" having parted company shortly before the second world war.

A reviewer should always declare an interest: here is mine. I grew up, in a manner of speaking, with Martin Amis. I read **The Rachel Papers,** covertly, in the school library, bought **Success** in my first term at university and thought **Money** the finest English novel of the 1980s. Even **London Fields,** for all its prolixity, still seems immeasurably better than the chaff that excluded it from the 1989 Booker shortlist. It is curious that **Time's Arrow,** despite its dexterous sleight of hand, the occasional elevation of its prose into something very near poetry and the conspicuous engagement with "maturity", should end up as a disappointment.

The explanation is, I imagine, half to do with Amis and half to do with the circumstances in which he writes; half to do with an awareness that the moral high ground that he occupies occasionally gets sacrificed to the joke, half to do with the whole postmodern prohibition of representational writing.

Here, for example, is an account of possibly the greatest act of inhumanity in the history of humanity, and it is done by means of a device—a telling and fruitful device, but a device all the same. All this is in keeping with the postmodern ukase, in which a supposedly extraordinary reality requires an extraordinary treatment. Or as Eva Figes once put it: "The English social realist tradition cannot contain the realities of my lifetime, horrors which one might have called surreal if they had not actually happened."

Novelists who continue to produce "realistic" patchworks of bygone experience commonly have critics lining up to inform them that it is impossible to write like that any more. Yet **Time's Arrow,** which employs any amount of modish trickery, has the odd effect of making the reader pine for a slightly staider technique—one which would provide an adequate vehicle for human feeling. With any luck, hindsight will show this to have been a halfway house between brilliant but flawed juvenilia and resplendent mid-period achievement. At the moment, it is only an entertaining conceit wound out to extravagant length.

### David Lehman (review date 17 November 1991)

SOURCE: "From Death to Birth," in *The New York Times Book Review,* November 17, 1991, p. 15.

[*In the following review of* Time's Arrow, *Lehman focuses on the reversed chronological order of the book's narrative and the intent of Amis's technique.*]

My 8-year-old son, an expert at videocassette recorders, wondered one day, "Why can't we rewind time?" The question in all its blunt naïveté suggests the imaginative conceit at the heart of Martin Amis's remarkable new novel, *Time's Arrow.* Mr. Amis explores how life would appear, how it would feel and what sense it would seem to make if it were a film running backward—if time's arrow were to reverse its direction and a recording angel, along for the ride, permitted us to watch history (which Lord Byron called "the devil's scripture") as it is unwritten, line by line, gesture by gesture, until the perpetrators of the 20th century vanish into their mother's wombs.

The vehicle for this experiment in chronology—you might call it a fictional deconstruction of time—is the backward narration of one man's life. Mr. Amis's protagonist is a shady character, a doctor known retrogressively as Tod T. Friendly, John Young, Hamilton de Souza and Odilo Unverdorben. There is a good deal of onomastic playfulness at work here, since "Tod" means death in German, a language of considerable importance in this short novel; "friendly" is life in America, land of benign forgetfulness, where no one inquires too closely about the suave European stranger in town; and "young" is what he gets to be as the book goes along.

*Time's Arrow* begins on Tod Friendly's deathbed in "affable, melting-pot, primary-color, You're-okay-I'm-okay America." Weeks go by. He is released from the hospital. Immediately he has a heart attack in his garden. Then comes a car crash, followed by "the first installment" of his love life, a fight with a woman named Irene, who tells him she knows his dark "secret" because he says it in his sleep. Irene visits more frequently. There are other women as well. Tod meets them where he works, in the offices of American Medical Services on a commercial strip somewhere in New England. It is clear that he is on the run. Every December he gets a letter in primitive code advising him that the weather continues to be "temperate" in New York. One year he reads that the weather, "although recently unsettled, is temperate once more!"

In time, Tod moves to New York, where he has an emergency meeting with a sinister clergyman who warns him of danger—the Immigration and Naturalization Service might act to revoke his citizenship. Backward he proceeds until, in the summer of 1948, he sets sail "for Europe, and for war." He continues to shed false identities until the narrative finally catches up with the horrifying secret deep in his past,

which holds the key to the riddles in his personality and life: Odilo Unverdorben was a Nazi doctor, a dealer of death in Auschwitz, where he administered the poison gas used to kill Jews. In the book's relentless backward logic, he "personally removed the pellets of Zyklon B [from the shower room] and entrusted them to the pharmacist."

For the tale to have maximum impact, Mr. Amis needs an utterly naive narrator who is ignorant of modern history and unaware that backward is not the way things are supposed to go. Postulating a split in his protagonist's personality, Mr. Amis tells the story from the point of view of the man's alienated psyche or soul, condemned to witness events without comprehending them. There is pathos in the widening discrepancy between the reader's knowledge and that of the ghostly narrator. From the latter's warped vantage point, Auschwitz is a culmination, the one place where the world makes sense. Previously, the world was illogical. On American streets, adults snatch toys from children and sanitation workers dispense rubbish. People are "always looking forward to going places they've just come back from, or regretting doing things they haven't yet done. They say hello when they mean goodbye."

Doctors and hospitals especially, mystify the narrator, for—in backward time—patients enter well and leave sick, while mothers go to the hospital to return their babies. In Auschwitz, however, creation is accomplished, since murder, at reverse speed, appears to be the giving of life. Out of ashes and feces, the Jews are assembled—"the bald girls with their enormous eyes. Just made, and all raw from their genesis." Indeed, for the spectral narrator, Auschwitz is where the medical profession works wonders, undoing death on an unprecedented scale.

Mr. Amis's vision of the Holocaust undone is particularly moving. In Auschwitz, the gold is restored to the corpses' teeth: "To prevent needless suffering the dental work was usually completed while the patients were not yet alive." Then the bodies return to life in the "Sprinkleroom." In this version of history, on Kristallnacht the Nazis "all romped and played and helped the Jews." The racial laws are repealed; the Jews have the rights of citizens. The novel ends with the annihilation of the Nazi doctor's consciousness—not by death but by birth—concurrent with the restoration to health and prosperity of the Jews in pre-Nazi Germany.

Since the definitions of *"verdorben"* in German include "corrupt" or "fallen." Mr Amis's name for his damnable doctor takes on a double meaning. In an inverted world, *"Unverdorben"* might be the word for corrupt. But the word can also mean the opposite—innocent, unfallen, as if original sin could be undone. As his wordplay suggests, Mr Amis—the author of *London Fields* and *Money* and the perennial bad boy of English letters—is a writer of wit and post-modernist invention, who sets traps of ironies for readers to stumble into. But there is a moral purpose to Mr. Amis's experiments with narrative strategy and metaphysical possibility. The novel's inversions of causality and chronology seem perfectly in keeping with the Nazis' inversion of morality. In this sense, *Time's Arrow* implicitly warns us against turning the world of logic upside down or inside out—the very thing Mr. Amis does in this fiction.

The backward structure allows Mr. Amis to solve several narrative problems. As in a detective novel or psychoanalytic session, the climax occurs with the reconstruction of events that took place long ago. In addition, with his ghostly narrator Mr. Amis gets the benefit of both the first-person and the third-person points of view. The effect is like that of schizophrenia or, in the religious terms Mr. Amis seems to prefer, the divorce of the soul from the rest of a man's being. Most audacious is Mr. Amis's appropriation of erasure—the definitive motif of deconstruction—which he applies to the genocide of the Jews. The very instrument of revisionist history is put to the service of heartbreaking fiction.

In *Time's Arrow*, Martin Amis has written a book rich in poignancy and savage indignation.

## Pearl K. Bell (essay date Spring 1992)

SOURCE: A review of *Time's Arrow*, in *Partisan Review*, Vol. LIX, No. 2, Spring, 1992, pp. 282-95.

[*In the following excerpt, Bell dismisses* Time's Arrow *as "offensive" and maintains that Amis "fails to comprehend" what he has "exploited" in his story about Nazi Germany.*]

Martin Amis's restless ingenuity trips him up in a more serious way in *Time's Arrow,* a laborious attempt to be "original" about the Holocaust—hardly a subject that lends itself to the artful devisings of literary contrivance, or the sardonic bray of satire that has characterized his earlier work. In his new novel Amis has literally bent over backwards to be different. Reversing the order of time, Amis's portrait of a Nazi doctor, assistant to Mengele in Auschwitz, begins with his death and ends with his birth, taking him from his final days in California through years of medical practice in Boston and New York, to hiding out in Portugal and Italy after the war, to Auschwitz, medical school, and birth in Solingen, where Eichmann, too, was born. Conversations run from end to start, seagulls fly in reverse, corpses come to life. Since the doctor is incorrigibly priapic, the sexual implications of the backward scheme are obvious.

Amis attempts to underscore the gravity of his undertaking by splitting the consciousness of his protagonist: The narra-

tor is the soul of the Nazi doctor—the confused, jauntily colloquial voice of conscience, unaware of the murderous, unrepentant body that maimed and destroyed its victims in the camps. Through the separation of body and soul Amis tries to drive home his point that the conscience of the doctor was totally cut off from, and thus unable to comprehend or atone for, the atrocities committed by his physical being. But does the backward narration in any way intensify the evil of this doctor's life? On the contrary, what the reverse action makes dismayingly clear is the bag-of-tricks gamesmanship that inspired this grievously misguided approach to the Holocaust. We can only wince, and worse, at the gallows facetiousness that brings dead bodies to life with poisonous injections and fire. "I saw the old Jew float to the surface of the deep latrine, how he splashed and struggled into life, and was hoisted out by the jubilant guards, his clothes cleansed by the mire." Such manipulative "irony" denies the essential horror of Auschwitz, which is that the Jews struggled not into life but into death.

As he informs us in his afterword, Amis leaned heavily on Primo Levi's *Survival in Auschwitz* in writing *Time's Arrow, or The Nature of the Offense.* The subtitle is in fact Levi's phrase. Indeed, the only genuinely chilling words in this novel—"Here there is no why," which begin the Auschwitz chapter—have also been appropriated from Levi. In his memoir of the camp, Levi recalls plucking an icicle from a window only to have it snatched away by a guard. When he asked "*Warum?*" the guard replied "*Hier ist kein warum.*" Those four simple words convey more about the Holocaust than all of Amis's backward-running narrative, which, in violating the order of cause and effect, trivializes what he has exploited but failed to comprehend. And that is the nature of his offense.

## Maya Slater (essay date Summer 1993)

SOURCE: "Problems When Time Moves Backwards: Martin Amis's *Time's Arrow*," in *English: The Journal of the English Association,* Vol. 42, No. 173, Summer, 1993, pp. 141-52.

[*In the following essay, Slater points to problems that occur in the narrative of* Time's Arrow *as Amis attempts to tell a story in reverse.*]

In his latest novel, *Time's Arrow,* Martin Amis takes up the challenge posed by Nabokov in *Look at the Harlequins!*: 'Nobody can imagine in physical terms the act of reversing the order of time. Time is not reversible'. Amis does perform this impossible task. His novel begins with the hero's death, and works back through his life more or less to his birth. The result is more eccentric than might be expected by readers familiar with flashbacks or works like Pinter's play *Betrayal*, whose scenes succeed each other in reverse chronology. For Amis moves backwards through time on a more fundamental level. We are given a minutely detailed account of the hero's life in reverse, as though we had pressed the reverse button on a video recorder. In the world of this book, people walk backwards to their cars, and the cars go off down the road backwards. Bunches of flowers are taken back to gardens, and reattached to plants. The plants grow smaller and finally disappear into the ground as seeds. Rain never falls, but is sucked upwards into the clouds. Collapsed piles of rubble rise as an earthquake shakes them, and in a trice become perfect buildings. This is how Amis puts it:

> I live on a fierce and magical planet, which sheds or surrenders rain or even flings it off in whipstroke after whipstroke, which fires out bolts of electric gold into the firmament at 186,000 miles per second, which with a single shrug of its tectonic plates can erect a city in half an hour.

The novel, then, is set in a kind of science-fiction world in which impossible conditions prevail because a fundamental commonplace of our existence is turned on its head. Amis is not the first writer to exploit this sort of reversal. It was used by Lewis Carroll in his novel *Sylvie and Bruno* and there are visual examples of it in films such as Jean Cocteau's *Le Testament d'Orphée*, where we see torn flower-petals regenerate into a perfect bloom. But this novel is the most sustained example of the technique that I know of. It is interesting not only as an isolated, eccentric achievement, but also because the problems the author has to solve cast an unexpected light on the writer's craft. In particular, the technique offers unique linguistic possibilities. It is Amis's handling of these and his solutions to the principal problems posed by reverse narrative that I want to explore here.

The first problem is that of narrative voice. The implications of telling a story backwards must have a major impact on the personality and approach of the narrator, particularly if, as in this case, a first-person narrator is selected. Logically, the narrator of a backwards narrative should start off with a complete store of knowledge, and progressively 'unlearn' the facts of the tale as he tells it. This would eliminate suspense: past events hold no surprises for narrator or protagonists, so how can they hold major surprises for the reader?

Amis solves this problem by endowing his Narrator with an extraordinary series of characteristics. He is an insubstantial being who materializes inside the protagonist at the moment of his death. The novel, beginning at that moment, is like an enactment of the often-repeated assertion that when a man is drowning the whole of his life passes before his eyes. But in this case the past life of the protagonist, Tod, is relived backwards not before his own eyes, but before those of the mysterious Narrator, the internal observer who appears to be curled inside Tod's head, looking at the world through Tod's eyes. Tod remains unaware of his presence. Amis lays down a set of rules to explain why the Narrator's perception encompasses some elements but not others. The Narrator is given the power to share Tod's emotions and dreams, but not this thoughts: '. . . I am awash with his emotions. I am a crocodile in the thick river of his feeling tone.' This rule is not arbitrary, but is explained in terms of Tod's emotional state. Because Tod wants to suppress the memory of his past, he avoids thinking about it, and locks it away in a private part of his mind, so that the Narrator cannot guess what it is. Tod never discusses his past with anyone. From the start the Narrator suspects that Tod has a horrible secret, but has to wait to find out what it is, and the reader, of course, must wait with him. In this way, suspense is generated.

But having a strange being with no corporeal dimension as a mouthpiece presents a number of further problems. In the bewildering backwards setting, the rules governing the responses and attitudes of the Narrator have to be made clear to the reader. We cannot take the Narrator for granted, or make any assumptions about him, since he is outside our experience. So despite his lack of a physical body the Narrator has to be given a distinctive personality. He comes into existence fully mature, with his perceptions clear ('fully formed, fully settled'). He has firm opinions and a sense of humour. He also has a decent moral code: he believes in kindness, generosity, fidelity and love. In this, he is frequently at odds with Tod, who is a loner and a womanizer. In addition, the Narrator has a considerable store of acquired knowledge:

> I'm not a complete innocent.
>
> For instance, I find I am equipped with a fair amount of value-free information, or general knowledge, if you prefer. $E=mc^2$. The speed of light is 186,000 miles per second. . . . I have a superb vocabulary. . . . and a nonchalant command of all grammatical rules.

The Narrator also seems to have evolved some attitudes that specifically relate to Tod's past. For example, he has, from the start, an unreasoning dislike of doctors, which comes to seem all too appropriate when Tod's secret is finally revealed. For Tod was originally a Nazi doctor at Auschwitz. And it is from the memory of his own past that he is trying to escape.

But the Narrator's most essential characteristic is that he himself experiences life forwards, like a normal person. Imprisoned within a life that is moving backwards, he applies the logic and the powers of observation of a normal mind to the bizarre, topsy-turvy circumstances of his new existence. Amis, like many classic science-fiction writers, chooses to observe the unusual from a standpoint that is congenial and familiar to the reader. This device is not explained by Amis; but the reader has a powerful incentive to accept it, since the Narrator sees life as we do, and enlists our sympathy as we observe him reacting as we might do to a reversed world. The technique also enables Amis to describe the backward-moving world in detail, to extract the interest from it, rather than taking it for granted, because it seems so strange to the Narrator.

> **The language that Amis has adopted to describe life in reverse . . . is idiosyncratic, over-technical, obsessional, the language of a madman. I suspect that reversed narrative imposes this sort of language.**
>
> **—*Maya Slater***

Furthermore, though we never learn why, the Narrator seems aware that he has readers, who need to have the situation explained to them. He assumes, too, that his readers are like himself, seeing things forward, experiencing backward speech as gibberish. Amis copes with the fact that all his characters talk backwards by first giving an example of backward speech, after which the Narrator explains how he is going to reproduce such speech in the future:

> . . . . It goes like this:
>
> 'Dug. Dug', says the lady in the pharmacy.
>
> 'Dug', I join in. 'Oo y'rrah?'
>
> 'Aid ut oo y'rrah?'
>
> 'Mh-mm,' she'll say, as she unwraps my hair lotion. I walk away, backwards, with a touch of the hat. I speak without volition, in the same way that I do everything else. To tell the truth, it took me quite a while to realize that the pitiable chirruping I heard all about me was, in fact, human speech. Christ, even the larks and the sparrows sound more dignified. I translate this human warble, out of interest. I soon picked it up. I know I'm fluent, now. . .

The impact on the language is already apparent: if Amis were to take his approach to its logical conclusion, every word spoken would be in this kind of gibberish, and the novel would be unreadable. Instead, he sketches in the implications of backwards dialogue, and then moves on to use words forwards.

But despite this concession, language in this novel is not the language of ordinary narrative. The Narrator explains with scrupulous care how the reversed world works, as if realizing that it will be difficult for the reader to appreciate what is going on unless he spells it out. So his language is more meticulous, and events are described in more detail, than would normally seem acceptable. For example, here is a description of the process of backwards eating:

> First I stack the clean plates in the dishwasher . . . then you select a soiled dish, collect some scraps from the garbage, and settle down for a short wait. Various items get gulped up into my mouth, and after skilful massage with tongue and teeth I transfer them to the plate for additional sculpture with knife and fork and spoon . . . Next you face the laborious business of cooling, of reassembly, of storage . . .

Quite apart from the strangeness of the activity, the language used here is abnormally precise, detailed and scientific. Imagine the normal, forwards process described in the same sort of language:

> You face the business of getting the foodstuffs out of storage, for dismantling and heating. I transfer them to a plate for division by knife and fork and spoon. I place various items in my mouth, and after skilful massage with tongue and teeth I swallow them. You settle down for a short wait, then dispose of the scraps in the garbage, take the soiled dish and then I stack the dirty plates in the dishwasher.

We see how inappropriate such language is for events that we take for granted in normal life. Reverting to the original passage, we can see that the concern to make the process completely clear to the reader means that the language is all wrong for a simple process like eating a meal. The words used are unexpected. They may suggest inappropriate contexts: 'reassembly' suggests a manufacturing process, 'sculpture' evokes the art world, 'massage' seems to involve the whole body. Or they may seem too impersonal and formal. It would be impossible in normal parlance to refer to bits of food on a plate as 'various items'.

The language that Amis has adopted to describe life in reverse, then, is idiosyncratic, over-technical, obsessional, the language of a madman. I suspect that reversed narrative imposes this sort of language. If one imagines a more ordinary account of eating, and reverses it, the result would be virtually incomprehensible. For example, I might say 'I cooked myself a scrambled egg, washed up and had a cup of coffee'. In reverse, this could be: 'I brought up a cup of coffee, dirtied up, unscrambled an egg and made it raw.' A novel written in this way, reversing ordinary language without adding any explanatory detail, would be unreadable.

Despite his obsessional style, the Narrator does not come across as mad; rather the reverse. I think this is just because his precision, his desire to make his topsy-turvy world clear to the reader, make him seem like the only sane being in a nightmare world. His language suggests a conscious attempt to make himself clearly understood by his forward-living readers. In a sense, then, the world of this novel is not truly reversed—it is a backwards world seen through forward-looking eyes. It is the Narrator's all too understandable estrangement from it, and his struggle to cope with it, that make it acceptable to us; without the Narrator the weirdness would become intolerable. The precision and unnaturalness of his language can also make the Narrator himself seem pathetic and vulnerable, a misfit doing his best when the outside world has gone badly wrong.

The Narrator himself occasionally gets things wrong, as though he were still writing from the perspective of one who knows which way the world should really be turning, and cannot come to terms with his predicament. His misinterpretation of what is happening can make him seem comical. This tends to happen when the complexities of his reversed world defeat him, and, by taking things far too literally, he misses something that is obvious to the reader. For example, he several times expresses annoyance at Tod's cleaner Irene because she comes in and dirties and untidies the flat. She is, of course, simply reversing the process of tidying and cleaning. At such moments we are induced to laugh at the Narrator, or alternatively to wonder at his failure of understanding, rather than finding his surroundings bewildering or distressing.

At other times, his inaccuracy in narrating an event backwards can endow it with a weird, haunting or nightmarish quality. For instance, the Narrator accepts at face value something that happens when Tod is practising as a doctor. The patients leave Tod's consulting-room, and as they depart, give us a strange and ghostly moment: 'They back off from me with their eyes wide. And they're gone. Pausing only to do that creepy thing—knocking, quietly, on your door'. The Narrator knows perfectly well that people knock on the door after leaving the room, since he is aware that the world is moving in reverse. He told us so at the start, commenting 'It just seems to me that the film is running backwards'. The weird, unreal atmosphere is created by the fact that we can both understand the original simple forwards action and appreciate the strangeness that results from reversing it.

Strictly speaking, the Narrator is not dealing honestly with us: sometimes he is a sophisticated observer who knows his situation, while at other times he plays the uncomprehending innocent. But this failing in his character enables Amis to include more vividly meticulous descriptions of processes in reverse. Much of the enjoyment of this book is in the detail with which the Narrator views the backwards world.

In his more lucid moments, the Narrator is well aware that language has to be used in a special way to render his surroundings. He comments: 'Apart from words denoting motion or process, which always have me reaching for my inverted commas ('give', 'fall', 'eat', 'defecate'), the written language makes plain sense, unlike the spoken.' This remark tells us two things. First, there is a complete dichotomy between the written and the spoken word. If you pick up a book in the Narrator's world, it will look exactly like a book from our normal world. The problem is, of course, that you are not free to read the book forwards; you must start at the end and read each word backwards. Amis has an amusing episode in which a Japanese delights the Narrator by opening his book at what an English-speaking reader would call the beginning. Another problem, and one which Amis neglects to tackle, is what you should do with the knowledge you have acquired during your reading. Strictly speaking, if you are reading backwards, you should start with your mind full of information from the book, and should progressively shed this as you un-read the book back to the beginning. When you finally close the book, you should have unlearnt everything it had told you. The Narrator does not do this: he builds up a store of knowledge about Tod's life as an older man as he accompanies Tod on his journey backwards through time. The Narrator's inappropriate knowledge results in weird anachronisms. For instance, at one point Tod is treating a child patient, and the Narrator wonders whether he recognizes this child from a point earlier in Tod's backwards life, that is to say, from long afterwards in real time.

The second point made by the Narrator in his comment is about the use of verbs. To repeat: 'words denoting motion or process . . . always have me reaching for my inverted commas'. This touches on the most crucial linguistic idiosyncrasy in this text. As all activity moves backwards, the verbs we would normally use for such activity become inappropriate. Here for instance is a description of Tod doing what in straightforward time would be giving a toy to a child:

> He takes toys from children, on the street. He does. The kid will be standing there, with flustered mother, with big dad. Tod'll come on up. The toy, the squeaky duck or whatever, will be offered to him by the smiling child. Tod takes it. And backs away, with what I believe is called a shiteating grin. The child's face turns blank, or closes. Both toy and smile are gone: he takes both toy and smile. Then he heads for the store, to cash it in. For what? A couple of bucks. Can you believe this guy? He'll take candy from a baby, if there's fifty cents in it for him.

In forwards time, Tod has gone to a shop, bought a toy, walked towards a child and given it to him, and the child smiles when he gets it. You can see that the verbs are reversed: 'give' becomes 'take'; 'take' becomes 'offer'; 'buy' becomes 'cash in'.

Reversing the verbs can also produce much more subtle effects than merely turning the narrative back to front. For instance, in the above passage, after Tod has taken the child's toy, he 'backs away.' This is simply a reversal of 'he walks up'. But the verb 'to back away' is not synonymous with 'to walk backwards'. It implies a strong negative emotion. One backs away through excessive fear, shyness or shame. In forwards time, Tod walks forwards, smiling. In reverse time, his grin seems frightened or propitiatory. The subtlety of this is that it suggests a subtext of unacknowledged unhappiness and fear, which may be imposed by the language but which is only too appropriate since Tod is tormented by the memory of his Nazi past and of the torture he inflicted on innocent children. The most interesting of the reversed verbs in the text make one feel that there is something sinister hidden in their meaning, while yet being a perfectly logical reversal of the normal process. To give another example, Tod crosses the Atlantic to Europe (in reality, of course, he was escaping from Europe and his Nazi past to build a new life in the USA). The ship, as we would expect, sails backwards. In real time, Tod prefers to stand at the stern of the ship, watching the wake, looking back towards Europe. Reversing this, Tod is standing watching the way the ship is going, and the ship goes over its own wake as it moves backwards. The Narrator puts it like this: 'We are successfully covering our tracks as we sail'. This is literally true of the process of backwards sailing, but it also exactly corresponds to Tod's activities, were they to be described in forwards time. As we will discover, he escapes from Auschwitz and moves slowly across Europe, obliterating clues to his past. He hopes that by sailing to America he will successfully put potential pursuers off the scent.

Complex verb effects like this are rare: by virtue of being so striking, they would detract from the flow of the narrative. A more common technique is to try to find verbs that are not too peculiar, so that the reader assimilates the backwards narrative without its seeming over-strange. Very often, the verbs could pass in a normal, forward-moving account. Tod 'tools along' or 'trudges' along the street, perhaps 'tugging' a shopping trolley. A girl hurries 'in through the door and across the room towards' him. A cab 'pulls up'; a car 'weaves at speed back up the street'. Tod 'settles down . . . with whisky glass'. But it is difficult for the verbs to seem completely normal when they are expressing the opposite of normality. Instead, they tend to impart a particular atmosphere to the narrative. Take for instance the verbs for drinking. We are told that Tod sits 'quietly snorting and drooling into [a] brandy balloon'. He describes getting drunk: 'We went out into New York City and staggered here and there through the Village and drooled it all out in bar after bar'. As drink-

ing backwards involves pouring liquid from the mouth into the glass, so these verbs for drinking, 'snorting' and 'drooling', provide a reasonably accurate account of the process. In addition, however, they have a pejorative flavour, so they introduce a nuance of contempt into the description. The overall tone of the narrative is detached scorn, mingled with sardonic humour. This effect is frequently achieved through the unusual verbs, which impose this mood on all the characters' actions simply because they are so unusual. There is good reason for this: we expect our everyday actions to be taken for granted, accepted without comment. If it appeared that someone was closely watching exactly how we set about drinking from a glass we would feel uncomfortable and under attack. If, in addition, the observer was selecting curious verbs to render our actions, we would feel as if we were being regarded as odd specimens, were being judged. At times, indeed, the Narrator does overtly judge Tod. But even in apparently unbiased descriptions there is an underlying element of criticism.

Perhaps because we are constantly measuring the descriptions of Amis's backwards world against our own, one effect of the reversed narration is to make us read particularly carefully. This attentive scrutiny is accompanied by a tendency to judge the text. The sheer sleight of hand required to tell a story backwards seems so difficult to achieve that one is constantly on the watch for the author to make mistakes, just as we watch a magician to try to discover the secret behind his tricks. During the course of Amis's particularly well-worked-out narrative, I did detect some wrongly described processes, where the verbs used clash with the apparent meaning. In the description of the reversed eating quoted earlier, Amis goes into the process of putting a dirty plate in the dishwasher: 'First I stack the clean plates in the dishwasher . . . then . . . select a soiled dish . . .' The word 'select' is wrong here. If he really were performing his actions backwards, Tod would not choose the plate from the dishwasher, but would lay his hand straight on it. (Imagine the normal, not reversed, everyday gesture of putting a dirty plate in a dishwasher: you remove your hand from it cleanly, without standing over it and deselecting it so that it blends in with the other dirty dishes.) It is as though the Narrator has simply tried too hard here, used too meticulous a verb for a casual process. Elsewhere, the verb is more strikingly wrong. Amis writes 'an ambulance . . . passes us and heads on down the street'. The ambulance should be 'backing', not 'heading', down the street. Although 'heading' involves facing the way one is going, this nuance scarcely impinges on a normal, forward-moving narrative. The fact that it sounds wrong when the narrative is reversed suggests that verbs in reversed actions will need to denote the precisely correct backwards motion. Any looseness of meaning will be noticed. With backwards narration, then, the author can expect an unusually attentive reading, an enhanced participation from the reader. I personally 'reran' much of the text in forward motion to check its accuracy. Felicitous solutions gave pleasure, and shortcomings were noted.

One respect in which Amis fails to exploit the narrative potential of his device relates to the magic of the world he has created. He invents an extraordinary universe whose laws can be logically worked out from our own. He arouses an exceptional degree of attention from his readers, focused on the words in his text. And yet, the overall mood is unemotional and flat, reflecting the emotionless world of reversed time, in which hope, anxiety and desire are by definition impossible. While this conveys the personality of the bewildered Narrator, clinging to logic to preserve his sense of reality, it fails to do justice to this new world, which is sometimes touched on rather than described, as if it were too disturbing to be detailed. At times, indeed, one can clearly see that a trompe-l'oeil similarity to our world is achieved at the cost of underplaying or even falsifying the magic of the Narrator's. To give examples: the magic is underplayed when you see Tod using a pen and paper. We are told 'Tod does his little stunt with the pen and pad'. What is actually happening is that Tod is un-writing. He takes a pad with a prescription written on it, puts his nib on the page at the end of the writing, and runs his pen back over the shapes of the letters, reabsorbing the ink into the pen. He finishes with a completely blank pad. To describe this as 'doing a little stunt' is not inaccurate but inadequate. This sketchy technique has one advantage: the narrative is not interrupted for the reader to wonder at the details of the 'stunt'. But an opportunity for describing something curious has been missed.

Elsewhere, the description is definitely inaccurate, and the mistake serves to make the narrative less strange and magical. For instance, here is a description of an old woman feeding the birds in the street, though backwards:

> An old lady descends from the black branches of the fire escape every morning and wearily gathers it all up and clambers home with it in paper bags: the food left for her by the birds.

The conceit of the birds coming and leaving food for a poor old lady is charming enough, and like a fairy tale. But the old lady's gesture as she picks up the bread is wrongly described when Amis writes she 'gathers it all up'. If we replay her action, but forwards, we see her coming down the fire escape, then getting out her paper bags, and scattering the bread by throwing it down. So the reversed narrative should be much more surreal. The bread left by the birds should jump up from the ground of its own accord to land in her hand. Amis's 'she . . . wearily gathers it all up' gives no hint of this magical process. In Amis's restrained account of this action, half the magic has been suppressed, creating a play between banality and surrealism that would have given

way to wonderment if a more accurate, hence stranger, account had been given.

Another category of language, in addition to verbs, lays itself open for close scrutiny in reverse narrative. This is the use of language to denote time, its passing and its sequence. Words like 'morning' and 'afternoon', 'before' and 'after', 'past' and 'future' take on new meaning in this novel. The reader is obliged to redefine them, and this may well give rise to reflections on the true meaning of such words. Take, for example, the following seemingly unexceptionable statement:

> [Tod] has acquired a taste for alcohol and tobacco. He starts the day with these vices—the quiet glass of red wine, the thoughtful cigar—and isn't that meant to be especially bad?

Bearing in mind the fact that time is reversed, we deduce that Tod is in fact ending, not starting, the day with a glass of wine, so that the verb simply denotes an opposite process. The effect is a sort of dramatic irony: we see that the Narrator's anxiety about morning drinking is groundless because he hasn't understood the time reversal. Much more complex is the noun 'day'. The Narrator uses it to describe a period that starts at bedtime and ends in the morning, when the backwards world gets into bed. This gave me cause to wonder whether this was a correct use of the word. The first meaning given by the OED [*Oxford English Dictionary*] is 'The time between the rising and setting of the sun'. What Amis gives us, reversing the time sequence, is 'The time between the setting and the rising of the sun', that is to say, the opposite of day. So that we cannot take the most common of nouns for granted. Another feature of this passage is the fact that the language of reversed time is systematically camouflaged. The problematic words are inserted in a text which is written simply, and in which the sentiments and their expression seem familiar and even banal. The Narrator appears at first sight to be expressing the common opinion that drinking in the morning is bad for you, using cliched adjectives (the *quiet* glass, the *thoughtful* cigar). Until the passage is examined closely, the impression is that one is reading about something ordinary. If, instead of half-concealing the impact of time reversal, Amis had consistently brought it to the forefront, the result would have been interesting as a short experiment but unreadable as a novel.

This, then, is a novel that plays tricks on the reader. It adopts a superficially matter-of-fact tone which gives us the impression that we are reading it as we would read a 'normal' novel. In fact, we are doing something that is almost the opposite of 'normal' reading. Amis, by reversing the order of events, has deprived us of our ease of reading. We can no longer read casually, because the mass of what we normally take for granted as readers has been swept away. Our only defence is not to let our guard slip, not to let anything past without scrutinizing it first. Proof-readers seeking out errors sometimes find it helpful to read a text backwards: they can concentrate on each individual word without allowing their eye to run on to the next. Amis, by reversing the text before we ever get to it, has turned us all into proof-readers of his novel.

## Chris Savage King (review date 1 October 1993)

SOURCE: "Bits of Rough," in *New Statesman and Society*, October, 1993, pp. 39-40.

[*In the following negative review, King calls* Visiting Mrs. Nabokov *"gossipy" and "egotistical," and dismisses the collection of journalistic pieces as "pretty miserable."*]

Martin Amis excites hero-worship and resentment in equal measure. From male writers, this is often a symptom of wanting to be him. This new collection of journalism covers a range of subjects that include snooker, fiction and Martin Amis. Being female, I should, in Amis' view, be "less baffled and repelled" in making critical judgments. Here we go, then.

It wasn't his fault that he was born into the literati, and *Visiting Mrs Nabokov* abounds in literary gossip. When Burgess and Borges met, they chatted in Anglo-Saxon! Excuse me: what a pair of nellies. Here's Amis on Saul Bellow at a conference in Haifa: "He was in stalwart attendance . . . on the day I gave my paper . . ." Or Amis on his friendship with Salman Rushdie: "I often tell him that if the Rushdie Affair were, for instance, the Amis Affair . . ." How about Martin reporting from the set of *Robocop II*? "Here's cold proof of how hip and classy this outfit is: nearly everyone had read my stuff." Or scolding Polanski for miscasting *Tess*? "Polanski shrugged and disagreed, showing no more than mild disappointment."

Most writers have egos the size of Mount Sinai. Amis' ego and ambition have also been his tragedy. Paperback editions of his early work were plastered in the kind of covers that wouldn't have disgraced Jacqueline Susann's oeuvre, with prose inside to match. He was in that league, then.

*The Moronic Inferno* was less a comment on the US, perhaps, than a way of describing its author's inflamed consciousness. Still, in that earlier book, Amis surveyed Brian De Palma, Aids and Hugh Hefner, when finer British writers wouldn't touch them. He had fame, money, pussy galore. He was loved—yes, but not revered. Like the Krays, like Keith Talent in *London Fields,* he wanted *respect*. But not in Aretha Franklin's sense.

In 1984, *Money*—a trash classic—was passed over in that year's Booker Prize, along with Angela Carter's *Nights at the Circus*. Headmaster's end-of-term report: no refinement, no intellectual rigour. Frightfully smutty mind. Must try harder. *Time's Arrow* followed, eventually. Here was the big subject: the Holocaust! Here was the pointless technical virtuosity: writing it *backwards*. Amis was correct in his estimate of the Booker panel's solemn idiocy. *Time's Arrow* was duly shortlisted, but didn't win.

Still, wasn't Martin Amis—old rugged chops, literature's bit of rough—really one of us? In *Visiting Mrs Nabokov,* we see him as a rosy-cheeked youth attending Battersea Grammar School: "practically Broadmoor". He was saved from this ordeal only by being swept off to the West Indies for four months' film work. "How can they afford the five-star prices?" he cries now, surveying holidaymakers in St Lucia. "Are they all betting-shops nabobs or coin-op kings?" He is startled, on meeting the winner of the darts world championship, that the man isn't "half-drunk in some roadhouse, smothered in tattoos". He is astonished, in China, to discover a Watford player "on his way from the ballet to the opera".

In a more gallant mood, here's Martin Amis, girl-watcher, on "Tennis: the women's game": "*Dynasty* with balls, bright yellow fuzzy ones . . ." Or on topless sunbathing in Cannes: "I had never seen so many breasts in my life, and all nonchalantly bared to the breeze." His piece on Madonna is a soft lament for the time when sexual trickery was something men did to women—one-way traffic, apparently.

A young Amis prepares for a Stones concert by ordering up two girls, and sullenly equipping himself with earplugs. Add a mention of a "dusky bongoist" accompanying Charlie Watts, and you have the spit of whichever John Junor type fulminated against noisy yobbos way back in the sixties.

"I *can* read and write, and to a high standard," he insists. And *Visiting Mrs Nabokov* has its share of cute phrases and observations. Trouble is, you have to wade through an awful lot of dated stuff, before you get to them. None of these articles is as good as his recent defence of Philip Larkin in the *Guardian*. Yet what was that about? More nostalgia for uglier times, when callow white men could be as sexist, racist or snobbish as they wished. The only response would be a wry chuckle over the brightness of the offence, and—with any luck—literary groupies would sink to their knees in breathless admiration. Outsiders were excluded, in the terms of this testimony, by having the wrong dinner jacket or liking naff songs.

In *Visiting Mrs Nabokov,* Amis and his chums drive themselves to hysteria, being clever-clever for its own sake. They form shifty poker schools, then "go home and sob in our wives' arms". Dear friends of Martin and "my father" are ceaselessly interviewed, but the only one he makes you want to read is V S Pritchett. Martin's head is still in the 1950s, and Amisland is a literary fantasy. Anyone who wants it is welcome to it. He seems less a hip, classy Mr Vain, and more like Hardy's Little Father Time.

I used to find Amis an entertaining writer. I found this collection pretty miserable. In the final straits, I had to buck myself up with active humour (Denis Leary's *No Cure for Cancer*), live fiction (Shena Mackay's *The Laughing Academy*), real literary criticism (D J Taylor's *After the War*) and a brilliant mind in top gear: Robert Hughes' *Culture of Complaint*. I'm thrilled they're repeating *Absolutely Fabulous*. I long for the TV *Buddha of Suburbia*. Contemporary culture isn't ugly; it's rich and beautiful. And none of it has anything to do with Martin Amis.

### Francine Prose (review date 27 February 1994)

SOURCE: "Novelist at Large," in *The New York Times Book Review*, February 27, 1994, p. 17.

[*In the following review, Prose lauds* Visiting Mrs. Nabokov *as light, unoffensive, and lively.*]

Written for British newspapers like *The Observer* and American magazines like *Vanity Fair,* and as an apparently welcome respite from writing fiction, the articles in Martin Amis's latest collection of essays have the range and appealing ragbag variety of work done on assignment. Indeed, as he writes in the introduction to *Visiting Mrs. Nabokov: And Other Excursions,* the only thing that unites these pieces is "getting out of the house."

In his forays away from his desk, Mr. Amis goes to China with a rowdy British soccer team whose patron and mascot is Elton John; he talks to Salman Rushdie in hiding, interviews Graham Greene in Paris and, in "one of the pillared public rooms of the Montreux Palace Hotel," visits Vladimir Nabokov's widow, Véra. He also attends a Rolling Stones concert, the Cannes Film Festival and the 1988 Republican National Convention, watches world championship chess and women's tennis matches, and plays poker with David Mamet and snooker with Julian Barnes.

Much of this is amusing, and it's perversely gratifying to see Mr. Amis irritated or horrified by things that we feel might annoy or appall us too: by the grim corporate architecture of Frankfurt or the crush of fans being herded into a rock concert. ("Once inside, panic and claustrophobia jockeyed routinely for one's attention. . . . In the high tradition of all the best rock concerts, you were treated as if you'd come to sate

some vile addiction rather than simply to exchange cash for entertainment.")

Several of the more successful essays are written in a tone strikingly unlike the ironic jeremiad we've come to associate with Mr. Amis's most recent novels, **London Fields** and **Time's Arrow**. Among these sympathetic studies is an incisive, rather loving essay on the brilliant, less than lovable poet Philip Larkin, who was a friend of Mr. Amis's father. An interview with—and appreciation of—J.G. Ballard makes one want to rush out and buy all of Mr. Ballard's novels.

In his introduction, Mr. Amis tells us that "writing journalism never feels like writing in the proper sense. It is essentially collaborative: both your subject and your audience are hopelessly specific." In fact, the most specific of these pieces are the strongest. There's a lively essay on the filming of *Robocop 2* and our eerily detached fascination with the *Robocop* films' bloody-minded bionic charm. And it pleased me to learn that Vladimir Nabokov was a "compulsive tipper" at the hotel where he lived, and that his widow insisted on picking up the check for drinks with Mr. Amis.

The blurrier pieces—including one on the nuclear weapons establishment in Washington—mean well enough, but keep tripping over grand statements and slightly awkward bons mots, like this observation occasioned by Mr. Amis's meeting with the chief scientist on the Strategic Defense Initiative project: "He is about Can Do. I am about Don't Do."

Such moments make one understand why Mr. Amis occasionally seems to chafe against the limits of his "hopelessly specific" subjects and audiences. Partly it's a problem of form, partly of expectation. The literary or celebrity interview, the 3,000-word article—these genres demand (that is, we readers demand) wit at the expense of depth, more facility than profundity. If some of the nonfiction collected here is clever and not much more, one understands that Mr. Amis was writing on assignment.

The essays in **Visiting Mrs. Nabokov** are bright; they move quickly; they don't ask much of us, or offend. And isn't that just what we're looking for as we lunge for the magazine rack on the airplane? In an essay on an alarming emergency landing during a flight to Spain, Mr. Amis describes himself as "a nervous passenger but a confident drinker and Valium-swallower." Those of us who don't much like to fly have always understood that there is something worthwhile—merciful, one might say—in writing something that pleasantly passes the time 30,000 feet above the ocean.

### Victoria N. Alexander (essay date Fall 1994)

SOURCE: "Martin Amis: Between the Influences of Bellow

and Nabokov," in *The Antioch Review,* Vol. 52, No. 4, Fall, 1994, pp. 580-90.

*[In the following essay, Alexander discusses the influences of Saul Bellow and Vladimir Nabokov in Amis's work, focusing on* London Fields, Money, *and* The Moronic Inferno.*]*

Martin Amis's novels feature heroes of playboy fantasies, unscrupulous upwardly mobile yobs, and charismatic murderers. With a mixture of anxiety and fascination, Amis chronicles the "cheapening of humanity," a phenomenon he attributes partly to the uniquely twentieth-century prospect of total annihilation and partly to the fact that much of American (and more lately British) life is dedicated to televised "event glamour"—a phrase borrowed from Amis's mentor, Saul Bellow. Both writers maintain that popular sporting/ religious extravaganzas give a false sense of collective life experience. Moreover, says Amis, channel-hoppers skip through tabloid journalism shows, cursory reports of sex scandals and riots, and mini-series on serial killers, delighting only in unsavory special effects. "It's a distracted age," Amis notes gravely; "the narrative line in human life is gone," and with it, he suggests, human decency.

Because the "decline of the West" is Amis's subject, he has earned an unfavorable reputation for playing the social critic, or if you prefer, for being a quixotic champion of bygone values. Amis's end-of-the-millennium novel, *London Fields,* tries but fails to explain how the nuclear threat has led to a disintegration of human decency, and *Money: A Suicide Note* tries but fails to prove that the distracting influences of fast food, pornography, and capitalism contribute to increases in gratuitous crime.

Trying to provide one's readers with advice on life may be a rather puerile inclination. Nevertheless, his statement regarding "the narrative line," of which the vicious and moronic are supposedly deprived, is intriguing. He proposes that people profit, intellectually and morally, by reading fiction, by gaining a sense of order and justice. He himself writes because he likes to impose order on chaos. But this is a limited explanation. What *does* Amis mean by "the narrative line"? Does he mean *the* narrative? Does he mean the human story, which once had an omniscient author, God, and a fairly well-contrived plot called Providence? I think he does. According to Bellow, his important advisor on the subject, distraction is a by-product of nihilism. Bellow, too, has spent much of his career giving his readers advice on life, most particularly encouraging the belief in the human soul.

The condition of distraction, for which Amis seeks a remedy, explains only Amis's motivation for writing. It does not explain why Amis, after offering Answers to big social problems, later rescinds them by stressing the fact of fiction. Amis, obsessed with apparent world-randomness, arranges

things the way he wants in his novels. At the same time, however, he is aware that his arrangement is only fiction, and he reminds readers of this by employing certain "postmodern" techniques such as involution, the inclusion of the author himself in the novel. Amis takes this cue from Nabokov, the renowned illusionist. In *Strong Opinions* Nabokov writes, "What I would welcome at the close of a book of mine is a sensation of its world receding in the distance and stopping somewhere there, suspended afar like a picture in a picture: *The Artist's Studio* by Van Bock" ("Van Bock" is an imperfect anagram of Nabokov).

Amis's aesthetic and moral principle, a queer hybrid of Nabokovian and Bellovian world-views, can be stated as: It is man's natural tendency to fictionalize, to bestow some kind of order—it is sometimes his comfort, sometimes his affliction, and at all times a quality of being human—but he should not deny the false truth of the narrative he creates.

Because Saul Bellow's narrators speak too closely to his own "truth," he could not discredit them by stressing the gap between fiction and reality. To Bellow, a venerable author has the power of vision, whereas Nabokov and Amis are quite happy to be characterized as illusionists or artists.

> **Amis's aesthetic and moral principle, a queer hybrid of Nabokovian and Bellovian world-views, can be stated as: It is man's natural tendency to fictionalize, to bestow some kind of order—it is sometimes his comfort, sometimes his affliction, and at all times a quality of being human—but he should not deny the false truth of the narrative he creates.**
>
> —*Victoria N. Alexander*

I spoke with Amis in 1993 about his two influences. I did not ask what bearing, if any, his "myth of decline" had on practical politics. Of more interest to me were his influences and the dynamics of faith/doubt and idealism/realism, which are a source of energy and artistic expression in his tragi-comedies. At the time, Amis himself seemed heedless of his paradoxical situation as a writer who believes in the value of faith, but has none.

Amis once said a writer is like a god—a predictable sentiment given the redeeming potential he attributes to literature. In an interview with Ian McEwan on "Writers in Conversation," Amis said he became a writer because "[Life] is all too random. [I have] the desire to give shape to things and make sense of things," and he added, "I have a god-like relationship [with] the world I've created. It is exactly analogous. There is creation and resolution, and it's all up to [me]."

Amis and I discussed the writer's essential business, whether it was the artist's function to "discover" meaning or to "give" meaning. Amis believes the artist "rearranges things to give point and meaning." He explained, "The difference between *In Cold Blood* and *The Executioner's Song*, say, and *Crime and Punishment* is that Capote and Mailer are just given the facts and cannot arrange them to point up a moral—or just arrange them to point up various ironies. What they're left with is *life*, which I say is kind of random."

Amis wrote about Truman Capote and Norman Mailer in *The Moronic Inferno.* From "a piece of event glamour"— that is, the execution of convicted murderer Gary Gilmore— Mailer assembled *The Executioner's Song,* a work of "fictoid" filled with "factoids," according to Amis. Mailer's work followed Capote's nonfiction novel *In Cold Blood,* which describes the pointless murder of the Clutter Family in Kansas. The American authors are not "artists" according to Amis's definition because neither has Amis's "god-like" control over material. The "narrative line" is absent from the "fictoid" genre because its "resolution" is not author-contrived. As Amis says, these facts "are given." Amis's preference for his own aesthetic model may prevent him from fairly judging the "true-life" novel. He has definite scruples against confusing life with fiction. Amis writes, "What is missing, though, is the moral imagination, moral artistry.... When the reading experience is over, you are left, simply, with murder—and with the human messiness and futility that attends all death."

Among Amis's designated "moral artists" is Saul Bellow. Any discussion of Martin Amis must include the Nobel-Prize-winning author who has greatly influenced Amis in terms of both subject and style. In Saul Bellow's "Jefferson Lectures," delivered in 1977, the John Self character is delineated in his description of "modern man":

> This person is our brother, our *semblable*, our very self. He is certainly in many respects narrow and poor, blind in heart, weak, mean, intoxicated, confused in spirit—stupid. We see how damaged he is, how badly mutilated. But the leap towards the marvelous is a possibility he still considers nevertheless. . . . He dreams of beating the rap, outwitting the doom prepared for him by history. Often he seems prepared to assert that he is a new kind of human being, whose condition calls for original expression, and he is ready to take a flier, go for the higher truth. He has been put down, has put himself down too, but he has also dreamed of strategies that will bring him past all this distraction, his own in-

cluded. For he knows something. . . . He is (or can be) skeptical, cant-free, heedful of his own intuitions.

This excerpt is so close to the story of John Self it could serve as *Money*'s synopsis. Amis acknowledges the collective influence of Bellow's work on the writing of *Money.*

Amis has written several articles on Bellow and his work. They have appeared in television interviews as a kind of twosome. Bellow looks ready to bequeath his literary mantle to Amis, who in turn seems eager to carry on a great tradition. Only upon further inspection does one begin to anticipate a "father-son" parting of the ways.

In *The Moronic Inferno,* Amis favorably reviews Bellow's *The Dean's December;* but, in fact, Amis modifies Bellow's perspective on a writer's essential business to suit his own. One gets the sense that Amis is slightly embarrassed for Bellow's sake when Bellow discusses transcendentalism, anthroposophy, or the existence of the human soul. Amis is something of an agnostic. For him, the writer is an artist-creator of a fictional world; whereas Bellow, whose strong faith pervades his writing, hints—warily sometimes, but more often with nerve—that the writer is a kind of prophet, visionary, or to be more precise, a medium who interprets this world.

The hero of *The Dean's December,* Albert Corde, like Bellow and Amis, is a writer concerned with the decline of social values and rise of gratuitous violence. Journalist Corde declares that "chronic lead insult" in urban populations has resulted in laziness, low intelligence, irritability, a predisposition to violence, insanity—social decay. Like a "new journalist" Corde is given the facts of his "story," but Corde notices the poetic coincidence that for centuries "leaden" has described the degenerate, and he insists the coincidence has metaphysical significance. Thinking objective facts could not communicate the oracular ramifications, he uses metaphor and poetry to communicate the deeper truth behind the report of chronic lead insult.

When discussing the writer's essential business, Amis made a distinction between the writer who "finds meaning" and who "gives meaning." It is debatable here whether Corde discovers meaning in the situation of chronic lead insult or invests it with meaning. I disagreed with Amis when he insisted that Corde's vision should be interpreted as "poetic" rather than "prophetic," an assertion that Corde is really a representation of an artist-creator, not a visionary-medium. In Bellow's Nobel Lecture, he clearly states his belief that great literature is not merely poetic. "There is another reality, the genuine one, which we lose sight of. This other reality is always sending us hints, which, without art, we can't receive."

Bellow insists upon "visionary truth" in literature, which, he says, "has always referred to a world beyond the threshold." With this in mind, one can assume Corde is supposed to be seen as a kind of prophet, who does not merely *invest* a situation with his own meaning, but who *discovers* a truth.

In Amis's review of *The Dean's December,* he writes that prior to 1976, "Bellow's heavy emphasis on illusory otherworlds had left him open to charges of crankery and self-indulgence"; however, in "Late Bellow," claims Amis, "transcendentalism has found its true function, which is Yeatsian—a source of metaphor." Amis redefines transcendentalism as "a system of imagery that gives the reader an enduring pang, a sense of one's situation in larger orders of time and space."

This definition seemed to suit his own writing more than Bellow's. Later, Amis elaborated, "What religion used to take care of was to give one a sense that one wasn't just living in a meaningless present, and that there were greater contexts. Religion won't quite do this for us anymore," said Amis. "If we're to believe in perfectibility or even improvement, then we need to be able to think of the human soul as an imperishable image of our potential and our battered innocence."

While Amis uses "soul" as a metaphor, he concedes that for Bellow the soul is not just a metaphor. It is a real belief in Bellow's case. "It's a rather weaker belief in my case," said Amis, "Not . . . a belief, but a kind of inkling, or suspicion."

Amis's other great influence, Vladimir Nabokov, claims a novelist is a "rival" to the "Almighty" and "must possess the inborn capacity not only of recombining but of re-creating the given world." Both writers betray a certain arrogance, likening themselves to gods. In fact, Amis confesses his ego is infinite; but it goes beyond idle boasting. The proud omnipotent writer duly exhibits his artistic prowess, and the nature of the novel is changed. Amis and Nabokov both emphasize the fact of fiction via involution. Amis includes himself as a character in *Money,* a character who is actually responsible for designing the plot. The reader's willing suspension of disbelief is discouraged, his awe of the artist-writer encouraged.

Amis has suggested literary otherworlds as tropes can do what religion no longer can, that is, "give a sense of one's situation in larger orders of time and space," or "a sense that one [isn't] just living in a meaningless present . . . that there [are] greater contexts." Ironically, in his fiction an intruding author rescinds the offer. It was all fiction, a sleight of hand. The author bows. John Self is left in a meaningless present.

Why does Amis do this? Out of maliciousness? To suggest that our sense of "greater contexts," like Self's, is, too, an illusion? Perhaps the temptation to reveal himself to his creation (to wink at the readers, to show off, really) is too great to resist. Or perhaps he feels he has a moral obligation to his readers à la Shakespeare's rustics in *A Midsummer Night's Dream.* Whatever the reasons, involution commonly occurs in the literature of postmodernism.

It should be obvious to the most gullible of readers that fiction is not "real life." So why bother? Given Amis's perception of the world as chaotic and brutal, one understands his compulsion to act as a kind of god. It is harder to understand why Amis restores randomness at the novel's close. At the end of *Money,* Amis reveals the author who explains "the game" to his tragic hero. In a very Nabokovian scene, the author figure and Self play chess. Amis forces his opponent into a suicide move, and Self finally realizes who has been controlling him all along.

The reasons Amis has given for including the author seem inadequate: "Many writers have started doing this, it is the way the novel has evolved." This is the explanation of an unthinking writer. Pressed further, Amis acknowledged Nabokov's influence, and he added, "It just feels inevitable that the illusion is broken, that one reminds the readers they are reading."

Nabokov maintained the reader should identify not with the characters of a novel, but with the author. The reader should always be aware of the author's intention. Amis said, "Perhaps involution is a way of making this unavoidable, making the reader constantly aware of the author's voice and personality." In other words, the writer should never let the reader suspend his disbelief.

It is true that credulous readers cannot fully appreciate an ironic novel. In *Money,* Self's tragic flaw is his credulity. He has been novelized by Amis and has undergone a willing suspension of disbelief. In the end, Self admits it all happened because he *"wanted to believe."* John Self is like any man who—to quote Bellow, as Amis is so fond of doing—"appears on the face of the Earth and doesn't know how he has come to be human." Naturally, he hopes that his existence has meaning, but at the same time he fears some agent controls his life.

In the opening pages of *Money,* Self exhibits superstitious behavior. He says, "Something is waiting to happen to me. I can tell. Recently my life feels like a bloodcurdling joke. Recently my life has taken on *form.* Something is waiting. I am waiting. Soon, it will stop waiting—any day now. Awful things can happen anytime." When he "chances" to meet Martin Amis, Self gets "the creeps." Throughout the novel, he intuitively refers to people on the streets of New York as "bit players," "extras," and "actors." Self is generally paranoid and is equally distracted by significant or random daily events.

Incidentally, Amis has similar "inklings." In *The Moronic Inferno,* he says coincidences make life feel "like a short story." Amis is visiting Bellow in Chicago; they will meet at the Chicago Arts Club. The art-supply store just outside Amis's motel window bears the sign "for the artist in everyone." Back at his motel after a day of discussing the nature of Art, he notes, "the black, bent, bald shoeshiner who slicked my boots with his fingers (he had his name on his breast, in capitals) was called ART." Vaguely suspicious at first, he decides his own preoccupations gave significance to unrelated particulars.

Amis's novels reflect a real condition; the average person often feels that he is in a novel, feels manipulated by an "author." Actually, "the common form now," said Amis, "the universal form, is television rather than [the] novel. People feel they are in some soap. That is the mild delusion that most people are suffering from." Amis called this a kind of modern superstition or credulity.

After surviving a heavy dose of pills, Self is finally "awakened." In the last section of the novel, he says, "*My life is losing its form. The large agencies, the pentagrams of shape and purpose have no power to harm or delight me now.*" Amis explained, "'*The large agencies*' are the ones that control the novel in which he has been enmeshed. Self has escaped the novel. He has escaped control of the author figure, me. The last section is in italics because it is, in a way, outside the novel. He really was meant to kill himself, but he screwed it up, as he screwed everything up. So, he is in a poorer but more controllable kind of existence."

Although Self is finally a crack-toothed, impoverished drunkard, according to Amis it is "a happy ending." Is Self happy because the "form" he lost was imposed or false? Self says, "Before my life was rich, now it's just present." Amis explained that Self feels that his existence is poorer "because it is without form. It is more random, but that does suit him more or less. At least he is not being manipulated." The "all-too-random" present must suit the author too since it inspires him to write.

In 1990 Amis told *Rolling Stone* he felt a "God-size hole" in his life, the terrible prospect of human mortality and insignificance. Amis said if the hole were filled one could "get through, but He's not available anymore." "Modernity," as Amis has described it, is this "poorer but more controllable kind of existence"; it is chaotic, godless, but has room for the gods of fiction to practice their art.

In Nabokov's *Pale Fire*, a novel that depends upon coincidences for its effect, the hero's brand of skepticism is par-

ticularly intriguing, perhaps because his name, "John Shade," seems playfully indicative of the author's other self, just as "John Self" seems suggestive of *his* author. Shade, who during a near-death experience sees a vision of a fountain, reads about a woman who had the same vision; however, he visits her and finds there was a misprint. She saw a "mountain" not a "fountain." Shade writes:

> Life Everlasting—based on a misprint!
> I mused as I drove homeward: take the hint,
> And stop investigating my abyss?
> But all at once it dawned on me that *this*
> Was the real point, the contrapuntal theme;
> Just this: not text, but texture; not the dream
> But topsy-turvical coincidence,
> Not flimsy nonsense, but a web of sense.
> Yes! It sufficed that I in life could find
> Some kind of link-and-bobolink, some kind
> Of correlated pattern in the game,
> Plexed artistry, and something of the same
> Pleasure in it as they who played it found.

It seems to suffice Amis to try and "find some correlated pattern in the game," which is, after all, the very thing a fiction writer does to temporarily fill that "God-size hole."

The "vein" of Nabokov that influenced Amis most includes *King, Queen, Knave, Despair, Laughter in the Dark, Lolita,* and *Transparent Things.* At first, it was hard to understand what Amis meant by "vein." The first three books mentioned were originally written in Russian, the last two in English. Too many other novels fall between these to make it a chronological "vein." Finally, I realized they have themes in common, the same themes that pervade *Money:* sexual deception, perverse greed, insane cruelty, and, in three of the four, murder.

It is worth noting that Martin Amis parts company with Vladimir Nabokov over several issues. First, Nabokov writes fiction because it is "an interesting thing to do. . . . I have no social purpose, no moral message; I've no general ideas to exploit, I just like composing riddles with elegant solutions." Second, Nabokov loathes social satire. He has "neither the intent nor the temperament of a moral or social satirist. Whether or not the critics think that in *Lolita* I am ridiculing human folly leaves me supremely indifferent. But I am annoyed when the glad news is spread that I am ridiculing America." Third, Nabokov doubts that "we can postulate the objective existence of a 'modern world' on which an artist should have any definite or important opinion."

Amis was criticized for his insistence upon the truth of his "myth of decline," whereas Nabokov was able to comment with impunity. Although he did not satirize philistines, perverts, and vulgar Americans, he did parody them. He abruptly explained, "Satire is a lesson, parody is a game." Nabokov knew the danger of applying the rules of a game of fiction to an everyday world. His "rules" work in a well-constructed tale, but bend and break in ambiguous, amorphous "reality."

Nabokov's villains, in fact, are artists-at-large who treat life like a game, who invent and enforce their own rules. Consider Hermann in *Despair*, whose art form is murder. Consider Kinbote, failed poet, exiled king or madman, who appropriates and distorts the meaning of John Shade's poem. As Martin Amis points out in "*Lolita* Reconsidered," Humbert is a failed artist who imprisons a child in his fantasy: "Humberts, because they cannot make art out of life, make their lives into art."

Perhaps this is all the explanation we need of why Amis underscores the fact of fiction at the end of his novels. He himself does not want to be an artist-at-large. He wants nothing in common with the self-deceived charismatic murderers, unscrupulous yobs, and playboy-fantasy heroes who populate his novels. Although Bellow is something of a well-meaning artist-at-large, he recognizes the risks of credulity when corrupt beliefs are involved, and he has argued Hitler was an inhuman artist whose medium was politics. Amis admittedly has less faith than Bellow, and in good conscience can only make art out of life, not life into art.

Martin Amis's father, the prolific and knighted author Kingsley Amis, detests the modern elements of *Money* and candidly informs reporters that he has never been able to finish it. He told *Esquire* that he blames "one of Martin's heroes—Nabokov. I lay it all at his door." He believes *Money* loses its artistic merit because of the author figure. "Martin Amis comes in, breaking the rules, buggering about with the reader, drawing attention to himself," complained Amis, Sr. to a *New York Times Magazine* reporter.

As a rule, Martin Amis plays down his father's literary influence. He said, "As a member of the same household and as a reader of his books he has influenced me. It is more a kind of humour really than anything else. I've always thought that if our birth-dates were transposed then he would have written something like my novels, and I would have written something like his."

Critic John McDermott claims that in Kingsley Amis's *Anti-Death League*, God's role is as a "sub-human joker responsible for catatonic states, limbless children and women's cancers." According to Martin Amis, this shows his father's birth-date is 1922 (his own is 1949). "A much more godless period," said Amis, "so I don't tend to think in that way. Although it is natural for him to do so."

As far as Martin Amis is concerned, today a Divine Being does not deserve the role of sub-human joker; the author

does. As intruding author, Amis is always "buggering about" with Self. A supreme example occurs when, near the end of *Money,* Self begins to realize, "*I'm the joke. I'm it! It was you. It was you.*"

Throughout the novel, Self yearns for his author's advice. Self says: "I long to burst out of the world of money and into—into what? Into the world of thought and fascination. How do I get there? Tell me, please. I'll never make it by myself. I just don't know the way." In an unlooked-for act of prudence, the would-be social critic/author does not tell Self the way, and in the end, Self is left outside the novel to fend for himself, like you and me, in the all-too-random world.

Although Amis has not been overly dependent upon his father for literary counsel, throughout his career he has relied heavily on his two mentors for guidance, instruction, and respectability. I found his latest collection of journalism, ***Visiting Mrs. Nabokov,*** and Bellow's new collection of journalism, *It All Adds Up*, lying side by side on the book store counter. To bolster his reputation as a writer, Amis has quoted Bellow and Nabokov and borrowed their phrases. Amis's choice of title for his most recent work makes one think of Amis hovering around the widow, hoping to come into possession of some of Nabokov's wisdom.

Amis has decisively positioned himself between both the cool, evasive Nabokov and the passionate, outspoken Bellow. Influenced by both great authors, Amis's writing exhibits the tensions between disbelief/belief, illusion/vision, which so far have provided for great comedy and marvelous energy in his writing. But his kind of high-strung comedy does not recommend him for the Nobel Prize, and Amis's ambition is to win the Booker and Nobel Prizes. When he stops trying to emulate his writing heroes, when he is in full possession of his own fame and his own wisdom, then he may develop his potential.

With the publication of his latest book, ***It All Adds Up,*** a title that sounds like the final equation, Bellow prepares for his death, getting his works in order, and modifying the tone of his lifelong message; rather than complaining about distraction, he encourages attentiveness. Coincidentally, Amis's reflection has turned to himself. Perhaps he is taking a final piece of advice from Bellow—to concentrate on his own attentiveness and not obsess about the world's power to distract. Recently, Amis has grown resigned and cautious, and if he has not lost his intensity in the process, perhaps his greatest work is yet to come.

**Roz Kaveney (review date 24 March 1995)**

SOURCE: "Energy and Entropy," in *New Statesman & Society,* March 24, 1995, p. 24.

[*In the following review, Kaveney asserts that* The Information *is a "generic" Amis novel, and claims the book to be "the overpriced sale of second-hand shoddy."*]

Nervous energy is not enough. Martin Amis has built a successful career on, and out of, fear of failure. His interest in that fear, like ours, is wearing thin. Sexual rebuffs in *The Rachel Papers,* having your credit cards cut up in smart New York restaurants in *Money*—these were intense moments because they are anti-sacraments, outward signs of an entire gracelessness thus far concealed.

The vehemence of this self-distrust underlay the obsession with bodily functions, which critics called Swiftian. Admit, pre-emptively, acne and dandruff, and people might stop at criticising your skin and your hair. Self-distrust also helped Amis produce interesting, if self-serving, responses to feminist critiques of male attitudes. Admit to this sin or that and you might get to plea-bargain the rest. He could be attacked for getting it wrong, but not for dodging the issues.

This was made easier by his interest in formal game-playing, derived from Nabokov, and his use of unreliable narration as the literary equivalent of dodgy alibis—I wasn't there, it wasn't me who did it, and I was drunk at the time. The crooked sexist slob of his best novel (*Money*) may be called Self, but there is a character called Martin Amis in it who wanders around virtuously observing; so that's all right, then.

*The Information* is the first clear example of the generic Martin Amis novel. It is an auto-pastiche in which old themes are endlessly enumerated to exorcise once and for all the demon of failure. Like *Success* and *London Fields,* its protagonist is split. Failed novelist Richard Tull has demonic Others in the shape of the glib, successful Gwyn Barry and demented criminal Steve Cousins. As in *London Fields,* the narrative is periodically broken off so that Amis can tell us about the astrophysics books he has been reading—an updating and inversion of the pathetic fallacy. If there is chaos and entropy in the life of Tull, it's because the universe is going to fall apart like a used tissue.

Richard, given an ultimatum by his wife about the sacrifices she has made so that he can write his increasingly unpublishable and over-technical novels, decides to punish his oldest and best friend Gwyn for success. Each attempt goes as wrong as Wile E Coyote's efforts to catch the Road Runner. Indeed, Richard inadvertently ensures Gwyn's greatest triumph, a major literary prize. Meanwhile, we realise that Gwyn has come to hate Richard and enjoys humiliating him. Gwyn too over-reaches and accidentally saves Richard from the worst consequences of his own actions.

This is an extremely formal plot, which must at some point have been laid out in Amis' head like a diagram. However, if you are writing a formal plot, whether tragedy or farce or this odd mixture of both, the form must impose disciplines. A sonnet, if you want to write one, had better have about 14 lines that (more or less) rhyme. The faults of *The Information* lie in just this area of high technique.

Specifically, Richard tries to ensure that Gwyn does not get the Profundity Requital award (Amis' ear for awful American pomposity, and villain's demotic, has deserted him) by privately telling each of the impeccably liberal judges lies about Gwyn's political attitudes. Unfortunately, the sexual harassment expert he tells about Gwyn's seduction of college servants is turned on by the darkly passionate heroes of Harlequin romances . . . One of the difficulties of comedy is knowing which jokes will run and run. When Amis repeats this gag with racism and public hanging, we learn—as he should have done—that this is not one of them. It would not have worked even from his father, who at least *believes* that all liberals are hypocrites.

Part of the plot turns on the fact that Gwyn's upper-class wife Demi has a trick of speech. Rather than do the old-fashioned thing of showing this in action over many scenes, Amis tells us about it. When Chekhov said you should not fire a gun in the third act unless you had hung it on the wall in the first, he did not mean that you should surround the gun with flashing neon lights and a sign that says *Ceci n'est pas un fusil.* But Chekhov, unlike Amis, did not have postmodern technique available as an excuse for laziness.

Amis has chosen to lack such old-fashioned virtues, and it's this lack that lands him in so much new-fangled political hot water. Demi is a sexist stereotype not because she sleeps with black coke dealers, but because she does so without any hint of inner life. Martin Amis will be accused of treating her as a sex object because he chose to treat her merely as a plot function. None of the women ever gets to be more than a funny voice, or a sexy one. It's not a matter of asking Amis to place Demi and the rest centre stage; just that, without some depth, their role in motivating the men—in whom he is more interested—is arbitrary.

Of course, there are splendid things here as well. Richard's relationship with his twin sons is admirably touching. Typically, one of them has a mild handicap in respect of understanding narrative. Richard writes short notices of vast biographies, and the running jokes about the horrors of literary life *are* funny. The descriptions of Richard's and Gwyn's books make one amusedly glad to be reading any other novel—even this one.

This is the novel Amis always feared he would eventually write: one in which the tricks and gambits that had always served him become threadbare, while those traditional virtues to which he had paid lip-service as reviewer become apparent by their absence. *The Information* is a very busy book, skipping between joke American publishers and joke pub quiz machines and joke HIV-positive punkettes. The nervous energy has to go somewhere and it is no longer going into technical control. No reviewer should blame Amis for making a lot of money. We are entitled to express concern that a brilliant career has come to this: the overpriced sale of second-hand shoddy.

## Michael Ratcliffe (review date 26 March 1995)

SOURCE: "What Little Boys Are Made Of," in *The Observer Review,* March 26, 1995, p. 17.

[*In the following predominantly negative review, Ratcliffe discusses some of the "bad writing" that is present in* The Information, *noting that while parts of the tale are sincere and "diversionary," much of the novel is "self-laceratingly autobiographical."*]

There are three ideas in Martin Amis's long and lugubrious revenger's comedy.

The first is that writers are, on the whole, a nightmare and, while he's sorry about that, it's much, much worse for them than for their nearest and dearest. The second is that men have a terrible time simply keeping up with other men, never mind the eternal struggle with their girlfriends, daughters and wives. (Women will ask questions so.) The third is that the universe is a pretty big place, and getting bigger all the time.

This is the worst news of all, because it means that, *sub specie eternitatis*, with an infinite cosmos of cold, hostile matter waiting to kill us out there, neither of the first two problems matters a toss. No wonder Amis is always photographed looking so solemn, moody and mean, the handsome face not even attempting to conceal some dreadful kind of inner crash.

I promised I wouldn't write about Amis the phenomenon, the face or the hype, since this is a review of *The Information,* the book, and not part of some imagined, miserably British campaign to break the brightest of British sons on a wheel of hysterical envy. But near-hysterical envy is the generating passion of the novel itself, and whether you will want to read about it for nearly 500 pages depends on your appetite for male menopause-frenzy and for writing which is sometimes brilliant and funny, but often, despite the carefully built-in tone of self-aware absurdity, heavy-handed and even downright bad:

Up and down his body there were whispered rumours of pain. In fact, physically, at all times, he felt epiphanically tragic.

And what about this?—

From a distance the grass had a layer of silver or pewter in it: the promise of the memory of dew.

Or this?—

Time passed. There was a transitionary period during which, no doubt, the women subliminally and approvingly assumed that Gwyn had set himself the stark and universal challenge of defecation.

Or this?—

The sniff he gave was complicated, orchestral. And when he sighed you could hear the distant seagulls falling through his lungs.

Since *The Information* is the story of two novelists, one a failure, the other a success, and of the deadly rivalry between them, quality of writing is the subject at its very heart, and it is impossible not to notice how clumsily much of the story is told.

Richard Tull, an unpublishable modernist of perhaps some originality (this is never made quite clear), makes a thin livelihood from reviewing fat biographies of mediocre writers, with titles like *The Soul's Dark Cottage: A Life of Edmund Waller* and *The House of Fame: A Life of Thomas Tyrrwhit.* (The ghosts of Eng Lit's Beazer Homes League float comically through the book.) He loves his seven-year-old twin sons, but not his wife Gina, although their sex life seems to remain active, despite his impotence (that, too).

They live in ungentrified North Kensington, and the dystopia of *London Fields*—dogshit, carbon monoxide, cowboy builders, hired teenage killers in smelly old vans—grumbles on.

Gwyn Barry, Richard's smuggest college chum, becomes a worldwide best-seller with a postmodern utopian novella that slips down easily in all languages; he dumps his long-time girl-friend (who goes mad in Swansea) and marries Lady Demeter, a distant cousin of the Queen. From their very grand house in Holland Park they make a TV programme praising the virtues of uxoriousness.

Demeter is pitied for her dimness, but Gwyn is a conceited and deceitful shit, and Richard—whose most recent manuscript, titled *Untitled,* variously induces migraine, double vision and suspected meningitis in those who attempt to read it—sets out to destroy him. First, his reputation as a writer, then perhaps the man himself. North Ken offers a Dickensian coven of willing intruders and assassins—useful to know that for the price of eight lead book reviews you can get anyone polished off—but most of their attempts collapse like Ealing comedy. Meanwhile, the rivalry continues over tennis, snooker and chess.

*The Information* is self-laceratingly autobiographical. That it is also in any way a *roman à clef* is vigorously denied by the novelist, who claims that Richard and Gwyn are simply the two halves of his own self. But it is, and they aren't. If they were really the two halves of Amis himself, then we should not only see Gwyn through Richard's eyes but also Richard through Gwyn's (which would have made a much more interesting novel). Instead, Gwyn is drawn with the wit, incisiveness and unforgiving hatred of Angus Wilson's early stories, while Richard, for all his awfulness ('I quite agree, what an asshole'), is given the benefit of the doubt as firmly as Lucky Jim was by Amis, K.

But where Dad has always made novel-writing look easy (and so, by inference, perhaps not very important), Martin Amis always strikes me as a novelist who struggles much too hard to be seen to be 'writing well' and to make novel-writing seem very important indeed. As a novel, *The Information* is all over the place. Rarely using one simile where two or three are to hand, never proceeding swiftly with a scene when the opportunity for decorative diversion presents itself, Amis blunts his comedy with poor timing and sententiousness.

Some of the diversions—a flight, a storm, a break-in, a circus, a country-house trip—provide great pleasure, but the best scenes by far are those between Richard and his small sons, for they are written without attitudinising or sentimentality, and come straight from the heart.

## Christopher Buckley (review date 23 April 1995)

SOURCE: "The Inflammation," in *The New York Times Book Review*, April 23, 1995, p. 3.

[*In the following review, Buckley discusses* The Information *and how Amis has evolved as a writer.*]

There's been a whole lot of keening in the British press lately about, Martin Amis's new novel, and some in our own. The cause of all this fuss and feathers is that—brace yourself—he fired one agent (the wife of his close friend, the novelist Julian Barnes), and hired another, Andrew Wylie, an American now referred to in the British papers as "the Jackal" and "the Robert Maxwell of agenting," who got him a juicy ad-

vance for the British edition, rumored to be close to $800,000. To a novelist like, say, Jeffrey Archer, $800,000 is a mere rounding error; but to a literary novelist like Mr. Amis it is giant clams indeed. Skeptics are already predicting that HarperCollins, the book's British publisher, will never earn that money back. At any rate, the result of all this has been an unseemly, indecorous and envious caterwauling such as has not been heard since William Golding won the Nobel Prize in 1983. As Gore Vidal famously put it, "Every time a friend succeeds, I die a little." Every now and then you're reminded what a teensy little sceptered isle Britain is. Maybe it's just a case of Amis envy. Still, you wonder: Don't they have anything *better* to worry about?

You have to hand it to Mr. Amis on a couple of counts. First, the tempest in this particular teapot perfectly befits the subject of the book, literary envy. Second—Americans will grasp this point without difficulty—if you can get $800,000 for your novel, *buddy*, go for it. Since he arrived on the scene in the 70's Mr. Amis has been the bad boy (English for *enfant terrible*) of the lit scene. All power to him if he can continue to pull it off at the age of 45. He's a novelist with a plan. There is arc and design to his career. He's said as much in interviews. Off to a frisky start with *The Rachel Papers* and *Dead Babies,* then a nice, steady build with *Money* and *Success;* turned a bit heavy in *London Fields* and the horologically challenged *Time's Arrow.* Now we have the midlife crisis novel. "Five years in the making," the jacket announces with a clash of cymbals, with kettle drumming by Saul Bellow, informing us that Mr. Amis is the new Flaubert, the new Joyce. Who's to argue? However you feel about it, you can't avoid it: Mr. Amis is his generation's top literary dog.

He comes highly pedigreed, but his terrain is the junkyard of the human psyche—in this case, the London literary scene. The main character is Richard Tull, 40-year-old book reviewer, editor and failed novelist, Salieri to Gwyn Barry's Mozart. Gwyn's latest novel has made him so hot that Richard, ostensibly his best friend, is positively melting within. He has a lovely wife, two swell young boys, one of whom he smacks when Gwyn hits the best-seller list. (Probably the only hilarious instance of child abuse in literature.) He has a job as editor of a small literary rag and also works at a vanity press. He has written a number of increasingly obscure novels. He smokes, does drugs, drinks, copes and cries himself to sleep at night. He is also impotent, which never helps. His latest novel, entitled *Untitled,* is so impenetrable that everyone who tries to read the manuscript is stricken with fearsome neurological problems before reaching page 10.

Gwyn—who, according to a recent exhaustive article in *The New Yorker* on the whole Amis fracas, is *not*, repeat not, modeled on Julian Barnes—has been Richard's closest friend since they roomed together at Oxford. He is Welsh. He is also "rich and Labor." *The New Yorker* article was at pains to establish that Mr. Amis, though rich, *still votes Labor,* apparently a dinosaur-sized bone of contention among his fraught British brethren. Clearly, the Barings bank scandal has provided diversion from *l'affaire* Amis in the very nick of time.

Except for saddling him with a weak bladder, the gods have smiled on Gwyn. He is as successful as Richard is not. Money is pouring in from his novels. Hollywood is holding on line two; he is a finalist for a prize called—Mr. Amis has perfect pitch—the Profundity Requital, a sort of mini-Nobel-cum-money-for-life. To top it off, he is married to the Lady Demeter de Rougemount, a rich and milky blonde with whom he appears to have frequent, sweaty sex. By now you're on Richard's side. Vidal was *so* right.

Richard's only consolation, in fact, is that Gwyn's writing is—well, put it this way: Gwyn's writing *stinks*. Which of course is why he is so rich and famous. Poor Richard finally can take no more. He resolves to inflict damage on Gwyn.

He starts out by searching all over London for a Sunday issue of *The Los Angeles Times,* and dumps it anonymously on Gwyn's doorstep with a note saying: "Something to interest you here. The price of fame! Yours ever, John," knowing that the vain Gwyn will spend hours—days—searching through the tonnage of newsprint for his mention.

This escalates to crunchier means of revenge, involving the usual Amis menagerie of dangerous proles, grimly amusing London netherworlders with names like Scozzy, Darko, Crash, RoosterBooster and 13. The law of unintended consequences kicks in with a bloody heel. One of the thugs gets things confused and goes after Richard instead of Gwyn. The game gets dicier, larger, more unpredictable. It becomes a game of chess—one of Martin Amis's passions.

Is an envious writer enough to sustain a whole novel? Surprisingly, yes. Mr. Amis is quite dazzling here, more so than he has been since *Money,* his delectable disemboweling of the movie business. *The Information* drags a bit around the middle, but you're never out of reach of a sparkly phrase, stiletto metaphor or drop-dead insight into the human condition. And there is the humor; Mr. Amis goes where other humorists fear to tread. Who but Martin Amis could make you laugh at someone with a cerebellum-busting, cocaine-and-plum-cherry-apricot-liqueur hangover sitting in Labrador retriever afterbirth?

Richard's indignation and resentments, his hatred, plotting, defeats ("Not even in his sweatiest . . . beriberis of facetious loathing had Richard ever seriously considered that he would one day be asked to face the prospect of a Gwyn Barry movie sale") and his *determination* to redress the cosmic imbal-ance make for gorgeous, dark inventions, such as his retyping Gwyn's novel so that he can—but I mustn't give it away.

Mr. Amis has chosen some grim venues before for his novels. *Time's Arrow* was about a Nazi death camp doctor. And the inside of the head of an impotent, failed writer isn't an alpine meadow in the sunshine. Reflecting on the suicide of a lover, Richard wonders "why so many writers' women killed themselves, or went insane. And he concluded: because writers are nightmares. Writers are nightmares from which you cannot awake. Most alive when alone, they make living hard to do for those around them." This brutal honesty seems at odds with Mr. Amis's strenuous hipness. He's the crown prince of literary hipness, the stud Beau Brummell of the blasé. But eventually hipness becomes tiresome. It becomes hollow, and nihilistic. Left to run its smug, self-referential course, hipness ends up turning the Ten Commandments into a David Letterman top 10 list.

Mr. Amis is one step ahead of this criticism. Richard muses that "women did all this feeling, and seemed to need guidance from the theater. Still, men were theatrical too, insomuch as they needed to be, feeling less. . . . Men attended only one school of acting (the method), that of the cool. That's men. That's men for you: hams of cool." It's a perfect, brilliant line, and self-knowing. It's these moments, aside from the cool prose, that make watching Mr. Amis evolve—look out, Flaubert! Look out, Joyce!—so interesting.

## Richard Eder (review date 30 April 1995)

SOURCE: "Pen Envy: The Baroque Obsessions of an Unpublishable Writer Character," in *Los Angeles Times Book Review,* April 30, 1995, pp. 3, 13.

[*In the following review, Eder lauds Amis as "dark, satirical and gifted with irascibility." However, he does find fault with Amis's lack of "inventiveness" and the aim of the author's satire.*]

The best-known male writers of Britain's postwar period wrote of a zero-sum island where rancor was the leading literary theme. The women writers, meanwhile, were beginning to find ways to move on: Iris Murdoch through pagan myth, Muriel Spark and Penelope Fitzgerald through different kinds of humor with a similar root in sadness.

In retrospect, perhaps "angry young men" was not quite the right term for John Osborne, Philip Larkin, Kingsley Amis and their contemporaries. Anger carries the implication that it will change something; in their case it was more a matter of chained resentment. The chains were rattled wonderfully well, sometimes; and the result was a stagy vitality that found its strongest expression, in fact, with the renaissance of British theater in the 1950s, '60s and '70s.

Murdoch, Spark and Fitzgerald kept on writing, and some of their freest and finest work has come in the past dozen years. Most of those male writers have died or fallen silent; only Amis, at a rate of a novel every couple of years, keeps on rattling his chain. Chains, of course, have two ends. Amis, moving to the right, has long since done his rattling from the proprietor's end while complaining about the help.

In the case of Kingsley's son, Martin Amis, the complaining has been passed right along, as well as the chain end. His writing is fancier, with an assortment of surreal and postmodern touches, and it is better paid—the size of the advance for his latest book set off a literary firestorm in London—but the family resemblance is overwhelming.

Both father and son write of intellectual phonies and pretenders, assorted degenerates and a rotted-out youth in an England of depraved popular culture and not the slightest social or moral structure. Martin portrays them more monstrously, but the outlook is remarkably similar.

Like his father, Martin Amis is dark, satirical and gifted with irascibility. But what we get under the satire is not a sense of protest but of contempt. It aims not so much to denounce the world in order to uplift it, as to exclude the world in order to uplift the writer and the circle he thinks he is addressing. With the Amises it has become less and less evident whom that circle includes. It is like standing with someone at a party and being talked above, or perhaps below, or perhaps the talker is talking to himself, more and more wordily.

Accumulating prolixity enfolds and deadens the witty turns and phrases that both writers are capable of producing. What has dwindled is an author's curiosity about his characters. In Kingsley's early work—*Lucky Jim, Take a Girl Like You*—this curiosity was exhilarating; with Martin it has never seemed very strong. He can create striking figures, but they emerge full-blown from their author's head, and begin to stiffen from that moment on.

They are stiff as straws, for the most part, in *The Information.* Like his last big novel, *London Fields,* it is a satirical jeremiad, a distant descendant of Trollope's very dark *How We Live Now.* Jeremiah operates on a smaller scale than in *Fields* panorama of a London in moral and material flames and ashes. Here the sprawling desolation of the times is strung onto a tiny ingrown framework.

*The Information* is powered by envy, a theme as specific to Britain's postwar writers—the male ones—as fatal passion was to Italian opera. It takes place in that well-worn fictional milieu where authors, critics, publishers, broadcasters and assorted intelligentsia talk, drink, fornicate, gossip and watch, for biting purposes, each other's backs.

Richard Tull, the narrator, is the author of two mildly praised avant-garde novels, followed by four unpublished ones of which the last, titled *Untitled,* is so painfully dense that by Page 10 or 11, any agent or editor who reads it comes down with migraine, double vision or worse. He earns a grubby living reviewing books and editing for a vanity press that takes on such projects as a dissertation claiming that the Nazi concentration camps were run by Jews.

He shares household and child-minding chores with his wife, Gina, who threatens to work full time—thus making him a full-time househusband—if he can't get his books to sell. Gina is admirable—or so it seems—and he lusts after her, but he is, of course, impotent.

Tull is burnt-out and obsessed. His buddy, Gwyn Barry, who had long been even more of a failure—worse manuscripts, grubbier hack jobs, uglier women—has suddenly become a literary celebrity, fabulously praised, richly rewarded, in demand all over the world, married to a beautiful earl's daughter, desired by other beautiful women, constantly interviewed. Tull let out an unearthly howl when Barry's utopian New Age novel, *Amelior,* first crept into the bestseller list; a devoted father, he hit one of his two sons. Now he lives to destroy the other man.

He thinks up schemes to prejudice the judges of a forthcoming literary prize that Barry is slated to win. He makes a feeble attempt to seduce his wife. He sends a depraved, AIDS-infected teen-age female punk to work on him. He researches feverishly a tell-all newspaper profile that will damn him. He engages in an elaborate scheme to make it appear that *Amelior* has been plagiarized. He negotiates with a degenerate drug-dealer who specializes in maiming and "frightenings" to disable him.

At the same time, he keeps Barry constant company (in his role of devoted old friend); takes every opportunity to put him down verbally (honest old friend); beats him regularly at tennis, pool and chess. He accompanies him on an author's tour of the United States. He nurtures, cherishes, warms his rage and prospective revenge. Since he is such an evident loser all along, it gives nothing away to say that here too, he loses.

*The Information* has its bright spots; mainly in the verbal energy and inventiveness with which Amis, through Tull, discharges upon his day and age. For much of the time, though, the inventiveness goes out. A whole section devoted to the U.S. tour is a tired rehash of what a great many satirical English writers—including Amis Sr. and Martin himself, in *Money*—have previously served up.

Tull's plotting is active but lifeless. None of the schemes is advanced or developed with any real conviction. It is not that we need necessarily to believe in a story of this kind, but the story has to believe itself. Far-fetched can be a fictional virtue, but we expect someone to do the fetching. Amis will take up a character or situation and then lose interest. The sadistic drug dealer, set up to be an effetely chilling figure, soon turns tepid. Gina, who shows signs of standing for some kind of human reality in the face of Tull's obsessions, is let to fall apart. Barry's wife, Demeter, has a faint starting mystery to her that goes flat.

Barry is a relentless caricature, a writer whose image has been created by publicity and is nothing but image. Battling this cartoon, Tull becomes little more than his own obsession. As most of the others do, he declines from being a character to being the author's remarks. Like an artist who possesses only crayon stubs, Amis quickly colors them down, and his book turns largely into his own fingerprints.

## Michiko Kakutani (review date 2 May 1995)

SOURCE: "Raging Midlife Crisis as Contemporary Ethos," in *The New York Times,* May 2, 1995, p. C17.

[*In the following review, Kakutani favorably discusses* The Information *as "ambitious" and "uncompromising," and predicts that the book will be favorably received.*]

Once in a while in some artists' careers, there comes along a work that sums up all their preoccupations, all their technical innovations to date. Sometimes, as in the case of Philip Roth's novel *Operation Shylock,* the work is simply a playful but solipsistic dictionary of familiar riffs and routines, a self-referential game of mirrors. Other times, as in the case of Ingmar Bergman's film *Fanny and Alexander,* the work is a wonderful synthesis of all that has gone before, a synthesis that not only serves as a kind of Rosetta stone to an oeuvre, but also transcends the sum of its parts.

While Martin Amis's new novel, *The Information,* is no *Fanny and Alexander,* it happily belongs to that second category of work. By turns satirical and tender, funny and disturbing, *The Information* marks a giant leap forward in Mr. Amis's career. Here, in a tale of middle-aged angst and literary desperation, all the themes and stylistic experiments of Mr. Amis's earlier fiction come together in a symphonic whole.

Like his first novel, *The Rachel Papers, The Information* features a horribly hapless hero, who's obsessed with bodily functions. Like *Dead Babies* and *Other People,* it purveys a willfully cynical view of modern life, a fascination with the seamy world of drugs and illicit sex. Like *Success,* it pits two old friends against each another in a competition for women and recognition. Like *Money,* it chronicles the spectacular fall of a not particularly likable hero. And like *Time's Arrow* and *London Fields,* it boasts a highly complex narrative that attempts to use the latest post-modern hydraulics to articulate an ambitious social vision.

In the past, Mr. Amis's narrative high jinks have often seemed awkward or merely gratuitous: *Time's Arrow* clumsily used a reverse-time sequence to relate the story of a former Nazi doctor, and *Money* featured silly cameo appearances by the author himself. In *The Information,* however, Nabokovian devices are not only employed to frame the story of a failed novelist, Richard Tull, but are also cunningly used to open out his hilarious tale of envy and revenge into a glittering meditation on the nervous interface between the real world and the world of art. At the same time, they transform his comical midlife crisis into a hard-edged satire of contemporary life.

> By turns satirical and tender, funny and disturbing, *The Information* marks a giant leap forward in Mr. Amis's career. Here, in a tale of middle-aged angst and literary desperation, all the themes and stylistic experiments of Mr. Amis's earlier fiction come together in a symphonic whole.
>
> —Michiko Kakutani

The vision of society delineated in these pages darkly (and presumably deliberately) presages the grim, futuristic one presented in *London Fields.* In that 1990 novel, London stood perched on the rim of millennial disaster, a victim of urban chaos theory and its own denizens' uncontrollable greed and lust. In *The Information,* which takes place in the present, racial and class tensions have already begun to escalate to a screeching new decibel level, and violence on the streets is dangerously random. There are burning mattresses on the sidewalks, sinister vans on the side streets, and menacing strangers watching the children play in the parks. Innocent-seeming old ladies turn out to be hit-and-run scam artists or telephone sex-line experts, and the "nasal insect drill of need and neurosis" fills the air at night.

For Richard, Mr. Amis's hero, the world has become a grim mirror of his own preoccupation with death, middle age and—last but not least—his rapidly unraveling career. Once upon a time, it seems, Richard was a promising young novelist with a bright future, a beautiful wife and lots of ambitious plans. He was happy feeling superior to his best friend and old schoolmate, Gwyn Barry, whom he even routinely beat at chess, snooker and tennis.

Recently, however, the two men have stepped onto escalators headed in opposite directions. Gwyn's progress is ever onward and upward: he has written a politically correct utopian novel that has become an international best seller; he has married a fabulously beautiful and wealthy woman who's related to the Queen, and he has become the No. 1 favorite to win a prestigious literary prize called the Profundity Requital, which would guarantee him a cushy income for life. All this success has turned Gwyn into an insufferable boor who spends the better part of his time preening for photographers and searching for his own name in the papers.

Richard, in the meantime, has fallen into an awful slump and appears headed for even further frustrations. His last few novels have gone unpublished, and his latest, unpromisingly titled *Untitled,* is now making the rounds of ever smaller and drearier publishers. His willfully difficult and allusion-filled work just isn't the sort of thing anyone wants to read. Richard's marriage has also hit an impasse (thanks, in part, to his impotence), and he finds himself increasingly baffled by his twin sons' noisy demands.

Even the two jobs that are supposed to help him eke out a literary living (reviewing obscure biographies and editing trashy manuscripts for a vanity press) are depressing him more than usual, and his former skills at chess, snooker and tennis are threatening to let him down. If people were planets, Richard thinks, he would be Pluto: the smallest and most pathetic, far away from the sun.

So what's Richard to do? He decides to ruin Gwyn's career—or failing that, his life. Some of Richard's strategies are purely literary: trying to ruin Gwyn's chances of winning the Profundity award by bad-mouthing him to the judges; scheming to write a nasty profile of Gwyn that would depict him as an untalented phony, and plotting to accuse Gwyn of plagiarism and manufacturing the evidence that would indict him.

These outrageous schemes are expertly rendered by Mr. Amis with the sort of light, high-spirited comic brio that distinguished *Lucky Jim,* the classic novel by his father, Kingsley, but Richard's plans soon take a darker—and more ominous—turn. Having decided that the literary world affords few truly satisfying opportunities for revenge, Richard turns to the real world, the world of sex and violence, to try to get even with Gwyn. He tries to seduce Gwyn's childless wife, Demeter, while sending a punked-out young woman to try to seduce Gwyn. He also retains the services of one Steve Cousins, a street hustler, hit man and drug dealer to the aerobically fit. Once summoned, however, Steve (or Scozzy, as he's known to his friends) will prove difficult to control; indeed he will

drag Richard and Gwyn out of their prim, self-absorbed world of books and introduce them to the mean streets of the London underworld.

Martin Amis's work has always reverberated with literary echoes, and in the case of *The Information.* It's easy to find dozens of allusions, debts and hidden homages to other books: from *Lucky Jim* to Richard Price's *Clockers,* from Saul Bellow's *Humboldt's Gift* to Tom Wolfe's *Bonfire of the Vanities.* Such references, however, are thoroughly subsumed here by Mr. Amis's own idiosyncratic vision and his ability to articulate that vision in wonderfully edgy, street-smart prose. He has written just the sort of novel his bumbling hero dreams in vain of writing: an uncompromising and highly ambitious novel that should also be a big popular hit.

## Julian Loose (review date 11 May 1995)

SOURCE: "Satisfaction," in *London Review of Books,* Vol. 17, No. 9, May 11, 1995, pp. 9-10.

[*In the following review, Loose discusses the themes, strengths, and weaknesses of Amis's novel* The Information.]

Clearly, for Martin Amis, enough is nothing like enough. To read him is to discover an author as voracious as his characters: like Terry in *Success,* who specifies that 'I want all that and I want all that. And I want all *that* and I want all *that.* And I want *all* that and I want *all* that.' Or like the fast-food, fast-sex junkie John Self of *Money,* who always gets less than he bargains for, yet keeps going back for more: 'I would cheerfully go into the alchemy business, if it existed and made lots of money.' Amis goes to any length to remind us of our whole-hearted addiction to the unwholesome—to alcohol, say, or nuclear weapons. The central character in his new novel, *The Information,* is so committed to smoking that he wants to start again before he's even given up: 'Not so much to fill the little gaps between cigarettes with cigarettes (there wouldn't be time, anyway) or to smoke two cigarettes at once. It was more that he felt the desire to smoke a cigarette even when he was smoking a cigarette.' Keith Talent in *London Fields* feels much the same way about pornography: 'He had it on all the time, and even that wasn't enough for him. He wanted it on *when he was asleep.* He wanted it on *when he wasn't there.*'

In *The Information,* a pitilessly professional literary agent explains that nowadays the public can only keep in mind one thing per writer. Authors need definition, 'like a signature. Drunk, young, mad, fat, sick: you know.' Amis's handle could well be: insatiable. And not just because he has become such a Post-Modern operation that, as we used to say of Madonna, even his publicity gets publicity. One of his favourite metaphors—for accumulating phone-calls, deals, anxieties—is of jets stacked in the sky above some fogbound airport (perhaps 'Manderley International Junk Novel Airport'), a consummate image for contemporary over-stimulation and over-supply, for what can barely be accommodated and yet won't nearly suffice. Amis once proposed 'never being satisfied' as Philip Roth's great theme, but it is the boundless nature of need that he, too, endlessly celebrates and satirises. And if Amis is the poet of profligacy, the expert on excess, it is because he is himself full of what he might call male need-to-tell, what John Updike has diagnosed as an urge 'to cover the world in fiction'. *Money* may have been the definitive portrait of Eighties materialism, but Amis has a sly suspicion that we haven't yet tired of reading about the things we cannot get too much of—like fame and money, sex and information.

Amis's latest anti-hero suffers from too much information, and not nearly enough fame, money or sex. Richard Tull, a 'charisma bypass', lives on the obscure margins of the literary world. The author of a clutch of difficult novels with hopeless titles like *Aforethought* and *Untitled*, he works as a shamefaced employee of a vanity publisher, edits the aptly named *Little Magazine*, and reviews ever-fatter biographies of ever-more second-rate writers (but at least 'when he reviewed a book, it stayed reviewed'). Richard's lot goes beyond the common unhappiness of the mediocre. The morning post brings demands from his publishers for the return of advances on unwritten books, and a solicitor's letter from his own solicitor; he is acutely impotent, and—plagued by intimations of his own mortality (having just hit 40)—cries to himself in the middle of the night. What twists failure's stiletto ever deeper is the corresponding success of his only friend, Gwyn Barry. Gwyn has written a blandly accessible novel about a New-Age utopia and, inexplicably, become an international bestseller. Richard is more than bitter: he is consumed beyond all reason, 'exhaustingly ever-hostile'. And so, in the best tradition of Amis characters, he formulates a plan, a mission: 'to fuck Gwyn up'.

Of course, Richard proves no better at revenge than at anything else. The over-laboured joke of the book is the comprehensiveness with which he fails, and the rashness with which he ever assumes 'this is the worst.' Richard doesn't just get charged with drunken driving, he drives his car head-on into a police station. His latest novel doesn't just prove unreadable, it gives people splitting headaches, double vision, lands them in hospital with *vasomotor rhinitis*. He sends Gwyn a random copy of the enormously fat Sunday edition of the *Los Angeles Times*, with an anonymous note pretending that it mentions him—and it does. He swallows his Larkinesque pride at never having been to America, and accompanies Gwyn on a publishing tour of the States, but his cunning attempts to sway the judges of the 'Profundity Prize' only ensure that Gwyn wins. He hires a professional thug to

do Gwyn some serious damage, but the professional turns out to be a psychopath, and it is Richard who gets beaten up, and his own family who are placed at risk.

As Richard's strategies variously fizzle out or detonate in his face, the narrative takes the form of one of the many books he's failed to write: 'The History of Increasing Humiliation'. We soon realise that all plot lines, all other characters exist only in so far as they serve to detain Richard in a never-ending 'Mahabharata of pain'. If Gwyn never quite seems a worthy subject of Richard's outsize fury, it is because he never carries much conviction as a subject. Similarly, the women in the novel remain mere objects of desire and disappointment. They may know all about tears (a woman crying is 'make-up in melt-down'), but they don't get to read Proust, write books or take any decisions: Amis frankly gives up on the attempt to make them more than two-dimensional, acknowledging 'difficulties of representation'. He also reminds us more than once that literary genres are in a muddle, now that 'decorum is no longer observed', but perhaps another decline is unintentionally mapped in this novel, a descent from black comedy to mechanical farce. For despite the ever-entertaining wit, the only twist is that there is no twist, and a terrible predictability sets in, as though Richard's chronic habit of failure had consumed the novel itself.

*The Information* makes much of rivalry and hatred between authors, but to describe the book's subject as literary rivalry seems a category mistake, of the kind Richard's son Marco repeatedly makes ('If you told Marco why the chicken crossed the road, Marco would ask you what the chicken did next'). Rather, *The Information* is a study of envy and egomania that happens to play itself out in the world of publishing. Nicholson Baker in *U and I* probed the devastating realisation that Updike 'writes better than I do and is smarter than I am'. Here, though, there is no sense of one writer warding off another's potentially crushing influence, or of the fragile accommodations made between near-equals. It has long been a tenet of Amis's writing that rivalry (like success) is something that American authors are particularly good at; he has written about the enmity of Gore Vidal and Norman Mailer, and now cites Berryman's unease at Lowell's pre-eminence ('Who's number one? Who's number one?'). But how does this relate to *The Information*? Richard writes Joycean novels on a scale of difficulty that would make even Gilbert Sorrentino blanch (his latest involving no less than 16 unreliable narrators). Gwyn's work, by contrast, is so politically correct and user-friendly that, as Richard outrageously comments, it would only be remarkable if he'd written it with his foot. If *The Information* has anything to say about literary rivalry it is because, for Amis, writing is an activity as inherently confrontational as tennis, or tag wrestling. Authors 'are competing for something there is only one of: the universal. They should *want* to go the mat.' There may seem something ludicrous about the notion of an exclusive 'universal', as though truths (like publishers' advances) are in limited supply. But then the author, according to Amis, is the one who wants it all, who cannot be satisfied: 'like all writers, Richard wanted, and expected, the reverence due, say, to the Warrior Christ an hour before Armageddon.'

If *The Information* fails to induce apocalyptic awe, it may be because, apart from the droll sketches of literary circles, this new novel is a very familiar Amiscellany. There's too much of the same: male envy, not least between authors and near twins; furious games of tennis ('you haven't got a backhand. It's just a wound in your side'); alcohol-fuelled trips to America, empire of trex; sad men staring disgustedly in bathroom mirrors at faces blasted with age and ridden with 'big boys'; villains who speak a post-Yardie patois and believe in getting their retaliation in first; talk of 'batch' and 'spinst', and orthodontic descriptions of urban decay ('the sound of fiercely propelled metal as it ground against stone . . . the whole city taking it deep in the root canal'). The cosmological interludes of *London Fields* return with a vengeance: 'The quasars are so far away and getting further away so fast. This is to put Richard's difficulties in context.' This is also to risk a sense of fatigue, for over-use can make such astronomic comparisons seem all too dull and sublunary, perhaps prompting us to recall the Total Perspective Vortex featured in *The Hitchhiker's Guide to the Galaxy*, that exquisite torture which does nothing more than show you your ultimate significance in relation to the rest of the universe.

Yet the loss of all sense of proportion is, of course, why Amis is so enjoyable to read. As the narrator of his first book, *The Rachel Papers,* at once laments and demonstrates, 'one of the troubles with being over-articulate, with having a vocabulary more refined than your emotions, is that every turn in the conversation, every switch of posture, opens up an estate of verbal avenues with a myriad of side-turnings and cul-de-sacs.' An improviser's sense of the possible is both a strength and a flaw: we may feel that with *The Information* Amis has ended up down a cul-de-sac, but his writing is still fantastically rich. There is no better place to find the spot-on perception: Americans call everybody 'sir', but manage to make the word sound like 'mac or bub or scumbag'; people's mouths 'nuzzle the necks' of cellular telephones, and bike messengers wear 'city scuba gear'; a flock of birds rears up 'like a join-the-dots puzzle of a human face or fist'; in prenatal classes, adults sit around on the floor and gaze up at teacher 'like the children they would shortly bear'.

The offbeam precision of the Martian poet is only one of Amis's modes, but it lends his writing such casual authority that frequent assumptions of the first person plural are unusually persuasive, even when 'we' would rather be included out: 'Bitter is manageable. Look how we all manage it.' 'We may think we are swearing at others, at traffic. But who *is* the traffic?' Hungry for the universal, and attentive to the

vagaries of excess, Amis will go places other writers won't: 'If we think about it, we all know the sneak preview of schizophrenia, with the toilet paper, those strange occasions when there seems to be no good reason to stop wiping.' Often, though, Amis's imagined reader seems more specific, a product of what Richard's son calls 'male-pattern boldness': 'The sense of relief, of clarity and surety a man feels, at the prospect of temptation, when he knows he has washed his cock before leaving the house.'

In his earlier novels, a more-or-less-recognisable 'Martin Amis' might appear and make playful remarks, such as: 'I really don't want to join it, the whole money conspiracy.' Martin Amis's presence in those books modishly alluded to Heisenberg's principle (an observed system interacts with its observer) and dramatised the unequal, even sadistic relationship between author and creation. *The Information* features more of 'Martin Amis' but less of the playfulness. Richard can't seem to decide if our present ironic age ends up with stories about writers, or with stories about 'rabble, flotsam, vermin'. Certainly it is the latter which allowed Amis and 'Amis' to come into their own. Where in *London Fields* we learn that Keith Talent went through his mid-life crisis at the age of 19, or read that 'in common with Leo Tolstoy, Keith Talent thought of time as moving past him while he just stayed the same,' the gap between the protagonist's lowlife awareness and the author's cruelly superior understanding was the joke, the ironic motor for the fiction. But *The Information* is dominated by Richard Tull, a figure who (success and readability apart) is much like Martin Amis. Admittedly 'Martin Amis' tells us about the very specific perils of teenage dating when you stand only 5-feet-six ('or 5' 6 1/2", according to a passport I once had'), but he, too, takes his kids to Dogshit Park, shares many of Richard's thoughts, and would seem to know what it is to experience a mid-life crisis—or, rather more grandly, 'a crisis of the middle years'.

That crisis finds narrative expression in a kind of theatrical throwing-up of hands: 'how can I ever play the omniscient, the all-knowing, when I don't know *anything*?' Amis-the-narrator keeps reminding us that he doesn't control his own characters ('To be clear: I don't come at these people. They come at me. They come at me like information formed in the night.') Where the unstoppable John Self knew he had our sympathy (even if he wanted 'much, much more of it'), 'Amis' makes a show of interrupting himself, dismissing language and fiction as inadequate to the task, losing his patience like a harassed teacher: 'We are agreed—come *on*; we are agreed—about beauty in the flesh.' But this forsaking of authority is everywhere betrayed by flexes of authorial muscle ('I think we might switch for a moment to the point of view of Richard's twin sons'), and by the sheer virtuosity of the writing. No one since Sterne has described impotence with such relish, even summarising the theme in literature ('as for Casaubon and poor Dorothea: it must have been like trying to get a raw oyster into a parking meter'). Perhaps the one thing Amis cannot do, we realise, is communicate a Beckettian sense of exhaustion, or a feeling that he is no longer in control. When he declares that 'the information is telling me to stop saying *hi* and start saying *bye*,' we can't help but note that only Amis would say it that well, with that vernacular spin—and, of course, want to say it at such length.

Redundancy is integral to the Amis project. Richard Tull delights in the self-defeating way in which abbreviations—MW for microwave, FWD for Four Wheel Drive—contain more syllables than the words they represent. Similarly, Amis flourishes three dazzling similes when one would do, or conjures up the perfect image, only to take it one step further: 'If the eyes were the window to the soul, then the window is a windscreen, after a transcontinental drive; and his cough sounded like a wiper on the dry glass.' Amis likens the beer-sticky streets of Ladbroke Grove to the darkness and fire of Pandemonium, and indeed his similes are increasingly Miltonic, always threatening to detach themselves from the main narrative and strike out on their own. Thus Richard, about to enter Gwyn's large and lavish house:

> Gwyn's set-up always flattened him. He was like the chinless cadet in the nuclear submarine, small-talking with one of the guys as he untwirled the bolt (routine check) on the torpedo bay: and was instantly floored by a frothing phallus of seawater. Deep down out there, with many atmospheres. The pressure of all that Gwyn had.

The primary pleasure of reading *The Information* is that of being regularly swept up in these epic, frothing digressions. The effect is like the description of an American interviewer Richard encounters, whose superficial 'warmth' and 'niceness' have been turned up on the dial 'as if these qualities, like the yield of a hydrogen bomb, had no upper limit—the range had no top to it—and just went on getting bigger and bigger and better as you lashed them towards infinity.' Such passages are so enjoyably overwhelming, so addictively all-consuming, that you feel you want to read a novel by Martin Amis even when you *are* reading a novel by Martin Amis.

## Merle Rubin (review date 17 May 1995)

SOURCE: "*The Information*—An Unpleasant, Familiar-Sounding Book," in *The Christian Science Monitor*, May 17, 1995, p. 14.

[*In the following review, Rubin examines* The Information *and states that despite the "unpleasant" nature of the story, Amis manages to contrive a "scathing satire of London literary life."*]

The publication of Martin Amis's eighth novel, *The Information,* stirred up considerable controversy in London literary circles, not only over the size of the advance its author demanded, but also over what some deemed his mistreatment of his literary friends and associates. (Amis replaced his former agent, Pat Kavanagh, wife of his longtime crony and fellow novelist Julian Barnes, with the far more aggressive agent Andrew Wylie, while allegedly using his soon-to-be-former friends as fodder for his fiction.)

Ironically, *The Information* happens to be a scathing satire of London literary life as epitomized in the covertly rivalrous relationship between two writers: successful, respected novelist Gwyn Barry and his increasingly envious and embittered friend Richard Tull, who obsessively schemes to damage Barry, both professionally and personally, in any way that he can.

Tull and Barry both started out as promising young writers, with Tull slightly in the lead. Better spoken, coming from a superior social class, more skilled at tennis, chess, and billiards, and—most importantly—far more of an artist than his less sophisticated friend, Tull is driven to distraction by the spectacle of his former inferior's run-away success.

Barry's breakthrough book, the one that brought him bestsellerdom and critical esteem, was a novel called *Amelior,* which dealt with the seemingly unpromising subject of a Utopian society: "... twelve youngish human beings forgathered in an unnamed ... hinterland. ... No holocaust or meteorite ... brought them there. They just showed up. To find a better way. ... In the place called Amelior, where they had come to dwell, there was no beauty, no humor ... no hate ... no love. And that was all."

Tull simply cannot fathom why the world should have taken *Amelior* to heart. His own career, meanwhile, has been a disheartening chronicle of ever-diminishing returns, which, perhaps, is less surprising when one learns that his most recent manuscript, titled *Untitled,* has induced various ailments in those who have tried to read it, and contains scenes of the sort in which "... five unreliable narrators converse on crossed mobile-phone lines while stuck in the same revolving door."

The fortune-favored Barry is married to an earl's daughter, and the happy couple has been featured on a television program illustrating the joys of uxorious-ness. The Barrys have not, however, publicized one of the rifts in their picture-perfect marriage: She wants children, and he does not.

The father of twin boys, Tull has become impotent with the

decline of his literary hopes. He ekes out his paltry earnings as a book reviewer with a job editing trash for vanity press. His pretty wife, Gina, who contributes more to the family income, has been urging him to give up his fruitless career as a novelist. Tull's response to his deep depression is to try to destroy his rival.

Much of *The Information* is taken up with various schemes Tull employs to damage Barry. Many of these schemes involve paying low-life criminals to harass and intimidate him. Others involve Tull himself in spreading vicious rumors (some false, some true) about his "friend." Tull's most ingenious scheme is a plan to frame Barry for the literary "crime" of plagiarism. Most of these schemes tend to backfire.

*The Information* is—and is meant to be—an unpleasant book: acrid, well-written, nastily clever.

It may also strike many readers as perhaps a little too familiar-sounding if they've read Mr. Amis's earlier books. The parts pertaining to the literary life are the liveliest. The lengthy excursions into the criminal world are even more of a bore than the play-by-play accounts of tennis, chess, and snooker games between the two rivalrous writers.

For the reader, there may be little to choose between the smug Barry and the rancorous Tull.

Once Amis has succeeded in delineating the tricky contours of their characters, the ugly details of plot—what does or doesn't happen to either or both of them—seem rather superfluous. Barry and Tull are like opposite halves of a single, narcissistic, self-hating person, a pair of bleak responses to the open-ended question: What do writers want?

## Ed Morales (review date 23 May 1995)

SOURCE: "Amis and Envy," in *The Village Voice*, Vol. XL, No. 21, May 23, 1995, p. 52.

[*In the following review, Morales discusses briefly the plot, themes, and autobiographical elements of* The Information, *praising some aspects of Amis's writing and faulting others.*]

With *The Information*, Martin Amis seems poised to make a profound comment on the nature of the writing business, the unnerving inevitability of aging, and, well, death itself. At least it appears that the information he refers to is Death; Death of the English Novel, Death of Western Civilization, Death of the White Guy. The word that's obviously missing from this title is *Superhighway*, but Amis, who still writes his novels in longhand, seems to want no part of postmodern

debate about technology and media, opting instead to offer this tidbit of crucial information: "The history of astronomy is the history of increasing humiliation." The sun doesn't revolve around Martin Amis!

The plot—there really exists very little plot—revolves around Richard Tull, a miserable, failed novelist turned book reviewer approaching 40, filled with envy toward his old friend Gwyn Barry, whose vapid, talentless prose has produced international bestselling novels about a p.c. Shangri-la called Amelior. Tull's obsessed with destroying Barry, by exposing him as a plagiarist, by sleeping with his wife, the Lady Demeter, by having thugs of dubious color beat the living crap out of him. It doesn't matter that all of these plots fail, for Tull is the living embodiment of failure, for his "history of humiliation was long—was long and proud." So it's not so surprising that Amis, who believes that "failure is more interesting than success," has Tull spend almost 400 pages wallowing in great "Gobis and Saharas" of failure.

*The Information,* which fails as the grand roman à clef that Amis's dual talent as novelist and journalist has promised, comes to us under a storm of attendant publicity about its roots in real life. All over Britain the headlines screamed of the infamous DENTAL IMPLANT SURGERY, paid for by the 500,000-POUND ADVANCE secured for *The Information* when Amis, after LEAVING HIS WIFE, dumped his long-standing agent, Pat Kavanaugh, and signed on with the loathsome Andrew Wylie, THE JACKAL, THE ROBERT MAXWELL OF AGENTING. That Kavanaugh was married to Amis's longtime novelist-pal and tennis buddy Julian Barnes, who was widely regarded as the model for the insufferable Gwyn Barry character, only fueled the hysteria in and around the Groucho Club.

Barnes and Amis are old friends and share games of snooker much as Richard and Gwyn do in *The Information,* but their real-life relationship is the inverse of the one in the novel. Gwyn, the alleged model for Barnes, has Amis's fame and wealth, while Barnes's work, although not as obscure as the hopeless Tull's, is certainly less surrounded by publicity circuses than Amis's. Amis insists in the *Guardian* that "both Richard and Gwyn are me," but it's hardly necessary to consult the overseas press to come to the same conclusion: Dividing oneself into any number of characters is a time-tested literary ploy, and Amis's meditation on the capacity for great success and dismal failure that coexists in most writers is one of *The Information*'s strong points—it's a kind of "There but for the grace of Kingsley go I" gambit, a bit of humility that is a clear victory for a writer whose most consistent and recognizable voice is that of a pissy crank with delusions of grandeur. The Richard/Gwyn dynamic also parallels the tortured dichotomy of the envier and the envied that functions as a motif in his earlier work, that is, John Self and

Fielding in *Money,* Samson Young and Mark Asprey in *London Fields,* and even the bifurcated narrator of *Time's Arrow.*

Just as the Nazi doctor central to *Time's Arrow* seems to be afflicted with a schizophrenia that produces a detached self who narrates against the flow of time, Amis seems to be detached from some unfashionable resentment that results from the current path of history. Having grown up liberal in the '60s—he reminds us early on that in England, "All writers, all book people, were Labour. . ."—as he enters middle age, he seems annoyed and frightened by the way the racial landscape is changing. There is an Oxford Posse paranoia going on here, apparently giving voice to his speculated frustration about not winning the Booker Prize, which of late, has gone mostly to the writers of color (Ben Okri, etc.,) who constitute a minimovement that's referred to as The Empire Strikes Back.

Hence Richard Tull's voluminous nervous titters over Lady Demeter's "distinct liking for—our colored bretheren"; whining sarcasm such as "How did people ever get the idea that *white skin* was any good at all, let alone the best?"; and Letterman-esque bombs like "I myself have a bro in my head—Yo!—who, after much ritual handslapping, takes over when I'm tired or can't come. . . ." While some might find this a self-deprecating reference to Tull's sexual impotence—and writers of color like Salman Rushdie and Hanif Kureishi are his friends—it's still pretty thinly disguised nastiness. And what am I to make of the assertion that one of the greatest of all of Tull's humiliations was to have his latest tome, *Untitled* ("with its octuple time scheme and its rotating crew of sixteen unreliable narrators"), picked up by the treacly multicultural Bold Agenda press, located on Avenue B, in my neighborhood? The big joke is that the other writers on board at Bold Agenda are named—*trés* p.c.—John Two Moons (nudge, nudge, a bloody American Indian) and Shanana Ormolu Davis (another colored lady). Poor Richard.

To be fair, the Tull saga is not the only focus of Amis's narrative—just before Tull's halting masochism gets old, Amis switches gears and goes with Barry for a while, which saves *The Information* from kissing the pavement like a 5 a.m. drunk. An impudent Welshman with no insight or talent, but a prodigious gift for seduction, Gwyn Barry represents the unabashed greed that Amis, being a proper Englishman, feels squeamish about claiming as his own—a squeamishness that might explain the British press's obsession with his cosmetic dentistry and his rich American girlfriend, the writer Isobel Fonseca. Carrying on an affair in his own house, right in front of Lady Demeter, and also providing the climactic shock of infidelity that allows *The Information* to lurch into its denouement, Barry, the winner, ties up all the loose ends, whereas Tull is about unraveling.

Still it's Tull who in the end provides the book's giddiest moment, literally stuttering as his battered intellect attempts to spit out the final humiliation: his assignment to do a magazine feature on Barry. "Although Barry was no. . . . He had a reputation as a. He made no secret of his love of. To him, the fairer," blurts Tull, on his information deathbed. And it's through Tull that we are treated to Amis's signature loping, polyrhythmic repetition, to his romps through the satire of Dogshit Park, to his incredible dexterity with language, all the while never forsaking the class struggle:

> Richard sat in Coach. . . . Hundreds of yards and hundreds of passengers away, Gwyn Barry, practically horizontal on his crimson barge, shod in prestige stockings and celebrity slippers, assenting with a smile to the coaxing refills of Alpine creekwater and sanguinary burgundy with which his various young hostesses strove to enhance his caviar tartlet, his smoked-salmon pinwheel and asparagus barguette, his prime fillet tournedos served on a timbale of tomato and a tampenade of Castillian olives—Gwyn was in First.

That's entertainment all right. So it would be nit-picking to mention the business about the "street kids" to whom Amis turns his ear in the goes-nowhere subplot—more nasty business about Tull having to resort to the "Other" to carry out one of his fiendish plots to "fuck Gwyn up"—and the shallow characterization of all the major female players: Tull's long-suffering wife, Gina; Tull and Barry's American-born literary agent, Gal Aplanalp; Tull's suicidal mistress, Anstice; and of course, Lady Demeter. Even when Amis spouts a lot of rot about nothing, he's worth waiting 20 pages for another mind-blowing, style-laden passage, and after slogging through to the bitter end, it was abundantly clear to me that Amis is not confused about whether he is the successful novelist or a failed reviewer. Still Amis should take more of a cue from his own journalism and provide a little more of the kind of information that gets us to read novels: stuff like plot and a character's transcendence.

### James Bowman (review date 29 May 1995)

SOURCE: "The Content of His Characters," in *National Review,* Vol. XLVII, No. 10, May 29, 1995, pp. 61-63.

[*In the following review, Bowman asserts that Amis's work is often lacking in plot but strong in prose.*]

Writers of fiction in the twentieth century can be divided into the champions of big texture and the champions of big content, and there can be no question that the texturalists have had the better of the conflict. The reassuringly Aristotelian beginning, middle, and end, which used to be thought a minimum requirement for a novel, have given way among the adepts of literary culture to what Ezra Pound called (and called for): "Beginning, Whoop! and then any sort of tail-off." Since Joyce at least, it has become a mark of the cognoscenti to admire prose fiction for its prose, rather than its fiction.

Martin Amis has become the star of his literary generation in Britain by leaving behind the fuddy-duddy Englishness of his father, Kingsley Amis, to adopt with enthusiasm the Hiberno-Continental view of the supreme literary virtue of a learned and coruscating prose style. He has worked very hard on his prose in *The Information,* as he has also done in his earlier books, and there has been little time left over for content. Plot has never been Amis's strong suit. Nor has characterization. Nor have ideas. They are still not. As for politics, he was recently quoted in the British press as saying that "every writer in England votes Labour; . . . there is nothing else to be."

> **[Amis] has worked very hard on his prose in *The Information,* as he has also done in his earlier books, and there has been little time left over for content. Plot has never been Amis's strong suit. Nor has characterization. Nor have ideas. They are still not.**
>
> —*James Bowman*

But if you want muscular verbs and striking adjectives, piercingly original images and highly wrought metaphors that make you laugh out loud, if you want to browse through a miscellany of information about astronomy—which, by the way, is not the even more metaphysically portentous "information" of the title—Amis is your man. His subject is the male mid-life crisis, blown up, in his distinctive style, to epic and indeed cosmic proportions.

Actually, that style is in some ways more American, partaking of the Yankee fondness for hyperbole, than British. Dour understatement in the British fashion is no more to Martin Amis's liking than simple storytelling—or than American intellectual life, to judge by the long passage in this novel given over to an American journey by his two British writers, Gwyn Barry, who is fabulously successful, and Richard Tull, who is fabulously unsuccessful.

> Like the lady who was of course still there between the mortarboard and the prosthetic legs (and what a moving acceptance speech she gave), like the laugh-

ing athlete who, after that mishap in the carpark, awoke to find himself running a network of charities from his padded rack, Richard had to see whether the experience of disappointment was going to make him bitter or better. And it made him bitter. He was sorry: there was nothing he could do about it. He wasn't up to better. Richard continued to review books. He was very good at book reviewing. When he reviewed a book, it stayed reviewed. Otherwise he was an ex-novelist (or not ex so much as void or phantom), the Literary Editor of *The Little Magazine*, and a Special Director of the Tantalus [vanity] Press.

Naturally, it is Richard with whom Amis, who has always had a penchant for the portrayal of failure on a heroic scale, identifies himself. But Richard and Gwyn are obviously literary and spiritual twins, whose convergence in the hurried final pages of the novel constitutes—insofar as it could be said to possess such a thing—its moral.

Actually, there is a shadowy Martin Amis figure who also appears here and there in the novel when it comes time for morals. It is he who explains all about astronomy and about "The Information"—the news of mortality and the middle-aged man's dawning realization of it. The information is: You will die. It is this Amis figure, rather than Richard, who tells us that "The information is telling me to stop saying hi and to start saying bye." There is meant to be an obscure connection between this sad awareness of death and Richard's obsessive envy and hatred of Gwyn, but Amis does not have the patience to spell out what it is. Instead, he frames deep thoughts in, more or less, his own voice, as when he reflects on how people read a certain kind of thin-textured, big-content novel in airports:

> Whatever junk novels were, however they worked, they were close to therapy, and airports were close to therapy. They both belonged to the culture of the waiting room. Piped music, the language of calming suasion. Come this way—yes, the flight attendant will see you now. Airports, junk novels: they were taking your mind off mortal fear.

Meanwhile, Richard is conspiring, for no very good reason, to get his friend beaten up, rejected, divorced, accused of plagiarism, or harried by petty worries—though all his plans, like his novels, fail and only serve to strengthen Gwyn further. Be he never so textural a writer, however, Amis cannot quite disregard the demands of character and of drama. And when we look for the Eliotic "objective correlative" we cannot help noticing that "mid-life crisis" is a pretty thin and a pretty glib explanation for the characteristically exaggerated hatred Richard feels for Gwyn. What is it he envies him for, anyway? Only money and celebrity, so far as we can see—

an appropriately vulgar counterpart to the cheap pop-psychology of the "mid-life crisis."

It is not as if we cannot believe in the titanic proportions of Richard's envy so much as that it is inspired by trivialities. It is not Gwyn's literary success but all its tawdry trappings—the army of worshipful fans, the rock video, the teenaged groupies at Gwyn's book signings who ask him to autograph the insides of their thighs. Oh man! Can life get any better than this? Well, yes it can, actually. And Richard knows that too, for he would really rather destroy Gwyn, bring him down to his own level, than enjoy the life that Gwyn enjoys. You begin to see why his authorial alter ego is convinced that "there is nothing else to be" politically but a socialist.

It is also richly ironic that Martin Amis has himself become such a self-conscious celebrity in Britain because of this book and his divorce and his expensive dental work and the controversy about his publisher's advance of some three-quarters of a million dollars. Clearly, Amis is more Gwyn than Richard.

There is another convergence here—a convergence of art and life—that is also present in the novel. After Richard's return from America, when all his remaining hopes for his own success are dashed, and all his plans to ruin Gwyn have come to nothing, he suffers a kind of terminal resignation which is reflected in the perfunctoriness of the novel's efforts to tie up its loose ends. Richard engages in one last scheme to ruin Gwyn by contriving, with infinite trouble, to have him accused of plagiarism, but he abandons it at the point of success in the last few pages—just as there is a shocking revelation about his wife and an even more shocking incident involving his son, Marco.

None of this potentially dramatic stuff is developed at all. It is as if Amis himself partook of the spiritual lassitude of his hero:

> It seemed to him that all the time he used to spend writing he now spent dying. His mind was free now. . . . This was the truth. And it shocked him. It shocked him to see it, naked. Literature wasn't about living. Literature was about not dying.
>
> Suddenly he knew that writing was about denial.
>
> Suddenly he knew that denial was great. Denial was so great. Denial was the best thing. Denial was even better than smoking.

Well, denial that takes the form of writing like this is certainly exhilarating. It excites us in the odd metaphor (the "dole quaffing fruit machines" in a sleazy pub), in the sensational simile (he imagines intercourse between old Casaubon

and Dorothea in *Middlemarch* as "like trying to get a raw oyster into a parking meter"), in unexpected reversals (Gwyn's hotel suite in New York contains "bouquets and bowls of fruit, presumably real but impressively fake-looking"), and in plain funny jokes (Richard finds it strange that he feels dizzy because he "was very good at the party and carefully counted his drinks: he'd had 17").

Sometimes this kind of brilliance is sustained over a whole paragraph, as when he tells of Richard's first reaction on meeting Gina, his wife-to-be, when she was a cashier in a museum:

> The world had not found out about her. How come? Because Richard knew it couldn't just be *him*. This was genetic celebrity, which had an audience and an essential value. In other times and climes her family would have kept her in a locked room and held an auction on her 16th birthday. Leaning forward at her desk, counting money, and sighing without weariness, she was ten years further on into womanhood—and the word, the phone calls and faxes, still had time to go out to the planet's playboys, all of them, from the pub spiv with his white-lipped salacities, up past the jodhpurred joke in his jeep, and right the way through to the kind of OPEC kleptocrat who blew half his GNP on his own Johnson. Richard felt the ignoble excitement of a Sotheby's smoothieboy buying a Titian from a tinker.

But, at the risk of proclaiming a philistine attachment to mere content, how much better the novel would have been if Amis had made some effort to create a character who could—as poor Gina, neglected as much by her creator as by her husband, never comes close to doing—live up to that description.

## David C. Ward (review date Summer 1996)

SOURCE: "Discussions of Recent Books: A Black Comedy of Manners," in *The Virginia Quarterly Review*, Vol. 72, No. 3, Summer, 1996, pp. 561-64.

[*In the following negative review, Ward faults* The Information, *saying it "does not have a plot, it has predicaments and events." He also declares that "none of the characters in* The Information *comes close to being sympathetic."*]

On its publication Martin Amis's *The Information* threatened to be avalanched by the various English literary and celebrity controversies of which its author was the lightning rod. Amis having his teeth fixed; Amis changing his agent thereby losing his friendship with author Julian Barnes who is the husband of Amis's now ex-agent; Amis hiring an American agent (nicknamed "The Jackal"!) and getting too much money for his next book(s); Amis divorcing; Amis generally getting too big for his britches; etc., etc. All this extra-literary brouhaha, which brawled over into the always decorous British tabloids, actually helped make people feel comfortable. It facilitated slotting *The Information* into easy categories: it was an expression of the author's "mid-life crisis" or a wicked literary *roman a clef* or Amis had "gone American." Since the subjects that Amis remorselessly anatomizes are so painful, displacement could be achieved by reducing literature to autobiography: "Boy, his teeth must have really hurt when he wrote this bit!"

But when A.S. Byatt castigated Amis for being money hungry, it is likely that her subtext, conscious or not, was her awareness that Amis was dynamiting not just the supposed gentility of the literary life but the very possibility of thought (including novels) and action. Byatt's *Possession*, after all, was a self-conscious homage to the novel, relying on a shared community of readers who could decode her lovingly recreated literary styles, solve the "puzzles," and resolve the narrative. Richard Tull, *The Information*'s main character, has written a novel, *Untitled*, which not only has no audience but which physically strikes down those who do attempt it with bizarre and paralyzing medical conditions! No one gets past page nine without going to hospital. So the news from *The Information* is much worse and therefore much better: Amis has written a perfectly pitched expression of our late 20th-century dystopia.

Although it takes place during the 40th year of its two protagonists, *The Information* does not have a plot, it has predicaments and events. The narrative drive is provided by Amis's coruscating style, and no one is better than he at eviscerating modern life. In British law, the "information" is the bill of particulars, the charge, the indictment and Amis indicts. Richard Tull and Gwynn Barry are writers. After a promising start, Tull is unsuccessful, eking out a living with literary odd jobs—reviewing, working at a vanity press, and a little magazine whose name is *The Little Magazine*—while writing and not publishing novels. Gwynn Barry, Tull's college chum, started out untalented, unsuccessful, and through some kind of cosmic accident has become not only fantastically best selling but critically well-received. His writes soppy novels about a utopian community or commune—Amelior (from amelioration)—whose optimistic perfectability is counterpoint to society's increasing awfulness and presumably the reason for their international popularity. Barry is married to a minor royal, short-listed for the "Profundity Requital," a fabulously endowed new literary prize, and gives interviews in which he discusses his writing's relationship to carpentry.

At its basic level *The Information* is a black comedy of lit-

erary manners (anyone who reviews books has to cringe at the progression of slab-like lives that Tull grinds through: *Love in a Maze: A Life of James Shirley* or *The Soul's Dark Cottage: A Life of Edmund Waller*) and literary jealousy. There is a fabulously rendered American book tour which no one who hopes ever to give a reading should read. Inevitably, Barry's success drives Tull wild and he concocts various plots of escalating violence against his rival. None of them work, most of them backfire, and just when you think things can't get any worse, they do. In farce, Kingsley Amis's *Lucky Jim* for example, the denouement is a boulversement which sets things right so that every one goes home happy; Jim does turn out, against the odds, to indeed be lucky. Here, Martin Amis sets things even more horribly wrong. Tull gets a final stamp to his cliff-hanging fingernails. Barry is revealed as not quite the benignly self-satisfied chump he appears to be. His shredding of Tull's illusions and hopes is shattering both to Tull and—however unlikable Tull is—the reader. The failure of Tull's escalating plots is skeined around by Amis's larger purpose to show the breakdown not just of a friendship but of all connection, including cause and effect. When Tull hires the autodidactic hard-man Steve Cousins (who is Richard's only reader and fan!) to beat up Barry things go haywire and Tull himself gets thumped by the confused thugs. Inevitably, Tull is impotent, promiscuously impotent.

"The Knowledge" is London cabbie slang for the ability, a prerequisite for a hack license, to find any address in the city by a route from any other address in the city. "The Knowledge" is learned by tireless application, the aspirant cab driver tracing city streets so that the pattern becomes wholly known and comprehended to the point of being synaptically imprinted. In this process, "The Knowledge" is reified, becomes a noun. The chaotic and bewildering arrangement of streets is ordered through an act of reason. "The Knowledge," then, is a paradigm of an almost 18th-century rationalism: a subject which is wholly known and comprehended by cognitive (and physical) application. The cabbie is Diderot in a car mapping the world for the *Encyclopedia*, like early doctors tracing veins.

Amis only mentions "The Knowledge" in a quick passage but it is key as the antithesis of "The Information." Instead of a body of knowledge which can be known and mastered, "The Information" is something inflicted on and endured by helpless men. It is not the workings of the conscious, rational mind (the cabbie on his bike learning every mews) but of sub- or even unconsciousness: "And then there is the information, which is nothing, and comes at night." In the scientific field of Information Theory, information has nothing to do with communication, rather it is synonymous with entropy. About the only scene we hear of in Richard Tull's *Untitled* is of "five unreliable narrators conversing on crossed mobile phone lines while stuck in the same revolving door," a tour de force image of cacophonous, incoherent entropy. Or as Amis writes in a perfectly balanced sentence of blockage: "The five lanes going out of the city were all blocked and the five lanes coming into the city were all blocked." So much for the efficient, rational progress implicit in "The Knowledge."

For Amis's fiction the paradox is that the obverse of Enlightenment ("The Knowledge") is not just the deconstructions of post-modernism but paralysis and collapse. We've built the enlightened city on the hill, lived in it for a while, and are now sliding inexorably off its dark side in terror. As Goya famously captioned *capricho* #43: "The sleep of reason produces monsters." One of *The Information*'s comic riffs showing irrationality triumphing over rationality is a driving school which teaches not just bad but anarchically irresponsible driving. Instead of following rules, the student is taught to "To impress your personality on the road." A not so comic riff is an anonymous driver who blasts at random intervals through Richard Tull's residential streets, scattering walkers and enraging him. In one of his bleaker poems, "The Life with the Hole in It," Philip Larkin defined life as "The unbeatable slow machine/ Which brings what you'll get." Well, Amis says, here's unbeatable life and here's the hole: try and tell them apart. Instead of the possibility of mastery, one can only submit to the inexorable. The speeding car will show up again and run over someone, probably you.

Amis's *London Fields* covered the destruction of civil society. Now he surveys the wreckage of the individual. There are Amis's now-familiar turns about the decrepitude and betrayal of the body, especially the bodies of fortyish men. Tull's bodily ills chart the progress of his failures to the point that he develops a phobia that he constantly smells of shit. More than this—if that's possible!—is a larger breakdown of feeling. None of the characters in *The Information* comes close to being sympathetic. Tull's self-regarding relief at an ex-lover's suicide ices the page. Barely able to conceive of the existence of others, let alone feel for or link with them, the characters have no clue about their own lives, work or emotions. We never actually hear what either's novel is about because neither can talk about them! Barry is at least sensible enough to come up with the hackneyed analogy with carpentry to "explain" his books to his public. Poor Richard Tull, attempting to uphold high art, is reduced to gibbering that the book is about what it is about and if he could talk about it he wouldn't have written it! In the end, Barry survives because his accidental success strokes his narcissism and cast-iron ego. For Tull, overloaded, all circuits fried, the only response is incoherence and a battered whimpering. The "information" leads men (this is a novel from which women are excluded both as characters and—perhaps—as readers) to "cry in their sleep and then say Nothing. It's nothing. Just

sad dreams." Men cry at night "because they don't know how to do it when they're awake."

The only redemption in *The Information* comes from Tull's children, and its a peculiar kind of redemption. First, Amis cutely draws the twins Marco and Marius so they are irresistable. They are unconditional in their love, no matter what Tull does or thinks, and Tull is weepingly grateful. But Marco has a learning disability—blockage again—so he has to read his children's stories with Tull helping him spell them out letter by letter. The scene where Marco and Richard laboriously decode "And the good boy and the bad boy went into the forest" is affecting but the point is that language devolving into fragmented symbols makes meaning impossible. And that Tull gives up trying to help his boy before they get to the word "forest." "Only connect?" Not bloody likely.

Words cannot express Martin Amis's achievement in *The Information*. I hate him.

---

## FURTHER READING

### Criticism

Diedrick, James. *Understanding Martin Amis*. University of South Carolina Press, 1995.

    A study of the themes and features found in Amis's work. Discussion of Amis's artistic vision, his journalistic experiences, and overview of the characteristics that make Amis's work unique. The book includes bibliographical references.

Doan, Laura. "'Sexy Greedy Is the Late Eighties': Power Systems in Amis' *Money* and Churchill's *Serious Money*." *The Minnesota Review* 34/35 (Spring/Fall 1990): 69-80.

    This essay compares power structures in Amis's *Money* to those in Churchill's *Serious Money*.

Harrison, M. John. "Speeding to Cradle from Grave." *The Times Literary Supplement*, No. 4616 (20 September 1991): 21.

    Compares the reverse-chronological time structure in *Time's Arrow* with several works by other authors that share the same organization, and praises the novel's originality and inventiveness.

Kermode, Frank. "In Reverse." *London Review of Books* 13, No. 17 (13 September 1991): 11.

    Examines the time structure of *Time's Arrow*.

Kessler, Jascha. "Reads Like Lightning." *American Book Review* 14, No. 4 (October/November 1992): 24-25.

Kessler's review provides a brief plot synopsis and analysis of *Time's Arrow* in which the critic lauds Amis's "compelling narrative," yet asserts that the subject matter of the work is controversial.

Mars-Jones, Adam. "Looking on the Blight Side." *The Times Literary Supplement,* No. 4799 (24 March 1995): 19-20.
Discusses similarities between some of Amis's previous works and *The Information.*

Michener, Charles. "Britain's Brat of Letters." *Esquire* 107, No. 1 (January, 1987): 108-11.
Based on an interview with Amis relating the author's views on his work, his life, and criticism of his writings.

Padhi, Shanti. "Bed and Bedlam: The Hard-Core Extravaganzas of Martin Amis." *Literary Half Yearly* 23, No. 1 (January 1982): 36-42.
An essay focusing on the lewd and sexual imagery in Amis's novels, where the critic is overly concerned with the "inappropriate" use of such material to sensationalize and commercialize the work.

Todd, Richard. "The Intrusive Author in British Postmodernist Fiction: The Cases of Alasdair Gray and Martin Amis." In *Exploring Postmodernism,* edited by Matei Calinescu and Douwe Fokkema, pp. 123-37. Amsterdam/Philadelphia: John Benjamins Publishing Company, 1987.
This chapter focuses on a comparison between uses of the device of the intrusive author in Amis's novel *Money* and Gray's novel *Lanark: A Life in Four Books.*

Updike, John. A review of *Time's Arrow,* by Martin Amis. *New Yorker* LXVIII, No. 14 (25 May 1992): 84-88.
Discusses the merits and faults of *Time's Arrow.*

Wood, James. "Paradox Pile-up." *The Times Literary Supplement,* No. 4724 (15 October 1993): 21.
Praises *Visiting Mrs. Nabokov,* commending both Amis's comic abilities and his powerful and concise descriptive prowess.

---

**Additional coverage of Amis's life and career is contained in the following sources published by Gale Research:** *Contemporary Authors,* Vols. 65-68; *Contemporary Authors New Revision Series,* Vols. 8 and 27; and *Dictionary of Literary Biography,* Vol. 14.

# José Lezama Lima
## 1910-1976

Cuban poet, novelist, short story writer, essayist, and critic.

The following entry presents an overview of Lezama Lima's career. For further information on his life and works, see *CLC*, Volumes 4 and 10.

## INTRODUCTION

José Lezama Lima is considered one of the greatest twentieth-century Latin American writers. His first and most famous novel *Paradiso* (1966) is the culmination of his lifelong work as a literary theorist and poet. In *Paradiso* and its sequel *Oppiano Licario* (1977), Lezama Lima embraces themes of sexuality and friendship, mythology and religion, to create an aesthetic world of his own: erudite, baroque, and rich in symbolism and allusion. When *Paradiso* was first published Lezama Lima's unorthodox depiction of family life sparked controversy in Fidel Castro's Cuba and led to official efforts to repress the work. However, the praise of other Latin American writers brought Lezama Lima's work to international attention.

### Biographical Information

Lezama Lima was born on December 19, 1910 in a military camp near Havana, Cuba. His father was a military officer who died at a young age in 1919. This haunted Lezama Lima throughout his life and served as a preoccupation of his writing. Lezama Lima formed an unusually close relationship with his mother and lived with her throughout her life. Chronic problems with asthma led him to spend much of his childhood reading in solitude. He studied Spanish literature before entering the Universidad de la Habana to pursue legal studies. The student protests against the dictator Gerarado Machado awakened his political consciousness and the school shutdowns which resulted from the protests led to a four-year hiatus during which Lezama Lima read widely and began to develop his interests in Cuban intellectualism and culture. In 1927 he began to write poetry and in 1937 he published his most important poem, *Muerte de Narciso (Death of Narcissus)*. From 1937 through the 1950s he edited a series of journals devoted to literature, politics, the arts, and culture in Cuba. At odds with the Batista regime, Lezama Lima became director of the department of literature and publications of the National Council of Culture after Castro's rise to power. In 1964, following his mother's death, he married Maria Luisa Bautista Trevino, an old friend of the family. The publication of *Paradiso* two years later brought trouble: authorities labeled the book pornographic due to its homosexual content, and in 1971 Lezama Lima was accused of antirevolutionary activities. He died in 1976, alienated from his friends and the Cuban culture to which he had devoted his life.

### Major Works

Lezama Lima's two best known works, the novels *Paradiso* and *Oppiano Licario,* build on his early work as essayist and poet. In poems and essays such as *The Death of Narcissus, Enemigo rumor* (1941; *Enemy Rumors*) and *La fijeza* (1949; *Persistence*) he explores themes such as the role of poetry and the poet, life, death, God, and religion. In *La expresión americana* (1957; *The American Expression*), Lezama Lima claimed that American culture, in contrast with that of Europe, creates an environment where neo-baroque aesthetics, ecstasy, joy, and magical realism converge to produce a uniquely American literary hermeneutic. In *Introducción a los vasos órficos* (1971; *Introduction to the Orphic Vases*) the author contended that the poet is the intermediary between God and humankind and alone can express the unlimited possibilities which exist in life. The somewhat autobiographical *Paradiso* follows the life of Jose Cemí as he comes of age in pre-Castro Cuba, exploring issues such as the connection between the material and spiritual worlds and the nature of family life. Cemí is taught by his friend and mentor Oppiano Licario that he must live his life through the eyes of a poet. *Oppiano Licario* and a collection of poems, *Fragmentos a su imán,* were published posthumously.

### Critical Reception

Lezama Lima has been labeled a "difficult writer" because of his use of arcane language and obscure imagery. However, many critics praise his aesthetic innovations, both in his poetry and his novels. *Paradiso* sparked negative comments from some critics in the United States—Michael Wood called the book "less a modern novel than a garrulous, old-fashioned treatise about a modern novel which hasn't been written yet"—but Latin American writers such as Julio Cortazar, Mario Vargas Llosa, and Octavio Paz argue that Lezama Lima's work represents some of the finest of twentieth-century writing and that he deserves to be considered one of Cuba's greatest writers.

## PRINCIPAL WORKS

*Muerte de Narciso* [*The Death of Narcissus*] (poem) 1937
*Enemigo rumor* [*Enemy Rumors*] (poetry) 1941
*Aventuras sigilosa* [*Secret Adventures*] (poetry) 1945
*La fijeza* [*Persistence*] (poetry) 1949
*Analecta del reloj* [*Analecta of the Clock*] (essays) 1953
*La expresión americana* [*The American Expression*] (essays) 1957; enlarged edition, 1969
*Tratados en La Habana* (essays) 1958
*Dador* [*Giver*] (poetry) 1960
*Paradiso* [*Paradise*] (novel) 1966
*Orbita de Lezama Lima* (selected works) 1966
*Posible imagen de José Lezama Lima* (poetry) 1969
*Poesía completa* (poetry) 1970
*La cantidad hechizada* [*The Bewitched Quantity*] (essays) 1970
*Esgeraimagen: Sierpe de don Luis de Góngora; Las imagenes posibles* (poetry) 1970
*Introducción a los vasos órficos* [*Introduction to the Orphic Vases*] (essays) 1971
*Obras completas,* 2 volumes (collected works) 1975
*Cangrejos, golondrinas* (selected works) 1977
*Fragmentos a su imán* (poetry) 1977
*Oppiano Licario* (novel) 1977
*Cartas (1939-1976): José Lezama Lima* (letters) 1979
*Imagen y posibilidad* (selected works) 1981
*El reino de la imagen* (essays) 1981
*Juego de las decapitaciones* (short stories) 1982
*Cuentos* (short stories) 1987
*Relatos* (selected works) 1987
*Confluencias* (essays) 1988

## CRITICISM

### J. M. Alonso (essay date Fall 1974)

SOURCE: "A Sentimental Realism," in *Review*, No. 74, Fall, 1974, pp. 46-7.

[*In the following essay, Alonso contends that while Lezama Lima's realistic writing style was influenced by the works of Ruben Dario and Maria Eugenia Gongora,* Paradiso *is sincere but unconvincing in its realism.*]

Perhaps, as the dust jacket claims, *Paradiso* was met with "unqualified enthusiasm" in Italy and France. But this was not the case here, and it is easy to see why.

Although comparisons can and have been made between *Paradiso* and *Ulysses* and *Remembrance of Things Past*, Lezama's book owes much more to the poetry of Dario and Góngora than to the novelistic breakthroughs of Proust and Joyce. Not surprising, perhaps, since Lezama is known as Cuba's premier lyric poet. However, this also means that *Paradiso* is rooted in precisely those literary traditions that, more than just foreign, have long been regarded in English with an open hostility as downright alien. They are considered, I think it is fair to say, decadent and in the worst of taste. It is true, of course, that Spanish literature has also struggled against this tendency, but it is not for nothing that the term Gongorism has an even more unforgivingly pejorative ring in English than it ever does in Spanish. In Latin America, however, this baroque strain has tended to remain alive, even gaining a new respectability with Alejo Carpentier, for example, declaring in the recent past that the baroque is a natural and legitimate mode of Latin American expression.

Therefore, quite within this baroque tradition, Lezama continually sacrifices narrative pull for the sake of stopping to display his lyricism. His style is an openly Dandyish cult of cultivations, unashamedly filled with long, elliptical sentences featuring a distinctly self-congratulatory inclination for the most learned if not arcane choices where simpler ones seem quite possible. And thus it parades itself for more than four hundred pages, dripping with all the junk jewelry left over from Modernismo, and then some, with the very charm of the book depending on it. Unfortunately, rendered into English, I believe it only succeeds in offending a puritanism that has progressively been dominating English writing since the days of the Royal Academy of Science and its battle against the Metaphysicals.

> Although comparisons can and have been made between *Paradiso* and *Ulysses* and *Remembrance of Things Past*, Lezama's book owes much more to the poetry of Dario and Góngora than to the novelistic breakthroughs of Proust and Joyce.
>
> —*J. M. Alonso*

But what makes *Paradiso* truly off-putting here, I believe, is what has caused it to receive a bad reception wherever else it has, which includes many quarters of the Spanish-speaking world. I refer now to Lezama's underlying but obvious protest of aristocracy which is at the heart of his distended and heavily cosmetized ornateness. Herein lies the reason why his characters, be they children, grandmothers or illiterate cooks will compulsively talk in floods of classical (n.b., European, quintessentially white) erudition, displaying familiarity not only with the supposed best of everything—anywhere—but especially with supposed European aristocratic customs. This is also why Lezama is continually making parallels between what is happening in, say, the daily family life he describes and something or someone grand out of classical antiquity or fabled histories. And here too, I regret, lies the key to those supposedly humorous incidents which have to do with race (e.g., how a Negro looks when frightened by a ghost or how a pompous Black traffic cop in a resplendent white uniform nevertheless "smells," etc.) or with the ignorance of less erudite people.

A simple protest of spiritual aristocracy would be one thing. Unfortunately, Lezama's heavy load of ornamental erudition, much like the ownership of jewelry and furs in many cases, ultimately means to signal the Cemí family's claim to actual sociological aristocracy, the kind once supposedly assigned by God. It means to say, as is obvious from the constant parallels, that these people, despite having to live in the leveling confusions of the New World, would find themselves quite at home in the fanciest courts of Europe that they can imagine. The regrettable result is an impression of very vulgar snobbery, the worse, of an unremitting provincialism which tends to embarrass more than offend.

From my point of view, however, *Paradiso* does not fail because of its hierarchical view of the world. And certainly not for being within that most highly literary tradition that includes such great Decadentists as Góngora and Darío. What I find fundamentally wrong here is what Lezama does with this tradition. Góngora, for example, with all his extraordinarily structured ornateness, pretended only to be making what the French sometimes call "mere literature" and sometimes "pure literature." His best work was indeed what Ortega called "a higher form of algebra done with metaphors," abstraction as well as a cult of Beauty. And as for Darió, with his fairy tale Versailles populated by Princesses and literary swans, we know he intended to create an artificial paradise in an attempt to escape from the world, which he confessed to detesting in his *Palabras liminares*. In fact, he not only said he disliked his moment in history, but just about everything else that had been his lot, despite his *"manos de marqués."* Lezama, however, seriously pretends to convince us that his *Paradiso* was not any such artificial paradise, some purely literary realm, but rather the world it was his to experience, filtered for us by his love for it. In a word, reality.

Therefore, despite his Gongorist, Decadentist plumage, Lezama turns out to be merely a kind of sentimental Realist. If Lezama had not initially pretended to anything other than presenting the reader with a loving fantasy, it might all have been different. This is the initial advantage that makes, for example, *One Hundred Years of Solitude* a viable fiction, which *Paradiso* is not. But, of course, such an early decision on the part of Lezama must have been out of the question,

considering that his intent was to convince the reader of exactly the opposite.

Lezama, to me, is thus neither convincing as a Realist nor as a Decadentist. Rather, his use of Gongorist cultivations as a social status-symbol while remaining essentially within a Realist intent strikes me as a perversion of two perfectly noble traditions which is condemned to being without the virtues of either. This fundamental flaw, however, is not caused by any lack of sincerity on Lezama's part. I am very confident he is that, and that he is so fervently. What *Paradiso* lacks as a work of art is the one difficult virtue which Gide congratulated himself for having, as an artist, at least, when he said he found himself much too honest to be sincere. Whatever else might be murky, this all comes through its English translation with an often painful clarity.

## José Lezama Lima (essay date Fall 1974)

SOURCE: "Confluences," in *Review*, No. 74, Fall, 1974, pp. 6-16.

[*In the following excerpt, Lezama Lima discusses his theory of poetics and philosophical views in regard to the creation of the plot and characters of* Paradiso.]

I saw night as a descent, as if something had fallen over the earth. Its slowness kept me from comparing it, for example, to something descending a staircase. One tide atop another, and so on incessantly, until it came within reach of my feet. I united the fall of night with the sea's unique extension.

The cars' headlights shone through in zigzagging planes and the "who goes theres?" began to be heard. The voices skipped from one sentry box to the next. The night began to be peopled, to be nourished. From afar, I saw it crossed by ceaseless points of light. Subdivided, fragmented, pierced by the voices and lights. I was far off and could only sense the signs of its animation, like a secret parley inside a closed brocade in the night. Distant and garrulous, master of its pauses, night penetrated into the room where I slept and I felt how it spread through my sleep. I rested my head on a wave that reached me in a wrinkle of ungraspable buoyancy. To feel myself as if resting on smoke, on rope, between two clouds. Night gave me a skin, it had to be the skin of night. And I, tossing and turning inside that immense skin; and while I revolved, it stretched out as far as the mosses of the beginning.

As a child I always waited for night with undeniable terror. Of course. For me, it was the room that does not open, the trunk with the lost key, the mirror in which someone appears at our side, a kind of temptation. It was not the challenge of an adventure, nor the fascination with the horizon line. I did not ride the night astraddle as it withdrew, nor did I have to reconstruct, for the other, diurnal, sleep, my fragments which the skin of night had left scattered on the bed.

The immense skin of night would leave me with numberless sensations for numberless comparisons. The dog that during the day had passed my side time and again almost without my noticing, now, at night, is at my side dozing, and it is then that I watch him most closely. I attest the wrinkles of his skin, how he flicks his tail and paws to drive off nonexistent flies. He barks in his sleep and angrily bares his fangs. In the night he has invisible enemies who keep bothering him. His earlier reactions of anger do not depend on the homology of his diurnal motivations. He does not depend on motivations in the night, but rather, without knowing it, he is generating innumerable motivations in the skin of night that covers me.

Night has reduced itself to a point, which begins to grow until it is night again. The reduction that I attest is a hand. The position of the hand within night gives me a time. The time in which that can happen. Night, to me, was the territory in which the hand could be recognized. I would say to myself, it cannot be waiting, that hand, it does not need my witness. And a weak voice, which must have been very far removed from some little fox's teeth, said to me: stretch out your hand, and you will see how night is there, and your unknown hand. Unknown, because I could never see a body behind it. Wavering in fear, then with inexplicable firmness, I slowly moved my hand forward, like a nervous passage across a desert, until I found my other hand, the other. I would say to myself: it's not a nightmare, and then more slowly: yet it could be that you're hallucinating, but at last my one hand corroborates the other. The evidence that it was there lessened my anguish until my hand returned once more to its solitude.

Now, after almost half a century, I am able to illuminate and even to separate into different moments my nocturnal search for the other hand. My hand fell upon the other hand, because the latter was waiting. If that hand had not been there, the failure, a fear of course, would have been greater than the fear generated because the hand was there. One fear hidden inside the other. Fear because the hand is there, and possible fear of its absence.

Afterwards I learned that Rilke's *Notebooks* also contained the hand, and afterwards I learned that it was in nearly all children, in nearly all manuals of child psychology.

There, already, was the becoming and the archetype, life and literature, the Heraclitean river and the Parmenidean unity. Does one withdraw the hand, lessen one's terrible experience because another has already suffered it, convert a decisive, terrible experience into a simple verbal game, into

literature? The time that had gone by taught me a solemn lesson: the conviction that what happens to us, happens to others as well. That experience of the hand on top of the hand would go on being extremely valuable even though all the outstretched hands might encounter all the hands

It was so crucial an experience that although the same thing is part of child psychology, there are still nights of the other hand, the ghostly one. There will always be nights when the other hand comes, and other nights in which the hand remains stiff and unvisited.

I expected not just the other hand but also the other word, which inside us shapes a continuous doing and undoing by instants. A flower that shapes another flower while the dragonfly lights upon it. To know that by instants something comes to complete us, and that by the expansion of breathing a universal rhythm is found. Inspiration and expiration, which are a universal rhythm. What is hidden is what completes us; it is the fullness in the length of the wave. The knowledge that it does not belong to us and the ignorance that it does belong to us comprise, for me, true wisdom.

The word, in the moments of its hypostasis, the whole body behind a word, a syllable, a pursing of the lips or an unexpected irregularity of the eyebrows. The residue of the stellar in each word was converted into a momentary mirror. An ink-sanding that left behind letters, directions. A solitary word that came to resemble a sentence. The verb was like an overly sweaty hand, an adjective was a profile or a face-to-face stare, eyes upon other eyes, with the tension of a buck's alert ear.

Each word was to me the boundless presence of the fixity of the nocturnal hand. *It's bath time, let's have lunch, go to sleep, someone's at the door*, were for me something like inscriptions that brought forth unceasing evaporations, the unchangeable and obsessive sketches of novels. They were the larvae of metaphors, developed in an undetainable chain, like a farewell followed by a new guest.

The expectation and the arrival of the hand began the verbal chain, or in the endless unfolding, the nocturnal hand was encountered. At times, waiting for the hand was fruitless and this separated one syllable from the next disproportionately, one word from its shipmate. It was a momentary void of distance that had sprung up in a wistful wait as much as in a paradoxical absence of good counsel. It was like a move overturned, or should I say precipitated, on an unfamiliar game-board. A disquieting verbal play, for something moved ahead, something challenged, threw out its call, over a net that sported a lone fish eager to befriend all the other fishes.

Thus, in each word I found a seed germinated by the union of the stellar and the verbal and, as at the end of all time, the pause and filling up of each instant of breathing will be occupied by an irreplaceable, unique word. Each word will contain a seed sown in the equilibrium tubes of the sentence, but in this world the verbal seed, as in the sequence of visible and invisible space in breathing, achieves in man the inborn surprise of a temporal coordinate. The stellar, what the Taoists named the silent sky, required the visceral transmutations of man, the oven of his innards, his secret and intimate metamorphoses to which the mysterious pineal eye was perhaps related, the extinct inner mirror reconstructed by the Greeks as being, like the Pascalian *moi haïssable*, like the *single nature* of the Alexandrians, which would later achieve its highest expression in the Augustinian *logos spermatikos*, each word's participation in the universal *verbum*, a participation treasuring breath, uniting the visible with the invisible, a metamorphic digestion and a spermatic progression exchanging the seed for the universal *verbum*, a complementary, protoplasmic hunger that generates the participation of each word in an infinite and recognizable possibility.

But man does not only generate, he also chooses. I would underline the resemblance between those two events, which to me are equally mysterious, for in choosing we originate a new seed, except that as it has a more direct relationship to man, we call it act. In the poetic dimension, to act and to choose are extensions of the seed, for that act and that choice are within the realm of the haptic sense of the blind, if I may use that term as a minimal approximation to what I mean.

It is an act that produces, and a choice that occurs, coded in supernature. An answer to a question that cannot be posed, that wavers in infinitude. A ceaseless answer to the terrible question of the demiurge: why does it rain in the desert? Act and choice taking place in supernature. Cities which man arrives at and cannot afterwards reconstruct. Cities built with millenial slowness and suppressed and razed in the twinkling of an eye. Made and unmade in the rhythm of respiration. Sometimes unmade by the sudden descent of the stellar and other times made like a momentary colonnade of the telluric.

What is supernature? The image's penetration into nature generates supernature. In that dimension I never tire of repeating Pascal's phrase, a revelation to me, that "because true nature is lost to us, anything can be nature"; the terrible, affirmative force of that phrase caused me to decide to juxtapose nature's determinism with the image replacing nature lost in that way: man responds with the total will of the image. And confronted with the pessimism of nature lost, man's invincible joy in the reconstructed image.

Do they live in a ruin? Are they strolling players on vacation? Is there a painter there? We observe Goya's *The Grotto*, one of his least known and best canvases. In the background, El Greco's livid sky and galloping clouds, contrasted with the calm flight of doves. Covered by the tablecloth, or hidden under the table, so that the doves will come closer. It is a coliseum in ruins, a deserted plaza, the crumbling wing of a convent. In front of this desolation, a coffeehouse has been set up; there, a ghost covered by a tablecloth pecked at by pigeons generates expectation and witty remarks. It is an unknown space and an errant time that will not come to rest on earth. And yet we stroll in that "here" and we move in that "now" and we manage to reconstruct an image. *That* is supernature.

Supernature does not only manifest itself in the intervention of man in nature; both man and nature, at their own risk, are present in supernature. Among the Tartars, dead children marry. On fine paper are drawn the wedding guests, the warriors, musicians, relatives bearing the amphorae for the libations. The witnesses sign, and their signatures are kept in closely watched archives. The relatives of both dead children join for companionship, living in the vicinity. They combine their fortunes and keep the holy days. Here is life seething up around the dead, and the dead child-couple penetrating into life. It is the answer to the assertion of the morphologists of the Goethian school that every species in perfecting itself generates a new species; in the same way, nature, growing with the image contributed by man, arrives at the new kingdom of supernature. . . .

Supernature has little to do with the *proton pseudos*, the poetic lie of the Greeks, since supernature never loses the primordiality from which it springs, for it combines the one with the nondual one; since man is image, he participates as such, and in the end finds the total clarification of the image; were the image denied him, he would remain completely ignorant of the resurrection. The image is the unceasing complement of the half-seen and the half-heard; the fearful *entredeux* of Pascal can be filled only with the image.

The *horror vacui* is the fear of being left without images, in the epochs in which the combinatorial, pessimistic finiteness of corpuscles predominated over the spiraloid rupture of the demiurge. In numerous medieval legends there appears the mirror that will not reflect the image of a wicked or demoniacal body: when the mirror will not speak, the demon sticks out its foul tongue. The innate conviction in man of knowing that the key also opens another house, that the sword guides another army in the desert, that the playing cards begin another game in the other region. Everywhere there is the reminiscence of an absolute that we do not know, generated by a causality in visibility, which we perceive as the lost city that we once again come to recognize. In reality, every basis of the image is hypertelic, goes beyond its finality and does not know it, and offers the infinite surprise of what I have called the *ecstasy of participating in the homogeneous*, an errant point, an image for the extension. It is a tree, a reminiscence, a conversation supporting the river with the forefinger's tracing.

Seed, act, and afterwards potential. Possibility of the act, the act on one point, and a point that resists. This point is an Argus, a sharp-eyed one, and it cleaves through the stellar. Its tracks remain, as if endowed with an invisible phosphorescence. In all of this there is a finite possibility which the potential interprets and unravels. Man's act can reproduce the seed in nature, and can make poetry permanent by a secret relationship between the seed and the act. It is a seed act that man can achieve and reproduce. The howling, piercing unity of a hunting party, a cry of exaltation, the permanent response of the orchestra in time, the warriors in the shadow of Troy's walls, the *grand armée*, what I have called the imaginary eras and also supernature, form, by an interlacing of seed, act, and potential, new and unknown seeds, acts, and potentials. Since to sow in the telluric is to sow in the stellar, and to follow the course of a river is to walk parting the clouds, as in the Chinese theatre a certain movement of the legs means to ride a horse.

When the potential is applied to a point or actuated in extension, it is always accompanied by the image, the most profound known unity between the stellar and the telluric. Were the potential to act without the image, it would only be a self-destructive act without participation, but every act, every potential is an infinite growth, an excess, in which the stellar supports the telluric. In participating in the act, the image provides a momentary visibility without which—without the image as the sole recourse within man's reach—an impenetrable excess would exist. Thus man takes possession of that excess, makes it rise up, and incorporates a new excess. All *poiesis* is an act of participation in that excess, man's participation in the universal spirit, the Holy Ghost, the universal mother.

Man as seed marks that development in his circumstance, he matches a broad-based tree trunk with his fervor for foundations, although we, by issuing from nature, will not know what causal series produce either splendor or poverty, nor at what moment the absolute will undetainably penetrate into those causal series. In some cities of Asia, at the passing from life to death, the dead man is not taken out by way of the door but rather a wall of the house is broken through, as if to prepare it for a new causality. In other Asiatic cities, at the moment of cremation, papers sketched on by friends are thrown in, jewelry, food, as if to grant protection and companionship for a voyage presumably into a new extension.

In rare vessels of choice—that is the expression the Bible uses—their development in life proceeds as if accompanied by a prodigious anticipation of the new extension. From the Castilian wasteland springs the Theresian fundament like an oblique experience: it is reproduced in Martì, locating in the

desert-like region the paradoxical seed of exile. After his imprisonment, Martì must have felt something like rebirth in the image of the resurrection, as after his death he rises up again in the flesh. The desert-like quality and his new, symbolic appearance in exile are equivalents, and for that reason in *Paradiso,* to propitiate the last meeting of José Cemì and Oppiano Licario, to reach the new causality, the Tibetan city, Cemì has to pass through all the occurrences and recurrences of night. The placental descent of the nocturnal, the balance pointer of midnight, appear as variants of desert (*desierto*) and exile (*destierro*), all the possibilities of the poetic system have been set in motion so that Cemì will keep his appointment with Licario, the Icarus, the new attempter of the impossible.

*Paradiso,* world outside time, equates itself with supernature, since time is also nature lost and the image is reconstructed as supernature. Liberation from time is the most tenacious constant of supernature. Oppiano Licario wants to facilitate supernature. Thus he moves on in his search through endless labyrinths. Chapter XII, denial of time, behind the glass case the dead centurion and boy endlessly switch faces, but finally, in Chapter XIV, the one behind the glass is Oppiano Licario himself. Denial of time attained in sleep, where not just time but also dimension disappear. I move the enormity of an axe, I achieve infinite speeds, I see the blind in the night-markets talking about the plastic quality of strawberries, in the end, the Roman soldiers rolling the astragals among the ruins, I achieve the tetractys, the four, god. Chapter XIII attempts to demonstrate a *perpetuum mobile*, to free itself from the spatial relative. The goat's head revolving on its pinion achieves that liberation, in Oppiano Licario's dimension of supernature, the figures of the child's past begin to reappear. It is the cognitive infinitude acquired at Licario's side, only the rhythm of the Pythagoreans is different from the systaltic rhythm, the violent one, that of the passions; they have passed into the hesychastic rhythm, into tranquillity, into sage contemplation.

Licario has set in motion the vast coordinates of the poetic system to propitiate his last meeting with Cemì. It was essential that Cemì keep this last appointment with Licario's words. *The image and the spider on the body,* says one of those sentences delivered the last night. His sister Inaca Eco Licario appears, proffering the poetic sentence like the promised land. The shade, the double, is what tenders the offering. The double makes the first offering, yields the first image, and Cemì ascends by the sacrificial stone to honor his name of Taino idol or image. Let us imagine a starry, Pythagorean night in 1955. I have been listening for several hours to Bach's *Art of the Fugue,* am drenched in the interlacings of the *fuga per canon.* Infinite relationships are achieved in the spiraloids of the nocturne. The constructions and expansions of the rhythm repeat themselves in each step we take and we grow while walking. We head down one of those streets that expand like paradisiacal rivers. The nocturnal lights in the funeral home must, without knowing it, detain the stroller, startling him. A merry-go-round's tune repeating keeps the stroller on a nocturnal path and urges him on. In its vertical dimension, like a maddened tree, the house hurls us the temptation of its back terrace, where, protected by the priapic god Terminus, two buffoons play chess. Here there is something like the repetition of a circular march. At the very edge of death, the coordinates of the poetic system flail out in desperation, when nature is exhausted, supernature survives, when the telluric image is broken, the endless images of the stellar begin. There, in the most untouchable remoteness, where the Pythagoreans gave the stars a soul.

### Emir Rodriguez Monegal (essay date Fall 1974)

SOURCE: "The Text in Its Context," in *Review*, No. 74, Fall, 1974, pp. 30-4.

[*In the following essay, Monegal compares* Paradiso'*s themes and structure to the works of Marcel Proust, James Joyce, and Dante, focusing on the novel's literal, allegorical, and spiritual elements.*]

It is easy to make the wrong assumptions when reading *Paradiso*. Originally published in Havana in 1966, the first and (until now) only novel of the great Catholic poet circulated almost clandestinely throughout the entire Hispanic world until 1968 when it was republished simultaneously in Mexico and Argentina. The original edition, by the Union of Cuban Writers and Artists (UNEAC), consisted of 4,000 copies, most of which never left the island. For some time, then, the novel was only known through enthusiastic and often raving supporters like Julio Cortázar, Mario Vargas Llosa and Severo Sarduy, and through polemics stirred by its many dazzling homosexual episodes. But the book did manage to circulate among the happy few who happened to get hold of a copy. Now that the book circulates freely in several languages, it may be pertinent to examine some of the traps into which the innocent reader might fall.

The most tempting of these traps is to assume that the novel is more or less autobiographical, like Proust's *A la recherche du temps perdu*, one of its most obvious and acknowledged models. In order to practice such a reading, it would be enough to observe that Lezama Lima, like José Cemí, the protagonist of the novel, was born in Havana; that his father was also a soldier who died when the writer was barely ten; that his mother (like Cemí's) was very loving; that Lezama was a student and a rebel during the same Machado dictatorship described in the second half of the novel. The author, like the protagonist, has suffered from asthma attacks since early childhood—the first chapter of the novel, which describes the horrors of suffocation, is a baroque elaboration of lived experiences, and not only another allusion to the Proustian texts. Like Cemí, Lezama is used to feeding upon his own visions and to seeing the world through thick metaphorical lenses. Future biographers will undoubtedly find many more subtle affinities between the author and his main character. What we already know permits a reading of *Paradiso* as a novelistic transformation of the childhood and youth of its author.

Although it exposes the reader to many dangers, an autobiographical interpretation ought not to be entirely discarded. *Paradiso* contains (among other things) a delightful chronicle of Havana during the first decades of the century. Throughout the entire first half of the book, an elaborate family gallery is presented. Several portraits clearly stand out; among them, the dark virility of Cemí's father, the all-pervading tenderness of his mother, the eccentric relatives and servants. If the text existed only at this level, the level of a family saga; if it were only a refined Cuban version of Proust's Combray, it would still be remarkable. Intense family passions—less explicit than the ones García Márquez chronicles in his *One Hundred Years of Solitude*, but no less incestuous—the undercurrents of Oedipal links, all constantly feed a labyrinthine narrative, in which food itself, in all its stages, from the elaborate cooking to the no less elaborate and ritual ingestion, plays an essential role.

> **The most tempting of these traps is to assume that the novel is more or less autobiographical, like Proust's *A la recherche du temps perdu*, one of its most obvious and acknowledged models.**
>
> **—*Emir Rodriguez Monegal***

In the second part of the book, with the notorious eighth chapter which proliferates in homosexual permutations, the novel loses a great deal of its local color. It becomes more schematic and it even takes on the air of a learned treatise. Cemí has now become an adolescent and his waking hours are occupied with the world of ideas, with endless discussions about the meaning of the universe, with the search for a rational explanation of all phenomena. Friendship becomes an exercise in nonstop conversations. Cemí is also a poet (like Lezama) and his own personal visions permeate the narrative until they actually supersede it. If Proust was the model for the first part, and even for some scenes of the second part (the sudden revelation of some character's homosexuality is as abrupt as the one practiced in *Sodome et Gomorrhe*), the second part of the novel follows more closely the pattern of James Joyce's *Portrait of the Artist as a Young Man*.

However tempting, that type of reading runs the risk of missing much of the book's real value. *Paradiso* is much more and much less than a *Bildungsroman*.

*The finger of God*

In *Il Convivio* (II, 1) Dante postulates four possible interpretations of a given text. Using the critical vocabulary of his time, he underlines the usefulness of starting with a literal interpretation: that is, the study of "the beautiful lie" which dresses up the work superficially; what we could call today its "fiction," or "fable." The second interpretation he indicates is the allegorical, the one that searches for a "hidden truth" behind the fiction. The third is the one from which the "moral" of the story is derived, a moral which will be useful to the readers. The fourth and last is the anagogic interpretation, the one that unveils the text's "sublime things," its final spiritual meaning. It is not necessary to be a specialist in order to recognize the imprint of Dante upon a book explicitly called *Paradiso*. Not unlike his master, Lezama suggests by the title he chooses different and successive readings of his work. We have already examined the one that would correspond to the "literal" one. It is both the easiest and the one that permits a greater consensus among its readers. Upon practising the second or allegorical reading, the reader becomes a co-author, and disagreement settles in.

The fact that the book contains, among many other things, an apology for homosexuality, was for a while a cause of dissent throughout Latin America; some of the first commentators (like Vargas Llosa) did not even mention the subject, as if it were too minor to draw any attention; others, like Cortázar, faced it squarely. As it is well-known, *Paradiso* not only describes sexual relations between men with a detail which is unusual in Hispanic literature, but it also contains very detailed discussions of the legitimacy of homosexuality in which the characters support their arguments with both classical and Christian texts. The book has been compared, from this point of view, with André Gide's notorious *Corydon*.

Needless to say, such a view is false. *Paradiso* does not defend homosexuality as *Corydon* does: it merely discusses it. Of the three main characters engaged in the discussion (Cemí and his two friends, Foción and Fronesis), only the second is a homosexual, frustratedly in love with Cemí. His frustration extends to his arguments: he is definitely not one of the most eloquent contributors to the debate. On the other hand, the narrative presents homosexual acts with a flourish for detail and metaphor that matches anything done previously. But the book also contains some descriptions of heterosexual activities. It could be argued, however, that the former are

presented with more linguistic artifice and that some of the episodes border on baroque perversity. But neither do the heterosexual passages escape from perversity. The point is that Lezama really does not make any distinction: sex (of any sort) is just sex to him. For that reason it is impossible to reduce *Paradiso* to a *Corydon* disguised as a novel.

This does not mean that the homosexual side of human nature does not occupy a considerable portion of the novel. There is indeed a constant preoccupation with homosexuality in the book and there is even an entire system of thought concerning it that has little to do with the superficial discussion of the problem. In his writings, Lezama has repeatedly referred to a stage of human nature that preceded heterosexuality, in which human reproduction was achieved androgynously, in a manner similar to that of a tree, whose branches fall off the main trunk and create new plants. In this and only in this sense, can *Paradiso* be allegorically interpreted as an exploration of the homosexual vision of the world: a vision which the Cuban author presents from the point of view of its mythical and metaphorical dimensions.

Although the mixture of extreme crudeness and poetic invention with which Lezama details intercourse seems to support the view of the book as an apology for homosexuality, in fact these same passages are the ones that hurt such an alleged cause the most because they underscore (as Saint Thomas puts it, according to Lezama) the pure bestiality of the act. On the other hand, in the discussion between the three main characters, it is possible to find a definitely allegorical interpretation of the world: an interpretation which is never made too explicit but one that holds the key to Lezama's final view of homosexuality.

Here we are indeed very far from any pornographic reading of a few selected chapters. In order to arrive at an allegorical level, one must cast off all prejudices and initiate an in-depth reading such as the one suggested (and to a certain point practised) by Julio Cortázar. By using as his point of departure a few subtle references to Jules Verne and his *Voyage au centre de la terre*, Cortázar did indicate an allegorical approach to *Paradiso*'s underlying poetic system. Unfortunately, the subject is too complex to be attempted here. In the words of one of the secondary characters, Oppiano Licario, Lezama has left the key to a complete decoding of this aspect of the novel. In another passage (curiously overlooked by Cortázar) the links between homosexuality as a subject and religion, are even more explicitly presented by Lezama. In a conversation, Cemí says to Fronesis: "The Greeks arrived at the pair of all things, but the Christian can say, from flower to phallus, this is the finger of God." That is: instead of the polarity of sexes, the unity of an androgynous God.

*Other types of misreading*

These belong to the level Dante called "moral," which today we may call "social," in the fullest sense of the word. Because *Paradiso* was originally published in today's Cuba, the novel cannot avoid being read as a critical description of the island's society before 1958; or as a critique of a certain type of bourgeois mentality which the Revolution has done its best to erradicate. Some Latin American critics who have read their Lukacs and Goldmanns more than they have read Lezama's works would undoubtedly dedicate many pages to demonstrate the testimonial value of the book. Who could doubt it? But then the newspaper accounts of the same period would be of equal or greater value.

It is also possible to imagine a last type of limited analysis of the book: one that would hinge upon the most external postulates of stylistics and would attempt to analyze it from the point of view of its purely formal structure. Then it would not be possible to avoid pointing to the distribution in three parts: fourteen chapters separated in two unequal sections—seven in one, six in the other—with a middle chapter, the notorious eighth, that works as a dividing line. Analogy enthusiasts could also point out that something similar happens in Proust's novel, since its first three parts are separated from the last four by a middle one in which, as in *Paradiso,* the hidden homosexual activity of the main characters is suddenly revealed. Another "structural" observation would indicate that the first part is more narrative than discursive, and that the second part reverses the proportion. A third and inevitable observation: in the second part, the presentation of events—that is: the narrative of what really happens to Cemí and his friends—is contaminated by "fantastic" episodes, either Cemí's own visions or interpolated literary texts which may constitute samples of his poetic exercises.

If we choose to add to these types of "external" criticism, the one that feeds on extensive notation of textual errors, misplaced quotations and even the all-pervading misprints, it would not be difficult to foresee (as Cortázar had already done) the hasty conclusion: *Paradiso* is another of these literary freaks irresponsibly promoted by Latin American writers and critics.

*The key to the system*

So many pitfalls should not discourage the common reader. Not only because it is possible to discover a lot of good and even marvelous writing in the novel, but also because *Paradiso* contains sufficient clues that lead to the type of reading Dante called "anagogic": a reading that underscores the "sublime things" the book truly deals with.

But first we must again underline the obvious: *Paradiso* is not the only work produced by Lezama. He is not just a writer who has spawned forth from revolutionary Cuba without any previous credits. On the contrary, years before *Paradiso* was published, Lezama had acquired a reputation among the best Latin American readers as the author of dazzling poems and essays as well as the coeditor (with José Rodríguez Feo) of the very important avant-garde magazine, *Orígenes*. Therefore, in order to place the novel in its true perspective and to practice with it a type of anagogic reading, there is no choice but to refer to Lezama's previous works, something which is easier said than done. First, because many of his early books have been out of print for a long time. Second, because even when they can be obtained, some of them make very difficult reading. Nevertheless, if one is determined to follow Lezama in all his labyrinthine progression, from poem to essay, and from essay to interview, the reward will be substantial. Lezama's poetic thought has a coherence and depth seldom seen in Latin American letters.

Some of his observations on his own poetry and poetics are worth quoting. In a letter he wrote to the editor of an anthology of his writings (*Orbita de Lezama Lima*, 1966), he points out:

> My work will always offer difficulties, the relativity of an obstacle, if you like; after various interweavings, after labyrinths that would burst out of a persecution that would make itself unceasing, after provocations at a certain point which resolved themselves in the most opposed latitudes, one would arrive at man's occupation of his own image in exile, of man without his own primeval nature. By means of the image, man recovers his own nature, he conquers exile, he acquires unity as a resisting nucleus in between that which ascends to the form and descends to the depths.

The phrase, even in its own morose and endless uncoiling, holds the key to Lezama's system: a system which has a center in the concept of salvation through poetic creation. Those who forget that Lezama is Catholic also tend to forget that he is a Catholic poet. Thus, the title of his novel is not exclusively designed to pay homage to another Catholic poet, his master. For Lezama, man has really been exiled from the paradise of childhood and is now living in exile. He can only be saved by poetry. Against the Heideggerian conception of man's being unto death, a conception which influenced so many of the poets of his generation (Lezama was born in 1910), he holds his own deep conviction that man's being is unto resurrection by means of poetry.

Poetic creation for Lezama is not, then, a simple literary activity, a production, as it is called. For him it is a road, a way. The poet's system, according to one of his best readers, is based on "the profound impression of childhood upon him," which "becomes the poetic; the poem burst forth from this, and poetry from both of them together; therefore, out of their reasoned totality one can extract the system." (See Armando

Alvarez Bravo, prologue to *Orbita.*) The experience of child-hood, Lezama's conversion of that experience into a poem, and then into poetry: such is the real, underlying way into *Paradiso* and all of Lezama's works. Thus the importance of the mysterious Oppiano Licario, the character who finally reveals the poetic (orphic) gift to Cemí.

---

**Poetic creation for Lezama is not, then, a simple literary activity, a production, as it is called. For him it is a road, a way.**

**—*Emir Rodriguez Monegal***

---

In an interview with Alvarez Bravo, also included in *Orbita*, Lezama points out his ultimate conception of what the poem is and does:

> I believe that the wonder of a poem is that it ends up creating a body, a resisting substance nailed down between a metaphor and a final image which assures the survival of that very substance, of that *Poiesis*.

According to this general interpretation, *Paradiso* is a poem, and because it is a poem, it is also a substance (a metaphor) that moves toward the final, unreachable, image. As such, the novel can only be understood in the full context of Lezama's work.

At this very point the anagogic reading begins: but it is also here where difficulties proliferate. Lezama himself has stated that "only the difficult is stimulating," and in the margins of a quotation by Pythagoras he adds:

> Long ago, Pythagoras made clear to us the different types of words there are. There is a simple word, the hieroglyphical and the symbolic. That is to say, the verb that expresses, that hides and that signifies.

Starting off with this statement it is possible to see how mis-leading can be a reading of *Paradiso* which takes into ac-count only the words that express (to follow Pythagoras' distinction) and which excludes the words that hide or sig-nify.

In one of the best essays included in his book, *Analecta del reloj* (1953), Lezama anticipated some of the difficulties of a complete reading of *Paradiso*. He says:

> On a Persian rug, a lion is roaring at a prawn which is shielded by a sheet of water in an artificial pond. What is our reading of such a paradoxical combina-tion? Are we to imagine, maybe, the shivers of the

lion if the end of his whiskers were to touch the sheet? Our reading is ironic and contains a pervad-ing sensitive delight before such a grouping, whose expression must have been originally perceived as symbolic and theocentric, and which now shows us the relative and pessimistic nature of any reading that belongs to a cultural cycle. And it is painful and tearing to know that the pessimism of such an im-possible reading begins with poetry.

These words were written by Lezama in an essay on Góngora. In reading his work, we have no choice but to recall the Per-sian figures in the carpet, in all the Jamesian implications of the formula. Before Lezama's text, and trying to place it into a context, it is impossible not to recall the absurd fate of Pierre Menard, the French symbolist poet who attempted to become the author of *Don Quijote*. Borges has already de-scribed his madness, underlying his one and only achieve-ment: the perhaps involuntary discovery that every reading of a text is a writing of it.

In attempting to summarize the possible different readings of *Paradiso* perhaps we have also discovered the obvious: that without an ironic reading of its text, the book has no valid meaning. This is a modest conclusion but the kind which ought to be reached more frequently.

## Raymond D. Souza (essay date 1976)

SOURCE: "The Sensorial World of Lezama Lima," in *Ma-jor Cuban Novelists: Innovation and Tradition*, University of Missouri Press, 1976, pp. 53-79.

[*In the following essay, Souza discusses the structure of* Paradiso, *focusing on Lezama Lima's symbolic use of char-acters and the story's themes, which include time, chaos, and freedom.*]

Carpentier's and José Lezama Lima's works are often con-sidered by critics as baroque, that is, complex and ornate. When used in this general sense, particularly with Lezama Lima, the term is an appropriate one, for *Paradiso* is the most complex novel ever published in Cuba. Indeed, it is perhaps the most intricate novel in Spanish America, and the author's imaginative genius both attracts and baffles the readers. This explains in part the mistaken proclivity of some to consider Lezama Lima as the Cuban answer to James Joyce. The works of both authors are complex, and Lezama Lima and Joyce reflect an amazing ability to use language in unusual and unexpected manners, but the essence of their art is different. Lezama Lima's work is as much an affirma-tion of one cultural context as Joyce's is a denial of another.

Lezama Lima was relatively unknown in Spanish America before the publication of *Paradiso* in 1966. As with Carpentier, international fame and recognition came to him late in his career. Prior to the appearance of *Paradiso,* Lezama Lima was mainly known to those interested in Cuban literature for his poetry and to those outside of Cuba for his distinguished editorship of the literary journal *Orígenes* (1944-1956). *Paradiso* won quick acclaim, for it gained the praise and support of writers such as Julio Cortázar, one of Argentina's and South America's most eminent and internationally accepted writers. The novel also received a great deal of notoriety for its frank and explicit exploration of homosexuality, a theme practically unheard of in Spanish-American letters. However, the homosexual theme has been greatly overemphasized, for it is not the most important motif in the novel. Rather, it is only one of the many ways the author explores an adolescent's movement from multiplicity to unity.

Lezama Lima narrates in *Paradiso* the fortunes and destiny of the Cemí family, a process that examines several branches of the family tree. In this respect, the novel represents a search for meaning in the past and a quest for significance in origins. The main events in the work take place between the waning years of the nineteenth century and the third decade of the present. A series of characters occupies central stage in *Paradiso,* but José Cemí, who is only five years old when the work opens, emerges as the main subject in the novel. Many of the excursions into the past that transpire in *Paradiso* investigate the origins of people who greatly influence José's life. His parents, important relatives, and intimate friends inspire or govern decisive phases of his development, and by the end of the novel José is ready to enter into the world alone and to embark on adventures of his own. Thus, *Paradiso* can be considered as a compendium of forces that move through time and space to converge on the living entity formed by José. Like Carpentier, Lezama Lima deeply respects the influence that the past has on the present and the future.

> **Lezama Lima narrates in *Paradiso* the fortunes and destiny of the Cemí family, a process that examines several branches of the family tree. In this respect, the novel represents a search for meaning in the past and a quest for significance in origins.**
>
> —*Raymond D. Souza*

*Paradiso* opens with José desperately struggling for air as he experiences a severe attack of asthma. His frantic efforts to breathe attract the attention of Baldovina, a servant who has been left to care for him while his parents attend an opera. Terrified and uncertain of how to cope with the situation, Baldovina seeks the help of two other servants. They respond to Baldovina's plea by performing a ritual that involves the formation of crosses on the sufferer's body. When they complete this strange ceremony, they suddenly and without explanation depart, leaving Baldovina to handle the situation as best as she can. She rubs José with alcohol and pours hot drops of wax on the welts that have appeared on his entire body. When José's parents arrive later, the attack has subsided, and after being informed as to what has happened, they conclude that their son "estaba vivo por puro y sencillo milagro."

There is much in the content and presentation of the introduction to Lezama Lima's novel and the way he creates and moves through it. After presenting the reader with José's critical situation, he gives an elaborate and poetic description of the Cemí family's home. It is not a description that is designed merely to give an objective picture of a certain material reality, but one that also captures the essence of the people who live there and their relations to one another. Baldovina, for example, is fearful of the consequences of her responsibility to care for José, and in her mind she has already suffered through the questioning that experience tells her she will be submitted to once again. Her feelings on the matter and her relationship to José's father, an army Colonel, are conveyed in a striking passage that uses sound and space as the basis of most of its images:

> Después llegaba el Coronel y era ella la que tenía que sufrir una ringlera de preguntas, a la que respondía con nerviosa inadvertencia, quedándole un contrapunto con tantos altibajos, sobresaltos y mentiras, que mientras el Coronel baritonizaba sus carcajadas, Baldovina se hacía leve, desaparecía, desaparecía, y cuando se la llamaba de nuevo hacía que la voz atravesase una selva oscura, tales imposibilidades, que había que nutrir ese eco de voz con tantas voces, que ya era toda la casa la que parecía haber sido llamada, y que a Baldovina, que era sólo un fragmento de ella, le tocaba una partícula tan pequeña que había que reforzarla con sus nuevos perentorios, cargando más el potencial de la onda sonora.

We are left with an impression of a timid and almost mute Baldovina, contrasted with the strength and loquacity of the Colonel and his authority. She is like a small echo of an autumn leaf whose destiny is controlled and ordained by the capricious nature of the wind.

As noted, the author opens the first chapter with José's attack of asthma and then pauses in the midst of it to describe the home. The description does not close in on itself but proceeds from a specific reality and then moves outward in a continual movement of expansion. For example, the author goes beyond merely enumerating the books in the Colonel's study, he evokes all the mystery and excitement of their contents. When his attention falls on some papers on the Colonel's desk, a whole new world is created. The Colonel is an engineer who uses his mathematical skills in the practice of artillery, a complex manipulation of time and space that the men under his command do not understand.

They are simply mystified by his ability, and their attitude toward the Colonel's domination of this enigma is captured in a masterful exercise of the imagination. "Sobre el pupitre, cogidos con alcayatas ya oxidadas, papeles donde se diseñaban desembarcos en países no situados en el tiempo ni en el espacio, como un desfile de banda militar china situado entre la eternidad y la nada." In one brilliantly structured sentence, Lezama Lima has humorously synthesized the preciseness of the Colonel's knowledge with the mystification that his ability produces in the soldiers under his command.

After such digressions, the author returns to the narration of José's attack of asthma. He has moved his reader's attention from a specific occurrence to the totality of the world of his characters. This is a creative process that he uses continually throughout the novel. It is something like circles that emanate when an object is dropped into a pool of water—a specific occurrence can open up one's awareness to a much greater area of reality. Lezama Lima continually moves in concentric circles, both in the process of exteriorization and interiorization, and once the reader has grasped this fact, his participation in the novel becomes more meaningful. Lezama Lima creates an entire world, and he does so, in part, by his attempts to portray the total essence of his characters and their surroundings. The reader feels somewhat as if he were blindfolded and on a snap-the-whip at an amusement park. He never knows when the movement will suddenly throw him outward from the center, or when it will cease and bring him back. But the experience is an exciting and stimulating one, as it is a creative process that continually challenges and expands the reader's awareness of the world in which he lives.

José's suffering and the symbolism of the crosses that are placed on his body are significant, for they set the stage for much of the novel's meaning. *Paradiso* can be taken as the narration of José's search for a basic understanding of the world and the universe. The association of his difficulty breathing during the attack of asthma with the application of the symbol of the cross to his body reveals human existence as a painful struggle, a struggle in which a search is made for a conjunction or synthesis of opposites. The servant's use of the cross represents an appeal to the spiritual world that contrasts vividly with the world of phenomena of José's

illness. The crosses can be taken as a symbol of the conjunction of life and death and of the earthly and celestial worlds, a symbol of the mystery and suffering of existence. José's recovery is regarded as a miracle, and no explanation is ever given of his sudden and spontaneous recovery from his bout with death. The setting for José's attempts to penetrate the mystery of life in the novel is really the narration of his process of becoming, his slow movement from a self-awareness that closes in on itself, to an appreciation of all that is exterior. It is a movement from unawareness to awareness, from multiplicity to unity, from chaos to form and order, and its narration is as fascinating to watch as a slow motion film of a blossoming flower. The act of creation mystifies and enchants and fills us with a sense of awe and appreciation for life that is difficult to convey except by means of art. The creative process of the novel is as important as the end result, and Lezama Lima constantly delights his reader with his startling and imaginative images.

The Colonel emerges in Chapter 1 as the center around which all the other members of his family revolve. He is a picture of strength and vitality, a man who knows how to enjoy life to its fullest. He fills the house with sound, and his jovial and forceful loquaciousness is only matched by his gastronomical feats. As the novel progresses, the sickly José, much to his dismay, discovers he cannot live up to his father's expectations. The Colonel finds it difficult to accept that his only son is asthmatic and not athletically inclined.

During the First World War, the Cemí family departs for Jacksonville, Florida, where the Colonel receives advanced military training. While there the Colonel is weakened by a virulent influenza and is hospitalized. His wife Rialta becomes terror stricken as the possibility of his death enters her mind:

> Había cobrado pavorosa conciencia de la magnitud del hecho familiar que se avecinaba. Empezaba a comprender lo que para ella resultaba incomprensible, la desaparición, el ocultamiento del fuerte, del alegre, del solucionador, del que había reunido dos familias detenidas por el cansancio de los tejidos minuciosos, comunicándoles una síntesis de *allegreto,* de cantante alegre paseo matinal.

The Colonel slips into an indescribable loneliness that he associates with death. "Estoy entrando en una soledad, por primera vez en mi vida, que sé es la de la muerte." Although afraid of his approaching death, he dominates his fear and refuses to have his family called to his side, as he does not wish to frighten them. As a result, he dies alone in the most abject loneliness, and Rialta is notified of his death by telephone. "De pronto, como una campanilla que se dilata el rocío de las hojas nocturnas, el teléfono pinchado desde el hospital, pareció querer hablar como un estrangulado." The news of his death and her loneliness remain in her memory and are associated with the sound of the windblown pine trees outside their Florida home. "Así como el coronel José Eugenio Cemí había muerto en la soledad sin término del hospital, Rialta recibía la más sombría noticia de su vida rodeada de extraños, alejada de su madre doña Augusta, oyendo como un hacha el viento lento del enero americano recorrer los pinares."

Rialta returns to Havana with her children and begins to reconstruct their lives, and she finds that she must now take the place of her dead husband. The image of the center and circle is often employed by Lezama Lima in *Paradiso*. It is perhaps the most significant image in the novel, and he uses this imagery in various ways. Often it is used to connote an individual who is the most important figure in another person's life, and during the novel we see the process of time and change at work, as we witness the dissolution of one circle and the emanation of another. This is the case when the Colonel dies and Rialta is forced to take his place. In another episode when doña Augusta, José's maternal grandmother, feels that she may die, she advises her children that "cada uno de aquellos fragmentos, de los que ella ocupaba el centro, tendría que comenzar en un nuevo centro con nuevas irradiaciones." In a sense, *Paradiso* can be considered as a set of spirals converging in a circle. Reading the novel is like tracing the course of several spirals, as they move through time and space and slowly come together.

The wedding of Rialta and the Colonel represents the circle image of the formation of an everlasting unified entity:

> José Eugenio Cemí y Rialta atolondrados por la gravedad baritonal de los símbolos, después de haber cambiado los anillos, como si la vida de uno se abalanzase sobre la del otro a través de la eternidad del círculo, sintieron por la proliferación de los rostros de familiares y amigos, el rumor de la convergencia en la unidad de la imagen que se iniciaba.

Rialta is pictured as the person who will form the center of a "trenzado laberíntico" during a period of fifty years, in a reference the reader does not fully understand until the Colonel dies. "Comenzaba un extenso trenzado laberíntico, del cual durante cincuenta años, ella sería el centro, la justificación y la fertilidad."

At other times rather than being a symbol of unity, the circle is used as a means of conveying the search for meaning that each individual must experience in his life, with its attendant confusion and chaos. In a fit of rage against a worthless son, Abuela Munda, José's paternal grandmother, states, "Eres un viejo accidente ya entre nosotros, y eso quiere decir que debes ir a buscar tu centro al extranjero." In a more com-

plex manifestation of the circle image, we see José at the age of ten leaving school with a piece of chalk. As he walks he drags the chalk on a wall, and as he does this someone attempts to grab the chalk. Behind the wall there is a large circular patio partially surrounded by small dwellings, and as José nears the end of the wall he is greeted by the shouts and taunts of a child who wants to harass him and to take the chalk from him. The sudden appearance of his tormentor startles him, and the transition is described as if the wall had disappeared and a circle had emerged. "Le parecía a Cemí aquello un remolino de voces y colores, como si el paredón se hubiese derrumbado e instantáneamente se hubiese reconstruido en un patio circular." The taunts of the child continue until an elderly woman recognizes José as the Colonel's son and rescues him. The association of the wall, a straight line, with the circular shape of the patio can be interpreted as a process of interiorization or search that José is to experience in the future. The shouting child could represent the confusion of the exterior world through which José must move; and the chalk, a writing instrument, his means to impose order on chaos—the written word.

The circle image also can represent a momentary escape from time and a return to unity. It is usually presented as a geometrical progression that begins with a square that changes to a circle. Thus, the multilateral shape of the square becomes a unified circle, an image of the movement from multiplicity to unity, from space to spacelessness, from time to timelessness. This progression is skillfully handled in an episode that evokes the memory of the dead Colonel. Rialta is watching her three children playing with a ball. They have formed a circle, and as they play the element of time is introduced:

> Los tres niños estaban tan abstraídos que el ascender de la pelota se cristalizaba como una fuente, y la fijeza de la mirada en el esparcimiento de los yaquis, los extasiaba como cuando se contemplan, en demorados trechos de la noche, las constelaciones. Estaban en ese momento de éxtasis coral que los niños alcanzan con facilidad. Hacer que su tiempo, el tiempo de las personas que los rodean, y el tiempo de la situación exterior, coincidan en una especie de abandono del tiempo, donde las semillas del alcanfor o de las amapolas, el silencioso crecer nocturno de los vegetales, preparan una identidad oval y cristalina, donde un grupo al aislarse logra una comunicación semejante a un espejo universal.

Rialta joins her children in the game, and the four figures form a square that begins to change into a circle. "El cuadrado formado por Rialta y sus tres hijos, se iba trocando en un círculo." The movement of the ball, the spontaneous mood of happiness the game produces, and the unity the formation of the circle gives them, produce an almost hypnotic state that momentarily erases time, and the memory of the Colonel becomes a living entity:

> El contorno del círculo se iba endureciendo, hasta parecer de un metal que se tornaba incandescente. De pronto, en una fulguración, como si una nube se rompiese para dar paso a una nueva visión, apareció en las losas apresadas por el círculo la guerrera completa del Coronel. . . . Y sobre el cuello endurecido, el rostro del ausente, tal vez sonriéndose dentro de su lejanía, como si le alegrase, en un indescifrable contento que no podía, ser compartido, ver a su esposa y a sus hijos dentro de aquel círculo que los unía en un espacio y en un tiempo coincidentes para su mirada. Penetrando en esa visión, como dejada . . . por la fulguración previa, los cuatro que estaban dentro del círculo iluminado, tuvieron la sensación de que penetraban en un túnel; en realidad, era una sensación entrecortada, pues se abría dentro de un instants, pero donde los fragmentos y la totalidad coincidían en ese pestañeo de la visión cortada por una espada.

The momentary spell makes Rialta feel her solitude even more intensely than usual, and she buries her face in her arms and cries. The spell is broken and the children scurry off.

The geometric progression from a square to a circle also appears during the sexual encounters of some of the other characters in the novel. It is used to convey the attempted movement from inner confusion to inner unity, or the movement from a pluralistic to a unified state. The sexual act becomes then one of many manifestations of the search for meaning in life and the control over chaos. Its appearance in the novel is mainly associated with friends and acquaintances of José during their adolescence. Two of José's closest friends during this period of his life are Fronesis and Foción, and the circle image appears in their lives as they struggle to free themselves from some fear or obsession.

Fronesis has difficulty having sexual intercourse with a young girl during one of his first exposures to sex. His inability to function adequately is related to some vague and illogical fear that he cannot express, or even bring to the awareness of his conscious mind. He resorts to a tactic that restores his virility. He cuts a circle of cloth from his undershirt; then, in this round piece of material he cuts a hole large enough for his penis and uses the piece of undershirt as an intermediary between his body and his partner's. When Fronesis leaves, he takes the shirt with him, and its presence constitutes a heavy psychological burden for him. He walks down to the sea wall that surrounds Havana, throws the undershirt into the sea, and watches it slowly disappear:

> La camiseta misma antes de anegarse, se fue

circulizando como una serpiente a la que alguien ha trasmitido la inmortalidad, pero al mismo tiempo en las concavidades gordezuelas del cuerpo del hombre fue apareciendo la serpiente fálica, era necesario crear al perder precisamente la inmortalidad. Así el hombre fue mortal, pero creador y la serpiente fálica se convirtió en un fragmento que debe resurgir. Fronesis sentía que los dos círculos de la camiseta al desaparecer en el oleaje, desaparecerían también de sus terrores para dar paso a la serpiente circuncidada. Desaparecían las dos abstracciones circulares, también desaparecían los yerbazales, las escoriaciones, los brotes musgosos, donde el nuevo serpentín del octavo día se trocaba en un honguillo con una pequeña corona planetaria en torno al glande de un marfil coloidal.

Fronesis has used the circle as a means of dominating and bringing under control psychic forces that threatened to destroy his masculinity. He experiences a fear of losing his identity by associating the sexual act, which can lead to a momentary loss of identity, with death. He successfully dominated these fears and is now ready to sublimate and direct them toward creative ends. He has imposed form on psychic chaos and has brought negative forces under control by the image of the circle. This enables him to begin the transition from adolescence to manhood and from potentiality to creativity.

Foción, José's other friend, is confronted with a problem similar to Fronesis's, but in his case it occurs after he has married. Foción proves impotent, and his father's ill-directed efforts to help him cause him to be influenced by a homosexual. As a result, Foción becomes a participant and exponent of this sexual practice. Fronesis explains much of Foción's background to José, "Foción tenía, por el abstracto desarrollo de su niñez y adolescencia, el complejo de la vagina dentada, veía la vulva de la mujer como una inmensa boca que le devoraba el falo." Foción's sexual orientation is presented as a chaos that he cannot dominate, "pues la naturaleza le regaló un caos pero no le dio la fuerza suficiente para luchar contra él. Se siente destruido, pero no tiene fuerza destructora."

Foción becomes, in effect, a symbol of primordial chaos, and his bisexual activities reveal the anarchy that precedes the organization of all creative forces. This is the basic meaning of the homosexual theme in *Paradiso,* for Foción's activities are a symbol of all the forces of the creative process. His anguish conveys the turmoil and confusion of formlessness, and his struggle to move from this state represents the movement from anarchy to order. Therefore, the treatment of sexuality in *Paradiso* is not an affirmation or denial of any particular sexual activity. Rather, sexual acts are exterior manifestations of inner conflicts or goals and the means by which the characters resolve their problems. Lezama Lima employs the homosexual theme as another way of dealing with the creative process.

Foción is greatly attracted to Fronesis to the extent of obsession. "Fronesis era para él un arquetipo de lo inalcanzable, cosa que sólo existía porque comenzaba por ponerlo a horcajadas en un punto errante que oscilaba en un claroscuro inmenso." His attraction toward Fronesis eventually allows him to escape from his inner chaos. José recognizes that the friendship between Foción and Fronesis is related to Foción's attempts to escape from his state of confusion and tells Fronesis, "Es un caos, el de Foción, que tú dominas, ordenas, distribuyes. Es un caos que tú necesitas para las hogueras de tu cosmos." Cemí's statements reveal that Fronesis has gained control over his own chaos, whereas Foción has not. Yet, Fronesis needs Foción in the sense that his own creative acts represent his imposition of form over the chaos that Foción represents.

Fronesis's father attempts to terminate his son's relationship with Foción. It is an effort that nearly provokes a rebellion in Fronesis, but his stepmother resolves the conflict between father and son. For the first time in her life, Fronesis's stepmother speaks freely of Fronesis's mother, who was her sister. This frank appraisal of origins restores harmony to the family, and Fronesis agrees to take a trip abroad.

This episode is followed immediately by one in which José visits a clinic where his grandmother, doña Augusta, is dying. While at the clinic, he discovers that Foción is a patient there:

> Al lado del álamo, en el jardín del pabellón de los desrazonados, vio un hombre joven con su uniforme blanco, describiendo incesantes círculos alrededor del álamo agrandado por una raíz cuidada. Era Foción. Volvía en sus círculos una y otra vez como si el álamo fuera su Dios y su destino. . . . La enorme cuantía de círculos que sumaba durante el día, la abría en espirales, tan sumergidos como silenciosos, mientras la nocturna lo acogía.

José concludes that the tree represents Fronesis. The next time he returns to the clinic, he discovers that a bolt of lightning has destroyed the tree and that Foción has disappeared. "El rayo que había destruido el árbol había liberado a Foción de la adoración de su eternidad circular."

The tree is a dual image. On the one hand, it represents Foción's obsession with Fronesis, and, on the other, it could represent the tree of life that embodies all the positive and negative aspects of existence. Foción's incessant circling of the tree reveals his attempts to control the chaos in his life and, by extension, to resolve the enigma of existence. It is

significant that the circle image is combined with the spiral, for the spiral indicates evolution, growth, and the movement from multiplicity to unity. Foción's motion is circular and spiral, suggesting a progression toward a solution to his problems. The bolt of lightning that releases Foción indicates the sudden gaining of an illumination and insight that frees him from his obsessive anguish.

Of all the characters in the novel, Foción represents, more than any other, multiplicity and chaos. His sexual activities are indicative of the disunity and formlessness that precede ordered creativity. His tumultuous emotions are like a primordial chaos, the earliest stage of disorganized creation. There is much in the novel to suggest that Lezama Lima regards the creative impulse as one of the underlying principles of existence.

The friendship that exists between Foción, Fronesis, and José is related in many ways to creativity. To a certain extent, it is possible to regard each one as a separate phase of the creative process. Foción represents primordial chaos, Fronesis the most elemental imposition of order on formlessness, and José the observation and refinement of the first two phases. When José visits his dying grandmother in the clinic, she comments on his ability to observe and remember "impresiones":

> Tu memoria les da una substancia como el limo de los comienzos, como una piedra que recogiese la imagen de la sombra del pez. Tú hablas del ritmo de crecimiento de la naturaleza, pero hay que tener mucha humildad para poder observarlo, seguirlo y reverenciarlo . . . la mayoría de las personas interrumpen, favorecen el vacío, hacen exclamaciones, torpes exigencias o declaman arias fantasmales, pero tú observas ese ritmo que hace el cumplimiento, el cumplimiento de lo que desconocemos. . . .

This conversation takes place immediately after Fronesis's decision to terminate his relationship with Foción and just prior to Foción's liberation from his obsession with Fronesis. After these events, Fronesis and Foción no longer appear in the novel, and José moves toward a fuller comprehension of his direction in life. A particular phase in José's development has ended, and he moves to another. Fronesis and Foción, having served as points of reference on his journey, now fade into the past as José's life embarks on a new path.

There are two other characters in *Paradiso* who have a decisive influence on José and his commitment to creativity. They are his Uncle Alberto and the shadowy and mysterious Oppiano Licario. Alberto resembles the Colonel, in that he is a strong-willed and assertive individual who is a picture of strength. On one occasion, he sends a letter to the family, and one of José's relatives invites José to listen to it,

> acércate más para que puedas oir bien la carta de tu tío Alberto, para que lo conozcas más y le adivines la alegría que tiene. Por primera vez vas a oir el idioma hecho naturaleza, con todo su artificio de alusiones y cariñosas pedanterías.

Although José does not display any reaction, the letter greatly impresses him and introduces him to the potentialities of language.

Alberto dies suddenly in an automobile accident, and his death, like the Colonel's, causes shock and consternation. It is hard for those who are left behind to comprehend why such young and active individuals should die suddenly. However, although the significance of death is not revealed, there are suggestions that it has meaning within a larger context that is unknown to the participants. In the last two chapters of the novel (13 and 14), Licario emerges as the central figure in José's reasoning of the enigma of death, for Licario knew Alberto and witnessed the death of the Colonel.

Death and time are the central concerns of the chapter that immediately precedes the reappearance of Licario. Chapter 12 represents an unusual flight of the imagination, for its contents are bizarre and, at first reading, much removed from the main content of the novel. There are four separate stories in the chapter, and they are presented in alternating segments that make it difficult for the reader to follow the sequence of events. The reader goes through the first segment of each story, and then the sequence repeats itself as the reader moves through the second part. The last three stories take place in Havana, but the first narration goes back to the exploits of the Roman general, Atrio Flaminio, in the second century B.C. The chapter begins with a specific historical orientation and moves to a highly imaginative realm. At the same time, however, the author moves his reader toward a consideration of time and eternity, and the separate stories converge on one point. Therefore, on one level he expands his reader's awareness, and, on the other, he focuses the attention on a certain problem of existence. In one of the stories, there is a vase that is broken into many fragments, reassembled, and later replaced. To a great extent, the vase parallels with what the author is doing in the chapter. He takes a subject, in this case, which is time, and breaks it down into several components or fragments and then rearranges them into a new form. Again, it is the process that is emphasized rather than the end result.

The first story narrates the exploits of Flaminio and his struggle and conquest over rational and irrational forces. His bearing depicts an open disdain for death. At one time, he announces to his troops, "Nada más que sabemos vencer,

desconocemos a la muerte, que tendrá que esforzarse hasta cansarse para reconocer a uno solo de nosotros." And his troops reply, "si se acerca la muerte la decapitaremos." Flaminio is the astute and courageous conqueror who lives so close to death that he seems to defeat it. His fondest wish is to die in battle, but he succumbs to an illness and loses the opportunity to die on his own terms.

In the second story, a small child breaks a large vase while he is cared for by his grandmother. The broken vase produces a great deal of concern, and the grandmother picks up the fragments and carefully puts them aside. The event is significant, and it is apparent that the vase is a symbol of wholeness and the integration of the morning of life (the child) with its evening (the grandmother). After the vase is broken, the child and the grandmother feel vaguely threatened, as if a unifying force in their lives has been destroyed. The child reappears in the third and fourth stories and serves as one of the several bridges that connect the four sections.

In the third story, an anonymous narrator relates his encounters with invisible forces in his home and the things he sees as he wanders through Havana. This section of the chapter conveys, better than any of the others, the mystery of existence and the secret working of forces that are only vaguely recognized. During one of his walks, he sees a man on a bench sewing. The man extracts an ivory egg from a stocking he is using, and he holds it up so it can be seen better. Soon after this, the narrator observes a sailor with a knife in his chest being removed from a bar.

The act of sewing could symbolize creation, as it is a process of accumulation and growth; and the egg, the mystery of life or the egg of the world. They are symbols of positive forces that are under control. The egg is contained in a stocking, and sewing requires the mastery of the materials being used. The shape of the egg suggests an organized reality that can be grasped and understood, and, therefore, one that has established limits. The dying sailor, however, is the victim of a knife wound, indicating the unleashing of primary and instinctive forces that are destructive and not under control.

Although the phenomena observed are open to interpretation, it is clear that the narrator has come in contact with forces or laws that govern existence, and that a definite organization and order exist. The geometrical progression from a square to a circle is also present in this section and attests to the narrator's movement toward an apprehension of the keys of existence. During one of his walks, he sees a child within a circle, and he attempts to approach him, as he wishes to see his face. He fails and the child disappears. We later discover that this child, and the one that appears in the second story, are the same.

The fourth story concerns an aging music critic, Juan Longo, whose young wife tries to impede the effects the ravages of time have on her aged husband by putting him into a cataleptic trance. His wife places him in a glass urn and carefully watches over him. As the years pass, she slowly becomes insane and is obsessed with the preservation of her husband's body. Longo's colleagues become curious about what happened to him, and they visit his home. His wife partially revives him, enough so that he can babble some nonsense that is taken as profound pronouncements. The delegation of music critics leaves, and Longo's wife dispatches him back to the world of dreams. The delegation unexpectedly returns and becomes fully aware of what is transpiring, and a decision is made to place Longo on public display. He is regarded as the "gran vencedor del temporal" and "el burlador del tiempo." Sensational statements are made about his unusual feat, and people flock to see him.

At this point, the four stories begin to merge, for among those who come to see Longo is the anonymous narrator of the third story. When he peers into the crystal urn, however, he does not see Longo but the child in the second story. And when Longo's wife glances into the urn, she is shocked to see a Roman warrior who is, in effect, the Atrio Flaminio in the first story:

> Al poner su rostro en la urna, se oyó tal chillido, que bastó también para astillar la noche y hacer que la cuidadora del sueño infinitamente extensivo descendiese al tenebroso Erebo. ¿Qué vio al asomarse a la urna? El rostro de un guerrero romano, crispado en un gesto de infinita desesperación, tratando de alcanzar con sus manos la capa, las botas, la espada de los legionarios que pasaban para combatir en lejanas tierras. El rostro revelaba una acometividad gimiente e impotente, lloraba por la desesperación de no poder sumergirse en el fuego de la batalla. En su lecho de paja, el rostro encendido por la piedra, cuando había jurado el devenir y las alas de las tropas transportadas hacia las pruebas de la lejanía, sentía que la sangre se negaba a obedecerle y se le enredaba en el rostro, formando falsos círculos negados a la movilidad. En lugar de un crítico musical, rendido al sueño para vencer el tiempo, el rostro de un general romano que gemía inmovilizado al borrarse para él la posibilidad de alcanzar la muerte en el remolino de las batallas.

Longo's wife begins to scream and disturbs him in his trance, causing him to die.

> Ya el crítico percibe las gotas de lo temporal, pero no como el resto de los mortales, pues la muerte, no el sueño, comienza a regalarle, ahora sí de verdad, lo eterno, donde ya el tiempo no se deja vencer, ha comenzado por no existir ese pecado.

Atrio Flaminio, Juan Longo, and the child represent different aspects of time. Flaminio is the past; Longo is the present; and the child is the future. They all die, but it is important to realize that death is presented as a means of passing from the realm of the temporal to the realm of the eternal. The temporal is an imperfect world ruled by change or time. Flaminio and Longo's wife attempt to control time by either suspending it or dictating how it should flow. Their error is in trying to control a realm ruled by change, and their attempts only result in the perpetuation of imperfection. Flaminio becomes a victim of suspended imperfection, encased in a moment that can only produce frustration. And Longo's victory over time is only an illusion that is easily destroyed by the disharmonic intrusion of reality. Their attempts to attain perfection in a realm of imperfection are doomed to failure, for they mistakenly regard death as their enemy, when in reality it is their passport to eternity. And eternity represents a realm in which time and imperfection do not exist. They have wronged in attempting to suspend the process of becoming, for it is a course that must be experienced on the road to being.

Chapter 12 ends with a vignette that is not directly related to any of the prior content in the chapter. The sketch is open to interpretation, but it is related to the creative process. Two centurions arrive at the ruins of a Christian temple, which was built over the remnants of an academy for pagan philosophers. They plan to entertain themselves with a game of dice. As they prepare to play, a bust of a geometrician holding a compass falls from one of the decaying walls. They pick up the bust and casually throw it aside, and it becomes wedged in an iron support that holds up the railing of a cupola. They begin to play with the dice, and the first numbers that appear are a two and a three. At this point, the bust of the geometrician falls again, and the point of the compass strikes a die showing the number three, causing the die to tumble over by the other one and both now show the number two. "El cuatro aportado por los dos dados, uno al lado del otro, como si las dos superficies hubiesen unido sus aguas." The two centurions cover themselves with a single cape, leave, and the sketch ends.

The numbers used in the vignette have symbolic meaning and most likely refer to the artistic organization of reality. The compass itself is symbolic of the creative process because it is the instrument with which circles are drawn. The number two most likely stands for duality or separateness, whereas the three denotes synthesis and unity. The creative act breaks down an image into its diverse parts and rearranges the different components into a new form. The unity symbolized by three is destroyed by the compass, and the formation of the four indicates the orderly arrangement of a new form. Therefore, a chapter that deals with man's war against time and his thirst for eternity ends with affirmation of the creative process. It can be surmised that daily and continual change is related to an overall process of creation. Birth and death, growth and decay are only aspects of this process, and man can live his life to its fullest by his own creativity. The essence of life then is to create rather than to preserve what was.

Chapter 12 brings into consideration questions concerning the structure of *Paradiso*, for the contents in this chapter are well removed from the main development of the novel. For the most part, *Paradiso* follows a traditional chronological approach and demonstrates great cohesiveness as it explores the Cemí's family tree. However, José's life has little to do with Atrio Flaminio or any of the other characters who appear in Chapter 12. Nevertheless, the chapter's theme can be related to the development of José's appreciation of time and death and his concern with creativity. These matters are presented as being common to all men at all times, and Lezama Lima succeeds in presenting a universal view that is valid in any setting. The chapter also serves as a good example of a technique used throughout the novel. The author begins with widely dispersed factors and unites them into a cohesive whole. He takes characters and events that are separated in time and space and telescopes them into a unified view of reality. As a result, the reader experiences a movement from multiplicity to unity as the fragments of the mosaic swirl into place.

The same technique is used in the presentation of Chapter 13. A disabled bus in Havana is the setting for the introduction of a number of people of diverse interests and backgrounds, and it serves as an ideal site for chance encounters. One of the persons that boards the bus is an old coin collector who turns out to be Licario. During a conversation in the bus, Licario states, "la vida es una red de situaciones indeterminadas, cada coincidencia es algo que quiere hablar a nuestro lado, si la interpretamos incorporamos una forma, dominamos una transparencia." Although life is viewed as a series of chance occurrences, it is asserted that it has form and can be understood. There is system and order in the apparent chaos of life that is accessible to those who will observe and reflect on what they see.

Shortly after the above statement is made, José boards the bus, and Licario notices the initials "J.C." on his wrist. Licario recognizes José as a descendant of the Colonel and concludes that he "ya no se moriría intranquilo, incompleto. Se había verificado el signo que le permitiría recorrer su último camino, con expresión para su pasado y con esclarecimiento para su futuridad." José, of course, does not know Licario, but fate brings them into contact. One of the passengers, Martincillo, picks Licario's pocket only to discover that he has stolen some ancient coins. Not knowing what to do with them, he decides to put them in another passenger's pocket. José witnesses the whole operation, takes the coins from the passenger, and returns them to Licario.

The following day José notices a note in his pocket from Licario. Licario thanks José for returning the coins, invites him to visit, and explains past events that link Licario to José's family:

> Conocí a su tío Alberto, vi morir a su padre. Hace veinte años del primer encuentro, diez del segundo, tiempo de ambos sucedidos importantísimos para usted y para mí, en que se engendró la causal de las variaciones que terminan en el infierno de un ómnibus, con su gesto que cierra un círculo. En la sombra de ese círculo ya yo me puedo morir.

The purpose of Licarió's life is closely linked to the destiny of the Cemí family. Having witnessed the death of the Colonel, he now has the opportunity to participate in José's development from adolescence to manhood. Since he knew Alberto, he is also aware of the great talent that was lost to the family by Alberto's untimely death, and he is greatly relieved to be in a position to preside over José's emergence into a full awareness of creativity. Vital creative forces that have been momentarily suspended by death are about to surface, and Licario feels that his destiny is to be fulfilled.

José enters Licario's apartment building and is "mistakenly" taken to the seventh floor by an elevator operator. As he is walking down the corridor, he runs his hand along the wall, an act that reminds the reader of José's episode with a piece of chalk in Chapter 2. He stops and looks out of a window and sees Licario several floors below. Licario is with some of the people who were on the bus, and they are involved in a strange game involving many of the arts. It is a scene of great diversity and confusion. For example, Martincillo, the pickpocket of the earlier part of the chapter, is present and is using a piccolo to poke a crab that is howling like a dog. Licario is presiding over the whole affair as he strikes a bronze triangle and exclaims "estilo sistàltico." The elevator operator says he has made a mistake and that Licario lives downstairs. They descend to the lowest floor, and Licario opens his door before José has a chance to ring and gives the impression he has been waiting for him. None of the individuals José had seen from the seventh floor are there, and, except for a table and the triangle Licario had been striking, everything is different.

> Oppiano Licario presentaba un pantaleón negro y una camisa muy blanca. Mientras se prolongaba la vibración exclamó:—Estilo hesicàstico." Cemí replies, "Veo, señor . . . que usted mantiene la tradición del *ethos* musical de los pitagóricos, los acompañamientos musicales del culto de Dionisos." Licario immediately comments, "Veo . . . que ha pasado del estilo sistàltico, o de las pasiones tumultuosas, al estilo hesicàstico, o del equilibrio anímico, en muy breve tiempo.

The episode conveys a movement from chaos to order and from diversity to unity. The reference to Dionysos is significant, as it is a deity that represents the unleashing of uncontrollable and immense creative energy. This explains Licario's use of the term "estilo sistàltico" during the ritual and his later reference to it as a symbol of "las pasiones tumultuosas." His "estilo hesicástico" refers to order and psychic equilibrium. José has gained control over his inner passions and is now capable of imposing order on chaos. He has, therefore, escaped from the dangers of self-annihilation and dissolution and can now affirm life and existence. This is the symbolism of the white shirt and black trousers, for they are symbols of the positive and negative. Black represents the chaos that precedes organized creativity, that is, the initial stage of the creative process. And white can be the purification of these forces through the imposition of guidance and form. The two colors form a duality in which white (the shirt) is the upper and superior force. Now that this equilibrium has been attained, José is ready to embark on his own career, and Licario ends the chapter with the comment "Entonces, podemos ya empezar."

Licario is a very important factor in José's development, as he connects both José's past and future. His acquaintance with the Colonel and Alberto represents an appreciation of the past that operates as a kind of self-knowledge for José, and his understanding of the creative process helps José to become more fully aware of the potentialities that the future can hold for him. A section of the last chapter in *Paradiso* is devoted to Licario's past, once again reflecting Lezama Lima's approach to the novel by examining the past so that an appreciation of the present can be gained. Reading *Paradiso* is like tracing the paths left by several spirals as they wander and swirl through space and slowly converge to form a circle. To a certain extent, Licario represents knowledge of the past in a cultural and historical sense and, therefore, is endowed with the aura of mystery and authority that such wisdom imparts.

> **Reading *Paradiso* is like tracing the paths left by several spirals as they wander and swirl through space and slowly converge to form a circle.**
>
> —*Raymond D. Souza*

Near the end of the novel, José takes a nocturnal walk. His strolling in the night is an allegory of his attempts to penetrate the mysteries of life. The enigmas of existence are presented as a challenge that must be answered and struggled against, for they are riddles that can only be unraveled by great effort. Much of what happens to José during his walk parallels the call to adventure, which is an integral part of the presentation of the hero archetype. José feels that some strange force is compelling him to struggle against the night, and he senses that he is being called to accomplish some feat:

> Cemí siguió avanzando en la noche que se espesa, sintiendo que tenía que hacer cada vez más esfuerzo para penetrarla. Cada vez que daba un paso le parecía que tenía que extraer los pies de una tembladera. La noche se hacía cada vez más resistente, como si desconfiase del gran bloque de luz y de la musiquilla del tiovivo. Le pareció ver un bosque, donde los àrboles trepaban unos sobre otros, como el elefante apoyando las dos patas delanteras sobre una banqueta, y sobre el lomo del elefante perros y monos danzando, persiguiendo una pelota, o saltando sobre un ramaje, para caer de nuevo sobre el elefante. La transición de un parque infantil a un bosque era invisiblemente asimilado por Cemí, pues su estado de alucinación mantenía en pie todas las posibilidades de la imagen. No obstante sintió como un llamado, como si alguien hubiese comenzado a cantar, o un nadador que después de unir sus brazos en un triángulo isósceles se lanza a la piscina, más allá de la empalizada. Era un ruido inaudible, la paràbola de una pistola de agua, una gaviota que se duerme mecida por el oleaje, algo que separa la noche del resto de una inmensa tela, o algo que prolonga la noche en una tela agujereada por donde asoman su cabeza de clavo unos carretes de ebonita. Era un pie de buey lo que pisaba a la noche.

The ox is usually a symbol of cosmic forces, and apparently it is used in this context in the above quotation. José is moving into a state in which his awareness of these entities is expanding. The process of becoming is greatly accelerated, and an apprehension of being is more accessible to him. The reference to "todas las posibilidades de la imagen" is important, because it indicates that the poetic image can become a challenge that must be approached with a keen sense of intuition combined with the force and strength of intellectual discipline. Lezama Lima gives the impression that these are the implements that are necessary to gain insight into existence, and that this process is re-created every time one approaches a poetic image. The poet then becomes a leading exponent and glorifier of life, continually challenging his listeners to participate fully in it by increasing and expanding their own awareness.

José continues to move through the night, and among the many things he sees is a mosaic of the Holy Grail located in the center of a circle formed by King Arthur's knights. This is another example of the circle image in the novel, for the quest for the Grail represents the search for the mystic center. José's wanderings finally lead him into a room where a wake is in progress and Licario's sister is waiting for him. Licario has died and as José contemplates the significance of this event, memories of his father and other members of the family come to him. Licario's sister hands him a poem that Licario wrote shortly before dying.

The poem concerns Licario's impending death and its significance to José. It expresses belief in an existence after death and affirms the importance of the spiritual in man's life. The last line reads, "Vi morir a tu padre; ahora, Cemí, tropieza." José is confronted by life's greatest enigma—death—with a poem written by Licario. The word re-creates the enigma of life and also indicates that José's time of trial and tribulation is at hand. Both his father and Licario are dead, and he must now make his own way in the world. However, he is armed with a basic understanding of life's challenges and a definite sense of belonging as he feels that he is part of a tradition formed by those who came before him. José has been bequeathed the most precious of gifts, a spiritual inheritance.

José leaves the wake and stops for a drink in a coffee shop. He begins to idly tap his glass with a spoon, and the sound reminds him of Licario saying "ritmo hesicástico, podemos empezar." With these words the novel ends, marking José's emergence from adolescence and his readiness to venture into the world. One cycle has drawn to a close and another begins.

*Paradiso* is a remarkable novel, complex, and difficult but extremely rewarding to the reader who expends the effort the novel demands. The world that Lezama Lima creates and his unique way of viewing it leaves an impression that lingers indefinitely, and with the passage of time the novel's magneticism has a persuasive influence on the reader. The world is not quite as terrifying after having read *Paradiso,* for the novel encourages its reader to see life in its totality. And the view that emerges from this perspective is one of cohesiveness in which there is meaning and purpose. In this respect, Lezama Lima's outlook is not unlike Carpentier's, as both present a panorama that captures essential truths of human existence. Both are very much aware of the vast cultural currents that are operating in human society and of the debt that each individual owes to the past. And both tend to view history as a struggle against formlessness in which man continually battles to impose order on chaos.

However, their emphasis is quite different, for Lezama Lima considers how all these forces focus on the individual, whereas Carpentier's concern is to integrate the individual into the currents that engulf him. The individual is much more a master of his fate in Lezama Lima's view than in Carpentier's. All of the characters in *El siglo de las luces,* even the formidable Víctor Hugues, are dominated and swept along by the forces operating around them. The characters in *Paradiso,* on the other hand, discover that true freedom involves the control of one's own inner passions, and that they are victims of themselves as much as by exterior forces. Carpentier's characters struggle to transcend themselves by attempting to create a more perfect social order and world. Lezama Lima's search for an adequate expression of their creative impulse and their integration with life is seen as a celebration of the creative act. Creativity and its relation to time and eternity is a main theme of *Paradiso.*

The two writers show intellectual discipline in their writings and control their creations. Lezama Lima is more imaginative, and his language is more suggestive than Carpentier's. Conversely, Carpentier's control of form is more polished than Lezama Lima's, and it is unlikely that Carpentier would ever have included a chapter such as *Paradiso*'s Chapter 12 into his works.

Lezama Lima's imagery tends to weaken the structure of his novel at times and would involve him in difficulties were it not for his remarkable control. *Paradiso* contains indications, however, of a development toward a free use of creative language at the expense of novelistic structure. The control he exercises over the creative process enables him to present his reader with a fairly uniform creation. It is not as cohesive a product as Carpentier's, but it is considerably more structured than Cabrera Infante's *Tres tristes tigres,* which was published one year later in 1967.

*Paradiso* and *El siglo de las luces* explore the workings of time in the historical process and the human psyche, and both works consider chaos to be a definite threat to human existence. It is fair to surmise that both authors are fascinated with, yet somewhat threatened by, the diffusion that chaos represents. Carpentier sees this breakdown of order as part of a cyclical pattern that creates and destroys a countless number of social forms. For Lezama Lima, the process is related to the creative impulse, but one senses a resistance to the destruction of a creative entity once it has come into being. In some respects, the baroque nature of their art seems to be a way of resisting the destructive diffusion caused by the flow of time, an intricate series of bulwarks that guard against the penetration of time's erosive forces. Carpentier finds solace in man's collective unconscious and Lezama Lima in the hermetic image. They both look to the past with nostalgia, when there existed a freshness of spiritual and psychic energy that has become more diffuse and weakened with time.

Although *El siglo de las luces* and *Paradiso* do not focus on the contemporary period, their struggles against formlessness reflect some of the basic dilemmas of the present, an era haunted by the specter of complete and total disintegration. It remains to be seen whether man's need for constraints can be balanced with his desire for complete freedom and self-expression. A degree of control is necessary for the orderly progress of humanity and the conservation of a sense of decency, but it can easily degenerate into cruel and stifling repression as in the case of Víctor Hugues. Personal and collective freedom are desirable goals, but it is difficult to ascertain where freedom ends and chaos begins. Foción's avowals of sexual freedom bring him to the brink of chaos and self-destruction, and Sofía's unrestrained desire to transcend the inequities of a social order results in the senseless deaths of Esteban and herself.

There has been a gradual breakdown of form in all the arts in the twentieth century, and in the novel the constraints of structure are weakened by the impulse of creative language. Signs of the beginning of this transition are seen in the novels under discussion in the movement from the presentation of chaos merely as the thematic content of a work to its incorporation into the artistic fabric of a novel. Carpentier considers the problems of formlessness by using them as a major part of the content of his work in his study of the revolutionary process. Formlessness is also a topic in Lezama Lima's novel, but in addition it finds expression in images and becomes partially incorporated into the novel's form.

Cabrera Infante's *Tres tristes tigres* represents an almost complete embodiment of formlessness into the very language and structure of the novel. This novel creates a world that seems chaotic and without any apparent form, a universe ruled by chance. I will attempt to ascertain whether its chaos is absolute or if there is a new order being created from the ashes of the old.

## Margarita Fazzolari (essay date May-August 1981)

SOURCE: "Reader's Guide to *Paradiso*," in *Review*, No. 29, May-August, 1981, pp. 47-54.

[*In the following essay, Fazzolari discusses the sequential development of* Paradiso's *storyline, focusing on Lezama Lima's use of a "poetic system" that utilizes metaphorical images and language, and symbolic characters and events.*]

*The Beginnings*

José Lezama Lima, the outstanding writer to appear in Cuba in this century, began his career as a founder of literary magazines. *Verbum, Espuela de Plata* (Silver Spur), *Nadie Parecía* (No One Appeared), and *Orígenes* (Origins) form a chain of magazines that rescued Cuba from aesthetic mediocrity and attracted the best Cuban talent of the period—in literature, art, and music—while at the same time introducing the public to the most significant innovations occurring in the arts

and letters of the rest of the continent and Europe. *Orígenes*, which enjoyed the greatest prestige and the longest life, gave its name to the two generations of Cuban authors who gathered around Lezama's editorial ventures. These magazines also carried his first works. *Verbum* published Lezama's first poem, **"Muerte de Narcisco" ("Death of Narcissus")**, which already manifests one of the poet's great obsessions, the Fall. Veiled in precious and enigmatic expressions, the perfect and spiritual man of the poem's first lines loses his homogeneity and acquires a body. Fall and materialization lead to time, sex, sickness and death, provoking a devastating anguish only consoled in artistic creation.

This theme and its accompanying anguish persist in *Enemigo rumor (Hostile Murmurs)*, Lezama's first poetry collection, which introduces his other two basic themes: resurrection and the *felix culpa* or fortunate sin, the two experiences that reconcile the poet with the world and its horrors and lead him to see the unity of the opposites good and evil, light and shadow, fall and resurrection. Artistic creation, which had been a consolation, now becomes a way to salvation as well.

In *Aventuras sigilosas (Quiet Adventures)*, his second volume of poetry, Lezama presents a kind of poetic autobiography, almost a novel, with a plot, personification of abstract principles, conflict, confessions, dialogue, and action. This poetic cycle prefigures *Paradiso*. The fictionalization undergone by the metaphors of *Aventuras sigilosas* suggested to Lezama his two novels about the apprenticeship of the poet—*Paradiso* and *Oppiano Licario* the first dealing with the family and life experiences that lead the poet to poetry, and the second, with the poet's learning of his craft.

The last prose poem of *Aventuras sigilosas* initiates a new project for Lezama, the search for a "poetic system" that claims to explain the universe through poetry and such poetic elements as the image and the metaphor. This system is developed most completely in the essays of *Analecta del reloj (Clock Analect)*, *Tratados en la Habana (Havana Treatises)*, and *La cantidad hechizada (The Enchanted Quantity)*. For its part, *La expresión americana (American Expression)* proposes an interesting theory of artistic expression in Latin America, praising the baroque as the most authentic and original style for the continent, triumphant over other styles and even over the European baroque. In two other collections, *La fijeza (Fixity)* and *Dador (Giver)*, appear some of Lezama's best poems, such as **"Arco invisible de Viñales" ("The Invisible Arch of Viñales")** and **"Para llegar a Montego Bay" ("The Approach to Montego Bay")**, whose hermeticism is matched by the brilliance and abundance of their metaphors. In his posthumous book, *Fragmentos a su imán (Magnet Fragments)*, Lezama returns to the simplicity and anguish of the poetry which he left behind with *Enemigo rumor*.

## The Paschal Lamb

**Paradiso** is, as we said before, an apprenticeship novel. Here we can find the family, life, and expressive circumstances that surround the child and form the poet. The innocent family stories recounted in the first half of the novel conceal a symbolic foundation beneath their relative simplicity, while the symbolism is much more obvious in the complexity of the second half.

José Cemí, gasping with asthma, his small body covered with a rash, is the first image we see. Subjected to a brutal cure and a cabalistic exorcism by Baldovina and two other servants, he awakes the next day completely restored. The two illnesses set the future poet apart from infancy. His asthma indicates a subtle sensibility, a breathing that seeks wider spaces, as if struggling to keep time with a far-away rhythm that only the poet can perceive, the rhythm of the universe. This struggle will translate into an ever-greater opening out of his life, first from the family circle to the world, in his school and university years, and then, when he becomes a poet, to the stars. The rhythm imposed by asthma will mark his poetry as well. From his first article, Lezama used skin as an emblem for poetic sensibility. On several occasions thereafter, he said that "the forces of attraction between men and things do not take hold between one pore and another, but between the pores and the stars." Hence, the delicate yet tough skin of the child prefigures communion with the stars. The spell cast by the three servants, an allegory of the trinity, confirms the transcendental meaning of the illness, which can only be cured by a sacred rite. The greatest significance of asthma lies, however, in the death and rebirth of the child in each attack, a process that forces on him the poetic rhythm *par excellence:* for Lezama, poetry is "the image of a resurrection that man can achieve."

Food, as corporeal and spiritual nourishment, also possesses a significance that transcends the trivial plot. Culinary conflict conceals a struggle between the forces of tradition, represented by Rialta and doña Augusta, Cemí's mother and grandmother, and the forces of innovation, headed by the cook, Juan Izquierdo. Colonel Cemí, arbitrator of the conflict, solves it by appealing to the memory of José's Basque grandfather, in the moment in which the old man took symbolic possession of his new homeland, until then obstinately rejected. The drama unfolds under a poinciana tree:

> Beneath those intermingled reds and greens a lamb
> was sleeping. The perfection of his sleep extended
> throughout the valley, led by the spirit of the lake.
> Sleep made me stumble and trip, obliging me to look
> around to find a resting place. Motionless, the lamb
> seemed to be dreaming the tree. I lay on his stom-
> ach, which moved as if creating a rhythm favorable
> to the waves of the dream. I slept the whole day long.

> When I got back, the family was searching for me,
> trying to follow my tracks, but all marks had been
> wiped out.

The lamb-symbol is obviously derived from Christianity, and the dream indicates a time different from human time, a time of origins, that belongs to the divine order. The Colonel, inspired by his Father, rehires Juan Izquierdo. Thus, the child is able to learn from the strictness and perfectionism of his grandmother, the creative innovation of the cook, and his father's flexibility in taking the best from each.

The grandfather episode serves as one of the corner-stones of the novel, for it takes place at the *axis mundi*, a sacred place where an overlapping of levels makes communication possible between earth, heaven, and hell. In the first part of **Paradiso,** the *axis mundi* takes the form of José Cemí's family tree, where the terrestrial element—the strong trunk—is represented in the Basque grandfather, the celestial element in the mother and the infernal element in Uncle Alberto.

## American Expression

In the second chapter, Cemí learns the lessons of the language of the people and explores the by-ways of "American expression." The "slum rooming-house" episode satirizes the literary world of Havana, setting it on a carnival stage across which parades a long line of picturesque characters. The piece of chalk symbolizes Cemí's poetic destiny: the child's arrival causes the scandal and disturbance that Lezama's own arrival must have caused in the Cuban literary scene, and the accusation made against him: "Here he is, the fellow who deprived us of a clock" alludes to the atemporal, hermetic, religious quality of his writing.

As part of "American expression," Lezama allegorizes the baroque, "America's first master," split into the figures of Tránquilo and Luba. While the former cleans a cut-glass lamp at the top of a stairway, the latter, teetering on a bench, scrubs vigorously at a mirror whose frame is decorated with tropical vegetation. The two reflect the vertical and horizontal movements which, according to Orozco, work together to balance the baroque: the ascending line or yearning for infinity which kindled the Counter Reformation, and the horizontal path, the curiosity about humanity and nature, dating from the Renaissance. Nevertheless, this is a European balance; in America it breaks down, to be reorganized and replaced by a new unity. As the author of **La expresión americana** puts it: "First, there is a tension in the baroque; secondly, a Plutonism, an originating fire that breaks the fragments apart and reunites them." The tension emerges between Luba's aggressivity and Tránquilo's elusiveness; the Plutonism, in the resulting disorder and damage, expressed with Lezama's usual stylistic brilliance:

Suddenly the unstable balance between Tránquilo's cautious ascent and Luba's fierce and jolly horizontal expansion was lost. The lamp fell, shattering on the top of the ladder, and simultaneously the animals and plants in the mirror frame, liberated from the bombardment of paper and alcohol, recovered their lost natural aspect and primal temperament.

The strange alloy that results is broken by Captain Viole's satirical tirade, in which he reproaches Tránquilo for his magical powers and his unorthodox method of taming horses. Tránquilo symbolizes the poet, as he spends his days on horseback drinking in the sun and his nights absorbing dew:

> His nocturnal porous opening up caused distance and starriness to reach into his marrow, giving him a secret and silent security.

Tránquilo works as a horse-breaker because, for Lezama, the "winged horse" is the emblem of poetry, tamed by an unlikely method that ends "with a soft copulative violence."

In contrast to Tránquilo's absorbent pores, the skin of Doctor Copek, who forms part of the staff sent with Colonel Cemí to Jamaica, rejects the sun and prevents it from penetrating to his bones. This rejection leads to a tragicomic episode in which the Doctor is possessed by a roguish divinity who lodges in his left armpit, from where he can be expelled only with a magic rite. Lezama has been accused of racial prejudice for introducing black culture in this way; but the main thrust of the satire here is directed against Doctor Copek's extremely white skin. If black odors are seen as a capricious demon, the excessive whiteness of the Doctor's skin, his inability to absorb the sun's rays, betray a lack of sensibility. Here there is neither white nor black racism, but rather allegoric necessity.

Indian expression—in the Colonel's trip to Mexico—is chthonian, subterranean, and diabolic; here the devil of the Christian tradition forms an alliance with the lords of Xibalbá, from the *Popul Vuh,* sacred book of the Maya. In a society of hidden, unshared pleasures, a Mexican diplomat keeps an enormous diamond in his watchcase; Taxco dancers conceal their faces behind masks assigned to each one from birth; and a blind man in Cuernavaca, who repeats "for the love of God" incessantly, whether or not anyone is passing by, seems "to be sitting there measuring the time of another eternity by a different standard." In this episode, the forces of light, personified by the Colonel, and those of darkness, symbolized by the Mexicans and Vivo (one of the Taxco dancers) lock into an allegorical struggle. Out of this conflict comes the above-mentioned Plutonism—"that breaks the fragments apart and reunites them"—forming the Mexican baroque, which attained such brilliance.

*Family History*

Chapters III and VII are dedicated to family history. This is the part that recalls Proust most strongly. Lezama has often been compared to Proust, not withstanding the fact that Proust recounts events which he has witnessed, while Lezama acts rather as listener to family stories, most of which took place before his birth, in order to retransmit the stories charged with symbolism to his readers.

While Proust tries to recapture a time once lived, with its accompanying sensations, and to fix it forever in his book, Lezama seeks to give his family's history, whether or not he witnessed it, a transcendent meaning. If, in doing this, he manages to write a magnificent chronicle of Cuban life at the turn of the century, so much the better.

During the War of Independence, Lezama's mother's family emigrated to Jacksonville, Florida. To this period belongs the vivid image of the child Rialta clinging to the topmost branches of a tree, reaching for an inaccessible nut. Second branch of the family-tree, Rialta puts it into communication with the sky. Rialta is a bridge to the divine:

> [she] stretched out along the branches that creaked loudest, to reach the aged shells filled with double concave foreheads, muzzling each other softly. . . . Suddenly the light began to pour in around her, safeguarding her once more in her secure earthly landing.

But the word used by Lezama, here translated as "landing," is neither "atterizaje" nor "caída," but "levitación"—"levitation"—the opposite of "descent." If the reader does not understand the role played by the little girl in the tree, the word "levitation" makes no sense nor will the other unlikely events which occur in this novel, which depends on symbolic meaning rather than verisimilitude.

The conversation between doña Augusta and Mr. Squabs, which follows, deals with willpower and illuminates one of the pillars of Lezama's poetic system—"oblique experience." The concept is based on the mysteries of the will as illustrated by this verse from Matthew's Gospel: "I reap where I sowed not, and I gather where I have not strewed." "Oblique experience" results when will is added to chance. Lezama has compared it to the act of a man who "flicks the light switch in his apartment and starts a waterfall in Ontario." Through connections that link things with no apparent relation, man can influence the supra-terrestrial world. But the gods are wilful: instead of lighting up our room, they may send us a waterfall, but in Ontario. Thus when doña Augusta asks Flery to describe the mouth of a canon on the evidence of his slippers, the girl replies without hesitation: "Small and very red." A poetic answer is thus extracted from a silly girl:

"Perhaps he wasn't like that," Augusta pondered, "but you can see now, Florita, how the act of giving those slippers produces miracles, so that your daughter can reconstruct his figure perhaps in the shape that the good canon wanted for the final appointment in the Valley of Jehoshaphat."

Lezama's verbal extravagance combined with his gift for observation deepens into metalanguage: this episode is riddled with comments on the magical power certain expressions have for the family. The verbal fertility overflows in the hermetic description of the orgies celebrated by Elpidio Michelena, the boss of Cemí's grandfather, Andrés Olaya. Out of the impenetrable obscurity emerges an impression of superabundant vitality, which is reflected, in its turn, by a superabundance of words. And behind the orgiastic vitality is the pathos of the death of Andresito, the first in a long chain of deaths in the novel: tragic and grotesque deaths, quiet and catastrophic deaths, expected and unexpected deaths, deaths that redeem and others that condemn; each different from the others and all part of the same death that leads to rebirth in light or darkness but always in accordance with the same fruitful mechanism.

The family history of Cemí's father parallels that of the country in its counterpoint between the Basque husband and the Creole wife, echoing the counterpoint of sugar and tobacco. This fragment reads like a poetic commentary on Fernando Ortiz' famous book, in which tobacco becomes the badge of the Indian and sugar-cane that of the Spanish conquistador:

> When your father packed us up and took us to the Central, he never imagined that he was ruining our whole family. We were used to the gentle labors of Vuelta Abajo, tobacco and honey. We had that refinement of inlanders devoted to the cultivation of the finest leaves and to divining the exterior signs of the insects in relation to the seasons. . . . One day the whole Méndez troupe arrived at Resolución from Pinar del Río, and those scandalous, foul-smelling expanses of green, those fields of vulgar cane, an effusion of nature to us who were used to a more varied panorama, at first disturbed us, but finally we succumbed to its overwhelming extent. Underneath it all lay the submission of my whole family to your father's brutal decision.

The response to doña Augusta's words about will-power can be found in the improbable dining-hall scene in José Eugenio's and Alberto's boarding school. The Director cuts the bread and throws the pieces at the students from his table, thus forcing them to concentrate on their work while remaining alert to whatever an unpredictable chance or grace might send them. This awareness of "the sudden" forms another pillar in Lezama's poetic system, complementary to "oblique experience." The "sudden" is the instantaneous achievement of poetic knowledge, comparable to Christian revelation or the concept of grace, or to Romantic inspiration.

Although the first half of *Paradiso* corresponds to innocence, this closed world potentially harbors both good and evil, light and darkness. These possibilities unfold in Chapter V, divided between José Eugenio who represents light and uncle Alberto who represents darkness. The process begins in the school toilets where Alberto has been sent as a punishment, with a hermetic, dream-like scene in which the boy feels the attraction of Angra Mainyu, the force of evil and darkness, the Ahriman of Persian dualism. Alberto escapes from the school and spends the night out in a series of adventures that add up to an initiation into hell:

> All around, those not under the infernal spell, those who rock their heads in the perfume of the blessed air, hear songs, the creaking of wheat carts. Only the furtive one, in the little hell of that neighborhood, hears the stony bell, the rotten clapper, the mosquitoes who scratch the stone to bite the archangelic horse of the blacksmith, its mouth full of fine sand.

These adventures include Alberto's sexual initiation by the girl with the cactus flower and his meeting with Oppiano Licario, the personification of poetry. The latter, however, is not named, for, although artistic creation results from the Fall and can be a way to salvation, Alberto's fate is already determined and there is no salvation for him.

### The Birth of the Image

Chapter VI, which begins with the celebration of the wedding of José Cemí's parents and ends with the Colonel's death, is full of anecdotes about the protagonist's childhood. Although the Colonel is frequently described as joyful and surrounded by a halo of clarity, the figure which emerges is neither as attractive nor as sympathetic as that of the demonic Alberto. The father is a strong man who strives for perfection and has little patience with the weaknesses of others, especially with that of his children. His lessons, his healing methods, and even his jokes are harsh and counter-productive to the point of cruelty, as in the episodes of the boat, the bathtub, the swimming pool, Demetrio, and the running joke of death behind the door. The Colonel only succeeds in terrorizing his entire family, including himself.

The boat episode prefigures the separation of death, and, indirectly, the break-up of the family. Julio Ortega has said that "the father's finger seems to repeat the gesture of God the Father giving form to Adam." The motifs of the finger and water multiply in Cemí's nightmares, and the boy seeks salvation first through the fish of Christianity and, later, through his mother. In this way, he is able to reconcile his own helplessness, his terror at his father's jokes, his illness, and his mother's role as intercessor. The answer lies in poetry:

> Then a broad fish swam up in ingenuous Christmas pinkness, moving its iridescent fins as if combing itself. The fish eyed the forsaken finger and laughed. Then it took the finger into its mouth and began to afford its protection. Towing him by the finger, it brought him to a patch of floating moss where the carefully calculated rhythm of his new breathing began. Then he no longer saw salvation in the fish, but instead his mother's face.

Here the pattern of **"Muerte de Narciso"** is repeated: separation, anguish, and salvation through poetry, the latter symbolized by "the carefully calculated rhythm of his new breathing." Another prophetic incident is the one of the grindstone and the student. The father shows the child two images, which the latter transposes; asked another day, "What is a student?", the boy answers with metaphors alluding to the grindstone, making his father marvel at "his son's rare gift of metaphor, his prophetic and symbolic way of understanding a profession." Prophetic and symbolic," Julio Ortega has commented:

> because, for Cemí, as his destiny unfolds, the opposition between the two images turns out to be false: he integrates them through language, thus replacing his father's didactic finger with his own transposing one.

At his father's death, José Cemí discovers his poetic vocation. From that moment on, he lives in the presence of an absence, his eyes alert to every appearance of the "image"—as Lezama calls the ineffable mysteries—and his ears sharpened for any expression—in Lezama's system, any "metaphor"—that can capture this image and embody it in round, solid words.

Thus "Image" and "metaphor" join the other two pillars of the poetic system, "the sudden" and "oblique experience." The "image" is a thread from the hidden and the invisible made palpable in "the sudden"; the "metaphor" is material things breaking their specific limits through "oblique experience" and making contact with the absent and invisible in such a way as to allow the "image" to show forth. Cemí receives his initiation into the secrets of the "image" and the "metaphor" in stages. The first stage is the game of jacks, a ritual in which the Colonel's image appears to his family, called up by the children's intense concentration, the presence of Rialta—bridge to the supernatural—and the sacred power of the home. Rialta, the children, the jacks, the ball, and the pavement serve as metaphors which, in a series of

changing combinations—squares, circles, vertical movements of the ball, horizontal hand gestures for sweeping up the jacks, and, no less important, the symbolism of the numbers—summon up the presence of the absent father:

> Suddenly, in a flash, the cloud broke up to make way for a new vision. On the tiles imprisoned by the circle the full tunic of the Colonel appeared, a darkish yellow that grew lighter, the buttons on the four pockets brighter than copper. Above the still collar, the absent face, smiling from a distance, happy perhaps, partaking in some undecipherable contentment that could not be shared, while he watched his wife and children inside that circle that united them in space and time under his gaze.

The second stage comes with Cemí's initiation into poetic language, into "language made nature." It includes two key moments: Alberto's letter on fish and the chess game. A hallucinatory description of tropical fish abounding in sexual allusions and humor, the letter erases the symbolic meaning given to the fish by Christianity and replaces it with a sexual one. Acting as officiant, Alberto, the family demon, here presents the option of salvation through sin, deeply rooted in the symbolist tradition:

> "'The north coast is protrusive, promontorial, phallic, the south coast is concave, like a woman's ass. Dry and damp, flute and horn, a grassless glans, a grassy vulva.'"

But the battle for salvation is not truly joined until later, in the chess game, through a brilliant outpouring of images. Lezama once described warriors as:

> a group of men who, in victory or in defeat, achieve a unity in which the metaphor of their bond produces one total image.

It follows that the chess game is an image of the image achieved by warriors in battle, and, in Lezama, the image is always linked to resurrection. In this sequence, Alberto suggests the Orphic descent which will make the struggle for salvation possible.

*The Fall*

The dinner-table scene brings the family together only to disperse it afterwards. As a farewell to childhood and innocence, it is loaded with dark omens: the beet-juice stains on the table-cloth resemble blood stains, the conversation turns to vultures and leprosy, sexual insinuations abound. However, the general tone of the scene is happy, centered around the joy of eating together. Alberto's unexpected death comes only after a long series of ominous and symbolic events. Dr.

Santurce announces doña Augusta's grave illness and probable death; the news crushes Alberto. Oppiano Licario tries to approach him, but fails, leaving him to his fate. Fate takes the form of a Mexican guitarist, emblem of death and the devil, who appears to challenge Alberto. The musician's first defeat is only temporary, for Alberto finds his death in the company of another guitarist during a car trip to Marianao. On the road the condemned man sees visions of glory arising from the counterpoint between the landscape and the guitar-player's songs:

> Some blue flamboyants under the waxing moon built arches beneath which the carp of the first-born were to pass, homage of the nobility to the progeny of the sainthood, blue created to intensify the passage of a fish on a tray of hammered copper.

Soon the vision changes into one of "a little worm with malignant horns," then into "Satan's hosts," and finally into "the plants that need fire to reach man." Diabolic allusions multiply, until the last song declares Alberto's fate: to spend eternity in darkness and to burn in the fire of hell. Of course, the prediction is indirect, for Lezama believed that "only the difficult stimulates" and tended to be more oblique as the ideas he wished to express became more transcendent.

Alberto's turbulent death drags the young protagonist to his fall and introduces him to a world of sex tinted in the most vivid colors. The adventures of Laregas and Farraluque, two exemplars of virility, run the gamut from simple exhibitionism to homosexuality, covering a range of nuances that includes the ridiculous and culminates in a grotesque absolute with the episode of the charcoal warehouse, an image of hell.

The results of the Fall are the break-up of the family after the trip to Santa Clara; Cemí's awareness of time, identified with the line of the horizon and the fragmentation of self. In Santa Clara, Cemí makes friends with Fronesis, and, on returning to Havana, with Foción. The three friends represent three archetypes, the three parts of the human soul, according to the German mystics: Foción stands for instinct; Fronesis, as his name indicates, for reason; and Cemí, for the divine spark which still burns in man after the Fall.

The *axis mundi*, personified in Rialta, the Basque grandfather, and Uncle Alberto, in the descent toward the Fall, now—in the second half of Paradiso—centers on these three figures, Foción, Fronesis, and Cemí, who participate in the ascending movement that culminates in poetry.

The story of Godofredo the Devil is the most tragic and absurd episode in this infernal chapter, and also the only one to end in punishment, a terrible one: madness, the loss of an eye, and death. Curiously, it is also the only story in which sexual contact plays no part. The villains are desertion, alcoholism, intrigue, infidelity, and sadomasochism. Lezama's attitude is neither that of an ascetic nor of a libertine but rather that of a humanist who looks upon the sexual excesses of youth with an understanding smile and condemns only those who allow cruelty to prevail over natural bodily attraction.

*Toward Poetry*

According to a principle similar to that of the fruitfulness of death, any chaotic situation, whether revolution or orgy, can open the way for a new revelation; that is why the revolution in Chapter IX has a special significance. When Cemí reaches home after the riot, his mother, who has awaited him anxiously, tells him:

> Don't reject danger and always try what is most difficult. . . . When a man throughout his days has tested what is most difficult, he knows that he has lived in danger, and even though the succession of its waves has been peaceful, he knows that a day has been assigned to him in which he will not see the fish inside the current, but the fish in the starry basket of eternity.

Son of a soldier and grandson of patriots, Cemí feels his ancestors urging him toward action. Yet his temperament, his tastes, and his experiences point him toward meditation and poetry. His mother's words force him to make a choice, to confirm his destiny as a poet. Suetonius' chapter on Nero warns Cemí against a vocation without talent, but his poetic ambitions are reaffirmed when he recognizes himself in Goethe's *Wilhelm Meister's Apprenticeship*.

Now Cemí faces another decisive crossroads, the question of sexual identity. It is posed in a scandalous episode that takes place in the university, in a long discussion about homosexuality, and in the two visions that frame the two incidents. In the debate, Fronesis maintains that homosexuality is an ancestral memory of the mythic age when man reproduced through dreams, without needing carnal union. Foción accuses him of justifying "something that can't be justified, because it's deeper than justification." Foción concludes that homosexuality is a "hypertely" of immortality, a yearning to create something beyond the flesh or even the spirit, something totally new and unknown. He cites several famous homosexuals in support of his belief that artistic works embody a mystery that no normal man can achieve. Fronesis' answer ends with a beautiful hymn to man and to the diversity of the senses:

> His body, the carrier of all impulses, reopens in the diversity of the senses, but vice and repugnance reach him only when he picks up a shred of the breeze,

and his experience turns to powder when he emphasizes a particular sense.

The discussion is cut short by the arrival of Lucía—a living example of "the diversity of the senses"—who comes to tempt Fronesis. He accepts the challenge more out of courtesy and the will to perform what he considers his duty to explore this diversity, than out of true pleasure. Cemí sees homosexuality as a trap set by the devil, creating "another fall within the fall." He concludes that sin lies in seeking out and persisting in vice, but vice is forgivable as long as it is treated as a stage to be overcome.

After the discussion, as he goes down the University steps, Cemí sees a cart with an enormous phallus and "facing it the vulva of an opulent woman" decorated with a large black bow. Two genies comically point the phallus toward its destination. The black bow links the fear of women to fear of death, two fears which, once overcome, lead to the creation of a new being in carnal union with a woman. This creation in turn becomes the emblem of literary creation and resurrection, the union of contraries, flesh and spirit, a true hypertely of immortality.

Fronesis, representing reason, avoids the pitfall of homosexuality in the episode with Lucía. He exorcises his fear of the *vagina dentata* by cutting two circles out of his undershirt—the circles of Ouroboros, symbol of immortality—and using them to cover Lucía's vulva. On his way home, he walks along the Malecón mourning the loss of his innocence, and throws the shirt into the sea:

> Before sinking, the undershirt coiled itself like a snake on which someone has conferred immortality, while at the same time in the fatty concavities of the man's body the phallic serpent was appearing; it was necessary to create precisely in order to lose immortality. Thus man was mortal, but creator, and the phallic serpent became a fragment that had to rise again.

Here, unfortunately, the translation betrays us. Immortality, in the original, is not lost with creation but regained, since creation is a substitute for surviving in children or works. However, the allusion to resurrection is spelled out in the image of man stripped of his intemporal homogeneity, becoming "a fragment that had to rise again."

By using a collage technique, Lezama is able to intercut scenes from the encounter between Lucía and Fronesis with Fronesis' family history and Foción's adventure with the red-haired boy. Fronesis' mother is presented as a two-headed dragon: the fleshly mother, tangled in the chaos of her instincts, manipulating, unscrupulous; and the spiritual mother, kindly and serene. By contrast, Foción is the product of an uncertain paternity shrouded in a fog of drugs and madness, and a mother who represents pure materiality, hopeless chaos. Foción's encounter with the red-haired boy, in which the former sinks deeper into his desperate chaos, contrasts with Fronesis' struggle with and final defeat of his fears. Fronesis' sacrifice, implying an acceptance of the Fall, allows him to understand creation. This theme will grow in importance and lead to Cemí's discovery of poetry. That is why, in a conversation on Nietzsche the next day at the University, Cemí tells Fronesis, "Ego te absolvo": the sacrifice has acted as a *felix culpa* or redeeming sin.

The fibrous heart tumor—"a dragon run through by a lance, by a ray of light"—for which Cemí's mother is operated sums up this sacrifice and symbolizes the union of contraries. Since "mother" and "matter" have the same root, the tumor becomes an emblem for poetry.

Lezama has called any combination of matter and image monstrous, especially when it occurs on a high level, as in poetry and orchestral music. The mother's operation repeats a sacrifice that opens the way to a new life, the first step toward literary practice.

"The ascent of number put to song," which Cemí and Fronesis achieve in the University, is the first example of this practice. Numbers, along with fractions and multiplication, pertain to the fallen man, and the Fall led to the sanctification of numbers practiced by Pythagoras and his disciples, and continued by the two friends. The dragon motif—symbolizing matter—has gradually changed its shape and now appears in the form of a chorus of students who surround Cemí and Fronesis, passing through successive transformations until they become a symbol of resurrection:

> But once again St. George with his miraculous spurs will alert his courser to jump and tire the dragon. Urged on by the terrestrial explosions of that day of resurrection. St. George, now astride Pegasus, will fall upon the constellation Draco, breaking his chains of stars, his ember head, his maw fattened with febrile moon.

St. George, astride Pegasus, is an emblem of the poet, for as he pursues the image of resurrection, he fulfills the function assigned to the poet in Lezama's system. Resurrection in the flesh, a Christian concept that overcomes the duality between matter and spirit, provides the model for this duty to unify which Lezama imposes on the poet. He proposes to rescue the flesh from the contempt in which it has been held and to present it as an integral part of the totality created in resurrection and in poetry.

The three young men redouble their literary exercises. Fronesis dedicates a poem to Cemí; Foción dedicates another to Fronesis; and Cemí experiments with images and space-time groupings like the one of the bacchante, the Cupid, and the silver cup from Puebla, and makes an important verbal discovery in the word *tamiela*, which he analyses into ten different meanings, two of which, 'treasure' and 'latrine,' are complete opposites:

> The site where one guards both the most valuable and the most insignificant or abjured, but which, nevertheless, favored the course of the seasons with its demoniac, sulphurous aid to the earth. This warns us to beware distinctions. It commends to us the great One, the treasure of excretion and the excretion of treasure.

This discovery by Cemí corresponds to Fronesis' conjuration and is inverted in Foción's incestuous and homosexual adventure in New York, when he, in his own way, manages to unite the contraries "sun, earth, and moon." Foción sinks into madness, Fronesis disappears, and doña Augusta's death marks Cemí's arrival at poetry.

## The Destruction of Time and Space

In the ecstasy of the poet, as in that of the mystic, time stops flowing and eternity takes its place, gathering all moments into one. Lezama expresses this passage of time into eternity and its contrary movement through a story with a spiral structure consisting of four anecdotes which illustrate four alternative ways to defeat time: by fame, in the story of Atrius Flaminius; by repetition, in the anecdote of the child and the vase; by insomnia, in the one of the wakeful man; and by sleep, in the story of the music critic. Two of these characters, the child and the insomniac, seem to be *alter egos* of Cemí's, part of another effort to cancel time by showing the same person at different moments in his life. But all of these attacks on time are literary. Time is finally and definitively destroyed only in death, where "that sin no longer exists," and that is why all of the characters in the story die: Atrius Flaminius, the child, the insomniac, the music critic, and his guardian. Their deaths are emblematic: they die to the world and submerge in the divinity reached through poetic or mystical ecstasy.

Space also disappears in the ecstasy of creation. Lezama annuls it in the perpetual motion of a magical omnibus guided by a bull's head rotating on a steel wheel. Like those medieval ships that carried the dead to their final port, the magical bus takes poets to poetry, personified by Oppiano Licario. Thus the Havana literary world left behind in Chapter II reappears with its almost forgotten characters. The stalled omnibus represents a literature paralyzed by routine. When it acquires a new bull's head and new passengers, it starts on its way again. Inside, Oppiano Licario—Icarus of the word—forms the center of a heterogenous group which lacks nei-

ther a Judas—Martincillo, who robs the treasure of poetry (Licario's coins) and abandons it when it proves worthless to him—nor a saviour, Cemí, who restores the treasure to its rightful owner. Here Adalberto, Vivino, and Martincillo represent the systaltic or tumultuously passionate style, while Cemí exemplifies the hesychastic alternative, spiritual equilibrium.

Oppiano's coins are stamped on one side with a Pegasus, emblem of poetry, and on the other with an Athena. The goddess testifies to the intellectual and balanced character of poetry, what Lezama has called "aristia," or "Athena's protection in the whirlwind of combat." The stolen coins belong to the elect, for, in the end, only those who have been chosen enter Oppiano's house.

## Attaining Poetry

The last chapter of *Paradiso* shows a complexity capable of upsetting any attempt at interpretation. Here we find Oppiano Licario's daily life, his poetic method, and the traps which he lays to lead Cemí into his mortuary chamber. Oppiano's poetic method is based on a magic in which words control reality. By means of "the shock of the poetic syllogism," his answers provoke a reality which can be either future, historic, or recent, because his words aim at the center of eternity, the very source of time. Just as the poet once transposed the student and the grindstone, so now he transposes places and epochs. "Oblique experience" and "the sudden" govern this poetic syllogism.

> **The last chapter of *Paradiso* shows a complexity capable of upsetting any attempt at interpretation.**
>
> **—*Margarita Fazzolari***

Sometimes the poet's sentences emerge incomplete and seek their complements. At other times, they burst out with overwhelming force and impose a complete picture of a situation or an epoch. Historic incidents are incessantly transposed with recent events—such as those following Cochrane's party—in order to illustrate Oppiano's method. The resulting stories—allegories of the struggle against the devil, Salado, the Salty One, the Destroyer—emerge from emptiness or from a phrase. For example, the story of Baron Rothschild and Kamariskaya is born when Oppiano reads a mysterious inscription in an empty vitrine *"Pieces belonging to a service marked with the kirimon or trifoliate paulownia of the Imperial Family of Japan, lost during the Baron's lifetime."* The anecdote of the Venetian senator's murder may come from *The Venetian Gazette* or from the

*Compilation of Notices for Amsterdam Merchants.* The story of Logakón derives from the phrase "next to him on the left" and from three empty spaces: the neighboring seat at the Opera during a performance of *Faust;* the room next-door at the boarding house; and the neighboring table in the café. The magic of these apparently simple words manages to call a man out of eternity and to give him flesh. His name, Logakón, comes from *Logos,* 'the word.' He is the word incarnate, although the reference is not to Jesus but to the poetic word that acquires its dazzling prestige through the reverberations of analogy.

After Logakón's suicide, Licario imagines his last adventure. He will plant himself head-down in the earth, sending forth roots, branches and leaves like a tree: an image of resurrection (from an aerial perspective) which prefigures Licario's own death and resurrection.

From death, Oppiano spreads the nets that lead Cemí into his funeral chamber. As he strolls through the night, Cemí sees a three-story house with all the windows lit (lost nature); then a playground and, on the merry-go-round, a caretaker looking like "the helmsman of some infernal machine" (fallen nature); and, lastly, a forest "where the trees climbed up over each other" surrounding a house which suggests the supernatural. Cemí enters the deserted house and on the terrace finds many emblems:

> And every trefoil showed a key as if nature and super-nature had been united in something meant to penetrate, to jump from one region to another, in order to reach the castle and interrupt the feast of the hermetic troubadours.

This is poetry, the crown of Lezama's system: an enchanted castle where the invisible and the palpable—what Lezama has called causality and the uncaused—lock in combat, from which there emerges a new "causality that unites man and divinity, or death and the circle." Cemí reaches poetry by closing up "the space of the Fall," for his encounters are punctuated by the same songs that followed Uncle Alberto to his death. Only one testimony remains from that overwhelming encounter: the poem which Licario's sister delivers to Cemí in the funeral chamber:

> Reason and memory by chance
> will see the dove attain
> faith in the super-natural.

In the funeral chapel, the rhythm of poetry makes itself felt together with the rhythm of the universe and the lack of response, for the poet shoots his arrow into the infinite without hope of any response, without any assurance of hitting the mark. Poetry is a stumble, a kind of madness which Cemí must now assume under the lead of his master Licario, whose last words—"rhythm of hesychasts, now we can begin"—belong to the ceremonies of initiation he will perform in the pages of the novel *Oppiano Licario,* where the three friends meet again in order to achieve a new and definitive unity.

---

## FURTHER READING

### Criticism

Cascardi, Anthony J. "Reference in Lezama Lima's *Muerte de Narciso.*" *Journal of Spanish Studies* 5, No. 1 (Spring 1977): 5-11.
    Discusses the poetic style, structure, and thematic content of *The Death of Narcissus.*

Cortázar, Julio. "An Approach to Lezama Lima." *Review,* No. 74 (Fall 1974): 20-5.
    Remarks on his reactions to *Paradiso.*

Firmat, Gustavo Pérez. "The Strut of the Centipede: José Lezama Lima and New World Exceptionalism." In his *Do the Americas Have a Common Literature?,* pp. 316-32. Duke University Press, 1990.
    Discusses *La expresión americana,* focusing on the role of American culture as a "landscape" in which neo-baroque aesthetics encounter worldly ecstasy, wonder, and joy, and converge to create a "uniquely" American hermeneutic of literary expression.

Goytisolo, Juan. Review of *Oppiano Licario,* by José Lezama Lima. *The Times Literary Supplement,* No. 4627 (6 December 1991): 14-15.
    Remarks favorably on *Oppiano Licario.*

Irby, James. "Figurative Displacements in a Prose Poem of Lezama Lima: A Commentary on *Peso del sabor.*" In *Essays on Hispanic Literature in Honor of Edmund L. King,* edited by Sylvia Molloy and Luis Fernández Cifuentes, pp. 123-39. London: Tamesis Books, 1983.
    Discusses the "apocalyptic" themes and structural elements of *Peso del sabor.*

Lutz, Robyn R. "The Tribute to Everyday Reality in José Lezama Lima's *Fragmentos a su imán.*" *Journal of Spanish Studies—Twentieth Century* 8, No. 3 (Winter, 1980): 249-66.
    Examines *Fragmentos a su imán,* focusing on the themes, structure, and literary devices used in several poems, including "La mujer y la casa," "El esperado," and "El pabellón del vacío."

Pellón, Gustavo. "Portrait of the Cuban Writer as French Painter: Henri Rousseau, José Lima's Alter Ego." *MLN* 103, No. 2 (March 1988): 350-73.

Examines the influence of the French painter Henri Rousseau on Lezama Lima's writings.

Pérez Firmat, Gustave. "Descent into *Paradiso*: A Study of Heaven and Homosexuality." *Hispania* 59, No. 2 (May 1976): 247-57.
Discusses homosexuality in *Paradiso*.

Schwartz, Ronald. "Lezama Lima: Cuban Sexual Propensities." In *Nomads, Exiles, & Emigres: The Rebirth of the Latin*

*American Narrative, 1960-80*, pp. 24-33. Scarecrow Press, 1980.
Examines the plot and characters of *Paradiso* and suggests that in spite of the novel's elaborate literary style, it remains "a linguistic tour de force."

Siemens, William L. "The Birth of the Author in the Recent Cuban Novel." In *La Chispa '87: Selected Proceedings*, edited by Gilbert Paolini, pp. 291-96. New Orleans: Tulane University, 1987.
Examines the development of the novel in Cuba since 1868.

# Cormac McCarthy

## 1933-

(Born Charles McCarthy Jr.) American novelist.

The following entry provides an overview of McCarthy's career through 1996. For further information on his life and works, see *CLC*, Volumes 4, 57, and 59.

## INTRODUCTION

McCarthy is regarded as an important contributor to the Southern Gothic tradition as exemplified by William Faulkner, Carson McCullers, and Flannery O'Connor. His novels are praised for their powerful, descriptive passages and for their extensive examinations of evil. His protagonists are typically either extreme outcasts or young adventurers confronted with tremendous adversities who struggle against a brutal, merciless world. Occasionally faulted for his recurring themes and character types, McCarthy has nevertheless been praised for his command of language. Charles McGrath observed: "Even his most staightforward passages have about them a shimmer of grandness—achieved sometimes by importing arcane vocabulary, sometimes by repetition or tinkering with word order, and sometimes just by stretching a sentence out with 'and's until it acquires the desired pace and gravity."

### Biographical Information

Born in Providence, Rhode Island, on July 20, 1933, McCarthy moved to Knoxville, Tennessee, at the age of four, and later attended the University of Tennessee. After completing his first year there, he served for four years in the U.S. Air Force. He returned to the university, then left in 1960 without a degree to pursue a writing career. When his first novel, *The Orchard Keeper,* was published in 1965, McCarthy had already been awarded a fellowship for a year of travel abroad by the American Academy of Arts and Letters. A William Faulkner Foundation Award followed in 1965. A grant from the Rockefeller foundation in 1966 and a Guggenheim fellowship in 1976 helped the reclusive author make ends meet throughout his early writing career. Annie DeLisle, McCarthy's second ex-wife, recalls his aversion to steady jobs and comfortable lodgings: "We lived in total poverty . . . [and] we were bathing in the lake. . . . Someone would call up and offer him $2000 to come speak at a university about his books. And he would tell them that everything he had to say was there on the page. So we would eat beans for another week." A "genius award" from the MacArthur Foundation in 1981 enabled McCarthy to purchase a small home in El Paso, Texas, and move out of the motel in which he was living in Knoxville, Tennessee. He has published several novels since then. In 1992 *All The Pretty Horses* (1992) won the National Book Award, the National Book Critics Circle Award for fiction, and landed on numerous bestseller lists. *The Crossing,* published in 1994, is the second installment in McCarthy's "Border Trilogy," and like the other novels, it has been praised for its portentous themes but faulted for, among other things, being "derivative, sentimental and pretentious."

### Major Works

*The Orchard Keeper,* McCarthy's first novel, is about an old man living in the mountains of Tennessee, and a young boy, John Wesley Rattner, whose father is killed by a whiskey bootlegger named Marion Sylder. A country bar burns down, young John saves a dog from an attack by a raccoon, and the boy is befriended by Sylder. Like all McCarthy's novels, *The Orchard Keeper* deals with a protagonist struggling against a brutal, hostile world. In *Outer Dark* (1968), Culla and Rinthy Holme are siblings who produce a child. Culla abandons the child in the woods and leaves his sister to fend for herself. Rinthy spends the rest of the novel wandering about looking for her child. Seeking work, Culla steals a squire's boots and subsequently flees four pursuers across a river in which he nearly drowns. The themes of murder, incest, and ignorance found in *Outer Dark* reemerged in many of McCarthy's later works. *Child of God* (1974) presents the story of Lester Ballard, a necrophiliac who drags corpses home, talks to them, and dresses and undresses them as he schemes to murder new victims. Man's capacity for evil is clearly demonstrated in such passages. In another passage, McCarthy describes the rape of a daughter by her father after he catches her having intercourse with a boy behind the barn. Providing readers with brutal and horrifying accounts, McCarthy's bleak vision of the world becomes appallingly real. To make Lester more empathetic, his farm is sold over his head, his cabin burns, and he is treated poorly at every turn. Here and in later novels, McCarthy uses the technique of portraying flawed or evil characters in a sympathetic way to achieve realism and authenticity. In *Suttree* (1979), McCarthy presents a character who has a degree of self-awareness and intelligence. Again, the setting of the novel is Tennessee, and Suttree, the hero, is a drunken loner who makes his living as a fisherman and resides on a houseboat. A floating body is discovered in the opening scenes and at the conclusion of the story Suttree returns to his houseboat to find a rotting corpse in his bed. A metaphysical theme runs throughout the novel, culminating when Suttree wanders about in the forest and undergoes a sort of transformation and rebirth. Foremost in *Suttree* are the themes of decay, death, and destruction, which were also prevalent in the earlier works. *Blood Meridian* (1985) is the violent and gory tale of "the kid"—a protagonist who finds himself in East Texas with renegade U.S. troops who are massacred by Comanche Indians. Falling in with American mercenaries after a stint in jail, the kid ventures into a gruesome journey filled with bloodshed, the defilement of corpses, and random slaughter. The dominant, towering, evil persona of Judge Holden further highlights McCarthy's theme of man's inhumanity to man. The novel is purportedly based upon actual people and events in history, making the violence especially unnerving. The setting of *Blood Meridian* departs from the Tennessee locales of earlier works, but the story follows McCarthy's pattern of using characters who struggle against a brutal, violent world. *All the Pretty Horses* carries on this tradition, as John Grady Cole leaves his home in Texas after the death of his grandfather and during the divorce of his parents. With his friend Lacey Rawlins, the two boys ride off into Mexico to experience a variety of adventures. John becomes entangled in a romance with a high-born, passionate, young girl named Alejandra, daughter of Don Hector and niece of a formidable aunt, Dueña Alfonsa. Relying on traditional Western props, *All the Pretty Horses* includes corrupt Mexican officials; a torturous jail term; long, dusty rides through the landscape; a murdered companion; and a fulfilling act of revenge at the conclusion. Following much the same story pattern of *All the Pretty Horses, The Crossing* focuses on two teenaged brothers, Billy and Boyd Parham, who leave their home in New Mexico and travel south. Billy traps a wolf and becomes determined to return her to Mexico; later he and Boyd attempt to recover horses stolen from the family ranch where their parents have been killed; and Billy returns to Mexico late in the novel to search for the missing Boyd. *The Crossing* contains a metaphysical theme apparent in the novel's abundance of fables, sermons, morality tales and figures who dispense wisdom. Combining elements of the picaresque adventure and metaphysical pilgrimage that were present in *All the Pretty Horses, Suttree, Blood Meridian,* and other novels, McCarthy weaves a riveting tale that comments on man's capacity for evil.

**Critical Reception**

McCarthy's early novels have not received much critical attention, and his first five books never sold more than 2,500 hard-cover copies in their first release. However, his later works have garnered more publicity, and he is emerging as a popular writer of bloody, violent, and richly detailed stories of the American West. McCarthy's prose style is a common topic among critics. Commenting on McCarthy's writing, Walter Sullivan states: "His prose is magnificent, full of energy and sharp detail and the sounds and smells of God's creation." McCarthy presents violence in his novels without

motivation, reflection, or moral debate, and reviewers have found this discomforting. Despite the many shocking and gruesome scenes in McCarthy's work, critics recognize his skill in composing a story. Quoting a passage from *Outer Dark* in which a child is murdered, Edwin T. Arnold writes: "[T]he effect causes some to throw the book to the floor." *Child of God* produced similar reactions with its scenes of necrophilia and rape, yet critics praise it for its lyrical prose. McCarthy's skill at making evil characters empathetic fascinated Anatole Broyard, who states: "An evil character brilliantly portrayed will awaken our empathy—even sympathy—more readily than a good one in a pedestrian description." Other critics found the subject matter appalling. *Suttree* is another example of a novel filled with violence and unscrupulous, evil characters. While some would find McCarthy's cast of characters repugnant, McCarthy's vivid descriptions are both authentic and moving. In a review of *Suttree,* Guy Davenport remarks: "[I]t is a thoroughly believable novel, its every gesture authentic. There are multiple plot lines, a small town's worth of characters, and enough episodes for a four-hour movie." In *All the Pretty Horses* critics again found McCarthy's descriptive prose to be both his strong point and his downfall. Richard Eder writes: "McCarthy wavers between the lovely and the ludicrous. . . [L]oftiness gusts like a capsizing high wind, and the writing can choke on its own ornateness." *The Crossing,* like *All the Pretty Horses,* is concerned with the adventures of two young men, and critics have commented on McCarthy's repeated use of formulaic plot and scenery. Reviewer Robert Hass writes: "*The Crossing* is a miracle in prose, an American original. . . it is a tale so riveting—it immerses the reader so entirely in its violent and stunningly beautiful, inconsolable landscapes—that there is hardly time to reflect on its many literary and cinematic echoes." The overwhelming violence and brutality in McCarthy's writing is thus received differently by different critics. Yet there is consensus that there are deeper currents running throughout his work, and that the violence is not gratuitous. While McCarthy's florid prose is often faulted, he is considered a master stylist and peerless in his ability to provide authentic setting and mood.

---

# PRINCIPAL WORKS

*The Orchard Keeper* (novel) 1965
*Outer Dark* (novel) 1968
*Child of God* (novel) 1974
*Suttree* (novel) 1979
*Blood Meridian, or The Evening Redness in the West* (novel) 1985
*All the Pretty Horses* (novel) 1992
*The Crossing* (novel) 1994
*The Stonemason* (play) 1994

# CRITICISM

## Walter Sullivan (review date October-December 1965)

SOURCE: "Worlds Past and Future: A Christian and Several from the South," in *The Sewanee Review*, Vol. LXXIII, No. 4, October-December, 1965, pp. 719-26.

[*In the following excerpt, Sullivan discusses* The Orchard Keeper *and the triumph of technology over man in the novel.*]

*The Orchard Keeper* is Cormac McCarthy's first novel, but at thirty-three, McCarthy has a more mature mind and is a more finished craftsman than Miss Tyler. His prose is magnificent, full of energy and sharp detail and the sounds and smells of God's creation. The sense of fulfillment one gets from reading *The Orchard Keeper* is difficult to convey, because when the book is broken down to its bare bones it is likely to appear to be a trite contraption. It is written squarely in the middle of the agrarian influence, and reading it, one thinks of Faulkner here and Lytle there, or of Madison Jones or Marion Montgomery. But such impressions are fleeting and prove to be false. McCarthy is like nobody so much as he is like all the writers who have gone before him and had sense enough to see in the land a source of human salvation. He is a kind of anachronism who celebrates the traditional values in the traditional way.

His locale is the mountains around Knoxville, Tennessee; his people are the moonshiners and hunters and lawmen and farmers who live there. The action is the tapestry woven by the infinite crossings and recrossings among the inhabitants of a small community. McCarthy begins with a sequence about a thieving drifter who is killed while trying to commit murder and highway robbery against the man who has given him a ride. He ends two decades later with the son of the drifter standing beside his mother's recent grave. Within this mortal framework, the boy and the man who killed his father become loyal friends. This is, of course, a cliche, but McCarthy endows the situation with freshness by ignoring the irony, by insisting upon nothing. Rather, our attention is directed to the changing seasons, to the ceremonies of life and death, to the violations and accommodations wrought between man and nature. Men hunt and fish, endure flood and freeze, make love, get drunk, walk the ridges, run whisky, fight, and finally die. And they talk. And they display their affections. Or rather, they do not display them, and that is why so much of *The Orchard Keeper* seems significant.

Everything here is so low-keyed—and therefore typical of the mountaineer temperament—that to paraphrase McCarthy is to exaggerate him. The surge of the book is in its physical movements, in the cars that go careening over mountain roads, in the sound of the panther's cry at night, in the struggle between dogs and coons, or in the running of the trap line. Beneath this, piquant and almost pristine because they are never forced, are the old stories of betrayal and fidelity, of disappointment and fulfillment, of all the joy and anguish of life.

The orchard keeper is an old man, and what he keeps are the bones of Rattner, the murdered drifter. Marion Sylder, his own shoulder broken from the fight, dropped the body in the old spray-pit where it was later discovered by children. The old man does not know whose remains he tends. Certainly, he has no inclination to report their existence to the authorities. But out of his humanity, he tends what was once human, periodically dropping in a fresh evergreen to cover the skull: willingly he serves a *memento mori*. But he will not abide the encroachment of civilization, which comes in the form of a giant storage tank erected by some government agency on the mountain top. ("The great dome stood complacent, huge, seeming older than the very dirt, the rocks, as if it had spawned them of itself and stood surveying the world, clean and coldly gleaming and capable of infinite contempt.") The old man shoots holes in the tank, and when he refuses to come quietly the police go after him in force. They surround his house and shoot out his windows, finally shoot one of their own number and leave. But the old man is captured at last and turned over to the social workers.

As always, technology is finally triumphant. The old man is sent to the home for the aged. Sylder is caught running moonshine: there is water in the gasoline he bought at the country pump and his engine stops. The boy goes to the army and most of the others die. This is the ending.

> They are gone now. Fled, banished in death or exile, lost, undone. Over the land sun and wind still move to burn and sway the trees, the grasses. No avatar, no scion, no vestige of that people remains. On the lips of the strange race that now dwells there their names are myth, legend, dust. . . .

## Anatole Broyard (review date 5 December 1973)

SOURCE: "'Daddy Quit', She Said," in *The New York Times*, December 5, 1973, p. 45.

[*In the following essay, Broyard discusses McCarthy's writing, and his ability to make readers empathize with evil, immoral characters.*]

It's interesting to see how a good writer can make us care about a "bad" character. I mean bad in a moral sense. Talent, it seems, can find the humanity behind the inhuman, the pathos that comes from being out of step with the world, the loneliness, like death, that is the wages of sin. In spite of our increasing disillusionment in fiction and in the social sciences with homo sapiens, he is still all that we've got and only the most obdurate misanthrope can resist him when he is presented in the round, when even his imperfections pulse with life and hope.

An evil character brilliantly portrayed will awaken our empathy—even sympathy—more readily than a good one in a pedestrian description. It seems that we hunger for vividness, that we are afraid of being engulfed in a gray anonymity. Give me character of any kind is an unspoken plea of our age, to which the "charismatic" craze bears witness. I think, for example, that the unprecedented hostility shown to President Nixon is not a response to his character or his politics, but to his insistence on concealing his character in his politics.

I suppose that Ballard, the protagonist of Cormac McCarthy's *Child of God* is evil, but I hesitate to call him that. It is not a philosophy of permissiveness or any diabolist leanings that inhibits me, but the fact that he is so real, coupled with the further condition that all of his actions flow so naturally from what he is. He murders, rapes, vandalizes corpses, sets fires and steals—yet Mr. McCarthy has convinced me that his crimes originated in a reaching for love. Now ordinarily such a statement—and there is no shortage of them—would make me feel very impatient with the person who made it. But art, apparently, hath charms to soothe the indignant breast.

I cared about Ballard and very nearly forgave him his sins because the author seduced me into feeling that he was someone I knew very well—so well that I felt like a reluctant neighbor being questioned by reporters about the fellow next door who had just committed a lurid crime. That's the magic of art. It can make you contradict yourself, surprise yourself, discover charities you blush to confront. When Ballard lugged a dead girl several miles to his freezing shack and thawed her out in front of the fire so that he could vandalize her, I felt not disgust but pity. "He poured into that waxen ear everything he'd ever thought of saying to a woman." Well, I temporized, it seems to be the best he can do.

When he goes out and buys clothes for the dead girl, so he can dress and undress her—first going outside so he can steal a look at her through the window—I could see the perverted poetry of it. It was the same sort of feeling that induced him to carry everywhere with him two huge teddy bears and a stuffed tiger he had won at a shooting gallery. When he began wearing the clothes of his other female victims as he went out to commit murder, his character took on still another dimension—one harder for me to feel but one that the author's conception of him could still afford.

Mr. McCarthy has the best kind of Southern style, one that fuses risky eloquence, intricate rhythms and dead-to-rights accuracy. I've often wondered whether this kind of writing—William Faulkner is the classical example—isn't partly a result of the black influence on Southern speech, a stress on sonorousness and musicality. Whatever its source, the author uses it to splendid effect in several flawless scenes. In one of them, Ballard is sleeping in his shack when a pack of hunting dogs, close on the trail of their prey, follows its scent through the doorless entrance and out the window, while he, first terrified, then enraged, strikes out at them.

When Ballard finds a rusty old axhead and takes it to the blacksmith to be sharpened, the smith croons a beautiful elegy to the lost instinct of workmanship, describing, again in infallible rhythms, each step of the process. "Some people will poke around at somethin else," he says, "and leave the tool they're heatin to perdition but the proper thing is to fetch her out the minute she shows the color of grace. Now we want a high red. Want a high red. Now she comes." In another scene, a father catches his daughter behind the barn with a boy and chases him off. But then he finds sex so strong in the air that before he realizes what he is doing, he has taken the boy's place. His daughter's response ought to go down in the annals of Southern history. "Daddy quit," she says.

To demonstrate that he is human too, Mr. McCarthy makes a few small mistakes here and there. He ought to resist words like strobic, palimpsest, mutant and inculpate, as well as inversions like knew not. And there's an apostrophe to fate on page 156 that belongs in somebody else's book. But these are overflowings, mere spills, from a brimming imagination. *Child of God* is no idle title. Ballard is one, like you and me and the author too, and this book isn't going to let us forget it.

## Guy Davenport (review date 16 March 1979)

SOURCE: "Silurian Southern," in *National Review,* Vol. 31, No. 11, March 16, 1979, pp. 368-69.

[*In the following review Davenport discusses the Southern influences in McCarthy's novels, and praises the novelist's originality and skill in rendering the "outrageous and the macabre."*]

In his fourth novel, Cormac McCarthy deepens his sounding of the Silurian depths of human nature. We are creatures designed and damned by the past. In an alley in Knoxville, all the animistic conjurations of West Africa thrive in their millionth year; the visionary mind of Wales and the stubborn will of Scotland, fueled by whisky and enraged by adversity, plunge the conduct of life in Tennessee into dark triumphs of irreality.

The people he writes about do not think, especially before they leap. He has subtracted from narrative tradition that running account, by author or character, of rationalization, opinion, and intent which reached an ultimate in Joyce's stream of consciousness and provides most novels with a large part of their matter ("She loves me, he reflected to his not ungainly image in the mirror, savoring the clean sting of the Aqua Velva").

In his second novel, *Outer Dark,* people move as in a silent film. Their actions are described as beautifully and fully as a camera sees. Voices speak. Awful things happen before our eyes. The denouement is shocking. But the adverbial element has been omitted. There is not even an ironic tone to guide us. And all motivation, all messages from minds, all reverie, all memory are kept from us as a dark secret.

McCarthy's first novel, *The Orchard Keeper,* won the William Faulkner Foundation Award for 1965. His third, *Child of God,* achieved as distinct a style as any in American writing, a harmony of vernacular and Renaissance English. In Tennessee, the setting of all McCarthy's novels, locutions survive from the bucolic English of two centuries ago, alongside the stuttering and depraved English all of us speak anymore.

Critics have sniped at McCarthy's studied prose rhythms and unfamiliar words, not seeing the need he has of them. He must summon his world before our eyes in all its richness and exactness of shape, because that is all he is summoning.

Cormac McCarthy's tales are all dark. Brother and sister beget a child; men who seem to lust to hurt everything in reach roam from murder to murder; a man copulates with corpses of his own killing, keeping them mildewed and cool in the depths of a cave. Such horrors are not offered as Grand Guignol; they are the doings of ordinary folk in an ordinary world. They are the doings of stubborn, willful, gaunt Tennesseans in overalls and aprons, chewers of tobacco and dippers of snuff.

In this new novel, Suttree is a fisherman who lives in a houseboat on the river that runs through Knoxville. He was somebody else once. He is, presumably, from a well-to-do family. He is just out of prison when we meet him; a good two hundred pages later we find out why he was there. He pals around with the fast sporting set that hangs out at the Greyhound Bus Station, with blacks who drink and gamble in back rooms, and with the derelicts who inhabit the arches of overpasses, sleeping in cardboard boxes.

What fascinates Cormac McCarthy about people is irratio-

nal intrepidity—unflappable stubbornness, inviolable muleheadedness. He treats it comically, heroically, even lyrically in this long novel which, in essence, rings and thuds with heads butted against ungiving oak. His protagonist (who is, for the first time in McCarthy's work, permitted a limited amount of interiority) is a stubborn will among stubborn wills of varying degrees of intelligence.

There is a hierarchy of these unlearning persisters. On the lowest rung is a chucklehead named Harrogate, a ratfaced adolescent, all bone and gall, who comes on the scene as a sexual violator of watermelons. He is a type in the South, one that can be characterized entirely by his prolonging his sentence on the chain-gang (raping watermelons is presumably bestiality under Tennessee law) rather than work in the prison kitchen. Masculinity is a finely graduated commodity.

Up from Harrogate on the scale we find various derelicts, scavengers, and professional pushers of their own luck. At the top, I'm not certain whether we are to understand an Indian who somehow still fishes in his native river, or a black who is a kind of chief to his people (a bootlegger and gambler otherwise) and whose brutal fights with the police exhibit a will that means never to knuckle under.

This is a violent novel, wild with fights and McCarthyan horrors, such as a body kept in an icebox for six months so that its welfare checks will continue. But it is a thoroughly believable novel, its every gesture authentic. There are multiple plot lines, a small-town's worth of characters, and enough episodes for a four-hour movie were the novel to be filmed. Though it seems to ramble from jail to river to alley, its structure is as tight as the strings on a guitar.

Cormac McCarthy is a Knoxvillian, and there is something of a portrait of the artist as a young man about this book. Coming after three objective novels with no trace of a self-portrait, there is nothing here of the author digesting his adolescence. Instead, it would seem that the author has projected himself into a character he might have been were circumstances otherwise, or that he is being autobiographical in an obliquely symbolic way. His protagonist has too subjective a cast to be an observed character. It is as if the author had asked what part of himself bears the imprint of the world in which he was raised, and answered himself by witnessing what these traits look like exemplified by a gallery of characters ranging from near-idiotic to noble.

Such a connoisseur of the outrageous and the macabre (and of the lyrically beautiful, when he wants to be) can be read for the story alone. One is soon won over, however, to Cormac McCarthy's radically original way with tone and his sense of the aloneness of people in their individuality. At the heart of *Suttree* there is a strange scene of transformation and rebirth in which the protagonist wanders in a forest, sees visions, and emerges as a stranger to all that was before familiar. This is a scene no one else could have written.

Very little of his work echoes other writers; where it does (Faulkner, for instance, and the King James Bible), the echo is in homage rather than imitation. Such originality and integrity are as rare as they are welcome.

## Jim Crace (review date 2 May 1980)

SOURCE: "Tribal Views," in *New Statesman,* Vol. 99, No. 2563, May 2, 1980, p. 682.

[*In the following excerpt, Crace discusses categorizing* Suttree *as a "tribal" work, and faults the novel for lacking an "overall social and allegorical context."*]

Cormac McCarthy's Big New Southern novel, *Suttree,* is also a fairly 'tribal' work if one can swallow the quaint dictionary definition of a tribe as 'a group of people in a primitive or barbarous stage of development'. His characters are city derelicts, rag pickers, possum hunters, and various junkyard angels who pass their days in bars (drinking Redtop beer and splo whisky) or in the work-house penitentiary (sipping moonshine). They break strangers' noses as frequently and with as little decorum as they break wind. Suttree, the keystone character of the novel, for all his college education and bouts of aristocratic Southern introspection, is no violet, either, when it comes to busting heads and cracking bottles.

Is this novel, then, a disguised pilgrimage to Faulkner's imaginary Yoknapatawpha County? Certainly McCarthy presents a similarly wide gallery of comic/brutal characters. But his bite is bigger than his chew: the string of anecdotes and incidents which comprise the novel lacks overall social and allegorical context and, because the plot is linear rather than integrated, it lacks design.

What is needed to tie this episodic package together is a distinctive and idiosyncratic narrative voice which links and advances the component tales *unselfconsciously.* What one, in fact, gets instead is swampy and often graceless prose:

> They lifted him onto the deck where he lay in his wet seersucker suit and his lemoncolored socks, leering walleyed up at the workers with the hook in his face like some gross water homunculus taken in trolling that the light of God's day had stricken dead instanter.

*Suttree* cannot recover, it seems, from that spirit-sinking, tangled and pretentious evocation of Knoxville, Tennessee,

in portentous italics ('*The river lies in a grail of quietude. . . .*' etc, etc.) with which it opens. Such a pity—because the action and dialogue of *Suttree* (particularly those sections which recount the schemes of Harrogate, 'the moonlight melonmounter. . .—a convicted pervert of a botanical bent',) are crackling with invention, irreverence, and ill-mannered humour.

It may be that Cormac McCarthy does not make of Tennessee what Faulkner made of Mississippi. He does succeed, though, in doing for Knoxville what Genesis XIX has done for Sodom and Gomorrah.

Compared to these two new American novels much of the current British fiction seems insipid and self-consciously discursive. Its characters *talk* moonshine—they don't drink it.

## John Lewis Longley Jr. (review date Spring 1985)

SOURCE: "*Suttree* and the Metaphysics of Death," in *The Southern Literary Journal,* Vol. XVII, No. 2, Spring, 1985, pp. 79-90.

[*In the following article, Longley Jr. provides an examination of the novel* Suttree, *discusses McCarthy's writing style, and comments on McCarthy's place in the literary world.*]

> Gods and fathers what has happened here, good friends where is there clemency?

Suttree is standing in the ruin of a great house where he may or may not have lived as a child. He is surrounded by warped parquetry, buckled wainscot, ruined plaster. We are reminded of another waif, crying for what is lost:

> Kennst du das Haus? Auf Saulen ruht sein Dach,
> Es glanzt der Saal, es schimmert das Gemach,
> Und Marmorbilder stehn und sehn mich an:
> Was hat man dir, du armes Kind, getan?

But there will be no Protector to take Suttree by the hand and lead him down the happy highway back to the land of lost content. He does not cry "Dahin! Dahin!" He is in his own country; he is standing in the actual house. The journey he has made is not one of space or distance or even time. He has put all his past life behind him, programmatically and totally.

> In my father's last letter he said that the world is run by those willing to take the responsibility for the running of it. If it is life that you feel you are missing I can tell you where to find it. In the law courts,

in business, in government. There is nothing occurring in the streets. Nothing but a dumbshow composed of the helpless and the impotent.

This dumbshow is what Suttree has chosen. He has flown by
many nets: religion, family, marriage, education, a job, respectability. He has taken himself out of the roles of son,
husband, and father. His associates are outlaws, alcoholics,
prostitutes, perverts, murderers, thieves. Of all the figures in
the dumbshow, Suttree is haunted most by the memory of
his twin brother who was stillborn.

> I saw how all things false fall from the dead. . . If
> our dead kin are sainted we may rightly pray to them.
> Mother Church tells us so. She does not say that
> they'll speak back, in dreams or out. . . .

> He lies in Woodlawn, whatever be left of the child
> with whom you shared your mother's belly . . . I
> followed him into the world . . . And used to pray
> for his soul days past. Believing this ghastly circus
> reconvened elsewhere for alltime. He in the limbo
> of the Christless righteous, I in a terrestrial hell.

This is more than apt description. Suttree is in Hell, and by
his own volition. Make no mistake; this is no hippie lying on
his back, growing hair and blowing grass. He has not taken
the simple slide along the path of least resistance. His is an
active life; the rules are hard but simple: exploit no one and
be not exploited, avoid money and steady employment, kiss
no one's ass. Know the limitations you have set. To escape
into memory or fantasy is dangerous. You will surely die,
but put it off as long as possible.

This is the here and now that Suttree lives in. It is, in its
brilliantly rendered surface, an actual place in a real time:
McAnally Flats, a slum area of Knoxville, Tennessee in the
early 1950's. McAnally was at that time a high-crime area,
with more than its share of blind pigs, aggravated assaults
and bootlegging. On that level, we can ask why anyone would
choose to live like this. On another level we may ask why
anyone has chosen Hell, but that is a very old question indeed. This essay will try to account for Suttree's choice.

Cormac McCarthy is the latest example of that most American of phenomena: a superb writer who is totally unknown
to the general public. Unknown, but not unrewarded. He has
received many grants and fellowships. He has published four
novels, and a fifth novel has been announced. *Suttree,* his
masterpiece, was published in 1979, and is already out of
print. Aside from reviews and brief mention in fiction
chronicles, there have been only a handful of full-dress essays on his work. One of these is "Further into Darkness:
The Novels of Cormac McCarthy," by Professor John Ditsky.
In this essay, Professor Ditsky assesses McCarthy's place in

the mainstream of Southern literature. He anticipates the
dreary litany we have heard so often: the subject-matter is
grotesque and the language is bombastic. He is able to demonstrate that subject-matter and language are great strengths,
not weaknesses. Indeed, McCarthy's fictional rhetoric would
be worth a book-length study of its own.

Equally fascinating areas for analysis would be a comparison of Suttree and the fiction of Dostoyevsky. The novel is
richly comic, and that element would repay close study. Much
can be made of family patterns, particularly the relationship
between father and children. Suttree has many doubles:
Harrowgate, the rag-picker, his stillborn brother. Some secondary characters are expansive enough to deserve a novel
of their own. Fascinating as these prospects are, they must
be put aside for the moment. I want to explain Suttree.

The novel is a seamless web of great complexity and richness. It is all texture and very little structure. In this regard it
is like *Finnegans Wake,* which is circular in form, and can
be entered at any point. There are several very large controlling metaphors which are omnipresent in the story; which
weave in and out of the flow of events. McAnally and Knoxville in general is one. Another is the river and by extension
its tributaries. The river represents the form of the novel:
flowing from day to day, but not always at the same speed,
and not always with the same debris in it. Under the surface
are uncharted swirls and eddies; dark and dangerous, which
are matched by the deep uncharted caves which underlie
Knoxville.

The Tennessee River at this time was arguably one of the
filthiest streams in North America. In spite of the many TVA
dams it was very muddy. It was heavily polluted by industry, and by human debris in general. Because of the dams,
there are many backwaters, and the water ebbs or flows only
as the river level changes. Because of this, flotsam and jetsam that backs up out of the main stream may stay around
for days or even years. This includes trees, crates and boxes,
discarded light bulbs, used condoms, and the random dead
body. The main channel is very deep and opaque. Very little
can live there except the catfish that Suttree catches for a
living. These creatures exemplify what it would take to live
in such a world: prehistoric, antediluvian, mindless; swimming easily in the ambient filth, or resting quiescent in the
frozen mud.

Another large metaphor is what might be called the pastoral
and its attendant dangers. East Tennessee is one of the most
beautiful places on earth.

Once outside the city there are green fields and rolling hills.
Go far enough upstream or into certain tributaries, and the
water becomes pure and cold. A little further away are the
peaks and coves of the Great Smokies. Truly every prospect

pleases and only man is vile. Or, more accurately, man and all his works: the abandoned mines, the junked cars, the rotting shacks, the endless shopping centers that rear their lovely heads. This contrast increases the power of another phenomenon: the degree to which a sensitive and perceptive human can move within the beauty of the visible world, seeing and feeling it all, and at the same time never forgetting that the world, at best, does not know or care. And, at worst, this beauty may conceal the thing that will kill him.

What is wrong with Suttree? We can easily visualize his relatives asking: What ails that boy? What ails Suttree is what ails us all; we are shown it on every page. After his long affair with Joyce, he returns to his houseboat, repairs it, re-establishes his trot-lines and his old life. It is not a happy experience. After the repairs are finished, he prepares his supper and eats it alone. He looks into the ovoid of lamplight and frames questions and answers to himself.

> Of what would you repent?
>
> Nothing.
>
> Nothing?
>
> One thing. I spoke with bitterness about my life and I said that I would take my own part against the slander of oblivion and against the monstrous facelessness of it and that I would stand a stone in the very void where all would read my name. Of that vanity I recant all.

This is not adolescent rebellion. The passage comes near the end of the novel; I would simply suggest that it may be the definitive statement of the Existential consciousness. To understand its sources, we may have to pull apart the fabric of the novel, unraveling its many threads and textures. There are a great many of these threads; I will single out only three: Suttree and family; Suttree and love; Suttree and death. They are not found in isolation in the novel, any more than they would be in life. All of them have major statements in the first few pages: the suicide and the rag-picker, the memory of the stillborn brother and the letter from Suttree's father.

Or, there is Suttree's own marriage. We are shown bits and pieces: his own fragmentary comments, the behavior of his wife's family at the funeral of Suttree's little boy, and the comments of the sheriff when he orders Suttree out of town. The wife's elderly parents attack Suttree physically and the father pursues him with a loaded shotgun. What has Suttree done to create such blind implacable hatred even in a time of bereavement? Was it a shotgun marriage? Were they ever divorced? On what grounds? The sheriff says Suttree has ruined her life. How? These details hardly matter. What matters is the power and magnitude of this episode in the

scant ten pages it covers. Suttree cannot attend the funeral of his son; he must watch the entire proceeding from a distance.

> The little bier with its floral offerings had come to rest on a pair of straps across the mouth of the grave. A preacher stood at the ready. The light in this little glade where they stood seemed suffused with immense clarity and the figures appeared to burn. Suttree stood by a tree but no one noticed him. The preacher had begun.
>
> When all the words were done a few stepped forth and placed a flower and the straps began to lower, the casket and child sinking into the grave. A group of strangers commending Suttree's son to earth. . . Suttree went to his knees in the grass, his hands cupped over his ears.

This marriage is one of the three pair-bond relationships in Suttree's life. All of them are terminated violently, and in each case, the "resolution" grows out of inner tensions in Suttree himself; powerful emotional and moral conflicts. At the moment his son's coffin is lowered into the ground his wife gives way.

> The mother cried out and sank to the ground and was lifted up and helped away wailing. Stabat Mater Dolorosa. Remember her hair in the morning before it was pinned, black, rampant, savage with loveliness. As if she slept in perpetual storm.

From this small glimpse we can infer something of what he has had and a great deal of what he has given up. The life he has built requires a hard-eyed realism; and unflagging rejection of those involvements which would be a danger to him. For the most part, he is able to fend off the demands put on him by the inept, the helpless or the actively criminal. Sometimes his better judgment is absent or not enough: Leonard with his father's unburied corpse; Harrogate and his criminal schemes. Suttree has already served a year in the workhouse because he was passed-out drunk at the wrong time.

Reese is a different cause. He is clearly in the classical redneck tradition. When he works, he follows the trade of mussel-brailing: a primitive technique for dragging freshwater mussels and harvesting the shells. Reese needs Suttree's boat and Suttree's physical strength. Reese's wife is never named, but considerable attention is given to her appearance: a potbellied slattern with lank hair. If she is not actually dirty, she looks dirty. She is, however, deeply religious. She will be revealed gradually as a true matriarch and the mainstay of the family. Reese and his wife have had four children. One by-product of mussel-brailing is fresh-water pearls. The union of Reese and his wife has produced the pearl which is Wanda. She is young; everything about her is fresh, clean, pretty. Inevitably Suttree is alone with her. Inevitably they make love. He feels some compunction, some concern. He forbids her to come to his blanket at night, and she sleeps with the rest of the family. A period of heavy rain and flooding ensues. The slate cliff crashes down on the sleeping family, and Wanda is killed.

Many months later, Suttree takes up with a high-priced whore named Joyce, and soon settles into the pattern of fancy-man. She showers him with gifts; he spends his days in idleness while she works her trade. They acquire an apartment in a middle-class neighborhood and a bright-red XK 120. Suttree knows perfectly what his duties are: to be constantly attentive and flattering. Then the trouble begins with a series of hysterical episodes. These culminate when Joyce kicks out the windshield of the Jaguar, tears their money to shreds, and attracts the attention of the police.

Placing these three relationships side by side develops some illuminating conclusions. We have seen a little of what Suttree's marriage turned into. Clearly, that experience has its influence in his treatment of Wanda. If they continue what they are doing, the consequences are clear enough: Pregnancy, a shotgun marriage, more children and no way to provide for them. In a dozen years she will look exactly like her mother. Suttree forbids her to come to him at night as she has done. If he had not done this, she would still be alive.

Joyce is simply Wanda turned inside out. She too must have been an innocent child-like being. Precisely how she was introduced into the Life does not matter: all such stories are very much alike. She is in the Life, and will continue in it until madness or violence puts an end to her. Suttree sees that he is not helping her; he is making her worse. He walks away.

On the first page and the last page of the novel the motif is stated: Death is always at hand; in the city, on the river, in the mountains. Often he is heard at a distance, on horse-back, accompanied by hounds and the sound of horns. Death is *the* controlling image: death as enemy, death as danger, death as omnipresent event. In "real" life, death is omnipresent, of course, but in the real life of McAnally Flats, the odds are considerably steeper. Simply to inhabit the place, with its blind pigs, its beer joints, its homicidal police, its brawling as a way of life; simply to drink its lethal illicit whiskey is to lay life on the line, and is a statement as well as an action. By the end of the novel, almost all of Suttree's friends are dead. He has survived several near-fatal events, and by the narrowest of margins.

*Timor mortis conturbat me.* One way or another, we all think about it. Professor Ditsky's essay accounts for the "enormous and disturbing energy and power to move the reader." This power resides, in part, in "the clash between near-in-

credible erudition and resources of diction and the actual subject matter—the characters, the action, the settings. . . ." One such clash between diction and event occurs when Suttree and Ab Jones consult with an ancient black fortune-teller who is a reputed witch.

> A hookbacked crone going darkly and bent in a shapeless frock of sacking dyed dead black with log-wood chips and fustic mordant. Her spider hands clutching up a shawl of morling lamb. Gimpen granddam hobbling through the gloom with your knobbly cane go by, go by.

Within her tiny house and all its silly bric-a-brac there is a group photograph of her extended family taken many years ago. Upon close examination, the ancient grandmother who is the centerpiece of the family groups is shown to be dead when the picture was taken; the family had kept her body unburied until the itinerant photographer could be found. In one corner of the photograph there is a blank. It is where the old witch, then a child, was standing. Ab Jones is there to secure the death of his great enemy, Tarzan Quinn. But when the bones are cast, the results are disquieting. It is not Jones or Quinn death is interested in; it is Suttree.

Another contrast is between the finality, the totality of death and insignificance, the mediocrity of death's agents. If at times he comes on horseback, at others he is cloaked in a shabby inanity. The list is very long. There are sheriffs and city police, who are often stupid and bored, but who wear badges and guns, and have the unquestioned authority to use them. A flip remark or a lifted eyebrow can make the difference. There is the sad collection of drunks, bums, and criminals that Suttree runs with; frequently he is drawn into near-fatal brawls for no good reason. Once we have learned the signs and portents, we can spot these agents easily.

One is a half-grown kid, a drifter Suttree runs into on a lonely road, at night, after his little boy's funeral. They fight, and Suttree barely escapes with his life. The most evident agents of this kind are the moronic twins Vernon and Fernon. They are possum-hunters and are replete with all the badges and accouterments. They are accompanied by hounds, and carry the instrument of death, a shotgun. They are not merely twins; they are telepathic and telekinetic. It is possible for a stranger to whisper a word in the ear of one of them, and the other will know what it is.

The next night Suttree eats a meager repast with the family again. He takes his blanket to the river's edge, and eases toward sleep.

> The next moment all this was changed forever. Suttree leaped to his feet. The wall of slate above the camp had toppled in the darkness, whole jagged

ledges crashing down, great plates of stone separating along the seams with dry shrieks and collapsing with a roar upon the ground below, the dull boom of it echoing across the river and back again and then just the sifting down of small rocks, thin slates of shale clattering down in the dark. Suttree pulled himself into his trousers and started up through the trees at a run. He heard the mother calling out. Oh God, she cried. Suttree heard it with sickness at heart, this calling on. She meant for God to answer.

Somehow they get the slate off Wanda's crushed and mangled body; Reese picks her up.

> He seemed to be making for the river with her but in the loose sand he lost his footing and they fell and he knelt there in the rain over her and held his two fists at his breast and cried to the darkness over them all. Oh God I caint take no more. Please lift this burden from me for I caint bear it.

Vernon and Fernon have not killed Wanda; they have simply brought her death to her.

The metaphysics of death receive their fullest orchestration in the episode of Suttree's journey into the other-worldly high country of the Great Smokies. This passage covers a very brief span in the total pagination of the book. It implies or subsumes the motif of the quest, the Grail legends, and the matter and vocabulary of chivalry. It is much like the solitary pilgrimage of a hermit who wanders the wilderness for forty years. We are never told his reason for going; perhaps we are being left free to imagine our own. He takes a home-made backpack, a blanket, a fishline and a little dried food. On the very first night the auditory and visual phenomena begin: true visions or delusions; it makes no difference. His food is soon gone; there are trout in the river, but they will not bite his hook.

> In the morning turning up the frostveined stones for bait he uncovered a snake. Soporific, sleek viper with fanged jawhinges. Fate ridden snake, for all stones in the forest this one to sleep beneath. Suttree could not tell if it watched him or not, little brother death with his quartz goat's eyes. He lowered the stone with care.

There is no way to paraphrase or convey the tapestry of this journey; it must be read for itself. Suttree moves unscathed through the wilderness; there is snow at the higher elevations but he is not cold. There are storms, but the lightning does not come near him. Ravens fly by but bring him no food. Hunger increases his delusions, or perhaps the delusions are real and hunger has nothing to do with it.

He passes under a stone bridge and remembers the legend of the horseman who galloped under it. The horse came out but the man did not. He had been skewered through the skull by a protruding steel rod and had hung there, swinging. Suttree goes deeper and higher into the mountains. His clothes rot away. He sleeps more, and spends hours gazing into his various campfires. He is accompanied now by his Doppleganger . . . "Some doublegoer, some other Suttree." He is afraid that if this double eludes him he will dodder here forever.

His visions become even more powerful. He is not surprised to see a procession of monks. He sees whole troops of ghost calvary colliding. The climax is reached when he watches a panoramic Walpurgisnacht. There are hags and illbedowered harlots, chimeras and cacodemons, trolls and gnomes. A mesosaur, a garfish, and a gonfalon float overhead. Even so, these creatures do not harm him. The snake under the rock did not harm him. The wilderness has treated him with a sublime indifference. He might have starved at last, except that he finds a human. It is a small man with a crossbow, hunting out of season. The dialogue which follows is comic, but we know this man to be the emissary of death; he is small, frightened, and insignificant, but he carries the instrument of death in his hands and threatens to use it. He sends Suttree into the nearest town. Here, in spite of weeks without food, he cannot eat what he is served. He is refused service in the ABC store. A black man warns him "they'll vag you here." Somehow he finds his way to the bus station and gets a bus back to Knoxville.

He is skin and bones and can barely walk. Mrs. Long takes him into her boarding house again. He lies awake in the night, listening to the shunting of switch-engines.

> Recurrences of dreams he'd had in the mountains came and went and the second night he woke from uneasy sleep and lay in the world alone. A dark hand had scooped the spirit from his breast and a cold wind circled in the hollow there. He sat up. Even the community of the dead had disbanded into ashes, those shapes wheeling in the earth's crust through a nameless ether no more men than were the ruins of any other thing once living. Suttree felt the terror coming through the walls. He was seized with a thing he'd never known, a sudden understanding of the mathematical certainty of death. He felt his heart pumping down there under the palm of his hand. Who tells it so? Could a whole man not author his own death with a thought? Shut down the ventricle like the closing of an eye?

Suttree recovers more or less. He goes on with his life. He lives past his experiences with Wanda and Joyce. His brushes with death are almost continuous; one by one his friends are killed. Then he is in big trouble with the police. The trouble begins when he finds Ab Jones huddled in an alley. Suttree has managed to get Jones onto his feet when the prowl car finds them.

One officer insults them, and Ab replies in kind. He runs down the alley with both officers in pursuit. Acting on impulse, Suttree gets into the police car, drives it to the south bank of the river and sends it into the river. Meanwhile, Ab is clubbed into insensibility after he has seriously injured several officers. He is placed in a cell, and Tarzan Quinn waits for him to regain consciousness. Ab will die as a result of this treatment.

The criminal offenses which Suttree can be charged with are accessory to assault on a police officer and theft and destruction of a police cruiser. Dell, Ab's wife, tells him: "Don't let em get on you. They never will get off." He sees Oceanfrog, who tells him the police are looking for him. Late at night he destroys his trot-lines, stashes his skiff and removes his things from his houseboat. He holes up under an assumed name in the same skid row hotel where he lived with Joyce. He stays there for some days and becomes very ill. J-bone finds him near death and takes him to the hospital.

In the long sequence that follows, Suttree is all but dead for many weeks. A priest comes to give him his last rites. There are many days and nights of delirium, in which he sees and talks to all his dead, both very new and long, long gone. At last he is able to totter to a telephone booth; the faithful J-bone comes and he is taken for one last time to the old house on Grand Avenue. Once again he lies in the same bed and listens to the city noises in the night.

But now there is something that can only be called a major change in Suttree's world. McAnally Flats is being removed by that most ruthless method of slum clearance—the building of a freeway. What law and the police could never change is being swept away in a few weeks by the wrecker's ball. Suttree watches the process more or less with equanimity. He has made his decision: all things considered, he is going to leave Knoxville forever. There is hardly anyone left to tell the news to; only Trippin Through the Dew, the black transvestite homosexual.

> Suttree held out his hand. Tell me goodbye, he said.
>
> Where you goin?
>
> I dont know. I'm leaving Knoxville.
>
> Shoot. He slapped at Suttree's outstretched hand. You aint goin noplace. When? When you goin?
>
> Right now. I'm gone.

> The black reached out sadly, his face pinched. They stood there holding hands in the middle of the little street. When you comin back?
>
> I don't guess I'll be back.

Two scenes remain in the novel, short and powerful. In one, Suttree has returned for one last look at his houseboat. The door is ajar. A body is in his bed. It has been there for sometime. On one level of mundane realism this is merely another homeless derelict. But we know better: death has come for Suttree and has found someone else instead. When the city ambulance comes for the body, a Greek chorus of commentary is provided by three tall young black men.

> Who sick? one said.
>
> There was a man dead in there, the driver said.
>
> They looked at each other. How long he been dead?
>
> A couple of weeks.
>
> Shoo, one said, wrinkling his wide nose. That's what that's been.
>
> You dont know who it was do you?
>
> No suh.
>
> Dont know who lived here?
>
> No suh.
>
> Come on Ramsey, we got to go.
>
> I heah you, man.
>
> The driver closed the door and motioned with his hand and the ambulance pulled away. The boys watched them go. Shit, one said; Old Suttree aint dead.

In the final scene, Suttree stands beside a dusty road in his cheap new clothes, holding his small cardboard suitcase. He thumbs many cars but no one stops. A construction gang is at work across the road, inside a deep ditch. A waterboy comes with his bucket and passes the dipper to the workmen. We see only their supplicating hands as they reach up out of the ditch for the life-giving water. Unbidden, the boy comes across the road and hands the dipper to Suttree. He drinks and thanks the boy. Suttree has been given the water of life. A car stops without being thumbed. Suttree gets in, and the city which contains the buried bones of friends and forebears begins to slip behind.

When he looked back the waterboy was gone. An enormous lank hound had come out of the meadow by the river like a hound from the depths and was sniffing at the spot where Suttree had stood.

Somewhere in the gray wood by the river is the huntsman and in the blooming corn and in the castellated press of cities. His work lies all-wheres and his hounds tire not. I have seen them in a dream, slaverous and wild and their eyes crazed with ravening for souls in the world. Fly them.

## Tom Nolan (review date 9 June 1985)

SOURCE: A review of *Blood Meridian, or the Evening Redness in the West,* in *Los Angeles Times Book Review,* June 9, 1985, p. 2.

[*In the following review Nolan discusses the "gruesome pilgrimage" undertaken by the protagonist and the writing style of the author.*]

The apocalyptic landscape of Cormac McCarthy's harrowing and remarkable fifth novel is a blasted purgatorial heath, a hellish waste of thorns and buzzards where a malevolent sun squats and pulses like some great fire at earth's end. Across this tortured region of death and fear moves a crew of loathsome brigands as foul and evil as the arid waste they seem condemned to roam.

*Blood Meridian* is a fiction purportedly based on historical events that took place in the Southwestern United States and in Mexico in 1849-1850. Its central antihero is "the kid," a nameless lad still in his teens when first he demonstrates his "taste for mindless violence."

Coming out of Tennessee, the kid makes his way to East Texas, casting his lot there with an ill-fated outfit of renegade U.S troops determined to annex part of Mexico despite conclusion of the war with that country. Once on the merciless plain, these adventurers are set upon and mostly destroyed by a party of Comanches, "a legion of horribles, hundreds in number. . . wardrobed out of a fevered dream." The kid escapes, is jailed in Chihuahua, then recruited into the ranks of American mercenaries commissioned by Mexico to take a quantity of Apache scalps.

Theirs is a gruesome pilgrimage into the howling wilderness where coyotes dig up the dead and scatter their bones. Nameless dread is followed by ritual slaughter. Bodies are hacked and splattered, corpses are defiled. Vivid and terrible visions tumble upon one another with biblical fury as the dreadful caravan bleeds across this *terra damnata* "like some helio-

tropic plague" out of a "heathen land where they and others like them fed on human flesh."

These cursed degenerates have names like Batchat and Toadvine, and their leader is one John Glanton. Most insidious is the hairless giant called Judge Holden, an ominous tempter and figure of depravity given to the telling of wicked parables and the quoting of legal Latin. The air around these men is rosy with doom, and in their wake can be heard "the cries of souls broke through some misweave in the weft of things into the world below." In this place of crimson light and nameless rage, where "all covenants are brittle," a man dare not seek to know his own heart, for it is not the heart of a creature "that is bound in the way that God has set for it."

The prose of the book is stripped of quotation marks and filled with locutions suitable to an antique text. Morbid and droll mottoes head each chapter, sardonic glosses on the actions to come. Gustave Dore's illustrations would be a fitting complement to this frightful phantasmagoria. One can imagine its original discovered in some old pioneer's attic trunk, its yellowed pages flecked with gore. One pictures its author as some unrelenting recording angel who has stared hard and long into the pit and whose face wears a curious expression.

*Blood Meridian* stands the world of Louis L'Amour on its head (indeed, heaps hot coals upon it), but it is not merely a perverse burlesque of the traditional Old West romance. There is a great deal of action in *Blood Meridian,* but to seek in it the pleasures of a hard-riding adventure novel would be like looking for belly laughs in the *Divine Comedy.* McCarthy's screed is a theological purgative, an allegory on the nature of evil as timeless as Goya's hallucinations on war, monomaniacal in its conception and execution, it seeks and achieves the vertigo of insanity, the mad internal logic of a noon-time nightmare that refuses to end. Abandon hope, all ye who open this one.

## Bill Baines (review date Spring 1986)

SOURCE: A review of *Blood Meridian,* in *Western American Literature,* Vol. XXI, No. 1, Spring, 1986, pp. 59-60.

[*In the following review, Baines comments briefly on the "cruelty," "inhumanity," and "gore" present in* Blood Meridian.]

Set in the Southwest of the mid-nineteenth century, *Blood Meridian* does not invite confusion with any romantic notion of the West prevalent in that century or this. Cormac McCarthy reconstructs that West as a Daliesque stage upon which characters and forces often resonant of Shakespeare and the Bible act out their roles. Loosely based upon, or more accurately, *around* the Yuma Crossing Massacre of 23 April, 1850, and some of its principals, the book rises from its beginning above the mean particulars of history to universal certainties and uncertainties, the stuff of serious fiction.

McCarthy's book focuses on cruelty, perhaps man's most apparent quality in the world the author creates. The book's inhumanity is not—as is often the case in Westerns—the cruelty of white to Indian or Indian to white, but the cruelty of human to human perennial to literature and to other affairs of mankind. Underlying that and often reinforcing it is the apparent callousness of fate, indifferently and inexorably putting each person in the place or time to die in whatever predestined cruel or ridiculous manner.

As befits such matters, McCarthy's strong and often apunctuative style blends neologism and archaism in a syntax sometimes drawing on the rhythms of the Bible, sometimes on the resources of Old English, always modern in a Joycean way. Strong images abound (". . . Callaghan's body floated anonymously down-river, a vulture standing between the shoulderblades in clerical black, silent rider to the sea," and later, "Downshore the dull surf boomed") and combine with the writer's cadences to give *Blood Meridian* both poetry and strength.

As the title might indicate, gore, the book's strongest image, dominates. If the reader has ever witnessed or cleaned up the results of a totally successful ambush, he (for most American women haven't) will be prepared for the atrocities man commits upon man in this story; if he has not, the book will slam into him like a Sam Peckinpah film.

The protagonist, a nameless and taciturn young Everyman known only as "the kid," runs away from home at fourteen to the West to keep, as it appears, his appointment with his particular destiny. The book ends in his twenty-eighth year, the time intervening filled with his wandering throughout the West from one scrape, adventure and encounter to more of the same.

It is not, however, the kid who dominates McCarthy's *terra damnata*, but "Judge" Holden, an enigmatic giant, a genius who proves, Renaissance-like, master of sciences, arts, crafts, war, languages—of the world. At once nihilist, absurdist, rationalist and irrationalist, the powerful judge is limned in heroic proportions, an embodiment of the evil too often inherent in the ways man handles his knowledge. Holden, the most "civilized" and rational character in the book, exhibits many of its greatest cruelties, psychological and physical, ordering, then destroying—like western man—the world without.

The reader learns little of import about the kid that is not filtered through or later interpreted by the judge. As Holden berates his sometime colleague for failure to dedicate himself wholly to war, the latter's dull, animal integrity becomes apparent. Immortality, the freedom to dance, evades him, says Holden, for it is only gained in the flux of combat through relentless cruelty and lack of mercy. Earlier in the story, another character asks about Holden, "What's he a judge of?" When in the final pages the judge thus indicts the kid, the reader learns that he is a judge of the protagonist and ultimately of all mankind.

A powerful yet dreamlike book, *Blood Meridian* will not appeal to the reader who either sees or seeks the nice and the pleasant in man and his world.

## Geoffrey O'Brien (review date 15 July 1986)

SOURCE: "Cowboys and Nothingness," in *The Village Voice*, Vol. XXXI, No. 280, July 15, 1986, p. 48.

[*In the following review, O'Brien discusses* Blood Meridian *within the context of the Western genre, noting differences and similarities between the two.*]

The Western, being the simplest of genres, is also the most protean, ever ripe for new variations. For a moment in the '60s, Sam Peckinpah and Sergio Leone appeared to have arrived at its logical dead end, but writers today are taking a fresh look at the genre. It attracts like a power source, a link to the limitless. Reinventing the Western means re-inventing America, turning the creation epic upside down to come up with a different end-product: a new Texas, a new Mexico, a new definition of reality. Notions of the real, of course, change with alarming swiftness, so that *The Wild Bunch* or *For a Few Dollars More*, billed in their day as cynical anti-Westerns, now seem as soaringly romantic as any of their predecessors. All that empty space is what does it. Almost as mechanically as a drug, desert and canyon and prairie elevate the squalidest occurrences into ritual splendors. Set a third-rate racketeer against infinite sky and he becomes Wyatt Earp. No wonder writers and filmmakers can't stay away from a genre that does half their work for them.

In *Blood Meridian* Cormac McCarthy reduces the Western to its essential components: landscape and killing. From the classic Hollywood variety he has preserved the hypnotic expansiveness of wide-screen vistas and the technical precision of large-scale bloodletting; and to compensate for the absence of a Fordian or Hawksian mise-en-scene, he has forged a distinctive prose which might be described as Hardboiled Biblical, a weird blend of cold-eyed photo-realism and prophetic diction. Reading the book is like watching a slowly unwinding painted panorama. From a distance it resembles a magnificent canvas by Bierstadt or Church, but as you peer more closely at its clefts and dells you find them crammed with hacked bodies and discarded torture implements: "The dead lay awash in the shallows like the victims of some disaster at sea and they were strewn along the salt foreshore in a havoc of blood and entrails. Riders were towing bodies out of the bloody waters of the lake, and the froth that rode lightly on the beach was a pale pink in the rising light. They moved among the dead harvesting the long black locks with their knives and leaving their victims rawskulled and strange in their bloody cauls." What disturbs is not so much the violence as its lack of resonance, the way the immense surroundings swallow up suffering.

As *Blood Meridian* traces the depredations and torments of a band of scalp-hunters roaming the Tex-Mex border in the 1840s, its welter of skirmishes and massacres feels like a single moment impossibly distended, a moment of absolute pain preparing to give way to nothingness. In most Westerns, violence is climactic; here it's as predictable as the passage of time, and the moments of high drama occur when the slaughtering is unexpectedly suspended. During the rest of the book, killers kill and are killed with such rolling repetition that the horrors begin to seem incidental twitchings of an essentially immobile landscape. McCarthy's drifters are "like beings provoked out of the absolute rock . . . in a time before nomenclature was." For them the articulations of language amount to no more than "the dull boom of rock falling somewhere far below them in the awful darkness inside the world." A mindless life-force asserts itself through violence in the face of imminent extinction.

The book imposes itself by sheer duration and reiteration. Its long-winded cadences testify that there is no limit either to the killing or to the barren territories through which the killers ride, stagger, and ultimately crawl. Dialogue is guttural and terminally inarticulate. When the lone survivors of a Comanche raid encounter each other amid gutted torsos and handfuls of viscera, they converse about as expressively as McCarthy's people ever do: "What kind of indians was them?" "I dont know." "Damn if they aint about a caution to the christians." These minimal exchanges are set off by the baroque profusion of language that McCarthy lavishes on their surroundings. The life of the book resides in its rocky underpinnings and spiky vegetation. On a single page we move among "gray lava dust" and "scalloped canyon walls," through "fallen rock and scoria and deadly looking bayonet plants," into "an old reliquary of flintknappings and ratchel"—pausing only for a moment by "a bush that was hung with dead babies"—to end up at "a village on the plain where smoke still rose from the ruins and all were gone to death."

This dominance of background pushes cowboy-picture aesthetics to their limit: between precisely described, usually

violent action and engulfing, luridly beautiful settings, there's no room for any privacy of thought or feeling. The human interior ceases to exist. But if *Blood Meridian* stakes out a domain of emptiness, the emptiness is dense, messy, a tangle of desperate and dying creatures. In a previous novel, *Child of God,* McCarthy dealt with similar material, but there the action was restricted to an east Tennessee backwater and most of the atrocities stemmed from a single deranged person. *Blood Meridian* encompasses all places and all people, going beyond the hermetic rigors of genre toward a theoretically unfinishable cavalcade, like a camera panning across an endless field of corpses.

In fact the book doesn't really end; it dissolves, in a manner I don't find altogether satisfactory. With most of the cast annihilated, the last few chapters threaten to veer from hallucinatory realism into a more allegorical mode. The Judge, a murderous intellectual madman who has quietly dominated the band of killers, takes on an increasingly supernatural air, and the drooling idiot who accompanies him across desert wastes evokes an unfortunate Shakespearean parallel—unfortunate because an appeal to literature can only weaken the unmediated intensity of the bulk of the novel. But whatever one makes of McCarthy's mode of withdrawal from his nightmare, the book's termination is curiously unimportant. The hell of endlessness McCarthy has taken us through is enough to convince us that if the book did not end inadequately it could not end at all. *Blood Meridian* has no more destination than its blood-spattered protagonists, only a relentless forward movement. The terror of that blind and arbitrary process—a process also known as history—soaks into every page. Like all Western heroes, McCarthy's mercenaries ride off into the sunset: and the sunset devours them.

## John Lewis Longley Jr. (review date Autumn 1986)

SOURCE: "The Nuclear Winter of Cormac McCarthy," in *The Virginia Quarterly Review,* Vol. 62, No. 4, Autumn, 1986, pp. 746-50.

[*In the following essay, Longley notes that every major episode in* Blood Meridian *is based on a real event in history. The critic comments upon the themes evident in every McCarthy novel: the "pervasiveness of evil," the "usurpation of authority," and the "denial of responsibility."*]

*Blood Meridian* is not for the tenderhearted. In his fifth novel, McCarthy presents us with a new locale and a different time frame. The action in each of his first four novels is centered in East Tennessee and takes place in the middle of the 20th century. *Blood Meridian* takes place in northern Mexico and what is now the American southwest. The time is 1848-1850 with an epilogue some years later.

One thing must be clearly understood from the start. Every major episode in this book is based on real events. The major characters are all people who actually existed. What they did, the actions they performed are to be found in the documents of the period. The basic situation is this: Governor Trias of Chihuahua province must confront the Apache, who are literally destroying the province by wiping out much of the Mexican population. The governor opts for the Final Solution; he declares open season and a bounty: $100.00 gold American for every Apache scalp, age and sex of the scalpee not a consideration.

The strike force is organized by Glanton. These men are not militia or police or wagon train guards. They are experienced, highly professional killers. Killing is what they do. Many of them are already under death sentence in other jurisdictions. When they find an encampment of Apache, the blood flows, and many scalps are brought in. The reward money is thrown away in an epic spree of drinking, rape, and looting. In a few days, graffiti begin to appear on walls: *Mejor los indios.* Other scalps must be obtained. The killers soon discover that once a scalp has been lifted and carted about for weeks, no one can tell if the scalp is Indian or Mexican. The killing becomes democratic: anyone with black hair is killed and scalped. The rest of the novel traces the rapid decay of group and personal discipline. At the end they are killing and robbing anything that moves.

So much for the historical record. The documents are in the archives if anyone cares to read them. But McCarthy is no more likely to rest with the historical record than he was to describe East Tennessee simply as he found it. What we have to consider is the work as fiction—what he has done with time, place, and people.

Several elements or conditions are present in any McCarthy novel. Chief among them are denial of responsibility, usurpation of authority, and the rejection of Grace. What is often most troubling to the general reader is not only the pervasiveness of evil, but even more the lack of any rationale, any motive for the things that people do. McCarthy has repudiated several attempts to make him into a philosopher, but there is a metaphysic working here: as with the Greeks, the sign of evil is the violence it brings forth. As so often is the case in his other fiction, landscape (whether it is a bucolic landscape filled with murderers, or a grubby slum like McAnally Flats) is landscape as metaphor. The landscape in *Blood Meridian* is like the landscape on the moon, or like the surface of the earth will be after a prolonged nuclear winter when everything is dead. On the prosaic level of factual realism, this landscape is simply the Great American Desert—desolate, arid, littered with the bones of animals and men. Its abiding characteristic is its enormous indifference to everything that happens: hope, travail, terror, death. At a wider and deeper level, this landscape is the landscape of Hell—the inevitable configuration of a world without Grace. Once this condition is understood, the incredible becomes commonplace and the unthinkable becomes routine.

This being true, no one escapes. There are no good guys anywhere—not the Indians, the Mexicans, the Americans, including the handful of black Americans who ride in Glanton's band. They are murderers all, by profession and by choice. The most that can be said for the Indians is that they kill and scalp for fun and glory, not for money.

In characterization, the novel is purely ensemble playing. There is no central character whose story waits to unfold. If there is a protagonist, it is "the Kid," not otherwise named, whose story begins and ends the novel. The Kid is introduced at age 14: "He can neither read nor write and in him broods already a taste for mindless violence." The Kid is perfect for the part he is fated to play: to cause suffering and to endure suffering. He is often used as a foil to play off the ideas and actions of Judge Holden.

The band of killers is led by Captain Glanton, a small man who is clearly insane. He can never return to the United States because of some dreadful action he has taken there. It is said that he is ". . . equal to whatever might follow for he was complete at every hour. . . . He'd long forsworn all weighing of consequence." He holds his gang of cutthroats together by iron discipline and simple fear. They know there is nothing he will not do, since most of them have already seen examples of what he does to deserters. If Glanton should be otherwise occupied, there is always the Judge. Tobin, the ex-priest, believes that Glanton and the Judge have some terrible secret covenant. Events will bear this out.

The Judge is an albino and is seven feet tall. His skills and accomplishments are endless; not only the frontier skills needful to thrive in an empty desert peopled by savages, but others: languages, music art, science, history, philosophy. He is a fanatical botanizer and archaeologist, but not for the usual reason. Asked what he plans to do with the artifacts he collects, he replies: "To expunge them from the memory of man."

Eventually, everything about the Judge will fall into place: he hates all living things. He says: "Whatever in creation exists without my knowledge exists without my consent." "The freedom of birds is an insult to me." He intends to be suzerain of all the earth ". . . and yet everywhere upon it are pockets of autonomous life. . . In order for it to be mine nothing must be permitted to occur upon it save by my dispensation." Hence the comment of the Kid: "You're crazy."

Of all forms of biologic life, the Judge hates humans the most, and children most of all. His own personal, exquisitely refined recreation is child-murder. His procedure is to rescue a child in a massacre, pet it, win its confidence, and then kill and scalp it. Tobin, the ex-priest, repeatedly warns the Kid that the Judge has singled him out for some long-range, particularly horrible fate. But the Kid does not listen, and the story winds on to its end.

The reviewers in the large national newspapers have been having a terrible time with *Blood Meridian*. One suggests that readers would not find the book compatible with their orange juice and corn flakes as though most serious fiction is read at the breakfast table before rushing off to the commuter train. Another admits that McCarthy is almost a genius, but he fails (alas) because of his *brutality* and his *excess*. *Blood Meridian* would be a masterpiece but for the excess. One is forcefully reminded of the remark about Thomas Sutpen's recipe for morality. If only McCarthy had measured the ingredients for his pie or cake a little more carefully.

Putting this novel in a context of corn flakes is a failure to deal with it. Instead of treating it like a Gothic romance or a novel by Stephen King, it ought to be confronted for what it is. The earlier novels were often compared to Faulkner, primarily because of rhetoric and subject matter (as though East Tennessee and Mississippi were identical and somehow interchangeable). What serious critics will have to do is look for other affinities—Melville, Conrad, and Dostoevski. The Judge invites comparison with Stagrovin and Svidrigaloff, or perhaps even Nechaev himself. Instructive parallels can be drawn with *Heart of Darkness*—what happens in a savage wilderness when all restraints are removed, and there is no one to say *Thou shalt not*.

Recently *The New Yorker* ran a series in which the reporter traced the march of W. T. Sherman through Georgia. The series concluded with some philosophical speculation about the relationship between that episode and what went on at (for instance) My Lai. The present writer grew up in an area devastated by Sherman, but even the most horrific folk tales of my childhood never accused Sherman of scalping women and children. The reporter in *The New Yorker* has an interesting (if somewhat obvious) thesis, but he is looking at the wrong sources. The precedents of My Lai are not found in Sherman's march, which was carried out against white Americans. The precedents have always been there in our national policy toward anyone with a darker skin and a more "primitive" culture, which is simple genocide. Some quick examples: "The Puritans first fell on their knees and then on the aborigines." "The only good indian is a dead indian." "Civilize 'em with a Krag." "Manifest Destiny." The events at Greasy Grass and Wounded Knee. The crop-headed young men on our military bases who wear T-shirts proclaiming "Kill 'em all—let God sort 'em out."

Mr. McCarthy is not trying to tell us about the Good Little Boy. The reviewers who object to the blood in *Blood Me-*

*ridian* either do not know what happens when several dozen people are shot, chopped, or scalped in a confined space, or they do not wish to think about it. In either case, their quarrel is with human physiology, not Cormac McCarthy's fiction.

### Mark Royden Winchell (review date April 1990)

SOURCE: "Inner Dark: or, The Place of Cormac McCarthy," in *The Southern Review*, Vol. 26, No. 2, April, 1990, pp. 293-309.

[*In the following essay, Winchell maintains that the "pyrotechnical use of language that is McCarthy's distinctive signature as a writer" is the author's greatest achievement. Winchell also discusses the influence of Faulkner on McCarthy's work and comments at length on the "revulsion" and "horror" found in the novels.*]

Cormac McCarthy may be the most highly respected unknown writer in contemporary southern letters. Vereen Bell estimates that McCarthy's five novels have sold no more than fifteen thousand copies in their various editions, and two of those novels (*Child of God* and *Blood Meridian*) are listed as "out-of-stock" by their publisher. If McCarthy has been shunned by the public, he has steadfastly resisted that sure refuge of the "serious" writer—academic patronage. (In fact, he flunked out of the University of Tennessee once and dropped out after a second try.) Although he has been sustained by private foundations, he seems never to have fed at the public trough, and he obviously prefers the company of skid row derelicts to that of professional literary types. He has guarded his privacy with the zeal of a J. D. Salinger or Thomas Pynchon without having their royalties as a buffer between himself and the critical establishment. When Mark Morrow finally tracked him down for a 1985 picture book on southern writers, he found McCarthy living in a ten-by-ten-foot room in the Colonial Motel on Kingston Street in Knoxville, his only visible possessions a portable typewriter and a '64 Rambler.

But eccentricity is so endemic to writers and would-be writers that no one would give McCarthy a second look if weird behavior were all he had to recommend himself. It is the stylistic brilliance of his five novels that makes Cormac McCarthy a writer's writer and would do so even if he were as truly unknown as B. Traven. McCarthy possesses a southern feel for character and dialogue (rendered without quotation marks) and a not-altogether-southern eye for the mystery and otherness of nature. His sense of the comic reminds one alternately of Flannery O'Connor and the best of the current "grit lit" crowd.

However, it is his pyrotechnical use of language that is McCarthy's distinctive signature as a writer. His cadences and syntax inevitably remind one of Faulkner, but McCarthy's working vocabulary leaves even Faulkner in the dust. (One can imagine the college dropout taking a perverse pleasure in sending erudite professors scurrying to the dictionary to verify the meaning of some arcane term used with astonishing precision.) As John Ditsky notes, "Though doubtless operating under some degree of Faulknerian influence, McCarthy writes as though Faulkner had never existed, as if there were no limits to what language might be pushed into doing in the last half of the twentieth century." Consider, for example, a not atypical passage from McCarthy's *Outer Dark:*

> What discordant vespers do the tinker's goods chime through the long twilight and over the brindled forest road, him stooped and hounded the windy recrements of day like those exiles who divorced of corporeality and enjoined ingress of heaven or hell wander forever the middle warrens spoorless increate and anathema. Hounded by grief, by guilt, or like this cheerless vendor clamored at heel through wood and fen by his own querulous and inconsolable wares in perennial tin malediction.

Only a college sophomore with a thesaurus or a supremely gifted and self-confident writer would have dared construct such a paragraph.

The mixed blessing of Faulkner's influence has been a commonplace of southern criticism at least since the time that Flannery O'Connor commented on the wisdom of getting off the track when the Dixie Limited comes through town. As Louis Rubin points out in his essay "On the Difficulties of Being a Southern Writer Today: or, Getting Out from Under William Faulkner," that sage advice has too often been ignored by writers who appropriate aspects of Faulkner's style "to describe an experience that was not really Faulknerian at all."

Although this specific observation was made about William Humphrey, it could very well apply to Cormac McCarthy, whose first novel was published two years after Rubin's essay. The echoes of Faulkner in McCarthy's prose serve not so much to remind us of stylistic similarities as to alert us to philosophical differences. For all of the degeneracy and pessimism in his novels, Faulkner was at heart a moralist who believed in an irreducible core of human dignity. His works possess a moral center, either explicit or implicit, that judges the evil and depravity of the world. In McCarthy's universe that center either doesn't exist or cannot hold. Had McCarthy written *The Sound and the Fury,* Dilsey would have been gang raped by a bunch of Klansmen on the way home from church.

A good part of the difference between Faulkner and McCarthy lies in the fact that Faulkner gave his characters a far richer interior life. McCarthy's people more often resemble the Darwinian creatures who inhabited the naturalistic novels of the late nineteenth and early twentieth centuries. (Even in his primitive emotional state, Benjy Compson seems less bestial than any half dozen of Cormac's cretins.) As we read McCarthy's descriptions of his characters and their natural habitat, sometimes blending into each other, we see a humanity that differs only in degree from the rest of the animal world. (When man and nature merge in Faulkner, as in *Go Down, Moses,* it is because nature has become more nearly human, man not less so.) When we do get inside McCarthy's characters, we find in *Suttree* a surrealistic dream world that exists outside the realm of reason, and in *Child of God* a cesspool of perversion that is not only unnatural but a grotesque parody of much that is human. And as we move back to the outside world, we find not even the rational jungle of Darwin but an absurdist wasteland where chaos and pointless brutality take the place of natural law.

In his first novel, *The Orchard Keeper,* McCarthy made a point of continually violating the comfortable expectations of his readers. Vereen Bell has noted how the novel's shifting, almost random, point of view defies even the illusion of authorial control. McCarthy so consistently avoids the transitions and connections of a well-made novel that we suspect neither accident nor ineptitude but some more insidious design to be at work. This design extends beyond the form of the novel to the story being told. At first glance, the basic outline of that story is what one might expect from the first novel of a contemporary southern writer. A young boy grows up in a rural setting besieged by the forces of civilization. With his father dead, the boy's two primary role models are a wise and fiercely independent hermit, from whom he learns the ways of nature, and a sociopathic bootlegger, from whom he learns defiance of authority. Years earlier, the bootlegger had killed a man who tried to steal his car and then dumped the body in an abandoned spray tank in an orchard near the hermit's cabin. What none of the three major characters knows is that the dead man was the boy's father.

In a conventionally plotted novel McCarthy might have had the young boy, John Wesley Rattner, torn between the two rather different forms of iconoclasm represented by the hermit and the bootlegger. Or he might have had the boy face a grave moral crisis by discovering that his bootlegger friend, Marion Sylder, killed the father he had sworn to avenge. Or John Wesley could have come to maturity by learning that his father was a tramp and a thief, not the sainted provider his widow made him out to be. McCarthy's steadfast refusal to turn any of these obvious tricks of plot may well be a higher form of realism, a fidelity to the disconnectedness of actual experience. The fact that this strategy is so disconcerting tells us something about the nature of art.

The greatest literature enables us to look into the very heart of darkness by making of the intolerable a thing of beauty. By giving coherence and articulation to human experience, art can make the fate of an Oedipus, a Kurtz, or a Benjy, an object of sublime contemplation, an occasion of catharsis. In the hands of a clumsy or indifferent artist, the materials of tragedy degenerate into soap opera or pornography. This is clearly not the case with Cormac McCarthy. Neither clumsy nor indifferent, he is presenting reality with a deliberate paucity of narrative structure—either conventional or experimental. Even when literary things happen, it is with the inconclusiveness of real life. Rebellion leads to suffering but not to martyrdom. Words of wisdom are spoken without conviction and with no long-lasting effect. Epiphanies change no lives. The final scene of the novel shows a grown-up John Wesley sitting on his mother's gravestone, concerned only about the wetness of his sock.

If there is a message in *The Orchard Keeper* it is profoundly naturalistic. The novel opens with a parable of three men cutting an elm tree that has grown up around a piece of fence. Obviously, this is a case of nature surrounding and obliterating a human construct. What is perhaps more significant, however, is that the men assume it is the fence that has grown up inside the tree. Not only are the effects of man less durable than the world of which they are a part, but human vanity frequently blinds us to that fact. At the end of the novel, we learn that the elm tree had been felled on the day that John Wesley visited his mother's grave and that the iron embedded in the tree had been part of the fence surrounding the cemetery. When he leaves, John Wesley walks through the hole in the fence oblivious to what it might teach him.

Near the end of McCarthy's second novel, *Outer Dark,* is an infinitely more grotesque instance of nature enveloping the merely human:

> The tinker in his burial tree was a wonder to the birds. The vultures that came by day to nose with their hooked beaks among his buttons and pockets like outrageous pets soon left him naked of his rags and flesh alike. Black mandrake sprang beneath the tree as it will where the seed of the hanged falls and in spring a new branch pierced his breast and flowered in a green boutonniere perennial beneath his yellow grin.

The difference between this nightmare landscape and the more pastoral image of the fence in the elm is a measure of the increasing horror of McCarthy's vision, or at least the increasing gothicism of his technique. William J. Schafer sees *Outer Dark* (and McCarthy's work in general) as a testament of the "hard wages of original sin." However, in a world where there is neither primal innocence nor a hope for

redemption, original sin seems somehow too positive a concept.

If, as we have long believed, a sense of place is one of the glories of southern literature, McCarthy again frustrates our expectations, for the setting of *Outer Dark* seems to owe as much to Beckett as it does to Faulkner. (In commenting on the opening paragraph of *The Orchard Keeper,* John Ditsky writes, "If this is the South, it is the South perceived by Vladimir and Estragon.") As in a dream, the locale of individual scenes is specific enough, often hauntingly so, without an identifiable context of period or region. We surmise only that we are someplace in the rural South toward the end of the nineteenth century. Beyond that, we know only that McCarthy's characters live in an outer dark of incest, murder, infanticide, and cannibalism.

The principal characters are a brother and sister, Culla and Rinthy Holme. Like a backwoods Adam and Eve (the comparison is William Schafer's), they couple and produce offspring—an infant whom Culla claims died at birth but whom he has really abandoned to the elements. When Rinthy finds no body buried in the child's ostensible grave, she correctly infers that the baby is still alive and in the custody of an itinerant tinker who sells household goods and pornographic postcards. Rinthy sets out in search of the child, and Culla in search of Rinthy. Although neither quest is successful, brother and sister continually cross paths with each other, the tinker and their baby, and three terrifying marauders whose behavior gives a whole new meaning to the concept of motiveless malignity.

Because he recognizes the taboo against incest (or at least against incestuous progeny), Culla is the more fully socialized of the two siblings. Rinthy is a far more innocent and elemental figure. She says, "I don't live nowheres no more . . . I just go around hunting my chap. That's about all I do any more." Her strong maternal instincts, including breasts that continue to lactate for her absent child, make Rinthy a positive symbol of the life force. However, her experience undercuts that life force at nearly every turn. Even when people take her in, which they are constantly doing, they are unable to help her find her child, and one of the homes where she briefly stays seems the very negation of family life. Although the husband and wife have produced five children, none lived to adulthood. The wife is reduced to churning butter to sell at the local stores (an ironic counterpoint to Rinthy's lactation). Not only is her husband unable to eat the butter, but he hurls an entire board of it at her in the midst of a pointless argument, as Rinthy beats a frightened retreat.

Culla encounters considerably greater peril in his travels. He sees graves robbed and men hanging from trees. In one unforgettable sequence, he crosses a river in a runaway ferry boat whose captain has been swept overboard. (During part of the crossing Culla frantically dodges a berserk horse he cannot see, until finally the horse gallops to his death in the swollen river.) Upon attaining the other shore, Culla encounters the three marauders, who insist on his sharing a sinewy and indigestible meat that may well be human flesh. He is then forced to exchange his nearly new boots for rotten old ones and left to fend for himself in the night. When Culla Holme (now ironically homeless) takes shelter in an abandoned house, he is arrested for trespassing and is sentenced by the local squire to ten days' labor to work off a five-dollar fine. When Culla asks to stay on later for no more than board, the squire tells him to get out of town.

Culla faces additional danger when he encounters a group of hog drovers. After the hogs inexplicably stampede and plunge over a cliff, taking one of the drovers with them, the surviving men conclude that Culla has somehow been responsible for the catastrophe and decide to hang him. They are even encouraged in a roundabout way by one of the many false prophet figures who populate McCarthy's fiction—a parson who looks as if he could have stepped right off the pages of "Snuffy Smith." Culla escapes this bit of irrational and undeserved punishment by leaping into the river after the hogs. The presence of the parson and the obvious parallel to the biblical story of the Gadarene swine makes this incident something more than just another example of gratuitous violence in an absurd world. Again, the surface comparisons are meant to highlight differences rather than similarities. Unlike Christ, Culla casts out no devils. (In McCarthy's world the demons are omnipresent and probably omnipotent.) He can save only himself, and that only by swimming with dead hogs.

McCarthy gives some sense of closure to *Outer Dark* when Culla Holme finally comes across the infant he had left for dead. The marauders have hanged the tinker (don't ask why) and stolen the child, and they seem to be waiting for Holme when he limps to their campfire after escaping from the hog drovers. Apparently having had a change of heart, Holme asks that the men give him the baby for his sister to raise. What follows is one of the most disgusting and harrowing scenes in contemporary literature:

> Holme saw the blade wink in the light like a long cat's eye slant and malevolent and a dark smile erupted on the child's throat and went all broken down the front of it. The child made no sound. It hung there with one eye glazing over like a wet stone and the black blood pumping down its naked belly. The mute one knelt forward. He was drooling and making little whimpering noises in his throat. He knelt with his hands outstretched and his nostrils rimpled delicately. The man handed him the child

and he seized it up, looked once at Holme with witless eyes, and buried his moaning face in its throat.

Although Holme has a too obviously symbolic encounter with a blind prophet a few pages later, the real end of the novel comes immediately after the butchering of the child. Arriving at the marauders' former campsite in the late afternoon (how many days later we do not know), Rinthy

> trailed her rags through dust and ashes, circling the dead fire, the charred billets and chalk bones, the little calcined ribcage. She poked among the burnt remains of the tinker's traps, the blackened pans confused among the rubble, the lantern with its skewed glass, the axle and iron wheelhoops already rusting. She went among this charnel curiously. She did not know what to make of it.

That Rinthy's quest for her child should end this way is almost as horrible as the murder itself. Not only is innocence incapable of overcoming evil, it is sometimes incapable of even perceiving it. However, nature itself outlasts both the good and evil that men do. McCarthy reminds us of this when, leaving the perplexed Rinthy, he describes the hanging tree growing up around the body of the tinker:

> He took the sparse winter snows upon what thatch of hair still clung to his dried skull and hunters that passed that way never chanced to see him brooding among his barren limbs. Until wind had tolled the tinker's bones and seasons loosed them one by one to the ground below and alone his bleached and weathered brisket hung in that lonesome wood like a bone birdcage.

If *Outer Dark* is a book of intermittent horror, McCarthy's third novel, *Child of God,* is calculated to produce revulsion on nearly every page. To take only one example, the incest that precipitates the action in *Outer Dark* is an undramatized given (sort of like the adultery in *The Scarlet Letter*). In *Child of God,* it is a merely incidental perversion—graphically described. When the local dumpman catches one of his slatternly daughters (offspring to whom he has given such names as Urethra, Cerebellum, and Hernia Sue) copulating in the woods, he chases the boy away and begins beating his child with a stick. "She grabbed it," McCarthy writes. "He overbalanced. Hot fishy reek of her freshened loins. Her peach drawers hung from a bush. The air about him grew electric. Next thing he knew his overalls were about his knees and he was mounting her. Daddy quit, she said. Daddy. Oooh." When he ascertains that her swain did not "dump a load" in her, "he pulled it out and gripped it and squirted his jissom on her thigh. Goddamn you, he said. He rose and heisted up his overalls and lumbered off toward the dump like a bear." Walter Sullivan hardly overstates the case when he says of this novel, "In spite of all the effective writing and the generation of dramatic tension, it is not a consummated work of art but an affront to decency on every level."

But McCarthy's reputation as a serious artist is such that critics are inclined to give him the benefit of the doubt and assume that some higher seriousness redeems his gross sensationalism. Perhaps like Leslie Fiedler in *Freaks,* he is simply trying to define the human by the marginal rather than the central. In the second paragraph of his novel, McCarthy describes his hideous protagonist as "a child of God much like yourself perhaps." Robert Coles finds this hint of theology quite convincing and writes of McCarthy, "He is a novelist of religious feeling who appears to subscribe to no creed but who cannot stop wondering in the most passionate and honest way what gives life meaning." While such a characterization accurately describes Coles, it begs several questions when applied to McCarthy. I am not convinced that Cormac McCarthy believes there is meaning in life or that the search for it is a worthwhile activity. Nevertheless, in a bizarre way, *Child of God* may well be the most human of his first three novels.

As we have seen, *The Orchard Keeper* and *Outer Dark* both demonstrate the powerlessness of humanity to withstand the forces of natural mutability. The central action of *Child of God* is the effort of one seriously depraved human being to defeat those very forces. As dialectical opposites, love and death have always been closely linked in life and literature. Undying love and no-longer-living loved ones are the stuff of both sentimental tearjerkers and the most sublime novels and poems of the Western world. No human sentiment is more understandable than the desire that passion should transcend death itself. Yet strictly speaking, this desire is profoundly "unnatural." Unchecked by a sense of reality, it can lead to morbid fixation and—at its most extreme—necrophilia. In fact, to some twisted minds, it may seem paradoxically necessary to kill the beloved in order to cheat death, or simple change, of its natural advantage. It was so for Porphyria's lover in Browning's poem and for Faulkner's Miss Emily. However, for sheer lunacy neither of these lovers of the dead can touch McCarthy's Lester Ballard.

For Browning and Faulkner necrophilia was the punch line (I hesitate to say climax) of the story, beyond which nothing need nor could be said. For McCarthy, it occurs at the center of the narrative, with its implications worked out in increasingly shocking detail. Before we even get to that narrative center, however, there is enough garden-level depravity to titillate the prurient imagination. In less than fifty pages, Lester threatens to kill an auctioneer, spies on a couple in lover's lane while spilling his seed on the fender of their car, kills a recalcitrant cow by throwing a rope around its neck and trying to pull it with a tractor, and strips the clothes off a woman who has been sexually assaulted and left by the side of the road.

We also learn that as a child Lester has bloodied a playmate who refused to fetch a softball for him and that he had walked into a barn where his father had hanged himself. In a particularly ghastly scene he gives a captured robin to the idiot child of a girl he is trying to woo. After leaving the child with the bird for a few minutes, they return to find "its mouth was stained with blood and it was chewing. Ballard went on through the door into the room and reached down to get the bird. It fluttered on the floor and fell over. He picked it up. Small red nubs worked in the soft down." Perhaps as a foreshadowing of Lester's future antics, the idiot has chewed the robin's legs off to keep it from getting away.

By the time Lester stumbles onto an abandoned car where a couple has been asphyxiated in the midst of coitus, less than ten pages after the incident with the robin, we are prepared for just about anything. McCarthy manages to heighten the ghoulishness of the scene by describing it in a matter-of-fact language that keeps our attention riveted to what is happening (here the resemblance is more to Hemingway than to Faulkner). While the dead man, his penis still sheathed in a wet yellow condom, appears to be watching him, Ballard kicks the man's feet out of the way, sniffs the girl's panties, and unbuckles his trousers.

> A crazed gymnast laboring over a cold corpse. He poured into that waxen ear everything he'd ever thought of saying to a woman. Who could say she did not hear him? When he'd finished he raised up and looked out again. The windows were fogged. He took the hem of the girl's skirt with which to wipe himself. He was standing on the dead man's legs. The dead man's member was still erect.

Baroque language would have ruined the effect here. Like the sick jokes that began circulating in the late fifties and early sixties, this scene shocks precisely because it makes the horrible mundane, if not exactly banal.

Lester is not only a child of God (whatever that may finally mean), he is something of a mad god himself, ruling a world of make-believe people. In addition to the human corpses he acquires, he has stuffed bears and tigers he has won at the fair. "[A]s aberrant as Lester progressively becomes," Vereen Bell notes, "he is ruled at every turn both by unspeakable appetite and by a warped compulsion to domesticate it." He plays house with his menagerie—first in a run-down shack and, when that burns, in a cave. He even goes to town to purchase clothes, including black and red underwear, for his favorite corpses. It may be that Lester's behavior is most alarming when it comes closest to parodying the normal (just as the news that Ted Bundy collected cheerleader magazines seemed kinkier than if he had been exclusively a connoisseur of hard core pornography). The point is not that there is no distinction between normality and abnormality but that in assaulting that distinction, mockery of the normal becomes a special kind of perversion.

To appreciate the particular quality of McCarthy's vision, one need only consider what other writers might have done with Lester's story. Flannery O'Connor would certainly have made a theological parable out of it. (Robert Coles notwithstanding, this is something that McCarthy does not do.) Faulkner might have turned it into another tale of the individual against the community. Richard Wright probably would have made Lester a black man who found necrophilia to be an existential political statement. And a liberal humanist such as William Styron could have shown how Lester's deprived background turned him into a criminal. Instead, we have a novel that seems to owe more to the tall-tale tradition than to any influence of the Southern Renascence. There is no single reliable narrative voice here, but seemingly omniscient accounts of Lester's behavior interspersed with first-person monologues from various residents of the area. After awhile, the wary reader begins to wonder how much of this he is to accept at face value and how much is pure fabulation.

In no facile sense are we to assume that Lester is simply a product of his environment or that he is really no different from ostensibly normal people. However, if McCarthy's mode of narration is meant to suggest that Lester has become a mythic figure for his community (this is Vereen Bell's contention), we have to wonder that it is about that community that causes it to make such myths. At least part of the legend of Lester Ballard is pretty conventional fare. Speaking of his ability to handle a rifle, a townsperson observes, "I'll say one thing. He could by god shoot it. Hit anything he could see. I seen him shoot a spider out of a web in the top of a big red oak one time and he was far from the tree as from here to the road yonder." Lester is even barred from the fair because he has won too many prizes. But, of course, that note of diminution is itself telling. Rather than being a hunter of wild beasts, he is a winner of stuffed animals. In this modern-day parody of the frontier, it is only a matter of time before Lester's firepower and cunning are turned against his fellow man. And even then, his prey are not real live enemies so much as human trophies.

McCarthy also manages to draw subliminal parallels between Lester and the community through scenes that eerily resemble each other. After Lester bags his first corpse and tries to carry her up to the attic, he discovers that she is too heavy for him. So, he brings in some lengths of old plow line, which he pieces together before the fire.

> Then he went in and fitted the rope around the waist of the pale cadaver and ascended the ladder with the

other end. She rose slump-shouldered from the floor with her hair all down and began to bump slowly up the ladder. Halfway up she paused, dangling. Then she began to rise again.

After Lester's underground cache of loved ones is discovered, a rope is thrown into the cave.

> When it descended they made it fast to the rope around the corpse and called aloft again. The rope drew taut and the first of the dead sat up on the cave floor, the hands that hauled the rope above sorting the shadows like puppeteers. Gray soapy clots of matter fell from the cadaver's chin. She ascended *dangling*. She sloughed in the weem of the noose. A gray rheum dripped (emphasis added).

These, however, are not the only two dangling corpses in *Child of God*.

Early in the novel, one of the townspeople surmises that Lester "never was right after his daddy killed hisself." This citizen was one of two men who cut the body down. "I seen his feet hangin," he recalls. "The old man's eyes was run out on stems like a crawfish and his tongue blacker'n a chow dog's. I wisht if a man wanted to hang hisself he'd do it with poison or somethin so folks wouldn't have to see such a thing as that." Much later in the story, an oldtimer recalls a public hanging from around the turn of the century. Obviously not sharing the squeamishness of the present generation, a crowd of spectators had streamed into town to see two malefactors brought to justice. It was the first of the year, and the streets were still decorated with holly boughs and Christmas candles. As the oldtimer remembers it:

> People had started into town the evening before. Slept in their wagons a lot of em. Rolled out blankets on the courthouse lawn. Wherever. You couldn't get a meal in town, folks lined up three deep. Women sellin sandwiches in the street. . . . [The sheriff] brung em from the jail, had two preachers with em and had their wives on their arms and all. Just like they was goin to church. All of em got up there on the scaffold and they sung and everybody fell in singin with em. . . . Whole town and half of Sevier County singin I Need Thee Every Hour. Then the preacher said a prayer and the wives kissed their husbands goodbye and stepped down off the scaffold and turned around to watch and the preacher came down and got real quiet. And then that trap kicked open from under em and down they dropped and hung there a jerkin and kickin for I don't know, ten, fifteen minutes. Don't ever think hangin is quick and merciful. It ain't.

These men had been White Caps, a vigilante group to which Lester's grandfather belonged.

Lester Ballard, who has defied the forces of mutability with such monomaniacal zeal, finally cheats the hangman. Never indicted for any crime, he is confined to a mental hospital in Knoxville near a man who used to open people's skulls and eat their brains with a spoon. (They did not converse because Lester had nothing to say to a crazy man.) With journalistic specificity, the omniscient narrator tells us that Lester contracted pneumonia in April of 1965 (the only way we have of dating the story). When this ailment proves fatal, his body is shipped to the state medical school and reduced to spare parts. The dissection is described with clinical detail. (John Ditsky is reminded of the dissection of Gary Gilmore in Norman Mailer's *The Executioner's Song*.) Then, "at the end of three months when the class was closed Ballard was scraped from the table into a plastic bag and taken with others of his kind to a cemetery outside the city and there interred. A minister from the school read a simple service." There is a certain poetic justice in the exploiter of corpses becoming an exploited corpse. At a more general level, however, Lester's end is simply another instance of the human person being reabsorbed into an indifferent nature. In that sense this child of God is indeed like all of us.

When we get to McCarthy's fourth novel, *Suttree,* we find three characteristics not evident in his previous work: a protagonist of obvious intelligence with a recognizable interior life, an affirmative sense of community, and a benign view of nature. The reason for these differences may simply be that McCarthy began *Suttree* before any of his first three published novels. Both thematically and technically, *Suttree* makes a good deal more sense if we see it as an earlier rather than a later product of McCarthy's muse. There is much of the apprentice novel about it and very little that resembles either *Child of God* or the more recent *Blood Meridian*. In fact, it seems hardly a novel of the seventies at all, but rather the sort of *tour de force* we might have expected in the sixties from an extremely gifted young man trying his damnedest to write like Faulkner, think like Steinbeck, and live like Kerouac.

Throughout a good part of the nineteenth century, southwestern humor featured a cultivated, upper-class observer thrown among barbarians. The humorists used this observer's superior sophistication as a means of judging the rabble while reaffirming conservative social values. In the character of Cornelius Suttree, we also have a representative of the upper class cast among the dregs of humanity. Suttree, however, is there by choice. Like many another sixties dropout, he finds life to be more authentic in the gutter than in the mansion. His entire life, and McCarthy's entire novel, is as much a social and political statement as the work of the southwest humorists. The difference is that McCarthy's vision is radical and proletarian rather than conservative and aristocratic. This is most evident on those few occasions when Suttree comes in contact with the world he left behind.

The most sustained of such encounters occurs when word arrives on skid row that Suttree's little boy has died. As this is the first inkling we have had that Suttree has left a wife and child behind, it comes as no surprise that he is not welcomed home with open arms. (Closed fists is more like it.) When he appears on the scene, his mother-in-law begins clawing and kicking him and tries to bite his finger off. His father-in-law clobbers Suttree in the head with his shoe and then goes into the house to fetch his shotgun. Later, the local sheriff, who could have walked off the set of any B movie about the South, buys Suttree a bus ticket and tells him to get out of town.

In the midst of all this rancor, Suttree manages to visit his son's open grave and pile dirt in with his bare hands while holding the cemetery tractor at bay. Given the man's obvious grief and his ill treatment by his in-laws, it would take a hard-hearted reader not to sympathize with Suttree. Since McCarthy tells us nothing about Suttree's married life and makes his antagonists into cartoon figures, we are not supposed to wonder why he abandoned this child he now seems to love so much. Nor does he seem to feel any guilt for having done so. Suttree's world is one where emotion crowds out moral responsibility. It reeks of a sentimentality lacking in McCarthy's other, harder and bleaker, novels.

Fortunately, we do not read Cormac McCarthy for dropout sociology any more than we read the southwest humorists for conservative politics. For whatever reason he may have taken up residence among the derelicts of the Knoxville waterfront, Suttree's adventures there hold our interest. Like the inhabitants of Steinbeck's Cannery Row, his cohorts are an assortment of whores, pimps, gamblers, and sons of bitches. By far the most memorable of these is a backwoods simpleton named Gene Harrogate. We first see Gene when he is arrested for sexually violating a patch of watermelons. Such wanton destruction of property earns him a stint on the chain gang (he would have been charged with bestiality had his lawyer not pointed out that watermelons are not beasts), where he meets our hero Cornelius Suttree. After becoming a free man (he prolongs his stay by refusing to work in the prison kitchen), Gene goes from one hare-brained scam to the next, until he is finally carted off to the penitentiary for stealing money from pay phones. The only other one of Suttree's associates who is almost as bizarre is a "pale and pimpled part-time catamite" named Leonard. When Leonard's father dies, the family doesn't tell anyone and keeps the body in an icebox for six months to keep the old man's welfare checks coming in.

Finding this book's humor its greatest virtue, I am simply

not convinced that there is enough to admire in its unfunny moments to warrant its incredible prolixity. Published after such a superbly crafted novel as *Child of God, Suttree* seems particularly lugubrious and overwritten. No doubt the rhetoric and vocabulary are meant to impose some sense of order and beauty on a world distinctly lacking in both. I fear, however, that McCarthy is simply asking language to do more than it is capable of doing. With Faulkner, one has a sense that the ornate language is matched by a largeness of vision. In McCarthy's work, absence of vision—a resolute inner dark—would seem to be the point. One cannot illuminate that darkness with fancy talk any more than one can permanently light up the night sky with Fourth of July fireworks. It's a good show, but the stars are a better guide.

The linguistic thickets in McCarthy's most recent novel, *Blood Meridian,* are not as formidable as in *Suttree,* but the moral landscape is considerably more harrowing. Having left his native South, McCarthy writes about a region that is native to the American imagination—the Wild West. As one might expect, however, McCarthy's West is not the mythic land we have come to know from pulp novels, movies, and television. Ever since Columbus's discovery that the world had a West, a new life (if not necessarily a new Eden) has seemed distinctly possible just beyond the horizon. Living in a country much larger and younger than those of Europe, Americans have tended to mythologize their experience in terms of space rather than time. Even though Frederick Jackson Turner announced the closing of the frontier a century ago (some four hundred years after Columbus had opened it), a belief in limitless space, personal freedom, and a second start remains an intractable part of the American Dream. Only in the past twenty-five years or so have we seen a substantial body of literature that can be regarded as anti-Western.

In his 1968 book, *The Return of the Vanishing American,* Leslie Fiedler argued that such writers as John Barth, Thomas Berger, Ken Kesey, David Markson, Peter Matthiessen, James Leo Herlihy, and Leonard Cohen were creating a new literary genre by exploiting and lampooning the pop Western. At the same time, the arbiters of middlebrow culture were also doing their best to debunk the West of our collective imagination. I recall reading in magazines such as *American Heritage* that Wyatt Earp really wasn't (in that marvelous redundancy) brave, courageous, and bold, but a cowardly bully who pistol-whipped drunken cowboys. Calamity Jane (or was it Belle Starr?) really wasn't a tomboyish actress whom one might one day marry, but a hideously ugly slut who copulated without regard to species or level of consanguinity. Even the movies got in on the act, giving us everything from the gentle spoof of *Cat Ballou* to the gut-bucket nihilism of Sam Peckinpah. *Blood Meridian* is very much in the Peckinpah tradition. In fact, it might even be regarded as a novelization (grotesque word for a grotesque phenomenon) of Peckinpah's West.

Set in the American Southwest and northern Mexico during the middle of the last century, *Blood Meridian* is loosely based on history. It follows a young man—known only as "the kid"—from his home in Tennessee to East Texas shortly after the Mexican War. From that point until the end of the book, some 330 pages later, we follow the kid's picaresque adventures among cutthroats so vile they would make a modern-day motorcycle gang look like a boys' choir. Although the titular leader of these free-lance killers is Captain John Glanton, the metaphysician of the group is a hairless behemoth named Judge Holden. Rather than seeing violence as a means to an end, the Judge regards brutality as its own justification. Throughout history, he argues, men have fought for a wide variety of causes and values. As a confirmed skeptic, he does not pretend to know whether any of these causes and values have objective validity. What is universal, however, is the act of fighting itself. Men make something valuable by fighting for it. According to this twisted logic, not only are all wars holy, but only war is holy.

Obviously, the pervasiveness of human evil is McCarthy's central point. (One of the book's epigraphs is an excerpt from the *Yuma Daily Sun,* noting the discovery of a 300,000-year-old skull that "shows evidence of having been scalped.") "To a remarkable degree," writes Vereen Bell, "the evil of suffering, which in *Suttree* merely impinged upon human life, in *Blood Meridian* has metastasized and become human." The problem is that the sustained and senseless violence of this book can shock for only so long before it begins to numb. The killing and maiming are finally so repetitious that action becomes the cause of boredom rather than an escape from it. In setting this tale in the old Southwest, McCarthy proves conclusively that it wasn't the Nazis who invented the banality of evil.

Whether Cormac McCarthy will continue to be "unknown" or eventually find a place in the mainstream of modern American (or at least modern southern) literature remains an open question. His books are too difficult and eccentric to woo readers away from Danielle Steele and James Michener, and unlike Harry Crews (the only other serious contender for "most degenerate southern writer"), he continues to shun the vulgarities of self-promotion. If McCarthy is to be discovered, it must be by the academic and critical establishment he has so far shunned. Although it is difficult to imagine a younger Malcolm Cowley preparing a Viking Portable McCarthy, Vereen Bell's recent book *The Achievement of Cormac McCarthy* (published as part of Louisiana State University Press's Southern Literary Studies) is an important first step toward canonization. The only problem is that Bell's book seems addressed to an audience that already understands and appreciates McCarthy's work. At present, that audience is probably too small to be anything other than a literary cult.

One cannot help admiring any contemporary writer of fiction who possesses sufficient self-confidence to go against the minimalist grain. Also, there is something refreshing about a novelist who still writes from experience and observation rather than from graduate courses in the Theory of Fiction. Of McCarthy's five books, however, only *Child of God* seems likely to outlive him. It is the sort of book that astonishes by testing the very limits of nihilism (pushing the outside of the envelope, as Tom Wolfe's test pilots would say). Such books (Joan Didion's *Play It As It Lays* is another) ask us to believe that the alchemy of style can transform patently offensive material into an object of aesthetic contemplation. The result is what Yeats might have called a terrible beauty, with the moralists among us italicizing the adjective and the aestheticians the noun. Whatever else one might say of him, the author of *Child of God* is a master craftsman with the courage of his perversions. But that distinction is probably not enough to earn him a place among the immortals. I suspect that Cormac McCarthy is what Faulkner would have been had *Sanctuary* been his greatest novel.

**Frank W. Shelton (review date Fall 1990)**

SOURCE: "*Suttree* and Suicide," in *Southern Quarterly*, Vol. 29, No. 1, Fall, 1990, pp. 71-83.

[*In the following essay, Shelton comments upon the existential themes within* Suttree, *and focuses on the protagonist of the same name. Shelton provides an overview of the novel, and discusses the Myth of Sisyphus, suicide, and other topics in his treatment.*]

Since the modern South possesses such a rich literary tradition, it is often customary to examine a contemporary southern writer from the point of view of his regionalism. However, Cormac McCarthy, in *Suttree* at least, can be rewardingly analyzed in the light of existential philosophy. The characters of his first three novels, *The Orchard Keeper, Outer Dark* and *Child of God,* are of such limited self-awareness, not to mention awareness of larger philosophical or religious issues, that whatever philosophical burden the stories bear is provided by the author and is deeply implicit in the novels themselves. With Suttree, and later with Judge Holden of *Blood Meridian,* McCarthy delineates characters who possess the intelligence, self-consciousness and articulateness needed to deal explicitly with his philosophical interests. It is as if, while deciding not to eliminate the primitiveness of his earlier characters and settings, in his recent novels McCarthy has felt the need to include educated and aware characters in order to confront more directly some of his abiding concerns. One of the concerns central to *Suttree* is the question of the meaning of life and the possibility of suicide, a possibility discussed by Camus in "The Myth of

Sisyphus," which is based on the proposition that, if there is no God then life has no ultimate meaning, and suicide is an option man must consider.

To portray McCarthy as a consciously or explicitly philosophical novelist in the tradition of, say, Dostoevsky or Camus, is not the point. His novels, *Suttree* especially, are too rich, seemingly chaotic and disordered and his sensibility too opposed to rationality for that. Vereen Bell, author of the best analysis of McCarthy's work to date, observes that "*Suttree* is carefully constructed to express its anti-metaphysical vision." Yet Bell describes McCarthy's anti-metaphysic in existential terms: "In McCarthy's world, existence seems both to precede and preclude essence, and it paradoxically derives its importance from this fact alone." Because of the many strands running through it, *Suttree* is certainly a very complex novel. Selecting the theme of suicide and tracing its manifestations and permutations in the novel will enable the reader to see how a work which seems disordered and lacking in linear plot does at least proceed to a resolution— a resolution to the very problem central to "The Myth of Sisyphus," and one presented with elements strikingly in common with that work. While many readers of *Suttree* have felt that the novel simply stops, it does resolve itself and does so in the same way as Camus's work: in an act of will rather than an act of rational thought.

McCarthy emphasizes the centrality of suicide to the novel by beginning with the suicide of a man who killed himself by jumping from a bridge into the Tennessee River. Suttree watches as the rescue boats troll the river and as the body is raised, dangling from a grappling hook lodged in the side of its face. Suttree feels a horrified fascination and cannot stay away, even coming close enough to the body to notice that the dead man's watch is still ticking. Then he takes a fish to the ragpicker, a character important to the theme of suicide in the novel. The following conversation occurs:

> You didn't see that man jump, did you? Suttree said.
>
> He shook his head. An old ragpicker, his thin chops wobbling. I seen em draggin, he said. Did they find him?
>
> Yes.
>
> What did he jump for?
>
> I dont guess he said.
>
> I wouldnt do it. Would you?
>
> I hope not.

At this very early point in the novel, then, McCarthy establishes in Suttree at least the potential for suicide. Subsequently, at the end of the first section, Suttree stands looking down into the water from the same spot on the bridge from which the man jumped, thinking, "To fall through dark to darkness. Struggle in those opaque and fecal deeps, which way is up. Till the lungs suck brown sewage and funny lights go down the final corridors of the brain, small watchmen to see that all is quiet for the advent of eternal night." Evident in Suttree's imaginative identification with the suicide is his horror of—yet attraction to—death and particularly suicide, a motif which runs throughout the novel.

Violence, sometimes of the most gruesome kind, runs through all McCarthy's novels, but *Suttree* is the only one to explore deeply the potential for violence against self. Even though the suicide described is the only literal one included in the novel, Suttree's own attraction to death and the actions of numerous other characters can be traced as part of this theme. Suttree, of course, does not actually commit suicide because, while he is "half in love with easeful death," he also half fears it. Suicide would be a definite act, requiring the kind of commitment and certainty which until the very end of the novel he does not possess. Yet the most basic reason death attracts Suttree is made clear: it would be a relief from the burdens and torments of consciousness. While wandering in a cemetery before the funeral of his son, he pauses before an old vault. "Inside there is nothing. No bones, no dust. How surely are the dead beyond death. Death is what the living carry with them. A state of dread, like some uncanny foretaste of a bitter memory. But the dead do not remember and nothingness is not a curse. Far from it."

Why does Suttree so yearn for escape from consciousness through death? Why has he decided to live in McAnally Flats, a slum area of Knoxville, among the derelicts and dregs of society? Unlike those among whom he lives, he has had alternatives. Scion of a prominent and prosperous family, he has turned his back on his past and his southern white background and is thus alienated by his own choice, not by irresistible social or economic forces as are most of the other residents of McAnally Flats. There are hints in the novel that his father is an aristocratic snob who looks down on his mother and anyone related to her even including their own son. Such acts are clear evidence to Suttree of the bankruptcy of social respectability, and he rejects it. Furthermore he can take no comfort from his family's past. When his aunt shows him the family picture album, he sees only people whose poor flesh has been beset by worms and death. Although this is one explanation of Suttree's death orientation, and perhaps the one that those looking at McCarthy from a southern perspective will most readily recognize, in the total context of the novel it is not the most essential one. Suttree chooses to live in a Waste Land for philosophical and ultimately religious reasons. And the world of the novel *is* waste land, with a number of specific parallels to T.S. Eliot's poem,

though lacking the potential for religious consolation which the end of "The Waste Land" provides. Polluted rivers and "unreal" cities are important images in both works. "Fear death by drowning" is central to the poem, and Suttree fears both the suicide's fate and the fate of his Uncle Milo, who drowned off the coast of South America. Finally Suttree is a version of the impotent Fisher King alienated from self and nature. Perhaps there is even an echo of another Eliot's poem in the hollowness of a city built on land honeycombed with caves. But however unattractive it is—the city is described as *"constructed on no known paradigm, a mongrel architecture reading back through the works of man in a brief delineation of the aberrant disordered and mad"*—the city manifests to Suttree reality, and he is unwilling to hide behind conventional social forms and structures as his family does.

Suttree is existential man facing the absurd, alien in a universe without meaning. According to Camus in "The Myth of Sisyphus," man has an irrational and wild longing for clarity, happiness and reason. "The absurd is born of this confrontation between the human need and the unreasonable silence of the world." A recognition of the unyielding silence and meaninglessness of the universe, Camus feels, leads man to contemplate suicide. Relevant is Kirilov's argument in Dostoevsky's *The Possessed:* "All man did was to invent God so as to live without killing himself." Though a lapsed Catholic, Suttree still feels an intense religious yearning. He haunts churches and admires the evangelists whom he encounters on the streets, people who at least have fervent beliefs. Suttree's problem is that of Camus's absurd man: without belief, why continue to live? Why not commit suicide? At one point in the novel he subjects himself to a violent storm.

> Suttree stood among the screaming leaves and called the lightning down. It cracked and boomed about and he pointed out the darkened heart within him and cried for light. If there be any art in the weathers of this earth. Or char these bones to coal. If you can, if you can. A blackened rag in the rain.
>
> He sat with his back to a tree and watched the storm move on over the city. Am I a monster, are there monsters in me?

Like King Lear on the heath or a character out of Dostoevsky, Suttree here confronts the universe with a demand either for answers or for death. Seeing little reason for living in an absurd universe, he defiantly calls extinction down upon himself.

The novel suggests that Suttree's orientation toward death began early in his life. When he visits the ancient ruined plantation house in which he probably once dwelt as a child, he recalls that even then he "had already begun to sicken at the slow seeping of life." Haunting his memory is the knowledge of his stillborn twin, and it is striking how many times in the novel Suttree is seen gazing at his reflection in mirrors, windows or water. During the latter occasions he usually expresses his self-contempt by spitting at his own image. In fact, one might say that with the awareness of his dead twin, he is born with the knowledge of death in his bones. His preoccupation with his double and with questions of identity suggests a radical incompleteness; there are times when he feels completion can only be attained through the death he desires and fears, through union with his twin, his other half.

While on the one hand Suttree sees more vitality in the city than in the respectable life of his family and his forebears, he also takes seriously the Conrad dictum, "in the destructive element immerse." *Suttree* is McCarthy's only novel to deal in any detail with urban life, and it is no coincidence that it is also one of his most explicitly philosophical and religious works. In his study of suicide, *The Savage God*, A. Alvarez associates technology (and by implication the city, a product of technology) with man's growing sense of estrangement and absurdity: "just as the decay of religious authority in the nineteenth century made life seem absurd by depriving if of any ultimate coherence, so the growth of modern technology has made death itself absurd by reducing it to a random happening totally unconnected with the inner rhythms and logic of the lives destroyed." If, as Camus maintains, in an absurd universe all usual codes lack meaning, no locale would better mirror that situation than the chaotic slums of the modern city. By living in McAnally Flats, Suttree makes an effort to confront a social and philosophical reality to which those living respectable lives blind themselves. Yet at the same time he is unable to cope with such a reality. His drinking and mindless fighting are attempts to blot out consciousness, which in its ultimate form could be accomplished only by death itself. His search for both heightened reality and escape from reality is yet another indication of the ambiguity and uncertainty in which he lives.

His uncertainty is further evident in the fact that, not only does he not succeed in killing himself, he never even makes an actual attempt. For just to attempt suicide would mean putting a stop to the drifting which is his mode of life through most of the novel. The act of suicide, paradoxically, involves a commitment, and Suttree is not capable of any kind of commitment. Many of his acts, however, are in essence invitations to death. So while not consciously willing or able to kill himself, certainly he subconsciously seeks death by immersing himself in the destructive element, in a city where death is ever present and, in Alvarez's words, "a random happening." Even in all his drinking and pointless brawling, he is more passive than active, never starting the fights but somehow frequently getting involved in them. If he does not

perish as a result, it is only because he is lucky. After all, he could as easily have been killed by the floor buffer which comes down on his head during a brawl as end up in the hospital with a mild concussion, as he does.

McCarthy's novel is particularly rich in character and incident. In the range of people portrayed, *Suttree* is impressive in its variety and vitality of life. These characters also offer a range of responses to absurd urban life, a range which encourages a more accurate evaluation of Suttree himself. Three characters are representative. Gene Harrogate, the "moonlight melon-mounter," the country mouse turned city rat, is life at its lowest denominator. Half-crazy but also half-shrewd with his many money-making schemes, he is completely oblivious to any concern other than prospering in the city. He is strangely appealing both to Suttree and to the reader, manifesting the vitality of life at the most primitive level. He is so committed to life that the idea of death never even enters his mind, though his style of life does lead him inexorably to prison. Perhaps not much further up the scale is Billy Ray Callahan, a drinker and a brawler whose only interest seems to be instant gratification. First encountered in the workhouse getting thrown in solitary confinement for fighting, he finally dies, shot through the head for stealing change from women's purses at a bar. He too has a kind of low-level vitality, but the incipient violence in his character makes his end inevitable. While he does not seek death, it seeks him, and surely being killed because of a few coins is meaningless and absurd. At the top of the spectrum of characters surrounding Suttree is Ab Jones, the black owner of a riverboat tavern. He is just as ready for violence as Callahan, but his violence has purpose and meaning. Determined to assert his manhood and dignity as a human being equal to any other, he is constantly harassed by the law because he refuses to back down and humble himself. Finally he is arrested and beaten to death while in jail. One could easily make the case that his death is a form of suicide, for in essence he persists in his way of life knowing full well the result will be fatal. Yet even if a suicide, his death, far from denying meaning and dignity, asserts it in the strongest terms. The deaths of Jones and Callahan occur near the end of the novel, and Ab's especially is very important to the transformation in Suttree's attitude toward death.

These characters, and others, illustrate the varieties of violence Suttree encounters in the city. He also is seen in a natural setting—when he takes a trip into the Smoky Mountains one November. While his motivation for the trip is not described, it is reasonable to assume on one level that he is attempting to purify himself through contact with nature. In McCarthy's cosmology, however, nature is not benevolent. and this trip too becomes a form of attempted suicide. He takes very little food and clothing with him, apparently not particularly concerned whether he survives or not. He does experience a kind of union with nature, but it is a union with an indifferent nature which can only be accomplished completely through death. "Everything had fallen from him. He scarce could tell where his being ended or the world began nor did he care. He lay on his back in the gravel, the earth's core sucking his bones. . . . He saw with a madman's clarity the perishability of his flesh." In fact union with nature leads to his wandering the mountains half-crazed, eating nothing, his clothes falling off his back. He could easily have wandered to his death, and it seems he would not have cared. It just so happens that he stumbles on a hunter with a bow and arrow, himself a figure of obscure menace who, rather than kill him, directs Suttree out of the woods. So as before, only chance or luck, not his will or desire for life, saves Suttree. As he lies in bed back in the city recuperating from this trip, he sums up its lesson to him: "He was seized with a thing he'd never known, a sudden understanding of the mathematical certainty of death. He felt his heart pumping down there under the palm of his hand. Who tells it so? Could a whole man not author his own death with a thought? Shut down the ventricle like the closing of an eye?" Again—or still—Suttree's thoughts run to suicide, to blotting out his life by willful act.

It may be Suttree's salvation that, although in his despair he chooses to live in an environment without stable values, he finally does not subscribe to the dictum of Ivan Karamazov: without God and the certainty of an afterlife, there is no morality and all is permitted. Or in Camus's rendering in *The Rebel* of Ivan's thought processes, "Long reflection on the condition of mankind as people sentenced to death only leads to the justification of crime." Callahan, Harrogate and others in the novel may by their actions implicitly adhere to such an idea, but McCarthy defers until his next novel, ***Blood Meridian,*** and the character of Judge Holden a full treatment of it. Suttree, even though he is in despair and attempts to isolate himself from all human contact, is frequently seen interacting with and showing concern for others. Here, as elsewhere, he is uncertain and ambivalent, wanting to withdraw from others but feeling some obscure need for contact. Often against his will he helps others: Harrogate, the junkman, the ragpicker, the railroader, even Leonard with the burial of his long dead father. He is thus certainly not beyond the pale of humanity; while attempting to live out the idea that in an absurd universe conventional moral codes are meaningless, he yet feels a common humanity with others. In his ambivalence, however, he cannot firmly commit himself to such an ethic. A motif recurs in the novel: someone invites him to share a meal, but he refuses and withdraws. The only satisfying meal he shares is with the Indian fisherman Michael, another outcast. After the episode Michael disappears from the novel, only to reappear much later knocking at his door. Suttree is so deeply asleep that he does not wake, and then Michael permanently drops from the book. This relationship too, one of the most fulfilling Suttree has, is abortive. In addition his latent morality is revealed by his attitude toward his mother and his son. In connection with them he

weeps for virtually the only times in the novel—when she visits him in the workhouse and he sees her deep grief and disappointment, and then when he makes the long trip to attend the funeral of his son, only to be forced to observe it from afar. The guilt he experiences in both instances is profound evidence that his humanity has not been destroyed, that even with his inclination toward and desire for death, he retains those feelings which make one human. Such feelings leave him receptive to experiences which near the end of the novel lead him away from death and toward life.

Vereen Bell is certainly correct to note in his essay that the form of *Suttree,* in which "rich episodes follow upon one another with chaotic improvidence, the timespans between them—their temporal relationships unmarked," mirrors a universe which lacks coherent structure and meaning. However one can trace in the last fifty or so pages of the novel a resolution to some of Suttree's dilemmas, particularly his problem of suicide. This resolution is presented in a non-linear, non-rational fashion, but even in this light the universe of the novel does not come to have coherence. The world remains as chaotic, meaningless and absurd as ever, but Suttree, in terms strikingly similar to those of Camus in "The Myth of Sisyphus," finds a way to live in it.

Suttree's movement toward such a resolution begins most directly with the death of the ragpicker, one of those derelicts whom Suttree visited and took care of when he could. He has some sympathy for him in his lonely and debased state, but Suttree seems primarily attracted to him because he expresses one aspect of Suttree's own character—the nihilistic side. For the ragpicker is a primitive, instinctive Ivan Karamazov, simultaneously accepting the existence of God but rejecting the world He made. He tells Suttree:

> I aint no infidel. Dont pay no mind to what they say.
>
> No.
>
> I always figured they was a God.
>
> Yes.
>
> I just never did like him.

Later he and Suttree talk about death, with the ragpicker repeating as usual that he is sick of living. Suttree responds:

> You told me once you believed in God.
>
> The old man waved his hand. Maybe, he said. I got no reason to think he believes in me. Oh I'd like to see him for a minute if I could.
>
> What would you say to him?

Well, I think I'd just tell him. I'd say: Wait a minute. Wait just one minute before you start in on me. Before you say anything, there's just one thing I'd like to know. And he'll say: What's that? And then I'm going to ast him: What did you have me in the crapgame down there for anyway? I couldnt put any part of it together.

Suttree smiled. What do you think he'll say?

The ragpicker spat and wiped his mouth. I dont believe he can answer it, he said. I dont believe there is a answer.

Then on a visit very late in the novel Suttree discovers the ragpicker's dead body, which is described in a suggestive way: "The old man lay with his eyes shut and his mouth set and his hands lay clenched at either side. He looked as if he had forced himself to death." Thus the man who at the beginning of the novel had affirmed that he would never kill himself like the drowned suicide has in effect done just that—he has willed his own death. An obviously upset Suttree mourns his death, but he rejects his way of dying. "He passed his hand through his hair and leaned forward and looked at the old man. You have no right to represent people this way, he said. A man is all men. You have no right to your wretchedness." The last pages of the novel are filled with the deaths of many other of Suttree's friends and acquaintances, and he feels more and more bereft. None of the other deaths, however, has the impact on him of the deaths of the ragpicker and Ab Jones. While the ragpicker's death is the passive, meaningless death of the almost-suicide, Jones's death provides Suttree a counter-example. It also is virtually sought out, but it comes as the result of the struggle for something of value. Suttree never becomes as active or as resolute a character as Ab, but near the end of the novel his attitude shifts from the passive nihilism of the ragpicker to the more purposeful rebellion of Ab Jones, as is suggested by his stealing the car of the policemen who arrested Jones and driving it into the river.

The deaths near the end of the novel emphasize forcefully to Suttree the finality and totality of death, but rather than immerse himself any longer in the destructive element he determines to live in the face of the absurdity of death. In fact, he undergoes not simply one but two resurrections, the first when he arises from his sickbed after almost dying of typhoid and the other when he abandons his houseboat, leaving inside the decayed corpse which might have been and which some identify with himself. These resurrections contrast with the two parody resurrections of Leonard's father, when he rises from the river in which Suttree and Leonard bury him and the at least threatened disinterment of the body for failure to make payments on the grave plot. Suttree's delirium during his illness reveals the change in him. Haunt-

ing him are images of corpses, decay and death. In his imagination he stands accused by a nun of wasting his life.

> Mr Suttree it is our understanding that at curfew rightly decreed by law and in that hour wherein night draws to its proper close and the new day commences and contrary to conduct befitting a person of your station you betook yourself to various low places within the shire of McAnally and there did squander several ensuing years in the company of thieves, derelicts, miscreants, pariahs, poltroons, spalpeens, curmudgeons, clotpolls, murderers, gamblers, bawds, whores, trulls, brigands, topers, tosspots, sots and archsots, lobcocks, smellsmocks, runagates, rakes, and other assorted and felonious debauchees.

> I was drunk, cried Suttree. Seized in a vision of the archetypal patriarch himself unlocking with enormous keys the gates of Hades.

He becomes aware that his way of life is the way of pure destructiveness, the unleashing of anti-life on the universe. When Suttree regains consciousness and lucidity, the priest who has been sitting with him and had administered the last rites to him observes,

> God must have been watching over you. You very nearly died. You would not believe what watches.

> Oh?

> He is not a thing. Nothing ever stops moving.

> Is that what you learned?

> I learned that there is one Suttree and one Suttree only.

He sees that the universe is not a fixed thing which one can ever expect to comprehend logically; it is process. In order to be a part of that process, Suttree must accept the necessity of choice, but a choice now for life instead of death. Only in such a way can he become himself, that one Suttree. Squandering his life was denial and abrogation of his responsibility to choose. While acknowledging the fact that his twin is dead and all men are mortal, he yet accepts that he is alive, with the consequent necessity of determining how to live. As he leaves Knoxville, "he'd taken for talisman the simple human heart within him. Walking down the little street for the last time he felt everything fall away from him. Until there was nothing left of him to shed." He manifests an awareness of pure existential being; in contrast to his attitude through much of the novel, he is now ready to embrace it wholeheartedly, not with the belief that only some transcendent reality can give life meaning, but simply because life is and man wills meaning on his own terms.

The final paragraph of the novel reads: "Somewhere in the gray wood by the river is the huntsman and in the brooming corn and in the castellated press of cities. His work lies all wheres and his hounds tire not. I have seen them in a dream, slaverous and wild and their eyes crazed with ravening for souls in this world. Fly them." Whatever the images of the hunter and the hound suggest—death, violence, the destructive element—Suttree's attitude has changed from the beginning of the novel. In the prologue the narrative voice asserts that inside its gates the city is beset by a thing unknown, wondering whether it might be "*a hunter with hounds or do bone horses draw his deadcart through the streets and does he call his trade to each?*" At the end Suttree will no longer live within the gates of the city and half-embrace death and oblivion. Learning that man can live meaningfully only by asserting his freedom in defiance of death and an absurd universe, he comes to reject suicide just as Camus does in "The Myth of Sisyphus":

> It is essential to die unreconciled and not of one's own free will. Suicide is a repudiation. The absurd man can only drain everything to the bitter end, and deplete himself. The absurd is his extreme tension, which he maintains constantly by solitary effort, for he knows that in that consciousness and in that day-to-day revolt he gives proof of his only truth, which is defiance.

His future life is uncertain, just as is the life of Camus's absurd man, but at least Suttree is now determined to live a life of flight and revolt, unreconciled to death and absurdity. Warmed by the human contact of the boy who, unbidden, gives him a drink of water and the man who, unbidden, offers him a ride away from Knoxville, Suttree is prepared to defy death and create his own meaning and joy through the human will to action.

## Andrew Bartlett (review date Fall 1991)

SOURCE: "From Voyeurism to Archaeology: Cormac McCarthy's *Child of God*," in *The Southern Literary Journal,* Vol. XXIV, No. 1, Fall, 1991, pp. 3-15.

[*In the following essay, Bartlett examines the novel* Child of God, *focusing on the various narrative perspectives within the book, most notably the voyeuristic perspective that is often employed.*]

Readers who find Cormac McCarthy's **Child of God** disturbingly powerful might well argue that this power results from the "raw material" of its antihero. Lester Ballard is a twenty-seven-year-old white native of Frog Mountain in Appalachian Sevier County, Tennessee: a cursing, spitting, vengeful, homicidal, necrophilic sociopath. This grotesque outsider could serve as stuff for a gratuitously shocking horror story. But Ballard represents a serious figure for McCarthy—not primarily a case study in psychology or criminology, but a fictional figure quite within the bounds of human possibility. Some degrees of human evil prove difficult to apprehend, must be seen to be believed. In its struggle with this difficulty, the aesthetic power of **Child of God** derives not so much from the force of Lester Ballard as subject or object but rather from the play of positions taken by the narrator through whom we see Ballard. Hunting, tracking, sighting, looking, watching, searching, exploring, examining—such processes dominate the story. Ballard demonstrates both a passionate attachment to the rifle he has carried since boyhood and an expert ability to sight and shoot, a faultless eye. The text is concerned not with a theological question, as the title might suggest, but with a problem of vision: how does a man such as Lester Ballard see the world? How might we, how ought we to *see* Lester Ballard? "He could not swim, but how would you drown him? His wrath seemed to buoy him up. Some halt in the way of things seems to work here. See him." I would suggest that McCarthy approaches this problem not merely by privileging Lester Ballard as an "objective" referential phenomenon but rather by playing with the rhetorics of visibility, ways of *seeing*. The aesthetic power of **Child of God** results from McCarthy's superb regulation of narrative distance and perspective, his command of four degrees of proximity to Ballard, four kinds of narrative position with differing visions: the voyeuristic, the oblivious, the blind (blinded by darkness), and—most inventive—the archaeological. These "visions" determine both rhetorical strategies on the surface of the text and dramatic structures in the elements of the story.

The voyeuristic counts as perhaps the most obvious mode of perspective in **Child of God:** its circumscribed field of vision frames space and focuses on some central object in which the watcher takes a serious, ambiguously perverse, interest. The narrator constantly watches Ballard watching another body oblivious to being watched: animals and people both dead and alive, potential prey and actual victims, atmospheric signs, landscapes, ruins. Ballard himself operates as a perverse conflation of hunter and voyeur. His demented sexual adventures begin when he eavesdrops on a couple making love in a parked car on the Frog Mountain turnaround. Because for Ballard erotic impulses are painfully confused with destructive impulses, the recurrent image of the voyeur in **Child of God** is that of a hunter who focuses on a presence or a scene of actual or potential death.

> Ballard took to wandering over the mountain through the snow to his old homeplace where he'd watch the

house, the house's new tenant. He'd go in the night and lie up on the bank and watch him through the kitchen window. Or from the top of the well house. . . . Ballard laid the rifle foresight on his chest. He swung it upward to a spot just above the ear. His finger filled the cold curve of the trigger. Bang, he said.

All elements of the voyeuristic converge in this scene: precise visual concentration on a relatively "literal" image, the reassuring presence of the object, pleasure in watching the oblivious watched figure, perverse motivation, a certain pathetic impotence, a sense of loneliness.

Watching something "really" present in the field of vision: that voyeuristic process dominates the text. Meaning in *Child of God* may seem inseparable from a scene of visual immediacy because the dominant perspective throughout the text is that of external focalization: narrative information is most often restricted to what characters say and do than what they think or feel. In the quantitative sense the text relies most steadily on such techniques, tending toward a discourse that is episodic, elliptical, laconic, rigorously metonymic, reliant on serial structures, exact in its taxonomic diction.

> He sits and dries the rifle and ejects the shells into his lap and dries them and wipes the action and oils it and oils the receiver and the barrel and the magazine and the lever and reloads the rifle and levers a shell into the chamber and lets the hammer down and lays the rifle on the floor beside him.

Such writing is about as "lean" and "simple" as one could wish; Ballard seated here is the frame, the rifle is the centre of attention. Even here, however, the effect is slightly comic: the repetition ("and . . . and . . . and") dramatizes Ballard's obsession with his rifle and the grammatical concentration of verbal and noun phrases with a single opening "he" mimics Ballard's concentration, his absorption in the task at hand. Ballard's perspective becomes synonymous with the narrator's, and thus with the readers, in a kind of voyeuristic tunnel vision. The most extended example of this maximized distance is the episode in which Lester Ballard rapes his first corpse—dark comedy at its most dark, but comedy inasmuch as Ballard appears so stupid, stupefied—as by gradual stages he decides to see the lovers poisoned by carbon monoxide and their remains as a kind of accidental windfall. The aesthetic quality of *Child of God,* however, is neither simple nor lean; the reader ought to resist overestimating the force of the voyeuristic perspective as a determining factor in the inventiveness of McCarthy's rhetorical strategy.

If Ballard's perspective often becomes ours by force of this voyeuristic logic, the different and differing perspectives and voices of the Appalachian folk living around Frog Mountain

gradually converge to a point we might call that of (relative) obliviousness. There is no question that McCarthy places a certain value on folk discourse, playing with its laziness, its inadequacy, its own ways of keeping the raw material of a Lester Ballard at a safe distance. Part I of the novel includes seven textual segments in which unidentified Appalachian folk from Sevier County tell what they know about Lester Ballard and the Ballard kin. The subtext would almost imply the unacknowledged presence of an inquirer who has arrived in Sevier County asking questions about Ballard, perhaps an aspect of the narrator's curiosity. One of these seven segments introduces the eye of the Sheriff, who becomes the ostensible representative of these civil folk. Part II employs no such voices, as is McCarthy's narrator has determined to follow Ballard without any local assistance, as if the folk voices served as gentle preparation for the horrible intimacies of Ballard's lonely struggle with the unusually cold winter. This increase in mediation of the narrator-proper counts most obviously as a necessary consequence of Ballard's increasing isolation, his necrophilia, his arson and murder, his retreat into the caves. In part III, again shorter and again divided again into fewer (eleven) segments, the narrator leaves Ballard's eye to follow the Sheriff's in three episodes. The Sheriff now occupies the role of Ballard's rival as hunter. The extended scene in which the Sheriff and his Deputy row about the streets of the flooded town and Mr. Wade tells the tale of Tom Davis functions as an ironic displacement of the seven separate segments in part I: its loquacious summariness, historical range, and traditional moralistic conclusion contrast sharply with the relative brevity, anecdotal quality, and fragmented diffusiveness of the earlier set of Ballard anecdotes. This gradual development of visual breadth mimics a certain approach to and apprehension of Lester Ballard. At one level the story functions as a parody of crime and detective fiction. Ballard leads the party of neo-vigilantes into the caves, escapes them and leaves them in the dark; this episode—the longest segment in the text—is profoundly symbolic of Ballard's peculiar status as one who cannot be confined or assimilated, either literally or figuratively, by agencies or discourses of social control.

The folk logic is diametrically opposed to that of the voyeuristic: one does not (really even care to) see what is there. Nobody in the Sheriff's world gets anywhere as near to seeing Ballard as we do, as "privileged" readers. Lovers who park their cars at Frog Mountain turnaround, storekeepers and clerks, officials of church and state, tend as a body to overlook or to underestimate Ballard's figure. In short, the people upon whom Ballard preys remain relatively oblivious to him. The discourse proceeding from their set of closely related positions consists of a somewhat casual dismissiveness based on a system of social law and theological assumption. Take, for example, the way in which the narrator closes an account of Ballard attending Sixmile church: the "strung heads" of the congregation turned together "like a cast of puppets" when Ballard entered late: "Ballard had a cold and snuffed loudly through the service but nobody expected he would stop if God himself looked back askance so no one looked." If the children of God believe the look of God "himself" is powerless to change Ballard, they will imitate that very powerlessness: this kind of resigned theology ironically perpetuates Ballard's isolation. Consider Ballard's release from a nine-day jail term.

> Ballard looked up and went through the gate and across the room toward a door with daylight in it and across a hall and out through the front door of the Sevier County courthouse. No one called him back.

The narrator here deviates from the strict empirical bounds of external focalization by virtue of a certain technique of negation, reporting the presence of an absence. Such a report implies a value judgement proper to the narrator: because they do not *see* him right, the forces of the law fail to call Ballard back. The Sheriff himself takes a vaguely paternalistic attitude to Ballard, calling him "man of leisure," seeing him as a "sullen reprobate." Ultimately the Sheriff proves either ineffective or strangely resigned—McCarthy aptly names him "Fate"—inasmuch as Ballard is "never indicted for any crime."

The folk would like to assimilate Ballard by framing him as an example of superlative "meanness." Mr. Wade, who recounts at some length the history of heroic lawman Tom Davis—Davis's pursuit, capture, and execution of the White Caps and Bluebills—sums up this legalistic attitude. When the deputy asks Mr. Wade whether he thinks people in older times "was meaner than they are now," Wade replies: "No . . . I don't. I think people are the same from the day God first made one." This firm principle does not constitute a satisfactory theodicy: original sin may dismiss, but it cannot explain the figure of a Lester Ballard. Take another similar example: what Wade says about the vigilantes Tom Davis corralled and executed.

> No, these were sorry people all the way around, every man jack a three hundred and sixty degree son of a bitch, which my daddy said meant they was a son of a bitch any way you looked at em.

This doctrinaire discourse would obliterate human evil simply by making it as such, by asserting that there does not exist "any way"—not a single perspective from any "degree" offered by geometry—to look at a "son of a bitch" such as Lester Ballard other than as a self-evidently damning figure. The reader ought to see the limits of such rotationally geometrical vision (one must confidently be placed at the center of the circle to see, like Wade's daddy, all the way around).

Earlier in the same scene the Sheriff speaks to a citizen by the name of Ed who comes wading down the street behind a rowboat that has emerged out of the hardware store; the hardware store has been robbed of some rifles. The Sheriff responds to Ed's query about how anyone could respond to the flood by causing even more trouble.

> Some people you cain't do nothin' with, the sheriff said.

> Ain't that the truth.

The fact is that McCarthy *does* "do something with" Lester Ballard—not in the sense of curing, containing, or converting him to social legitimacy, but in the sense of *seeing* Ballard from other perspectives outside and beyond these ones, this one (inasmuch as it points to a "unified" social vision). If the perspective of relative and interrelated obliviousness would ignore Lester Ballard by casting him out of the field of vision as a legendary example of original sin, then churchgoing, lawkeeping, and traditional storytelling—some of the ways in which this perspective is systematized and maintained—are not the only "ways" available either to Lester Ballard or to the narrator who makes Ballard his interest.

The third narrative perspective faces the blindness of darkness: there is nothing to see in the visual field because that field is a scene of death and darkness—you find yourself inside an underworld utterly devoid of light. If the voyeur frames and sights a specific object in a field of vision; if the oblivious perspective uses frames of reference too limited and circumscribed (frames *outside* which the voyeur is located); in this region we can not see because it is too dark, too dark for comfort. This is the kind of perspective that Lester Ballard himself barely escapes, wandering lost inside the caves, after he has escaped the neo-vigilantes: because there is almost nothing to see, the sense of hearing displaces that of sight. Inasmuch as there is little to see in it, there is little to say about it. In somewhat the same way that Ballard finds his way out of the caves—by virtue of digging, a peculiar combination of pagan luck and random struggle—so does McCarthy surpass the blindness of darkness.

This brings us to a fourth kind of narrative perspective, the one most interesting—interesting perhaps because it seems to betray a kind of wish to redeem Lester Ballard from the impoverished villainy of his "literal" status—to McCarthy's narrative practice in *Child of God*. This perspective relies on what we might call a discourse of archaeology. It positions itself at a distance from any authoritative pretensions to transcending suffering or mortality by attachment to allegorical theology or to conventional traditions of (fictional) moral decency. Inasmuch as it insists on accuracy and concentrates on precisely describing the material remains of the dead culture it studies (and a culture of death in the case of

Ballard as antihero), archaeological vision mimics voyeuristic vision. However, its methods must add to the clinical neutrality of external focalization because those remains, the visualized objects, are precisely remains: they do not speak only of themselves but speak for something other than the empirically self-evident—something ancient, vanished, obscure, enigmatic.

The logic of this mode of vision operates from an impulse to see what is *not* there, by virtue of a certain (authorial) suggestiveness. If the voyeuristic attitude toward the object is intensely attached to the presence of the object while remaining disrespectful of the object's proper status as other, the archaeological attitude is relatively detached from the object, detached enough to permit an attitude of associative freedom that becomes oddly respectful, that looks twice, as it were. In the logic of the voyeur, distance dictates a perpetual perversity: the voyeur acts as if he would possess and consume the object, and yet to "possess" the object (in the tactile sense) would be to destroy his status as voyeur. The archaeologist would possess the object only because it serves as remains, as fragmented evidence of a greater and imagined object, as the precious sign of a vanished, though possibly once-whole presence. Objects seen through archaeological vision necessarily force a relatively metaphorical discourse of reconstruction, of supplementarity.

As is the case with voyeuristic behaviour, Ballard seems to share something of an archaeological inclination with McCarthy's narrator.

> At the far end of the quarry was a rubble tip and Ballard stopped to search for artifacts, tilting old stoves and water heaters, inspecting bicycle parts and corroded buckets. He salvaged a worn kitchen knife with a chewed handle. He called to the dog, his voice relaying from rock to rock and back again.

If woods, waters animals, birds and fish animate some of the scenes of Ballard's territory, scenes of abandoned rubbish such as the above reminds us of the lifeless underside of that territory—they situate Ballard as the refugee of a vanishing, wasting human culture. Seeing what is not there, acting as if the dead were alive, founds the perverse logic of Ballard's necrophilia. When Ballard first copulates with a corpse, the narrator allows for the possibility of otherworldly spectators—as if he must necessarily distance himself from Ballard's perversion of archaeology. "A crazed gymnast laboring over a cold corpse. He poured into that waxen ear everything he'd ever thought of saying to a woman. Who could say she did not hear him?" This logic also helps explain why Ballard so often speaks into a void, as it were—speaks in spite of the void. This logic operates at its most absurd and "innocent" when Ballard aims his rifle at targets and declines to shoot, but says "Bang" anyway. Ballard sights a bass in one of Waldrop's ponds: "Ain't you a fine fat son of a bitch, he said." He loses patience during a henhouse robbery when the animals squawk: "You son of a bitch, said Ballard, to the chicken or Greer or both." Ballard has this habit of addressing an absent or a nonhuman body as if it were human, and the habit becomes more ambiguous when he speaks to the forces of nature and when—the narrator dialogically implies—nature responds, as if Ballard were the antitype of a providential divinity.

> Ballard crammed brush and pieces of stumpwood right up the chimney. He made coffee and leaned back on his pallet. Now freeze, you son of a bitch, he told the night beyond the windowpane.

> It did. it dropped to six below zero. A brick toppled into the flames. . . .

On that night, the night of his first adventure as necrophilic, the abandoned cabin burns down. The same perverse logic motivates Ballard in a reverse situation after he has shot Ralph's daughter: the imperative addressed to the night proved unintentionally effective, but the imperative addressed to this victim is intentionally cruel, a demented verbal overkill: "She was lying in the floor but she was not dead. She was moving. . . . Ballard gripped the rifle and watched her. Die, goddamn you, he said. She did."

Ballard's actions carry him to his worst extremities whenever Ballard himself perverts the logic of archaeological vision. But the narrator's field of vision—and therefore field of verbal reference—becomes, on the contrary, most "creative" when it situates Ballard in a frame which goes beyond the strictly empirical, strays outside the way of literality. The corresponding discourse tends toward the metaphorical, the allusive, the "literary." One might begin with an inventory of the similes littered throughout the text, many of which refer to Ballard himself. For example, Ballard and Darfuzzle squatting in the yard look "like constipated gargoyles." The morning after the cabin burns down Ballard climbs onto the hearth—the hearth is all that remains of the cabin—and sits there "like an owl." We see Ballard clambering up the mountain "like some crazy winter gnome"; carrying his final corpse off into the caves he looks "like a man beset by some ghast succubus"; emerging from the caves the next morning he peers about "like a groundhog before committing himself to the gray and rainy daylight." Or consider this passage in which Ballard fails to cross the flooded creek.

> Ballard and the log bore on into the rapids below the ford and Ballard was lost in a pandemonium of noises, the rifle aloft in one arm like some demented hero or bedraggled parody of a patriotic poster come aswamp. . . .

Warming his frostbitten feet in creekwater in the caves, the echoes of his gibbering come back "like the mutterings of a band of sympathetic apes." When Greer shoots Ballard, Ballard flies back from Greer's doorway in a violent dramatic reversal.

> He looked like something come against the end of a springloaded tether or some slapstick contrivance of the filmcutter's art, swallowed up in the door and discharged from it again almost simultaneously, ejected in an immense concussion backwards. . . .

The mention of cinema (the storyteller referring to a rival medium itself preoccupied with powers of vision has, as with the reference to "patriotic poster," its own ironic level of significance) brings us to another technique characteristic of McCarthy's archaeological discourse: the phrasal fragment that operates like a cinematic freeze frame. The metonymic pace of serial external action is interrupted and the narrator pauses to hold Ballard still, in a kind of animated suspension. Some such freezes are performed in a single sentence: "A gothic doll in illfit clothes its carmine mouth floating detached and bright in the white landscape"; "Ballard's shadow veering dark and mutant over the cupped stone walls." This discourse is just as obsessed as the voyeuristic with seeing Ballard, seems equally to imply the demands of an exacting accountability of vision, but it deploys an allusive metaphoric diction that goes beyond the strictly taxonomic and denotative: "gothic doll," shadow," mutant." The lengthier freezes gain from complexity.

> Ballard among gothic treeboles, almost jaunty in the outsized clothing he wore, fording drifts of kneedeep snow, going along the south face of a limestone bluff beneath which birds scratching in the bare earth paused to watch.

One of the ironies in the above is that even the birds regard Ballard as an alien, worthy of their curiosity, and ultimately harmless—inasmuch as they do not fly away (cf. the fate of the frozen robin Ballard catches as "playpretty").

> He looked about the room. Some stainless steel pots on a steel table. A pitcher of water and a glass. Ballard in a thin white gown in a thin white room, false acolyte or antiseptic felon, a practitioner of ghastliness, a part-time ghoul.

Here there are no birds to figure as comic displacements of the narrational voyeur, but noun phrases accumulate an alliterative intensity. Parison and asyndeton produce an effect of urgency, as if the narrator were struggling to contain the enigma of Ballard in metaphors that remain inadequate. In each case above, Ballard is contained by an external frame (*among* gothic treeboles, *in* a white room and gown), but the

effect surpasses mere voyeurism because the motive behind the freeze is to supplement the visualized object with a metaphoric discourse which refers to absent objects: alluding to a gothic world, for example, or to the world of medical horrors.

Although McCarthy's narrator seldom intrudes as a commentator on the action, when he does he speaks of a past which is primordial, permanent, strangely sacred—but equally vague, ambiguous, and provisional. Such commentaries produce a sense not of nostalgic lamentation but of material permanence that belongs to a mute, perhaps nonhuman natural world—that world to which Ballard most readily belongs. Ballard has excavated his way out of the caves and is walking toward the hospital in the third to last segment of the text.

> As he neared the town the roosters were calling. Perhaps they sensed a relief in the obscurity of night that the traveler could not read, though he kept watch eastward. Perhaps some freshness in the air. Everywhere across the sleeping land they called and answered each to each. As in olden times so now. As in other countries here.

This passage both universalizes the landscape and mystifies it. McCarthy's narrator chooses not to name any determinate cause for the rooster's enigmatic communication ("perhaps. . . .perhaps"); nevertheless, there is an affirmation of the similarity of this event to events in other, absent landscapes ("olden times . . . other countries"). Given the many precious moments in the text when Ballard's curses echo against a blank void or when demonic noises echo down the mountain, there is something of closure in this passage: here we have conversation, not the geometrical emptiness of echoes.

This archaeological discourse—the ways this discourse plays against the dominant, "purely" empirical discourse of external focalization—determines the specific aesthetic power, the peculiar quality of McCarthy's invention in *Child of God.* We see in Lester Ballard the remains of a certain spirituality, an inverted, voided Christian theodicy: Ballard is the ironic child of God, a walking threat and insult to human innocence, a grievous case against the gods, an apostate whose language is curses and whose knowledge of God is next to nothing. We see in Ballard the remains of a genealogically specific set of human kin, "Saxon and Celtic bloods," the grandson of a depressed vigilante and the son of a suicidal "lonely piper," traces of a social inheritance of deviance and marginality. We see the animality of Ballard: a protohuman simian creature, an ape, a caveman who defecates, urinates, spits, hunts, kills, eats, and—most habitually—*squats;* who sees in animals, trees, rocks, caves, stars, rubbish, the inexplicable fragments of his own shattered image. The text also sees Ballard as gnome, troll, ghoul, monster, hermit—as an anti-pastoral demonic figure who makes, takes, loves, and treasures female corpses, who threatens all enlightened common sense and lives in a fearful, pagan, fantastic realm. It is the subtle power of the condensation in McCarthy's archaeological vision that both permits and produces the terribly haunted discourse of these irreconcilable traces—traces of a Christian spirituality, of a wasting Appalachian society, of a bewildered and deprived animal nature, and of a strange pagan enigma.

But Lester Ballard remains a human animal, a human figure: "a child of God much like yourself perhaps."

> It was all lit up and the faces within [the churchbus] passed each in their pane of glass, each in profile. At the last seat in the rear a small boy was looking out the window, his nose puttied against the glass. There was nothing out there to see but he was looking anyway. As he went by he looked at Ballard and Ballard looked back. Then the bus rounded the curve and clattered from sight. Ballard climbed into the road and went on. He was trying to fix in his mind where he'd seen the boy when it came to him that the boy looked like himself. This gave him the fidgets and though he tried to shake the image of the face it would not go.

Previously, Ballard has looked intently at the posters of the wanted in the town post office, perhaps for his own face. He has almost touched his own image, Narcissus-fashion, in a pool on the Blount county side of Frog Mountain. But not until this relatively random visual confrontation—only relatively, because the churchbus is appropriately ironic, and the exceptional boy's puttied nose directing the vision out the back window instead of straight ahead like all the others is suggestive—not until this mirroring event occurs does the direction of Ballard's actions change. He returns to the hospital: "I'm supposed to be here, he said." Make no mistake: resignation or repentance, this choice is a kind of suicide, because Ballard belongs to the ancient mountain and not to modern society. This enigmatic conversion leads ultimately to his evisceration, to medical archaeology, as Ballard's corpse itself becomes remains: "the four young students who bent over him like those haruspices of old saw monsters worse to come in their configurations." Some might find it capricious that McCarthy's narrator tells us only that the "monsters worse" are possible—given the "perhaps," this is neither reassurance nor prophecy. I would grant the archaeologist those degrees of uncertainty that follow from incomplete evidence.

McCarthy's fictional discourse in *Child of God* refuses to rest on first principles, and celebrates what can be seen—seen by means of the threatening precision of the voyeur's eye looking through the sights of the beloved rifle, or seen by means of the creative expertise of the archaeological vision. The complacent perspectives based on a society of armchair storytellers or a system of principled theological uniformity tend to exclude or to overlook the evidence outside their necessarily circumscribed fields of vision. It seems that properly to recognize the strangely beautiful world of Lester Ballard, one must live by—perhaps must live on and must live with—traces and remains. Such remains produce their own peculiar necessities. Cormac McCarthy's discourse of archaeology in *Child of God* may be the only fictional response which respects—enough to see—those outsiders who find themselves too much at home among the dead, threatened by the absolute blindness of darkness and death.

## Richard B. Woodward (interview date 19 April 1992)

SOURCE: "Cormac McCarthy's Venomous Fiction," in *The New York Times Magazine*, Vol. CXLI, No. 48,941, April 19, 1992, pp. 28-31, 36, 40.

[*In the following article, Woodward conducts an interview with the elusive McCarthy, and gains many insights into the author's writing habits, his personal life, and his thoughts on his own fiction.*]

"You know about Mojave rattlesnakes?" Cormac McCarthy asks. The question has come up over lunch in Mesilla, N.M., because the hermitic author, who may be the best unknown novelist in America, wants to steer conversation away from himself, and he seems to think that a story about a recent trip he took near the Texas-Mexico border will offer some camouflage. A writer who renders the brutal actions of men in excruciating detail, seldom applying the anesthetic of psychology, McCarthy would much rather orate than confide. And he is the sort of silver-tongued raconteur who relishes peculiar sidetracks, he leans over his plate and fairly croons the particulars in his soft Tennessee accent.

"Mojave rattlesnakes have a neurotoxic poison, almost like a cobra's," he explains, giving a natural-history lesson on the animal's two color phases and its map of distribution in the West. He had come upon the creature while traveling along an empty road in his 1978 Ford pickup near Big Bend National Park. McCarthy doesn't write about places he hasn't visited, and he had made dozens of similar scouting forays to Texas, New Mexico, Arizona and across the Rio Grande into Chihuahua, Sonora and Coahuila. The vast blankness of the Southwest desert served as a metaphor for the nihilistic violence in his last novel, *Blood Meridian,* published in 1985. And this unpopulated, scuffed-up terrain again dominates the background in *All the Pretty Horses,* which will appear next month from Knopf.

"It's very interesting to see an animal out in the wild that can kill you graveyard dead," he says with a smile. "The only thing I had seen that answered that description was a grizzly bear in Alaska. And that's an odd feeling, because there's no fence, and you know that after he gets tired of chasing marmots he's going to move in some other direction, which could be yours."

Keeping a respectful distance from the rattlesnake, poking it with a stick, he coaxed it into the grass and drove off. Two park rangers he met later that day seemed reluctant to discuss lethal vipers among the backpackers. But another, clearly McCarthy's kind of man, put the matter in perspective. "We don't know how dangerous they are," he said. "We've never had anyone bitten. We just assume you wouldn't survive."

Finished off with one of his twinkly-eyed laughs, this mealtime anecdote has a more jocular tone than McCarthy's venomous fiction, but the same elements are there. The tense encounter in a forbidding landscape, the dark humor in the face of facts, the good chance of a painful quietus. Each of his five previous novels has been marked by intense natural observation, a kind of morbid realism. His characters are often outcasts—destitute or criminals, or both. Homeless or squatting in hovels without electricity, they scrape by in the backwoods of East Tennessee or on horseback in the dry, vacant spaces of the desert. Death, which announces itself often, reaches down from the open sky, abruptly, with a slashed throat or a bullet in the face. The abyss opens up at any misstep.

McCarthy appreciates wildness—in animals, landscapes and people—and although he is a well-born, well-spoken, well-read man of 58 years, he has spent most of his adult life outside the ring of the campfire. It would be hard to think of a major American writer who has participated less in literary life. He has never taught or written journalism, given readings, blurbed a book, granted an interview. None of his novels have sold more than 5,000 copies in hardcover. For most of his career, he did not even have an agent.

But among a small fraternity of writers and academics, McCarthy has a standing second to none, far out of proportion to his name recognition or sales. A cult figure with a reputation as a writer's writer, especially in the South and in England, McCarthy has sometimes been compared with Joyce and Faulkner. Saul Bellow, who sat on the committee that in 1981 awarded him a MacArthur Fellowship, the so-called genius grant, exclaims over his "absolutely overpowering use of language, his life-giving and death-dealing sentences." Says the historian and novelist Shelby Foote: "McCarthy is the one writer younger than myself who has excited me. I told the MacArthur people that he would be honoring them as much as they were honoring him."

A man's novelist whose apocalyptic vision rarely focuses on women, McCarthy doesn't write about sex, love or domestic issues. *All the Pretty Horses,* an adventure story about a Texas boy who rides off to Mexico with his buddy, is unusually sweet-tempered for him—like Huck Finn and Tom Sawyer on horseback. The earnest nature of the young characters and the lean, swift story, reminiscent of early Hemingway, should bring McCarthy a wider audience at the same time it secures his masculine mystique.

But whatever it has lacked in thematic range, McCarthy's prose restores the terror and grandeur of the physical world with a biblical gravity that can shatter a reader. A page from any of his books—minimally punctuated, without quotation marks, avoiding apostrophes, colons or semicolons—has a stylized spareness that magnifies the force and precision of his words. Unimaginable cruelty and the simplest things, the sound of a tap on a door, exist side by side, as in this typical passage from *Blood Meridian* on the unmourned death of a pack animal:

> The following evening as they rode up onto the western rim they lost one of the mules. It went skittering off down the canyon wall with the contents of the panniers exploding soundlessly in the hot dry air and it fell through sunlight and through shade, turning in that lonely void until it fell from sight into a sink of cold blue space that absolved it forever of memory in the mind of any living thing that was.

Rightful heir to the Southern Gothic tradition, McCarthy is a radical conservative who still believes that the novel can, in his words, "encompass all the various disciplines and interests of humanity." And with his recent forays into the history of the United States and Mexico, he has cut a solitary path into the violent heart of the Old West. There isn't anyone remotely like him in contemporary American literature.

A compact unit, shy of 6 feet even in cowboy boots, McCarthy walks with a bounce, like someone who is also a good dancer. Clean-cut and handsome as he grays, he has a Celtic's blue-green eyes set deep into a high-domed forehead. "He gives an impression of strength and vitality and poetry," says Bellow, who describes him as "crammed into his own person."

For such an obstinate loner, McCarthy is an engaging figure, a world-class talker, funny, opinionated, quick to laugh. Unlike his illiterate characters, who tend to be terse and crude, he speaks with an amused, ironic manner. His involved syntax has a relaxed elegance, as if he had easy control over the direction and agreement of his thoughts. Once he had agreed to an interview—after long negotiations with his agent in New York, Amanda Urban of International Creative Management, who promised he wouldn't have to do another for many years—he seemed happy to entertain company for a few days.

Since 1976 he has lived mainly in El Paso, which sprawls along the concrete-lined Rio Grande, across the border from Juarez, Mexico. A gregarious recluse, McCarthy has lots of friends who know that he likes to be left alone. A few years ago *The El Paso Herald-Post* held a dinner in his honor. He politely warned them that he wouldn't attend, and didn't. The plaque now hangs in the office of his lawyer.

For many years he had no walls to hang anything on. When he heard the news about his MacArthur, he was living in a motel in Knoxville, Tenn. Such accommodations have been his home so routinely that he has learned to travel with a high-watt light bulb in a lens case to assure better illumination for reading and writing. In 1982 he bought a tiny, white-washed stone cottage behind a shopping center in El Paso. But he wouldn't take me inside. Renovation, which began a few years ago, has stopped for lack of funds. "It's barely habitable," he says. He cuts his own hair, eats his meals off a hot plate or in cafeterias and does his wash at the Laundromat.

McCarthy estimates that he owns about 7,000 books, nearly all of them in storage lockers. "He has more intellectual interests than anyone I've ever met," says the director Richard Pearce, who tracked down McCarthy in 1974 and remains one of his few "artistic" friends. Pearce asked him to write the screenplay for "The Gardener's Son," a television drama about the murder of a South Carolina mill owner in the 1870's by a disturbed boy with a wooden leg. In typical McCarthy style, the amputation of the boy's leg and his slow execution by hanging are the moments from the show that linger in the mind.

McCarthy has never shown interest in a steady job, a trait that seems to have annoyed both his ex-wives. "We lived in total poverty," says the second, Annie DeLisle, now a restaurateur in Florida. For nearly eight years they lived in a dairy barn outside Knoxville. "We were bathing in the lake," she says with some nostalgia. "Someone would call up and offer him $2,000 to come speak at a university about his books. And he would tell them that everything he had to say was there on the page. So we would eat beans for another week."

McCarthy would rather talk about rattle-snakes, molecular computers, country music, Wittgenstein—anything—than himself or his books. "Of all the subjects I'm interested in, it would be extremely difficult to find one I wasn't," he growls. "Writing is way, *way* down at the bottom of the list."

His hostility to the literary world seems both genuine ("teaching writing is a hustle") and a tactic to screen out distractions. At the MacArthur reunions he spends his time with scientists, like the physicist Murray Gell-Mann and the whale biologist Roger Payne, rather than other writers. One of the few he acknowledges having known at all was the novelist and ecological crusader Edward Abbey. Shortly before Abbey's death in 1989, they discussed a covert operation to reintroduce the wolf to southern Arizona.

McCarthy's silence about himself has spawned a host of legends about his background and whereabouts. Esquire magazine recently printed a list of rumors, including one that had him living under an oil derrick. For many years the sum of hard-core information about his early life could be found in an author's note to his first novel, *The Orchard Keeper,* published in 1965. It stated that he was born in Rhode Island in 1933; grew up outside Knoxville; attended parochial schools; entered the University of Tennessee, which he dropped out of; joined the Air Force in 1953 for four years; returned to the university, which he dropped out of again, and began to write novels in 1959. Add the publication dates of his books and awards, the marriages and divorces, a son born in 1962 and the move to the Southwest in 1974, and the relevant facts of his biography are complete.

The oldest son of an eminent lawyer, formerly with the Tennessee Valley Authority, McCarthy is Charles Jr., with five brothers and sisters. Cormac, the Gaelic equivalent of Charles, was an old family nickname bestowed on his father by Irish aunts.

It seems to have been a comfortable upbringing that bears no resemblance to the wretched lives of his characters. The large white house of his youth had acreage and woods nearby, and was staffed with maids. "We were considered rich because all the people around us were living in one or two-room shacks," he says. What went on in these shacks, and in Knoxville's nether world, seems to have fueled his imagination more than anything that happened inside his own family. Only his novel *Suttree* which has a paralyzing father-son conflict, seems strongly autobiographical.

"I was not what they had in mind," McCarthy says of childhood discord with his parents. "I felt early on I wasn't going to be a respectable citizen. I hated school from the day I set foot in it." Pressed to explain his sense of alienation, he has an odd moment of heated reflection. "I remember in grammar school the teacher asked if anyone had any hobbies. I was the only one with any hobbies, and I had every hobby there was. There was no hobby I didn't have, name anything, no matter how esoteric, I had found it and dabbled in it. I could have given everyone a hobby and still had 40 or 50 to take home."

Writing and reading seem to be the only interests that the teen-age McCarthy never considered. Not until he was about 23, during his second quarrel with schooling, did he discover literature. To kill the tedium of the Air Force, which sent him to Alaska, he began reading in the barracks. "I read a lot of books very quickly," he says, vague about his self-administered syllabus.

McCarthy's style owes much to Faulkner's—in its recondite vocabulary, punctuation, portentous rhetoric, use of dialect and concrete sense of the world—a debt McCarthy doesn't dispute. "The ugly fact is books are made out of books," he says. "The novel depends for its life on the novels that have been written." His list of those whom he calls the "good writers"—Melville, Dostoyevsky, Faulkner—precludes anyone who doesn't "deal with issues of life and death." Proust and Henry James don't make the cut. "I don't understand them," he says. "To me, that's not literature. A lot of writers who are considered good I consider strange.

*The Orchard Keeper,* however Faulknerian in its themes, characters, language and structure, is no pastiche. The story of a boy and two old men who weave in and out of his young life, it has a gnarliness and a gloom all its own. Set in the hill country of Tennessee, the allusive narrative memorializes, without a trace of sentimentality, a vanishing way of life in the woods. An affection for coon hounds binds the fate of the characters, who wander unaware of any kinship. The boy never learns that a decomposing body he sees in a leafy pit may be his father.

McCarthy began the book in college and finished it in Chicago, where he worked part time in an auto-parts warehouse. "I never had any doubts about my abilities," he says. "I knew I could write. I just had to figure out how to eat while doing this." In 1961 he married Lee Holleman, whom he had met at college; they had a son, Cullen (now an architecture student at Princeton), and quickly divorced, the yet-unpublished writer taking off for Asheville, N.C., and New Orleans. Asked if he had ever paid alimony, McCarthy snorts, "With what?" He recalls his expulsion from a $40-a-month room in the French Quarter for nonpayment of rent.

After three years of writing, he packed off the manuscript to Random House—"it was the only publisher I had heard of." Eventually it reached the desk of the legendary Albert Erskine, who had been Faulkner's last editor as well as the sponsor for *Under the Volcano* by Malcolm Lowry and *The Invisible Man* by Ralph Ellison. Erskine recognized McCarthy as a writer of the same caliber and, in the sort of relationship that scarcely exists anymore in American publishing, edited him for the next 20 years. "There is a father-son feeling," says Erskine, despite the fact, as he sheepishly admits, that "we never sold any of his books."

For years McCarthy seems to have subsisted on awards money he earned for *The Orchard Keeper*—including grants from the American Academy of Arts and Letters, the Will-

iam Faulkner Foundation and the Rockefeller Foundation. Some of these funds went toward a trip to Europe in 1967, where he met DeLisle, an English pop singer, who became his second wife. They settled for many months on the island of Ibiza in the Mediterranean, where he wrote *Outer Dark,* published in 1968, a twisted Nativity story about a girl's search for her baby, the product of incest with her brother. At the end of their independent wanderings through the rural South the brother witnesses, in one of McCarthy's most appalling scenes, the death of his child at the hands of three mysterious killers around a campfire: "Holme saw the blade wink in the light like a long cat's eye slant and malevolent and a dark smile erupted on the child's throat and went all broken down the front of it. The child made no sound. It hung there with its one eye glazing over like a wet stone and the black blood pumping down its naked belly."

*Child of God,* published in 1973 after he and DeLisle returned to Tennessee, tested new extremes. The main character, Lester Ballard—a mass murderer and necrophiliac—lives with his victims in a series of underground caves. He is based on newspaper reports of such a figure in Sevier County, Tenn. Somehow, McCarthy finds compassion for and humor in Ballard, while never asking the reader to forgive his crimes. No social or psychological theory is offered that might explain him away.

In a long review of the book in *The New Yorker,* Robert Coles called McCarthy a "novelist of religious feeling," comparing him with the Greek dramatists and medieval moralists. And in a prescient observation he noted the novelist's "stubborn refusal to bend his writing to the literary and intellectual demands of our era," calling him a writer "whose fate is to be relatively unknown and often misinterpreted."

"Most of my friends from those days are dead," McCarthy says. We are sitting in a bar in Juarez, discussing *Suttree,* his longest, funniest book, a celebration of the crazies and ne'er-do-wells he knew in Knoxville's dirty bars and poolrooms. McCarthy doesn't drink anymore—he quit 16 years ago in El Paso, with one of his young girlfriends—and *Suttree* reads like a farewell to that life. "The friends I do have are simply those who quit drinking," he says. "If there is an occupational hazard to writing, it's drinking."

Written over about 20 years and published in 1979, *Suttree* has a sensitive and mature protagonist, unlike any other in McCarthy's work, who ekes out a living on a houseboat, fishing in the polluted city river, in defiance of his stern, successful father. A literary conceit—part Stephen Daedalus, part Prince Hal—he is also McCarthy, the willful outcast. Many of the brawlers and drunkards in the book are his former real-life companions. "I was always attracted to people who enjoyed a perilous life style," he says. Residents of the city are said to compete to find themselves in the text, which has displaced *A Death in the Family* by James Agee as Knoxville's novel.

McCarthy began *Blood Meridian* after he had moved to the Southwest, without DeLisle. "He always thought he would write the great American western," says a still-smarting DeLisle, who typed *Suttree* for him—"twice, all 800 pages." Against all odds, they remain friends. If *Suttree* strives to be *Ulysses*, *Blood Meridian* has distinct echoes of *Moby Dick*, McCarthy's favorite book. A mad hairless giant named Judge Holden makes florid speeches not unlike Captain Ahab's. Based on historical events in the Southwest in 1849-50 (McCarthy learned Spanish to research it), the book follows the life of a mythic character called "the kid" as he rides around with John Glanton, who was the leader of a ferocious gang of scalp hunters. The collision between the inflated prose of the 19th-century novel and nasty reality gives *Blood Meridian* its strange, hellish character. It may be the bloodiest book since *The Iliad*.

"I've always been interested in the Southwest," McCarthy says blandly. "There isn't a place in the world you can go where they don't know about cowboys and Indians and the myth of the West."

More profoundly, the book explores the nature of evil and the allure of violence. Page after page, it presents the regular, and often senseless, slaughter that went on among white, Hispanic and Indian groups. There are no heroes in this vision of the American frontier.

"There's no such thing as life without bloodshed," McCarthy says philosophically. "I think the notion that the species can be improved in some way, that everyone could live in harmony, is a really dangerous idea. Those who are afflicted with this notion are the first ones to give up their souls, their freedom. Your desire that it be that way will enslave you and make your life vacuous."

This tooth-and-claw view of reality would seem not to accept the largesse of philanthropies. Then again, McCarthy is no typical reactionary. Like Flannery O'Conner, he sides with the misfits and anachronisms of modern life against "progress." His play, *The Stonemason*, written a few years ago and scheduled to be performed this fall at the Arena Stage in Washington, is based on a Southern black family he worked with for many months. The breakdown of the family in the play mirrors the recent disappearance of stoneworking as a craft.

"Stacking up stone is the oldest trade there is," he says, sipping a Coke. "Not even prostitution can come close to its antiquity. It's older than anything, older than fire. And in the last 50 years, with hydraulic cement, it's vanishing. I find that rather interesting."

By comparison with the sonority and carnage of *Blood Meridian*, the world of *All the Pretty Horses* is less risky—repressed but sane. The main character, a teen-ager named John Grady Cole, leaves his home in West Texas in 1949 after the death of his grandfather and during his parents' divorce, convincing his friend Lacey Rawlins they should ride off to Mexico.

Dialogue rather than description predominates, and the comical exchanges between the young men have a bleak music, as though their words had been whittled down by the wind off the desert:

> They rode.
>
> You ever get ill at ease? said Rawlins.
>
> About what?
>
> I dont know. About anything. Just ill at ease.
>
> Sometimes. If you're someplace you aint supposed to be I guess you'd be ill at ease. Should be anyways.
>
> Well suppose you were ill at ease and didnt know why. Would that mean that you might be someplace you wasn't supposed to be and didn't know it?
>
> What the hell's wrong with you?
>
> I dont know. Nothin. I believe I'll sing.
>
> He did.

A linear tale of boyish episodes—they meet vaqueros, are joined by a hapless companion, break horses on a hacienda and are thrown in jail—the book has a sustained innocence and a lucidity new in McCarthy's work. There is even a budding love story.

"You haven't come to the end yet," says McCarthy, when asked about the low body count. "This may be nothing but a snare and a delusion to draw you in, thinking that all will be well."

The book is, in fact, the first volume of a trilogy; the third part has existed for more than 10 years as a screenplay. He and Richard Pearce have come close to making the film—Sean Penn was interested—but producers always became skittish about the plot, which has as its central relationship John Grady Cole's love for a teen-age Mexican prostitute.

Knopf is revving up the publicity engines for a campaign that they hope will bring McCarthy his overdue recognition. Vintage will reissue *Suttree* and *Blood Meridian* next month, and the rest of his work shortly thereafter. McCarthy, however, won't be making the book-signing circuit. During my visit he was at work in the mornings on Volume 2 of the trilogy, which will require another extended trip through Mexico.

"The great thing about Cormac is that he's in no rush," Pearce says. "He is absolutely at peace with his own rhythms and has complete confidence in his own powers."

In a pool hall one afternoon, a loud and youthful establishment in one of El Paso's ubiquitous malls, McCarthy ignores the video games and rock-and-roll and patiently runs out the table. A skillful player, he was a member of a team at this place, an incongruous setting for a man of his conservative demeanor. But more than one of his friends describe McCarthy as a "chameleon, able to adjust easily to any surroundings and company because he seems so secure in what he will and will not do."

"Everything's interesting," McCarthy says. "I don't think I've been bored in 50 years. I've forgotten what it was like."

He bangs away in his stone house or in motels on an Olivetti manual. "It's a messy business," he says about his novel-building. "You wind up with shoe boxes of scrap paper." He likes computers. "But not to write on." That's about all he will discuss about his process of writing. Who types his final drafts now he doesn't say.

Having saved enough money to leave El Paso, McCarthy may take off again soon, probably for several years in Spain. His son, with whom he has lately re-established a strong bond, is to be married there this year. "Three moves is as good as a fire," he says in praise of homelessness.

The psychic cost of such an independent life, to himself and others, is tough to gauge. Aware that gifted American writers don't have to endure the kind of neglect and hardship that have been his, McCarthy has chosen to be hardheaded about the terms of his success. As he commemorates what is passing from memory—the lore, people and language of a pre-modern age—he seems immensely proud to be the kind of writer who has almost ceased to exist.

## Madison Smartt Bell (review date 17 May 1992)

SOURCE: "The Man Who Understood Horses," in *The New York Times Book Review*, Vol. XCVII, No. 20, May 17, 1992, pp. 9, 11.

[*In the following review, Bell discusses the differences be-* *tween* All The Pretty Horses *and McCarthy's previous novels, and calls the book the "most accessible" of his works.*]

Cormac McCarthy has practiced the Joycean virtues of silence, exile and cunning more faithfully than any other contemporary author, until very recently, he shunned publicity so effectively that he wasn't even famous for it. By his single-minded commitment to his work and his apparent indifference to the rewards and aggrandizements quite openly pursued by the rest of us, he puts most other American writers to shame. The work itself repays the tight focus of his attention with its finely wrought craftsmanship and its ferocious energy.

The magnetic attraction of Mr. McCarthy's fiction comes first from the extraordinary quality of his prose; difficult as it may sometimes be, it is also overwhelmingly seductive. Powered by long, tumbling many-stranded sentences, his descriptive style is elaborate and elevated, but also used effectively to frame realistic dialogue, for which his ear is deadly accurate. This mixture builds on Faulkner's work, yet, more than Faulkner ever did, Mr. McCarthy seems to be pulling the language apart at its roots. He's noted for archaisms so unfamiliar they appear to be neologisms. His diction and phrasing come from all over the evolutionary history of English and combine into a prose that seems to invent itself as it unfolds, resembling Elizabethan language in its flux of remarkable possibilities.

All these qualities make *Suttree* and *Blood Meridian,* the two long novels that precede his latest book, more than a little challenging to the uninitiated, and the world of violence that these and his earlier, shorter novels so brilliantly depict can seem, on casual inspection, to be senseless. *All the Pretty Horses,* the comparatively brief first volume of a planned trilogy, is probably the most accessible of Mr. McCarthy's six novels, though it certainly preserves all his stylistic strength. Although its subject and approach are superficially more palatable, the essence of his unusual vision also persists.

Where *Suttree* and *Blood Meridian* are deliberately discontinuous, apparently random in the arrangement of their episodes, *All the Pretty Horses* is quite conventionally plotted. Another distinction from Mr. McCarthy's earlier work is the presence of a plainly sympathetic protagonist, John Grady Cole, a youth of 16 who, in the spring of 1950, is evicted from the Texas ranch where he grew up. He and another boy, Lacey Rawlins, head for Mexico on horseback, riding south until they finally turn up at a vast ranch in mountainous Coahuila, the Hacienda de la Purisima, where they sign on as vaqueros. There, in magnificent scenes that make Faulkner's story "Spotted Horses" seem almost forgettable, John Grady's unusual talent for breaking, training and understanding horses becomes crucial to the *hacendado* Don Hector's ambitious breeding program.

For John Grady, La Purisima is a paradise, complete with its Eve, Don Hector's daughter, Alejandra. Their relationship is Mr. McCarthy's first excursion into romance since his 1973 novel, *Child of God,* in which all the female lovers are dead. Infinitely more sympathetically rendered, John Grady's affair with Alejandra ends badly nonetheless. When Don Hector and his aunt, the formidable Duena Alfonsa, discover it, they arrange for John Grady and Rawlins to be arrested for acts of murder and horse theft actually committed by another American runaway they met on the trail. The rest of their journey brings them closer and closer, though not fatally near, to the vortex of violent anarchy that swirls up toward the surface of all of Mr. McCarthy's writing.

In the hands of some other writer, this material might make for a combination of *Lonesome Dove* and *Huckleberry Finn,* but Mr. McCarthy's vision is deeper than Larry McMurtry's and, in its own way, darker than Mark Twain's. Along with the manifold felicities of his writing goes a serious concern with the nature of God (if God exists) and, almost obsessively, the nature of something most readers have assumed to be evil. The decay of Western civilization throws a long shadow over all his work. "We're like the Comanches was two hundred years ago," John Grady's father remarks. "We dont know what's goin to show up here come daylight. We dont even know what color they'll be."

The novel opens and closes with eerie images of American Indians that suggest our civilization may be swallowed up as completely as theirs. For John Grady, meanwhile, the issue is the using up of the country; he heads for Mexico because too much of Texas has been fenced in or foreclosed on. Mr. McCarthy's descriptions of the landscape are breathtakingly beautiful, but anyone who thinks he is sentimental about nature need only read *Blood Meridian* for a permanent cure.

Cormac McCarthy must be acknowledged as a talent equal to William Faulkner, but whatever he may owe to Faulkner's style, his substance could not be more different. Faulkner's work is all about human history and all takes place in mental spaces, while in Mr. McCarthy's work human thought and activity seem almost completely inconsequential when projected upon the vast alien landscapes where they occur. Human behavior may achieve its own integrity—it's John Grady's conscientious striving for this quality that makes him Mr. McCarthy's most appealing character—but it generally seems to have little effect. It's unusual for a writer to adopt such a disinterested posture toward human beings, but Mr. McCarthy, like John Grady, seems to hold a higher opinion of horses:

In his sleep he could hear the horses stepping among the rocks and he could hear them drink from the shallow pools in the dark where the rocks lay smooth and rectilinear as the stones of ancient ruins and the water from their muzzles dripped and rang like water dripping in a well and in his sleep he dreamt of horses and the horses in his dream moved gravely among the tilted stones like horses come upon an antique site where some ordering of the world had failed and if anything had been written on the stones the weathers had taken it away again and the horses were wary and moved with great circumspection carrying in their blood as they did the recollection of this and other places where horses once had been and would be again. Finally what he saw in his dream was that the order in the horse's heart was more durable for it was written in a place where no rain could erase it.

What order there may be in the world is not, Mr. McCarthy suggests, of our devising and is very likely beyond our comprehension. His project is unlike that of any other writer: to make artifacts composed of human language but detached from a human reference point. That sense of evil that seems to suffuse his novels is illusory; it comes from our discomfort in the presence of a system that is not scaled to ourselves, within which our civilizations may be as ephemeral as flowers. The deity that presides over Mr. McCarthy's world has not modeled itself on humanity; its voice most resembles the one that addressed Job out of the whirlwind.

As for himself, Mr. McCarthy has told a French journalist that the fact that he writes is incidental to his life, that he spends his time with equal profit gazing at the toes of his shoes. What for another writer would be a silly pose is for Mr. McCarthy the natural consequence of his view of the world and the people in it. It is an uncomfortable vision, but one that has a strange power to displace all others.

## Richard Eder (review date 17 May 1992)

SOURCE: "John's Passion," in *Los Angeles Times Book Review,* May 17, 1992, pp. 3, 13.

[*In the following review, Eder discusses* All the Pretty Horses, *provides a plot synopsis, and comments on McCarthy's descriptive prose.*]

When John Cole's grandfather dies in 1947, leaving the 18,000-acre Texas ranch he spent his life to assemble, the 16-year-old begs his mother to lease it to him. She is determined to sell out; she is an actress, likes a good time and cannot stand the place. So John and his buddy, Rawlins, take two horses, two guns and a little money, and light out for Mexico.

Cormac McCarthy's *All the Pretty Horses* is the ambitious first part of a trilogy. It tells how John, in love with the disappearing world of horses and infinite horizons, comes violently to manhood in a place and culture where the Old West survives in a Spanish configuration of passion, honor and a sense of the sacramental.

Horses are its heart and John's passion. He wins his place on a Mexican ranch, and the respect of the wealthy rancher, by breaking 16 wild ponies in four days. His torrid affair with the rancher's daughter, for which he will pay in blood, is launched when he rides a stallion, steamy from covering a mare, up to her fine-schooled Arabian mount. John is a half-centaur who strives, more urgently than for women, to regain his other half.

It is a mythic urgency. McCarthy is writing an epic about lost values. Horses, freedom, the spirit of the land, the deep and spontaneous humanity of the Mexicans, traditional manly prowess—all these stand in different ways for what has faded from American life. On their way south past highways and whizzing trucks, the boys can't find oats for their horses; they have to feed them packaged oatmeal dished out in hubcaps.

"Epic" is pretty close to "hiccup" spoken backward. McCarthy wavers between the lovely and the ludicrous. He has written a horse grand opera; Parsifal comes to mind. It is expansively moving at times, and—when the grand opera recedes to more modest but more artful glimpses of riding, horse-taming, Mexicans and boys ruminating—wonderfully engaging. But loftiness gusts like a capsizing high wind, and the writing can choke on its own ornateness. *Horses* is a novel entirely surrounded by language.

Here is a high-temperature rendition of John's sensibility:

> What he loved in horses was what he loved in men, the blood and the heat of the blood that ran them. All his reverence and all his fondness and all the leanings of his life were for the ardenthearted and they would always be so and never be otherwise.

Heat becomes meltdown. John "sat a horse not only as if he'd been born to it which he was but as if were he begot by malice or mischance into some queer land where horses never were he would have found them anyway. Would have known that there was something missing for the world to be right or he right in it and would have set forth to wander wherever it was needed for as long as it took until he came upon one and he would have known that that was what he sought and it would have been."

There is a hyper-inflated hint of Hemingway in this and other cadences, and there is absolute hyper-inflation in the use of Spanish to evoke a Hispanic place and culture. There are numerous two-line, four-line, eight-line exchanges in Spanish, and at one point, nearly a whole page. Spanish words are liberally slipped in, not just in dialogues but in the author's own voice, and for no apparent reason. John walks past not the room but the "cuarto" where a Mexican is sleeping, for example. In other cases, English is twisted into a Spanish syntax. I wonder how a Spanish translation of *Horses* would be managed.

It would be nice to say that such ornateness and bilingual mannerisms are defects in an otherwise splendid book. They are more than that; they seriously compromise it. But what they compromise is a moving and often enthralling story, a compelling portrait of a young man's hungers, a profound empathy for a different culture and a sweet skill in portraying it. McCarthy has a cunning narrative sense, except for one section near the end, where John gets his revenge on a brutal Mexican police captain, and movement is brought to a halt by sheer strenuous activity.

As John and Rawlins ride south into Mexico, their happiness in being on horseback and on an adventure, in frying bacon, eating beans out of a can and shooting and cooking a rabbit, their rambling reflections on the universe—all these have a Huck Finn-like buoyancy, with the desert as their river and the horses as a raft. There is humor, subtlety and finally a tragic wildness in a young boy who attaches himself to them, and is finally killed through pure untameability.

McCarthy's elevated prose does wonders for deserts, mountains, freezing winds, night landscapes and the tangibility of food, a bath and clean clothes. The section in which John, assisted by Rawlins, ropes and breaks a string of wild ponies has an exultant detail in the tradition of Melville's whale work and clambakes.

Pinpointing the essential of horse-breaking—converting a herd into individuals—the author's elaborate writing works well. He describes the ponies, some tied, some still racing back and forth, as "coming to reckon slowly with the remorselessness of this rendering of their fluid and collective selves into that condition of separate and helpless paralysis which seemed to be among them like a creeping plague."

McCarthy has a sure instinct for the worlds of men and their work. He writes with delicacy and art about Mexicans and their culture; a conversation between John and a group of children is grave, comic and supremely perceptive. He can describe the camaraderie in a Mexican bunkhouse, warm and marked by dignified reserve. There is the surreal horror of the Mexican prison in which John finds himself after his affair with Alejandra is revealed to her father, Don Hector, the owner of the ranch, and he is arrested on a trumped-up charge.

The women, on the other hand, are mainly cliches. John's mother is a wisp of frozen superficiality; the Mexican wives are sentimentally nurturing and deep-rooted. Alejandra is fiery and passionate and not much more; the lovemaking is all temperature and no flesh. Only Alejandra's great-aunt has an interesting individuality. Her confrontation with John is taut and unexpected, and her condemnation of the lovers is far more than a traditional one.

John himself is partly revealed and partly obscured by McCarthy's ambitious intentions. There is a disconcerting contrast between his down-home speech and the baroquely elaborate thoughts which the author puts in his head. As a spirited youth seeking out the world, he is convincing and engaging; but he becomes weighed down by McCarthy's epic plans for him.

For one thing, he is simply too good at everything. He does all the horse-breaking; Rawlins more or less holds the ropes. When they race, he wins and then he wins once more when he and his sidekick exchange horses. He discusses horse-breeding as equal to equal with Don Hector; when he plays chess with the aunt, he beats her two times out of three. Stalked by a professional killer in jail, he prevails in a lethal knife fight. And having bested in different ways the wild horses, Alejandra, Don Hector, the assassin, and a corrupt police captain, he sensitively confesses his moral scruples to a Texas judge who befriends him.

Parsifal, in short; and quite a lot to swallow. At the end, he literally rides off into the sunset, a man now, and ready for a new cycle of symbolic adventures. I would rather like to follow him, but I wish McCarthy would let me travel on foot.

## Irving Malin (review date 25 September 1992)

SOURCE: "A Sense of Incarnation," in *Commonweal*, Vol. 119, No. 16, September 25, 1992, p. 29.

[*In the following review, Malin discusses imagery, characterization, and the spiritual quest found in* All the Pretty Horses. *Malin comments on the language used in the novel, and on the "juxtapositions of beauty and blood, 'prettiness' and terror."*]

Cormac McCarthy is one of our best—if least known—writers. In this, his fourth novel, he uses the archetypal journey to discuss important spiritual themes. He is primarily interested in the origins of evil; the search for redemption; the meaning of our brutal existence.

Although his latest novel deals with the relatively simple characters of three adolescents—Cole, Rawlins, Blevins—who light out for the unknown territory of Mexico to find their mixed fortunes—the year is 1949—he is less interested in their characterizations than in their spiritual recognitions. The plot involves various adventures, misfortunes, coincidences. It is, for the most part, merely an excuse to look for epistemological answers. On one level the novel resembles the traditional initiation we find in *Huckleberry Finn* or, for that matter, in Faulkner's *The Reivers*. (The novel seems particularly "American" because of its underlying structure; it is our kind of *adolescent picaresque*.) But on a second (and deeper) level it is an occult narrative of the ultimate meanings—if there are any—of these adventures. There are echoes of a religious quest, a trip to discover the Holy Grail.

McCarthy's imagery is, perhaps, more important than his characterization. (It is, of course, difficult to separate the two.) The imagery is one of hovering presences, secret omens, perverse signs. I quote at random: "it was like looking through something and seeing its heart." Another passage on the nature of earth-bound horses: "Lastly he said that he had seen the soul of horses and it was a terrible thing to see. He said that it could be seen under certain circumstances attending the death of a horse because the horse shares a common soul and its separate life only forms it out of all horses and makes it mortal. He said that if a person understood the soul of a horse then he would understand all horses that ever were." Cole leaves Mexico; his exit is described in poetic terms. "After a while he pulled his hat down over his eyes and stood and placed his hands outstretched on the roof of the cab and rode in that manner. As if he were some personage bearing news for the countryside. As if he were some newfound evangelical being conveyed down out of the mountains. . . ." These examples are visionary, mystical, ghostly. They suggest that there is another world which somehow influences ours. They, indeed, offer a sense of *incarnation*.

McCarthy's language ranges from the laconic conversations of the three adolescents—even these conversations seem to hold ambiguous "presences"—to the almost biblical cadences of the following passage. "He thought that in the beauty of the world were hid a secret. He thought the world's pain and its beauty moved in a relationship of diverging equity and that in this headlong deficit the blood of multitudes might ultimately be exacted for the vision of a single flower."

I assume that this brilliant novel will force readers to view McCarthy as an original stylist, as one of the best contemporary writers. It will, indeed, assume its place as an example of the great religious novels written by any American. It will, without doubt, disturb us by its violent juxtapositions of beauty and blood, "prettiness" and terror.

## Vereen Bell (review date October 1992)

SOURCE: "Between the Wish and the Thing the World Lies Waiting," in *The Southern Review*, Vol. 28, No. 4, October, 1992, pp. 920-27.

[*In the following essay, Bell discusses the desires of McCarthy's characters to live in a world uncomplicated by the influences and demands the contemporary world places on them.*]

Cormac McCarthy's most sympathetic characters wish to live only in the mode of description—the less narrative the better—but the God that rules their world—an editor, clearly—likes stories and, either for his own amusement or to test them, he imposes plots upon them. Take this case of John Grady Cole, in *All the Pretty Horses*. The plot for him begins before he is born and with someone else's kin:

> It runs in the family, said Blevins. My grandaddy was killed in a minebucket in West Virginia it run down in the hole a hunnerd and eighty feet to get him it couldnt even wait for him to get to the top. They had to wet down the bucket to cool it fore they could get him out of it, him and two other men. It fried em like bacon. My daddy's older brother was blowed out of a derrick in the Batson Field in the year nineteen and four, cable rig with a wood derrick but the lightnin got him anyways and him not nineteen year old. Great uncle on my mother's side—mother's side, I said—got killed on a horse and it never singed a hair on that horse and it killed him graveyard dead they had to cut his belt off him where it welded the buckle shut and I got a cousin aint but four years oldern me was struck down in his own yard comin from the barn and it paralyzed him all down one side and melted the fillins in his teeth and soldered his jaw shut.

From thirteen-year-old Jimmy Blevins's fear of lightning—and from his not being afraid of anything else—otherwise inconceivably evil consequences for John Grady and his friend Lacey Rawlins ensue. Blevins, who has taken up with them on their ride into Mexico, loses his horse and his gun one night when he frantically dismounts and takes shelter in an arroyo during a thunderstorm. When against their better judgment the older boys help him repossess the horse in the next village—and later because Blevins goes back to repossess his gun as well—persecution and misfortune hound them as they ride on, seeking the good life that home in Texas no longer offers them. Worst of all, they are discredited and exiled from the ancient place of the good life, the Hacienda de Nuestra Senora de la Purisima Concepcion, that they believe they have found.

These circumstances, which the boys endure stoically and resourcefully, are generated not only by the plot that comes upon them out of nowhere but by their own generous impulses and honorable conduct. John Grady is asked at a point later in the story if he does not fear God and he says, "I got no reason to be afraid of God. I've even got a bone or two to pick with him." A kindly cafe proprietor says to him later "that it was good that God kept the truths of life from the young as they were starting out or else they'd have no heart to start out at all." This turns out to be the real point: whether John Grady can endure such gratuitous tribulation with his hardheaded boy's idealism intact. By the time he makes his way back to Texas—on Thanksgiving Day—he has good reason to fear the God of such plots; but he is also sobered and stronger, so he does not. He also now knows what the main question is even if it takes the form of an answer.

> He remembered Alejandra and the sadness he'd first seen in the slope of her shoulders which he'd presumed to understand and of which he knew nothing and he felt a loneliness he'd not known since he was a child and he felt wholly alien to the world although he loved it still. He thought that in the beauty of the world were hid a secret. He thought the world's heart beat at some terrible cost and that the world's pain and its beauty moved in a relationship of diverging equity and that in this headlong deficit the blood of multitudes might ultimately be exacted for the vision of a single flower.

The word *being* still means something in McCarthy's writing—after all this time since Heidegger—and his finest and simplest characters set their bearings by it in a way that determines their lives. It is greater than God Himself, and it is sacred. It is also elusive and perhaps illusory, and human beings are wholly incidental to it, if not its nemesis. McCarthy's nature exists wholly on its own, indifferent to human purpose or desire; his vivid, austere landscapes seem mysteriously to be gazing at us rather than the reverse. In this novel even horses, in some sweetly comic way, reflect upon the issue. When the boys, drunk off a canteenful of a Mexican moonshine called sotol, become sick and commence vomiting:

> The browsing horses jerked their heads up. It was no sound they'd ever heard before. In the gray twilight those retchings seemed to echo like the calls of some rude provisional species loosed upon that waste. Something imperfect and malformed lodged in the heart of being. A thing smirking deep in the eyes of grace itself like a gorgon in an autumn pool.

At best, human understanding and language can mediate being only imperfectly and, in action, only intuitively and in dreams or through the feeble agency of objective correlatives.

This is why McCarthy's narratives always seem to verge upon, without ever moving wholly over into, allegory: everything is potentially meaningful (even puking). It is also why the photorealistic details of processes or landscape and the substance and speech of ordinary human life ("The waitress brought their dinner, thick china lunchplates with steak and gravy and potatoes and beans. 'I'll get your alls bread'") are enveloped in an aura of stylization and romance. The aforementioned Alejandra Rocha y Villareal, for instance, with whom John Grady falls hopelessly in love as only a boy of seventeen can, is barely represented and, at that, only through John Grady's eyes; and yet she and her thwarted romance with John Grady are credible because of that special dimension of desire she inhabits which not only John Grady's infatuation but the novel itself creates. On the surface this central episode of the novel seems quite conventional, but its conventionality is animated by McCarthy's writing, which makes it new, and by the larger purpose that gives it value. The scene in which the two part for the last time is like a thousand others in film and literature and yet somehow redefines the genre. For John Grady it is like this: "He saw very clearly how all his life led only to this moment and all after led nowhere at all. He felt something cold and soulless enter him like another being and he imagined that it smiled malignly and he had no reason to believe that it would ever leave." And we believe him because we have been there before, in real life and in other fiction—not, precisely speaking, in love for the first time, but where love reaches. Love's having failed will change John Grady's reality, as the war and now cancer have changed his father's.

The deepest continuity with life in this novel is through horses:

> His father rode sitting forward slightly in the saddle, holding the reins in one hand about two inches above the saddlehorn. So thin and frail, lost in his clothes. Looking over the country with those sunken eyes as if the world out there had been altered or made suspect by what he'd seen of it elsewhere. As if he might never see it right again. Or worse did see it right at last. See it as it had always been, would forever be. The boy who rode on slightly before him sat a horse not only as if he'd been born to it which he was but as if were he begot by malice or mischance into some queer land where horses never were he would have found them anyway. Would have known that there was something missing for the world to be right or he right in it and would have set forth to wonder wherever it was needed for as long as it took until he came upon one and he would have known that was what he sought and it would have been.

What John Grady is said to love in horses is what, when he finds it there, he loves in men, "the blood and the heat of the blood that ran them. All his reverence and all his fondness and all the leanings of his life were for the ardenthearted and they would always be so and never be otherwise." The deepest offense in this story is to steal another's horse, and much of the novel's action is devoted to the obsession with recovering those that have been stolen and restoring them to their rightful owners, for such a theft is not simply a crime but the desecration of a type of invisible bond with the powers of the earth. When John Grady has dreams he dreams of horses, and those dreams are of sacred order:

> That night he dreamt of horses in a field on a high plain where the spring rains had brought up the grass and the wildflowers out of the ground and the flowers red and blue and yellow far as the eye could see and in the dream he was among the horses running and in the dream he himself could run with the horses and they coursed the young mares and fillies over the plain where their rich bay and their rich chestnut colors shone in the sun and the young colts ran with their dams and trampled down the flowers in a haze of pollen that hung in the sun like powdered gold and they ran he and the horses out along the high mesas where the ground resounded under their running hooves and they flowed and changed and ran and their manes and tails blew off of them like spume and there was nothing else at all in that high world and they moved all of them in a response that was like a music among them and they were none of them afraid horse nor colt nor mare and they ran in that resonance which is the world itself and which cannot be spoken but only praised.

McCarthy's symbols are never less than artfully naive, and their simplicity allows the reader to bear in mind that though this is a boy's story—in a richer but similarly ironic way that *Huckleberry Finn* is—it is deeply serious about the uncomplicated, romantic values that the boy's point of view keeps before us. We are not encouraged by the slightest inflection of the style to look upon John Grady and his friends with amusement or condescension. John Grady's youthfulness, and its associated idealism, is a correlative in itself—less a point of view than a private *episteme,* and one that refuses to be diminished. It is challenged persuasively both by experience and by a compelling history lesson in which John Grady is set straight by Alejandra's protective great-aunt; but it is never quite undone and we are not meant to think that it should be.

The Duena Alfonsa, Alejandra's great-aunt, is friendly toward and admires John Grady, but in the end she opposes him as a suitor for her niece not because he is of the wrong class or nationality or because he is penniless but, in effect, because his luck is bad—or more precisely because he has not been hardened in the ways that would give him more control over his—and by extension Alejandra's—destiny. The old woman's agenda is pragmatic and revolutionary and—allowing for the culture she speaks through and against—resolutely feminist:

> Society is very important in Mexico. Where women do not even have the vote. In Mexico they are mad for society and for politics and very bad at both. My family are considered gachupines here, but the madness of the Spaniard is not so different from the madness of the Creole. The political tragedy in Spain was rehearsed in full dress twenty years earlier on Mexican soil. For those with eyes to see. Nothing was the same and yet everything. In the Spaniard's heart is a great yearning for freedom, but only his own. A great love of truth and honor in all its forms, but not in its substance. And a deep conviction that nothing can be proven except that it be made to bleed. Virgins, bulls, men. Finally God himself.

Her own history encapsulates the horror and pathos of Mexico's history and because of that—because her story is a version of her culture's story—she has learned that the greatest tragedy is the cowardice of self-betrayal, and that self-betrayal occurs when one permits oneself to be diverted from the truth:

> It may be that the life I desire for her no longer exists, yet I know what she does not. That there is nothing to lose. In January I will be seventy-three years old. I have known a great many people in that time and few of them led lives that were satisfactory to them. I would like for my grandniece to have the opportunity to make a very different marriage from the one which her society is bent upon demanding of her. I wont accept a conventional marriage for her. Again, I know what she cannot. That there is nothing to lose. I dont know what sort of world she will live in and I have no fixed opinions concerning how she should live in it. I only know that if she does not come to value what is true above what is useful it will make little difference whether she lives at all. And by true I do not mean what is righteous but merely what is so.

In this respect, for the old woman, no matter how courageous and honorable he might be otherwise, John Grady is dangerously unfinished. "In the end," she says, "we all come to be cured of our sentiments. Those whom life does not cure death will. The world is quite ruthless in selecting between the dream and the reality, even when we will not. Between the wish and the thing the world lies waiting." This long Conradian monologue is presented through dramatic writing as chilling and as resonant as anything McCarthy has yet achieved.

The Duena Alfonsa's position in John Grady's story brings to the foreground its profoundest irony. The ruling desire of McCarthy's strongest characters, from Arthur Ownby in *The Orchard Keeper* to Cornelius Suttree in *Suttree,* is to live in some place that is not yet touched by the complications of the modern world, where it is possible to be one with the earth and to live in a genuine human communion. In practice this means that they want not so much to reverse history as to transcend it. It is no coincidence that when Cornelius Suttree is leaving Tennessee for the last time he stands above a roadbed where the new Knoxville expressway system is being built, connecting to the interstate system that will cause towns to die and cities to become indistinguishable. It is also no coincidence that he sees himself momentarily reflected and reclaimed in the blue eyes of a boy who has climbed the embankment to offer him water from a tin dipper.

John Grady Cole is Arthur Ownby in another time at a different age and also that reflection of himself younger that Suttree is permitted to see. Until now, in 1949, his grandfather's 18,000-acre cattle ranch has insulated him from history, but now that it is to be sold from around him, he can see the future coming. "People don't feel safe no more," his father says to him. "We're like the Comanches was two hundred years ago. We don't know what's goin to show up here come daylight. We don't even know what color they'll be." The father has given up, but John Grady is not waiting around to find out, and this is why he and Rawlins set out on horseback—how else?—meaning, without thinking or saying it in so many words, to move back in history by riding south. The great irony, as Senorita Alfonsa's story underscores, is that some kind of history is everywhere. The boys are too young to understand this yet (and many novelists and poets who should know better still don't): that there is no human place outside of time, and where human places are there are also the constructs and institutional artifacts of history. The fleas come with the dog. John Grady and Rawlins escape for a time the dissociating effects of the technology and capital of the new American order, but what they get from their adopted ancient culture is an attractive but totalitarian hierarchy—the autocratic rule of families, at best, and at worst, of brute power instead of law. In Enlightenment terms, a dignified ancient culture is also, inescapably, a primitive one.

It is not difficult at all to lapse into thinking of this story as taking place in the nineteenth century, or even earlier. The occasional battered truck and an especially ominous plane are surrealistically incongruous. John Grady and Rawlins bring an uncomplicated if wary democratic spirit into this old world which the system is unwilling to accommodate—itself stranded between past and future. What promises to be a dialectic turns out to be unproductive. What the outcome might have been imagined to be is, in the end, beside the point, for as the Duena Alfonsa says, in history there are no control groups—there is nothing but what happens—and her own paradigmatic reading of history is grounded in the authentic tragedy of Francisco Madero's rise and fall—a story for her for all time of what results when intellectual idealism and political reality collide.

The story of Madero (his brother had been a suitor of Senorita Alfonsa's) seems to be a paradigm for McCarthy as well. There can be no doubt by now that McCarthy is a genuine—if somehow secular—mystic. This novel along with *Blood Meridian* shows him to be also a serious student of history, and that he reads history's lessons clearheadedly without the slightest chance of projecting politically correct or utopian back-formations upon it. His project is like Conrad's Marlow's, to continue to be able to believe in a numinous value at the heart of existence while remaining wholly without reassurance about this project from the realities of political life. Nor are there any practical hopes that what we can imagine in our moments of concentrated intuition has any chance at all of flourishing in the institutions—using the term advisedly—of men. In his writing, too, McCarthy must therefore always wrestle with the deconstructive angel, seeking to represent in mere words the "resonance . . . like music . . . which is the world itself" while knowing full well that language and music cannot be the same and that to try to represent this presence through a medium which is hopelessly grounded in material nature is to fail, and that to fail in this dedicated way is to enact, yet again—a human fractal—the whole problem in itself of being in the world.

So as a writer McCarthy's story is exactly the same as John Grady Cole's, except in a different time. John Grady in turn is clearly intended to be a saint of this project, and humorous and ordinary as he is at one level, he is inhumanly demanding at another, both of the world and of himself. When he reconnoiters with Rawlins back in Texas for the last time, his friend tries halfheartedly to talk him into staying on, maybe going to work on the oil rigs where the money's good. "This is still good country," he says. "Yeah. I know it is," John Grady says. "But it ain't my country." "What is your country," says Rawlins. "I don't know," John Grady says. "I don't know where it is. I don't know what happens to country." So he rides on out, as each unaccommodated visionary must inevitably do. Riding on in McCarthy's world gets to be a habit. His characters remain both medieval and irredeemably American.

On the other hand almost all of the foregoing is both reductive and redundant, for this time around a McCarthy novel speaks lucidly and eloquently for itself. *All the Pretty Horses* is being described as more accessible than his other novels, and that is certainly the case. And that being the case no doubt accounts for its position (as of this writing) on the

*New York Times* bestseller list. Probably this novel has already sold more copies than all of McCarthy's previous novels combined. The editors at Random House who stuck by him during the lean years deserve knighthood. Now that Random House / Knopf sees that they have a promotable book, they are promoting it and McCarthy. This has required him to emerge briefly from hiding and, not surprisingly, he has conducted himself with a dignity one could wish upon other authors. The faint of heart will be pleased to discover, too, that in *All the Pretty Horses* the overpowering ratio of evil to good that we have come to expect from McCarthy's fiction has been pretty much reversed. This may bode well for the next two volumes of what is being represented as a trilogy. On the other hand it is the very essence of tragedy that, as the Duena Alfonsa expresses it, "the world is quite ruthless in selecting between the dream and the reality, even when we will not." The God who loves plots works in mysterious ways, and He stays busy. So we shall see.


## Denis Donoghue (review date 24 June 1993)

SOURCE: "Dream Work," in *The New York Review of Books,* Vol. 40, No. 12, June 24, 1993, pp. 5-6, 8-10.

[*In the following review, Donoghue discusses* All the Pretty Horses *in relation to McCarthy's other novels, asserting that McCarthy is at his "best with what nature gives or imposes, rather than with the observations of culture."*]

**All the Pretty Horses,** which won the National Book Award for fiction in 1992, is the first volume of The Border Trilogy, and Cormac McCarthy's sixth novel. The earlier ones are *The Orchard Keeper, Outer Dark, Child of God, Suttree,* and *Blood Meridian or The Evening Redness in the West.* McCarthy has been regarded as a writer's writer, a craftsman, a rhetorician, but not likely to be popular. *All the Pretty Horses* has changed that impression: it has gained critical approval, and become a best seller. Reviewers are comparing him with Faulkner. McCarthy may be a recluse, but he is a famous one.

He was born in Rhode Island in 1933, spent most of his childhood in a town near Knoxville, Tennessee, moved about a good deal, joined the air force, took some courses at the University of Tennessee, and since 1976 has lived in El Paso, Texas. He has been married and divorced twice and has a son. That is all I know about him biographically. His first four novels are set in the vicinity of Maryville, Tennessee. *Blood Meridian* sends its characters from Texas to Mexico and California, *All the Pretty Horses* keeps them in Texas and Mexico. I assume that the remaining volumes of The Border Trilogy will stay in the same region.

These novels are hard to describe. It may help a little, but not much, if I give the gist of their stories. **The Orchard Keeper** is set in mountainous Tennessee in the years between 1918 and 1948, by my count. It tells of an old man, Arthur Ownby, living a grim life by himself in a mountain cabin; his dog, Scout; a boy, John Wesley Rattner, whose father has been killed in a fight with a whiskey bootlegger, Marion Sylder. A country bar burns down, the boy saves a dog from attack by a coon, and is befriended by Sylder. There are vivid descriptions of weather, snow, six days of rain, and sundry hardships. The book ends with an elegiac passage I find unconvincing:

> They are gone now. Fled, banished in death or exile, lost, undone. Over the land sun and wind still move to burn and sway the trees, the grasses. No avatar, no scion, no vestige of that people remains. On the lips of the strange race that now dwells there their names are myth, legend, dust.

In **Outer Dark** Rinthy Holme has a child by her brother Culla. Culla abandons the child in a local wood where it is found and taken away by a tinker. Rinthy wanders about trying to find the child or the tinker. Culla goes off to look for work, steals a squire's boots, is pursued by four men, takes a ferryboat to cross a river in high flood, and is nearly lost along with a terrified horse. Eventually he comes upon three men and the child—one of his eyes gone—at a campfire. One of the men cuts the child's throat:

> The man took hold of the child and lifted it up. It was watching the fire. Holme saw the blade wink in the light like a long cat's eye slant and malevolent and a dark smile erupted on the child's throat and went all broken down the front of it. The child made no sound. It hung there with its one eye glazing over like a wet stone and the black blood pumping down its naked belly.

There are further horrors in **Child of God,** the story of Lester Ballard, whose father hanged himself when the boy was nine. Lester grows up a crazed necrophile. "Were there darker provinces of night he would have found them," the narrator says of him. Lester kills several women, brings them to a cave where he adorns their corpses and makes love to them. This one, for instance:

> He would arrange her in different positions and go out and peer in the window at her. After a while he just sat holding her, his hands feeling her body under the new clothes. He undressed her very slowly, talking to her. Then he pulled off his trousers and lay next to her. He spread her loose thighs. You been wantin it, he told her.

The characters in these three novels are like recently arrived primates, each possessing a spinal column but little or no capacity of mind or consciousness. A few of the minor characters are ethically precocious; that is, they are kind by nature and instinct, like the doctor who helps poor Rinthy. But most of them, and especially Culla, live upon a subsistence level of feeling and cognition. They meet the world without the mediation of law, morality, religion, or politics, and therefore they assume that its power is absolute and arbitrary. In *Democracy in America* Tocqueville says that "the social conditions and institutions of democracy impart certain peculiar tendencies to all the imitative arts,. . . The soul is often left out of the picture, which portrays the body only; movement and sensation take the place of feeling and thought; finally realism takes the place of the ideal." McCarthy's first novels imply that these dispositions are innate and incorrigible; that they obtain even where democracy has not yet been practiced.

This may explain why McCarthy appears to have little interest in plot, the development or complication of a story. His novels are episodic, rampant with incidents, but each of the incidents is placed at the same distance from the reader. The effect of this procedure is that a scene of violence and bloodshed, excruciating while it is going on, seems to compose itself almost at once into a *nature morte,* and it is amazing to see this occur. I am reminded of Freud's account of the work of dreaming in *The Interpretation of Dreams.* He says that the dream-work "does not think, calculate or judge in any way at all; it restricts itself to giving things a new form." The incidents in McCarthy's novels are not discriminated, adjudicated for significance, or pointed toward a climax, a disclosure, or a resolution. The new form they are given is that of being released from the observances of morality or other judgment.

In **Child of God** we read of "old buried wanderings, struggles, scenes of death . . . old comings and goings." But we are not encouraged to ask what these might mean or whether they entail a motive other than survival. As Elizabeth Bishop wrote in "Over 2,000 Illustrations and a Complete Concordance," "Everything only connected by 'and' and 'and.'" Not by and then and then and then. McCarthy's novels don't make me ask: What is to happen next and is a significant pattern or form to be disclosed at last? His episodes are produced not to be interrogated or understood within some large myth or other system of value. They are there to be sensed, to be seen. The appalling quality of each deed is its emptiness, as if it were done before anyone thought of any meaning it might have. Conduct is predicated upon some primitive energy, and when it is vicious beyond need it is merely a splurge of force that knows nothing else to do. In **Blood Meridian** the Judge buys two pups and immediately drowns them. The deed is of no account, like the earth itself in these books, which has presence and force but not a trace of meaning.

Even when the scene is genial, we are invited to look at it without thinking beyond the thing seen. As in *The Orchard Keeper:*

> Light pale as milk guided the old man's steps over the field to the creek and then to the mountain, stepping into the black wall of pine-shadows and climbing up the lower slopes out into the hardwoods, bearded hickories trailing grapevines, oaks and crooked waterless cottonwoods, a quarter mile from the creek now, past the white chopped butt of a bee tree lately felled, past the little hooked Indian tree and passing silent and catlike up the mountain in the darkness under latticed leaves scudding against the sky in some small wind.

This narrative procedure is Dutch rather than Italian, according to a distinction Svetlana Alpers makes in *The Art of Describing,* her study of Dutch painting. An Italian painting is narrative, dramatic, theatrical, "a framed surface or pane situated at a certain distance from a viewer who looks through it at a second or substitute world." A Dutch painting gives the look of things and assumes that that is enough, it does not incite the eye to go beyond or through the canvas to divine a story behind it. Meaning coincides with what is offered as visible. Each of McCarthy's early novels conveys a multitude of scenes, often loosely affiliated or not at all, and soon we start feeling that the world or life has presented itself in these ways without human intervention and is not to be asked why or wherefore. If human action in the world of these novels is arbitrary, occasionally kind but mostly red in tooth and claw, there is no point in looking further for causes and explanations. In *Blood Meridian* again the Judge finds an Apache child, keeps it with him for three days, dandling it on his knee, and then with motiveless malignity scalps it. There is no merit in looking for a reason.

Yet in *Suttree* and *Blood Meridian* there is also a revision of these assumptions. These books, too, are panoramic, picturesque, one picture gives way to the next. We are not to assume that each object of attention is organically or otherwise related to the next one as a phase in a story being told. But to the spinal column there has been added in at least a few specimens a brain capable of self-consciousness and wit. *Suttree* is set along the banks of the Tennessee River at Knoxville, where Cornelius Suttree, a dropout, has made himself a shantyboat and gets a poor living by selling fish to local eating-houses. He spends most of his time "in the company of thieves, derelicts, miscreants, pariahs, poltroons, spalpeens, curmudgeons, clotpolls, murderers, gamblers, bawds, whores, trulls, brigands, topers, tosspots, sots and archsots, lobcocks, smellsmocks, runagates, rakes, and other assorted and felonious debauchees." His friend Gene Harrogate lives on his wits and odd jobs: robbing telephone boxes, poisoning bats for sale to the authorities, removing the upholstery from

wrecked cars (under the seat of one of which he finds a human eye).

People in this book tend to get shot or to turn up dead in the river or to cause mayhem with bottles in the Indian Rock roadhouse. Near the end, Suttree takes to the Gatlinburg mountains, hallucinates, nearly goes mad, but survives to see the world as if it might at least sustain a question or two:

> It seemed to rain all that winter. The few snowfalls turned soon to a gray slush, but the brief white quietude among the Christmas buntings and softlit shopwindows seemed a childhood dream of the season and the snow in its soft falling sifting down evoked in the city a surcease nigh to silence. Silent the few strays that entered the Huddle dusting their shoulders and brushing from their hair this winter night's benediction. Suttree by the window watched through the frosted glass. How the snow fell cherry red in the soft neon flush of the beersign like the slow dropping of blood. The clerks and the curious are absent tonight. Blind Richard sits with his wife. The junkman drunk, his mouth working mutely and his neck awry like a hanged man's. A young homosexual alone in the corner crying. Suttree among others, sad children of the fates whose home is the world, all gathered here a little while to forestall the going there.

Later, Suttree is allowed a highfalutin soliloquy in which he claims to repent of one deed only:

> One thing. I spoke with bitterness about my life and I said that I would take my own part against the slander of oblivion and against the monstrous facelessness of it and that I would stand a stone in the very void where all would read my name. Of that vanity I recant all.

*Blood Meridian,* one of the most powerful American novels I have read, achieves its grandeur by not letting the world and life utter themselves without incurring rebuke. The story starts in 1849 when a boy, "the kid," arrives in Nacogdoches, Texas, having run away from home. He joins a pirate army to fight in Mexico. There are appalling scenes of carnage when they confront a band of Comanches. The kid survives to join the Judge and other killers, led by one Glanton, as mercenaries, hired by Governor Trias to kill the Apache leader Gomez; $1000 for Gomez's scalp, $100 a head for scalps of other Indians. These men live to kill or be killed. They range through the Southwest for murder and pillage, killing anything that moves, with guns for the distant work, knives for close work upon Apaches, Gilenos, and Yumas.

Meanwhile the Judge emerges as chief personage, a scholar

of sorts, Darwinian note-taker, amateur biologist, reader of sign, a Nietzsche before he could have read Nietzsche, and so psychologically opaque that he seems a force of demented nature. One of the most remarkable images in the book has the Judge and an idiot boy pursuing the kid and the ex-priest Tobin:

> More strangely he carried a parasol made from rotted scraps of hide stretched over a framework of rib bones bound with strips of tug. The handle had been the foreleg of some creature and the judge approaching was clothed in little more than confetti so rent was his costume to accommodate his figure. Bearing before him that morbid umbrella with the idiot in its rawhide collar pulling at the lead he seemed some degenerate entrepreneur fleeing from a medicine show and the outrage of the citizens who'd sacked it.

Given to high rhetoric, the Judge sounds like Melville's Captain Ahab or a crazed philosopher of the Enlightenment:

> Whatever exists, he said. Whatever in creation exists without my knowledge exists without my consent.
>
> He looked about at the dark forest in which they were bivouacked. He nodded toward the specimens he'd collected. These anonymous creatures, he said, may seem little or nothing in the world. Yet the smallest crumb can devour us. Any smallest thing beneath yon rock out of men's knowing. Only nature can enslave man and only when the existence of each last entity is routed out and made to stand naked before him will he be properly suzerain of the earth.
>
> What's a suzerain?
>
> A keeper. A keeper or overlord.
>
> Why not say keeper then?
>
> Because he is a special kind of keeper. A suzerain rules even where there are other rulers. His authority countermands local judgements.

At the end it is the Judge who speaks for justice by despising it; who denounces and pursues the kid to the last murder because the kid could have killed the Judge and chose not to. The Judge visits him in prison:

> He spoke softly into the dim mud cubicle. You came forward, he said, to take part in a work. But you were a witness against yourself. You sat in judge-

ment on your own deeds. You put your own allowances before the judgements of history and you broke with the body of which you were pledged a part and poisoned it in all its enterprise. Hear me, man. I spoke in the desert for you and you only and you turned a deaf ear to me. If war is not holy man is nothing but antic clay. Even the cretin acted in good faith according to his parts. For it was required of no man to give more than he possessed nor was any man's share compared to another's. Only each was called upon to empty out his heart into the common and one did not. Can you tell me who that one was?

Here as earlier in his pre-Nietzschean mode, the Judge insists that "moral law is an invention of mankind for the disenfranchisement of the powerful in favor of the weak" and that "historical law subverts it at every turn." Like Hitler, the Judge gulls his people into the conviction that they have been chosen to lead the march of historical destiny and that no moral consideration can impede them. Only the kid knows and acts otherwise, and he is inarticulate except in deed to the end.

Who speaks, then, for reality and justice in these novels? The narrator; or, rather, the narrative voice, since no character in the stories is given the role of narrator, except for a while in *Child of God,* where the narrator is a local resident, gossip, and mythmaker. In the other novels we have impersonal narration or—it amounts to the same thing—"free indirect style" which recalls for modern use the ancient styles, often biblical or epic, that have served a similar genre. As in the *Blood Meridian* description of Apaches riding across the playa to attack the mercenaries:

> The riders were beginning to appear far out on the lake bed, a thin frieze of mounted archers that trembled and veered in the rising heat. They crossed before the sun and vanished one by one and reappeared again and they were black in the sun and they rode out of that vanished sea like burnt phantoms with the legs of the animals kicking up the spume that was not real and they were lost in the sun and lost in the lake and they shimmered and slurred together and separated again and they augmented by planes in lurid avatars and began to coalesce and there began to appear above them in the dawn-broached sky a hellish likeness of their ranks riding huge and inverted and the horses' legs incredibly elongate trampling down the high thin cirrus and the howling antiwarriors pendant from their mounts immense and chimeric and the high wild cries carrying that flat and barren pan like the cries of souls broke through some misweave in the weft of things into the world below.

Some readers have felt that McCarthy's high style, even with the examples of Melville, Dostoevsky, Conrad, and Faulkner to warrant it, is bombastic. Here are the mercenaries from *Blood Meridian:*

> They wandered the borderland for weeks seeking some sign of the Apache. Deployed upon that plane they moved in a constant elision, ordained agents of the actual dividing out the world which they encountered and leaving what had been and what would never be alike extinguished on the ground behind them. Spectre horsemen, pale with dust, anonymous in the crenellated heat. Above all else they appeared wholly at venture, primal, provisional, devoid of order. Like beings provoked out of the absolute rock and set nameless and at no remove from their own loomings to wander ravenous and doomed and mute as gorgons shambling the brutal wastes of Gondwanaland in a time before nomenclature was and each was all.

That is English or American written as if it were Spanish, and if it were Spanish one would call it Gongorism, *gongorismo,* "a style in imitation of the ornate style of Gongora y Argote 1561-1627," the dictionaries say. But it is English or American, so a question of bombast arises.

But I would defend many, most, nearly all of McCarthy's high passages by noting how much they have to do. They have to speak for characters who cannot speak as eloquently for themselves, as in *All the Pretty Horses:*

> He lay on his back in his blankets and looked out where the quartermoon lay cocked over the heel of the mountains. In that false blue dawn the Pleiades seemed to be rising up into the darkness above the world and dragging all the stars away, the great diamond of Orion and Cepella and the signature of Cassiopeia all rising up through the phosphorous dark like a sea-net. He lay a long time listening to the others breathing in their sleep while he contemplated the wildness about him, the wildness within.

McCarthy's styles have also to speak up for values the characters could not express; for regions, places, landscapes, vistas, movements of the seasons, trees, rain, snow, dawn, sunset, outer and inner weather; and for times not our time. For such purposes, McCarthy commands many styles and dictions. Reading these novels, I was often lost among unfamiliar words, like the mercenary with suzerain. In *Suttree* alone I was grounded by these and had to go to the dictionaries: mordant (a reagent for fixing dyes), muricate (covered with many short spikes, and therefore used by McCarthy of Christ's crown of thorns), trematode (a kind of worm), soricine (of a shrewmouse), and tribades (lesbians: "the some-time cries of buckled tribades in the hours toward dawn when trade was done"). Most of these are in the third edition of the *American Heritage Dictionary of the English Language,* more useful than the *Oxford English Dictionary* when reading McCarthy's Tex-Mex fiction. The hard words are always accurately used, I gather from the dictionaries, and they help McCarthy to control the pace of one's reading and therefore the duration and quality of the attention one pays. A hard word slows you down, keeps you looking. As here, when Suttree visiting his Aunt Martha looks through her photograph album:

> Old distaff kin coughed up out of the vortex, thin and cracked and macled and a bit redundant. The landscapes, old backdrops, redundant too, recurring unchanged as if they inhabited another medium than the dry pilgrims shored up on them. Blind moil in the earth's nap cast up in an eyeblink between becoming and done. I am, I am. An artifact of prior races.

"Macled," I find, means blurred. Note, too, that the eyeblink-state is not between "becoming" and its customary affiliate, "being."

"So he thought about horses and they were always the right thing to think about," we read of John Grady Cole in *All the Pretty Horses.* As it turns out, horses are also the right thing to dream about, far safer objects of vision than women:

> That night he dreamt of horses in a field on a high plain where the spring rains had brought up the grass and the wildflowers out of the ground and the flowers ran all blue and yellow far as the eye could see and in the dream he was among the horses running and in the dream he himself could run with the horses and they coursed the young mares and fillies over the plain where their rich bay and their rich chestnut colors shone in the sun and the young colts ran with their dams and trampled down the flowers in a haze of pollen that hung in the sun like powdered gold and they ran he and the horses out along the high mesas where the ground resounded under their running hooves and they flowed and changed and ran and their manes and tails blew off of them like spume and there was nothing else at all in that high world and they moved all of them in a resonance that was like a music among them and they were none of them afraid horse nor colt nor mare and they ran in that resonance which is the world itself and which cannot be spoken but only praised.

The story involves to begin with two boys. John Grady Cole and Lacey Rawlins light out for Mexican territory and meet up with a still younger boy, Jimmy Blevins, who is riding a beautiful horse he may have stolen. In any case it is bound to arouse someone's greed and make for trouble. The first and best part of the book deals with the loss and further theft of the horse and the boys' plans to recover it. The relations between Jimmy, John Grady, and Lacey are convincingly delineated, and they point ahead to further discrepancies when life starts dividing them. Jimmy is lost, and the two boys ride into Mexico. They find jobs as ranch hands for the wealthy Don Hector. For a while, things go well. John Grady has a remarkable feeling for horses, their capacities and moods. Paradise for him, up to this point, consists of horses and the mesas on which he rides them. The boys round up wild horses and John Grady breaks them, talking to each horse as he presses himself against its shoulder. This world of horses, land, mountains, dawns, and sunsets is the ultimate good, or so it seems.

Unfortunately for the novel and for John Grady, Don Hector has a beautiful daughter, Alejandra. The first stages of courtship between boy and girl are conducted on horseback. Symbolic portent is provided by John Grady's riding a stallion bareback while the girl rides a black Arabian. Trouble begins when Alejandra insists on riding the stallion and Don Hector's informants bring the new back to him and to the Duena Alfonsa, the girl's grand-aunt and guardian. When John Grady and Alejandra become lovers, he must be punished. And Rawlins, too, who has warned John Grady off the girl but is now in trouble just as deep. The boys are arrested and taken off for jailing and interrogation to Encintada, where they meet Jimmy, in jail for shooting the man who stole his gun. So the story proceeds.

In the third part, John Grady and Lacey are released, bought out of jail by the Duena because she intends bribing John Grady to stay away from Alejandra. Rawlins decides he's had enough of Mexico and goes home. John Grady makes an operatic hero's decision to go back to the ranch and settle matters with the Duena and Alejandra. The Duena gives him money but in return he has to listen to a tedious recital of the history of Mexico and the Duena's more personal story. There is much intimation of class, ambition for one's children, family honor, and would John Grady please take a strong hint and a fistful of pesos and clear off, please? Not so: he insists on meeting the girl, who has no scruples about sex but in consideration of family honor won't go away with him. The dialogue at this point is the kind regularly heard in old-fashioned films from high-born girls living in historically oppressed countries. At one point Alejandra narrates the death of her heroic grandfather instead of engaging with John Grady in reasonable conversation:

> He died in this strange place. Esquina de la Calle del Deseo y el Callejon del Pensador Mexicano. There was no mother to cry. As in the corridos. Nor

little bird that flew. Just the blood on the stones. I wanted to show you. We can go.

> Quien fue el Pensador Mexicano?

> Un poeta. Joaquin Fernandez de Lizardi. He had a life of great difficulty and died young. As for the Street of Desire it is like the Calle de Noche Triste. They are but names for Mexico. We can go now.

After that, the novel has only fifty pages in which to recover its presence of mind, and that is not enough. There is a strong scene in which the bereft John Grady arms himself, returns to Encintada to punish his old interrogator and get back Rawlins's horse. But the novel otherwise has gone soft. John Grady has to prove in court that he is the true owner of the horse he is leading about. He tells the whole story in thirty minutes. Society, in the person of a benign judge, not only assigns ownership to John Grady but tells him how wonderful he is:

> The constable is instructed to return the property in question to Mr Cole. Mr Smith, you see that the boy gets his horse. Son, you're free to go and the court thanks you for your testimony. I've sat on the bench in this county since it was a county and in that time I've heard a lot of things that give me grave doubts about the human race but this aint one of em.

The novel has gone awry. In other passages the high rhetoric, for lack of answerable substance, virtually sinks poor John Grady, to whom metaphysical intimations are belatedly assigned:

> He thought that in the beauty of the world were hid a secret. He thought the world's heart beat at some terrible cost and that the world's pain and its beauty moved in a relationship of diverging equity and that in this headlong deficit the blood of multitudes might ultimately be exacted for the vision of a single flower.

It is hard to believe that this paragraph, the love story, the Duena's lecture, and the scene in court were written by the author of ***Blood Meridian*** and ***Suttree***. What has gone wrong with his prose since the first part of the novel, the superb scenes between the three boys, where the dialogue is just as good as Twain's in *Huckleberry Finn?* As in the scene where Jimmy Blevins offers to shoot anything that Lacey Rawlins throws in the air:

> He stood with his back to the sun and the pistol hanging alongside his leg. Rawlins turned and grinned at John Grady. He held the billfold between his thumb and finger.

You ready, Annie Oakley? he said.

Waitin on you.

He pitched it up underhanded. It rose spinning in the air, very small against the blue. They watched it, waiting for him to shoot. Then he shot. The billfold jerked sideways off across the landscape and opened out and fell twisting to the ground like a broken bird.

The writing is as good as the shooting. I can only think that McCarthy, who has appeared to be able to imagine anything, can't bring himself to imagine the forms of civil life. He alludes to them, but not with credence or conviction. He is not good with village Romeos and Juliets or indeed with any lives that have entered upon communities, cultural interests, attended by customs, proprieties, and laws. In this respect he is closer to Kafka and Beckett than to Faulkner. He is one of those writers who exhibit in their truest work, however they act as citizens, a refusing imagination: it refuses to give credence to the world as it has come to be in its personal, social, and political forms. Lionel Trilling noted that "Kafka's work gives very little recognition, if any at all, to the world in its ordinary actuality, as it is the object of our desires and wills, as we know it socially, politically, erotically, domestically; or, if it recognizes the world at all, it does so only through what it perceives of the radical incompatibility of world and mankind." In McCarthy's fiction the world is nature, deserts, mountains, rivers, snow, and lightning, and he writes of it in that character with reverence and wonder. His sense of the incompatibility of world and mankind arises from the human presence in that world. The presence has been wrong from the beginning. Original Sin, the Fall, is not man's first disobedience, as Christianity says, but a fault in the character of the human presence in the world. The fault issues in violence, hatred, bloodshed, to which McCarthy gives not moral consent but imaginative credence. He has sympathy with that abyss.

*All the Pretty Horses* may indicate McCarthy's desire to come in out of the cold of those Tennessee mountain winters, but his imagination is at its best there with Arthur Ownby or with the monstrous Judge of *Blood Meridian* drowning dogs. He is best with what nature gives or imposes, rather than with the observations of culture. The sex, for instance, between Suttree and Wanda is far more authentic than the love affair of John Grady and Alejandra. Wanda is as free of acculturation as Suttree would like to be. McCarthy's imagination knows that state and that desire. But when Alejandra emerges from the shower wrapped in a towel and says to John Grady, "I love you. But I cannot," we know that McCarthy is writing adrift from his talent. Any average Hollywood screenwriter could do that scene better.

So we have the first of three projected volumes. I look for-
ward to the complete work but wish I could be assured that the trilogy has now disposed of the only doomed lovers we are to sigh over.

## Kerry Ahearn (review date August 1993)

SOURCE: A review of *All the Pretty Horses,* in *Western American Literature,* Vol. XXVIII, No. 2, August, 1993, pp. 182-184.

[*In the following review, Ahearn provides a brief analysis of* All the Pretty Horses, *discusses the protagonist's quest, and calls the work "a must read."*]

After his first four novels, from *The Orchard Keeper* through *Suttree,* Cormac McCarthy's regional reputation was Southern, and his renown primarily stylistic. Commentators made comparisons with artists as diverse as Sam Peckinpah and Jorge Luis Borges. Then the Protean McCarthy produced *Blood Meridian,* a tale of the West that mixed grotesque violence and grotesque humor and delineations that both drew on and mocked the conventions of eighteenth-century novels and epic plots in general, altering his regional identification and adding to his reputation as a prose-wizard and an original visionary. *All the Pretty Horses,* winner of the 1992 National Book Award, is the first volume of a promised border trilogy, and will attract much attention to McCarthy as a writer of the West, and one who seeks to combine the impulses of the Modernist and the nineteenth-century traditions. This novel is a must-read.

McCarthy's story is elemental: at once abandoned and freed by the death of his grandfather, the divorce of his parents, and the sale of the family ranch near San Angelo, sixteen-year-old John Grady Cole sets out in the late 1940s with a friend on a journey south, crossing on horseback into the last great approximation of a dry frontier, Mexico. Into this traditional quest paradigm, McCarthy puts elements of western-on-the-road picaresque, and later the purest pastoral-and-romance interludes, the dense accretions of social-manners realism, the horror of captivity narratives, the suspense of the cross-country chase, the necessity of an ending. His particular skill is to draw energy from each of these sources without giving allegiance to any of them. His two most memorable characters, in fact, spring from very different traditions. The first, Jimmy Blevins, a pre-pubescent Achilles, draws impetus from the inflexibility of that heroic model so inadequate in complex circumstances, and yet lingers with the aura of a savior to the end. The second, the aging duena Alfonsa, also figures as a kind of destructive and saving force, but comes from a very different source: her long conversation with John Grady seems a deliberate and ironic echo of Christopher Newman's with Madame de Bellegard—he is the interloper, and she is the exacter of a terrible promise and the defender of a tradition, but also a woman of deep sensitivity, cursed with a tragic past which has given her the habit of philosophical speculation and the authority of grief. Her ten-page soliloquy, one of the densest self-contained sections in this novel, connects her personal history with that of Mexican radicalism and early feminist frustrations, and yet she cannot be satisfactorily described or comprehended by any political formulas.

John Grady Cole comes to life, as do many quest heroes, out of a shadowy past but carrying some great hurt. He is McCarthy's most difficult creation, an often surprising combination of innocence and experience. In the first third of the novel, his youthful stoicism might be seen as a liability too great for the narrative, but if the novel seems at this point too much Hemingway—the politicized grammar that avoids subordination, the characters that avoid speaking of emotion and live on rhetorical irony—it develops both stylistically and dramatically with echoes of Faulkner, Katherine Anne Porter, and Henry James. John Grady Cole becomes. *All the Pretty Horses* is a regional and an international situation, and ambitiously combines the personal and the political.

Cormac McCarthy seems to be doing what the young Larry McMurtry promised to do: explore the complex human implications of a time when the old life was passing away in the Southwest, and make us feel that the issue is not merely of the region, or of the past.

## Michael Dirda (review date 5 June 1994)

SOURCE: "At the End of His Tether," in *Washington Post Book World,* Vol. XXIV, No. 23, June 5, 1994, pp. 1, 13.

[*In the following review, Dirda comments on the broad scope of* The Crossing, *lauding the craftsmanship of McCarthy's writing but faulting the "heavy-handed" and "grandiloquent" aspects of the work.*]

Two years ago *All the Pretty Horses,* the first installment of Cormac McCarthy's "Border Trilogy," rounded up raves from the critics, landed on the bestseller lists, deservedly won major literary prizes (National Book Award, National Book Critics Circle Award for fiction) and proved Scott Fitzgerald wrong.

"There are," said Fitzgerald on one of his gloomy afternoons as an author, "no second acts in American lives." For most of his career, Cormac McCarthy (born in 1933) roamed the literary fringes as a frisky Southern Gothicist, a nephew to William Faulkner, Flannery O'Connor and Tennessee Will-

iams at their most outrageous: In McCarthy's *Child of God,* for instance, the protagonist develops a liking for sex with dead girls and occasionally wears a wig made out of a woman's scalp; in *Outer Dark* a sister bears her brother's child. But after *Suttree* appeared in 1979, McCarthy left his native Tennessee, moved to El Paso, and unexpectedly remade himself into what one might call a Tex-Mex novelist.

In *All the Pretty Horses* 16-year-old John Grady Cole travels south into Mexico with his friend Lacey Rawlins. Much of that novel's action resembles the most conventional western: long, dusty rides through a gorgeous landscape, an idyll on a big ranch, the doomed love affair with a passionate high-born senorita, a compadre murdered because of his valuable horse, false arrest by unshaven, corrupt Mexican officials, a hellish term in prison and, in the end, a satisfying act of revenge, followed by our hero riding off into the sunset. No doubt some of the widespread success of *Pretty Horses* derives from its use of these familiar props and costumes. But what makes the novel so extraordinary is, of course, its language.

Languorous yet exact, stately, wistful, occasionally humorous, McCarthy's sentences achieve a kind of epic serenity, as if Homer were to sing of cowboys instead of Achilles. At times, the methodical detailing of men at work—breaking horses, rounding up cattle—echoes the rhythms of good Hemingway, especially the grave, symbol-laden stories like "Big Two-Hearted River." Though its characters are hardly deep thinkers, *All the Pretty Horses* exudes an air of intimacy and introspection. It possesses an almost sacerdotal gravity. John Grady suffers, endures and ultimately earns that greatest of masculine compliments: He proves himself a serious man. Just so, one might call Cormac McCarthy a serious novelist.

None of the characters from *Pretty Horses* appears in *The Crossing,* so one must presume that "The Border Trilogy" is a thematic sequence, three western "novels of education" (unless of course John Grady Cole and Billy Parham team up in the last volume). Like its predecessor, the new book follows the adventures of two young men—the teenaged brothers Billy and Boyd Parham—as they leave home, in this case New Mexico, and travel south to meet their destinies. For McCarthy, Mexico spills over with primitive energy, spiritual mysticism and an unrelenting menace: It is an annealing furnace, a testing ground. In *The Crossing* the ordeal takes place in four stages: In the first Billy traps a wolf and decides to return her to the Mexican mountains; on their way he and the animal suffer various misfortunes; later Billy and Boyd pursue the horses stolen from their family's small ranch; and in the last section, Billy, unable to enlist to fight in World War II, returns to Mexico to search for his younger brother.

As before, McCarthy's language exemplifies the careful precision of a craftsman, and he is at his best in describing how a professional sets a trap, carries a pack or mounts a horse. "The traps were packed in the splitwillow basket that his father wore with the shoulderstraps loosed so that the bottom of the basket carried on the cantle of the saddle behind him." Such telling and precise detail generates a nearly sensual pleasure, like that one feels in watching an athlete perform with grace and ease.

Less pleasing, however, are McCarthy's purple flights, as when he expatiates about the wolf as "the beast who dreams of man and has so dreamt in running dreams a hundred thousand years or more. Dreams of that malignant lesser god come pale and naked and alien to slaughter all his clan and kin and rout them from their house." Such rhetorical cornpone breaks the continuous revery that prose aspires to. McCarthy works his magic best without flourishes: "The traps leapt mightily. The iron clang of the jaws slamming shut echoed in the cold. You could see nothing of their movement. Now the jaws were open. Now they were closed."

Throughout *The Crossing,* though, McCarthy always seems to be straining toward a grander level of significance, preferring ideas to things; he jumps for the metaphysical at any opportunity: "The indians were dark almost to blackness and their reticence and their silence bespoke a view of a world provisional, contingent, deeply suspect. They had about them a wary absorption as if they observed some hazardous truce. They seemed in a state of improvident and hopeless vigilance. Like men committed upon uncertain ice." Redeemed by that last sentence, this whole passage belabors, rather beautifully, the same point while skirting perilously close to the pseudo-philosophical.

Indeed, the novel as a whole is criss-crossed with fables, sermons, morality tales and lessons. Billy meets an old priest who talks to him of God's inscrutable ways; he encounters a former revolutionary who has had his eyeballs sucked out of their sockets, and who relates his life of blindness and insight; even Gypsies detail their world-view, while an elegant old cowboy discourses about the meaning of life: "People speak about what is in store. But there is nothing in store. The day is made of what has come before. The world itself must be surprised at the shape of that which appears. Perhaps even God." Some women found *Pretty Horses* boringly macho, too much a boy's adventure. This one may remind them, in places, of a magic-realist issue of Field and Stream.

To my mind, *The Crossing* would have been a more effective book had it been leaner, less grandiloquent, more focused on Billy and Boyd. But clearly McCarthy preferred to widen his scope and to take up, somewhat heavy-handedly, the hard question of how one lives in a brutal world. To me, the homely philosophers that Billy encounters sound windy

and abstract, especially when compared to the magnificent opening account of the boy and the wolf—though even this goes on too long. Still, it feels wrong to complain too loudly when there's so much to admire: McCarthy's artful reticences, for instance. One never learns the identity of two vicious murderers or the fate of Boyd's Mexican girlfriend. And no one can better describe the unforeseen irruption of violence—"he put up one hand as if to reach for the first of the horses as they came up out of the trees and then his shirt belled out behind him redly and he fell down on the ground"—or the beauty of a naked woman washing her hair in a river:

> She bent once more and trailed her hair in the water with a swaying motion sideways and then stood and swung it about her in a great hoop of spray and stood with her head back and her eyes closed. The sun rising over the gray ranges to the east lit the upper air. She held one hand up. She moved her body, she swept both hands before her. She bent and caught her falling hair in her arms and held it and she passed one hand over the surface of the water as if to bless it and he watched and as he watched he saw that the world which had always been before him everywhere had been veiled from his sight. She turned and he thought she might sing to the sun. She opened her eyes and saw him there on the bridge and she turned her back and walked slowly up out of the river and was lost to his view among the pale standing trunks of the cottonwoods and the sun rose and the river ran as before but nothing was the same nor did he think that it would ever be again.

This might be Joyce, an alternative epiphany to Stephen Dedalus's glimpse of the wading girl at the end of *Portrait of the Artist.*

Above all, despite its occasional longueurs and excesses, *The Crossing* generates an immense and sorrowful power, especially in its implicit parallels between Billy's relationship to the she-wolf and to Boyd. By its last page the reader will have suffered a great deal—this is not a happy book—and will return, as one sometimes does with a soul-shaking novel, to its opening sentences, saddened by the knowledge of what's to come:

> When they came South out of Grant County Boyd was not much more than a baby and the newly formed county they'd named Hidalgo was itself little older than the child . . . He carried Boyd before him in the bow of the saddle and named to him features of the landscape and birds and animals in both spanish and english. In the new house they slept in the room off the kitchen and he would lie awake at night and listen to his brother's breathing in the dark

and he would whisper half aloud to him as he slept
his plans for them and the life they would have.

"If people knew the story of their lives," wonders an old
vaquero to Billy much later, "how many would then elect to
live them?"

## Gregory Jaynes (review date 6 June 1994)

SOURCE: "The Knock at the Door," in *Time,* Vol. 143, No.
23, June 6, 1994, pp. 62-64.

[*In the following review, Jaynes comments on McCarthy's
reticent nature and the author's emergence as a recognized
best-seller, and touches briefly on his life and career.*]

When Cormac McCarthy's sixth novel, *All the Pretty Horses,*
won the National Book Award last year, journalists naturally wanted a word with the author. McCarthy possesses a
lifelong habit of refusing questions, however. As a Texas
lawyer buddy says, "He solicits publicity like a man evading
process." A prestigious literary honor did nothing to change
his mind; for that matter, he didn't go pick up the award. It
made for a good story all the same. Here was a man with a
fine hand with the language and a clear scope on the darkness out there, an impoverished artist on the high rim of his
middle years, a writer whose books until *Horses* had never
sold more than 2,500 copies in hard-cover, and here, with
recognition and cash at last on his cheap tin plate, he wouldn't
talk.

As a result, the press in many cases diminished McCarthy's
great value by making him out to be some sort of hermit
caballero and by all but ignoring his remarkable prose. Not
that any of it bothered him enough to respond. He just kept
working, and this week bookstores are receiving copies of
*The Crossing,* the centerpiece in a trilogy that began with
*Horses.* The hero of that book was a boy ahoof in Mexico in
1950, to whom it was easy to give your heart. *The Crossing*
moves two orphaned brothers on horseback across the same
spare terrain, this time just before World War II. Violence,
raw land, unlettered people, love, loss and a throat-slit dog
have something to do with the new narrative; or you could
say it is about that mean crossing from child to man, told as
cleanly as you'll find.

But don't expect to hear McCarthy talking about it. It does
the heart good to report one of life's little constants: he still
won't speak. With basically one exception, McCarthy has
never drummed for himself. The exception came with the
publication of *Horses* two years ago. At the time McCarthy
was 58 and unknown outside a small mob of readers, quite a
few of them critics, English professors or writers, who

thought he was God. Being God didn't pay spit, though, and
after five books and 30 years, McCarthy had his first agent,
Amanda Urban, and a new editor, Gary Fisketjon, two of
publishing's more glamorous figures. They impressed upon
him the idea that a little publicity never hurt. "It was very
simple," Fisketjon remembers. "He had no interest in it."
They leaned on him. "He said, 'If you start making exceptions. . .' He said, finally, 'If it will help—and I trust you in
thinking it will help—but never again.'"

McCarthy allowed the *New York Times* to seek him out in El
Paso, where he hangs his hat more days than not, but the
paper didn't gain much purchase on the novelist. Meanwhile,
due in the main to old-fashioned word of mouth, *All the Pretty
Horses* broke free, sold some, won some awards and was
acquired by Mike Nichols for the movies. The author bought
a new pickup truck, set to work on *The Crossing* and
clammed up.

Here, then, is what we know of Cormac McCarthy: He was
the eldest of six children. His father was a lawyer for the
Tennessee Valley Authority in Knoxville. He didn't feel he
fit in his family or his schools. He tried the University of
Tennessee twice and the U.S. Air Force once. He married a
young woman from college named Lee Holleman, the first
of his two wives, and they had a son, Cullen, who is an architect in Spain. The elder McCarthy's first book was *The
Orchard Keeper,* an unsentimental, striking, powerful, lovely
commemorative to a gone way of life in the old Tennessee
hills that ended so portentously it made you want to snatch
Faulkner from the grave and choke him for his influence.

McCarthy got some grant money for *The Orchard Keeper*—
the William Faulkner Foundation, the Rockefeller Foundation, the American Academy of Arts and Letters—and there
is no account of his having hit a lick at anything but novel
writing since. His second wife, Anne de Lisle, recalls living
in a barn with him outside Knoxville for eight years, bathing
outdoors, eating beans, her husband rejecting $2,000 offers
to speak at universities because everything he had to say
was available in those books that no one was buying. The
repellent could have been subject matter, but then only a
simpleton would think that *Outer Dark* was just about incest
or *Child of God* just about necrophilia. More likely, the villain was the complexity of language and thought that refused to meet the reader halfway.

McCarthy roved west in the early '70s, looking for a spot
that hadn't been written out. The second Mrs. McCarthy
wasn't invited along. Published words about the South were
everywhere, thick as clematis on a mailbox. This border territory, though, offered room. And it came with a history. As
McCarthy writes in his new novel, "A good deal of what
could be seen in the world had passed this way. Armored
Spaniards and hunters and trappers and grandees and their

women and slaves and fugitives and armies and revolutions and the dead and dying. And all that was seen was told and all that was told was remembered."

As he dug in and began to write in Texas, McCarthy's published work remained a hard slog for readers who couldn't cut through his syntactical thornbush, but in 1979 he brought out *Suttree,* apparently the last book set in the South he had in him, and it was rough, gnarly, funny as hell and, for the first time, accessible. Here is the novel on the Big Question:

You told me once you believed in God.

The old man waved his hand. Maybe, he said. I got no reason to think he believes in me. Oh I'd like to see him for a minute if I could.

What would you say to him?

Well, I think I'd just tell him. I'd say: Wait a minute. Wait just one minute before you start in on me. Before you say anything, there's just one thing I'd like to know. And he'll say: What's that? And then I'm goin to ast him: What did you have me in that crapgame down there for anyway? I couldn't put any part of it together.

Suttree smiled. What do you think he'll say?

The ragpicker spat and wiped his mouth. I don't believe he can answer it, he said. I don't believe there is an answer.

The MacArthur Foundation got wind of McCarthy about the time *Suttree* was coming along, and in 1981 he was awarded one of its genius grants. Shelby Foote said, "I told the MacArthur people that he would be honoring them as much as they were honoring him." Saul Bellow mentioned his "absolutely overpowering use of language, his life-giving and death-dealing sentences." Part of the grant money went to free the author from tumbledown motels: he bought a dog-eared little stone-and-stucco affair the color of mayonnaise left out too long, a dirt yard out front and no space in back to speak of, on Coffin Avenue.

In 1985 McCarthy brought out *Blood Meridian,* an apocalyptic epic, his *Moby Dick,* about a scalp hunter in the 1840s; to read it is to say goodbye to peace. Few did read it. McCarthy continued to live close to the bone in El Paso, a close-to-the-bone kind of town, just across the Rio Grande from Juarez, Mexico. He golfed, shot pool, ate modest portions of simple food at a cafeteria nearby and at a clattery coffee shop, hung with a couple of lawyers, an artist, an academic and a Nobel-prizewinning physicist next door in New

Mexico, saw some young women ("He's not a real terrible rounder," says a local gossip who knows him), let the natural world claim him and continued to produce world-class literature that somehow got sweeter-tempered, as though it had occurred to him that nasty dispositions were unattractive in a book.

El Paso let him be until *Horses* made the best-seller lists and the local paper took stock of what was in town. Then came the dreaded rap at McCarthy's door. The reporter, Robert Nelson, young and just out of school in Nebraska, had been by four or five times, had knocked until his knuckles hurt, but no one had answered. This time a face, a high forehead, came moonlike to the black copper screen:

"Who are you?"

"Mr. McCarthy, my name is Bob Nelson, and I'm with the El Paso Times, and I wanted to know if there was any chance you would spend any time with me or in any way let me write anything about you."

"I can't do that, Bob." The door stayed shut, deadbolted.

"Would you play golf with me or something?"

"Oh, don't do this."

"All right, I tried."

"Yes, you did."

Bob Nelson went away—went back to Lincoln, Nebraska, in fact, after a brief tour with the newspaper. A year passed, and then the other day a Fleet Street reporter took a run at McCarthy at Luby's Cafeteria, where he sat with his coffee and his soup and his periodicals. "I'm sorry, son," said McCarthy, "but you're asking me to do something I just can't do."

With every good wish, this correspondent drove past the Casa McCarthy this morning, waved so long and hollered hasta luego.

## Richard Eder (review date 12 June 1994)

SOURCE: "Cormac McCarthy's Next Pilgrimage," in *Los Angeles Times,* June 12, 1994, pp. 3, 12.

[*In the following review, Eder discusses* The Crossing, *lauding the descriptive passages but faulting both the portrayal of Mexico and the use of the Spanish language in the novel.*]

In the second part of Cormac McCarthy's epic trilogy, as in the first, the border between the United States and Mexico plays the same role as the rabbit-hole and the looking-glass in Lewis Carroll's two books of Alice. The young adventurers—McCarthy uses a pair—set out from a real though vividly charged Arizona and New Mexico, and cross into a world where realism, folklore, outsized passions and gnomic myths swirl in stormy colors.

Here is the difference: What is remarkable in the Alices lies at the bottom of the hole and the far side of the mirror. McCarthy's writing, powerful on this side of the border, frequently overpowers itself once it gets to Mexico. His imagination advances in conquistador mode, seeking the gold of Mexican rural traditions, manners, beliefs—and the very language itself—to adorn the dull tin-cannery of the modern American soul and the flatness of American speech. Like other tourists and invaders, he can make an illness out of a hunger. McCarthy writes as if feasting, only to have his lavishly nourished prose deteriorate, at times, into a literary equivalent of La Turista.

Like *All the Pretty Horses* (the first book of the trilogy), *The Crossing* sends two young ranch boys south of the border. The time is not long before World War II, when Arizona and New Mexico were crossed by trailer trucks and crisscrossed by men on horseback; and Mexico could be seen, from this side of the trucks, as the great dreaming past that the American Southwest was losing.

As in the previous book, the story has elements both of a picaresque adventure and a metaphysical pilgrimage. In *The Crossing,* in particular, we catch an occasional breeze from Don Quixote and Sancho Panza, crossing Castille with a lofty and wrongheaded purpose. Even more strongly, there are echoes of the Arthurian cycle. Billy and Boyd Parham, like Sir Gawain and Sir Perceval, engage in bloody and terrifying exploits that carry hints of a higher purpose, a Grail. McCarthy's spirit is closer to the fabulous prophetics of the Celtic legend than to the melancholy comedy of the Spanish satire. Among his conspicuous gifts—their conspicuousness can be a defect—humor and skepticism play little part.

*The Crossing* is divided into three sections. In the first, Billy traps a she-wolf that has wandered across the border and is marauding among the cattle on his family's ranch. Something in her fierceness and solitude—"the reckonless deep of loneliness that cored the world to its heart"—touches the boy. He takes her into Mexico to release her in the mountains. Instead, he is stopped by the police; his wolf is confiscated and taken to a *hacienda* to fight dogs in a ring. Billy shoots her to end the indignity, trades his gun for her corpse, takes it into the mountains and, after hardships, the quiet kindness of peasants and Native Americans, and an encounter with a sage or two, makes his way home.

Bandits have killed his parents and stolen the horses. Billy collects his younger brother, Boyd, and they make their way back to Mexico. They find three of the horses, steal them back, and fight a succession of battles with the men who have acquired them. Boyd, skeptical and reluctant up to then, less skilled and favored than Billy, has come into his own. Recovering from a gunshot wound, he disappears with a young Mexican woman who has joined them. Billy, after more hardships and a long detour through the story of a wise blind man, returns once more to the United States.

Two years later he makes his last trip, this time searching for Boyd. He comes upon him first in a local ballad about a young American who came to find justice and was killed. Eventually he locates the body and returns to New Mexico to bury Boyd on the family land. The book ends with Billy spending a night in a desert hovel in the company of a misshapen stray dog, and waking to a dawn that grows darker instead of lighter. It is a partial solar eclipse, perhaps, but it plays the role of the mists into which legends disappear so as never to end.

McCarthy is a strong writer and he can be a magical one. Like Hemingway and Faulkner he has forged an utterly individual style, an order of passions, tastes and values, and a way of looking at the world. Like them he has the virtues of his idiosyncrasy and the defects as well; though I find the virtues, real ones, smaller and the defects quite a bit larger.

There are splendid passages in *The Crossing.* In two scenes at the start, McCarthy could be Hemingway on fishing or Faulkner on hunting. In one, Billy and Boyd come upon a Native American hiding near the family ranch, and the tension and veiled threat of the encounter are memorable; in the other, the art and ordeal of tracking and trapping a wolf are told with glistening authority. In general, the parts that take place in the United States are clean and powerful; so is anything that portrays work or horses; so are the voices of Billy and Boyd, laconic and dry no matter what they are going through. There is a splendid fight or two; and the painstaking work of a village doctor on the wounded Boyd is a masterpiece of evocative realism with a haunting touch of mystery. Suddenly in the doctor there is a glimpse of Arthur's Merlin.

What is painfully weak is much of McCarthy's portrayal and use of Mexico; and it is a very serious weakness. McCarthy's problem is not insensibility or superficiality. On the contrary, he regards his Mexicans with such a passionate, penetrating and appropriating glance that he all but obliterates them. He understands them to the point of invisibility. He has understood them and now he creates them. And they fall into categories: wise and gnomic old men, warm and generous *campesinos,* knife-wielding bad guys, brave and life-enhancing women who supply meaningful helpings of torti-llas and beans.

It is wrong to wish that, just once, they would serve Spa-ghetti-O's. The point is that McCarthy gives them no room, within their categories, to be individuals. They are the hu-man frieze against which the spiritual pilgrimage of Billy will be played, and against which he will hear the three alle-gorical lessons that are the book's thematic heart. They are delivered ponderously by a former priest and by a blind man's companion and, quite enchantingly—perhaps it is the book's best sequence—by philosophical Gypsies. The message to the purposeful and struggling young man is, essentially, to struggle and intend less and to contemplate more.

Of all McCarthy's appropriations, though, the worst, as it was in *Horses,* is his voluminous use of Spanish, whole sen-tences and paragraphs at a time. It cheapens the English, it cheapens the Spanish. But even worse: His Spanish is largely unidiomatic, often awkward and scattered with glaring mis-takes. It makes no sense if he is writing for people who don't know Spanish; it makes less sense if he is writing for people who do.

## Robert Hass (review date 12 June 1994)

SOURCE: "Travels with a She-Wolf," in *The New York Times Book Review,* Vol. CXLIII, No. 49, 725, June 12, 1994, pp. 1, 38-40.

[*In the following review, Hass praises* The Crossing *as an "American original." This in-depth discussion of the novel focuses on description and craftsmanship, and Hass briefly examines McCarthy's play,* The Stonemason, *with respect to craft.*]

How does a writer like Cormac McCarthy—if there is any writer like Cormac McCarthy—follow up on the immense critical and popular success of his novel *All the Pretty Horses,* which won a National Book Award for 1992 and accumu-lated extraordinary praise? Mr. McCarthy got compared to William Faulkner—he has often been compared to Faulkner—Mark Twain, Herman Melville and Shakespeare. The answer provided by *The Crossing,* the second novel in his projected Border Trilogy, is that he writes an even better book.

*The Crossing* is a miracle in prose, an American original. It deserves to sit on the same shelf certainly with *Beloved* and *As I Lay Dying, Pudd'nhead Wilson* and "The Confidence-Man," and if it will put readers in mind of Faulkner, Twain, Melville and Shakespeare, it will also put them in mind of Ernest Hemingway, Flannery O'Connor, Miguel de

Cervantes, Samuel Beckett. Joseph Conrad and, for good measure, John Ford, Sam Peckinpah and Sergio Leone. But *The Crossing* is a tale so riveting—it immerses the reader so entirely in its violent and stunningly beautiful, inconsolable landscapes—that there is hardly time to reflect on its many literary and cinematic echoes or on the fact that Mr. McCarthy is a writer who can plunder almost any source and make it his own.

The novel begins on a small cattle ranch in a New Mexico valley in the last years of the Depression. A wolf has come down out of the Sierra de la Madera to the south and begun to attack grazing cattle. Father and sons set about trapping the wolf, but it is an emblem of their moment in the history of the West that the last trapper who might know how to go about it is gone. They acquire a key to his cabin, long shut down, and the boys are given entry to the workshop of a cruel, immensely practical and almost obsolete art: longspring traps for coyote; larger traps for cougar and bear and wolf, iron-toothed, brutal and jagged; springs and chains and stakes greased with lard and packed in wooden boxes; fruit jars and apothecary bottles in which swim the liver and gall and kidneys of animals, elixirs for the purpose of scenting the traps. From this sudden, arcane, unexpected view into the settling of America the novel proceeds.

Billy Parham, the protagonist, who has dreamed of wolves; finally stumbles on a method and traps the wolf and, also unexpectedly, hogties it, muzzles it, leashes it with a catch-rope—all of this heart stopping to read—and sets off south across the unfenced land to return it to the mountains of Mexico from which it came. And at once we are in the world of romance. If an old man in antique armor on a bone-thin horse, followed by a fat would-be squire on a mule, was once a strange apparition on the highways of Cervantes's Spain, then a young man on a cow pony dragging behind him a wild and recalcitrant she-wolf through ranches, American and Mexican, where wolves are a remembered tale of raven-ous ferocity and terror, may well seem to replay that story, with the same mix of comedy, cruelty and philosophical wonder.

This first section of the book reads, indeed, like a cross be-tween Faulkner's novella *The Bear* and *Don Quixote.* It is about the length of a novella, and it is written with such force and momentum—the reader is so ransacked emotionally by the end of it—that it seems, one-third of the way into the book, that Mr. McCarthy can have nowhere to go.

And what the novel does at this point is to take a deep breath and repeat itself. Billy Parham, this time accompanied by his brother Boyd, makes the crossing into Mexico again. And in the final section of the book, he makes it again. It is part of the boldness—or obsessiveness—of Mr. McCarthy that *The Crossing* tells very nearly the same story as *All the Pretty*

*Horses.* In that earlier novel, set on the Texas-Mexico border in 1949, a young man leaves home and crosses into Mexico in search of his fate. But in *The Crossing,* fatality has entered the tale. If John Grady Cole, the hero of *All the Pretty Horses,* heads out like Huck Finn in search of open-ended adventure, Billy has elected, or been elected, to perform a nearly impossible task.

Billy's first crossing is intended to perform this wildly improbable and Quixotic act of—what? honor, reparation—toward the world of his dream. The second is meant to reclaim a patrimony. The third is to complete these two tasks in a different form. All three quests seem impossible, and they are undertaken as if Billy had no choice, and in this they are like fate, like all the things that people have done in their lives that they couldn't not have done, and it is in its meditation on this circumstance that some of the deepest energies of the book reside.

Mr. McCarthy, because he is interested in the mythic shape of lives, has always been interested in the young and the old or, if not the old, then those who have already performed some act so deep in their natures (often horrific, though not always) that it forecloses the idea of possibility. "Doomed enterprises," Mr. McCarthy's narrator remarks, "divide lives forever into the then and the now." So *The Crossing* is full of encounters between the young boys, who look so much like the pure arc of possibility, and the old they meet on the road, all of whom seem impelled, as if innocence were one of the vacuums that nature abhors, to tell them their stories, or prophesy, or give them advice.

Some of these episodes are quite long, and take the form of those stories-within-the-story that the old romances and the earliest novels were so fond of. Others are quite brief, and they are among the most indelible scenes in the book, partly because, reading them, we are put in the position of the traveler, especially the youthful traveler, for whom the world glimpsed has the quality of revelation. As the young riders traverse poor, rural northern Mexico, in the wake of a bitterly failed revolution, in a landscape of barren and tortuous beauty, what they see on the road becomes an emblem of what the world is. And it is a world of inexplicable kindness, inexplicable cruelty. The kindness—since this is a book of desperate wanderings—often takes the form of shared food, and it is part of the power of the book that the reader, reduced to something like mendicant vulnerability by its more nerve-wrenching moments, reads these scenes as gratefully as if he were eating.

Some of the moments are pure encounter: two people only looking at each other, or exchanging a few words as they pass by, and they stay etched in the mind like blue-period Picassos. Or, to multiply analogies, like throwaway scenes in Bunuel or Fellini. Indeed, if this book is to be filmed, it is

a western directed by Fellini or Bunuel that one imagines giving visual equivalents to these portraits of beggars, wanderers, holy fools, the insulted and the injured, and their vatic sayings: an old Mexican trapper dying in a room of half light and necrotically stale air, who tells the young hero that the wolf is a hunter and "a being of great order and that he knows what men do not: that there is no order in the world save that which death has put there"; a kindly Yaqui drover on a mountain road, switching the rump of an ox, who offers the information that "the ox was an animal close to God as all the world knew and that perhaps the silence and the rumination of the ox was something like the shadow of a greater silence, a deeper thought" and that in any case "the ox knew enough to work so as to keep from being killed and eaten and that was a useful thing to know." And there is the world-ravaged prima donna of a down-and-out commedia dell'arte troupe, whom Billy later sees naked, bathing enormously pale breasts in a clear stream, who tells him that "the road has its own reasons and no two travelers will have the same understanding of those reasons." A blind man, who lost his eyes as an object lesson in revolutionary retribution and then outlived his despair, tells Billy that he believes that "the light of the world was in men's eyes only for the world itself moved in eternal darkness and darkness was its true nature and true condition and that in this darkness it turned with perfect cohesion in all its parts but that there was naught there to see" and that it was "sentient to its core and secret and black beyond men's imagining."

One of the most fetching and emblematic scenes in the book is a brief encounter at roadside, when Billy is dragging the wolf beside him and meets and old peasant woman and her 14-or-15-year-old sullen (and probably pregnant) companion. Nothing much happens in the scene. The women smoke—"the way poor people eat which is a form of prayer." They exchange words, the women ask about the wolf, which they take to be a dog, and they spar with each other a little, finding themselves suddenly in the theater of a stranger's eyes. It is like stumbling suddenly onto an allegory of youth and age from a medieval pastoral, or like the emblematic figures turned up on a tarot card, and it catches something of Mr. McCarthy's sense of the comic.

The old woman explains that the young one is married to her son, but not by a priest. The girl offers the view that priests are thieves. The old woman rolls her eyes and says that the girl thinks she is a revolutionary, and that those who have no memory of the blood shed in the war are always the most ardent for battle, and that during the revolution priests were shot in the villages, and that women dipped their handkerchiefs in the blood and blessed themselves and that the land was under a curse.

The young woman tells Billy that the old woman is always talking about priests and curses and that she is half crazy.

The old woman says that she knows what she knows. And the young woman says that at least she herself knows who the father of her child is, and the old woman says, ay, ay. Then she remarks that the wolf is pregnant and that she will have to be unmuzzled to lick the pups and that all the world knows that this is necessary. The young woman regards the wolf and says that she would like to have a watchdog like that to drive off anyone at all who was not wanted. And she makes a gesture, Mr. McCarthy writes, "that took in the pines and the wind in the pines." Then the boy says he has to go, and the scene is over, except that Billy Parham looks back and sees that they have not moved, they sit staring at whatever they were staring at when he appeared, and they seem diminished by his departure.

There are more than a dozen of these scenes in the book. They seem to have no meaning other than the human gesture they describe, and at least half of them have a vividness, a sense of mystery that is the mystery of a thing or person being nothing other than itself—as if the road made all of life a parable. The book teems with action, and with spectacle and surprise; the life of the towns, the work camps, the haciendas, the peasants and miners and cowboys and drovers. Indians and Gypsies lives ruined, thriving, bent under labor, bent to every conceivable shape by circumstance. And the boys travel through this world, tipping their hats, saying "yes sir" and "nosir" and "si" and "es verdad" and "claro" to all its potential malice, its half-mad philosophers, as the world washes over and around them, and the brothers themselves come to be as much arrested by the gesture of the quest as the old are by their stores of bitter wisdom and the other travelers, in the middle of life, in various stages of the arc between innocence and experience, by whatever impulses have placed them on the road.

Mr. McCarthy is a great and inventive storyteller, and he writes brilliantly and knowledgeably about animals and landscapes—but finally the power and delight of the book derive from the fact that he seems incapable of writing a boring sentence. Reading him, one is very much in the hands of a stylist. His basic mode in this book—it is a considerable intensification of the manner of *All the Pretty Horses*—is a version of high modernist spareness and declarative force. The style comes from Joyce and Hemingway out of Gertrude Stein. It is a matter of straight-on writing, a veering accumulation of compound sentences, stinginess with commas and a witching repetition of words: "He was very cold. He waited. It was very still. He could see by his breath how the wind lay and he watched his breath appear and vanish and appear and vanish constantly before him in the cold and he waited a long time. Then he saw them coming. Loping and twisting. Dancing. Tunneling their noses in the snow. Loping and running and rising by twos in a standing dance and running on again."

Once this style is established, firm, faintly hypnotic, the crispness and sinuousness of the sentences of what would otherwise be quite ordinary description gather to a magic: "The snow in the pass was halfway to the horse's belly and the horse trod down the drifts in high elegance and swung its smoking muzzle over the white and crystal reefs and looked out down through the dark mountain woods or cocked its ears at the sudden flight of small winter birds before them." These rhythms pass into even the most workmanlike business of the novel, getting from here to there, moving characters about: "There was still snow in the upper stretches of the road and there were tire tracks in the road and horse tracks and the tracks of deer. When he reached the spring he left the road and crossed through the pasture and dismounted and watered his horse."

Of course, Mr. McCarthy is capable of lifting out of this hypnotic and lapidary directness into high Faulknerian crash-and-burn:

> He woke all night with the cold. He'd rise and mend back the fire and she was always watching him. When the flames came up her eyes burned out there like gatelamps to another world. A world burning on the shore of an unknowable void. A world construed out of blood and blood's alcahest and blood in its core and in its integument because it was that nothing save blood had power to resonate against that void which threatened hourly to devour it. He wrapped himself in the blanket and watched her. When those eyes and the nation to which they stood witness were gone at last with their dignity back into their origins there would perhaps be other fires and other witnesses and other worlds otherwise beheld. But they would not be this one.

A curiosity and signature of the style is the occasional use, faintly mocking, of something like antique legal diction. It gives Mr. McCarthy's descriptive prose an odd taste of necessity and judgment. The wolf again: "Her eyes did not leave him or cease to burn and as she lowered her head to drink the reflection of her eyes came up in the dark water like some other self of wolf that did inhere in the earth or wait in every secret place even to such false water holes as this that the wolf would be always corroborate to herself and never wholly abandoned in the world."

This language could easily seem affected but it rarely does; or, as with Faulkner, readers will find themselves yielding to the affectation and to the barren landscapes it describes, and to the carnival of figures encountered on the road. Who make a world that is at once unlike anything in American fiction and deeply familiar, since it is the site of one of the oldest of stories, the one about having a task to perform in the world and learning what the world is from trying to perform it.

It is Mr. McCarthy's gift that he can signal his literary intentions to his readers without archness. If he seems post-modern in his sense that everything is a quotation of a quotation, he parts company with post-modern practice in thinking, not that everything therefore refers to nothing, but that in human life certain ancient stories are acted out again and again. A writer's moral relation to these stories is like nothing so much as a craftsman's relation to his tools, and nothingness is not to be counted for the pleasure of merely circulating, but built against, sentence by sentence—and here certain Faulknerian adjectives might come into play—if hopelessly, in the knowledge of the doom of all human intention, then indefatigably, in the knowledge of the skills of a trade that has been passed down to one and that will be passed in turn to other hands.

This is a male ethic. It may be *the* American male ethic, but it descends to us from sources as old as the *Odyssey* and the *Aeneid*—those primers of maleness—and it came to the heroes of our popular fiction, cowboys and urban detectives by way of Joseph Conrad before it got to Hemingway and Faulkner. Mr. McCarthy has apparently chosen in his Border Trilogy to examine it yet again.

*The Crossing* is, in this way, a book about the artist's task, or any workman's task. This is also the subject of *The Stonemason,* a play by Mr. McCarthy also just published, as if to emphasize the prodigality of the author's talent and nerve. It concerns several generations of a black family in Louisville in the 1970's, all living under the same roof, and it reads, perhaps, like a version of *A Raisin in the Sun* conceived by Eugene O'Neill.

The main character is Ben Telfair, a college-educated 32-year-old man, who has taken up, from love of his 101-year-old grandfather, his trade of freestone masonry. A good part of the play is concerned with Ben's descriptions of the beauty and saving power of his grandfather's art. It is not a play about race. The main character's name, which seems a pun on "tell fair," suggests that it is as much about the novelist's craft and the passion of that craft as is about the mason's. To make the world. To make it again and again. To make it in the very maelstrom of its undoing." And future critics are likely to interpret Ben Telfair's relation to his grandfather as a kind of ironic, morally ambiguous allegory of Mr. McCarthy's relationship to William Faulkner and to the traditions of the novel.

I can imagine that some African-American readers may feel that Mr. McCarthy has displaced his own concerns onto his black characters. The rhythms of Ben Telfair's speech seem distinctly Irish Catholic, rather than African-American. But the play certainly avoids stereotypes, and it tries to think about work in America. The grandfather, perhaps because he has nothing else to call his own, practices his craft as lovingly as if it were a religion. Like the genes of the timber wolf in *The Crossing* (and the art of the trapper), his craft, with its lore and its fidelities, is passing away.

In one lovely scene, the old man refuses to lay an honorary cornerstone in Louisville because the Old Testament enjoins against building with hewn stone and because he knows, from the story of the Hebrew people in Egypt, that such labor is the work of slaves. The old man's son, Ben's father, has made a business of the craft and sent his son to college, and the son has rejected whatever his education might have given him and taken up the old man's art. And the play is about what this old ethic of work, a male ethic undertaken in pity and desperation, can and cannot sustain.

It is very near to the ethic that leads Billy Parham of *The Crossing* and John Grady Cole of *All the Pretty Horses* to cross over a border from what they know to what they need to know. I can also imagine some readers feeling that Mr. McCarthy has displaced the epidemic of violence in American culture onto a half-legendary state of Chihuahua. Displacement has always been a condition of the romance. And the Mexico in Mr. McCarthy's novels, if it is half dreamscape, is not unlike the Mexico of the novelists Juan Rulfo and Carlos Fuentes. Perhaps the western, which was always a sort of American Protestant morality tale, a *Pilgrim's Progress* made out of simple virtues and simple tests, needs, as the century ends, an older and darker Arcadia in which to be enacted. In any case, it is clear that the form is not through teaching us, since it has given us in *The Crossing* a masterwork. And, most interesting of all, Mr. McCarthy is not through yet. We can await the conclusion of the Border Trilogy.

### Malcolm Jones Jr. (review date 13 June 1994)

SOURCE: "Brightening Western Star," in *Newsweek*, June 13, 1994, p. 54.

[*In the following review, Jones lauds McCarthy as a "master prose stylist," and calls* The Crossing *"emotionally satisfying." A portion of the review is spent discussing McCarthy's emerging status as a prominent writer, and his growing fan following.*]

Cormac McCarthy's fans divide into two camps. The first and much smaller group fell for McCarthy years ago, when he was writing Southern Gothic novels distinguished by creepy plots full of necrophilia and incest, told in prose so rich it could rot your teeth. The second set of customers came along with the publication in 1992 of *All the Pretty Horses.* That novel, full of cowboys and horses, had its hair-raising moments, but it is nowhere near as nerve-racking as the rest of McCarthy's work. Ironically, this anomalous work made McCarthy a literary star. Launched by an enthusiastic promotion campaign by his new publisher, Knopf, *All the Pretty Horses* sold 180,000 copies in hardcover and 300,000 in paperback. The movie rights went to Mike Nichols for a six-figure advance. Winner of both the National Book Award and the National Book Critics Circle award for fiction, the novel was the first installment of what McCarthy calls "The Border Trilogy." Now comes the second volume, *The Crossing,* with a first printing of 200,000 copies, an enormous initial print run—perhaps the largest ever—of a purely literary book. Plainly Knopf hopes to lure all of McCarthy's new fans back for second helpings. If they come, they're in for a big surprise.

Superficially, *The Crossing* is a rewrite of *All the Pretty Horses.* The period is still mid-20th century, although the second book takes place a few years before the first (and none of the first book's characters reappears). Again, two teenagers on horseback travel from the American Southwest into Mexico. There they pursue violent and vivid adventure. And there the comparisons stop. Where the first book was—by McCarthy's standards—an almost bucolic romance, a hymn to the pluck of youth and the allure of the Western landscape, the second remorselessly chronicles a boy's journey from youth to bitter experience.

McCarthy's hero, Billy Parham, makes three forays into Mexico. His first is an ill-fated attempt to return a wolf to her mountain home. When he goes back to his family's ranch in New Mexico he finds that thieves have murdered his parents and stolen their horses. Accompanied by his younger brother, Boyd, he goes back to Mexico to retrieve the herd. On his third journey he goes looking for Boyd, who has run off with a Mexican girl. Hardheaded and determined, Billy proves a gritty hero, but the tough lesson of *The Crossing* is that gumption, though admirable, is not sufficient to carry the day. At every step of his journeying, Billy loses something he loves—horses, kin, even his way of life. In the end, "he seemed to himself a person with no prior life. As if he had died in some way years ago and was ever after some other being who had no history, who had no ponderable life to come." Where *All the Pretty Horses* was about the making of a man, *The Crossing* chronicles the making of a ghost.

McCarthy's longtime fans will feel more at home in *The Crossing* (just as they must have felt discomfited in the almost sunny confines of *All the Pretty Horses*). McCarthy once again cleaves to his vision of the world as a place where evil is as common as dirt while goodness is only an ideal, something to be sought after. But onto this iron core, McCarthy welds the tenderness, the affection for his charac-

ters that he seemed to discover for the first time in *All the Pretty Horses.* So, while this is not a happy story, it is an always emotionally satisfying tale. And beautifully wrought: the first long chapter alone, describing Billy's adventures with the wolf, could stand as a novella worthy of comparison with Faulkner's *The Bear* and Katherine Anne Porter's *Noon Wine.*

Though he is a master prose stylist—he speaks of a tarantula's "measured octave tread" and a villain's eyes "like lead slag poured into borings to seal away something virulent or predacious"—McCarthy is best appreciated for his utter unpredictability. Concurrently with the appearance of *The Crossing,* for example, Ecco Press is publishing McCarthy's only play *The Stonemason,* which centers on, of all things, the domestic troubles of a middle-class black family in Louisville, Ky., in the '70s.

A writer of such vaulting ambition is bound to stumble now and then. McCarthy's predilection for opaque philosophizing periodically stops the narrative cold, and his ear for dialogue, fine as it is, is not flawless. More than once the Parham boys sound like Hoss and Little Joe chewing the fat on the Ponderosa. But these are piddling misdemeanors. McCarthy has proved beyond a doubt that he can take a hackneyed genre, the cowboy novel, and elevate it to the level of literature. No writer now working elicits greater pleasure in his readers or prompts keener anticipation for what he'll do next.

## Michiko Kakutani (review date 21 June 1994)

SOURCE: "Border Crossings, Real and Symbolic," in *The New York Times,* June 21, 1994, p. C21.

[*In the following negative review, Kakutani discusses the influence of Faulkner on McCarthy's writing and compares* The Crossing *to Faulkner's story,* The Bear. *Faulting* The Crossing's *"self-importance" and "pretentious prose," Kakutani dismisses the novel as a "loose variation" on the themes of* All the Pretty Horses.]

Though it's billed as Volume II of "The Border Trilogy," Cormac McCarthy's latest novel, *The Crossing* is less a sequel to his award-winning book *All the Pretty Horses* than a loose variation on its themes of loss, exile, violence and fate. Once again, Mr. McCarthy gives us the story of two resourceful boys who leave their home in the States and make the dangerous crossing into Mexico. And once again, their crossing becomes a kind of metaphor for the emotional traversing of borders between civilization and nature, order and chaos.

In his earlier books, Mr. McCarthy's debt to Faulkner—in terms of both language and violent subject matter—has been feociously clear. In *The Crossing* that debt has not only been pushed to the point of parody, but it has also been ornamented with gratuitous borrowings from Cervantes, Hemingway, Gabriel Garcia Marquez, Larry McMurtry and assorted John Ford westerns. Although the novel achieves isolated moments of emotional grandeur, the overall result is not a mythic, post-modernist masterpiece, but a hodgepodge of a book that is derivative, sentimental and pretentious all at once.

The first portion of *The Crossing* reads like a sophomoric retelling of the Faulkner classic *The Bear*. This time, the teenage boy, who is to embark on a rite of passage, is named Billy Parham (though he is repeatedly referred to like the Faulkner hero, as "the boy"), and the symbol of the wilderness is a she-wolf, instead of a bear. One of the many wise men Billy will meet in the course of his adventures tells him "that the wolf is a being of great order and that it knows what men do not: that there is no order in the world save that which death has put there."

Sent by his father to trap a wolf that has been killing the cattle on his family's New Mexico ranch, Billy duly catches the animal, then impulsively decides to return it to its home in the Mexican hills. He muzzles the wolf, puts a collar and leash around its neck, and sets off for the border with the wolf training, doglike, behind his horse. On the road to Mexico, the boy and his wolf will meet assorted friends and foes, who tend to talk in pidgin English or pidgin Spanish and say Hemingwayesque things like "the wolf's time was very near at hand."

When the wolf meets an unfortunate and violent end, Billy closes his eyes and imagines her in heaven, imagines "deer and hare and dove and groundvole all richly empaneled on the air for her delight, all nations of the possible world ordained by God of which she was one among and not separate from." Though this is touching in the way that children's books about noble animal heroes are touching, it ultimately diminishes and sentimentalizes Faulkner's fierce, uncompromising vision of nature.

Having buried the wolf, Billy makes the long trip home to his family's ranch, only to discover that horse thieves have killed his mother and father. Once again Billy saddles up his horse and, accompanied by his younger brother Boyd, he sets off again for the border to retrieve his family's stolen horses.

A series of picaresque adventures ensue, in which Billy and Boyd meet up with a succession of gypsies, bandits, ranchers and peasants. Some of these strangers are kind, offering food and medicine and a place to rest. Some of them are cruel, threatening to kill, maim or hurt the boys. Indeed, Boyd will be seriously injured in the course of their wanderings,

and Billy will have to make a heroic effort to try to save his wounded brother, a mission that will culminate in a long, perilous journey, reminiscent of Captain Call's final pilgrimage at the end of Larry McMurtry's *Lonesome Dove*.

The people Billy meets during his peregrinations are a motley lot, including a blind old man who relates a horrifying tale about how he lost his eyes, a singer with a touring opera company, a frightened young girl and a lapsed priest.

However different their circumstances, almost all these people speak in the same portentous, prophetic terms. "The road has its own reasons," says one, "and no two travelers will have the same understanding of those reasons." Another asks, "What remedy can there be for what is not?" A third says: "Things separate from their stories have no meaning. They are only shapes."

Mr. McCarthy's own prose, particularly in the first half of the book, is similarly heavy, announcing its own significance and the significance of the author's intents. Sometimes it sounds like bad Hemingway: "He said that while the huérfano might feel that he no longer belonged among men he must set this feeling aside for he contained within him a largeness of spirit which men could see and that men would wish to know him and that the world would need him even as he needed the world for they were one."

Sometimes it sounds like bad Faulkner, crossed with bad Thomas Wolfe: "For this world also which seems to us a thing of stone and flower and blood is not a thing at all but is a tale. And all in it is a tale and each tale the sum of all lesser tales and yet these also are the selfsame tale and contain as well all else within them."

Toward the end of *The Crossing* this mannered writing gradually gives way to less pretentious prose, as Mr. McCarthy begins to allow the drama of Billy's story to take over. This shift in style serves no discernible purpose, however, and it makes for a disjointed, inorganic book. In any case, the reader has by then already wearied of the novel's affectations, its grab-bag derivativeness, and most of all, its self-importance.

### Bruce Allen (review date 26 June 1994)

SOURCE: "The Land of the Wounded Men," in *Tribune Books*, June 26, 1994, p. 5.

[*In the following favorable review, Allen praises the descriptive prose in* The Crossing, *and the "vividly rendered conflict" of* The Stonemason. *Comparing McCarthy to Melville and Faulkner, the critic lauds these two works, while acknowledging their frequent melodramatic passages.*]

Cormac McCarthy, who was born in 1933 and has been publishing novels since 1965, was until only two years ago an obscure name to the larger reading public, burdened with a reputation as a writer's writer. McCarthy's dark and violent fictions, set in the American South and Southwest and redolent of earlier times and more primitive ways, were almost equally praised for their lyrical force and damned for their relentless pessimism.

Then came *All the Pretty Horses,* a resonant tale of initiation set in southwestern Texas and Mexico, which won both the National Book Award and National Book Critics Circle Award and was accorded virtually unanimous nationwide and international acclaim. No longer was McCarthy the property of the cognoscenti, although he has maintained his taciturn separation from the literary establishment.

McCarthy is currently represented by two new books: *The Crossing,* the middle novel in his "Border Trilogy" (of which *All the Pretty Horses* was Volume 1), and *The Stonemason,* a full-length play, originally written more than 15 years ago, since revised and thus far unproduced.

Part spoken reverie and part dramatic action, *The Stonemason* portrays a black family, the Telfairs of Louisville, through the eyes of Ben Telfair. A former schoolteacher, Ben has turned from that vocation to the path followed by his beloved grandfather ("Papaw"), who has remained throughout his long life (of 102 years) devoted to the craft in which his grandson perceives a sustaining moral example—and from which the succeeding Telfair generations have drifted away into financial collapse, infidelity, drug abuse and suicide.

Expertly constructed and limpidly written, the play offers several incisive brief characterizations, and it triumphs in its presentation of Papaw, whose earthy wisdom McCarthy makes altogether credible. (Papaw is undoubtedly modeled on the ageless Indian guide Sam Fathers of Faulkner's novella *The Bear.*)

Ben Telfair is a mouthpiece, and his solemn celebration of the workingman's ethos provokes the other Telfairs ("You think his opinions are valuable because he's worked all his life. Isn't that a pretty romantic notion?") and occasionally lapses into sententiousness. But McCarthy has set traps and springs them remorselessly. Ben's adherence to the ideal of stonemasonry leads him to misunderstand and unintentionally betray others who deserve his devotion ("I've questioned the rightness of loving that old man beyond all other souls," he ruefully concludes), and he contributes his own share to the destruction of the family he has labored to save.

Like all McCarthy's work, *The Stonemason* is a mixture of vividly rendered conflict and complex discursive commentary. Compared to his novels, it's minor work but seems to this reader both skillfully fashioned and eminently playable. One hopes that McCarthy's current high reputation will encourage somebody to stage it.

*The Crossing,* which surely will enhance that reputation, contains numerous echoes of *All the Pretty Horses,* though its characters, plot and setting are new. Once again we are thrust into a barren landscape in which man and animals alike labor to comprehend and survive a universe that is at best indifferent, at worst charged with a phlegmatic menace.

The setting is southwestern New Mexico and Mexico in the three years just before, then after America's entry into World War II. In the first of the novel's four long segments, Billy and Boyd Parham, aged 16 and 14, help their father track a marauding she-wolf—an almost unheard-of anachronism in their relatively peaceful cattle-ranching corner of the world.

Discovering the wolf caught in their trap and acting on a bone-deep impulse he only half understands, Billy carries the wounded animal across the border into Mexico, pledged to return it to the mountains whence it came. But his mission is thwarted, and Billy does what he must to salvage the integrity of the creature.

In part two, after long weeks away and perhaps heeding the admonition of a traveling stranger who urges him to "cease his wanderings and make for himself some place in the world," Billy returns home—to a scene of devastation and loss, and reunion with the younger brother for whom he now declares himself responsible. Another journey ensues: this one in search of justice, if not revenge. There are more "crossings" and an encounter with a wandering adolescent girl, who joins them.

Part three focuses on the boys' efforts to recover horses stolen from them. A violent confrontation sows the seeds of later, more grievous trouble. Billy loses Boyd, finds him, then loses him again.

Part four finds Billy alone, trying to enlist in the army but being rejected when he's diagnosed with an irregular heartbeat. He drifts from one temporary job and unwelcoming place to another, never at peace ("the one thing he knew of all things claimed to be known was that there was no certainty to any of it"), daring danger, courting death. Finally, learning of his brother's whereabouts, Billy manages, against overpowering odds, to reclaim him—although he remains thereafter rootless and purposeless, seeking some kind of connection that he seems perpetually fated to lose or drive away.

This powerful story is captured in imagery of great beauty and precision. The metaphor of crossing, for instance, perfectly encapsulates both the maze-like rites of passage the

Parham boys endure and their restless, prickly inability to settle or belong.

The sonorous density of McCarthy's Faulkner-derived prose is seen at its best in his eerie presentation of the captive wolf (whose "eyes burned . . . like gatelamps to another world"), and in dozens of breathtakingly imaginative descriptive passages (for example: "the thin horned moon lay on its back in the west like a grail and the bright shape of Venus hung directly above it like a star falling into a boat").

McCarthy is a matchless describer of processes (preparing, and setting wolftraps, cauterizing a bullet wound, etc.), and a superbly visual writer whose images are truly seen (a boy dressing at night "held [his] boots to the window-light to pair them left and right"; a rider having dismounted "stood down into the snow and dropped the reins and squatted and thumbed back the brim of his hat").

He pays his readers the compliment of rendering much of the novel's dialogue in untranslated Spanish (we're thus forced to pay close attention, and can almost always understand the sense, if not every word, of such conversations).

What McCarthy says of a tribe of nomadic Indians—that "their reticence and their silence bespoke a view of a world provisional, contingent, deeply suspect"—might apply to all this novel's characters. Yet he enters fully into the heart and mind of Billy Parham and makes believable and moving his helpless love for all he cannot but lose.

This novel's intricate view of human travail embraces both blunt fatalism ("death is the truth") and the stoical conviction that we do not, after all, wander in a meaningless void. ("Deep in each man is the knowledge that something knows of his existence. Something knows, and cannot be fled nor hid from.")

*The Crossing* abounds with action that some will declare melodramatic, and there's no question that McCarthy lets the brothers encounter a few too many mysterious strangers possessed of numbingly gnomic wisdom. Oppressive literary echoes include not just McCarthy's homage to Faulkner but also awkwardly re-imagined simulacra of the opening of *Great Expectations* and the Father Zossima passages of *The Brothers Karamazov*.

But these are only blemishes. On balance, this ambitious novel offers a masterly display of tonal control and some of the most pitch-perfect rapturous prose being written these days. The opening section, focused on the dramatic symbiosis between captured animal and emergent boy-man, is a magnificent piece of writing, in every way comparable to the best of Melville as well as Faulkner.

There's enough going on in this brilliantly imagined book to lure a reader into racing eagerly through its pages. But don't skim. You won't want to miss a single sentence.

## C. Carr (review date 5 July 1994)

SOURCE: "True West," in *Village Voice*, Vol. XXXIX, No. 27, July 5, 1994, p. 81.

[*In the following review, Carr focuses on the deeper meanings within the bleak and desolate settings and occurrences in* The Crossing. *Acknowledging that there is purpose to the bloodshed and evil in McCarthy's novels, Carr comments on the themes of loss and the human condition in the works.*]

A boy is traveling through Mexico on horseback, leaving the Southwest, leaving home. That's a bald outline of Cormac McCarthy's new novel, *The Crossing.* In his last novel, *All the Pretty Horses,* two boys traveled from the Southwest into Mexico. As did a boy in his previous book, *Blood Meridian, or, The Evening Redness in the West.* Yet the voyages are as different as if set on separate continents.

In *The Crossing,* a 16-year-old named Billy Parham makes three trips south of the border. There he both endures tragedy and encounters the tragic—people who try to impart to him whatever lessons they've learned the hard way. Among other things, he hears that there is only one story, and a narrator's task is never to choose one tale from among many, but to make many tales of the only one there is. *The Crossing* is McCarthy's most powerful version yet of the western he seems to write again and again.

He used to be thought of as a southern writer. The first McCarthy novels I ever bought were reprints from Ecco Press labeled "Neglected Books of the Twentieth Century," and these early books, set in either Tennessee or some nameless rural South, teem with moonshiners, thrillkillers, and most of all, poor white folks—the lonely, the righteous, and the crazed. Critics compared him with Faulkner; sometimes they still do. His prose is both lush and precise, his diction antique. But he out-grotesqued Faulkner. He out-monstered him. *Child of God, The Orchard Keeper, Suttree* and *Outer Dark* include necrophilia, incest, serial murder, and lots of cruelty-for-the-hell-of-it.

So if brutality, depravity, and beautiful writing were standard, if an angel had set out to illumine parts of hell, it was easy to see *Blood Meridian* as more of the same. In a rare 1992 interview with McCarthy, *The New York Times Magazine* suggested that *Blood Meridian* "may be the bloodiest book since *The Iliad.*" A protagonist called "the kid"—he's never named—joins a gang of scalphunters riding into

Mexico around 1850. The novel moves from one act of nihilistic violence to the next, on waves of rich, almost biblical, prose. The book has no plot and, apart from "the kid," no center, just a trail of gristle and rue, crusted clothes, perished animals. True west. But *Blood Meridian* turned out to be a transitional book, the gory prototype of his border novels.

McCarthy's Border Trilogy properly began with his next work, *All the Pretty Horses,* which won a National Book Award and thrust a "writer's writer" out of obscurity at the age of 59. This second McCarthy western, set exactly a hundred years after the events of *Blood Meridian,* remains the most accessible of his books. Sixteen-year-old John Grady Cole rides into Mexico for freedom and adventure—for fewer fences of all kinds. He's traveling with his best friend, he's uncannily skilled with horses, he even finds romance. When events turn deadly near the end of the story, the reader senses that they will scar Cole but not break him.

*The Crossing* is much darker. On each of his three trips into Mexico, Billy is trying to set something right, restore a certain order. But these are doomed enterprises. Deciding on impulse to take a wolf he's trapped to the Mexican mountains so she can run free again, Billy sets off on the first journey with no money, no food, not even a blanket. We never learn what compels him to do this. McCarthy doesn't psychologize. But here, for the first time, he philosophizes. For example, a dying man who counsels the boy on how to trap a wolf says he can do this by finding a place "where acts of God and those of men are of a piece" because there "God sits and conspires in the destruction of that which he has been at such pains to create." The man also tells Billy that wolves know "there is no order in the world save that which death has put there."

Indeed, death keeps appearing to show Billy this order, but he doesn't comprehend it. "Men wish to be serious but they do not understand how to be so," the dying man has told him. "Between their acts and their ceremonies lies the world and in this world the storms blow and the trees twist in the wind and all the animals that God has made go to and fro yet this world men do not see. They see the acts of their own hands or they see that which they name and call out to one another but the world between is invisible to them."

Naturally, this concept becomes a gloss on Billy's own story, and McCarthy keeps refining the idea as other people the boy encounters tell him that the world is a story, that it exists in men's hearts, that its picture is all we know. But Billy keeps trying to hold what can't be held, thereby suffering grievous loss. Though he doesn't die, he isn't saved.

As the second book in the Border Trilogy, *The Crossing* suggests that McCarthy has more in mind than a geographic division between the U.S. and Mexico. He is also describing that liminal area where connections, or transitions, are made: boy/man, animal/human, innocence/experience, even English/Spanish (the boys in these books are bilingual and the Spanish is never translated). However, Mexico *is* depicted here as a place of possibilities, danger: the frontier. The events that unfold there seem timeless, while life in the States is dreary and predictable.

We're suffused with a keen sense of what's about to be lost in all of McCarthy's westerns. In the first sentences of *The Crossing,* set a couple years before World War II, Billy and his family have moved to a new county in the bootheel of New Mexico where "you could ride clear to Mexico and not strike a crossfence." But a neighbor soon complains that the country is "crowdin up." And wolves have disappeared along with any idea of how to catch them. (The one Billy traps has wandered out of Mexico.) *All the Pretty Horses* begins in Texas a couple of years after the war. The last time Cole sees his father before leaving for Mexico, the father tells him that things will never be the same: "We're like the Comanches was two hundred years ago. We don't know what's goin to show up here come daylight." And *Blood Meridian* ends with an image of a man digging holes across the prairie for fenceposts. Free riding over the range, for scalphunters or anyone else, is a thing of the past long before the trilogy even starts.

The Border books are not only revisionist westerns, but literary ones. In fact, they are very Leslie Fiedler-ish, with their boy-heroes "lighting out for the Territory." Like Huck. Like Ishmael. How is it that in all of American literary history—despite the importance of the western in our national culture, mythology, and self-image—no one has ever written a "great" western novel? (I mean a book that might enter the canon alongside *Huckleberry Finn* and *Moby Dick.* Fiedler makes a case for The Leatherstocking Tales as the first westerns, and canon fodder they may be, but they're not great literature. Willa Cather? She wrote about pioneers, about domesticating the frontier. But her books aren't westerns, which deal with masculinity, confronting the wild, and the ambiguity inherent in that encounter.) Somehow, the western has been confined almost exclusively to the realm of popular culture, from dime novels to *Dances With Wolves.*

In reviews of *The Crossing,* some critics have been enthralled by the portentous themes while others have wearied of the portentous sentences. (For example, the Sunday *Times* praised the book as "a miracle in prose" while the daily *Times* panned it as "derivative, sentimental, and pretentious.") But I think *The Crossing* might be the first great western. At the same time, it turns the genre inside out; for one thing, it defuses potentially dramatic confrontations or disappearances, giving us instead a flat line: "[Billy] rode out the gate before his father was even up and he never saw him again." As if certain things are simply fated. As if that fate were more important than what actually happens to bring it about. McCarthy does not show or even describe most of the violent deaths that change Billy's life. The reader discovers them after the fact, as the boy does. In a pop western, the encounter with death (the gunfight, the Indian raid) would be what the book is about. Here, the impact of death is what the book is about. However the canon makers finally judge *The Crossing,* it is certainly pivotal to McCarthy's oeuvre, a volume with the power to change how we read his earlier work, and the first in which he goes beyond his astonishing descriptive powers to get at something deeper.

Near the end of *The Crossing,* Billy is set upon by robbers who injure his horse. Sitting near the animal, wondering what to do, Billy suddenly sees what could be a scene from a Fellini film; gypsies with a team of six yoked oxen pulling the remains of an ancient airplane through the wild. The gypsies stop to help, telling Billy that the plane crashed in the mountains almost 30 years ago, killing the pilot. The pilot's father had hired them to recover the plane. But there was a sister plane that also crashed. Do they even have the right plane? One of the men tells Billy that this question is of consequence—and that is just the trouble.

> A false authority clung to what persisted, as if those artifacts of the past which had endured had done so by some act of their own will. Yet the witness could not survive the witnessing. In the world that came to be that which prevailed could never speak for that which perished but could only parade its own arrogance. It pretended symbol and summation of the vanished world but was neither. He said that in any case the past was little more than a dream and its force in the world greatly exaggerated. For the world was made new each day and it was only men's clinging to its vanished husks that could make of that world one husk more.

What all McCarthy's books share is a sense that humans are at best narrow, often insensate or crude, and sometimes evil. So the dialogue between humans is spare, while the writing around nature, animals, the world runs from lyrical to florid. In *The Crossing,* Billy learns in very specific ways about the human condition. For one thing, humans want borders. That's why we name things, frame things with stories, hang on to the past. And still, we are always lost.

## Sven Birkerts (review date 11 July 1994)

SOURCE: "The Lone Soul State," in *The New Republic,* Vol. 211, No. 4147, July 11, 1994, pp. 38-41.

[*In the following review, Birkerts notes similarities between* The Crossing *and* All the Pretty Horses, *and comments on the differences between these two works and previous novels.*]

The myth of Cormac McCarthy is the myth of hard knocks endured and surmounted. There were long, lean years when novels now seen as brilliant were unable to find an audience. The author acquired a reputation as a drifter, a misfit and an uncompromising solitary. And then, in 1992, came a double play. *All the Pretty Horses,* the first volume of McCarthy's projected Border Trilogy, won two of the major fiction prizes. All of a sudden everybody knew the writer and always had. Through the alchemy of retrospect, the sorry sales figures became dues paid, and McCarthy emerged as one of our grizzled eminences.

McCarthy's arrival at highbrow stardom may have seemed like a happy accident, but of course there are good reasons why it happened. Through sheer persistence, the author had begun to attain critical mass within the literary establishment. No less important, a decade or so ago the prose style changed, became more action-centered and accessible. Finally, that inchoate thing known as public taste seems to be shifting in McCarthy's favor, our fluctuant appetite for hard-bitten realism spiking up as hard-biting nature itself disappears.

Born in 1933, raised mostly in East Tennessee, McCarthy published his first novel, *The Orchard Keeper,* in 1965. It was a dense book, disturbing and lyrical. McCarthy found few readers and most of the reviews he got compared him to, inevitably, Faulkner and O'Connor. But to make this point about a Southern writer is to make no point at all. The critics might just as usefully have invoked Melville, Beckett, Joyce—or for that matter, any one of the whole dark chorus from Sophocles and Jeremiah to Nelson Algren and Juan Rulfo. Truer still would have been to downplay the genealogies and say, as Robert Coles (one of McCarthy's few perceptive early readers) did, that here was an author with a deep imagination of evil, a sharp sense of human limitation and a love of both austere and grandiloquent expression. But critics are generally uneasy without their slots and readers have never cottoned in large numbers to any grim vision of the truth of things. McCarthy's trio of Appalachian mountain folk—a murderous bootlegger, a fatherless young man and a half-addled old orchard-keeper—was left to wander in the limbo of the written about but unread.

The same fate befell his subsequent two novels, *Outer Dark* and *Child of God.* The oeuvre was tending from brutal and pitiless to more so. McCarthy stayed in the Tennessee mountain setting, concocting scenarios as primal and stark as anything in literature. In *Outer Dark* a baby born of incestuous coupling and left to die in the woods is rescued; it lives long enough to draw its parents, brother and sister into a web of horrifying consequence. *Child of God* inverted the sense of its title, tracing the gruesome track of an accused rapist after his release from prison. There was nothing in any of these books to suit the predilections of a refined readership. Nor did McCarthy do anything to further his cause—he gave no interviews, made no exertions toward wooing a public.

Brutal and harsh as these first novels were, they were also stunningly well-written. From the first McCarthy has commanded a prose style of singular precision and intensity, a style that draws upon two very different idioms. One is unadorned yet finely graded and seems to extend onto the page from the landscape itself:

> Half a mile farther and the road turned up a hill, emerging from the woods to poke through a cornfield where a brace of doves flushed out and faired away to the creek on whistling wings. Beyond the field and set back up from the road was a small board shack with the laths curling out like hair awry, bleached to a metalgray.

Then there is the more ornate style, a studied baroque, that every so often threatens to choke the more solid growth like some kudzu:

> . . . a dozen jerry-built shacks strewn about the valley in unlikely places, squatting over their gullied purlieus like great brooding animals rigid with constipation, and yet endowed with an air transient and happenstantial as if set there by the recession of floodwaters.

To talk about McCarthy is to talk about style every bit as much as subject matter. His novels, for better and worse, are not much occupied with the intricacies of plot. Things do happen, of course, important things, but so often it seems as if they happen because the writer has willed it so. His gift, and his true fascination, are for beholding the world; for establishing page by page the densities of presence—of people as well as places and things. McCarthy meditates on creation, stares at it. He does not look past appearances, he looks through them. Describing a pair of boots, he writes: "They were cracked and weatherblackened and one was cleft from tongue to toe like a hoof." It is as if we are looking at the famous Van Gogh painting: we see the boots, but what we register are the weary miles, the human sorrow. The dynamics of this are hard to explain, but readers of McCarthy often testify to his ability to create a spell. He works by a process of steady engulfment, first putting new ground under the reader's feet, then a sky; then he pulls forth his myriad particulars from some place of dreamlike familiarity.

In 1979 McCarthy published *Suttree,* a massive novel in every way different from the pared-down works that had come before. He moved his setting from back-country to city, in this instance Knoxville, and at the same time indulged to the maximum his penchant for the hypertrophied style:

> He could hear the river talking softly beneath him, heavy old river with wrinkled face. Beneath the sliding water cannons and carriages, trunnions seized and rusting in the mud, keelboats rotted to the consistency of mucilage. Fabled sturgeons with their horny pentagonal bodies, the cuprous and dacebright carp and catfish with their pale and sprueless underbellies, a thick muck shot with broken glass, with bones and rusted tins and bits of crockery reticulate with mudblack crazings.

Like the earlier novels, *Suttree* is less an orchestrated set of plot developments than a serial progression, sequence after sequence showing forth the damnations of modernity—the waste, the venality, the hypocrisy—all images and episodes held together in the battered psyche of Cornelius Suttree, wastrel son of a wealthy Knoxville family. Suttree lives on his ramshackle houseboat on the Tennessee river and studies the world, suffering along with the derelicts he tries to help out, immersing himself in the tides of corruption until he can stand it no longer and must leave.

*Suttree* can be viewed as McCarthy's valediction to the Appalachian settings of his early career. In the 1970s he moved to El Paso, Texas, and took his fiction with him. In 1985 he published *Blood Meridian,* a violent chronicle of scalping raids in mid-nineteenth-century Texas and Mexico. This was his most savage expression yet and it may have effected a kind of purge, for the novels that follow are conspicuously different in focus and vision. With *Blood Meridian* there is also a distinct change in style, as if the new terrain were calling forth a new way of setting sentences to the page. From this point on McCarthy begins writing in a more tightly flexed and more colloquially rooted idiom—a complete turnaround from the language of *Suttree.* Now he builds his scenes with quick strokes, mostly outward narration and unpunctuated conversation; when images are used, they are charged and evocative. McCarthy's terse economy suggests a worldview by turns unsentimental and pitiless. The effect is—to resort to those traditional poles of comparison—more Hemingway than Faulkner:

> The kid lay listening. There were no new riders. After a while the judge called out again. Come out, he called. There's plenty of water for everybody.
>
> The kid had swung the powderflask around to his back to keep it out of the creek and he held the pistol up and waited. Upstream the horses had stopped drinking. Then they started drinking again.

But this is mild. More characteristic might be a passage like this: "The explosion filled all that sad little park. Some of the horses shied and stepped. A fist-sized hole erupted out of the far side of the woman's head in a great vomit of gore and she pitched over and lay slain in her blood without remedy." The reviewers of the novel spoke of it as a revisionist Western, Louis L'Amour rewritten with a bloody pen. But again McCarthy seemed to be using history to look beyond history—as if what really drove him were the desire to see human nature plain. Which, to judge by that novel, meant exacting a look at the worst.

In the two novels written since *Blood Meridian,* first *All the Pretty Horses* and now *The Crossing,* the writer seems to have changed his approach. Not that he has softened his estimate of the human capacity for evil, but he has established that estimate within a larger spectrum, one that also has room for redemptive forces. *All the Pretty Horses,* his story of two teenaged boys riding through the countryside of northern Mexico in search of stolen horses and adventure, is distinguished far less by scenes of bloodshed or intimations of horror than by the frank exuberance of the narration and the breathtaking descriptions of the natural world. We find violence, of course, and scenes of gratuitous cruelty, but also moments of tenderness and humor. Battered by circumstance, John Grady and his friend, Rawlins, never lose a certain expectant readiness. McCarthy reminds us of his darker view of things only at strategic moments, though when he ends the book it is with an ominous intimation:

> He touched the horse with his heels and rode on. He rode with the sun coppering his face and the red wind blowing out of the west across the evening land and the small desert birds flew chittering among the dry bracken and horse and rider and horse passed on and their long shadows passed in tandem like the shadow of a single being. Passed and paled into the darkening land, the world to come.

*The Crossing* is in many ways similar to *All the Pretty Horses.* The characters may be different, but the terrain is the same, and the narrative inscribes the same vast circle: departure from home, extended wanderings in Mexico and return. And so long as we think of narrative as essentially incident and complication, as action tending toward a resolution, McCarthy's can be recounted quite concisely.

The novel basically tells the coming-of-age story of Billy Parham, a young man we first see growing up with his family in the rough range country of New Mexico in the early 1940s. In the opening scenes Billy is obsessed with trapping a marauding she-wolf that has crossed over from the mountains of Mexico and is attacking their cattle. He begs his father to be allowed to set the traps himself and one morning has success. With the extreme restraint that has become char-

acteristic, McCarthy writes: "He rode out the gate before his father was even up and he never saw him again."

When Billy reaches the trap, the wolf is there. But instead of killing her—he sees that she is pregnant—he is moved to take her back over the border and free her. In this wrinkle of his character, this feeling for the maligned creature, lie the seeds of his fate. The journey that he undertakes is harsh, full of privations and difficult makeshifts. McCarthy stays with the external narration. We learn about Billy only by reading the signs of his actions. But through these we gradually arrive at a comprehensive sense of who he is. When the wolf is taken from him by a group of self-appointed authorities—hijacked for bloodsport—he follows. He watches the wolf fight off savage dogs for as long as he can bear it, then makes his move: "He stepped over the parapet and walked toward the wolf and levered a shell into the chamber of the rifle and halted ten feet from her and raised the rifle and took aim at the bloodied head and fired." The string of conjunctions in that sentence gives us a precise sense of how Billy wills his action forward in stages.

After killing the wolf Billy journeys back home, arriving to find the farmstead empty, suspended in a desolate silence. He walks from room to room, looking:

> He walked into his parents' room and stood. He stood for a long time. He saw how the ticking of the mattress bore the rusty imprint of the springcoils and he looked at that for a long time. Then he hung his hat on the doorknob and walked over to the bed. He stood beside it. He reached down and got hold of the mattress and dragged it off the bed and stood it up and let it fall over backwards. What came to light beneath was an enormous bloodstain dried near black and soaked so thick it cracked and splintered like some dark ceramic glaze. . . . He looked at it all and he fell to his knees in the floor and sobbed into his hands.

Billy understands now. His parents have been killed, the horses have been stolen; if he cannot find his brother, Boyd, he has nothing in the world. But miraculously Boyd *has* survived—Billy tracks him down—and the two brothers set off on Billy's horse, back to Mexico.

In the long sections that follow, the brothers patrol the mountain country of northern Mexico. McCarthy creates what feels like a dream of slowly unfolding days lived through hour by hour, mile by mile. The boys ride themselves to exhaustion, make camp. They eat when they can, mostly when some good person takes pity and offers them a plate of beans or some bread. During the course of their obscure journey, they find some of the horses and steal them back. Later they find others—there are standoffs, skirmishes with marauders. We find ourselves in a kind of frontier version of *The Trial*. It is never clear who serves whom or where the power comes from. Men on horseback ride up in clouds of dust, pistols are brandished. And with a minimum of conversation—never once speaking about the murder of their parents—the brothers push on.

The shape of the journey is determined by certain developments. Boyd falls in love with a 14-year-old girl, another of McCarthy's drifters, and she joins their entourage. Then Boyd is shot in a raid and nearly dies. When he is finally mended, when Billy has reunited him with his girl, he and she disappear, never to be seen again. Billy drifts disconsolately north, returns to the United States and tries to join the army. But the doctors discover a heart murmur and he is turned away. With a shrinking sense of options, Billy heads back to Mexico. When he arrives he learns that Boyd has been killed. The novel ends as he completes his last mission, finding his brother's bones and bringing them back home for burial.

Described thus, in terms of core episodes, *The Crossing* might not sound terribly compelling, especially since the characters do not interact on any level of sophistication; nearly all of the affect must be inferred. The theme, moreover, is one familiar from previous books: McCarthy maps again the brutal terms of existence and argues the unceasing need to be stoical and resourceful in the face of pain and certain loss. And yet, like *All the Pretty Horses*—more, I would say—*The Crossing* achieves resonance. By structuring the narrative as he has, by writing with such unflagging lyrical power, McCarthy displaces our focus from the outer events to the primal archetypes that underlie them. The novel shifts us constantly from the physical to the metaphysical, creating a recursiveness of action in which we suddenly catch the ozone whiff of human souls eking their way forward under an indifferent sky. *The Crossing* is only incidentally about the wolf or the horses or the many unexpected encounters. The message is more chillingly basic. An old man whom Billy meets unfolds the truth:

> He told the boy that although he was *huerfano* [an orphan] still he must cease his wanderings and make for himself some place in the world because to wander in this way would become for him a passion and by this passion he would become estranged from men and ultimately from himself.

He tells this to Billy before the boy discovers that he is literally an orphan. The old man is speaking in the Heideggerian sense: we are all solitary, plunged into being and made to suffer it.

The power of the novel depends entirely on McCarthy's ability to immerse us in the time and place, and this he does through his prose—through the cadences and word-sounds

and the rightness of the images. The world is set before us with fever-dream clarity. McCarthy establishes density and mass; he incises detail as with an engraver's needle. And then, with simile and metaphor, he sweeps everything into profound animation. His descriptions can range from the earthbound and homely ("The wolf was standing bowed up in the road with its hair all wrong like something pulled backwards out of a pipe. . . .") to the more ethereal: "When the flames came up her eyes burned out there like gatelamps to another world." This is poetry, and one reads it with a sort of covetousness, returning to passages just for their beauty:

> The sun was low in the west and the shape of the light from the window lay suspended across the room wall to wall. As if something electric had been cored out of that space.

> His eyes were very blue and very beautiful half hid away in the leathery seams of his face. As if there were something there that the hardness of the country had not been able to touch.

> The horse's ears quartered the compass for the source of the noise.

> He was perhaps a mile out and he approached in a series of thin and trembling images which in those places where the foreground was flooded would suddenly augment in their length and then shrivel and draw up again so that the rider appeared to advance and recede and advance again.

McCarthy is writing entirely against the grain of our times, against the haste and the distraction and the moral diffusion. This doubtless has much to do with his appeal: we crave what we hasten to evolve from. As we lose the deeper sense of space and time, as we become riders of the information highway, creatures of call-waiting and tax-deferred annuities, we cannot but see works like this as a kind of amber in which older ways of life have been immobilized. We become aware as we read of weather, distances, the grain and heft of implements; we feel the envelope of silence around each person. And how eloquent are McCarthy's encounters and partings—they define a sense of space most of us have never even glimpsed. Men and women in doorways, watching as riders reduce to pinpoints in the distance, and watching still. As an old, more spacious world rises up, we experience a more vivid and consequential feeling about human destiny. We are in a place where questions about good and evil and matters of the spirit do not sound forced or literary.

McCarthy has been, from the start, a writer with strong spiritual leanings. His orientation is Gnostic: he seems to view our endeavors here below as a violation of some original purity. But a sensibility so attuned to earthly beauty cannot be oblivious to the higher promptings of the soul. His intuitions are of the most primary sort, never even remotely doctrinaire. In the early books we heed his exacerbated awareness of violence and cruelty, of evil, without finding much place for the good. But now, in these most recent works, we meet up quite often with decency. There are venal killers, yes, but they are outnumbered by the poor who emerge from their dwellings to offer succor. Time and again Billy and his brother are taken in, fed and humanly honored:

> At dawn the day following while he saddled his horse the workers came out bringing gifts of food. They brought tortillas and chiles and *carne seca* and live chickens and whole hoops of cheese until they were burdened with provisions beyond their means to carry them. The Muoz woman gave Billy something which when she stepped back he saw was a clutch of coins knotted into a rag.

At moments like this, McCarthy attains the dense simplicity of parable. Indeed, he includes in the novel an extended interlude that could have come directly from one of the God-possessed writers of an earlier day. Before he returns from his ill-fated mission to free the wolf, Billy meets another old man, a hermit of sorts, who tells him a lengthy tale about a priest and a visionary outcast. It is given to the latter to embody the true holy spirit and the priest must humble himself considerably before he can learn the lesson intended for him:

> The priest saw that there is no man who is elect because there is no man who is not. To God every man is a heretic. . . . Every word we speak is a vanity. Every breath taken that does not bless is an affront. . . . In the end we shall all of us be only what we have made of God. For nothing is real save his grace.

One would think such words would sit strangely in this rude context of vigilantes and drifters, but they don't. McCarthy's vision of silences and spaces consorts readily with the movements of the religious imagination. It is for us to square the sense of the embedded parable with Billy's meandering track. We must factor in as well these words from a mysterious rider Billy meets on his way back north. In what is one of the last exchanges of the novel, the man addresses him: "This world will never be the same, the rider said. Did you know that?" Billy replies: "I know it. It ain't now." We can read this as a secular counterpart to the visionary's message: it identifies the principle of change and rebirth without ascribing it to a deity. The two perspectives stand like shifting background panels. In the foreground Billy Parham, who has fought and ridden and looked for a way home, lays his brother's bones to rest in a small graveyard. Then, like John Grady, he sets off again, more orphaned than ever.

## Edwin T. Arnold (essay date 4 November 1994)

SOURCE: "Blood and Grace: The Fiction of Cormac McCarthy," in *Commonweal,* November 4, 1994, pp. 11-16.

[*In the following essay, Arnold provides an overview of McCarthy's works, discussing how the novels address the issues of contemporary society. Focusing on the religious themes of the works, Arnold examines McCarthy's sensibilities and the deeper messages within the novels.*]

Cormac McCarthy's novels compose an extended journey. His characters travel the mountain roads and forests of east Tennessee, the city streets of Knoxville, the deserts and hills of Mexico and the Southwest. For the most part, their wanderings seem without immediate purpose, or purpose of the vaguest sort: an undefined desire to withdraw or to explore or to escape. They are descendants of Ishmael, both the biblical outcast and Melville's nomadic seagoer. I can think of no other author who so carefully charts his characters' movements from street to street or town to town—you can follow them on maps if you wish. And yet his novels usually cease their telling in the midst of journeys, still on the road, short of destination, for, in the world of McCarthy, the only true destination is death.

"He spoke as one who seemed to understand that death was the condition of existence and life but an emanation thereof." This is the author's description of a gypsy encountered by his protagonist Billy Parham in McCarthy's new novel, *The Crossing,* but it could apply equally well to McCarthy, who himself seems fascinated, at times even exhilarated, by the multiple manifestations of doom. In his novels, death is portrayed with astonishing variety in the constant violence men do to men. "Holme saw the blade wink in the light like a long cat's eye slant and malevolent and a dark smile erupted on the child's throat and went all broken down the front of it," reads a passage in *Outer Dark,* and the effect causes some to throw the book to the floor. In *Child of God,* death is amatory, a means for the necrophile-murderer Lester Ballard to "[pour] into that waxen ear everything he'd ever thought of saying to a woman. Who could say she did not hear him?" In *Blood Meridian,* a tale of Western scalp hunters, death is all butchery and business, murder for profit in a landscape of *terra damnata:*

> They moved among the dead harvesting the long black locks with their knives and leaving their victims rawskulled and strange in their bloody cauls. . . .Men were wading about in the red waters hacking aimlessly at the dead and some lay coupled to the bludgeoned bodies of young women dead or dying on the beach. One of the Delawares passed with a collection of heads like some strange vendor

bound for market, the hair twisted about his wrist and the heads dangling and turning together.

And yet it should not be surprising that a man so taken with death should prove equally passionate about life, for each, he argues, makes the other possible. McCarthy turns to the wild to revel in the majesty of unnegotiated vitality. In his first novel, *The Orchard Keeper,* he embodies this fierce joy in the hawk which the boy, John Wesley Rattner, traps for bounty, only later to comprehend that such an act is sacrilege. "I cain't take no dollar," he tells the clerk. "I made a mistake, he wadn't for sale." In later books, those set in the Southwest, McCarthy employs the horse, whose physical vitality he extols in lofty, mystical celebration:

> While inside the vaulting of the ribs between his knees the darkly meated heart pumped of who's will and the blood pulsed and the bowels shifted in their massive blue convolutions of who's will and the stout thighbones and knee and cannon and the tendons like flaxen hawsers that drew and flexed and drew and flexed at their articulations and of who's will all sheathed and muffled in the flesh and the hooves that stove wells in the morning groundmist and the head turning side to side and the great slavering keyboard of his teeth and the hot globes of his eyes where the world burned.

In *The Crossing,* it is the wolf that stands as emblem of a fierce, uncompromised wisdom which sees the balance of life in death, and death in life:

> He said that the wolf is a being of great order and that it knows what men do not: that there is no order in the world save that which death has put there. Finally he said that if men drink the blood of God yet they do not understand the seriousness of what they do. He said that men wish to be serious but they do not understand how to be so. Between their acts and their ceremonies lies the world and in this world the storms blow and the trees twist in the wind and all the animals that God has made go to and fro, yet this world men do not see. They see the acts of their own hands or they see that which they name and call out to one another but the world between is invisible to them.

It is the "world between," the invisible place of blood and grace, that lies at the heart of McCarthy's fiction.

McCarthy, now sixty-one, is the author of seven published novels, one published five-act play, and one filmed screenplay. His first four books—*The Orchard Keeper, Outer Dark, Child of God,* and *Suttree* are set largely in the first half of the century, in Tennessee around Knoxville, where McCarthy attended Catholic high school and, without graduating, the University of Tennessee. His screenplay, *The Gardener's Son* (directed by Richard Pearce, and shown on PBS in 1977), is based on an 1876 murder in Graniteville, South Carolina. His drama, *The Stonemason* (published in 1994 but written earlier, apparently around 1980) takes place in Louisville, Kentucky, in the 1970s.

Shortly before the publication of *Suttree,* McCarthy left his second wife (he is twice divorced) and moved to the Southwest, first Tucson and then El Paso, which he has since used as his home base. His subsequent books have been Westerns, although to label them as such is no more accurate than to call his earlier books Southern or Appalachian; McCarthy's writings, for all their detailed accuracy of speech and custom and place, easily transcend any notion of region. *Blood Meridian: Or the Evening Redness in the West,* is a hyperviolent tale of scalp hunters in the 1840s, based on historical record and rendered with such realism that many readers cannot get past the first third of the book. *All the Pretty Horses,* the first volume of The Border Trilogy, is set one hundred years later and, in effect, reconstructs the world of *Blood Meridian* in more romantic and forgiving terms (for McCarthy, at least); it is not surprising that it has proved to be his one best-seller, although the scope of its success (it sold over 100,000 copies in the first year; won the National Book Award and the National Critics Circle Award and was a finalist for the Pulitzer Prize; the screen rights were bought by Mike Nichols, filming set for next year) is astonishing, indeed. The second volume of the trilogy, *The Crossing,* was published last spring in an initial printing of 200,000 copies, and the book was a main selection of the Book of the Month Club. A darker, sadder, but also deeply compassionate work, *The Crossing* denies its readers the conventional plot satisfactions found in *Pretty Horses,* although it tells essentially the same story, paralleling its sixteen-year-old protagonist Billy Parham's journey with that of sixteen-year-old John Grady Cole in the first volume (and, inevitably, with the sixteen-year-old "kid" in *Blood Meridian*). Whether this somber, less engaging but, I believe, more significant novel will hold the readers of *All the Pretty Horses* remains to be seen. So far, however, it has sold well.

Incest, infanticide, necrophilia; drunkenness, debauchery, sacrilege; physical deformity and spiritual morbidity: this is a bleak place McCarthy explores in his fiction. But it has been too easy, especially of the books leading up to The Border Trilogy, to categorize McCarthy as an unusually talented purveyor of nihilistic Southern Gothic horror shows and to miss the essential religiosity at the core of his writing. Denis Donoghue, following earlier critics like Vereen M. Bell, the author of *The Achievement of Cormac McCarthy,* describes the characters in the first novels as "recently arrived primates, each possessing a spinal column but little or no capacity of mind or consciousness." And while it is true that Culla Holme in *Outer Dark* or Lester Ballard in *Child of God* and, to jump ahead, the kid in *Blood Meridian* are unlikely to put their feelings of despair and alienation into reasoned words, Culla *dreams* of himself standing before a prophet, crying "Me. . . Can I be cured?"; from his cave Lester watches the "hordes of cold stars sprawled across the smokehole and wondered what stuff they were made of, or himself"; and the kid, after his year with the scalpers, "began to speak with a strange urgency of things few men have seen in a lifetime and his jailers said that his mind had come uncottered by the acts of blood in which he had participated." In later time he wanders the Southwest carrying with him a Bible he cannot read, moving inevitably toward his final judgment.

The kind of spiritual devastation suggested in these novels is detailed at length in *Suttree,* considered by many to be McCarthy's *magnum opus.* The remnants of his Catholic education and sensibilities are displayed most clearly in this lengthy work. Suttree is a lapsed Catholic but a haunted one, hounded by the specter of death, especially that of his still-born twin brother: "If our dead kin are sainted we may rightly pray to them. Mother Church tells us so. . . . I followed him into the world, me. . . . And used to pray for his soul days past. Believing this ghastly circus reconvened elsewhere for all time. He in the limbo of the Christless righteous, I in a terrestrial hell." Having abandoned his wife and own child, having broken with his well-to-do family, Suttree passes his days fishing on the polluted Tennessee River which runs near the slums of Knoxville. "He said that he might have been a fisher of men in another time but these fish now seemed task enough for him," McCarthy writes.

*Suttree* is a brilliant book by many measures, a hugely comic, extravagantly written, richly told epic of bedraggled humanity. Peopled by over 150 named characters (some actual figures from 1950s Knoxville), it concentrates on Suttree and on the country youth Gene Harrogate, whom he meets in prison and who follows him to the big city. Harrogate (an extraordinary creation, echoed by Jimmy Blevins in *All the Pretty Horses* and, to a lesser extent, Boyd Parham in *The Crossing*) brings out Suttree's sense of responsibility; he tries to save the boy from his own innate foolishness. But Harrogate is hell-bent, beyond rescue, and finally Suttree can try to save only himself. By the end of the novel, he has nearly died, faced judgment in his delirium, and been granted a kind of grace (it is mother's name: he comes to refer to himself as "son of Grace"). Given last rites by a young priest, he is asked, "Would you like to confess?" "I did it," he answers, and the truth embraces his whole life. "God must have been watching over you. You very nearly died," the priest says. "You would not believe what watches," Suttree answers. "He is not a thing. Nothing ever stops moving."

Although each of the earlier books (with the possible excep-

tion of *The Orchard Keeper,* a novel which suggests mystical truths but is largely devoid of outright religious considerations) questions the relationship between man and God, in *Suttree* it becomes a main theme. (The book was apparently written over a twenty-year period, and the three other novels can be read as offshoots of the larger work.) Starting with *Blood Meridian* (and including his play *The Stonemason*), McCarthy's writings have become increasingly solemn, his style more stately, his concerns more overtly theological. The world is a wild place in McCarthy's fiction, and its God a wild and often savage and mostly unknowable God, but a God whose presence constantly beckons. In *Blood Meridian,* the former priest, Tobin, says of the "Almighty": "Whatever could it mean to one who knows all? He's an uncommon love for the common man and godly wisdom resides in the least of things so that it may well be that the voice of the Almighty speaks most profoundly in such beings as lives in silence themselves. . . . No man is given leave of that voice."

"I ain't heard no voice," the kid spits in reply.

"When it stops. . . you'll know you've heard it all your life," Tobin answers.

It may be surprising to think of marauding scalp hunters debating the existence of God, but, as if in response to the muteness of his earlier characters, McCarthy's more recent ones engage in lengthy conversations discussing the issues of life and death and God's role in both. As another former priest tells Billy Parham in *The Crossing,* "Men do not turn from God so easily you see. Not so easily. Deep in each man is the knowledge that something knows of his existence. Something knows, and cannot be fled nor hid from. To imagine otherwise is to imagine the unspeakable." He continues:

> Nor does God whisper through the trees. His voice is not to be mistaken. When men hear it they fall to their knees and their souls are riven and they cry out to him and there is no fear in them but only that wildness of heart that springs from such longing and they cry out to stay his presence for they know at once that while godless men may live well enough in their exile those to whom he has spoken can contemplate no life without him but only darkness and despair.

There are godless men aplenty in McCarthy's novels, and many of them are evil, ranging from the three dark ghoulish figures who roam the land of *Outer Dark,* haunting Culla's path, to the "sooty-souled rascal" Judge Holden in *Blood Meridian,* who finally calls the kid to judgment, to the strange Indian who brings violence to Billy Parham's home and sets him journeying in *The Crossing.* But for each man there is always also the possibility of grace. "You think God looks out for people?" Lacey Rawlins asks John Grady Cole in *All the Pretty Horses.* He answers himself, "I do. Way the world is. Somebody can wake up and sneeze somewhere in Arkansas or some damn place and before you're done there's wars and ruination and all hell. You don't know what's going to happen. I'd say he's just about got to. I don't believe we'd make it a day otherwise." Or, as a Mexican bandit tells the kid in *Blood Meridian,* "When the lambs is lost in the mountain. . . . They is cry. Sometime come the mother. Sometime the wolf."

McCarthy's protagonists are most often those who, in their travels, are bereft of the voice of God and yet yearn to hear him speak. This is especially true in the first two volumes of The Border Trilogy. "Long voyages often lose themselves," a traveling actress tells Billy Parham. "The road has its own reasons and no two travelers will have the same understanding of those reasons. If indeed they come to an understanding of them at all. Listen to the *corridos* of the country. They will tell you. Then you will see in your own life what is the cost of things."

The "*corridos,*" the stories of the country: these are the messages, the lessons, the parables McCarthy tells. As a character says in *The Crossing,* "For this world also which seems to us a thing of stone and flower and blood is not a thing at all but is a tale. And all in it is a tale and each tale the sum of all lesser tales and yet these also are the selfsame tale and contain as well all else within them. So everything is necessary. Every least thing. . . . Of the telling there is no end. . . . Rightly heard all tales are one." For both John Grady Cole and Billy Parham, the tale is very much the same, and the "cost of things" unusually high; and by his book's end, each boy seems depleted, shriven, leading one to contemplate their possible meeting in volume three and the consequences of that meeting.

Indeed, rightly seen, all of McCarthy's works take the same journey, tell the same tale, posit the same moral and spiritual questions. Everything is necessary, nothing ever stops moving, and when God speaks, in gift or in blood, all fall to their knees. As the priest tells Billy Parham, "In the end we shall all of us be only what we have made of God. For nothing is real save his grace."

## Jean Richey (review date Winter 1995)

SOURCE: A review of *The Crossing,* in *World Literature Today,* Vol. 69, No. 1, Winter, 1995, pp. 140-141.

[*In the following review, Richey comments on McCarthy's obsession with violence and evil in* The Crossing, *and lauds the author's great descriptive abilities.*]

*The Crossing* is the second novel in Cormac McCarthy's Border Trilogy following *All the Pretty Horses,* which brought this reclusive writer great popular acclaim when it was named the winner of both the National Book Award and the National Book Critics Circle Award and was even optioned for film. Post-*Horses* readers may not realize that McCarthy is not only someone who may possibly be America's greatest descriptive writer but is also an author uniquely obsessed with violence and evil. Sociopaths, serial killers, necrophiliacs, and murderers populate pages wherein mayhem, blood, and generally prevalent malevolence dominate his early works: *The Orchard Keeper, Outer Dark, Child of God, Suttree,* and *Blood Meridian. Blood Meridian* is a culmination of themes and skills, a genuine masterpiece with stunningly visualized landscapes and characters whose evil McCarthy presents as a natural process. This fictional realm is dramatically offset by the sympathetic protagonists in the Border Trilogy.

Like *All the Pretty Horses, The Crossing* is set in the southwestern United States and Mexico, featuring, as does the first novel, rites-of-passage adventures of adolescent boys riding horses into Mexico and finding themselves caring, losing, and learning what the dimensions of life mean. In *The Crossing* Billy Parham makes three trips to Mexico. First he goes to return a she-wolf to a mountain setting where it can survive, but he finds he can protect neither the animal nor his own feelings when Mexicans seize the wolf to fight dogs as entertainment. Next Billy goes back to Mexico with his younger brother Boyd after having returned home to New Mexico to face an existence that has been wiped out when his parents were murdered in his absence. For Billy this foray is to recapture stolen horses, but for fourteen-year-old Boyd the goal is to obtain justice. Billy's third journey into Mexico is to try to find his brother, who had run off with a young Mexican girl. Billy's search ends in a graveyard, where he digs up Boyd's remains to return them to New Mexico for burial.

The events leading up to and including the first Mexican crossing create a wonder of great writing. The story of how Billy comes to respect the wolf and to recognize and love the freedom of its natural state is beautiful and heart-rending:

> He squatted over the wolf and touched her fur. He touched the cold and perfect teeth. The eye turned to the fire gave back no light and he closed it with his thumb and sat by her and put his hand upon her bloodied forehead and closed his own eyes that he could see her running in the mountains, running in the starlight where the grass was wet and the sun's coming as yet had not undone the rich matrix of creatures passed in the night before her.

The second trip, when Billy and Boyd go to Mexico together,

is very much like *All the Pretty Horses* in both narrative and style. In the third part of the novel, often verbose and contrived commentaries substitute for action, dialogue, and reader response. Characters briefly encountered again and again present metaphysical views disguised as personal histories.

McCarthy's metaphysical assumptions are existential. Human consciousness of the past exists within each person in memories and contacts, held in an ongoing meaning by individuals as fragments, subject to loss as memory dims and subject to arbitrary changes without order or meaning. What underlies and transcends personal reality is the natural world, beautifully depicted in the wolf story at the beginning and throughout the book in descriptions of nature. Verbose "tales" told within the main story line are disjunctive; characters whom Billy meets in all sorts of places discourse with the same tones, saying the same things about time, loss, and man's place in the world. Sometimes indeed these characters speak in Spanish—far more often than in *All the Pretty Horses*—but much of the Spanish commentary is paraphrased in English for those many readers who see this work as a western story more than as a merging of realities metaphysical and cultural.

Cormac McCarthy is as good as a writer can be in his use of description, certainly better than any American now living and possibly even better than Faulkner or Melville. He uses this great talent to try to come to terms with the omnipresence of evil in man's nature, as he understands and presents it. Whereas the Border Trilogy has toned down evil incarnate in characters—so fully realized in *Blood Meridian*—these themes are much stronger in *The Crossing* than in *All the Pretty Horses*. McCarthy is obsessed with blood as a symbol of life—both for the living and, in violence, as part of dying. This shows up in repeated references throughout his work relating to the sun, light, shades, reflections, events, et cetera. In earlier works McCarthy was content simply to refer to blood; in *The Crossing* he is in the process of connecting that awareness to his sense of time and man's place in the world. Billy shoots a hawk in one scene and finds a droplet of blood; he then cuts his hand to let the blood drip. This focus on loss and survival as part of living is shifting in McCarthy's style, and readers will be truly interested to see what the final volume in this trilogy will be like.

For McCarthy, blood clearly symbolizes life as a mean end, and for him its connection is constantly threatened by the reality of evil portrayed in violence. The two Border Trilogy novels have shown characters who love and weep and seem to have much in common with that part of the human species not labeled as murderers and evildoers. Once McCarthy works out his own world view about how to narrate these elements, perhaps the excessive lectures that flaw much of the last section of his wonderful new book will not intrude either on his narrative or on readers' responses.

## FURTHER READING

### Criticism

Bell, Vereen M. *The Achievement of Cormac McCarthy.* Baton Rouge: Louisiana State University Press, 1988.
> Criticism and interpretation of McCarthy's works, includes bibliography.

Coles, Robert, ed. *That Red Wheelbarrow: Selected Literary Essays.* Iowa City: University of Iowa Press, 1988, 352 p.
> A collection of essays on various authors that reprints an article originally published in the March 22, 1969, issue of *New Yorker* focusing on the novel *Outer Dark.*

Hall, Wade, and Rick Wallach, editors. *Sacred Violence: A Reader's Companion to Cormac McCarthy.* Texas Western Press, 1995.
> A selection of essays presented at the first McCarthy conference in Louisville, Kentucky, October 15-17, 1993.

Hicks, Granville. Review of *Outer Dark,* by Cormac McCarthy. *Saturday Review* 41, No. 51 (21 December 1968): 22.
> Hicks provides a brief review of *Outer Dark* in which he faults certain parts of McCarthy's "gaudy prose" and praises other parts which he deems "austere and colloquial."

Luce, Diane C., and Edwin T. Arnold, eds. *Perspectives on Cormac McCarthy (Southern Quarterly).* University Press of Mississippi, 1993, 217 p. (Originally printed in *Southern Quarterly* Vol. 30, No. 4, Summer 1992.)
> Ten essays explore the work of McCarthy. Topics include historical and philosophical sources, the moral center of his works, continuities in his fiction, and other aspects. Includes bibliographies.

Phillips, Dana. "History and the Ugly Facts of Cormac McCarthy's *Blood Meridian.*" *American Literature* 68, No. 2 (June 1996): 433-60.
> An essay discussing the influences and forces that shape *Blood Meridian,* and attempts to explore the novel's point of view.

Rudman, Frank. A review of *Suttree. Spectator* 244, No. 7924 (24 May 1980): 21.
> A brief review of *Suttree* in which Rudman praises McCarthy's ear for dialogue, writing ability, and style.

Sepich, John Emil. "The Dance of History in Cormac

McCarthy's *Blood Meridian.*" *The Southern Literary Journal* 24, No. 1 (Fall 1991): 16-31.

This essay examines the historical sources and basis of *Blood Meridian,* and attempts to answer why "the kid" (the protagonist of the novel) is killed at the conclusion.

————"A 'bloody dark pastryman': Cormac McCarthy's Recipe for Gunpowder and Historical Fiction in *Blood Meridian.*" *Mississippi Quarterly* 46, No. 4 (Fall 1993): 547-63.

An essay focusing on the historical basis of *Blood Meridian* and the character of Judge Holden.

Sullivan, Walter. "About Any Kind of Meanness You Can Name." *The Sewanee Review* 93, No. 4 (Fall, 1985): 649-56.

Sullivan compares *Blood Meridian* to Lewis Green's *The Silence of the Snakes* and William Hoffman's *Godfires.*

---

**Additional coverage of McCarthy's life and career is contained in the following sources published by Gale Research:** *Contemporary Authors New Revision Series,* **Vol. 42;** *Dictionary of Literary Biography,* **Vols. 6 and 143; and** *DISCovering Authors Modules: Popular Fiction Module.*

---

# Katherine Anne Porter

## 1890-1980

American short story writer, novelist, essayist, and nonfiction writer.

The following entry provides an overview of Porter's career through 1995. For further information on her life and works, see *CLC,* Volumes 1, 3, 7, 10, 13, 15, and 27.

## INTRODUCTION

Katherine Anne Porter is widely recognized as one of the foremost twentieth-century American writers of short fiction. Noted for her stylistic originality and technical mastery, Porter produced a small but formidable body of work that set new standards of achievement for American fiction. Superior sensitivity, irony, and uncompromising artistry characterize her best work, especially as displayed in *Flowering Judas* (1930), *Pale Horse, Pale Rider* (1939), and *The Leaning Tower and Other Stories* (1944). Porter is distinguished for her penetrating psychological studies and unique feminine perspective, particularly regarding the complexities of love, relationships, and mortality. She won a large popular audience with the publication of her first and only novel, *Ship of Fools* (1962), and received crowning accolades with *The Collected Stories of Katherine Anne Porter* (1964). Often associated with the leading figures of the Southern literary tradition, including William Faulkner, Flannery O'Connor, and Eudora Welty, Porter's meticulously crafted short stories influenced a generation of writers and remain consummate examples of that genre.

### Biographical Information

Born Callie Russell Porter in Indian Creek, a small town in Texas, Porter was the fourth of five children. Her mother died when she was two, upon which the family moved to Hays County to stay with their grandmother until her death in 1901, then resettled in San Antonio where Porter received her education at Thomas boarding school. Her humble origins in the South, frequent dislocations, and the emotional insecurity caused by an inattentive father and the deaths of her mother and grandmother would later find expression in her writing. In 1906 Porter left school and married John Henry Koontz, a railway clerk whose Roman Catholic faith she adopted as her own. This was the first of four marriages that all ended in divorce. Seeking an outlet for her creative aspirations, Porter left Koontz in 1916 and travelled to Chicago to pursue an acting career as Katherine Anne. Shortly thereafter Porter found work on the staff of newspapers in Fort Worth and Denver until suffering a near-fatal bout with in-

fluenza in 1918. This illness, and an earlier episode of tuberculosis, inspired her subsequent fascination with themes of death and rebirth. After a brief residence in New York City and ghostwriting *My Chinese Marriage* (1921), Porter left for Mexico in 1920 where she accumulated valuable new experiences, participated in revolutionary politics, and would remain for extended periods until 1930. She published "Maria Concepción," her first story, in *Century* magazine in 1922, later collected in *Flowering Judas* which, along with *Hacienda* (1934), reflect the lasting influence of her years in Mexico. In 1931 Porter visited Europe with the first of two Guggenheim fellowships where she witnessed Nazi Germany, remarried, and settled in Paris. Upon returning to the United States in 1936, Porter ended this marriage and retreated to Pennsylvania to finish *Noon Wine* (1937). With the publication of *Pale Horse, Pale Rider* and *The Leaning Tower and Other Stories,* Porter received widespread critical recognition. Beset by the constant distraction of university teaching, lectures, and romantic interludes, however, Porter struggled to produce new material. After twenty years of intermittent effort, she published *Ship of Fools* at age seventy-two, the long anticipated novel that became an instant best-seller and was made into a popular film. Four years later she won both a National Book Award and Pulitzer Prize for *The Collected Stories of Katherine Anne Porter.* Porter finished *The Never-Ending Wrong* (1977), an account of the Sacco-Vanzetti affair, three years before her death in Silver Springs, Maryland.

**Major Works**

Porter's short fiction is highly regarded for its remarkable form and style, each work marked by the author's insightful and largely unsentimental renderings of people and places, particularly when set in the American South and Mexico. Porter's interest in family dynamics and the role of women in patriarchal society is recognizable in her earliest writings. *Flowering Judas* contains several stories that feature strong female characters who confront weak or selfish men, as in "Maria Concepción" and "Rope." The title story describes a young woman's threatening involvement with a corrupt Mexican revolutionary who attempts to seduce her with his songs. Here Porter draws on the symbolism of betrayal and evokes an atmosphere of pervasive hostility in which the two main characters indifferently move toward self-destruction, ending in a dream sequence that reveals the woman's deep guilt and fear of death. "The Jilting of Granny Weatherall," another notable story from Porter's first collection, describes a dying woman's unrelenting resentment for the man who left her at the altar much earlier in her life. As in many of her stories, Porter examines marital strife and the female struggle for identity and autonomy, revealing an underlying distrust of love and relationships. In *Hacienda,* Porter creates an ironic and perhaps autobiographical story involving the production of a documentary on Mexican life headed by a Russian communist filmmaker and an American. Reflecting Porter's disillusionment with revolutionary activity in Mexico, an unnamed female narrator describes the awkward and often satirical interaction between natives and Westerners as they attempt to realize the humanitarian and artistic objectives of the project. *Pale Horse, Pale Rider* contains several examples of Porter's best writing, including the title story, "Old Mortality," and "Noon Wine," published separately two years earlier. "Pale Horse, Pale Rider" features Miranda, a familiar character who appears in other stories and is recognized as the author's alter ego. Here Miranda survives a near-fatal illness and experiences haunting dreams that signify her struggle with her own mortality and the death of her boyfriend, Adam, who is prepared to serve in the First World War. Though she recovers, Adam succumbs to the illness, which he himself contracts while nursing her. The story is both highly autobiographic and symbolic, referring to Porter's own severe illness while working as a journalist and the fate of prelapsarian Eden. As in "Flowering Judas," Porter employs dream sequences to enhance the psychological complexity of her characters and to add layers of symbolism. *The Leaning Tower and Other Sto-*

*ries,* inspired by her visit to Europe, contains the balance of Porter's most significant short stories, including "The Old Order," "The Downward Path to Wisdom," and the title story. Almost twenty years passed before she produced her next substantial work of fiction, *Ship of Fools,* a novel based on a fifteenth-century Christian allegory of the same title. Drawing directly from the experiences of her European travels and foreshadowing the atrocities of the Second World War, Porter describes a fictitious voyage to Germany in 1931. The large international cast of characters includes German, American, Mexican, Cuban, and Spanish passengers, presenting a microcosm of world affairs on the eve of Hitler's ascent and the national and religious stereotypes that paved the way. As in much of her fiction, Porter invokes complex symbolism to convey profound irony and psychological profiles of the characters as they continue on their tragic course.

**Critical Reception**

Porter enjoyed generous critical attention and wide popular appeal during her life. Her short stories continue to serve as prime examples of the form she mastered. "Flowering Judas" and "Pale Horse, Pale Rider" are the subject of frequent praise, though agreement as to which of her stories stands in highest regard is inconsistent. Among the various collections and recollections of her fiction, *Flowering Judas, Pale Horse, Pale Rider,* and *The Leaning Tower and Other Stories* contain Porter's most successful and best-known work, gathered together in the award-winning publication *The Collected Stories of Katherine Anne Porter. Ship of Fools,* Porter's most ambitious creative endeavor, was initially hailed as her magnum opus. Upon further consideration, however, the didactic novel became the subject of criticism, particularly directed at Porter's caricatures of Germans and Jews and shallow understanding of the historical and political causes of the Second World War. Despite the shortcomings of her long fiction and relatively small lifetime literary production, Porter's best short fiction has been favorably compared to that of James Joyce and Anton Chekhov. Her acclaimed technical superiority and highly perceptive treatment of women and relationships distinguish her literary reputation and sustain critical interest in her life and work.

# PRINCIPAL WORKS

*My Chinese Marriage* [as M.T.F.] (nonfiction) 1921
*Outline of Mexican Popular Arts and Crafts* (nonfiction) 1922
*Flowering Judas* (short stories) 1930; revised edition published as *Flowering Judas and Other Stories,* 1935
*Hacienda* (novella) 1934
*Noon Wine* (novella) 1937
*Pale Horse, Pale Rider: Three Short Novels* (novellas) 1939
*The Leaning Tower and Other Stories* (short stories) 1944

*The Days Before: Collected Essays and Occasional Writ-
    ings* (essays) 1952; revised edition, 1970
*A Defense of Circe* (nonfiction) 1955
*The Old Order: Stories of the South* (short stories) 1955
*Ship of Fools* (novel) 1962
*The Collected Stories of Katherine Anne Porter* (short sto-
    ries) 1965; revised edition, 1967
*The Never-Ending Wrong* (nonfiction) 1977
*Letters of Katherine Anne Porter* (letters) 1990

# CRITICISM

## *The New York Times Book Review* (review date 28 September 1930)

SOURCE: A review of *Flowering Judas,* in *The New York Times Book Review,* September 28, 1930, p. 6.

[*In the following review, the critic notes the strength of Porter's technical skill and offers brief assessments of each of the short stories in* Flowering Judas.]

Katherine Anne Porter is of that youngest generation of American artists from which one dares hope much. The generation—called "our own generation" by Malcolm Cowley, who is 33 years of age—includes Elizabeth Madox Roberts, Glenway Wescott, Yvor Winters and Kenneth Burke. What distinguishes this group from older groups in American letters—the groups that included Dreiser, Anderson and others—is its working practice of putting nothing creative forward until it has been weighed and polished and given the benefit of a hundred second thoughts. This may be evidence, carefully hidden under the fetish of "discipline," of a lack of creative vitality; but, in any event, it has resulted in a small body of work that is technically perfect. Four of the six stories in *Flowering Judas* are additions to this body of work; they are carefully wrought, devoid of clichés, distinguished for their technical originality. And behind these four stories there is power to feel, a power that is kept always under control. The ardor-in leash of **"Maria Concepción," "Rope," "He"** and **"The Jilting of Granny Weatherall,"** imparts to the stories an intensity that is lacking in much fiction that, superficially, seems more emotional.

One of the stories, **"Rope,"** is wrought out of a simple enough situation. It concerns a period of emotional tension between husband and wife. The wife has a case of "nerves"; she blows up when the husband brings home a useless strand of rope from the village store. The husband has forgotten the coffee; and the piece of rope stands as symbol to the wife of all that she must endure in selfishness and forgetfulness on the part of the male. To the husband, the rope signifies the freedom, the carelessness, that marriage has inevitably curtailed. There is nothing unusual about this situation, but Miss Porter focuses it in an unforgettable way. Her knowledge of the psychology of the situation is uncanny and she brings it out by putting the entire story in indirect discourse. Instead of actual conversation one gets the overtones of conversation. This is far more important than the reporting of speech could possibly be, for we get a series of insinuations, of implications, a sense of things left unsaid, that actual dialogue could not bring out.

Two of the stories, **"Maria Concepción"** and **"Flowering Judas,"** are set in Mexico. They mirror—the first more than the second—a cruelly ardent vision of life that one likes to think of as Mexican. Certainly one gained a similar idea of Mexican character from the stories of D.H. Lawrence. But whatever their spiritual truth, they are distinguished by a scrupulous distinction of phrase. Maria Concepción, for example, walks away from a glimpse of her husband's infidelity with "her ears strumming as if all Maria Rosa's bees had hived in them." When the husband and Maria Rosa leave the village for war, it is to enter a theatre of battle that eventually "unrolled itself, a long scroll of vexations, until the end had frayed out within twenty miles of Juan's village."

**"Flowering Judas"** is less successful than **"Maria Concepción."** It fails because at the end it slips into a dream symbolism that is confused, and the result—which may be the fault of the reader's insensitiveness—is that we get only a confused sense of what the woman, Laura, is like. **"The Jilting of Granny Weatherall"** slips in and out of a dream state with far more convincing reality. In this story, through the distortions and confusions of a dying woman's mind, we get a knowledge of a superb old lady who has lived imperiously and nobly. **"He"** tells the story of the effect of an imbecile son upon a family. It escapes sentimentality by reason of its careful objectivity. The only bad story in *Flowering Judas* is **"Magic,"** which is simply a five-finger exercise on Miss Porter's part.

## Louise Bogan (review date 22 October 1930)

SOURCE: "Flowering Judas," in *The New Republic,* Vol. LXIV, No. 829, October 22, 1930, p. 277-8.

[*In the following review, Bogan praises* Flowering Judas.]

Miss Porter's stories, here collected for the first time, have appeared during a period of some years in Transition, "The American Caravan" and in commercial magazines appreciative of distinguished writing. In each of the five stories in the present book [*Flowering Judas*], Miss Porter works with that dangerous stuff, unusual material. Two stories have a

Mexican locale. Two contain passages which describe lapses into the subconscious and the dream. **"Magic"** briefly explores the survival of frayed but savage superstition. **"Rope"** follows the rise and fall of an hysterical mood, and **"He"** sets against simple human devotion an idiot's non-human power and suffering.

It is to Miss Porter's high credit that, having fixed upon the exceptional background and event, she has not yielded, in her treatment of them, to queerness and forced originality of form. With the exception of **"Magic"** (which I should prefer to think of as an experiment, since its effect is false, for reasons only too easily defined—the use of the fustian maid-to-mistress monologue, for one), the stories do not lean upon the doubtful prop of manner for its own sake. Miss Porter has a range of effects, but each comes through in its place, and only at the demand of her material. She rejects the exclamatory tricks that wind up style to a spurious intensity, and trusts, for the most part, to straightforward writing, to patience in detail and to a thorough imaginative grasp on cause and character. She has "knowledge about reality," and has chosen the most exacting means to carry her knowledge into form.

The fact, and the intuition or logic about the fact, are severe coordinates in fiction. In the short story they must cross with hair-line precision. However far the story may range, the fact and its essence must direct its course and stand as proof to the whole. The truth alone secures form and tone; other means distort the story to no good end and leave within the reader's mind an impression far worse than that produced by mere banality. Joyce's "Ivy Day in the Committee Room" depends wholly upon the truth of the fact; Chekhov's greatest stories, say "The Duel" and "Lights," have command of reasons in the first place, of emotion, taste and style secondarily. The firm and delicate writing in Miss Porter's **"Flowering Judas,"** a story startling in its complexity, were it not based on recognizable fact, would be to no purpose. As it is, its excellence rises directly from the probity of the conception. It is as impossible to question the characters of the fanatical girl and the self-loving man—the "good revolutionist," who, softened to a state beyond principle, is fit only for a career—as it is to find a flaw or lapse in the style that runs clear and subtle, from the story's casual beginning to the specter of life and death at the end. **"Rope,"** after **"Flowering Judas,"** is perhaps the most remarkable story in the book. It makes no claim; its integration becomes apparent only when the reader tries to recount it to himself in any other form than its own. The mood is put together so accurately that its elements cannot be recombined.

**"Maria Concepción"** does not entirely come up to Miss Porter's standard. A slight flavor of details brought in for their own sake mars its intensity, and one does not entirely trust Maria's simplicity of motive. For the most part, how-

ever, the stories in *Flowering Judas* can claim kinship with the order of writing wherein nothing is fortuitous, where all details grow from the matter in hand simply and in order. Miss Porter should demand much work of her talent. There is nothing quite like it, and very little that approaches its strength in contemporary writing.

### Charles A. Allen (essay date Summer 1956)

SOURCE: "Katherine Anne Porter: Psychology as Art," in *Southwest Review*, Vol. XLI, No. 3, Summer, 1956, pp. 223-30.

[*In the following essay, Allen examines psychological devices and symbolism employed by Porter to illustrate hostility and frustration.*]

Katherine Anne Porter has published, as her admirers announce apologetically, three slim volumes of stories and novellas. A half-dozen of her stories equal the best written by any twentieth-century American. Usually her theme is the betrayal of life through the hostility that develops if physical and social needs are repeatedly and consistently frustrated.

**"The Downward Path to Wisdom,"** included in *The Leaning Tower* (1944), is one of her best stories. And it is her most elaborate study of hostility, largely because the origin of the hostility is explored in detail. Whereas most of her work begins with the fact of adult hostility, **"The Downward Path"** indicates how the adult has been molded to an aggressive pattern as a child—a central vision of contemporary psychology.

**"The Downward Path to Wisdom"** shows how the child Stephen is made uncomfortable and guilty about his body, uncomfortable and guilty about his social relationships. The adult failure to give the four-year-old boy understanding and love takes many forms in the story, varying from forthright rejection, such as the father exhibits in the opening pages, to the inconsistencies of attitude (alternate concern and dismissal) revealed by the grandmother and mother.

Hostility, caused by the frustration of social and physical needs, always expresses itself, sometimes directly, usually indirectly. The expression may take the form of immediate and open aggression, as it does when Stephen dashes his dish against the floor. Or, if the frustration is not released if it is turned inward, it breeds anxiety, feelings of inadequacy and depression or of confusion and fear. Often anxiety takes a physical or somatic form. Pushed out of his parents' bedroom, Stephen "hurt all over." Accused of stealing a lemon and a few balloons, he wishes "he might go to sleep"; but it would "be wrong to go to sleep while Uncle David was still talking." Escape through sleep blocked, Stephen forces himself to listen to Uncle David's harangue, "but the sounds were strange and floating just over his head."

The anxious person always attempts to defend himself against his uncomfortable feelings of tension. A possible defense for Stephen is sleep, but as this is "wrong" and no doubt dangerous, he becomes listless, inattentive, really half asleep. He has adopted a simple defense, lethargy, to make his anxious tension more bearable, less threatening. But his tension has simply been shifted—it has not been dissipated. The meaning of **"The Downward Path"** is found in the genesis of hostility and its expressions in anxiety and defense. In scene after scene, one or more of these elements are brought into sharp view, dramatized, elaborated through repetition to produce the final unity of statement: aggression is instilled into the child by his family. At the key moment of the story Stephen says: "I don't want to go home. I want to go to school. I don't want to see Papa, I don't like him." Mama lays her hand over his mouth: "Darling, don't." A little later, at the moment of climax, Stephen, through the pressures of hostile adults, is forced to

> a quiet, inside song so Mama would not hear. He sang his new secret; it was a comfortable, sleepy song: "I hate Papa, I hate Mama, I hate Grandma, I hate Uncle David, I hate Old Janet, I hate Marjory, I hate Papa, I hate Mama. . ."

Before he is much older, Stephen will be incapable of such an honest admission. He will gradually build up unconscious feelings of love and hostility for his elders, become anxiously guilty about these conflicting feelings, and in consequence grow to hate both himself and the world.

Although **"The Downward Path"** is an accurate study of the genesis of hostility, the story is in some respects defective. The primary weakness is the portrayal of Grandma, who can be, and frequently is, misread as a harmless, even loving victim of her quarreling and hostile children. For Grandma is simply photographed; the author's studied refusal to judge the significance of her words and acts forces the burden of judgment entirely on the reader. Unless he knows a good deal of contemporary psychological theory, the burden is apt to be a little heavy.

**"The Downward Path"** demonstrates that Miss Porter knows the genesis of hostility. Yet, in most of her work, she is unwilling to dramatize her knowledge. One might insist that she is not obliged, any more than was Hawthorne or Henry James, to reveal the origin of adult hostility. But her omission is a little disappointing, since her artistic intention is heavily dependent upon psychological validity; and it is especially disappointing when she interprets adult hostility as

simply the result of adult frustration, as she does in **"The Cracked Looking-Glass."**

**"The Cracked Looking-Glass"** sings of frustrated love and its resultant defensive behavior. Why ever did Rosaleen marry a man thirty years her elder, what childhood insecurity prompted such an act? Rosaleen is a handsome Irish woman, proud of her looks and vitality, and filled with a need for a younger man's love. Most of the time she manages to conceal her frustration by compulsive talking and daydreaming; in consequence she can hardly distinguish, in her vanity and need for attention, between the real and the unreal. As she concocts romantic visions of the past or future, she weeps in gentle self-pity; as she contemplates her neighbors, who are likely to be un-Christian "natives" or "foreigners," she self-righteously preens her own virtue. Unable to escape her plight, she lives on the food of quixotic hope and imagination.

The portrait of Rosaleen is both complex and vigorous. Its strength derives from a skilful use of incremental repetition; the firm establishment of such compulsive personality motifs as talking, crying, weeping, dreaming; and the probing of these traits by qualification, redefinition, and elaboration. But language is almost as important as method. Controlling metaphors simultaneously describe the scene and allude obliquely to personality traits, conscious and unconscious.

Although the story is largely Rosaleen's, Dennis is also roundly developed. He is impatient of his wife's noisy theatricality and just as prone to self-pity as she, all of which enriches the humor and allows the author to maintain an attitude compounded of gentle irony and wry sympathy. The tone, the method of incremental repetition, and the use of metaphor demonstrate the character and largely make the structure and meaning. This is the pattern most frequently found in Miss Porter's work, one which depends very little on the use of symbol. In fact, a cracked looking-glass which distorts Rosaleen's image in such a way as to imply the grotesquerie of her defenses is the only important symbolic element in the story.

**"María Concepción"** is similar to **"A Cracked Looking-Glass"** in language and method. The subject of **"María"** is a Mexican Indian village, a "primitive" village in which the feelings of love and hostility run close to the surface. More specifically the subject is María: her marriage, her desertion, her jealous suffering, her murder of her rival in love, her exoneration by her husband and the villagers, and her fulfillment as a mother. Miss Porter succeeds in making the village and María synonymous by letting them represent elemental life struggling to survive and propagate the race. It is an old and simple theme, but dramatized with force and clarity.

The theme does not demand, as does that of **"The Down-ward Path,"** an interpretation of unconscious motivations. Yet in their actions all the characters are hostile, and explo-ration of the origins of María's hostility might have produced a more satisfying piece. In fact, the author's attitude toward her secondary characters—a delicate balance of admiration, irony, and compassion—is a perfect instrument for a light probing of unconscious motivations.

The story's vigor depends primarily on the originality and use of image. Image is responsible for atmosphere: an atmo-sphere of sharply contrasted darkness and bright color, and of dust (death). And image is used to dramatize María's feel-ings, as in the sentence, "She burned [in jealousy and hu-miliation] all over now, as if a layer of tiny fig-cactus bristles, as cruel as spun glass, had crawled under her skin." The last paragraph of the story is perhaps the finest example of such imagistic statement of emotion.

**"The Jilting of Granny Weatherall"** introduces a method more dependent on the use of symbol than on that of image, a method encountered only three times in Miss Porter's work. The novella *Pale Horse, Pale Rider* is a confused and ob-scure attempt. **"Flowering Judas"** and **"The Jilting of Granny Weatherall"** are successful in their use of densely packed symbolic connotations.

The subject of **"The Jilting"** is one woman's experience with death. Granny is unprepared: her will unmade, her love let-ters undestroyed. Pestered by doctor and priest, by the imagi-nary but vexing whispering of her daughter Cornelia, she clings desperately to her final hope: immortality and God's love. As the thin flame of life and frantic hope wanes, she is engulfed by an infinity of blackness—betrayed by God as she has been betrayed by life.

For, as we learn during Granny's final hours, she has weath-ered much in her desperate search for love. As a young woman, she loves George, but is frustrated when he fails to appear for the wedding. In shame and humiliation and spite-ful pride she marries John, whom she dutifully serves, even in the long years after his death, by nurturing his four chil-dren and by managing efficiently the economy of household and farm. But, without awareness, she is serving mainly her lost lover. Fearfully, her conscious mind repeats: "Find George. Find him and be sure to tell him I forgot him. I want him to know I had my husband just the same and my children and my house like any other woman. . . . Tell him I was given back everything he took away and more." In her delirium the repressed unconscious floods to the surface. Her youngest child is named Hapsy, the child who "should have been born first, for it was the one she had truly wanted." Hapsy is symbolically equated with George, with George's child, with herself—in brief, with true love, the truly loving family.

It was Hapsy she really wanted. She had to go a long way back through a great many rooms to find Hapsy standing with a baby on her arm. She seemed to her-self to be Hapsy also, and the baby on Hapsy's arm was Hapsy and himself and herself, all at once, and there was no surprise in the meeting. Then Hapsy melted from within and turned flimsy as gray gauze and the baby was a gauzy shadow, and Hapsy came up close and said, "I thought you'd never come," and looked at her very searchingly and said, "You haven't changed a bit!" They leaned forward to kiss, when Cornelia began whispering from a long way off, "Oh, is there anything you want to tell me? Is there anything I can do for you?"

The key to this passage is found in the phrases "gray gauze" and "gauzy shadow," and the word *whispering*. Gray is a frequently repeated motif, emblematic of fear and betrayal and frustration. Gray is the color of threatening fog and smoke; and gray is George's color, for he is literally "the smoke of hell." And so when Hapsy says, "I thought you'd never come,... you haven't changed a bit!" the reader knows that Hapsy is now symbolic of Granny and George speaking in unison. The kiss that follows is broken by Cornelia's *whis-pering* the world's knowledge of Granny's humiliation and failure. This moment of illumination is even more impres-sive when one recalls that poor, misused Hapsy is later imag-ined by Granny to be standing by the bed "in a white cap." "Cornelia, tell Hapsy to take off her cap. I can't see her plain." Whiteness is a heavily laden symbol (the white wedding cake, uncut; the white wedding veil, unlifted) which represents fear, betrayal, humiliation, frustrated love. In other words Hapsy, like George, is ambivalently loved and hated.

Thus the method of the story depends upon an incremental repetition of images, individual images which are gradually endowed with dense symbolic meaning. There are, in addi-tion to the images of gray and white, the images of light (lamps, candles, matches) which mean security, love, order, and life itself. There is the image of dark (night) which rep-resents fear and death. There are the images of water (puddles, damp hands, perspiration, cold water) which mean "clammy death." Such symbolistic images, and a few less obvious but related ones, "float" down the corridors of Granny's haunted mind. At times they stand in sharp isolation, at times they coalesce to symbolize the key facts of Granny's personality: frustration, anxiety, and defense. This symbolistic method brilliantly explores the complex theme of betrayal; for Granny has been betrayed not only by her hope for secular and di-vine love but also by compulsive efforts to believe in her rigidly "ordered" service to the family.

Most of Miss Porter's best work is found in the first edition (1930) of *Flowering Judas.* The title story is an exploration of hostility which beautifully merges all the elements of symbol, tone, atmosphere, point of view, language, character, and theme.

Laura teaches young Indian children (the setting is Mexico) during the day and works for Braggioni's revolution by night. For a month of evenings, as the story opens, she has resisted "tenaciously without appearing to resist" the "slow drift" of Braggioni's destructive intention: Laura fascinatedly recognizes the threat not only of seduction but also of murder. She opposes Braggioni through flattery, plays on "the vast cureless wound of his self-esteem" by allowing him night after night "to sing passionately off key" as he "scratches the guitar familiarly, as though it were a pet animal." As he sits before her inviolable detachment, Laura "notes again that his eyes are the true tawny yellow cat's eyes." Braggioni is both cruel and ominous. "Laura feels a slow chill, a purely physical sense of danger, a warning in her blood that violence, mutilation, a shocking death, wait for her with lessening patience."

Throughout the story the author maintains this atmosphere of threat. Both Laura and Miss Porter view the possibility of catastrophe with a consistent irony. There is an admirable fusion of tone and atmosphere—a fusion which flashes with a sparkling density of impressionistic image, an easy combination of colloquial and formal idiom, a rush of precise action verbs qualified by contradictory adjectives and adverbs. Language, atmosphere, and tone merge, and it is the fine control of these elements in combination with symbolic and mythic references which largely accounts for the richness of connotation and unity of effect.

As Ray B. West, Jr. has demonstrated (in an article in *Accent*), religious, material (machine), and love symbols are extremely important in the characterization of Braggioni, Eugenio, and Laura and for the thematic implications of the story. Braggioni is a callous Christ: "A hungry world saviour," "punctured in honorable warfare," "a professional lover of humanity." Laura is a Waste Land figure, a female model of Eliot's Gerontion, without "sight, smell, hearing, taste, and touch," incapable therefore of passion and love, divine or human. "'It may be true I am as corrupt, in another way, as Braggioni,' she thinks in spite of herself, 'as callous, as incomplete,'" and if this is so, any kind of death seems preferable." This is a key sentence; it implies the central meaning. Laura and Braggioni are hostile beings, incomplete in different ways, but both lost, incapable of faith and love.

Braggioni is bent on dynamiting the world; Laura is unconsciously determined to dynamite herself, for she is conspiring with Braggioni to bring about her own death. When Braggioni leaves her at the end of the first scene, having temporarily laid aside his slow intention under the pressure of an aroused vision of destruction, Laura realizes the possibility of freedom: "I must run while there is time." Yet she

does not go. Fearing death, she is ambivalently frozen in a death yearning. In brief, Laura has turned her aggression inward, and Braggioni has focused his outward. This is the difference between them, this and the fact that Laura, unlike Braggioni, can see herself with an entirely clear vision.

To dramatize Braggioni's lack of insight into his own hostility is, I imagine, the primary purpose of the brief second part of the story, the episode which shows Braggioni returned to his wife after a month's absence. She accepts him gratefully and washes his feet. Mr. West, with Christ still in mind, gives the foot washing a significance of purification ritual, and suggests that Braggioni, touched by pity for his weeping wife, is capable of love and redemption. I am unable to accept such a reading.

There is little reason to believe that the foot-washing ceremony is anything more than a matter of Laura's satiric (and envious) vision of Braggioni's homecoming. Whether the scene is read as an act of Laura's imagination (as I believe it should be) or is presented from the point of view of omniscient author or observer-reader, Miss Porter succeeds in emphasizing the main difference between Braggioni and Laura. Because Laura sees through him as perceptively as she sees through herself, one might hazard a guess that Laura's redemption is more nearly possible than Braggioni's. Not only protagonist, she promises to become heroine!

In any event, this second scene recapitulates the "vast wound of self-esteem," a wound which is a delicate and dangerous equilibrium of self-pity, theatricality, selfishness, opportunism, and sadism, exactly the traits Braggioni exhibits earlier in the story.

The final scene, the dream vision, highlights Laura's ambivalent fear of and desire for death and her guilt feelings about her betrayal of herself and the world. The ghost of Eugenio offers her guidance to death:

> No, said Laura, not unless you take my hand. Then eat these flowers, poor prisoner, said Eugenio in a voice of pity, take and eat: and from the Judas tree he stripped the warm bleeding flowers, and held them to her lips. She saw that his hand was fleshless, a cluster of small white petrified branches, and his eye sockets were without light, but she ate the flowers greedily for they satisfied both hunger and thirst. Murderer! said Eugenio, and Cannibal! This is my body and my blood. Laura cried No! and at the sound of her own voice, she awoke trembling, and was afraid to sleep again.

Laura's "one holy talismanic word" throughout is *no*, not only *no* to the Braggioni-revolutionary situation (one, ironically enough, which she justifiably negates), but *no* to *any* situation involving faith, love, and life itself. This is the final meaning of Laura's hostility, of her entranced death impulse. This death drive is repeatedly emphasized, and because of it there is the clear implication that Laura will not remove herself from the "ominous" grasp of Braggioni. The atmosphere of threat and danger which is so central to the structure of the narrative is a reality, a reality which Laura clearly perceives and which she is unconsciously bending to her obsessed need for annihilation. In her hostile depression she will continue to betray life as she waits for the "hungry world-saviour" to cart her to his "feeding trough."

**"Hacienda"** is a fast-paced, charming comedy of manners. The setting is Mexico; the time is any year of the 1920's or 1930's. Although the first-person observer is not named, she is obviously the autobiographical protagonist who is later to be named Miranda.

In the first scene the observer, whom I shall call Miranda, is guest of Andreyev, a Russian Communist movie-maker; and of Kennerly, a rigid, opinionated American who hates the disorder, dirt, and disease of Mexico as much as the incomprehensible Mexicans. The men are returning to an hacienda to continue their work on a documentary film of Mexican life. The scene is designed primarily to contrast the confused Kennerly with a trainload of stoical natives. A tone of mischievous mockery is brilliantly sustained in this opening section, as it is throughout. It is a tone that directs its skepticism toward the frailties of native as well as Western culture. Although Miss Porter is more sympathetic with the Indians than with the Europeans and Americans, one of her major themes is that both of the cultures are sick.

As the story progresses, Kennerly, overwhelmed by too many chocolates and too much beer, falls asleep, thus giving Andreyev an opportunity to expatiate on the Mexican character, the film project, and life at the hacienda of Doña Julia and Don Genaro. Life has been quite unpredictable at the hacienda, what with all the difficulties with the Mexican censors and Doña Julia's infatuation with her husband's mistress, Lolita; but when an Indian boy from the hacienda boards the train to announce that two Indian lead characters in the unfinished film are in grave trouble, one is prepared for still more difficulty and excitement. For Justino has shot and killed his sister Rosalia—they have accomplished line for line in real life a scene they had played for the film a couple of weeks before! Ah, poor Rosalia, poor Justino! And how can the film now be completed?

Arriving at the hacienda, Miranda quickly meets her hosts and a half-dozen other lost characters. Betancourt is supercilious and mean in a hundred petty ways; a favorite target of his malice is the song writer, his old friend Carlos Montaña. Stepanov looks with contempt on everything but billiards and other sport. Uspensky has "a monkey attitude towards

life": "'Ah, yes, I remember,' he said gallantly, on meeting some southern women, 'you are the ladies who are always being raped by those dreadful negroes!'" Don Genaro finds his meaning in mad, exhibitionistic charges across the landscape: "speed and lightness at great expense was his ideal." Almost anything "exciting" pleases Doña Julia, especially flirtations and love affairs—and sweetmeats. The hacienda overseer epitomizes the emptiness and ridiculousness of all the characters:

> The Spanish overseer, who had been cast for the rôle of villain—one of them—in the film, came out wearing a new pair of tight riding trousers, of deerskin and silver embroidery, like the saddles, and sat slouched on the long bench near the arch, facing the great corral where the Indians and soldiers were. There he sat nearly all day, as he had sat for years and might sit for years more. His long wry North-Spanish face was dead with boredom . . . [he] had already forty pairs of fancy charro trousers, but had thought none of them quite good enough for the film and had caused to be made, at great expense, the pair he was now wearing, which were entirely too tight. He hoped by wearing them every day to stretch them. He was miserable, entirely, for his trousers were all he had to live for, anyhow. "All he can do with his life," said Andreyev, "is to put on a different pair of fancy trousers every day, and sit on that bench hoping that something, anything, may happen."

"Action was their defense against the predicament they were in, all together . . ." This is, I think, the main theme—a point which the author presses against both cultures.

Here in **"Hacienda"** is exquisite satire on one aspect of the "catastrophe of our time": the defensive need in the absence of faith and love to seek self-importance through compulsive activity for activity's sake—especially activity which is rationalized in terms of humanitarian symbols. Like the best of Hemingway's and Faulkner's work, the best of Miss Porter's carries a subtle humanistic implication: man's first duty is to understand himself rather than to try to save the world.

## Stanley Kaufmann (review date 2 April 1962)

SOURCE: "Katherine Anne Porter's Crowning Work," in *The New Republic*, Vol. 146, No. 2474, April 2, 1962, pp. 23-5.

[*In the following review, Kaufmann cites shortcomings in*

Ship of Fools, *particularly concerning theme and character development.*]

Katherine Anne Porter has published her first novel at the age of 72, and since she spent 20 years on it, we must assume it will be her only novel. She forecast the book in 1940 in the preface to the Modern Library edition of *Flowering Judas:*

> [These stories] are fragments of a much larger plan I am still engaged in carrying out. . . . All the conscious and recollected years of my life have been lived to this day under the heavy threat of world catastrophe, and most of the energies of my mind and spirit have been spent in the effort to grasp the meaning of those threats, to trace them to their sources and to understand the logic of this majestic and terrible failure of the life of man in the Western world.

Here at last is the fruit of the effort. **Ship of Fools,** whose title is taken from a 15th-Century German allegory, is so complex that it must be described briefly. It narrates the voyage of a German passenger ship from Vera Cruz, first to Havana, then to some European ports, and finally to Bremerhaven in August, 1931. The large cast of characters includes several German couples and individuals; a Swiss family; several Mexicans; two young American artist-lovers, an American divorcée, an American engineer; a troupe of Spanish dancers; a group of Cuban medical students; the captain and the ship's doctor; a Swede; and a Spanish countess deported from Cuba. In steerage there is a mass-character: 876 Spanish workers being returned from Cuba—men and women—who sicken, fight, murder, and give birth below decks during the crossing. About 30 of the first-class passengers are principals in the story.

The formal symbolism is so patent and so "very old" (as Miss Porter says in her foreword) that it is a quickly assumed bond between her and us. Her use of "this simple almost universal image of the ship of the world on its voyage to eternity" tells us that she is too concerned with large issues to devise small novelties. Its familiarity helps to place her work in a historical continuum and helps the reader to focus on content rather than form.

The first point basic to an understanding of this novel is the significance of its date: August, 1931. The United States was writhing in the Depression. Latin America was erupting through a 400-year-old crust of Castilian cruelty. To name the two European countries relevant to this book, in Germany the Nazi Party had leaped from 800 thousands votes (1928) to 6.4 million votes (1930); in Spain the Bourbons had been deposed, and the country had been made an arena for fratricidal left factions whose quarrels eventually invited

the Falange. In short, Western man was beginning to run the fever that resulted in the collapse of a society founded on Judeo-Christian ideals. Five thousand years of ethical monotheism, two thousand years of compassionate saviorism had produced a 20th Century that began with a world war and Fascism; now it was hastening towards Nazism and a vaster war. The seal was soon to be set on the fact that this particular spiritual and moral effort of the human race had not succeeded; that the relics of outward forms and *nostalgie de dieu* were no proof otherwise; and that another way must be found. Midsummer 1931 is a good place to mark the start of the last great landslide; what was always latent begins here to be visible.

The second basic point is a truth often obscured by Miss Porter's reputation as a writer concerned with sensibility and subtlety. She is a social-political artist as well. *Flowering Judas* and *Hacienda* are examples of this, as is the novella that is the clearest antecedent of the present book: *The Leaning Tower,* which deals with a young American painter in Berlin in 1931. In life as well as art Miss Porter has not been immured in ivory. Apropos of Jenny, this novel's young American painter ("She had picketed dozens of times . . . and had been in jail several times"), it can be noted that Miss Porter was arrested as a Sacco-Vanzetti picket in Boston in 1926. Throughout her life the spheres represented by the novels of Virginia Woolf and of Malraux have concerned her simultaneously.

It would be easy and superfluous to ticket each of this novel's characters. The doctor, duel-scarred and Catholic, represents what is traditional, proud, reticent in Germany; the young American pair represent the license for neurosis inherent in the New World's liberalism. And so on. As for the principal events: the grotesque flirtation between Herr Rieber and Lizzi Spoeckenkieker represents the sexually and socially frustrated elements that surged to support Nazism; the carnival masks are the truth about the maskers; the births in steerage en route symbolize the persistence and growth of the vindictive proletariat. All this, like her use of the ship image, is patent. Miss Porter has set no puzzles to be solved; the microcosmic symbols in her novel are crystalline.

It is more pertinent to discuss the book's achievements with those symbols. In substantial part this, unfortunately, means discussing its shortcomings, for, to me, the book is a disappointment. This was inevitable, of course. No book by any mere human being could be awaited as long and as fervently as Miss Porter's novel and then fulfill all expectations. But it is more of a disappointment than allowance for mortality explains.

To begin where any novel first meets us, before themes or characters are manifest: its style. Recently I re-read all four of Miss Porter's collections, and I understand Edmund

Wilson's bafflement about commenting on their style: "a surface so smooth that the critic has little opportunity to point out peculiarities of color or weave." The style is neither stunning nor in itself poignant; it is inconspicuous at the same time that it serves the highest demands. It can rarely be quoted for itself, yet is rarely banal.

---

**[Porter's] style is neither stunning nor in itself poignant; it is inconspicuous at the same time that it serves the highest demands. It can rarely be quoted for itself, yet is rarely banal.**

*—Stanley Kaufmann*

---

But in the novel there is a small yet radical change of texture, more of an enameled richness with paradoxical lapses which, like cracks in a table, reveal the veneer; and (to shift metaphors) for all the faintly plummy diet, there is a certain lack of sustenance. Its general feeling as against her past work, is one of somewhat more labor and slightly less certainty. No excerpts can adequately convey the effect of Miss Porter's prose, but these passages from the description of La Condesa may be some indication of what I mean. "She was slender except for a lazy little belly, and her clothes were very expensive-looking." The first half is masterly, the second is commonplace and involuted. Why not "looked expensive?" It is at least simpler. "On her right [hand] she wore what appeared to be a light-colored much-flawed emerald." The implication of "what appeared to be" is misleading; in the event the sentence would be both cleaner and more accurate with the phrase deleted. "These hands, very narrow, fine, heavily veined and old-looking, were in constant movement." Besides the excess of "very" and "looking" in one paragraph, why not "moved constantly"?

This is not to apply the marking-methods of a composition class to a distinguished writer. Only because she has been so exceptional a stylist does the prose of the present book seem less pure—moderately ornate with the attendant penalties of ornament. If previously there were few quotable master strokes, there were also few heavinesses.

There is no central character. Because Jenny, the American painter, seems in some measure autobiographical, we suspect at the beginning that she is the pivot of the book, but this does not turn out to be so. The book's view is impartial, divine. The tapestry structure that Miss Porter has chosen— the frequent interweaving of numerous character and narrative strands—is a difficult one to handle at such length. As far as transitions are concerned, Miss Porter manages it well—which is to say that, in a sense, she ignores the problem. She lets her interest in the next character she approaches take the reader with her. Only when she uses vaguely cinematic methods (we are "inside" A and walk past B; we then go "inside" B and watch A walk past), when she is worried about a transition and draws our attention to it by using a device, only then is there a slight jar. Otherwise this rigorous structural juggling is well executed.

The snare of this method, which Miss Porter by no means escapes, is compulsive rotation. After A and B have been absent for a while, Miss Porter returns to them, subjectively, whether or not she has anything to add to their portraits or has new action in which to involve them. She gives them further scenes merely to keep them alive for the reader, which leads to considerable repetition and duplication.

This duplication underscores a kinetic lack in the book. The characters are well perceived and described, but we know all that Miss Porter has to say about most of them after the third or fourth of their episodes. We know that Jenny and David are going to quarrel, although they would like to love each other; that Denny, the engineer, is going to be stupidly vulgar; that Frau Rittersdorf is going to write stuffily in her journal; that Professor and Frau Hutten are going to behave like George Grosz characters. Once they are established, there is little development of them in depth and only for a few of them has Miss Porter devised modest narrative. At the end the doctor knows more about himself as a result of his encounter with La Condesa; Freytag, the German with the Jewish wife, sees his position more clearly; perhaps the American couple are a little wiser about each other. As for the others, barring a few mild adventures for some, they are pretty much where they were in the first half of the novel. Although we have recognized them all very early as valid human beings, we are not much illuminated past what we initially recognize. The book is a portrait gallery, not the morality play or allegory it promises to be.

This fact—that we are given a cross-section of European and American characters and characteristics rather than a progressively meaningful drama—takes us to the largest criticism that must be made of the work.

The sign of a masterpiece (and surely Miss Porter's novel must be judged as masterpiece or no) is the creation of extra life; under such analyzable matters as style, structure, character there is a deep oceanic swell. It is a supra-real effect, the bright intangible circle made by the spinning tangible wheel. That effect is not made here; always we see only the hub, spokes, rim. We can see how (generally) well made the novel is and well written, how well observed in terms of surface and immediately sub-surface elements; but the most we ever get from it is magnified recognition, never extension or exaltation. Partially this may be because Miss Porter, unlike Tolstoy, Stendhal, Malraux, sees no further into the heart of the several intrinsic mysteries than we do, thus can only set down more superbly than we could what is more or less common knowledge. There are other reasons, too.

One does not quite presume to tell Miss Porter how she could have achieved profundity, but it is possible to point out a few ways in which she cut herself off from it. First: two-thirds of her principal characters are German, and with the exception of the doctor—who, doomed by heart trouble, is an enforced philosopher—they are uniformly repulsive. Sometimes this repulsiveness is imposed with black-board-and-pointer observations: "The Captain, from his eminence of perfectly symmetrical morality, a man who steered by chart and compass, secure in his rank in an ascending order of superiors so endless the highest was unknown, invisible to him, took deep pleasure in his apocalyptic vision of the total anarchic uproar of the United States, a place he had never seen. . . ." Mostly it is evoked with conventional accurate touches: creases of fat on the back of the neck, smug *gemutlichkeit,* sentimentality about animals. ("'Go away, get out,' commanded Herr Rieber . . . but because Bébé wore a hairy hide and was on all fours he was therefore sacred, there was no question of using sterner measures.") All through the book run prognoses of Nazi action: Nuremberg laws, gas chambers, euthanasia, world conquest. Although all of it is true enough, it is hardly completely representative of Carl von Ossietzky's country; and it turns the book into something of a thirty-year-old anti-German tract.

Second, a similar point, the only Jew in the book is Herr Loewenthal, who is a believable character: whining, aggressive, fearful, the product of the centuries' ghettos. (The scene in which Freytag is forced to sit at table with him for the first time is a small gem of misadventure.) Miss Porter, I think, wanted to use Loewenthal's cringing behavior with his cabinmate and others as a foretaste of the fact that still staggers young Israelis: that German Jews rarely resisted their oppressors. But as her group of Germans is too unrelievedly dark, so her single Jew gives too mean and sullen a picture. (Freytag's wife is described otherwise, but she is not present as a force in the book.)

These two criticisms merge in a greater issue. Miss Porter is writing of the "majestic and terrible failure" of Western man, but all one can feel on finishing this book is that if this is Western man, it is high time that he failed and there is little majesty or terror in it. As with the Germans and Jews, on a larger scale her portrait is incomplete if she meant Western man, entire, to be her protagonist. There is scant hint in it of what makes his failure worth regret, scant trace of lost possibilities of grandeur. The book is thus less tragic than satiric; but satire about a huge complex of civilizations ceases to be satire and becomes misanthropy.

One does not urge a more sanguine view on Miss Porter; this

in only to note some of the elements that keep us from the edge of the abyss she presumably wanted to show us. In his monograph on her four previous books, Harry John Mooney, Jr. writes of her autobiographical character, Miranda, and of Upton, the hero of *The Leaning Tower:* "Both Miranda's tragedy and Charles Upton's horror spring from contemporary history; they are the result of those hostile elements, only dimly perceived in the order of the world, which spell death for the individual plan for happiness." There is little of this tragedy or horror for any of the characters in this novel. Either they are satisfied with the world or (like the dancers) contemptuous of it or (like Jenny) flirtatious with its responsibilities. The title of the book becomes more literal than figurative, and the whole effect is smaller than we anticipated from Miss Porter's crowning work.

## M. M. Liberman (essay date Fall 1966)

SOURCE: "The Responsibility of the Novelist: The Critical Reception of *Ship of Fools,*" in *Criticism,* Vol. VIII, No. 4, Fall, 1966, pp. 377-88.

[*In the following essay, Liberman examines the critical reception of* Ship of Fools *and considers the essential characteristics of the novel as a literary form.*]

The title of this essay is, I suppose, somewhat misleading, in the way that a title can be, when it seems to promise a discourse on an arguable concept. In this instance it suggests a certain premise: namely, that the question, "What does the author owe society?" is one which still lives and breathes. In fact, I think it does not. I suspect, rather, that its grave can be located somewhere between two contentions: Andre Gide's that the artist is under no moral obligation to present a useful idea, but that he is under a moral obligation to present an idea well; and Henry James's, that we are being arbitrary if we demand, to begin with, more of a novel than that it be interesting. As James uses the word *novel* here, I take it to mean any extended, largely realistic, narrative fiction, but his view is applicable as well to fiction in other forms and modes.

If a literary work is more than immediately engaging; if for example, it stimulates the moral imagination, it is doing more than is fairly required of it as art.

Why, then, if I think it is in most respects dead, do I choose to raise the question of the writer's responsibility? The answer is that I do not choose to raise the question. The question is continually being raised for me, and because literature is my profession, it haunts my house. Thus, I am moved to invoke certain commonplaces, as above, of a sort I had supposed to be news only to sophomore undergraduates. This was the case markedly on the occasion of the publication of Katherine Anne Porter's *Ship of Fools* in 1962. Twenty years in the making, a book club selection even before it was set up in type, restlessly awaited by a faithful coterie, reviewed widely and discussed broadly almost simultaneously with its appearance on the store shelves, this book caused and still causes consternation in the world of contemporary letters to a degree which I find interesting, curious and suspect. The focus of this paper will be on the critical reception of this book and I hope that the relevance of what remains of the responsibility question will issue naturally from it. Finally, I must quote at awkward length, in two instances, in order to be fair to other commentators.

The first brief wave of reviews were almost unanimous in their praise of *Ship of Fools* and then very shortly the many dissenting opinions began to appear, usually in the most respectable intellectual journals where reviewers claim to be, and often are, critics. These reviews were characterized by one of two dominant feelings: bitter resentment or acute disappointment. A remarkable instance of the former appeared in the very prestigious journal, *Commentary* (October, 1962) as its feature article of the month, under the byline of one of its associate editors. That Miss Porter's book should have been originally well-received so rankled *Commentary*'s staff that a lengthy rebuttal was composed, taking priority over other articles on ordinarily more pressing subjects, such as nuclear destruction and race violence. The article progresses to a frothing vehemence in its later pages. I will quote from the opening of the piece which begins relatively calmly, as follows:

> Whatever the problems were that kept Katherine Anne Porter's *Ship of Fools* from appearing during the past twenty years, it has been leading a charmed life ever since it was published last March. In virtually a single voice, a little cracked and breathless with excitement, the reviewers announced that Miss Porter's long-awaited first novel was a "triumph," a "masterpiece," a "work of genius . . . a momentous work of fiction," "a phenomenal, rich, and delectable book," a "literary event of the highest magnitude." Whether it was Mark Schorer in the *New York Times Book Review* delivering a lecture, both learned and lyrical, on the source, sensibility and stature of the novel ("Call it . . . the Middlemarch of a later day"), or a daily reviewer for the San Francisco *Call Bulletin* confessing that "not once (had) he started a review with so much admiration for its author, . . ." in the end it came to the same thing.

Riding the crest of this wave of acclaim, *Ship of Fools* made its way to the top of the best-seller lists in record time and it is still there as I write in mid-September. During these four months, it has encoun-

tered virtually as little opposition in taking its place among the classics of literature as it did in taking and holding its place on the best-seller lists. A few critics . . . wound up by saying that *Ship of Fools* fell somewhat short of greatness, but only after taking the book's claim to greatness with respectful seriousness. Some of the solid citizens among the reviewers, like John K. Hutchens, found the novel to be dull and said so. Here and there, mainly in the hinterlands, a handful of independent spirits . . . suspected that the book was a failure. But who was listening?

Prominent among the circumstances which have helped to make a run-away best-seller and a *succés d'estime* out of this massive, unexciting, and saturnine novel was the aura of interest, partly sentimental and partly deserved, that Miss Porter's long struggle with it had produced. Most of the reviews begin in the same way: a distinguished American short-story writer at the age of seventy-one has finally finished her first novel after twenty years of working on it. As this point was developed, it tended to establish the dominant tone of many reviews—that of an elated witness to a unique personal triumph, almost as though this indomitable septuagenarian had not written a book, but had done something even more remarkable—like swimming the English Channel.

The *Commentary* critic goes on to charge Miss Porter with having written a novel contemptible in two decisive ways: (1) badly executed in every conceivable technical sense, particularly characterization and (2) unacceptable on moral grounds, being pessimistic and misanthropic; "But the soul of humanity is lacking," he says, quoting still another reviewer sympathetic to his own position. Why Dostoievsky, for example, is permitted to be both massive and saturnine and Miss Porter not is a question spoken to later only by implication. The critic's charge that her writing is "unexciting" is curious considering his own high emotional state in responding to the work. The charge of misanthropy is, of course, directly related to the alleged technical failure of the characterization, which he says "borders on caricature" in the way it portrays nearly every human type as loathsome and grotesque, with hardly a single redeeming feature. In considering the charge of misanthropy we are, perforce, confronted with the question of the writer's social responsibility in the moral sphere, for the attribution of misanthropy to a writer by a critic is typically a censure and is seldom merely a description of the writer's stance. The writer is usually, as in this case, denied the right to be misanthropic on the ground that it is immoral to hate and, given the writer's influential function, it is deemed irresponsible of him to clothe such a negative sentiment as hate in intellectually attractive garb.

In my efforts at synthesis, I will get back to these questions. But for the moment I should like to point out that *Commentary*'s view of **Ship of Fools** as depicting mankind in a hatefully distorted, therefore, untruthful, therefore, immoral way, is in fact the view of the book commonly held by the normally intelligent and reasonably well-educated reader of fiction, if my impressions are accurate; these impressions are based, in small part, incidentally, on the way the book was received on the Grinnell College campus, where it was required reading for freshmen in a week of panel discussions before the onset of formal instruction. The book was selected, I was told, because it was thought controversial and dealt with themes of human import. Scarcely three of my colleagues could stomach the book and even fewer, I understand, blushed to inform the new students of its putative unfortunate characteristics.

I turn now to the other mode of reception: acute disappointment. One of the most clearly and intelligently presented of this group was Professor Wayne Booth's critique in the *Yale Review* (Summer, 1962) from which I quote, in part, as follows:

> Katherine Anne Porter's long-awaited novel is more likely to fall afoul of one's bias for finely-constructed, concentrated plots. In this respect her own earlier fiction works against her; part of the strength of those classics, **Pale Horse, Pale Rider** and **Noon Wine,** lies in their concision, their economy, their simplicity. *There* is *my* Katherine Anne Porter, I am tempted to protest, as she offers me, now, something so different as to be almost unrecognizable—a 225,000-word novel (more words, I suppose, than in all of the rest of her works put together) with nearly fifty characters. What is worse, the manner of narration is fragmented, diluted. Her plan is to create a shipload of lost souls and to follow them, isolated moment by isolated moment, in their alienated selfishness, through the nasty, exasperating events of a twenty-seven day voyage, in 1931, from Veracruz to Bremerhaven. She deliberately avoids concentrating strongly on any one character; even the four or five that are granted some sympathy are kept firmly, almost allegorically, subordinated to the portrayal of the ship of fools ("I am a passenger on that ship," she reminds us in an opening note).

> Her method is sporadic, almost desultory, and her unity is based on theme and idea rather than coherence of action. We flash from group to group, scene to scene, mind to mind, seldom remaining with any group or observer for longer than three or four pages together. While the book is as a result full of crosslights and ironic juxtapositions, it has, for me, no steady center of interest except the progressively

> more intense exemplification of its central truth; men are pitifully, foolishly self-alienated. At the heart of man lies a radical corruption that can only occasionally, fitfully, be overcome by love . . .

> Once the various groupings are established—the four isolated, self-torturing Americans, two of them lovers who hate and fear each other when they are not loving; the sixteen Germans, most of them in self-destructive family groups, and all but two of them repugnant almost beyond comedy; the depraved swarm of Spanish dancers with their two demon-children; the carefree and viciously irresponsible Cuban students; the half-mad, lost Spanish countess; the morose Swede; and so on—each group or lone traveler is taken to some sort of climactic moment, most often in the form of a bungled chance for genuine human contact. These little anti-climaxes are scattered throughout the latter fourth of the book, but for most of the characters the nadir is reached during the long "gala" evening, almost at the end of the journey. . . . Such a work, lacking, by design, a grand causal, temporal sequence, depends for complete success on the radiance of each part; the reader must feel that every fragment as it comes provides proof of its own relevance in its illustrative power, or at least in its comic or pathetic or satiric intensity. For me only about half of the characters provide this kind of self-justification. There are many great things: moments of introspection, including some masterful dreams, from the advanced young woman and the faded beauty; moments of clear and effective observation of viciousness and folly. But too often one finds, when the tour of the passenger list is undertaken again and again, that it is too much altogether. Why, why did Miss Porter feel that she should try to get everything in? Did she really think that it would be more powerful to give forty instances of depravity than twenty, or five? . . . it is only because she tries for a canvas large and busy enough to defeat the imaginative genius of a Shakespeare that she gets into trouble.

> Trouble is too strong a word. Even if all of my reservations are sound, which I doubt, the book is more worth having than most fully-successful but less ambitious novels . . . what I hope most of all is that you'll find me completely mistaken in asking for a more rigorous or an inappropriate economy, and that, unlike those who have praised the novel in public so far, you'll explain to me how to read it better on my next try. For now, honesty requires a timid vote of admiring, almost shamefaced disappointment.

Since a useful version of Aristotle's *Poetics* has been available to us, there have been critics who have been engaged in what has been called criticism proper, the task of determining what literature in general is, and what a given work of literature in particular is. One fundamental assumption of criticism proper is that by a more and more refined classification, according to a work's properties, all literature can be first divided into kinds and sub-kinds. Ideally, and as such a process becomes more and more discriminating and precise, and as the subdivisions become small and smaller, criticism will approach the individual work. Accordingly the proper critic assumes that all questions of evaluation, including, of course, moral evaluation, are secondary to and issue from questions of definition. Or to put yet otherwise, the proper critic asks: How can we tell what a work means, let alone whether it's good or bad, if we don't know what it is to begin with? At this turn, I call attention to the fact that in none of my own references to *Ship of Fools* have I spoken of it as a novel. The *Commentary* editor calls it a novel and Mr. Booth calls it a novel and in the very process of describing what it is about this alleged novel that displeases them, they go a long way toward unintentionally defining the work as something else altogether. But instead of evaluating *Ship of Fools* on the grounds of their own description of its properties, both insist on ignoring this analytical data, making two substitutions in its stead: (1) the publisher's word for it that *Ship of Fools* is a novel and (2) their own bias as to how the work would have to be written to have been acceptable as a novel. Mr. Booth is both candid and disarming in making explicit his bias for finely-constructed, concentrated plots. To entertain a preference for *Pride and Prejudice* or *The Great Gatsby* over, say, *Moby Dick* or *Finnegans Wake* is one thing and legitimate enough in its way. To insist, however, that the latter two works are inferior because their integrity does not depend on traditional plot structure would be to risk downgrading two admittedly monumental works in a very arbitrary and dubious way. Finally, to insist that every long work of prose fiction should be as much like *Pride and Prejudice* as possible is to insist that every such work be not only a novel, but a 19th century one at that.

The *Commentary* critique has its own bias which is not, however, stated explicitly. It is the bias of the journal itself as much as of the critic, and is one it shares with many another respectable publication whose voice is directed at an audience it understands to have a highly developed, independent, post-Freudian, post-Marxist, humanitarian social consciousness. Neither especially visionary, nor especially doctrinaire, such a publication has, typically, nevertheless, a low tolerance for anything that smacks of the concept of original sin, having, as this concept does, a way of discouraging speculation about decisively improving the human lot. Miss Porter's book appears to take a dim view of the behavior of the race and that is enough for the intellectual journal, despite its implied claim to broad views and cultivated interests, including an interest in fiction. The aggrieved critic

cannot come down from high dudgeon long enough to see that a view of literature as merely an ideological weapon is in the first place a strangely puritanical one and wildly out of place in his pages. Secondly, there are a few more commonplaces about literature which are usually lost sight of in the urgency to claim that people are not all bad and therefore can and must be portrayed in fiction as likely candidates for salvation. Most works of fiction, *as anyone should know,* are not written to accomplish anything but themselves, but some works of fiction are written to demonstrate to the innocent that there is much evil in the world. And others are written to demonstrate to the initiated, but phlegmatic, that there is more evil than even they had supposed and that, moreover, this evil is closer to home than they can comfortably imagine. In any case, since fiction is by definition artificial, the author is within his rights in appearing to overstate the case for the desired results. It is nowhere everlastingly written that literature must have a sanguine, optimistic and uplifting effect. Is there not sometimes something salutary in a work which has the effect of inducing disgust and functioning therefore as a kind of emetic? Had the critic given Miss Porter her due as an artist he might have seen that *Ship of Fools* condemns human folly, but it never once confuses good and evil. It is one thing to be a writer who smirks at human decency and argues for human destruction (Marquis de Sade)—it is another to be a writer who winces at human limitations and pleads by her tone, her attitude towards her readers, for a pained nod of agreement. Said Dr. Johnson to the Honourable Thomas Erskine some 200 years ago: "Why sir, if you were to read Richardson for the story, your impatience would be so much fretted that you would hang yourself. But you must read him for the sentiment." In the case of *Ship of Fools,* this sentiment is so consistent and so pervasive as to make us wonder how anyone could have scanted or mistaken it. It is the very opposite of misanthropy in that far from taking delight in exposing human foibles, in "getting" her characters' "number," Miss Porter's narrative voice has the quality of personal suffering even as it gives testimony. It seems to say: "This is the way with the human soul, as I knew it, at its worst, in the years just prior to the second World War. And alas for all of us that it should have been so." By way of illustration, recall the characters Ric and Rac. I select them because Miss Porter's readers of all stripes agree that these two children, scarcely out of their swaddling clothes, are probably as thoroughly objectionable as any two fictional characters in all literature in English. Twin offspring of a pimp and a prostitute, they lie, steal, torture, attempt to murder a dumb animal, cause the death of an innocent man and fornicate incestuously; they are not very convincing as ordinary real children and for a very good reason. They are not meant to be. I cite a passage from that section where, having made a fiasco of their parents' larcenous schemes, they are punished by those parents:

Tito let go of Rac and turned his fatherly discipline

upon Ric. He seized his right arm by the wrist and twisted it very slowly and steadily until the shoulder was nearly turned in its socket and Ric went to his knees with a long howl that died away in a puppy-like whimper when the terrible hold was loosed. Rac, huddled on the divan nursing her bruises, cried again with him. Then Manolo and Pepe and Tito and Pancho, and Lola and Concha and Pastora and Amparo, every face masking badly a sullen fright, went away together to go over every step of this dismaying turn of affairs; with a few words and nods, they decided it would be best to drink coffee in the bar, to appear as usual at dinner, and to hold a rehearsal on deck afterwards. They were all on edge and ready to fly at each other's throats. On her way out, Lola paused long enough to seize Rac by the hair and shake her head until she was silenced, afraid to cry. When they were gone, Ric and Rac crawled into the upper berth looking for safety; they lay there half naked, entangled like some afflicted, misbegotten little monster in a cave, exhausted, mindless, soon asleep.

For 357 pages, a case has been carefully built for the twins' monstrous natures. The reader has been induced to loathe the very sound of their names. Suddenly the same reader finds himself an eye witness to the degree of punishment he has privately imagined their deserving. But even as they are being terribly chastised they demonstrate an admirable recalcitrance and suddenly it is the adult world which appears villainous, monstrous and cruel. Finally, in the imagery of our last view of them, they are not demons altogether, or even primarily, but in their nakedness, which we see first, they are also merely infants and this is what does—or should—break the reader's heart. The reader is meant to sympathize, finally, with these hideous children, but more than that, his moral responses have been directed to himself. He has been led to ask himself: Who am I that I should have for so long despised these children, however demonic they are. Am I, then, any better than their parents?

---

***Ship of Fools*** **condemns human folly, but it never once confuses good and evil. It is one thing to be a writer who smirks at human decency and argues for human destruction (Marquis de Sade)—it is another to be a writer who winces at human limitations and pleads by her tone, her attitude towards her readers, for a pained nod of agreement.**

**—M. M. Liberman**

---

When I contend that Ric and Rac are not meant to be taken as real children, I am agreeing for the moment with the *Commentary* critic who spoke of Miss Porter's method of characterization as caricature, as if to speak of this method so, were, *ipso facto*, to condemn it; as if realism were the only possible fictional mode and the only category into which a long fiction can be cast. But if *Ship of Fools* is not a novel, what would a novel be? I rely on the recent study by Professor Sheldon Sacks, *Fiction and the Shape of Belief*, to define it as follows: a novel would be an action organized so that it introduces characters about whose fates the reader is made to care, in unstable relationships, which are then further complicated, until the complication is finally resolved, by the removal of the represented instability. This plainly is not *Ship of Fools*. Our most human feelings go out to Ric and Rac, but we cannot care further about them precisely *not* because we are made to hate them, but because they are clearly doomed to perpetual dehumanization by the adult world which spawned and nurtured them. In the same image in which Miss Porter represents them as helpless infants, she also declares them "mindless." The generally unstable relationships which define the roles of most of the other characters in the book remain unstable to the very end and are not so much resolved as they are revealed. The resolution of the manifold conflicts in the work is part of the encompassing action of the work, that which the reader can logically suppose will happen after the story closes. The Germans will march against Poland and turn Europe into a concentration camp. The others will, until it is too late, look the other way. This is a fact of history which overrides in importance the fact that no one on the ship can possibly come to good.

Nor is *Ship of Fools* a satire which is organized so that it ridicules objects external to the fictional world created in it. Rather, it is, I believe, a kind of modern apologue, a work organized as a fictional example of the truth of a formulable statement or a series of such statements. As such it owes more than its title to the didactic Christian verses of Sebastian Brant, whose *Das Narrenschiff, The Ship of Fools,* was published sometime between 1497 and 1548. Brant's work was very influential and no one thinks of it as misanthropic when he reads:

> The whole world lives in darksome night,
> In blinded sinfulness persisting,
> While every street sees fools existing
> Who know but folly, to their shame,
> Yet will not own to folly's name.
> Hence I have pondered how a ship
> Of fools I'd suitably equip—
> A galley, brig, bark, skiff, or float,
> A carack, scow, dredge, racing-boat,
> A sled, cart, barrow, carryall—
> One vessel would be far too small
> to carry all the fools I know.

Some persons have no way to go
And like the bees they come a-skimming,
While many to the ship are swimming,
Each one wants to be the first,
A mighty throng with folly curst,
Whose pictures I have given here.
They who at writings like to sneer
Or are with reading not afflicted
May see themselves herewith depicted
And thus discover who they are,
Their faults, to whom they're similar.
For fools a mirror shall it be,
Where each his counterfeit may see.

As an apologue Miss Porter's work has more in common with Johnson's *Rasselas* than with *Gone with the Wind.* As an apologue it not only has the right, it has the function by its nature to "caricature" its actors, to be "saturnine," to have a large cast, to be "fragmented" in its narration and above all, to quote Mr. Booth again, to achieve "unity based on theme and idea rather than coherence of action . . . [to have] no steady center of interest except the progressively more intense exemplification of its central truth. . . ."

In addition to calling attention to its formal properties for evaluating Miss Porter's book not as a novel but as something else, one ought to stand back a bit to see how the work fits a reasonable definition of the novel historically, that is, according to traditional and conventional themes and types of action. Recall that though the English word novel, to designate a kind of fiction, is derived from the Italian *novella,* meaning "a little new thing," this is not the word used in most European countries. That word is, significantly, *roman.* One forgets that a work of fiction, set in our own time, and thus bringing us knowledge of our own time, that is, news, is not, however a novel by that fact alone, but may be a literary form as yet undefined and, therefore, unnamed. For, in addition to bringing us news, the novel, if it is such on historical principles, must pay its respects to its forebears in more than a nominal way. It must do more than bear tales and look like the *Brothers Karamazov.* It must, I suspect, as a *roman,* be in some specific ways romantic.

We understand that the novel is the modern counterpart of various earlier forms of extended narrative. The first of these, the epic, was succeeded in the middle ages by the *romance* written at first like the epic, in verse, and later in prose as well. The romance told of the adventures of royalty and the nobility, introduced a heroine and made love a central theme. It relocated the supernatural realm from the court of Zeus to fairyland. The gods were replaced by magical spells and enchantments. When magical spells and enchantments were replaced, in the precursors of contemporary fiction, by the happy accident, the writer took unto himself a traditional given and the romantic tradition continued in the novel. When

Henry James arranged for his heroine, Isabel Archer, to inherit a substantial sum of money from a relative who didn't know her, this was very Olympian of him; at any rate it was a piece of modern magic, legitimately granted to the novelist. Realist though he was, James recognized that the romantic element gets the novel going, frees the hero or heroine from those confinements of everyday life which make moral adventure undramatic. When in the most arbitrary way James makes Isabel an heiress he launches her on a quest for self-realization. He gives her her chance. Now in this connection, I quote again from *Ship of Fools:*

> While [Freytag] shaved he riffled thru his ties and selected one, thinking that people on voyage mostly went on behaving as if they were on dry land, and there is simply not room for it on a ship. Every smallest act shows up more clearly and looks worse, because it has lost its background. The train of events leading up to and explaining it is not there; you can't refer it back and set it in its proper size and place.

When Miss Porter, who could have put her cast of characters anywhere she wanted, elected to put them aboard ship, she made as if to free them, in the manner of a romance, for a moral quest; that is, they are ostensibly liberated, as if by magic, precisely because they *are* aboard ship—liberated from the conventions of family background, domestic responsibility, national custom and race consciousness. Theoretically, they can now emerge triumphant at the end of the journey, over duplicity, cruelty, selfishness and bigotry. But they do not.

Freedom they are incapable of utilizing for humane ends. Freedom Miss Porter can grant them, but since they are men of our time, they cannot, in her view, accept it responsibly. That is, they cannot make good use of their lucky accident because their freedom is only nominal. On the one hand, history has caught up with them; on the other hand, psychology has stripped their spiritual and emotional lives of all mystery. In Miss Porter's world the past is merely the genesis of neurosis (there is no point in pretending we've never heard of Freud) and the future, quite simply, is the destruction of Isabel Archer's Europe of infinite possibilities (there is no point in pretending we've never heard of Neville Chamberlain). *Ship of Fools* argues that romantic literary conventions do not work in the modern world, and emerges as even more remote from the idea of the novel than a study of its formal properties alone would suggest. One can see it finally as anti-novel.

In her 1940 introduction to *Flowering Judas,* Miss Porter says that she spent most of her "energies" and "spirit" in an effort to understand "the logic of this majestic and terrible failure of man in the Western world." This is the dominant theme of *Ship of Fools* as it is of all her writing. Nearly every character in the work is a staggering example of an aspect of this failure. And here is the only passage in the work emphasized by italics:

> *"What they were saying to each other was only, love me, love me in spite of all! Whether or not I love you, whether I am fit to love, whether you are able to love, even if there is no such thing as love, love me."*

## Charles Thomas Samuels (review date 7 March 1970)

SOURCE: "Placing Miss Porter," in *The New Republic,* Vol. 162, No. 10, March 7, 1970, pp. 25-6.

[*In the following review, Samuels offers a mixed assessment of Porter's* The Collected Essays and Occasional Writings, *praising the author's technical skill while finding weakness in the substance of her writings.*]

*The Collected Essays and Occasional Writings* contain all of Katherine Anne Porter's previous volume of nonfiction, *The Days Before,* as well as an equal amount of essays, reviews, letters, and journal entries not gathered in the earlier book. Of the new material, we should welcome **"St. Augustine and the Bullfight,"** a masterly memoir with the shapeliness of good fiction, **"A Wreath for the Gamekeeper,"** which passionately and comically denounces *Lady Chatterley's Lover,* one chapter (**"A Goat for Azazel"**) from an uncompleted biography of Cotton Mather, and scattered instances of wit and perception. Little of the rest, however, warrants reprinting, especially in a ponderous tome with a $12.50 price-tag and little or no editorial apparatus (no explanation of why just these letters and journal entries were selected, no notes on unfamiliar people or places, scant information on the occasion or magazine that inspired many of the pieces). Nevertheless, this book should help us to comprehend the elusive nature of Miss Porter's talent.

In perhaps the first important review of her fiction, Edmund Wilson remarked, "Miss Porter is baffling because one cannot take hold of her work in any of the obvious ways," and nearly all subsequent critics have complained that no writer so often praised has been so rarely illuminated. Placing Miss Porter has been rendered difficult by several myths that have swaddled her away from the probing touch of criticism, and *The Collected Essays* can dispel at least two of them.

For a long time now, Miss Porter has been reputed a sort of priestess of art, who regards writing as a religious vocation and thus manifests its mysteries with the infrequency of revelation. Or, in the words of John Aldridge, her "paucity of production has come to be regarded as the mark of a talent so fine that it can scarcely bring itself to function." Instead, Miss Porter is a thorough professional, as *The Collected Essays* suggests, with its generous supply of craftsmanlike trivia apparently written on demand. Not writing itself but the writing of fiction seems to preclude copiousness, so we are reminded by this volume to look further for the causes of her slender output of stories and her single novel written over a period of twenty years.

The other myth protecting her reputation is that she is a stylist, a maker of stories in which we contemplate the surface rather than probe the depths. But in her *Paris Review* interview Miss Porter herself deplores this characterization ("I've been called a stylist until I really could tear my hair out. And I simply don't believe in style"); and *The Collected Essays* constantly reiterate her belief that art is statement, the insight that style merely manifests. For this reason, the style of her fiction is scarcely less discursive than that of her nonfiction. After painstakingly inspecting the former, Robert Heilman (one of her supporters), has validated the author's self-appraisal: "The difficulty of describing a style without mannerisms, crotchets, or even characteristic brilliances or unique excellences leads one constantly to use such terms as *plain, direct, ordinary, unpretentious, lucid, candid."*

---

**I've been called a stylist until I really could tear my hair out. And I simply don't believe in style.**

**—Katherine Anne Porter**

---

The myth of Katharine Anne Porter the stylist, for all the positive implications, tends to reduce her to the status of a minor word-player, whereas her numerous admirers insist that she isn't "minor" at all. What, then, can be adduced in behalf of her acceptance as a major writer? Something, one would think, that relates to profundity of vision, the powerful conviction that can make, let us say, Emily Bronte major, though her output was even smaller than Miss Porter's. The trouble in Miss Porter's case is that the sensibility aspiring toward statement is almost constitutionally unable to assert anything. She does not, so much have a "vision," a point of view, as a suspicion of people less uncommitted. As Robert Penn Warren argues, the center of her work is irony, skepticism, "a refusal to accept the formula, the ready-made solution, the hand-me-down morality, the word for the spirit."

The positive side of this is Miss Porter's tonic contempt for cant and fanaticism, of which the best example in *The Collected Essays* is a scintillating put-down of Gertrude Stein (**"The Wooden Umbrella"**). On the other hand, Miss Porter's skepticism can also become rigid, her contempt for fanaticism so sweeping as to ironically resemble its target.

In her nonfiction, these traits are exemplified by the unfinished book on Cotton Mather, where her rage seems almost out of control. Within the compass of a single sentence she indicts the Mather family for "natural personal arrogance . . . theological pride [and] jealous vanity." Her poor hero can scarcely enjoy a meal without having to digest her ironic laughter at his belief that eating was seductively pleasurable. As a result, we begin to wonder not only why the author bothered to tell his story but how he could have achieved sufficient stature to make it important that she expose him.

Miss Porter's unqualified hostility sometimes produces similar problems in her fiction. As for Puritans, she feels for Germans a hatred too deep to encourage insight. This is what makes her novella **"The Leaning Tower"** so unenlightening (with, for example, its tired linking of German brutality and the duelling code) and her novel *Ship of Fools* so enervated (with its trite irony of a pet-loving anti-Semite).

What disturbs in her negativism is not the attitude itself but its tendency to preclude characters and events of any convincing complexity. With admiration, Eudora Welty asserts, "Katherine Anne Porter shows us that we do not have to see a story happen to know what is taking place"; but the absence of reported behavior and the presence of asserted criticism can produce the effect of straw men burned by the author's private anger. Something like this is true even of the beautifully written story **"Flowering Judas,"** in which the fake revolutionary Braggioni is fully exposed by Laura's initial view of him. Therefore, since we do not actively discover his unsoundness, we do not deeply feel her final understanding—also rhetorically expressed—that she is not measurably superior.

In discursive comments on her own fiction, Miss Porter always maintains that her stories originate in actual experience; she is not, so far as we can tell, a writer of rich imagination, and this fact, more than any other, seems to account for her difficulty in producing much fiction. Therefore, although she is always clear, she is only forceful when dramatizing an experience that was forceful to begin with. Distinctive neither in style nor vision, Miss Porter, after all, is at the mercy of her material. Only when she touches something truly rich is her skepticism undiminishing and her rhetorical clarity a pure advantage.

The experience need not be personal. This we see from a fine story like **"The Jilting of Granny Weatherall,"** about an old woman who cannot forget the man who rejected her even on her death bed. Here the imminence of death, superbly realized by Miss Porter, transfigures what might have been mere vanity, and Granny Weatherall becomes a serio-

comic representative of man's will to perfection. Another of Miss Porter's smaller successes is **"Magic,"** in which the former inmate of a bordello tells about the forced return of an errant colleague without realizing that it was poverty and not voodoo that brought the girl back. This is no more scenic than most of Miss Porter's stories, but its brevity (five pages) and the counterforce of the teller's incomprehension cause the facts to reach us with maximum impact.

Her great novella **"Noon Wine"** is scenic—the most unrhetorical, dramatically vivid of her fictions, the only one which is allowed to play itself out before our eyes so that we, and not the author, articulate its meanings. For once, Miss Porter had material that could be so trusted: a violent murder committed for obscure motives, complex characters, neither wicked nor foolish, a tangle of implications defying the neatness of epigram. In her account of the tale (**"Noon Wine: The Sources"**) included in *The Collected Essays,* she makes clear the extent to which these marvels were not invented but were rendered from life.

Another great achievement is the novella **"Old Mortality,"** a work whose autobiographical immediacy we may infer from other stories that feature her alter ego, Miranda. With astonishing economy, it compresses both the history of an entire family and its heroine's movement, as she goes from child to wife, through immersion in the family's romantic myth about itself to mature awareness that it is a myth. Yet, as in **"Noon Wine,"** Miss Porter establishes the complexity of life here, instead of settling for easy irony. Miranda is forced to face not only the falsity of romanticism but the contrary excess of an astringent perspective on romantic delusion that is so characteristic of her creator.

In the review to which I have earlier alluded, Edmund Wilson was "tempted to say that the effect [of her writing] is pale," but he was "prevented by the realization that Miss Porter writes English of a purity and precision almost unique in contemporary American fiction." Rereading her stories alongside the prose makes it clear that precision and pallor can go together, if precision works to evade the mystery of real people and situations. In too much of her fiction, Katherine Anne Porter is indeed the essayist, or critic, for whom the greatest goods are consistency and clarity—both of which she purchases at too high a price. Those who esteem her should forebear inviting us, because she wrote so little, to consider everything she wrote; for Miss Porter is admirable only when her material pushes her beyond an irony that is always lucid but often without resonance.

## M. M. Liberman (essay date 1971)

SOURCE: "Symbolism, the Short Story, and 'Flowering

Judas,'" in *Katherine Anne Porter's Fiction,* Wayne State University Press, 1971, pp. 70-9.

[*In the following essay, Liberman explores the significance of symbolism in "Flowering Judas" and addresses previous critical readings of the story.*]

If one opens Jean Stafford's *Collected Stories* to, say, "The Lippia Lawn," which begins, "Although its roots are clever, the trailing arbutus at Deer Lick had been wrenched out by the hogs," he is promised the work of a poet, and this promise the other stories generally keep. It is the "clever," employed for all its worth, including *its* root sense, that does it almost all, and this is as it should be if, as I suppose with a few others, the short story is, in crucial ways, most like the lyric in that its agent is neither plot nor character, but diction. When its language is felicitous, decorous, and evocative, the tone and feeling will cradle characterization, enhance idea, and imply action which the novel must nearly always dramatize or fail. But this is not to say that the short story *is* a poem and here, too, is where many fledgling writers and not a few experienced critics have gone wrong.

The short story is not quite a poem any more than it is a short novel boiled conveniently down to bite size. So it cannot, therefore, be done with sounds, sights, and symbols alone. Surely he was correct who contended that "the storyteller must have a story to tell, not merely some sweet prose to take out for a walk." And so was that editor who wrote to Katherine Anne Porter, "No plot, my dear, no story," although how he supposed that stricture to apply to *her* work I can imagine only in a way that does him no credit.

Commentators and editors have grouped Miss Porter's stories in a variety of ways: early—late, Miranda—Laura, new order—old order, and Mexican—non-Mexican, to name a few. This habit is conventional and usually harmless enough; it does not mislead if one keeps in mind that it is usually more a descriptive than a critical practice. It is more to the point of criticism, however, to see a "story" as falling naturally into two groups which are explicitly evaluative according to degree of formal accomplishment: realized stories with sufficient verbal efficacy to compensate adequately for the absence of the explicit causal-temporal logic essential only to most longer fictional forms; and alleged stories which no amount of verbal magic can rescue from a poverty of implied plot and other indispensable narrative features.

"During the 1940's, it was as symbolist that Miss Porter was most effusively praised by totemist critics," James William Johnson reminds us. "In fact, criticism of her work became tantamount to an intellectual parlor game: 'Let's see who can find the most abstruse symbols in **"Flowering Judas.'"** Her work survived this craze, which was largely unnecessary, since the truth is that her symbols operate on the most

direct level and, where she intends a multiplicity of meaning, Miss Porter almost always tells the reader so." It ought to be added to Mr. Johnson's refreshingly commonsensical observation that although her work has survived "this craze," the "craze" itself dies hard. The neo-euhemerism of the thirties and forties seems down but by no means out, and the readings of **"Flowering Judas"** which can serve as paradigms of that era's notorious and, often, hilarious symbol-mongering have, to my knowledge, never been recanted. Moreover, the epigones of the totemists are still publishing critiques of Miss Porter's stories founded on the assumption that there is nothing, given sufficient ingenuity, that cannot be read as metaphysical verse.

**"Flowering Judas"** is, to be sure, a highly figurative composition. The modern short story almost invariably is, because, perhaps paradoxically, its author is likely to write in a realistic mode. For whereas the publicly verifiable in the novel requires extended treatment, partly in order to represent time sequentially, the familiar in the short story, dealing as it does with the moment, can be represented best by a good deal of shorthand. The result has been a "symbolic realism" where the most ordinary events are imitated, but by a selective process so scrupulous as to evoke at least what the novel might show or tell. When most successful, as in **"Flowering Judas,"** the evocations are practically symbolic in that they stand for more than themselves. It follows that, mistaking the means for the end, the amateur is forever producing the unwritten. In the place of the authentic story there is fobbed off something between an impressionistic hodge-podge and a bastard lyric, known at times as the "mood piece" and at others as the "prose poem." There is also the "slice-of-life," and, more recently, the "open-ended" story, a legitimate enough form, if it is not open at both ends, top and bottom. Since on the contrary **"Flowering Judas"** is so plainly a fully realized effort to tell a tale classically, that is, to move a serious theme through implied time by means of characters who act on ethical choices, and to do this, moreover, without failing to accommodate to theme, wherever possible, the details of image and fable, it might, therefore, be wise to be a bit warier than most critics have been of reading this story as if its meaning partook of its figuration rather than, as I believe to be the case, the reverse.

There has been no slackening of published interest in **"Flowering Judas,"** but the standard reading continues to be the West-Stallman analysis which appeared in a college anthology of short fiction in 1949. I know of no reading that does not take off from it, at least in its basic assumption of the accessibility of theme and meaning through symbolism. The text is incorrectly titled "The Flowering Judas." If one believed that the causes of error are unconscious but real, the accident would be seen as a true mistake. For West and Stallman, *the* flowering Judas is virtually *the* story. The analysis itself is titled "Theme through Symbol," which, I contend, is not a viable concept for narrative fiction. The West-Stallman reading asks what the purpose of the individual symbol is, and replies that it is to "signify the theme." "In the title itself" the "most important" symbol "occurs," and the source is given as Eliot's "Gerontion." "This is scarcely a coincidence," we are told, "since Eliot's passage so clearly suggests Laura's activity at the end of the story." The five lines in which the words "flowering Judas" appear are quoted as if they are proof. The Judas tree is seen quite simply as "a symbol for the betrayer of Christ." Laura's eating the buds is a "sacrament . . . of betrayal." If we put aside the question of failure to cite evidence of Miss Porter's specific debt to Eliot in this instance, we are nonetheless free to grant her known interest in Eliot and the obviousness of the betrayal theme in both poem and story do, admittedly, constitute presumptive evidence of source. But to go further in lining up the story with the poem is to jump to conclusions about the use of the symbol, based mistakenly on the assumption that symbols are used in stories quite as they might be in poems, that is, to signify theme. In fact, in Miss Porter's story, the symbol of the flowering Judas is employed to enhance theme and finally to reiterate theme, but not to be a sign of theme as if theme had not been established by other means. Laura is found wanting from beginning to end, and the meaning of the story does not wait on a final symbolic revelation to make accessible what would otherwise be mysterious. "I have a great deal of religious symbolism in my stories," Miss Porter recently allowed, "because I have a very deep sense of religion and also I have a religious training. And I suppose you don't invent symbolism. You don't say, 'I'm going to have the flowering Judas tree stand for betrayal,' but of course it does." Of course, it does, because given the association of the name Judas it can. But it does only if the author, in effect, employs it to that end. If the reader can recognize the Judas tree as a symbol of betrayal, he can do so legitimately, and not arbitrarily, only if he has been permitted to see betrayal in the story's action. It is the story, all in all, that makes of this particular tree a working symbol of anything whatever. In a work as psychologically realistic as this one, concerned as it is with the levels of a young woman's harassed consciousness (Laura's mind is in fact the work's arena), the Judas tree does not stand primarily and independently as the figure of pagan treachery, analogous to Laura's treachery. Rather it illuminates, dream image that it is, the natural depths of the bedeviled feelings of a woman who cannot, when awake, come to terms with those feelings. Seen this way, **"Flowering Judas"** is not a symbolic story in the sense that it depends on symbols to pull its thematic irons out of the fire. The entire work is in a way "symbolic" insofar as it impels the reader to attend to one striking detail and not another. But within this sense of symbol the Judas tree as a figure is not the most important. It cannot, logically, be more important than any other narrative detail which gives us insight into Laura's character. It may seem crucial because of its strategic location, that is, at the end. Thus placed, how-

ever, it can astonish only a reader who has paid little attention to the work's beginning, as might astonish the figurative phrase "my eyes burned" at the conclusion of Joyce's "Araby," a story which begins, "North Richmond Street, being blind, was a quiet street. . . ."

Miss Porter has written of **"Flowering Judas"**:

> All the characters and episodes are based on real persons and events, but naturally, as my memory worked upon them and time passed, all assumed different shapes and colors, formed gradually around a central idea, that of self-delusion, the order and meaning of the episodes changed, and became in a word fiction.
>
> The idea first came to me one evening when going to visit the girl I call Laura in the story, I passed the open window of her living room on my way to the door, through the small patio which is one of the scenes in the story. I had a brief glimpse of her sitting with an open book in her lap, but not reading, with a fixed look of pained melancholy and confusion in her face. The fat man I call Braggioni was playing the guitar and singing to her.
>
> In that glimpse, no more than a flash, I thought I understood, or perceived, for the first time, *the desperate complications of her mind* and feelings, and I knew a story; perhaps not her true story, not even the real story of the whole situation, but all the same a story that seemed *symbolic truth* to me. If I had not seen her face at the very moment, I should never have written just this story because I should not have known it to write. [Italics mine]

**"Flowering Judas"** owes its greatness not at all to some opportunistic employment of a conventional religious symbol to signify theme but to a brilliant narrative practice throughout, one capable of representing a feeling that, once apprehended by the reader, permits him to see with what overriding intelligence Miss Porter knew her Laura, "the desperate complication of her mind" and what it meant.

The celebrated dream sequence on which the story ends and which is supposed to be central in its resolution and revelation through the symbol of the tree and the buds follows:

> The tolling of the midnight bell is a signal, but what does it mean? Get up, Laura, and follow me: come out of your sleep, out of your bed, out of this strange house. What are you doing in this house? Without a word, without fear she rose and reached for Eugenio's hand, but he eluded her with a sharp, sly smile and drifted away. This is not all, you shall

see—Murderer, he said, follow me, I will show you a new country, but it is far away and we must hurry. No, said Laura, not unless you take my hand, no; and she clung first to the stair rail and then to the topmost branch of the Judas tree that bent down slowly and set her upon the earth, and then to the rocky ledge of a cliff, and then to the jagged wave of a sea that was not water but a desert of crumbling stone. Where are you taking me, she asked in wonder but without fear. To death, and it is a long way off, and we must hurry, said Eugenio. No, said Laura, not unless you take my hand. Then eat these flowers, poor prisoner, said Eugenio in a voice of pity, take and eat: and from the Judas tree he stripped the warm bleeding flowers, and held them to her lips. She saw that his hand was fleshless, a cluster of small white petrified branches, and his eye sockets were without light, but she ate the flowers greedily for they satisfied both hunger and thirst. Murderer! said Eugenio, and Cannibal! This is my body and my blood. Laura cried No! and at the sound of her own voice, she awoke trembling, and was afraid to sleep again.

It has been prepared for by a single reference to the Judas tree earlier in connection with a "brown, shock-haired youth" who pleaded for her love in vain. Laura, for her part, "could think of nothing to do about it."

The sense one gets of Laura's emotional stinginess is not so much that, Judas-like, she has betrayed the young man in withholding human warmth but that, like the central figure of **"Theft,"** Miss Porter's story of another young woman who is seen explicitly to have stolen life's spiritual riches from *herself,* Laura has betrayed Laura. We know next to nothing of the young man, but we know how desperately Laura needs to fulfill herself. The young man will fare badly, but it is not inevitable. Laura, on the other hand, is doomed forever to suffer her own starving soul, a fact confirmed by a negation and fear of life and truth, the note on which the very last image is played out. But nothing of what is given to the reader anywhere in the dream sequence is unprepared for, and is, moreover, explicitly *reasoned* by the narrator the moment it is possible to intrude sufficiently to explain Laura. In a work of fiction in which the narrator tells the reader what he needs to know, no symbol so arbitrary as to liken a frightened nunlike girl to the historical Judas is artistically allowable. Nor is Miss Porter guilty of such faulty aesthetic judgment.

If Miss Porter is a symbolist only in the sense we have described, that is, as a writer whose choices of vocabulary, of levels of diction, and of varieties of image work insistently to induce one to read beyond mere denotation, she is also a symbolist in **"Flowering Judas"** in the sense of her own

phrase "symbolic truth," which I take to be synonymous with "meaning."

Finally, the West-Stallman reading has it that

> Laura is not redeemed, even though she desires it, as the eating of the buds of the Judas tree suggests. Her sacrament is a devouring gesture and Eugenio calls her a cannibal, because she is devouring him (Man). She is, like Judas, the betrayer—the destroyer; and her betrayal, like his, consisted in an inability to believe. Without faith she is incapable of passion, thence of love, finally of life itself.

> This is the "moral" of the story, translated as it is into the language of Christian theology: "Man cannot live by bread alone." Distilled even beyond that, into the language of statement, we might say that the theme is this: "Man cannot live if he accepts only materialistic values"; or, to put it into a positive statement: "Only in faith and love can man live." This does not, however, represent the "meaning," for the meaning is, as we have said, the total embodiment—the form. The statement is only an inadequate attempt on the part of the reader to seek out the author's intention. The question the student should ask next is, "How much does it leave unsaid?"

It is a little like shoveling sand in a windstorm to so much as begin to take issue with this crowd of New Critical pieties: the historical Christian assumptions as the ground for reading a "moral" statement; the fudging of the question of meaning by equating it simply with "form"; and the raising of the old specter of "intention." Miss Porter makes it quite clear that her intention is to elucidate the "desperate complications of her [the protagonist's] mind" and that the "meaning" of the story is in whatever general human nature can be discerned from such an elucidation. The "symbolic truth" Miss Porter speaks of is precisely in the way Laura's career corresponds to the ambiguous and paradoxical condition of recognizable modern man. Laura "is not at home in the world." In this configuration the most crucial fictional device is not the Judas tree but Laura herself. The theme, then, can hardly be stated as "man cannot live if he accepts only materialistic values." **"Flowering Judas"** dramatizes nothing so much as the fact that modern man, especially modern political man (Braggioni), lives and thrives, but more like a pig than a human. As for Laura, who has been enlisted in Braggioni's cause, she is so far from being materialistic that, in her "notorious virginity," she has even disowned her body. She is the most spiritual of women, but her spirit has been given over to a crusade founded not on a faith in the soul of man or the love of God but on the mindless force of history. In surrendering herself thus, she has surrendered everything.

If one must state a theme, it would be that of *self*-betrayal, and, more interestingly for a fictional construct, the way in which anomic modern life can be made of it.

> But she cannot help feeling that she has been betrayed irreparably by the disunion between her way of living and her feeling of what life should be, and at times she is almost contented to rest in this sense of grievance as a private store of consolation. Sometimes she wishes to run away, but she stays.

In their haste to see the meaning of **"Flowering Judas"** as inhering in its "most important" symbol, as it "occurs," commentators after the New Critics have failed consistently to distinguish the foreground of the narration from its shadowy, memorial background, where a series of rather theoretical and underdramatized "betrayed" characters have compromised Laura's Mexican life. Even Braggioni, despite his imminence and despite his taking part in the most affecting of scenes (his homecoming), curiously resides as almost exclusively an evil presence in Laura's desolate consciousness. There is, in fact, only one character upstage, Miss Porter's thrillingly intelligent narrative voice, guiding us over the landscape of Laura's mind, making sense for us of its "disunion." This she does in the historical present, so that the truth may be held up for inspection in life's continual moment.

### Thomas F. Walsh (essay date Fall 1979)

SOURCE: "The Dreams Self in 'Pale Horse, Pale Rider,'" in *Wascana Review,* Vol. 14, No. 2, Fall, 1979, pp. 61-79.

[*In the following essay, Walsh explores the significance of Miranda's dreams in "Pale Horse, Pale Rider," noting allusions to fear of death and the author's own personal experiences.*]

Deriving its title from an old spiritual, Katherine Anne Porter's **"Pale Horse, Pale Rider"** tells how Death carries off Adam, "a sacrificial lamb" who is "committed without any knowledge or act of his own to death," leaving Miranda the "one singer to mourn." Therefore some critics have read the story as a tragedy of circumstances in which war and disease doom its star-crossed lovers. Wayne Booth writes that the reader is united with Miranda "against the hostile world around her" as she travels "alone toward the discovery that the man she loves has died." He also stresses her "moral superiority": "She must be accepted at her own estimate from the beginning," for "the slightest suggestion that she is at fault" or "that the author and reader are observing [her] from above rather than alongside will destroy, at least in part, the quality of our concern and hence of our final revelation." Yet, in the story's five dream (or delirium) sequences, we do observe Miranda "from above" without sacrificing our concern for her. They are the most subjective parts of **"Pale Horse, Pale Rider"** because they reveal the hidden undercurrents of her mind, but they are also the most objective because they enable the reader to understand her in a way that she never understands herself. Miranda's dreams offer convincing evidence that the agonizing circumstances of war and disease trigger rather than cause her despair at the end of the story, bringing to the surface what lay submerged in her character prior to their event. She seizes upon the circumstances but never completely grasps the underlying causes of her discontent.

Examining the story's five dreams in detail, I shall show that: the opening dream of the Pale Rider establishes the ironic pattern of the story and reveals early symptoms of Miranda's discontent that strongly resemble those of the ontologically insecure person of R. D. Laing's *The Divided Self;* Adam is a narcissistic projection of Miranda, this discussion relating to Laing's study and encompassing a reading of the second, third and fourth dreams; Miranda's long fifth dream dramatizes the crisis of her desperate physical and psychological struggle with life and death, resulting in her Pyrrhic victory over influenza and in her alienation from the world of the living; and Porter, like Miranda, came to consider her own near-death from influenza more significant to her than her love, her story indirectly serving as a justification of her conception of herself as artist.

The story's opening dream reveals Miranda's chronic inner struggle with life and death. She envisions herself in her childhood home, readying for a pre-dawn journey that she does not "mean to take": "Daylight will strike a sudden blow on the roof startling them all to their feet; faces will beam asking, Where are you going, What are you doing, What are you thinking, How do you feel, Why do you say such things, What do you mean? . . . How I have loved this house in the morning before we are all awake and tangled together like badly cast fishing lines . . ." She wonders where "that lank greenish stranger" is, as if she were looking for him, and then decides to saddle her horse and outrun "Death and the Devil." The stranger then appears and rides with her, "regarding her without meaning, the blank still stare of mindless malice that makes no threats and can bide its time," but she tells him to ride on, after which she "slowly, unwillingly" awakens, waiting "in a daze for life to begin again." Then "a gong of warning" reminds her of the war which she had "happily" forgotten.

Not remembering her dream, Miranda thinks that sleep is a happy escape from the war: while bathing, she "wished she might fall asleep there, to wake up only when it was time to sleep again." Later in the day her desire to escape becomes an explicit death wish: "There's too much of everything in this world right now. I'd like to sit down here on the curb . . . and die, and never again see—I wish I could lose my memory and forget my own name. . . ." But her dream of the Pale Rider suggests that Miranda's fear and insecurity are rooted, not in the present circumstance of war, but in her childhood. The young Miranda awakes before her family to escape their demands which she considers a threat to the self; her escape is from the human condition, conceived in terms of sleepers who are shocked into an unhappy resurrection by the sun and become hopelessly entangled with each other as it runs its course until they can sleep and forget again. Her fluctuating attraction and aversion to the Pale Rider reveal her paradoxical attempt through death to preserve the self from extinction by others and her determination to live on despite her fears. She rejects the Pale Rider and with him the dream-escape itself as she waits "in a daze for life to begin again," just as the sleepers in her dream would be "startled" to life by a "blow of daylight." The irony is that her forgotten dream of escaping the war has played out the hopelessness of her escaping anything, which she learns at the end of the story: having been shocked back to life on Armistice day, "she folded her painful body together and wept silently, shamelessly, in pity for herself and her lost rapture. There was no escape."

The opening dream is a paradigm of Miranda's unbearable dilemma throughout the story; fearing life and death, she reluctantly chooses life which she likens to death. Her condition is similar to that of Laing's ontologically insecure person who "may feel more unreal than real; in a literal sense, more dead than alive; precariously differentiated from the rest of the world, so that his identity and autonomy are always in question." Particularly relevant is the insecure person's feeling of "engulfment," in which he fears that he will lose his identity and autonomy in any relationship with another or "even with himself." "Engulfment is felt as a risk in being understood (thus grasped, comprehended), in being loved, or simply in being seen."

Miranda's flight from the well-meaning questions of her family is an explicit example of her fear of being understood. Just as she seeks sleep as an escape from war, a temporary death which preserves her life, so in the dream she wishes her family temporarily dead because awake they and she become "tangled together like badly cast fishing lines," an image of her fear of losing her autonomous identity. In an essay Porter quotes with approval Willa Cather's fear of the family: "Yet every individual in that household . . . is clinging passionately to his individual soul, is in terror of losing it in the general family flavor. . . . Always in his mind each member is escaping, running away, trying to break the net which circumstances and his own affections have woven about him."

The common ingredient in Miranda's dream and in Cather's passage is the fear of engulfment or entrapment, expressed by the fishing line and net images. Cather implies that this fear in some form is a common experience. Laing would agree, pointing out that in the "comprehensible transition" from the sane to the psychotic, *"sanity or psychosis is tested by the degree of conjunction or disjunction between two persons where one is sane by common consent."* The key word is "degree." I find that the degree of Miranda's disjunction between herself and the world is remarkable enough to view her symptoms in light of Laing's study, but not as remarkable as, for example, Mr. Helton's disjunction in **"Noon Wine,"** the second story of *Pale Horse, Pale Rider*; obviously Miranda is sane and Helton is not.

Another symptom of Miranda's engulfment is her dread of relatedness even with herself which she expresses in her uncertain response to the Pale Rider as Death and the Devil: "Ah, I have seen this fellow before, I know this man if I could place him. He is no stranger to me." Miranda confronts an aspect of herself which she fears and hates and for that reason is not quite able to recognize. The Pale Rider as Death symbolizes her death-wish. As the Devil he symbolizes her pervasive fear that she is evil to others as they are to her.

Miranda's sense of mutual danger and distrust between herself and others is reflected by the Pale Rider's "blank still stare of mindless malice" and by her preoccupation with eyes throughout the story. His stare is matched by the "really stony, really viciously cold" stare of the Liberty Bond salesman and by the "malign eyes" of the rainbow-colored birds of her second dream. The "unfriendly bitter" eyes of the hospitalized soldier anticipate Miranda's own "covertly hostile eyes of an alien" as she too lies in a hospital bed at the end of the story. Her eyes reveal her sense of betrayal, yet the hostility of all the eyes has a common source in her mind; without realizing it, the betrayed are self-betrayed. Her remark that "the worst of the war is the fear and suspicion and the awful expression in all the eyes you meet . . . as if they had pulled down the shutters over their minds and their hearts and were peering out at you, ready to leap if you make one gesture or say one word they do not understand instantly" applies equally to her. The "hard unblinking point of light" of her last dream represents her loveless determination to survive in a hostile world against which she has formed her defense. Laing notes that to the insecure individual "every pair of eyes is in a Medusa's head which he feels has power actually to kill or deaden something precariously vital to him. He tries therefore to forestall his own petrifaction by turning others to stone." Miranda's preoccupation with hostile eyes obviously does not assume such an extreme form although she notes the "really stony" stare of the bond salesman. Her hostile eyes, if they do not petrify others, serve defensively to counteract their hostility.

Miranda's dream and painful recollection of the preceding

day are partially offset by her love for Adam, who "was in her mind so much, she hardly knew when she was thinking about him directly." Although the first fifteen pages of the story offer no evidence that he was in her mind, we still must question how Miranda in love is like the engulfed person who "regards his own love and that of others as being as destructive as hatred." One answer is that he longs for and needs love, but, as Laing points out, his longing and need are not enough to overcome his dread. This applies to Miranda, the poignancy of whose story does not lie only in Adam's death, but also in her belief that she could love him if he had lived.

One disturbing note in Miranda's love for Adam is the frequency with which she expresses her pessimism about their future together: ". . . he was not for her nor for any woman, being beyond experience already, committed without any knowledge or act of his own to death"; she "faced for one instant that was a lifetime the certain, the overwhelming and awful knowledge that there was nothing at all ahead for Adam and for her"; "Pure, she thought, all the way through, flawless, complete, as the sacrificial lamb must be." The uncertainties of wartime alone cannot account for Miranda's insistence on Adam's death; her frequent premonitions betray her unconscious desire that he die, for she fears love: "'I don't want to love,' she would think in spite of herself, 'not Adam, there is no time and we are not ready for it and yet this is all we have—.'"

Miranda's ambivalent response to love also explains her idealization of Adam as pure and flawless, a prelapsarian Adam who cannot survive in the fallen world of war, disease, and human love. Her inclination to idealize him out of existence reveals not only her fear of accepting him as real, but also her idealization of herself. Adam does not seem real because he is a narcissistic projection of Miranda—that is, her double.

The clues to the doubling relation are that Miranda and Adam are "twenty-four years old each, alive and on the earth at the same moment," both are Texans, are vain about their appearance, indulging in the purchase of expensive clothes, keep "unwholesome" hours, and like to swim, dance and smoke. Like many doubles Adam almost seems a hallucination: he keeps company with Miranda in the late evening and is alone with her during the day, even in public places, talking exclusively to her except for a brief exchange with her landlady.

Miranda's vanity touches on the reasons for the doubling relation. Adam tells her, "I think you're beautiful" and when she later returns the compliment in almost exactly the same words, he objects to the inappropriate adjective, but the point is that she unconsciously applies it to herself, seeing her beauty in him. Significantly, the sentence telling us that Adam's "image was simply always present" in her thoughts is immediately followed by "She examined her face in the mirror. . . ."

Miranda's vanity is a manifestation of that narcissism which Otto Rank defines in its broadest sense as self-love in which is "rooted the instinct for self-preservation, and from which emerges the deep and powerful longing to escape death, or the submergence into nothingness, and the hope of awakening to a new life. . . ." In this sense all are narcissistic, but narcissism becomes extreme to the degree that a person, in his inordinate fear of aging and death, is unable to accept his own limitations in time. His consuming preoccupation with self prevents him from loving another. Desperately attempting to realize his ideal self, he may provoke the appearance of his double who represents that self or hated aspects of his personality which fall short of the ideal.

Miranda's narcissism in its purest form appears in her fifth dream as the "minute fiercely burning particle of being that knew itself alone, that relied upon nothing beyond itself for its strength . . . composed entirely of one single motive, the stubborn will to live." After her recovery she thinks that "her hardened, indifferent heart . . . had been tender and capable of love," but it is doubtful that she was ever capable of truly loving Adam, who appears as a projection of her desire to escape time, and of her fearful knowledge that she cannot escape, that she is doomed to grow old, lose her beauty, and die.

Miranda's concern for her appearance and her "uneasiness" at the first symptoms of influenza pertain directly to Adam's function as her double. She projects his "beauty" and perfect health because she desires eternal youth, but the reality of her situation ("I have pains in my chest and my head and my heart and they're real") causes her to transform him from a god into a time-doomed victim of her fears of old age and death. When Adam first greets Miranda, "She half noticed . . . that his smile faded gradually; that his eyes became fixed and thoughtful as if he were reading in a poor light." It is as if Adam's eyes become "fixed" in death. The word recurs twice more: his eyes are "fixed in a strained frown"; "his face [is] quite fixed and still." At the end of the same day Miranda completes his transformation from god to mortal as he sits in a restaurant "near the dingy big window, face turned to the street, but looking down. It was an extraordinary face, smooth and fine and golden in the shabby light, but now set in a blind melancholy, a look of pained suspense and disillusion. For just one split second she got a glimpse of Adam when he would have been older, the face of the man he would not live to be."

Miranda's glimpse of Adam grown old gives her a premonition of herself in the same condition. Having created his image out of her desire for immortality and then infected it with fear of aging, she finally denies him the aging process, as if his death were, paradoxically, a defense against the ravages of time. Her shifting images of him anticipate her own worst fears at the end of the story. His "blind melancholy" and "look of pained suspense and disillusion" precisely describe her mental state after her recovery from influenza. Even the "dingy" window and "shabby light" of the restaurant foreshadow the "melancholy wonder" of the hospital scene, "where the light seemed filmed with cobwebs, all the bright surfaces corroded. . . ." Miranda's physical transformation, wrought by disease, embodies all her earlier fears of aging. She is like one of the "old bedridden women down the hall," her trembling hands tinted "yellow . . . like melted wax glimmering between the closed fingers." It is as if she has aged as rapidly as she imagined Adam aging in the restaurant.

Miranda's narcissistic fear of aging also colors her views of those who have aged. We are less surprised than Adam at her overreaction to the bond salesman: "I hate these potbellied baldheads, too fat, too old, too cowardly, to go to war themselves. . . ." She also overreacts to Danny Dickerson, the pathetic has-been performer with his ten-year old clippings: "He might have been a pretty fellow once, but now his mouth drooped where he had lost his side teeth, and his sad red-rimmed eyes had given up coquetry." Chuck doesn't understand why Miranda bothers to mention "the also-rans" in her reviews, nor would he understand the unconscious connection she has made between the "very beautiful" Adam and the once "pretty" Dickerson.

Miranda, then, projects Adam as dead or soon to die to protect herself from the engulfment of his love and to express her death wish through him. Identifying with him as good and mortal, she unconsciously wishes him dead because he reminds her of what will happen to her in time. Also, by removing him from time, she can preserve him as god and, at the end of the story, evoke him unchanged as "a ghost but more alive than she was." He becomes her "sacrificial lamb" because he enacts her death wish, allowing her to follow her stronger instinct of self-preservation.

Miranda's sexual fears also express her fears of engulfment and aging, as the symbolic relation between her influenza and her love of Adam suggests. Eleven days elapse between the couple's first meeting and the day influenza forces her to bed. Since the incubation period of the disease is from ten days to two weeks, her love and her disease develop simultaneously, although to Miranda "it seemed reasonable to suppose [her headache] had started with the war." Her flashback of the first nine days shows that she and Adam were frequently together without expressing any strong feeling for each other. But on the tenth day she is preoccupied with her love for him and with her malaise. She holds hands with him in the theater, apparently for the first time, and goes dancing with him: "They said nothing but smiled continually at each other, odd changing smiles as though they had found a new language." But their clearly expressed love is counterpointed against the Wasteland conversation of the girl at the next table who recounts her rejection of a former date's advances. In an abrupt transition we then discover Miranda in bed, gravely ill with influenza. But the point of the girl's rejection of her date is not lost, for Miranda sinks into her second dream which indirectly involves the rejection of her own date of the night before.

Miranda's second dream is a mixture of memory and delirium. She first evokes "cold mountains in the snow," the frigid Denver landscape of the present which she will associate, after her recovery, with deadened, loveless reality. She then evokes the past of her childhood, "another place she had known first and loved best," of warm skies, tropical trees and a "broad tranquil river," made slightly ominous by the "hovering buzzards." But this landscape suddenly changes into a hideous jungle, "a writhing terribly alive and secret place of death, creeping with tangles of spotted serpents, rainbow-colored birds with malign eyes . . . screaming long-armed monkeys tumbling among broad fleshy leaves that glowed with sulphur-colored light and exuded the ichor of death, and rotting trunks of unfamiliar trees sprawled in crawling slime." Miranda, waving gaily to herself in bed, enters the jungle and hears "the hoarse bellow of voices" warning her of danger and war.

As in the first dream Miranda's childhood landscape of warmth and security turns nightmarish, expressing her fear of the war and of life itself. First, the dream anticipates her death-in-life recovery from influenza, the "sulphur-colored light" of the leaves relating to the "sulphur colored light [that] exploded through the black window pane," and the exuding "ichor of death" relating to "the sweetish sickening smell of flesh and pus" of her body. The "hoarse bellow of voices all crying together, colliding above her head" is also picked up in the later passage: "Bells screamed all off key, wrangling together as they collided in mid air, horns and whistles mingled shrilly with cries of human distress . . ." The voices in the dream cry of danger and war whereas the other voices are celebrating the Armistice, but for Miranda it is all the same: "the far clamor went on, a furious exasperated shrieking like a mob in revolt." Her nightmare of death is really her nightmare of life.

The jungle landscape also reveals Miranda's sexual fears. The "writhing terribly alive and secret place of death" reverses the connotations of the womb; life and death are juxtaposed because the "long march" to death, "beset with all evils" begins at birth. The phallic imagery in the passage suggests a terrifying version of the sex act. The seminal "ichor of death" and "crawling slime," extending the life-death paradox, relate to "the sweetish sickening smell of flesh and pus" of the passage describing her recovery because sex is a disease, just as marriage to the younger Miranda of **"Old Mortality"** is "an illness that she might one day hope to recover from."

The dream does not directly mention Adam although the phallic serpents may relate to his statement, "Where I'm going . . . [you] crawl about on your stomach here and there among the debris." However, this imagery shows that the prostrate Miranda unconsciously responds to his sexuality, her influenza an infectious accompaniment to her growing awareness of their love. After returning to her room after her dream, Adam, although "shy of the word *love*," finally tells Miranda that he loves her, his coat off, lying in bed with her, his arm under her shoulder and "his smooth face against hers," and "Almost with no warning, she floats into the darkness, holding his hand" only to dream of killing him. There is a causal relation between their intimacy and the content of her third dream.

Like the first two dreams the third is set in a wood, "an angry dangerous wood of inhuman concealed voices singing sharply like the whine of arrows," reminding us of the voices of the second dream and of the Armistice. Adam is struck in the heart by flights of arrows, but rises each time "in a perpetual death and resurrection," but when Miranda "selfishly" interposes between him and the arrows, they pass through her heart and kill him: ". . . he lay dead, and she still lived, and . . . every branch and blade of grass had its own terrible accusing voice."

The dream, as critics point out, expresses Miranda's guilt in exposing Adam to her contagion, but it also confirms the ambivalence of her love for him, seen earlier in her frequent predictions of his death. His "perpetual death and resurrection" repeat the pattern of her own escape from life to death to life, and again reveal her desire for immortality in her projection of him as a god, impervious to the onslaught of war and love. But again the image of the unchanging god gives way to Adam's human reality. His death, caused by her interposition, proves her own fear of endangering him by the contact of her love as well as her unconscious desire to escape his love by killing him. Laing points out that the insecure person "regards his own love and that of others as being destructive as hatred," causing him "to destroy 'in his mind' the image of anyone . . . he may be in danger of becoming fond of, out of a desire to safeguard that other person . . . from being destroyed." The bowdlerized version of the dream which Miranda gives Adam when she wakes—"There was something about an old-fashioned valentine" with "two hearts carved on a tree, pierced by the same arrow"—directly equates his death with the interlinking of their hearts. The arrows of her dream represent war, pestilence, love, and sexual contact. To Miranda they are all equally lethal.

When Adam leaves shortly after Miranda's third dream, he is replaced by Dr. Hildesheim, who carries her to the ambulance: "'Put your arms around my neck,' he instructed her. 'It won't do any harm and it's a great help to me.'" His simulated affection and allusion to harm reinforce Miranda's ambivalence toward love, making him a fit substitute for Adam in the fourth dream. This dream, set in a "landscape of disaster," pictures Hildesheim as Boche, "his face a skull beneath his German helmet, carrying a naked infant writhing on the point of his bayonet" and a huge pot of poison. He throws the infant and poison into the "pure depths" of a once dry well on her father's farm, causing "the violated water" to sink back into the earth. Miranda emerges from her dream screaming, "Hildesheim is a Boche . . . kill him before he kills you."

This dream reveals Miranda's unconscious surrender to the war hysteria which she so abhors in her waking hours (the "baby on a bayonet" occurs in a Liberty Bond speech), but it also reveals hidden fears that existed before the war. Like the first two dreams it depicts Miranda's attempt to return to her childhood. Because he poisons her purified childhood memories and because his skull makes him another Pale rider, Hildesheim is the enemy while Miranda is the baby whose retrogressive escape he prevents. Later she accuses him and others of conspiring "to set her once more safely in the road . . . to death." Whether projected as a monster by the unconscious or as well-meaning bungler by the conscious mind, Hildesheim is a scapegoat whom Miranda can conveniently blame, in her self-pity, for her unwillingness to accept her mortality.

The dream is also a condensation of Miranda's fearful version of life. Born naked into the world, helpless and pure as the living water of the well, she is subject to war (poison, bayonet), disease (poison), and death (skull), making Hildesheim as Hun and Pale Rider her enemy. Also subject to love and sex, equated with war and disease, she is "violated" by Hildesheim, a substitute for Adam and perhaps for all men. His phallic bayoneting recalls the Liberty Bond speech and Adam's earlier description of how he used the bayonet, gouging the "vitals" out of sandbags and watching the sand "trickling out," while the instructors cried, "Get him, get that Boche, stick him before he sticks you."

After her fourth dream Miranda's semi-conscious mind "split in two . . . her reasoning coherent self [watching] the strange frenzy of the other coldly, reluctant to admit the truth of its visions, its tenacious remorses and despairs." The splitting continues in a different form in the two main parts of her fifth dream. Both parts are extreme expressions of her isolation from life, yet completely opposite each other regarding the role her consciousness plays. In the first part she attempts to blot out experience by becoming insensate while in the second part she attempts to purify experience to make it conform to the dictates of her feelings.

In the first part Miranda, thinking about oblivion, finds herself "on a narrow ledge over a pit that she knew to be bottomless." When she is certain that "Death is death . . . and for the dead it has no attributes . . . she sank easily . . . until she lay like a stone at the farthest bottom of life, knowing herself to be blind, deaf, speechless, no longer aware of the members of her own body, entirely withdrawn from all human concerns . . ." At this point she has dehumanized herself, "all ties of blood and the desires of the heart" dissolving and falling away from her except her "stubborn will to live."

Miranda is indeed at "the farthest bottom of life" physically and psychologically, her mind split away from her body and from her painful guilt over Adam and Hildesheim. It is her most extreme form of escape, an escape into nothingness in which she sheds her humanity and becomes an inanimate stone. Her struggle is best explained by Laing's comments: the insecure person, once he has successfully destroyed in his mind the image of anyone he loves and reduced all his wants to nothing, "sets about murdering his 'self. . . . He descends into a vortex of non-being, but also to preserve being from himself." He notes elsewhere, ". . . to forgo one's autonomy becomes the means of secretly safeguarding it; to play possum, to feign death, becomes a means of preserving one's aliveness. To turn oneself into a stone becomes a way of not being turned into a stone by someone else."

The first part of Miranda's dream ends with her stubborn will to live, out of which springs her vision of a more hopeful and seemingly more human state of being. The setting is a "deep clear landscape of sea and sand, of soft meadow and sky," another landscape evoked from childhood memories, but with the difference that this one is peopled with "all the living she had known": "Their faces were transfigured . . . beyond what she remembered of them, their eyes were clear and untroubled . . . and they cast no shadows." Miranda later refers to this vision as "her paradise," "a child's dream of the heavenly meadow," but she has not envisioned an afterlife, for eternity to her is "unknowable." Rather she has projected an idealized version of this life, where all the "living" and "transfigured," their "untroubled" eyes without the "awful expression of fear and suspicion" of which she had complained earlier. Yet all the living are so idealized that they are not human; they are "pure identities" who cast no shadows in a timeless world where it is "always morning." Miranda, "desiring nothing," "within touch but not touching" anyone, has purified human relationships out of existence in an attempt to render them harmless.

As her dream fades, Miranda resumes her painful journey back to life and death: she "felt without warning . . . some small flick of distrust in her joy . . . somebody was missing. . . . There are no trees, no trees here, she said in fright. . . . We have forgotten the dead, oh, the dead, where are they?" Some interpret this difficult passage to mean that Miranda

has resisted death to return to Adam since later she complains, ". . . I wish you had come back, what do you think that I came back for, Adam, to be deceived like this?" But the passage states that she returns because the "somebody" missing from the "company of the living" is dead. And when she does return, she makes no inquiry about him; not until she reads many days later the letter informing her of his death, does she complain of being deceived.

The passage is better interpreted as part of the entire fifth dream, which moves downward to the farthest bottom of life and then upward and back to life. Miranda's vision of paradise is a stage between her desire to protect herself by turning into a stone, and her counter-desire to return to life from which she has fled. Her paradise fades, as did her vision of Adam as god, because it is unreal and cannot be sustained. Having fled from life which threatens death to states of non-life too similar to death, she returns to life defined by the presence of death. Miranda needs the dead to know that she is alive despite the grief it causes her.

Miranda's need of the dead is symbolized by her alarm at the absence of trees in her dream of paradise, which "the same monotonous landscape of dulled evergreens" replaces. The evergreens are symbols of life in death like the woods in her first three dreams. The "angry dangerous wood" of the third dream in which she kills Adam is probably inspired by Belleau Wood, patriotically evoked by the hated Liberty Bond salesman, who prompts her to think, "What's the matter with you, why aren't you rotting in Belleau Wood? I wish you were. . . ."

After her recovery Miranda exhibits all the symptoms of Laing's insecure person. Awakening to the smell of death in her body, she thinks, "The body is a curious monster, no place to live in, how could anyone feel at home there? Is it possible I can ever accustom myself to this place?" To her "all objects and beings" are "meaningless, ah, dead and withered things that believed themselves alive!" She is "not quite dead now . . . one foot in either world," but she assures herself that she will "cross back and be at home again." "Condemned" to this life by those who have "conspired" to restore "her disordered mind," she views them with the "covertly hostile eyes of an alien." Although she knows that people will say that they love her, "her hardened, indifferent heart shuddered in despair at itself, because it had been tender and capable of love." Similarly, the insecure person feels "more dead than alive" and unable "to experience himself 'together with' others or 'at home in' the world"; he lives "in despairing aloneness and isolation," an incomplete person "'split' in various ways, perhaps as a mind more or less tenuously linked to a body. . . ." Obviously, Miranda would not view herself in these terms since she feels fortified by a knowledge gained at a terrible price in her struggle with death in her fifth dream.

Miranda's vision of paradise is crucial to her view of herself and of the world. It confirms her despair of ever finding happiness, but it also reinforces her "stubborn will to live." Knowing that there is no escape from the world, she is stoically determined to live in it but not be part of it. She will disguise her face with make-up and mask her inward feeling with a smile so as not to "tamper with the courage of the living." Their courage is based on the illusion that happiness can exist, but her brush with death has given her an insight into the "truth" which they are not privileged to share. Thus her secret knowledge which she considered the source of her despair makes her unique in her own eyes. As she prepares to reenter the world in "the dazed silence that follows the ceasing of the heavy guns," she almost covets that despair because to her it defines a courage superior to that of the living.

---

**Miranda's vision of paradise [in "Pale Horse, Pale Rider"] is crucial to her view of herself and of the world. It confirms her despair of ever finding happiness, but it also reinforces her "stubborn will to live." Knowing that there is no escape from the world, she is stoically determined to live in it but not be part of it.**

*—Thomas F. Walsh*

---

Miranda's constricting fear of self and others does not allow me to accept her at her own estimate as Wayne Booth and some other critics do. Yet Porter's comments on her own experiences, which became the basis for **"Pale Horse, Pale Rider,"** seem to justify their interpretation. She reports that while working for Denver's *Rocky Mountain News* in 1918, she almost died of the influenza that carried off her friend Alexander, who had nursed her in the first stages of her illness. During her illness she had a "vision" which eventually became Miranda's "dream of the heavenly meadow":

> It took me a long time to go out and live in the world again. I was really "alienated," in the pure sense. It was, I think, the fact that I really had participated in death, that I knew what death was, and had almost experienced it. I had what the Christians call the "beatific vision," and the Greeks called the "happy day," the happy vision just before death. Now if you have had that, and survived it, come back from it, you are no longer like other people, and there's no use deceiving yourself that you are.

We can never know to what extent Porter transformed her vision of 1918 into her fiction of 1938, or to what extent her

fiction transformed, in the next thirty years, her conception of her original experience. She has so mythologized it that her account of her own return from the dead seems more literal and mystical than that suggested by Miranda's playful dialogue with herself: "Lazarus, come forth. Not unless you bring me my top hat and stick. Stay where you are then, you snob. Not at all, I'm coming forth." Yet the close identification between author and character allows the reader to view **"Pale Horse, Pale Rider"** as a personal statement of Porter's self-perception as artist. The biographical, as well as thematic, key to the story is the old spiritual that gives it its title. When Adam summarizes the many verses about the rider's carrying off the whole family including the lover, Miranda responds, "Death always leaves one singer to mourn. 'Death, . . . oh leave one singer to mourn—.'" Death grants character and author their wish. Allowing her her vision, he leaves Porter to mourn her loss in her art. **"Pale Horse, Pale Rider"** is her new spiritual, justifying her role as artist and assuaging her guilt over her survival at the cost of another. It may also justify her detachment from any who might come between her and the practice of her art, for she has made her priorities clear: "But this thing between me and my writing is the strongest bond I have ever had—stronger than any bond or any agreement with any human being or with any other work I've ever done."

The close identification between author and character seems to indicate that Porter consciously intended the reader's acceptance of Miranda's estimate of her vision. My interpretation runs counter to her intention on *this* point, and implies that Miranda's fears, to some extent, originated in the author's own. Porter's statement, "When I was a child, I was always running away," relates to Miranda's escape from her sleeping family in the first dream, and the alienation "in the pure sense" that Porter experienced after her vision may have been an extreme manifestation of a condition that unconsciously existed before her own exposure to war and influenza.

Porter's comments pertain to Miranda's vision, but other comments reinforce my reading that Miranda deceives herself into thinking that, like Juliet, she has returned to her beloved only to find that he has died in her service. Such a motive is in the best tradition of romantic love, on which Porter theorizes in a letter to her nephew in 1948. In "love at first sight," the lover

> is instantly transfigured with a light of such blinding *brilliance all natural attributes disappear* and are replaced by those usually associated with archangels at least. They are *beautiful, flawless* in temperament, witty, intelligent, charming, of such infinite grace, sympathy, and courage, I always wonder how they could have come from such absurdly inappropriate families. . . . It is a disaster, in fact. We are in love and while it lasts—. . . . And when it

is over. And when *I have recovered from the shock,* and . . . *put my mangled life in order,* I can then begin to remember what really happened. It is probably the silliest kind of love there is, but I'm glad. . . . there were times when I saw human beings at their best, for I don't think by any means that I lent them all their *radiance.* . . . Lightening makes the most *familiar landscape* wild, strange, and *beautiful,* and *it passes.* It was all my fault, though. If one ever treats a man as if he were an archangel, he can't ever, possibly, consent to being treated like a human being again. He cannot do it, it's nonsense to expect it. It begins to look as if I had never wanted it.

The words I have italicized recall Miranda's description of Adam, her dream of paradise, and her subsequent disillusion. The passage suggests that Miranda's very act of idealizing Adam is proof that she, like Porter, never wanted a lasting love relationship at all. Although Porter wrote her letter ten years after she published her story, she may have intended Miranda's self-deception. In an interview she remembered telling a friend in Mexico that Alexander was the only man she could have spent her life with. "And he replied, 'Just think, now he can never disappoint you.' And I suppose if there is anything at all good about it, that's it, but it does seem an awfully high price to pay to keep one's illusions, doesn't it?" Her friend, who could not have made his sardonic remark later than 1931, the last year of her stay in Mexico, exposed her self-deception which she had probably tried to sustain since her recovery from influenza. By 1938 she must have known that her attempt was futile. If she did intend that the reader accept Miranda's estimate of her love for Adam despite her own suspicions about Alexander and romantic love, her suspicions crept into her story nevertheless, as an examination of Miranda's dreams reveals.

Porter's near identification with Miranda illuminates but cannot resolve the problem of whether the reader should accept her at her own estimate, although it helps explain why critics are divided on the issue. In this paper we have viewed Miranda "from above" because we know more about her than she knows about herself, but that does not diminish the force of our sympathy for her as unwitting victim of overwhelming circumstances and of her ontologically insecure personality.

**Mary E. Titus (essay date Spring 1990)**

SOURCE: "The 'Booby Trap' of Love: Artist and Sadist in Katherine Anne Porter's Mexico Fiction," in *The Journal of Modern Literature,* Vol. 16, No. 4, Spring, 1990, pp. 617-34.

[*In the following essay, Titus explores sexuality, gender politics, and the objectification of women in Porter's early published and unpublished writing.*]

"Her eagerness to be beautiful in their eyes, to draw them to her, made her ache. Her nerve ends boiled and bubbled. But she kept her face calm as she watched them, serpent-feminine enough to know that her attitude of calm pleased them." Inscrutable without and turbulent within, Alma, the silent, erotic center of Katherine Anne Porter's unfinished story, "The Evening," resembles several of the female characters in Porter's 1920s Mexico fiction. "The Evening" belongs with four other early narratives, all originating in Porter's relationship with the Mexican artist community: **"Flowering Judas"** (published in 1930), **"Virgin Violeta"** (1924), **"The Martyr"** (1923), and its unpublished counterpart, "The Lovely Legend" (manuscript dated 1925). These biographically related texts focus on the relationship of male spectator and female spectacle, often through an artist and his model/muse, and expose the sadomasochism that Porter saw fueling the transformation of women into symbolic and erotic objects. Read together and then set in the context of essays and unpublished journals, they reveal that during the 1920s Porter was intently exploring the issues of power underlying the tradition of romantic love.

> In Porter's early Mexico fiction, interactions between the sexes are presented as sexualized struggles of dominance and submission. The male characters share the same sadistic goals: to subject the women to their will, consume them as sexual objects, or use and then discard them in the service of some creative act.
>
> —*Mary E. Titus*

In Porter's early Mexico fiction, interactions between the sexes are presented as sexualized struggles of dominance and submission. The male characters share the same sadistic goals: to subject the women to their will, consume them as sexual objects, or use and then discard them in the service of some creative act. Yet, although threatening, even monstrous, these men are powerful and thus, the texts suggest, dangerously attractive. Confronted with the physical and emotional threat implicit in the presence of the male artists, the passive women respond in a complex manner. They do not imagine a different, active existence; rather, their desires are either for safety, escape from or protection against the controlling male gaze, or, more frequently, pleasure, the pleasure which

Porter suggests accompanies self-objectification and which can be gained by further attracting masculine admiration.

Except for "The Evening," these stories adopt either the woman's point of view, exploring the mingling of desire and terror aroused by a powerful man's attention, or the man's point of view, exposing his combined obsession with and exploitation of the woman. All share an atmosphere of erotic tension and employ images of gluttony, suffocation, and entrapment.

Perhaps Porter never finished "The Evening" because she was unable to settle on a point of view for the text. Some passages ("Her eagerness to be beautiful . . .") follow Alma's thoughts as her nerves "boil and bubble" in her violent desire to arouse violent desire. She longs to fulfill her romantic fantasy: "To dance with one man while another stared in another direction with murder in his heart . . . that was the way she described it to herself." Other passages move into the minds of the men surrounding her, and in these Porter reveals how men, either artists or parasitical aesthetes, use women as the passive medium out of which they shape their aesthetic. Their argument—that all beauty requires the presence of some ugliness—is punctuated by unspoken feelings of desire or hostility for Alma. They think of the silent woman as an object exchanged among men and employ the dualistic imagery that characterizes the imaginations of all the men in Porter's artist stories. According to Gordito, for example: "She would not go back to Ciro or to Roberto—no she would not go back, she would go on to Vicente . . . little whore, adorable angel." Because the manuscript of "The Evening" shifts about in point of view and is incomplete, it is not possible to state with any assurance Porter's final goals. But the text underscores her explorations of the sexual/sadistic bonds between passive women and controlling men, a theme which arose out of her experiences in 1920s Mexico. In fact, among Alma's admirers, little Lino, who scrawls "obscene caricatures," is easily identified as Miguel Covarrubias, the young caricaturist who, with other members of Mexico's artist community, helped Porter organize an exhibition of Mexico folk art in 1922.

"Flowering Judas" stands at the center of Porter's Mexico fiction, and at its center is the eternal present, where Braggioni watches Laura with the patience of a predator. Told from the woman's point of view, this story explores the combination of attraction to and fear of her own objectification which keeps Laura frozen and silent throughout the narrative. Although "nobody touches" Laura, she appears surrounded by men who watch and desire her, and she defends herself against the sexual threat implicit in their gaze by erecting barriers. Like Alma, she maintains an "attitude of calm" and conceals her sexuality: her lips are "always firmly closed"; her "great round breasts" are covered "with thick dark cloth." Yet despite these measures, Laura's most ordinary actions take on the quality of performance under the eroticizing gaze: "No dancer walks more beautifully than Laura walks, and she inspires some amusing and unexpected ardors" as she passes silently through the streets.

Laura's defenses mask desire as much as resistance. She is "full of romantic error" and enjoys being a spectacle. When a young man begins daily to follow her, "she is pleasantly disturbed by the abstract, unhurried watchfulness of his black eyes which will in time turn easily towards another object." She finds the kind of masochistic pleasure under the male gaze that E. Ann Kaplan identifies in her discussion of the erotic in film: "Assigned to the place of object (lack), she is the recipient of male desire, passively appearing rather than acting. Her sexual pleasure in this position can thus be constructed only around her own objectification." Through her long, tense confrontation with Braggioni, Laura holds herself still, frozen like an erotic image for his contemplation.

Laura's pleasure in her own objectification—like Alma's in "The Evening"—is combined with an "insatiable thirst" for "excitement." Her marginal participation in the Revolution rises from this attraction to the erotic: what is dangerous is also sensual. Thus, she lives tantalizingly close to impending violence, whether it be the revolution's chaos or Braggioni's physical assault. Hers is a "liminal state" between yielding and flight, an exciting, sustained tension. Seated across from Laura, Braggioni is the mirror in which she views what she fears and desires. His physical appearance suggests the combination of sensuality and violence which secretly attracts her. Gluttonous, oily, with yellow eyes like a cat, he exudes an erotic threat. Like Laura's masking clothing, Braggioni's costume forms a central symbol of his sexuality:

> Over his lavender collar, crushed upon a purple necktie, held by a diamond hoop: over his ammunition belt of tooled leather worked in silver, buckled cruelly around his gasping middle: over the tops of his glossy yellow shoes Braggioni swells with ominous ripeness, his mauve silk hose stretched taut, his ankles bound with the stout leather thongs of his shoes.

Braggioni's silk and leather clothing suggests the implements of bondage in sadomasochistic sexual fantasies. His gasping body is "buckled cruelly" inside his heavy belt; his feet are bound. Braggioni represents the erotic dangers and pleasures of love for Laura, as yielding to desire requires subjection of the self.

Cruel and vain, Braggioni pins Laura beneath his gaze and assaults her with his song. He plays the guitar as though it were her body, expressing through it the sexual violence implicit in his costume: "under the rip of his thumbnail, the strings of the instrument complain like exposed nerves." Braggioni as singer resembles the other artist figures in Porter's fiction; not only is woman his subject and his inspiration, but the goal of his art is her submission. Thus his song, which transforms Laura into a figure in a romantic legend, legitimizes his hunger: it represents an effort to control her by controlling the language which defines her. "'O girl with the dark eyes,' he sings and reconsiders. 'But yours are not dark. I can change all that. O girl with the green eyes, you have stolen my heart away!'" Braggioni remakes the song as he would like to remake Laura; his words are a mask over his predatory gaze, the "cat's eyes" which, as he sings, mark "the opposite ends of a smoothly drawn path between the swollen curve of her breasts."

Knowledge of Porter's source for Braggioni's song further reinforces the fact that Porter views the gluttonous revolutionary as an artist and Laura as his passive medium. Thomas Walsh has identified the song as "A la Orilla de un Palmar," a ballad in which a male speaker recalls meeting a beautiful woman and singing her lament: "I am a little orphan, alas. I have no father and no mother, nor even a friend who comes, alas, to console me." As Walsh rightly points out, "the song is obvious male fantasy with the promise of sexual conquest lurking just below its sentimental surface." In Braggioni's ballad, sung to the tune of his sadistic guitar, the male artist speaks the woman's desire; she is his creation, part of his fantasy of seduction and control.

Laura's half-willing attraction to the combination of sensuality and danger in Braggioni becomes most apparent as she oils and loads his pistols. Although until this point she has resisted him entirely, keeping an "open book on her knees," as "her knees cling together" under her heavy skirt, she takes his ammunition belt when he asks and "spreads it laden across her knees" and "sits with the shells slipping through the cleaning cloth dipped in oil." The guns and the oil, the two elements of Braggioni's erotic appeal—violence and sensuality—occupy her completely. And when he asks her why she has no lover, "a long, slow faintness rises and subsides in her," suggesting that her conscious defenses briefly yield to unconscious desire. The wave passes, but in that moment Braggioni's sensual but dangerous hold has tightened. Again the guitar represents Laura's passive body: "Braggioni curves his swollen fingers around the throat of the guitar and softly smothers the music out of it." The moment is both climax and murder, a soft smothering. While Braggioni "strokes the pistol lying in [Laura's] hands," his hypnotic voice describes the violent explosions that will accompany the revolution.

**"Flowering Judas"** has biographical ties to Porter's other 1920s fiction which explores sadomasochism and romantic fantasy. Braggioni's blonde curls and his youth as an impassioned poet suggest that his character is based partially on

one of her admirers, the Nicaraguan poet Salómon de la Selva, with whom she was involved in 1922. Publicly, Porter claimed that she combined "four or five objectionable characters into . . . one" when she created Braggioni, and privately she was even more explicit about Carlos, the poet with the predatory eyes in **"Virgin Violeta."** In unpublished notes on her *Collected Stories,* Porter wrote that Carlos was "Based on looks, character, and malicious ways of Salómon de la Selva." De la Selva's poetry participates in and perhaps influenced the atmosphere of her 1920s fiction. His collection *Tropical Town and Other Poems,* published in 1918, explores themes of religious and sexual devotion, often mingling the Christian and the erotic with suggestions of violence. In these poems, sacred ecstasy, a dying in passionate communion with God, is connected with sexual ecstasy, a losing of the self in another. Some of de la Selva's poems recall the experiences of such mystics as Saint Teresa; others use language suggesting the rituals and implements of sacrifice; still others are explicitly sexual, the sexuality emphatically stained with sadomasochism. One man's caresses are burning flames in the night; another lover is "afevered for the torture" of his beloved's touch; dawn brings death to passion; in several poems, the beloved herself is dead.

Porter's papers also link de la Selva with two other acquaintances in 1920s Mexico: Diego Rivera and his model and wife, Guadalupe Marin. According to Porter's notes, the 1924 story **"The Martyr"** was directed at "Diego Rivera and his wild-woman Lupe Marin." Among her unpublished papers is a description of an evening with Rivera, Marin, and de la Selva from which she drew material for **"Virgin Violeta":**

> The night at Los Monotes . . . Lupe the Savage. Diego. Salómon de la Selva. Our pilgrimage to the Nino Perdido . . . The old convent in the old street, the cobblestones and broken glass, the rattle of the tinny orchestra from the pulquerria around the corner. A danzon. We dance, and afterward he makes a poem . . . something about the nuns in that convent who looked out on dancers in other days . . . and tonight their ghosts with ghostly partners, come and dance again—the nuns are dancing with small bare feet, over broken glass in a cobbled street . . . for me, he said.

De la Selva's nuns dancing barefoot on broken glass—a characteristic image of erotic sacrifice—reappear in these 1920s stories, in both **"Virgin Violeta"** and the unpublished "The Lovely Legend." In the latter, Amado, de la Selva's fictional counterpart, weeps briefly over a woman's masochistic devotion. "'She did, she did,' he sobbed. 'She danced for me on broken glass with her white feet bleeding. I knelt and kissed the wounds through the cold iron grill of the gate.'" The image deserves attention, for it clearly fascinated Porter. Like Laura, the nuns wear clothing which both covers their sexuality and ostensibly announces its repression or denial. External identity is erased; they are blanks awaiting the inscription of male desire, either the fantasy accompanying the erotic gaze or, in the case of the nuns, the patriarchal Word.

Like Laura too, the nuns are silent. The poet both interprets their actions and claims them for his own pleasure. Yet their blankness is a mask worn over a potential sensuality which, when released, finds expression in masochistic display. Dancing on glass, the nuns simultaneously reveal their sexuality—the blood suggesting defloration or menstruation—and receive punishment for it. Their expression of desire is simultaneously self-sacrifice. The nuns enact this erotic ritual for the male observer—"for me," the poet says. The dancing nuns are de la Selva's supreme romantic fantasy, a spectacle of adoration, submission, and sexual sacrifice.

In **"Virgin Violeta,"** the image of dancing nuns becomes central to Porter's exploration of a young girl's seduction by a male poet's text. Violeta's awakening sexuality leads her from romantic fantasies of masochistic devotion, fed by Carlos's poems, to a terrifying experience of her actual entrapment and victimization within these fantasies. As in **"Flowering Judas,"** in **"Virgin Violeta"** the point of view belongs to the silent woman. Thus, the story shares the same erotic tension of withholding and desire and has the same slow movement, a sense of unendurable time spent in a liminal state between boredom and arousal. From the beginning, romantic love is entwined with religious ecstasy, violence, and abasement in the text. Carlos's poetry speaks of the "torment of love," and the picture above Violeta's head shows St. Ignatius before an aloof Virgin Mary, "grovel[ling] in a wooden posture of ecstasy."

Entering puberty, Violeta becomes infatuated with her cousin, Carlos. He fascinates and attracts her both as a man and as a poet; she longs for his approving looks and studies his poetry seeking the images of his desire. The power of Carlos's text contends with that of the Church for Violeta, giving her another version of what it means to be good. She conceals his poems in her missal, memorizing them during religious service. Throughout the long, slow evening, Violeta dreams of a masochistic sacrifice, combining ecstasy with self-abasement. She is enthralled by Carlos's description of "the ghosts of nuns . . . treading with bared feet on broken glass as a penance for their loves" and shakes all over when she reads the poem, imagining that it had been written for her: "'The nuns are dancing with bared feet / On broken glass in the cobbled street.'. . . She was even one of the nuns, the youngest and best-beloved, ghostly silent, dancing forever and ever under the moonlight to the shivering tune of old violins."

Placing herself within Carlos's text, Violeta imagines herself as the "best-beloved" object of Carlos's desire. Like

Laura, she finds looking and being looked at absorbing and stimulating. She feels intensely exposed to Carlos's critical gaze as she sits at her mother's knee. And watching the poet watch her sister, Blanca, she becomes increasingly aroused. As spectator, Violeta identifies herself with Blanca, the focus and actual passive recipient of Carlos's desire. This excited identification resembles the potential pleasure that E. Ann Kaplan assigns to the female spectator of an erotic film: "[l]ocating herself in fantasy in the erotic, the woman places herself as either passive recipient of male desire, or at one remove, as *watching* a woman who is passive recipient of male desire and sexual actions." In Porter's text, Violeta's identification with her sister is so complete that she participates in her physical experiences. When Blanca's shawl slips from her shoulder, "A tight shudder of drawn threads played along Violeta's skin, and grew quite intolerable when Carlos reached out to take the fringe in his long fingers."

Violeta alternates watching with fantasy. She imagines a "beautiful and unexpected" future in which she becomes "miraculously lovely," all-desirable. In common with Alma in "The Evening," she longs to be a performer in a clichéd romantic scene, with an audience of excited, admiring men. She imagines that "she would dance with fascinating young men . . . would appear on the balcony above, wearing a blue dress, and everyone would ask who that enchanting girl could be." The center of the fantasy is, of course, Carlos; he is the most important of the admiring observers. In Violeta's mind, her sudden desirability is proof that she has devoted herself to his text. Looking at her displayed on the balcony, "Carlos . . . would understand at last that she had read and loved his poems always." For Violeta, memorizing the poet's text is one with becoming the text. Transformed into the perfect object of desire, she becomes a poem. Just as Braggioni's guitar stands for Laura's body in **"Flowering Judas,"** so Violeta becomes Carlos's poem in her imagination, the perfect actualization of his romantic texts.

Finally unable to restrain her desire, Violeta intimates to Carlos her knowledge of his poems. The confession immediately brings what she both desires and fears: her transformation into an erotic object. When she rises to retrieve his book, the poet follows her down the dark hall, the predatory *pad-pad* of his rubber heels close behind her." Finally, he traps her in the moonlight and kisses her. Although Violeta receives only a kiss, the impact of Carlos's act is equal to a rape; she is, as her name suggests, a virgin violated.

Carlos's unexpected kiss constitutes a terrifying violation for several reasons. Violeta dreams of Carlos's love and turns to him expecting "to sink into a look warm and gentle." What she confronts instead is the blank gaze of the predator: "His eyes were bright and shallow, almost like the eyes of Pepe, the macaw." Rather than offering a communion between equals, Carlos seeks to possess and devour. Like Braggioni's predatory gaze, which belies the superficially compassionate content of his song, Carlos's eyes expose the sadistic desire underlying his poetry. "Staring at her, fearfully close," their blank rapacity alarms Violeta, and she struggles to escape, feeling as if she is "about to smother."

No matter how she turns, however, the young girl confronts another image of herself as she is perceived by the poet. She cannot escape his text: it surrounds her like a mirror, and she possesses no other language except that which defines and thus controls her. Although Violeta feels violated by the poet's act, she continues to watch herself as if through his eyes, and in the next moments her sense of self is repeatedly transformed as she struggles to accept the changing images that Carlos provides. The poet first calls Violeta an innocent child, chiding her for overreacting to "a little brotherly kiss." When he tells her that she "smell[s] like a nice baby, freshly washed with white soap," his voice "tremble[s] in a strange way," revealing that her innocence excites him. Violeta, longing for adulthood, cannot fully understand Carlos's fantasy, the pleasure he takes in imagining her innocence as a blank, whitewashed and inviting inscription. Although she accepts his image, she does so with shame and horror. "She saw herself before him, almost as if his face were a mirror. Her mouth was too large; her face was simply a moon; her hair was ugly . . . 'Oh I'm so sorry!' she whispered." In her own mind, Violeta feels transformed into a round-faced infant by the poet's controlling language and look. To be undesirable, she feels, is to be without value, to not exist, and she suddenly longs "to run away," to kill herself.

However, Carlos's next words again transform Violeta: "What did you expect when you came out here alone with me?" he asks, suggesting that she invited the kiss. Suddenly she is seducer rather than child—she has provoked her own violation. "He turned and started away. She was shamefully, incredibly in the wrong. She had behaved like an immodest girl." Buffeted between the twin poles of male fantasy, Violeta becomes in moments both the virgin and the prostitute, the temptress and the victim: like Alma in "The Evening," she is simultaneously "little whore" and "adorable angel." "It was all bitterly real and unbelievable," she thinks, "like a nightmare that went on and on and no one heard you calling to be waked up."

Laura and Violeta form a still center in their stories, surrounded by men who perform the actions and do most of the speaking. Willing objects of fantasy, they alternately yield to and struggle against the defining language and erotic gaze of the more powerful male characters. In their identification with vehicles of the imagination—musical instruments, poetry—Laura and Violeta resemble artist's models whose nude bodies provide image and inspiration. In this context, in two other stories dating from the 1920s, **"The Martyr"** and "The Lovely Legend," Porter more explicitly explored the sado-

masochism which she saw underlying the tradition of romantic love. Of the two, she published only **"The Martyr,"** a text that uses ironic reversal to make its point: the artist is his model's victim. Both **"The Martyr"** and "The Lovely Legend" are told from the male artist's point of view. Both expose, with underlying irony and anger, each artist's exploitation and objectification of the passive woman in the making of his art.

In creating Ruben, the artist in **"The Martyr,"** Porter drew on her acquaintance with Diego Rivera. Isabel, Ruben's model, resembles Lupe Marin, Rivera's wife and model, known for her violent temper, and the painting in the story corresponds to Rivera's mural "Creation," which he painted in 1922 at the Preparatoria School. However, Porter draws Ruben, her artist, with the exaggerated strokes of a cartoon. The martyr of the story, he can speak only of his passionate adoration of Isabel. When she leaves him for another artist, he gorges himself to death, between bites mourning the moments when "she used to kick my shins black and blue." Ruben's steady, destructive feeding not only reveals his self-destructive tendencies but also suggests his powerful desire to repossess Isabel. Thus, Porter repeatedly links his eating to his loss: while he laments Isabel's absence, he fills himself with substitutes: "Crisp sweet cakes," "sweet wine," and "soft Toluca cheese, spiced with mangos." "[E]ating cheese and gazing with wet eyes at the nineteenth figure of Isabel" on his easel, Ruben longs again to devour his model with his eyes but now must satisfy his hunger for her in other ways.

Ruben's "consuming" desire for Isabel is apparent even before she runs away, in his obsession with her as his model. She would often "stand all day . . . while Ruben made sketches of her." His mural is to contain twenty figures of Isabel, twenty reinterpretations of her significance. In the flesh, the single focus of the artist's gaze, Isabel becomes the sole subject of his language after her departure. Here she appears in characteristic dual terms—innocent child and evil temptress. "[My] poor little angel Isabel is a murderess," Ruben mourns. She is a killer in the diminutive: "Ah Isabelita, my executioner!" Ironic and exaggerated, **"The Martyr"** parodies the male artist's obsession with the meaning of woman. Yet even as parody, Ruben's gluttony suggests the artist's desire to control and consume his model through language and image. (At the same time the story alludes to Rivera's own voracious appetite for both food and sex.) His frequent relations with his models—perhaps including Porter—are public knowledge. Isabel's response can be inferred from her flight, as can her boredom and sense of entrapment before she escapes with her lover. Yet in describing the new relationship, Porter reveals that Isabel is as addicted to her objectification as is Laura in **"Flowering Judas"**: Isabel has left Ruben for a man who will create a "mural with fifty figures [of her] in it, instead of only twenty."

The mocking tone of **"The Martyr"** disappears in "The Lovely Legend," replaced by a clear sense of underlying rage. Here Porter portrays two artists, friends, both using the same woman as image and inspiration in their art. The painter Rafael's relationship to this model is both overtly exploitive and sadistic; in contrast, the poet Amado is foolishly infatuated with his own fantasies of the woman. Rafael, occasionally referred to as Ruben, is clearly based on Diego Rivera; Amado, a poet and lover, takes his character from Salómon de la Selva. The story opens with the two men discussing women as erotic objects. Amado is describing at length the color and odor of women he has desired or made love to; Rafael seems bored, mentioning finally his need for a particular type of woman to serve as a model:

> I need a model for the Maya fresco, said Rafael. I want a lean tall woman who does not simper or paint her finger nails. She must have long hard hands and feet, and a nose with a hooked bridge. Her hair must be black.

According to Amado, Rosita, a dying tubercular prostitute living at Calle de la Palma, meets Rafael's need exactly. Like Isabel in **"The Martyr,"** or like Lupe herself, according to Porter's notes, Rosita is aloof and bold, gaunt but physically powerful and often violent. Rafael takes her home as his model and paints her during the increasingly infrequent lulls between her violent rages and physical attacks.

Because of Rosita's profession and her increasing violence, the reader is unable to share the complacency with which the male characters view her objectification. In fact, her original role as prostitute suggests the truth about her second role as model. In both roles she is powerless, an object that may be possessed and then discarded. Whether standing before the two men in the artist's studio or at Calle de la Palma, in the men's minds she has value only insofar as she stimulates both their erotic fantasies and their art: the two seem inextricably linked. Her violent attacks on Rafael suggest that Rosita resists her completely passive status. Although she does not speak, by throwing pots at the painter's head she clearly upsets the terms of their relation and attempts, unsuccessfully, to assert her presence as more than a passive medium.

Rafael, however, remains entirely indifferent towards his model, unlike Ruben in **"The Martyr."** He does not recognize her violence or rage in any way. Her protest is merely an annoyance, and he makes no effort either to understand or to resolve it. For him, Rosita is an object, not a person, a more or less useful means for expressing his creative powers. As he tells Amado, "this empty creature, useless as a human being, has for me the value of a work of art." On the other hand, Amado, the poet, is deeply affected by Rafael's images of Rosita, "recreated in splendor, her likeness raised to the stature of a goddess." Stimulated by his fellow artist's work, he begins to construct increasingly obsessive romantic fantasies about the model until, unable to overcome his infatuation, he flees to Nicaragua, rewrites all of his poetry, and dreams of Rosita's "magnified portraits." During the poet's absence, Rafael tires of the model's violence, perhaps because he unconsciously recognizes it as an effort at self-expression. As he later tells Amado, Rosita had acquired an increasingly irritating tendency to regard "those gorgeous bones as her own property." Her usefulness over, he returns her to the brothel at Calle de la Palma. When an unsubdued Amado returns, Rafael tells him Rosita is dead. The poet mourns Rosita passionately and composes a lengthy ballad of her life, transforming her into "The Lovely Legend." But then, upon learning that she has been returned to her former profession, he visits Calle de la Palma only to experience an inexplicable yet complete collapse of his fantasy. She ceases to be a significant object for him, and he feels, suddenly, "as if she were really dead."

In Rafael's last speech to Amado, Rosita's status as an object to be appropriated and discarded becomes entirely evident. According to Rafael, Rosita herself had no identity; she existed and had value only through the forms given her by the artist's desire. When that desire disappeared, she became a thing of no value. "Why mourn?" Rafael asks his friend:

> You have your poem, I have my fresco: they are the ends, what else is in the least important? Rosita? pah, dead or alive, how does she figure in this now? [. . . .] I tell you, you loved some fancy you had of her, nothing more. She is not a woman to love, she is a bitch and ugly to her core, any beauty she possesses you added to her yourself. I clothed my idea with her outlines, and I love that: but I never confused the two things.

As prostitute, bitch, and ugly woman, Rosita is nothing—she has no significance except as a passive physical vehicle for the artist's vision. In Rafael's speech, Porter exposes the sadistic appropriation of Rosita by poet and painter alike. Rosita herself has no voice in the story—the men articulate her significance and insignificance. Her only recourse is inarticulate rage. Ironically, what is produced through or by means of this silent woman are more texts: a poem, a fresco, a "Lovely Legend." These transform a dying prostitute, like an orphan wandering on a shore, or a nun dancing on glass, into a romantic victim.

When "The Lovely Legend" is grouped with Porter's other published and unpublished stories from 1920s Mexico, it becomes apparent that in her early fiction she repeatedly explored the sadomasochism which she saw underlying relationships in which women are transformed into symbolic and erotic objects. All of her male characters are artists: poets, painters, singers. Their poems, paintings, and songs originate in a relationship to a woman that is both violent and sensual. And their art is implicated in that violence; although alternately seductive poetry and obsessive fantasy, it is always predatory, seeking to define, objectify and ultimately control its female subject. In those narratives written from the woman's point of view, the combination of attraction and danger surrounding the male artist creates such ambivalence that the female character is frozen between desire and terror, yielding and flight. On the other hand, narratives written from the man's point of view expose an attitude toward the woman that is either so fatuous or so coldly exploitative that the female characters respond with violence.

Although the connections among these several narratives become clear when they are examined as a group, what remains unclear are Porter's possible motives for exposing and exploring the sadomasochistic potential in these relationships. Her 1921 essay, **"The Mexican Trinity,"** provides one clue. Here she condemns contemporary Mexican literature for ignoring the revolution and adhering to the old themes of "romance and the stars, and roses and the shadowy eyes of ladies, touching no sorrow of the human heart other than the pain of unrequited love." Romantic love is neither modern nor revolutionary, Porter implies; it is distinctly unliberating. The Mexico stories develop a more complex and even more condemnatory statement on art that portrays romantic love. By focusing on the relationship of male artist and female subject, these stories expose the origins of the tradition, showing the varying postures of seduction, infatuation, and sacrifice which are celebrated as love rises out of oppressive, violent relationships and which are, in actuality, postures of domination and submission. The poems, paintings, and songs in these stories either originate in the exploitation of a woman or express a lover's desire to possess the beloved: a desire which finds correspondence in her unacknowledged wish to be possessed. "Possessing," as Porter points out in her essay, **"Marriage Is Belonging,"** is too often "the basis of many contracts" between men and women.

A book review from 1925 provides another important clue to Porter's concerns in her Mexico fiction. In the review, she touches on a related subject: art is made predominantly by men, and in it women have a predominantly passive role as muse or model. This, Porter argues, is a wrong that must be remedied. "Why did woman allow herself to be used as a symbol by man?" she asks in the review. Why is woman an actress, "a plastic medium for the expression of someone else's idea"? "If this difference is biological," she continues, "then it may be said that nature is the implacable enemy of woman and it is the duty of intelligence to combat this destructive law."

These statements, bolstered by the feminism of other 1920s reviews, support the reading that Porter's early fiction attacks the conventions of a male-dominated literary tradition in which women perennially served as passive subject rather than active creator, and in which one goal of art—whether it be Braggioni's song, Carlos's passionate poems of sacrifice and adoration, or Amado's "Lovely Legend"—is their submission to men's creative and erotic fantasies. Thus, the fiction condemns the male artists who perpetuate and benefit from the tradition of romantic love.

Yet this answer is also incomplete. For the women in Porter's Mexico stories do not blindly comply with the demands of their male companions. Laura is well aware of the violence under Braggioni's oily song, and both Isabel and Rosita throw pots at the painters' heads. What these stories (told from the woman's point of view) make absolutely clear, in fact, is that women are seduced by the romantic love tradition and often find their own objectification exciting. Porter's terms in the review—"nature" and "intelligence"—illuminate Laura's position between yielding and flight. Her mind tells her that she should flee, but her body stays firmly in place. In a brief, undated journal entry, Porter laments her own upbringing in the tradition of romantic love and the shock she encountered—perhaps like Laura's terrible disillusionment—when she entered "real life" in the twenties:

> LOVE. My earliest notions of love were founded, alas, for me in the world I was about to encounter, not on Freud, but on Harry King's poem to his dead wife, on Heloise's letters to Abelard on Wuthering Heights . . . and on my father's perpetual mourning for my mother, who died young and fair and never faded as mortal women do. This is no preparation for what we are pleased to call real life as I was to learn.

In "The Making of Flowering Judas," Thomas Walsh suggests that Laura's defensive pose reflects her author's fears: "Porter identified with . . . Laura's 'notorious virginity,' expressing her own fear of violation in a world in which men were used to having their way with women." Yet as much as Laura expresses Porter's fear, she also expresses her desire. As a public reviewer, Porter condemned artistic conventions of sexual objectification, but privately she acknowledged her own romantic desires. Like Laura, she was poised between two worlds, one of "romantic error," which she found impossible to relinquish, another of modern disillusionment, in which she could see that the tradition of romantic love perpetuated oppression in every relation of men and women, from that of artist and subject—the scheme in which the fantasies first find expression—to that of lovers, as the fantasies are acted out. As a scrap written in the third person among her papers states: "She suffered a great deal from love, or rather, the impossibility of finding an adequate substitute for illusion."

Caught up in the Mexican art community, Porter must have felt great contradictions between her attraction to and emotional involvement with the men she knew and her simultaneous recognition that both their art and their culture exploited women sexually. Romantic herself, she records with pleasure, "Salómon repeating his poems, lightly melancholy, full of a false nostalgia, oddly enchanting." Yet elsewhere her notes explicitly condemn the poet's romantic code: "I detested his attitude toward love and women." She comments wryly, "If Salómon met the Virgin Mary, he would introduce himself as the Holy Ghost." "Symbols"—"little whore, adorable angel"—or models and muses—"plastic medium[s] for the expression of someone else's ideas"—the women in Porter's Mexico fiction are objectified and exploited. Yet to grind paints and perhaps model for Diego Rivera and to dance with Salómon de la Selva and have that dance transformed into a poem were undoubtedly experiences which Porter was unwilling to relinquish.

Throughout her life, Porter's fiction as well as her letters, journals, and essays, records an unresolved struggle between desire for romantic love and desire for freedom: it seemed impossible for her to achieve these two together. This struggle was probably extremely acute during the 1920s. Porter turned thirty in 1920, and her unpublished personal notes from the next ten years record forcefully her recurring frustration with emotional relationships. "Not one of them wished me to live as I must live, given my nature and my vocation," she once wrote in her notes. "They wished to put my whole life to uses for which it simply was not intended." Conditioned by her upbringing and culture and, moreover, impelled by her own desires for love, she often complied willingly with her companion's expectations. The results were painful: she saw herself, like a model or muse, transformed by the other's fantasy of her: "under the strain of trying to live in the vise in which they could fit me," her notes record, "I took on, you might say, the shape of their own distorted desires." Lovers consumed or destroyed her, Porter's journals from the twenties suggest, leaving her "withered" and "mangled." As for Laura in **"Flowering Judas,"** the alternative to seemingly inevitable subjection is flight. In a journal entry dated Monday, February 27, 1928, Porter describes her struggle between these two unsatisfactory alternatives and vows to end a period of self-imposed isolation and "face the world." "I found much there to frighten and discompose me," she writes, "but only because my sexual impulses led me into situations that I could not control or battle with. . . . Certainly my doubts of human beings and their motives is [sic] founded in a fear of their power over me."

The mingled violence, hatred, and desire which infuse sexual relations in Porter's 1920s fiction become a consistent characteristic of her vision, apparent in much of her work through *Ship of Fools.* Finally, all romantic relationships are seen as stifling and destructive. From Miranda's sudden recognition,

"I hate loving and being loved, I hate it," to Jenny Brown's impassioned attack: "I think it is a booby trap . . . I hate it and I always did," spoken "with a violence that made her shake all over," rejections of love chime repeatedly in Porter's writing. This early group of Mexico stories about artists and desire reveal that in the 1920s Porter was exploring the materials out of which this "booby trap" is created and maintained, perhaps in an effort to control her own victimization by love. The stories not only expose the violence underlying the symbolic, erotic objectification of women, but they also, with intense honesty, explore the ways in which women have been attracted to or participated in their own objectification.

### Reynolds Price (review date 27 May 1990)

SOURCE: A review of *Letters of Katherine Anne Porter*, in *New York Times Book Review*, May 27, 1990, pp. 1, 23.

[*In the following review, Price praises the publication of Porter's correspondence for offering new insight into the life and work of the author.*]

Katherine Anne Porter wrote letters of an astonishing intellectual sinew and clarity with an ease that escaped when she turned to fiction. Despite the fact that the best of her stories, short novels and essays are as strong as any in American letters—**"Noon Wine"** alone can stand, calm, shoulder to shoulder, with anything in Tolstoy or Chekhov—her work has yet to win the wide and steady attention it earns and rewards. Most years I read her collected stories with students at an excellent university; and given the fact that their experience of past writers is generally meager, I unfailingly discover that almost none of them—even those women interested in the work of other women—have ever heard of Porter, much less consumed her adamant shelf of books.

Strange and regrettable as that is, I can think of interesting reasons why. First, her supreme skills were for short forms; and one of the puzzling realities of the literate American public, pressed as it is for time, is a relative refusal to buy and read short stories. Then from here it can also be seen that the worst piece of luck in an unlucky career struck Porter late. It was only in 1962 that she published the novel she had worked on for more than 20 years.

*Ship of Fools* was a brush-fire commercial success—huge sales, book clubs, a movie, interviews, prizes and the ensuing mud-wrestle of a wildly intemperate critical response, pro and con. In no time the book was one of those frequent hapless phenomena—the novel that sells like hot cakes but is soon abandoned as unreadable. In retrospect, it seems a little less mechanical and embittered than it did; but the backwash of her *Ship*'s launching still laps at Porter's best work. And bad luck has dogged her posthumously.

She shares the fate of Hemingway in being the victim of at least one biography of the sort few political villains deserve, much less benevolent artists. With no sustained attempt at comprehension, Joan Givner's 1982 *Katherine Anne Porter: A Life* retailed Porter's commitment to personal secrecy and mythmaking, her four unhappy marriages and numerous affairs with young men, her world-roaming restlessness and grim depressions as if they were symptoms of an inbred viciousness, not the common agony of millions who lack Porter's piercing mind and language.

But the final reason for her neglect is larger still; and not at all paradoxically, it is the chief source of her power. The quality of her mind and of the stories she told is fearless, steely and lethal to the most widely cherished illusions of the species—our poisonous grip on romance and self-regard, our panicked insistence on overinflating the bounds of masculinity, femininity, matrimony and parentage. Porter's stories take an aim as accurate and deadly as Nathaniel Hawthorne's, and her prose is leaner, for dissecting deeper. The results are dazzling.

---

> **Porter's stories take an aim as accurate and deadly as Nathaniel Hawthorne's, and her prose is leaner, for dissecting deeper. The results are dazzling.**
>
> —*Reynolds Price*

---

*Letters of Katherine Anne Porter,* the first selection of her apparently voluminous correspondence, marks the fact that she was born 100 years ago on May 15. Despite a lifetime of chronic ailments, she proved a hardy product of her Texas origins and lived to 90. These letters demonstrate how sleeplessly she shaped her relation to family and home, her friendships, business dealings, all aspects of her world perhaps except for her own romances (only one of which figures here). Whether she writes to a young godchild, a long-unseen brother, an editor or to President John F. Kennedy about his inauguration, the unique keenness of her actual and mental eyes charges her headlong prose with the rare hum of a welcome but dangerous magnetism, heard only when such a splendid witness delivers her findings.

Her encounter with the poet Hart Crane is an early example. Porter had lived and worked in Mexico at intervals for more than a decade when Crane arrived in 1931 on a Guggenheim fellowship. She had known him slightly in New York and offered him hospitality at the large house in Mixcoac that she shared with others. Soon, however, Crane's drunken disorder and Porter's revulsion precipitated a break; and her letter of June 22 is, in its cool fury, an unanswerable depiction and denunciation of the alcoholic life:

> You know you have had the advantage of me, because I share the superstition of our time about the somewhat romantic irresponsibility of drunkenness. . . . Therefore I have borne to the limit of my patience with brutal behavior, shameless lying, hysterical raving, and the general sordid messiness of people who had not the courage to be as shabby as they wished when sober. . . . I believe a drunken mood is as good a mirror as a sober one. . . . Your emotional hysteria is not impressive, except possibly to those little hangers-on of literature who feel your tantrums are a mark of genius. To me they do not add the least value to your poetry, and take away my last shadow of a wish to ever see you again. . . . Let me alone. This disgusting episode has already gone too far.

More than a year later, at the news of Crane's suicide, she tries to draw back for a gentler look; but her mind barely lets her: "I did not look at all upon him as some one who must be saved and spared at the expense of every one around him. . . . And besides, all this talk of 'saving' him—he did not want to be saved, he could not be. All that was worth touching in him he put into his poetry, and it is this I wish to remember, and keep and foster. Not that living corpse, who wrote his poetry almost in spite of himself, and who, if he had stayed in the world, would have come to worse ends."

Though the letters collected here seldom call for such blowtorch intensity, it is a continual sign of Porter's open-eyed sanity that again and again she tries to turn the same gaze on her own failings—her restlessness, her paralyzing depressions, her knack for blinding herself to herself: "I have a deep, incurable (apparently) painful melancholy, night and day, which just sits on my neck. Its nobody's fault except my own, if it is even that. . . . So now I sit in the sun as if I hoped that would cure me. I think maybe work will cure me."

It was only a common human tragedy that her understanding was powerless to surmount such a deep inner division and bafflement. Many decades passed—romances, loves, teaching, performing, homeless wandering. The melancholy cruelly prevailed, as it had in her father's life. Letters streamed freely, but it was only in short near-miraculous bursts that she was able to write fiction. In a feat worthy of legend, the great works of her life—three long stories in *Pale Horse, Pale Rider* (1939)—were completed in little more than a week's work for each. And *Ship of Fools* though nearly complete in the early 1940's, was only finished in a concentrated few weeks of 1961.

Fortunately, this wide selection of letters provides the best possible antidote to any suspicion that the whole of her life was wretched, a rudderless voyage. Now we have hundreds of pages of firsthand evidence that—whatever her struggles with work, love and a means of subsistence—Porter was rarely less than a solid kind help to a broad range of friends, from children and fellow artists to relatives older than she. The potentially merciless stamina of her scrutiny could shift with ease to an affectionate and witty domestic attention, and her full discussions of religion, politics, American racism and the rise of fascism are brave and eloquent. Till old age dims her zest, the single most constant note she sounds, in the midst of trials and failure, is a burning joyful vitality—a love of the world, its creatures and things.

I mentioned the (unexplained) omission of what may well be hundreds of surviving love letters. They seem the only large strand of her life not represented and may yet appear. A decidedly spotty "Who's Who" of correspondents is provided, and the absence of explanatory notes is occasionally regrettable. Otherwise, the editing by Isabel Bayley, Porter's friend and literary trustee, is admirably unintrusive. Without access to the originals, I cannot speak for the accuracy of the text; I can only affirm that every sentence sounds like Porter in at least one of her large range of voices—glad or consoling love, help for artists younger than she, delight in the world, righteous but sober and justified rage at evil and ignorance and the final exhaustion of age.

Katherine Anne Porter would be the first now to grant that life and her own responses to it kept her from much that she meant to do—who says less? But any sane reader could soon assure her that what she did, in her art alone, still waits among us—tall, profound and as unassailable as time allows. In 1943 she wrote to her nephew: "Ah dear, how pleasant it would be to a writer if only he could know that after years of neglect and evil criticism during his life time, and all sorts of complete misunderstanding of what he was trying to do, he would find his hundredth birthday being celebrated the whole year long." This bountiful volume begins at least to answer that hope for a writer who more than earned celebration.

### Roseanne L. Hoefel (essay date Winter 1991)

SOURCE: "The Jilting of (Hetero)Sexist Criticism: Porter's Ellen Weatherall and Hapsy," in *Studies in Short Fiction,* Vol. 28, No. 1, Winter, 1991, pp. 9-20.

[*In the following essay, Hoefel provides a feminist interpretation of "The Jilting of Granny Weatherall."*]

A central issue in the criticism of **"The Jilting of Granny Weatherall"** is that of Hapsy's identity and her role in the life of Ellen Weatherall. The analyses dealing with this question are based on various assumptions, treated as facts, regarding who/what took precedence in Ellen's life. Among these assumptions are the following: (1) that Ellen is still grieving over the jilting at the altar by George sixty years ago; (2) that she is being totally sincere when she thinks she's had everything that any "normal" woman would want; (3) that the reference to something "not given back" is either a reference to her former fiancé George or to the general unhappiness that issues from loneliness or a lack of love; and (4) that all the names she mentions are those of her husband or children.

These assumptions are not simply sexist in origin, but heterosexist. They result from a view of the world, which is the privileged view, that places primary importance on relationships between men and women. Such assumptions have led to the widely held inference that Hapsy is one of Ellen's children and that, as a few critics maintain, she is the favorite because she reminds Ellen of George. This latter reading in particular seems to minimize women's importance by subordinating them to a wish for a man. And clearly, if Hapsy is not Ellen's child but is, rather, a friend, both readings diminish the potential importance of women in each other's lives. Yet the text reveals that Hapsy's significance in Ellen's life supersedes that of all the others, including George, John, and her children. Hapsy, I argue, was not Ellen's child, nor was she an uninvolved servant or midwife, as critics have surmised. She was, instead, Ellen's close friend, with whom Ellen shared an emotional, spiritual, and perhaps intellectual bond.

A re-visionary reading of this work—which so many have deemed a tragic story or tragic triumph of a woman's jilting by one man—is made possible and best served by what Adrienne Rich calls a lesbian/feminist focus:

> lesbian/feminist criticism has the power to illuminate the work of *any* woman artist. . . . Such a criticism will ask questions hitherto passed over. . . . It will thus identify images, codes, metaphors, strategies, points of stress, unrevealed by conventional criticism which works from a male/mainstream perspective.

This perspective, which may or may not include—and is certainly not limited to—loving in the sexual sense, can illuminate the "codes, metaphors, strategies [and] points of stress" in **"The Jilting of Granny Weatherall."** Precisely *because* this particular vantage point is not restricted to lesbian sexual expression, its application to the works of an avowedly heterosexual woman artist should not be, in fact is not, problematic. Given Porter's obvious feminism, a feminist reading of this story will be instructive, especially since Joan Givner includes **"The Jilting of Granny Weatherall"** among the three stories containing a thematic pattern that reverses the weak, passive woman motif by substituting in its stead a woman asserting her rights.

While many critics, particularly John Hardy, William Nance, and Joseph Wiesenfarth, note in various ways that Porter heroines search for identity and independence, their arguments are not developed from a feminist perspective. Hardy may be partially correct in saying, for example, that Ellen Weatherall dies wanting sexual satisfaction; but he does not mention the possibility that she was fulfilled in other, perhaps more important ways, through her intimate relationship with, memory of, and search for Hapsy. And while William Nance—who takes this presumed lack of sexual gratification one step further—argues that Ellen used the jilting in order to reject men thereafter, his analysis does not consider her viewpoint apart from a single humiliating experience imposed by one man, George.

An irony in these critics' arguments—in which they contend that Ellen is one among many Porter heroines searching for an identity and independence (e.g., Nance goes so far as to claim that "she keeps her hard-earned domination to the end, when she blows out her own light,")—is that they repeatedly refer to her as "Granny" Weatherall rather than as Ellen. While some may argue that this is merely being consistent with the story's title and some references in the narrative, the fact that Porter does provide her first name, and has "Ellen" refer to herself that way, is extremely important. Classifying her as a "granny" implicitly denies her existence independent of her family, while using only her surname negates her identity separate from her marriage.

To be more specific about the missing links of previous criticism, most assessments have been plausible, yet overlook, ignore, or repress evidence in the story that might moderate—if not totally contradict—their conclusions. As Judith Fetterley poignantly states:

> When only one reality is encouraged, legitimized, and transmitted and when that limited vision endlessly insists on its comprehensiveness, then we have the conditions necessary for that confusion of consciousness in which impalpability flourishes. . . . To examine American fictions in light of how attitudes toward women shape their form and content is to make available to consciousness that which has been largely left unconscious and thus to change our understanding of these fictions, our relation to them, and their effect on us. It is to make palpable their designs.

Charlotte Goodman provides one example of the way in which vision can be limited. In her comparative analysis of women's and men's attitudes toward death as portrayed in

literature, she concludes that Ellen is a victim of decisions made by the men in her life, and thus dies feeling unfulfilled. This interpretation implies that women in general and Ellen in particular cannot overcome victimization or empower themselves or each other. On the contrary, Ellen and Hapsy play supportive roles in each other's lives and are strong in the face of many setbacks.

Regarding Ellen's relationships with men, critics like William Nance dismiss Ellen's reasons for defying male authority figures—doctor, priest, or husband. But this dismissal belittles or refuses to acknowledge her existence as an individual capable of living, surviving, loving, and dying according to her own desires. Porter foreshadows Ellen's justified resistance to male "authorities" at the outset of the story when a male doctor (ironically, a care-taker) insults Ellen's dignity by his condescending tone and manner:

> Doctor Harry spread a warm paw like a cushion on her forehead where the forked green vein danced and made her eyelids twitch. "Now, now, be a good girl, and we'll have you up in no time."

And after she reprimands him for speaking to her disrespectfully "just because she's down"—and because she is an elderly woman and thus deemed doubly dispensable—he replies, "Well, Missy, excuse me," and pats her cheek, compounding the insult. Porter thus provides at the beginning of her story an image of men who trivialize women. Ellen's reaction to Dr. Harry's condescending attitude suggests that such diminutive treatment by men caused, at least in part, her reaction to them and formed her character.

In addition, "Ellen used to think of [her husband] as a man," but "he would be a child beside her if she saw him now. It seemed strange and there was something wrong in the idea." Besides a literal interpretation of the memory that would indicate that John died young, here, two inferences support a picture of a more independent and critical Ellen: (1) she sees John as a "dwarfed" man, suggesting that men declined in her esteem, perhaps in response to their patronizing treatment of her or their inadequacies as providers; and (2) what Ellen deems "wrong" in that image is that she cannot see herself beside him, in his childlike state; or, in her matured state, she has grown beyond him in more than only the sense of aging. Perhaps she could see herself beside someone else, someone not in any sense a child.

The "someone" beside whom Ellen visualizes herself seems to be Hapsy. Ellen has chosen not to be vulnerable to men, who might abandon or patronize her; yet the notion of her having a choice has been obscured by or, at best, has escaped most critics. Joseph Wiesenfarth contends that Ellen never dared to love again after the jilting, since her heart never healed. Such a claim, again, seems based upon a heterosexist view which, as the privileged one, can often marginalize other equally—if not more—plausible interpretations. Clearly, Ellen did love again, not only in loving her children, but also in loving Hapsy, and continuing to love her after painfully losing her.

Significantly, Ellen's seeing herself beside someone *not* her husband or her child implies that she has not only deviated from the conventional "norm" that views women's identity as formed and expressed in relation to husband and children, but also that she has changed her opinion about the roles allotted to women and the expectations of them. We do see her initially in her traditional role as mother where she is a woman serving others:

> When she thought of all the food she had cooked, and all the clothes she had cut and sewed, and all the gardens she had made—well, the children showed it. There they were made out of her, and they couldn't get away from that.

But later we learn that she believes that her deceased husband "couldn't possibly recognize her" since:

> She had fenced in a hundred acres once, digging the post holes herself and clamping the wires with just a Negro boy to help. *That changed a woman.* John would be looking for a young woman with a peaked Spanish comb in her hair and the painted fan. Digging post holes *changed a woman.* (emphasis added)

Traditional interpretation of this passage accurately claims that Ellen has matured, learned to accept responsibility. But the repetition implies a more substantial change. Ellen has assumed a new identity, no longer confined to the conventional sphere delineated for women. In fact, Ellen frequently expresses her desire for independence. On one occasion she says to the doctor, "Don't tell me what I'm going to be. I'm on my feet now, morally speaking"; and on another, "I pay my own bills." Yet she often vacillates between this desire for independence and her need for others, for tradition (especially that embodied by the Catholic religion), and for family.

The only time one does not find such ambivalence is in her love for another woman, Hapsy; only in this relationship is she not self-sacrificing. Porter's narrative method (including her use of uncoded and encoded discourse, ambiguity, and scrambled chronology) both provides textual evidence supporting Hapsy's prominence over George, John, or Ellen's children, and indicates that Ellen is not the desperate, frustrated woman that many readers try to make her out to be; that she grew after the jilting—leaving men behind; and that her hope for happiness lies in reunion (again, not necessarily sexual) with Hapsy.

First, through the stream-of-consciousness technique, Porter is able subtly to reveal Hapsy's identity and her relationship with Ellen. Frequently, when Ellen shifts in and out of consciousness, the encoding of thought also shifts, from the quoted—when she is speaking, or at least imagines she is speaking—to the unquoted, those times she knows she is not articulating aloud her thoughts, or perhaps can or will not do so for other reasons: namely, a need to repress certain thoughts.

In one of the most telling unquoted passages of the stream-of-(un)consciousness narrative, Ellen advises, "Don't let good things rot for want of using," and "Don't let things get lost. It's bitter to lose things . . . don't let me get to thinking." Obviously, she is obsessed with losing things; but George is not the prime loss of her life. Of course, one cannot deny that George was a loss, for Ellen says (more than half-way through the story), "I want you to find George and tell him I forgot him," thus attesting that she has been concerned with this loss for some time. Indeed, immediately following this passage about bitter loss are Ellen's memories about being jilted at the altar, and one is tempted, therefore, to connect the two causally. But in many of the dialogues with herself, Ellen freely associates ideas that are certainly connected but not necessarily directly. So the juxtaposition of bitter loss and jilting does not absolutely indicate that George is what she is most bitter over losing.

For example, the paragraph following this reminiscence of the "hell"-ish jilting, which she eventually deems a "nightmare," has as its first thought: "Hapsy?" And it is Hapsy's name that precedes even George's as well as those of the children: Lydia, Jimmy, and Cornelia. "Did you send for Hapsy, too?" possibly indicates that Hapsy is one to be considered apart from the children. Again, it is significant that each of these passages is unquoted, for the encoded style reflects that Ellen's thoughts about Hapsy are kept private and unspoken. Attempting to discover Hapsy's identity and her relation to Ellen, and to explore further the evidence that Hapsy is not Ellen's child, is aided by Ellen's references to "riding country roads in the winter when women had their babies" and "sitting up nights with sick horses and sick Negroes and sick children and hardly ever losing one." The ambiguity of this crucial passage opens up several possible interpretations. First, the understatement of "hardly ever" indicates repression or avoidance of a painful reality. Second, the pronoun "one" need not refer to children, as critics have often concluded since Hapsy seems to have died or disappeared; nor does it necessarily refer to horses. Given the structure of the sentence, this phrase could as easily refer to sick Negroes. This ambiguity, combined with the portrayals in Porter's fiction of close relationships between black women and the white women for whom they work (for example, Nannie and Sophia Jane in the Miranda stories), might suggest, although not definitively establish, that Hapsy was one of the "sick Negroes," a confidante of whom Ellen had grown quite fond, but had somehow lost. Together with other similar allusions to Hapsy's absence, this reference confirms that Ellen lost Hapsy (whose name invokes the notion of happenstance in that she proved the exception to whom Ellen refers in her phrase, "hardly ever losing one").

Barbara Carson's analysis of Nannie, especially in relation to Sophia Jane, in Porter's Miranda stories, is instructive here. Similar to Nannie, Sophia Jane—and by extension, because they lived at the same time in similar societies, Ellen—is bound by social conditioning to her religious/domestic tradition and family. Just as Nannie in her dutiful service eventually comes to be seen as a part of Sophia Jane's family, so too might have Hapsy in Ellen's family. Carson suggests that Nannie and Sophia Jane are both in "the terrible race of procreation." Perhaps similar inferences can be made regarding Hapsy and Ellen: they participate in the same enterprise and, thus, it is less difficult to understand their seeing reflections of each other in a child born to one of them—as expressed in the following passage, where we learn that if Ellen went back far enough in memory, she would find:

> Hapsy standing with a baby on her arm. She seemed
> to herself to be Hapsy also, and the baby on Hapsy's
> arm was Hapsy and himself and herself, all at once,
> and there was no surprise in the meeting.

Here Ellen interchanges identities with Hapsy, as though she feels integrally a part of her and of the baby Hapsy is holding. Not surprisingly, on the same page we find: "It was Hapsy she really wanted." But regardless of whether Hapsy was a servant in the tradition of Nannie, she can (must?) certainly be seen as Ellen's close friend.

Ellen's search for Hapsy continues throughout the story and, indeed, intensifies as she nears death. After remembering Hapsy with the baby on her arm, Ellen has an apparition of sorts in which she is beside Hapsy: "Hapsy came up close and said, 'I thought you'd never come,' and looked at her very searchingly and said, 'You haven't changed a bit!' They leaned forward to kiss, when Cornelia began whispering from a long way off." Cornelia's forbidding whisper aborts this mutual welcoming with—at this point—ironically loaded questions: "Oh, is there anything you want to tell me? Is there anything I can do for you?" One wonders, perhaps, what Ellen might have said aloud or mumbled in her sleep, as her subconscious surfaced during this dream reunion, that prompted such pleas. Or at least one ponders the powerful effect of this dream, which possibly made her incoherent enough to elicit such pleas.

Here, sequence is important, for only upon recognizing anew that her love lies with Hapsy can Ellen then decide that she would like to find George and let him know she has forgot-

ten him. Even if, as Mooney argues, Ellen had married John and had his children "out of spite," that certainly was not the reason she loved Hapsy. Clearly, Hapsy is one who means something beyond the family, as revealed by the following lines which, because they come after the vivid memory of Hapsy and the imagining of their reunion, seem to be associated with Hapsy:

> Oh, no, oh, God, no, there was something else be-
> sides the house and the man and the children. Oh,
> surely they were not all? . . . Something not given
> back. . . . Her breath crowded down under her ribs
> and grew into a monstrous, frightening shape with
> cutting edges; it bored up into her head, and the
> agony was unbelievable.

Undeniably, (the memory of) this loss is incredibly painful. Critics have suggested that the something not given back could be any one of the following: George, Hapsy as an unborn or stillborn child, a jilted faith, Christ (e.g., as argued from the reference to the "Bridegroom"), God, Heaven. While each of these is possible, more plausible, given the importance Ellen assigns to Hapsy, is that Hapsy—not as child, but as close companion—is the something else not given back. And even though why or how Hapsy was taken away is not given, one can surmise an approximate *when*. This is provided by two parallel passages referring to giving birth (which follow and thus occur within the same one-and-one-half page span). The first is initiated in Ellen's memory by excruciating pain ("the agony was unbelievable"), the second by a scream.

But more significant in establishing a time sequence than even the shared suffering of these two passages are two requests to John to get the doctor: "Yes, John, get the doctor now, no more talk, my time has come," and "John, get the doctor, Hapsy's time has come." The repetition—varied only by whose time has come, Ellen's or Hapsy's—reinforces the common experience of childbearing and indicates that Ellen lost Hapsy soon after she bore one of her own children and also after Hapsy bore a child. This passage not only helps to explain the earlier memory in which Ellen merges with Hapsy and the baby on her arm; but also, when viewed in conjunction, the two memories suggest that it is not only the common experience that bonds the two women: Ellen feels fundamentally connected to Hapsy.

Equally important for ascertaining the roles Hapsy played in Ellen's life is the reference to Hapsy as a nurse, which reinforces the deepening of the bond created initially by such common experience; that is, Hapsy possibly participated in Ellen's childbearing as a sort of midwife, or at least as some kind of helpmate or caretaker. For, directly following "Hapsy's time has come," one learns: "But there was Hapsy standing by the bed in a white cap." This is the image of a nurse. (Seeing Hapsy as midwife elucidates also Ellen's memory of Hapsy holding the baby.) But Ellen "cannot see her [Hapsy] plain," not because she isn't accustomed to seeing Hapsy in that role—for it is Ellen who links these ideas sequentially, leaving readers to infer connections, consequences, and importance between the seemingly disparate images in her mind. Rather, Ellen's sad inability to see clearly the one she thinks is her long-awaited love standing near the bed stems from a combination of other factors: the fact that Ellen has not yet fully, or perhaps at all, opened her eyes (which does not occur until the beginning of the subsequent paragraph); the possibility that she is extremely disoriented from her pain, medication and—although she denies it until the very end—the growing realization of impending death; and finally, the chance that Ellen has associated Hapsy with another (nurse) who is actually, physically present, perhaps a nurse accompanying the doctor on his evening visit to Ellen.

When Lydia, who has driven as fast as she could, tells her mother that they have arrived, Ellen responds, "Is that you, Hapsy?" Upon realizing that Lydia, Cornelia, and Jimmy are there, Ellen thinks, "my children have come to see me die." She does not qualify this statement by saying instead, "My children, except Hapsy, have come." While she knows that Hapsy is dead and thus may not include her among those who have come to see her die, one of her next thoughts indicates that Ellen still sometimes fantasizes that Hapsy is alive and wearing jewelry she would like to bequeath to her. For even though Ellen feels compelled, partly out of duty to a dutiful daughter, to will her prized amethyst set to Cornelia, she means for Hapsy to wear it "whenever she wants."

In addition to reinforcing the urgency of Ellen's search for Hapsy, the passage involving the amethysts also combines two social meanings of exchanging precious stones: passing them down from generation to generation as an heirloom or keepsake and exchanging them between love(r)s or intimate friends as symbolic of timeless bonding. While the former interpretation has been used to argue that Hapsy is another daughter, the latter suggests that Hapsy and Ellen shared an intimate friendship. In her final moments, then, Ellen—even though feeling unprepared for death—finds solace in the thought of Hapsy, as the telling interior monologue of the story's penultimate paragraph reveals:

> You'll see Hapsy again. What about her? "I thought you'd never come." Granny made a long journey outward, looking for Hapsy. What if I don't find her? What then? Her heart sank down and down, there was no bottom to death, she could not come to the end of it.

Death and the promised afterlife will have meaning and promise only if Ellen can find Hapsy; not finding her, death would become bottomless, symbolic of hell—with, paradoxically,

infinite "depth," but without true "depth" for which the soul, heart, and mind yearn. From a fetal position (Ellen "lay curled down within herself"), she begs God for a sign of hope, a hope that includes the finding of Hapsy. Two possibilities arise here: one, finding Hapsy is simply a sign that heaven exists, a sign of eternal life (Happiness); the other, for Ellen, heaven exists only if she meets Hapsy again, for just as life without Hapsy was hard, so would afterlife be. But either way, rather than George (who may or may not be dead) or John (who is dead), Hapsy is *the* important figure in Ellen's life.

---

**Our understanding of Porter's "The Jilting of Granny Weatherall" changes dramatically when we recognize that Ellen is a victim of the (hetero)sexist sociocultural expectations imposed by patriarchy, but maintained in part because of women's collusion with them.**

**—*Roseanne L. Hoefel***

---

Thus the union of her soul with Hapsy's, a spiritual "wedding" of sorts, calls up the image of the Biblical bride*groom,* understandably cited by many critics as an allusion to Christ. Indeed if Christ as bridegroom is Redeemer of eternal life, as argued by critics who conclude that either Christ or Ellen's faith has jilted Ellen—or Ellen them—this poignant metaphor implies another possibility: that her despair in not finding eternal unity with her lost love is what is too cruel, unforgivable, and unfathomable all at once: "She could not remember any other sorrow because this grief wiped them all away. Oh, no, there's nothing more cruel than this—I'll never forgive it." She proceeds to blow out the light of a lifetime hope upon which she had thrived.

In sum, our understanding of Porter's **"The Jilting of Granny Weatherall"** changes dramatically when we recognize that Ellen is a victim of the (hetero)sexist sociocultural expectations imposed by patriarchy, but maintained in part because of women's collusion with them. Lesbian/feminist criticism is one means of defying such collusion with male/mainstream interpretations. Non-complicity can take other, perhaps related, shapes also. For instance, as Barbara Carson observes, Porter's women search for the prize she calls a "valid selfhood":

> If the words are vague, the concept is not. At its center are the recognition and use of one's own powers and abilities even in the face of custom, the discovery of truth for oneself (including the truth of

one's own desires), and the strength to face that truth and act from that basis. It is, in short, the creation of an essence for oneself through self-initiated actions, rather than the passive acceptance of a role assigned by others.

Hence, Ellen's final act of blowing out the light is triumphant because defiant, emphasizing that she has recognized her own choices, especially regarding the significance of Hapsy in her life and in her death.

A feminist perspective on Porter's story thus challenges previous readings and by necessity resists criticism that perpetuates the mythology of heterosexual romantic love, an enterprise that maintains male power by attributing the desires and happiness of the female characters' (and authors') lives to their relationship with men. A feminist revisioning encompasses, in Ellen's own words, "always a little *margin* over for peace" (emphasis added), and provides space for new readings when the old prove insufficient or unsatisfactory. It demonstrates how heterosexist perceptions—even, or perhaps especially, when we do not recognize them—obscure or limit our vision. Jean Kennard perhaps puts it most succinctly: "we need a way of reading/writing about any literature that does not reconfirm the universality of heterosexual experience. . . . Our critical work can expose the assumption of universal heterosexuality for what it is, a false assumption." This analysis suggests, I hope, areas to which this long overdue direction can lead.

## Robert E. Hosmer Jr. (review date 19 April 1991)

SOURCE: "One Fixed Desire," in *Commonweal*, Vol. CXVIII, No. 8, April 19, 1991, pp. 266-7.

[*In the following review, Hosmer praises the publication of* Letters of Katherine Anne Porter.]

W. H. Auden was "an unusually stinking and opinionated sodomite"; Charlie Chaplin "an odious little beast"; T. S. Eliot "a dry damned soul who packs an awful wallop"; Edmund Wilson "a mere goon"; and as for Carson McCullers, well, her first book was the product of "a peculiarly corrupt mind, a small stunted talent incapable of growth, and her further work has borne this out in my mind." Whose mind? Katherine Anne Porter's. And so it goes in this six-hundred-page collection, a mere selection from the letters of an important American writer: in her editor's note, Isabel Bayley, Porter's literary executor since 1974, informs us that there were "thousands" of letters from the period of 1930 to 1963, the writer's major working years. Bayley's work is exemplary, not only in her choices, but in her scholarly attention to detail and textual apparatus; her chronology, "who's who"

list, introduction, and index provide consistently accurate and helpful information.

What Porter disliked, she disliked with ferocious intensity; what she liked, she embraced with unqualified enthusiasm: Henry James was "the very greatest artist and novelist this country ever produced"; Marianne Moore, "my favorite living poet and one of the most delicious persons alive"; Eudora Welty, "very seriously gifted, very imaginative and bold and complex." And despite a pervasive loathing for homosexuals, she brought herself to praise Auden: "I know of no gifted human being of whose morals, manners, whole way of life and conduct of life, I disapprove of more entirely than I do of Auden's—I think he is perfectly awful. And how I love his poetry."

> What Porter disliked, she disliked with ferocious intensity; what she liked, she embraced with unqualified enthusiasm.
>
> —*Robert E. Hosmer Jr.*

The letters Isabel Bayley has chosen with such care and resonant precision chronicle the wanderings of Porter's person and spirit during her most creative phase, for it was this time period that saw the publication of her major fiction from *Flowering Judas and Other Stories* (1930) to *Ship of Fools* (1963), with *Pale Horse, Pale Rider* (1939), *The Leaning Tower and Other Stories* (1944) appearing along the way. We follow Porter's restless odyssey from home to Mexico, Germany, Switzerland, France, Italy, Belgium, and back home again. From these various places she maintained a steady stream of correspondence with a who's who of American literary life and legend: Glenway Wescott, Ezra Pound, Josephine Herbst, Robert Penn Warren, Allen Tate, Caroline Gordon. To read her correspondence is to live some of that life.

Certainly, some of Porter's letters reveal her as harsh, intolerant, and unforgiving, particularly toward Catholics (they are "Fascists" and "we are in danger of being taken over by Catholics"), homosexuals ("this whole city [New York] now simply swarms with every little pervert . . . they are really taking the place, speaking of termites . . . the most depraved and tiresome set of half-humans I ever saw"), and writers of whom she disapproved, not only McCullers but others like "poor Malcolm Cowley [who] never was anything but cold oatmeal from the neck up" and Hemingway, "such a bore of a man really and such an incomplete artist . . . so completely uninteresting and insignificant." Yet so many other letters illuminate a sweet, gentle, and compassionate woman for whom life was not easy; most impressive is her generous encouragement to younger writers like Eudora Welty, and the palpable affection manifest in her extended correspondence with her nephew Paul.

It is the artistic dimension of Katherine Anne Porter that emerges with an expected fullness in this collection, for she has always been known as a woman so dedicated to her art as to consider it as a monastic vocation. In a letter to Glenway Wescott, written in 1941, she declares what has always been her "one fixed desire: to be a good artist, responsible to the last comma for what I write." And nothing will stand in her way—no divorce suit, no critic, no editor, no publisher. In her dealings with the latter, Porter is ruthless, driving a hard bargain with every contract signed. Throughout, these letters show that Porter stuck to that intention, declared in a letter to Albert Erskine, her fourth husband: "my job now is to keep on my feet and keep working. And I feel pretty ferocious about it. I would slit the throat of a six-months-old infant who got in my way."

Nowhere does Porter's solitary dedication to her art come across more strongly than in the story of her writing her only novel, the long-awaited *Ship of Fools*. These letters record a labor decades-long, for what was begun as a twelve-page ship's journal written as a letter en route from Mexico to Germany in 1931 did not find final, published form as *Ship of Fools* until 1962; Porter's letters are studded with references to her false starts, delays, postponements, and disappointments in the process. The novel's million-dollar success failed to make up for its being judged something far less in literary terms. Thirty years' labor on a work that many critics scorned.

Life was a struggle for Porter—against so many forces, but particularly against ill health (she was plagued by respiratory and pulmonary problems), a self-acknowledged tendency to melancholia, and a deeply unsettled personal life. Numerous love affairs and four broken marriages littered her life, and she assessed it all: "love, for me, has been rather more as if I were a bundle of wheat going through the threshing machine than anything else. When I came through I was clean winnowed"; "marriage for me has meant pure disaster, and a strange cruel starvation of the heart." Nonetheless, a difficult, dislocated life did not embitter her; in a letter to her nephew, she opined that, "all life worth living is difficult, nobody promised us happiness; it is not a commodity you have earned, or shall ever earn. It is a by-product of brave living, and it never comes in the form we expect, or at the season we hoped for, or as a result of our planning for it."

May the publication of these *Letters* renew and refresh Katherine Anne Porter's presence among us as a writer of substance and very considerable grace.

## Ruth M. Vande Kieft (essay date 1993)

SOURCE: "The Love Ethos of Porter, Welty, and McCullers," in *The Female Tradition in Southern Literature,* edited by Carol S. Manning, University of Illinois Press, 1993, pp. 235-43.

[*In the following excerpt, Kieft explores Porter's attitudes toward love and romantic relationships as shaped by her personal experiences and reflected in her writing.*]

Since love is a central theme in much fiction, especially that of women writers, it is not surprising to find the theme dominant in the fiction of Katherine Anne Porter, Eudora Welty, and Carson McCullers. What is surprising, given their time and place in the most conservative part of the country, the South (Texas, Mississippi, Georgia) in the first half of the twentieth century, is the extent to which each writer, though she could not totally escape conventional codes and attitudes toward love, essentially subverted them in her life as a fiction writer. Their contrasting lives and fictional projections of love reveal how as artists they individually fulfilled their destinies and escaped from the common female destiny, the stories society might have written for them, and they for their characters, as lovers, wives, and mothers.

In my essay, I analyze and relate these two sets of stories, the biographical and fictional "love lives" of the three writers. I am aware of the hazards of my undertaking: chiefly its magnitude and the impossibility of sorting out facts from fiction. For in what other area of a woman's life is reality more infused with fantasy, is language more "loaded" and ungovernable, are assumptions, actions, values more charged and elusive in their meanings?

I face these difficulties squarely and attempt to deal with them in two ways. First, I use the term *mythos* because it implies a pattern of attitudes and experiences that are both individual and yet shared with others in smaller or larger groups. For each of the three writers, there is, in addition to a unique personal history, a set of "conventional" (religious, archetypal, literary) sources of the mythos that the writer either wholly or partially accepts or rejects. Each has her own relationship to "the truth," each a different way of conducting her life and using it in her fiction, a different mix of the realistic with the fantastic. Each writer's "mythos of love" is the intricately woven pattern of several components: (1) her early experiences within the family setting; (2) her "love history" as a woman; and (3) her imaginative assimilation of both traditional and modern attitudes toward love acquired through formal education, reading, observation. Each component is to some extent cloaked in its own language and reference system, the community's encoding of attitudes and assumptions. Since I cannot treat all elements consistently or at equal length, I shall stress what seem the most important formative influences on each writer.

Second, I have limited my study to the fiction itself and material essentially biographical rather than critical. Fortunately, for two of the writers we have long, definitive, authorized biographies written by sympathetic women: Joan Givner's of Porter and Virginia Spencer Carr's of McCullers. In Welty's case, we have a slender autobiography, *One Writer's Beginnings,* itself a work of art, though not, I think, another of her works of fiction, for I believe it to be as honest as it is beautiful, moving, and amusing, however selective in its personal revelations. These biographical sources being different from each other in kind and approach, I make no claims for their comparative objectivity, or that of my own conclusions. Since the territory I hope to survey is thickly wooded, I intend to be wary, flexible, and suggestive rather than definitive or doctrinaire.

1

Porter's mythos of love seems the most perilous of the three to describe because, though convoluted, it is easiest to reduce to a formula: the Freudian one of the wholly determining effects of early childhood on all of a writer's work. In an extraordinary feat of fact-gathering and reconstruction, Givner has told Porter's life story and revealed her life-long habit of interweaving fact, fantasy, and fiction. Porter invented for herself a Southern aristocratic past and early family history. She assumed and played out the dual roles of Southern belle modernized and liberated, and legendary femme fatale. Her beauty, love of finery in clothing and decor and exoticism in food and drink, her four marriages and countless love affairs, her self-infatuated conversations, her restless traveling and adventures, her uncanny timing in being in the right place at the right time to involve herself with important historical persons and events—all this is the stuff of a legend she self-consciously created, a legend more usually associated with Hollywood stars than one devoted to a craft that invites what Welty once referred to as "the intimacy of strangers."

Givner's "uneasy sense," expressed in the prologue to her biography, "that the revelations about [Porter's] life constituted some cruel kind of exposure," seems justified, for it is an often vain, selfish, capricious, exploitive, irresponsible, deceitful character that emerges. Yet Givner salvages respect and admiration for Porter, whose actual life she found "more heroic than anything [Porter] invented," for it is the story of a sensitive child named Callie whose mother died when she was two years old; who was raised in miserable poverty and overcrowding in a large household by a strict Methodist grandmother; who was neglected, erratically treated and unloved by a weak and self-indulgent father; whose amorous adventures were the compulsive attempts of a love-starved woman to find what she could not possibly attain. Givner's commissioned biography seems the fruit of Porter's decision to "come clean," make a truthful final confession, not only to a priest but to the world. Yet whatever her relation to the truth, in her personal legend making, Porter was exhibiting a characteristically Southern trait.

The encoded rhetoric that lies behind Porter's ethos of love has both a popular and a traditional source, each of which I think she had unconsciously assimilated, insofar as the rhetoric fed some impossible idealism about romantic love that she seems never to have lost. The popular source is best illustrated by excerpts from letters Porter's father, Harrison, wrote shortly after the death of his wife, Alice, samples of the kind of sentimental graveyard rhetoric satirized by Mark Twain in *Huckleberry Finn.* The first letter, to his oldest daughter, was sent with a picture:

> Gay: This is your mother. She is buried near Brownwood. It is a holy place for us all. There I saw the star of all my earthly hopes go down in an endless darkness and there is no light in my heart even at noonday. In this strange twilight I try to trace the narrow road I must walk to reach this city of the dead and lie down in the long night beside my love. But this star is not extinguished altogether for it shed the rays of its purity and love over the waste landscape of my life, gave meaning to Nothingness and left memories that not time nor death itself can take away.

To a close friend of Alice he wrote: "I loved her better than my own life, aye, better than I did my God. . . . If there is, after this turmoil, a halcyon period, a golden place somewhere 'en vista' of the golden dawn, I know my spirit will seek hers there, though but a season. Hell thenceforth with the companionship of the Dragon of the Apocalypse will not torment me worse than the pangs that now rend me."

From this graveyard rhetoric it is a short leap to that of the poem Uncle Gabriel writes to memorialize his beloved Amy in **"Old Mortality"** ("A singing angel, she forgets / The griefs of old mortality"). Noteworthy about Harrison Porter's rhetoric, in addition to its self-indulgence, is its "literary" pretension and the mixing of religious language with that of human love. Harrison plays out his drama as mourner on a cosmic stage against a backdrop of time and eternity, heaven and hell, salvation and damnation. And Porter played out her drama on the same cosmic stage.

The other encoded rhetoric is that of the ancient noble literary tradition of Courtly Love, the Age of Chivalry. The love ethos is often adulterous, thriving most when unconsummated, product of fevered imaginations, high codes of morality and tests of bravery, celebrated by poets of stature from the Middle Ages to the nineteenth-century Romantics. Actually, this noble tradition reached the South, and doubtless Porter, more by way of Sir Walter Scott than Dante, Shakespeare, and Keats. Porter had little formal education and was not an inveterate reader as a child. Her fictional portrayal of what had become of the Western world's and the South's version of love is negative: she shows love traduced and betrayed, relentlessly exposed and rejected, yet also as inescapable and hopelessly victimizing. The romantic and antiromantic are constantly at war in Porter's fiction; her pages are strewn with the combatants wounded, dying, and dead of that mortal struggle.

It is instructive to look closely at the battle in its formative stages, to Miranda's, that is, Porter's generation as it appears in **"Old Mortality."** Miranda and her sister Maria, eight and twelve years old, are deeply impressed by the story of Aunt Amy, who, though now only a "ghost in a frame," had once been "beautiful, much loved, unhappy, and had died young." Though somewhat skeptical about the romantic legends told by their elders, the little girls enjoy "patching together . . . fragments of tales that were like bits of poetry, and music . . . with the theatre." The romance of their Uncle Gabriel's "long, unrewarded love for [Amy], her early death," was a story linked for them with books they thought of as "unworldly . . . but true, such as the Vita Nuova, the Sonnets of Shakespeare and the Wedding Song of Spenser; and poems by Edgar Allan Poe." Thus an ancient and noble lineage of love poetry is provided for Porter's fictional counterpart, Miranda, though there is little to indicate that these greatest of love poets were early a seriously formative part of Porter's actual reading and thinking. Yet as central to her fictive world, they provided her with the norm for the lofty and unattainable ("unworldly") ideal of love she saw everywhere traduced.

Amy is presented as willful, capricious, a type of La Belle Dame Sans Merci. She dresses and behaves scandalously, has many beaus while resisting the courtship of Miranda's profligate Uncle Gabriel, has a duel fought over her and compensates for life's dullness by running off, half-sick, on a three-day lark to the border with her brothers. She perversely accepts Gabriel when he loses his family inheritance, marries him in a gray wedding gown, and dies within ten days, not only of chronic illness, but, it is hinted, an overdose of medication. Miranda is impressed by this history, and although she already knows how far reality is from the romantic legends enshrined in the family memory, she persists in her addiction to the romantic gesture, as in her rebellion against conventional morality. Her alternately strict and indulgent rearing makes satirical comedy of the emphasis on character training taught by the nuns in the convent school in which Miranda and her sister are "inured." Their father reinforces the superficiality of the Catholic moral codes by stressing his daughters' need to be good chiefly in order to win the reward of being swept off to the races on certain "blessed Saturdays."

Miranda elopes from out of the convent at sixteen and flees from the marriage within two years. Desperately in love, Porter herself married at sixteen in a double wedding with her sister, a civil ceremony conducted by a Methodist minister. Though the marriage lasted nine years, the longest of her marriages, the relationship was a disaster. Porter later referred to her husband, John Koontz, as a "monster"—a term she applied to all her husbands and lovers. Givner speculates that Porter's "inability to find any pleasure in sex . . . aggravated furthermore by her discovery that she was not able to bear a child" was the cause for her romantic disillusionment. In the final section of **"Old Mortality"** Porter has Miranda think, after her divorce, "I hate loving and being loved. I hate it," and then suffer "a shock of comfort from the sudden collapse of an old painful structure of distorted images and misconceptions."

Yet Miranda rejects also her ugly, chinless, peppermint-breathed feminist cousin Eva in Eva's reductive assessment of Amy's romantic history as "just sex!" What else but desire for romantic love—with its rich fantasy, brief and ambiguous pleasure, and almost inevitable disillusionment and pain—could have induced Porter's fictional characters to act as they did? **"Old Mortality"** ends with Miranda's thinking, "I don't want any promises, I won't have false hopes, I won't be romantic about myself. . . . At least I can know the truth about what happens to me, she assured herself silently, making a promise to herself, in her hopelessness, her ignorance." The final word shows how little Porter believed that Miranda, or anyone, *could* find the truth for herself, unshackle herself from the past or even settle for the bleak reductions of the present. Porter found her truth only in the realm of what she created, the means and end of her integrity and her personal salvation, her fictional art. And in her choice of the free, bohemian existence and refusal of the traditional roles of strong, supportive wife and mother, she became a prototype of the modern woman artist.

The Miranda stories tell a bitter story about love—with one exception, **"Pale Horse, Pale Rider."** But that story presents romantic love as mythical, Edenic. Miranda's soldier-lover is named Adam—obviously prelapsarian; he is described as being round, firm, and beautiful as an unbitten apple; he is even compared to the sacrificial lamb. The pale horse and rider of the Apocalypse, death, carries him off sinless, and before his and Miranda's love is consummated. There is no grand passion: only the sweet elusiveness of an ideal lost love. The encoded language is religious—hymns, prayers, the Bible—from Genesis to Revelation, Eden to the fourth horseman of the Apocalypse (death) to a viewed and missed Paradise beyond; the love language is innocent—that of simple Western ballads.

The finality of death is the seal on a perfect love that might be viewed as Porter's imaginative reenactment of the love of her mother and father. In later life Porter idealized the young man on whom she modeled Adam—apparently a young English soldier who lived in the same rooming house, looked after her before a hospital bed could be found, kissed her once, and died of influenza while she was ill. She made of this casual acquaintance the man she might have trusted and been happy with all her days. "This lifelong devotion," says Givner, "should properly be seen as the love of a writer for a favorite character, the love of an artist for the created object. There is, therefore, an ironic truth in her assertion that he was the one man she could have loved."

Miranda, the survivor, denied her bright vision of death, is seen in the end as a silver-gray ghost, though a very smartly dressed one, with her beautiful smooth gray gloves. Salvation through style: that too was Porter's modus vivendi as she took up her life after her rub with death. In stories based more purely on her own experience, Porter achieves a group of painfully authentic, psychologically acute portraits of the failures of modern love. Givner describes how the patterns of confusion, tension, and dissolution developed from a "fatal ambivalence" in Porter's nature. She craved an adoring, protective kind of masculine love she never got from her weak father, or for a great length of time from any of her husbands and lovers, since it would have been one requiring a docile and obedient wife or mistress to complete on the receiving side. Yet she also had the desire to be a strong, dominant and independent woman like her grandmother. Her apparent distaste for the sexual relationship and her apparent inability to bear children further threatened her fragile sense of her femininity and desirability.

In story after story, Porter presents stormy quarrels between lovers and the unconvincing calms or reconciliations that follow them; she shows destructive fury striking out blindly. To the heroine of **"Theft,"** survivor of many painful love affairs, the loss of a beautiful, golden cloth purse reflects "the long patient suffering of dying friendships and the dark, inexplicable death of love" in a landslide of remembered losses." In the end she thinks, "I was right not to be afraid of any thief but myself, who will end by leaving me nothing." In these stories love is elusive and illusionary yet eternally revived as though in answer to some demon of obsession.

This misanthropy and cynicism about love reaches a series of frenzied peaks in *Ship of Fools.* The feeling between David darling and Jenny angel passes quickly and irrationally from loving passion to fierce hatred, the flux of emotion touched off by the slightest impression, such as the couple's reactions to Jenny's appearance in a fresh white dress. When David sees her as lovely, and tells her so, the narrator says, "She believed it with all her heart, and saw him transfigured as he always was in these mysterious visitations of love be-

tween them—reasonless, causeless, having its own times and seasons, vanishing at a breath and yet always bringing with it the illusion that it would last forever." Yet, after seeing Jenny drunk in another man's embrace, David comes to think that "the girl he thought he knew had disappeared so entirely he had almost to believe he made her up out of the odds and ends of stuff from his own ragbag of adolescent dreams and imaginings. . . . There never was, there couldn't possibly be, any such living girl as he had dreamed Jenny was."

Dr. Schumann, the ship's physician, loves La Condessa but does not comfort her by giving any sign of his love until very shortly before she leaves the ship in political custody. The irony is that he is illicitly feeding the Condessa's drug addiction and thus killing her. A Mrs. Treadwell, divorced and bitter, remembers her "despairs, her long weeping, her miserable grief over the failure of love." She unleashes such mindless fury against aggressive male sexuality that she makes pulp of the face of a young man with the sharp pointed heel of her evening slipper when he comes to the cabin in lustful pursuit of her young cabin-mate. All three of the "heroines" of *Ship of Fools,* as Givner points out, are avatars of Porter at some state of her life in a typical love relationship.

Whereas this psychologically acute fiction is painful, often self-lacerating in its personal revelation, in other stories Porter makes the imaginative leap into persons unlike herself, relating their experiences with empathy and compassion as well as fidelity to the particulars of their time and place. In **"Flowering Judas"** she shows the plight of a modern young woman who has lost the Catholic faith of her childhood and can replace it neither with the Socialist faith of the Mexican Revolution nor the personal faith and purpose of romantic or maternal love. In **"Noon Wine"** she portrays a weak poverty-stricken woman, Mrs. Thompson, testifying against her conscience, in support of her morally weak husband. She is defeated by fate and social codes in a society as dominated by male supremacy as is Sicily or Mexico.

In other of Porter's stories, however, women are far from weak and defeated in relation to their men. Maria Concepcion accomplishes her own revenge on her sexual rival by killing her and taking the girl's child as her own. **"Granny Weatherall"** nourishes a life-long grievance against the man who jilted her and risks hell rather than surrender that hatred, even on her deathbed. These women are strong enough to take risks that may cost them their lives, for time and eternity. In their fight against male hegemony, they might appear to be champions of female independence until one looks closely at what each of these women desires. It is the love of her man, the fulfillment of the promise or vow he made and broke; it is position in the community, marriage, the child by him she expects. These are women who embrace traditional feminine roles with a vengeance. Porter knows much of woman's consciousness and dilemmas in love but nothing of their cure, and she does not fictionalize her own personal "cure" of self-realization through her art.

What fascinates in Porter's personal and fictional love experiences, finally, is the tension between extreme idealism and scepticism, traditional romance and realistic modern attitudes. A clear-eyed appraisal of herself told her how foolish and brief were her many affairs, how much based on fictions spun out of the imagination. And yet she had a faith that there was also, in the love object, an actual love and beauty that answered her need and capacity for discovering and offering her own; and that, when this idealization was mutual in a relationship, it was wonderfully transforming. When she fell in love, her partner was "instantly transfigured with a light of such blinding brilliance all natural attributes disappear[ed]" and an "archangel" appeared, "beautiful, flawless in temperament, witty, intelligent, charming, of . . . infinite grace, sympathy, and courage." This is the golden god of romantic love. It was inevitable that such great expectations should again and again suffer disillusionment. She called it "'probably the silliest kind of love there is, but I am glad I had it. I'm glad there were times when I saw human beings at their best, for I don't think by any means I lent them all their radiance.'"

Porter was a fierce and often intolerant woman, requiring impeccable manners but failing in trust and fidelity. Legendary in all things, she was above all that in her primary dedication to her art. Admired and hated with equal fervor, she has been accused of many character flaws but never of being a less than committed and formidably gifted fiction writer.

## Mary Gordon (essay date 16 April 1995)

SOURCE: "The Angel of Malignity: The Cold Beauty of Katherine Anne Porter," in *The New York Times Book Review*, April 16, 1995, pp. 17-9.

[*In the following essay, Gordon draws attention to the literary accomplishments of Porter.*]

A writer pressing the case of the neglected hero gone before has a difficult role: part night nurse, part hit man. Tenderly we protect the wounded one, aggressively we search for someone we can blame. We are, of course, thinking about ourselves. The neglected writer of the past is our own feared specter, our double, thrust into the darkness of the future, the ghost of what we tell ourselves will never happen but know is to come.

A kind of love grows up between these writers, one living,

one dead. This can be trying if the writer you love is probably not a person you would have liked. I am in the situation of thinking that Katherine Anne Porter wrote like an angel, but is someone I'm glad I didn't have to know.

She was almost certainly not a nice person. She was a great beauty, but all her young photographs have a self-conscious, self-dramatizing quality that makes them difficult to approach. She lied brilliantly on a variety of subjects, from her place of birth to her age. She was born in West Texas in 1890, but often suggested she was a daughter of the Old South, and a younger one at that. She lied about rather crucial things to two of her four husbands, neglecting to tell one she had had a hysterectomy and revealing her true age to another only on their wedding day. She was slippery in business dealings; one of her favorite words—"shady"—could not inaptly be applied to her. She also loved the word "bitter," and both shadows and bitterness contributed to her difficulties in working and to the vexed nature of her relationships.

She was an anti-Semite, although she produced devastating portraits of anti-Semites, and she was a racist who believed that darkies were happy on the old plantation, although she wrote a story full of understanding of the buried longings of former slaves. She dated Hermann Göring at least once, and was disappointed when he didn't call back, but later said she was the first among her friends to grasp the horrors of Nazism. She betrayed one of her best friends, Josephine Herbst, to the F.B.I., which suspected Herbst of being a Communist. It was done casually, alcoholically, on a "date" with an agent set up to get her drunk and make her talk. Porter forgot having "talked," then resented Herbst for her political recklessness, which she saw as a danger to herself.

But none of this has to do, really, with why Katherine Anne Porter is not more widely read. Being read has not, thank God, rested on good behavior, loyalty to friends, sobriety or straight dealings with publishers. Think of the case of Ernest Hemingway, like Porter a beauty, a poseur, a betrayer and a drunk—but certainly not unread.

The image of Hemingway inevitably comes to my mind when I think of Porter. They were the reverse sides of each other— one so traditionally masculine, one so traditionally feminine. Both were deeply American yet ill at ease in America, both wrote with a passionate eye and a reckless insistence on getting things said. But it was Porter's bad luck to be a near-contemporary of Hemingway's. His spare, stripped-down style set a tone for what it was to write as an American. The problem was that it set *the* tone, so that others were drowned out or considered deficient, improper, overdone.

Now I must admit here that I enjoy blaming Hemingway for things. On a bad day, I lay at his feet overpopulation, air pollution and harmful additives in foods. On a good day, I admire his descriptive powers and the integrity of his plain style. But let us, however reluctantly, put blame aside and consider that Hemingway was surrounded or enveloped or covered by a historical cultural accident outside his control. He precisely fit the bill of American fantasy after World War I. Partly it was his war record, partly it was his looks—what Edmund Wilson is said to have called his Clark Gable smile. And then there was the athleticism, the sexual adventurism and being in Paris at the right time.

Certainly, he added to American prose a needed and on the whole healthful styptic touch. There was, beginning in the age of Victoria, a kind of sickly overabundance that affected everything from furniture to the poetic line. It was also an age of increased female power and feminization of culture. Perhaps for that reason, the choking fustiness that characterized the taste of the age became associated with the female—the maternal, unsexual female, that is. And she was the one who, in the provincial towns of America, ran culture. How exhilarating Hemingway's sentences must have seemed to a claque of young men who feared death by antimacassar.

The novel—all prose fiction for that matter—is the love child of two deeply incompatible parents. It has journalism for a father, poetry for a mother. For Hemingway and all his sons, the goal was to make of prose an Athena: sprung full blown from the head of the father, the mother swallowed up and kept from sight. "Good" prose was to have the sharp, telegraphic punch of newspaper language; "bad" prose was ornamented, gilded as the Gilded Age. This determination became the boot that flattened the face of American prose. It had many victims, including, perhaps most notably, F. Scott Fitzgerald, who died virtually unread, most of his books out of print. Later, other voices, particularly William Faulkner's, swelled the American chorus. But Porter's combination of cold realism and an unmistakably female point of view made her an uncomfortable passenger on what Flannery O'Connor called Faulkner's "Dixie Express" at the same time that she was marginalized as a "Southern writer."

> **Porter's combination of cold realism and an unmistakably female point of view made her an uncomfortable passenger on what Flannery O'Connor called Faulkner's "Dixie Express" at the same time that she was marginalized as a "Southern writer."**
>
> —*Mary Gordon*

Added to these accidents affecting Porter's status is the formal prejudice that insists that the novel is the real thing and shorter forms only pathetic country cousins. So for many years, Porter took her place as a writer of perfect short stories, admirable but somehow outside the big picture. She had no traceable ancestors and spawned no followers. Her stories resisted easy categorization. Their finished shape belied their originality. They combined ferocity and tenderness, opulence and precision, voluptuousness and chastity. It was easier to treat her as a curiosity, a fragile and perhaps overwrought china doll, than to acknowledge the importance of what she had produced. And she produced very little—three collections of stories, *Flowering Judas* (1930), *Pale Horse, Pale Rider* (1939) and *The Leaning Tower* (1944). Her collected stories, published in 1965, are only 495 pages long: in a career of nearly 50 years, that's 10 pages a year.

Publishers kept asking for *the novel,* and she put her mind to it, adopting a course that was both personally and formally a torment to her. She began *Ship of Fools* in 1941, and worked over it, seized by reluctance and boredom and self-hatred, for more than 20 years. When it finally appeared, in 1962, it brought her a fame and a financial success her stories had never achieved, it became, for younger readers, the way that they knew Katherine Anne Porter. Which meant they did not know her at her best, as a writer of stories. And if they knew her only as the author of the book a much-hyped movie was based on, they would wonder what any shouting had ever been about.

*Ship of Fools* has a kind of greatness, but it is not the kind associated with the traditional greatness of the novel. We expect that in a novel characters will move and grow, and the characters of *Ship of Fools* appear in a series of static snapshots. There is an overlay of melodrama: a drug-addicted "Condesa," a saintly doctor, an alcoholic aging belle, a dwarf. But the novel is fearless in its facing of the possibility that the true nature of human beings is malign. To act with malignity would seem, in Porter's mind, to be as natural to humans as drawing breath. There is the thick malignity of the Germans, the careless, coarse malignity of the Americans. But most frightening of all is the troupe of Spanish dancers who are utterly outside the web of moral consideration. They will do anything for profit, to get their way or to experience the joy of humiliating. There are two children in the troupe, twins from hell called Ric and Rac after two dogs in a comic strip, who live only to cause harm, and one night they throw the beloved white bulldog of a childless German couple overboard, simply out of boredom.

We see over and over again in *Ship of Fools* a technique of which Porter is a master: the ability to describe gesture and manners, to use them as a nest in which to enclose a statement of general, even metaphysical, significance. This is evident in her description of a scene in which a drunken husband beats his wife in the same room in which their child is supposedly asleep. Then in a fit of morose mutual lust, the parents make love in the bunk above their son's head. In the morning, another passenger sees them bowing and holding the door for each other and remarks:

> That sad, dull display of high manners after they had behaved no doubt disgracefully to each other and their child was intended no doubt to prove that they were not so base as they had caused each other to seem. That dreadful little door-holding bowing scene had meant to say, You can see, can't you, that in another time or place, or another society, I might have been very different, much better than you have ever seen me. . . . What they were saying to each other was only, *Love me, love me in spite of all! Whether or not I love you, whether I am fit to love, whether you are able to love, even if there is so such thing as love, love me!*

Lost in the bitterness and cynicism with which Porter wrote *Ship of Fools* is the joy in nature and in simple living that marks her greatest short stories. This pleasure suffused the breathtaking **"Holiday"** (1960), which took her more than 30 years to write. It is the story of a suffering young woman's vacation with a family of German immigrant farmers. The center of the story is a hideously afflicted young serving girl, who the narrator only gradually realizes is one of the children of the family. She sees that the forgetfulness, the brutal using of this girl is not a cruelty but a down-to-earth understanding that a dreadful tragedy has occurred, that something must be done with it and life must go on. Ottilie, the damaged girl, is portrayed in all her grotesqueness, surrounded by her family's intensely healthful and fecund business. But around these two aspects, like a shimmering envelope, is the narrator's enchantment with the land and the coming of spring. She describes one of her first rides across the property:

> There was nothing beautiful in those woods now except the promise of spring, for I detested bleakness, but it gave me pleasure to think that beyond this there might be something else beautiful in its own being, a river shaped and contained by its banks, or a field stripped down to its true meaning, plowed and ready for the seed. . . . The leaves were budding in tiny cones of watery green.

After a disastrous thunderstorm, in which everybody in the family works to the utmost to try to save what is being ruined by the overwhelming waters, the mother (whom Porter has described, with one of her delicious aphorisms, as a "matriarch in men's shoes") simply takes to her bed and dies. The family goes off in a caravan of wagons for the funeral; only the narrator and Ottilie are left at home. Ottilie begins to weep, to howl with weeping. The narrator assumes that she is grieving because she hasn't been included in the fu-

neral procession, and she takes her in a rickety wagon to try to catch up with the others. She discovers that what Ottilie wants is not to join the others but just to go for a ride. What she wants is a holiday. In her realization, the narrator is shocked into a deep understanding:

> Ottilie, now silent, was doubled upon herself, slipping loosely on the edge of the seat. I caught hold of her stout belt with my free hand, and my fingers slipped between her clothes and bare flesh, ribbed and gaunt and dry against my knuckles. My sense of her realness, her humanity, this shattered being that was a woman, was so shocking to me that a howl as doglike and despairing as her own rose in me unuttered and died again, to be a perpetual ghost. Ottilie slanted her eyes and peered at me, and I gazed back. The knotted wrinkles of her face were grotesquely changed, she gave a choked little whimper, and suddenly she laughed out, a kind of yelp but unmistakably laughter. . . . The feel of the hot sun on her back, the bright air, the jolly senseless staggering of the wheels, the peacock green of the heavens: something of these had reached her. She was happy and gay, and she gurgled and rocked in her seat, leaning upon me and waving loosely around her as if to show me what wonders she saw.

Porter earns her right to speak about humanity, about life and death, because she has so firmly rooted her perceptions in the soil of the particular. The mention of Ottilie's stout belt, the touch of the narrator's fingers on her dry flesh, makes us understand that the voice of the narrator is entirely trustworthy; if she says this is the nature of life, we will believe it.

And we believe Porter when she takes us in **"Pale Horse, Pale Rider"** into the territory not only of death, but of dying. The strength of our belief is connected to the fact that we are not reading just a story about dying. We learn, as well, about sexual love, the war at home, pleasure in weather and clothing and animal aliveness, the manners of people who work at a minor newspaper in a minor American town, the precarious position of a woman who must earn her way with no one behind her to break her fall.

The lovers in the story are named Adam and Miranda: the first man, the untainted daughter of Prospero. He is a soldier about to leave for World War I. Adam expects not to return, so the few days he has with Miranda have a great preciousness. But she can't take time off from work on the newspaper to spend the day with him. So we see her in her rather cheerful office, with the colleagues who sit on her desk and let their feet dangle. There is a brilliant set piece about a hoofer to whom Miranda has given a bad review. He insists on confronting her and insists that she tell him why she doesn't think he's any good. "I've been called the best in the business and I wanta know what you think is wrong with me," he says in an agonizing display of bravado that ends in tears.

In the course of Miranda's daily rounds, we meet types who are caught on the exhilarating hook of Porter's aphoristic wit. A thuggish Liberty Bond salesman is introduced: "He might be anything at all . . . advance agent for a road show, promoter of a wildcat oil company, a former saloon keeper announcing the opening of a new cabaret, an automobile salesman. —any follower of any one of the crafty, haphazard callings." Another patriotic fund raiser is said to have a face "in which nothing could be read save the inept sensual record of 50 years."

Miranda's attraction for Adam is recorded in a prose that is oddly arousing in spite of its formal strictness. His uniform, his shoes, his watch, his hands are all the locus of a tremendous masculine force. And yet, when Miranda falls sick, he nurses her with the tenderness of the mother she still yearns for. It is not, after all, the war that cuts into their time together: it is the influenza epidemic, which brings Miranda to the brink of death.

And it is at this moment that Katherine Anne Porter performs one of the riskiest feats in American literature. She dares to use the language of transcendence and of dream to describe what is supposed to be indescribable: the experience of dying. She approaches it breakneck, on the back of a horse that is always on the verge of bolting. But it does not, even for a moment, resist her control. Then, the heart-stopping fence is taken, with the inevitable arc of perfect flight:

> There it is at last, it is very simple. . . . Granite walls, whirlpools, stars are things. . . . None of them is death, nor the image of it. Death is death . . . and for the dead it has no attributes. Silenced she sank easily through deeps under deeps of darkness until she lay like a stone at the farthest bottom of life, knowing herself to be blind, deaf, speechless, no longer aware of the members of her own body, entirely withdrawn from all human concerns, yet alive with a peculiar lucidity and coherence; all notions of the mind, the reasonable inquiries of doubt, all ties of blood and the desires of the heart, dissolved and fell away from her, and there remained of her only a minute fiercely burning particle of being that knew itself alone, that relied upon nothing beyond itself for its strength; not susceptible to any appeal or inducement, being itself composed entirely of one single motive, the stubborn will to live.

Grammatically, this last sentence is a matchless piece of virtuosity: 12 clauses that rise, fall, meander, rise again, then

crash. The sentence is followed by a much quieter diction: we learn that Miranda will live but that Adam has died—not of a German bullet but of the influenza he caught from her. Reluctantly, Miranda understands that she must go on living. She plans her resurrection in a traditionally feminine way: she makes a shopping list. "One lipstick, medium, one ounce flask Bois d'Hiver perfume, one pair of gray suede gauntlets without straps, two pairs gray sheer stockings without clocks. . . . A jar of cold cream. . . . No one need pity this corpse if we look properly to the art of the thing."

Katherine Anne Porter was heroic in her commitment to looking properly to the art of the thing. This commitment allowed her to look in the face of such unimaginables as evil, death, the irreparable blows of fate, and force them to turn themselves beautiful. It was an exhausting and perilous enterprise, one that made it almost impossible to live. She reached 90, but for many of the years of her long life she produced no writing. What she did produce has the clarity and inclusiveness of the art we have proclaimed great. She once sent a message to a high school class in Oklahoma: "Practice an art for love and the happiness of your life—you will find it outlasts almost everything but breath."

---

## FURTHER READING

### Bibliography

Bixby, George. "Katherine Anne Porter: A Bibliographic Checklist." *American Book Collector* 1, No. 6 (November-December 1980): 19-33.
   Provides a list of first editions of Porter's works.

Hendrick, George. "Selected Bibliography." In *Katherine Anne Porter,* pp. 161-71. New York: Twayne Publishers, N.D.
   Provides a list of Porter's collected and uncollected works.

Machann, Clinton, and William Bedford Clark. "A Texas Bibliography of Katherine Anne Porter." In *Katherine Anne Porter and Texas: An Uneasy Relationship,* pp. 124-82. College Station: Texas A & M University Press, 1990.
   Provides a list of Porter's Texas related texts and criticism.

### Criticism

Bloom, Harold. "Introduction." In *Modern Critical Views: Katherine Anne Porter,* edited by Harold Bloom, pp. 1-5. New York: Chelsea House Publishers, 1986.
   Explores aspects of narcissism in "Flowering Judas."

Brinkmeyer, Robert H., Jr. "'Endless Remembering': The Artistic Vision of Katherine Anne Porter." *Mississippi Quarterly* 40, No. 1 (Winter 1986-87): 5-19.

Examines the role of memory in Porter's fiction.

Cheatham, George. "Fall and Redemption in *Pale Horse, Pale Rider*." *Renascence* XXXIX, No. 3 (Spring 1987): 396-405.

Examines the Christian concept of fall and redemption as evident in *Pale Horse, Pale Rider*.

Core, George. "The *Best* Residuum of Truth." *The Georgia Review* XX, No. 3 (Fall 1966): 278-91.

Provides an overview of Porter's work based on contents of *The Collected Stories of Katherine Anne Porter*.

Hafen, P. Jane. "Katherine Anne Porter's 'The Old Order' and *Agamemnon*." *Studies in Short Fiction* 31, No. 3 (Summer 1994): 491-3.

Examines allusions to Aeschylus' *Agamemnon* in "The Old Order."

Hinze, Diana. "Texas and Berlin: Images of Germany in Katherine Anne Porter's Prose." *Southern Literary Journal* XXIV, No. 1 (Fall 1991): 77-87.

Examines the influence of Porter's geographic surroundings in her fiction.

Gibbons, Kaye. "Planes of Language and Time: The Surfaces of the Miranda Stories." *The Kenyon Review* 10, No. 1 (Winter 1988): 74-9.

Explores the depth and complexity of the Miranda character in Porter's fiction.

Gottfried, Leon. "Death's Other Kingdom: Dantesque and Theological Symbolism in 'Flowering Judas.'" *Publications of the Modern Language Associations* 84, No. 1 (January 1969): 112-24.

Explores the theological underpinnings and allusions to Dante's *Inferno* in "Flowering Judas."

Jefferson, Margo. "Self-Made." *Grand Street* 2, No. 4 (Summer 1983): 152-71.

Provides an overview of Porter's life and literary production.

Jorgensen, Bruce W. "'The Other Side of Silence': Katherine Anne Porter's 'He' as Tragedy." *Modern Fiction Studies* 28, No. 3 (Autumn 1982): 395-404.

Provides discussion of "He" as tragic drama.

Kirkpatrick, Smith. Review of *Ship of Fools*. *The Sewanee Review* LXXXI, No. 1 (January-March 1963): 94-8.

A favorable review of *Ship of Fools*.

Moddelmog, Debra A. "Narrative Irony and Hidden Motivations in Katherine Anne Porter's 'He.'" *Modern Fiction Studies* 28, No. 3 (Autumn, 1986): 405-13.

Critical and psychological interpretation of the mother-son relationship in "He."

Richardson, Phyllis. "Southern Belle From a Log Cabin." *Times Literary Supplement* No. 4840 (January 4, 1996): 6-7.

Offers commentary on Porter as portrayed in Janis P. Stout's biography *Katherine Anne Porter: A Sense of the Times*.

Ruoff, James. "Katherine Anne Porter Comes to Kansas." *The Midwest Quarterly* IV, No. 4 (June 1963): 305-14.

Describes a visit by Porter to the University of Wichita.

Ryan, Marjorie. "Dubliners and the Stories of Katherine Anne Porter." *American Literature* XXXI, No. 4 (January, 1960): 464-73.

Comparative analysis of James Joyce's *The Dubliners* and Porter's short stories, noting thematic similarities and differences in tone, particularly Porter's greater sympathy for her characters.

Stout, Janis P. "Miranda's Guarded Speech: Porter and the Problem of Truth Telling." *Philological Quarterly* 66, No. 2 (Spring, 1987): 259-78.

Character analysis of Miranda in "The Old Order," "Old Mortality," and "Pale Horse, Pale Rider," noting the development and significance of her character in Porter's stories.

Tate, Allen. "A New Star." *The Nation* CXXXI, No. 3404 (October 30, 1930): 352-3.

A favorable review of *Flowering Judas*.

Unrue, Darlene Harbour. "Katherine Anne Porter and Henry James: A Study in Influence." *Southern Quarterly* 31, No. 3 (Spring 1993): 17-28.

Examines the significance of Porter's personal interest in the life and work of Henry James.

Walsh, Thomas F. "Xochitl: Katherine Anne Porter's Changing Goddess." *American Literature* LII, No. 2 (May 1980): 183-93.

Explores the significance of the Aztec goddess Xochitl in "The Children of Xochitl" and "Hacienda," noting the development of related themes in "Pale Horse, Pale Rider" and *Ship of Fools*.

——. "The Making of 'Flowering Judas.'" *The Journal of Modern Literature* 12, No. 1 (March 1985): 109-30.

Examines the origin and development of characters and theme in "Flowering Judas" as inspired by Porter's personal experiences in Mexico.

———"'That Deadly Female Accuracy of Vision': Katherine Anne Porter and *El Heraldo de Mexico*." *Journal of Modern Literature* 16, No. 4 (Spring 1990): 635-43.

> Examines Porter's contributions to the Mexican publication *El Heraldo de Mexico*.

Welty, Eudora. "My Introduction to Katherine Anne Porter." *The Georgia Review* XLIV, No. 1-2 (Spring-Summer 1990): 13-27.

> Welty's reminiscences on friendship and correspondence with Porter.

## Interviews

Bufkin, E. C. "An *Open Mind* Profile: Katherine Anne Porter Talks with Glenway Wescott and Eric F. Goldman." *The Georgia Review* XLI, No. 4 (Winter 1987): 71-95.

> Porter comments on the creation and themes of *Ship of Fools* while reflecting on formative events in her life and the creative writing process.

Thompson, Barbara. Interview with Barbara Thompson. *Paris Review* 8, No. 29 (Winter-Spring 1963): 87-114.

> Porter discusses her background and writing.

---

**Additional coverage of Porter's life and career is contained in the following sources published by Gale Research:** *Authors in the News,* **Vol. 2;** *Contemporary Authors,* **Vols. 1-4R and 101;** *Contemporary Authors New Revision Series,* **Vol. 1;** *DISCovering Authors; DISCovering Authors: British; DISCovering Authors: Canadian; DISCovering Authors Modules: Most-Studied Authors and Novelists Modules; Dictionary of Literary Biography,* **Vols. 4, 9, and 102;** *Dictionary of Literary Biography Documentary Series,* **Vol. 12;** *Dictionary of Literary Biography Yearbook,* **Vol. 80;** *Major Twentieth-Century Writers; Something about the Author,* **Vols. 23 and 39; and** *Short Story Criticism,* **Vol. 4.**

# Theodore Roethke

## 1908-1963

(Full name Theodore Huebner Roethke) American poet.

The following entry provides an overview of Roethke's career through 1991. For further information on his life and works, see *CLC*, Volumes 1, 3, 8, 11, 19, and 46.

## INTRODUCTION

Theodore Roethke is distinguished as one of the most gifted and innovative American poets of the 1940s and 1950s. He is widely acclaimed for his inventive use of language, facile technique, and highly imaginative metaphorical description of the natural world. With the publication of *Open House* (1941), his first book of poetry, Roethke received critical attention and rose to prominence with *The Lost Son and Other Poems* (1948), *Praise to the End!* (1951), *Words for the Wind* (1957), and *The Far Field* (1964). Roethke's most effective work is characterized by recurring childhood memories and striking primordial imagery that elevate autobiographic detail to archetypal significance. His dynamic and often playful verse relies heavily on intuitive word associations and careful structure for sonic effect. Roethke's penetrating exploration of the past and the subconscious mind reflect a lifelong quest for harmony sought in self-acceptance and transcendence. Highly regarded for his originality and ability to evoke the universal in personal experience, Roethke exerted an important influence on the development of post-war American poetry.

**Biographical Information**

Born to German-American parents in Saginaw, Michigan, Roethke's rural upbringing centered around the family's prosperous greenhouse business. His early experiences among the acres of sprawling flora ended abruptly during adolescence with a series of tragedies—the sale of the family greenhouse business, his uncle's suicide, and his father's sudden death. The last caused him considerable anguish and would have a profound effect on his writing. Roethke earned an undergraduate degree at the University of Michigan and, after trying a semester of law school, undertook graduate studies in English at Harvard University. A university teaching career followed, first at Lafayette College, then Michigan State University, Pennsylvania State University, Bennington College, and finally at the University of Washington where he remained from 1947 until his death. During the 1930s Roethke began to establish his reputation as a poet by publishing work in several prestigious journals, including *Poetry, The New Republic,* and *The Saturday Review.* In 1935

he suffered a serious mental breakdown that resulted in hospitalization and cost him his teaching position at Michigan State University. Roethke would suffer from recurring episodes of manic depression for the rest of his life, a source of intense creative inspiration that disrupted his academic career and weakened him emotionally. He produced *Open House,* his first volume poetry, in 1941, and received a Guggenheim Fellowship four years later. *The Lost Son and Other Poems* followed in 1948, resulting in a second Guggenheim Fellowship that allowed him to finish *Praise to the End!* in 1951, another success rewarded with large grants from the Ford Foundation and National Institute of Arts and Letters the next year. In 1953 Roethke married Beatrice O'Connell, a former student from Bennington, and published *The Waking* (1953), which won a Pulitzer Prize, followed by *Words for the Wind* in 1958, the winner of several major awards, including the National Book Award and the Bollingen Prize. In the next several years he also published two volumes of children's verse, *I Am! Says the Lamb* (1961) and *Party at the Zoo* (1963). After a period of lecturing and extensive travel in Europe on a Ford Foundation Grant, Roethke suffered a fatal heart attack in 1963. He left a substantial body of new work that appeared posthumously in *The Far Field,* winner of the National Book Award in 1964, and *The Collected Poems* (1966).

## Major Works

Roethke's artistic development is marked by persistent efforts to attain self-knowledge and unity in nature through the reconciliation of individual experience and revelation. His early poems in *Open House* are studied adaptations of conventional forms that display his mastery of meter and rhyme, though evince an intellectual rather than sensuous approach to his material. Roethke reveals his affinity for nature imagery and adumbrates the subconscious personal tensions that found expression in his later work. The title poem, "Open House," is a self-referential incantation that anticipates Roethke's regression into the psyche and cathartic inner journeys. With *The Lost Son and Other Poems* Roethke broke sharply with his contemporaries and began his innovative work, abandoning the restrained structure of his previous poetry for more expressive free verse steeped in irregularity and the irrational. The vivid imagery of the first section, referred to as the "Greenhouse Sequence," is among Roethke's most powerful, reflecting a deep connection to the vegetative world of his early life and evoking Jungian archetypes in pre-conscious experience. Through the symbolism of cultivation and harvesting, Roethke exposes the paradox and reality of life and death. This volume also contains "My Papa's Waltz," which portrays the terrifying godlike stature of Roethke's father, and "The Lost Son," which describes the complex and disillusioning process of individuation in a circular pattern that became characteristic of Roethke's metaphysical explorations. In *Praise to the End!* Roethke ventured further into the surreal, experimenting with the non-grammatical language of pre-verbal childhood with great effect. Alternating between nonsense verse and oracular declaration, Roethke celebrates self-discovery and the union of body and spirit. The title poem, "Praise to the End!," incorporates elements of nursery rhyme and Freudian imagery of sexual awakening to evoke the sensual joy of worldly experience and metamorphosis. *The Waking* contains selections from earlier volumes and Roethke's well-known "Elegy for Jane" and "Four for Sir John Davies," inspired by the influence of William Butler Yeats. Their lyrical tone, though less associative than that of the previous two volumes, reaffirms the primacy of intuitive perception and faith over reason. *Words for the Wind* includes *The Waking* in its entirety along with a series of love poems and two important longer pieces, "The Dying Man" and "Meditations on an Old Woman." Returning to the meter and rhyme of his earlier work, Roethke explores female consciousness and the contradictions of love and mortality with both empathy and wit. *The Far Field* contains additional love poems, "Sequence, Sometimes Metaphysical," and "North American Sequence," considered Roethke's last great achievement. In this expan-

sive series of meditative passages, Roethke employs the journey motif to juxtapose emotional self-exploration and reclamation with sweeping description of the continent and its varied flora and fauna.

## Critical Reception

Roethke is widely acclaimed as one of the most important American poets of the twentieth century. In the tradition the Romantic poets and Americans Ralph Waldo Emerson and Walt Whitman, Roethke evokes the mystical and visionary in solitary experience and sustained introspection. Though criticized for derivative aspects of his work, particularly the overt influence of Yeats, Roethke assimilated and extended the modernist contributions of Wallace Stevens and T. S. Eliot to establish a poetic voice of his own that reached further into the depths of the individual psyche. *The Lost Son and Other Poems* and *Praise to the End!* are regarded as his best collections, along with "North American Sequence" from *The Far Field.* Despite frequent allusion to his emotional life and childhood, Roethke's poetry aspires to the universal and is essentially ahistorical, ignoring social and political events of his time. His diverse work, with its many styles, themes, and moods, defies simple classification, though his effective synthesis of autobiography, playful idiom, and archetypal symbolism was a major influence on beat, confessional, and deep-image poets in subsequent decades. Roethke's innovative attempt to discover psychic origins and to achieve transcendence through intuitive language and organic imagery remains a significant achievement in contemporary American poetry.

---

## PRINCIPAL WORKS

*Open House* (poetry) 1941
*The Lost Son and Other Poems* (poetry) 1948
*Praise to the End!* (poetry) 1951
*The Waking: Poems 1933-1953* (poetry) 1953
*The Exorcism: A Portfolio of Poems* (poetry) 1957
*Words for the Wind* (poetry) 1957
*I Am! Says the Lamb* (poetry) 1961
*Party at the Zoo* (poetry) 1963
*Sequence, Sometimes Metaphysical* (poetry) 1963
*The Far Field* (poetry) 1964
*On the Poet and His Craft: Selected Prose of Theodore Roethke* (essays) 1965
*The Achievement of Theodore Roethke* (poetry) 1966
*The Collected Poems of Theodore Roethke* (poetry) 1966
*Selected Letters of Theodore Roethke* (letters) 1968
*Theodore Roethke: Selected Poems* (poetry) 1969
*Straw for the Fire: From the Notebooks of Theodore Roethke, 1943-1963* (notebooks) 1972

*Dirty Dinky and Other Creatures: Poems for Children* (poetry) 1973

## CRITICISM

### M. L. Rosenthal (review date 21 March 1959)

SOURCE: "Closing in on the Self," in *The Nation,* Vol. 188, No. 12, March 21, 1959, pp. 258-60.

[*In the following review, Rosenthal offers tempered criticism of* Words for the Wind.]

Pick up one of Theodore Roethke's longer poems and you are confronted with a stunning mishmash of agonized gibber, described by the poet himself in an essay written some years ago as "the muck and welter, the dark, the *dreck*" of his verse. The same essay (**"Open Letter,"** published in Ciardi's *Mid-Century American Poets*) asserts that he nevertheless counts himself "among the happy poets." And indeed, Roethke at his best throws all kinds of dissimilar effects into the great, ceaseless mixer of his sensibility, stirring together notes of driving misery and hysterical ecstasy, of Rabelaisian sensuality and warm, wet regressiveness:

> Believe me, knot of gristle, I bleed
>   like a tree;
> I dream of nothing but boards;
> I could love a duck.
> Such music in a skin!
> A bird sings in the bush of your
>   bones.
> Tufty, the water's loose.
> Bring me a finger. . . .
>
> **("Give Way, Ye Gates")**

Some of the allusion here is a little too private. ("Tufty, the water's loose," for example, has all sorts of obvious physiological connotations but probably has something to do with Roethke's boyhood experiences helping out in his father's greenhouse. And it would take more than a feather to knock me over if I were suddenly to learn that "Tufty" was a family nickname for Theodore.) But the passage as a whole, which begins the poem, is a wildly bawdy outcry of desire, thinly and wittily veiled in euphemism.

Later in the poem all this exhilaration withers up and is replaced by language of frustration and suffering, and then of a sort of minimal self-consolation. The over-excitement of the first part, in which the pain of the need behind desire was muted or hidden in humor, is balanced off by a gross, almost infantile desolateness. The images now are of impotence and shame:

> Touch and arouse. Suck and sob.
>   Curse and mourn.
> It's a cold scrape in a low place.
> The dead crow dries on a pole.
> Shapes in the shade
> Watch.

This projection without comment of opposed psychological states is characteristic of Roethke's most interesting work. A desperate exuberance that seems at one moment unrepressed joy of life, at the next the pathetic hilarity of the unbearably burdened, makes the manic-depressive mood-spectrum the law of life. Each opposite is implicit in the other, and that is the only necessary logic at work here. The universe of Roethke's poems is a completely subjective one—not what source of meaning the speaker has outside himself but how he feels within is the key to everything. The private sensibility is a mad microcosm; the speaker responds violently to everything that touches it; and he struggles frenetically to win through to a moment of calm realization in the sunlight of "wholeness." The ebullient anguish of poems like **"My Papa's Waltz," "Child on Top of a Greenhouse,"** and **"The Shape of the Fire"** is a triumphant realization of the aesthetic of hypersensitivity. Consider the opening stanzas of **"The Shape of the Fire."**

> What's this? A dish for fat lips.
> Who says? A nameless stranger.
> Is he a bird or a tree? Not everyone
>   can tell.

Water recedes to the crying of spiders. An old scow bumps over black rocks. A cracked pod calls.

> Mother me out of here. What more
>   will the bones allow?
> Will the sea give the wind suck? A
>   toad folds into a stone.
> These flowers are all fangs. Comfort
>   me, fury. . . .

The reader will come somewhere near the poet's intention, I think, if he imagines the speaker to be giving a voice to the fire and responding to it. It crackles and whispers—what is the secret of its voice? There is a horror in that devouring sound that considers the wood or coals (or anything else) "a dish for fat lips"; the second stanza gives further images for that dry, merciless sound and its terror—the receding of waters before the "crying of spiders" perhaps the most nightmarish of them. The third stanza shows the speaker overwhelmed with the sheer dread of mutability and annihilation that has been accumulated through all these impressions. The whole process is not so much conceptual as it is self-hypnotic. This is the shaping sensibility in operation, and in this sort of thing Roethke is brilliantly successful.

But it is not his only sort of thing, for in addition he often does try to conceptualize, and he tries to give his poems a further implication of victory over the frenzy through a Freudian rebirth of the Self. These efforts are not, by and large, very convincing. Thus, the last two movements of **"The Shape of the Fire"** are attempts to soar and transcend in the old sense—like the ending of "Lycidas": "To-morrow to fresh woods, and pastures new." But Milton had a vision of "the blest kingdoms meek of joy and love," and the mourner of his poem speaks to a completely different scale of values— that of the macrocosm ruled over by "the dear might of him that walk'd the waves." That is not the universe of Roethke's poems, and so his ending is contrived, though in its way lovely and delicate.

Something similar happens in **"The Lost Son,"** whose title suggests the psychoanalytical, inward turning of the poet's eye. Roethke's essay **"Open Letter"** says of this poem that it is at first "a terrified running away—with alternate periods of hallucinatory waiting . . . ; the protagonist so geared-up, so over-alive that he is hunting, like a primitive, for some animistic suggestion, some clue to existence from the sub-human." So be it—this panicky hunt for pre-intellectual sources of the sense of being truly alive is without doubt one of the real, if uneasy, enterprises of the modern mind. But the poet is not ruthless enough to carry the hunt through— any more than he was able to remain true to the realizations at the beginning of **"The Shape of the Fire."** He finds another clue to salvation, an easier one, than the frenzied beginning would imply was possible. It is the "lost son's" psychological re-entry into the world of his most vivid childhood memories—the world of the "long greenhouse" which he has called "my symbol for the whole of life, a womb, a heaven-on-earth."

Re-entry into this paradisal womb, one gathers, is the necessary preliminary for a rebirth of the Self. The true "coming-through" into mature, calm reconciliation has not yet occurred, but faith is expressed that it will do so—

> A lively understandable spirit
> Once entertained you.
> It will come again.

The promise is too pat and wishful—of a Freudian romance with a happy ending. As in most of Roethke's longer work, the dénouement does not live up to the poem's initial demands. Shorter poems like **"The Return," "The Minimal,"** and **"The Exorcism"** are really better in the way they sustain a sometimes Dantean close-up of minutely detailed, realistic horror on the terms with which they began. I would add also the beautiful **"The Visitant,"** the guilt-filled **"The Song,"** the deeply sad and very original **"Dolor,"** the dream-like **"Night Crow,"** and the sweatily, feverishly, embarrassedly alive greenhouse poems from Roethke's 1948 volume *The Lost Son and Other Poems*. Together with certain passages in the longer poems, such pieces constitute Roethke's more lasting achievements.

## Karl Malkoff (essay date 1966)

SOURCE: "The Greenhouse Land," in *Theodore Roethke: An Introduction to the Poetry,* Columbia University Press, 1966, pp. 1-17.

[*In the following essay, Malkoff provides an overview of Roethke's life and work, noting developmental influences, recurring themes, and his major publications.*]

The "lost world" of childhood experience plays a crucial part in the work of many contemporary writers. This is particularly true in the case of Theodore Roethke, who derived much of his poetic power and originality from his attempt to interpret adult life in terms of a permanent symbolism established in childhood. Roethke was born in Saginaw, Michigan, on May 25, 1908. His father and uncle owned one of the largest and most famous floricultural establishments in the area at that time. There were twenty-five acres, most of them under glass, in the town itself; and beyond that, farther out in the country, the last stretch of virgin timber in the valley; and finally, a wild area of second-growth timber which the Roethkes converted into a small game preserve. As a child, Roethke would tag after his father as he made his rounds, or wander alone among shoots that dangled and drooped in the silo-rich dark of a root cellar, playing in a pulpy world of beetles, worms, and slugs. Growing older, his relation to the greenhouse world became more active; work and play were combined in hacking at black hairy roots under concrete benches, gathering moss in the swampy field at the edge of the forest, or triumphantly climbing to the roof of the fragile greenhouse. In short, all the joys and fears of growing up were experienced as part of this kingdom of dynamic plant life; and so, it is not surprising that in later years the greenhouse became for Roethke the focus of most childhood memories, his "symbol for the whole of life, a womb, a heaven-on-earth."

But although the womblike greenhouses were dark and protective, they must have had threatening aspects as well, for Roethke later revised this description in favor of greater complexity. "They were to me, I realize now, both heaven and hell, a kind of tropics created in the savage climate of Michigan, where austere German Americans turned their love of order and their terrifying efficiency into something truly beautiful."

Symbol of creation and the strict imposition of order upon chaos, on the one hand, of the protective, fertile womb, on the other, the dual nature of the greenhouse corresponds to Roethke's feelings toward his father and mother respectively. Otto Roethke, "a Prussian through and through," was strong and firm, the personification of *Ordnung;* but this strength was, for his son, a source of both admiration and fear, of comfort and restriction. His father's mixture of tenderness and brutality comes across clearly in Roethke's **"My Papa's Waltz."** There he describes how Otto, a bit drunk, would roughly waltz him around while his mother looked on disapprovingly, and he himself was both afraid and joyful. On another, soberer occasion, Theodore, who was seven years old at the time, saw his father bring two poachers to a halt with rifle bullets, and then, leaving his gun behind, walk over and slap them both across the face, these men who had broken the natural order.

Roethke's references to his father, no matter what emotional coloring they are given, have one thing in common: they always convey a sense of awesome, godlike power. This is the man who made the flowers grow, a rainbow at his thumb as he held the watering can; this is the man who established law and enforced it. In Roethke's case, the use of the father as symbol of God (as in **"The Lost Son"**) is more than an artificially conceived literary image: it is charged with experience.

Roethke's mother, the former Helen Marie Huebner, appears less frequently, and in less specific terms, through the poet's work, than his father. She is, however, the central figure in one of Roethke's important series of contemplative poems, Meditations of an Old Woman. "The protagonist is modelled, in part, after my own mother, now dead, whose favorite reading was the Bible, Jane Austen, and Dostoevsky—in other words a gentle, highly articulate old lady believing in the glories of the world, yet fully conscious of its evils." Although this is not a childhood recollection, there is a definite sense of continuity between this quiet, literate old woman, and the young mother who, with the nurse, used to sing Theodore to sleep with nursery rhymes in English and German.

***Praise to the End!,*** another of Roethke's sequences, in which he attempts to recapture his childhood world, is filled with representations of this young mother, but they are generalized and archetypal, rarely as individualized as those of the father. Conceivably, since the mother is shown at the apex of an Oedipal triangle, Roethke never learned to deal with the sexual connotations of specific memories. In any case, however simplified the image of the mother may be in Roethke's poetry, it is necessary to keep in mind that she

was a complex figure to her son, and often usurped the father as an establisher of values. "My mother," wrote Roethke, "insisted upon two things—that I strive for perfection in whatever I did and that I always try to be a gentleman." And Roethke had also told friends "the story of a brutal fist fight from which he dragged himself home bruised and bleeding, and how it was his mother who refused to let him into the house, ordering him to go back and thrash the boy who had just thrashed him."

Roethke attended Arthur Hill High School. There he wrote a speech for the Junior Red Cross which became part of an international campaign and was translated into many languages. But in spite of the glow of this success, chief among many similar prize-winning achievements, he intensely disliked the high school, the town itself, and (with the exception, at times, of the land owned by his father and uncle) that entire area of Michigan. Like many adolescents, Roethke was very much disturbed by the hypocrisy of the adult world, by the venom of small-town gossip, its pettiness, its sugary destructiveness. Roethke ended by being convinced that the most "respectable" and "human" members of the community were the gangsters and bootleggers who operated out of Saginaw at that time. He would go to all lengths to have a drink with one of his idols; for Roethke, in spite of his genuine affection for the small and helpless of the world, had great, perhaps excessive, respect for power and for those who wielded it.

Roethke received his A.B. from the University of Michigan in 1929, and attended Michigan Law School and Harvard before finally earning his M.A. at Michigan in 1936. He seems to have disliked all of these schools impartially, but it was at Harvard that Roethke showed his poetry to Robert Hillyer, and received encouragement—"Any editor who wouldn't buy these is a damn fool!"—crucial to his career. It was at this point that he abandoned all ideas of a future in law or advertising. He was studying law, and had already written advertising copy which had been used in a national campaign—his first love, after all, had been prose. However, soon after the meeting with Hillyer, Roethke's poetic career was fully under way, and by the mid 1930s he was contributing regularly to numerous periodicals.

From 1931 until 1935, Roethke was an instructor at Lafayette College, and from 1936 to 1943 he was at Pennsylvania State College (becoming assistant professor in 1939). At both schools, he not only taught English, but coached the tennis teams as well. This should serve to remind us of another aspect of Roethke's personality. He wrote of flowers, of the delicate and small things of the world, he sang the spirit as he found it manifested in man and nature; but he himself was anything but delicate—he stood six feet three inches tall and weighed well over two hundred pounds—and he was very much aware of his own physicality. In tennis, or in any game, he was a fierce competitor, quite likely to sulk and storm if he lost. He was a big bear of a man. But that is only a partial truth; he was not slow, and, if he was not light-footed, neither was he totally clumsy. In later years, for example, when Roethke was at the University of Washington, there was once a fire in the waste basket in the English office that left everyone else flatfooted and gaping while Roethke ran for an extinguisher and put the fire out. If Roethke was a bear, he was a dancing bear, not only in physical movement, but in his life as a whole. By the alchemy of his poetry he transformed a gross and ugly material world into an image of the spirit; he created something graceful out of an awkward reality.

By the time Roethke was thirty, the pattern of his life as poet and teacher was set; but the real struggle had only begun. Throughout his adult life, Roethke was subject to periodic breakdowns within a broader cycle of manic-depressive behavior. His torment was compounded, at least for many years, by the need to cover up these breakdowns in order to survive in the academic community, and he suffered an acute sense of humiliation and defilement as a result of both the illness itself and the position in which it put him. However, he was ultimately able to make of this liability one of his chief assets.

Early poems treat the breakdowns from an objective point of view; they are talked about and intellectualized rather than directly experienced. In particular, Roethke says he is going to salvage what he can, and use the illness to move beyond himself, to a greater awareness of reality. Now these poems do not succeed as representations of Roethke's experience because they lack particularity, they are vague rather than universal; but Roethke is not here interested in exploring the nature of insanity itself, but rather the relation of periods of insanity to normal life. He has not yet learned to turn this concern into good poetry, but this point of view is at the heart of his later work. Insanity, for Roethke, is not a phenomenon divorced from life; it is rather incorporated into it. It is an aspect of experience from which one can perhaps learn a good deal more than from one's routine existence.

In later poems, such as **"The Pure Fury," "The Renewal,"** and **"The Exorcism,"** the mental anguish is not simply talked about, but is directly experienced. Roethke manages this with the aid of vastly improved techniques; but the great power of these poems is ultimately due to the vision of insanity as an integral part of life implicit in his earliest work. The anxiety experienced during a psychotic episode, the dissociation of personality, become in Roethke's hands not states of mind peculiar to the insane, but rather more intense perceptions of the human condition as it is experienced by any man.

There is an equally important corollary to this. If insanity involves more acute as well as distorted perceptions of real-

ity, then, in certain areas, the insane man holds a privileged position; he is in the forefront of human consciousness partly by virtue of his insanity, and, if he can control the tools of language, he can write the poetry of prophecy, he can give to the rest of mankind the insight necessary to change one's life so that it will be more in accord with reality than our mind-dulling society allows. In his last years, Roethke was convinced that there was a close relationship between genius and insanity, and he saw himself in the company of those poets who turned their madness into verse. "What's madness," asked Roethke, in one of his final poems, "but nobility of soul / At odds with circumstance?" This nobility, according to Roethke, is a product of heightened awareness; it is the tragic vision of life which transforms a meaningless sequence of events into something greater than itself.

In 1941, Roethke's first volume of poems, *Open House,* was published. (The name, and the very existence, of the title poem were suggested by Roethke's close friend, Stanley Kunitz.) The forty-nine poems represented only a little more than half of the poet's published work. In later years, even most of these began to "creak," and Roethke preserved only seventeen of the poems of his first eleven years of writing in *Words for the Wind.* Nonetheless, the book was well received, and its apparent conventionality made possible the near universality of praise never accorded his more controversial later work. Roethke used traditional lyric forms, his content tended to be intellectual rather than sensuous; poets such as the metaphysicals, Auden, Léonie Adams, and Elinor Wylie loomed in the background as reasonably well assimilated influences. Although we can now look back on this work and trace the origins of what were to become Roethke's major themes (e.g., the tension between flesh and spirit, the exploration of the self as a search for identity), there was little indication to someone reading his poems at the time of what was to follow.

In 1943, Roethke started teaching at Bennington. Two of the circumstances of his stay there are of note: he no longer taught tennis; and one of his students was Beatrice Heath O'Connell, whom Roethke met again several years later and ultimately married.

In 1947, Roethke arrived at the University of Washington (where he taught until his death) as associate professor. The next year, he was made full professor; and his second book, *The Lost Son and Other Poems,* was published. It contained several lyrics in the mode of *Open House,* but the greenhouse poems at the beginning, and the four long developmental poems at the end, were startlingly new, for contemporary poetry as well as for Roethke. The notion that the world of plants might be used as an emblem of human growth was traditional, but not until the greenhouse poems had anyone—not even D. H. Lawrence—combined this with Roethke's concentrated sensuality of imagery and adept manipulation of a subterranean, Freudian universe. The long poems were even more original. Using a framework provided by Freud and Jung, Roethke presented the development of the individual not by means of rational discourse, but in terms of the imagery and symbolism of the natural world, of the world of myth and legend, and the prerational consciousness from which it springs.

In 1951, Roethke published *Praise to the End!,* a sequence of developmental poems built around the nucleus of the last four works of his previous volume. So successfully did Roethke achieve his goal of finding an adequate symbolism with which to communicate the process of individuation directly, that he found himself in the practically unique position of having instituted, perfected, and finally exhausted a genre. Grumbling critical voices were beginning to make themselves heard; but the disapproval came largely from England, which was busy lowering the reputation of other nondiscursive poets, such as T. S. Eliot and Dylan Thomas. In general, acclaim was resounding.

One of the most important years of Roethke's life was 1953. He brought out *The Waking,* which received the Pulitzer Prize; he began the readings in philosophical and religious works which were to play so important a part in his later poetry; and, on January 3, he married Beatrice O'Connell.

*The Waking* included a selection of poems from *Open House,* almost all of *The Lost Son,* and the entire *Praise to the End!* There were also several new poems, in one of which Roethke announced a new source of inspiration: "I take this cadence from a man named Yeats; / I take it, and I give it back again . . ." Unquestionably, a certain Yeatsian influence was present in the stanzaic forms, the use of slant rhymes, the lyrical expression of public, philosophical themes. But while the critics were only too glad to believe that Roethke had borrowed something from Yeats, many were reluctant to admit that he had given anything back. The question of whether or not Yeats's influence was properly assimilated will be taken up later in this study. In any case, these reservations were not pronounced enough to prevent Roethke from receiving the Pulitzer Prize in 1954. Awards were not new to Roethke; he had, for example, received from *Poetry* the Eunice Tietjiens Prize (1947) and the Levinson Award (1951). But this, his first recognition on a popular and national scale, was vastly important to a man whose competitive instincts were not limited to the tennis court, who had committed himself fully to the struggle for recognition, and who, only a few years before his death, was able to refer to himself sardonically as "the oldest younger poet in the U.S.A."

Roethke's marriage seems to have been for him a kind of joyous reawakening. His feelings toward his wife are represented in his poetry from the beautiful epithalamion, **"Words for the Wind,"** written during the honeymoon visit to Auden's villa on an island off Naples, through the playful fear of Beatrice's anger in **"Her Wrath";** but his final word was the moving **"Wish for a Young Wife,"** his prayer that she live without hate or grief after his death.

The various other aspects of Roethke's life should not be allowed to overshadow the fact that he earned his living as a teacher. However, his concern with teaching went much further than that; he compared good teaching to the dance—a significant experience that cannot be recaptured—and was always concerned with ways of improving his own performance. **"The Teaching Poet,"** an essay, clearly reveals the sympathetic, sensitive nature of his approach. But far more telling than this was the almost universal regard he received from his students: they considered him a great teacher.

As for the faculty, Roethke felt that it should contain more "screwballs"; he certainly seemed one himself, especially during his high periods, and he was not always an easy person to get along with. He could rage unnecessarily against a particular teacher in private. But he was immensely (and honestly) glad when someone had received recognition for achievement, and his public praise for the department as a whole was endless. He was, insists his chairman, more profoundly concerned about the department than most of those who took their "good citizenship" for granted.

Roethke's feelings toward those with whom he worked, and those with whom he competed, were, to say the least, ambivalent. Sometimes, his rage and hate would grow to intolerable levels; he finally came to publish wave after wave of invective in frenzied, Joycean prose, using the pseudonym Winterset Rothberg. In **"Last Class,"** he attacked the members of "Hysteria College," the mindless, impenetrable students, the isolated, passionless faculty. **"A Tirade Turning,"** published posthumously, contains a similar storm of language, directed this time against Roethke's peers: critics, teachers, and poets. But the significant fact is that the tirade does after all turn, the outburst of hate leads to love: "Behold, I'm a heart set free, for I have taken my hatred and eaten it." Identifying his present competitors with the cousins with whom he competed as a boy in Saginaw, Roethke dissipates his rage. It is poetry used as therapy. Possibly, as John Ciardi has suggested, this process is behind much of Roethke's good verse: "This is poetry as a medicine man's dance is poetry. The therapy by incantation. Roethke literally danced himself back from the edge of madness."

In this manner, then, a ranting, dancing bear, Theodore Roethke approached the last, great years of his career. *Words for the Wind,* which still must be considered his most important single volume, was published in England in 1957, and in this country the following year. It contained *The Waking* in its entirety, and an equally long selection of new poems. In Love Poems and Voices and Creatures, the psychological quest for the self is given new depth and meaning in philosophical and religious terms. Existentialist thinkers such as Kierkegaard, Buber, and Tillich, and both western and oriental mystics, become the starting points of frenzied metaphysical lyrics. The Dying Man is Roethke's most direct tribute to Yeats, a brilliant sequence of poems that seem to be in Yeats's style, and yet are unmistakably Roethke's; no man who was simply imitating could have written them.

The book concludes with five—four in the British edition—longer poems, collectively entitled Meditations of an Old Woman. These poems, avoiding rational discourse, like those of *Praise to the End!*, are organized psychologically, in terms of association of imagery, and musically, in terms of alternating themes. The Meditations are the search for the self with new implications, the search for an identity that transcends the temporal limits of the material world; like all of Roethke's more powerful work from this point on, they are pervaded by a growing awareness of imminent nonbeing, of the fact of approaching death. T. S. Eliot has often been cited as having influenced the structure, and, to some extent, the content of these poems. At this suggestion, Roethke was highly indignant (as he was not when Yeats was invoked). Perhaps he was protesting too much. But certainly with regard to content, the points of direct contact with Eliot seem to indicate, as we shall learn, a direct opposition rather than imitation.

There is, however, one sense in which Roethke would not have minded being compared to Eliot; he too had the "auditory imagination," and frequently insisted that his verse was above all meant to be heard. For some years, Roethke had been giving poetry readings whenever he could, and experimenting with recordings. The strain on him was enormous, but he always managed to put on a good show. His major recording, the only one widely available, is *Words for the Wind,* readings of a selection of poems from that book.

*Words for the Wind* earned for its author both the National Book Award and the Bollingen Prize. It had even become the Christmas selection of the Poetry Book Society when it appeared in England, and Roethke was overjoyed at finally having been accorded that degree of recognition there. There was even more adverse criticism than before, most of it from English poets provoked by Roethke's larger exposure on that side of the Atlantic, and a number of cries of "pseudo-Yeats"; but both criticism and praise were louder than ever before, which itself gave weight to Roethke's claim to acceptance as a major poet. In addition, he was at the center of what Carolyn Kizer called the "School of the Pacific Northwest," a school united not so much by form or intellectual content as by "the feeling area" of their work and by a sense of artistic community. Yet, for a man like Roethke, the apparent security of his position could in an instant give way to limit-

less extremes of anxiety. Each new successful poem was viewed with terror as possibly the last of its kind. Each comment in which a contemporary was praised could be interpreted as a slight to his own stature. So the struggle did not cease; it barely paused. At times appearing so confident he would bully his friends and guests, at times filled with self-loathing and self-depreciation, he danced on.

Some of his last years were spent at the house of Morris Graves, while Graves painted in Ireland; some were spent at the home the Roethkes later bought at nearby Puget Sound. There was another trip to Italy, which Roethke did not like, partly because of his inability to master Italian or any other foreign language, and a trip to Ireland which, because of his easy adaptability to the pubs, he liked to excess. It was at a neighbor's pool, near the house at Puget Sound, that Roethke died of a heart attack on August 1, 1963. He was only fifty-five years old, but he had been sick for some time. The film made shortly before his death, *In a Dark Time* (Poetry Society of San Francisco, 1964), shows him old beyond his age, and the poems of his last years are filled with premonitions of death.

*The Far Field* appeared posthumously in 1964, including most of the poet's serious verse since *Words for the Wind.* This volume, which received the National Book Award in 1965, is devoted to the perfection of old forms rather than to the development of new ones. North American Sequence is a series of long contemplative poems, in the mode of Meditations of an Old Woman, with the author this time using himself as persona. Psychological and religious imagery are interwoven in this final revery in search of the self, in search of transcendent identity. The Love Poems once again have a Yeatsian touch, but this time in the vein of lyrics such as *Words for Music Perhaps,* rather than the more abstract philosophical poems. Mixed Sequence, for the most part less concentrated in its diction, provides an essential change of pace. And the last part, Sequence, Sometimes Metaphysical, is the culmination of the volume, and of Roethke's career. The sequence begins by describing a mystic experience (in **"In a Dark Time"**), and then explores its implications for the poet's life. Psychology and theology, madness and mysticism, have drawn very close together in this last phase of Roethke's work. The sequence is similar in intent to Roethke's early explorations of the relation of a nervous breakdown to "ordinary" life. But that is the end of the similarity. In content, Roethke has passed from platitudes to a full awareness of the complexities of the human condition; and, in technique, which makes full use of the powerful and exact archetypal imagery of the meditative poems combined with the density of meaning achieved through expert manipulation of form, Roethke is completely equal to these complexities.

With the publication of his collected poems and selected prose, most of the essential materials upon which a fair estimation of Roethke's poetic worth must be based have become available. Allan Seager is preparing a biography, and several full-length studies of Roethke, including a collection of essays edited by Arnold Stein, are published or underway. This present study is intended as a beginning of the detailed examination of the full scope of Roethke's serious verse necessary to its fair evaluation.

## Richard A. Blessing (essay date 1972)

SOURCE: "Theodore Roethke: A Celebration," in *Tulane Studies in English,* Vol. 20, No. 0, 1972, pp. 169-80.

*[In the following essay, Blessing examines technical devices employed by Roethke to evoke dynamic energy and movement, particularly as evident in his elegies.]*

Theodore Roethke was ever one to appreciate the process by which complaint becomes celebration, by which a tirade turns to kissing. He would have understood, I hope, my beginning a celebration of his poetry with a complaint—another man's complaint—against it. "We have," writes M. L. Rosenthal,

> no other modern American poet of comparable reputation who has absorbed so little of the concerns of his age into his nerve-ends, in whom there is so little reference direct or remote to the incredible experiences of the age—unless the damaged psyche out of which he spoke be taken as its very embodiment. But that was not quite enough. The confessional mode, reduced to this kind of self-recharging, becomes self-echoing as well and uses itself up after the first wild orgies of feeling.

Rosenthal is no straw man, though I believe he is dead wrong here. There are, as always, straw men enough to be found. John Wain offers a comically conceived Soviet critic who denounces Roethke's failure to mention "the bread-lines, the war, the racial upheavals," and I might offer a student or two who would venture to say that Roethke is not "relevant." But Rosenthal is a good reader, and other good readers— some of them quite sympathetic to Roethke—have, in gentle ways, intimated that he does not give one "a sense of total participation in life," or that he is "almost untouched by public happenings or by history."

Nonetheless, I think it might be more accurate to say that few, if any, other modern American poets of comparable reputation have absorbed more wholly the concerns of our age into the nerve-ends, nor have more adequately represented in their art the incredible experiences of the age. If, as I believe, the essential experience of modern life is speed, movement, energy, whirl, a sense of unceasing and often

violent motion, Roethke surely took it all into the nerve-endings, into the blood and pulse, into the rhythms of his giant body which became the rhythms of his poetry. "Live," he told his classes in verse writing, "out in your fingers." His fingers and their nerve-endings told him that his world was in motion, and he was wise enough to sense that the historical events that swirled around him were but varied forms of the same energy which drove him in his personal evolution as a man and an artist. In fact, I think the root metaphor in all of Roethke's work is the historical event, provided that one understands that any action with all of its context—its total sweep backward into the past and forward into the future— is an event in history. The teaching of a class, the death of a student, the journey out of the self, will serve as well to give a sense of the complexity and dynamism of life—of history— as will the battle of Gettysburg, the assassination of a president, a visit to China. The poet's task—and Roethke's genius—is to make his words become an event, to arrange them in such a way as to create in their reading the sweep and energy of the experience of our time.

Because Roethke was a teaching poet who labored lovingly to help his students discover the secrets of his craft and art, and because many of the notes from which he taught have been preserved, one may with some confidence theorize about what the poet tried to do in his poetry and how he went about doing it. Time and time again the jottings which became the classroom performance demonstrate the vocabulary of dynamism. The key words, repeated in varying forms and combinations, are "energy," "intensity," "speed," "flow." There are lists of devices for heightening intensity in a poem, for speeding the imagery, for creating energy in rhythm. There are aphorisms. "What is the most important element: energy." "Style: What is style but matter in motion?" "A poem means an extra, a surplus of energy." "The enemy of intensity: grandiloquence." There are questions, apparently from students, and hastily scribbled answers:

> Q. What do you want in the way of a rhythm, Mr. R.?
> A. It's the nervousness, the tension, I think I value most. Blake's bounding line and old Willie's high imperial honking.
> Q. You speak of energy in rhythm. What are the factors that seem to enter into, or contribute to, this force?
> A. They are so multiple that they constitute the whole art of writing; but I feel what comes to the aid are alliteration of initial sounds and a manipulation and a variation of interior sounds, (repetition of words) particularly vowels. The line—but the verbal forms particularly, particularly the "ing" participial form, impart, as would be expected, movement. *This may be because I see the world in motion,* but I don't think so. [Italics added.]

There is also the testimony of Roethke's former students, for he seems to have been unforgettable in the classroom. One of the best of his pupils, David Wagoner, has told me that he remembers Roethke's saying, perhaps quoting someone else, that in poetry "motion is equal to emotion." Another, Oliver Everette, writes that Roethke used to snarl, "You've got to have rhythm. If you want to dance naked in an open barndoor with a chalk stuck in your navel, I don't care! You've got to have rhythm. I don't care how you get it." He also remembers that Roethke stressed "motion in poetry," telling the class that "Motion or action should be found in every line. The poetic mind sees things in motion."

It seems to me that Roethke's problem as a classroom teacher was essentially the same problem with which he wrestled as a poet. Given that the poetic eye sees things in motion, given that energy is all, by what techniques does one transfer a sense of that motion and energy to the page or to another's ear? How does one "teach" energy? Not, I think, entirely by telling people to alliterate initial sounds and manipulate interior ones, though I do not wish to undervalue the importance of just such devices. A better clue, I believe, to Roethke's success as a teacher comes from the coed who once told him, "I don't understand a word you say, but I just watch your hands." Or from Richard Hugo, now a fine poet in his own right, who says that he learned at least as much from Roethke's actions—from the boundless energy, what Hugo calls the "overstance," of the teaching performance—as he did from Roethke's words. In Roethke's classroom, apparently, the medium was, to an unusual degree, the message. How do you teach a beat? You don't. But many a student seems to have been surprised to find his foot tapping in time to Roethke's bear-like professorial dance.

"Talent talks," Roethke wrote in one of his notebooks. "Genius does." And Roethke was more than talented. Therefore, the critic who concerns himself primarily with what one of Roethke's poems "talks about," with a paraphrase of the "thinky-think," as Roethke called it, has only a part—and not the best part—of the poem. In his great poems Roethke's "meaning"—never mind the ostensible subject—is always a celebration of the energetic dance of being. To meet his own standards for genius he had to create a revelation of that dance for his audience, and he had to do it by means of his words. In short, he had to make the experience, not talk about it.

As Roethke himself suggested, the devices by which all this is accomplished are "multiple," surely too multiple to be discussed adequately in an article-length study. Nevertheless, a critical thesis ought to be followed by "pages of illustrations," and I have rather arbitrarily decided to illustrate this one by examining the techniques which present dynamism in a few of Roethke's elegies. Energy, the thrust and surge of life, is perhaps most clearly revealed by contrast, most felt when its way is blocked by obstacles or when its motion and sweep are set off against the perfect stillness of death. It is not surprising, then, that Roethke is often at his best in the elegiac mode. **"Elegy for Jane, My Student, Thrown by a Horse," "Frau Bauman, Frau Schmidt, and Frau Schwartze,"** and the little piece called simply **"Elegy"** in *Words for the Wind* are some of his more successful attempts to represent the rhythm and pace of life.

Roethke's elegies always celebrate those who have been most active, those in whom energy has been most intensely present. I suppose he was naturally drawn to such people, and he seems to have identified the energy expressed by their bodies, the speed with which they moved and acted, with the creative energy that he prized above everything. The trick is to re-create that energy with words so that the bodily rhythms of the dead move again and breathe again and *are* again for so long as the poem is remembered. If the trick is brought off, the poet has, in a way, triumphed over death by creating a symbolic and immortal equivalent to the energetic rhythms of the human body.

The first stanza of the **"Elegy for Jane"** comes close to achieving just such a triumph:

> I remember the neckcurls, limp and damp as
>     tendrils;
> And her quick look, a sidelong pickerel smile;
> And how, once startled into talk, the light
>     syllables
>         leaped for her,
> And she balanced in the delight of her thought,
> A wren, happy, tail into the wind,
> Her song trembling the twigs and small branches.
> The shade sang with her;
> The leaves, their whispers turned to kissing;
> And the mold sang in the bleached valley under
>     the rose.

The passage is a catalogue of memories expressed as images; it is a bombardment of the senses creating an experience greater than the sum of its parts, for the speed with which those parts are juxtaposed becomes an additional "meaning" given to the recollected portrait of the girl. Jane is a protean figure, evolving through shifting imagery from plant to fish to bird as Roethke's mind leaps from metaphorical association to association. She is clearly not idealized as a physical beauty. Few coeds would be pleased to have their neckcurls likened to tendrils and fewer still would appreciate having their quick sidelong glance bring to mind a "pickerel smile." It is not beauty, however, that Roethke is after here, but energy—the tendrils' thrust toward light, the violent rush of the pickerel. It is the sense of quickness, of startled leaping, of balancing, of motion so contagious that it causes all the world about to tremble in tune with the song Jane sings. There is much that appeals purely to the kinesthetic sense—a feeling of lightness and quickness, of rising and falling, of precarious balancing against the thrust of the wind.

There is an abundance of just that sort of "alliteration of initial sounds and manipulation of interior sounds" which Roethke suggested might contribute to the energy of a poetic rhythm. "Neckcurls" and "tendrils," "quick look" and "pickerel," "wren" and "wind," "startled" and "syllables," and "light" and "leaped" are among the more obvious examples of Roethke's continuous playing of sound against sound, of manipulation and variation of vowel and consonant. There is also the simple, almost primitive diction—a heavy preponderance of monosyllables, a careful avoidance of "grandiloquence." And there is, primarily in the choice and placement of verbs, the sense of the enormous activity of all things—of leaves that whisper and kiss, of mold and shade that sing.

The passage is primarily a hymn to the power of Jane's talking, to her ability to give the quickness of life to the "light syllables." She is the natural poet, her promise never to be fulfilled, and as such she serves as a kind of Edward King to Roethke's Milton. Just as Milton imaginatively gives King the power to move with his singing "The willows, and the hazel copses green," so Roethke imagines Jane's song to be answered by the shade and by the mold "in the bleached valleys under the rose." And, as in "Lycidas," the energy of the elegiac voice is the assurance that the power to make the light syllables leap is imperishable. Though he denies paternity, in one sense the poet is father to the Jane of the poem. His breath becomes the breath of her startled talking; his verbal energy becomes the rhythm to which her body sways.

One of Roethke's most effective devices for suggesting the flickering speed of life is that by which, as in a kind of double vision, he has Jane be both present and not present at the grave. "My sparrow, you are not here," he says, "Waiting like a fern, making a spiny shadow." The bird, the singer with tail into the wind, is not a creature to wait, to be still. Yet she is, at once, "My maimed darling," the Jane who goes to the earth, and "my skittery pigeon," the Jane whose birdlike energy endures in the memory and in the cadence of the poet.

Just as Jane is "not here" and very much "here," the poet is neither father nor lover and yet something of each. In many ways the poem is about a relationship with a student, a relationship which is fully disclosed by the word "love," a shocking four-letter word in this context. Neither the rights of love nor the rites of love allow for such a relationship. We honor the grief of fathers, sympathize with the grief of lovers, but there are no "rites" (surely the pun is deliberate) by which a male professor may speak the words of his love for his student Jane. Yet Roethke affirms and expresses his rights even as he denies that he has them. His role in the ceremonial

mourning exists in motion of its own sort, flickering between the role of the father he was not and the role of the lover he was not, existing only in the nameless spaces gaping between those solid, respectable pillars in the house of grief.

**"Frau Bauman, Frau Schmidt, and Frau Schwartze"** manages to convey something of the same sense of an elusive, darting "reality," for the three ladies move so swiftly as to manage to be in two places at the same time, to be "Gone" and "still hover[ing]" simultaneously. The ladies, like Jane, have the power to transfer their energy creatively into the life around them, and it is that power which commends them to the memory and to the apotheosizing power of the imagination. The fraus are glimpsed through a flurry of active verbal forms—creaking, reaching, winding, straightening, tying, tucking, dipping up, sifting, sprinkling, shaking, standing, billowing, twinkling, flying, keeping, sewing, teasing, trellising, pinching, poking and plotting. Even nouns such as "Coils," "loops," "whorls," "nurses," "seed," "pipes" and others are potential verbs, suggesting that the names of greenhouse things are squirming with metaphorical action. The ladies are never still, for even when they stand astride the greenhouse pipes, their skirts billow and their hands twinkle "with wet." Their movement is always that of "picking up," and the movement of the poem, like the movement of the climbing roses, is upward from the earth toward the sun. So swiftly do the ladies scurry that the memory blurs fact into fiction, the historical ladies into the mythic. Flying "like witches," they become more and more enormous in their activity until at last they trellis the sun itself, giving support to that strange flower which is the life of our planet.

As the remembered ladies become apotheosized into mythic figures, Roethke imagines them to take on the fecund powers of earth mothers. They straddle the phallic pipes of the greenhouse, pipes belonging to Roethke's father, until their skirts billow "out wide like tents"—as if someone might live there. They have, we are told, the power to "tease out" the seed, to undo the lifeless "keeping" of the cold. And, finally, they give the poet himself a symbolic birth. Acting as midwives to themselves, they pick him up, pinch and poke him into shape, "Till I lay in their laps, laughing, / Weak as a whiffet." The ladies, trellisers of the sun, also trellis "the son," the boy fathered by the greenhouse owner.

Though the ladies are, as the first word of the poem insists, "Gone," they "still hover" in the air of the present. All of the verbs in the first stanza are, as one would expect in a remembrance, in the past tense. Nevertheless, Roethke refers to the fraus as "*These* nurses of nobody else" as if they were present, as if the memory had managed to recapture in part that which had been totally lost. And, of course, he says that "Now, when I'm alone and cold in my bed, / They still hover over me, / These ancient leathery crones. . . ." The relationship between poet and crones is a highly dynamic one. On the one hand, the hovering mothers "still" have the power to give him life. He lies like a seed, cold and in his bed, and they breathe over him the breath of life, a snuff-laden blowing that lifts him from the keeping of the cold into a life that manifests itself in poetic blossoms. On the other hand, it is the poet who "keeps" the fraus alive, whose breath gives to the dead the power to move and be again. Their energy is entirely dependent upon his ability to intensify the language until their movement becomes tangible in empty air, becomes an event in the viscera of the reader. The poem itself takes its cadence from those German fraus, takes it and gives it back again.

As for the poet, he has, by the end of the poem, lost himself in two places at once. He is in his bed and the time is "Now," yet the crones who hover above him breathe "lightly over [him] in [his] first sleep," presumably that sleep from which one wakes at birth. They are the remembered gateway to the past, these witches capable of collapsing time so that the cold sleep of the adult is at one with the first sleep from which he wakened into life. They are the means by which Roethke demonstrates the sweep of the "Now" in which we always live; for through the fraus who were, through the fraus mythologized and through the fraus who remain as a felt presence, he has made a poetic representation of the living extension of the past into the ever-moving present.

The poem called **"Elegy"** is short enough to quote entirely:

1

Should every creature be as I have been,
There would be reason for essential sin;
I have myself an inner weight of woe
That God himself can scarcely bear.

2

Each wills his death: I am convinced of that;
You were too lonely for another fate.
I have myself an inner weight of woe
That Christ, securely bound, could bear.

3

Thus I; and should these reasons fly apart,
I know myself, my seasons, and I KNOW.
I have myself one crumbling skin to show;
God could believe: I am here to fear.

4

What you survived I shall believe: the Heat,
Scars, Tempests, Floods, the Motion of Man's
Fate;

I have myself and bear its weight of woe
That God that God leans down His heart to hear.

**"Elegy"** is a poem that took several titles as Roethke worked it into its final shape. The piece was first called "Humility, Its Coarse Surprises Can," after the opening line, a line followed by "Undo the virtues of a carnal man." In that early form the poem was apparently intended as a tribute to an aunt, Julia Roethke. All of the pronouns referring to the dead person are feminine, and another draft, apparently of the same period, has as its subtitle "In Memoriam: Julia Roethke." Underneath her name Roethke had written and lightly crossed out "Dylan Thomas." In many drafts the poem is called "The Stumbling," and Roethke seems to have decided that it suited Thomas better than his aunt, after all. But in final form the poem is, wisely, I think, unassigned, and the neuter pronoun "you" replaces the limiting "he" or "she" which had referred to the dead person in the earlier versions. As it stands in *The Collected Poems,* **"Elegy"** celebrates the memory of everyman, all who have been begotten, born and died.

It is a difficult poem, one easily misread. I believe Karl Malkoff, for one, misreads it in his study of Roethke. According to Malkoff, "Guilt is precisely the theme of '**Elegy**'. . . . Indeed, the universe as man knows it is defined by the passage of the seasons, . . . by the passing out of existence of all life. Once this dissolution has occurred, man can no longer atone for his guilt; his 'essential sin,' his condemnation, is fact forever." The poem does, indeed, open with an admission of heavy guilt, but such an admission demonstrates that sense of humility which may bring even a "carnal man" to salvation by the means of God's grace and with the help of His mercy. It is a poem, I think, that moves from near despair to comfort, from a weight of scarcely bearable woe to a weight that "God leans down His heart to hear."

The form of the poem supports this reading, for as Roethke manipulates his quatrains, they become highly dynamic, suggesting change and development rather than the static hopelessness of Malkoff's interpretation. **"Elegy"** has the soul of a villanelle; that is, the third and fourth lines of each quatrain act as refrain lines of a sort and give to the poem that satisfying effect of repetition that is the essential pleasure of, say, Thomas' "Do Not Go Gentle" or of Roethke's own **"The Waking."** With Roethke, however, refrain lines are always similar, but rarely the same. He manipulates such lines so that the reader is arrested by their continuous alteration as much as by their repetition. The ear is set up for an echo that never quite arrives; instead, the ear is teased by words that move about, altering meaning and value in every stanza.

Stanza one is an admission of the narrator's worthlessness, his sinful condition. If all creatures are like himself, he speculates, then the idea of original sin is rational enough. Indeed, his own sinful nature and the woe of the world he inhabits may well seem to make irrational any doctrine which does not begin by acknowledging some "essential sin" as explanation for the fallen nature of the world. Pondering such a creation and his sinful place in it, the poet skirts dangerously near despair, believing that his weight of sin and woe is such that "God himself can scarcely bear." Nonetheless, God "can" bear that weight, and the basis for future hope is established.

In the second stanza, Christ, God become man, takes upon Himself "the weight of woe," and does so "securely bound," as if with *both* hands tied behind His back. There is a possible pun here, in that Christ, bound on the cross, is bound for Heaven, and thus "securely bound" in a way that precariously bound man is not. In any case, God the Father, the harsh judge who tolerates with difficulty the foolishness of man, has taken on His more merciful aspect, the aspect of the savior who offers Himself as a full, perfect and sufficient sacrifice for the sins of the world.

The third stanza marks a significant change in the attitude of the narrator, a change marked by a shift in rhyme scheme and the substitution of the word "fear" for the word "bear" that ended the first two stanzas. Essentially, the narrator turns from one kind of knowing to another, from the reasoned to the intuitive. He can bear his "inner weight of woe" because Christ could and did bear it; and should his carefully reasoned doctrine of essential sin fly apart, still he knows what he KNOWS. At the last, a man knows only what his experience tells him—and experience may tell him that he KNOWS some things beyond the need for "reasons." God could believe that the poet lives, is "here," for the purpose of being fearful. We do not ordinarily think of fear as a positive emotion, but in this case it seems to me that it is God Himself who is feared. And the fear of the Lord is the beginning of wisdom, a further step in humility for the spiritual stumbler toward grace. God is feared because of the narrator's awareness of his own sinfulness and of the enormous strain of such a weight upon the mercy of God. He knows that he is a sinner in a crumbling skin and that Eternal Justice for such as he has been would be terrible indeed.

But if God can believe in the narrator's humility before Him, the narrator will believe in "the Motion of Man's Fate," in the human power to survive "the Heat, / Scars, Tempests, Floods." If it is the glory of God to show compassion to such woeful creatures as men, it is the glory of men to act creatively in the face of immense suffering, to survive the Tempests and sing (as Dylan Thomas sang) beneath a weight of woe. The poet who believes in the power of human survival and yet remains humble, fearing the Lord, possesses himself ("I have myself") and is capable of bearing the woe that is his portion of Man's Fate. And, for such a one, "That God that God leans down His Heart to hear." Because the narrator has moved from reasoning to KNOWing, because he has

come to a contrite admission of his own fear, God has changed from the God who "scarcely" can bear (tolerate) human sinfulness to that God who bends compassionately toward man and listens, not with His judging mind, but with His merciful heart. It is a poem, like the other two elegies, about a dynamic relationship, in this case one in which man and God change as they interact with one another. Within the confines of a tight formal pattern, Roethke has managed to convey an impression of enormous motion and process, an impression heightened by shifting refrain lines, altered rhyme schemes, associative leaps that all but fracture syntax, and by changing the length of the final line, filling it out to five beats after closing the other quatrains with lines that were short a foot. If the poem works, and I think it does, it works because form and meaning are one, because Roethke's technical skill has been equal to the task of presenting process and change in his poem.

It would be foolish to suggest that these elegies represent an adequate sampling of Theodore Roethke's lifetime of poetry. Nonetheless, I think they do illustrate a few of his better techniques for presenting dynamism in a work of art. The propulsion, the forward thrust, of the free verse comes from the intensification of verbs, the frenetic lists of actions, the energetic rhythms, the associative leaps from image to image and the playing off of sound against sound, phrase against phrase. In the more formal piece, Roethke uses his modified repetition to underscore change and development, and he shifts rhyme scheme and line length to suggest shifts in mental or spiritual development. In all three poems the relationships between the poet and the dead or between the poet and God are highly dynamic ones, relationships which alter even as the poet speaks the words of his love. In these poems, as elsewhere in his work, Roethke manages to transfer the rhythm, the motion, of life from his pulse to the printed page. It is this energetic, dynamic quality which I find the essential characteristic of his craft and which makes his poetry worthy of celebration.

## John Vernon (essay date 1973)

SOURCE: "Theodore Roethke," in *The Garden and the Map: Schizophrenia in Twentieth-Century Literature and Culture,* University of Illinois Press, 1973, pp. 159-90.

[*In the following essay, Vernon explores Roethke's affinity for garden imagery and the symbolism of sexual development, personal growth, and self-consciousness.*]

In Marvell's "The Garden" there is a well-known passage that recalls one of the points Eluard's poem "You Are Everywhere" makes:

The Mind, that Ocean where each kind
Does straight its own resemblance find;
Yet it creates, transcending these,
Far other World, and other Seas;
Annihilating all that's made
To a green Thought in a green Shade.

Marvell begins by citing the classical doctrine of perception, which says that sense images of external objects are accompanied by images in consciousness and that the latter resemble the former as mirror images resemble real things. But then, as Eluard did with the line "you are its resemblance," Marvell undercuts that doctrine by giving the mirror image a kind of integrative autonomy, by annihilating the absolute two-term map relationship and asserting a dynamic unity of external and internal, of subjective and objective: "a green Thought in a green Shade." This is the condition of the garden, as I have been describing it. And the world of Roethke's poetry is above all a garden.

As we have seen, the garden is not the polar opposite of the map; rather the garden embraces and transforms the map, temporalizes it, unfolds it in time. The garden is not total mergence and confusion, a scrambling of all things and all objects together, but unites mergence and separation, unity and multiplicity. This is why the garden in Roethke's world is often a greenhouse, the meeting place of the human and nonhuman, the organic and the rational, the natural—Kenneth Burke has said—and the artificial. Or as Roethke himself put it in his notebooks: "What was this greenhouse? It was a jungle and it was paradise. It was order and disorder." Even when the setting of Roethke's poems is not a greenhouse, his world has this feature of uniting the garden and the map. It is the perfect illustration of the symbolic world described in the previous chapter, of the world that unites space and time, body and world, discreteness and mergence, Being and Nonbeing.

It is also the perfect illustration of the schizophrenia that unites madness and sanity. The first of Roethke's many bouts with "insanity" that landed him in the hospital, and earned him such titles as "manic-depressive neurotic," "manic-depressive psychotic," and "paranoid schizophrenic," occurred in 1935. One night he wandered into the woods near his apartment in University Park, Pennsylvania (he was teaching at Pennsylvania State). He got lost, cold, and wet, but eventually found a highway and thumbed home. He returned to the same woods the next morning, skipping his classes; later in the day he appeared at the dean's office in a disheveled condition, told off the dean, and was sent to the hospital. Roethke's own description of what happened to him in the woods is also a description of the world of his poetry, the "insane" world of the child, the primitive, and the schizophrenic: "For no reason I started to feel very good. Suddenly I knew how to enter into the life of everything around me. I

knew how it felt to be a tree, a blade of grass, even a rabbit. I didn't sleep much. I just walked around with this wonderful feeling."

This is "madness." But as Roethke showed in the poems he wrote ten years later (those published in *The Lost Son* and *Praise to the End!*), this is the world of everyone, stripped of repression; it is the world of the child, not as we leave the perceptions of childhood behind, but as those perceptions underlie our continuing experience; it is the world of the garden, and it is the garden itself as the world. The irony of the attempts of others to treat Roethke's schizophrenia, to analyze him, to "help" him, is that they are the very ones who needed help, for their inability to see and feel as Roethke was able to, for their inability to enter into the life of everything around them. Roethke's perception is normal; theirs, and by implication ours, is abnormal, since it neutralizes the primary experience of the symbolic world, of the garden, with the forms of the map and of objectivity, by which here and there, inside and outside, are absolutely separated.

In Roethke, the garden is not only a place; it is also a mode of experiencing, an organization of experience, or better, a process, a way experience happens. And it is a process exactly the same as what Laing calls the healing voyage of schizophrenia. In the previous chapter we saw that the experience of time in this voyage is simultaneously a rising and a falling, a going forward and a going back. Roethke makes precisely this point about his *Lost Son* and *Praise to the End!* poems in a notebook entry: "To go back is to go forward." In these poems, regression is also progression; time loops back to gather itself as it goes forward to meet itself. The "itself" that time loops back to gather lies in the prehistory of the world as well as in Roethke's childhood. The landscape of the poems is both the greenhouse operated by Roethke's father in Saginaw, Michigan, and the primordial garden previous to the rise of civilization; and the inscape of the poems is both the emotional state of Roethke as an adult and the childhood experience of life as an undifferentiated whole previous to the emergence of adult consciousness. Children lose this undifferentiated whole as they grow into adulthood. One must go back and recover it in order to become a full man. "To go back is to go forward."

The *Praise to the End!* poems are a developmental sequence of fourteen long, experimental poems about childhood and the growth out of childhood into adolescence first published completely in *The Waking: Poems 1933-1953* (1953). Four of the poems were initially published in *The Lost Son* (1948), and the whole sequence except for the last poem, **"O, Thou Opening, O,"** was published in *Praise to the End!* (1951). In Roethke's arrangement (which was not followed in the posthumous *Collected Poems*), the sequence is divided into two major sections, the first consisting of **"Where Knock Is Open Wide," "I Need, I Need," "Bring the Day!" "Give**

Way, Ye Gates," "Sensibility! O La!" and "O Lull Me, Lull Me," and the second consisting of "The Lost Son," "The Long Alley," "A Field of Light," "The Shape of the Fire," "Praise to the End!" "Unfold! Unfold!" "I Cry, Love! Love!" and "O, Thou Opening, O."

Taken as a whole, the sequence represents one long poem, each part of which (that is, each poem) contains and reaffirms that whole. The movement of progression and regression, of expansion and deflation, occurs rhythmically in each poem and in the overall sequence in such a way that the sequence sways as a tree does, with a unified gradation of movements and countermovements, from the small and quick to the large and ponderous.

The sequence gains its vitality from its regressions that carry the poet and the reader—and the language of the poems—back into that timeless childhood experience of life as an undifferentiated whole, being a radical means of recovering that experience for everyday life. "Whole" is an abstract word; as an experience, however, it is real and tangible, and not always pleasant, as Roethke shows. In Roethke's sequence the human body often regresses to its polymorphous wholeness, its being as a blob, to the womb, just as the world often regresses into a confusion of all its objects together, into slime, and just as language often regresses into nonsense and playing with sounds. These three regressions are inseparable; they are one in structure and feeling in portions of the sequence. Roethke's most explicit description of them occurs in **"The Shape of the Fire"**:

> Who, careless, slips
> In coiling ooze
> Is trapped to the lips,
> Leaves more than shoes;
>
> Must pull off clothes
> To jerk like a frog
> On belly and nose
> From the sucking bog.
>
> My meat eats me. Who waits at the gate?
> Mother of quartz, your words writhe into my ear.
> Renew the light, lewd whisper.

In this passage, the mergence of the world—mud—threatens to swallow and merge with the body, and both these images of mergence are followed by a regression of language into nonsense. One is reminded of Burroughs and of all the instances of mergence, especially those occurring in canals or swamps, in his novels. But unlike Burroughs, Roethke emerges from this primordial confusion and liquid mergence of all things, not by flying toward the opposite polarity, toward atomistic separateness, but by combining mergence and separateness in the unity of opposites that is the condition of the garden: by channeling into the world, into separateness, and carrying the wholeness from which that separateness is descended into every manifestation of it.

In terms of temporality, this means that the sequence is about the evolution out of timelessness into that world which unites Being and Nonbeing in time, which unites timelessness and time, the continual absence and presence of time, the sway and countersway that is time. The sequence, more specifically, is about the child's growth in time, and about how growth is that act which is always leaving and simultaneously falling back into itself. The best image of this is the child's literal growth into his limbs, hands, feet, eyes, mouth, penis—and the point of this growth is that the child always both retains himself and moves out of himself, always unites his "parts" with his original and continual wholeness, his body. This is impossible to picture in a map space; it is impossible to "picture," period. In the realistic novel, we saw that "plot" in its basic sense is characterized spatially by a sequence of convergences and divergences; and in *The Octopus,* we saw the mechanical image of this structure in the railroad and the chutes and elevators that channel wheat into bins. In a map space, the whole is always separated from its parts, or at most is the sum of them. But in Roethke, the whole—whether it be language, world, body, or time—overflows into each of its parts, into the variety of its forms, into each small thing, in the becoming act of growth. This is why Roethke's world is a world of small things—pebbles, petals, slugs, leaves, cinders, seeds, tongues, fingers—but it is also why that world is a whole world.

Since each poem reflects the whole in Roethke's sequence, I will examine the first poem in detail and then move more quickly through the succeeding ones. The first poem says all that needs to be said—but only because the rest follow.

Here is the first section of the first poem, **"Where Knock Is Open Wide"**:

> A kitten can
> Bite with his feet;
> Papa and Mamma
> Have more teeth.
>
> Sit and play
> Under the rocker
> Until the cows
> All have puppies.
>
> His ears haven't time.
> Sing me a sleep-song, please.
> A real hurt is soft.
>
> Once upon a tree
> I came across a time,

It wasn't even as
A ghoulie in a dream.
There was a mooly man
Who had a rubber hat
And funnier than that,—
He kept it in a can.

What's the time, papa-seed?
Everything has been twice.
My father is a fish.

The first thing to be noted about these lines is their quality of nonsense and play. Roethke has begun his sequence as close to the condition of primordial mergence as possible, and the casting around of the language, the ranging of it in play, and its decided lack of "meaning" in the usual sense are expressions of this mergence. This is language at its most silent because it is language with little reference outside of itself. It is language as almost pure gesture, as a mouth, where the condition of all the body is that of a mouth. Thus the oral images in the first four lines are most appropriate; the child is truly at an oral stage of development, where everything, including language, partakes of that total narcissistic union for which a baby at his mother's breast is the most apt image. This is why, spatially, most of the images in these lines have to do with being enclosed and with the feeling of softness: play *under* the rocker, a hat *in* a can, "A real hurt is soft."

But the language in this section, for all its narcissistic play and its self-enclosedness, is not without a referential function. Indeed the hard edge of reality is beginning to impinge upon the soft primordial wholeness of the child's world; thus the mention of teeth or a hurt or a can, and also the matter-of-fact, almost abstract statements such as "Everything has been twice." This is also the feeling of the section's rhythm and movement: the casting around, the play and flow of language, is twice brought to an abrupt halt by some rather prosaic, flat lines. The language play and nonsense verse occur in four-line units, each line of which has two or three stresses and is not end-stopped; these flow smoothly until they are halted by three-line units with three or four stresses in each line, all of which are end-stopped. This is the beginning of the strophe-antistrophe movement, the sway and countersway, evident throughout the whole sequence. Out of narcissistic play, Roethke pulls up short at the plain fact of the world: "His ears haven't time."

The awakening sense of time is perhaps the most important aspect of this opening section. The word "time" is mentioned three times in this section, the point being that out of a timeless condition of play and self-enclosedness, the child is losing himself into time and is beginning to feel a past grow behind him and a future come toward him. One of the mentions of "time" is born out of that very playfulness, out of the child's casting around with words: "Once upon a tree / I came across a time." These lines should "normally" read, of course, "Once upon a time / I came across a tree." Roethke's shifting of the normal syntax of words, which occurs throughout the sequence, is indicative of the unsettled state of the child's consciousness; a tree is just as new and unfamiliar to him as a time, and both are part of the new world he is inadvertently creating by tossing his words around. It is only natural that the child should come across a time while playing with his words, since that play is simply the birth of the poem itself and since the poem thus born can exist only in the falling away of its words, in time.

The closing three lines of this section accumulate most of the above themes and discoveries, and introduce some new considerations that are to be important in the sequence. The narrator asks, "What's the time, papa-seed?" a question that is to be taken literally: what is time? The appropriateness of asking papa this question is in the fact that the very awareness of the father *as* father constitutes a time consciousness, a historical consciousness. The latter is made explicit by the ensuing two lines: "Everything has been twice. / My father is a fish." These lines open up the particular nature of that time consciousness, and its difference from the primordial mergence the child is leaving behind. Everything has been twice; there is a dual mode to the world-in-time, as opposed to the self-enclosed nature of play and timeless mergence. Most of the rest of the sequence will be an attempt to unite that dual mode with the previous wholeness of the child, a unity prefigured by the father's being and not-being of himself as a fish.

Throughout the sequence, the father is identified with the male generative principle, what penetrates the amorphous wholeness of preexistence and infuses it with form, gives it parts, limbs, separations. This is why papa is "papa-seed" and why he is also a fish. The fish image in Roethke represents the only formed thing in the undifferentiated mass, the "body without skin," or water: it is the root of that body, which means it is also the father of that body. The identification of the fish with the penis, and thus of the father with the penis, is a natural one. Images of the penis—the fish, the rat, the foot, the worm—are a central focus of many of the sequence's conflicts and resolutions, and can be arranged opposite images of the vagina—holes, nests, gates, caves, water. The unity of male and female becomes the perfect image of the unity of separation and wholeness, of discreteness and mergence, that is the final condition of Roethke's world. This unity is equally a unity of father and mother and a unity, an integration, of the self. This is why a common image of the unity of male and female, the act of fishing, is expressed in one of the last poems of the sequence as a self-directed act of integration: "Fishing, I caught myself behind the ears."

Section two of the poem continues much of the playing with words that constitutes section one, but also introduces several new considerations:

> I sing a small sing,
> My uncle's away,
> He's gone for always,
> I don't care either.
>
> I know who's got him,
> They'll jump on his belly,
> He won't be an angel,
> I don't care either.
>
> I know her noise.
> Her neck has kittens.
> I'll make a hole for her.
> In the fire.
>
> Winkie will yellow I sang.
> Her eyes went kissing away
> It was and it wasn't her there
> I sang I sang all day.

The sensual richness of the child's language play reveals a world that is itself sensually rich, a world that plays with and tosses around each of the various senses that open upon it. The world of the child is synesthetic, and all his sense perceptions are present in each separate one, just as the whole of the body is present in each of its parts; thus "I know her noise. / Her neck has kittens," and "Her eyes went kissing away."

Synesthesia has been called a sign of schizophrenia, and as such it reveals the sense in which our most primary experience is schizophrenic. Merleau-Ponty says, "the senses intercommunicate by opening on to the structure of the thing. One *sees* the hardness and brittleness of glass, and when, with a tinkling sound, it breaks, the sound is conveyed by the visible glass." In this respect, "synaesthetic perception is the rule, and we are unaware of it only because scientific knowledge shifts the centre of gravity of experience, so that we have unlearned how to see, hear, and generally speaking, feel. . . ." The experience of the child in Roethke's sequence is the opposite. He is learning how to see, hear, and feel, and is thus able to retain the undifferentiated wholeness of experience that converges upon and fills out each separate perception of the world.

These lines also contain the first ambiguous references to "her" in the poem. "Her" is in a certain sense the child's mother, the living representation of his primordial wholeness, and the ultimate object of his regressions. But as the sequence proceeds, "her" obviously comes to indicate another woman, who becomes the focus of all the vaginal im-

ages in the poems and thus represents a separate being whom the child, growing out of childhood, must unite with.

Two more points about this section: first, death is experienced for the first time by the child and handily disposed of in play—something that will become increasingly difficult to do as the sequence proceeds. Second, the phrase "I know" is repeated twice, an indication of the child's rapid growth in time. "I know" constitutes in both cases a kind of recognition, and recognition implies that the child possesses a past that is not simply a primordial mergence but a history, an accumulation of experiences.

"I know" triggers the next section, which in feeling, rhythm, and theme is substantially different from the first two.

> I know it's an owl. He's making it darker.
> Eat where you're at. I'm not a mouse.
> Some stones are still warm.
> I like soft paws.
> Maybe I'm lost,
> Or asleep.
>
> A worm has a mouth.
> Who keeps me last?
> Fish me out.
> Please.
>
> God, give me a near. I hear flowers.
> A ghost can't whistle.
> I know! I know!
> Hello happy hands.

If the sequence is structured on a kind of expansion-deflation rhythm, the meaning of "deflation" is made clear in the first two stanzas of this section. In the first section the expansive play of the child stopped at the hard edge of the real world; here that stoppage is given the explicit emotional character of fear and the temporal and spatial character of being lost. It is rhythmically expressed by the fact that all the lines are end-stopped, and some even have full stops in the middle. The lines have a kind of atomistic quality, a feeling of things broken apart and lying beside each other. In terms of time, this is to say that the growing time-awareness of the child has suddenly hit a nerve in consciousness that reveals time is slipping away as well as going forward. A kind of fear is produced in the child, a fear that makes him clutch at whatever is at hand in order to stop the passage of time.

This is "being lost," not the loss of orientation that can occur in a map space, but the loss of self in time that necessarily occurs in growing up. The loss of self in time is always accompanied by a coming toward one's self, but either may be experienced more intensely than the other, and in this case the former is. This is why the child grabs at things: in order not to slip away into the past. But the irony is that whatever he reaches for slips away itself—as if he were being blown backward, and reached out of desperation for doorknobs and handles that loosened and came off in his hand. Heidegger's description of fear is apt here: "When concern is afraid, it leaps from next to next, because it forgets itself and therefore does not *take hold of* any definite possibility." Thus these lines:

> Eat where you're at. I'm not a mouse.
> Some stones are still warm.
> I like soft paws.

This feeling of jumping from one thing to the next is echoed throughout the sequence. In **"The Lost Son,"** for example: "What a small song. What slow clouds. What dark water. / Hath the rain a father? All the caves are ice. Only the snow's here." Or in **"Give Way, Ye Gates":**

> Touch and arouse. Suck and sob. Curse and
>    mourn.
> It's a cold scrape in a low place.
> The dead crow dries on a pole.

The further irony is that this jumping from thing to thing in order to stop time leads finally to regression. The child clutches at everything around him as time slips away, but nothing works, nothing is rooted, until he finally clutches at himself and his world once again becomes self-enclosed. Since the feeling of time slipping away is also a feeling of losing oneself, the solution is to embrace oneself, to root oneself. This is the "near" the child asks God for. His world is not near, because he is being blown away from it, and all its handles come loose. But his hands are near, what he uses to clutch at the world: "I know! I know! / Hello happy hands." The hint of masturbation is unmistakable, especially given the accompanying references to "fish" and "worm." All that is necessary is for the child to direct the use of his hands toward himself, allowing himself to be blown totally back through time, to regress.

Masturbation is an ambiguous act throughout the sequence. On one hand, it is a dead end, a desperate attempt to stave off being lost. The penis itself is a perfect image of the separateness into which the primordial wholeness of the child's world has been channeling; to fasten upon it is to acknowledge the fragmentation of the world that being lost results in. It is to relinquish the world as such, to let it pass by, and to enclose oneself like a snake swallowing its tail. On the other hand, the act of enclosing oneself leads back to that pool of narcissistic and maternal wholeness out of which the child has been thrust, and therefore leads back to the original mergence with the world. The paradox is that the image of separation and isolation, the penis, leads to wholeness, and thrusts the child back into the world he has just relin-

quished. Masturbation becomes the act by which the child can connect with the erotic nature of his environment, with the life of nature itself. The child says, "I hear flowers," when masturbation is hinted at. This kind of fundamental erotic connection between the child and his world is made more explicit in passages where masturbation is made more explicit, in **"Praise to the End!"** for example:

> It's dark in this wood, soft mocker.
> For whom have I swelled like a seed?
> What a bone-ache I have.
> Father of tensions, I'm down to my skin at last.
>
> It's a great day for the mice.
> Prickle-me, tickle-me, close stems.
> Bumpkin, he can dance alone.
> Ooh, ooh, I'm a duke of eels.
>
>> Arch my back, pretty-bones, I'm dead at both
>>    ends.
>> Softly, softly, you'll wake the clams.
>> I'll feed the ghost alone.
>> Father, forgive my hands.
>
> The rings have gone from the pond.
> The river's alone with its water.
> All risings
> Fall.

The "near" the child asks for becomes the natural things of the world, as well as his own skin: "It's a great day for the mice. / Prickle-me, tickle-me, close stems." The being lost that had forced the child back on himself has become its own opposite, a being found. The deflation that is being lost has become, of its own movement, an inflation, both literally and figuratively, a mutual embrace of the child and his world.

But as the final lines of the above passage and the following section of **"Where Knock Is Open Wide"** make clear, that very inflation of the child's world, which is centered in the penis, becomes of its own movement a deflation; thus "All risings / Fall," and the emphasis at the end of that passage upon being alone: "I'll feed the ghost alone," and "The river's alone with its water." Similarly, in section four of **"Where Knock Is Open Wide,"** the narrator says:

> That was before. I fell! I fell!
> The worm has moved away.
> My tears are tired.

The sway and countersway of time in the sequence, and the sense in which those two movements are born out of each other, is primarily felt in this recurring rhythm of being lost, regressing, and then out of that very regression, expanding and embracing the world erotically, and in turn out of that very expansion, finding oneself lost again. The emphasis at the beginning of the sequence is upon being lost, and at the end upon embracing the world and being found, but each is also present in the other.

The rest of **"Where Knock Is Open Wide"** reemphasizes, after the brief countermovement of embracing the world, the being lost and being alone of the child's fall into time. Here is section four:

> We went by the river.
> Water birds went ching. Went ching.
> Stepped in wet. Over stones.
> One, his nose had a frog,
> But he slipped out.
>
> I was sad for a fish.
> Don't hit him on the boat, I said.
> Look at him puff. He's trying to talk.
> Papa threw him back.
>
> Bullheads have whiskers.
> And they bite.
>
>> He watered the roses.
>> His thumb had a rainbow.
>> The stems said, Thank you.
>> Dark came early.
>
> That was before. I fell! I fell!
> The worm has moved away.
> My tears are tired.
>
> Nowhere is out. I saw the cold.
> Went to visit the wind. Where the birds die.
> How high is have?
> I'll be a bite. You be a wink.
> Sing the snake to sleep.

The bulk of the section is given as a kind of reverie, a memory, perhaps the only one the child could fasten upon to prevent the recurrence of being lost. The feeling of the passage is a kind of uneasy stasis: there is no intensely felt fear and no radical regression, but neither is there any embracing of the world and progression.

And yet this section does contain the climax of this first poem: "That was before. I fell! I fell!" Out of the realization that the reverie is a reverie issues a temporal self-consciousness, a kind of being inside and outside of oneself that is the basis of time as falling. "I fell!" also refers to the child's sexual sin and to the correlation between the child's sin and that of the race, by calling to mind the fall of Adam. The traditional equation between the penis and the snake in the Garden is

made in the next line: "The worm has moved away." The image of the penis also appears three stanzas earlier, and as in the first section of the poem, it appears in terms of a close connection between father and fish:

> I was sad for a fish.
> Don't hit him on the boat, I said.
> Look at him puff. He's trying to talk.
> Papa threw him back.

Not only is this passage another instance of the fact of death, but it is also an allegory which in general displays the authority over life that the father possesses, and in particular displays his displeasure with the son's attempt to express his sexuality, to "talk" with his penis. As in Eden, the child's sin is a sin of disobedience of the father; "Father, forgive my hands," he says in **"Praise to the End!"** His salvation, as the rest of the sequence shows, will be an attempt to reconcile himself with the father.

The end of the poem, section five, shows the final break with the father that is necessary before reconciliation is possible:

> Kisses come back,
> I said to Papa;
> He was all whitey bones
> And skin like paper.
>
> God's somewhere else,
> I said to Mamma.
> The evening came
> A long long time.
>
> I'm somebody else now.
> Don't tell my hands.
> Have I come to always? Not yet.
> One father is enough.
>
> Maybe God has a house.
> But not here.

The father's death dramatically heightens the son's sense of separation from himself, from his original mergence with the world. Time now is "a long long time" since it has fallen out of itself, and the son is "somebody else" since he has done the same. Nothing is in fact present, nothing is here. "Kisses come back," the son says; God is "somewhere else," and even God's house, the world itself, is "not here." The father's death shows that the narrator's reconciliation with the father will be in an important sense a reconciliation with everything, with God, with the world. Thus the line "One father is enough" will find an answer in the last poem of the sequence: "A son has many fathers."

The dominant theme of **"Where Knock Is Open Wide"** is

being lost. There is a momentary interlude, an awakening and being found in section three—"I know! I know!"—but this quickly recedes, and the poem ends on a note of absence.

Being lost is the intense experience of time slipping away. There is an experience related to being lost that equally concentrates on only one aspect of time and therefore produces a similar sense of incompleteness, and that is desire. If being lost is the realization of time slipping away, desire is the realization of time slipping ahead, of time always eluding our grasp. The dominant theme of the next poem in the sequence, **"I Need, I Need,"** is this experience of desire, as its title makes clear. Grammatically, most of the poem is concerned not with what has happened but with what may happen, or should happen. Thus many of the sentence forms are commands or wishes; in section one, for example:

> Whisper me over,
> Why don't you, begonia,
> There's no alas
> Where I live.

There's "no alas" because in this new orientation in time to the future there's no pausing to reconsider or catch one's breath. There is a kind of restlessness in this section, not exactly a searching but a quizzical wandering:

> Went down cellar,
> Talked to a faucet;
> The drippy water
> Had nothing to say.

This wandering breaks out into pure playful wish in the next section, followed in turn by a conscious realization that the leaping ahead of time means the world is always essentially incomplete:

> I wish I was a pifflebob
> I wish I was a funny
> I wish I had ten thousand hats,
> And made a lot of money.

> Open a hole and see the sky:
> A duck knows something
> You and I don't.
> Tomorrow is Friday.

The image of the hole in these lines and the realization that time is slipping ahead combine in the poem to form the essential structure of desire. Desire is a hole that is always being filled but never retains anything; it is a constant and pure progression, a continual outstripping of itself. It is pure mouth, which is why the predominant imagery of the poem is oral ("Sit in my mouth" at the beginning of the poem, and

"My hoe eats like a goat" at the end). Desire is eating, and it is that particular eating, like fire, whose sustenance passes through it instead of being retained.

The images of eating—and of fire—congregate at the end of the poem and become explicitly sexual. At the poem's beginning, oral images appear in terms of the mother, but at the end they are presented in terms of the "her" introduced in **"Where Knock Is Open Wide."** It is almost as if in order to stop the ceaseless passing through and slipping ahead that constitute desire, the narrator had to invent an object of desire. This is the structure of all sexual awakenings: they are not precipitated by a "her," but the desire already existing casts around until it finds a "her" it can anchor in:

> Who's ready for pink and frisk?
> My hoe eats like a goat.

> Her feet said yes.
> It was all hay.

> I said to the gate,
> Who else knows
> What water does?
> Dew ate the fire.

> I know another fire.
> Has roots.

The anchoring of desire succeeds to such an extent that the final image of eating is of desire itself being eaten: "Dew ate the fire." The recurring use throughout the sequence of water and fire to represent the female and male principles indicates that this devouring of desire is simply the inevitable result of sexual fulfillment. It is anything but permanent; "another fire" already exists, its roots are already down, and it will inevitably burst forth to start the cycle over again.

But the last two lines—"I know another fire. / Has roots."—have a further possible meaning, a meaning more indicative of the direction the rest of the sequence will take. If fire, as an image of desire, represents a kind of pure becoming and pure progression, a temporality that always leaps ahead of itself, then a fire with roots represents, paradoxically, a becoming that has a permanence at its heart, a progression that retains itself. It represents the full structure of temporality, the structure for which being lost on the one hand and desire on the other are only partial manifestations. The fire with roots is the very act of growth that is temporality in its most complete sense.

The next poem, **"Bring the Day!"** is the shortest of the sequence, and represents a kind of peaceful interlude before the emphasis in the sequence shifts to growth and embracing the world. The dominant image of this poem is the kiss, again an oral action, but that particular oral action that is neither a devouring nor a being devoured but rather a kind of floating on the surface of both. The kiss is the image of gentle and mutual appropriation, of the cooperative alliance of things. Thus the poem opens with these lines:

> Bees and lilies there were,
> Bees and lilies there were,
> Either to other,—
> Which would you rather?
> Bees and lilies were there.

The feeling in the poem is one of compatibility. Except for a brief brush with being lost, there is no sense of incompleteness. Rather the images are of things that suit and complete each other:

> Leaves, do you like me any?
> A swan needs a pond.
> The worm and the rose
> Both love
> Rain.

The space of both being lost and desiring was a kind of atomistic space, a space broken up into the separate objects the narrator clutched at to steady and fix himself. Here the space is one that funnels through things and enables them to gently manifest themselves, to introduce themselves:

> The herrings are awake.
> What's all the singing between?—
> Is it with whispers and kissing?—
> I've listened into the least waves.

Things hold themselves out in this poem, as we hold objects out on our hands. Their space is a buoyant one that allows them to float before us, to stretch and feel themselves awakening:

> O small bird awakening,
> Light as a hand among blossoms,
> Hardly any old angels are around any more.
> The air's quiet under the small leaves.
> The dust, the long dust, stays.
> The spiders sail into summer.
> It's time to begin!
> To begin!

The peace of the poem is that quiet that exists before a storm, that stasis out of which beginnings proceed and which even the most violent kind of becoming and progression has to continually carry with it and have at its heart if it isn't to outstrip itself and swallow itself as pure desire.

This becoming with a stasis at its heart is the dominant theme

of the next poem, and the continual resolution of the rest of the sequence. The title, **"Give Way, Ye Gates,"** refers to floodgates but also has obvious sexual overtones. Throughout the sequence the gate is an image of the vagina, as in the line "My gates are all caves," in **"The Long Alley."** The gate is particularly a symbol of the forbidden nature of sexual union, since its function is to block entrance. But in this poem the gates literally give way, and the result is a reawakening and a rebirth of the narrator into the world, both sexually and existentially. Birth is an important theme in the poem, of equal importance to the theme of sexual union. The two themes are collapsed in the line describing the actual giving way of the gates: "Tufty, the water's loose." Tuft means a clump of hair, so refers to the female sexual organ; "the water's loose" calls to mind a release of stored sexual impulses on the one hand and a pregnant woman's breaking water on the other. Together these two meanings indicate the sense in which the giving way of the gates is a surge of energy that carries the child out of the womb into sexual union with another. The giving way of the gates is that surge of energy which is the child's act of growth.

Throughout the sequence, the two kinds of images that best reveal the structure of this act of growth are of openings—gates, holes, mouths, caves—and of water—streams, ponds, lakes, the amniotic fluid. With regard to the images of water, a flood is the most explicit image of growth, for that forward movement always accumulates itself; this is precisely what growth is, the movement forward in time that accumulates itself, the falling that is also a rising. Growth is that activity which never leaves itself behind and yet always goes forward. In this sense, not only a flood but any movement of water embodies the structure of growth, since water always carries its source—water—with it when it moves. The movement of water, precisely like growth, is that flow out of itself which retains itself. This is the point of the closing lines of **"Give Way, Ye Gates"**:

> The deep stream remembers:
> Once I was a pond.
> What slides away
> Provides.

Just as water partitions itself out of an original wholeness into more and more refined parts—rivers and streams—but retains that original wholeness, carrying it into each of those parts, so growth is the activity of partitioning one's body into its parts, while always retaining that original mergence, that original wholeness, that "pool," out of which it came.

The imagery of holes reveals a similar structure. In the sequence, the concept of "hole" is used in two senses: as an enclosure, e.g., a pit, and as an opening out of an enclosure. The imagery of enclosures indicates regression and a return to the original condition of mergence. "Who stands in a hole

/ Never spills," says the narrator in **"Give Way, Ye Gates,"** a sentiment echoed throughout the sequence in all the images of mergence and sinking, of pouring into one's self and filling one's self, that result in a kind of blob existence familiar from Burroughs' novels; thus, in lines already quoted:

> Who, careless, slips
> In coiling ooze
> Is trapped to the lips,
> Leaves more than shoes.

The "coiling ooze" is one's own body as well as the amorphous body of the earth; thus it is one's body as a hole or pit in which one is trapped. Similarly, the lines "Everything's closer. / Is this a cage?" in **"Bring the Day!"** or the phrase "I'm lost in what I have" in **"O, Thou Opening, O"** refer to the body as it funnels back into itself and fills the hole of itself, to a kind of regressive growth that never leaves itself. Opposed to these images in the sequence are all those of emerging from a hole, of flowing out of one's self. "I've crawled from the mire, alert as a saint or a dog," the narrator says in **"Praise to the End!"** a line echoed in **"O, Thou Opening, O":** "I've crept from a cry." This imagery of emergence is related to the experience of desire, of always leaping out of and ahead of one's self. And both are expressions of the becoming aspect of growth, of the structure of human existence as a continual progression; we are always "Looking toward what we are," Roethke says in **"Give Way, Ye Gates."**

The concept of growth embraces both these aspects of the imagery of holes. Growth is that activity in which we are always being filled and yet always emerging from ourselves; it is the grave and the nest united. Growth is time as falling, and particularly, in terms of the body, time as a falling into and a simultaneous rising out of ourselves. This is growth: we lose and gather ourselves, we slip by ourselves in the very act of falling into ourselves, and we always overflow ourselves without spilling. Roethke's most stunning image of a kind of overflowing that doesn't spill occurs at the end of **"The Shape of the Fire":**

> To know that light falls and fills, often without our
>   knowing,
> As an opaque vase fills to the brim from a quick
>   pouring,
> Fills and trembles at the edge yet does not flow
>   over,
> Still holding and feeding the stem of the contained
>   flower.

This is precisely the condition of the body in growth, a fact made clear by Roethke's description, several lines before this passage, of a rose "Rising slowly out of its bed, / Still as a child in its first loneliness." Growth is a perfect unity of stasis and silence with continual becoming, is sustained fullness that trembles at its own brim and simultaneously leaves itself in order to feed itself. That unity of the timelessness of the child's world with the successiveness of adulthood enables time to embrace both presence and absence, both passing and becoming. This is why Roethke's narcissism, evident throughout the sequence, is not idle self-indulgence but that perfect excess of being which is also perfectly trim, that complete absorption in one's self which is also completely impersonal. "Fishing, I caught myself behind the ears," he says in **"Unfold! Unfold!"** indicating that the reach into one's self, into the narcissistic pool, is also an emergence out of one's self.

In Burroughs, by contrast, the two aspects of growth in time—flying and sinking, emerging and submerging—exist beside each other, with no fundamental connection or unity between them. In Roethke's sequence they exist united, in that perfect unity of Being and Nonbeing which also preserves their separation. To submerge is to emerge in Roethke's poems, or as Roethke said about the entire sequence, to go back is to go forward. Growth is that activity in which one always falls back into the hole of the self, fills that hole, and is consequently impelled forward—all in one motion.

Growth is the activity that organizes all the countermovements of the poem, the sway and countersway of its rhythm, the progression-regression, expansion-deflation movement of the child's wanderings in the world. Growth unites being lost and desiring or needing—it is that fire with roots by which we are what we become, and it thus unites being lost and being found. The emphasis upon being found in the rest of the sequence is equally an emphasis on coming toward oneself in the world.

The emphasis is also upon uniting with the world, upon filling the world as one fills one's self, while always not-being the world as well, while always flowing out of it. The ambiguity of masturbation in the sequence reflects this being and not-being of the self and the world, and indicates its connection with the concept of growth. Masturbation is a kind of ecstatic self-enclosedness, a being-filled that is also outside of itself and specifically is outside of itself by being in the world, by erotically plugging into nature. Growth is that very excess of being which overflows into the world, into the objects of the world, and enables the body both to define itself on the "ground" of the world and to unite with the world. This is the further significance of the image of catching oneself while fishing: to catch oneself is to generate oneself, to become the father of oneself, and this is possible only because one is united with "mother" earth, with the world. This is why all I have said about growth also applies to the world: the world overflows its objects while retaining itself among them, a phenomenon for which plant life offers the best illustration.

Growth, in other words, is the fundamental condition of the garden, that continual, becoming unity of mergence and discreteness, of unity and multiplicity, that is the full sense of the garden. This is the significance of the images of water and light in the final two poems in this first section of the sequence. Water and light are symbols of that wholeness which impregnates the world and fills it out, which holds things in their separateness while connecting them with everything else. Lines like "The lake washes its stones" in **"Sensibility! O La!"** and "Light fattens the rock" or "The sea has many streets" in **"O Lull Me, Lull Me"** all express the intimate reciprocal relationship between wholeness and separation in the natural world. The final poem, **"O Lull Me, Lull Me,"** explicitly connects this organization of the natural world with the ongoing process of growth that the child is experiencing:

> The poke of the wind's close,
> But I can't go leaping alone.
> For you, my pond,
> Rocking with small fish,
> I'm an otter with only one nose:
> I'm all ready to whistle;
> I'm more than when I was born.

As a symbol of that wholeness and continuity which informs the process of growth, the pond in these lines is also a symbol of the world itself. The narrator "can't go leaping alone" because growth that isn't fed by the world and that doesn't simultaneously overflow back into the world is no growth at all. This is why, in the same poem, images of the connection between inside and outside and between body and world become prominent for the first time in the sequence:

> I see my heart in the seed;
> I breathe into a dream,
> And the ground cries.
> I'm crazed and graceless,
> A winter-leaping frog.

This is the kind of resolution that will occur often at peak moments in the second half of the sequence.

However, the resolution is still only partial at this particular point in the sequence; the process of growth has begun, but has not yet filled itself out completely. Thus in **"O Lull Me, Lull Me,"** the narrator says: "Soothe me, great groans of underneath, / I'm still waiting for a foot." As in much of the rest of the sequence, the foot is an image of the penis. Roethke's fixation with the penis throughout the sequence is in many respects a fixation with growth, since as the body channels into its limbs, it channels most noticeably into the penis. (In another poem in the sequence, Roethke sings a song of encouragement to his penis to grow: "Be large as an owl be slick as a frog, / Be good as a goose, be big as a dog,

/ Be sleek as a heifer, be long as a hog,— / What footie will do will be final.") In the line "I'm still waiting for a foot," however, the indication is that the process of growth is still in its beginning stages; the "foot" by which he is to grow forward and connect with the world, like his whole body, is "more than when I was born," but not quite enough yet.

The references to "her" in these last two poems make the same point. In **"Sensibility! O La!"** the opening lines are:

> I'm the serpent of somebody else
> See! She's sleeping like a lake:
> Glory to seize, I say.

Clearly "she" is no longer the mother, but is another, the very symbol of otherness that the poet must connect with in order to truly grow. But at the end of the poem there is a slipping back, not exactly a regression, but certainly a failure to achieve the other and a recognition that such achievement is difficult:

> My sweetheart's still in her cave.
> I've waked the wrong wind:
> I'm alone with my ribs.

And further on: "Mamma! Put on your dark hood; / It's a long way to somewhere else." The double function of growth, to retain itself and leave itself, is always in danger of slipping exclusively into one or the other. Particularly with regard to the world outside and to the most important manifestation of that world, another person, there is a temptation to draw back; thus "I'm alone with my ribs" and "It's a long way to somewhere else."

Despite these obvious setbacks, the emphasis of the rest of the sequence is upon union with the world in the act of growth. In Roethke's radical insistence upon the full meaning of this union, he abandons the references to "her" and "she" that occur in the first half of the sequence. It is as if before taking the step that most of us take—sexual union—he wanted to explore it fully in a more fundamental way, in terms of our relationship to the objects we encounter every day, at every moment. This is why the dominant emphasis in the rest of the sequence is upon the sexual nature of the world—upon the sexual nature of Being in general. Roethke's vision is of that gap in Being, that Nonbeing which passes through and fills Being out, and requires that the body and the world always mutually embrace and penetrate each other so both can truly grow. The peak moments of the rest of the sequence occur when the narrator and the world slip into each other's skin through the common hole they share, the hole in time that is growth. I will conclude by examining some of these peak moments.

The first occurs in **"The Lost Son"** and climaxes with a dizzy plunge into the hole of the world, into that pure Nonbeing at the heart of everything:

> These sweeps of light undo me.
> Look, look, the ditch is running white!
> I've more veins than a tree!
> Kiss me, ashes, I'm falling through a dark swirl.

This passage occurs several stanzas after a description of being lost in which the narrator says, "My veins are running nowhere." By contrast, the "running" of his veins in this passage, the new infusion of life, is the opposite of being lost; it is an intimate connection with the things of the world: "I've more veins than a tree!" The same dizziness that is found in the extreme state of being lost is there, but it moves in exactly the opposite direction; it moves toward the world, penetrates the world: "I'm falling through a dark swirl." The next poem, **"The Long Alley,"** contains lines that express a similar kind of dizzy union, except in this case the world penetrates the protagonist. Here is the entire passage, perhaps the most beautiful one in the sequence, or even in all of Roethke's poetry:

> Shall I call the flowers?
> Come littlest, come tenderest,
> Come whispering over the small waters,
> Reach me rose, sweet one, still moist in the loam,
> Come, come out of the shade, the cool ways,
> The long alleys of string and stem;
> Bend down, small breathers, creepers and
> winders;
> Lean from the tiers and benches,
> Cyclamen dripping and lilies.
> What fish-ways you have, littlest flowers,
> Swaying over the walks, in the watery air,
> Drowsing in soft light, petals pulsing.
> Light airs! Light airs! A pierce of angels!
> The leaves, the leaves become me!
> The tendrils have me!

As in **"The Lost Son,"** this incident occurs after a period of being lost and regressing. Here the things of the world, their vegetal, sexual aspect, literally plunge through the body of the poet, and the result is a totally ecstatic experience of being-in-the-world: "The leaves, the leaves become me!" It is this kind of ideal metamorphic moment for which the whole sequence exists. One more example should suffice, from **"Praise to the End!"**:

> Arch of air, my heart's original knock,
> I'm awake all over:
> I've crawled from the mire, alert as a saint or a
> dog;
> I know the back-stream's joy, and the stone's
> eternal pulseless
> longing.

> Felicity I cannot hoard.
> My friend, the rat in the wall, brings me the
> clearest messages;
> I bask in the bower of change;
> The plants wave me in, and the summer apples;
> My palm-sweat flashes gold;
> Many astounds before, I lost my identity to a
> pebble;
> The minnows love me, and the humped and
> spitting creatures.

This is that complete openness which is also completely filled; it is that total self-effacement in the presence of the world which is equally a complete self-fulfillment, a complete realization of the self. Roethke disperses himself, loses himself into even the most inanimate objects, stones and pebbles, and by that very dispersal finds himself fully and collects himself. And this losing and finding oneself in intimate union with the world is the "bower of change" that the poet basks in; it is growth itself.

The space of this union with the world is that perfect unity of space and time which is the space of the garden. Each thing presents itself as autonomous and independent, as something with its own space, and yet all things participate in each other and are drawn together in a common space; they are drawn together by that particular hole in Being which is the body's link with the world, by that mutual temporality of body and world by which they fall into and out of each other, by growth. The space of Roethke's world unites fullness and emptiness, plenitude and nothingness, as growth itself does. All of this can be seen in a passage in **"A Field of Light"**:

> I touched the ground, the ground warmed by
> killdeer,
> The salt laughed and the stones;
> The ferns had their ways, and the pulsing lizards,
> And the new plants, still awkward in their soil,
> The lovely diminutives.
> I could watch! I could watch!
> I saw the separateness of all things!
> My heart lifted up with the great grasses;
> The weeds believed me, and nesting birds.
> There were clouds making a rout of shapes
> crossing a windbreak
> of cedars,
> And a bee shaking drops from a rain-soaked
> honeysuckle.
> The worms were delighted as wrens.
> And I walked, I walked through the light air;
> I moved with the morning.

The "separateness of all things" is preserved in Roethke's world, and so the space of that world is not one absolute objective block; but neither is it an atomistic space, as in

Burroughs, in which each thing is confined totally to itself. Rather it is a space that gathers up objects in all their separateness, as a wave gathers up stones, and integrates them by virtue of that separateness—a space in which objects are always falling into place, a space that simultaneously contracts and expands, a becoming, temporal space.

This space both anchors things and releases them for the grasp of the body; it thus perfectly unites here and there, the subjective point of view and the absolute, objective world, fantasy and reality. It is a space that flows out of itself, as the body leaves itself in growth, and that simultaneously fills and impregnates itself. The image of things leaving themselves is common in Roethke, and the most general example of it, which reveals it as a basic structural principle of his world, occurs in **"The Lost Son"**:

> From the mouths of jugs
> Perched on many shelves,
> I saw substance flowing
> That cold morning.

The space of all Roethke's poetry is a metamorphic space, dynamized by time, a space that leaves itself and becomes, changes, as the clouds in the previously quoted passage make "a rout of shapes crossing a windbreak of cedars."

We saw in Chapter One that the schizophrenic world of the map is one in which holes open up, holes such as absolute space or absolute consciousness, both of which are hermetically sealed and are of a different order of being from what they exclude. The space of Roethke's world also contains holes, but they are holes that are both continually being sealed and continually opening. It is space as a collection of mouths, not atoms. As he puts it in **"Unfold! Unfold!"**:

> Easy the life of the mouth. What a lust for
>     ripeness!
> All openings praise us, even oily holes.
> The bulb unravels. Who's floating? Not me.
> The eye perishes in the small vision.

Oral images opened the sequence and expressed the primordial wholeness of the child's world. Here they express that wholeness as it is carried into the growing world of everyday experience and united with each separate entity in that world. "The eye perishes in the small vision" because it is drawn into the bottomless hole of each separate thing, thus is drawn into the world itself. This is possible only because the space of Roethke's world—of the garden, and of schizophrenia as the most ideally sane state of consciousness—is one in which all things open upon each other and upon the body, in which subject and object, fantasy and reality, are perfectly united. Space is a hole and things are holes in Roethke's world, but space is also a medium and things are

also things, and the pure potentiality of both is also pure actuality.

This metamorphic space, this space of mouths, is the reason Roethke's world, as in Baudelaire's sonnet, is a world of correspondences—correspondences between things and between the body and things. It is also the reason the objects of that world so often speak and sing, not only to the protagonist but also to each other. As Kenneth Burke points out, Roethke prefers verbs of communication to any others in describing the things of the world. Weeds whine, a cracked pod calls, "Even thread has a speech." The world of Roethke's poetry is engaged in a constant energetic exchange with itself and with the body; it is the symbolic world in the fullest sense:

> Sing, sing, you symbols! All simple creatures,
> All small shapes, willow-shy,
> In the obscure haze, sing!
>
> A light song comes from the leaves.
> A slow sigh says yes. And the light sighs.

Each thing in Roethke's world manifests itself in every other thing, and even—or especially—all opposites exist in and of each other. Roethke says in **"Unfold! Unfold!"**: "Speak to the stones, and the stars answer." Or as he puts it more generally in **"O, Thou Opening, O"**: "The Depth calls to the Height."

This unity of opposites indicates the way in which Roethke's world is a total alternative to the dualistic structures of classical Western thought, an alternative that is manifest in our most primary, everyday experience. Body and world, subject and object, time and space, fantasy and reality, child and man, all exist in a perfect unity, a unity given previous to any reflection, and a unity that couldn't conceivably be otherwise. But each exists also as perfectly autonomous; each is bounded and liberated by itself; each is a hole, a mouth. The garden, Roethke's world, is the condition of growth; it is open-ended, a mouth, since it leaves itself and fills itself in the becoming motion that is growth. This includes the world of inanimate as well as animate things, since the life of that world is the perfect unity of life and death, of Being and Nonbeing, that infuses every moment of our lives. The "other condition" that Roethke claims in the last poem of the sequence to be king of is the schizophrenia of the garden, the condition of the symbolic world, which embraces and unites the garden and the map, unity and multiplicity, life and death, fantasy and reality, while falling and rising in the single flow of growth:

> I sing the green, and things to come,
> I'm king of another condition,
> So alive I could die!

## Harry Williams (essay date 1977)

SOURCE: "Poets and Critics on Roethke," in *"The Edge of What I Have": Theodore Roethke and After,* Bucknell University Press, 1977, pp. 13-36.

[*In the following essay, Williams provides a survey of Roethke's critical reception among contemporary poets and reviewers.*]

Throughout Theodore Roethke's middle and late career and after his death in 1963, poets have enthusiastically praised his work, while major critics have generally ignored or slighted him. Not until the fifth edition of the well-known anthology, Sanders, Nelson, and Rosenthal's *The Chief Modern Poets of England and America* (1970), was Roethke included; and only recently in a collection of essays, *Profile of Theodore Roethke* (1971), the editor, William Heyen, pointed out that nine of his ten contributors were themselves poets (the single exception being Roethke's biographer, the late novelist Allan Seager), thus again reminding one that Roethke is essentially a poet's poet.

What later poets particularly admired in Roethke's work was the unusual intensity of the lyric voice, the projection of a preconscious self into the life of plants and animals, using highly original free-verse patterns that presented the speaker, the *I* in the poems, as unmasked—the poet himself asserting an oracular voice that tries to sound out archetypal themes, often probing the child-parent relation through a selective use of surrealistic imagery, that is, the "deep image." Carolyn Kizer quoted the poet himself in his role of teacher at the University of Washington (1947-63): "I teach a beat"; and she went on to underscore one of Roethke's characteristic rhythms—the end stopped, strong stress trimeter line, to which the poet continually returned throughout his career. Largely because of Roethke's presence in Seattle, she surmised, a significant number of talented poets gathered there.

If Roethke was revered for his mastery of the short line, he was equally revered for his mastery of the long line. His "great verbal sophistication," as Howard Nemerov describes it, manifests itself, not in the unit of the line, but in the strophe. James Wright, once a student of Roethke's, captures this twofold lyrical quality when, in his own poetry, he writes, praising his teacher: "And sweet Ted Roethke, / A canary and a bear," or elsewhere in referring to Swift's poems: "These are the songs that Roethke told of, / The curious music loved by few." It is this lyricism defining an epic theme—what Stanley Kunitz calls the poet's protean journey of transformation out of the self—that accounts for Roethke's particular appeal and influence. For Kunitz, Roethke's lyrical journey out of the self is a real achievement because he does not indulge his ego, and as a result he "was the first

American bardic poet since Whitman who did not spill out in prolix and shapeless vulgarity."

Leslie Fiedler sees Roethke's work as seeking out myth and image in the privacy of dreams rather than in a decaying culture. Roethke's journey is a returning, not to a lost culture, but to the greenhouse of his youth where his father watched over and cared for a floral culture; and it is a return, as Fiedler perceptively describes it, "to all that is truly subversive in the line that comes down to us from Poe by way of *symbolisme*." Delmore Schwartz, who sees Roethke as original and important enough to be compared to Yeats and Valéry, notes Roethke's genuine awareness of the "abyss," the depths of the unconscious to which all romantic poets must return for self-definition and value. Because this return to the unconscious is dangerous, courting psychic disaster, achievement of self-renewal is at best precarious. Failure is always close at hand, yet self-renewal "is what we want: to be gathered together once more," says James Dickey, quoting from the end of Roethke's **"The Long Waters."** Roethke extends into modern times that Wordsworthian sense of *being,* of reunification with nature and one's self, and for this reason alone Roethke is for Dickey the greatest American poet there has ever been.

Perhaps C. W. Truesdale has best summed up Roethke's appeal by equating Roethke's second volume, **The Lost Son and Other Poems** (1948), to Whitman's "Song of Myself"—an extension, in fact, of Whitman's poetics, exhibiting a controlling metaphor of organic growth and a progress from darkness to light: "Most of what we call the American archetypes find themselves again in his work (in unexpected ways), and above all the sense of the land—the vast, the particular, the wasted, the utterly beautiful and the utterly exploited landscape of America, the motherland of Thoreau, Whitman, Twain, even Cooper." Truesdale does not identify the major works, as such, other than **"The Lost Son"** sequence of poems, but it is the theme of resurrection in that sequence that, for Truesdale, defines Roethke's appeal: "the poet is always the 'lost son' seeking a fresh birth in a new America."

In reviewing Roethke's first collection of verse, **Words for the Wind** (1958), John Berryman compares Roethke with Robert Lowell; the two "possess the most powerful and original talents that have emerged during the last fifteen years." If Lowell is Latinate, formal, rhetorical, massive, historical, religious, impersonal, then Roethke is "Teutonic, irregular, colloquial, delicate, botanical and psychological, irreligious, personal"—a formidable list of comparisons, indeed, but comparisons that perhaps Roethke would have agreed with, since he had remarked at one time about Lowell's excessive concern with formal structures, and about his lack of intuitive perception. Berryman also singles out the longer poems in **"The Lost Son"** sequence as Roethke's largest achievement, one of the "fixed objects" in American poetry.

In addition to praise, one is not surprised to find some of these poets acknowledging a direct influence. Kunitz candidly admits that Roethke had taught him a way of coping with affliction. Galway Kinnell insists that no one really had any influence on his work, "until I ran across Theodore Roethke's poems." In accounting for Ted Hughes's poetic power, W. E. Snodgrass sees Hughes doing the same thing as Roethke.

Anne Sexton remembers "writing to Sylvia [Plath] in England after *The Colossus* came out and saying something like '. . . if you're not careful, Sylvia, you will out-Roethke Roethke,' and she replied that I had guessed accurately and that he had been a strong influence on her work."

Just what these poets saw in Roethke's work that the critics found convenient to ignore raises interesting questions that I shall try to answer throughout the ensuing pages. Why, for example, should so many critics have remained cool for so long to the romantic archetypes and lyricism that attracted the poets to Roethke in the first place? Perhaps it is the lack of a well-defined terminology for the motive and effect involved in any exchange between two or more poets—as Richard Wilbur has recently suggested in an essay on the subject of poetic influences. Wilbur reminds one that poets do borrow, steal, adapt, translate, impersonate, and parody one another, and that it is the business of other poets and also of the critics to account for this behavior. Wilbur himself discusses the beneficial effects of the Yeatsian influence on Roethke in the early fifties, an influence that Roethke literally documented in **"Four for Sir John Davies"** and **"The Dying Man,"** as well as the poem later added to the greenhouse sequence in *The Lost Son,* **"Frau Bauman, Frau Schmidt, and Frau Schwartze."** In fact, the trimeter line Carolyn Kizer speaks of is a product of this Yeatsian influence. Of course, an influence can become merely derivative if it is not transformed in the younger writer's imagination, for in reading any poet the reader is always put into that position where he must distinguish between what is wholly belonging to the poet—what is stolen, to use Eliot's phrase—and what is merely borrowed. Without referring to particular poems, Wilbur sees Roethke's later poetry, after the "Yeatsian poems," showing an absorption of the older writer's influence, and hence a perfection of the Roethkean voice.

Although many of the major critics were silent about Roethke at mid-century and after, there were some critics who raised specific objections. In his study of modern English and American poets, *The Shaping Spirit* (1958), A. Alvarez defines the "unmannered," confessional mode of the American poet who writes from a sense of his own isolation within

a classless, unstructured society. Speaking about *The Lost Son* in general, Alvarez argues that Roethke failed to succeed as a confessional poet. Roethke's talent "of a kind" (of a much lower caliber than that of Lowell's or Eberhart's) is delicate and direct in its treatment of the poet's "private troubles" (Alvarez refers to only one of the greenhouse poems, **"Cuttings"**), but because there is no sense of embarrassment, there is offered only an immediate purity and not that "overbearing, claustrophobic intensity" that Alvarez would have. In Roethke's subsequent volume, *Praise to the End!* (1951), Alvarez sees the poet as merely exploiting his material, using his verse "as though it were an analyst's couch." Roethke's artistic identity is a matter of nonconformity and being different: "He ends where the important writers begin, in that sense of isolation from which they create an impersonal artistic order."

M. L. Rosenthal's first critical introduction, *The Modern Poets* (1960), also treats Roethke as part of the confessional school of American writing. The greenhouse poems of *The Lost Son* volume are (contrary to Alvarez) "embarrassedly alive," yet, "as in most of Roethke's longer works, the dénouement does not live up to the poem's initial demands." Generally a defender of the "new poetry," Rosenthal is severely critical of Roethke's personal manner, "the private sensibility of a mad microcosm" that seeks unity and wholeness that, in the case of **"The Lost Son,"** is merely wishful thinking. In his second study of poetry since World War II, *The New Poets* (1967), Rosenthal reiterates his position and further extends his remarks to Roethke's posthumous volume, *The Far Field* (1964), which he sees as "often marred by verbosity, cliché, and derivativeness." Admitting that Roethke came into his own as a poet in his group of greenhouse poems, "that his youthful experience around his father's greenhouse in Michigan provided just the vivid, squirmingly uncomfortable, and concrete focus his poetry needed to channel," that these poems enabled him to objectify for a time his "uncontrolled, riotous psyche," Rosenthal nevertheless objects to Roethke's seeming inability to absorb "so little of the concerns of his age into his nerve-ends . . . so little reference direct or remote to the incredible experiences of the age." In Roethke's hands, then, the confessional mode is reduced to self-recharging and self-echoing.

The charge that Roethke's poetry is outside the experiences of the age is repeated by Monroe K. Spears in his study of modern poetry, *Dionysus and the City* (1970). Referring generally to **"The Lost Son"** sequence, Spears admits that Roethke's poetry at its best has a "deep inwardness and closeness to the Unconscious," yet because the Dionysian element is so strong, the poetry refuses to deal with "the world of normal adult experience." As a result, much of the verse tends toward incoherence and "real obscurity."

It has been demonstrated how some poets revered Roethke's

lyricism, his voice of the self proclaiming a drama of the new self, but certain critics have found this preoccupation with the self too narcissistic. Discussing the nature of the modern lyric, William Pritchard looks upon Roethke as a representative figure of the "somnambulistic" poet devoid of irony and changing tone of voice. Pritchard would advance the cause of a Frost, or a Lowell—despite the singular tones of a Milton, or a Blake, as Pritchard himself admits—the cause for a lyricism that gestures between lyric impulse and the "wryly satiric." These "negative" critics appear to agree on at least two points: Roethke's limited theme that makes him (embarrassed or not) merely a personal, self-conscious poet, and his lyric form or lyrical monotone. These negative criteria, however, can be turned to Roethke's account.

In his seminal essay, "The Vegetal Radicalism of Theodore Roethke" (*The Sewanee Review,* Winter 1950), Kenneth Burke offered for the first time a challenging structural approach to *The Lost Son* volume. Burke recognizes at once the symbolic importance of the greenhouse for Roethke (in Roethke's words: "A womb, a heaven-on-earth"), and from the thirteen-poem greenhouse sequence (now fourteen), he singles out that poem about the greenhouse itself, **"Big Wind,"** as being representative of Roethke's method in all of these poems—his "intensity of *action*" whereby the poem develops from stage to stage, with the "unwinding of the trope." It is not the close description of flowers that makes these poems succeed—although this is clearly part of Roethke's intention—but the fact that Roethke can make his flowers suggest analogues to human behavior and motives quite like the figures of animals in Aesop's fables. In exploiting the floral image, even as a conceit, as Burke sees it, Roethke could develop these analogues on different levels of meaning (root, sprout, blossom), all the while amplifying his theme by a regressive withdrawing of the self ("the most occult of early experiences"). In this greenhouse world with its "peculiar balance of the natural and the artificial," there is almost a perfect symbol for that mystery that relates the individual with the social: "In hothouse flowers, you confront, enigmatically, the representation of status. By their nature, flowers contribute grace to social magic—hence, they are insignia, infused with a spirit of social ordination." In establishing Roethke's radicalism, Burke distinguishes between Eliot's aesthetic and that of Roethke's—the latter, for example, expressing an intuition of sensibilities having a minimum of ideas and a maximum of intuitions, hence a poetry of impulse rather than motive. In this way Roethke's vocabulary is shorn of the abstract—words with -ness or -ity endings—that characterize much of Eliot's poetry. Eliot meets the modern problem of identity in terms of doctrine, while Roethke grapples with that problem in opposite terms, regressing as thoroughly as he could, "even at a considerable risk, toward a language of sheer 'intuition.'" Moreover, Roethke's images become symbolically intuitive when they interchange their meanings through repetition in varying contexts; thus fish, water, flower, or girl might form a symbolic cluster by the repetition of each of these images in related contexts. In this way the images fuse their respective meanings: "They are 'fusions' if you like them, 'confusions' if you don't, and 'diffusions' when their disjunction outweighs their conjunction."

In dealing with the longer sequences, including **"The Lost Son,"** Burke touches on two important techniques that have come to characterize Roethke's method in all of his long poems, as shall be seen later. The first is Roethke's shifting voice, extending the *I* of the speaker into a "cosmically communicating 'voice.'" The second is the way the imagery brings into tension the concrete and the abstract by almost always invoking the notion of "edge" (also suggested by the disjunctive qualities of the truncated, and endstopped lines): "the constant reverberations about the edges of the images give the excitement of being on the edge of Revelation (or suggest a state of vigil, the hope of getting the girl, of getting a medal, of seeing God). There is the pious awaiting of the good message—and there is response to "the spoor that spurs." Burke reprinted his essay in his collection, *Language as Symbolic Action* (1966), without changing it, for, as he was to say in a note appended there, "I cannot better contrive to suggest the rare, enticing danger of Roethke's verse as I felt it then, and still do."

Nothing of critical importance appeared in the decade following Burke's essay. Perhaps the publication of one notable volume of poetry (*The Lost Son*) coming seven years after Roethke's first volume, *Open House* (1941), was not enough of a production to attract serious attention. Also, the radicalism that Burke proclaimed may well have cautioned critics, for Roethke was to become more experimental (as the poems juxtaposed to Burke's essay were to show) in his next volume, *Praise to the End!,* which effectively extended **"The Lost Son"** sequence. Moreover, consistency was not Roethke's habit: he introduced a neo-Yeatsian mode in *The Waking* (1953) and extended it further into *Words for the Wind* (1958), all the while carrying over poems from one volume to the next. But in the sixties, especially after Roethke's death and his posthumously published *The Far Field* (1964), a number of important critics began to give this poet their attention. Arnold Stein edited a collection of essays in *Theodore Roethke: Essays on the Poetry* (1965), the first collection that indicates Roethke's new-found acceptance by the critical establishment. Most of the essays tend to support Roethke's growth as a poet, but because of the breakthrough made by *The Lost Son* and the radical experiments of the related poems in the *Praise to the End!* sequence, two questions naturally suggest themselves: do these two volumes—and specifically the former—constitute Roethke's achievement? Is there no growth and development in the later poetry?

Stephen Spender, W. D. Snodgrass, John Wain, and Louis Martz argue for a decline in poetic strength. Spender, for example, acknowledges Roethke's nonegotistic search of the *I* in **"The Lost Son"** sequence from these two volumes—hence the title of his essay, "The Objective Ego"—yet in the later poetry Roethke exhibits "the Yeatsian grand manner, he becomes the egotist who burdens the reader with his problems." A perpetual beginner, Roethke could not extend his childlike visions of organic nature into the world of society as everyone must come to know it; "he was not a free enough intellect to dominate the Yeatsian mode." Snodgrass's particularly incisive essay, "'That Anguish of Concreteness,'" similarly sees a failing in the later Yeatsian poems; but if Roethke, "who had invented the most raw and original voice of all our period," had misused the formal and elegant voice of Yeats, he had not done so with Eliot's voice (a less confining influence), which is behind the long sequence, **"Meditations of an Old Woman,"** for here the Roethkean voice clearly emerges. In the later poems from *The Far Field,* the mystical and religious rationale and the borrowed cadences become too pervasive for Snodgrass, as does Roethke's penchant for rejecting form as he creates it in his seeking a unity with all objects. Eliot's ideas and Yeats's cadences have become models of form, "have rushed in to fill the vacuum of the father-model." Rejection of form, then, becomes itself a form, a convention, and the language then becomes weakened through slackness and "expectability." John Wain, in his essay, "The Monocle of My Sea-Faced Uncle," similarly praises **"Meditations of an Old Woman,"** more for its originality and evocation of a genuinely feminine personality. Roethke is the only poet of the century who successfully refuses compromise between inner and outer reality by insisting on his intensity of vision, and to write about those things "that the mind apprehends only through the intuitions of the body." For these reasons *Praise to the End!* occupies a central place in the Roethkean canon. Louis Martz, on the other hand, sees Roethke's originality in terms of mind rather than bodily intuition. Applying Wallace Stevens's lines, "The poem of the mind in the act of finding / What will suffice," to Roethke's manner, Martz reveals a meditative mode displaying a speaker/actor who "seeks himself in himself in order to discover or to construct a firm position from which he can include the universe." Roethke's meditative manner develops out of the greenhouse poems—"one of the permanent achievements of modern poetry"—and reaches its zenith in the longer sequences making up the last section of *The Lost Son,* "The Greenhouse Eden" (Martz's title), to which Roethke would return in his later poetry, but never surpass.

The later poetry receives more sympathetic treatment from Ralph J. Mills, Jr., Frederick J. Hoffman, William Meredith, Denis Donoghue, and Roy Harvey Pearce. Mills's essay, "In the Way of Becoming: Roethke's Last Poems," treats the Roethkean journey as a quest for mystical illumination, a quest that alternates between contrary states within the "re-flective consciousness" of the speaker—between ecstasy and despair—as in **"Meditations of an Old Woman"** and **"North American Sequence."** However, it is not until **"Sequence, Sometimes Metaphysical,"** constituting the last section of *The Far Field,* that Roethke reaches his peak in the process aimed toward "a union with or experience of the Divine." Unlike the freer, Whitmanesque rhythms with their breath-controlled strophes in "North American Sequence," the lyricism in **"Sequence, Sometimes Metaphysical"** is taut and economic, "capable of containing and concentrating immense pressures of feeling," (the two sequences exemplifying Roethke's opposing rhythmic forms). What Snodgrass sees as a weakness in this last volume, Roethke's desire to escape *all* form and shape, is precisely what Mills commends as "Roethke's mystical perceptions by striking inward steadily with little recourse to external affairs . . . approximating the instant of naked revelation."

Donoghue, Meredith, and Pearce approach the poetry as an ordering of chaos, both inner and outer, private and public. Donoghue's perceptive essay, "Roethke's Broken Music," follows the Burkean example in tracing Roethke's "intuition of sensibilities" to define that ordering process. If the early poems held out the common romantic idea of the opposing self, the middle and late poems develop the sense of losing one's self at the edge of the abyss, and "the abyss is partly the frog-spawn of a blind man's ditch, partly a ditch of his [Roethke's] own contriving, partly the fate of being human in a hard time, partly the poet's weather." This is the way to innocence; the poems are intuitive directions, akin to spiritual exercises, "all the better if they are caustic, purgative, penitential. The exercises are never finished, because this is the way things are, but once they are well begun the soul can proceed; the energy released is the rage for a sustaining order." Donoghue stresses Roethke's universal appeal, insisting that he is never merely a regional or American poet. He gives two valid arguments: first, Roethke's eclectic influences (Eliot, Hopkins, Joyce, Whitman, Stevens, Yeats) preclude such labeling and, second, Roethke's response to the parental figures (and the wife or lover in the love poems) is so vivid it engrosses all other responses that would better define a regional or local poet. In the poet's search for value and meaning there is an assumption on Roethke's part that this search is only interesting insofar as it is representative, and of no interest when it ceases to be. "Roethke set himself to work toward lucidity and order without turning himself into a case study entitled, 'The Still Complex Fate of Being an American'. . . . But," Donoghue adds, avoiding a seeming contradiction, "Roethke's way of being an American is an eminently respectable way, and part of his achievement is that he makes it available to others." It is just this availability, the nature of Roethke's influence, that is studied in the last chapter of this text.

In Meredith's essay, "A Steady Storm of Correspondences:

Theodore Roethke's Long Journey Out of the Self," the assertion is again encountered that the *Praise to the End!* volume is central, "an anatomy of Roethke's imagery and sensibility" in which he explores the self without egotism. Flirting with "the slow rhythm of chaos," Roethke makes knowledge felt by means of syntax and rhythm; human speech becomes instinctive, "primarily involuntary, an animal cry." Pearce, on the other hand, is concerned with what he calls "the power of sympathy" in the later poetry. Roethke "could not understand the compulsive twentieth-century quest for identity via the route of alienation"; yet there is alienation in the poetry, but it is often associated with violence and only by means of sympathy is that violence transformed into power, thus, "alienation into identification." The argument of Roethke's **"North American Sequence"** is "to unify and make all of a piece, the world which has invaded the poet, so as to allow him to invade it." In this way the poet comes "to comprehend the full range of the other, that chain of being which moves from the minimal to God." Finally, there is Hoffman's incisive essay, "Theodore Roethke: The Poetic Shape of Death," stressing Roethke's dual language, the metaphysical and the natural. It is Roethke's particular success—unparalleled in modern American poetry—to have kept the two so well balanced, so reciprocal. Similar to Louis Martz, Hoffman regards Roethke's work as a poetry of the mind. The mind entering itself is Roethke's "steady concern," and to effect this metaphysical extension of himself he had to go beyond the greenhouse and the "papa principle" in *The Lost Son,* even though a sense of return was always imminent. The Roethkean persona looks into death's possibilities, he sees dying as "continual becoming," a knowledge "of growth as a move toward mortality," which finds its best expression in **"Meditations of an Old Woman."** In *The Far Field* Roethke develops metaphors of transcendence, that is, the will to transcend the particularity of the temporal process in order to define the self, and it is in the late poem, **"In a Dark Time,"** that Roethke resolves "the mazes caused by life and the problems created by the expectation of death."

As excellent as many of these essays are, they are inevitably concerned with only the general qualities of Roethke's poetry. Within the compass of a brief essay, one can offer little structural criticism of specific poems, although what is provided is a needed emphasis on the Roethkean theme—the journey out of the self.

Aside from Burke's criticism of **"The Lost Son,"** the earliest work done on a specific poem is Hugh Staples's essay, "The Rose in the Sea-Wind: A Reading of Theodore Roethke's 'North American Sequence'" (*American Literature,* May 1964). Stapes traces the sequence's structural pattern, describing the first poem of the sequence as an overture introducing the thematic imagery that will operate as leitmotifs throughout the sequence. The middle four poems alternate between sets of opposing images, earth and water,

for example, or light (fire) and darkness; thus **"Meditation at Oyster River"** is dominated by water imagery, **"Journey to the Interior"** by earth imagery, the cycle repeating itself with the next two poems, **"The Long Waters"** and **"The Far Field."** A final version is then offered in the last poem, **"The Rose,"** which presents the rose as the symbol of form, and here the sequence reconciles and resolves all the thematic images of the previous poems, gathering them together as a final achievement of unity.

Staples's method is both explicative and critical, and it may be that together with Burke he inspired further explication, the most notable example being the only book-length study so far, Karl Malkoff's *Theodore Roethke: An Introduction to the Poetry* (1966). Malkoff's thoughtful explication of the entire range of Roethke's poetry falls short of any critical assessment of the poet's style and structure, but it does serve a most useful purpose in explicating key themes from a psychoanalytical point of view. The longer poems from the last of *The Lost Son,* for example, show Roethke's "adept manipulation of a subterranean, Freudian universe," and in so doing are original for contemporary poetry at that time. In viewing the poetry from psychological perspectives, Malkoff stresses the poet's personal sense of guilt—sexual in **"The Lost Son,"** and in the form of a personal mysticism trying to take over in **"Meditations of an Old Woman"** and **"North American Sequence."** In assuming that guilt operates the controlling theme, Malkoff is forced to account for what appears to be Roethke's ambivalence (between the personal and the impersonal) in conceptualizing terms of myth and legend, and by using Freud and Jung, or other writers of consequence. As a result, Malkoff sometimes belies an impatience with Roethke's poetic strategies, as in the case of **"Four for Sir John Davies":** "The victory over the powers of darkness and nonbeing . . . is at best tentative; and this sets the pattern for the bulk of Roethke's remaining poetry, which is characterized by a tormenting vacillation between hope and despair rather than any consistent point of view."

Extending Staples's structural approach and enlarging upon Malkoff's basic explications, a few good studies of individual poems have appeared over the past several years. William Heyen in his essay, "Theodore Roethke's Minimals" (*Minnesota Review,* 1968), shows how Roethke's random selection of minimals (worms, mice, dogs, children, crows, and the like) is not meant to offer a development or hierarchy, as in a great chain of being, but rather is made to support the poet's varying moods. Most of the images represent stages of becoming and being, as in **"Meditations of an Old Woman"** where the woman's alternate moods of elation and despair are reflected in the way she interprets the bird and its song during the entire sequence. Heyen's criticism favors a mystical approach to the poetry, and a year later one finds him writing toward that end in a second essay, "The Divine Abyss: Theodore Roethke's Mysticism" (*Texas Studies in*

*Language and Literature,* Winter 1969). Heyen concentrates on **"The Abyss"** from *The Far Field* in order to develop Malkoff's assertion that Roethke was quite familiar with Evelyn Underhill's *Mysticism.* That the poem's five-part structure corresponds to Underhill's outline of five phases of mysticism (awakening of self; purification of self; illumination; the dark night of the soul; union) is somewhat weakened by Heyen's admission that the fourth phase, the dark night of the soul, finds little correspondence in the poem. Yet the poem is the "prototypical" mystical poem, and the mystical journey it suggests is the very essence of many of Roethke's later poems in *Words for the Wind* and *The Far Field.*

Another essay of a more explicatory mode than Heyen's is James McMichael's "The Poetry of Theodore Roethke" (*The Southern Review,* Winter 1969). McMichael again emphasizes the Roethkean predicament—the journey out of the self, and particularly its relationship to the meaning of God for Roethke, the desire to find one's God: "I have emphasized," says McMichael, "that the *sine qua non* of Roethke's journey out of the self is his commitment to the mindless part of God's creation." Woman and animals are the mediators of this "mindless part" because they are closer to the "soil." In **"North American Sequence,"** however, woman is precluded from the hierarchy of mediators of this "his most complete definition" of the journey out of the self. McMichael follows Staples's treatment of leitmotifs in the sequence as a hierarchy of elements within an earth-air-water framework. The final poem of the sequence is an ambitious attempt to define the paradoxical relationship between self and other and achieve as much resolution as possible. The rose, as symbol, is outside the hierarchy of mediators that has been at work in the preceding five poems; yet the value of the rose is somehow related to the transiency of this hierarchy, and the fact that this commitment might sink to nothingness leaves the poet (and the reader) with an acute sense of man's central dilemma.

Reworking Burke's ideas about Roethke's "intuition of sensibilities," Jerome Mazzaro develops a linguistic/psychological metaphor to explicate a sampling of the poetry in his essay, "Theodore Roethke and the Failures of Language" (*Modern Poetry Studies,* July 1970). Again, Mazzaro underscores the success of Roethke's intuitively directed language because it is symbolically informed. But something is lost in the process, and that is language's failure to communicate cognitively when it is intended to function symbolically. Roethke exemplifies that peculiar energy that depth psychologists claim an American culture creates, an energy "emanating from the tensions produced by the distance between the high level of her conscious culture and an unmediated unconscious primitive landscape." Mazzaro's account for the unintelligibility of some of the poetry, particularly in *Praise to the End!,* amounts to an apology for the poet: "for com-

plete interaction, his [the reader's] sensitivity to symbolic language must equal the poet's."

As if to exemplify Mazzaro's pronouncement about psychic parity between reader and poet, John Vernon offers his explication of **"The Lost Son"** sequence in *Praise to the End!* in his essay, "Theodore Roethke's *Praise to the End!* Poems" (*The Iowa Review,* Fall 1971). In attempting to account for the entire **"Lost Son"** sequence (not to be confused with the greenhouse sequence of an equal number of poems), Vernon discusses the first few poems, particularly the opening poem, **"Where Knock is Open Wide,"** giving very little attention to the central poem, **"The Lost Son"** (until Vernon's essay very little, if nothing, of critical significance had ever been done with the "nonsense poems" making up part of this sequence). Vernon sees the dynamism of the child's world depicted in these poems; it is a synaesthetic world in which the imagery is predominantly sexual and parental. Father, mother, and self define a trinitarian identity that is always fluid because it is always holding in tension notions of separateness and mergence, of time and timelessness, of presence and absence.

In writing about the rise of a sacramental visionary mode in literature replacing the "supernaturalist figuralism" of the past, Nathan A. Scott, Jr., in his recent book, *The Wild Prayer of Longing: Poetry and the Sacred* (1971), devotes a chapter to Roethke as the exemplary poet of the sacred. Scott refers to Roethke's Blakean remark that everything that lives is holy, and he sees Roethke's sacramental verse as peculiarly American, promoting a sense of awe or wonder in the tradition of Whitman, Twain, Melville, or Thoreau. Roethke's praise of the small, calling upon snails, weeds, birds, and the like, keeps him away from the mystical, the supernatural, the "Supreme Fictions," even "God." Despite the fact that Roethke's sacramental vision is primarily limited to the nonhuman world, he deserves to be included "among the major poets using the English language in this century" because he knew "the very essence of the sacramental principle—namely, that nothing may be a sacrament unless everything is."

Brendan Galvin's "Theodore Roethke's Proverbs" (*Concerning Poetry,* Spring 1972) has given some needed attention to the proverbial, axiomatic quality of Roethke's poetry. A poem is seen as an aggregate of lines, of proverbs, separately recorded at various times in the notebooks, and it is the proverb that, for Roethke, was a way of ordering experience, "strategies" to cope with the problem of identity and to "induce his courageous plunges into the mire of the preconscious, and his subsequent returns."

What can be concluded from this criticism? Perhaps only two or three agreed-upon assertions at most—namely, that Roethke's controlling theme is the journey out of the self, that his lyric mode draws upon those of Yeats and Whitman, and that **"The Lost Son"** and the related poems forming **"The Lost Son"** sequence are central to his poetry. The rest is controversy—his mysticism, his symbolism, his range, his objectivism, his influence. Why this controversy persists (a healthy sign in itself) may be due to the absence of any thorough treatment of the poetry itself, that is, a critical assessment of more than one poem or sequence that would help establish the Roethkean mode of identity without reducing the poems to Freudian puzzles as Malkoff does. There is, of course, Burke's incisive but brief treatment of **"The Lost Son,"** but nothing more of any consequence, except perhaps Staples's analysis of a decade ago of that other longer sequence of poems, **"North American Sequence."** Burke's analysis of **"The Lost Son"** sequence is directed to the greenhouse poems, **"The Lost Son"** itself receiving only selected criticism and not an extensive analysis of the entire poem. Staples's analysis of the later sequence is not only good, but also thorough and, therefore, difficult to improve upon; yet there still remains the job of tying this last sequence into the earlier ones, a job that Staples could not have contemplated, focusing almost exclusively, as he did, on the single sequence itself. Allan Seager reports that the long poems making up **"North American Sequence"** came easily "with an unwonted confidence," that Roethke "knew what he wanted to say and he was sure of his means." If this is true, accepting the centrality of **"The Lost Son,"** the longest poem in the *Praise to The End!* sequence, then surely the one is an outgrowth of the other. There is, however, that other long sequence, **"Meditations of an Old Woman,"** that comes between the two in time and that is quite similar in technique to the later sequence. There are, then, three long poems (the shorter of the three, **"The Lost Son,"** is some seventy-five lines longer than the nearest contenders for length, the Yeatsian poems) that readily offer themselves for critical assessment as a group.

There are other reasons for treating these long poems as major pieces defining the Roethkean mode; for one, they exemplify in their own way that trinitarian sense of identity that John Vernon observed in the *Praise to the End!* sequence— the death of the father theme structuring the first poem, perhaps that of the mother the second (since Kunitz believes it was written immediately after the death of the poet's mother), and then the third poem finally concentrating on the mature self. Second, Roethke's greenhouse world, initially explored in the fourteen-poem sequence that makes up section one of *The Lost Son,* is never absent from these long poems; in fact, the greenhouse image is significant in each poem, making the group itself a unit for that reason alone. Third, each of these poems is somehow concerned with the urban world, the city, outside the "natural" world. In an essay entitled, **"On 'Identity,'"** Roethke describes his principal concerns as follows: "(1) The multiplicity, the chaos of modern life; (2) the way, the means of establishing a personal identity, a

self in the face of that chaos; (3) the nature of creation, that faculty of producing order out of disorder in the arts, particularly in poetry; and (4) the nature of God Himself." He goes on to refer to his own poem, **"Dolor,"** as a footnote to the inanimate sterility of the institution; "the 'order,'" says Roethke, "the trivia of the institution is, in human terms, a disorder, and as such, must be resisted." Resistance is precisely the method these long poems use. It might be said that they resist "false" trivia (institution trivia) with what Roethke would call "true" trivia (the trivia of "natural shapes"). It is the natural shapes running through these poems that contribute to their metric and thematic unity, but it is important to note the presence of an opposing "unnatural" imagery— in other words, intrusions from the city that become more pronounced, developing chronologically through these poems. The "kingdom of bang and blab," the disjunctive and sacred world of moss, mole, and stone depicted in **"The Lost Son,"** can become profane and deadly as, "A kingdom of stinks and sighs, / Fetor of cockroaches, dead fish, petroleum" in the later poem, **"North American Sequence."** Thus, there is money creeping into the first of these poems; there are "the self-involved" and "those who submerge themselves deliberately in trivia," on the borders of the speaker's mind in the second poem; and there is the waste and decadence "at the edge of the raw cities" in the background of the third poem.

It is not usual to stress the social aspect of Roethke's poetry; indeed his ostensible neglect of the social theme has caused critics to assume that his range is limited, even as Robert Lowell seemed to do in a rather glib remark for *The Paris Review* (1961): "The things he knows about I feel I know nothing about, flowers and so on"—although Lowell drops glibness for reverence in his poem, "For Theodore Roethke." Roethke's apparent dearth of societal referents in his poetry, however, is really no reason to assume a lack of concern for "the incredible experiences of the age"; on the contrary, his concern can be said to condition and inspire the poetry.

Finally, Roethke's poetry has a tragic dimension so far ignored by all who have written about him. Burke alludes to it when he describes Roethke's verse as having that "rare, enticing danger" about it; and Donoghue, as well, when he speaks about the loss of self as "partly the fate of being human in a hard time," that Roethke's poems, in the middle and late period, are spiritual exercises, a way toward innocence, "never finished" in their "rage for a sustaining order." I am reminded of Yeats's remarks, for he saw the tragic dimension as a controlling form in all artistic expression: "Tragic art, passionate art, the drowner of dykes, the confounder of understanding, moves us to reverie, by alluring us almost to the intensity of trance," and it is this trancelike condition that Roethke leads one to and away from in these major pieces, "for the nobleness of the arts"—to continue with Yeats's words—"is in the mingling of contraries, the extremity of sorrow, the extremity of joy, perfection of personality, the perfection of its surrender, overflowing turbulent energy, and marmorean stillness." Above all, it is this perfection of personality *and* the perfection of its surrender that Roethke accomplishes in these poems.

Joyce Carol Oates has admirably restated the problem of tragedy in modern times, and I have accepted her assumptions about the nature of tragedy—namely, that the art of tragedy grows out of a break between self and community; that at its base is fear; that although actual human life may in large part be valueless ("the multiplicity, the chaos of modern life"), tragedy asserts itself as a valuable and unique human passion, "risking loss of self in an attempt to realize self"; that if the death of God means the death of tragedy, "then a redefinition of God in terms of the furthest reaches of man's hallucinations can provide us with a new basis for tragedy." Because Roethke's three longest poems are themselves an expression, among other things, of this search for God (". . . the nature of God Himself")—a redefinition of God really—they share in the search, as well, for a tragic form.

It is the tragic form inherent in these three poems that perhaps in some way defines Roethke's appeal to later poets. What Staples calls "a dimension curiously suggestive of the epic," in referring to **"North American Sequence,"** might be Roethke's assertion of a tragic form in addition to the appeal of his deep or intuitive imagery and his verbal rhythms, especially in an age of tragic failure, an age more of pathos and nihilism. Certainly, the controversy over the essence of tragedy is healthfully active today, and that Roethke should address this controversy through his art is a testament to his appeal.

In the following three chapters I shall take up, respectively, each of these three long poems in terms of the ideas discussed so far, and in the final two chapters the question of Roethke's influence in terms of the themes and lyrical qualities of the poetry discussed as well as in the poetry of some major contemporary poets. For this purpose I have chosen James Wright and Robert Bly as representative together of one facet of the Roethkean mode of experience; James Dickey by himself representing another vision of Roethke; and Sylvia Plath and Ted Hughes representing yet another.

It would not be wrong to suppose that many contemporary poets were reacting against the studied ironies and tensions in much of the poetry of Eliot, Stevens, and Auden—perhaps Frost and some of Lowell (and one thinks, too, of Tate and Ransom)—that these poets took a second look at Roethke's romantic stamp that bore the impressions of Wordsworth, Whitman, and Yeats. What they found—the profundity of the lyric forms in the greenhouse poems and the remarkable sequences that followed—proved to have enormous appeal for them; here again was a new voice.

## Sandra Whipple Spanier (essay date Spring 1979)

SOURCE: "The Unity of the Greenhouse Sequence: Roethke's Portrait of the Artist," in *Concerning Poetry*, Vol. 12, No. 1, Spring, 1979, pp. 53-60.

[*In the following essay, Spanier examines autobiographic allusions to the creative process revealed in the* "Greenhouse Sequence" *from Roethke's* The Lost Son and Other Poems.]

Simplicity is deceptive in Theodore Roethke's "greenhouse sequence," which includes the first thirteen poems of *The Lost Son and Other Poems* (1848) plus one other poem inserted in two later editions of the group. The works are short and descriptive. They contain few, if any, abstract or philosophical statements. On first reading, the sequence may appear to be little more than an album of snapshots—true in color and sharply focused, to be sure—taken in and around the greenhouse that Roethke's father operated in Saginaw, Michigan throughout the poet's childhood. Roethke seems to have arranged the snapshots in a careful order, though (even his later addition is precisely placed within the group), and it is only when we view the sequence as a whole that the full significance of this body of poems emerges.

There appears to be a general movement forward through the sequence, from the pre-natal life of the cuttings in the first poem to the crisp, perfect blossom of the carnation in the last. Though he is not speaking here specifically about the greenhouse sequence, Roethke's own comments support a cyclical reading of the poems:

> Each poem . . . is complete in itself; yet each in a sense is a stage in a kind of struggle out of the slime; part of a slow spiritual progress; an effort to be born, and later to become something more. . . . At least you can see that the method is cyclic. I believe that to go forward as a spiritual man it is necessary first to go back. Any history of the psyche (or allegorical journey) is bound to be a succession of experiences, similar yet dissimilar. There is a perpetual slipping-back, then a going-forward; but there is *some* "progress."

As I see it, the fourteen greenhouse poems run the gamut of human experience in more or less chronological order: birth, the struggle to survive in a harsh environment, growth, death, eternity. But the sequence can also be read more specifically as a documentary of the process of artistic creation, from the first pre-conscious stirrings of thought, through the artist's struggle to resist the forces which work against his creation and to develop it fully, to the finished product, which may either fail and be rejected or succeed in achieving perfection and, thereby, eternal existence, Grecian-urn fashion. In this reading, the greenhouse sequence becomes Roethke's "portrait of the artist."

Several critics have sensed that these poems, though they are concrete and simple, might also be read symbolically or allegorically. Kenneth Burke writes that they are "clearly the imagistic figuring of a human situation." He likens them to Aesop's fables featuring flowers instead of animals, saying, "The poet need but be as accurate as he can, in describing the flowers objectively; and while aiming at this, he comes upon corresponding human situations, as it were by redundancy." Richard Blessing adds that "in the greenhouse sequence the reader is asked to supply the abstractions himself—or to leave them out, if he prefers." Theodore Roethke himself invites a symbolic reading, or, rather, demands one, when he calls the greenhouse "my symbol for the whole of life, a womb, a heaven-on-earth."

It becomes evident, then, that these simple poems have been crafted precisely enough and arranged carefully enough to be able to bear the weight of abstraction, just as a perfect crystal goblet, if placed properly, is said to be able to bear the weight of a person standing on it. I will take Roethke at his word that the greenhouse represents "the whole of life" and will examine the sequence as a microcosm of human life, and, more specifically, as an allegorical depiction of the process of creating a work of art.

In my view, the poems fall into several groups, each marking a stage in the "life cycle" of a work of art: (I) pre-conscious beginnings; (II) the "struggle out of the slime"—crude, but tenacious existence; (III) obstacles to survival; (IV) nurture and growth; (V) soaring beyond ordinary experience—striving for perfection; and (VI) products of the effort.

Consistent with the complexity of their subject, these poems are packed with paradox and the tension of opposites. In them there is dynamic interplay between life and death, beauty and ugliness, fecundity and decay, creation and destruction, activity and stillness, past and present. The greenhouse itself is a paradoxical image, as Burke has remarked, embodying "a peculiar balance of the natural and the artificial."

In looking at these poems, then, I will try to "supply the abstractions," as I believe we are permitted and even invited to do, focusing on the part each poem plays in the allegory and considering the paradoxical imagery which Roethke employs to depict the complex, dynamic, often messy and painful process of artistic creation.

I have called the first phase of the creative process "preconscious beginnings," and the poems **"Cuttings"** and **"Cuttings (later)"** belong in this group. Very little "happens" in these poems; in the eight lines of **"Cuttings,"** we simply view sticks planted in loam slowly awakening to life:

> One numb of growth
> Nudges a sand-crumb loose,
> Pokes through a musty sheath
> Its pale tendrilous horn.

**"Cuttings"** describes the first stirrings of vegetal life on a microscopic scale: we can even see the "intricate stem-fur" on the sticks and their "small cells." The only motion here is the loosening of a grain of sand, yet Roethke has managed to endow such a still scene with a sense of potential vigor in his choice of action verbs: the sticks "droop," small cells "bulge," slips keep "coaxing up" water, a nub of growth "nudges" and "pokes." Thus, in this simplest of poems, we can see Roethke's dynamic and paradoxical imagery operating. In stillness and dormancy there is activity and life.

**"Cuttings (later)"** continues the description of the sticks slowly coming to life, but here Roethke explicitly relates "This urge, wrestle, resurrection of dry sticks" to human experience by asking

> What saint strained so much,
> Rose on such lopped limbs to a new life?

He tells us that he feels the stirrings of life in himself; we are witnessing the rejuvenation of a stilted, "lopped" human being beginning a new way of life. To begin to supply abstractions, this could well be a portrait of the artist himself, whose soul has been dried out and pruned by conventional existence and who is beginning to recognize an inner calling to his art. He feels new life coming to him from within, independent of his will, "sucking and sobbing" in his veins and bones. As the artist traditionally looks backward and inward to encounter life at its most basic, so the speaker tells us, "I quail, lean to beginnings, sheath-wet." Again, there is a tension of opposing forces in the imagery. There is simultaneous movement of growth in both directions: the saint "*rose*" to a new life and small waters are "seeping *upward*," while the stems are "struggling to put *down* feet" (italics mine). Similarly, the sprouts "break out" into an external environment, yet there is movement backward and inward as the speaker leans to beginnings. This imagery reinforces the allegorical applications of this poem to the experience of the artist in that an artist's work involves both out-reaching communication and private introspection.

The second group of poems—**"Root Cellar," "Forcing House,"** and **"Weed Puller"**—abounds with crude but tenacious life, depicting "the struggle out of the slime," to use Roethke's terms. On the allegorical level, we witness in this group the artist's determination that this germ of a work of art will survive. **"Root Cellar"** presents a vivid description of vegetal abundance and fecundity in a dark cellar. We are told that

Nothing would sleep in that cellar, dank as a ditch,
Bulbs broke out of boxes hunting for chinks in the
    dark,
Shoots dangled and drooped,
Lollying obscenely from mildewed crates,
Hung down long yellow evil necks, like tropical
    snakes.

Again, the concrete description calls up more abstract associations with human life. In the root cellar we may be reminded of the abundance and tenacity of human life, of people striving and struggling to survive in the most adverse conditions. More specifically, the activity in the root cellar parallels the gestation of a work in the artist's mind. Like the shoots and bulbs, the poet's thoughts and feelings at this stage are chaotic, ineffectual, unpresentable, maybe even a little obscene, but, nevertheless, struggling hard to survive. There is little order but much life:

Nothing would give up life:
Even the dirt kept breathing a small breath.

Paradoxically, this poem about fecundity and the will to live is set in an environment of darkness and decay, amid "a congress of stinks," just as much art emerges from unpleasantness, pain, and confusion.

In the **"Forcing House,"** there is a feeling of unnatural vigor as the plants are shot with nutrients and pulse with forced steam. The vines, scums, mildews, and blossoms

All pulse with the knocking pipes
That drip and sweat,
Sweat and drip,
Swelling the roots with steam and stench,
Shooting up lime and dung and ground bones,—
Fifty summers in motion at once,
As the live heat billows from pipes and pots.

The mechanisms in the greenhouse mercilessly manipulate nature, trying to improve upon it, just as a poet may not-so-gently "work over" his budding creation in order to perfect it. Language and experience are removed from their normal, natural states and are artificially manipulated, compressed, and intensified by the poet, who, like the operator of the forcing house is perfectly capable of putting "Fifty summers in motion at once." As in the poems already discussed, there is paradox here, too, with nature and artifice in opposition. In the greenhouse and in the artist's mind, natural entities are roughly and sometimes cruelly handled, precisely because the "torturer" (the florist or the artist) cares for them and wants them to improve and thrive.

In **"Weed Puller"** there is a contrast between the lovely public spectacle of

Lilies, pale-pink cyclamen, roses,
Whole fields lovely and inviolate,—

and the weed puller's private view of the underside as he, "down in that fetor of weeds," is

Hacking at black hairy roots,—
Those lewd monkey-tailes hanging from drain
    holes,—
Digging into the soft rubble underneath.

This underneath view seems analogous to the sometimes messy "root layer" of the artist's mind, filled with things repressed, forgotten, or decayed, but very much alive and the breeding ground for beautiful creations. While others view only the pretty public blooming of the finished work, the artist, like the weed puller, must engage in a private struggle, grovelling in the messy source of it all, trying to create beauty and order out of chaos:

Tugging all day at perverse life:
The indignity of it!—
With everything blooming above me.

The artist, too, may find his subterranean work treacherous going, in terms of his own mental health, for the poet describes himself as

Crawling on all fours,
Alive, in a slippery grave.

**"Orchids," "Moss-Gathering,"** and **"Big Wind"** are included in the group I call "obstacles to survival" because they depict some stumbling blocks in the creative process, both external and internal. **"Orchids"** is a poem of quiet seduction and deadly beauty. The orchids are sensuous and alluring, and they seem almost human: they lean out over the path in the greenhouse and sway close to the face, they are "delicate as a young bird's tongue," they have "soft luminescent fingers," their "musky smell comes even stronger" when the heat goes down and the moonlight falls on them through the glass, and they slowly draw in air through "their fluttery fledgling lips." Lovely as they are, though, the flowers are insidious and must be resisted. The imagery points up their treachery and the need for caution when dealing with them. The orchids are "adder-mouthed," they come out "soft and deceptive," and they drift down from their beds of moss like "devouring infants." The sensuous yet sinister descriptions suggest that the orchids may represent sensuous, worldly pleasures, which, however pleasant-seeming and attractive, may divert the artist from his real work and eventually destroy him.

In **"Moss-Gathering"** the obstacle to creation is a sense of guilt within the artist himself. Pulling up naturally-growing moss to be used in a cemetery basket, a "made" object, makes the speaker feel mean:

> As if I had broken the natural order of things in
>     that swampland;
> Disturbed some rhythm, old and of vast impor
>     tance,
> By pulling off flesh from the living planet.

The conflict and danger here are within the artist. In order to create an art object, any artist must somewhat destroy "the natural order of things," and in this creation there is a sense of loss, "As if I had committed, against the whole scheme of life, a desecration." These conscientious pangs may not be completely undesirable—things to be erased from the artist's mind—but they are potentially crippling to him and do represent an obstacle to creative productivity and, therefore, must be reckoned with.

**"Big Wind,"** analyzed in detail by Kenneth Burke, is a metaphorical narrative of survival as the greenhouse rides out a violent rainstorm just as a ship would ride out a storm at sea. This poem is a portrait of endurance, of something battling against an external assault and finally emerging unscathed. While the owners help by draining the manure machine, watching the pressure gauge on the rusty boilers, and stuffing burlap into holes left by blown-out glass, the greenhouse "hove into the teeth of it, / The core and pith of that ugly storm." The fragile glass house, which finally "sailed until the calm morning, / Carrying her full cargo of roses," may be likened to the delicate (or, at least, sensitive) mind of the artist, as it struggles to survive the attack of a harsh and hostile world upon its sensibilities and emerges from the battle intact, carrying its "full cargo of roses"—its beautiful and cherished creations.

Assuming that the artistic impulse has germinated, clung stubbornly to crude existence, and surmounted the obstacles of insidious distraction, potentially crippling inner reservations, and overt external assault, the time has come for care and nurture so that its fullest growth may be realized. The next three poems in the sequence—**"Old Florist," "Frau Bauman, Frau Schmidt, and Frau Schwartze,"** and **"Transplanting"**—explore the theme of care and growth.

**"Old Florist"** is a portrait of a man close to life, nurturing, caring for, and protecting the flowers. Again, there is paradox in that his loving care often consists of destruction. The same "hump of a man" who gently fans life into wilted sweetpeas with his hat and stands all night watering roses also stamps dirt into pots, flicks and picks leaves, pinches back asters, and drowns a bug "in one spit of tobacco juice." Creation and destruction are juxtaposed in the greenhouse as they are in art; the artist must prune and selectively destroy parts of his work in order that it be sound.

**"Frau Bauman, Frau Schmidt, and Frau Schwartze"** depicts three "ancient ladies" bustling about the greenhouse caring for the flowers. It did not appear in the first edition of the greenhouse poems but was later inserted between **"Old Florist"** and **"Transplanting"** in the volume *The Waking* (1953) and more recently in *Words for the Wind* (1958). Louis Martz has complained that this poem with its "Yeatsian" flavor is an "intrusion" and is out of place in the simple greenhouse sequence: "it breaks the natural, intimate presence of those earlier poems, and it ought to be printed elsewhere in future editions of Roethke's poetry." But when the sequence is viewed in terms of the groupings I have outlined, it does belong here, for the three ladies are also nurturing creatures, sometimes even called "earth mothers." We are told that they straightened blossoms, tied and tucked the stems, "teased out the seed that the cold kept asleep," and "They trellised the sun; they plotted for more than themselves." These vigorous, vigilant "nurses of nobody else" are peacemakers, bustling along rows, "keeping creation at ease." Past and present come together in the final lines, as the mature poet remembers how they picked him up, "a spindly kid," and nurtured him, and he tells us.

> Now, when I'm alone and cold in my bed,
> They still hover over me,
> These ancient leathery crones,
> With their bandannas stiffened with sweat,
> And their thorn-bitten wrists,
> And their snuff-laden breath blowing lightly over
>     me in my
>         first sleep.

**"Transplanting,"** too, is a poem of care and nurture. We watch sure hands swiftly and skillfully transplant the young plants into loam and set them in the warm sun. In this poem, the last of the "nurturing" group, we finally view the triumphant culmination of this tender care, dramatically, as though in slow motion photography:

> The young horns winding and unwinding,
> Creaking their thin spines,
> The underleaves, the smallest buds
> Breaking into nakedness,
> The blossoms extending
> Out into the sweet air,
> The whole flower extending outward,
> Stretching and reaching.

"Stretching and reaching" is the central motion of the next poem, **"Child on Top of a Greenhouse,"** though we have moved from the realm of plants to that of human beings. In this seven-line poem, quite simply, a child has climbed to the top of a greenhouse and is looking down through the glass at the flowers below and at the people on the ground looking up at him and shouting. The child's climbing where no one has ventured before (much to the alarm of those bound to the earth by aging joints or common sense) is much like the artist's striving to soar above the known and ordinary. The analogy is strengthened when we remember that Roethke called the greenhouse the "whole of life." The poet, like the child, wants to stand atop it, to conquer and master the summit, but it is a terrifying, lonely, and thrilling quest, baffling and upsetting to the less ambitious. Roethke has captured the terror and exhilaration by packing a tremendous amount of action into this very short poem. All is in violent motion with the wind billowing out the child's britches, splinters of glass and dried putty cracking under his feet, flowers "starting up like accusers," the glass "flashing with sunlight," a few clouds "all rushing eastward," elms "lunging and tossing like horses," and "everyone, everyone pointing up and shouting!"

The final two poems depict the possible end products of this artistic quest: the reject on the junk heap and the enduring perfect creation. In **"Flower-Dump"** we view the junk heap. The flowers, weeds, molds, dead leaves, and clumps of roots which have been "pitched" and left to decay are topped by

> One swaggering head
> Over the dying, the newly dead.

This tulip is like the latest literary addition to the artist's wastebasket. Happily though, Roethke does not end on the teeming trash heap his series of poems about artistic creation. Instead, he leaves us with **"Carnations,"** a poem about this crisp, intricate, classically perfect flower. The description of the carnation evokes images of the classic age of Greece: the leaves are "Corinthian scrolls," the air is cool "as if drifting down from wet hemlocks," and the poem ends with the description of

> A crisp hyacinthine coolness,
> Like that clear autumnal weather of eternity,
> The windless perpetual morning above a Septem
>    ber cloud.

This still life of cool perfection and timelessness is the perfect culmination for this series of poems about artistic creation, for producing such a classic *objet d'art* is the goal of any artist.

In the greenhouse sequence Roethke has led us through the whole creative process. We have witnessed the most primitive stirring of an artistic impulse, its first crude but determined efforts to exist, the obstacles to its survival, the nurturing and development of the work, the artist's soaring beyond everyday existence, his failures, and the culmination of his effort in the creation of a classic, eternal work of beauty.

Roethke called his greenhouse his symbol for the whole of life. I would offer a more particular metaphorical equivalent for the greenhouse as it appears in this sequence of poems. As it is a place in which nature is imitated, artificially cultivated, and improved upon, it is much like the mind of the artist, who draws upon nature as the source of his art but manipulates and stylizes it, and, if he is successful, fashions a product which may be more "real" and enduring than the piece of nature it imitates. A work of art, like a hot house flower, may be more perfect than its uncultivated counterpart in nature. Luckily for us, too, the greenhouse is transparent, so that we may look with Roethke into the artistic mind as it creates a work of art.

### Kermit Vanderbilt (essay date 1979)

SOURCE: "Theodore Roethke as a Northwest Poet," in *Northwest Perspectives: Essays on the Culture of the Pacific Northwest,* compiled and edited by Edwin R. Bingham and Glen A. Love, University of Washington Press, 1979, pp. 186-216.

[*In the following essay, Vanderbilt examines Roethke's regional self-identity and distinct American voice, particularly as influenced by his Midwestern origins and later years in Seattle.*]

To explore the relationship between Theodore Roethke and the Northwest is very satisfying for several personal reasons. I was Roethke's colleague in his late years at the University of Washington. He knew I admired his poetry, but I was somehow unable to accord him the repeated and fulsome praise I knew that he deserved and almost insatiably required. I now intend to give proper homage to Roethke and make amends for the perversity of my earlier restraint. I shall also atone for my failure in never having shared with Roethke the regional impulse in his later poetry. After his posthumous **The Far Field** appeared in 1964, I began to discover how important the Northwest was to Roethke. Since then, I have followed the steady flow of critical analyses, revaluations, and rising estimates of his lyrical virtuosity and dynamic vision. (How the insecure Roethke would have savored this belated recognition!) Still absent in this criticism is the importance for Roethke of what D. H. Lawrence termed "the spirit of place."

The neglect is understandable. Testimony abounds that Roethke was in no sense to be mistaken for a regional poet. The evidence is formidable enough that I want to assemble it rather fully at once. I shall then argue the positive case for Roethke as a man and poet whose total career can be understood as a growing possession of his American geography and selfhood. Finally, I want to offer a few comments about

Roethke in the light of standard conclusions which so often appear in discussions of literary regionalism, at least since recognition of Faulkner. I mean the *pro forma* consideration of regionalism as *initial* response. The writer of major talent then dissolves, transforms, and transcends this regionalism and moves outward to the national, international, and cosmic reaches of his sensibility. That a literary region in American might claim a healthy autonomy through its own shaping myths and archetypes, a unique reason for being that is fully realized in its own necessary form—this possibility has seldom been entertained seriously by our literary historians and critics. Allen Tate observed in 1929, for example, that American regionalists like Lindsay, Sandburg, and Masters, let alone the would-be epic poet like Hart Crane, suffered from the absence of a truly national literature, a "homogeneous body of beliefs and feelings into which the poet may be educated." In particular, "the spiritual well-being of the West," said Tate, "depends upon its success in assimilating the cultural tradition of the older sections." But Tate then hoped that future writers in the "provinces" could help somehow to solve the problem of a national literature by releasing local wellsprings and creating ancillary pipelines into an eventual mainstream culture (my imagery, not Tate's). Only recently, one of our best poetry critics, Fred Moramarco, reviewed a collection of dubiously "Western" poetry and then went on to advance the companion, or universal, theory of regional offerings. The best author will select his local materials with an eye and ear responsive to significant universals. Unlike Tate, Moramarco does not foresee a vital literary regionalism in the future from which larger "verities" can emerge, for he doubts that the distinctive region itself any longer exists. Instead, we live in "post-McLuhan media saturated global village uniformity." The sad result is that "the idea of a regional literature in any meaningful sense died in this country with the passing of Frost, Faulkner, Jeffers and a few other major literary talents who were able to isolate regional qualities and discover the universal verities within them." Compulsively echoed and rephrased by lesser critics over the past fifty years, these demands for significant national and universal expression have encouraged a fair amount of misdirected ambition in the careers of American authors who might otherwise have been content to embrace and vitalize the particular history, folklore, and landscape of their region. Among the victims of this confused purpose, I am afraid, was our poet Theodore Roethke.

## I.

No interpreter of Roethke, biographer or critic, has discovered that in his life or poetry Roethke drew either a strong identity or consistent nourishment from his locale. He was above all, we are told, a private, meditative, hermetic sort of man and poet. He derived from his natural surroundings a stream of correspondences to express the agonized progress of the lonely self in its mysterious and sometimes wondrous drive toward transcendence and beatitude.

Biographer Allan Seager writes, for example, that for Roethke, "It was himself he had to sing, not the circumambient world. He only used that." And Seager confirms his judgment with the testimony of Stanley Kunitz, whose friendship dated from Roethke's first teaching job at Lafayette College in the early thirties: "Stanley Kunitz says [Roethke] was not a really close observer, and, of course, he did not need to be since everything around him was useful to him only as signatures of himself." When Roethke traveled, he was interested in meeting a few interesting people rather than touring the monuments or natural wonder of historic places. Many of his friends and colleagues—from Lafayette to Michigan State to Pennsylvania State to Bennington and (after 1947) the University of Washington—would probably concur with Denis Donoghue that Roethke was the autonomous poet who never attached himself to an ideology or a geographical region: "He never set up shop as a Left Wing poet or a Right Wing poet or a Catholic poet or a New England poet or a Southern poet or a California poet; he never claimed privilege in any region of feeling."

Donoghue's regional list was casual. We may inquire into his two prominent omissions—the Michigan Saginaw Valley of Roethke's childhood and the Pacific Northwest of his final sixteen years. Ample data suggests that Roethke felt no spirit of place in the environs of Saginaw. Seager puts it this way:

> There is no memory of Roethke hanging around the old folks listening, like Faulkner, and his old folks were German, anyway. Their stories would have led him back to the Old Country which never interested him. He also ignores all the vivid racy tales of the lumber boom, tales that expressed courage, will, and cunning that might have engaged another man. Unlike Allen Tate or Robert Lowell, he ignores in his poetry the events of his region's history. He must have been aware of the Indians, for he collected a shoebox full of flint arrowheads in his rambles along the riverbanks. But, of course, many boys did that.

Years after, during the first mental breakdown in late 1935 that terminated his brief teaching stint at Michigan State University, Roethke recorded the following insight about himself in a long medical questionnaire: "Afraid of being localized in space, i.e. a particular place like W. E. Leonard in Madison. Question: What is the *name* of this? Hate some rooms in that sense, a victim of claustrophobia (sp)? Wasn't Dillinger a victim of this? Aren't many of the criminal leader types of this sort [*sic*]." The illuminating reference to Dillinger connects with Roethke's poetic self-image as the outsider and points to his regional alienation even earlier. In one of his college essays at the University of Michigan, Roethke had discussed "the poet as criminal," the instance being François Villon. Early on in Michigan, then, Roethke felt himself a lonely poet and species of outrageous free spirit. Or as Seager provocatively sees it, Roethke "may have begun to suspect that poetry, having no voice in the community where he lived, was antisocial. . . . Poetry was akin to crime. Strange and unwelcome in middle-class America, the poet was a criminal." Though he admired Whitman, the young Roethke would not emulate the people's bard and camarado. He was, instead, the tough-guy poet. "I may look like a beer salesman, but I'm a poet," he announced defensively by way of introduction to the president of Bennington College at a job interview in New York early in the forties. Even through the fifties and into his final years, he continued to fashion and embroider the fiction of the gangster element in his life. He would relate how he had once been on close terms with the Detroit underworld and that the notorious Purple Gang had once "offered to bump my Aunt Margaret off for me. As a favor, you understand." The cadences here might have been lifted directly out of one of the fabrications of Jay Gatsby.

Seager effectively discounts these "memories" of regional outlawry. "In the Thirties, Ted was not near Detroit long enough to ingratiate himself with the gang lords." Excepting the one year in Michigan during the mid-thirties, he was successively at Harvard, Lafayette, and Penn State, safely out of touch with Michigan and its urban underworld.

His first two books of poetry firmly support the thesis that Roethke was never a midwestern regionalist, either by sympathetic identity or literary example. Before *Open House* appeared in 1941, ten of the poems were anthologized in a volume titled *New Michigan Verse* (1940). Hungry for a reputation, Roethke was delighted to be published but, says Seager, "he had a few misgivings also because he did not want to be known as a regional poet." Roethke rather explicitly denies, also, any regional impulse in the Saginaw greenhouse poems which create the celebrated breakthrough in the mid-forties and dominate his second book, *The Lost Son* (1948). When he comments on this work in progress to Kenneth Burke, Roethke stresses not the significance of local place but rather the intention to "show the full erotic and even religious significance that I sense in a big greenhouse: a kind of man-made Avalon, Eden, or paradise." The inspiration and metaphor of the organic greenhouse world appeared to be mythic and not regional. Outside the childhood greenhouse, to be sure, were a community and a region, but the growing youth came to feel this area as annihilating space, either a claustrophobic "particular place" or a pitiless waste land. In a vivid notebook jotting later in the fifties, Roethke remembered "the Siberian pitilessness, the essential ruthlessness of the Middle West as I knew it."

Roethke came to the Northwest in 1947 to join the English faculty at the University of Washington, and it remained his academic address until his death in the summer of 1963. Yet some colleagues who were closest to him there have told me that he was never a chamber of commerce spokesman for the Northwest. Even before he took up residence in Seattle, Roethke in the East expressed "misgivings about going even further into the provinces" than ever before. When he arrived in mid-September of 1947, he mentioned his initial fears to Kenneth Burke: "I'm afraid I'm going to be overwhelmed by nice people: it's a kind of vast Scarsdale, it would seem. Bright, active women, with blue hair, and well-barbered males. The arts and the 'East' seem to cow them." Neither pub life nor cafe society had much of a chance in this Northwest outpost. "I found, to my horror," Roethke continued, "that you have to go a mile from the campus even to get beer, and there are no bars for anything except beer and light wines in the whole of Seattle, except in private clubs. And there are no decent restaurants, either, as far as I can find out."

Several months later, he wrote again to Burke. Living in the Northwest, it was now clear, amounted to a sort of physical and spiritual exile. "I tell you, Kenneth," he wrote, "this far in the provinces you get a little nutty and hysterical: there's the feeling that all life is going on but you're not there." Within the year, he had reverted to the earlier self-image of the poet as at best an outlaw celebrity in his tame middle-class community. "As the only serious poet within 1,000 miles of Seattle," he wrote another friend in the East, "I find I have something of the status of a bank robber in Oklahoma or a congressman in the deep south."

In 1951 he moved out of the University district to North Edmonds, where the house offered a splendid view of Puget Sound. "But oddly enough," he wrote to Babette Deutsch, "it's lonely and I resent the 30 minutes drive each way." After his marriage in 1953 he lived in Bellevue on Lake Washington and finally bought a house across the lake nearer to the University in 1957. But one should not easily conclude that Roethke had slowly become a loyal Northwesterner. Throughout his tenure at the University of Washington, he was inquiring into jobs elsewhere or applying for Fulbrights and other grants that might bring him relief or delivery from the scene at Seattle and the University.

This alienation was caused, in part, by what to him was a depressing climate in the Northwest. In his first or second year, he entered the following verses in a notebook.

> What eats us here? Is this infinity too close,
> These mountains and these clouds? On clearing
>     days
> We act like something else; a race arrived
> From caves . . . [*sic*]

> Bearlike, come stumbling into the sun, avoid that
>   shade
> Still lingering in patches, spotting the green
>   ground.

Writing to Princess Marguerite Caetani (founder and editor of *Botteghe Oscure*), he ruefully exclaimed in 1954, "Such a stupid letter!—even worse than usual. But it's partly the weather, I think—the sun hardly ever gets out in these parts. (San Francisco and Berkeley were wonderfully warm & non-foggy the week I was there.)" The climate affected not only his disposition. His physical health also deteriorated. Seager writes: "His arthritis grew worse and became more painful in Seattle's damp climate. (He kept trying to get a job in California for the winter terms where he could be in the sun. He liked the sun.) He seemed to have a permanent bursitis in his elbow, and what he called 'spurs' in his shoulder for which he often got cortisone injections."

Small wonder, then, if Roethke in his later poetry appears not to celebrate the Northwest but, instead, meditates upon death and the Roethkean soul's "drive toward God." Frederick Hoffman recalled that in the summer of 1957, Roethke confided "that he was much concerned with the mysteries and paradoxes of death, and that his new poetry reflected these concerns. It did just that. . . ." Even in the **"North American Sequence,"** William Snodgrass eloquently dismisses the native and regional note and hears instead a predominant urge to regression and death. The "burden" of such poems as **"Meditation at Oyster River"** and **"The Long Waters,"** says Snodgrass, is "a desire to escape *all* form and shape, to lose all awareness of otherness . . . through re-entrance into eternity conceived as womb, into water as woman, into earth as goddess-mother."

Other critics have echoed this conclusion, and some have gone on to remark that Roethke in the Northwest years scarcely seems to have acknowledged the ordinary human life of his community and region, let alone the political and social crises of the nation and world. Perhaps the capacity to respond to a regional *ethos* in America is linked to the capacity to respond to a national *ethos*—to feel the pulsebeat of the nation in the whole and in its distinguishing parts. The people of Washington State after the War were affected not only by the Canwell Committee political witchhunts, or logging and aircraft prosperity, but more broadly by Little Rock, McCarthyism, Eisenhower and Nixon, and a standardized civilization exploding with machines, gas pumps, and supermarkets. Where does this life appear in the poetry of Roethke? Simply, it is not there. But in recent years we have glimpsed, in the published notebooks, a Roethke to some degree conscious of both the humdrum and "provincial" and also the national temper of Cold War life in the Eisenhower fifties. But he appears through it all a man tormented by his incapacity to absorb this life, either concretely or abstractly,

into his imagination, to ventilate his airtight broodings of self with poems ranging from his Seattle A & P to the shoddy goings-on of Joseph McCarthy and Richard M. Nixon. Being aware of a regional America, he muses, is to be sensitive to the lonely limits of the "provincial" experience lived simultaneously within an American civilization of major shortcomings and meager returns. In short, he cannot go the poetic route of a Hart Crane, Williams, Lowell, or Ginsberg. The following prose excerpts from the published notebooks reveal something of the distinguishing tone of the postwar decade—from Seattle to the nation's capital—which a lonely Roethke heard and felt but was unable to convert into his poetry.

> Me, if I'm depressed, I go down to the A & P and admire the lemons and bananas, the meat and milk.

> Crane's assumption: the machine is important; we must put it in our lives, make it part of our imaginative life. Answer: the hell it is. An ode to an icebox is possible, since it contains fruit and meat.

> Perhaps our only important invention is the concept of the good-guy.

> After Mr. Richard M. Nixon, I feel that sincerity is no longer possible as a public attitude.

> . . . there are intense spiritual men in America as well as the trimmers, time-servers, cliché-masters, high-grade mediocrities.

> Democracy: where the semi-literate make laws and the illiterate enforce them.

> Was it my time for writing poems about McCarthy or my time for sending out fresh salmon or the time of playing happy telephone or my time for dictating memoranda about what's wrong with America? . . . or my time for crying.

> I think no one has ever spoken upon the peculiar, the absolute—can I say—cultural loneliness of the American provincial creative intellectual. I don't mention this as something to be sighed over, worried about, written about—simply say it is simple fact that the American is alone in space and time—history is not with him, he has no one to talk to— Well, the British do.

> As a provincial, an American, no fool, I hope, but an ignoramus, I believe we need Europe—more than she needs us: the Europe of Char, of Perse, of Malraux, of Michaux, those living men with their sense of history, of what a freeman is.

An argument can be fashioned, nevertheless, that despite his poetic escape from the ordinary or critical affairs of his fellow earthlings, Roethke in Seattle was, in the most expressive and traditional manner, the poet of his place and time. In his dark confessional pages he spoke powerfully of the poet's spiritual despairs and searchings. Were they not shared, however diffusely, by Northwest folk and in fact, by all addled Americans whose lives were without ties and ballasts in the new global chaos of the mid-twentieth century? Another vivid notebook entry, presumably self-descriptive, supports this view of Roethke's American career and might aptly serve as the poet's own modern epitaph:

> The grandeurs of the crazy man alone,
> Himself the middle of a roaring world.

## II.

Other Roethkes insistently emerge from the biographical pages. They blur together to suggest the man and poet who related himself positively to a place of birth, a region of his formative youth, a native land, and finally, a second region of his mature years. Allan Seager underplays this opposite story. The temptation is familiar to all who have conceived or labored to write the coherent biography of a complicated human being. Roethke's shifting masks and identities were varied and complex. He was a man of fierce, self-rending ambivalences. In addition to the previous examples of disaffection from region and country, leading to final escape into the metaphysical, one discovers also Roethke's embracement variously of the communal, the regional, and the national.

Though I am in search of a Northwest Roethke, I should briefly touch the earlier years for the evidence that he felt a certain positive spirit of place and attachment in America before 1947. In the early forties when Roethke arrived at rich and presumably sophisticated Bennington, Seager was struck by his new colleague's "ambiguous fear and admiration of the rich, his ambiguous fear and admiration of the East" which seemed to stir "all sorts of atavistic and Middle Western antagonisms" in the man. Seager did not know then that this Midwest identity had recently become a central concern for Roethke. He had applied for a Guggenheim grant just before. The poetry would advance beyond the private rejection and anger he had earlier expressed in regard to provincial Michigan and the "hideous" life of his youth. "A series of poems about the America I knew in my middle-western childhood," he wrote, "has been on my mind for some time; no flag-waving or hoopla, but poems about people in a particular suburbia." Though he failed to receive the grant, Roethke persisted, and in his successful Guggenheim application three years later he described two of his three projects to be the writing of a distinctly regional verse:

(1) a dramatic-narrative piece in prose and verse about Michigan and Wisconsin, past and present, which would center around the return of Paul Bunyan as a kind of enlightened and worldly folk-hero.

(2) a series of lyrics about the Michigan countryside which have symbolical values. I have already begun these. They are not mere description, but have at least two levels of reference.

To William Carlos Williams, who would understand this regional programme, Roethke worried over "the Paul Bunyan idea. The more I think about it, the less I like it. But I've got to get some device to organize some of my ideas & feelings about Michigan, etc.—not too solemn or God bless America or Steve Benétish. Maybe it's worth trying, anyway." When *The Lost Son* appeared in 1948, readers would find that Roethke had organized his "ideas & feelings about Michigan" not within the Bunyan myth but rather in a primordial myth of the child's Edenic greenhouse world. In the "Michigan" poetry, Roethke did not fulfill his intensely regional undertaking after all. Nor did the outer vegetal life register on the inner Roethke except largely as a human metaphor, to be equated, shaped, verbalized. But the urge to regional description and symbolization, as well as to natural immersion and union, had begun. It remained a part of his creative impulse which he would continue to explore and ultimately frame and express in the Northwest.

In a 1953 appearance on BBC's "The Third Programme," Roethke introduced himself as a poet of unmistakably regional origins. "Everyone knows that America is a continent," he said, "but few Europeans realize the various and diverse parts of this land." He then described his own Saginaw Valley and termed it "a wonderful place for a child to grow up in and around."

Again in an interview shortly before his death, Roethke fondly reminisced about Michigan scenes of his childhood which "still remained in his mind" to influence his poems. Other testimony is now at hand to support this version of Roethke who clearly felt a decisive part of his identity as a man and sensibility as a poet had received salutary strength from the region of his earliest years. It remained as a residue of positive and cherished memory to sustain the maturing poet and enrich the strong poems in his last book which I shall turn to in a moment.

Sometime in his early development, as Roethke understood himself to be an Upper-Midwesterner, he also sensed another part of his identity which should be noted before we enter the Northwest phase. He came to feel his roots as an American. The process is too subtle to trace with absolute certainty. After he became assured of a reputation, Roethke almost emphatically portrayed himself as having been, early on, a national poet in the American grain. Though he was an avid reader of the English poets and dramatists, he recalled first of all his American masters whom, he said, "*early,* when it really matters, I read, and really read, Emerson (prose mostly), Thoreau, Whitman." And to a degree his memory is corroborated by student documents. His notes from a college course in American literature at Michigan in the late twenties include these releaving comments on Whitman:

> What are we to say of Whitman as poet? Selection? Defied rules. Can art be formless NO!
> 1) An undying energy of life—a tang—vitalizing something.
> 2) A certain largeness—deals with deep things in life on a large scale.
> 3) Most great poetry is primal?

In a composition for his rhetoric class, Roethke's theme was his strong response to nature. Again are the hints of a developing American consciousness: "I know that Cooper is a fraud—that he doesn't give a true sense of the sublimity of American scenery. I know that Muir and Thoreau and Burroughs speak the truth." One can scarcely detect these "American" influences in the deeply private poetry that would soon come from Roethke's pen in the early post-college years. No doubt he had to discover other aspects of selfhood—his personal, sexual, and family identity—before he possessed any version of a representative Roethke, Mid-westerner or American.

Soon after *Open House* appeared in 1941, Roethke seems to have felt a new growth away from the tight limits of this early poetic form and experience as well as, so we may infer, a movement toward a larger, a more inclusive identity. "My first book was much too wary," he wrote Kenneth Burke a few years later, "much too gingerly in its approach to experience; rather dry in tone and restricted in rhythm." And in a pair of anecdotes to Allan Seager in the mid-forties, Roethke illuminates the early making of a self-consciously national poet. The first is a letter after he arrived at Bennington: "It seems I was hired because, according to the president, Lewis Jones, I'm 'a grass roots American with classic tastes.' So, simple fellow that I am, I'm to teach a course in American literature (just people that interest me) next year." Though he is amused by this American version of himself, the man and poet with an as yet plastic and uncertain self-image regarded the comment revealing enough to remember and repeat.

The other occurrence, however, made him belligerently nationalistic. In July, 1946, a less amusing version of the American Roethke had arrived from England. The London *Horizon* had returned his new greenhouse poems. "It seemed to us that your poetry was in a way very American," the rejection letter announced, "in that it just lacked that inspiration, in-

evitability or quintessence of writing and feeling that distinguishes good poetry from verse." Seager comments that "this letter made him wrathy and he was still fulminating against the 'god-damned limeys' when I saw him later in the summer."

The sting of this criticism may still have festered when Roethke presently wrote an introductory comment on *The Lost Son* poems to be included in John Ciardi's *Mid-Century American Poets* (1950). He now insisted that this poetry was very American and possessed a strong inspiration, inevitability or quintessence of feeling.

> Some of these pieces, then, begin in the mire; as if man is no more than a shape writhing from the old rock. This may be due, in part, to the Michigan from which I come. Sometimes one gets the feeling that not even the animals have been there before; but the marsh, the mire, the Void, is always there, immediate and terrifying. It is a splendid place for schooling the spirit. It is America.

So much for American beginnings. In his Northwest years, when Roethke was bidding for and finally winning the cherished poetry prizes against his native competition, we can recognize a highly attuned "American" poet. Indeed, the competitiveness in the old tennis coach (incredibly, one of his duties at Lafayette and Penn State) had fully surfaced in the poetry career the year before the Seattle period began, when the leading influence on American poets was England's top seed, T. S. Eliot. Roethke had sent a manuscript copy of his poem **"The Lost Son"** to Eliot's current archenemy, William Carlos Williams. Roethke included the following comment: "It's written . . . for the ear, not the eye. . . . And if you don't think it's got the accent of native American speech, your name ain't W. C. Williams, I say belligerently." But Roethke's adversary was not Williams; it was the influential exile in England who irritated both men. "In a sense [**"The Lost Son"** is] your poem, yours and K. Burke's," he continued to Williams, "with the mood or the action on the page, not talked about, not the meditative T. S. Eliot kind of thing. (By the way, if you have an extra copy of your last blast against T.S.E., do send it to me. I can't seem to get a hold of it anywhere.)" Roethke clearly understood that the Eliot cult must be discredited in America before the judges could hear and consider Roethke's (and Williams') native accents. By 1949 he was encouraged. He wrote to Kenneth Burke of new signs that "the *zeit-geist,* ear-to-the-ground boys in England" were coming over to his side and now calling it Roethke over Eliot: "[They] think I'm the only bard at present operating in the U.S. of A., that everybody is tired of Tiresome Tom, the Cautious Cardinal."

One of Roethke's gratifying intimations of a growing reputation in Eliot's country came in 1950 when John Malcolm

Brinnin told him that Dylan Thomas, on his first American tour, wanted especially to meet America's Theodore Roethke. Roethke was very proud of that and enjoyed Thomas immensely. Here was an authentic "roaring boy," a British admirer, and no rival for the American prizes. Finally in 1954 Roethke won his first big award, the Pulitzer, for *The Waking*. (But he remained envious when Aiken, not Roethke, won the National Book Award that year.) The following year, Roethke was Fulbright lecturer in Florence. Like many American writers before him, he now comprehended his native land more keenly from the vantage point of Europe. His concern, predictably, centered not on the characteristic travails of political democracy in an election year, but rather on the state of American letters. He sized up once again the relative strengths of modern American poets:

> Sometimes I think the fates brought me here for my own development: to see my contemporaries, and elders, in their true perspective. And some of the American biggies have dwindled a good deal in my sight. For instance, Hart Crane, whom I once thought had elements of greatness. Except for the early poems, he now seems hysterical, diffuse—a deficient language sense at work. Williams, for the most part, has become curiously thin, self-indulgent, unable to write a poem, most of the time, that is a coherent whole. (This last saddened me a good deal, since I'm really fond of Bill.) Etc. People who *have* held up are Bogan, Auden, and of course old Willie Yeats, whom I'm not lecturing on; and Tate, for instance, looks better all the time, as opposed to Winters, whose work is often dead, rhythmically, and so limited in range of subject-matter and feeling.

After *Words for the Wind* (1958) won him most of the major prizes in America he had not yet claimed, including the National Book Award, Roethke was clearly preparing now to beat the world. He was ready to go, finally, after the big one, "to bring the Nobel in poetry to America," as he said with a veneer of patriotism. But the egotism was not far behind. He wrote his editor at Doubleday, "Certainly I'm a vastly better poet than Quasimodo, and this French man [Perse] is good but does the same thing over and over. I think Wystan Auden should be next, then Pablo Neruda, then me...." He had arrived at this "cold, considered objective judgment" of his native genius after a final repudiation of "the Pound-Eliot cult and the Yeats cult." As he told critic Ralph Mills, neither "Willie" Yeats nor "Tiresome Tom" Eliot was ever Roethke's master:

> In both instances, I was animated in considerable part by arrogance: I thought: I can take this god damned high style of W.B.Y. or this Whitmanesque meditative thing of T.S.E. and use it for other ends, use it as well or better. Sure, a tough assignment.

> But while Yeats' historical lyrics seem beyond me at the moment, I'm damned if I haven't outdone him in the more personal or love lyric.... Not only is Eliot tired, he's a [expletive deleted by editor] fraud as a mystic—all his moments in the rose-garden and the wind up his ass in the draughty-smoke-fall-church yard.

The next year, in a London interview, Roethke named the American poets he most admired: Auden, Elizabeth Bishop, and Stanley Kunitz. The last two certainly were no threat to his ambitious climb to the top of the heap. And Auden might be seen not only as a poet ambiguously American, but also a leader of the Roethke cheering section. The year before, as Roethke recalled, Auden had passed along to a mutual acquaintance the compliment that "at one point he was worried that I was getting too close to Yeats, but now he no longer did because I had out-done him, surpassed him, gone beyond him."

One formidable American remained to challenge Roethke in the poetry sweepstakes. This was Robert Lowell, whom Roethke met in summer of 1947 at Yaddo Writers Colony. He had grimly vanquished Lowell in all the recreational contests. "I was croquet, tennis, ping-pong and eating champion," he reported at the end of the summer. Seager writes perceptively here of the distinctly American myth of success and ardor for combat that lay within Roethke's hunger for greatness: "He was like Hemingway. To view literature as a contest to be won is a Saginaw Valley, Middle-Western, American set of mind, and throughout Ted's career he saw Lowell loom larger and larger as his chief opponent." In this contest with Lowell, Roethke received the most punishing defeat publicly in July of 1963 shortly before his death. An admirer of Lowell, the Irish poet Thomas Kinsella, was in Seattle at Roethke's invitation, staying as Roethke's houseguest until later in the week when he gave a poetry reading. Seager recreates the harrowing climax of that evening:

> Ted sat in the front row. The reading was well-received and afterward Kinsella permitted a question-and-answer period. Someone asked, "Mr. Kinsella, who do you consider the greatest living American poet?" With Ted in the front row at the high tide of his renown, this was not, in a way, a genuine question but a solicitation of a compliment.

> But Kinsella, helplessly candid, hypnotized into tactlessness by his honest opinion, said, "Robert Lowell."

> Ted did not explode, but at the party he and Beatrice were giving for Kinsella later that evening, he grumped to his other guests, "That bastard, damn

him. Did you hear what he said?" until Beatrice told him it would look better if he just shut up, and, oddly enough, he did. Later, calmer, more sober, Ted realized that Kinsella had a right to his opinion, forgave him and they parted friends.

Perhaps one can rightly infer that the competitive Roethke traced Lowell's national success to his impressive roots in his American region. If so, the challenge to the leading younger poet of the Northeast might come in one manner, then, if Roethke could square off as the leading poet of the Northwest. But aside from the national ambition, Roethke for a number of years had been discovering the natural—and poetic—resources of the Northwest with that "obsessive quality of emotional ownership" that Richard Hugo looks for in the authentic regional poet.

I have recorded earlier Roethke's negative reactions to the environs of Seattle. Once more, the response to place in the mercurial Roethke has a dynamic, positive side as well. One of his first references to a possible academic residence in the Far West comes in a letter of late 1946 when he was on his first Guggenheim Fellowship and afraid that Bennington would not invite him to return (he was technically still on leave from Penn State). He admitted that he had been "brooding about the West Coast." Shortly after, he wrote to George Lundberg, sociology professor at the University of Washington whom he had known at Bennington. Lundberg recommended him to the English department chairman, Joseph Harrison. After some of his characteristic haggling about salary, Roethke arrived in Seattle in September 1947 to become associate professor of English at $5,004.

The Northwest had one salutary effect on him at once. Some eleven years before, a bookless Roethke in Michigan had lamented to Louise Bogan on his twenty-eighth birthday, "No volume out and I can't seem to write anything. You can say what you want, but *place* does have a lot to do with productivity." An ounce of rationalization in the frustrated poet may be present here. By contrast, however, he exploded with ideas and poems after he arrived in Seattle. Seager speculates on the causes: "Whether it was the stimulation of a new setting, the West Coast with its opulence of natural life in its almost English climate, or whether he felt that he had been idle too long (and 'idle' meant not that he had not been writing but that he had gone too long without publishing a book) . . . he filled more notebooks and more loose sheets with poetry in these two years than in any period of his life." He moved out to Edmonds after several years of residence in the University district, finding it "more Northwestern." And for all his restless applying for grants or other jobs to take him away from the University of Washington, Roethke in spring of 1957 did buy the Seattle house on Lake Washington, an act which most money-conscious Americans make when they

confirm a place as their home. Roethke was assuredly money conscious.

He was also, by then, *the* reigning poet of Seattle. I met him not long afterward, and can attest to the fertile results of his presence. He was no longer the only serious practicing poet for one thousand miles around. Poetry readings seemed to be happening almost nonstop-usually on the second floor of Hartman's Bookstore in the District or on campus in the Walker Ames Room of Parrington Hall. Roethke's local students were appearing, while ex-students were returning to Seattle to read from their work. I recall the reading appearances of such visitors as Marianne Moore, Snodgrass, Merwin, Kunitz, Wright, Langland, Ginsberg, Bogan, and Leonie Adams—all of them come to Seattle or detoured there en route down or up the coast because Roethke had made the Northwest a vital corner of American poetry. Roethke himself, not to be outdone, made his own flamboyant public performances, now legendary in Seattle, appearing as the Northwest bard and declaiming his verses to his fellow townspeople, from savants to bourgeoisie, with an effect that would have cheered and amazed the bardic Whitman himself.

A "Northwest Renaissance" in poetry was proclaimed by Seattle poet Nelson Bentley, one of the Roethke faithful. During 1963 in San Diego, where I had gone to teach in a somewhat sunnier climate, I asked John Ciardi when he came through, "Are you conscious in the East of a 'Northwest Renaissance'?" He replied, "I don't know about any Northwest movement, but we all know that one poet named Theodore Roethke is out there."

How intensely Roethke was engaged in his private Northwest movement, a love-hate affair with a locale in which the critical citizen helped to form the integrity of feeling in the poet, we can now begin to gauge in the published notebooks. I mentioned earlier the entries where he comments on the isolation of a "provincial creative intellectual" in America and records the sterile, prosy observations of a frustrated citizen in Seattle. The notebooks also reveal the exhilarating process of a poet exploring his adopted Northwest landscape and converting it into usable tropes and images. But I leave this examination of the notebooks, a fruitful subject, to future students of Roethke and regionalism and turn instead to the published poetry itself.

### III.

Roethke's first book of poems in the Northwest appeared in 1951. ***Praise to the End!,*** his "tensed-up" version of Wordsworth's *Prelude,* carried nine new poems which can be read, in one sense, as Roethke's completing the "lean to beginnings" in the previous ***Lost Son*** collection. Once more he tracked his voyage of the mind's return to the dream logic, Mother Goose rhythms, and purposeful gibberish of childhood, and then back again to the varieties of rebirth after these mythic descents. He will return to this early Michigan in the late Northwest poems, but the goblin fears of childhood are no longer present. To a degree, then, he was ready, after *Praise to the End!,* to experiment with a new stage of poetic expression that had lain in embryo within the first Northwest notebooks.

A promise of the regional poems to come begins to appear in the new verses of his next book, *The Waking: Poems: 1933-53* (1953). **"A Light Breather,"** to select one, reveals a joyous dynamism of the spirit, "small" and "tethered" as before but now "unafraid" and "singing." Together with the unhurried grace of the title poem, these lines point to the dearly earned resolutions shaped in the Northwest settings of his final long poems. Symptomatic of a new phase, too, are poems like **"Elegy for Jane,"** which Seager calls "the first of his poems to have its whole origin on the West Coast" (though one will discover "a sidelong pickerel smile" in Roethke's 1938 notebook). Finally are the more ambitious efforts of the 1953 volume which show a Roethke who is escaping from his prison of the self to engage the ambient world and the being of other living creatures. **"Old Lady's Winter Words"** is one instance, and Roethke will enlarge this empathy in the **"Meditations of an Old Woman"** sequence of his next book. Of equal significance in 1953 is the first great sequence of metaphysical love poems, **"Four for Sir John Davies."** Here Roethke at last is able to reach outside the dance of the solitary self, merge with a partner, and experience a quasi-Dantean transcendence into mature love, the "rise from flesh to spirit." Not surprisingly, these love poems forecast an imminent involvement for Seattle's forty-four-year-old bachelor-poet. Any colleague at the University who read these poems in earlier journal publication might have advised Roethke that he was beginning to sound increasingly vulnerable to the presence of any marriageable woman. On a December evening in 1952 on his way to a reading in New York City, he inadvertently met along the street a former Bennington student, Beatrice O'Connell. He courted her every day thereafter, and at the end of a month they were married. Allan Seager believes that Roethke's marriage presently led him to a heightened awareness of the Northwest world. As his capacity of feeling reached out to his young Beatrice, "hesitantly, even reluctantly perhaps, he admitted her into those labyrinths within himself where his father still lived, and he began to love her, not in the same way that he loved his father but with a true love nevertheless. And from this time forward, she participated in his growth, encouraged and supported it. Then he could see the mountains, the siskins, the madronas, and begin to use them."

Viewed in this regard, the **"Love Poems"** segment of the next book, *Words for the Wind: Collected Verse* (1958), is considerably more than occasions for Roethke to range through his varieties of lecherous punning, metaphysical wit,

and Dantean love of a modern Beatrice. The love poems, thoroughly studied for their passionate metaphors of wind and seafoam, light and stones and rippling water as "spirit and nature beat in one breastbone," will perhaps reveal the true beginnings of that distinctive Northwest sensibility which fully emerges in Roethke's last book. Useful also to that end, although for other reasons, are the final three sections of *Words for the Wind,* with their natural stream of correspondences tallying the movements of the soul, downward to the spiritual DTs and harrowing plunges and upward to the ascensions and harmonious resolutions with an "agency outside me. / Unprayed-for, / And final."

And so we arrive at *The Far Field* (1964), the final volume which Roethke, almost providentially it now seems, had lived to write. At this zenith came his death. There would be no descent, no failing of creative energy. *The Far Field* becomes the logical culmination of Roethke's poetic and American sojourn out of the Midwest and through his native land to maturity and reconciliation in the Northwest.

The year before his death, Roethke wrote to Ralph Mills, Jr.: "I am still fiddling with the order and composition of certain final poems." Only weeks before his death, he settled on a structure of *The Far Field* in four parts: **"North American Sequence," "Love Poems," "Mixed Sequence,"** and **"Sequence, Sometimes Metaphysical."** The first, or **"North American,"** sequence of six poems includes the title poem, **"The Far Field."** (An original title for the book, "Dance On, Dance On, Dance On," had come from the final poem.) Perhaps I am swayed unduly to believe that in changing the book's title, Roethke was signalling the reader that the opening section with **"The Far Field"** would carry the crucial burden of the entire volume. In any event, the **"North American Sequence"** has become the great achievement in Roethke's last book. It might properly be called the "Northwest Sequence" for reasons I hope will be apparent in fairly short order. The genesis of this sequence may be traced, in one fashion, to the summer of 1950. Roethke had bought his first car and had driven it back to Seattle. The trip created the stirrings of a "symbolical journey," his own spiritual version of a Northwest passage. It suggested "for next or possibly later book . . . a happy journey westward"; but there would be a uniquely Roethkean variation of this traditional passage—"in a word, a symbolical journey in my cheap Buick Special toward Alaska and, at least in a spiritual sense toward the east of Russia and the Mongolian Plains whence came my own people, the Prussians, those poop-arse aristocrats, my father called them, who fed their families into the army or managed the hunt for Bismarck and Bismarck's sister—all this in Stettin in East Prussia, now held by the Poles."

By the end of the decade, Roethke had modified this journey. It was now an exclusively North American and ultimately regional experience. He told Zulfikar Ghose in an interview in London in 1960, during his Ford Foundation fellowship, about his shifting conception and emphasis: "My imagery is coming more out of the Northwest rather than the whole of America." The nature of the journey had changed. In Ghose's words, it was "not like driving a car across America, but an exploration of the North-West."

He had, in fact, developed a triple motif of outer-inner journeys. First is the Northwest passage to the dark oceanic "stretch in the face of death," and the periodic resolution experienced at the Pacific Coast shoreline, a journey out to the physical "edge" and metaphysical "beyond" and then back to reconciliation "where sea and fresh water meet" in the Northwest corner. The second passage or journey is a return to his origins, a movement eastward to the Michigan of his father's greenhouse and Roethke's childhood. Gone in this experience, as I hinted earlier, are "the muck and welter, the dark, the *dreck*" which burden the poems in *The Lost Son* and *Praise to the End!* Third is a "journey to the interior," imaged in an inland American geography perhaps equivalent, temporally, to the middle period of Roethke's initial breakdown in that "Siberian pitilessness, the essential ruthlessness of the Middle West." Here he moves beyond the child's insulation from time and death and forward to the mature man's encounter with the voids and abysses and multiplicity of challenges to his spiritual growth. But he does not attain to the outer thresholds of vision, the achieved moments of outer-and-inner union and transcendence that belong to the Northwest passage. Ranging forward and back across the American landscape in the **"North American Sequence,"** then, Roethke's speaker can understandably admit in **"The Far Field"**: "I dream of journeys repeatedly."

Of the three journeys, the Northwest passage is by far the richest and most dominant in the six poems of the sequence. Roethke gathers within it the shifting motifs of selfhood within the Northwest's natural plenitude, identifications with birds, fish, trees, and flowers (and occasionally as relief, with the stillness of rocks, clam shells, driftwood, and nature's minimals); the imagery of edges, abysses, and thresholds; the desire for convergence, resolution and union with the natural scene of salt water, fresh water, air, and earth; and on occasion, when blessedly aided by the soft regional light and wind, the speaker feels the shimmerings of immanence which create a felt convergence, a moment of transcendence and beatitude. By entering upon the other two journeys inland from time to time, he enriches and paces the sequence in alternating rhythms of charged meditation and dynamic movement across American space. The speaker, classically a migratory American, travels inward and outward across the North American terrain in pursuit of his total selfhood. But he returns always to the Northwest shoreline for an ultimate synthesis.

These interlacing journeys and themes and alternating

rhythms are sounded in the first poem, **"The Longing,"** and then are centered on a longed-for passage, finally with an American Indian vigor of exploration, to the threshold of full spiritual awareness. Just as this initial poem becomes, musically, a prelude, almost an overture, to the entire sequence, the final poem, **"The Rose,"** will climax and recapitulate the sequence.

**"The Longing"** opens "In a bleak time, when a week of rain is a year." (We can assume the speaker is in Seattle.) But this is not life-giving rain. The speaker's spirit is in a slump amid the reigning "stinks and sighs, / Fetor of cockroaches, dead fish, petroleum" and the pointless angst of nightclub crooners and their self-pitying, lust-fatigued audience, an unsavory scene of

> Saliva dripping from warm microphones,
> Agony of crucifixion on barstools.

In a regressive aside, he associates pure joy only with children, dogs, and saints. The Roethkean interrupting question focuses the list and impels the poem onward: "How to transcend this sensual emptiness?" The Northwest scene, natural and manmade, fumes in its putrefaction. In bleak contrast to the free-soaring gull we remember at the onset of Hart Crane's *The Bridge,* Roethke's Northwest seagulls "wheel over their singular garbage." Images which later will foreshadow immanence—the regional light and wind—are invoked in this spiritual torpor to deepen our sense of their absence.

> The great trees no longer shimmer;
> Not even the soot dances.

The spirit, slug-like, recoils. But it retains the hunger for a new start, like "a loose worm / Ready for any crevice, / An eyeless starer."

So the sequence begins in one of the bleak rainy spells with which Roethke in Seattle was all too familiar. In the two remaining sections of **"The Longing,"** we follow the Roethkean voyage of the modern soul in its tormented quest for light and wholeness. He conducts this soul-search initially by going back to the beginnings of elemental life. The clues of the way toward transcendence are sensed in the spareness of the natural world.

> The rose exceeds, the rose exceeds us all.
> Who'd think the moon could pare itself so thin?

A sign is also received in the unnatural light that cries out of the "sunless sea" in the same measures of longing.

> I'd be beyond; I'd be beyond the moon,
> Bare as a bud, and naked as a worm.

Roethke captions this retrogression and desire in the final lines of the section: "Out of these nothings / —All beginnings come."

The conclusion is introduced with a Whitman catalog of the speaker's longing for identification and convergence with the plenitude and beneficence he now feels he may possess in the world, by contrast with the opening section and the ascetic vacuity that followed upon it. In the poems to follow, the desire to pace his spiritual growth in harmony with his natural surroundings will be, at the same time, an esthetic search for a shaping, concrete language that will also express the inexpressible: "I long for the imperishable quiet at the heart of form." But as of now, the speaker has received only the intimation of future thresholds. He anticipates, meanwhile, a rite of passage through the North American interior.

> . . . the mouth of the night is still wide;
> On the Bullhead, in the Dakotas, where the eagles
>    eat well,
> In the country of few lakes, in the tall buffalo
>    grass at
>          the base of the clay buttes . . .

Does the aging spirit dare to go primitive? No, if subjected to the ruthless plains of the interior. Yes, if sustained amid the inland waters.

> Old men should be explorers?
> I'll be an Indian.
> Ogalala?
> Iroquois.

**"Meditation at Oyster River,"** the second poem of the **"North American Sequence,"** begins at twilight on the east coast of Vancouver Island. Roethke's explorer looks eastward to the "first tide-ripples," briefly immerses his feet in the water, and then partakes of earth and air as well by ascending to a perch on the cliffside. In the Northwest "twilight wind, light as a child's breath," the spirit quivers with alertness. A soundless pause has readied the time for meditation after urgent longing in the previous poem.

Section two finds the speaker half in love with easeful death, persisting "like a dying star, / In sleep afraid." He yearns for escape from the lonely self, for oneness with the deer, the young snake, the hummingbird—the shy and alert creatures of land and air. "With these I would be. / And with water." At this threshold of poised awareness, "In this first heaven of knowing," Roethke takes us, in section three, on a backward motion toward the source, to "the first trembling of a Michigan brook in April." He feels the old quickenings of a younger spirit which, like the melting Tittebawasee in early spring, could awaken, expand, and burst forward into a new season of becoming.

The meditation finally returns to Oyster River and closes with the harmonious resolution of youth and age as he is "lulled into half-sleep" in a Whitman-like sea-cradle. After his journey back to Michigan and forward once more to the waters of the Northwest, he merges now in quiet joy with the waves and the intrepid shorebirds. The poem closes in a radiant, although not fully composed, vision:

> In the first of the moon,
> All's a scattering,
> A shining.

Arrivals on the threshold of naturalistic grace are momentary and precarious. In the third poem, **"Journey to the Interior,"** the speaker returns to the yawning mouth of the night which awaited him at the close of **"The Longing."** He now embarks on that second American journey into the past, between Michigan beginnings and Northwest consummations.

As in **"The Longing,"** he begins in dislocation, though not, this time, in spiritual dullness. Roethke initially presents "the long journey out of the self" in a vague, geographical metaphor: to pass through the perplexed inner workings and torments of the emerging self is like steering a lurching automobile through detours, mud slides, dangerous turns, flash floods, and swamps "alive with quicksand." Finally, the way narrows to a standstill, "blocked at last by a fallen fir-tree, / The thickets darkening, / The ravines ugly."

From this introductory standstill, he sets forth on a new soul's journey. In section two, this exploration takes the form of an actual trip westward through the North American interior. The explorer, appropriately, is neither child nor man now but a reckless youth careering over gravel at full throttle, scorning to "hug close" like the fear-ridden older motorist he would become in the previous stanza. With the arrogant confidence of youth, he courts danger and death on the American roadway head-on: "A chance? Perhaps. But the road was part of me, and its ditches, / And the dust lay thick on eyelids,—Who ever wore goggles?" (Roethke is here falling back on his own self-made legend that he had been once the extroverted American roaring boy. In fact, the hypersensitive youth from Saginaw had grown beyond forty before he owned a car and made this western journey through the interior. For an emerging identity, however, Roethke knew well that fantasy is as powerful and "true" as fact.) The second section concludes as the trip advances through the western prairies and beyond the Tetons. The past merges with the present, the random fluidity of the land journey is abated, and "time folds / Into a long moment" for the youth become, in the remembrance, confident father of the troubled man.

In the final section, the speaker can still feel his "soul at a still-stand," but this time with a difference. Thanks to the remembered journey through the American interior which has intervened, he again moves to the edge of water in the Northwest. Reconciled to change and death, united with the soft elements of his region, he can "breathe with the birds" while he stands "unperplexed" looking out on the Pacific scene. All extremes dissolve on that "other side of light," and

> The spirit of wrath becomes the spirit of blessing,
> And the dead begin from their dark to sing in my
>     sleep.

**"The Long Waters"** was apparently written after but appears before **"The Far Field."** Presumably, Roethke felt the need for a tranquil, sustained meditation piece to separate **"Journey to the Interior"** from **"The Far Field"** (which was originally titled "Journeys"). **"The Long Waters"** occurs in a setting closely resembling Oyster River. The poem moves quietly among three Roethkean stages—retrogression (closing at times to infantile regression), thresholds, and convergence. These movements are experienced largely in Northwest images without the backward journey motifs of the previous poems. Roethke creates, instead, an alternating rhythm of gentle ebbing and flowing, action and reaction. In a transparent outline modeled and elaborated after Roethke's own example, we may see the internal structure of the five sections to develop this way:

1. *Initial retrogression (II. 1-12).* The speaker celebrates the joyous minimals of earth, water, and air—the worms, minnows, and butterflies. He confesses his childlike "foolishness"—his "desire for the peaks, the black ravines, the rolling mists," but also the opposite need for security amid "unsinging fields where no lungs breathe, / Where light is stone."

*Threshold to convergence approached (II. 13-19).* He returns to a firecharred "edge of the sea . . . Where the fresh and salt waters meet, / And the sea-winds move through the pine trees" in near-concert with the burnt-yellow grass and peeling logs.

2. *Retrogression again (II. 20-32).* He invokes protection of a Blakean mythic mother against the quietly distressing motions of the worm and butterfly and the "dubious sea-change" but he knows that change and death are also the mothers of pleasure and beauty.

3. *Convergence approaches unawares (II. 33-48).* The abundant varieties of Northwest coastal images—the leaping fish, the ivy rooting in saw-dust alongside the uprooted trees, the casual osprey and dawdling fisherman, and a sea surface full of imagined flowers both alive and dead—bring the casual speaker almost to a reconcilement of extremes, to feelings of beatitude and immanence.

> I have come here without courting silence,
> Blessed by the lips of a low wind,
> To a rich desolation of wind and water,
> To a landlocked bay, where the salt water is
>     freshened
> By small streams running down under fallen fir
>     trees.

4. *Threshold reappears (II. 49-53).* "In the vaporous grey of early morning / . . . . A single wave comes in."

*Retrogression once more (II. 54-59).* But when the wave reaches "a tree lying flat, its crown half broken," the speaker, vaguely troubled, recalls "a stone breaking the eddying current / . . . in the dead middle way, / . . . A vulnerable place."

5. *Convergence followed by a light transcendence is briefly achieved (II. 60-78).* His receptive "body shimmers with a light flame" in the sea wind as the "advancing and retreating" sea, which images the risings and fallings of the poem, now yields up a visionary "shape" of "the eternal one." The undulant long waters attenuate in the long poetic line, shaping for the speaker a transformed moment of union and renewal.

> My eyes extend beyond the farthest bloom of the
>     waves;
> I lose and find myself in the long water;
> I am gathered together once more;
> I embrace the world.

With **"The Far Field"** the sequence now returns to the opening of **"Journey to the Interior"**—the metaphorically "narrowing" trip by automobile to a final stalling "in a hopeless sand-rut." (One glimpses in the images the American affliction of Poe and the late Mark Twain.) From this still-stand of the spirit, Roethke again searches the way out by going back. The journey in this case will not be to the interior but an extended return to a timeless childhood, to moments of immanence in that "far field, the windy cliffs of forever, / The dying of time in the white light of tomorrow." In that field, "one learned of the eternal" in the child's world of dead rats and cats, of life-nestings in the field's far corner. For nature's casualties, his young "grief was not excessive." The warblers always heralded Maytime renewal and nature's plenitude. With similar ease, the child could ponder the evolution of mindless shells or indulge his innocent fancies of reincarnation.

Returning to the adult's present, the speaker, no longer constricted, can sense "a weightless change, a moving forward." The earlier narrowing of section one is repeated, but in an image of release, "As of water quickening before a narrowing channel / When banks converge." He emerges to face outward to sea. Like the philosopher's man of Wallace

Stevens, he is able to confront an ultimate Protean reality, with more insouciance, even, than the wondering child he once was.

> The murmur of the absolute, the why
> Of being born fails on his naked ears.
> His spirit moves like monumental wind
> That gentles on a sunny blue plateau.

The poem rises into gentle transcendence. The "finite things" which in previous lines of the sequence recalled "a vulnerable place" or a disturbing juxtaposition of death and life, now compose in a constellation of Northwest images that the tranquil mind discovers to be the shape of "infinitude":

> The mountain with its singular bright shade
> . . . . .
> The after-light upon ice-burdened pines;
> . . . . .
> Silence of water above a sunken tree:
> The pure serene of memory in one man,—
> A ripple widening from a single stone
> Winding around the waters of the world.

The final poem, **"The Rose,"** sums up and completes the **"North American Sequence."** All three of the American journey-motifs are here, together with all of the inner stages of the soul and their supporting images. More fully than any of the preceding single poems, **"The Rose"** is Roethke's Northwest poetic creation par excellence. It appeared in *The New Yorker* the month before his death. The thorough critic of Roethke's poetry would want more than a score of pages to explicate this beautiful poem and account for it within the entire sequence. I shall try to manage a fraction of the assignment in a few pages.

Appropriately with these verses that close the sequence, Roethke can begin with near-feelings of convergence that by now have been earned. We understand his opening assertion about the Northwest seacoast:

> There are those to whom place is unimportant,
> But this place, where sea and fresh water meet,
> Is important—

He then draws the bountiful natural life into this ultimate song of himself. In the next fifteen lines, he describes some dozen Northwest birds and at the same time, predictably, he unites them to air, earth, and water. He no longer requires the agonizing interior journey through and out of the perplexed self. He can "sway outside myself / Into the darkening currents" with the quiet grace of the intrepid hawks he has just described (lines 4-5).

Section two advances the easy motions of grace onto a pa-

cific ocean "As when a ship sails with a light wind— / . . . dipping like a child's boat in a pond." Still, in its apparently buoyant ease of passage, his spirit feels obscurely troubled, somehow adrift and incomplete. The realization he is seeking now approaches on the Northwest shoreline before his feet. His guide to this knowledge, both fact and symbol, is the single "rose in the sea-wind," the transcendent rose he had briefly invoked in **"The Longing."** Its own excuse for being, the wild rose silently instructs by a dynamic staying "in its true place," by "flowering out of the dark," widening in noonday light, and stubbornly resisting encroachment upon its solitary life. The meditation upon the individualized wild rose leads the speaker associatively to one final journey to the greenhouse world of his childhood. In the reminiscence, the aged man repossesses the glories he had known when "those flowerheads seemed to flow toward me, to beckon me, only a child, out of myself." The child had merged with the roses and both had flourished in the bountiful Eden created by his sufficient, protective father:

> What need for heaven, then,
> With that man, and those roses?

The childhood memory then triggers the other, or later, journey into the past. Section three first echoes the early morning "sound and silence" of the Northwest scene in the opening lines of the poem. We are then taken on a last journey into the "interior," to gather up and catalog the inland "American sounds in this silence"—a Whitman excursion among industrial noises, the bravuras of birds, "the ticking of snow around oil drums in the Dakotas, / The thin whine of telephone wires in the wind of a Michigan winter," and more. His second journey eastward into the past completed, the old explorer has reached the final definition of himself. His longing for "the imperishable quiet at the heart of form" had first occurred within the fluid Whitman catalog of the first poem. He now hears the imperishable quiet in the "single sound" that issues in the Northwest setting of **"The Rose"** at the heart of this Whitman free form. Phrased another way, his question in **"The Longing"** had been "How to transcend this sensual emptiness?" He has discovered the answer: the sensual emptiness has been transcended in the sensual fullness of the Whitman-Roethke gatherings of American plenitude, as in these fluid interior "American sounds in this silence." And this possession, be it noted, has occurred within a primary context of the regional. After extended longing, he has found the place of his desire. It is glimpsed, significantly enough, not as an ultimate paradiso or a child's insular garden of flowers, but as a transcendent landscape of earth composed both of languid shimmerings and Roethkean edges. The moment then dissolves in the precarious balance of a rapt instant of earthly beauty. The closing lines of the penultimate section of **"The Rose"** suspend an image of life wakening into, or indistinguishable from, death.

And a drop of rain water hangs at the tip of a leaf
Shifting in the wakening sunlight
Like the eye of a new-caught fish.

The speaker emerges from the vision to explain himself in the final section. Thanks to the final journeys of private and native—and esthetic—self-realization that were stimulated by the rose's expansive self-containment, he has again embraced his present world, his Northwest, and can accept even

    the rocks, their weeds,
Their filmy fringes of green, their harsh
Edges, their holes
Cut by the sea-slime . . .

Like the space-time curvature of this journey poem, the poet's spirit matching the condition of the rose in the sea-wind, he has "swayed out . . . / And yet was still." He can also rejoice equally with the bird, the lilac, and the dolphin in the calm and change which they accept in air, land, and water. In the lovely closing lines, he absorbs in his controlling solitary symbol the diversity of experience and imagery in this climactic poem.

[I rejoiced] in this rose, this rose in the sea-wind,
Rooted in stone, keeping the whole of light,
Gathering to itself sound and silence—
Mine and the sea-wind's.

So ends an intensive drive toward definition of the many Roethkean selves, of the perplexed American in his country and his region. The **"North American Sequence"** can be read as Roethke's final portrait, not unlike those late photographs of the poet in a Northwest landscape, his face variously lined with what Robert Heilman read as "suffering endured, dreaded, inescapable, and yet survived and, in an ever maturing art, surmounted." Even Roethke's "drive toward God" was climaxed in the ultimate landscape of the Sequence. The northern coast and oceanic far field of his adopted region served him perfectly to frame and extend his religious journeys in and out of time and space and even to resolve them in fleeting moments of joyous, tranquil union.

Finally, this sequence enabled Roethke the poet to assimilate those American peers who meant the most to him without permitting the national echoes to disturb or overpower the regional tonalities. The mastery of this casual plagiarism offers one of the surest signs of the major poet coming into possession of his own definable voice. Merely the final lines of **"The Rose,"** which echo the close of "When Lilacs Last in the Dooryard Bloom'd," show how well Roethke had learned his poetic orchestration from Whitman. The larger motifs of the sequence—the passages through nature and America and beyond to a total selfhood—are indebted similarly to Whitman, especially the "Song of Myself," "Out of

the Cradle," and "Passage to India." Echoes of the symbolical American journeys of Hart Crane, likewise a transplanted Midwesterner, and William Carlos Williams's immersion in a local America also abound, as do the parallels and instructive differences with the experimental Eliot of *The Waste Land* and the Tiresome Tom of the *Four Quartets*. Clearly important to Roethke, too, are the sensual Stevens of "Sea Surface Full of Clouds" and the more philosophical Stevens of "Sunday Morning," "Asides on the Oboe," and "Notes Toward a Supreme Fiction." And we hear the Emily Dickinson of seasonal thresholds, nuances of light, and the edges of death. Sounding clearly, also, are the American nature notes of Emerson's "Rhodora" and Frost's "West-Running Brook," as well as the correspondences of New England coast and self in Robert Lowell—less transcendental but historically richer than Roethke's. But enough. An annotated **"North American Sequence,"** obviously, would extend the references almost endlessly. Astonishing, then, for all Roethke's allusive and emotional range and intensity in this late sequence is the account from his biographer that these culminating long poems "came easily with an unwonted confidence—he knew what he wanted to say and he was sure of his means."

Roethke's American debts for this regional achievement lead naturally, in turn, to the question of his own possible influence on the younger practicing poets of the region. Richard Hugo, William Stafford, Carolyn Kizer, and David Wagoner have carefully evaded the idea of any Roethke "school" in the Northwest while they praise his brilliant example of the verbal pressures and cutting edges possible in a highly disciplined poetry. Surely this is a healthy and necessary spirit of poetic autonomy. The "school" with its intimidating master voice has more often curbed than liberated vital literary expression, regional and otherwise. I suspect, however, that Roethke's regional experience at the end had been fashioned too powerfully not to have become a part of the consciousness of poets writing today in the Northwest. If so, this need not be totally bad. The Roethke idiom has generated intimations, if you will, of a receivable and emerging heritage. But the nature of Roethke's contribution to a Northwest poetry will obviously not be known for some time to come, just as anything nearing a definitive notion of a Northwest ethos awaits the regional intuitions of individual poets, novelists, scholars, and memorializers to come.

## IV.

Had he lived, would Roethke have continued to mine the Northwest vein of his **"North American Sequence"**? Elsewhere, the final volume only clouds a possible answer. He had gone on to include more of the torments, the voids, and the self-disintegrations of the past. The best of these metaphysical lyrics include **"The Abyss," "In a Dark Time,"** and **"In Evening Air."** He did extend himself, however, in the rare sequence of final love poems. With the same daring that led him earlier to create the feminine voice of his **"Medi-tations of an Old Woman"** (feminists today might call the effort ill-advised) he aimed in his final love poems to ex-press the perhaps more difficult voice of a sensitive young woman in love. But in previous years he seemed always too restless, too experimental and ambitious to repeat many of his successful innovations. He would throw most of them out the window, as James Dickey once said, and then start anew. In his continuing art as in his religious meditations, Roethke would probably have strained again to "go beyond," "to be more," to outdo himself. The new love lyrics or the **"North American Sequence,"** then, had been tried and com-pleted. Perhaps it would be time, once again, to move on.

One exciting possibility remains on record to point a way that Roethke might have taken had he lived. His wife re-ported that when Roethke once visited the grave of Chief Seattle, "he knelt in the grass and [crossed himself] seriously." The gesture may tell how soberly he had assumed his late ambition to write an epic of the North American Indian. His structural device would be, once more, a passage across the nation's heartland. The speaker would stop to commemo-rate the scenes of tragic undoing which various tribes suf-fered at the hands of the white marauders and military. In this epic drama, which Roethke hoped to create, he said, "through suggestive and highly charged symbolical lan-guage," the heroic figures, indicated in his notes, were to include the Nez Perce's Chief Joseph, the Oglala's Black Elk and Crazy Horse, as well as white adversaries like Gen-erals Custer and Crook. The theme would be "the guilts we as Americans feel as a people for our mistakes and misdeeds in history and in time. I believe, in other words, that it be-hooves us to be humble before the eye of history."

Such a culminating work, as I suggested at the beginning, would have been utterly *de rigueur* in the eyes of literary critics and Nobel committees—the regional writer impres-sively widening his range to become the national epic poet and, even more, an American conscience in the world's his-tory. The Nobel-haunted Roethke was all too aware of the required pattern. A passage he entered in the late notebooks almost completely mirrors his anguish. He defiantly justi-fies his major work as faithfully "American" despite, or even because of, its being "provincial" (he continues to use, some-what wryly, this pejorative term for the regional). Implicitly and belligerently he is advising the Nobel people to stuff their award.

> There's another typical stance: only *I* hear it. Then just listen: hump, schlump, bump—half the time: a real—did I say real?—I mean *unreal,* unnatural—thumping away in stupid staves, an arbitrary lop-ping of lines, rhythms, areas of experience, a turning away from much of life, an exalting of a few limited

areas of human consciousness. All right, I say, make like that, and die in your own way: in other words limited, provincial, classical in a distorted and—I use the word carefully—degraded sense; "American" in the sense American means eccentric, warped, and confined.

But we can set aside this too-obvious concern over obliga-tory soarings upward and outward to national epic, univer-sal archetype, and the larger "areas of human consciousness" and indulge our pride in the native poet whose versatile pow-ers and range of vision expanded *within* the Northwest land-scape and seascape. Immersion in the local and the "confining," the "exalting" of the solitary self in our own "true place," the poet Roethke is saying at last, brings us intermittently to experience in the only way that knowing is finally possible—that is, privately in the desire of the heart—those deep responses and truths that others may wish to el-evate with the abstract labels "American" or "Universal." This distinctive regional expression, which he bled for and slowly earned over the years, is what we have overlooked or undervalued in Roethke. By *The Far Field,* he was virtually creating the Northwest as a regional source of poetic truth. Inevitably with Roethke, expressing the spirit of place also had to mean a revealing of his mature identity as a man and poet. In the transcendental vision of the important last po-ems, Roethke and his Northwest had finally come to One.

## Cary Nelson (essay date 1981)

SOURCE: "The Field Where Water Flowers: Theodore Roethke's 'North American Sequence,'" in *Our Last First Poets: Vision and History in Contemporary American Po-etry,* University of Illinois Press, 1981, pp. 31-61.

[*In the following essay, Nelson examines theme and image of* "North American Sequence" *in* The Far Field, *drawing attention to Roethke's pastoral tone, American sensibility, and frequent allusion to the infinite and rebirth.*]

> I think of American sounds in this silence:
> On the banks of the Tombstone, the wind-harps
>   having their say,
> The thrush singing alone, that easy bird,
> The killdeer whistling away from me,
> The mimetic chortling of the catbird
> Down in the corner of the garden, among the
>   raggedy lilacs,
> The bobolink skirring from a broken fencepost,
> The bluebird, lover of holes in old wood, lilting its
>   light song,
> And that thin cry, like a needle piercing the ear,
>   the insistent cicada,

> And the ticking of snow around oil drums in the
> 　Dakotas,
> The thin whine of telephone wires in the wind of a
> 　Michigan winter,
> The shriek of nails as old shingles are ripped from
> 　the top of a roof,
> The bulldozer backing away, the hiss of the
> 　sandblaster,
> And the deep chorus of horns coming up from the
> 　streets in early
> 　　morning.

My decision to place a chapter on Roethke after a discussion of the influence of the Vietnam war on American poetry may first appear improbable. A far less public poet than those I have just discussed, Roethke rarely shows interest in events in American history; indeed, until late in his career he gives little overt evidence of an attempt to come to terms with his national origin. Of course the obliteration of historical references in Roethke's early pastoralism may itself be a response to history, but that is not my immediate concern here. My concern is rather with the way in which Roethke's work, partly because of these differences, offers a strategic perspective on the poetry of the last two decades.

Roethke's career in several respects parallels those of the poets I will discuss in subsequent chapters. Even more than any of them, his vision was quite fully articulated before he began openly to engage his sense of American history. Like Kinnell and Duncan, he does so in open forms very much in the Whitman tradition. I will emphasize the last phase of Roethke's career, particularly his **"North American Sequence,"** where, as the epigraph above suggests, he opens his greenhouse world to a more literal American landscape. Partly because of the power of Roethke's vision, partly because the period in which he worked was a less traumatic one, the conflict between poetic aspiration and a constrained sense of historical possibility is less intense in **"North American Sequence."** Nonetheless, like the poets I examined in the first chapter, Roethke finds his vision threatened by its exposure to American culture. The result is a poetry, grounded in loss and courting failure, that in many ways anticipates the poetry of the 1960s.

Midway in Roethke's career, a playful ambivalence enters his poetry. This ambivalence, in which previously secure images become either unattainable or ambiguous, foreshadows the more radical uncertainty of his final poems. In his enigmatic little poem **"The Beast,"** for example, the speaker approaches a great, overgrown door and sees beyond it "a meadow, lush and green" where a "sportive, aimless" beast is playing. Watching the beast, he catches its eye; thereupon he hesitates, falters, and falls to the ground. He attempts to rise, but collapses again. When he is able to stand at last, the beast with its great round eyes has gone: "the long lush grass

lay still; / And I wept there, alone." The narrator never actually enters the meadow; he falls "hard, on the gritty sill," and does not go beyond. The reader never learns where the meadow is, nor the identity of the ambiguous beast. These things are evocative precisely because they are so gnomic. The poem's symbols have the open-ended quality of dream images. Indeed the meadow may be the multireferential field over which dreamers fly; for the poet it is simultaneously the external world and a forgotten terrain within himself. Other passages in *Words for the Wind* suggest much the same duality:

> On a wide plain, beyond
> The far stretch of a dream,
> A field breaks like the sea;
>
> A field recedes in sleep.
> Where are the dead? Before me
> Floats a single star.
> A tree glides with the moon.
> The field is mine! Is mine!

Field, meadow, and plain—with their ravishing openness—make up one end of Roethke's polarized poetics of nature. At the other end are spaces of enclosed germination—including, of course, the famous greenhouse poems. Both types of space have their characteristic inhabitants. To the fields belong the many species of birds who fly above them; to the greenhouse, the tiny animals who cluster there—snail, slug, and worm: "When I was a lark, I sang; / When I was a worm, I devoured." These animals embody the emotive qualities of their respective spaces, and they suggest thereby what human use those spaces have. The greenhouse provides both a retreat and an organic resource; there the self, "marrow-soft, danced in the sand." It is a kind of evolutionary swamp which nurtures the self until it can embrace its wider surroundings. Kenneth Burke has superbly catalogued the "vegetal radicalism" of the dense, vital "realm of motives local to the body" which animate Roethke's greenhouse world. Among the wrestling thatches of damp stems, Roethke discovers "severedness, dying that is at the same time a fanatic tenacity; submergence (fish, and the mindless nerves of sensitive plants); envagination as a homecoming."

The fields offer suitably more expansive possibilities for both growth and threat. If the greenhouse presents a smothering, claustrophobic death, the fields proffer the risk of death through over extension. The fields challenge us to attempt an excess of becoming; if we accept that challenge, the self may be sacrificed to the landscape: "I fear myself in the field, / For I would drown in fire." Yet death in Roethke's poetry—whether in greenhouse or field—is always a rite of passage toward rebirth. Often it is willing and even deliberate. The old woman who meditates over her death declares, "I'm wet with another life," and her words point to the self-delivery implicit in rebirth. The new life she is wet with is her own:

> The sun! The sun! And all we can become!
> And the time ripe for running to the moon!
> In the long fields, I leave my father's eye;
> And shake the secrets from my deepest bones;
> My spirit rises with the rising wind;

In these open fields, the secret reserves of the self fertilize a new poetry of expansion. The old woman leaves her father's eye, for in nature's setting she is self-born. But Roethke's lines also have an autobiographical context; the greenhouse and a field beyond it mapped the natural borders of his childhood—the one a protected space overseen by his father, and the other a joyous but threatening exposure to the world.

If history were to enter Roethke's poetry at all, it would clearly be most likely to appear during encounters with the second kind of landscape. Put simply, it is easier to forget America in a greenhouse than it is on the prairies. Moreover, in order to personalize landscapes of distance, Roethke would have to take into himself more than their idealized correlatives. Indeed, in *Open House,* where his poetry tries to be ahistorical, the personalized versions of open space are rather strained and awkward, while intimate spaces already show some of the convincing intensity they achieve in the first section of *The Lost Son and Other Poems.*

Roethke's whole career moves toward a poetry that can encompass both these locations simultaneously—toward a textuality extending the body's privacy to an immense landscape and, at the same time, harboring the world within the body's space. In their most conclusive form, the introspective values associated with the greenhouse—meditation, repose, retreat to the womb, death and germination in darkness—are condensed in the image of stone. The values associated with the fields—motion, flight, ravishment, ecstatic self-realization through risk—are condensed in the image of light. Between stone and light, between the earth and the air, stands a poet whose vertical flowering would link them both. "I live in air; the long light is my home; / I dare caress the stones, the field my friend; / A light wind rises: I become the wind." By verbally mediating between stone and light, the poet can link the landscapes they represent. The movement toward a poetry where greenhouse and field can coalesce culminates in **"Meditations of an Old Woman"** and **"North American Sequence,"** Roethke's masterpieces. In the second, especially, Roethke seeks a language which will give voice to "the unsinging fields where no lungs breathe, / Where light is stone."

**"Meditations of an Old Woman"** is the more accessible of the two poems. It has a clear narrative persona, with which the reader can easily identify, and a meditative context that prevents associative leaps and structural breaks from seeming too disruptive. It even, retroactively, makes the more fractured associativeness of **"The Lost Son"** less threatening. To the extent that Roethke presents a convincing image of an old woman's consciousness, the poem appears to be a *tour de force* of empathic identification. Yet the woman's hesitation between passivity and action, with naturalistic correlatives of pool and river, is really an elaboration of Roethke's own polarity of enclosure and openness. Moreover, giving the two alternatives sexual force and making the choice between nesting and flying a woman's problem is an entirely traditional decision. Roethke's human vision is less new than his excited sense of discovery would lead us to believe. The femaleness of protected resources and the maleness of energy in motion are a poetic given.

These perceptual categories inhere in the language; to fuse them is not so much a narrative or psychological problem as a verbal one. Yet Roethke, as Allan Seager's biography of him demonstrates, saw his poetic enterprise more competitively than his green mysticism suggests. More, perhaps, than he may have known, he was an ideal poet to confront the ground reality of language directly.

It is not until **"North American Sequence"** that Roethke fully realizes his own combative need for sheer verbal performance. In that poem, he also accepts the cultural pressure behind his art. **"North American Sequence"** is a more faulty achievement than **"Meditations of an Old Woman"** because it risks much more, but it is also, finally, a greater poem. It is the only major poem in which Roethke accepts his specifically American roots. Because of that, the poem cannot wholly succeed, but that is its strength. The willingness to fail becomes for Roethke the aesthetic equivalent of his temptation to die. For the first time in his career, it is not merely the mystical speaker who would die, but the poem in which he speaks.

In **"The Longing,"** the first poem in **"North American Sequence,"** the search for light incarnate begins in a demonic version of the greenhouse world. Vitality has degenerated into corruption: "A kingdom of stinks and sighs, / Fetor of cockroaches, dead fish, petroleum." This resembles the landscape Roethke mentions in his **"First Meditation,"** where the self and the world converge in despair: "I have gone into the waste lonely places / Behind the eye; the lost acres at the edge of smoky cities." Here again "the slag-heaps fume at the edge of raw cities" and "the gulls wheel over their singular garbage." This is a specifically American vista and its concomitant sense of a jaded, guilty sexuality is equally American. The speaker calls himself "a loose worm / Ready for any crevice," and the sexual image is not accidental. In **"The Longing"** this sense of physical revulsion is particularly intense. It is as though the greenhouse life has been distributed all over the landscape, exposed to cultural forces, and left to decay. More significantly, perhaps, the inside of the poet's own body is now vulnerable to the body politic. The once potent vegetable shoots, and those sheath-wet sproutings in the poet himself, have succumbed to an unfulfilled lust that "fatigues the soul"; the figure of the worm now offers a cowardly reversion to shapelessness.

"How," Roethke asks, "to transcend this sensual emptiness?" His answer is his own version of America's ever more belated cultural optimism. Despair, we convince ourselves, is the foreknowledge of our oncoming joy. The very proximity of death will return us to our revitalized origins. For Roethke, then, the very decomposition of the spirit presages its salutary immersion again in the world of the flesh. "What dream's enough to breathe in?" he asks, "A dark dream"—a dream illuminated by the dark light of eyes turned toward the body's depths, a dream of "a body with the motion of a soul." Thus the worm and slug, verging on formlessness and insensate matter, suggest a new beginning for a self ravaged and vulnerable. Shapelessness becomes universality and self-transcendence: "I'd be beyond; I'd be beyond the moon, / Bare as a bud, and naked as a worm." Purgative journeys are apparently pre-eminently *cleansing;* spiritually on the other side of the moon, he recovers a virginal sexuality. Reduced to the empty vertical shape of a man—"to this extent I'm a stalk"—the poet is open to an influx of life outside himself. And the life outside will have to revive him, for even an industrial swamp is democratically procreative. Like Whitman, he pleads simply to participate in unselfconscious becoming: "I would with the fish, the blackening salmon, and the mad lemmings, / The children dancing, the flowers widening."

The wish for otherness is just that—a wish, but it appears to be sufficient. The shift from slag heaps to salmon streams is entirely willful and arbitrary. It is sanctioned by a cultural fantasy that now has post-Freudian justification—the wilderness is still psychologically accessible in all of us. Not in *each* of us, but in *all* of us; collectively we still harbor the continent in its original fertility: thus the plea for otherness and the inclusive listing. One can believe the same thing elsewhere, of course, though Conrad thought the journey to origins needed the analogy of a trip to the Congo, and Lawrence thought it might help to come to the New World. In America, however, one simply embraces all things and places. Nowhere else could a poet be thought other than foolish for flinging together fish, children, flowers, "great striated rocks" and even "buffalo chips drying."

**"North American Sequence"** alternates rhythmically between periods of emotionally-charged self-exploration and precise though kaleidoscopic descriptions of nature. These different types of discourse are so readily identifiable that a reader could collect and rearrange them to make several more consistently coherent poems. Yet the result would not be so

powerful. It is precisely the willed rhythm of movement between inside and outside, between the self and the world, and the complementary alternation between depression and joy, which propel poet and reader into the final vision. The introspective personal sections become increasingly ecstatic and mystical as the poet tries to move more deeply into the organic world he contemplates within himself, but this movement is checked by continuing reversals. The self is repeatedly nullified or emptied; nature again presents its dying face. As a poetic device, this kind of rhythm is unavoidably imprinted with echoes of Whitman's *Song of Myself;* Roethke, then, is compelled to find some way to repossess this rhythm and make it his own. He cannot entirely succeed, however, and his accomplishment here, contrary to Harold Bloom's analysis in *The Anxiety of Influence,* is founded on this very limitation.

Roethke brings this tension to the surface, exploiting it to dramatize the poem's verbal battle. In **"Meditations of an Old Woman,"** he has his title character say that "the body, delighting in thresholds, / Rocks in and out of itself." In **"North American Sequence,"** the Whitmanesque assurance that this rhythm is preeminently biological is abandoned. The juxtaposition of self and other parallels natural rhythms because the language has usurped nature; nature is a felicitous manifestation of will. The poem itself becomes the "Beginner, perpetual beginner" that the old woman proclaims herself to be.

The poem's continuous rhythm of expansion and withdrawal is reinforced when Roethke watches the tide at the beginning of **"Meditation at Oyster River."** Since the dying salmon, the mad lemmings, and the opening flowers of the first poem would fulfill themselves as inevitably as the tide, it is appropriate for young crabs and tiny fish to ride the tide shoreward in the second poem of the sequence. Nature begins to respond to the poet's call; the water surrounds him momentarily, and we anticipate his joining the tide, but instead he retreats to a safer perch. The decision is a partial rejection. He resists the natural world even while reaffirming his need for it. Then suddenly he unveils a full experience of the tide that could only be achieved from within the water. Not, however, the literal water at the shoreline, for the tides have been reconstituted in the water of words. The pull and tug is now inherent in the temptation to speak. Perched on his rock, he verbalizes the inward stresses of the oncoming waves—the forward thrust of the tide, the water sculpted by sandbars and fringed by beds of kelp, "topped by cross-winds, tugged at by sinuous undercurrents." He receives the benediction of the tide when the water laps his toes, but only that. Then he appropriates the energy, internalizes it, and dreams of a final cleansing. It would be like ice melting in the spring—weakening, shattering, and flowing, suddenly unburdened of both its human and its natural debris:

And I long for the blast of dynamite,
The sudden sucking roar as the culvert loosens its
    debris of
        branches and sticks,
Welter of tin cans, pails, old bird nests, a child's
    shoe riding a log,
As the piled ice breaks away from the battered
    spiles,
And the whole river begins to move forward, its
    bridges shaking.

In a few lines, we move from the "tongues of water, creeping in quietly," to this image of violent evacuation. The shock is considerable, not only because the passage is intrinsically destructive but also because it is a deliberate aggression against the Whitmanesque listing in **"The Longing."** The import is difficult to escape: there will be no loyalty to nature here except as it can be used to suit the poet's spiritual imperatives. This is an aesthetic alternative to the more literal historical usurpation of the American wilderness—rather less damaging, of course, but in service of needs no less dark. "I have left the body of the whale," Roethke writes, "but the mouth of the night is still wide." Free from the self's restrictive darkness, there is yet the wider darkness of the communal self. Emptied of himself, the poet comes into "the first heaven of knowing," a knowledge revealed when the poem celebrates its power. The power is a freedom to remake nature, almost to obliterate it. Like Whitman, Roethke reconstitutes nature in his speaking voice, though Roethke makes the violence of the process more visible. The poem summons its landscapes only to discard everything but their essential energy. It is not only a mystical, trance-like tone we hear in the poem's final meditation; it is an assertion of priority: "I rock with the motion of morning; / In the cradle of all that is." To this impersonal voice, the tide is now an intimate otherness that originates within: "Water's my will, and my way, / And the spirit runs, intermittently, / In and out of the small waves." For an instant his body seems part of the mutual vibrancy of landscape and self, though it is really the text that is holding them together in its net. There his consciousness is dispersed over its own perceptual field: "All's a scattering, / A shining."

The third poem begins by reversing this euphoric mood. The self retreats to its anguished territory and bodily darkness closes in again, through darkening thickets and contorted ravines. The poem juxtaposes its title, **"Journey to the Interior,"** with its first lines: "In the long journey out of the self, / There are many detours." It is a paradox the poem will nullify by force. The journey out of the self will proceed into a true interior we will share with the heart of a new world.

When we start the third poem, we assume that the poet has symbolically cleansed himself of civilization. The bleak clut-

ter of an industrial wasteland in the first poem was exchanged for a world of sandpipers and herons in the second. Though a collection of trash intrudes again, it is carried away on a flood of water. The problem would seem to be solved, so we expect Roethke's experience to be less compromised. Thus the car that introduces **"Journey to the Interior"** is divisive and unsettling. Surprisingly, Roethke does not reject this standard symbol of the contemporary wasteland; he embraces it. Roethke provides what for him would seem an unlikely tribute to the teenage myths of the late 1950s. He recalls risking his life to drive eighty miles an hour on a dangerous road, and his celebration of this bravado is no less loving than his catalogues of natural life: "A chance? Perhaps. But the road was part of me, and its ditches, / And the dust lay thick on my eyelids,—Who ever wore goggles?" By now this memory would be hopelessly sentimental, but **"Journey to the Interior"** was first published in 1961, and Roethke just manages to be innocent of the specific cultural self-consciousness that would have made the passage impossible. Instead, the homage to America's mechanical fantasies is more general; on that level, Roethke is quite aware of his inverted pastoralism. The poet has traded in his greenhouse for an automobile. Nonetheless, at the still center of his car ride he finds the greenhouse again.

Through the windows of the car, Roethke discovers that "all flows past"—dead snakes and muskrats, hawks circling above rabbits, "turtles gasping in the rubble," and even "a buckled iron railing, broken by some idiot plunger." All this detritus of nature's cruelty gathers in a catalogue evoking the rhythms of universal change. The passage obviously extends the breaking of the ice-jam passage in **"Meditation at Oyster River."** There he wished the self, like thawing ice, could be freed as though blasted by dynamite. Here the violence is more literal and commonplace; it is thereby at first more resistant to visionary synthesis. If this landscape "exceeds us all" it does so only by asserting a brute reality beyond our intervention. That, of course, is exactly Roethke's intention—to demonstrate that even the Darwinian side of America's landscapes can provide the raw material for textual transformation. Thus it would be a mistake to conclude that this "detour" into rude violence is peripheral to the poem's chief ambitions. Structurally and rhetorically, "Journey to the Interior" parallels all the poems in the sequence with its movement through descriptive catalogues to a visionary moment. Its dark world of dying things is not a lapse into a negative apocalypse that the sequence later overcomes; it is a necessary stage in the poem's development. It captures the one purgative experience essential to all visions of American communality—trial by visual fact.

What we see tends simply to contradict what we believe. Moreover, in a nation obsessed with the desire to create an ideal community, belief is generally codified before it is tested against reality. That was very much Roethke's artistic situa-

tion when he came to write **"North American Sequence."**
His poetic world had been mapped out long before, and there
was little if anything he could discover about it in his last
years. What he could do, however, was to expose his vision
to history, to open his greenhouse to the world at large. That
is what he does most daringly in **"North American Sequence."** The result is a poem whose visionary synthesis
must virtually contradict the catalogues of loss on which it is
founded. The poem's transcendent moments depend so much
on sheer assertion that they are always on the verge of becoming merely manic artifice. Yet Roethke's power of conviction just manages to sustain our trust in his vision. He
convinces us that on the edge of our cultural hysteria is a
zone of beneficial calm:

> I rise and fall, and time folds
> Into a long moment;
> And I hear the lichen speak,
> And the ivy advance with its white lizard feet—
> On the shimmering road,
> On the dusty detour.

Roethke succeeds for a moment in fusing a traditional opposition in American culture. The machine and the garden are
brought together and shown to have a common core. Indeed,
the machine is hurled into what is left of the garden and, at
least as a metaphor, gets closer to the garden's source than
did any of America's historical expeditions. Roethke's vision from the car is almost a mechanistic recapitulation of
Wordsworth's boyhood memories in *The Prelude* of running, then stopping short to see the earth still whirling past
him. For a moment, Roethke believes that not he but the
things around him are moving.

The poem builds to a new pastoral ecstasy, though it is an
ecstasy dependent on a poetic will symbolized by an on-
rushing car. As so often in his work, Roethke describes his
meditative immersion in the physical world in terms of elemental transformation—earth to water, air to fire, stone to
light. In **"The Dream,"** where sea and shore meet wood and
meadow, the image of a woman changes a field to a glittering sea. Here in this willed poetic space where all dying things
commingle, he declares, "I rise and fall in the slow sea of a
grassy plain." These wide plains of vision gather the separate things of America into a common dance of death. In the
territory of her poem, Roethke's old woman recovers all her
past in her present, both love's worst day when "the weeds
hiss at the edge of the field" and the meadows where she
remembers herself as a young girl—"running through high
grasses, / My thighs brushing against flower-crowns." In
**"North American Sequence,"** the prairie recalls the more
public fuming wastes at the opening of the sequence and
foreshadows the far field of the eternal near its close. Floating on this field of American locations, the poet tries to find
them all a place in his greenhouse Eden. Outside history, the

new greenhouse will nurture a set of landscapes themselves
imprinted with history's image. Each time is to be a collection of times, each moment a whole cycle of moments. Each
voice and every movement will be democratic. Making himself the stage for this drama of simultaneous events, Roethke
gives voice to America's special version of negative capa-
bility. He is bereft of purposeful motion—"beyond my own
echo, / Neither forward nor backward, / Unperplexed, in a
place leading nowhere"—committed to being only one
unique vehicle for the country's self-expression. Roethke
verges on an image of himself emptied, almost unborn, yet
ripe, with the nation's earth filling his mind. He wants, as
Galway Kinnell has described it, to make himself "vacant as
a / sucked egg in the wintry meadow, softly chuckling, blank
/ template of myself." For Roethke, to unveil this empty,
original form would be to see his own face reflected in a
generalized image of the genesis of the nation's natural life.

In the closing stanzas of **"Journey to the Interior,"** Roethke
begins to articulate the shape and texture of an image that
has hovered, half-voiced, throughout his career—the central
form of forms. As we shall see, the notion of a form of forms
runs through Robert Duncan's work as well. For Roethke it
is not so much a mystical talisman, though if Roethke's visionary passages are severed from his descriptive reveries,
the form of forms would be reduced to that; it is more his
obsessive creation and re-creation of a central project that
can never be wholly achieved because our history continually denies it. This primary form must combine erosive, temporal flux with subsuming, atemporal pattern. His phrase
for this aboriginal goal is "the flower of all water." In the
midst of the natural processes gathered together by the poem's
advancing and retreating tide, Roethke asserts that these opposing rhythms are fulfilled in a single place: "I see the flower
of all water, above and below me, the never receding, / Moving, unmoving in a parched land, white in the moonlight."
Every fluted wave, all the endless curving arcs of water, rise
up through him to turn inward on a central flowering. The
passage suggests that he has discovered the hidden paradigm
of sheer fluidity, but the image is really a fiction sustained
by intratextual associations. "I rehearse myself for this," he
admits, for "the stand at the stretch in the face of death."
Each poem in the sequence is a new rehearsal, and the sequence as a whole is a series of rehearsals. Roethke's verb
implies not so much a preparation for the inevitable as an
elaborately staged ritual that will enable him to possess the
inevitable within the poem.

Throughout **"Journey to the Interior"** our anticipation of
that end is partly anxious. From the opening car ride, "where
the shale slides dangerously / And the back wheels hang almost over the edge," through the descriptions of a conventionally picturesque town rendered foreboding, to the
catalogue of vulnerable or dying creatures, a sense of threat
continues. His images are adaptations of his more secure

pastoralism, but with a new nervousness. Earlier in his career, he could write of a wish to hear "a snail's music," and we could accept this as an extension of his greenhouse attentiveness to minute and soundless motion. Now a surreal uneasiness invades these dreams. When he claims to "hear the lichen speak, / And the ivy advance with its white lizard feet," we may reasonably wonder if these images communicate not only heightened awareness but also a sense of inexorable violation.

A similar ambivalence is at work in Roethke's evocation of the flower of all water; it is set against a sterile background— "a parched land, white in the moonlight." The flower, it seems, both opposes and fulfills its surroundings. Roethke casts his vision as an affirmation; "the spirit of wrath," he writes, "becomes the spirit of blessing." Yet the final line extends Whitman's dream of a democratized, luxuriant death to an image whose joy could easily turn to terror: "And the dead begin from their dark to sing in my sleep." Ten years later W. S. Merwin would be writing lines like these to summon the communality of collective dread.

At its moment in time, the end of the 1950s and the beginning of the 1960s, Roethke's poem can offer these images of collective renewal straightforwardly; they are not yet totally undermined by their historical context. Within a few years, Roethke's optimism would have appeared complicit with more dubious cultural enthusiasms. To maintain some independence for his vision, Roethke might have had to distance himself from arguments for open forms outside the world of poetry, at the risk of damaging his vision by its own defensiveness. By the mid-1960s **"Journey to the Interior"** would have been undone by too many bitter ironies. As at other points in American history, the image of a hawk circling above its prey would have had a military correlative. Similarly, the ruined landscape of **"The Longing"** and the catalogue of dying things in **"Journey to the Interior"** would have been ineluctably demonic in five years, merely commonplace in ten. By then, Roethke could hardly describe the rippling tide as "burnished, almost oily" without being literal and therefore unintentionally comic. Yet I am not arguing that **"North American Sequence"** would not have succeeded had it been written later; I am saying it could not have been conceived at all. Like the car Roethke recalls driving, the poem's route skirts disaster; it travels the edge of his historical moment, hanging halfway over the abyss. From our perspective, the poem is filled with poignant vulnerability. Like many credible American affirmations, it is designed to age instantly, to appear from the outset to have been written in the past. We can believe, then, that the dead have sung in Roethke's sleep, even though we know that their voices in our darkness would be more harsh.

**"North American Sequence"** draws its strength from Roethke's acceptance of the categorical frailty of its vision.

Like us, he knows that the poem's Edenic pastoralism is already a nostalgic artifice. It exists in the poem's "long moment" and nowhere else; it is, Roethke writes in the next poem, "a vulnerable place, / Surrounded by sand, broken shells, the wreckage of water." This place is Whitman's shoreline, the narrow vantage point where continent and sea may be exchanged so rapidly that neither seems troubled by its past. Roethke returns to this territory in **"The Long Waters"** to show us that he, like Whitman, can still perform this aesthetic sleight of hand. Moreover, he tells us, he can play this game with the same ingenuous rapture: "How slowly pleasure dies!" he exclaims, then later: "I embrace the world."

If there is excessive bravado in these claims, it is touched with saving self-mockery. This playfulness is made possible by the poem's confidence in its own textual ground. As we enter the fourth poem, **"North American Sequence"** now contains its own reserve of organic life. Like the country at large, the poem is itself a wellspring of energy. When Roethke returns to descriptive reverie in **"The Long Waters,"** he is recovering familiar poetic territory. Indeed it is territory now incorporated in the poem's form. When he moves from meditation to description, he is no longer duplicating a transition from the self to the external world; instead he is balancing two kinds of poetic language. The rhythm of excursus and return is a verbal rhythm. As the language moves forward, the natural settings already detailed are carried along as well. Each particular animal and place, exact in its isolation, echoes the other things the poem describes. It is therefore no longer necessary to worry that the land is finally unknowable. Whatever can be seen and named suffices: "Whether the bees have thoughts, we cannot say, / But the hind part of the worm wiggles the most." The part of nature that can be aesthetically co-opted serves, synecdochically, to redeem the rest. It is not only the poem, then, which is renewed by these successive visual catalogues; nature itself is revitalized when the poem gives attention to its changes.

The catalogues in **"The Long Waters"** are variously humorous and reverent. Thus "the worm's advance and retreat" comically invokes the motion of the tides, and Roethke even proceeds to ask protection from such essential rhythmic force. Yet there are also intense and almost overawed descriptive celebrations: "A single wave comes in like the neck of a great swan / Swimming slowly, its back ruffled by the light crosswinds." Both these images draw attention to the poem's power of vision, to its ability at once to specify and to exaggerate. Whatever the poem sees, it changes and perhaps also fulfills. Throughout **"The Long Waters"** Roethke is supremely confident of his transformative resources. That security enables him to move between the comic and honorific without disrupting the poem's tone. Overshadowed slightly by the darker vision of **"Journey to the Interior,"** yet also partly freed by that preceding poem's purgative fear, **"The Long Waters"** establishes a new perspective of bemused respect. In that gaze, both "the butterfly's havoc" and "the heaving sands" are at home.

Roethke has generalized his greenhouse ambience. What was once a quality of perception dependent on a particular place has been adapted to any location. That alone would not represent a radical development in Roethke's aesthetic. We might expect that he would, in Bachelardian fashion, internalize the greenhouse world and become capable of extending its nurturing warmth to the rest of his experience. A series of little greenhouse poems about different miniature landscapes would naturally follow. But a long poem sequence, moving rapidly through a wide range of settings and emphasizing the act of poetic transformation, is another matter. It asks whether the American landscape at large can become a greenhouse for the questing self. That is one of our culture's founding questions. Roethke's private greenhouse space thereby suddenly becomes both characteristic and public.

That sense of larger ambitions lends a covert uneasiness to the first four sections of **"The Long Waters."** The uneasiness is anticipatory. We know that the variations in mood are building to a need for another visionary synthesis. Another verbal resolution will have to draw these new images together. Salmon leap for insects, ivy puts down roots, a fisherman dawdles over a bridge. Each of these things is unique, yet they share a common rhythm; their separate actions verge on communality. That union will have to be verbal, for it is not given to us in the natural world. Indeed, our sense of verbal expectation is increased by allusions to the language of resolution used earlier in the sequence. Roethke names the gestures of plants, animals, and men, then he summarizes those names in the poem's demonstrated rhetoric: "These waves, in the sun, remind me of flowers." This statement can be rationalized—trout and pine trees may gesture as instinctively as unfolding flowers; they can register on the eye as successive waves of phenomena. Yet the memory Roethke invokes is really of a relation to the poem's language. In these descriptive sections, Roethke relaxes into a daydream of naming in order to gather energy for a new articulation of the poem's depths. Once again, he will speak of the flower of all water.

As with each of the first three poems, the penultimate moment is one of self-abnegation. He claims to be merely the passive recipient of the vision, to be first the land's breath and only then its voice. "I have come here," he writes, "without courting silence," and the irony in a poet's making that particular assertion is apparent. Yet he is in a sense merely the vehicle of imagery already present in the landscapes described. Of course, he has selected, arranged and vocalized those settings; he has given them whatever imperative toward communal form they now display. Nonetheless, the poem increasingly communicates a sense of inevitable force that gives Roethke's posture of passivity some justification.

Having set all this in motion, he can step back and pretend innocence. "I remember," he writes, "the dead middle way, / Where impulse no longer dictates."

Roethke would have us believe that he is no longer governed by the fatal self-pity of the first poem. His need to be reborn is collective, involuntary, and it can be realized through the instinct of the elements to play at metamorphosis. Nature, or at least nature apprehended, is a series of analogies. Moreover, those analogies converge on one another in the poem's space. There they do not merely clarify one another, they touch. And in touching they waken to a new life, "as a fire, seemingly long dead, flares up from a downdraft of air in a chimney." Roethke wants to speak from the point where these forces meet. He wants to occupy the verbal shoreline, the textuality, between self and other. Ambiguously, then, he can be both witness and agent, actively propounding a vision of selfless empathy. The destination of all he sees and describes, he is also the point of departure for its fresh emergence. He will consummate all nature in a single form, while scattering everywhere seeds of himself. The eyes of his poem see inwardness everywhere:

> I see in the advancing and retreating waters
> The shape that came from my sleep, weeping:
> The eternal one, the child, the swaying vine
>     branch,
> The numinous ring around the opening flower,
> The friend that runs before me on the windy
>     headlands,
> Neither voice nor vision.
>
> I, who came back from the depths laughing too
>     loudly,
> Become another thing;
> My eyes extend beyond the farthest bloom of the
>     waves;
> I lose and find myself in the long water;
> I am gathered together once more;
> I embrace the world.

These are the last two stanzas of **"The Long Waters,"** and they present what is so far Roethke's fullest vision of the form of forms. Rather than a single unifying figure, his vision is a series of parallel and perhaps equivalent images. In that sense, it merely testifies again to the poet's desire to make multiple images seem simultaneous. Yet this "shape" that rises out of the poem's "advancing and retreating waters" does carry the impulse further. Part of that effect is simply cumulative, but the cumulative force still requires suitable language with which to stage its re-emergence. Roethke makes several passes at that language here, and they provide a dramatic glimpse of the synthesis toward which he is working.

The passage is a kind of retrospective and anticipatory summary of Roethke's poetic goals. It reaches back through **"North American Sequence"** and uses it to gather together the poet's previous work. The sequence of equivalent descriptions serves to conjoin all the paired opposites Roethke has celebrated during his career. At their center is this ambiguous "shape" now openly used to contain a variety of restorative images. Like Yeats's image of the dancer, from which Roethke drew inspiration, the shape he sees is paradoxically both an object and an action. In two of his most well known love poems, Roethke saw this universal form manifested in a woman's body; he called it "a shape of change, encircled by its fire" and marvelled at "the shapes a bright container can contain." Here the shape is encircled as well by the play of light and movement about an opening flower; it is an eternal figure, summoning child and vine branch to its common ground. Like the body of the old woman in Roethke's **"Meditations,"** the form of forms is at once dense and airy. It is a universal shape of change through which all birth and death must pass.

The figure Roethke wants to describe is partly a very abstract and generalized extension of a body image primitive enough to represent all embodiment. Like the shape of the human body bent by age or curved in foetal sleep, it would resemble the earliest curled form shared by men, animals, and plants. To the extent that the image is organic and relatively static, Roethke's early greenhouse poems account for its imperatives toward growth and change. Yet Roethke also extended this archetype to inorganic matter. Through much of the middle part of his career, therefore, bodily process is used to draw the elements into association with the body image. When we breathe, for example, the body fills with air, and when we sleep, the body acquires the heaviness of stone. As stone and light, earth and fire, permanence and change coalesce verbally in the body image, it becomes an increasingly representative figure—the enduring and decaying house where each of us lives.

Yet the body that is so verbally allusive is not really the natural body but the body of the poem. The rapturous and playful catalogue in the conclusion to **"The Long Waters"** dramatizes the collective force of the poem's language. We are to imagine, with Roethke, that the descriptive and exclamatory appositives in the first of these two stanzas impinge on a single figure. They do so here, in the text we read. With the poem's senses dispersed in several landscapes, the poem itself is at once the poet's body and the thinking of the world's body. "Small waves," he wrote earlier, "repeat the mind's slow sensual play." Now he has learned that the poem that counterpoints such likenesses between external physical movement and his own perceptual processes can create and contain their entire interaction: "So the sea wind wakes desire. / My body shimmers with a light flame." "I roam elsewhere," he writes, "my body thinking." The poem draws

each of these elsewheres together, so that the rhythm of the tides is transferred to the poem's breathing.

The shape emerging from the poem's waves seems both familiar and separate, both a friend and the poet himself. It reflects everything of himself he had forgotten, yet makes him "become another thing." It is both personal and archetypal. Thus it emerges at once from the poet's sleep and from the ocean's depths. It is greeted with tears of relief and benediction that flow from himself and from the ocean's salt water. The poet is himself, he is a stranger, and finally he is everyone. Only through the poem's disguise can he maintain this multiple role. It is a role that American poets have often assumed in more blatantly prophetic form. Nor is this the first time Roethke himself has sought to become a representative and unifying figure. Yet **"North American Sequence"** is perhaps the first time he hints that the slug and worm of his private greenhouse poems are actually vestigial culture heroes, explorers working toward the source of a greenhouse Eden that belongs to all of us.

The "I" in the last two stanzas of the fourth poem in the sequence stands not only for Roethke and for the poem itself but also for a broad American audience. We too are gathered into the poem's voice. As a speaker, the poet fills the traditional American role of prophetic witness. That role had been functioning covertly in Roethke's poetry for some time, but **"North American Sequence"** makes it considerably more apparent. As a result, the quality of sheer performance becomes central to the experience of the poem. Roethke is trying for a definitive reintegration of self and nature, and we watch him try over and over again. That sense of continual recapitulation, of assaying yet another time the same textual synthesis, makes his creative effort here more patently self-conscious and deliberate than it has ever been before. What some critics experience in Roethke's poetry as embarrassing self-promotion, too artificially orphic, becomes the actual subject of **"North American Sequence."** In the process, Roethke's vision acquires a new credibility. We no longer have to believe that the vision exists outside the poetry, that it is so pervasively real it is "neither voice nor vision." We only have to recognize that Roethke wants the vision to succeed and that his desire is characteristically American.

The composite landscape of **"The Long Waters"** is unashamedly synthetic. It is a made place where the poet can summon all of nature's seasons to one mind. By shuffling together a collection of natural sites, the poem would create a varied but harmoniously accessible textual space, a continent on the printed page open to all of us. The project, of course, cannot literally succeed. Yet Roethke accepts the provisional status of his poem's solution, and he even admits that its implicit contradictions are as much comic as mystical. That gives the poem a genuine poignancy; it cannot achieve what it sets out to do. Moreover, each time the poem makes large claims for its vision, the purely verbal quality of those claims will make them seem mere posturing.

The ecstatic synthesis of these two stanzas gives us a glimpse of a personal and cultural unity that will not be. It echoes the partial and anticipatory conclusions of the first two poems in the sequence, recovers the more dramatic synthesis at the end of **"Meditation at Oyster River,"** and leads us to expect yet more radical summations from **"The Far Field"** and **"The Rose."** Yet these parallel statements of formal apotheosis are also equivalent and even interchangeable. Delayed, diverted, repeatedly almost achieved, the poem's form is imminent throughout. It is a tentative form in continuous motion, at once scattered and whole. "I lose and find myself," Roethke writes, and the poem too is "gathered together" and dissolved in "the long water."

Roethke would like to exist simultaneously in visionary transcendence and ironic deflation. Thus it is appropriate, though unsettling, that each of his verbal resolutions is discarded when the next poem in the sequence begins. As Richard Blessing has observed, "The narrator has slipped back into spiritual despondency in the space between poems." Each of these regressions brings us up short, yet they are implicit in the precarious rapture of the preceding vision. If we can learn to move back and forth between the dark and light of vision at will, we will have internalized the poem's lesson. It is a lesson addressed both to Roethke's own sometimes violent emotional reversals and to the country at large. For the American dream of a humanized wilderness must have its darker side as well.

Into that darkness once again the sequence descends at the beginning of the fifth poem, **"The Far Field":** "I dream of journeys repeatedly: / Of flying like a bat deep into a narrowing tunnel." This repeats the movement toward and into closed space that opened **"Journey to the Interior."** The visionary synthesis at the end of **"The Long Waters,"** then, is not a natural given; it is a feature of the poem's performative force, and Roethke will have to work his way toward it again through fear and loss. We have, however, brought with us a sense of the potential interchangeability of human artifacts and natural life, so the car of **"Journey to the Interior,"** which returns as well, no longer seems to violate the poem's wider focus. Roethke imagines being trapped in a sand-rut "Where the car stalls, / Churning in a snowdrift / Until the headlights darken." The image of the car wheels churning echoes the description in **"Meditations of an Old Woman"** of a "journey within a journey," lost, "the gate / Inaccessible," possessed of tremendous futile energy, like "two horses plunging in snow, their lines tangled." It is a paralysis of fear endured in slow motion, yet savored, as when Roethke (elsewhere in the same volume) imagines that

a meadow mouse which escapes after he captures it must now live under the owl's eye, like a "paralytic stunned in the tub, and the water rising."

The feeling of paralysis amidst danger, one of the most common dream events, puts Roethke in touch with one of his childhood memories—the field "not too far away from the ever-changing flower-dump," whose end drops off into a culvert. There collects, as in the ice-flow passage of **"Meditation at Oyster River,"** a mixture of human and animal debris: tin cans, tires, and "the shrunken face of a dead rat, eaten by rain and ground-beetles." There too he finds a tomcat, shot by a watchman, "its entrails strewn over the half-grown flowers." A few years later, Galway Kinnell describes a similar scene more vividly in "The Porcupine"; its effect on both poets is comparable, as Roethke begins to think of himself emptied, simplified by death.

First, however, he needs to elevate these specific images into a general image of death that can be a more manipulable verbal resource. "At the field's end," he writes, "one learned of the eternal"; these deaths are the common voice of all the worldly things the poem has assembled. He suffers for them, but his "grief was not excessive," for there are also "warblers in early May." The natural rhythms of life and death give him, in the poem, a context for contemplating himself with "another mind, less peculiar." Perhaps, he muses with a playfulness resembling that of the poetry he wrote for children, he'll return in another life as "a raucous bird, / or, with luck, as a lion." The choices are all willed and fanciful, even the more primitive ones. He writes of lying naked in sand, "Fingering a shell, / Thinking: / Once I was something like this, mindless," and he thinks he might "sink down to the hips in a mossy quagmire." The image of envagination and the empty shell invoke both the evacuated, archetypal template of the self and the moist greenhouse where it acquires its face. Yet the birds and far field suggest the vast reaches of air and the self opened to the infinite. **"The Long Waters"** laid the ground-work for a figure unifying self and world; "The Far Field" extends that synthesis to the two poles of nature introduced early in Roethke's life—the close greenhouse and the wide field.

Roethke is working to create a far field, deep and open but as close as the page he writes his poem on, whose verbal rhythms can unify greenhouse and field and do so not for himself but for all of us:

> I learned not to fear infinity,
> The far field, the windy cliffs of forever,
> The dying of time in the white light of tomorrow,
> The wheel turning away from itself,
> The sprawl of the wave,
> The on-coming water.

This is the far field where the poem's many waters will gather to flower together. There all outward movement returns to itself, folding disparate things into a single flowering: "The river turns on itself, / The tree retreats into its own shadow." The field will fold together all North American landscapes, as mountain meadow water and a glacial torrent flow together in the alluvial plain. Thus each distant spring, each American tributary feeds our inward reservoir, while the self, brimful of its inwardness, overflows everywhere. From the center of this Whitmanesque self, as from a single stone, spread concentric rings of water, carrying reflected and diffused light ever outward: "The pure serene of memory in one man,— / A ripple widening from a single stone / Winding around the waters of the world." This outpouring water is also a benediction and an embrace, both freeing and bringing home what it touches. The poet's vision, conferring on each thing the dignity of its single name, meanwhile draws each thing within its reach to possess it. In the final lines of **"The Far Field,"** a collective consciousness can appear to be cleansed of longing, for it contains everything. An omnipresent force in nature, the poet's will suffuses inanimate matter and sets it to dream in words: "A man faced with his own immensity / Wakes all the waves, all their loose wandering fire."

"I have come to a still, but not a deep center," he writes, "a point beside the glittering current." There "My mind moves in more than one place, / In a country half-land, half-water." This mediating land, the territory between self and world, between earth and water, is the textuality the poem maps out for itself. Into this land, and into his poem, he must die to be reborn as a collective figure. "I am renewed by death, thought of my death." Yet there is not one death, but many, and each is a renewal. Each time the self is lost, it is regained in the image of the world, in every immediate dying change before his eyes: "The dry scent of a dying garden in September, / The wind fanning the ash of a low fire." "He is the end of things, the final man," the first and last man—Adamic, for the end of things is foretold by a true beginning; each final man begins his life anew. The self—mysterious sea-cave in which the world drowns to breathe again—will be repeatedly buried and uncovered by the tides. In the body of the poem he can become, as he puts it elsewhere, "A phoenix, sure of my body, / Perpetually rising out of myself."

At the field's end, hovering over the ever-renewing grave of the sea, Roethke recovers the lost innocent self in a new image of his text as a body. Now the sea-shape of this body, foolish and ancient, green and dying ("In robes of green, in garments of adieu"), can forgo all anxious postures. Its form, sea-blessed, is not imprisoning slime or unmoving stone. It is the site of all changes, the nexus where movement must pass whether to be contained or freed. "The body," he writes elsewhere, is "but a motion in a shoe." All movement is thereby imprinted with this image of the empty self—all

things fulfill themselves under the sign of the body, whose shape of change is the sign of the form of forms. "Flesh, flash out of me," he writes in a notebook, but the need to be free of a body is supplanted by the discovery of his body anywhere in North America he looks. "The flesh," he once wrote, "can make the spirit visible." Thus "the flesh fathers dream" as wide as the world. "And I became all that I looked upon." The greenhouse body grows until the far field itself is enfleshed.

The greenhouse world of his childhood, which Roethke explicitly summons to his side in **"The Rose"**—the final poem of the sequence—now nurtures even the farthest bloom of the waves. "The leafy mind" of his early poems "that long was tightly furled" has thick leaves opening in every elsewhere. Roethke thinks of roses in a tiny childhood world at last granted its true space, in greenhouses six hundred feet wide. He remembers his father lifting him high over the elaborate hybrids: "And how those flowerheads seemed to flow toward me, to beckon me, / Only a child, out of myself." In **"The Rose,"** the distant field flowers through the poet—out of the ground on which he stands. "There are those to whom place is unimportant," he writes in the poem's first line, "but this place, where sea and fresh water meet, / Is important." The rose of baffled wonderment in the first poem ("The rose exceeds, the rose exceeds us all") is transformed into a figure for a self exceeding the limits of time and space, yet supremely flowering in its place:

> But this rose, this rose in the sea-wind,
> Stays,
> Stays in its true place,
> Flowering out of the dark,
> Widening at high noon, face upward,

This place is the collective sign of all the sites the poem celebrates and engenders. Roethke therefore catalogues anew the beach and the meadow, the sea and the air, filling **"The Rose"** with diverse American places in the culmination of his sequence. So that any place, any moment, is the scene of the entire continent's survival. He lists the songs of several birds, "the mimetic chortling of the catbird" and "the bobolink skirring from a broken fencepost," then orchestrates a cacophony of sound—cicadas, the shriek of nails ripped from a roof, horns and bulldozers. But he absolves the raucous clatter of its variety in a comprehensive gesture:

> I return to the twittering of swallows above water,
> And that sound, that single sound,
> When the mind remembers all,
> And gently the light enters the sleeping soul,
> A sound so thin it could not woo a bird,

"Beautiful my desire," he continues, "and the place of my desire." When desire is deeply rooted in its immediate place, it can surpass self-mortification to voice the collective will of the land, but only the poem has so flexible and representative a location. The sequence of poems began in a paralyzed "agony of crucifixion on barstools" where "not even the soot dances." It ends when the crown of thorns smiles and takes flight: "I sway outside myself / Into the darkening currents . . . Was it here I wore a crown of birds for a moment?" "I played in flame and water like a boy / And I swayed out beyond the white seafoam":

> Near this rose, in this grove of sun-parched, wind-
>     warped
>         madronas,
> Among the half-dead trees, I came upon the true
>     ease of myself,
> As if another man appeared out of the depths of
>     my being,
> And I stood outside myself,
> Beyond becoming and perishing,
> A something wholly other,
> As if I swayed out on the wildest wave alive,
> And yet was still.
> And I rejoiced in being what I was:
> In the lilac change, the white reptilian calm,
> In the bird beyond the bough, the single one
> With all the air to greet him as he flies,
> The dolphin rising from the darkening waves;
>
> And in this rose, this rose in the sea-wind,
> Rooted in stone, keeping the whole of light,
> Gathering to itself sound and silence—
> Mine and the sea-wind's.

The rose is a universal figure, but here it is also uniquely American, symbolizing the cohering self-expression of North America's land. The America that flowers here is, of course, largely a visual one. Roethke has not opened his poetry to specific historical events but rather to a variety of sites, including those that have become industrial wastelands. The landscapes, then, represent both possibilities lost and possibilities yet untried. This attributes a static, spatialized character to American history, a tendency Roethke shares with many other American writers.

The resolution Roethke offers us in **"The Rose"** is exclusively verbal, almost gratuitously so, yet this fragility increases its force. Culturally and personally, the poem offers a momentary way of attaining a harmony the world does not offer. As Adrienne Rich will do ten years later, Roethke works out verbally a synthesis not available elsewhere in human experience. Unlike Rich, however, Roethke does not really expect the poetry to change his life. For a man at times unhinged by guilt and self-doubt, the poignancy and necessity of a vision that is wholly a willed artifice should be apparent.

**"North American Sequence"** is an artifice that also reaches out to gather all of Roethke's poetry together. We can hear in it echoes of images recurring throughout his career, though that is true of almost any of his poems. More important is the poem's effort to be the apotheosis of that imagery, liberating its heaviness and its edge of despair. If the rose in the final poem is rooted in stone, then stone thereby flows and looses the weight whereby "his thought is tied, the curving prowl of motion moored to rock." There is energy in even that absolute repose: "I touched the stones, and they had my own skin." "My flesh," he wrote earlier, "is breathing slower than a wall." "I know . . . the stone's eternal pulseless longing," "I know the motion of the deepest stone." He has lodged himself verbally at the center of the earth's most eternal substance, and he feels his spirit, too, bound up in the body's unyielding matter. But the immobility of body and stone is only a thickening of the circle of changes; so the spine, emblem of the body's rigidity, is the vortex of a new unfolding. "I turned upon my spine, / I turned and turned again," he writes, so as to become a rose, "a blaze of being on a central stem."

In the deepest stone starts that slow-moving curve traced later by the opening flower and the cresting wave. The original poles of nature are abandoned for a continuum in motion, where the elements are interchanged and self and other become one another unpredictably. Yet in the final moments of the poem, a further resolution appears. Water and flame, stone and light, the fecund "lilac change" and sterile "reptilian calm," seem almost to coalesce. Here, where world and body interpenetrate the poem's flesh, **"North American Sequence"** holds its forces in momentary stasis. In the image of the rose unfolded in the sea-wind, at once vulnerable and eternal, intimate and indifferent, the poem voices a dream of all motion taken up by form. Deep within the self, and everywhere outside us, is this far field where water flowers in stone.

## Peter Balakian (essay date 1989)

SOURCE: "Our First Contemporary," in *Theodore Roethke's Far Fields: The Evolution of His Poetry,* Louisiana State University, 1989, pp. 1-13.

[*In the following essay, Balakian draws attention to Roethke's influence on modern American poetry, particularly his synthesis of autobiographical detail and transcendental consciousness reflected in the subsequent work of beat, confessional, and deep image poets.*]

Poets' reputations rise and fall with the currents of aesthetic fashion, the prevailing winds of critical methodology, and the vicissitudes of religious and philosophical world views.

321

Of course reputations are not always an indication of artistic achievement, and the complex cultural processes that canonize writers and cast others into oblivion are not always just or reliable. No artist is immune from the relativism of a historical moment, yet I believe that truly significant art of a previous era will continue to define a part of the present and in doing so will transcend the relativism of any historical moment.

The complex reasons for the present decline in Roethke's reputation as a poet are not my concern here. Yet I find it odd that the judgments of some of our most influential critics of twentieth-century poetry find him to be a poet of lesser importance and do not accord him the value a poetic harbinger deserves. No doubt the current trend toward critical methodologies based on linguistic theory and tied to a tradition of French rationalism has had something to do with a milieu that is not particularly sympathetic to the kind of poetry Roethke has written. His intuitive psychology, lyrical language, and suprarational view of the universe do not seem suitable for critics engaged in the rational methods of linguistic analysis. It may be true, too, that Roethke's shifts in style and idiom—what may appear to be a lack of external harmony within the body of his work—during the five decades in which he wrote have made him difficult for critics to categorize. Although I do not see Roethke through a hagiographer's lens, I do believe his rightful place is that of an innovative poet who has been a major source of influence on the poetry of our time.

One can argue forcefully, as I wish to, that no single book of poems is as important to the evolution of the idioms that have dominated American poetry in the four decades following World War II than is *The Lost Son and Other Poems,* published in 1948. Most of these poems were written and published in American magazines and journals in the early and mid-forties.

Hyatt H. Waggoner and James E. B. Breslin have portrayed accurately the shift in American poetry that became apparent by the mid-fifties and marked an end to the final phase of modernism that was waning by the late forties. Certainly Allen Ginsberg's *Howl* (1956) and Robert Lowell's *Life Studies* (1959) are landmarks in their rejection of the autotelic, symbolistic, and purportedly impersonal poetry of late modernism. Ginsberg and Lowell were concerned with breaking down the barriers between life and art and finding a representative identity that was more subjective and personal than that which T. S. Eliot, Ezra Pound, Robert Frost, William Carlos Williams, or Wallace Stevens had created. By the late fifties and early sixties Ginsberg, Lowell, John Berryman, Sylvia Plath, Anne Sexton, Denise Levertov, James Dickey, James Wright, and Robert Bly, to name several, were proceeding along new lines. They were writing poetry that was more openly autobiographical and personally emotional; their

poems reflected a sense that poetic language was part of a life process; their language was more demotic and their diction more colloquial. As Breslin puts it, they sought "ways of ordering poetry that [would] not stifle consciousness" and "new ways of binding form and flux so that temporality will not seem to have been violated."

Not only did the subject of the poet's past become important, but also material of the poet's family became significant to this new poetry. In the way that inherited Western cultural myths, symbols, and history were crucial to the modernist poet's sense of the past, experience derived from personally inherited history—blood history—became central to the postmodern poet's idea of the past. The impact of World War II, the nightmare of the Holocaust, and the terror created by the atomic and now nuclear age, seem to have discredited for poets much of the meaning and viability accorded Western civilization. For example, the overarching Western myths and texts that stand behind "The Waste Land," "The Cantos," or "The Bridge" became far less meaningful and therefore less usable to American poets after World War II. And if it can be said, as I believe it can, that familial history has supplanted a good deal of cultural history for the poets of our time, then certainly Roethke's *The Lost Son,* Ginsberg's *Kaddish,* and Lowell's *Life Studies* emerge as the seminal family cycles of the era. Each book in its own way is groundbreaking, each uses autobiographical and inherited familial sources to shape a myth out of history, and thus each marks a break with the modernist idea of the past.

Breslin maintains that the evolution of American poetry after modernism can be best understood by dividing the period into five major groups: the beat, confessional, deep image, Black Mountain, and New York schools. In a broad sense, the poetry of these five groups, he argues, characterizes the major poetic reorientation of our period. Although such a paradigm may be too schematic, it gives a perspective on our age and helps make historical sense of Theodore Roethke. If we look at our era in terms of these five movements, which in sum can be said to give definition to the dominant trends, it becomes clear that Roethke in *The Lost Son* had anticipated many of these new directions. (Oddly enough, Breslin fails to discuss Roethke as a significant force in this historical evolution.) For no single book of poems, written at such an early date—a good decade before Lowell and Ginsberg had their breakthroughs—incorporates more of the innovative forms and poetic assumptions that have come to define the contemporary idiom in American poetry.

In *The Lost Son,* Roethke is confessionally Freudian in the manner that would become important to poets like Lowell, Berryman, Plath, Sexton, and Ginsberg. Yet the psychic identity of his persona, the lost son, is based predominantly on Jungian psychology. And it is, of course, the Jungian idea of consciousness that would be embraced by the deep imagists like Bly and Wright and by other poets such as Galway Kinnell, W. S. Merwin, and Charles Simic in their attention to the idea of collective mind. What Roethke described as his "telescopic" method of presentation contains several of the assumptions that lie behind the deep-image technique. And Roethke's protean experiments with form anticipate various elements of the dynamism of open-field form that would become important to the Black Mountain poets.

Roethke's confessional voice in *The Lost Son* grew from the painful experience of his private life. Unlike his modernist predecessors, he did not attempt to transform his personal suffering into a medium that was impersonally mythic or aesthetically self-contained. If emotional trauma and psychic pain are apparent in "Prufrock," "The Broken Tower," or "Sunday Morning," for example, the origins of Eliot's, Crane's, and Stevens' suffering and the private details that would uncover their unique personalities were not their poetic concerns. Conversely, Roethke's poems confront the intimate self and turn the bald sources of experience into grist for the poet's transforming power. Roethke's childhood in his father's greenhouse and his history of mental breakdowns are the central autobiographical events which inform the creation of the lost son.

His father's twenty-five acres of greenhouses in the Saginaw Valley and the hothouse world of peat moss, plant cuttings, carnations, roses, cyclamen, and compost organisms was the loamy place out of which he would shape his mind and delve into his psychic and familial past. The greenhouse became the glass womb in the mind where a lifetime's source of figurative language blossomed into a concept of self. Roethke lived much of his adult life in the throes and cycles of manic depression for which he was periodically hospitalized and on occasion given shock treatment. His battle with life at the mind's edge was a passageway for him into the wilderness of his psyche and soul. With Roethke one is forced to restate an old truth: his mental instability was a source and fuel for his art.

The Freudian kind of confessionalism in *The Lost Son* is realized, to a large degree, in Roethke's ability to make use of traumatic and ecstatic childhood experience and his need to probe his private dream world in order to release psychic tensions and relieve himself of past burdens and repressed guilt. By wrestling with his painful past, he sought a way to confront his father, the greenhouse keeper who haunted his imagination. Although Freudian notions were not unknown to modernists like Eliot and Crane, such a confessional psychology was at most only obliquely associated with the poet's personal life *in the poems*. By contrast Roethke's poetry of confession makes use of the details of autobiography in a way that is significantly different from the modernists.

The psychic life of his persona, the lost son, is defined by

the family landscape of Roethke's greenhouse childhood: his father, Otto, whose untimely death left Roethke at age thirteen a lost son; those Old World employees, Max Laurisch, Frau Bauman, Frau Schmidt, and Frau Schwartz, who were horticulturists and extended kin in the poet's memory; and the greenhouse chores—like weed pulling, moss gathering, and transplanting—that as a boy Roethke performed ritualistically and assiduously for his father. The grounding of a poetic cycle in such highly personal concerns would become a common assumption for poets such as Plath, W. D. Snodgrass, Sexton, Lowell, Berryman, and Ginsberg by the late fifties and early sixties. Roethke—like Lowell with his New England Protestant family and Ginsberg and his politically radical Jewish family—is concerned with the mythic shape of his family past and with the archetypal and cultural significance of that past. This psychological and cultural way of transforming family history into confessional poetry also differs significantly from another kind of domestic poetry, often more simple (meditations on wives, husbands, sons, daughters, etc.), that is prevalent in Romantic and Victorian poetry and that has become popular again in the past decade. In short, much of what is innovative about *The Lost Son* stems from Roethke's pioneering this postmodern form of familial confessionalism, which contained at least part of the new era's "new confession," as Emerson once put it. Roethke wrote in a notebook entry:

> I was crazed
> Into meaning more profound than what my fathers
>     heard,
> Those listening bearded men
> Who cut the ground with hoes; and made with
>     hands
> An order out of muck and sand. Those Prussian
>     men
> Who hated uniforms.

This new kind of confessionalism could be successful only if the unveiling of the private life could achieve universality. The naked self and the representative nature of that self must constantly overlap—sometimes fully merged and at other times in a necessarily uneasy tension. It has been well documented that Roethke had, especially during the forties, a deep interest in Jungian psychology, and this interest served his evolving poetics. In creating the lost son, he wished to unite a deeply personal consciousness (a Freudian concept of the mind) with an impersonal or collective idea of the psyche which was based largely on a Jungian concept of the unconscious. This unique merging of Freudian and Jungian psychology in *The Lost Son* anticipates both the Jungian proclivities of Robert Bly's deep imagism and the Freudian confessionalism of Lowell, Ginsberg, Berryman, Plath, and many others.

Numerous times during those years, Roethke recorded his

feelings about the nature of the collective mind in the "lost son" poems. He came to believe that one could move forward spiritually only if one returned first to the origins of one's psychic life. He asserted that his new poems oozed out of an "older memory" and "dribbled out of the unconscious." A world of cosmogonic occurrences and a state of primal feeling defined the evolving personality of the lost son. And his wonderful depiction of his Jungian crow of chaos became a veritable emblem for his art:

> When I saw that clumsy crow
> Flap from a wasted tree,
> A shape in the mind rose up:
> Over the gulfs of dream
> Flew a tremendous bird
> Further and further away
> Into a moonless black,
> Deep in the brain, far back.

> ("Night Crow")

This peculiar blend of Freudian and Jungian concepts evolved out of Roethke's approach to the natural world. Nature became his objective correlative, that medium through which he could forge a confessional voice able to contain a personal self and a representative version of that self—something mythic. Given the realities of Roethke's childhood, nature would always be a vehicle of the evolving self and a container for the spirit's life and the mind's form.

For Roethke, nature was not only religion brought down to earth, a container of emblematic meanings and an embodiment of human consciousness as it was for Emerson; nature was the script of his life—myth and autobiography bound into one. The natural world was the reality in which his childhood was lived and his family's drama acted out. His Freudian relationship to his parents could not be separated from the stuff in the greenhouse. Because he invented his lost son—the myth of himself—out of the hothouse world his father created, nature became both an emblem of autobiography and the container of a universal soul. He referred to his greenhouse as a "womb, a heaven-on-earth."

This compelling and idiosyncratic relationship with nature was crucial to his ability to make of the lost son a confessional voice and a mythic mask—a poetic character with what one must term an ontogenetic and a phylogenetic identity. This myth making thus allowed him to turn the lost son into a character with an archetypal heritage whose identity resonates with that large cast of lost sons who have preceded him: Jesus, Job, Oedipus, Telemachus, Hamlet, Huck Finn, Ishmael, Quentin Compson, Stephen Dedalus, to name a few. In seeking his own father and his spiritual Father, the lost son is, in every sense, on a pilgrimage—on a passage at once out of the self and into its mucky interior.

Roethke's ability to create a phylogenetic identity for the lost son and to dramatize a "racial memory" derived to a large degree from his ability to "telescope image and symbol," as he put it. His acute awareness of this technique discloses the degree to which he felt he could penetrate the human psyche and face the mystery in things.

> I believe that, in this kind of poem, the poet, in order to be true to what is most universal in himself, should not rely on allusion; should not comment or employ many judgment words; should not mediate (or maunder). He must scorn being "mysterious" or loosely oracular, but be willing to face up to the genuine mystery. His language must be compelling and immediate: he must create an actuality. He must be able to telescope image and symbol, if necessary, without relying on the obvious connectives: to speak in a kind of psychic shorthand when his protagonist is under great stress. He must be able to shift his rhythms rapidly, the "tension."

It is precisely through this "psychic shorthand" and "telescoping" that he created images "deep" enough to hold and express his protagonist's primordial identity. Delmore Schwartz addressed this quality of psychic depth in Roethke with great insight when he noted: "The reader who supposes that Roethke is really a primitive lyric poet loses or misses a great deal. Perhaps the best way to describe what is under the surface is to quote Valéry's remark that the nervous system is the greatest of all poems."

Thus Bly's insistence that deep images unlock the unconscious mind was a discovery Roethke had made in the mid forties in the first four "lost son" poems. During the late fifties and early sixties, Bly would advocate a poetry that transcended the constraints of the human ego and allowed man to participate *with* nature and be at home in the universe. Calling for an alternative to the cerebrally oriented and rationally enclosed literature characteristic of writers like Lowell, Arthur Miller, and Saul Bellow, Bly singled out only Walt Whitman and Roethke as American poets who have brought us "news of the universe." Bly's belief that deep images lead us back to the primary connections between the human self and the animistic world was in some way an emanation of Roethke's poetics of two decades earlier. For Roethke had created a sacred and numinous nature and an archetypal mind that embodied what Bly later called a "poetry that reaches out in waves over everything that is alive." Bly was advocating what Roethke had accomplished in *The Lost Son:* a poetry that was aesthetically and ontologically organic—free of a dualistic human identity. Perhaps no protagonist in American poetry learns to overcome the dualisms of the Western rational mind with more happy passion than the lost son, who cries at the closing of **"A Field of Light"**:

My heart lifted up with the great grasses;
The weeds believed me, and the nesting birds.
There were clouds making a rout of shapes
crossing a windbreak of
  cedars,
And a bee shaking drops from a rain-soaked
honeysuckle.
The worms were delighted as wrens.
And I walked, I walked through the light air;
I moved with the morning.

Roethke is not a projectivist in the post-Poundian way that Charles Olson lays out in his famous "Projectivist Verse" essay. Roethke's sense of form and intent is different from that of poets like Robert Duncan, Robert Creeley, and Denise Levertov. However, his kinetic language, his bardic feeling about the spoken quality of the poem, and his organic and dynamic concept of consciousness dovetail with the forms of inclusive openness that Olson and the Black Mountain poets would be practicing and preaching by the early fifties. Roethke, who was older than Olson, shared one major source of influence with him—William Carlos Williams. The impact of Williams on Roethke accounts for some of the kinetic language and protean form in the "lost son" poems, and several of the poetic principles that Olson would advocate in his 1950 projectivist verse manifesto had, in the "lost son" sequence, already become second nature for Roethke, who wrote with both the compulsive containment of a metaphysical and the discursive openness of a Poundian.

Many of the essential ideas in Olson's projectivist essay indicate the degree to which Roethke's experiments intersect with the Black Mountain orientation. Olson calls for a "revolution of the ear" and "the *kinetics* of the thing." "The poem itself must," he says, "at all points, be a high energy construct," for "it is from the union of the mind and the ear that the syllable is born." For Olson, the poem has to unite linguistic rhythms with physiological rhythms, and he insists that "verse will only do in which a poet manages to register both the acquisitions of his ear and the pressures of his breath."

Olson's idea of organic free verse form leads him to think of the poem as a field in which the words that embody objects create a "necessary series of tensions." In this dynamic idea of form it is essential that the poet not dissipate his linguistic energy in any way. "The descriptive functions generally have to be watched, every second, in projective verse, because of their easiness, and thus their drain on the energy which composition by field allows into a poem. *Any* slackness takes off attention, that crucial thing, from the job at hand." The kinetic field, Olson believes, is shaped to a large degree by the relationship between linguistic sound and the movement of the poet's consciousness. Thus the poet can, "without the

convention of rime and meter, record the listening he has done to his own speech." And the success of such an effort rests largely with the ear—"the ear, the ear which has collected, which has listened, the ear, which is so close to the mind that it is the mind's, that it has the mind's speed." This dynamic kind of poetic language, Olson believes, could carry the kind of energy poetry has not "carried in our language since the Elizabethans."

Roethke's own breakthrough to the principles of organic form occurred, of course, in the forties when he began working on *The Lost Son*. In a letter he wrote to Williams while he was at work on the poem **"The Lost Son,"** he proclaims an idea of dynamic poetic speech that sounds a good bit like Olson. He has written a poem, he says, "for the ear and not the eye . . . with the mood or the action on the page, not talked about, not the meditative, T. S. Eliot kind of thing." This letter and the others Roethke exchanged with Williams in the forties reveal his enthusiasm for Williams' idea of organic form. Thus, in a historical sense Williams becomes a common source for Roethke and Olson.

A comic aphorism Roethke recorded in a notebook of the mid-forties indicates how deeply he felt about the importance of the ear: "All ear and no brain / Makes Teddy inane." Like Olson, Roethke has no use for slackness or lack of linguistic pressure. His notebook entries of the mid-forties stress his commitment to a dynamic and organic free verse, and, like Olson, he complains that "so much of modern verse seems tensionless." Although Roethke was not a theorist as Olson was, his belief that if the poet "can't make the words move, he has nothing," is similar to Olson's advocacy of dynamic language in an open field. In discussing the influences on the "lost son" poems, Roethke points to "German and English folk literature, particularly Mother Goose; Elizabethan and Jacobean drama, especially the songs and rants." Oddly enough, but not coincidentally, we find Roethke and Olson both appealing to the dynamism of Elizabethan English in their desire to reclaim some original energy for contemporary free verse.

In his desire to write "a poem that is the shape of the psyche under great stress," Roethke created an organic form that flexed its syntax. The protean shape of the lost son's mind is, to a large degree, generated in the euphonic qualities of Roethke's ear which in turn shape the kinetic force of the line. The dimensions of the lost son's psychic experience create—in the most organic way—the stresses in the lines and the nature of the lines that constitute the stanzas in the four lost son poems. Like Olson, Roethke disdains artificial syntactic connectives and the use of traditional metaphor and simile. His goal is to create a language that embodies in every aspect of its form the content of the mind. That moment of manic frenzy in section 3 of **"The Lost Son"**—which is followed by the two lines made up of "money" and "water" that disclose the matter-spirit duality in the protagonist—exemplifies this kind of protean organicism.

> All the windows are burning! What's left of my
>   life?
> I want the old rage, the lash of primordial milk!
> Goodbye, goodbye, old stones, the time-order is
>   going,
> I have married my hands to perpetual agitation,
> I run, I run to the whistle of money.
> Money money money
> water water water

A poet of consequence to the evolving direction of his art is naturally a beneficiary of a given moment in history. As a poet coming to maturity in the waning phase of modernism, Roethke was able to have a perspective on that great generation. He could make selective use of the innovations of the period and absorb what he had to of writers like Eliot, Stevens, Williams, James Joyce, and William Faulkner—to name several who influenced him. Unlike poets of the generation to follow him, who often felt antagonistic about the modernist masters, Roethke felt both connected to and yet, I think, shrewdly distanced from the age of Eliot and Pound.

Roethke's maturation during the middle decade of the century gave him a healthy and creative perspective on modernism as well as a broad cultural vantage point. For as a mid-century American poet, he was able to bring together—to synthesize in his idiosyncratic way—dominant post-Christian intellectual movements: Romanticism, Darwinism, and modern psychology (Freudian and Jungian). Roethke had enough historical distance from these intellectual world views to be able to create out of them a set of assumptions and ultimately an aesthetic myth from which his language and poetic concerns could evolve.

Critics have examined at length the importance of British Romanticism, American Transcendentalism, and Freudian and Jungian psychology in Roethke's work. But Roethke's organic aestheticism is also, at least in part, an emanation of Darwinism. He is, of course, in no way a Darwinist; in the obvious sense, he is neither secular nor deterministic. Rather, proceeding from certain Darwinian assumptions, he extends his own version of what can be called post-Darwinian myth. Darwin's organic conception of life, growth, and evolution, and his idea of an organic architecture unifying the entire scheme of plant and animal life, had immense meaning for Roethke. His ability to identify with the subhuman world of plants, stones, and microorganisms in **The Lost Son** and **Praise To The End!,** his assertion in **"The Waking"** that "the lowly worm climbs up a winding stair," and his sense of phylogenetic origins in **"The Far Field,"** where we find him "Fingering a shell, / Thinking: / Once I was something like this, mindless, / Or perhaps with another mind, less pe-

culiar," exemplify how thoroughly he absorbed a vision of the Darwinian cosmos.

Viewing Roethke from the vantage point of the century's final decade, one might say that he pioneered our first important postmodernist poems. In creating a mythic autobiography out of his vision of certain intersecting intellectual forces that shaped America at mid-century, he was able to find a relationship between an idea of the transcendent, a modern notion of the natural world, and a concept of the contemporary human self. In forming a new script from the intellectual realms his imagination filtered to the supple language of his rhetoric, the greenhouse keeper's son and the spiritually driven manic-depressive poet forged our first contemporary confessional persona.

It is important to keep in mind that behind these three modern intellectual trends lies Roethke's idiosyncratic but deep commitment to a Judeo-Christian tradition. The more orthodox idea of God that he presents in his final group of poems, **"A Sequence, Sometimes Metaphysical,"** discloses a persistent sense of otherness—a pre-Romantic sense of the separateness that exists between man and God—which is evident at various points in various forms throughout Roethke's poetry. His interest in Christian mysticism, his use of mystical ideas and tropes, and his thorough reading of Evelyn Underhill's *Mysticism* underscore this dimension in Roethke's work. Numerous notebook entries reveal Roethke's spiritual zeal, among them "Those damned old mystics have got me despising myself," and "If God does not exist, neither do we." Finally, this Judeo-Christian aspect of Roethke's art in no way contradicts or adds confusion to the modern sensibility he created out of Romanticism, Darwinism, modern psychology, and literary modernism. That his Judeo-Christian strain could be also an integral part of his vision is a testimony not only to his genius but to the largeness of his poetry and the permanence of the myth he made for our time—a myth he created out of both his personal past and our cultural past.

## Mary Floyd-Wilson (essay date January 1991)

SOURCE: "Poetic Empathy: Theodore Roethke's Conception of Woman in the Love Poems," in *South Atlantic Review,* Vol. 56, No. 1, January, 1991, pp. 61-78.

[*In the following essay, Floyd-Wilson examines Roethke's representation of women in his poetry, noting Roethke's idealization of the female persona and attempt to transcend self by portraying women as the dual embodiment of the universal and particular.*]

In a poetic universe teeming with greenhouse life and distinctly lacking in human beings, Theodore Roethke's two series of "love poems" have a conspicuous presence in a complete collection of his work. While an "utter assent to other people, other lives . . . marks the best poetry" of his contemporaries, Roethke concentrates on the lower rungs of the evolutionary ladder. His early verse focuses on the "I," and in a self-described "journey out of the self" the poet explores primordial memories, subhuman life and a child's perception of the world. Stephen Spender describes the development of Roethke's work as a movement "from the child's absorption in the physical nature around him, to confrontation with the polarity of people and things outside—women, the woman!—and at the end the separation of spirit from body, the confrontation of death." Roethke emerges from *Praise to the End!*'s (1951) "interior life of childhood" to discover "woman" as lover for the first time in the 1958 volume *Words for the Wind*. Loving another person becomes a process of self-awakening for a man who heretofore rarely stepped out of his own consciousness, and found his comfort and identity in "[t]he gradual embrace / Of lichen around stones." To ease the awkwardness and fear inherent in this self-expansion, the poet feels "most drawn to the woman of the Love Poems when she is least human, most animal." "She" is woman in the absolute sense—a general, almost mythic figure.

Although written before the love poems, Kenneth Burke's essay "The Vegetal Radicalism of Theodore Roethke" sets the tone for the critical debate concerning Roethke's portrayal of women. Burke notes that even Roethke's early verse courts an absolute woman and that it lacks what he terms "personalization." According to Burke, Roethke confronts and individualizes human relations successfully in his poem **"Elegy for Jane,"** but fails to "personalize" in most of his other verse. While several critics have debated over the influence of Burke's criticism on the love poems of *Words for the Wind,* it is my contention that the neglected love poems of *The Far Field* show a more overt achievement of personalization.

Roethke's female in these first love poems may be a "creature of spiritual and mythological proportions" who helps him achieve "harmony with the cosmos," but she is not "affirmed as herself" or a "person in her own right." The second series of love poems, contained in the posthumous *The Far Field* has received little critical attention compared to its predecessors. Although overshadowed by **"The North American Sequence"** and **"Sequence, Sometimes Metaphysical"** in the same volume, these thirteen poems "have a simplicity . . . openness," and "personal quality not often found" in Roethke's verse. Although Roethke did not arrange these love poems, six of them do imply an intended series: he dons the mask of a young female, creating a series which Coburn Freer calls "meditations of a young woman." In the only full-length essay devoted exclusively to Roethke's

love poems, Freer asks, rhetorically, "Why should this mask have appealed to Roethke at this particular stage of his development?" In answer to Freer's question, I believe that Roethke needed to enter the female's consciousness, much in the way he did in **"Meditations of an Old Woman,"** in order to personalize her. Not only does assuming the female voice provide "the needed focus for a more personal love lyric," it gives Roethke a sense of a woman individualized. Once he reassumes his own voice, he depicts her objectively as a whole other person in a manner that reveals an "inward blessedness" and a "plain tenderness" lacking in his first love poems.

Theodore Roethke's idealization of "woman" originates from a guileless wonder rather than an inculcated web of traditions and symbols. Unlike many other poets, Roethke's main poetic interaction with a female occurs in a few isolated works relatively late in his career. In contrast, Roethke's "toughest mentor," William Carlos Williams, wrestles with the "ineluctable mystery of Woman" incessantly; Williams's idealization of women stems from a conscious obsession "to find out about them all." By insisting that "[a]ll women are not Helen, / I know that, / but have Helen in their hearts" ("Asphodel"), Williams implies that the tradition of a feminine ideal haunts him as a modern poet. Roethke, on the other hand, only responds to the enigma of woman, or any person for that matter, "when a specific human relation touch[es] him and he grasp[s] it." By comparing him to Williams, one discovers an elemental simplicity in Roethke's experience with women. While Williams builds upon the complexity of culturally emphasized sexual differences, Roethke finds poetic power through regression. He derives inspiration from a "realm of pure impulsiveness" that predates "motives" and the significance of difference, freeing his responses of "all *arrière-pensée,* all ulterior purpose." His "discovery" of woman moves him toward a recognition of a self differentiated from the world. Although Williams's poetry may, in fact, travel along a parallel track, moving from the abstract "muses of *Patterson* to a celebration of his wife and marriage in 'Asphodel'," his interest in women often takes the impersonal and highly developed form of "fascinating experimentation." The sensations of individual human love overwhelm Roethke, and in a defensive effort not to "drown in fire," he writes his first love poems for "a woman with an empty face." The final love poems, therefore, mark a personal achievement in emotional maturity and wholeness in terms of Roethke's approach to the female. While in *Words for the Wind* Roethke's love poems explore the self, portraying woman as an abstraction, in *The Far Field* the poet recognizes woman as another "I," equal, actual, and particularized.

As Randall Stiffler and other critics note, the "major source of conflict" in the love poems of *Words for the Wind* "is in the lover himself, and love for him is a dynamic emotional continuum." The conflict concerns a desire for the woman, love's power of "self-discovery," and a fear of the possible "self-annihilation" inherent in both physical and spiritual intimacy. Beginning with a dream of woman and the delights of love, the poems move through ambivalence, desire, fear and rage, exploring the opposing allurements of spiritual and physical fulfillment. Coburn Freer interprets the poems through the Prodigal Son parable: "[T]he person who is loved [the poet] must bear the entire burden of being forgiven and receiving," and to avoid this "psychic burden, the beloved, the Prodigal, has an almost obsessive desire to retain his own identity." In order to maintain his own identity in the face of love, the speaker alternately idealizes and belittles the woman, never recognizing her as an equal. He views her and love as invading impurities that will destroy his sense of self, without acknowledging the woman as an individual with her own selfhood.

Roethke meets his beloved in **"The Dream"** from *Words for the Wind,* and states that "Love is not love until love's vulnerable," revealing both comprehension and fear of the paradoxes of his newly found passion. Throughout the sequence he portrays the woman as powerful, unknowable— sometimes encompassing eternity and sometimes, nothingness, depending on the stability of his own identity. In **"Words for the Wind"** he calls her a "substance" and a "[c]reaturely creature," depicting her as almost subhuman. According to Stiffler, by "making her less human and more animal, Roethke's desire for her grows. He assimilates her to the intimacies of his Greenhouse worldview, and he can therefore more easily approach her." In **"All the Earth, All the Air"** she is as "easy as a beast," and in **"Words for the Wind,"** "[s]he frolicks like a beast." By portraying her as a lower "creature" Roethke places distance between himself and the woman; he achieves the same goal by raising her to the status of goddess and worshiping her from afar. In **"I Knew A Woman"** the poet plays the adoring suitor to a woman whose movements mesmerize and dazzle him. He nibbles meekly "from her proffered hand," and follows behind her "for her pretty sake." She *teaches* him the joys of touch, taking the superior role, and he admits (with tongue in cheek perhaps), "I'm martyr to a motion not my own." In **"The Dream,"** she magically turns "the field into a glittering sea," which he plays in "like a boy." As the sequence progresses, "She wakes the ends of life," and "knows all" that the poet is. By portraying himself as a "fond and foolish man," and the woman as both bestial and divine, the poet establishes an unequal relationship wherein he claims to "see and suffer" himself "[i]n another being, at last."

Seeing and suffering himself in another being leads to a sense of expansiveness for the speaker. In his essay **"On 'Identity'"** Roethke speaks of breaking from "self-involvement, from I to Otherwise" and of becoming aware of another being in order to bring on "mysteriously, in some instances, a

feeling of the oneness of the universe." Throughout the love poems, Roethke's love for the woman has an element of universality. Since she represents both change and eternity to the poet, his union with her symbolizes his movement from the "I" to the "Otherwise." "All things bring [him] to love," and all things—the rose, the oyster, the star, and the leaf—"[a]re part of what she is." He finds "her every place," and feels "her presence in the common day." In **"The Sententious Man,"** he even tastes his sister when he kisses his wife. She is a "shape of change," and in her presence he "start[s] to leave [himself]." For the woman to act as the agent by which the poet achieves this sense of interconnection, she must necessarily remain both aloof and indefinite in character.

As the sequence progresses, Roethke characterizes the woman in more negative terms, illustrating his growing fear of her effect on his consciousness. In the poem appropriately entitled **"The Other,"** he implies than his identity has become too entangled in the woman. "What is she, while I live?" he asks, complaining that he feels "plague[d]" by "her Shape." His desperation grows as he wonders, "Is she what I become? / Is this my final Face?" **"The Pure Fury"**'s speaker finds himself on the edge of psychic disintegration, and he blames his "darling" for his despair and mental instability. In the first stanza he recalls another "fearful night" when "every meaning had grown meaningless," yet he had found unity and restoration in the morning through the minimal world: "I touched the stones, and they had my own skin," he says. In the second stanza he asserts that the "pure" live alone, implying that the relationship contaminates him and engenders his mental degradation. The speaker's "fear of losing his self in the woman leads him very near a state of derangement." He explains that he loves "a woman with an empty face" and when she "tries to think," nothingness "flies loose again." He scorns the philosophers who theorize on nothingness, since he actually lives "near the abyss," and is keenly aware that the "self can be . . . annihilated." When his "darling squeaks in pure Plato," she seems to represent the very nothingness he dreads. The third stanza equates "the need for solitude" with an "appetite for life," a need which ironically intensifies his despair to a state of "pure fury." In the final stanza he explicitly blames the "she" for his near loss of self: "Dream of a woman, and a dream of death," he exclaims, and then asks "When will that creature give me back my breath?" Far from being personalized, the woman in this poem seems as mysterious and ominous as death.

The poet admits that his fear actually stems from "those shadows" that "start from [his] own feet," and love of a woman intensifies the vulnerability and unsteadiness of his own identity. In **"Love's Progress"** he ends the poem, "I fear for my own joy; / I fear myself in the field, / For I would drown in fire." The poet fears the expansiveness and unity that love entails and that the woman represents. As Coburn Freer notes,

"No problems have been solved" in the sequence. Not only does the woman remain vague and dehumanized, the poet senses a loss in his own identity. In **"The Renewal"** he seeks a reintegration of self: "I know I love, yet know not where I am; / I paw the dark, the shifting midnight air. / Will the self, lost, be found again? In form?" Without mentioning the woman, he claims a moment of "[i]llumination" that leads him to love and expansiveness, ("I find that love, and I am everywhere"). Love, and not the woman, becomes the focus for the poet. In the concluding poem **"Memory,"** the speaker says the woman "knows all I am," but that "[l]ove's all. Love's all I know." Since Roethke treats love as a search for his own identity, and conceives of the woman as almost psychologically parasitic, the "she" fails to materialize as a human being equal to the poet in this sequence of poems. While Roethke has incorporated "other people" in his poetry with this first series of love poems, in my opinion he has yet to individualize relations in the manner Burke suggests.

In his earlier poem **"Elegy for Jane,"** Roethke proves that he has the ability to utilize his intimacy with the natural world while individualizing human relations. In contrast to the situation of the love poems, the dramatic situation of an elegy poses little threat to the poet's identity. The girl's young age and her lifelessness increase her approachability for the poet. The final lines of the poem explain that he has "no rights in this matter, / Neither father nor lover," and this *lack* of a relationship provides the necessary objectivity for Roethke to express tenderness for a particularized female:

> If only I could nudge you from this sleep,
> My maimed darling, my skittery pigeon.
> Over this damp grave I speak the words of my
>     love. . . .

In contrast to the woman of the love poems, Jane is no longer a "shape of change." Not only does Roethke give specific physical details of the girl ("the neckcurls, limp and damp as tendrils; / . . . a sidelong pickerel smile," but he also acknowledges her proper name, a concrete label that helps to distinguish the specific from the general. He compares Jane to a wren, a fern, and a pigeon, characterizing the "light syllables" of her talk, her "spiny shadow," and the absence of her "skittery" movements respectively. Unlike those in the love poems, these nature metaphors accentuate Jane's human qualities rather than overwhelm them.

The poet's relationship to Jane is an inherently unequal one of teacher to student, which gives him some connection to her while maintaining a safe distance between them. Although Roethke despairs over the ambiguity of his connection to the girl, her distance allows him to keep his own identity intact. The last two stanzas emphasize his ability to confront human relations; through his use of the second person, a technique practically absent from the first sequence of love po-

ems, Roethke breaks from self-involvement, moving "from I to . . . Thee" (**"On 'Identity'"**), and successfully individualizes Jane. While Roethke achieves "personalization" in this poem, Jane's non-threatening (and unequal) state, and his vague relationship to her help separate this elegy from the love poems. The Roethke who has rights in the matter as a lover fails to particularize the woman of *Words for the Wind* in this manner.

**"Meditations of an Old Woman"** concludes the volume *Words for the Wind,* and Freer conjectures that Roethke chooses this feminine mask "to imply that the demands of the lover can only be handled through this perspective." The poem stands as Roethke's first extended use of a female persona, and employing the mask appears to be a step in the poet's progression towards confronting woman (and his fears of love) through poetic empathy. As in **"Elegy for Jane,"** Roethke again creates a dramatic situation in which the female poses little threat to the male's psyche. Not only is the old woman incapable of making "sensual gifts to and demands of a man," Roethke bases the character on his deceased mother, dissociating her from the woman of the love poems. Nevertheless, it seems possible that entering the consciousness of a female brings Roethke closer to recognizing his lover as a person in her own right. Roethke may, in fact, have had Burke's notion of personalization in mind when he composed **"Meditations of an Old Woman."** While critics have acknowledged the possible effect of Burke's criticism on the first love poems, the influence of "personalization" on **"Meditations of an Old Woman"** and the second series of love poems has received little attention. In a 1952 epistolary response to Burke's essay, Roethke, referring to the poem **"Old Lady's Winter Words,"** asks the critic to "take a look at the current *Kenyon.* There's a piece (by me) that may bear out your prophecy: about a person. . . ." It seems significant that this poem stands as the only predecessor to **"Meditations of an Old Woman"** spoken from the perspective of an elderly female.

The adoption of a female persona makes **"Meditations of an Old Woman"** a transitional piece between the two series of love poems. Although Roethke protects his own identity by creating a non-threatening character, he does have the old woman ask, "What is it to be a woman?" The question confronts the very perceptions of woman that Roethke perpetuates in the love poems. In **"I Knew a Woman,"** the speaker characterizes the female as a "bright container." The old woman of the **"Meditations"** asks if being a woman means "To be contained, to be a vessel?", seemingly referring to the woman as merely a sexual recipient or a bearer of children, and asking if these aspects of the female make up her whole self. As a living female well past her fertile years, the old woman knows that her "being" has a "flame" and a spirit beyond the utilitarian connotations of a "container."

Fascinated by the movement of the mind, Roethke creates for himself an accessible persona in the old woman in terms of her wisdom and intellectual approach to life. In contrast to the woman of the love poems, who has bestial traits and often seems indistinguishable from the natural elements, Roethke dons a female mask whose articulate, intelligent, and defined presence overshadows any exclusively "feminine" qualities that might intimidate a male by their sheer foreignness. In describing the old woman, Roethke says, "she's tough, she's brave, she's aware of life and she would take a congeries of eels over a hassle of bishops any day." In other words, Roethke empathizes with and admires a woman who can say, "I was always one for being alone, / Seeking in my own way, eternal purpose." She relishes both her solitude and her search. In **"Meditations of an Old Woman,"** Roethke creates a female within himself, yet he deemphasizes the aspects of woman which most frighten him. Dissimilar to the female figure in the love poems, the old woman confesses that she has "become a strange piece of flesh," indicating a disconnected condition of mind and body. Even her youthful memories seem confined to the "[f]lesh-awkward" adolescent years when one's physicality seems to have a life of its own. Underplaying the physical and augmenting the intellectual spirit allows Roethke to form and enter a relatively permeable female consciousness.

Donoghue notes that the "answers come too easily" to Roethke in **"Meditations of an Old Woman."** In his estimation, Roethke assumes a serene wisdom and stability, or an "autumnal calm" without "really earning it." In my assessment, the true autumnal calm comes in Roethke's posthumous volume, *The Far Field.* Rosemary Sullivan appraises *The Far Field* as a "book of reconciliation and atonement, of final statements on themes that have preoccupied [Roethke] from the beginning—themes of love, [and] identity. . . ." Biographer Alan Seager observes that at this time Roethke's mind and poetry seem "to have forgiven everyone everything, demolished its hatreds, and solved all its discords." The mature Roethke sounds less angry when he concludes in **"Journey to the Interior"** that "[t]he spirit of wrath becomes the spirit of blessing," in contrast to his earlier lament, "Where's my eternity / Of inward blessedness? / I lack plain tenderness." The love poems of *The Far Field* reveal a more generous spirit and emotional maturity than their predecessors. Not only does he adopt the persona of a young girl, he achieves a level of "personalization" equal to that attained in **"Elegy for Jane."** In the poem just preceding the love sequence, Roethke writes,

> Among the half-dead trees, I came upon the true
> ease of myself,
> As if another man appeared out of the depths of
> my being,
> And I stood outside myself,
> Beyond becoming and perishing,

> A something wholly other. . . .

This passage describes a successful journey out of the self—of moving from the "I to Otherwise." In his late poems, Roethke discovers that not only can the lost self be found again, but it can also become less fragile by moving away from self-absorption.

Experiencing the "true ease" of his self gives Roethke the stability to don the mask of a woman who resembles the female of *Words for the Wind* in terms of age and vitality. In six love poems from *The Far Field,* Roethke charts the young girl's own journey out of the self, confronting through the persona female experiences that mirror *his* past struggles with love. By creating the persona of a young girl, Roethke enters the "consciousness of woman, an 'I' different . . . from the center of consciousness of the earlier love poems. . . . In the process the poet's separate identity is not lost, but put aside." Roethke's ability to "put aside" his own identity illustrates his progression. As the final love poems indicate, Roethke's sense of self has strengthened to the point that he can move beyond the "I", and individualize his relations with his female lover.

**"The Young Girl"** begins the sequence and establishes that her spiritual journey has begun. "What can the spirit believe?," she asks, echoing her poetic ancestor of **"Meditations of an Old Woman,"** who exclaims, "The soul knows not what to believe." The young girl, on "coming to love" seeks an understanding of her own identity that encompasses the body and the spirit:

> What can the spirit believe?—
> It takes in the whole body;
> I, on coming to love,
> Make that my study.

She recognizes that the spirit "takes in the whole body," and she plans to "study" the relationship between the two. In the second stanza, she skips on the shore with such a sense of newness that she seems almost to have just emerged from the sea—the source of all beginnings. Her eyes wander without focusing and her thin arms move without purpose, emphasizing her unformed state and lack of direction:

> We are one, and yet we are more,
> I am told by those who know,—
> At times content to be two.
> Today I skipped on the shore,
> My eyes neither here nor there,
> My thin arms to and fro,
> A bird my body,
> My bird-blood ready.

Intuitively (perhaps through the power of innocence) she has a sense of her body and soul in harmony. Malkoff notes that the bird is a "symbol of soul in Roethke—and blood—symbol of body—," thus "bird-blood" connotes this unity. The girl admits that she has been "told by those who know" that "[w]e are one, and yet we are more," recalling the speaker of the earlier love poems—"Each one's himself, yet each one's everyone." As Roethke repeatedly asserts, feeling this "oneness of the universe" (**"On 'Identity'"**) remains inextricably linked to the journey out of the self. Paradoxically, the process of discovering one's identity can bring on the fear of self-annihilation. The young girl implicitly acknowledges this fear when she observes that we are "[a]t times content to be two," confessing that a state of separateness may ensure a more peaceful existence. Nevertheless, the young girl is "ready" to embark on the trip "from self-involvement, from I to Otherwise" (**"On 'Identity'"**).

In **"Her Words,"** the second poem in the sequence, Roethke removes the mask momentarily and refers to the young girl in the third person. The poem describes an encounter between the girl and "her true love," and hints at the complexity of loving while attempting to retain one's identity. By comparing the girl to a cat, Roethke draws upon the distinction made in **"Meditations of an Old Woman"** between the "self-involved" women and those who feel "the soul's authentic hunger." The young girl of **"Her Words"** believes she can "'delight in a lover's praise, / Yet keep to [herself her] own mind. . . .'" This separation of the soul from one's actions resembles the behavior of those selfish "cat-like immaculate creatures" the old woman describes. But **"Her Words"** concludes with a "'storm, the storm of a kiss,'" indicating that the power of the lovers' union may overwhelm the young girl beyond her anticipation. As the other poems in the sequence reveal, the young girl does experience the "soul's authentic hunger" despite her efforts to keep her "own mind."

The immediately following poems, **"The Apparition"** and **"Her Reticence,"** seem to parallel *Words for the Wind*'s **"The Pure Fury"** in terms of the speakers' fears of psychic disintegration. The title **"The Apparition"** could apply to the "soft-footed one / Who passed by"—(her lover)—or to the girl, sans heart, sans soul. She wonders if she should grieve or mourn in reaction to both her lover's disappearance and the death of her own identity. In **"Her Reticence,"** the girl wishes to send her beloved an unconnected part of herself:

> If I could send him only
> One sleeve with my hand in it,
> Disembodied, unbloody,
> For him to kiss or caress.

Her imagination seeks a way to give something to her lover, yet protect the self. In **"The Pure Fury"** the poet asks "When

will that creature give me back my breath?" and, similarly, in **"Her Reticence"** the young girl fears losing her "whole heart" and "soul" to her lover. She feels vulnerable, physically and spiritually, and dreads the consequences of revealing her growing dependence on him.

The next poem, **"Her Longing,"** illustrates the transformation that the self undergoes when it needs another being. Sustaining a correspondence to Roethke's own struggle for identity, the poem relies heavily on the world of smaller creatures to describe the renewal of the young girl's ego:

> Before this longing,
> I lived serene as a fish,
> At one with the plants in the pond,
> The mare's tail, the floating frogbit,
> Among my eight-legged friends,
> Open like a pool, a lesser parsnip,
> Like a leech, looping myself along,
> A bug-eyed edible one,
> A mouth like a stickleback,—
> A thing quiescent!

Before she had yearned for another, the young girl had "lived serene as a fish" without a sense of identity or a need for self-definition. Her existence within the minimal world had been one of *part* to *whole*—the "tail" of a mare, a "frogbit," and the parasitic "leech." The second half of the poem describes her conversion to a bird that "the sea itself cannot contain," and metaphorically the change mimics natural evolution. Her longing engenders a power and vitality within that sends her soaring with "the gar-eagle, the great-winged condor." The poem climaxes with her metamorphosis into a phoenix, the ultimate symbol of rebirth. Not only does the young girl escape the soulless existence of the "self-involved" criticized by the old woman, but also as a "phoenix" she "flame[s] into being" through her desire for another. By beating her wings "against the black clouds of the storm," the girl proves herself willing to confront the darkest aspects of "[p]erpetually rising out of" herself. She moves away from the serenity of solitude to embrace the tumultuous but spiritually revelatory "other."

**"Her Time,"** the last poem in the sequence, attempts to describe (to the extent that language can) an epiphanic instant that stands outside of time. In a flash of understanding, the young girl conceives of herself as simultaneously unified with and disconnected from the external world. The poem flows in a continuous sentence, yet Roethke strives to pinpoint the revelatory instant with recurrent time qualifications of "when" and "before":

> *When* all
> My waterfall
> Fancies sway away

From me, in the sea's silence;
*In the time*
*When* the tide moves
Neither forward nor back,
And the small waves
Begin rising whitely,
And the quick winds
Flick over the close whitecaps,
And two scoters fly low,
Their four wings beating together,
And my salt-laden hair
Flies away from my face
*Before* the almost invisible
Spray, and the small shapes
Of light on the far
Cliff disappear in a last
Glint of the sun, *before*
The long surf of the storm booms
Down on the near shore,
*When* everything—birds, men, dogs—
Runs to cover:
I'm one to follow,
To follow.

(emphases added)

When the girl's "[f]ancies sway away" and when the "tide moves / Neither forward nor back," she seems a part of the natural elements. Her mind moves with the water. The vast range of her vision makes her exact location indeterminable. Although she is only "near shore," she feels the spray of water. She seems closest to the "two scoters" flying low. In the same moment that she appears indistinguishable from the external world, she realizes her separateness and individuality. She emphasizes her individuality by making it clear that she follows "everything"; after the "birds, men, dogs . . . [run] to cover," then she is "one to follow." The repetition of "follow" gives significance to the fact that she is momentarily alone and the very last to seek shelter. Conversely, her following stresses her connectedness to others. She must remove herself from the elements and join the others before the "storm booms / Down on the near shore." The girl has learned first-hand of her concurrent state of dependence and independence. In the process of loving another being, she has come to understand that "[w]e are one, and yet we are more, . . . [a]t times content to be two."

In this sequence of poems, the young girl experiences a journey out of the self and a process of self-definition akin to Roethke's own. By adopting a female persona Roethke creates a woman with an inner life—a consciousness—and in doing so, his lover becomes personalized. Seager mentions that Roethke wrote these poems out of concern for his wife, Beatrice. Although referring to the landscape poems of *The Far Field,* Seager makes an important observation pertain-

ing to a change in Roethke towards his wife in these last years: "[H]e had ceased to regard Beatrice as an acquisition whose beauty would enhance his reputation every time he appeared with her. . . . [H]e came to see what she meant to him as a woman, how great his dependence on her was . . . and he began to love her . . . with a true love." This biographical information helps mark the distinction between the love poems of *Words for the Wind* and those of *The Far Field.* By assuming the mask, Roethke recognizes his lover as a fellow human being who seeks and suffers in a life analogous to his own.

The remaining love poems "comprise a very mixed bag." Two lyrics, **"Light Listened"** and **"His Foreboding,"** recall the *Words for the Wind* series in terms of their approach to love. **"Light Listened"** echoes **"All the Earth, All the Air"** and **"I Knew a Woman,"** two of the more celebratory love poems of their sequence. The woman appears in touch with the elements, and as the last line has it, "Light listened when she sang." She moves and changes "with changing light," and nothing "could be more nice / Than her ways with a man." **"His Foreboding"** presents a darker side of love, stressing the speaker's dependence on the woman as an "incommensurate dread / Of being, being away / From one comely head." In this line, the poet equates the dread of "being" with "being away" from his beloved, a correspondence that encompasses the paradoxes of living and living. For the speaker, being alone means returning to "nothingness," and the "loneliest thing" he knows is his "own mind at play."

The lyric **"Song"** demonstrates the progression of Roethke's approach to love since *Words for the Wind.* His "wrath" and "rage" have faded with time. In the first stanza, the speaker sees "wrath" as the "edge" or sharpness of his thoughts that he had "carried so long / When so young." The second stanza questions a future that lacks one's self-protecting rage: "Will the heart eat the heart? / What's to come? What's to come?" Roethke's reconciliation to his dependence on his beloved shows itself in the last stanza. In contrast to the earlier love poems, the poet speaks directly to his lover, and asks her for the answers; while in *Words for the Wind,* he mocks his lover who "squeaks in pure Plato" and has "an empty face," *The Far Field*'s speaker acknowledges the value of the woman's inner self by seeking her wisdom. Freer notes that "the woman has the transcendent knowledge that the poet lacks, and also has the knowledge of the present and its possibility of fertile regeneration." The poem shows that the speaker still has doubts concerning his own strength of mind, but he also has the courage to confront his loved one on an equal level.

**"Her Wrath," "The Shy Man,"** and **"The Happy Three"** have no counterparts in *Words for the Wind.* They approach love in a lighter manner, and each contains examples of personalization. **"The Happy Three"** depicts a domestic quarrel humorously. His "darling wife" nags and frowns in a typically human fashion. The poet leaves the house in irritation "[t]o drink some half-and-half / On the back lawn" in the company of their pet goose, Marianne, "[n]amed for the poetess." By reporting a dialogue and providing domestic details, Roethke creates a slice-of-life poem that personalizes the characters involved. Although he describes a scene of discord, he does it comically, and admits that his "banked-up vertigo / Vanished like April snow; / All rage was gone." The final lines celebrate the lovers' reconciliation, as he, his wife, and Marianne romp "out again, / Out again, / Out again, / Three in the sun."

**"Her Wrath"** also characterizes anger through humor. Not only does the poem recognize the woman's emotions (a circumstance completely absent from *Words for the Wind*), but it also names the poet's lover—"Beatrice." While Roethke does compare his Beatrice to Dante's idealized Beatrice, she remains many steps removed from the earlier "absolute woman." In **"The Shy Man,"** Roethke calls his lover O'Connell's daughter," O'Connell being Beatrice's maiden name. While the poem may be a "mannered imitation of Irish song," it illustrates Roethke's improved ability to confront human relations in a traditional manner. "'I am not alone,'" he says, "'For here close beside me is O'Connell's daughter.'" Roethke particularizes his loved one, and acknowledges in simple terms the support she provides.

**"Wish for a Young Wife"** makes an appropriate conclusion to Roethke's last sequence of love poems. It stands as the only love lyric that reaches the level of personalization of **"Elegy for Jane,"** yet surpasses the elegy in emotional maturity:

> My lizard, my lively writher,
> May your limbs never wither,
> May the eyes in your face
> Survive the green ice
> Of envy's mean gaze;
> May you live out your life
> Without hate, without grief,
> And your hair ever blaze,
> In the sun, in the sun,
> When I am undone,
> When I am no one.

In this poem, Roethke speaks directly to his wife, recognizing their age difference and offering a tender prayer for her future. With unmatched generosity, Roethke wishes her eternal youth and happiness, understanding that he will someday be "no one." Roethke's hope for his wife's prolonged existence in the face of the inevitable dissolution of his own identity reflects an unprecedented sense of emotional security and spiritual wholeness. In contrast to the **"The Pure**

**Fury"** in which Roethke blames woman for the death of self, **"Wish for a Young Wife"** celebrates the woman's life while the poet accepts his own mortality. In wishing that her "hair ever blaze, / In the sun, in the sun," Roethke echoes the climax of **"Meditations of an Old Woman,"** in which the speaker equates "The sun! The sun!" with "all we can become!" Not only does Roethke successfully confront human relations and realize a particularized female, but he also wishes her the joys of "becoming" even after he is "undone."

The whole of Roethke's work charts his progress as a spiritual man, as well as his development as a human being. His poems record the painful process of maturation, of breaking from "self-involvement," and seeking the relationship between the self and the not-self. Loving his wife increases the complications of his struggle for identity. In *Words for the Wind,* intimacy with a woman poses a threat to the poet's psyche, causing him to dehumanize the female out of self-preservation. Personalizing and objectifying another person, or recognizing the *other*'s reality as equal to his own becomes an important step in Roethke's journey out of the self. By personalizing Jane and donning the mask of the old woman, Roethke makes significant advances towards the "inward blessedness" of *The Far Field.* The young-girl sequence expands Roethke's poetic empathy for his beloved. As a final word, **"Wish for a Young Wife"** shows an unselfish Roethke who in the face of his own extinction exults in the vitality of an individualized woman.

## Don Bogen (essay date 1991)

SOURCE: "'The Method is Cyclic': The 'Lost Son' Sequence and *Praise to the End!*," in *Theodore Roethke and the Writing Process,* Ohio University Press, 1991, pp. 54-73.

[*In the following essay, Bogen explores the process of self-discovery and maturation as expressed by Roethke in "The Lost Son" and* Praise to the End!, *especially as influenced by parental relationships and sexual awakening.*]

If Roethke became a "master of description" in his composition of the greenhouse poems of the early '40s, his work during the rest of the decade was focussed on developing powers of "suggestion." The four-poem **"Lost Son"** sequence which concludes Roethke's second book is the first manifestation of this new development. While the greenhouse poems lead to self-discovery through the examination of specific memories, the later work is concerned with underlying patterns behind the memories; in it Roethke begins to delve directly into the unconscious, without the mediation of greenhouse description. The result is complex, highly experimental work unlike anything Roethke had done before. In Chapter 5 we will take a close look at the new ways of writing behind an example of this work, but first it is necessary to consider the material as a whole. The four-poem **"Lost Son"** group is the first of the sequences of longer poems which become increasingly important in Roethke's career, including **"Praise to the End!,"** **"Meditations of an Old Woman,"** and **"North American Sequence."** It is also the only group of poems to be incorporated in two separate volumes: as the conclusion of *The Lost Son and Other Poems* in 1948 and as the opening of Part II of *Praise to the End!* in 1951. In Roethke's development of the **"Lost Son"** poems and *Praise to the End!* as sequences we can see the overall process of self-discovery he underwent from the mid-'40s to the early '50s.

Writing about **"The Lost Son"** in his essay **"Open Letter,"** Roethke summarizes the general movement of the poem and the sequences in which it is included:

> This crude account tells very little about what actually happens in the poem; but at least you can see that the method is cyclic. I believe that to go forward as a spiritual man it is necessary first to go back. Any history of the psyche (or allegorical journey) is bound to be a succession of experiences, similar yet dissimilar. There is a perpetual slipping-back, then a going-forward; but there is *some* "progress." Are not some experiences so powerful and so profound (I am not speaking of the merely compulsive) that they repeat themselves, thrust themselves upon us, again and again, with variation and change, each time bringing us closer to our own most particular (and thus most universal) reality? We go, as Yeats said, from exhaustion to exhaustion. To begin from the depths and come out—that is difficult; for few know where the depths are or can recognize them; or, if they do, are afraid. (Roethke's emphasis)

The two-level description of the greenhouse poems points to the "depths" Roethke mentions here in its connections between the self and the primal world of natural processes. The drive toward "beginnings" Roethke announces in **"Cuttings (*later*)"** leads the poet back to the "slippery grave" (**"Weed Puller"**) where life starts and ends, and Roethke's original title for the greenhouse poems, "News of the Root," suggests a thorough examination of these depths. But in 1945 Roethke complained that the greenhouse poems were "not sufficiently related." The greenhouse experience is obviously one of the "powerful" ones Roethke mentions in **"Open Letter,"** and we see its repetition "with variation and change" in each poem. But the greenhouse poems do not, in the end, develop a "*succession* of experiences" that would reveal a "history of the psyche." Though some critics have since found broad patterns in the greenhouse poems—a progression from physical description to meditation, "a general sense of growth," a movement toward transcendence of the past—

Roethke's own dissatisfaction with the relations among the greenhouse poems led him toward a much more deliberate concept of progression in the **"Lost Son"** sequence. If the greenhouse poems are like separate photographs of memories carefully arranged in an album, the **"Lost Son"** sequence is like a movie. The sequence of longer, multisectioned poems allows the poet to undertake a kind of "journey" in the process of writing, to extend his self-discovery beyond the bounds of specific scenes and memories.

This extended self-discovery involved changes not only in the idea of progression among poems but also in style. While the two-level nature of the greenhouse poems anchors the poet's discoveries about himself in images from the natural world, the sequences of Roethke's middle period are considerably more dense symbolically, with more complex relations between the physical and psychological dimensions. As Roethke moved from "description" to "suggestion," he began to work more "intuitively," as he put it; and the result is poems which develop a whole range of suggestions in different images. A worm, for example, functions simultaneously as a literal creature used for fish bait, an archetype of mortality, a phallic symbol, and an image of regression and lowliness. This associative richness, with its abundance of psychosexual connotations, reflects Roethke's extensive forays into "the depths" of the unconscious, which we will see in more detail in Chapter 5. In the completed texts, the wealth of suggestions is augmented by the poet's predominant interest in what he called "dramatic" expression in this period. In the greenhouse poems Roethke wanted to "be true to the actual," but his development of the poems in the sequences as dramatic pieces changed the context of images considerably:

> All these states of mind were to be rendered dramatically, without comment, without allusion, the action often implied or indicated in the interior monologue or dialogue between the self and its mentor, or conscience, or, sometimes, another person.

By removing comments, allusions, and direct action in the physical world in his drive for the dramatic, the poet creates difficult, often disjointed work in which images are liberated from their standard contexts. Meaning is expressed in a fundamentally new way, as Roethke notes in **"Open Letter":**

> If intensity has compressed the language so it seems, on early reading, obscure, this obscurity should break open suddenly for the serious reader who can hear the language: the "meaning" itself should come as a dramatic revelation, an excitement. The clues will be scattered richly—as life scatters them; the symbols will mean what they usually mean—and sometimes something more.

This new, more suggestive approach is vital to the poet's more complex self-discovery in the sequences. With it, Roethke is able to develop, as he put it, "a genuine imaginative order out of what comes from the unconscious."

As Roethke noted in the seminar on identity, "The human problem is to find out what one really *is:* whether one exists, whether existence is possible. But how?" (Roethke's emphasis). The greenhouse memories respond to the first part of this comment, showing the poet "what he *is*"; in the sequences that follow these poems, Roethke goes on to consider the broader question of "whether existence is possible" for him. The sequences trace what Roethke called the "mental and spiritual crisis" of confronting his own experience, of integrating the world of the greenhouse—including his father's death and his own maturation—into a clear sense of his identity in the present. The process of engaging the past and incorporating discoveries from it in a deeper sense of self is at the heart of Roethke's work on the **"Lost Son"** sequence and *Praise to the End!* "To begin from the depths and come out" was his overall goal. As the sequences take shape we can see the poet gradually moving toward a resolution of his confrontation with the past.

Roethke's work of the mid to late '40s divides roughly into two periods: from 1945 to the fall of 1947, during which he composed the four-poem sequence included in *The Lost Son* while teaching at Bennington and Pennsylvania State; and from fall of '47, when Roethke moved to the University of Washington, to the completion of *Praise to the End!* in 1950. Within these two periods the poet developed the sequences in several stages. First came a three-poem version of the **"Lost Son"** sequence, without **"A Field of Light."** This was followed by the four-poem version published in *The Lost Son.* In late 1947 Roethke completed the title poem of *Praise to the End!* He then went on to the eight other new poems in this book, conceiving them as a single sequence in the following order: **"Where Knock Is Open Wide"**; **"I Need, I Need"**; **"Bring the Day!"**; **"Give Way, Ye Gates"**; **"Sensibility! O La!"**; **"O Lull Me, Lull Me"**; **"Unfold! Unfold!"** and **"I Cry, Love! Love!"** The last stage of Roethke's work involved dividing this group into Parts I and II of the finished text and integrating the original **"Lost Son"** sequence in the new volume. Looking at these stages in order, we can see how Roethke's understanding of himself and his past evolved in the process of writing.

As **"Open Letter"** explains, Roethke's progress on this journey of self-discovery is "cyclic." This cyclic quality is reflected in the repeating five-part structure Roethke uses for three of the four poems in the **"Lost Son"** sequence. The pattern of self-exploration in **"The Lost Son,"** described in detail in **"Open Letter,"** involves an initial sense of stagnation, flight from it, regression to an irrational level, then re-creation of a childhood greenhouse experience, leading to a

more satisfying vision of self and world. This pattern is followed, with some variation, in the two poems written immediately after **"The Lost Son"**: **"The Long Alley"** and **"The Shape of the Fire."** **"The Lost Son," "The Long Alley,"** and **"The Shape of the Fire"** were all completed by February, 1947 and represent Roethke's first sense of the sequence; in a letter at this time he wrote that the finished manuscript of his new book contained only "three long poems." This first group of three poems is a highly coherent unit which exemplifies the kind of cyclic progress Roethke describes in his essay. Though the process of self-discovery is repeated in each poem, the poet's self-understanding increases as the sequence progresses; he gradually becomes more aware of how the process works, more confident of its final outcome. From a state of calm expectation—"Wait"—at the end of **"The Lost Son"** (5.25), Roethke moves toward self-acceptance and a desire for active confrontation with reality—"I'll take the fire"—in **"The Long Alley"** (5.10), and then on to what Louis Martz calls "full maturity and conscious power" in **"The Shape of the Fire."** The titles of the three poems, all from the world of the greenhouse, reflect this movement: The poet starts out as a **"Lost Son,"** then perceives **"The Long Alley"** ahead of him, and finally comes to know **"The Shape of the Fire"** at the heart of the greenhouse and his past.

Added to the **"Lost Son"** sequence in the fall of 1947, **"A Field of Light"** involves the same general movement from a sense of personal stagnation to a new vision of self, but there are several important differences between this poem and the three composed before it. Unlike the other **"Lost Son"** poems, **"A Field of Light"** is written entirely in the past tense; it thus seems less dramatic and chaotic than the other works. The title of the poem does not suggest the intensity of the enclosed greenhouse, as do the others, but rather a sense of freedom and spiritual illumination in the open field. In fact, the specific greenhouse experiences which surface in the fourth sections of the other poems are completely absent from **"A Field of Light."** The five-part structure is replaced by a more compact three-part organization which leaves no room for a long, irrational "Gibber" (**"The Lost Son,"** Part 3) or a "Return" (**"The Lost Son,"** Part 4) to the greenhouse. The stress in the later poem is not so much on the process of self-discovery as on the vision of self attained after the process is completed. In contrast to the other poems, **"A Field of Light"** has its longest, most developed section at the end, in which we see a man at peace with himself and nature:

> I could watch! I could watch!
> I saw the separateness of all things!
> My heart lifted up with the great grasses;
> The weeds believed me, and the nesting birds.
> There were clouds making a rout of shapes
>      crossing a
>           windbreak of cedars,

And a bee shaking drops from a rain-soaked
  honeysuckle.
The worms were delighted as wrens.
And I walked, I walked through the light air;
I moved with the morning.

                      (3.14-22)

All of these differences suggest an increased distance on Roethke's part from his past and a slight movement away from the regressive and irrational aspects of his personality. These changes may reflect the temporary therapeutic effect of completing the original three-poem sequence. Roethke was certainly aware of the potential for psychic progress through writing. Commenting on his work in 1955, he described his poems as an attempt to "transmute and purify my 'life,' the sense of being defiled by it." **"A Field of Light"** seems a more "purified" poem than the ones written before it. The differences between **"A Field of Light"** and the other three poems may also reflect changes in Roethke's life. During the two-year period in which the first three poems were written, Roethke spent a great deal of time in his hometown. He worked there on the original **"Lost Son"** sequence in the summer of 1945 and from January, 1946 until the completion of the three-poem series in February of the following year. A few entries from the poet's notebooks of this period suggest the kind of immersion in his past Roethke was undergoing during the months in Saginaw:

> Long, fruitless introspection, characteristic of the German, relieved by occasional dim flickers of insight. Like a half-blind animal that at best can see no colors but gray, he broods and broods. My memory, my prison.

> I am nothing but what I remember.

> What was the greenhouse? It was a jungle, and it was paradise; it was order and disorder: Was it an escape? No, for it was a reality harsher than reality.

> The long mind roves back.
> I wear between my eyes the image of death.
> I carry death in my mouth.

> Blundering man, gentle with birds,
> Whom the caterpillar caressed,
> Whom the snake kissed.

> I was never his son, not I.

In his notebooks the poet constantly examines his memories, trying to determine his true relation to the greenhouse, to his father, to aspects of himself. Even the process of

memory itself is called into question. This is a considerably more intense process than the "looking" at the past Roethke had done in the greenhouse notebooks; it involves not only gathering material from the past but critically judging it and trying to determine its meaning. Memories are developed not so much as narratives important in their own right but as tools for self-scrutiny. As we will see in the next chapter, Roethke works continuously at liberating unconscious material in these notebooks, not just remembering events but actually creating whole worlds of psychic imagery from his plunges into "the depths." This kind of intense introspection was often painful for Roethke, as the reference to "my memory, my prison" and the description of himself as a "half-blind animal" suggest.

In addition to this immersion in the past, Roethke suffered his second mental breakdown during this period—after Christmas, 1945—which may be reflected in some of the more irrational parts of the sequence. However, it is important not to exaggerate the role of Roethke's breakdowns in his poetic work. To compare Roethke with Sylvia Plath and Rimbaud, as one critic does, is to romanticize mental derangement and reduce these poets' vastly different work to a form of inspired—or induced—madness. To suggest that writing about himself was psychologically "dangerous" for Roethke, as another critic does, is romanticization of a different sort which conjures up a distorted image of the poet as martyr to his own sensitivities. Roethke's biographer Allan Seager gives a plausible interpretation when he suggests that the five-part structure developed in **"The Lost Son"** reflects the pattern of the poet's breakdown, with the second and third sections expressing "the terror, the physical and psychic exhaustion of his stay in the hospital." But Seager goes too far in implying that Roethke's mental illness provided the "substructure" for the entire poem. Neither **"The Lost Son"** nor the other two poems in the group I have been discussing describe or arise directly from Roethke's breakdown. Rather, they are based primarily on an intense imaginative reliving of the past, as Roethke's comments in notebooks and the essay **"Open Letter"** make clear.

**"A Field of Light"** was written during a much calmer period in the poet's life, the summer of 1947, a month of which Roethke spent at the Yaddo Writer's Conference in rural New York. Roethke's physical distance from Saginaw and his past, the relaxed atmosphere of Yaddo, and the friendship and support of other writers, notably Robert Lowell, are reflected in the brighter, more peaceful tone of the poem Roethke eventually came to see as an "interlude" in the **"Lost Son"** sequence. Roethke's decision to insert this "interlude" in a group of poems he had originally considered complete is a choice which suggests an increased sense of control over the personal material from which the poems are derived. With **"A Field of Light"** added, the sequence no longer reflects its own chronological development in Roethke's life; a re-ordering of personal experience is involved. This re-order-ing implies an ability to see how the sequence presents the self and a desire to arrange that presentation in a certain way.

Though the last of the four **"Lost Son"** poems to be written, **"A Field of Light,"** is more self-accepting than the others, Roethke is not satisfied with the kind of "progress" involved here. If he were, he would have kept the poems in their order of composition, concluding the series with the least "troubled" of the four. Roethke's final arrangement of the sequence links the later vision of self in **"A Field of Light"** back to the poems which gave rise to it and changes it from an endpoint to an interlude in a cycle. Kenneth Burke sum-marizes the value of this kind of cycle-making in "The Veg-etal Radicalism of Theodore Roethke":

> The dangers inherent in the regressive imagery seem to have received an impetus from without, that drove the poet still more forcefully in the same direction, dipping him in the river who loved water. His own lore thus threatened to turn against him. The endur-ing of such discomforts is a "birth" in the sense that, if the poet survives the ordeal, he is essentially stron-ger, and has to this extent *forged himself* an iden-tity. [Burke's emphasis]

What new sense of identity has Roethke developed by in-serting **"A Field of Light"** in the **"Lost Son"** sequence? The self we see in the completed sequence seems less troubled, less obsessed with specific childhood experiences than it does in the original three-poem series. The intensity built up in the first version of the sequence through repeated patterns in structure, style and subject matter is now inter-rupted by a poem that offers what Louis Martz calls "a retro-spective view of the development of the entire sequence." **"A Field of Light"** shows the enlightenment and ease to-ward which the sequence as a whole has been headed.

Inserted in the middle of the group, this "retrospective view" adds a suggestion that the poet will eventually be able to put the intense experiences of the earlier poems into perspec-tive. At a future time he will presumably see these psychic processes in the relatively calm way he looks at them in **"A Field of Light,"** and in retrospect the most vivid aspects will not be the "dark" ones—the terror, the irrationality, the re-gression to childhood—but the "light" at the end of the ex-perience. The position of **"A Field of Light"** between the second and third poems of the original sequence also modi-fies the structure of the group, setting up a new balance be-tween two poems focussing on "darkness"—**"The Lost Son"** and **"The Long Alley"**—and two poems focussing on "light"—**"A Field of Light"** and **"The Shape of the Fire."** Though this re-ordering of the poems does not eliminate the "darker" passages in the concluding work, the inclusion of a new poem in the sequence "brightens" the group as a whole.

Stressing in **"A Field of Light"** that the final illumination, not flight or regression, is the most lasting part of the pro-cess of self-discovery, Roethke makes the affirmative vision at the end of the four-poem sequence all the more powerful.

The addition of **"A Field of Light"** to the middle of the **"Lost Son"** sequence is the first major step in Roethke's cyclic progress. The self-discovery involved here comes not from new understanding of a specific memory, as it had in the greenhouse poems, or from progressive repetition of a pat-tern of psychic development, as it had in the first three **"Lost Son"** poems, but from complex interactions among the dif-ferent sides of the poet's experience seen in the works. **"A Field of Light"** comments on the other poems in the se-quence from the distance of its retrospective vision; but this vision, set in the middle of the group, is then modified by its new role as an "interlude" rather than a summary. Cycle-making of this sort demands constant re-evaluation of po-ems and the experiences they describe. This includes returns to the "depths" even after they seem to have been left be-hind, in the "perpetual slipping-back" that is part of the cy-clic process. Burke's "birth" metaphor is appropriate for this intense, laborious process. In a reading of the four-poem **"Lost Son"** sequence, Roethke mentioned that the last poem of the group, **"The Shape of the Fire,"** was originally an attempt to conclude the exhausting process of self-explora-tion he had been undergoing as he was writing these works.

This attempt was not successful. By the fall of 1947 Roethke had completed the four-poem "Lost Son" sequence and had begun teaching at the University of Washington. *The Lost Son and Other Poems* was due to be published the follow-ing year, but the poet was still immersed in the cyclic pro-cess of self-discovery he had begun two years earlier. Its first manifestation after the move to Washington was the poem **"Praise to the End!"** Commenting on this piece in a letter to Kenneth Burke, Roethke stresses its close thematic relation to the **"Lost Son"** sequence:

> I've just finished a long (97 lines) poem, the last probably from the dark world. The tone of some of the passages is somewhat the same; but what is said (dramatically) is different. The thing is much "clearer," I think, than the other: can really be worked at as equations: There's a more complicated "ec-stasy" passage, which resolves into death-wish.

Though **"Praise to the End!"** in its final version has four sections, an explanatory outline Roethke provided for it sug-gests the five-part structure of the three original **"Lost Son"** poems:

1) Act
2) Reaction to act (quiet, sense of impotence)
3) Song: reasons for act reaction again

4) Two flashbacks related to act, then the present again

5) Sublimation (The fact that there are few human symbols here isn't accidental.)

The middle sections here seem particularly close to the earlier five-part model, including the sense of exhaustion in the second section, the irrational song of the third part, and the regressive flashbacks in the fourth part. From these similarities it might seem that **"Praise to the End!"** represents a return to the obsessions of the first three **"Lost Son"** poems, and that Roethke, in effect, learned nothing from his composition and arrangement of the four-poem sequence. However, the differences between **"Praise to the End!"** and the **"Lost Son"** sequence indicate some important developments in the poet's understanding.

Though Burke's "Vegetal Radicalism" essay provides an excellent analysis of the *Lost Son* volume, his assertion that **"Praise to the End!"** and other poems written directly after *The Lost Son* "repeat the regressive imagery without the abysmal anguish" undervalues the persistent element of despair in some of these works. The cause for this despair can be seen in the "equation" Roethke felt summarized **"Praise to the End!"**: "onanism equals death." Unlike the **"Lost Son"** poems, **"Praise to the End!"** begins not with general stagnation but with a specific masturbatory "act." The poet's reactions to this act—despair, flight into irrationality, regression—are reminiscent of the **"Lost Son"** sequence, but the final ecstasy is now seen as a "death-wish." The return to the past in Part 3, instead of refreshing the poet and leading him to a revitalized sense of self, now involves him with "graves" (3.25), "ghosts" (3.28), "owls" (3.21), and dreams of being "all bones" (3.13) as the father's death looms imminently over adolescent experience. In **"Praise to the End!"** the past is not a greenhouse but a grave.

The despair underlying **"Praise to the End!"** also colors the father's presence in the poem. The role of the dead father as a judgmental figure—"Father Fear," as Roethke calls him—had been hinted at in the "Gibber" section of **"The Lost Son"** (3.16-17). In **"Praise to the End!"** this aspect becomes dominant, as the poet begs mercy for his autoerotic transgression: "Father, forgive my hands" (1.12). But the father also has a benign side: his role as a loving guide who can help the son in his progress toward maturity. This ambivalent vision of the father is at the heart of the two sequences. While the judging father arises from the son's masturbatory guilt and is bound up with a death-wish, the loving father represents the hope of successful progress toward resolution of the problems of identity and sexuality. When the judging father appears, the poet is mired in his own failures, the bleak world of onanism and death. The loving father, in contrast, is a model who can lead the poet from masturbation toward genuine love, from fear and guilt toward a renewed sense of self.

In the **"Lost Son"** sequence as a whole the potentially destructive aspect of the father is gradually overshadowed by his nurturing abilities, and he becomes a "lively understandable spirit" (**"The Lost Son,"** 5.21) who can guide the poet to a kind of maturity. But in **"Praise to the End!"** these positive qualities are gone; the poet must beg forgiveness of a "Father of tensions" (1.4), a "ghost" (1.11) whose condemning presence leads him eventually toward death.

The change in the role of the father from the **"Lost Son"** sequence to **"Praise to the End!"** reveals some basic limitations in the final resolution of the four-poem sequence. The incompleteness of the vision of self attained in the **"Lost Son"** group is dramatized by the contrast between the last four lines of the sequence—

> To know that light falls and fills, often without our knowing,
> As an opaque vase fills to the brim from a quick pouring,
> Fills and trembles at the edge yet does not flow over,
> Still holding and feeding the stem of the contained flower.
>
> (**"The Shape of the Fire,"** 5.15-18)—

and these lines from the beginning of **"Praise to the End!"**:

> The rings have gone from the pond.
> The river's alone with its water.
> All risings
> Fall.
>
> (1.13-16)

In the first passage the stress is on containment, security, constant nurturing; the long lines with their smooth, regular rhythms and the half-rhymes at the ends of the lines augment this emphasis. The lines from **"Praise to the End!"** illustrate a situation in which this security breaks down; the enclosing "rings" of the calm "pond" are gone, and the "river" takes over, breaking the smooth order of the verse form as it pushes toward a "Fall." The "river" here is clearly sexual and points to a problem which is not adequately resolved in the **"Lost Son"** sequence.

Though **"The Lost Son"** and other poems in the sequence hint at sexual activities in references to "serpents" (**"The Long Alley,"** 1.1), "eels," "mouths of jugs" (**"The Lost Son,"** 1.55, 3.22), and other suggestive images, sexuality generally remains on the level of infantile fantasy in these poems. Though masturbation is mentioned, the conflict between easy autoerotic gratification and the desire for sex with another person does not predominate; and the fact that the poet is by himself in the ecstatic scene at the end of the sequence seems to have no negative connotations. However, when more adult sexual needs are considered in **"Praise to the End!"** the absence of another person in the concluding vision of self is connected with onanism and death. Roethke mentions this in his letter to Kenneth Burke:

> I've been astonished to find that in the last 24 lines of affirmation
> there is not one reference to anything human except the line:
>
> "I've crawled from the mire, alert as a saint or a dog."
>
> And a saint is hardly human. All the other images are fish, birds, animals, etc . . . Onan's folly. (Roethke's ellipsis)

In another letter he refers to the union with nature at the end of the poem—a union which is similar in tone and imagery to that at the end of **"A Field of Light"** or **"The Shape of the Fire"**—as "Ecstasy-death wish, etc. (Sublimation carried to its ultimate end)." The ecstatic vision of harmony becomes, like masturbation, a flight from confronting real sexual needs and a disobedience of the father. While the nurturing father in the **"Lost Son"** sequence leads the poet toward personal security and self-acceptance, the judging father in **"Praise to the End!"** shows what Roethke has *not* achieved: intimate relations outside the self. The poet's first response to this new challenge is flight and a longing for death.

Though **"Praise to the End!"** depicts a failure to attain a level of social and sexual maturity, the conclusion of this work is not completely hopeless. In **"Open Letter"** Roethke says the following about the end of the poem:

> Is the protagonist "happy" in his death-wish? Is he a mindless euphoric jigger who goes blithering into oblivion? No. In terms of the whole sequence, he survives: this is a dead-end explored. His self-consciousness, his very will to live saves him from the *annihilation* of the ecstasy. (Roethke's emphasis)

"Self-consciousness" and a "will to live" are qualities the poet has gained by the end of the **"Lost Son"** sequence. Though the self-acceptance achieved here gives the poet the confidence to "explore" masturbation and its consequences, Roethke eventually comes to consider the attempt to deal with sexual needs exclusively through the self-oriented vision of the **"Lost Son"** sequence a "dead-end." The cyclic process of self-discovery involves continual re-thinking of previous conclusions in this way. As Roethke noted in **"Open Letter,"** each poem is "complete in itself; yet each in a sense is a stage." As former endpoints become stages in a cycle,

the poet's awareness of self grows. "Transcend that vision. What is first or early is easy to believe. But . . . it may enchain you" [Roethke's ellipsis], the poet wrote in a notebook during this period. **"Praise to the End!"** points out a kind of enchainment in self, in which the sexual excitement of the "duke of eels" (1.8) is always followed by a sense of despair, impotence and death, a feeling of being "asleep in a bower of dead skin" (2.31), and "All risings / Fall" (1.15-16). Later poems will attempt to transcend this lonely pattern of arousal and sorrow. This transcendence, however, does not involve discarding the earlier sense of self but rather including it in a newer, broader vision.

Written after **"Praise to the End!"** in 1949-1950, the remaining eight poems in Roethke's third book were conceived originally as a sequence tracing the poet's growth from early childhood to maturity. A letter indicates that the six-poem sequence making up Part I of the published text at first also included **"Unfold! Unfold!"** and **"I Cry, Love! Love!"** Later these two poems were removed from the sequence and placed at the end of Part II. In February, 1949 Roethke sent a draft of the first poem of the group, **"Where Knock Is Open Wide,"** to Kenneth Burke, outlining his initial plans for the eight-poem sequence in a letter:

> This piece is conceived as the first of a sequence of dramatic pieces beginning with a small child and working up. A kind of tensed-up *Prelude*, maybe: no comment; everything in the mind of the kid.

The title **"Praise to the End!"** is from *The Prelude* and suggests an interesting link between the new sequence and the poem Roethke wrote just before it. Here are the lines from which this title is taken:

> How strange that all
> The terrors, pains, and early miseries,
> Regrets, vexations, lassitudes interfused
> Within my mind, should e'er have borne a part,
> And that a needful part, in making up
> The calm existence that is mine when I
> Am worthy of myself! Praise to the end!
> Thanks to the means which Nature deigned to employ;
> Whether her fearless visitings, or those
> That came with soft alarm, like hurtless light
> Opening the peaceful clouds; or she may use
> Severer interventions, ministry
> More palpable, as best might suit her aim.

Referring to the title in another letter, Roethke tells Burke that "Ambiguities, ironical and otherwise, are intended." Wordsworth's confident, assertive lines stand in clear contrast to a poem in which **"Praise to the end!"** becomes a death-wish.

Though Wordsworth's position is treated ironically in Roethke's poem, the lines from *The Prelude* also suggest a goal for Roethke: self-acceptance and harmony with nature. The first attainment of this goal at the end of the **"Lost Son"** sequence was shattered by the emergence of powerful sexual needs in **"Praise to the End!"** In the "tensed-up *Prelude*" which follows it, the poet attempts to trace his own sexual development as he dramatically reconstructs "The terrors, pains, and early miseries" of childhood and adolescence. The cyclic development of the sequence takes another turn here. In a misjudgment typical of his work on sequences, Roethke had believed **"Praise to the End!"** to be the last poem "from the dark world." But the new issues this poem raised sent him back again for new answers. This return to the past is an extended and more self-critical version of the returns in the **"Lost Son"** poems; it puts the past we have seen in the earlier sequence under a microscope by separating it into different periods and focussing more directly on the sexual issues raised by **"Praise to the End!"** The fact that the new sequence is made up entirely of dramatic monologues gives Roethke's encounter with the past an added intensity. He is not only returning to childhood as he had earlier but actually reliving it, speaking with the child's voice as he seeks to express everything "in the mind of the kid." This more intense and detailed treatment of past experience represents for Roethke another step in the cyclic progress toward "The calm existence that is mine when I / Am worthy of myself!"

The eight-poem "tensed-up *Prelude*" breaks naturally into four units. Roethke published the second, third and fourth poems of the series under the single title **"Give Way, Ye Gates"** in 1950. At the conclusion of this group he added the following note:

> I wish to have these three poems considered as an entity, the group making one poem from childhood into a violent adolescence: a caterwauling.

If this three-poem group is taken as the core of the sequence, the opening poem of the volume, **"Where Knock Is Open Wide,"** takes the sequence back from "childhood" toward infancy, while **"Sensibility! O La!"** and **"O Lull Me, Lull Me"** move forward from "violent adolescence" toward young adulthood. The last two poems of the sequence, **"Unfold! Unfold!"** and **"I Cry, Love! Love!,"** represent an adult perspective, which helps explain why Roethke eventually separated them from the rest of the series. Briefly, the first four poems of the sequence trace the child's development from infantile confusion and fear of his parents' power—

> A kitten can
> Bite with his feet;
> Papa and Mamma
> Have more teeth.
>
> (**"Where Knock Is Open Wide,"** 1.1-4)

—through the first awareness of his own independent sexuality—"I know another fire. / Has roots." (**"I Need, I Need,"** 4.15-16)—with its attendant anxieties; to a sense of sexual readiness—"It's time to begin!" (**"Bring the Day!,"** 3.7)—based on a faith that "What slides away"—parental nurturing, a childhood sense of security—will, in the end, "provide" (**"Give Way, Ye Gates,"** 4.16-17). The next two poems examine the autoerotic stage of "John-of-the-thumb" (**"Sensibility! O La!,"** 2.4) as the young man develops a clearer sense of self and other through sexual fantasies. The last two poems depict conflicts in the adult between a genuine desire to love and the death-wish derived from guilt Roethke noted earlier in **"Praise to the End!"**

The arrangement of the poems for the completed volume is the last stage in Roethke's cyclic progress. When it was published in 1951, *Praise to the End!* was divided into two sections: Part I contained the first six poems in the "tensed-up *Prelude*" while Part II included the **"Lost Son"** sequence, followed by **"Praise to the End!,"** **"Unfold! Unfold!,"** and **"I Cry, Love! Love!"** As I mentioned, Roethke originally wrote **"Unfold! Unfold!"** and **"I Cry, Love! Love!"** as the concluding part of the eight-poem "tensed-up *Prelude*," but these poems have enough similarities to the **"Lost Son"** series and **"Praise to the End!"** that they do not stand out awkwardly in Part II of the finished volume. Both poems are written from an adult perspective, and we see in both the old progression from stagnation, through regression, to a new vision of self. Stylistically these two poems are indistinguishable from the others in Part II; the short lines and sing-song rhythms that mark the early poems in the sequence gradually disappear as the series progresses. Richard Blessing points to these stylistic and thematic similarities among the poems of Part II:

> Poem after poem begins with the thought of death and with the language of death. . . . The voice is anxious, the sentences terse and frequently truncated, without subjects. The imagery is oppressive, establishing a kind of wasteland as spiritual landscape. But out of such beginnings the poet sets about making a verbal gesture of cherishing, a gesture celebrating life and its motion.

In their position at the end of Part II in the finished volume, **"Unfold! Unfold!"** and **"I Cry, Love! Love!"** complete this "gesture," capping the volume and linking both sections. They respond to the insufficiencies **"Praise to the End!"** revealed in the **"Lost Son"** sequence by going beyond the vision of self-acceptance at the conclusion of **"The Shape of the Fire"** to include a new understanding of sex and death.

We can see this new attitude in the secure, assertive tone of the last poem of the sequence, **"I Cry, Love! Love!"** The poet's confidence here is not based on an exaggerated idea of his own importance or a delusion of complete self-knowledge, as lines like "Bless me and the maze I'm in!" (2.7) and "Behold, in the lout's eye, / Love" (2.25-26) indicate. Neither is it based on mere "reason," as the opening of the poem's second section makes clear. Rather it is grounded in an expanded sense of self-acceptance which has developed over the course of the "tensed-up *Prelude*." In **"Open Letter"** Roethke stresses the personal validity of the final vision of identity here:

> None the less, in spite of all the muck and welter, the dark, the *dreck* of these poems, I count myself among the happy poets. "I proclaim, once more, a condition of joy!" says the very last piece.

The line following this proclamation, "Walk into the wind, willie!" (2.16), prepares us for the confident confrontation with death that occurs in the last section of the poem:

> I hear the owls, the soft callers, coming down from
>   the hemlocks.
> The bats weave in and out of the willows,
> Wing-crooked and sure,
> Downward and upward,
> Dipping and veering close to the motionless water.
>
>                                        (3.1-5)

The scene here, with its "bats," "owls," and "hemlocks," is even more evocative than the one at the conclusion of **"Praise to the End!,"** and Karl Malkoff finds an "implicit acceptance of the death wish" at the end of **"I Cry, Love! Love!"** However, viewing this poem in the context of the sequence it originally completed, we can see that **"I Cry, Love! Love!"** is not a recapitulation of **"Praise to the End!"** but the culmination of the poet's response to it; the death-wish of the solitary onanist is replaced by a new perspective which confidently reaches out toward union with another person. The landscape of death at the beginning of the section is converted into a scene which compounds birth and procreation:

> Who untied the tree? I remember now.
> We met in a nest. Before I lived.
> The dark hair sighed.
> We never enter
> Alone.
>
>                                        (3.15-19)

Though sex is seen as a symbolic return to the womb, this new "entrance" does not represent the end result of a solitary man's wish for death but rather a union between two people which produces life.

In Part II of the final text, then, the isolated security of the "contained flower," at first countered by the onanism and death of **"Praise to the End!,"** eventually grows into a "condition of joy" which points toward entrance into new life through sexual union. This vision is not reached directly by the adult mind of Part II but rather comes from a dramatic reliving of the poet's development from infancy to maturity. After this "tensed-up *Prelude*" has been written, the original ironic aspect of the title *Praise to the End!* is changed. The quotation from Wordsworth is no longer primarily a reference to the death-wish in a single poem but rather an allusion suggesting what the collection as a whole has accomplished: an inclusion of all the "terrors, pains, and early miseries" of past experience into a more accurate and secure sense of self-worth.

In the complex process of writing *Praise to the End!* Roethke proceeded, as he put it, "from exhaustion to exhaustion." Each apparent conclusion he reached—in the three-poem and later four-poem **"Lost Son"** sequences, in **"Praise to the End!,"** and in the "tensed-up *Prelude*" that followed it—was incorporated in a broader cyclic pattern which then demanded new work as issues were raised through new juxtapositions of poems. Repeated plunges into "the dark world" of the past and the unconscious are at the heart of this process, gradually leading the poet toward deeper self-awareness. This work in cycles allowed Roethke to enrich and expand the process of self-discovery begun in the greenhouse poems, as he progressed from the careful examination of individual memories to an extended "history of the psyche."

---

# FURTHER READING

### Bibliography

McLeod, James Richard. *Theodore Roethke: A Bibliography.* Kent, OH: Kent State University Press, 1973, 241 p.
    Provides a comprehensive listing of Roethke's works, including primary sources, contributions to periodicals, translations of his works, film and musical adaptations, and critical sources about Roethke.

### Criticism

Beaman, Darlene. "Roethke's Travels: An Overview of His Poetry." *Green River Review* XIV, No. 2 (1983): 79-90.
    Explores the inner journey motif and quest for transcendence in Roethke's poetry.

Blessing, Richard Allen. "The Dying Man." In *Theodore Roethke's Dynamic Vision,* pp. 161-70. Bloomington, IN: Indiana University Press, 1974.
    Offers analysis of Roethke's use of language in "The Dying Man."

Davis, William V. "Fishing an Old Wound: Theodore Roethke's Search for Sonship." *The Antigonish Review,* No. 20 (Winter, 1974): 29-41.

Examines the development and significance of Roethke's relationship with his father as revealed in his poetry.

Gunn, Thom. Review of *Words for the Wind. The Yale Review* XLVIII, No. 4 (Summer 1959): 623-6.

A generally unfavorable review of *Words for the Wind.* Gunn cites shortcomings in examples of Roethke's nonsense verse and admonishes the obvious influence of William Butler Yeats in this volume.

Hoey, Allen. "Some Metrical And Rhythmical Strategies in the Early Poems of Roethke." *Concerning Poetry* 15, No. 1 (Spring 1982): 49-58.

Examines Roethke's characteristic free verse form, meter, and use of sonic device in poems from *The Open House* and *The Lost Son and Other Poems.*

Johnson, Julie M. "'Dance On, Dance On, Dance On': Dance as Image in the Poetry of Theodore Roethke." *Massachusetts Studies in English* IX, No. 1 (1983): 64-76.

Explores the significance of dance motifs in Roethke's poetry, particularly as such imagery reveals Roethke's poor self-image and longing for unity in physical, psychological, and mystical terms.

Kalaidjian, Walter B. "Understanding Theodore Roethke." In *Understanding Theodore Roethke,* pp. 1-28. Columbia, SC: University of South Carolina Press, 1987.

Provides an overview of Roethke's life and major works.

La Belle, Jenijoy. "Archetypes of Tradition." In *The Echoing Wood of Theodore Roethke,* pp. 84-103. Princeton, NJ: Princeton University Press, 1976.

Examines the influence and synthesis of literary tradition and Jungian archetypes in Roethke's poetry.

Mazzaro, Jerome. "The Failure of Language: Theodore Roethke." In *Postmodern American Poetry,* pp. 59-84. Urbana, IL: University of Illinois Press, 1980.

Examines Roethke's effort to establish his own poetic voice through imitation and innovation, reflecting both the necessity and burden of his artistic influences.

Molesworth, Charles. "Songs of the Happy Man: Theodore Roethke and Contemporary Poetry." *John Berryman Studies* II, No. 3 (Summer 1976): 32-51.

Discusses the characteristic qualities of Roethke's poetry, particularly form, imagery, and aspects of self-analysis, noting his influence on subsequent American poets.

Parini, Jay. "Theodore Roethke: The Poetics of Expression." *Ball State University Forum* XXI, No. 1 (Winter 1980): 5-11.

Examines Roethke's idea of poetry and the poet, noting his relationship to the Romantic tradition.

Pearce, Roy Harvey. "Theodore Roethke: The Power of Sympathy." In *Historicism Once More: Problems & Occasions for the American Scholar,* pp. 294-326. Princeton, NJ: Princeton University Press, 1969.

Examines Roethke's identification with and expression of sympathy, violence, power, and control.

Pinsker, Sanford. "An Urge to Wrestle / A Need to Dance: The Poetry of Theodore Roethke." *CEA Critic* XLI, No. 4, pp. 12-7.

Discusses Roethke's mystical fascination with the joy of life and rebirth.

Ramakrishnan, E. V. "The Confessional Mode in Theodore Roethke: A Reading of 'The Lost Son.'" *Indian Journal of American Studies* 11, No. 1 (January, 1981): 58-65.

Explores Roethke's struggle with personal experience and self-consciousness in "The Lost Son," particularly as expressed in the dynamics of perception and harmony.

Rohrkemper, John. "'When the Mind Remembers All': Dream and Memory in Theodore Roethke's 'North American Sequence.'" *Journal of the Midwest Modern Language Association* 21, No. 1 (Spring 1988): 28-37.

Offers interpretation of the "North American Sequence" as a meditative reconciliation of past and present, noting Roethke's painful childhood memories and the psychic fragmentation caused by mental illness in his adult life.

Scott, Nathan A., Jr. "The Example of Roethke." In *The Wild Prayer of Longing: Poetry and the Sacred,* pp. 76-119. New Haven, CT: Yale University Press, 1971.

Examines Roethke's sacramental voice and ecstatic vision, especially as expressed by appeals to wonder, instinct, and the sense of "otherness" in reality.

Smith, R. T. "Critical Introduction to the Poetry of Theodore Roethke (1908-1963)." *Green River Review* XIV, No. 2 (1983): 11-6.

Provides a summary of major themes and symbolism in Roethke's poetry.

Stein, Arnold. "Introduction." In *Theodore Roethke: Essays on the Poetry,* edited by Arnold Stein, pp. ix-xx. Seattle, WA: University of Washington Press, 1965.

Provides a laudatory overview of Roethke's creative life and poetry.

Sundahl, Daniel James. "Theodore Roethke's 'The Lost Son': Solipsism and The Private Language Problem." *Essays in Arts and Science* XVII (May 1988) 41-61.

> Explores self-referential allusions in Roethke's "The Lost Son," especially as related to Ludwig Wittengstein's conception of language and the limits of expression.

Thurley, Geoffrey. "Theodore Roethke: Lost Son." In *The American Moment: American Poetry in the Mid-Century*, pp. 91-105. London: Edward Arnold, 1977.

> Provides a reassessment of Roethke's literary career, noting the effect of uncritical public sympathy for Roethke and the academic and imitative qualities of his poetry.

---

**Additional information on Roethke's life and career is contained in the following sources published by Gale Research:** *Concise Dictionary of American Literary Biography, 1941-1968; Contemporary Authors,* **Vols. 81-84;** *Contemporary Authors Bibliographical Series,* **Vol. 2;** *Dictionary of Literary Biography,* **Vol. 5;** *DISCovering Authors Modules: Poets Module; Major Twentieth-Century Writers;* **and** *Poetry Criticism,* **Vol. 15.**

---

# Tchicaya U Tam'si
## 1931-1988

(Born Gérald Felix Tchicaya; surname also spelled Tchikaya) Congolese poet, dramatist, novelist, and short story writer.

## INTRODUCTION

Considered by many as one of the most influential modernist African writers, Tchicaya is relatively unknown in the English-speaking world due to the paucity of translated editions of his work. He chiefly wrote poetry but turned to drama and fiction toward the end of his career. Despite having spent nearly a lifetime abroad in France—a move which marked his early works with an overwhelming sense of loss—Tchicaya reflected on life in newly independent Africa in his poetry, addressing the effects of Christianity, colonialism, and European pedagogy on his native continent through rich imagery, African symbols, and rhythms derived from African oral literature. Critics have observed the influences of French surrealism and *négritude,* a literary movement that championed blackness, in his writing style, and they have compared his verse to that of French poets Aimé Césaire and Arthur Rimbaud and African poets L. S. Senghor and Diop Birago. Tchicaya's novels and short stories juxtapose Christian and African cultural and religious values, often blending elements of surrealism and fantasy, while his dramas concern modern African struggles for power.

### Biographical Information

Born August 25, 1931, in what is now the People's Republic of the Congo, Tchicaya was the son of the Congolese first deputy to the French National Assembly in Paris, and he finished his secondary education at Paris's Lycee Janson de Sailly. Afterwards, he remained in France, working at various odd jobs as a laborer, draftsman, and messenger. During the early 1950s, Tchicaya began writing poetry, and in 1955 he published his first verse collection, *Le Mauvais sang (Bad Blood)*, which attracted little critical or popular attention. His succeeding volumes, *Feu de brousse* (1957; *Brush Fire*) and *A triche-coeur* (1958; *By Cheating the Heart*), however, garnered him recognition as an important new African voice. In the late 1950s he produced more than one hundred radio programs based on adaptations of African legends that he later collected as *Légendes africaines* (1968). After a brief stint in Leopoldville, Zaire, in 1960 as editor of the newspaper *Le Congo,* he returned to Paris and worked with the United Nations Educational, Scientific, and Cultural Organization (UNESCO) as a permanent official for the rest of his life. Tchicaya solidified his reputation as a leading proponent of *négritude* with the publication of *Epitomé* (1962) which

earned him the grand prize for poetry at the Festival des Arts Nègres at Dakar in 1966. By 1970 Tchicaya was considered a major African writer following the appearance of *L'Arc musical* (1970; *Bow Harp*) and the English-language translation of *Selected Poems* (1970). During the late 1970s he focused his literary skill on drama, producing the plays *Le Zulu* (1976), *Vwène le fondateur* (1977), and *Le Destin glorieux du Maréchel Nnikon Nniku, prince qu'on sort* (1979; *Glorious Destiny of Marshal Nnikon Nniku*). In the 1980s, Tchicaya diversified his canon further by writing fiction, including the short story collection *La main sèche* (1980; *Dried Hand*) and the novels *Les cancrelats* (1980; *The Cockroaches*), *Les Méduses, ou les orties de mer* (1982; *The Madman and the Mermaid*), and *Ces fruits si doux de l'arbre à pain* (1987). Tchicaya died April 21, 1988, at Oise, France.

### Major Works

*Bad Blood* concerns the poet's emotional response to his awareness about the human condition and the black man's status as a victim. Using images of children and birds, the collection's passive, despairing tone alternates with one of aggressive revolt. Tchicaya characteristically uses irony to temper intensity. *Brush Fire* explores the consequences of European colonialism, articulating the ways foreign systems of education and religion have alienated Africans from their culture and undermined native spiritual traditions. *By Cheating the Heart* emphasizes the poet's search for a purpose in life and addresses the suffering in Africa caused by slavery and colonialism. The fable-poem "Exquinoxiale," for instance, portrays Africa as a mother who has lost her child, yet prepares her body for the birth of another. *Epitomé*, widely regarded as Tchicaya's masterpiece, "reads like a poetic diary" of the Congolese uprising in 1960 and 1961, according to Gerald Moore. Christological imagery and language are vital in the collection, as the poet identifies himself with Christ and draws parallels between the exploitation of the Congo with the crucifixion. In *Le Ventre* (1964; *The Belly*), the Congo experience again dominates, with the author contemplating the life and death of his country. This collection contains some of Tchicaya's most difficult poetry due to its concentrated language, grammatical structure, and limited use of punctuation. *Bow Harp* and *La Vests d'Intérieur suivi de Notes de Veille* (1977) contain few references to public events but plenty of religious imagery. The more lyrical *Bow Harp* attempts to define the poet's faith, and *La Veste d'Intérieur* explores the isolation of the artist who lives in exile in a foreign culture. His novels are more political in nature. *The Cockroaches* details the lives of a French colonial and his African servants, and *The Madman and the Mermaid* investigates the mysterious deaths of two Congolese villagers. The stories of *Dried Hand* feature a surreal style, a mixture of French and African storytelling conventions, and a proverbial tone. *Ces fruits si doux de l'arbre à pain* focuses on family relationships, African mysticism, and Congolese politics.

**Critical Reception**

Tchicaya's literary work—no matter what the genre—has met with nearly universal critical acclaim, despite little attention from critics of African literature and general readers. Thomas R. Knipp called Tchicaya "the most prolific and gifted of the second generation of francophone poets," adding that "he is also the most difficult. . . . an old-fashioned poet—even bookish and academic." The difficult nature of Tchicaya's poetry is a recurring theme in criticism of his work, however, Tchicaya's "mastery of his medium precludes his being dismissed as obscure or unintelligible," remarked Betty O'Grady. Many commentators have viewed Tchicaya as the most successful poet of *négritude,* although his verse as a whole has had little impact on the black world for reasons "more closely related to the political evolution of Africa than to literary merit," according to Clive Wake. Others have sensed a difference in Tchicaya's style of *négritude,* because it is more focused on the changing present rather than the traditional past. Chaibou Elhadji Oumarou suggested that Tchicaya's verse attempts "to build a cultural identity from within, that is, an identity geared toward the future. Such an identity has to be informed not by literary patterns imposed from without, but by pages of African history." Generally, critics have commended Tchicaya for the authenticity and universality of his work. Because of the religious nature of many of his poems, commentators have often attempted to reconcile the Christian and African elements to determine each poem's or collection's primary influence. Susan Erica Rein suggested that his poetry conveys a transcendent religiosity constituting nothing less than a unique "Tamsien religion," which combines features of African spiritual traditions and Catholicism. Tchicaya's fiction also has garnered praise similar to his poetry. Eric Sellin found that the novel *The Cockroaches* "significantly enriches the corpus of Francophone African literature," and that his stories "deserve the most careful intellectual scrutiny.

# PRINCIPAL WORKS

*Le Mauvais sang* [*Bad Blood*] (poetry) 1955
*Feu de brousse* [*Brush Fire*] (poetry) 1957
*À triche-coeur* [*By Cheating the Heart*] (poetry) 1958
*Epitomé* (poetry) 1962
*Le Ventre* [*The Belly*] (poetry) 1964

*Légendes africaines* [editor] (radio scripts) 1968
*L'Arc musical* [*Bow Harp*] (poetry) 1970
*Selected Poems* (poetry) 1970
*Le Zulu* (drama) 1976
*La Veste d'Intérieur suivi de Notes de Veille* (poetry) 1977
*Vwène le fondateur* (drama) 1977
*Le Destin glorieux du Maréchel Nnikon Nniku, prince qu'on sort* [*Glorious Destiny of Marshal Nnikon Nniku*] (drama) 1979
*Les cancrelats* [*The Cockroaches*] (novel) 1980
*La main sèche* [*Dried Hand*] (short stories) 1980
*Les Méduses, ou les orties de mer* [*The Madman and the Mermaid*] (novel) 1982
*Ces fruits si doux de l'arbre à pain* (novel) 1987

# CRITICISM

**Thomas R. Knipp (essay date Summer 1974)**

SOURCE: "Negritude and Negation: The Poetry of Tchikaya U'Tamsi," in *Books Abroad,* Vol. 48, No. 3, Summer, 1974, pp. 511-15.

[*In the following essay, Knipp examines the themes of negritude and the alienation of the modern African in Tchicaya's poetry.*]

The Congolese Felix Tchikaya U'Tamsi is the most prolific and gifted of the second generation of francophone poets. He is also the most difficult. His surrealism reaches back through Aimé Césaire to André Breton and others in the 1920s. In this sense he is an old-fashioned poet—even bookish and academic. But his poetry, which in the hands of Gerald Moore, Sangodare Akanji and others seems to translate well, is oblique, fluid, suggestive, and replete with private symbols and symbolic motifs which accumulate meaning as they appear in poem after poem. Moore describes this process as a "spiral, exploratory movement."

It is easy to read U'Tamsi as a poet of Negritude—as the most successful example of Negritude at work in the second generation. Senghor insists upon such a reading. He attributes to U'Tamsi "A single passion, to bear witness to *Negritude*. [U'Tamsi] is a witness whose sole end here [in *Epitomé*] is to manifest *Negritude*. We have seen that he has all the negro virtues, but above all he assumes the mingled hope and despair of the negro, the epical suffering." U'Tamsi himself speaks of Negritude as of a movement in which he is participating. At the Dakar festival he stressed the link between it and the universal civilization in the best Senghor tradition: "The fruits of Negritude should not be picked by black hands alone but also by the hands of men of good will everywhere."

On the other hand Moore wonders if surrealism (what Senghor calls *une syntaxe qui déraisonne*) can be made to serve the cause of an ideology. The conception of Negritude as an ideology is, of course, inadequate even as a critical convenience. Negritude is so many things that its opponents cannot isolate it long enough to kill it. Among other things it is a state of mind—and a very flexible, durable one. In U'Tamsi's case it is indeed a state of mind, and surrealism is a technique used by a poet whose mind and experience are encapsulated within the boundaries of Negritude. Therefore the sentiments of Negritude will surface periodically and will underlie and infuse much of the poetry.

A reading of his poetry—particularly **Brush Fire**—reveals that U'Tamsi does combine the surrealism associated with the Caribbean origins of Negritude with the themes and historical perspective of Senghor and David Diop.

U'Tamsi's African suffers.

> je vous ai dit ma race
> elle se souvient
> de teneur du bronze bu chaud

> My race
> remembers
> the taste of bronze drunk hot

Because of their suffering his Africans have acquired a moral superiority to the white Europeans, who were the cause of the misery. In *Epitomé* the white man is portrayed as a criminal—not only exploitative, but hypocritical and sadistic.

> La mer obéissait déjà aux seuls négriers
> des nègres s'y laissaient prendre
> malgré les sortilèges de leurs sourires
> on sonnait le tocsin
> à coups de pied au ventre
> de passantes enceintes

> Already the sea obeyed the slave traders
> The Negroes let themselves be taken
> Despite the spell of their smiles
> The alarm bell was sounded with a kick in
>     the bellies of pregnant women.

Elsewhere, where his anger against the Europeans is less intense, he still indicts them because "they could not wait / until I proferred my own hand to them." He complains that "they set their technical constellations against me" and that the harmonious nature of Africa—the mangrove and weeping willow—could not resist their onslaught. However, whether the anger is mute or intense, the roles assigned to European and African correspond to the roles found in Senghor, Dadié and the two Diops.

In the poem **"Erect,"** U'Tamsi rejects the roles assigned to the black man by the conqueror—the roles of slave and *evolué*. "No slave's lament nor the Marseillaise either." And the African himself, liberated by the retreat of colonialism, will determine his new role.

> voici le serpent fuit devant la sève mûre
> qui surgit des flammes
> une nuit fit des noeuds dans toutes les mémoires
> je sais des danses qui sont d'atroces tragédies
> mes nègres dansent
> ton nègre danse
> le serpent en fuyant libère nos mémoires

> Here the serpent flees before the ripe sap
> that wells up in flames
> a night knotted together from all memories
> I know dances that are atrocious tragedies
> My negroes dance
> Your negro dances
> the fleeing serpent frees our memories

**"A Mat to Weave"** is a fairly long poem which establishes a counterpoint between the social and the personal. The poet speaks of the unique black contributions: "he came to deliver the secret of the sun." But he is rejected:

> il avait l'âme mûre
> quand quelqu'un lui cria
> sale tête de nègre

> His soul was ready
> when someone called him
> dirty wog.

And he remains unaccepted, still in possession of his secret. "Still he is left with the gentle act of laughter." The later lines of the poem seem autobiographical. He describes the Westernizing process through which he has passed:

> ici commence son poème-de-vie
> il fut traîné dans une école
> il fut traîné dans un atelier
> et il vit des chemins plantés de sphynx

> here begins the poem of his life
> he was trained in a school
> he was trained in a studio
> and he saw roads planted with sphinxes

But he emerges from the process with the vital African residue—nature and joy—still intact.

> il lui reste l'arc suave de son rire puis
> l'arbre puis l'eau puis les feuilles.

he is still left with the soft arch of his
laughter then the tree then the water then
the leaves.

However among these rather positive assertions of Negritude, U'Tamsi weaves other themes and visions. The search for identity which one finds in Lenrie Peters, the sense of alienation that one finds in Kofi Awoonor, the apocalyptic visions found in Frank Parks—all these surface in *Brush Fire*. U'Tamsi speaks of the African's identity quest as the search of a desolate man—a man, as he says in *Epitomé*, with "soul and body naked," a "man without a history." If these phrases seem to refer to the generic Negro, the following apocalyptic lines from **"Still Life"** seem painfully personal as well:

si je vous dis
mon père ignore le nom de ma mère
je suis témoin de mon temps
et j'ai vu souvent
des cadavres dans l'air
où brûle mon sang

If I tell you
my father does not know my mother's name
I am the witness of my age
I have often seen
carcasses in the air
where my blood burns.

Under such conditions and in such a world it is heroic not merely to know one's identity but also to contribute, and U'Tamsi takes on this heroic task in **"Abortive Joy."**

j'essaie de sauver ma peau
et d'agrandir le monde
d'une mesure de deux mains

I am trying to save my skin
and to enlarge the world
by the measure of two hands

But the last three lines of the previous quotation suggests that for U'Tamsi there are moments of suffering when Negritude and the contribution of two hands are burned away by the apocalyptic vision of the modern world in all its violent hopelessness—a modern world in which to carry the Negro's unique message of laughter and the universal rhythm is not to redeem men but only to intensify through irony one's own agony. The following lines are from **"Against Destiny"**:

il n'y a plus de soleils couchants
il y a l'herbe vorace
il y a le feu plus vorace
les peines poilues des bras pauvres

les transes
mimées
quelle agonie.

There are no more setting suns
There is ravenous grass
There is more ravenous fire
The hairy sorrow of impoverished arms
and trances
mimed
what agony.

These last quotations illustrate themes more commonly found in anglophone than in francophone poetry. They are part of the cry of the lonely African, not part of the assertion of Negritude. Perhaps this thematic duality is explainable environmentally in terms of U'Tamsi's time and place. He is the inheritor of the poetic tradition of Senghor and Césaire, but he is also, like Peters, Awoonor and Parks, an African who came of age as a man and an artist in the troubled 1950s. If he shares a tradition with Senghor, he shares an experience—a moment in time—with Peters and the others. But whatever the causes, his poetry does possess a tension and a density resulting from the counterpoint and interpenetration of the two themes. The result is, perhaps, the richest poetic achievement in modern Africa.

## Clive Wake (essay date 1975)

SOURCE: "Tchicaya U Tam'si," in *A Celebration of Black and African Writing,* edited by Bruce King and Kolawole Ogungbesan, Oxford University Press, 1975, pp. 124-38.

[*In the essay below, Wake provides a thematic overview of Tchicaya's works, suggesting "ways in which one might gradually penetrate the mysteries" of his poetry.*]

Tchicaya U Tam'si is a major African poet, the most outstanding French-speaking African poet of the younger, or what one might perhaps call the post-Négritude, generation. His work has not, however, made the same impact on the black world as Senghor's, for reasons which are more closely related to the political evolution of Africa than to literary merit.

Tchicaya's poetry, like Senghor's, is deeply rooted in an African consciousness torn by colonialism (although unlike Senghor, Tchicaya is also profoundly affected by the memory of slavery). Their attitude of mind is, however, very different. Whereas Senghor knows who he is and where he is going—it was part of the essential confidence and optimism of Négritude—Tchicaya is frustrated by the apparently insuperable difficulty of finding his identity, in relation both to the past and to the present, and has no certainty at all about his future either as a black man or quite simply as a man. It is precisely because he is unsure about the ability of man in general to overcome his weaknesses that he can feel so little confidence in his future as a black man. Senghor, starting from an absolute confidence in his own race, is able to face the rest of humanity with an equal confidence. The tone of their writing is therefore very different. Senghor's poetic diction embodies the calm dignity of the poet's self-assurance, with which the almost biblical rhythms of his verse are very much in keeping. Tchicaya's sense of frustration, anger and loss produces a more aggressive diction which expresses the ups and downs of an unsatisfied self-exploration. Sure of his links with the African past, Senghor constantly refers by name to the heroes of African history and to the particularities of the traditional culture. Such references are almost totally absent from Tchicaya's poetry. For him, there are the general images of a suffering past—slavery and colonialism—and the particular images of twentieth-century misery—the lynched black American Emmet Till, the murdered political leader Patrice Lumumba and the Congo: the Congo, a river as well as a place, above all. This is the region where he was born in 1931 and the scene of one of Africa's most traumatic experiences of the twentieth century. Although he was born on the Brazzaville side of the Congo, he identifies in his poetry with the nightmare of the other Congo's history between 1959 and 1961, both because of the significance of the events themselves and because they reflected with symbolic intensity his own sense of violation and loss. The specific events of the period find their place almost naturally in a poetic universe which was by then ready to receive them. This was a poetic universe made up of two primary elements, the suffering human body in all its parts and the Congolese landscape of savannahs, forests, rivers (and chiefly one river), birds, animals, sun and sky. These are the realities of his world, and the necessary sources of his imagery and his symbolism.

> **Tchicaya's sense of frustration, anger and loss produces a more aggressive diction which expresses the ups and downs of an unsatisfied self-exploration.**
>
> —*Clive Wake*

Tchicaya writes a difficult poetry. Much of it remains impenetrable to even the most assiduous and sensitive of readers, although there is little doubt about the main lines of his thought. Tchicaya has, however, with justification, denied the charge of hermeticism: '. . . personally I do not think myself hermetic. I admit I have a big nose, I admit I have a club foot, but I do not admit being hermetic. It is quite easy

to read my poetry if one takes time, if one is careful to pause in the right places; there is no trick about it' [*Cultural Events in Africa*, no. 60 (1969)]. There is no evidence that the poet is deliberately trying to make his work inaccessible to the reader. The poetry is constructed around a very vivid, startling use of imagery and symbolism of a chiefly visual kind. One is tempted to define it as Surrealist, but this would be a mistake. The use of enigmatic visual imagery, largely without referents, along with ellipsis, non-linear argument, ambiguity, lack of punctuation and a refusal generally to make allowances for the reader are common to much modern French poetry which is not Surrealist. Surrealist poetry is concerned with subconscious experience and ought, if it is genuine, to be based on spontaneous (called 'automatic') writing. The structure and imagery of all of Tchicaya's poetry are very carefully controlled, and throughout his work there is broadly the same recurring pattern of images, phrases and themes. Moreover, Tchicaya seems to be much more concerned with conscious experience than with the subconscious; he is anxious for the self-knowledge which will tell him where he stands in relation to other men. This would certainly be in keeping with Tchicaya's rejection of the description of his poetry as hermetic. He goes on to say: 'It is as when I say: I lend a pack of cards to a passer by. I lend. I give. One must visualise the pack of cards and one must visualise the hands of the passer-by, and the passer-by himself. And if the passer-by is a Fortune-teller one must wait for the prognostication . . . nothing could be more direct.' He is stressing here the conscious quality of his poetic experience. The purpose of this essay will be to try to suggest some of the ways in which one might gradually penetrate the mysteries of this complex, highly-charged but very immediate poetry.

Tchicaya has so far published six volumes of poetry: *Le Mauvais Sang* (1955), *Feu de Brousse* (1957), *A Triche-coeur* (1960), *Epitomé* (1962), *Le Ventre* (1964), and *Arc Musical* (1970). The first three volumes were re-issued (with a number of significant alterations to *Le Mauvais Sang*) in a single volume, in 1970. *Epitomé*, which also incorporated a number of significant textual amendments, as well as additions, was re-issued in the same volume as *Arc Musical*.

In his first volume, *Le Mauvais Sang (Bad Blood)*, the young poet evokes the emotional impact made on him by the realization that the human condition, and in particular that of the black man, condemns him to the role of victim, not hero. Although the black man's situation in the world is central to his theme (it is mentioned in the very first poem and the notion of 'bad blood' refers to the black man's supposed congenital inferiority), it is not again directly referred to until the end of the volume, and in the final poem it literally explodes into prominence. This approach has the effect of strengthening Tchicaya's point by bringing us to the poet's awareness of himself as a black man via his awareness of himself as a human being first and foremost. But Tchicaya is not so much concerned with his lot as a black man as with that initial realization of his human condition. Like his admired predecessor Rimbaud, Tchicaya expresses it very aptly through the image of the child, and occasionally through the image of the bird, when he wants to stress more the idea of the poet as a singer and a lonely figure. The child's imagination is particularly sensitive to the experience of alienation and hostility. Family ties are important to him, so Tchicaya's child has no family, 'neither father, nor mother, nor brothers', he is 'a bird without feathers, a bird without a nest'. He has an instinctive longing for joy, purity and love ('sun', 'gold', 'love', 'heart' are all words carrying these ideas which recur frequently), but he seems to be held by a 'destin' ('destiny') which is corrupted at source; he is led to believe that his very life blood, his very blackness are impure. In his quest for an answer to the riddle of this paradoxical conflict between aspiration and hopelessness, he is torn alternately by hope and despair, by apparent success and a profound sense of defeat. He meets a fortune-teller who describes his life as 'a long journey at the end of which you will be hanged'. His frustration provokes intense resentment, emotions which come very forcefully through the imagery and the rhythms. Passive sadness, in verses perhaps deliberately reminiscent of the nineteenth-century French poet Verlaine, alternates with outbursts of aggressive revolt which are in turn reminiscent of Verlaine's companion Rimbaud. The intensity of the emotion is maintained by its being held tautly in check, its only outlet an irony which makes no allowances for the unwary.

The volume is not, however, merely a random collection of mood poems. There is a unity of imagery and theme, but also an evolution in the poet's attitude to his predicament. A poem of hope seems to be cancelled out by a poem of despair and so on, like a pendulum. But as the volume nears its close, the feeling of hope comes to dominate more and more. In the poem **'Espérance, o savanes'**, while the penultimate stanza ends with the exclamation 'Défaite!', the last stanza ends with a resounding 'Espérance!'. The first and last poems of the collection themselves indicate the distance covered by portraying exactly opposite states of mind through the same image of 'le mauvais sang'. The first poem asks a question without any hope of an answer:

> Heave your song—Bad Blood!—how then to
> survive the soul bloomed with shit. . . .

In the last poem, [**'Le Signe du Mauvais Sang'**], rather like Césaire in the *Cahier*, the poet ironically accepts the squalor and ugliness of his physical and moral condition as it has been presented to him. He rejects the temptation of self-pity and fatalism. 'A toad's destiny is pure enough', he exclaims. Another of the last poems is entitled **'Le Gros Sang'**, where 'bad' (or 'impure') is replaced by 'big' as the qualification

for 'blood'. This poem contains an important line which expresses the mood of the final poem: 'I am the tempered steel, the fire of the new races'. The poet acknowledges the virtue of pride: "In the memory of man pride has been a vice I make it a God . . . I am a man I am black'. Along with the transition from defeatism to a more aggressive self-assertion comes the realization that what he has so far seen as a private predicament is one he shares with all the 'new races'. The poet's sense of isolation disappears and he is able to declare: 'I create Brotherhood'. Where he had once taken seriously the idea of the inherent impurity of his blood, he now uses the phrase 'le mauvais sang' with an irony which indicates his new state of mind:

> That's it they are of course tractors grumbling
>     across my savannah.
> No it is my blood in my veins!
> A bad blood it is!

Tchicaya's concern with colonialism is more explicit in *Feu de Brousse (**Brush Fire**)*. Although he tells us his 'love is sad', this volume has none of the passive sadness, with its hint of self-pity, to be found in *Le Mauvais Sang*. Instead there is a much greater firmness of purpose, already evoked in [**'Le Signe du Mauvais Sang'**]. The central theme of *Feu de Brousse* is the idea that the black man has been deprived of the spiritual continuity of his African tradition, and without it it seems he cannot find his identity. Colonialism, coming in the wake of slavery, and bringing with it the cultural arrogance of Christianity, has undermined his tradition and created in him a sense of rootlessness; in terms of the book's symbolism, the fishermen have abandoned the river. In the poem **'Long Live the Bride'**, he illustrates his argument by taking what was at the time one of the great events of Africanized Christianity. The *Messe des Piroguiers* ('The Fishermen's Mass') had recently been performed in the Cathedral of Saint Anne in Brazzaville. Less well-known than the *Missa Luba*, it was nevertheless one of the fashionable 'African' masses of the day:

> uncle nathanael writes to me of his astonishment
> at hearing the drums
> over radio-brazzaville.

Tchicaya was not to be taken in by the novelty of drums in a Christian church. In allowing their use, the missionaries had been careful to exclude any of the 'lewdness' they associated with traditional African dance and music. Tchicaya regards this emasculation as a travesty:

> my catafalque is ready
> and I lie dead murdered on the altar of christ.

Tchicaya returns constantly in his work to the way European education and religion have alienated him and Africans in general from themselves, and at the same time destroyed the links that once bound Africans of different tribes together. The poems of this volume evoke the poet's attempts to rediscover his own lost spiritual continuity with his people. There are false solutions: he pretends to accept the white man's ways, but this leads to a hypocrisy which can only give him 'the life that kills'. He seeks the answer in the vision of an ideal, represented here by the love of a woman, especially Sammy; the theme and Sammy recur throughout his work. But idealism is no solution either. He comes finally to realize that he has to stand on his own two feet and walk, as the titles of the last two poems in this volume indicate: **'Debout'** (**'On your feet'**) and **'Marche'** (**'Walk'**).

---

**Tchicaya returns constantly in his work to the way European education and religion have alienated him and Africans in general from themselves, and at the same time destroyed the links that once bound Africans of different tribes together.**

**—Clive Wake**

---

This summary is a gross oversimplification, inevitably, of a complex and subtle exposition in poetic terms of the poet's conception of his predicament. Imagery drawn from the human body, especially the various associations with blood, is significant, but he expresses his theme mainly through the medium of imagery suggested by the Congo landscape. The river itself is the central symbol, standing for the continuity of life and the spirituality it ensures. Often the poet identifies himself directly with the river:

> His river was the gentlest dish
> the firmest
> it was his most living flesh.

Some of the images, such as the dish in this quotation, seem odd at first. The dish can be associated with the later image of the matrix, equated with the poet's eyes, the symbol of the true self.

The river must be bridged, the two banks linked again, and the spiritual continuity of his soul in space and time restored. It seems to him that only the rainbow—perhaps an image of the ideal—can achieve this. The last poem, **'Marche'**, draws the imagery and themes of the volume together in the form of a fable which seems to suggest ultimate success for the poet. The river Congo is created from the eyelash of a waking child, and the banks of the river are joined by time; the poet crosses and is restored to his origins, able to undergo the purification by fire which will clean away his shame.

> the bell tolls it is time
> across time and river
> time fords the tolling of the bell
> on its mounts of silence
>   and crosses
> my soul is ready
> peace on my soul
> light the fire that washes away shame.

*A Triche-coeur* (*By Cheating the Heart*) stresses the theme of the poet's quest for purpose. In the opening fable-poem, **'Agonie'**, the poet ('the black boatman') crosses the river to a bird on the other bank who represents his soul. Filled with his ambition to 'heal with the mud of his sad eyes / the lepers of their leprosy', he learns that he must instead set his sights much lower. The bird tells him:

> I am your soul farewell
> my body is only a shadow farewell
> your arms will be untied
> I am not a leper
> do not die waiting for me
> with your arms stretched out in a cross.

A later poem, **'L'Etrange Agonie'**, develops the theme of the poet's quest more fully and in a more intensely personal way. The outcome is, however, the same: his future will not be that of a conqueror but a club-foot.

The poet's concern with the purpose of his own life is always inextricably tied up with his awareness of 'the orphan' Africa's three centuries of suffering through slavery and colonialism. In a very vivid and moving fable-poem, **'Equinoxiale'**, Africa is portrayed as a mother who has lost her child and during her centuries of mourning ploughs and sows her body in readiness for the birth of a new child. In several poems, Christianity's role is developed more fully, in readiness almost for the next volume, *Epitomé*. It enables the poet to exploit the image of the cheating heart. The Christianization of Africa by men who use methods that betray Christ also leads to duplicity on the part of the poet who hides his real preoccupations from them and even from his own people:

> Devoted to my illusions
> I never laughed
> I never showed my teeth to anyone . . .
> I pretended they were bad.

In turn he betrays the betrayed Christ (who is later to be presented as the betrayer himself) and turns back to the pagan Sammy, whose pure song rises from among the devastated trees of Africa like a clear river flowing through green fields. In the title poem of the volume, Tchicaya contrasts the apparent sterility of his own suffering and his sense of having betrayed Africa by his cheating and hypocrisy with the falseness of Christ's sacrifice (Christ is symbolized as a wild boar), for did he not instruct the 'corner-stone' Peter to bring into being a religion of violence?

> with the sword break bread
> stretch forth your hand make love.

The unifying idea of this volume is the moment of death (agony) and death itself, for death sums up a man's life and, as the Gospels say, inaugurates a new life. Christ dies so that a religion based on violence and violation might emerge; the mother mourns for her child while she prepares her body for a new birth; the death of the orphan Africa is evoked in yet another fable-poem, **'Le Corbillard' ('The Hearse')**; and so too is the mystery of the poet's own agony as he strives to free himself from a destiny that prevents him from realizing the real purpose of his existence.

*A Triche-coeur* reads like a prologue to *Epitomé*, although all three volumes so far discussed reach their climax in this last one. *Epitomé/Les Mots de Tête pour le Sommaire d'une Passion (Epitome/Epigraphs for the Summary of a Passion)*, published in 1962, is perhaps Tchicaya's most important work to date, the two subsequent volumes notwithstanding, not only in terms of the poet's artistic development, but also, as it is clear from the title, in terms of his awareness of the stage reached by his intellectual and emotional development. 'Epitome' indicates a quintessential bringing together, or summary, of the elements that constitute his 'passion' (in the religious sense), and the word 'summary' in the sub-title on the one hand reinforces this intention and on the other it includes the now less common meanings of *summa*, the 'sum or substance of a matter', to quote the OED, and the notion of the highest point or climax of an experience. This is clear from Tchicaya's use of the preposition in the title of the poem's first section: **'Au Sommaire d'une Passion' ('At the Summary of a Passion')**. These intentions are made very relevant when we consider the events which provided an essential element in the inspiration of the poem. These were the events that followed on the outbreak of violence in Leopoldville (which Tchicaya refers to throughout his work as Kin) in 1959 (the date is mentioned in the text), a year before the country's independence. Something like two hundred African civilians lost their lives in clashes with the Belgian forces of order. These events, in all their brutal reality, force the poet to come face to face with himself, to confront the introspection of a perhaps too theoretical poetry with the facts of life.

In **'Préface'**, Tchicaya acknowledges the ambiguities of his attitude to the world around him. During the course of the poem, he refers to himself as the man with a limp, anxious to do what is right, but imperfect and aware of his own treach-

ery. People, he says, demand purity, but he is not pure in the accepted sense. There are sides to his personality and his behaviour which deserve criticism. He has seemingly identified with the white world, spent time on that 'society beach' which crops up from time to time in his poems. But real purity, he argues, comes from the experience of all aspects of life, with its many pressures and temptations. They are the cause of the 'headaches' that constitute the matter of his poems. 'Nothing is pure which excludes a mixture of everything; I shall say that real purity doesn't care a damn for purity. . . . The darkest night has greater brightness than the flash of lightning that shatters it.'

The poet is faced with two main problems. Firstly, there is the urgent need to know who and what he is, the nature of his destiny. This is the continuing anxiety. He wants to find the roots of his 'genealogical tree', which is his tree of life. This quest remains an apparently hopeless one. He is reluctant to opt for the artificial answers provided by movements like Négritude—

> The cross the banner négritude in overalls
> who wants to get involved?

Secondly, he senses a conflict between his quest for his racial and cultural roots and the intense anger he feels about the events taking place in Leopoldville. There is, in fact, a shift of emphasis from the hitherto essentially egocentric nature of his quest to the poet's relationship with the here and now of the African situation and the problem of the poet's commitment to it. The long first section of the poem, **'At the Summary of a Passion'**, poses the problems and indicates the poet's hesitations. In the last section, he seems to reach a conclusion. He rejects the attitude of mind that is represented by van Gogh and Matisse who withdraw from 'the noises of the city' in order to create an art which has nothing to do with everyday realities. They work in isolation—perhaps to some extent he has also done so up until now—while

> on the pavements the passers-by
> have a deluge in their hearts.

His own passion—the word already indicates this—is paralleled with Christ's, and he too assumes the suffering of his fellow men. But, whereas he has so far tended to reflect mostly on the pain caused to himself by the wearing of the poet's crown of thorns, he will instead now concentrate on the pain felt by others, and thus in a true sense assume their suffering:

> by the salt of a wine
> explain the weather as it is
> turn away from all the sores that condition
> the growth of thorns on my crown.

The poet's commitment is to an awareness of the suffering of others, not his own, and to its poetic expression:

> From what love
> at what cost
> I die with each song of love.

The poet becomes a Christ whose passion and death are the poem, the verbal realization of the people's suffering. This brings him back, as so often is the case with this poetry of exploration, to the first poem, **'Préface'**: 'Nothing is closer to the Word than the word when it is made to resound'.

Much of the imagery and many of the key phrases of the earlier volumes are present in *Epitomé*, which is a bringing-together in a special way of all that has gone before. More stress is laid in this volume, however, on the image of the sea, the symbol of 'the human adventure', than on that of the river, the symbol of an individual culture, ultimately only part of the whole into which it flows. The shift is in line with Tchicaya's anxiety to decide whether his duty is to all men or to those who make up his own people. He is fascinated by the figure of the salt-gatherer, working on the sea-shore, gathering the essence of all things. In the end he decides, 'I shall no longer go down to the sea'. This is, too, the volume in which Tchicaya's Christological imagery plays its most important role, for, not only does he deliberately parallel 'the analysis of his suffering' with Christ's, using the imagery and terminology of Christology throughout the poem, but he also makes a bitter attack on Christ (especially in the section entitled 'The Scorner'), who is contaminated by association 'with the bourgeois', and Christianity, which is epitomized in the Cathedral of Saint Anne at Brazzaville. He plays on the ambiguities of Christ's betrayal of Africa and his own, but finally shifts the true dignity of the Cross from the white man's God to the black poet.

*Le Ventre* (*The Belly*) is Tchicaya's most difficult poem; the concentration of the poem's language makes the text often intractable. Although it is based on the by now familiar imagery of the human body, the belly of course in particular, and although many other key images and phrases return, if with less insistence, there is an air of unfamiliarity which must strike the reader who has followed Tchicaya's poetry this far. He is clearly still preoccupied with the development of the situation in the now independent Congo-Kinshasa (Zaïre), between the date of independence on 30 June 1960 (once again, the date is given in the text) and Lumumba's assassination in February 1961: violence continues, the African leadership is compromised with international big business and the former colonial power has sent in troops to protect its interests (there is specific reference to the landing of Belgian troops at Kamina and Kitona). The name Kin recurs almost obsessively,

> the town
> where the river has its hand
> on my heart.

Nor is Katanga forgotten. The opening section recalls the imagery of the closing section of *Epitomé:* the rain continues to fall, and there is 'nothing to take away from that crown (of thorns)'.

Lumumba is not mentioned by name in the text, although he is given as the author of an epigraph: 'I am the Congo'. He is, however, the poet's central preoccupation, the basis of his angry reflection on the political and human situation and on leadership and sacrifice. Continuing the imagery of *Epitomé*, he presents Lumumba as a Christ figure, betrayed by his own people for money:

> Ah the jews know too well
> that this messiah was for sale.

(Tchicaya often refers to himself and black people metaphorically as Jews.) Money dominates:

> at Kin where blood
> has its exchange rate I don't know what it is:
> Is it measured by the dollar?

The poet even foresees the time when his own poetry will be quoted on the stock-exchange.

Gerald Moore suggests that 'in *Le Ventre* there is less reference to external events or to the past. The poet is here involved in a long interrogation of himself.' The past certainly does have little place in the poem, and the quest for the genealogical tree has disappeared (although the river symbol remains). However, it is because the pressure of the present is even more overwhelming than it was in *Epitomé,* and it determines the nature of the self-interrogation; this becomes a reflection on the life and death of another person with whom the poet identifies. The dominating image of the belly (closely linked with blood, which is perhaps the second most powerful image in the poem) suggests concern with the most basic of everyday human experiences, with the elemental human realities of sexuality and birth, greed and generosity, the physical satisfaction of hunger and thirst. As an image the belly is a kind of visible presence in a way that the more traditional symbols of the heart and the head cannot be. The latter remain curiously abstract because they are dominated by what they stand for, whereas the belly, unusual, almost grotesque as a poetic image, seems to have a physical reality which imposes itself on the imagination. The poet's reflections range from:

> the belly. For sale everywhere with that pestilential heat of old charnel houses,

to Lumumba's death:

> He died with his back to the wind:
> turn over his belly:
> if his belly is hard
> it shows he died on his feet!
> Do not weep.
> Walk erect!

In the opening section of the poem we are presented with the vivid, startling picture of upturned bellies floating among the water hyacinths in Stanley Pool. The upturned belly is likened to the visible part of a seamark, for which he uses the word *voyant*, normally associated with the idea of prophecy. But prophecy does not seem to be his preoccupation here. He is using the more down-to-earth meaning of the word to stress a very down-to-earth meaning of martyrdom: the inspiration that the martyr gives through his example. Tchicaya uses the image to bring the poem to an end, associating the marker with the dead martyr:

> But love for life
> the love one gives from the belly
> the earth takes care of that
> Thank God markers fall
> mostly on their back
> mostly with their arms outspread
> mostly with their belly facing the sky!

During the course of the interview quoted earlier in this essay, Tchicaya mentioned his feeling of sadness at the failure of men of different races to form community: 'An overflow of misery, undisguised and physical, a moral misery I would like to call it, and there was this odd impression of forlornness, of utter solitude, a barred horizon. Certainly there is in my writing this universe, this loneliness, sadness of man—man everywhere, whether he be black, white, yellow etc.' He had spoken of his 'sad love' before in his poetry, especially in *Epitomé*, but it is with *Arc Musical* (*Bow Harp*) that the feeling itself comes through. In earlier volumes, the sadness was spoken of but not evoked; it was kept in the background by the more imperious nature of the poet's anger and frustration. The tone of *Arc Musical* is strikingly different from its predecessors. We are made to share his sadness that

> a cry cannot pass
> unless it is covered in blood,
> unless it promises its blood . . .
> but this cry is
> there has been enough bloodshed!

His whole work is haunted by the spilling of human blood, so the need for love is what becomes most urgent for the poet now, 'love, love at last satisfied'. With it goes an equally urgent longing for peace:

> The treasure . . .
> is in the voice of the man
> where no storm rages
> over the corn in the plains at dawn.

In the first of two poems entitled **'Communion'**, Tchicaya evokes his own discovery of communion with men, a discovery which, to his surprise, was not painful, which did not dismember him, and for which he would now be prepared to suffer anything. The second poem of this title opens with one of those striking lines which one constantly meets with in Tchicaya's poetry:

> Quand l'homme sera plus féal à l'homme
> (When man will be more loyal to man).

When this happens, 'life will rediscover my body'.

There is a lyrical quality about most of these poems which is sometimes reminiscent of *Le Mauvais Sang*, but it is a parallel which only serves to show how far Tchicaya has come both as an artist and as a man since that first volume. His style is now very much his own. There is no trace of Verlaine or of Rimbaud, and there is, above all, a depth of feeling and a depth of sincerity which could only have come after the experience of suffering recorded in the previous volumes. The confrontation between the egocentric poet and external reality at the heart of *Epitomé* seems to have come to complete fruition. Similarly, Tchicaya is able to transcend the specifically racial concerns of his earlier poetry to write poetry which is unambiguously universal in its representation and understanding of the human condition. He is not afraid to go down to the sea. He does not, however, fall victim to sentimentality, as could so easily happen. He is very much aware of the human realities, and it is his recognition of the fact that love and peace are not often enough preferred to hate and bloodshed that forms the basis of his sadness and prevents sentimentality. He constantly reminds himself of the need to return to reality from the world of music in which he would prefer to live. These poems are about the interplay in the poet's life of his dream and reality. In the final poem of the collection, entitled **'Sinaï, bis'**, he offers to inscribe a new decalogue on the cheeks of the men of peace, the poem he cannot set down on the printed page:

> the poem I have seen
> the poem this page suppresses
> which would have saved the blood
> so that a hand might dash
> both sphinxes and wanderers
> so that birds might trust
> in the innocence of man.

## Eric Sellin  (review date Autumn 1981)

SOURCE: A review of *Les cancrelats,* in *World Literature Today,* Vol. 55, No. 4, Autumn, 1981, p. 715.

[*In the following review, Sellin praises Tchicaya's literary achievement in* Les cancrelats.]

African fiction of French expression has tended, since the early 1950s, to conform not only to French linguistic stringencies but also to French literary models. The African writer adopted certain forms which conformed to his predilections, notably the diary, the epistolary exchange, the autobiography and the short story or fable.

A new, more boisterous fiction, which made the French language and consequent literary tradition bend to its will rather than vice versa, emerged in the late 1960s with the publication of Ouologuem's irreverent *Le devoir de violence* and Kourouma's *Les Soleils des Indépendances.* This free-wheeling assault on the French love of order and conformity—paralleled in North Africa by the writings of Kateb, Boudjedra and Khaïr-Eddine—seemed to herald a new and vital African idiom. Two swallows do not, however, make a summer, so to speak, and the arrival of another major novel in this lineage may therefore be viewed as something of a literary event.

*Les cancrelats* is a first novel by Tchicaya U Tam'Si, a world-renowned Congolese poet. The plot is labyrinthine and contains subplots, but essentially it deals with the activities of two generations in a French colonialist family and in the family of the elder colon's servant. The precise nature of the plot is almost incidental, however, to the texture of *Les cancrelats,* a texture which is deliberately rough and abstract, like one of those experimental wall hangings by weavers. The main pattern interweaves missionary-style Christianity (in the novelists mentioned above Islam is a major force, but in the Congo we are south of the reach of Islam's proselytizing), the proverbial wisdom of traditional African culture and a highly charged style with a unique vocabulary.

Tchicaya has bent the French language to fit his narrative without breaking it. There is a sense of translucence in which the African proverbial diction glows vigorously through the otherwise Cartesian light of the French language. Tchicaya has written fables and stories and retold African legends, but with *Les cancrelats* he establishes himself as a novelist of major proportions and significantly enriches the corpus of Francophone African literature.

## Eric Sellin  (review date Winter 1982)

SOURCE: A review of *La main sèche,* in *World Literature Today,* Vol. 56, No. 1, Winter, 1982, pp. 162-63.

[*In the favorable review below, Sellin maintains that the stories in* La main sèche *"deserve the most careful intellectual scrutiny."*]

Tchicaya's short stories [in *La main sèche*], published the same year as his first novel, *Les cancrelats,* have the same triple thrust as that novel. First, there is the surreal and fascinating style; second, there is the blend of Western Christianity and African tradition; and third, there is the proverbial tone to the diction. Particularly salient in these tales is the fascinating blend of Christian elements and the personal African optics of the narrator. A black baby who takes the place of a papier-mâché Jesus in a crèche has been abandoned by its mother. Or are we actually witnessing the Second Coming? In another story a talking mouth (**"noire et lippue, bien sûr"**) retraces the evolution from sea organism to Homo sapiens.

Tchicaya has often been assimilated into the surrealist movement because of his unusual imagery and his interest in Rimbaud. Now, with the stories of *La main sèche,* Tchicaya reinforces that association, especially in the oneiric passages of **"Rebours"** and in the plotless urgency of several other stories. These tales are not slices of life but rather slices of consciousness lent a palpable dimension. The major coordinates of Tchicaya's world are African and French conventions. If Tchicaya *is* a "surrealist," it is on his own terms. His devotion to the Rimbaldian tradition of the *hallucination simple* is embraced somewhat cynically, and his prime world view remains African—namely natural rather than supernatural. Tchicaya brilliantly reverses one of Europe's most famous existentialist quotations when he speaks of people entering a judge's chambers, including "un certain Pascal qui, dit-on, enseignait aux arbres la mauvaise foi des humains." In this reversal lies the clue to the fundamental difference between European surrealism and African surreality.

Tchicaya's stories, which at first appear casual, deserve the most careful intellectual scrutiny.

## Victor Carrabino  (review date Spring 1984)

SOURCE: A review of *Les Méduses, ou les orties de mer,* in *World Literature Today,* Vol. 58, No. 2, Spring, 1984, pp. 310-11.

[*Below, Carrabino compares* Les Méduses, ou les orties de mer *to a detective novel.*]

Within twenty-four hours, two friends, Elenga and Muendo, die. Their third friend, Luambu, is found comatose between the two friends' graves, yet he appears and disappears, much to the dismay of the people. André Sola, supervisor of the C.F.C.O. where Luambu was employed, goes through great pains to uncover the mysterious death of the two friends. Obviously, there are two versions of the story: the story told by the "civilized people," who blame the war, and that told by the villagers, who delve into the world of magic to explain the evanescent presence of Luambu—a sorcerer who is solely responsible for the death of the two friends. There is a reason for his vengeance:

> "[Luambu] avait fait mourir parce que [Elenga] ne voulait pas, pour sa soeur, quelqu'un qui n'était pas de son ethnie, qui pouvait bien être son ami mais pas son beau-frère. . . . On ne plaisante pas avec un lari. . . . Muendo, avec ses ancêtres sénégalais . . . Luambu l'avait endormi, fait ami-ami et vlan! l'avait scié. Littéralement scié."

André Sola, the investigator of the novel [*Les Méduses, ou les orties de mer*], is convinced that Luambu is a revenant, having himself benefited from the magic of Luambu: "À la suite du cadeau de Luambu, il avait perdu son bégaiement." Luambu is as mysterious as the night with which he is symbolically associated. Sorcerers exist. The white man will never understand the story as André Sola sees it: "Comment expliquer au Blanc ce qui se passait; il dira: superstition de sauvage." Sola's fear is intensified when he finds out that his own boss, M. Martin, may be involved with the magic spell of Luambu: "Il se voyait pris dans un cercle de magie blanche, tracé autour de lui par M. Martin et Luambu. M. Martin, Luambu, complices, acolytes." M. Martin's diabolic laughter strengthens Sola's fear, for he is convinced that Luambu and M. Martin "étaient complices." M. Martin, a white man, is associated with the "Malin parce qu'il se présente sous la peau d'un Blanc."

Evil and malefic forces then become linked to the arrival of the white man, for

> "l'histoire que voici se passe à peu près à l'époque où, disait-on, un Blanc parcourait de nuit le Village Indigène de Pointe-Noire et qu'avec une baguette magique, il transformait hommes, femmes, enfants et chiens en viande de corned-beef . . . communément appelé singe." Once evil has entered, it will lurk over and over again, like Medusa's head. And like Medusa's head or the "orties de mer," evil will constantly nettle and prick the sacred world of the black man. The two worlds are thus juxtaposed in a blend of poetic images that transport the reader to a world of mystery and unknown, which, no doubt, Tchicaya prefers.

[*Les Méduses, ou les orties de mer*] could easily pass for a detective novel, though often bathed in the irrational pursuit of something intangible, unattainable. The past can be captured by the oral tradition. Tchicaya U Tam'si fortunately perpetuates it through his art.

## Kenneth Harrow (review date Spring 1988)

SOURCE: A review of *Ces fruits si doux de l'arbre à pain*, in *World Literature Today*, Vol. 62, No. 2, Spring, 1988, pp. 322-23.

[*In the following review, Harrow briefly comments on the family relationships, mystical aspects, and Congolese politics of* Ces fruits si doux de l'arbre à pain.]

Tchicaya U Tam'si's first two novels, **Les cancrelats** and **La main sèche**, both appeared in 1980. Now, after a lacuna of seven years, we have a third novel in the vein of the first two. Three elements characterize U Tam'si's latest efforts [in **Ces fruits si doux de l'arbre à pain**]. The first is the focus on family relationships as a vehicle for developing the characters and the story. Here the family head is an upright and caring paterfamilias whose role as judge embroils him in the snares of Congolese politics and corruption during the early years of independence. His wife and children belong to the new generation of the educated class. Much care is given to developing the close feelings of this family; the society in which they live, however, is scarcely evoked. The light banter, the chic tone, and the isolation of the action act to remove the sense of historical specificity; the setting could as easily have been Paris for much of the novel.

In a sense the same could be said of the second element, the novel's mystical aspect. Here the discourse, in contrast to that involving the family scenes, is typically dense, poeticized, stiff with symbolic overtones. The poet who established himself as one of the major voices in contemporary African writing here continues the vein of his earlier work. Death, madness, extraordinarily introspective contemplation—all are dimensions added to the political and familial relationships which acquire a text of their own and which reduce the mundane to a surface reality. However, for all the surrealistic qualities evoked, no sense of a concrete African tradition emerges. Conjointly, U Tam'si gives a parallel, folklore text to this hermeneutic, augmenting the subjective discourse with its own reverberations of unreality, recalling his earlier publication, **Légendes africanes.**

Lastly, U Tam'si gives us his most overtly critical portrayal of the political scene in contemporary Africa, damning not only the actors at the time of the 1963 coup and its aftermath, but also their hypocritical, unjust, and pitiful counterparts in the ruling classes of Africa since the suns of independence rose. Poet, playwright, and novelist of force and style, Tchicaya U Tam'si remains one of the most gifted African writers of our time.

## Irving Malin  (review date Fall 1989)

SOURCE: A review of *The Madman and the Medusa,* in *Review of Contemporary Fiction,* Vol. 4, No. 3, pp. 223-24.

[*Below, Malin considers* The Madman and the Medusa *"as an epistemological and linguistic mystery."*]

Although Tchicaya's brilliant novel [*The Madman and the Medusa*]—part of the acclaimed Caraf series—can be read in several ways, I would like to look at it as an epistemological and linguistic mystery. From the very first page we see the uncertainty principle at work. We are told in an "introduction" that "this story took place about the same time when, so they said, a white man used to wander at night through the native village of Pointe-Noiri and with a magic wand turn men, women, children and dogs into corned beef which people called monkey meat." There is an opposition between the white man and the natives—the novel is set in Africa—which suggests the warfare against colonials, but the emphasis seems to be upon magical transformation. Can we believe the story? Is it "true"? Is it a symbolic tale or an African sermon?

We are ready for the mysterious atmosphere of the rest of the novel—that story which serves, if you will, as a parallel text or an extended commentary upon the introduction. The novel gives us the stories of the deaths of Elenga and Muendo and (possibly) Luamba-Lufwa Lumbu—the events preceding their deaths, the events following their deaths—but there are many gaps that are never filled, many mysteries that remain unsolved. And the imagery continues to disturb us: it stresses changing perspectives, perverse displacements, incomprehensible occurrences. The result: we are placed in a discontinuous world that engulfs our conscious attempts to order it. If we consider the discontinuities, disappearances, and discrepancies of the text (and the texts within the text), we begin to go mad. We cannot explain character, plot, cause and effect. We are told to "pull ourselves together," but at the same time we are informed that we do not have distinct selves.

The novel is brutal for several reasons: it describes (if only ambiguously) the painful deaths of two (or three?) men; it subtly undermines the possibility of knowledge; it apparently questions itself because it is filled with disappearances, secrets, and visions. Thus the novel, in a metaphoric sense, attacks its very existence and madly destroys all order. But the artistic triumph is clear. Tchicaya suggests that language itself is a displacement—an incomplete world that refuses to be conquered. After we attempt to define things, we are left with the idea that only questions, omens, and signs can ever help us to admit: "No, no, it's not here. Look . . . it's over there." But where are "here" and "there"? And *how* should we look?

## Betty O'Grady  (essay date Winter 1991)

SOURCE: "Tchicaya U Tam'Si: Some Thoughts on the Poet's Symbolic Mode of Expression," in *World Literature Today,* Vol. 65, No. 1, Winter, 1991, pp. 29-34.

[*In the essay below, O'Grady assesses Tchicaya's literary achievement, analyzing the imagery, symbolism, rhythms, and sociopolitical context of his poetry and prose.*]

The death of Tchicaya U Tam'Si on 22 April 1988 at the age of fifty-seven sent shock waves through the world of African literature. Tchicaya, the oldest of a generation of important Congolese writers, is one of the few whose reputation has reached beyond the confines of Francophone Africa and France. During his lifetime, however, he never reached the wide audience that he deserved, not only as a poet but also as novelist and playwright. Despite the fact that *Epitomé* (1958) won him the first prize for poetry at the Festival des Arts Nègres at Dakar in 1966, his reading public has remained limited. While recognizing him as one of the leading contemporary African poets, critics and readers remain strangely reserved. In a recent publication Théophile Obenga puts his finger on one of the main reasons for this reticence: "U Tam'Si n'est l'héritière de personne et de rien: à souhait, et non sans belle ironie" (U Tam'Si inherits from nobody and nothing: by choice and not without beautiful irony). Tchicaya's writing defies classification. His intensely personal world view and poetic expression create his own individual mythology, which sets him apart from all neat literary categories. His poetry is often described as hermetic, which is, in reality, the literary critic's terminology for admitting that it is not easily understood. At the same time the poet's obvious mastery of his medium precludes his being dismissed as obscure or unintelligible. Who then is this poet? What is his significance as a writer?

Perhaps U Tam'Si owes the initial recognition of his work by Western critics to fortuitous historical circumstances. In France the surrealist revolt against traditional poetic norms had opened the way for experimental form and expression, and poets such as André Breton and Robert Desnos had enthusiastically supported the Negritude poets. In his preface to the 1947 edition of Aimé Césaire's *Cahier d'un retour au pays natal* Breton recognized in Césaire's poetry "cette exubérance dans le jet et dans la gerbe, cette faculté d'alerter sans cesse de fond en comble le monde émotionnel jusqu'à le mettre sens dessus dessous qui caractérisent la poésie authentique." At times U Tam'Si's own words would seem to confirm this link with the surrealists, although he himself has said that he had not read their poetry at the time of writing his own first poems: "I lack the intoxication to understand what is plausible. And yet the world is as it appears to the lark: a distorting mirror." However, as this study of U Tam'Si's imagery and symbolism will attempt to make clear, fundamental differences distinguish his verse from that of the French surrealists, who, in advocating automatic writing, deliberately refused all restraint imposed by logic. The surrealist poet's highly individualistic message was "dictated" by his subconscious being, which he believed to be the echo of the universal consciousness. It was expressed by an arbitrary association of words which, at first reading, the poet often understood no better than the reader. This is very different from U Tam'Si's dense and at times esoteric imagery, by which he expresses his profound and passionate identification with the suffering of Africa and, more particularly, of the Congo. U Tam'Si's imagery is distinguishable from that of the surrealists because of its coherent scheme of reference and world view. His poetic universe is that of an individual who expresses both consciously and unconsciously his sense of a collective identity. This will become apparent when a closer look is taken at his image-symbols.

In general, U Tam'Si's merit as a poet was judged in terms of criteria that had evolved out of the European experience, which meant that the full extent of his creative inspiration and originality was not appreciated. This is perhaps still true today. By virtue of his early schooling under the French colonial administration and his having lived almost exclusively in France since the age of fifteen, U Tam'Si inherited from a dual cultural tradition. Nevertheless, his early writing in particular was strongly marked by his non-Western experience, thought modes, speech patterns, and thematic concerns. Although he was in no way traditionalist or limited by a uniquely African perspective, it is no doubt this unfamiliar world of reference which, on first reading, makes his poetry appear impenetrable to the Western reader or even to the Congolese reader who, through the process of "acculturation" has lost touch with "the cultural heart of the land." U Tam'Si is uncompromising in the demands he makes upon his reader: "When I write, I do not recount, I don't chew your food for you. I say to you 'There you are,' and according to the habits that you have acquired, you may take more or less." He has also noted, on the other hand: "If one makes a literal reading of what I write, one understands what I am saying." Similarly, he has indicated that the key to his poems can be found in the titles, just as the proverbs that run as a leitmotiv through his novels point to the meaning.

However, the "literal reading" advocated by U Tam'Si is

based on an important assumption: that his work will be read as a whole. This is a crucial factor in "decoding" U Tam'Si's creative writing. Unfortunately, it is very difficult to make the necessary global reading of his work so as to appreciate the extended imagery and thought patterns; not only does little of his work exist in translation, but much of it is out of print as well—the fate suffered by a high proportion of valuable African writing. Perhaps, following upon U Tam'Si's untimely death, there will be a resurgence of interest in his writing, leading to the reprinting of those works that are presently unobtainable.

It is important to read U Tam'Si's oeuvre not only as a whole but also chronologically, in the order of composition. His novels illustrate this very well; the first three, each over 250 pages long, form a trilogy that paints a vast human and sociopolitical fresco of the Congo, although spanning only fifty-some years in the life of the main protagonists, Sophie and Prosper. In fact, it was conceived of as a single narrative and was divided into three in order to satisfy the editors. Thus, although each novel may be read and enjoyed in isolation, characters and events in one of the three may be alluded to in another or may reappear without explanation, with the result that the full significance is lost on the reader. Similarly, certain recurrent images become key symbols, an understanding of which is essential in order to release the full meaning of the text. One such image-symbol is that of the *cancrelat* or cockroach, which lends its name to the first novel, *Les cancrelats.* The word first appears in the enigmatic proverb which introduces the novel: "Le cancrelat alla plaider une cause au tribunal des poules!" (The cockroach went to plead its cause before the hens' court). Both the proverb and the cockroach image reappear at significant points in the first and last of the three novels, illuminating the meaning of the text and themselves acquiring new connotative dimensions. The semiological role of *le cancrelat* is lost on the reader who reads *Les phalènes* without having first read *Les cancrelats.*

When viewed globally, the overall shape and development of U Tam'Si's poetry and prose can be compared to that of an orchestra. In fact, the importance of music as a structural element is consciously emphasized by the poet in his first collection of poems, entitled *Le mauvais sang,* which has musical terms as subtitles to the two main sections. In a piece of orchestral music the part for a single instrument may be extracted from the score and enjoyed in isolation, but it only acquires its full meaning when integrated into the orchestrated whole. Similarly, the full force of a single poem's expression and vision is released only when it is read in the context of the whole body of U Tam'Si's poetry. His poetic discourse works extendedly: an idea or image, initially introduced almost unobtrusively, will be picked up in successive poems, where a different context or emphasis will add new layers of meaning, until, as with the *cancrelat* image, it attains the value of a symbol. U Tam'Si's discourse at times reads like a form of poetic shorthand, where a single word-sign signifies a complexity of meaning, intelligible only if the reader has followed its development.

---

**When viewed globally, the overall shape and development of U Tam'Si's poetry and prose can be compared to that of an orchestra.**

—*Betty O'Grady*

---

The importance of the overall shape or structure as a signifier in U Tam'Si's poetry can be illustrated by the collection entitled *Le ventre*. The final poem, **"le ventre reste,"** takes up successively and almost line by line the titles of the thirteen poems that make up the collection, so that each phrase releases the complexity of emotion and meaning that was developed in the poem of that little. The whole is woven together in a perfectly controlled and unified statement which, in the final stanza, ends with a vision of hope: "God be thanked the prophets fall / most often on their backs / most often with their arms opened wide / most often / their bellies to the sky!"

A study of the way in which the image of *le ventre* is developed into a key symbol reveals the dialectical nature of U Tam'Si's symbolism. Typically, the final statement of "le ventre reste" (quoted above), which is also the final statement of the collection, is not definitive, for U Tam'Si refuses to be categorical. "To identify a thing is to limit its possibilities," he says in *Les cancrelats*. It is by taking cognizance of the dialectical complexity of an idea or an image that one comes to some sort of understanding. U Tam'Si's refusal to simplify is illustrated in the image-symbols that constitute the framework not only of his poetry but also of his prose. It is thus worth making a brief semiological study of the complex *ventre* symbol.

In divinatory practices the opened belly of an animal or fowl reveals the future to the seer. This is particularly significant, for in his poetry and prose U Tam'Si makes frequent allusions to the prophetic vocation of the poet. Furthermore, in traditional African society the storyteller was often believed to have prophetic vision, and, conversely, the seer would express himself in poetic or esoteric language. Lying on his back, open to the sky or the heavens, arms wide and receiving, the seer-poet offers himself to divine inspiration. Yet the opened belly means death, both for the sacrificial animal and for man caught up in violent conflict. Yet again, the belly is associated with fertility and regeneration (*bas-ventre* means "womb"). The navel symbolizes the biological and

the cultural link with the mother, Mother Earth/Africa, and therefore the Ancestors. Indeed, the collection entitled *Le ventre* has been interpreted as the poet's attempt to understand his own identity in terms of his origins and his relation with his mother and Africa. The belly is associated too with warmth, with passion, and, particularly in Africa, with dance: "Dance is the best language / in which to make of two bodies / the two parts of a single phrase / which writes the perfect verb to love!"

The concept of the brotherhood of man and, more particularly, of a united Congo, informs all Tchicaya's creative writing; it is something he believed in passionately, and his disillusion and bitterness were all the greater as he witnessed the internecine fighting that crippled the Congo Republic. He was deeply shocked by the assassination of Patrice Lumumba, with whom he had worked and whose ideals he shared. The martyred political leader, epitomized by Lumumba, is the major thematic concern of *Epitomé* (1962) and *Le ventre*. It is a theme which links up with that of the Christ, betrayed and betrayer, and the suffering poet-prophet, thus forming another complex image-symbol, which finds its origin in his first collection of poems: "Christ trahi voici ma croix humaine de bois" (Christ betrayed here is my human cross of wood).

Still, whereas the belly is often associated with warmth and life, refrains such as "The belly / always with that sickening warmth / as of the charnel-house" serve as a reminder not only of death but also, significantly for the Central African countries such as the Congo, of cannibalism: "We shall live no more on flesh or blood / I am eating a dish of meat this evening / why not the flesh of my brothers / burnt in the holocaust?" The belly is associated with greed, the voracious appetites of the exploiters of Africa, both the colonialists and the neocolonialist dictators of the newly independent states.

It is not possible here to do more than touch on some of the main dialectical themes and connotations contained in the symbol of the belly; as one progresses through the poems of *Le ventre,* one is struck by the rich density of allusion, the play and replay of word and image, and one becomes aware that it is probably impossible to give a complete exegesis of the symbol. To define is to limit, to simplify is to falsify—that is what U Tam'Si would seem to be saying.

Another important factor that contributes to the dynamic force of U Tam'Si's creative writing but is unfortunately lost in a piecemeal or incomplete reading of his work is the role played by rhythm, in terms of both structure and language. The importance of rhythm in African poetry has been more than adequately explained by Léopold Senghor, himself one of the greatest lyric poets of Africa. Like the poets of the *Anthologie*, U Tam'Si is, in the words of Senghor, an "auditory" poet; his poems are to be spoken aloud, not read silently. In a 1986 interview in Paris, U Tam'Si stated, "Everything that I have written is oral." Thus assonance, alliteration, and echoing reverberations reinforce the repeated images, refrains, and ideas. This makes his poetry extremely difficult to translate satisfactorily.

Again it is important to make a chronological reading of U Tam'Si's poetry in order to appreciate the semiological significance of rhythm. As he frees himself of conventional metric form, it is rhythm that determines the shape and progression of the poem. In *Feu de brousse* the insistent and syncopated rhythm of the drum predominates. A selective reading destroys the cumulative effect of the repeated words and phrases, which mark time and then advance the poem, which echo an image from a previous line or poem and then surge forward with a new thematic element. At times the effect is incantatory, creating a profound emotion that in turn releases the poem's significance. In his later poetry rhythm plays a more subtle role; less semiologically significant in itself, it serves to underscore and develop the meaning of the image-symbols. Flexible yet controlled, the dynamics of repetition and variation, suspense and advance, create a complex pattern of sound and movement, which is an integral part of the poem's meaning.

In U Tam'Si's writing, repetition and rhythm are not only semiologically but also structurally significant. The collection *Le ventre* represents one of the most striking illustrations of this. The dialectical nature of the word-symbol *le ventre* has already been discussed, but it is important to consider the *ventre* symbol in the context of the collection as a whole in order to appreciate how the contradictions and contrasts make up a synthetic unity. Space does not allow for the required detailed study of this high-frequency word. However, a chronological reading of the poems in the collection would reveal how the development of the referential value of the *ventre* symbol mirrors the organically integrated structure of the whole. This rhythmic pattern is a constant in U Tam'Si's writing, a structural technique which can be found in his first collections of poems and which is developed to a striking degree in his later works. For example, repeated semiological and linguistic elements link the poems in *Le mauvais sang*, and key recurrent images such as blood, water, the woman/mother/Africa, and the Christ are introduced. In later volumes the title of a poem is often anticipated in the preceding poem, thus reinforcing the sense of pattern in ideas and sounds. This repetition is not static; each reappearance of an image brings to it a new dimension, and its development can be traced through U Tam'Si's work as a whole. It is significant that many of the key images in his verse are important signifiers in his prose.

To understand how repetition determines progression, it is important to consider African music. There the repetition,

which is often monotonous to the Western ear, is in fact made up of constant slight variations that mark the forward movement of the song or dance. The development takes place over an extended time span.

One of the most important effects of the rhythmic repetition of image and sound is to give U Tam'Si's work both consistency and homogeneity. As has already been shown, certain core ideas or images inform his entire work, not only as leitmotivs but as part of the structural and referential framework. These images, anchored in the real, material world, are developed by association and correspondence, and they signify at several levels. Thus in *Le mauvais sang*, a chain of ever-widening reference is created, beginning with "blood" and the "wound," through "water" to "thoughts" and "memories," "diving" (back into the stream of time, the past), to "skiff" (canoe), "river" (the Congo River), and "shipwreck." Each of these links in the image chain acquires greater resonance as it is picked up and developed in a later poem or collection. Thus "wound" is inseparable from the Christ figure, which, introduced in *Le mauvais sang*, becomes a dominant image in *Epitomé* and *Le ventre*.

Water and rain link with the immense Congo River, which reflects the past and potential grandeur of the country, the dream of a nation reunited, just as the tributaries of the Congo River link across the land. The Congo River is also the source of identity: "There remains a river and the key of dreams in its flanks." Furthermore, it represents the total giving of self, the poetic vocation, commitment to an ideal (the throwing of oneself into the water). Elsewhere U Tam'Si has compared his poetry to the Congo River, "qui charrie autant de cadavres que de jacinthes d'eau" (that carries along as many cadavers as water lilies). Water, like blood, is a sacrificial and cleansing element, and as the river leads to the ocean, so it links up with another very important and complex image-symbol in U Tam'Si's discourse, the ocean/salt/waves/sea gull. Again, space does not allow an adequate treatment of these images, each of which requires close analysis in the context of U Tam'Si's creative writing as a whole.

It is not possible to appreciate the full depth and breadth of U Tam'Si's symbolic universe without taking cognizance of his dual cultural heritage. His early, formative years in the Congo would have had an indelible effect on his thinking and imaginative mind, but at an early age he accompanied his father to France and, from that time, spent most of his life away from Africa, primarily in Paris. An important facet to the study of his poetic imagery would be to trace the gradually increasing incidence of semiological elements originating in the European context. Right from the start of his literate life, however, elements of a French subculture would have influenced his thinking, for all his schooling was in French. In fact, his mother tongue, Vili, was not and still is not taught anywhere, not even at junior school. It is important, then, not only to take into account the way in which language patterns influence thought, but also to remember that the French colonial policy of "assimilation" consistently aimed at imposing a French subculture at the expense of the African cultures.

For a non-Congolese reader, U Tam'Si's writing cannot be understood out of its sociopolitical context. This is not always easy, since few detailed historical, geographic, or sociocultural studies of the Congo are available, and of those that do exist, the majority are written by European historians and ethnologists. U Tam'Si does not make it easy for the non-Congolese reader. He has said that he does not write for a Western public: "That would denaturalize my thinking. I speak of my country to those of my country . . . and then to those who might be led to live there." Thus he assumes a knowledge of the political events leading up to independence in 1960 and the turbulent years that followed. His language is elliptic; images follow each other in quick succession, often specifically Congolese or regional in origin. Even universal images such as the sun or rain or trees must be read in the context of the Congolese heat and tropical rain forests. For example, no European experience of rain can release the full resonance of "The belly trembles, the deluge approaches" or of the lines "the rain is clinging, sticky, / gummy, insistent, petrifying, excreting, / shitty and distressing." It is impossible to convey adequately the musical reverberations of the original French, which reinforce U Tam'Si's earthy, ironic humor as he speaks of the chaos that engulfed the Congo after independence.

In his preface to the 1962 edition of *Epitomé* Senghor speaks of the "kaleidoscope" of images, which erupt with the force of a "geyser." He refers to the "syntax of juxtaposition," which "explodes the hinges of logic." U Tam'Si's poetry translates the "movements of a passion, in offbeat rhythms and syncopation," like African music. At times the asymmetric parallelisms, the enjambments, the breaks and returns make it difficult to follow the movements of the poet's mind and passion. What appear to be linguistic "gymnastics" in fact find their origin in the oral tradition. Learning to understand and use proverbs and *devinettes* (riddles) was as important a part of the young African child's "schooling" as was the learning of mythological and historical stories and fables. Riddles depend upon the clever use of sound and words to create a symbolic language, behind which lies the "hidden" meaning that must be guessed at. Through these games a certain mental and linguistic dexterity is learned. Many of U Tam'Si's poems open with a gnomic utterance which, while not explained, is never gratuitous; it plays an important semiological role, just as the titles of the poems or the lines set in proem serve as an epitome for the poem. This use of proverbs and enigmas is equally significant in U Tam'Si's prose works. For the non-Congolese or even non-Vili reader, the meaning of some of the aphorisms and eso-

teric utterances will remain hidden. For example, only someone familiar with African and more particularly Congolese or Vili custom would realize the full dialectical force of the phrase "They have spat on me," since spitting or unction by saliva is a form of benediction.

Two interesting attempts have been made to categorize the major images that inform U Tam'Si's poetry, but the danger of this method is that the essential and dynamic homogeneity of his symbolism is lost. To classify separately such complex symbols as water, blood, and the woman/mother figure is to splinter the "substance" of the writer's creative universe. Théophile Obenga gives a better understanding of the intrinsic unity of U Tam'Si's poetry through a detailed study of the blood image (*Le sang*), which he sees as U Tam'Si's "literary fancy," the key to both the logical and the imaginary universe of his poetry. The work of Gaston Bachelard and, more recently, that of Gilbert Durand suggest a similar approach. Their investigations into the psychology of the imagination and their analysis of archetypal and mythical imagery represent a synthetic treatment of image and symbol, whereby contradictions and contrasts form a harmonious whole. Durand demonstrates the inadequacy of the structuralist approach for the analysis of imagery, in that it does not take sufficient cognizance of the dynamic and unifying creative mind behind the poetic discourse, an understanding of which requires an organic rather than a mechanistic approach. Although one would not claim that a piece of creative writing can be fully understood only in the light of the author's personal life and psyche, there is nevertheless a general motivating force behind the symbolism that emanates from a particular emotional and mental universe.

There exists a symbiotic relationship between, on the one hand, the mythical universe created by the poet and augmented with each new piece of writing, and on the other the writer's own mental universe; symbols, rhythm, and structure acquire a dynamism of their own and inform the writer's own philosophical and emotional development. Speaking about his writing, U Tam'Si said: "A creative work should take root in you. The more it takes root in you, the more chance it has of affecting others." This is not a new idea, but its significance is not always taken into account by contemporary literary critics.

U Tam'Si's work is of particular interest in this respect, for his highly integrated poetic universe reflects a holistic world view that stands in sharp contrast to the Manichean Western world view. U Tam'Si's thought processes are firmly rooted in a sense of rhythmic pattern, the cycles of life and man's collective identity. His poetic discourse is strongly individualistic in terms of image and language, yet his concern is for understanding the meaning of "existential anguish" not for the individual alone but for the individual as part of a corporate body, past, present, and future. His poetry is the concrete expression of his conception of the poet-prophet, whose role in the life of society is as important as that of the mason or the carpenter: "The poet is above all a man, a man in the full meaning of the word, a conscious man. A conscious man is he who dreams, and the dream is only a projection into the future of what can be realized." The poet, like Christ and the political martyr, lays himself open to the conflicting forces of life. U Tam'Si's creative writing constitutes the commitment of a life to this task. In his poetry the poetic "I" represents a constant dialectic, an intensely personal expression that crystallizes the experience of a people. He expresses this in an observation from *Notes de veille*; the final ironic comment is typical of his blend of mocking self-deprecation and dedicated belief in the poet's vocation:

> "En fait l'homme s'élabore dans un temps trop court dans lequel il lui est impossible d'assimiler tous les éléments extérieurs qui pourraient faire de lui une unité solvable. Peu y sont arrivés: Christ, Rimbaud . . . moi ma gloriole défunte" (In fact man develops in too short a time, during which it is impossible for him to assimilate all the external elements which could make of him a creditable unity. Few have managed it: Christ, Rimbaud . . . I, my defunct vainglory).

## Chaibou Elhadji Oumarou (essay date Summer 1995)

SOURCE: "Writing a Dynamic Identity: Self-Criticism in the Work of Tchicaya U Tam'Si," in *Studies in Twentieth-Century Literature*, Vol. 19, No. 2, Summer 1995, pp. 223-37.

[*Below, Oumarou explores the rationale behind the critique of Négritude and Africa in Tchicaya's works, determining that such self-criticism functions to "free [oneself] both from the vestiges of colonialism and from the stifling African traditions."*]

> Je suis en rupture avec la tribu, je suis en rupture avec l'ethnie, je suis en rupture avec l'Afrique.
> 'I broke with the tribe, I broke with ethnicity, I broke with Africa.'
>
> —Tchicaya

Thus spoke Tchicaya U Tam'Si in an interview with Tahar Bekri (1988). Very few Africans have had the courage to express their outrage at the stifling African traditions with the vigor and consistency of U Tam'Si. The break with the tribe, the ethnic group, and Africa is an expression of his anger and frustration at himself as reflected in the practices of his society.

In fact, self-criticism is a major theme in Tchicaya's work as he strives to build a dynamic identity through a dynamic writing style. A dynamic identity changes with time and it is directed toward the future as opposed to static identity, which is concerned with only the past. The former is an attempt to live the present, an opening up of self to reality and the necessities of life. The latter is an attempt to escape reality in order to swim in the stagnant waters of an idyllic past.

U Tam'Si's attempt to face up to the present, to confront it in order to change it, permeates all his work as he tries to teach and educate his readers about the danger of a return to a mythic past:

> Car en réalité il faut savoir rompre avec le passé lorsque celui-ci croupit dans les eaux stagnantes de la turpitude. Les nations, les peuples meurent de leur identité figée. Ce qui est vie est nécessaire dans le changement. Je veux être une civilisation et non un vestige.
>
> For in reality one must know how to break with the past when it grows foul in the stagnant waters of turpitude. Nations and people die of their set identity. What is life is necessary in change. I want to be a civilization, not a vestige of the past.

This essay is an attempt to problematize Tchicaya's efforts to create a dynamic identity for himself, his country and Africa. The focus on self-criticism is meant to further explore the rationale behind his attempted break away from the stifling African traditions. It seeks to know whether or not U Tam'si is hiding behind self-criticism to please a particular audience or whether he is expressing legitimate concerns about Africa.

In order to understand his position better and find appropriate answers to these questions, it is imperative to place him and his work in historical context. Born before the independence of Africa, he grew to witness and experience colonization and the struggle for independence in his native Congo. As a matter of fact, he worked closely with Patrice Lumumba to gain political independence for the country. Thus, his personality as a writer must have grown out of those difficult moments in the history of the continent, and one should expect his work to reflect his personal take of the events.

In addition to the political events, Tchicaya could not ignore the literary activities of his contemporaries. He had to communicate with them in one way or the other since each writer is the product of his or her epoch. In this respect, Négritude was one important literary event he could not circumvent. Founded in Paris in the thirties by Léopold Sédar Senghor, Aimé Césaire and Léon G. Damas, it was then their attempt to create an image for and about Africa with which they could identify with a sense of pride.

An exact definition of Négritude is difficult to find, partly because the founders' distinct personalities influenced their respective philosophies and works. But Senghor soon became the spokesperson for the movement, and he has been credited for giving it a wider application. In *Ce que je crois* (1988), Senghor defines it as "l'ensemble des valeurs de la civilization noire" 'the sum total of the values of black civilization.' But as translator Melvin Dixon claims in the introduction to his *The Collected Poetry By Léopold Sédar Senghor* (1991), the latter's search for the essence of Blackness has led discussions of the movement "to come dangerously close to validating racial stereotypes. . . ."

Of particular relevance to this essay is Dixon's remark that "the most powerful African elements in Senghor's poetry are in fact images from the past rather than verbal constructions of a present reality: the past in its lush, abundant, luxuriant, erotic diction. . . ." The poem, "Night of Sine," is a case in point. In it the poet tries to remember his past, but by so doing he also constructs and expands what he sees as an African identity. Listen to him:

> Woman, place your soothing hands upon my
>   brow,
> Your hands softer than fur.
> Above us balance the palm trees, barely rustling
> In the night breeze. Not even a lullaby.
> Let the rhythmic silence cradle us.
> Listen to its song. Hear the beat of our dark blood,
> Hear the deep pulse of Africa in the mist of lost
>   villages.
> Now sets the weary moon its slack seabed
> Now the bursts of laughter quiet down, and even
>   the storyteller
> Nods his head like a child on his mother's back
> The dancer's feet grow heavy, and heavy, too,
> Come the alternating voices of singers.
>
> Now the stars appear and the Night dreams
> Leaning on that hill of clouds, dressed in its long,
>   milky pagne.
> The roofs of the hut shine tenderly. What are they
>   saying
> So secretly to the stars? Inside, the fire dies out
> In the closeness of sour and sweet smells.
>
> Woman, light the clear-oil lamp. Let the Ancestors
> Speak around us as parents do when the children
>   are in bed.
> Let us listen to the voices of the Elissa Elders.
> Exiled like us

> They did not want to die, or lose the flow of their
>   semen in the sands.
> Let me hear, a gleam of friendly souls visits the
>   smoke-filled hut,
> My head upon your breast as warm as tasty *dang*
>   steaming from the fire,
> Let me breathe the odor of our Dead, let me gather
> And speak with their living voices, let me learn to
>   live
> Before plunging deeper than the diver
> Into the great depths of sleep.

Rather than be concerned with such a past, U Tam'Si opts for the creation of a new dynamic identity that focuses on the present. His break with Africa is not a total rejection of his roots or an absolute refusal to keep usable elements of the past. On the contrary, it is an attempt to build a cultural identity from within, that is, an identity geared toward the future. Such an identity has to be informed not by literary patterns imposed from without, but by pages of African history. Seen from that perspective, his break with ethnic can be interpreted as an effort to break free from the chains of ethnicity in order to reach out to and accommodate the other.

As a matter of fact, Africa is now coming to grips with postcold war problems such as famine and civil unrests that contrast with the peace in "Night of Sine" and further complicate divisions along ethnic lines. In this respect, Tchicaya's verbal construction of reality carries some dose of nationalist concerns and his self-criticism is just the other side of his dream of fraternity.

It is unfortunate that he has received so little attention from critics of African literatures. Whether their relative silence is the result of his position vis-à-vis the stifling African traditions and Négritude or of the difficulty in penetrating his work is uncertain. But there is no doubt that he is one of the most modern African writers, as George Lang (1985) has already noted, and one of the greatest as well.

Among the critics who have studied him, most see him as unruly and rebellious. In the novel *Les Cancrelats,* a voice expresses doubts about the past of Loango, a metaphor of Congo and Africa. Says the voice:

> Ce passé de Loango est peut-être une légende. Une
> légende perdue au fond d'un précipice mauve et sombre. Ne vous approchez pas, ne vous penchez pas
> sur cet abîme, les argiles pétrifiées au fond, parmi
> les broussailles, ont la couleur de blessures
> purulentes. . . .

> This past of Loango is perhaps a legend. A legend
> lost at the bottom of a mauve and gloomy precipice.
> Do not go near it, do not lean on that abyss, the pet-

rified mud at the bottom, among the bushes, has the color of purulent sores.

Against this background of a gloomy and dirty past, the petrified mud is a sign of decay that indicates that the past in question is about to die. What is more, instead of a stone or concrete wall as found in many brilliant dead civilizations, Loango's past has mud in the bush. This ugly picture contrasts sharply with glorious pasts that one can be proud of. The association of that ugliness with the African past shows U Tam'Si's intention to denounce exaggerated embellishments of the African past.

It is an attempt to say that Africa also has its dark side which has almost gone unnoticed by the Négritude romantics. In *Le ventre,* a collection of poems, he makes it clear that his focus is the ugly facet of himself: "Je dialogue avec ce qui est pollué en moi" 'I hold a dialogue with the defiled part of me.'

As pointed out earlier, it will be a mistake to consider this dialogue as a denial of self in order to please a particular audience. In an Africa facing all sorts of social problems, the pollution Tchicaya talks about is likely to refer to the collapse of religious and ethical values. Ill-digested western values coupled with ignorance and poverty have indeed led to corruption and lack of morality. Thus by choosing to address with the ugly facets of modern Africa, U Tam'si magnifies the issue so that it can receive the attention it deserves.

In other words, he is just saying that he is not perfect, nor does he expect anyone else to be. In his collection of short stories, *La main sèche,* he criticizes those writers who embellish their past to make it look more glorious and perfect. There is no such past in the history of civilization as far as the present author is concerned. For Tchicaya, there is nothing to be ashamed of as long as one faces the truth and uses it as a basis for positive and constructive action.

In this respect, running away from one's culture to embrace a foreign one is not the solution to the problem. Tchicaya laughs at the so-called "évolué(e)s," who, as the result of their contact with Western civilization, have lost confidence in their own. To them he has this advice: "Je tus mon dégoût. Je me dis qu'il y a lâcheté à fuir le monde tel qu'il se revèle" 'I silenced my disgust. I tell myself that there is cowardice in running away from the world as it is' (*Main*).

Tchicaya wants everyone to face their world as it is, to look at themselves critically in order to see their reality. His self-criticism has cost him his credibility in the eyes of many people in Africa. Yet as Emil Magel (1980) claims, Tchicaya is critical of both Europeans and Africans. His criticism of them, in the process of the search for the truth, has been seen as unfaithful, treacherous, and disloyal. Despite his awareness of the criticism, U Tam'Si persists against what Magel calls the normative rules of the game. They consist of the unspoken prohibition against providing ammunition to racist enemies by exposing the ugliness of Africa.

> **Tchicaya wants everyone to face their world as it is, to look at themselves critically in order to see their reality.**
>
> **—*Chaibou Elhadji Oumarou***

But for Tchicaya, the search for the truth is more important than whatever the searcher happens to find. Thus in *Les Cancrelats,* Damien, whose daughter is murdered, goes to search for the killer. In the process, he makes important discoveries about himself and the conditions of his life. The authorial voice comments:

> La révolte, née de cette recherche, l'aurait conduit à l'avant vers un acte. Qu'importe quel acte? Chaque acte étant l'affirmation d'une liberté!

> The revolt, born of this search, would lead him forward toward an act. Does it matter what kind of act? Each act being the affirmation of a liberty!

The search is therefore essential in U Tam'Si's philosophy and it should be considered as such. To his counterparts who undertook the search for their identity in a remote past, he warns that the search ought to be exhaustive as well as objective:

> C'est une chose d'aller à la source, une autre de voir venir l'eau à vous. Dans le dernier cas, c'est que ça déborde de quelque part. Savoir ce que c'est ce quelque part est important, si vous tenez à la vie; sinon il vous reste votre soif ou pire. . . .

> It is one thing to go back to the sources, another thing to see water coming up to you. In the last case, it is because it overflows from somewhere. To know that somewhere is important, if you hold to life; if not, there remains your thirst or worse. (*Cancrelats*)

There is no doubt that the water is a metaphor for the identity the writers in question are looking for. The quotation is almost a direct attack on those writers of whom Prosper, a character in *Les Cancrelats,* is a representative. Under "Le Cauchemar" 'Nightmare,' Tchicaya, in describing Prosper, says that he:

> vivait dans un perpetuel compromis, à ce qu'il disait.

Une formule creuse à laquelle il voulut donner un
sens. Tout son malaise était que ce compromis
devenait irremediable. Et qu'il fallait s'en faire une
raison. Mais ce qui le chiffonnait de plus, c'était qu'il
ne savait de quoi était fait ce compromis. Il était
revenu au pays. . . .

lived in a perpetual compromise, as he said. A hollow formula to which he wanted to give meaning.
And it had to be a good reason for him. But what
annoyed him most was the fact that he did not know
what the compromise was about. He came back to
his country. . . . (*Cancrelats*)

Prosper epitomizes the dilemma of African writers in general. The above accusation points to the external influences
on African literature through some literary patterns on which
it has been modelled. The perception of a negative influence
of Europe on Africa is not new, however. Various critics
(Ingeborg Kohn 1980; Mike de Llew 1973, 1979) have discussed the influence of European anthropologists on African writers at the beginning of the 20th century.

The essence of their criticism has been summarized by Cheikh
Anta Diop and Paulin Hountoundji, as quoted by Eileen Julien
(1992). In her critique of Négritude, Julien points out the
rampant racism in the movement whose "terms of definition
. . . are . . . precisely those of Gobinau [a French racist], with
this difference that they are now seen as positive and essential to world humanism."

Senghor's idyllic past has indeed a lot to do with the influence of the early European anthropologists and other scientists. The negative consequences of the scientific revolution
on European societies had given birth to a love for nature
known as Romanticism. Under this movement, the "savages"
of Africa and elsewhere were considered as living in paradise. The notion of the "Noble Savage" became popular and
more anthropologists became interested in Africa. Leo
Frobenius was influential on the work of Senghor, who
readily acknowledges his debt to him.

Yambo Ouologuem's *Devoir de violence* [*Bound to Violence*]
is one of the African responses to the influence of anthropologists who, it should be noted, were not all bad.
Hountoundji is also noteworthy for his sharp criticism of
those early anthropologists and African writers whom he
accuses of complicity in many respects. According to Julien,
he:

refers to the complicity in the 1930s and 40s between Third World nationalists and 'progressive'
Western anthropologists. For years they will assist
each other, the former using the latter in support of
their pluralistic theses.

Tchicaya is therefore not the only one to have criticized the
external influences on the African writers and the African
identity they have attempted to construct on foreign literary
models. He refers to Négritude as a "formule creuse" 'hollow formula' to which Prosper has attempted to give meaning. He also defends himself against the accusation that he
destroys Africa by exposing its ugliness to the world. A voice
that may be considered as his says to Ndundu:

Ndundu, je suis . . . je n'oublie pas, je suis tien, mais!
Tu es mien et je te dis encore: mais! Comprends ce
que tu voudras, regardetoi, regarde-moi. Je me
regarde, je te regarde. *Le ciel ne nous voit pas
autrement que tu te vois, autrement que je me vois.
Là est la vérité. Hausser les épaules, c'est se tourner
le dos et se dire innocent! Quelle innocence est la
mienne? Je m'accuse, oui! Je m'accuse!*

Ndundu, I am . . . I do not forget, I am yours, but. . .!
You are mine and I say again: But. . .! Understand
what you want, look at yourself, look at me. I look
at myself, I look at you. *The heavens do not see us
differently from how you see yourself, differently
from how I see myself. In that lies the truth. Shrug-
ging one's shoulders, that is turning one's back and
proclaiming oneself innocent! What innocence is
mine? I accuse myself, yes! I accuse myself!*
(*Cancrelats,* emphasis mine)

This self-accusation is certainly a balance to the exaggeration of the African romantics whose idylls have not cured
the ills of their societies. B. M. Ibitokun (1981) has defended
Tchicaya on the ground that his "mauvais sang" 'bad blood'
has nothing to do with congenital inferiority. At best, it is
his historical situation that can best explain it. Unhappy about
that condition, the poet "covers himself up with a mask of
humor in order not to give up way to despair and nihilism."

U Tam'Si calls upon his people to live in the present and to
be more responsible. He makes this point most clearly and
eloquently in his interview with Tahar Bekri, expressing his
outrage at:

Cet angélisme qui veut que nous n'ayons aucune
part de responsabilité dans toutes les catastrophes
qui sont cause de tant d'indigences. Bouter le feu à
tout cela.

that sainthood which wants us to have no share of
responsibility in all the catastrophes which are the
cause of so much indigence. Set fire to all this.

The call to set fire to the stifling African traditions is reminiscent of his other collection of poems, *Feu de brousse*
(*Brush Fire*). Used to clear farms seasonally in Africa, the

bush fire is, as Tchicaya says, an exorcism meant to destroy anything that could hinder the sowing of good seeds. In other words, the collection is meant to be an action of weeding and seeding, an act of the construction of a better future.

To reach that goal, he calls upon people to be more active, more involved, in taking constructive initiatives if they want to get out of the desperate conditions in which they languish. He urges them all, especially the youth, not to simply follow the steps of their parents:

> Parce que c'était ce qui était désormais permis: qu'un fils pouvait marcher devant son père et *non suivre son père* . . . Mais ceux-là qui disent, qui s'indignent qu'un fils . . . qu'ils s'indignent après tout!. . . Qu'un fils pouvait précéder son père sur un chemin périlleux.

> Because that was what was allowed from that time onwards: that a sibling could walk in front of his father and *not follow his father* . . . But those who say, who are indignant with the sibling . . . let them be indignant after all!. . . That a sibling could precede his father on a perilous road. (*Cancrelats,* emphasis mine)

The dangerous road is the one that leads to innovative and positive thinking and action. And because there is no easy way to freedom, he wants to shake the people, especially the youth, out of their resignation and docile obedience. As mentioned earlier, any act is, in the view of U Tam'Si, an affirmation of liberty. On the contrary, silence is an acceptance of oppression and an exercise of cowardice.

As Katheryn Wright (1991) suggests in her article on satire and censorship in *Le destin,* central to the climate of his work is the theme of the death of life, a wounding of the spirits that have led to resignation. Because of his repulsion at the general state of things, he dedicated *Le destin glorieux du Maréchal Nnikon Nniku, prince qu'on sort*

> à la jeunesse Congolaise avec l'espoir de la voir partager avec moi la sainte horreur que j'ai des petits caporaux faiseurs de coups d'états.

> *The Glorious Destiny of Marshal Nnikon Nniku,* Prince to be deposed to the Congolese youth with the hope to see it share with me the holy horror that I have for the small corporals makers of coup d'états.

This is a sad commentary on modern Africa, where military regimes still preside over the destiny of many nations. The play is in fact a dramatization of the various problems facing the continent. It magnifies and criticizes neo-colonialism, which still operates through political, economic and cultural

channels. Very satiric, the play exposes the corrupt African regimes, which are more eager to serve foreign interests rather than those of their own countries. Finally, the satiric laugh it causes is meant to move Africans out of their, passive acceptance of exploitative regimes.

To this effect, Tchicaya is determined to get everybody out of the "mauvais sommeil" 'bad sleep' and to break with the chain of the "solidarité tacite, dans le pire" 'tacit solidarity, at its worst.' He takes recourse to the techniques outlined above in order to sensitize the people and lead them to revolt against the yoke of the living death. No wonder that he employs several aesthetic devices to transform ugliness into awareness, silence into voices, and passivity into action. The scatological device is used not because he likes the filth in Africa, but because it is too repulsive to live with:

> Il arrive qu'on se bouche le nez. . . . L'air a mauvaise haleine. Des carries qui troublent les bouches! . . . Les gens ne savent plus vivre, . . . on aimeraient que certaines bouches n'aient jamais raison! Tout depend de la place que l'on fait dans la vie.

> It happens that one closes the nose. . . . The air has bad breath. Tooth-decay which troubles mouths!. . . People do not know how to live anymore, . . . one would like that certain mouths never be right! It all depends on the place one makes in life. (*Cancrelats*)

While tooth-decay suggests a state of mental and physical corruption, the polluted air shows how the corruption penetrates all aspects of life, political and cultural in particular. It is therefore a general contamination that invites a serious and urgent treatment that U Tam'Si is trying to offer through his work. To that end, his satiric pen is like a magnifying glass which helps everyone who can read to see the social ills they are living with.

Wright has contended that Tchicaya has the ability to transform political oppression into a successful surrealistic vision by supporting its meaning with satire and its attendant ironies. She defines irony as a "type of literary censure" which is used to criticize and correct a given situation. To do so, the satirist has to strike a difficult balance between aesthetic features and those of attack. Although most of her observation is based on *Destin,* much of it can be applied to his entire work.

In this respect, irony, humor, and satire are the most important tools of his sharp criticism. *Les Cancrelats (The Roaches)* is an ironic title whose meaning unfolds as one reads the novel. It is the story of cockroaches (Africans) taking their case to the tribunal of a hen (France). Set against the background of colonialism and neo-colonialism, the novel is a satiric laugh at those naive Africans who believe that they can get a fair trial at the tribunal of a judge who happens to have interest in the case they defend.

Apart from the self-criticism, this novel contains some of U Tam'Si's most acerbic attacks on colonialism. Casting the latter in the same mold with Christianity, Tchicaya has condemned the wrongs done to Africans in the name of Christ. Using a mixed couple (African woman and White male) as an example, he describes their love-making as a metaphor for the rape of Africa by Europe. It has also been a plunder of the former by the latter. Thus after they finish their intercourse, an authorial voice comments that "Jean a pillé Sophie . . . Saint Jean a pillé Sainte Sophie. . . ." 'John has looted Sophie . . . Saint John has looted Saint Sophie. . . .' (*Cancrelats*). Is it not ironic that Saint Jean loots Saint Sophie in the name of Christ?

But as Jacques Chevrier (1988) argues, despite Tchicaya's apparent bitter attacks on Christianity, he is not against the Christian religion as such. He is against the false Christians preaching a false Christianity supported by mercantilistic interests. Chevrier reports that the Bible was Tchicaya's bedside book, and the title, *La main sèche* (*Dried Hand*), borrowed from St. Matthew's gospel, supports his claim.

U Tam'Si is a realistic writer whose critique of Négritude and Africa is not as negative as many would like to think. The writer is very concerned about the future of his continent with regard to the present. He worries about his culture as it faces the invading French culture and civilization. Yet he criticizes those who think that the stifling African traditions and other symbols of oppression should continue to be worshipped.

---

**[Tchicaya] criticizes those who think that the stifling African traditions and other symbols of oppression should continue to be worshipped.**

**—*Chaibou Elhadji Oumarou***

---

His courageous move away from the mythic past and Négritude, which, according to Chevrier, are synonymous with obscurantism and immobilism, is also seen as his willingness to accept a compromise whose reality is dictated by the history of Congo, which many critics associate with the Congo River as well. Godard quotes U Tam'Si as saying that "Le Congo c'était la quête politique de mon père, c'est la mienne" 'Congo was the political quest of my father, it is mine.'

The history of Congo is the history of all colonized African countries. It is the history of the encounter between the Christian God and the local divinities of Africa. The result of the encounter is the fusion of two different and often conflicting world views. As a result, a new barbarian has been born out of that encounter, a barbarian defined by Tchicaya in the foreword (Avant-propos) to *La main sèche* (*Dried Hand*). His argument is that every civilization is:

> une rencontre syncrétique de deux mondes, au moins, barbares l'un pour l'autre, barbare l'un et l'autre. Et cela produit de toute évidence *un nouveau barbare* si controversé lui-même que c'est forcement un être tragique, fatal, parce qu'habité par deux morts, celle de deux mondes qui l'ont enfanté. Ici, le monde paien et le monde Chretien.

> a syncretic encounter of two worlds, at least, barbarians to each other, barbarians both. And that produces obviously a *a new barbarian* so controversial that he is by force tragic and fatal as a carrier of two deaths, that of the two worlds which gave birth to him. In this case, the Pagan and Christian. (*Main,* emphasis mine)

This argument is reminiscent of Samba Diallo's tragic character in *L'aventure ambiguë* (*Ambiguous Adventure*) by Cheikh Hamidou Kane. The new barbarian and Diallo share the same tragic destiny of living in a world where different value systems come together, sometimes with conflicts. They consist of Christianity and Paganism in the case of the new barbarian, Western values in addition to Christianity and Islam in the case of Samba Diallo.

The death of Samba Diallo after the fatal blow dealt by the fool leaves open the question of whether or not his death means opting for a choice, that of dying in the name of Islam in order to avoid the paradox of a tragic destiny. In fact, the voice of the Light which talks to Diallo in his grave may be interpreted as a sign of welcome to him.

In the case of the new barbarian, he is said to be the child of two dead worlds: African and European. So despite his being fatal and tragic, the new barbarian seems to be the phoenix born out of the ashes of his parents. A syncretic synthesis seems to have been achieved, unlike in the case of Samba Diallo. In the foreword to *La main sèche,* U Tam'Si says that the collection is "Le portrait à facettes d'un être qui se cherche une identité de synthèse" 'The portrait of a multifaceted man looking for a syncretic identity.'

This may be interpreted as part of U Tam'Si's struggle to live a significantly productive life, an attitude well summarized by Katheryn Wright when she says that for Tchicaya, "Fate itself may not be controllable, but to yield to a contrived destiny is to accept the prison of oppression." He has proven that philosophy through his personal writing style, which invites readers to adopt a self-questioning or critical attitude. Not content with his identity, he looks for a dynamic model that would help him free himself both from the vestiges of colonialism and from the stifling African traditions. The only true identity is created through (self-) questioning, Tchicaya U Tam'Si answers in his work. Without sure and dynamic identity, there is no sure stance from which one can look at oneself with the smile of a free person.

---

## FURTHER READING

### Criticism

Ibitokun, B. M. "The Hemorrhage of Time in Tchicaya's *Le Mauvais sang.*" *Ufahamu: Journal of the African Activist Association* 10, No. 3 (Spring 1981): 29-41.

> Explores the ways *Le Mauvais sang* presents and dramatizes the historical effects slavery and colonialism.

Moore, Gerald. "The Politics of Negritude." *Protest & Conflict in African Literature,* edited by Cosmo Pieterse and Donald Munro, pp. 26-42. New York: Africana Publishing Corporation, 1969.

> Discusses Tchicaya's contributions to the negritude movement.

Moore, Gerald. "Tchicaya U Tam'si: The Uprooted Tree." In his *Twelve African Writers,* pp. 146-69. Hutchinson University Library for Africa, 1980.

> Thematic and stylistic analysis of Tchicaya's poetry and plays in relation to the poet's biography.

Rein, Susan Erica. "Religiosity in the Poetry of Tchicaya U Tam'si." *Journal of Religion in Africa* X, No. 3 (1979): 234-49.

> Discusses religious themes and imagery in Tchicaya's poetry, proposing that the poet's concept of religiosity unites aspects of both "African religion" and Catholicism.

Spronk, Johannes M. "Chaka and the Problem of Power in the French Theater of Black Africa." *The French Review* 57, No. 5 (April 1984): 634-40.

> Examines the historical and ideological influences of Chaka, nineteenth-century king of the African Zulu tribe, on a number of playwrights, including Tchicaya.

Yewah, Emmanuel. "Political Rhetoric in/and the African Text." *Research in African Literatures* 21, No. 2 (Summer 1990): 67-78.

> Examines the speeches in *Le Destin glorieux du Maréchal Nnikon Nniku prince qu'on sort* in terms of the text's rhetorical elements, demonstrating how the "phraseological and ideological planes help create an image of the speech maker."

---

**Additional coverage of Tchicaya's life and career is contained in the following sources published by Gale Research:** *Contemporary Authors,* **Vols. 125 and 129.**

# François Truffaut
## 1932-1984

French screenwriter, filmmaker, and critic.

## INTRODUCTION

Truffaut is considered one of the most innovative filmmakers in the history of French cinema. He was at the forefront of the French New Wave style of filmmaking and is best known as a proponent of the auteur theory, that the director should be involved in the creation of the film from the writing of the script to the direction of the movie. He also worked throughout his life as a film critic, attacking the pretention of French cinema and praising American filmmakers. Although his life was relatively short, Truffaut made numerous films which achieved both critical and public success.

### Biographical Information

Truffaut was born on February 6, 1932, in Paris. Not wanted by his parents, he spent his youth as a delinquent, skipping school and attending the cinema. Truffaut dropped out of school at the age of 15, about the time he met the film critic André Bazin. Bazin was instrumental in having the youth released from a juvenile detention center and later in helping him avoid criminal charges for desertion from the army, as well as influencing him about the cinema. Truffaut wrote an important essay for Bazin's journal *Les Cahiers du Cinema,* "Une certain tendance du cinema francais" which discussed the concepts of the auteur style. Truffaut married Madeline Morgenstern, the daughter of an influential film producer, and her dowry allowed him to establish a film production company. In 1957 he made his first film, *Les Mistons,* and in 1959 he released his best-known film, *Les Quatre cents coup (The 400 Blows).* He continued to make films at the rate of approximately one per year. The father of three daughters, Truffaut divorced his wife and in the last years of his life lived with the actress Fanny Ardent; he died of a brain tumor in 1984.

### Major Works

Throughout his lifetime Truffaut created 21 feature films, 3 shorts, 10 books, and hundreds of articles and reviews. He was influenced by the filmmakers Renoir and Hitchcock and his films addressed subjects such as youth and misfits. His first critical and commercial success *The 400 Blows* was an autobiographical account of a neglected, abused and misunderstood boy, Antoine Doinel. The film won Truffaut the 1959 Cannes Film Festival award for best director and brought him public recognition. He continued the story of

Doinel in the films *L'Amour à vingt ans* (1962; *Love at Twenty*), *Baisers voles* (1968; *Stolen Kisses*), *Domicile conjugal* (1971; *Bed and Board*), and *L'Amour en fuite* (1980; *Love on the Run*). *Tirez sur le pianiste* (1962; *Shoot the Piano Player*) reflected Truffaut's deep love and respect for the American cinema, particularly of B movies. It was an unusual blend of many genres and was both serious and comical. *Jules et Jim* (1962; *Jules and Jim*) is an intense character study, the product of a wide range of cinematic devices, and is somber and introspective. In *La Nuit americaine* (1973; *Day for Night*), which won the New York Film Critics' award for best picture and an Oscar for Best Foreign Film, Truffaut considers the nature of filmmaking. It is again autobiographical and Truffaut plays the role of a film director in the movie.

### Critical Reception

Critics agree that *Jules and Jim, Shoot the Piano Player* and *The 400 Blows* are Truffaut's best works. There is less agreement about the rest of his work. Some critics believe that Truffaut's first films are his best and the quality of his work decreases over time. Others point out that *Day to Night* and

*L'Enfant sauvage* (1970; *The Wild Child*) are among his best work. Most critics agree that *Fahrenheit 451* (1966), based on the Ray Bradbury novel, and *La Sirene de Mississippi* (1970; *Mississippi Mermaid*) are his least successful works. Despite criticism, he is praised for his approach which, while affectionate, does not sink into sentimentality. He is also known for his ease in filmmaking and for his natural style and balance.

## PRINCIPAL WORKS

*Une visite* [with Jacques Rivette and Alain Resnais] (screenplay) 1954

*Les Mistons* [adapted from a short story by Maurice Pons] [*The Mischief Makers*] (screenplay) 1957

*Une Histoire d'eau* [with Jean-Luc Godard] (screenplay) 1958

*Les Quatres cents coups* [with Marcel Moussy] [*The Four Hundred Blows*] (screenplay) 1959

*Jules et Jim* [adapted from the novel by Henri-Pierre Roche] [with Jean Gruault] [*Jules and Jim*] (screenplay) 1962

*Tirez sur le pianiste* [adapted from the novel *Down There* by David Goodis] [with Marcel Moussy] [*Shoot the Piano Player*] 1962

*Tirez au flanc* [adapted from a vaudeville farce] [*The Army Game*] 1963

*L'Amour à vingt ans* [with Yvon Samuel] [*Love at Twenty*] (screenplay) 1963

*La Peau douce* [with Jean-Louis Richard] [*The Soft Skin*] 1964

*Mata Hari* [with Jean-Louis Richard] (screenplay) 1965

*Fahrenheit 451* [adapted from the novel by Ray Bradbury] [with Jean-Louis Richard, David Rudkin, and Helen Scott] (screenplay) 1966

*Le Cinema selon Hitchcock* [*Hitchcock*] (interviews) 1966

*La Mariée était en noir* [adapted from the novel *The Bride Wore Black* by Cornell George Hopley-Woolrich] [with Jean-Louis Richard] [*The Bride Wore Black*] (screenplay) 1968

*Baisers voles* [with Bernard Revon and Claude de Givray] [*Stolen Kisses*] (screenplay) 1969

*L'Enfance nue* [with Claude Berri, Mag Badard, and Guy Benier] [*Me*] (screenplay) 1970

*La Sirene de Mississippi* [adapted from the novel *Waltz into Darkness* by Cornell George Hopley-Woolrich] [*Mississippi Mermaid*] 1970

*L'Enfant sauvage* [adapted from the journals *Memoire et Rapport sur Victor de L'Aveyron* by Jean Gaspard Itard] [with Jean Gruault] [*The Wild Child*] (screenplay) 1970

*Domicile conjugal* [with Claude de Givray and Bernard Revon] [*Bed and Board*] (screenplay) 1971

*Les Deus Anglaises et le continent* [adapted from the novel by Henri-Pierre Roche] [with Jean Gruault] [*Two English Girls*] (screenplay) 1972

*La Nuit americaine* [with Suzanne Schiffman and Jean-Louis Richard] [*Day for Night*] (screenplay) 1973

*Une Belle Fille comme Moi* [adapted from the novel by Henry Farrell] [with Jean-Loup Dabadie] [*Such a Gorgeous Kid Like Me*] (screenplay) 1973

*L'Histoire d'Adele H.* [adapted from *Le Journal d'Adele Hugo* by Frances V. Guille] [with Jean Gruault, Suzanne Schiffman, and Jan Dawson] [*The Story of Adele H.*] (screenplay) 1975

*Les Films de ma vie* [*The Films of My Life*] (reviews) 1975

*L'Argent de Poche* [with Suzanne Schiffman] [*Small Change*] (screenplay) 1976

*L'Homme qui aimait les femmes* [with Michel Fermaud and Suzanne Schiffman] [*The Man Who Loved Women*] (screenplay) 1977

*La Chambre verte* [adapted from the stories by Henry James] [with Jean Gruault] [*The Green Room*] (screenplay) 1979

*L'Amour en fuite* [with Marie-France Pisier, Jean Aurel, and Suzanne Schiffman] [*Love on the Run*] (screenplay) 1980

*Le Dernier Metro* [adapted from the story by Truffault and Suzanne Schiffman] [*The Last Metro*] (screenplay) 1981

*La Femme d'à côté* [with Suzanne Schiffman and Jean Aurel] [*The Woman Next Door*] (screenplay) 1981

*Vivement Dimanche* [adapted from the novel *The Long Saturday Night* by Charles Williams] [with Suzanne Schiffman and Jean Aurel] [*Confidentially Yours*] (screenplay) 1982

*Correspondence* (letters) 1988

*The Little Thief* [with Claude de Givray] (screenplay) 1989

*Truffaut also directed these films.

## CRITICISM

### Penelope Houston (review date Spring 1961)

SOURCE: "Critic's Notebook," in *Sight and Sound*, Vol. 30, No. 2, Spring, 1961, pp. 62-6.

[*In the following excerpt, Houston reviews* Tirez sur le pianiste, *commenting that although the critics and public disliked the film, it reflects Truffaut's dedication and devotion to the art of filmmaking.*]

Left-wing critics in this country seem to have been thrown distinctly off-balance by Truffaut's *Tirez sur le pianiste*. No one has had the nerve to write, though some people have said, that Truffaut may have to be written off as a serious film-maker if this is the way he intends to carry on. Apparently the audience which saw the film at a meeting of the French Federation of Ciné Clubs towards the end of last year shared some of these reservations. At any rate, *Cinéma 61* in its January issue published Truffaut's detailed answers to the questions asked him; answers which are revealing of the artist's position, and not irrelevant in relation to the critic's.

The basis of these critics' dissatisfaction is nothing more or less than a sense of let-down. *Les Quatre cents coups* was humanist, engaged, autobiography with a conscience. It was also a film which satisfied everyone, arousing instantaneous sympathy and liking. Yes, Truffaut says rather bitterly, "I started out to make a little film, something which the press would quietly encourage but which people wouldn't go to see. Then I saw this modest little family enterprise become a big international success . . . It belonged to the public which has no affection for the cinema, to the man who goes to the pictures once a year to see *Bridge on the River Kwai* or the new Clair film, the public I mistrust most in the world." And so: "This time I wanted to please only the real enthusiasts . . . and my only rule in making *Tirez sur le pianiste* was my own pleasure . . . I would call the film a respectful pastiche of the Hollywood B-film, from which I have learnt such a lot."

"I know," Truffaut says, "that there is nothing the public dislikes more than abrupt changes of mood, but I have always loved them . . ." Practically speaking, the remarkable thing is that he was able to carry out this disregard for audience tastes, to make the film as he wanted. And what did he want to make? A record, almost, of a love affair with the cinema, a film full of jokes and allusions and tricks and charm. Godard's dedication of *A Bout de Souffle* "to Monogram Pictures" and Truffaut's avowed desire to do a pastiche of the B-picture are very personal variations on the French intellectuals' passionate attachment to a dream America. Truffaut has clearly haunted the cinema since his childhood. *Tirez sur le pianiste* exists so much in the context of other films that you feel anyone who hasn't followed at least something of his own route to it could only be mystified.

To be pompous about a film like this, treating its director like a youth club leader who has been caught carrying a flick-knife, is merely trying to dragoon the artist into one's own camp. He has no intention of being pinned down, as his film makes sufficiently clear. His answer to the second question asked him—"why dodge the big issues of our time?"—is even more specific.

"You can," he says, "find my film useless, a misfire, a negation, anything you like. What I don't accept is your right to tell me that I ought to have been making something else in-

stead . . . When a journalist asks me 'Why aren't young filmmakers doing pictures about Algeria?', what I'd like to answer is 'Why don't you write a book about Algeria?' Because you wouldn't know just what to write? Well, then, I wouldn't know what to film!" He goes on to attack the Stanley Kramer type of problem picture, with its holier than thou self-righteousness, its lack of urgency or desperate conviction. "You can only," he says, "talk of the 'big problems' with devastating sincerity if they really keep you from sleeping at night." And consequently: "If, being what I am, I had tackled one of these 'big subjects' you want me to film, approaching it from the outside, I would have been dishonest since there would still have been in my heart a sleeping *pianist* . . ."

One's sympathies are all on Truffaut's side. This is the way an artist functions; and for the critic to stand on the sidelines and try to shout the players down is not only futile but mannerless. Truffaut has chosen an obvious example to quote against his critics: films like Kramer's *The Defiant Ones* and *On the Beach,* so respectable, so genuinely well-meaning, so unassailably correct, are empty precisely because the sense of involvement at a personal level is missing. The element of evasive smugness in the social conscience film has itself become a cliché, from Kazan's *Pinky,* which made it easy to sympathise with its Negro heroine because, after all, she was really Jeanne Crain, to Guy Green's *The Mark,* which appeals for a more tolerant attitude to sex criminals but won't take the risk of making its hero guilty of anything more substantial than an impulse.

All the same, Truffaut is really taking us down a false trail. No one expects the filmmaker dutifully to sit down with a list of "big subjects" and tick them off one by one. What one could say is that his understandable retreat from the intimidating difficulty of the social subjects needn't lead him all the way to a private fantasy world of his own. We can't, again, presume to tell him that he ought to be concerned with some aspect of social reality; but we can ask why he isn't, what is the condition of the society he's living in which makes him so unwilling to come to grips with it. *Tirez sur le pianiste* is almost a classic example of the kind of work John Berger means, I think, in the quotation I've used earlier in these notes. To enjoy it fully you must "accept what the artist himself is trying to do . . . that it is necessary for him to create a kind of tidal world of flux . . ."

It isn't very difficult to do this: to enjoy the mixture of character study, gangster fantasy, comedy and pathos; to take Truffaut's film precisely at his own evaluation of it and to recognise the honesty as well as the impudence which has gone into its making. It throws off sparks like a catherine-wheel, a fizzing, dazzling, short-lived divertissement. It comes not from an uncommitted artist, but from an artist who recognises in himself the necessity to be committed all the way. And his emphasis on the difficulty (the emotional, rather than the economic problem) of this is something on which critics of the left might usefully comment.

## Roger Greenspun (essay date Spring 1963)

SOURCE: "Elective Affinities: Aspects of *Jules et Jim,*" in *Sight and Sound,* Vol. 32, No. 2, Spring, 1963, pp. 78-82.

[*In the following essay, Greenspun discusses the cinematography in* Jules et Jim *and the way in which the film's images illustrate the problems in the characters' lives.*]

The forms of life flourish within the protective circles of François Truffaut's **Jules et Jim.** Whatever is reflected in the kindly eyes of Jules "*comme des boules, pleins d'humour et de tendresse,*" tadpoles squirming in a round bowl of water, the slow sensitive circling of a room by hand-held camera taking careful inventory of the pleasant labours of a reflective and observant man's life—circles enclose to promote and enhance the abundant vitality of this film's world and its creatures. Files of dominoes meander across circular tables. A young woman imitating a locomotive triumphantly puffs her way around Jules's room with a cigarette inverted in her mouth, followed in close-up by a rapidly circling camera. The camera races through an even more rapid circle in a café when the young woman, Thérèse, deserts Jules for another man. But after the camera's dizzy 360 degrees; pan Jules sits down, and draws on a round table top the face of another girl he might love. A figure of speech, the "family circle," becomes an image when the camera follows smiling glances from eye to eye at the German chalet. For the ways in which the film sees life, the cosmos itself according to Catherine's German authority being a great inverted bowl, the growing family ideally nurtures and extends possibility; the family circle can even improve the time, making a balance between an abstract symbol of perfection and all the inevitable signs of dissolution. Finally the protective charm is lost when through the broken arc of a circle, a ruined bridge, Catherine plunges herself and Jim to death.

While life in **Jules et Jim** naturally expands in circles, the patterns human beings impose on it tend often to be triangular. The central *ménage à trois* enforces the idea of a triangle, and in the artful arrangements of characters and above all in the opposition of camera lenses to the many corner settings the idea is subtly realised. To be caught in a corner is to be miserable; Jim and Gilberte, who are generally miserable together (and who are rarely alone except in the implicit presence of a third party), are usually to be found in corners—sitting glumly in their café, or lying in Gilberte's bed. In a film so devoted to celebrating the freedom and grace of broadly sweeping movements, and to seeing life, in Albert's ballad for Catherine, as a whirl, the rigid triangular

figure, the cramped corner setting, are traps. Typically Catherine, although she never quite succeeds with circles, manages in spite of being repeatedly an impulsive party in a love triangle, never to be cornered. But often, in the placing of her various beds, in where she sits while the men play dominoes, you will find her up against a wall.

Catherine is conjured into view through an insistence upon the powers of seeing. First she is a photograph projected by concentrated light in a darkened room, then a carved stone head in the bright Mediterranean sun, and finally a living presence in a Paris garden. From the first her beautiful smile attracts, and at the end a subdued version of that smile is the last to be seen of her. She flashes the smile most brilliantly during the post-war reunion between Jules and Jim, when she tells Jim that though Jules thinks his future will be bright it may not be spectacular. As it turns out, she makes his future both bright and spectacular. Catherine's last act, the shaping of a destiny, confirms the slightly more than natural role she plays in the film. The enigma within her smile, which defies all the camera's clever attempts to hold it still, ultimately defines her. Jules, who is always willing to establish essences, says she is "une vraie femme," but before we are through with her we see the true woman costumed as "Thomas" in pre-war Paris, in high boots for the German countryside, and in extremely mannish shirt and tie in Paris of the 1930s. Variously identified as daring thinker, emancipated woman, "true woman," wife, mistress, mother, innovator in love, queen, almost a man—Catherine seems compelled to act out the contradictory impulses implicit in such a confusion of roles.

At their most mysterious the complications in her life serve aspirations towards a higher disorder in natural forces. She appears in a glow of light after a shower of water (in the camera's passage up from a gymnasium shower room, through an overhead glow, into Jules's garden), and after death by drowning she disappears in flame. Her first leap into the Seine produces fiery rings of reflected light upon water. When she pours liquid down a drain, smoke rises up in response. She is more than a little prone to catching fire herself. An enterprising witch, she does very nearly manage to combine fire and water, only to be defeated in each try by the violence of her means. Her direct assaults upon the elements contrast with the imperfect contact the men make, shivering in a shower, playing cautiously with the sea on a sunny holiday, sawing firewood against the winter cold. But those contacts, if not perfectly comfortable, are nevertheless viable, as Catherine's attacks are not. (On one of the best of days, during the foggy walk along the lake, when sky, earth, and water are very close to one another in natural harmony, Catherine has the men skimming stones over the surface of the water.) Attempts to realign the elements, particularly ones so traditionally antithetical as fire and water, produce not a new nature, but rather destruction in this one.

For each of her whims she has a reason: being quits, keeping the balance. Jules has known few women; she has known many men: they might cancel out to make a good pair. A few hours with an old lover before her marriage pays off a few insults from Jules's mother. To justify her infidelities to Jim, *"Gilberte égale Albert."* But Catherine's reasons are never reasonable; being quits shades over into seeking revenge. In this she closely reflects the world in which she lives, imitating in her own sphere some of the statecraft games that modern Europe plays in its sphere, and finally going sour as everything around her goes insane. The instruments at her disposal increase in potential efficiency, from a quaintly mysterious bottle of vitriol at the beginning to the fatal automobile at the end. In a sense she is doomed by the way in which her wilful inventiveness finds its too ready match in the development of the world's inventions.

Between her delightful "Thomas", who as symbol so strangely moves the young men, and the masculine pose of her last scenes, there are ominous differences—age, increasing respectability, the styles of the times, and above all a simple change in the elements of disguise from a moustache playfully drawn on to a pair of steel-rimmed spectacles. At the end she has lost some of her flair for being a man. She has substituted for it an impressive technical proficiency, which the camera closely records, in handling the knobs and levers of her automobile. Catherine *herself* is a deeply moving symbol, of the eroding demands of simply living (she seems to bear all the burden of ageing in the film), of boredom, of incessant wilful change, of whatever signifies the slipping away of life in time—in the times through which you live and which, with a smile if you are very lucky, will see you to your death. Destructive, with her fires and her burning liquid, desperately asserting balance and yet repeatedly losing it, Catherine is sadly fated at the same time that she seems to *be* fate; hiding behind pencilled moustache, prim spectacles, and a beautiful smile.

Catherine's role as it were emerges from within the mysteries of her appearance. For the two men the conventions of their appearance almost hide the mysterious humanity of their roles. People call them Don Quixote and Sancho Panza, and to some degree people are right. But Jim more nearly resembles the type of the Romantic hero—tall, dark, full lips, low voice, cape coat. At times he is betrayed into parodying the type, as in the struggle with Catherine over her pistol and the escape from the old mill. More often, however, he translates the traditional role into what must of course be its modern equivalent: the adventurous pragmatist whose "occupation" consists in seeing for himself, and whose special gift is an appreciation of the influence of conditions.

Jules, the little clown, saddened as his life continues, is almost as conventionalised in his appearance, even to wearing the same jaunty striped suit and string tie to his wife's cre-

mation as he had worn for a game of leapfrog with Jim thirty years before, when the film began. He thinks of himself as an absolutist: Catherine *is* a queen; Baudelaire says that woman is abominable, and Baudelaire means what he says "metaphysically." Jim succeeds in romantic love; Jules fails. Jim goes exploring (Catherine even tells him to go see for himself what is beyond the earth's crust in her cosmology); Jules, a lovable Buddha, withdraws into contemplation. As he retreats from it a little, Jules's ways of valuing life increase in their scope and coherence. Some day, he says, he may become ambitious and write a love story—about insects. The comment is rueful, but not bitter. The semi-comic frustration of so many of his desires combines with the love with which he approaches his naturalistic researches, to relieve him from the necessity for self-interested involvement in the world he so conscientiously observes. Catherine's last request is that Jim come with her in her automobile, and that Jules watch them carefully.

The three central characters largely are defined through the complexity and delicacy of the ways in which the film insists upon seeing them, in relation to a continually widening, life-sustaining round of outside contexts. Jules and Jim are writers and intellectuals, and they do a great deal of quoting and translating. Thérèse disappears while they argue about Shakespeare; Catherine on the other hand teaches all men—about Shakespeare—though she jumps into the Seine after too many quotations from Baudelaire. Jules will translate Jim's autobiographical novel into German, and he does translate Catherine's English quotation from a German author into French for Jim; but later Jim has apparently learned enough German to tell Gilberte that he is translating an Austrian play into French. Jim's very name, pronounced "Djim *à l'anglaise,"* carries over from another language. To the political turmoils of the great world the interlingual activities of these ideal friends offer an ironic contrast. Literature and translation affirm a community, but *not* a simple identity, of human experience through letters, and show a better way to Frenchman and German than the national aspirations of their two countries. So far as the film's montage presents it, World War One is declared as if to interrupt Jules's rendition of the *Marseillaise* without an accent.

Near the very beginning Thérèse gets things going when she runs away from an anarchist painting a fence slogan that reads "MORT AUX AUTRE(S)." When the two men meet after the war, Jules at once asks, how are the others? A little later he tells Jim to give his regards to the others. The question of "the others" is complicated because while they are the ones who fill the cemeteries, they are also the ones who put them there; they write the books and paint the pictures, but they also burn the books and hate bohemian artists. "The others" are everybody, and they may excite concern, compassion, fear, or loathing. But no matter what the nature of their claim they direct attention to a larger view of the world, a corrective to the tightly involuted emotional tangle that runs through *Jules et Jim*. They are a reminder that beyond the tiring fascination of one woman's shuttling between her men there are other things to look at and care about: people, and in the smallest, most familiar, most surprising ways, the surrounding life of nature.

In the newsreel and old film footage of the First World War there are a few startling moments, during the sequences of horizontal distortion, when flattened soldiers scampering up the barren hills of no man's land look like insects. Later, to signify the end of the war, a field of tall flowers suddenly sprouts helmet-waving soldiers greeting the news of the Armistice. These begin a series of images that continue into the final moments of the film. There is of course some irony in the man-insect relation that pervades the middle portion of the film: Catherine as queen bee of the hive (earlier Jim had said that marriage made her less of a grasshopper and more of an ant, but it is Jules we shortly see sawing wood with ant-like industry while his wife and best friend kiss in the chalet); the love story about insects; an insect in the background wandering down a windowpane during part of a lyrically romantic sequence, Catherine's and Jim's *"premier baiser, qui dura le reste de la nuit."* The last example is instructive, because Jim's sensitive outlining of Catherine's profile in the half light is not seriously undercut by the insect's tentative journey; rather the two explorations are complementary in their delicacy.

The most important thing about the encompassing plant life is that it does totally surround; that it so interpenetrates the film's action that a fern branch comes naturally to Catherine's hand during her long night talk with Jim, or that the way of knowing the time or kind of day is to observe the quality of light upon trees—the early morning light on dense leaves near a window to mark the ending of Catherine's and Jim's first night; the harmonious misty closeness of trees, land, sky and water during the peaceful visit to the lake. Quietly significant moments for people seem to include plants: a vase full of them by Catherine's head as she sings her ballad, another vase beside her and Sabine as they sit knitting while the men play dominoes. The cremation sequence opens through a shot of funeral palms.

Although it includes death the natural world is almost always idyllic. At their best—a meal in Jules's Paris garden before the war, the south of France, much of the time spent in the German countryside—the affairs of human beings approximate that idyllic order. When they do not, the advantage always lies with nature. Towards the end of the film Jim concedes the failure of his and Catherine's attempt to live by new laws. The trouble with espousing any kind of revolutionary change is that it implicitly puts one in opposition to an environment that in all aspects demonstrates the rightness of gradual evolution. Tadpoles, insects, plants—

all offer a lesson in the survival of ancient forms. Whatever thrives lives peacefully; flower-pattern shell bursts that destroy the land prohibit life.

Truffaut has compared his films with circuses:

> My films *are* circus shows, and that's what I want them to be . . . I'd like people to boo the sequences that have gone wrong and clap the ones they enjoy. And since people who come to see my films have to shut themselves up in the dark, I always like at the end to take them out into nature—to the sea, or the snow—so that they'll forgive me.

Quite apart from the sophistications inherent in the relation Truffaut sees between audience and film (and apart from the charm of thinking of the final scenes of *Les Quatre Cents Coups* and *Tirez sur le Pianiste* as nature excursions), the idea of a circus show with its open assumption of putting on an act is especially relevant to *Jules et Jim*. Thérèse's locomotive act, Jules's and Sabine's equestrian act, Catherine's sloppy kid costume for "Thomas," the old film slapstick behind the opening titles, the elaborate double take of Jules' and Jim's Paris reunion near the end—all these suggest two frames of reference; one looking inward to the development of the film's action, and the other looking outward to an emerging insistence upon an idea of "theatre" as such. It is crucial to the film's method that it call attention to the various arts and their kinds (in houses, bridges, songs, statues, plays, paintings, novels, poems, films, etc.) so that it may make allusion to them when it wishes, and ultimately so that it may add all of them to the demonstration of marvellous diversity that is its meaning.

For a small example of the method, consider a very minor vignette. While the camera circles Jules's room in the introduction to the German chalet, Catherine's voice explains the arrangements of the household. At one point she mentions a local girl who comes in to help with the housework and serving, and the camera lifts slightly to observe on the wall a small painting of a girl and a man kissing. Obviously the point is not that Jules and the girl are having an affair (the painting has already been seen in Jules's Paris apartment); it is rather that just in passing here is a way of thinking about young servant girls established in the conventions of genre painting. The reference has nothing more to say about the girl; its context is not her life, but the life of art. While a voice describes the way things are, the camera finds for them a pictorial tradition.

There are other still pictures: drawings of spiders, Jules as a Romantic Mozart, posters advertising art exhibits and films, Jules's period photographs of German beauties, Albert's slide collection of odd stone faces, the many Picassos, snapshots of Jules and Jim miserable in their uniforms, and of course still photographs made by stopping the moving pictures. There is even a sense in which moving pictures themselves are remarkable for being pictures that move, as in the curious conclusion to Jim's account of a soldier who in the midst of the Great War won a girl by letter, only to be killed before he could consummate his love:

> I will show you a series of photos
> of him . . . if you look at them
> quickly, he seems to move.

The story about the soldier and his personal combat is one of several more formal tales: Thérèse's story of her adventures, Jim's autobiographical novel, Catherine's side of the story of her marriage with Jules, Jim's account of how he came to his profession, the story of Don Quixote and Sancho Panza, *Elective Affinities*. The "story" of *Jules et Jim* both contains and stands in series with all the many stories that are told in the course of the film. The exceptional persistence of a narrator's voice itself draws attention to the integrity of narrative with its typical resources and devices. Thus "story", like "motion picture", is one aspect of the total film. Stories even have a special function of their own; an inartistic function by most modern judgment. Stories are for moral lessons: Jules's little fable of the ruler who was unhappy because he had two wives, Jim's indictment of Catherine based upon the story about a woman on a ship who wanted always to make love to a new stranger, the questionable morality of the Scandinavian dramatist who wallows in vice to preach virtue, what Baudelaire or Shakespeare teach, the significance of burning the books.

> **Sound and sight, story and picture, example and image, learning and pleasure—related pairs that not only help explain but in their very doubleness construct the world of *Jules et Jim*.**
>
> **—Roger Greenspun**

While literature teaches us the life of right conduct and tells us how to prepare for its trials, the visual arts, including the art of the film in historical perspective, give us a sense of style—a feeling for the ways in which we may most gracefully come to terms with the imperfections of external reality. A general notion of the efficacy of style as such seems to be behind all the demonstrations of particular styles of filmmaking, periods of Picasso, fashions in dress, even parodies of sculptural style in Albert's slide collection and in the outdoor museum. To the major subject of the relation between art and life, the film brings a new appreciation of the old aesthetics according to which the dual functions of a work

of art are to instruct and to delight. Sound and sight, story and picture, example and image, learning and pleasure—related pairs that not only help explain but in their very doubleness construct the world of *Jules et Jim*.

Jules watches the time pass through a triangular-circular hour glass that tells him when he is to do—whatever it is he wants to do when he turns it over to apportion the day to his own needs and uses. This combination of geometric figures, like an accommodation of time's demands to the expression of personal vitality, seems a characteristic symbol for Jules, who wants Catherine *and* Sabine *and* Jim, and will do whatever he can not to see his circle disintegrate. While Catherine's fantastic, boring, sometimes frantic plans to force new combinations fail (though even as they fail they disclose at least a perverted understanding of her world's demands, if not its methods), Jules's quiet, intelligent, flexible inclusion of as much as possible within the circle of his nurture succeeds as well as anything can succeed in an existence in which personal visits to cemeteries must follow the larger actions.

The narrator says that after Catherine and Jim were cremated Jules might have mingled their ashes, but chose not to. At the end, close but separate, and not scattered over everything as Catherine wanted hers to be, their remains seem deeply and a little humorously a memorial to the best of the film's values. All the genuine combinations of this film, even the unsuccessful ones, are happy in some degree. German and French, short and tall, fair and dark, withdrawn and involved—Jules and Jim preside over a world of valuable disparities. Given the demands of the fiction and of the life it portrays, Jules's heroic attempt to hold all things together, no matter how ill sorted, is bound to fail. But beyond the fiction there can be at least momentary success for an analogous attempt in the privileged universe of a work of art. The burden of a work that is so at pains to distinguish the integrity of each of its several elements is exactly a love of multiple relations, tolerance, elemental order, gradualism, plenitude, the inclusion of all of "*les autres*." Upon the contrapuntal inventions of this Solemn Music neither any one nor any other, nor the submergence of one into another, but *all* the several forms and creatures that squirm, struggle, dance into life, in this great sustaining bowl their mixt power employ.

## T. J. Ross (essay date July 1973)

SOURCE: "Wild Lives," in *Literature/Film Quarterly*, Vol. 1, No. 3, July, 1973, pp. 218-25.

[*In the following essay, Ross analyzes* Fahrenheit 451 *and* The Bride Wore Black, *and suggests why the critics and the public have not considered them to be among Truffaut's best work.*]

The three films made by Truffaut after his major triumph with *Jules and Jim* were met with increasing reserve by both critics and general audiences. Undeniably, *The Soft Skin, Fahrenheit 451,* and *The Bride Wore Black* lack the sweet-and-sour charm of *Jules and Jim* (or *Shoot the Piano Player*), let alone the more consistently affable charm of the semi-autobiographical sequels to *The Four-Hundred Blows*. Nor are these films, even *Fahrenheit 451,* as obviously rife with cultural significance. They are also surprisingly conservative in form, their melodrama and violence unredeemed by a counterpointing play of visual gags (such as we find in *Shoot the Piano Player*). Nor, in their compact and straight-moving scenarios do they pretend to the ascetically severe, documentary-like realism of a later—and better received—work like *The Wild Child*. These are, in contrast, fictional films based deadpan on pop genres: science fiction, the crime thriller, the romance of adulterous passion and intrigue. Thus, they comprise a line of Truffaut's which we might call (using Pauline Kael's yardstick) his "movie-movies."

Yet they remain relatively unpopular, not seeming to fulfill their possibilities either as outright pot boilers or as serious statements in popular forms. There is in fact a clear thematic consistency between the movie-movies (including the later *Mississippi Mermaid*) and the rest of Truffaut's work. Not only *The Wild Child,* where the approach is most direct, but each of Truffaut's films is concerned with the experience of various kinds of "wild life" as these kinds of life—and feeling—struggle against being brought to bay in the social environment. The central conflict in Truffaut's films is between the brutality of an untamed human creature and the taming brutalities of civilization. It would be a false lead, therefore, to set the genre works in a category apart from those presumably aimed at more serious levels of the game.

The level of the game of the movie-movies proves in fact to be as intensive as anything to be found in Truffaut's work. But though *The Soft Skin* has been gaining ground over the years with university and art house audiences as one of Truffaut's best films, *Fahrenheit 451* and *The Bride Wore Black* still wait their due appreciation. In this essay both films are discussed mainly with a view to defining their particular qualities and levels of appeal; at the same time the discussion may help to focus some of the leading critical questions about Truffaut and the nature of his achievement so far.

Ray Bradbury's *Fahrenheit 451* is one of that small group of pop classics which everyone, whatever the height of his browline, has read. It is when a novel is both famous and familiar that scriptwriters are most likely to produce scenarios fatally "faithful" to its contents: the least stilted adaptations most often derive from novels not deemed to be special but rather plucked out of common garden variety. Happily, Truffaut's adaptation of Bradbury is loose. He drops the love plot and also omits the mechanical giant dog that provided much of the novel's gut-level of suspense and thrills. Truffaut also works against the grain of the conventional appeal of his stars, Oskar Werner and Julie Christie. The latter for once is not seen as swinging girl-of-the-people, mod and matey. Nor does Werner appear in his usual get-up as solemnly romantic bourgeois cashmere sweater boy. Like such of his English counterparts as Leslie Howard or Rex Harrison, Werner is the perfect matinee idol: the character-type he projects is one of banked yet certain powers who, like the very rich, can afford with impunity to be "shy" or moody. This sort of "shyness" as a means of warding off or holding at bay—or in their place—the importunate or the extraneous, serves to support rather than contravene an innate sense of command over a scene. And this is the image of the standard romantic lead of stage or screen: the man in command of circumstance, however "retiring" he might otherwise appear.

But in Truffaut's film, Werner is seen as a man whose feelings sway mostly between perplexity and terror. Under pressure from Truffaut (a pressure which led Werner himself into an emotional state of perplexity and consternation) Werner plays—and with a hard-edged conviction—a man groping his way: the complete anti-hero. Julie Christie plays two contrasting parts. In one, she is a lover of books who is, however, so grim in her dedication that she, too, appears to be groping her way as tensely as our anti-hero. In the other, she plays a character to whom books are entirely alien. This character is seen as being too self-alienated ever to find her way back to herself. Yet the very numbness of her manner reflects a core of feelings also compounded mainly of perplexity and fear.

The perplexed citizens of *Fahrenheit 451* exist in a world where book-burning is the norm, so much an accepted part of the way of life that to be for books is to be anti-social. Truffaut's visual rendering of this situation, variations on which abound in the literature of science fiction, leads to some of his most affecting images. In one shot, for example, people in a park being frisked for concealed books by patrolling firemen stand with feet apart and arms negligently raised as if being frisked for concealed weapons. The metaphor of "ideas as weapons" is here conveyed with a low-keyed yet resonant pathos.

In his *Loss of Self in Modern Literature and Art,* Professor Wylie Sypher plainly notes that "culture means criticism." It is precisely this point of view which is stood on its head by the rationale of the fire chief (Cyril Cusack) when he explains that books are corrupt because they encourage a critical responsiveness to experience. What is wanted, he further explains, is not the life of culture but rather the universal attainment of happiness. Nor is he in doubt about the essential requirement for this end: ". . . the only way to be happy is for everybody to be made . . . equal."

Feeling "equal," however, depends on remaining doped: by way of pills or wall-to-wall television. Through such means the emotions are deadened: for to be awakened from emotional torpor: means inescapably (as in *Brave New World* and all its offshoots) to discover one's unhappiness, since anyone with the least emotional development could not be happy in the sort of world overseen by the fire chief. Because books "make us emotional" by bringing intimations of mortality and possibility close to our nerves, books must be effaced as "unnatural."

Again, a familiar theme, on which Truffaut rings the changes with a deft economy. With his opening shots he establishes the TV set in its function as one of the family—as indeed the key member of the family since, in always being there, it provides a steady drug against loneliness. Also functioning as key extensions of the family are the three telephones, the third located in the bathroom. When Werner's emergency call to a hospital after his wife has taken an overdose of sleeping pills is answered by the droll "Poisoning speaking," the moment proves as unspeakably telling as when the befuddled department head of *Lucky Jim* answers his office phone with: "History speaking. . . ."

Werner plays a fireman named Montag who, after reading a book, gets hooked, begins hoarding books in his own house, is betrayed by his wife (Julie Christie) to the authorities, flees for his freedom, and then is guided by another general reader (Christie once more) to a mysterious book resort whose members spend their time memorizing literary classics. The titles of their exercises are flashed on screen in the finale in an orgy of name-dropping: Stevenson paired with Genet; Austen with Proust; etc. It all offers a merrier reading list than what could be hoped for in any lit. survey course—an unsystematic cultural romp reflecting the sensibility of autodidact and *auteur* Truffaut.

And it is surely the voice of the *auteur* we hear blending with that of his protagonist when the latter asserts, of the value of his reading habit: "Behind each of these books there's a man, that's what interests me!" Through his reading in the identities of others, Montag comes to discover his own, is roused to a consciousness of the reality of his own nature. In his excitement he interrupts his wife and her friends, clustered before the TV, to read them passages from Dickens' most autobiographical fiction, *David Copperfield*. His reading causes one of the circle to weep: "I'd forgotten about those things!" Another, the realist in the group, objects: "Filth! novels aren't like life." She is right insofar as novels act to disturb the peace of that sort of daily living that itself

is the ultimate drug. Thus Montag retorts: "She cried because it's true."

Montag's reading dissipates his concern for his impending promotion in the fire department, a prospect by which he had been controlled as much as his wife by her TV "family." As he says to his wife when she mentions the prospect: ". . . that was *before*. . . ." In his conversion to the life of culture he goes so far as to become a saboteur against the fire teams of happiness. This toughness of response conforms to the style of the other people of the culture camp (whose combative militance is stressed in the film, though it is not a part of the scheme of the novel). Montag's way of fighting fire with fire is to plant books in his co-firemen's houses, then denounce them. And when he is found out, we will see him turn his flame thrower on the fire chief. What is released in Montag by his reading proves indeed to be "wild" (and poses a problem to be returned to later).

One of the film's most remarkable scenes concerns the self-immolation of a reader whose house is invaded by the firemen. The lady of the house stands at the center of her great library, its contents all flung in a heap for burning, and herself lights the pyre, crying out: "These books were alive; they spoke to me." And so she chooses to perish with them.

The victim is heroine Julie Christie's aunt; in contrast to her niece (the earnest and stilted manner of whose cultural dedication adds a piquant touch to her beauty), the aunt is absolutely plain in appearance and manner, lacking even in the glamour of some special kind of vulnerability. She is presented as in no way "special." This focus on a character with whom the audience is least likely to identify serves all the more to drive home the plight and pathos of the common reader in a time of outrage. The objective focus further strengthens the scene's humanist assertion, an assertion which is in harrowingly exact balance to the fire chief's venal line on making everyone "equal."

And yet—this scene of self-destruction is inescapably extreme and brutal, and points to an undercurrent of brutality in this film the source of which would seem to lie outside the exigencies of plot. The culture camp itself, as was noted, turns out to be no nest of doves. Unlike his master Renoir, in whose films death is also frequent and sudden, Truffaut is no creator of pastorals. The pressures of present time unfailingly impinge, whatever the period or place; and where death in Renoir, however sudden or ironic, is invested with the dignity of its intrinsic relation to plot, death in Truffaut is either of an absurdist arbitrariness or else (in what is but the other side of the same coin) strikes out of the vagaries of an essentially ideological passion (the one kind of passion to which a Renoir or a Hitchcock tends to remain aloof). Deaths through violence, suicide, heart attack, abound in Truffaut's films, but perhaps no film of his is so fierce and brutal in its moods and events as *Fahrenheit 451,* his homage to the culture of books.

Consider the house-burning that follows soon after the one just described. This time Montag's own house is the target, and it is his recently collected books we see piled up for burning. Chief Cyril Cusack gestures with a "triumphant leer" to Werner-Montag to turn on the flame. Montag turns it first, with rather a vehement relish, on the cold bed shared by him and his wife; then points his torch with an equal vehemence on the TV wall; and then, with the same calculated intensity, right on the fire chief, who has enough time to cry out in terror before disappearing in the flames. Montag's movements are not shown as being either spontaneous or trance-like—but rather as steady and remorseless as the fast draw of the hero of a Western. The action is all the more barbarous for its being so conscious, anticipating in this the frightening awareness of the murderess-heroine of *The Bride Wore Black.*

This fury of attack on the outrage of the times is as characteristic of the New Wave as of other late vanguards. We would expect nothing less in a film by Godard. It is often overlooked that Truffaut is as prone as his peers to such brutal effects and, like them, capable of overkill in his retaliatory thrusts.

The allegiance to culture of this film is not markedly liberal; it is more akin to the moods of Modernist art in its self-consciousness and ferocity. Nowhere is the film more double-edged and problematic in effect than in its concluding scenes at the book resort. The people of the camp are shown to be so busy memorizing and reciting their texts that they have no time to spare for each other. On a bleak midwinter's day, a dying old man listens while his son recites to him in their tent a passage out of Stevenson: the passage is about the death of a cold-hearted father in the dead of winter. The boy looks eagerly to his father for some sign of feeling, some word, but receives only an impatient tug as signal of a word skipped in the reading. Surely dedication is here being pushed beyond the limits of cultivation to the barbarism of a cult; and surely Truffaut is on to this. He can't intend his *Weir of Hermiston* episode unironically. Yet the sort of query raised by this distancing irony seems off key. Questions which had nagged round the edges of *Fahrenheit 451* (and are also in play in *The Soft Skin*) are now directly posed with an unbalancing belatedness. They seem to want another film for closer, more integrated treatment—and that film is *The Bride Wore Black,* a film in which a great human commitment—romantic love—is avowed through acts of murder. The protagonist of this film begins at that point of violence to which Montag in his newfound humanism is finally pressed.

The typical "wild child" at the center of Truffaut's films is not a child of the forest but rather one whose passions find

their source in the staple myths of Western culture: like the artist-hero of *Shoot the Piano Player,* around whom dead bodies pile as high as in Mickey Spillane; or the obsessively liberated heroine of *Jules and Jim* who literally takes herself and her unwitting lover over the edge; or the betrayed wife of *The Soft Skin* who mows down her husband in her outrage (and who remains one of the most interestingly considered studies of a woman in Truffaut). These are characters—none more so than the bride dressed in black—who manifest in their rampages that merciless spirituality (and consequent assertiveness of Style) which has been characteristic of the arts in our century. In this gallery a top spot would go to the self-immolating lady in *Fahrenheit 451,* whose action depends on an extremism as despairing as it is uncompromising; it is certainly far from encompassing all possible options. Truffaut's homage to literature is not free of vulgarity; and like those vulgar "flaws" inseparable from the more imposing qualities of the tragic hero, the vulgarity of Truffaut's film inheres in the emotional imperatives of the action, in the pathos of its logic. The same holds for the homage to romantic passion in *The Bride Wore Black*; and it is probably the evident streaks of vulgarity in the pattern of this film which stirred critics, especially those not much at home with movies, to overheated reactions. Thus, Marvin Mudrick, writing in the *Hudson Review* (Winter, 1968-69), fumed over the film as "A high camp existentialist French insult to the intelligence." Why he felt that a mere adjectival planting of "high camp," "existentialist" and "French" (!) before a capping cliché would be enough to raise shudders all round must remain a puzzle. In face of a film adaptation of a Cornell Woolrich thriller of 1940, the statement would seem to be excessive; we do not, after all, anticipate here a pitch out of the Great Tradition.

The story begins when a bridegroom is accidentally shot to death at the altar on his wedding day. His betrothed then devotes herself to tracking down and destroying the five men responsible, through their carelessness with firearms, for his death. There is a macabre poetic justice (and feminist assertion) in the way she takes advantage of and manipulates her prey according to how each in his turn seeks advantage over her in the name of Romance. Her vengeance thus takes on a general aspect as the vengeance of Woman, uptipping in the very process of epitomizing, the myth of romantic love—a myth which the more dogmatic of women's liberationists would see as a sexist myth created by the male imagination.

Each of the bride's victims is shown to be a self-centered mediocrity. The group consists of: (1) a playboy-socialite; (2) a down-at-heels reclusive bachelor; (3) a smug suburbanite on his way up the political slope; (4) a happy-go-lucky, rather gurgling artist; (5) an oafish gangster. It is on the afternoon of his own wedding party that our heroine (Jeanne Moreau) gets the playboy. As a mystery guest at the festivities, she teases the groom out to his penthouse balcony, and as he gaily reaches over the rail to catch her scarf being blown away in the breeze, she shoves him off.

The reclusive bachelor is picked up by the lady at—where else?—a concert. And it seems further appropriate that he should get his by way of a dose of poison in his cheap champagne. The lady gains entry to the suburbanite's house in the guise—how else?—of a school teacher, come to give Junior a make-up lesson while his mother is away. She wins over Junior, who never in his days had seen such a teacher, and gets him off to bed, to leave her alone with Dad preparing his maiden political speech. A second look at teacher causes Dad to stray over to her from his homework. Like a blue movie bunny, she teases him into playing a game of hide-and-seek; once he has hidden himself in a thickly panelled cupboard she locks him in, then takes off to leave him to his fatal confinement.

The longest of these vignettes is devoted to the painter. To enter his scene, of course, neither the guise of school teacher nor concert-goer would be apt. The obvious role is that of model; and for model Moreau, the artist obligingly falls hard, enticed all the more by her glacial self-possession. He struggles to break through, to "reach" her. And we in the audience are fully caught up in the suspense, anticipating the relief we will feel when he circumscribes our heroine's sinister and murderous will. Unlike the others, this genial character seems a likely bet to succeed. But even as we are held in suspense about Moreau's powers of endurance for running out her set course, even as our wonder grows over the extent—the enormity—of her passion, we find ourselves guiltily hoping that she will in fact go the course, hold out. We are thus brought into emotional complicity with Truffaut's protagonist and her passion. At best we remain ambivalent, held in rather a mortified state of suspense up to the ultimately teasing moment when Moreau, posed as Diana, goddess of the hunt, stands on a pedestal with bow and arrow primed and aimed straight at the painter's heart. As her idolater smiles up at her, she lets loose her shaft.

Meanwhile, the gangster had got himself jailed and so appears to be safely out of harm's way. But Moreau plants clues that lead to her own imprisonment for the artist's murder, and we next see her as volunteer meal dispenser at what would appear to be a co-ed penal compound. In the last scene she enters the gangster's cell with a tray of food; a butcher knife attached to her belt dangles at her side like a sword in its sheath. The door hardly clangs shut on her when a scream of surprise and agony is heard. The door remains mercifully shut, sparing us the sight of the slaughter taking place behind it.

In his quest for the right word, the one Mr. Mudrick ought to have found is: decadent. *The Bride Wore Black* is an amoral triumph of style: a beautiful and disconcertingly satisfying film. The impassivity of the film's style is in itself a commitment to the style—engendered by her savage loyalty to principle—of the heroine. In the novel the heroine does not destroy the fifth man, though she baits a trap for him with a sawed-off shotgun. The whole point of the film, however, is the consistency of an action in which each fox is bagged. The completion of this action is the completion of the film. The style of the heroine, then, is the film. Nor does the film dawdle over the gruesome effects of her actions—in contrast to the novel, the sensationalist ingredients of which led Gershom Legman to include it among his examples of a sexless-sadistic literature of "bitch-heroines" of the Forties. Thus Legman describes the killings in the novel as "studiously gruesome." In place of such studious and random lingering over details, the film offers a grim, and perhaps more shocking, wit. The last death is the most perfunctorily treated; in the attention paid to the other four, the focus is on how the heroine each time manipulates the frenzies and calculations of romantic feeling in order to slay those who had short-circuited hers.

In *Fahrenheit 451,* the point of view on the cultist tendencies of cultural aspiration remained hazy in focus, tangential. There was also a certain haziness of definition in the focus on romantic feminism in *Jules and Jim* Precisely how far were we to see its heroine as justified in her leaps and tumbles? With *The Bride Wore Black* the focus is sharp and sustained: Truffaut sees the cult of passion, to which he here offers homage, as essentially barbarous. As barbarous as it remains none the less in continuing play in the culture of Europe. Truffaut's work further reinforces and updates the thesis of Denis de Rougemont's study, *Love in the Western World*; but where the scholar takes a critically adverse view of his subject, the artist is both more immediate and dispassionate in his involvement. His own cool devotion to styles and anti-careers which express a "terrible beauty" bears all the signs which have long been identified with the temperament and style of the aesthete.

---

**In a celebrated essay, Thomas Mann developed an equation between aestheticism and barbarism; and we may note of Truffaut's most memorable protagonists that they are both barbarous and fascinating.**

**—T. J. Ross**

---

In a celebrated essay, Thomas Mann developed an equation between aestheticism and barbarism; and we may note of Truffaut's most memorable protagonists that they are both barbarous and fascinating. They are characters whose hopes, based on the most intimate, intuitive and private forms of cultivated experience like reading stories or being in love, are violently wrenched into the principled, inflexible, and remorseless passions of an ideologue. Moreau in *The Bride Wore Black* is seen entirely as an ideologue of passion, driven by her sense of loss, rather than as a passionate lover (this is also mainly the case with her role in *Jules and Jim*). In mourning for her dream she becomes a killer of other dreamers, reducing her own relation to the variety of options and promises in human experience to the one-note, perversely consistent assertion of a "life-style." As we have seen, the anti-hero of *Fahrenheit 451* is brought, in the development and assertion of his style, to a similar ascetic desperation. So, too, it would seem, has Truffaut in his art: which remains brilliant yet crucially limited in its range and purview.

## Marsha Kinder and Beverle Houston (essay date Winter 1973-74)

SOURCE: "Truffaut's Gorgeous Killers," in *Film Quarterly*, Vol. XVII, No. 2, Winter, 1973-74, pp. 2-10.

*[In the following essay, Kinder and Houston consider the changing roles of women in Truffaut's films.]*

The central character in many of Truffaut's films is a profoundly seductive woman steeped in the archetypal mystery of the *belle dame sans merci*; she uses her sexual liberation like a *femme fatale,* to destroy a hero who is either sensitive and needy, or who mistakenly believes that his rationality will enable him to cope with her magic. Truffaut's earliest films present a combination of attraction and hostility in response to this kind of woman. In *Les Mistons* (1957), a group of boys tease and torment a young woman who is awakening their adolescent desires; they cannot forgive her amorous behavior with her fiancé, who later dies in an accident. In *The 400 Blows* (1959), the young boy is most vulnerable to his seductive, adulterous mother, who ends up by coldly rejecting him and confining him in an institution. In *Soft Skin* (1963), even the loving wife and mother finally turns and shoots her unfaithful husband. The *femme fatale* dominates *Jules and Jim* (1961), *The Bride Wore Black* (1968), *Mississippi Mermaid* (1970), and *Such a Gorgeous Kid Like Me* (1973). All these films reveal the magnetic power of the romantic fantasy, which is held in tension with a deflating comic irony. Though the power of this woman remains unabated throughout these films (in fact, she is completely triumphant in *Gorgeous Kid*), there is a shift in balance between the romanticism and the irony. After *Jules and Jim,* though the heroes are still hopelessly drawn into the seductive fantasy, Truffaut does not evoke a parallel reaction in the audience. The *femmes fatales* are presented with increasing ironic distance and the struggling heroes become more and more

absurd. This trend is continued in *Day for Night* (1973), Truffaut's latest film, where the ridiculous male victim is even more dangerous than the seductive female. As in *Gorgeous Kid,* their relationship is an object of mockery; but it no longer merits the central focus, for Truffaut at last introduces viable alternatives.

*Jules and Jim* is unique in its even balance between the two forces and between two views of Catherine (Jeanne Moreau) as the liberating muse and the irresponsible tyrant. This combination gives her omnipotence over the lives of Jules (Oskar Werner), the delicate German whose rationality leads him to study entomology, and Jim (Henri Serre), the tall, dark Frenchman who develops into the sensitive writer-adventurer. After tormenting the two of them with her changes of heart, she plunges her car off the end of a bridge in a fit of pique, taking Jim along for the fatal ride. Jules, though astonished, is basically relieved. Hitchcock provides the conventions and tone for *The Bride Wore Black,* where Truffaut moves further into irony, focusing on the aesthetics rather than the ethics of murder. Julie (again played by Jeanne Moreau) kills with style and verve, suiting the seduction and the *modus operandi* to each victim's tastes. As the "wronged woman" whose bridegroom was accidentally shot on the church steps by a group of men cleaning a gun, Julie is romantically justified in her vengeful hunt (one of her victims paints her as Diana, conveniently providing bow and arrow). When she is finally arrested, the only man left unmurdered is the one who actually fired the shot; however, she takes care of him in prison with a carving knife. Though she ends up behind bars, no one has escaped her power and, in her own terms and those of the film, she's a smashing success. In *Mississippi Mermaid,* the romance is provided by Catherine Deneuve's exquisite person, her clothes, and the exotic settings. Her appearance—in flowing white, and carrying a birdcage—delights the lonely plantation owner (Jean-Paul Belmondo) who has acquired his bride by mail. Later he learns that not only is she an impostor, but, in cahoots with her ruthless lover, she has murdered the real bride. Yet love conquers all, bringing forgiveness from her husband, who is moved to aid her in another murder. His continuing adoration becomes profoundly absurd as this divine Julie tries several times to murder *him*. Finally, he succeeds in being alone with his beloved in a mountain retreat—which she transforms into a deadly trap. In *Gorgeous Kid,* the audience is not for one moment allowed to share the romantic illusion of Stanislas Previn (André Dassolier), who longs to see the vulgar and utterly selfish Camilla Bliss (Bernadette Lafont) as a helpless but redeemable victim of a nasty childhood, and as a great *artiste* on her way to stardom. While she has the sexual energy and comic resilience of a Moll Flanders, the sociologist hero, to his ruination, forgets that she is a potent maneater who began precociously by killing daddy. After heroically proving her innocence for the one murder she didn't commit, this poignant fool winds up in jail, betrayed into taking the rap for her latest killing. In *Day for Night,* Alphonse (Jean-Pierre Léaud), a babyish movie star, is jilted by a scriptgirl named Liliane (played by Dani) who runs away with a stuntman in the middle of the shooting schedule. Although she is deceitful, irresponsible, and self-centered, Liliane is not a killer. Her actions, words, and clothes (she wears a T-shirt that labels her as a "Wild Thing") all clearly indicate that she is not the marrying kind. Early in the film she warns Alphonse, "It's stupid to be jealous, or else go all the way and commit murder." Yet, he constantly clutches at her snatch, insisting, "That's mine, keep it for me, in sacred trust." Her reasons for not wanting to marry him are sound: "He's a spoiled brat who won't grow up. He needs a wife, a mistress, a wet nurse, and a maid. . . . He wants the whole world to pay for his unhappy childhood." When she leaves him, he sulks like a baby and wallows in his misery. Clearly he loves to be the victim and chooses his women accordingly: "My affairs have always ended badly. I thought women were magic." His indulgent masochism makes him dangerous: he petulantly holds up the movie and tries to destroy the marriage of the woman who comforts him. While confirming this pattern, his role within the inner movie takes him all the way. He plays the young husband whose wife falls in love with his father; in the end, he shoots his father in the back.

In all of these films, a second important contrast is created between willfulness and accident. The films move toward a more skeptical view of chance, implying a rejection of the romantic view of lives shaped by fate. Prepared for their kismet by having seen the stone sculpture of the "eternal female," Jules and Jim meet Catherine and recognize the face; inevitably she becomes their muse, the feminine force destined to shape their lives. The film is full of chance meetings, especially the one where the three are joyfully reunited after finding each other in a movie theater. Catherine insists that the future of her relationship with Jim be determined by whether he succeeds in getting her pregnant. Although Catherine feels she can transform chance into a kind of creative spontaneity (as when she jumps into the Seine, electrifying the complacent men), this quality is revealed as a destructive willfulness, fully realized in the impromptu suicide. *The Bride Wore Black* focuses on a series of deliberate murders, framed by two accidents—the shooting of the bridegroom, which triggers the plot, and the final coincidence that brings hunter and hunted into the same jail. Yet, the single-minded determination of Julie's revenge somehow denies that her husband's death was accidental, and her extraordinary prowess suggests that the bizarre final encounter is also exactly as she planned it. As in these two films (as well as *Shoot the Piano Player* and *Two English Girls,* both of which open with comic accidents), the events of *Mississippi Mermaid* are launched by the fortuitous shipboard meeting of mail-order bride and the pair of killers. While pursuing Julie, the husband just happens to see her on TV.

Yet these accidents are overshadowed by the elaborately evil plotting of Julie and her lover, and the apparently willful masochism of the husband. *Such a Gorgeous Kid* places even stronger emphasis on the dangerous machinations of the killer, in contrast to the self-destructiveness of her victim. Camilla rationalizes her murders by calling them "fate bets" (e.g., take away daddy's ladder—will he notice or not?). In the 2-to-1 fate bet where she tries to exterminate husband and lover, she hears Fate whispering: "On your way, sister. Get the lead out and move!" Comic repetition reveals that this attitude is completely self-serving, allowing her to evade responsibility for her action. Similarly, Arthur, the puritanical exterminator, uses chance to rationalize his sexual transgressions; every time he and Camilla have sex, they must re-enact the accident that first brought them together. But on that occasion (as in most of her sexual exploits), Camilla is willing to take credit for her performance: "Fate was doing her part and I reckoned I must do mine." The sociologist, on the other hand, tries to exonerate her for both sex and murder. He uses clichés of love and psychosocial causality to ignore the blatant facts and deny Camilla's responsibility; finally, this attitude blinds him to what the audience clearly sees—that sooner or later she will do him in. From a romantic perspective, *la belle dame* in each of these films could be seen as the embodiment of Fate for her male victim. But Truffaut seems to move toward a psychological inevitability implicit in *Jules and Jim* and blatant in *Gorgeous Kid* and *Day for Night*; the selfish woman will manage to find a man who likes to suffer, and *vice versa*. In *Day for Night* the conflict between willfulness and accident is placed in the context of art. The director of the film (played by Truffaut) struggles against countless unforeseen circumstances in the attempt to shape and control his movie: the personal lives of the actors and crew keep intruding—marital problems, love spats, pregnancy, a dying son and mother. Finally, one of the stars (Jean-Pierre Aumont) is killed in an automobile accident, forcing the director to change the ending. At first he sets out to make a great work of art; but as the problems mount and he is pressured by time, finances, and people, his aspirations grow more modest—he hopes only to finish the film. Yet as we watch the process, we see that Truffaut knows how to take advantage of the accidents. As the players meet their crises, he incorporates their feelings and their dialogue into his script, enriching the meaning and value of his film. As an artist, he must develop a balance between control and spontaneity.

Truffaut carefully controls settings and environment to create the tone and particular interplay between romance and irony unique to each film. In *Jules and Jim,* the vulnerability of the young men is linked to the nostalgic setting where they formed their friendship—Bohemian Paris with its narrow stairways, miniature courtyards, picturesque streets and cafés. In the country, the romance is emphasized by the impressionistic visuals; sunny settings and sweeping long shots create a dream-like quality. The freeze shot is used to capture fleeting moments. The World War I footage and the Nazi book burnings of the late thirties provide a sharp contrast, reminding us that the romantic dream can lead to its own destruction. In *The Bride Wore Black,* each set is a test for Julie. She must select the appropriate costume and personality to dominate whatever scene she enters. At a swank cocktail party, she is dazzling in white. Going low-profile in a school teacher costume, she takes over the suburban household of her third victim, locking him in a narrow cupboard to suffocate. Her reclining portrait totally dominates the studio of the artist (victim #4); proud of her portrait (and her other accomplishments) she leaves it intact, which leads to her arrest. *Mississippi Mermaid* presents a series of extremely romantic settings: the lush vegetation and intense sunlight of the Reunion Islands; the charming old French house in the country; the decayed Antibes night club; the isolated mountain cabin. These environments provide a dreamy or exotic surface behind which the scheming, the sordid, and the deadly are played out.

---

**Truffaut carefully controls settings and environment to create the tone and particular interplay between romance and irony unique to each film.**

*—Marsha Kinder and Beverle Houston*

---

The opening visuals of *Gorgeous Kid* immediately contrast the worlds of Camilla and Stanislas. Behind the titles, color-filtered negative images rush by to light, bouncy music, evoking Camilla's superficial gaiety. Then suddenly, the film cuts to an image of a shelf of books and a quiet sound track, evoking the traditional humanism of the sociologist. The contrast is further developed through the two groups of sets. Scenes involving Stanislas take place in the musty confinement of an empty courtroom within the barred prison, or in his small, crowded office. In both locales, the camera frequently focuses on his tape-recorder, emphasizing the sociological investigation. Instead of soft visuals evoking romance, as in *Jules and Jim* and *Mississippi Mermaid,* the detailed realism of *Gorgeous Kid* invites irony. Camilla's life (developed largely through flashbacks) also takes place in the world of everyday reality, but with much greater color and variety. The first house she encounters is messy and crowded, and the lower portion is full of large, dangerous machines; later she chooses a rat-infested gothic castle for the scene of her double murder attempt. Other important sets present tawdry, sleazy version of the conventionally glamorous world of show biz: Sam Golden's night club (this third-rate European parody of an American rock star is immortalized in a huge billboard); ugly, crowded dressing rooms; back-stage

scenes with dancers grotesquely wigged and made up. When she escapes from prison and is running away from the high, grey walls, the camera suddenly pulls back, revealing her in the middle of a huge, utterly empty field, implying that her freedom will be as desolate as her confinement. This shot evokes the final image in *400 Blows* where, after the boy has fled from prison, the camera reveals him standing at bay; but the sea behind him is more romantic, more fruitful than this barren landscape. *Gorgeous Kid* is also full of symbols used with irony: the innocent white lamb that crosses little Camilla's path after she has finished off daddy; the neon sign of future promise that appears over her husband's shoulder as she is about to abandon him; the flexible piping wielded by her exterminator lover. Truffaut leads us to scorn both these heavy-handed symbols and our impulse toward psychologizing when Stanislas responds to Camilla's desire for a banjo as sublimated penis envy.

This spirit of parody extends to the whole process of sociological investigation. Frequently Truffaut offers glaring comic contradictions between the visual flashbacks and Camilla's account of her life (so carefully preserved on tape) as in the patricide where she innocently asks, "How could I know my father was up there?" or her "dignified" reaction to her husband's violence, when she claims she acted like the Queen of England, but in the flashback she screams, "You crummy motherfucker!" But Stanislas *never* learns the truth of the flashbacks, and even flees to avoid the corroborating evidence of the prison guard from Camilla's home town, who smacks his lips over her early sexual exploits. The film's typical shot is a zoom in to the face of a character, but this investigative technique is unrevealing. As the lawyer begins to seduce Camilla, the camera pulls in for a tight close-up of his earnest, smitten face. Only much later do we learn the extent of his exploitive corruption.

In many ways, *Gorgeous Kid* is the farcical flip-side of *The Wild Child*. Both films focus on scientific investigation, but treat it very differently. In the earlier film, the highly contrived, elegant, spare interiors emphasize the positive, humanistic values of rational inquiry, and the woodland exteriors are beautiful in their moon-lit mystery. Both films present an encounter between two people possessing entirely different bodies of knowledge—the civilized and the wild. *The Wild Child* focuses on what the nature boy has to sacrifice in order to acquire the benefits of civilization, thereby stressing the values of both worlds (and developing a tragic vision, since both choices involve loss). But the darkly comic *Gorgeous Kid* emphasizes the inadequacies of both worlds; the professor's civilized naivete does not protect him from Camilla the predator. As she tells him, when they've reversed positions around the prison bars: "Jail's funny. There's them that know and those that don't. So now you know, like me." On the other hand, Camilla's wild days are ruthless and homicidal; in a world like hers, no one would be safe.

In *Day for Night* the wildness and humanism are combined in the world of movies. As in *Gorgeous Kid,* show biz is a zany world full of tantrums and sexual antics. The jealous wife of the production manager shrieks at the big shots, "Your movie world, I think it stinks." Both stars proclaim that it's "a rotten life" and decide to quit movies for good. But we don't believe them—partly because the film stresses, in contrast to the wildness of their private lives, the great vitality and satisfaction in the creative effort. Practically everyone on the crew works hard from early in the morning to late at night. Instead of focusing on the glamour of the movie sets, Truffaut treats them with romantic irony. We go behind the scenes and see in action the cranes, weather machines, cameras, trick candles, and prompter cards, and then the camera moves in, hiding the equipment and emphasizing the illusions it can create. This comic breakdown of illusion not only deflates the sentiment (as we watch them shoot the climactic kitchen scene through a window streaked with phony rain, Truffaut shouts, "Remember, no sentimentality in this scene"), but also wins our admiration for the ingenuity and wit of the operation. After hearing that Liliane has run off with the stunt man, Joelle (who has just enjoyed a quickie with one of the crewmen who happened to help her change a flat tire) quips: "I'd drop a guy for a film. I'd never drop a film for a guy." Like Truffaut, she knows not only how to take advantage of fortuitous accidents, but also where the real satisfactions of show business lie. At the peak of Alphonse's absurdity, he steps into the hotel corridor in his nightshirt and poutingly declares to Truffaut: "I need money to go to a whorehouse." Instead, Truffaut gives him some good advice: "People like you and me are happy only in our work." As in *Wild Child* and *Gorgeous Kid,* we again see images of books in the hands of a civilized man; but instead of a scientist, this time it is Truffaut, the film-maker, exploring his roots in the works of Buñuel, Godard, Welles, Hitchcock, Bergman, Bresson, Rossellini, and Dreyer, with whom he helps to form an impressive cinematic tradition. *Day for Night* is Truffaut's *8 1/2,* his *Contempt,* his *Immortal Story,* his *Discreet Charm,* his Passion of *Anna,* and he explicitly places his work in the proper context, dedicating it to the Gish girls. The recurring dream sequences suggest that he has civilized his own "wild child" through his art. At first we see an anxious child with a cane running down a dark, deserted street (reminiscent of the opening in *Shoot the Piano Player*); in the next version the child is impeded by an iron gate (evoking images from *400 Blows* and *Wild Child*); but in the final dream sequence we discover that the gate is guarding a movie theater, which the boy successfully invades in order to rip off promotional stills from *Citizen Kane,* the masterpiece of a precocious genius.

In Truffaut's films, the basic polarities are developed along sexual lines: the men rely on will, civilization, and reason; the women are the wild, natural creatures who rely on chance. But paradoxically, the rational men are more susceptible to fantasy, and the women, who are the romantic objects, are more capable of cynical irony. The primary problem for most of Truffaut's men is that they never quite grow out of adolescence. Growing up is the main theme of *Les Mistons* and the autobiographical series, in which Jean-Pierre Léaud grows up in real time. His vulnerable sensitivity and his need for love are most sympathetic in *400 Blows* because he *is* a child who cannot be expected to deal with the selfishness and corruption of the world around him. As we watch him age in *Love at Twenty* and *Stolen Kisses,* he is clearly trapped in adolescent yearning. In *Bed and Board,* now married, he tries to live out his fantasy in an affair with an Oriental woman, but returns to wife and child. Actually, he is drawn to her parents, suggesting that his conception of maturity is a comfortable, static, bourgeois existence. In *Two English Girls,* Léaud provides an alternative to these films; though he still bears an autobiographical connection with Truffaut (being the author of a novel about two men in love with the same woman), he portrays a different character. The darling of an over-protective momma, responsive to every woman he encounters, he moves back and forth between burning passion and cool detachment. His feelings become the subject matter for his art, but his personal growth is stunted. Leaud is least sympathetic in *Day for Night* as the totally self-indulgent baby, who at one point retreats to carnival dodg'em cars as a means of expressing his frustration. In *Shoot the Piano Player* all the men are dangerous babies including Charlie, who manages to commit murder without dropping the role of kid brother. Truffaut seems to identify strongly with the child, which may be the source of his extraordinary skill with child actors. In *Gorgeous Kid* he mocks himself through the baby film-maker, whose unedited footage (which he is at first unwilling to release) documents Camilla's only innocence. The precocious film buff is treated more seriously through the dream sequences in *Day for Night,* where he is identified with the mature film-maker. (In one transition, the dream gate becomes the entrance to the film studio.) No matter what their age or experience, Truffaut's men are always capable of losing themselves in an adolescent passion that proves to be their downfall. In fact the only grown-up men in Truffaut's films are Dr. Itard in *The Wild Child* and the director in *Day for Night*—the only roles played by Truffaut himself. In *The Wild Child,* the boy is externalized and becomes a foil for the rational humanist. Truffaut abandons sexual romance, and confronts directly the conflict between the wild and the civilized, the child and the adult. This dualism is rendered more personal in *Day for Night,* which combines the autobiographical films with the others. Truffaut's two sides are separated and exaggerated: Léaud plays the ridiculous adolescent while Truffaut himself is the mature authority figure.

In developing his female characters, Truffaut has usually focused on the threat posed by women who try to break through social conventions and live out their own desires.

Until *Day for Night* Truffaut was unable to explore this aspiration without focusing on destruction. In his earlier films, as he moved from *Jules and Jim* to *Gorgeous Kid,* his attitude grew increasingly negative. This pattern is reflected in the women's names. In *Jules and Jim,* Catherine, who identifies with Napoleon, is linked by her name with the Empress of Russia, one of the greatest female tyrants of all time. Through her resemblance to the stone carving, Catherine is also infused with a timeless, mythic, female power that can manifest itself in any age or nation. In *The Bride Wore Black* and *Mississippi Mermaid,* the woman is called Julie, evoking Strindberg's play *Miss Julie*—which moved Catherine to jump into the Seine in protest; its freedom-loving heroine is, of course, destructive to men. The women in the later films no longer possess Catherine's mystic force; their power comes from either diabolical cleverness or ethereal beauty. In *Gorgeous Kid,* the heroine has sunk from empress to whore. Her combination of names—Camilla Bliss—evokes not Garbo's languid lady, but a comic sexuality, which is exactly the source of her power. Camilla's dreadful performances with banjo and song are grotesque in comparison with Catherine's charming little performance with guitar and lover in *Jules and Jim.* Camilla as siren could lure only the deaf, but the people seem to love it.

---

> **In Truffaut's films, the basic polarities are developed along sexual lines: the men rely on will, civilization, and reason; the women are the wild, natural creatures who rely on chance. But paradoxically, the rational men are more susceptible to fantasy, and the women, who are the romantic objects, are more capable of cynical irony.**
>
> —*Marsha Kinder and Beverle Houston*

---

In relationship to other women, Catherine is polarized with Gilberte, Jim's patient girlfriend, who is clearly no match for the heroine. The promiscuous young girl who smokes like a choochoo train deflates the seriousness with which Catherine takes her own adventures. But in *Gorgeous Kid,* only other women can see through Camilla. At first, Clovis's mother seems like a worthy opponent, but she is ultimately done in by Camilla's death trap. Sam Golden's explosive wife, however, kicks Camilla out of her husband's bed, and later tricks her with the corrupt lawyer. The prison matron can control Camilla, but only with institutional paraphernalia. Camilla is polarized with the mousey secretary who, though helpless, is able to see right through her. After their first encounter, she calls her a slut, and constantly tries to tell Stanislas what she really is—a tramp, a whore, a nymphomaniac. Far more accurate than the scientist, she pre-

dicts, "I bet she even raped the exterminator," and tries to convince him: "She's not a victim. She's a menace." But like Gilberte, she can only sit and wait.

These *femmes fatales* have in common a profound selfishness and irresponsibility, which make them a menace to everyone, especially men. The question arises, then, is it possible in Truffaut's vision for a woman to exercise seductive power and break out of conventional limitations without becoming a wild killer? If a basically "nice girl" transgresses sexual lines, either through self-sacrifice (like the wife in *Shoot the Piano Player* who goes to bed with a man to help her husband's career), or through a deliberate attempt to gain freedom (like the artistic sister in *Two English Girls*), she may have to pay with her life. And even nice girls are capable of being bitchy. In *Shoot the Piano Player,* the hyper-sensitive Charlie is horrified by the way Lena torments her lecherous boss. She helps to provoke the fight in which Charlie unwillingly kills him. Yet, like his wife who committed suicide, Lena is the one who is accidentally killed; again Charlie is the sensitive survivor.

There are, however, some exceptions. Truffaut's first positive unconventional heroine is the teacher (Julie Christie) in *Fahrenheit 451* (1966), a film that stands outside both lines of Truffaut's work. She succeeds in luring the book-burning hero (Oskar Werner) away from a dehumanizing, repressive society. But her rebellion serves a return to books, Truffaut's favorite symbol of traditional humanism. Not until *Day for Night* do we find a heroine (played by Jacqueline Bisset) who really takes an important step forward. At first, we suspect she's going to be another siren. Her name is Julie, and that usually means trouble in a Truffaut movie. She is a famous movie star who, after a serious "breakdown," married her doctor. Thus, when we see her interviewed by reporters, we expect her to conform to the stereotype of the neurotic, childlike sex symbol (epitomized by Anita Ekberg in *La Dolce Vita*). But instead she turns out to be a strong, independent, mature woman who works hard and well as a professional actress. Unlike other Truffaut heroines, she is noncompetitive and friendly with other women. Even though she is critical of Liliane's abrupt departure, Julie defends her to Alphonse and perceptively predicts that she will become the victim in her relationship with the stunt man. Julie's one mistake is sleeping with baby Alphonse—to keep him from falling apart or leaving before the film is completed. It may be adultery, but it's also team spirit. Her value system conforms to that of Truffaut and the costume girl—work and humanism above bourgeois mortality. But naughty little Alphonse responds to this mercy-fucking by calling her husband next morning to say: "I love your wife. I slept with her. Set her free." In this crisis, Julie suffers pain and guilt, for her older husband had left his wife and children in order to devote himself to her and to "make her into a responsible adult." Apparently he has succeeded, for Julie is able to cope with the situation, continue her work without holding up production, and even be forgiving and sympathetic with poor Alphonse. When her husband offers her a pill to calm down her nerves, which she tries to refuse, we begin to suspect that she really doesn't need him anymore; she seems to take it to reassure him of her dependency. Yet her generous spirit may again be somewhat self-defeating, for she has already told Truffaut that she's decided to live alone and he has quickly incorporated this decision as the right ending for his script. In the film within the film, she plays a young English girl who rejects her young husband (played by Alphonse) when she falls in love with his father (played by Alexander, the actor who dies in the car crash). She decides to leave them both; the deaths of her elderly lover in the film and the actor who plays the role suggest that in her own private life she may, indeed, live out this independence. The name of the inner film is *Meet Pamela,* which may evoke the 18th-century English novel *Pamela* (just as *Two English Girls* brought to mind the Bronte sisters, as several critics have suggested); in Richardson's novel, as in Truffaut's *Day for Night,* we meet a new kind of heroine.

In the earlier films dominated by *femmes fatales,* these lethal women seem to represent not womankind but a romantic individualism that is both seductive and dangerous. This vision is powerful because it encourages the individual to live out pure instinct and overcome limitations imposed by civilization. But what if the instincts are flawed? What if sublime intensity (through love and art) is also an invitation to violent death? These issues are developed most explicitly in *Jules and Jim,* but they are of central concern even in the farcical *Gorgeous Kid* where the habits of love are subtly linked with war. The film ends with the secretary sitting at the typewriter, sweetly waiting for her lover to emerge from prison, while the sound track offers the strains of "J'Attendrai," the famous French waiting song of World War II. In the midst of the melodramatic scramble to save the "innocent" Camilla, the camera gives us close-ups of Kodak kittens and puppies, reminding us how easily we can be manipulated by art. Truffaut pursues this mockery in *Day for Night* where the crew struggles to get a shot of an adorable fluffy kitten lapping up milk in a love scene. (Finally, they are forced to bring the scrawny studio cat as a stand-in.) Even on the set, no one can resist the helpless and adorable. If we are foolish like Stanislas, this is how we will react to Camilla. The power of art is further undermined when we meet the baby *auteur* who comes up with redeeming evidence. Camilla abdicates responsibility for her own acts and her betrayal of Stanislas in the name of art: her "sufferings" have made her an *artiste,* she claims, and Stanislas (if he survives) will be able to write the great novel.

*Day for Night* holds a very important position in Truffaut's canon. As content, the filmmaking process becomes his vehicle for expressing kindness, wit, and wisdom, the values

which must tame the wild. The film functions as a reaffirmation of art, allowing the full realization of Truffaut's powers that were present in his finest films—*Shoot the Piano Player, Jules and Jim,* and *The Wild Child.* It also succeeds in integrating the autobiographical films with the others and striking a balance between wildness and humanism, chance and willfulness. This development is also reflected in his treatment of men and women. Both Truffaut the director and Julie the actress are successful professional artists and responsible adults whose generous social virtues transcend the romantic illusion and selfish cruelty so pervasive in the earlier films.

## Gerald Mast (review date 2 April 1977)

SOURCE: "From 400 Blows to Small Change," in *The New Republic,* Vol. 176, No. 14, April 2, 1977, pp. 23-5.

[*In the following review, Mast compares* Small Change *to Truffaut's earlier film* The 400 Blows. *Mast states that although both films have similar subject matter,* Small Change *has a lighter tone.*]

Perhaps the most remarkable thing about François Truffaut's *Small Change* is that it was made by the same man who made *The 400 Blows.* In his most recent film, Truffaut returns to the subject and setting of his first feature film—the world of children and the schoolroom, the contrast between that world as children see it and as adults see it. But as opposed to the bitterness, the pain, the sarcasm in Truffaut's earlier contrast of childhood innocence with the shades of the adult prisonhouse, *Small Change* is a benign, bemused and accepting view of the inevitable contrast. The difference between *Small Change* and *The 400 Blows* is the distance that man has traveled.

> *Small Change* **is a thoroughly sunny film—literally and figuratively. Almost every scene has been shot in bright sunlight, dominated by the sparkling colors that sunlight produces on film.**
>
> —*Gerald Mast*

*Small Change* is a thoroughly sunny film—literally and figuratively. Almost every scene has been shot in bright sunlight, dominated by the sparkling colors that sunlight produces on film. It is a song of summer—of tanned faces, sparkling flowers, lush grasses, blue skies. When the children remove their outerclothing for medical examination, even their underwear becomes a visual sea of blazing color, silky, multi-colored mass of dazzling flags, banners and pennants.

The film's spiritual sunshine is as bright as its visual imagery. Rather early in the film a delightful four-year-old child plays near an open window on the fifth floor of an apartment house. The child's kitten walks gingerly on the ledge of the window sill, pushed there by the child himself, who is blissfully innocent of the cause-and-effect relationships of windows, heights and gravity. Using the classic devices of the cinema to build suspense (prolonging the slow but steady movement of the child toward that window ledge, viewing the child's progress from carefully edited, disturbing angles), Truffaut builds our fears for the safety and survival of the child.

And the child does fall (in the same kind of slow motion that Truffaut used for the climactic death plunge into the lake of *Jules and Jim* or the climactic death slide through the snow of *Shoot the Piano Player*). But in *Small Change* the slow motion summons not death but life. The tiny child turns a magnificent somersault in mid-air only to land safely on his back, as if he were executing some ordinary gymnastic stunt, tumbling on a soft mattress or bed of flowers rather than solid ground. The child giggles, unhurt, and exclaims, "I go boom."

Several images of this sunny film speak directly to those of Truffaut's less sunny past. One is a shot in the schoolyard where we briefly see a row of old wooden desks, standing on their sides, that have crossed the path of the clean, modern ones which are replacing them in the schoolrooms. Those old desks—dark, dull and inky brown (as compared to the shiny lightness of the new desks), with the traditional slits for pens and a hole for the inkwell, misshapen with age, defaced by the carvings and cravings of the generations who sat behind them—are of course a symbol of the older, traditional French education.

But they also specifically recall the desks that dominated the schoolroom of *The 400 Blows,* the identical kind of desk behind which the tortured and lonely Antoine Doinel was forced to sit. (And the identical kind of desk served the same function in Jean Vigo's *Zero de Conduite,* a major influence on Truffaut's original depiction of the schoolroom as a prison cell). Although the arrival of those new desks may imply the humane changes in the French educational system, they also imply the changes in Truffaut. In *Small Change* those old desks, and the resentment they imply, have been flushed out, exorcised, purged from the filmmaker's soul as well as his schoolrooms.

A parallel purging of the demons of his past underlies Truffaut's image of the dark, dilapidated, black-tar-paper house of Leclou, the maltreated boy. The house is an ugly

and drab anachronism in this film of bright colors and modern apartments, where the boy must leave the sunlight (which he prefers) to retreat into the cave. Significantly, Leclou is about the same age as the young Antoine Doinel. And significantly, Truffaut never permits his camera inside the dark house; its contents remain a mystery throughout the film.

Instead, Truffaut brings the darkness of that house into the sunlight, flushing out the witchlike mother and grandmother who torture the boy, exposing them to the light, and, apparently, packing them (rather than the boy) off to prison. Whereas *The 400 Blows* dwelt exclusively with the child's feelings of torture and pain—in effect, inside that witch's house—*Small Change* seems the filmmaker's final release of those dark phantoms within him to the light, where they can be exposed and erased in the same way that sunlight bleaches a roll of unexposed film.

This metaphoric link of light and film to Truffaut's autobiographical imagery is no accident, for Truffaut brought about his spiritual transformation by falling in love—with the cinema. Or rather, he accomplished it by being allowed to indulge his love, by discovering things about his love and thereby deepening it, and by his lover's rewarding him with both material and spiritual favors. The earlier *Day For Night* (1973) is, of course, Truffaut's most explicit sonnet to the cinema, in which he plays a film director who lovingly converts his life into his art and his art into his life.

The recurrent dream sequence of this earlier film leads directly to the sunny imagery of *Small Change.* The director's dream begins agonizingly enough, resembling the *angst*-laden dreams of such prototypic "art films" as *Wild Strawberries* and *8 1/2.* Like those earlier "art films" (and like his own earliest films), the dream is in black and white (although the rest of the movie is in color), and the boy in the dream looks decidedly like Antoine Doinel of *The 400 Blows* (and, like Leclou, is about the same age as Antoine in that early film). But the anxious, "art film" dream turns into a joke (like the child tumbling from the window); its ominous mood dissolves into laughter, for the great spiritual crisis is merely the theft of some stills from a theater showing *Citizen Kane.* Even the director's childhood memories are of the cinema (just as, in *The Clowns,* Fellini's are of the circus).

Truffaut's first three feature films, which established his reputation (*400 Blows, 1959; Shoot the Piano Player, 1960; Jules and Jim, 1961*), looked and felt enough like the other "art films" of that period to be taken as part of the same movement. They were moody, somber, dark, filled with tortured human souls for whom beauty, love and joy were extremely fragile and inevitably ephemeral. But immediately after this trio of critical successes (and commercial successes on the American "art circuit"), Truffaut's career went into a deep decline. His *The Soft Skin* (1965) was so elliptically told and so critically condemned that he feared he had lost touch with his public. He tried to regain that touch with a more commercial, technicolor adaptation of a literary property, Ray Bradbury's *Fahrenheit 451,* which constricted him with its demands to literary fidelity (and which was the only major literary work he was ever to adapt). And *The Bride Wore Black* (1968) was such an homage to Hitchcock, virtually a film dissertation, that the director seemed more chained to cinema that he loved than fired by his love of cinema.

Truffaut's work could only move forward by moving backward. In *Stolen Kisses* (1968) and *Bed and Board* (1970) Truffaut returned to Antoine Doinel. (He had previously glimpsed back at Antoine in a single episode of *Love at Twenty,* 1965, one of those multi-director, multi-episode movies that the "art movement" inexplicably spawned in the '60s.) Truffaut, like Antoine, and like Jean-Pierre Léaud who played him, was now 10 years older. Antoine was no longer a child, and the director no longer saw and spoke as a child.

Instead, Truffaut showed Antoine making the transition—sometimes clumsy, sometimes comic, sometimes touching—between the world of children and the world of adults, a world which tormented him so much when he was a child. Antoine found a vocation (after several bungling attempts), found sexual fulfillment (after several bungling attempts), and eventually found the meaning of home, wife, mistress, job, and all the other values of adult life. As Antoine matured, the director grew up with him, although Truffaut steadily kept several wry, ironic, and wise steps ahead of him (as opposed to his almost complete identification with the child's world in *400 Blows*).

Truffaut's autobiographical summation of the process is *The Wild Child* (1970), a film which does not seem autobiographical at all. On its surface, the film is a costumed case-study of an 18th century child who survived as a creature of the jungle, as one of Rousseau's noble savages, for his first 12 years, who was then captured by civilization and taught to live according to its rules. But Truffaut himself plays the teacher in the film, the man who trains and tames the child because he is committed to his beliefs, his vocation, and his love for the boy. The potential link between teaching and film directing becomes explicit in *Day For Night,* in which the director Truffaut plays resembles that earlier teacher in his love, patience, commitment, wisdom and control; it becomes implicit in *Small Change,* in which M. Richet, the sympathetic teacher played by Jean-François Stevenin, is clearly a surrogate for the director himself with similar spiritual and physical qualities to the director's previous screen roles. (Indeed, Stevenin played Truffaut's assistant director in *Day For Night.*)

*The Wild Child*'s autobiographical link is also clear in Truffaut's dedicating it to Jean-Pierre Léaud, the boy who was originally, like the director himself, a "wild child," and

was about the same age as this Wild Child, who grew up with the director while the director grew up with him. In *The Wild Child* Truffaut realizes that the life of natural spontaneity and pure freedom may seem fine from a child's point of view, but for adult human beings the "noble savage" is a poetic idealization. For people, civilization and society *are* nature. Wild children can't communicate with others; wild children don't feel love. (They certainly don't make movies.)

And so *Small Change* is not a Wordsworthian study of the child's world of spontaneity and innocence, imprisoned by adult society—and Antoine is literally imprisoned in *The 400 Blows*. Rather, it is a study of the way that education (in the schoolroom or the movie house, by school teachers or film directors) joins the child's sensibility and imagination with the community of human beings, to which all adults belong. True, the children still feel the adults as aliens in their world; they have more fun with Molière's *L'Avare* when the teacher is out of the room, for the play becomes part of their world of play. But Truffaut now sees "education" (be it in school, at the movies, or simply by growing up) as the means of bridging the gulf and effecting the synthesis of nature and civilization, spontaneity and society.

Such a thematic statement brings Truffaut's concerns very close to Jean Renoir's, the director who has been his greatest influence and inspiration. Like Truffaut, Renoir earned his early reputation with somber, philosophically disturbing films in black and white, and then made much sunnier late films in color. Like Truffaut, Renoir developed the conflicting claims of art and nature, claims which seemed mutually exclusive in the earlier films but came to be synthesized in the later ones—primarily by the director's realization that his commitment to his art was capable of making such a synthesis. Like Truffaut, Renoir was extremely prolific, a man who had fun making films, giving them a perpetual spirit of breezyness, casualness, easyness, and apparent artlessness.

This spirit has led many critics of both Truffaut and Renoir to dismiss several of the films (particularly the sunniest ones) as "minor" in comparison to the heaviest ones against which they are inevitably measured. But these comic works of acceptance, synthesis and sunshine (say, Renoir's *The River, The Golden Coach,* and *French Cancan* or Truffaut's *Stolen Kisses, Day for Night,* and *Small Change*) are perhaps as "minor" as *The Marriage of Figaro, A Midsummer Night's Dream,* or *City Lights.*

*The 400 Blows* ended without an ending—with what was, at the time, a startling and rare visual effect (subsequently debased into the most obligatory of movie and television clichés). Antoine Doinel has been ceaselessly running, away from the prison of his childhood life, toward what?—he doesn't know. He finally arrives at the edge of the sea and stops, for he can run no further. He turns back toward the land, in the direction from which he has been running. And the moving image suddenly freezes, stops, loses its motion and becomes a still photograph. Where can he go? What can he do? What is to come? What will he become? What is there to become? Truffaut's first feature film ends with a question mark—for us and for himself. *Small Change* is the most recent of his answers.

## François Truffaut with Hélène Laroche Davis (interview date January 1980)

SOURCE: "Reminiscing about *Shoot the Piano Player*: An Interview with François Truffaut," in *Cineaste*, Vol. XIX, No. 4, January, 1980, pp. 30-3.

[*In the following interview, Davis questions Truffaut about the making of* Shoot the Piano Player.]

At the end of a little street, filled with the voices of children playing in the schoolyard, are the offices of Les Films du Carrosse, François Truffaut's production company in Paris. This is where we first met in 1978 to discuss a project for a book on *Shoot the Piano Player*. Images of *The 400 Blows* and *Small Change* came to my mind as I entered the building. The walls of Truffaut's office were lined with books. He had a genuine love for books, especially old and rare books. After a warm and friendly welcome the conversation focused on *Shoot the Piano Player* and he responded with characteristic enthusiasm to the project. He immediately began searching for material about the making of the film— newspaper clippings, documents, and photographs, as well as his own recollections. He spent time telling me anecdotes about the actors, anecdotes always tinged with affection. He even began to design a cover for the book. This stimulated a renewed interest in the film on his part and resulted in a revival of it in 1982 with beautiful new prints made possible by the financial success of *The Last Metro*.

After several meetings in Paris and California, and an extensive correspondence, we decided to tape a formal interview in his office at Les Films du Carrosse in January 1980 (with technical assistance by Robert Ernest Tompkins). What follows is a translated and edited version of the interview. It deals with the making of *Shoot the Piano Player,* the casting of actors, the reaction of the press, and the affinity of Truffaut for the novels of David Goodis.

[*Cineaste:*] *What place would you give* **Shoot the Piano Player** *in relation to your other films?*

[François Truffaut:] No place. Simply, the second film I made. I have said before that this film was made in reaction

to *The 400 Blows,* which was so French, I needed to show that I had also been influenced by American cinema. It is so true that, at the time when I used to see Rossellini a lot—I had worked with him for years, and he had loved *The 400 Blows*—he told me he was going to see *Shoot the Piano Player*. I said, "Do me a favor, do not see *Shoot the Piano Player*," because I knew deep down that I had made this film almost against him, maybe.

*Was* **Shoot the Piano Player** *a victim of criticism against the New Wave rather than against the film itself?*

Yes. There was a polemic. I did receive the Young Critics Prize, a prize that existed only for two or three years. A few critics used to get together; Françoise Sagan was among them. They gave the prize to *Shoot the Piano Player* so they must have liked it. Other critics attacked it, as they did all the second films of New Wave directors. The idea was that these young men were capable of making a first film because they told the story of their childhood. But they could not make a second film. Thus we were refused entry into the profession.

*Your first three films—***The 400 Blows, Shoot the Piano Player,** *and* **Jules and Jim**—*were shot in CinemaScope. Why did you start with the large screen? Are you satisfied with the results?*

When we were critics at the *Cahiers du cinéma*, we defended CinemaScope against older critics and some French directors. In *The 400 Blows,* as in the first New Wave films, we were shocked by the simplicity of our technical means for shooting. We had only a noisy camera. We did not record the sound directly, only a vague test sound. We were shooting on real locations, with a reduced crew. Our means were so limited that we thought the result would not be a real movie. I was very surprised when *The 400 Blows* was selected for the Cannes Film Festival, because I told myself that at Cannes they should not show a film that had not been shot with direct sound. (However, if we go back to 1946, at the first Cannes Film Festival, they showed René Clément's *La Bataille du rail,* which must have been shot under these same conditions.) Yet it is strange to think that in 1959 in Cannes the three French films presented—*Orfeu Negro (Black Orpheus),* **The 400 Blows,** and *Hiroshima, mon amour*—had been shot without direct sound and outside a studio. In spite of the fact that he liked our films, Jean Renoir reproached us for not defending direct sound and was not satisfied with postsynchronization. In *The 400 Blows* it worked rather well because children are easily dubbed and Jean-Pierre Léaud is so well dubbed that you can't tell. With the parents it is not so good. Besides, there are parts shot with direct sound. For instance, the interview with the psychologist, which could not have been dubbed. I used this silent film system with postsynchronization up through *Jules and Jim*. Afterwards we switched to direct sound.

To answer your question on CinemaScope: by shooting *The 400 Blows* in scope, I had the rather naive feeling that the film would look more professional, more stylized; it would not be completely naturalistic. CinemaScope has this strange peculiarity of being an oblong window that hides many details. When someone moves in a room, if you have a square frame (1.33:1) you have all the details, what is on the table, on the wall, you judge the decor at the same time. Whereas in a CinemaScope room, the character moves abstractly, almost like in an aquarium. It is very clear in *Shoot the Piano Player,* during Théresa's confession, for instance. You are left with a face moving against a grey background. It becomes more abstract. And I liked that. I thought that in movies, we give actors absurd motivations to justify their movements, for instance, "Go over there to put out your cigarette in the ashtray." And I did not like these motivations. I believed that we could ask actors to move without a reason. That is why I liked CinemaScope. But afterwards, I abandoned CinemaScope when I learned that for *The 400 Blows* and *Jules and Jim,* 16mm reproductions were made, reducing the film to a flat screen. So CinemaScope, which had been invented to fight against television, was completely assimilated into the system; it was even harmed . We ended up seeing our favorite films massacred in movie theaters, with the top and bottom of the frame cropped. At first I thought that shooting a film in scope meant preserving it. Now that my films are shown on television cropped right and left, we know that there is no other solution than the 1.75:1 screen, which is the format used for most American films.

*What made you decide to adapt Goodis's novel?*

I read the book when it came out. It must have been at the time I was shooting *Les Mistons.* I had just written the scenario of *Breathless,* which I did not think I would make myself, but I didn't really know what I would do with it. It was a true story that happened in the Pigalle district, where I was born. At that time I discovered *Shoot the Piano Player* and I was enthused by the dialogue, the poetic tone of the book, the love story, the evocation of the past. I gave the novel to Pierre Braunberger, who was the only producer to take an interest in the young directors, and he liked it a lot and bought the rights to it. Then, while working on the adaptation, I felt that it was not right to start with this film. So I offered the script of *The 400 Blows* to him and he turned it down. He preferred *Shoot the Piano Player.* So I made *The 400 Blows* with my father-in-law who was a retired producer. My experience with *Les Mistons* had taught me that I worked well with children, that I was not quite ready for adults, and that I would work better on a subject close to me. After I discovered *Shoot the Piano Player* I started reading all of Goodis's books, looking for what they had in common. When we talk about the attraction that hard-boiled detective novels have for French people, we have to remember that it is

not only the American material in which we find a certain poetry, but, because this material has been transformed by the translation, we get an almost perverse pleasure out of it. For instance, I believe that the version of *Johnny Guitar* dubbed in French is more poetic than the original film, because there is a certain style, a theatrical style that touched us in France, a sentimental style. I think that Americans like *Johnny Guitar* now in retrospect, after the French reaction. For instance it is the only Western in which the characters say "*vous*" to each other. "*Jouez-nous un air, Monsieur Guitare.*" The French text of *Johnny Guitar* leads the film in the direction of classical tragedy.

There is also a rhythm of synchronization. When we like a book like *Shoot the Piano Player* it is difficult to explain why to an American audience. We even like the distortion. When I wrote an article for *Cahiers du cinéma* on Humphrey Bogart, I not only described what I liked in Bogart, but also paid homage to the two actors who used to postsynchronize his voice. Dubbing, like subtitling, is a technique that distorts and sometimes enhances the meaning. The printed word reinforces and makes things funnier. This is what happened to some of my films when they were shown at the New York Film Festival. It is the only time I ever saw my films in the States. I noticed more laughter than in France at certain points, just because of the printed words.

*Is that what happened with "Avanie et framboise," the Boby Lapointe song?*

It's quite different. Boby Lapointe's song was an accident. Pierre Braunberger didn't like this singer. He said that he did not understand a word he was saying and wanted to cut the scene. So, I said that I would subtitle the song so he could understand. I remembered the Canadian films of Norman McLaren that I loved. In these films, people in the audience were supposed to sing along. The words appeared syllable by syllable with a little ball bouncing on the syllable at the time it was to be sung. I had the syllables appear at the time Boby Lapointe pronounced them.

*Did you plan the changes of tone in* **Shoot the Piano Player** *because they appear in the novel, or did this style come spontaneously during the shooting?*

They were planned but they were reinforced in the shooting because I realized that I was faced with a film without a theme I clearly understood. In a movie like *Adele H.,* I know that I have the same idea repeated, that the heroine must be excessive in her character, which becomes obsessive. Whereas with a film with an unclear subject, such as *Stolen Kisses* or *Love on the Run,* some days I stress the comical side, other days the dramatic side. It is only when the film is finished that I know what it is about. The first time I showed *Shoot the Piano Player* to Jacques Rivette, he told me something that upset me. He said: "Do you realize that the main character of your film is a bastard?" I suppose that he said it because the character is a complete introvert who never expresses his thoughts, who is withdrawn, who refuses to intervene when he sees that women are victimized. Later on Rivette liked the film. But it is unusual to have so little control over what one is doing. The scenario was really a compromise between what I liked best in Goodis and other things I wanted to say. I found Goodis's book too chaste. The film is not as chaste as the book. I was advancing instinctively, according to the actresses, too. I was what was appropriate for these three very different women. I consciously wanted to show three portraits of women who can pass through a man's life. That part was planned.

Two years before making *Shoot the Piano Player,* I was a critic at the *Cahiers du cinéma* and *Arts.* There had been such an exaggerated reception and publicity for *The 400 Blows* at the Cannes Film Festival. We were in the news and were interviewed over and over. It did not go to my head, but it created a certain agitation in my mind after this disproportionate success of *The 400 Blows.* Afterwards in *Shoot the Piano Player,* there was an echo of the notion of celebrity and obscurity. It is reversed in *Shoot the Piano Player* since it is a famous person who becomes unknown. There are touches here and there of this feeling that troubled me. For instance, a small detail, when Aznavour is sitting and there are photographers who call him in a more and more familiar way: "Monsieur Saroyan, Charles, Charlie . . ." It is something that had struck me at the Cannes Festival, where Cocteau insisted that I go up the stairs with him before the showing of *The 400 Blows.* And Cocteau, who was very popular with the photographers, was hailed in that manner: "Cocteau, *Maître,* Jean . . ." It made me laugh. And the scene with Aznavour is an echo of this.

*Why did you choose to stress the poetic atmosphere of Goodis's novel?*

In spite of my admiration for Ernst Lubitsch, I have to disagree with him when he says "In a film one must never speak of the past." He thinks it is wasted time and we lose the audience. As for me I have always been moved by scenes that are told but not seen, or when there is a reference to the past. So there is that style of interior monologue in *Shoot the Piano Player* that excited me, and I wanted to reproduce it in the film. I was very meticulous. In a first version, I used Aznavour's voice. Later I realized that his voice was good for dialogue but not for voiceover, because his voice was not soft enough. Maybe we can see here something that is in several other films I made, that is, an attempt to include literary forms in the soundtrack of my films because I like commentary, flashbacks, and evocations of the past. Even the imperfect tense of a verb: when Marie Dubois says "You were here, you started playing piano again," it is very liter-

ary. It is funny because this film is an homage to American cinema, and at the same time this verb tense is not used in American cinema.

*What about the superimposed images in their first intimate scene, where this very literary dialogue takes place?*

The superimposed image expresses the passage of time. I liked the idea of intimacy being born. Also, because Aznavour's voice was not soft enough, I used only her words and no words from him. It emphasized the feelings and was rather well done.

*What about the role of Marcel Moussy in the writing of the screenplay of* **Shoot the Piano Player** *?*

His role was not as important as for *The 400 Blows* because *The 400 Blows* corresponded to the work he had done on television for a program called *If It Were You (Si c'etait vous),* which presented problematic social situations. For *Shoot the Piano Player,* I had not been able to explain to him why I liked the book, and he wondered why I wanted to make this film. In our first discussion, he wanted to establish social roots for the characters, to situate them socially. I realized that I could not answer his questions, because I felt like making an abstract film. In the script, there were precise references to places in Paris or in France and during the shooting I changed that, I decided to remain abstract; I wanted to say "the town," "the snow," to stress more the *Série Noire* aspect. There was an attempt on my part to oppose certain French films that adapted novels by James Hadley Chase taking place in America and transposed them to the French Riviera. That transposition was always done in bad taste. I did not want to give French equivalents for the locations. I wanted to remain abstract.

*So Marcel Moussy did not continue?*

After a few weeks, we gave up, and we said that we would work together on another script, some other time. Then I went to the Colombe d'Or at Saint Paul de Vence, and I wrote the script alone, up until the part when the characters have to leave Paris, because it was urgent to start shooting.

*How did you develop the character of Fido?*

There is a link with the previous film. The little boy had a part in *The 400 Blows.* He was in the classroom, tearing his notebook page by page because he had blotted the pages. Finally he had only three pages left. He made us laugh a lot. Also when he tried out for *The 400 Blows,* he imitated Aznavour, and he has a scene in *Shoot the Piano Player* where he imitates a singer as he walks away from the school.

*How did you choose the other actors?*

I had been moved by Aznavour [Charlie] when I saw him in Franju's film *La Tête contre les murs* (*Head against the Wall*). I liked his face, the way he moved. Nicole Berger [Théresa] I had known for a long time. She was Braunberger's stepdaughter. She had acted in several films, even, when she was very young, in *Le Blé en herbe* (*The Game of Love*) by Autant-Lara. She was a very sensitive girl, sad and interesting. Michèle Mercier [Clarisse] was not well known. She was a dancer in a few films.

Marie Dubois [Léna] was the result of a search. I was looking for someone to convey the idea of purity. I looked at many actresses and photos. Then Marie Dubois's picture came to my attention, but she never came to our appointments because she was very busy. Her agent told me that she was going to appear on TV and, when I saw her, I was sure she was the right one. She finally came at the last minute. We hardly had time to buy her a raincoat for her part and she started right away. Actually I named her Marie Dubois, because her name was not good for an actress. Her name was Claudine Huzé. [*In French Huzé is pronounced like* usé, *and means "worn out."*—H.L.D.] Since I liked that novel by Jacques Audiberti entitled *Marie Dubois*, which is a great portrait of a woman, I proposed that name to her, and she agreed to be named Marie Dubois. And Audiberti was very happy.

Albert Rémy [Chico] was the father in *The 400 Blows,* and I felt like giving him a nice role, because he was my friend and I was embarrassed to have him this harsh role in *The 400 Blows.* There was also a clown side to him, very innocent, pure comic, which I wanted to show.

The gangsters are Daniel Boulanger [Ernest], who had played a small part in *Breathless* by Godard and was Philippe de Broca's scriptwriter, as well as being a novelist. Claude Mansard [Momo] was from the theater. He had acted in many plays by Ionesco, a very emotional actor. The two gangsters looked like two big cats. I was ill at ease with these gangsters. I had grown up in Pigalle and I only had bad memories of them. One night when I was very young, I was alone at home because my parents had gone out. There were guys making noise under my window, so I threw a pan of water on them. They took it badly and came up and kicked the door. I was dying of fear, and I pushed a heavy armoire against the door. When my parents came home I got in trouble because the door had been damaged. Those guys were gangsters. Often there were shots in the middle of the night in Pigalle. It is snobbism on the part of artists to like gangsters. There is no reason to like them, they are bad guys. During the war, they often worked with the Gestapo. That is why I made them comical. I never included gangsters in my later films, even those taken from the *Série Noire*, like *The Bride Wore Black* and *Mississippi Mermaid.*

The scene in the street with the passerby is taken from another book by Goodis. The title escapes me. Catherine Lutz [Mammy] had never acted before; I liked her a lot. She worked in a movie theater, I found her beautiful, with a Marlene Dietrich look. Her facial structure was beautiful. She acted again in *Stolen Kisses,* where she was a detective. Serge Davri, who played Plyne, was crazy. I first noticed him in the music hall, where he is still doing the same act after thirty years. He breaks plates on his head as he recites poems. Sometimes he is funny, and sometimes it is a fiasco. He made me laugh, that's why I chose him. But it was difficult to work with him, because some days he refused to work.

*We noticed a difference in the timing of the various copies of* **Shoot the Piano Player**. *How do you explain that?*

People are not accurate in the timing, they print anything. But I did make mistakes and changed a few scenes. I was ashamed of the dialogue in the car [*when the gangsters discuss women*—H.L.D.], which I found too raw. So I put so much traffic noise in the scene that one could not hear the dialogue. People blamed me for it, and I made a second cut where you could hear better. There may be other short scenes cut or moved. There was a scene in which you saw Aznavour in a Monoprix buying a pair of stockings for Marie Dubois. That scene was to be accompanied by a song in the Monoprix, a very famous song by Tino Rossi called "*Petit Papa Noel*." But it took very long to obtain the rights for this song and, when we finally got them, I was in the middle of editing and I had decided to cut the scene. Probably those timing differences are due to small things like this. It is also very difficult to make films with Pierre Braunberger at the Films de la Pléiade because it is quite disorganized. It often happens that there are several versions of a film. One time **Shoot the Piano Player** was on French television, and for four minutes a scene was shown with the soundtrack from another scene. Nobody noticed, because they thought it was another pretentious experiment of the New Wave. I was furious. But this illustrates the chaos of the Films de la Pléiade and Pierre Braunberger—in spite of his love of cinema, which is real.

*How much did the film cost?*

I think the film cost $150,000 at the time.

*So a budget was imposed on you?*

Yes, but although I was not working in luxury, it was all right. In black and white we do not pay so much attention. Of course some sets were ugly. Everything was done sparingly. At one point, we needed a cocktail party in the film; we needed a crowd. It was decided to use a cocktail party that had been organized to publicize the film. People had to be filmed secretly.

*In general did those restrictions hinder you?*

No. I was rather carefree and happy then. I had made *The 400 Blows* with a lot of anxiety because I was afraid that the film would never come out, that people would say that, after having insulted everybody as a critic, I should have stayed home. Whereas *Shoot the Piano Player* was made in euphoria thanks to the success of *The 400 Blows.* It was the discovery of some unusual material that I did not master, that I did not understand. But there was a great pleasure in filming, much greater than in *The 400 Blows,* where I was concerned about Jean-Pierre Léaud. I was wondering if he would show up each day, or if he had had a fight and would have marks on his nose. With children we worry more because they do not have the same self-interest as adults.

## Stuart Y. McDougal (essay date 1981)

SOURCE: "Adaptation of an Auteur: Truffaut's *Jules et Jim* (1961) from the novel by Henri-Pierre Roché," in *Modern European Filmmakers and the Art of Adaptation,* edited by Andrew Horton and Joan Magretta, Frederick Ungar Publishing, 1981, pp. 89-99.

[*In the following essay, McDougal argues that Truffaut's adaptation of Henri-Pierre Roché's novel* Jules et Jim *is both true to the novel and contains autobiographical aspects of Truffaut's life.*]

> The film of tomorrow seems to me even more personal than a novel, individual and autobiographical, like a confession or a private diary.
>
> *François Truffaut, 1957*

In 1956, François Truffaut was browsing in a Paris bookstore when his eyes fell on a copy of *Jules et Jim* by Henri-Pierre Roché. He was immediately drawn to the title and, as he studied the jacket, intrigued to discover that it was a septuagenarian's first novel. At the time Truffaut was twenty-four and supporting himself by writing film criticism for *Cahiers du Cinéma* and *Arts.* He purchased the novel, took it home, and pored over it until, like a character in *Fahrenheit 451,* he knew it by heart. Later that year, in a review of Edgar Ulmer's film *The Naked Dawn,* he wrote:

> One of the most beautiful modern novels I know is *Jules et Jim* by Henri-Pierre Roché, which shows how, over a lifetime, two friends and the woman companion they share love one another with tenderness and almost no harshness, thanks to an esthetic morality constantly reconsidered. *The Naked Dawn* is the first film that has made me think that *Jules et Jim* could be done as a film.

Henri-Pierre Roché received a copy of the review and sent Truffaut a note of thanks. Thus began a lengthy correspondence. Among the subjects discussed was the possibility of filming *Jules et Jim.* Like many of the *Cahiers* critics, Truffaut was already dreaming of putting his ideas into action.

The following year, Truffaut adapted "Les Mistons," a short story by Maurice Pons about a group of adolescents in the south of France who discover the mysteries of sexuality during the course of a summer. Roché viewed the film and found that it confirmed his belief that Truffaut had the proper sensibility to adapt his novel. However, because of "circumstances and economic arguments," Truffaut filmed his own work of autobiographical fiction, *Les Quatres Cents Coups* (*The 400 Blows*; 1959), rather than Roché's. During the filming, Truffaut gave a copy of *Jules et Jim* to Jeanne Moreau. She was most enthusiastic about the book and saw a strong role in it for herself. Truffaut mailed her photograph to Roché, who immediately replied: "I absolutely must meet her: bring her to me." Shortly thereafter he died, without meeting the living embodiment of Catherine and without ever seeing Truffaut's first feature film, *The 400 Blows.*

Several years later, Truffaut was able to film *Jules et Jim.* Although Roché's novel forms the basis of his film, Truffaut also draws upon incidents in his own life and in particular his relationship with Roché. *Jules et Jim* becomes both an adaptation of Roché's novel and the "confession of private diary" of its director. This film shows how an auteur can adapt the work of someone else and still make a very personal statement.

In the second half of the film, Jim recounts to Jules and Albert a story about a soldier who meets a girl briefly on a train and begins a correspondence with her. The girl responds to the soldier's letters by sending her photograph. As the weeks pass, the exchange of letters becomes more and more frequent and their relationship becomes increasingly intimate. They decide to marry, and the soldier requests permission from the girl's mother. Then, suddenly, the soldier receives a head wound. He dies in the hospital the day before the armistice, without ever seeing the girl again.

To many viewers this story seems out of place, and yet it is central to an understanding of Truffaut's movie. The soldier was Guillaume Apollinaire, and the incident is related in his letters to Madeleine Pagès, collected in *Tendre Comme le Souvenir.* An accomplished poet and friend of painters in addition to being a prodigious correspondent, Apollinaire could easily have served as a model for the Jules and Jim of prewar Paris. Apollinaire's story, as Truffaut presents it, leads us in two directions: both inward to the world of the film, and outward to Truffaut's personal experience.

The incident is changed in one significant respect: Truffaut makes the soldier die before being reunited with the girl, and thus his dreams are never tested by reality. Apollinaire did die from a war wound, but at the time of his death he was married to a woman he had met while convalescing, after he had severed his relationship with Madeleine Pagès. By altering the story, Truffaut creates a strong parallel to his relationship with Roché. Like the soldier in Jim's anecdote, Roché died before he could see the dreams of his correspondence realized.

Throughout the film, Truffaut identifies Jim with Roché and Jules with himself. Jim remains close to Roché's characterization in the novel, but Truffaut makes him, rather than Jules, the novelist. Jules is no longer Jewish, as he is in the novel, nor nearly so neurotic as the suicidal character of Roché's creation. Jules shares Truffaut's fascination with language and finds expressions of his own emotions in literary sources (such as Baudelaire and Goethe) at crucial moments in the film. Although awkward with women, he is clearly "the man who loved women," capable of sketching his beloved's face on a restaurant table à la Matisse. His fantasy about writing a novel with insects as characters (and the profusion of metaphors in the second half of the film comparing Catherine to an insect) is less surprising when one learns that Truffaut had used some of the profits from his first films to produce a film on the sex life of insects for none other than the son of Henri-Pierre Roché.

Catherine's character has undergone the greatest change. While Roché's Kate is German, Truffaut has made Catherine French to align her more closely with Jim. Throughout the film, she identifies with Napoleon and therefore *La France*. The many women of different nationalities who surround Jules and Jim in the novel have been dropped, and Catherine's role has been made correspondingly larger. Incidents involving deleted characters (*e.g.*, the burning of the letters or the translation of Goethe's poem) have been transferred to Catherine. Whereas in the novel two women represent "sacred love [and] profane love" to Jim, Truffaut's Catherine is both sacred and profane, "a woman," in Jules's words, "we all love . . . and whom all men desire." She speaks the first words in the film: The screen is dark and we hear her unidentified voice, intoning lines not from *Jules et Jim* but rather from Roché's later novel, *Les Deux Anglaises et le Continent,* which Truffaut filmed in 1971. The viewer is immediately disoriented since it is impossible to identify either the speaker or the subject, but the lines articulate a major theme of the film as well as asserting the importance of the verbal in a visual medium. In a sense Catherine has the final word as well, since her song ("Le Tourbillon") echoes in Jules's head as the movie ends.

Although Truffaut has simplified Roché's novel, he has retained an astonishingly large amount of its language.

Truffaut's love of words nearly equals his love of film, and here his fidelity to Roché is the greatest. Indirect discourse becomes direct speech, and important speeches, like incidents, are transferred from deleted characters to one of the principals or to the narrator. It is a tribute to Truffaut's skill that his characters remain consistent.

Truffaut has retained Roché's narrator, but his presence naturally becomes much more obtrusive in the film than it was in the novel. He distances us from the action and makes us continually aware of the artifice involved in the storytelling. His is a frequent voice in the film—summarizing action, providing transitions, and giving us access to the thoughts of Jules and Jim.

Truffaut is faithful to the general outlines of Roché's novel, but he condenses, selects, and even adds, all the while developing the material in a very personal way. The initial encounter between Jules, Jim, and Catherine is taken from Roché's novel, but Truffaut makes significant alterations and additions. Roché has the pair spend months studying at the Bibliothèque Nationale in Paris before they feel prepared to visit Greece. Once in Athens, they perceive resemblances everywhere between statues and the women in their lives: "The Wingless Victory reminded them of Lucie; a female combatant on a pediment, of Gertrude; and a dancing girl on a vase, of Odile." After a month there, they are joined by Albert, a friend of Jules who is a painter. Among his collection of sketches and photos is one of a "goddess being abducted by a hero." The trio seek out this statue and are captivated by it. Jules and Jim return to Paris "feeling sure that the divine was within human reach." Months pass, and Jules receives a visit from three German girls. One of them, Roché notes, "had the smile of the statue on the island," and Jules falls in love with her immediately.

Truffaut makes the discovery of Catherine symptomatic of the confusion of art and life which pervades his protagonists' lives. The sequence opens in Albert's Paris apartment, where Jules and Jim have come to view a slide show. Truffaut spent his own childhood in darkened cinemas, and it is appropriate that he should have Jules and Jim discover their ideal woman in a similar environment. Her model is revealed through the successive refinements of different artistic media: the photographic reproduction (slide) of an "imitation" (statue) of a woman dead for many centuries. As spectators, we experience this process with them through yet another medium: film. To heighten our awareness of the distances involved here and to emphasize the element of artifice, Truffaut has the second half of the sequence narrated entirely. Jules and Jim pursue this statue at once; Truffaut dissolves directly from the slide of the statue in Albert's apartment to a shot of Jules and Jim on the island, and the juxtaposition substantiates our feelings about their impetuosity. Then, through a subjective camera, we participate in their exploration of the terrain until the statue is located. A series of shots of the statue recapitulates the shots in Albert's apartment, while the narrator assures us that if ever they met such a statue, "they would follow it."

Truffaut adds an important scene before the meeting with Catherine. Jules and Jim are boxing in a gymnasium. Jim offers to read from his novel, which, it becomes clear, is quite autobiographical. Jules listens intently and then declares that he would like to translate it into German. In Roché's novel, Jules is also writing fiction, but without the autobiographical intent of this scene. Truffaut makes Jim the novelist to identify him with Roché; the novel he reads from resembles nothing more than *Jules et Jim*. Jules, like Truffaut, chooses to "translate" the work from one language (or medium) to another. Their activities here contribute to their own characterizations, but also illuminate the life of their creator and his problems in the making of this film.

For the meeting with Catherine, Truffaut takes a scene from early in the novel, in which Jules proposes a toast to the abolishment of all formalities while drinking with Jim, Lucie, and Gertrude in Munich, and transfers it to Jules's apartment. As the three women descend the steps, the camera lingers on Catherine's face. Here is the actualization of the ideal they have discovered in art. A series of close-ups duplicates the earlier shots of the statue, which duplicated the slides in Albert's apartment. Once again the viewer participates in their discovery. To strengthen the visual parallels, the narrator comments on the likeness, noting that "the occasion took on a dreamlike quality." The scene is a perfect fusion of the literary and the purely cinematic.

Truffaut's adaptation of Roché's novel reflects strongly his relationship with Roché, but it is personal for other reasons as well. Through his use of cinematic allusions and through an extraordinary variety of cinematic techniques, Truffaut presents the viewer with a cross-section of some of the films in his life: Renoir's *Une Partie de Campagne* (1936), in the early shot of Jules and Jim rowing with two women on the river; Welles's *Citizen Kane* (1941), in the sequence at the theater as well as the use of musical themes identified with characters; Murnau's *Sunrise* (1927), in the scene where Jules saws logs on the terrace of his German home; Ophuls's *La Ronde* (1959), in the scene before the mirror when Jim and Catherine spend a night at a hotel before his return to France; Chaplin's *The Kid* (1921), in Catherine's masquerade; Hitchcock's *Under Capricorn* (1949), in the use of the moving camera when Catherine tries to seduce Jules after she has taken Jim for her lover; Hitchcock's *Shadow of a Doubt* (1943), with the superstition of the hat on the bed; and Griffith's *Intolerance* (1916); among others. Moreover, there is a production still accompanying both the French and English editions of the film script showing Truffaut directing in a costume which recalls D. W. Griffith, just as there is a painting within the film of Jules as Mozart. And Jules, as he is leaving the Left Bank's Cinéma des Ursulines with Catherine, pauses momentarily before a 1928 cover from the French periodical *Du Cinéma* an important predecessor of *Cahiers du Cinéma,* which helped support Truffaut as a young critic. Truffaut has lived his life in and through films, and *Jules et Jim* chronicles some of these privileged moments.

The tribute to Chaplin builds upon separate incidents in Roché's novel: Catherine's masquerade, and her footrace with Jules and Jim. Truffaut combines a homage to *The Kid,* by dressing Catherine like "the kid," with a homage to its creator, by giving her a mustache like Chaplin himself. In addition, the music helps evoke the period of the great silent films. The scene captures Catherine's need to dramatize and to masquerade. But with all its gaiety, it is filled with ominous undertones. The setting contrasts markedly with the early shots of Jules and Jim frolicking over a bridge in the countryside, where the simple, pastoral beauty of nature was an appropriate metaphor for their relationship. Here the trio passes a barred fence and then enters a totally enclosed industrial bridge with iron girders and chain-link fencing, suggesting confinement and entrapment. Catherine's behavior substantiates the feeling created by the *mise-en-scène*.

Catherine's first leap into the Seine foreshadows the plunge with which the film concludes. Here too, Truffaut takes significant liberties with his text and incorporates several important homages. Truffaut prefaces the sequence with an original scene at a theatrical performance to which Jim has invited Jules and Catherine. At the conclusion of the play, Catherine claps with an enthusiasm and persistence that recall a similar scene in *Citizen Kane* (1941). The three leave the theater, and Catherine states the reasons for the heroine's appeal in terms which define her perfectly: "She wants to be free. She invents her life at every moment." Catherine identifies with the liberated heroines of Strindberg, an identification which also points to her propensity to dramatize, and that is exactly what she does in the scene which follows. Jules and Jim pay little attention to her and instead discuss the play in a cerebral manner, with Jules quoting Baudelaire on the nature of women. To regain their attention, Catherine takes a dramatic jump. Truffaut has provided a motivation for Catherine's action which is lacking in the novel; it is a protest against both the crippling intellectualism of Jules and the personal neglect which accompanies it. Roché's woman calls for help after jumping, but Truffaut's Catherine manages extremely well on her own. She succeeds by this gesture in becoming once again the focus of their attention and in inspiring Jim to attempt to capture this magnificent action in a drawing. Truffaut's characters continually make art out of the materials of their lives, and model their lives on works of art.

Truffaut's love of film also reveals itself in his use within *Jules et Jim* of actual footage from earlier films. Old footage of Paris, for example, adds an important note of authenticity to his period recreation. The lengthy footage of World War I marks a decisive break between the gaiety of prewar Paris and the more somber life which follows. The war, which plays a negligible role in Roché's novel, looms large in the film. Truffaut stretches this footage to the dimensions of his wide screen, and projects silent footage at sound speed; as a result, the images become distorted and the movement of the figures appears mechanized. Not only does this increase our sense of distance from the war, but it becomes a telling comment on the futility of combat.

Truffaut also uses the war metaphorically. The war separates Jules and Jim, who fight on opposite sides, each with the fear of killing the other. Yet when peace comes, their relationship becomes strained because of Catherine, and their own personal warfare begins. Tensions are symbolized by the difficulty of communication, and failure by the inability to create. Again, the relationship between art and life is close.

> [In *Jules and Jim*,] Truffaut . . . uses the war metaphorically. The war separates Jules and Jim, who fight on opposite sides, each with the fear of killing the other. Yet when peace comes, their relationship becomes strained because of Catherine, and their own personal warfare begins.
>
> —*Stuart Y. McDougal*

Truffaut makes the different nationalities of the trio serve as bonds and barriers. At one point in the novel, Jim laments that he and Catherine "only communicated in translation," and this becomes the case in the film both with Jules and Catherine and with Jules and Jim. Catherine is capable of translating Jules's recitation of a stanza of Goethe's "Rastlose Liebe" into French for Jim, but she prefers to read Goethe in French and has a copy of *Les Affinités Électives* in Germany which Jim borrows. In Germany, Jules discourses at length to Jim on the difficulty of translation and the importance of this activity for communication: "You will note that the words cannot have the same significance in two different languages as they don't have the same gender. . . ." He then invites Jim to transcend national boundaries and learn "to appreciate German beer," but typically, Catherine interrupts: "Jim is like me, he's French, and he doesn't give a damn about German beer." She follows this by reciting a litany of French wines, which serves as a preface to a quiet taunt: "Catch me," she murmurs to Jim as she flees from the house. Thus, her relationship with Jim begins on a note of linguistic and

nationalistic unity. But the importance of translation as an activity with strong parallels to cinematic adaptation has been reaffirmed.

In Roché's novel, the problems Catherine and Jim encounter are principally legal, as they struggle endlessly with the Germanic legal system while she and Jules seek a divorce. Truffaut symbolizes their difficulties by their inability to create a child. Their failure to conceive separates them. When, surprisingly, Catherine becomes pregnant, she suffers a miscarriage. As the narrator notes soberly: "Thus between the two of them, they had created nothing."

For Catherine, having a child by Jim would be a way of transcending time. When she is unable to do this, she steps out of time by committing suicide and taking Jim with her. Like Jules, we bear witness with horror as her car plunges downward in a broken arc. At significant moments in the film, such as this one, Truffaut is able to do what none of the characters can achieve in their lives: manipulate time cinematically by slowing and freezing the moments of descent, just as he had done in Catherine's earlier jump into the Seine, which this scene evokes. In the quickly paced first half of the film, time seems to stand still. Characteristically, Jules records the passage of time with an hourglass, whose form remains the same while the sands shift from one side to another. Neither he nor Jim appears to age during the more than twenty years chronicled by the film. Jim is living with Gilberte and still thinking of getting married, as he was when the film began. Jules attends the cremation in the same striped suit he had worn on his first outing with Jim and Catherine. Jules and Jim live for art and thus seem to be eternally young, as Roché must have appeared to Truffaut. Only Catherine expresses a fear of aging, and her appearance gradually alters from one of romantic lushness to Nazi severity in the more slowly paced second half of the film. Truffaut signals the passage of time not by changes in his characters' appearances but by the presence of works of art which transcend time.

Chief among these are the different paintings by Picasso, which can be dated only by the time of their creation. The other means are the films we see within this film—the newsreels of the war and the burning of books.

Jules and Jim make creation a part of their daily lives: Jim attempts to capture his early experiences by creating the Jim of his novel, Jules sketches the woman he loves on a cafe table, Jim observes Catherine's first plunge into the Seine and desires to make a drawing of it. Catherine shares their continual need to shape the incidents of their lives into anecdotal stories, and few films contain as many narrated stories as this one. But while it is salutary to transform the materials of one's life into works of art, there is a danger in doing the reverse. Jules and Jim's discovery of Catherine is a good example of this, and Catherine herself aspires to model her entire life after works of art. In Roché's novel, Catherine keeps a diary and later achieves some success as a writer and illustrator. Truffaut eliminates this aspect of her creativity and instead shows her attempting to make her life a work of art. Albert's song, "Le Tourbillon" ("The Whirlwind"), is both about her and characteristically performed by her; it is a perfect summation of her enticing and capricious nature. But Catherine realizes that her life, however artful, is transient, and she seeks to overcome this by having a child with Jim.

Within the world of the film, none of the characters succeeds in creating a lasting monument, yet their aspirations are realized by the work of Roché and then Truffaut. We have no way of evaluating Roché's fidelity to his own experience, although his preoccupation with the subject of fidelity in the novel demonstrates its importance for him. It clearly has a bearing on the nature of adaptation, and on this score we are able to assess Truffaut's achievement. Truffaut adheres to the contours of Roché's plot and displays an extraordinary fidelity to the book's language. He also honors his relationship with Roché by creating strong parallels between it and Jules's relationship with Jim. His film resembles a series of reflecting mirrors: a semiautobiographical film creating a work of art out of a semiautobiographical novel which creates a work of art out of the lives of the author's friends, who themselves are engaged in the same process. Truffaut's film is an affirmation of the powers of art to immortalize experience, and it joins the august company of those timeless works which he has incorporated into it.

## Bart Testa (essay date 1982)

SOURCE: "François Truffaut," in *Religion in Film,* edited by John R. May and Michael Bird, University of Tennessee Press, 1982, pp. 210-18.

*[In the following essay, Testa considers religion and spirituality in Truffaut's work, contrasting his cosmology with the beliefs of his mentor André Bazin.]*

Among film makers whose work has received treatment by critics considering the religious dimension of cinema, a particularly complex figure is François Truffaut. The leading student of André Bazin, Truffaut reflects in his films his own belief that human consciousness and experience must be bound to language and culture. For Bazin, human consciousness is directly grounded in Being, and for him the special role of film is to express this grounding in a manner free of "those piled-up conceptions, that spiritual dust and grime," which our culture has imposed upon our grasp of reality. In contrast to his mentor, Truffaut believes rather that experi-

ence is always mediated by culture and that human consciousness is constituted by language. This conviction is increasingly evident during the progress of Truffaut's career, attaining mature expression in *Fahrenheit 451* and *The Wild Child.*

> The leading student of André Bazin, Truffaut reflects in his films his own belief that human consciousness and experience must be bound to language and culture.
>
> —*Bart Testa*

Bazin's film theory was evolutionary. He argued that the tradition of "faith in reality" exerted pressure on the history of film such that there was a gradual withering away of cultural accretions on the essential photographic realism of the film medium. Bazin expressed this theory by writing a history of film style that showed the realist tradition progressively displacing the tradition based on "faith in montage and the image." Certain of Bazin's views come to forceful expression in Truffaut's critical writings, as, for example, in his discussion of two adaptations of Georges Bernanos' novel *The Diary of a Country Priest,* one by the leading French scenarist Jean Aurenche (it was never filmed) and the famous version later made by Robert Bresson.

In his comparison, Truffaut reveals how close he is to Bazin and even establishes his argument by drawing upon Catholic phenomenological film criticism that had extended Bazin's realism into an explicitly theological approach to film. He draws on this critical school's position that film can go beyond psychology to express religious consciousness. Truffaut adapts this view to support his own contention that the *auteur* can share and express Bernanos' religious sensibility in film. Conventional French film makers, represented for example by Jean Aurenche, had thought such a sensibility in a novel to be "unfilmable."

The "certain tendency" Truffaut uncovers is that the French cinema of the fifties is dominated by a tradition of quality in which the work of a few scenarists determines the aesthetics of French film as a whole. The position developed by Aurenche and others is that many classical novels are at least in part impossible to convey to the screen unless mediated by psychological realism, a system of equivalents devised by the scenarist. Nevertheless, as Truffaut points out (citing Bazin's "The Stylistics of Robert Bresson"), the finished Bressonian adaptation of Bernanos is totally faithful, thus proving that the "unfilmable" is but a determination made within the narrow confines of certain formulas. Truffaut then sarcastically suggests that the whole tradition of quality is but an impoverished set of formulas that allows script writers to dominate the directors who shoot their scripts. Consequently, when adaptations are made, says Truffaut, all novels seem to be the same novel since they have to conform to the same formula and their vision of human nature is limited to psychological realism. In contrast, the *auteur* like Bresson, when he sets out to do an adaptation, struggles to find true filmic equivalents and achieves greater fidelity because, paradoxically, he exercises greater freedom.

Truffaut's first three feature films indicate the kind of cinema he was to make over a twenty-year span. *The 400 Blows* (1959) opens the autobiographical Antoine Doinel cycle starring Jean-Pierre Léaud, to which Truffaut returned periodically through the 1960s, concluding with *Love on the Run* (1979). *Shoot the Piano Player* (1960) initiates the series of genre films that run through the 1960s and seem to have ended with the nearly self-parodic disaster *Such a Gorgeous Kid Like Me* (1972). *Jules and Jim* (1961) is the first of two Henri-Pierre Roché adaptations; the second is *Two English Girls* (1971). Both works deal with the agonized passage from the romanticism of the nineteenth century into the modern period. Close to the Roché films are the curious *The Story of Adele H.* (1975), based on the journal of Adele Hugo but thematically treated as a gloss on both the Roché films and the Doinel cycle, and *The Green Room* (1978), based on Henry James' "The Altar of the Dead." *The Wild Child* (1969) stands somewhat apart from the kinds of films Truffaut has made, almost as a thematic essay, though it too is a film based on a journal, from the eighteenth-century Doctor Itard, whom Truffaut himself plays in the film. *Day for Night* (1973) and *The Last Metro* (1980), appearing after several lesser works, are Truffaut's *hommages* to film and theater respectively.

Seeds are planted in *The 400 Blows* that spring up in the subsequent Doinel films and separate Antoine from the tradition of the Bazinian realist hero. The love of the child Antoine for Balzac anticipates the growth of the character into a "symbolizer" who does not confront his reality but dreams and insists on his romantic projections. Truffaut both sympathizes with and chides this later Antoine. The sympathy is everywhere—in Antoine's quirky loves, in his comic eagerness and aching seriousness, and in his immersion in the working world around him, most often figured by Truffaut as a social collective (a figure borrowed from Renoir), such as the detective office in *Stolen Kisses* and the courtyard in *Bed and Board.* The recurring critique of Antoine is placed by Truffaut in those privileged moments where Antoine's direct encounters with women divest him of the enchanted image he has projected on them.

In *Bed and Board,* Antoine becomes a novelist of autobiographical persuasion. This not only cues the viewer to his cultural self-interpretation and to the privileges of language

as his special medium, but Antoine's novel-writing also doubles the process of the Doinel cycle as a whole, reflecting the ethical problems of Truffaut's autobiographical cinema. James Monaco in *The New Wave* (1976) sees this doubling as a self-reflexive meditation on the role of the film maker; one might also add that it expresses Truffaut's deliberate "fall" from the aspiration of a direct realism into the complexities of the languages of writing and film. The reflexivity of Antoine, however self-involved, points out that the films, too, are the products of reflection, that they are constructed bits of language: in short, that they are writing.

Monaco observes, "Our main sense of [Antoine] in *Bed and Board* as in *The 400 Blows* is deeply colored by his isolation." But this isolation is of a new sort, for it is grounded in Antoine's novel-writing rather than on his bold dash for freedom as in the earlier film. Still, the novel itself is being written in service to that dash, for Antoine is now reinventing himself through memory, through writing. In this way, *Bed and Board* recalls the solitude of *The 400 Blows* not only to remind us of Antoine's irreducible humanity, but also to acknowledge his growth from an unguarded child into a self-mythologizing artist. And that artist is now re-creating the child just as Truffaut himself re-created himself as Antoine.

That Truffaut has refused to allow the cycle's resolution in *Bed and Board* to stand, but takes it back with *Love on the Run,* marks just how far he has moved from Bazin, for whom a character's growth should lead to a reconciliation with Being, to facing reality itself. Truffaut never allows this final reconciliation; his characters remain forever self-complicating. Why? Because for Truffaut there is no humanity outside culture, no "really real," no "ground of being" to which human consciousness has access. There is for Truffaut only the ethically frail, much-flawed means of language that we have all inherited from our culture.

Outside the Doinel cycle, Truffaut also mounts a somewhat more systematic consideration of his concerns with the exploration of characters as inheritors of culture and users of language, and he sometimes does so with greater urgency than is found in the gently unfolding story of Antoine. It is in *Fahrenheit 451* and *The Wild Child* that Truffaut's theological anthropology is most fully thematized. At stake here is the question of what constitutes the human and what connects the individual to reality. For Truffaut, reality is always mediated by culture, the "producer" of meaningful language, even though its results are ambiguous: for language loses the reality that it opens to love at the same moment it discloses it. This is why Truffaut at once celebrates and criticizes Antoine's romanticism, for Antoine's love would be impossible without a specific cultured language to evoke it and give it form even as it distorts love and has to be corrected-by, humanly enough, the beloved.

The expository sequences of *Fahrenheit 451* are surprisingly undramatic. The absence of books and of all but the most functional language has reduced the people of the future into unfeeling, sedated monads, typified by the hero Montag (Oscar Werner) and his wife, Linda (Julie Christie). In films within the dystopian subgenre of science fiction movies (like *THX 1138* or *Nineteen Eighty-four*) to which this Truffaut film belongs, interpersonal love, the bearer of authentic humanity, is conventionally placed in rebellious opposition to the inhuman coldness of the futurist society. But Truffaut sets up a conflict on a very different plane, between culture and society. The characters in this film remain as impersonal as the society around them. The acting is muted and even Montag's relationship with Clarisse (also played by Julie Christie) is cold.

The film narrates Montag's discovery of literature through which he discovers his human identity. Eventually, he and Clarisse move to the fringes of society where they join the book-people, those who individually memorize a single book and become that book, even changing their names. And it is there, among the book people, that human discourse, and with it humane existence, is resumed as recitation. Not human nature or its usual manifestations, love, rebellion, or freedom, but human *work,* the work of culture and language, is the basis of humanity discovered and cultivated in *Fahrenheit 451.*

Truffaut treats the same theme, though with far greater depth and grace, in *The Wild Child.* Some have seen the life of Victor before his capture as a nature idyll. But Truffaut clearly does not. Although, as Monaco reports, Truffaut has toned down the violence originally planned for the opening sequences, the finished film still shows Victor either desperately struggling to survive or rocking back and forth in his tree-top perch in an autistic trance. The middle of the film, while hardly a paean to civilized society, shows that the boy is reviled as subhuman precisely because he fails to live up to the myth of the noble savage—the very myth that predisposes viewers to misread the film's opening as an idyll.

Dr. Itard (Truffaut himself) proves to be the serious representative of human culture. Itard conceives humanity to be the product of work, the labor of education. Once Victor arrives at Itard's home-laboratory, and his senses are loosened from the rictus his constant struggle for survival has induced, *The Wild Child* becomes the story of the acculturation of the boy, a process that consists of his learning language (broadly understood to include table manners, dress codes, and so on) and each step in this process is accompanied by Victor's emergence as a human personality.

Itard's journal, read off-screen to cover ellipses and to double for narrative with commentary, at times expresses the doctor's doubts about the benefits of civilization, but the film moves inexorably toward the disclosure of Victor's soul, the final experiment Itard performs. This is the painful sequence in which Itard unjustly punishes Victor during one of his lessons. The boy rebels, thus showing he has the power to tell right from wrong. It is no accident that this episode should become the final experiment, for the emergence of personhood in Truffaut's cinema does not occur through any exfoliation of human essence but through the power of language to expose the soul.

*The Story of Adele H.,* also from a "found text," the solipsistic journals of Adele Hugo, reverses the process of *The Wild Child.* We are told through titles that Adele invented her own language. She is shown writing obsessively throughout the film, inventing a whole universe of romance for herself and the military officer who has already jilted her—and will do so again and again. Eventually, Adele leaves the real world, which she physically wanders through like a specter, and enters wholly into a fantasy universe. In a sense, she is an extreme version of what Antoine could have become had he lived in a period of high romanticism as Adele did. Next to *Two English Girls* and *The Green Room, Adele H.* is easily the darkest, most pessimistic of Truffaut's films, for it relentlessly traces, with immense tenderness and detail, a descent into what for this director could only be a damnation—the delusion of language itself. Its inevitable successor, *The Green Room,* is a long meditation on a dying sensibility that seems in space to exist in the anteroom of hell, in time to teeter on the edge of muted apocalypse. Julien Davenne (Truffaut) sinks into an obsessive contemplation of his dead wife; another woman, Cecilia, speaks to him of life and the future, but unlike so many Truffaut heroines, she fails to draw Julien out of his symbolized universe.

Over the span of two decades, and a diversity of film themes and subjects, Truffaut has constructed a cinematic opus that both derives from and departs from his mentor André Bazin. The spirituality of these varied works, beginning in psychological realism, tends toward an evocation of a religious transcendence (or depth) through images of fugitive flights, the act of writing (a re-invention through memory), the struggle between a romantic past and a modern present, between rapture and realism. There is no articulated spirituality in that there is no readily recognizable relationship of events and images to an ultimate reality or ground of being. Rather what emerges is the gently latent possibility that one comes face to face with the problem of individual and collective destiny only when confronted with the catastrophic threat of the deterioration and ultimate loss of language and culture. Truffaut's ambiguous evocations invite, in fact require, bringing to these films an independent theological judgment which for Bazin and the films of the Neorealists and Bresson would have been inherent in the artistic work itself.

## Eugene P. Walz (essay date Winter-Spring 1983)

SOURCE: "Antoine's First and Final Adventure," in *Mosaic,* Vol. XVI, Nos. 1-2, Winter-Spring, 1983, pp. 139-43.

[*In the following essay, Walz discusses Truffaut's short story* "Antoine and the Orphan Girl," *which he describes as a pastiche of Jean Cocteau's work.*]

Antoine Doinel was to acquire a last name and a police record in *The Four Hundred Blows* (1959), his first girlfriend and job in *Antoine and Colette* (1962), a dishonorable discharge from the military and several more jobs in *Stolen Kisses* (1968), a wife, a child and a mistress in *Bed and Board* (1970), and a divorce in *Love on the Run* (1979). The "adventures" of this amusingly pathetic cinematic character were first chronicled, however, not on film or in a film script but in print—in **"Antoine and the Orphan Girl"** (**"Antoine et l'orpheline"**). This little-known story . . . was published in a small and now defunct monthly, *La Parisienne,* in May 1955—two years before François Truffaut embarked on his filmmaking career. It is the only fiction that Truffaut wrote solely for print.

"Every artist begins with a pastiche," Paul Gauguin once observed, and so it is with Truffaut. When **"Antoine and the Orphan Girl"** was published, François Sentein, one of the editors of *La Parisienne,* appended a preface in which he pointed out that the story was an homage to Jean Cocteau and that, in writing a pastiche, Truffaut was reviving an outdated form. He also noted that the story was composed with affection and without irony, that it was "innocent, almost naive, and content to be so." His conclusion was that "a pastiche which deprives itself of irony interests us by itself. Its value does not come from the skill with which it broadcasts its tricks but in the natural way it keeps using them."

Although Truffaut's debt to Cocteau, as both writer and filmmaker, was not as great as was his debt to other writers and filmmakers, it is also noticeable in his first feature films. In *The Four Hundred Blows,* when Antoine runs away from home he stays in the apartment of his best friend, René Bigey, an apartment that features a stuffed horse and other grotesque furnishings and that Truffaut acknowledged was constructed "à la Cocteau." That *Les enfants terribles* was a specific model in this film is apparent from several direct allusions (the scene, for instance, in which Antoine and René flap the bedcovers to clear away their cigarette smoke) and from the fact that Truffaut quotes Cocteau in his introduction to the anthologized scripts for the Doinel cycle. In **"Antoine and the Orphan Girl"** there are a number of obvious references to *Les enfants terribles* (Antoine's room, his childish games, and the description of his father's apartment as "an empty theater" for their lovemaking). A more likely source is Cocteau's "Le grande écart" ("The Miscreant") with its use of asterisks

and discontinuous narrative, its sad-wise aphorisms, and its anti-feminist overtones. As Sentein implies, however, it is not the specific allusions that make this an effective pastiche but the feeling generated by the story that the author has steeped himself in Cocteau's works.

More noteworthy than the literary allusions, and more recognizable to a contemporary audience than they would have been to Sentein, are the story's autobiographical elements. Antoine Doinel has long been recognized as Truffaut's cinematic alter ego, as has the fact that Truffaut utilizes details from his own life in all of his films. **"Antoine and the Orphan Girl"** proves that this is not just a cinematic tactic but part of his total esthetic.

Truffaut's childhood was not a happy one. Both of his parents worked, and they spent their spare time pursuing his father's passion for camping and the outdoors. Thus he felt unwanted at home, particularly by his mother who was, it seems, almost pathologically sensitive to any noise or disruption he might make. Although his father was an outdoorsman, Truffaut did not share his enthusiasms. He once admitted, for instance, "I never show people swimming because I don't know how to swim." As a teenager he was rarely at home and rarely in school. When he was about fifteen, his father turned him over to the police for vagrancy. The boy was consequently sent to *le centre d'observation des mineurs delinquants* at Villejuif. Truffaut was rescued from this prison-asylum by the noted film critic André Bazin—who performed a similar "miracle" in getting him released from military service in 1952. All of these figure in **"Antoine and the Orphan Girl."** The only detail that is, from existing evidence, untrue to Truffaut's life is the death of his mother; she died only recently, not when he was twenty. In *The Four Hundred Blows,* however, Antoine performs a similar "execution," using the supposed death of his father as a way of excusing his many absences from school.

"Cinema of the First Person Singular" is a phrase that has been used to describe Truffaut's career, but it is clearly more than just this autobiographical quality that characterizes both his films and the preceding story. When he uses details from his personal life he injects these into popular genre forms. And it is this conflict, this dialectic, between the personal and the conventional, the auteur and the genre, which gives his films their distinctiveness.

Yet even this is not precise enough. Jacques Rivette, Truffaut's friend and colleague at *Cahiers du Cinema* during the 1950s, made a comment concerning *The Four Hundred Blows* that can be applied to all of Truffaut's work but has never been given sufficient emphasis. He observed that Truffaut "humbly reconstructs from personal experience a reality which is equally objective, and which he then films with absolute respect." It is this feature, the combination of subjectivity and objectivity, which gets to the heart of Truffaut's esthetic.

This quality of objective subjectivity is partly a function of Truffaut's peculiar use of point of view. In "**Antoine and the Orphan Girl**" he combines the intimacy of a confession with the detachment of a sociological analysis. Although the story is told from the point of view of a superior, "limited-omniscient" narrator, the sentiments expressed indicate that this narrator is also, if not identical to Antoine, then entirely in sympathy with him. As in his films, Truffaut plays with the idea of multiple perspectives. At times the narrator provides the audience with first-hand, privileged access to certain intimate disclosures. At other times information is withheld; things are left unspoken or unrevealed. Ellipses are used. (At their most extreme the ellipses in this story are the literary equivalent of a jump-cut—the disjunctive cinematic device for which Truffaut and his colleagues in the French *nouvelle vague* were to be so celebrated.)

---

**"If a man has character he will," according to Nietzsche, "have the same experience over and over again." The experience that keeps recurring in Truffaut's films is estrangement.**

**—*Eugene P. Walz***

---

Furthermore, at various points in the narrative Truffaut abandons the third-person for another tactic he has repeatedly used in his movies. He has described it as a "first-person confidential tone," and its main feature is a form of direct address. Near the beginning of the description of the budding romance between Antoine and Henriette the narrator asks: "Have I made it clear that with Henriette Antoine was not living his first adventure?" This attempt by Truffaut to bring the reader into the story is the literary equivalent of, for instance, Antoine's responding to the psychologist's questions in *The Four Hundred Blows* by talking directly to the camera. Voice-over narration in his films is often used for the same effect—to create an intimacy, an immediacy, between audience and characters. One of the models Truffaut admits to having used as a source of this tactic is the film version of *Les enfants terribles.*

"If a man has character he will," according to Nietzsche, "have the same experience over and over again." The experience that keeps recurring in Truffaut's films is estrangement. Every story that Truffaut has written for or adapted to the screen has in one way or another dealt with the termination of a relationship, either familial or romantic. What fascinates him most is not the termination itself but the conflicting attitudes of the people involved and the effect the ending of a relationship has on the more sensitive and/or naively romantic person—the dreamer, the idealist. Truffaut believes that for some people love is provisional (temporary or relative) and for others it is definitive (permanent or absolute). Rarely do two people share the same attitude at the same time. And, if they do, circumstances conspire against them. The idealist, therefore, is made to suffer. For idealists do not change; they do not learn from experience.

Such is the case with the central character in "**Antoine and the Orphan Girl**." Antoine is the role model for at least two dozen Truffaldien movie characters. "Accustomed to miracles" and believing in destiny, he is blind to his obsessions and his inevitable fate (a fate that we the readers are privy to from the opening paragraph where dreams dissolve into reality, where a "suit of armor [is] just a pair of wool trousers"). His actions are rendered more poignant by the fact that he is "rejected" by both his family and his lover—and by the momentary realization of his dreams. Furthermore, his is not a lofty quest but simply a yearning, however urgent, to be accepted, to be normal. Antoine goes swimming, for instance, because of a "desire to do-as-others-do."

Truffaut orchestrates his story about Antoine into four straightforward sections: one in which he provides a quick character sketch, a second in which he spells out the situation, and two longer sections detailing the ecstasy and the agony of romantic love. Clearly, it is the latter two sections in which he is most interested, especially the final section which delays a result that is inevitable to the audience while it underlines the irony of Antoine's actions. In Henriette's absence Antoine reinforces his romantic obsessions in the funny yet sad way that is characteristic of Truffaut's best films. In Pigalle he "imagines ideal couplings, with perfect actors and actresses." He is inspired by a vision in a movie house to such an amusing extent that he overvalues its importance to others. He and his best friend belittle women, not realizing the callow and contradictory nature of their observations, and reaffirm their friendship without acknowledging the inadequacy of it to their present situations. Obviously, as the abruptness and irony of the last two words of the story indicate, Antoine does not learn from this affair. That he should be doomed to repeat these encounters with almost Sisyphean regularity in the Antoine Doinel cycle of films is entirely consistent with this initial story.

From the vantage point of the fifties, the value of "**Antoine and the Orphan Girl**" was calculated by the ease with which Truffaut executed his homage to Cocteau. Today the value of the story comes from the way it anticipates so completely his filmmaking career: his methods of storytelling, his concerns about the fragility of love, and his fascination with characters who are, to use John Dryden's phrase, "but children of a larger growth." Over the years of his evolution at the hands of his creator and Jean-Pierre Leaud, the actor who portrayed him on screen, Antoine has grown to be less easily identified with Truffaut—who declared that with *Love on the Run* he was ending the screen life of his long-time alter ego. "**Antoine and the Orphan Girl**," therefore, provides the final link in the chain of Antoine's "adventures." Ironically it was also the first.

## Raymond Cormier (essay date February 1990)

SOURCE: "The Metaphorical Window in Truffaut's *Small Change*," in *The French Review,* Vol. 63, No. 3, February, 1990, pp. 452-63.

[*In the following excerpt, Cormier discusses the merits of Truffaut's film* Small Change *as a vehicle for the study of French.*]

> Et je me couche, fier d'avoir vécu et souffert dans d'autres que moi-même . . . —Baudelaire, *Les Fenêtres*, 1869.

With *L'Argent de Poche* (*Small Change*), which saw its premiere in March 1976, François Truffaut has given us a charming, bittersweet, funny and sad film about childhood. The story, it may be recalled, leisurely follows the interlocking "careers" of about a dozen youngsters in the village of Thiers (20-odd miles east of Clermont-Ferrand) during the last month of the school year. Not unlike the mood in his quasi-autobiographical *La Nuit américaine* (*Day for Night,* 1973), the narrative is bathed in typical Truffautian authenticity: optimistic human images of a new mother feeding her baby with her breast milk contrast with those of a young adolescent's first hesitant kiss; within all there lurks as well a dark side of cruelty—"les enfances abîmées," as Truffaut put it.

*L'Argent de poche* offers the patient viewer much more than the vapid shallowness that anodyne critics have allowed the work. In fact, the film singularly achieves what it sets out to accomplish, especially if one studies carefully its subtle, transparent, and often self-referential imagery. Unified in time and space, this "evergreen" film is, I believe, a near-perfect vehicle for intermediate French classes. . . .

Those familiar with Truffaut's little gem may agree it deals with anything but "small change;" in fact, merely from the point of view of censorship in the history of American cinema (especially 1922-1960), it offers a controversial and shocking portrayal of a victim of child abuse. Children are not just petty, expendable beings—society's "pocket money." Rather, as Wordsworth puts it, "The Child is the Father of

the Man" (they represent the future of mankind). Both young adult and older students readily grasp and appreciate this compelling insight. In fact, the multitude of children featured in the film recall, for Truffaut, "une foule chinoise." Truffaut renders justice to betrayed children, for the film is "la revanche définitive du miston, le quatre cent unième coup qui fait oublier tous les autres, la sauvagerie vaincue par la clarté lumineuse du regard. L'enfance enfin vue de face . . . , l'enfance comprise, aimée et non plus hypocritement caressée, . . . ."

Besides this, *Small Change* stresses several key ideas, for example, the compensatory nature of human development, the indispensability of a mother's love to human happiness, and especially the child's need for autonomy. The film also bears the unmistakable imprint of Hitchcock's superb thriller, *Rear Window* (French title, *Fenêtre sur cour*). For instance, a handicapped character (Patrick Desmouceaux's father), like Hitchcock's L.B. Jefferies (Jimmy Stewart) also spends time looking out the window each day. References to money—as another "sign"—seem to abound as well (e.g., Nicole's lost wallet, Richard's 10 franc "haircut money," Julien's guileless errand, etc.); they occur unexpectedly in many shots. Tracking down allusions and sleuthing such as this makes for greater classroom enjoyment of the film.

Moreover, students are delighted to observe that, of the 150-odd shots in the film, more than half in fact include windows of various types (and many doors, door-frames and a variety of enclosures are featured as well).

Once we assess the major signs in *Small Change,* it becomes clear that windows, insofar as they isolate and exclude, suggest semiotically the exclusion of children from adult society. In the metaphorical terms of psychohistory, childhood mirrors and predicts in part the arrangement of society. As Insdorf has revealed in writing of *The Wild Child,* the window is the operative frame, ". . . simultaneously enclosing and leading out".

> **Once we assess the major signs in *Small Change,* it becomes clear that windows, insofar as they isolate and exclude, suggest semiotically the exclusion of children from adult society.**
>
> **—*Raymond Cormier***

The following survey of window imagery hopes to grasp more fully the esthetics of Truffaut's obviously non-aleatory cinema. In this "collective chronicle [*unanimiste*]," as

Truffaut called his film, denotative and connotative action and thought are fused in a single unique mosaic.

We will turn now to a selection of the more important sequences. One of the first windows to appear in the film involves a direct, self-conscious, and obtrusive homage to Hitchcock (Hitch always played a cameo in his films). In this sense, Truffaut's presence as New Wave film director intrudes.

The 12 year-old blond Martine, travelling with her father, is visiting Bruère-Allichamps in the exact center of France. Her appearance here opens the "envelope" of the film, just as the final epilogue involving her and Patrick at Camp Mérindol, recounted in a letter, closes the story. Martine sends a postcard to her cousin Raoul who lives in Thiers (a pretext to get us to the main setting for the film; cf. the deceptive postcard in *Rear Window*).

Sitting in the car and seen behind the glass windshield, waiting for her to place the postcard in the postbox is Martine's approving father—played by François Truffaut.

A second interesting episode involving a window occurs when Lydie, the pregnant wife of elementary school teacher Jean-François Richet (the film's main character), visits her husband's classroom to ask for the keys to their apartment. Framed by the doorway, Lydie peeks hesitantly into the classroom to look at the students, who return her stare, equally curious about her. Richet gives her the keys, then awkwardly closes the classroom door with its cathedral glass window and bestows a 9-second kiss on his wife. This sexual intimacy, dimly perceived by viewer and student alike, is punctuated by the childrens' giggles of embarrassed amusement.

Another truly unforgettable window scene, involving the toddler Grégory Félix, both amazes and amuses students. Recalling the crowning fall of "Jeff" (in Hitchcock's *Rear Window*), the episode pinpoints a second major thematic idea, hinted at by the original working title of the film, *La Peau dure*. Children may "go boom" literally or figuratively, but, for some reason—as Lydie explains it to her husband later, whether it be by their state of grace, innocence, or tough skin—they rarely get seriously hurt.

During his mother's momentary absence, Grégory, trying to reach his kitty which had fallen onto a window landing below, falls out of his apartment window, nine stories down. Truffaut shoots the sequence with Griffith-like deftness (at least four cameras). The observers on the ground look up but are unable to help. Luckily, little 24 month-old Grégory falls into a bush, makes a soft landing, then stands up, gurgles aloud, and walks away from the accident completely unhurt!

Later, what might seem at first to be an amusing sketch, upon reflection shows that a moral may be drawn also from Sylvie's Sunday afternoon adventure. Her parents leave her behind and go to dine at a local restaurant. (Sylvie is abandoned over a dispute involving a pocketbook; cf. the famous alligator purse in *Rear Window*!) Like a stage, the window of little Sylvie's apartment becomes the setting for her to call out on her father's police megaphone to all her neighbors in the courtyard—"J'ai faim! J'ai faim!" Coming as it does at the structural midpoint of the film, the dramatic scene suggests more than just a capricious child's cuteness. Her own physical hunger—for food *and* attention here—stands in regard to both Patrick Desmouceaux's and Julien Leclou's desperate yearning and need for maternal love, tenderness, and especially autonomy. One might speculate that Truffaut hungered, too—for freedom, "the freedom," writes Jameson nostalgically, "to kick over whatever traces custom and usage had imposed on the imaginative spirit, and to lunge after beauty and truth wherever the chase might lead".

With Sylvie in deep focus, the foregrounded Deluca brothers come to the rescue. All the neighbors, in a bonded community, watch this event from their apartment windows. Like the confused observers on the ground below who watch Grégory, the neighbors look out onto the building's inner courtyard and talk to each other. They are clearly drawn together by this "shameful" crisis involving the daughter of the police chief, and are delighted when the Deluca brothers invent a solution, and the device of sending Sylvie abundant food in a basket on ropes and pulleys—through the window—recalls also a poignant sequence in *Rear Window* (involving a dog, later killed by the villain—a "potent scene" for Truffaut). Sylvie's imprisonment is thus converted to a moral spectacle.

If Julien Leclou is the film's dark "outsider," or "wild child," the blond Patrick Desmouceaux represents "the stranger" figure, as in **Stolen Kisses**. Not unlike the ski holiday advertisement in **Les 400 Coups,** the Wagon-Lits "Confort sur le rail" poster in the beauty shop offers Patrick a romantic window within a window (it shows a man and a woman preparing for bed in a train compartment). As Insdorf has remarked,

> Patrick is a stranger to maternal love and, therefore, develops a crush on a woman who represents both a mother and an idealized romantic figure. The object of his affections is his friend's mother, Madame Riffle, who bestows kisses on her son Laurent as Patrick looks on hungrily. His infatuation is nurtured in her beauty shop, where he meets Laurent for school every day.

That is, by confusion in Patrick's mind between Madame Riffle and the beautiful blond woman in the poster, the exotic setting reminds him of "motion and passion, escape and love, trains and sleep." The dreamy couchette offers as well both the warmth of a home and a way out of Thiers, or confining village life, where Patrick's hunger for love can be filled (as it _will_ be at summer camp, in Mérindol).

In the poster, one sees, outside the train through the compartment window, the quiet night, nine or ten stars, and, below them, some mountains. For commentative sound, soft, sweet _pizzicato_ music accompanies the scene in which Patrick gets lost in contemplation of the poster. During the film, Patrick enters the windowed, starry world of the poster more than once; one might almost say he prays before this "great image." Bachelard, constructing a kind of "anthropology of the imagination," describes such images in his influential _Poétique de l'espace:_

> Les grandes images ont à la fois une histoire et une préhistoire. Elles sont toujours à la fois souvenir et légende. On ne vit jamais l'image en première instance. Toute grande image a un fond onirique insondable et c'est sur ce fond onirique que le passé personnel met des couleurs particulières.

Another major sequence involving a window could be called the "beginning of the end." In their _cinéroman,_ Truffaut and Schiffman name the chapter "Julien se révolte." Just before this _dénouement_ (an ironic cut that will jerk us away), there occurs perhaps the most peaceful, empowering, and snug moment in the film. Here, Lydie Richet breastfeeds her newborn Thomas as Jean-François reads aloud to her from Bruno Bettelheim about the symbiosis between the breastfed baby and its mother (real warm "comfort on the rails of life!"). Intimacy and satisfaction prevail. In the next shot, we see the newborn Thomas Richet fully lighted in his white crib. Lydie, accompanied by sweet Bach-like string music, softly answers Richard Golfier's repeated Saturday afternoon questions about the baby's age, smile, the shape of his ears, his grasp, etc.

Suddenly, we are confronted with an ominous, dark, and ugly rainstorm. Into the dilapidated shack referred to as Les Mureaux, a real "bleak house," enters Julien Leclou, obviously soaked from the pouring rain (we never see the inside of his home). We vaguely hear the savage shriek of his mother's voice, and suddenly he is thrust outside, back into the rainstorm. Now the door is locked. Julien stoops, picks up a stone, and hurls it—like some latter-day, Baudelairian "good poet"—through the dark window of the door.

This act of revolt appears to be a Truffautesque visual echo of the moment when the beastlike Wild Child, thrust into a dark room, "yearns so much for the outdoors that he smashes a window with his head." It may be recalled here that the child's preferred place was near the open window, seen as a

boundary between . . . constriction and mobility,

affection and freedom. When the boy successfully completes an exercise, Itard rewards him with a glass of water which he drinks by the window. His teacher realizes that "this child of nature was trying to reunite the only things that survived his loss of liberty: a drink of fresh water, and the view of the sun and the country."

With the sound and picture of the crash of the glass at Les Mureaux, Julien begins a kind of anarchical adventure, a downward journey where chance and struggle prevail. He moves through the dark, wandering sequence at the _fête foraine,_ or carnival, then on to the all-nighter spent asleep on the cold sidewalk; these images provide an ironic counterpanel first to the warm enclosure _chez les Richet,_ then to the mocking classroom scenes that occur earlier, when Julien first appears in the film.

Julien, solitary, miserable, cold, and hungry, walks around the fair (we seem to be watching him from the window of the ticket booth/guard house). He sees and hears a colorful child's merry-go-round, but cannot think for a moment about taking a ride on any of these amusements: he has no money, literally. But there is another level of meaning, if we take the idea of "money" in a figurative sense, certainly made apparent by the school courtyard scene when the mysterious and uprooted Julien first materializes.

His classmates-to-be are at that moment reciting from Molière's _L'Avare_ (Act 4, Scene 7); it is Harpagon's tirade— _Au voleur, au voleur_—"A l'assassin, au meurtrier/ Justice, juste ciel! Je suis perdu, je suis assassiné/ On m'a coupé la gorge, on m'a dérobé mon argent./ Où est-il? Où se cache-t-il? . . ."

By means of rapid, Chaplinesque intercutting between the sounds of these words and the sight of Leclou's tired rags and strange E.T.-like emotionless face, Truffaut suggests— only vaguely at first—that, like Harpagon's treasure, Julien's inner spirit, his vitality and youthful fantasies have all been inexorably stolen away. One recalls here the harsh and painful aspects of the adult world in _Les 400 Coups_—with, as Petrie asserts, its "casual and callous destruction of human potential."

This interpretation of the Harpagon scene becomes clearer once we see the miserable Julien wandering around the amusement park, alone, broke, and as silent and dumb as the Wild Child in isolation.

The final important window scene in the film involves an obtrusive, voyeuristic camera shot that still shies away from showing all the details (just as Hitchcock never shows the gory, sawed-up parts of the murdered body in _Rear Window_).

Julien is brought in to an examination room at school for the annual medical checkup. He is reluctant to undress, so, in the half light, the doctor and the school nurse assist him. At window height, the camera is poised just outside. Then as Julien is (apparently) prepared for an x-ray, it zooms in to investigate—very slowly, yet still outside the window. Scarcely visible, the figures in the claustrophobic darkness seem to freeze. Time seems to stand still as the film's sound stops.

It is as a result of this medical examination that the authorities discover Julien's bruises, cuts, and burns. Even when the doctor actually describes the situation to the police, i.e., that Julien is an abused, "butchered" child, the camera hesitantly approaches the window but does not enter inside the school principal's office, perhaps because what is being revealed is too horrible to record. (Just as, in the hospital, Jean-François finds himself unable to photograph his wife in childbirth: he watches ecstatically, mouth open, frozen in wonder before the singularly unbanal miracle of birth—too beautiful to record?)

During the film, the martyred Julien is depicted with facial bruises; he is sullen, generally unresponsive to the youngsters around him, and only marginally compliant to the world of adults. Petty thievery and deception seem to fuel his fire: the desire, need for, or lack of money (he gets no "spending money" at home!) drives him to pick pockets, steal, and sneak into the cinema without paying. A brief but unsettling scene shows him at the side of a street, intentionally placing his foot out into traffic and watching the passing cars swerve away with screeching tires to avoid hitting him. This is not a sign of "masochism" (as some of my students mistakenly inferred). Julien gets no pleasure from this activity; rather, he is acting out a tragic "death wish"—to escape further beatings from his crazed, hateful mother.

Significantly, for this tightly-knit and closed village community, the townspeople of Thiers, when they witness Julien's handcuffed mother and grandmother through the police van windows, are angry enough to lynch the two of them.

The window figures prominently in French thought, especially in Symbolist poetry. For example, in a prose poem, *Les Fenêtres*, Baudelaire writes:

> Celui qui regarde du dehors à travers une fenêtre ouverte ne voit jamais de choses que celui qui regarde une fenêtre fermée ... Ce qu'on peut voir au soleil est toujours moins intéressant que ce qui se passe derrière une vitre. Dans ce trou noir ou lumineux vit la vie, rêve la vie, souffre la vie.

It is a cinematic convention that windows, like the voyeuristic eye of the camera, may provide an opening onto the private, or at least non-public, activities of others. Like the camera, too, windows allow limited access to what is going on "inside." Much can be left out of the picture, as the banality of everyday life attests. This is the paradox of the camera-as-window—it limits yet helps us see all we missed! In the film, such is the case with cinema itself, and the Sunday family visits to the movies in Thiers suggests an escape, a "Sesame" that opens onto another world. The movie screen in the theater functions at once as a transparent opening through which all of life (as pre-selected by the filmmaker!) may be interpreted, and as a secure "self-enclosed cosmogony" that allows us to travel to unknown, strange, or even dangerous worlds—right in the comfort of our reclining seat.

The poetic glass window can also mirror or reflect and draw into itself what is placed before it. As suggested, and as R.G. Cohn shows for Mallarmé, this seems to be the case for Baudelaire, and even Rimbaud (in *Les Chercheuses de poux*). Here the iconic window becomes a loop of transcendence and escape, a path toward freedom from unthinking, limited, or habitual emotional responses. Similarly, if the viewer projects him or herself into a representation of a window, one might say that the image itself offers an opportunity for daydreaming. As Bachelard puts it prophetically in *La Poétique de l'espace:*

> Quel bel exercice ... de la fonction d'habiter la maison rêvée que le voyage en chemin de fer! Ce voyage déroule un film de maisons rêvées, acceptées, refusées ... Sans que jamais, comme en automobile, on soit tenté de s'arrêter. On est en pleine rêverie avec la salutaire interdiction de *vérifier*.

The film works as well as it does because of one crucial character, Jean-François Richet. This sympathetic teacher provides the kind of serene harmony needed to help the viewer tolerate the story of Julien. Richet's warm and open classroom style (note, for instance, the spontaneous use of the postcard for a lesson in geography) contrasts sharply with the harsh portrayal of school, teachers, and learning in *Les 400 Coups*. In this sense, *Small Change* represents to a certain extent a redemption, Truffaut's mitigation and mellowing vis-à-vis his bitter first feature (Petrie 68). Whereas Antoine Doinel, with a mean-spirited schoolteacher, studied "'ludicrously incongruous love poems about hares'" (Allen 35), Julien's teacher, Mademoiselle Petit, at least tries to reach him, and Julien does try to learn a little also. Besides, the constricted spatial patterns and limiting atmosphere of *Les 400 Coups* are replaced by a certain amount of schoolyard freedom, noisy children playing leapfrog in the sunlight, etc. (Allen 68), not to mention the total abandon in the very opening of *Small Change*—hundreds of school-boys running wildly through Thiers to exhilarating music.

*L'Argent de poche* is a more lighthearted film. Richet, about to become a father, brings to the story a balance of elation and comedy that contrasts with the traumatic, impersonal, and hostile world of Julien and the difficult one of Patrick.

Truffaut has backed up his camera to the classroom window (again); extra students are crowded around and sitting on windowsills. Richet's stunning and unforgettable speech makes an eloquent appeal for children's rights: in the cruel, indifferent, and selfish world of politics, children are forgotten. They have no vote and therefore no say in matters that directly affect them. Richet emphasizes to his students that, faced with the injustices and difficulties of life, they must "'s'endurcir pour pouvoir l'affronter,'" but they must not "'become callous'"(*se durcir.*) "'La vie est dure, mais elle est belle puisqu'on y tient tellement.'" By some kind of ironic "'balance'" ("compensatory law"), those who experience hard knocks end up somehow more resilient, better equipped to face life's loneliness and sadness.

"Things that hurt, teach," is the paradoxical aphorism of Benjamin Franklin. It is no surprise that one early film critic referred to the film as a "hymn to joy," a "miraculous *summa*," a work "touched by grace"; nor that a Swedish writer referred to Truffaut not as a pessimist, but as trusting in the possibilities of human communication—especially through the language of film!

Metaphorical windows—filmic, intimate, voyeuristic, symbolic, poetic, sympathetic, and reticent—form a major system of signs in this artful work. Not a masterpiece; just a little, breezy film about small people's "small moments;" unfailingly cheery, glowing with apparent artlessness and spontaneity and love for children, Truffaut's *L'Argent de poche* is a small French film with a big message. It offers many insights—cinematic, humanistic, epistemological, and even psychohistoric. For the thoughtful and attentive viewer, the rewards are great since it offers so many opportunities for extensive interpretation and discussion.

## John Simon (review date September 1990)

SOURCE: "François Truffaut: Saved by the Cinema," in *The New Criterion*, Vol. 9, No. 1, September, 1990, pp. 35-43.

[*In the following review, Simon considers Truffaut's life and philosophy about filmmaking.*]

There are good, questionable, and bad reasons for wishing to read someone's collected letters. The sound reason is simply wanting to know that remarkable person better; to become, at least vicariously, a confidant and friend. The more dubious reason is wanting to impress people who haven't read the book with juicy anecdotes—human, all too human. The unsound reason is trying to derive some previously secret formula for success and fame. No one became lastingly famous for aping someone else: originality is the minimum requirement.

Readers embarking on *François Truffaut: Correspondence 1945-1984* will be foiled utterly in their baser expectations. Not only is there no formula for success, there isn't even much gossip. For the latter, the reason is twofold. Truffaut, who—like many, if not most, film directors—is known to have conducted love affairs with some of his stunning leading ladies, stipulated that none of his love letters be published for quite some years to come; and Truffaut's family (for which read ex-wife) saw to it that the present editors, Gilles Jacob and Claude de Givray, omit passages or letters that might be considered embarrassing. After referring to the many Truffaut letters that were lost or thrown away (André Bazin, the critic who was Truffaut's mentor and a sort of adoptive father, never kept any letters), they mention that some "letters were, rightly or wrongly, judged too intimate for publication."

> **Truffaut was extremely talented, intelligent, quick-witted, generally outspoken, hard-working, enthusiastic, woman-crazy, generous, fierce when angered, and, on top of that, nice.**
>
> **—John Simon**

It is easy to overhear the plaintiveness in that "rightly or wrongly," which refers, of course, also to the many omissions indicated by ellipses. Yet one can often infer from the very placement of the lacunae that the stuff cut could not have been all that terrible, and that it is only the vanity of the ex-wife, Madeleine Morgenstern, that is at stake. Still, there is enough left in these 500-odd pages (573 if you count the footnotes and pictures) to give a fair idea of what Truffaut was like. And what he was like—be prepared for something rare in a film director—is *nice*.

But, of course, not nice the way people about whom one can say nothing much else are deemed nice by default. No. Truffaut was extremely talented, intelligent, quick-witted, generally outspoken, hard-working, enthusiastic, woman-crazy, generous, fierce when angered, and, on top of that, nice. Yet this man started out as something close to a juvenile delinquent, army deserter, manic-depressive. He was quite literally saved by his love of books and film, as he himself was first to admit. And that love of books, by the way, was the second unusual thing about this filmmaker.

The third, though in France after World War II this was not so rare, was that he began as a film critic. However, in my view, the letters are more persuasive and better written than the criticism.

The letters, I repeat, tell a good deal, and much is neatly filled in by the editors' preface, notes, and chronological table. About all matters French they are perfectly informed and informative; about foreigners, in good French fashion, somewhat less so. Thus the actress Nora Gregor was Austrian, not German; *fumetti* are not dialogue balloons, but a kind of photographed Italian comic strip; Tom Jones is not a producer of Broadway musicals, but their librettist; Charles T. Samuels was a scholar and critic rather than a journalist. But these are trifles.

François Truffaut was born in 1932, the son of an architect and a secretary at *L'Illustration.* The parents farmed the boy out successively to his grandmothers (one in Paris, the other in the suburbs), until, on the death of the second, the eight-year-old boy came home again. Shunted from school to school, he was a miserable student, excelling only at French. Sitting at the back of the classroom, he'd often do crossword puzzles. Whenever possible, he and his friend Robert Lachenay would play hooky: they'd read books or hang out at the movies. They even stole a typewriter from Truffaut senior's office and hocked it for movie money. François founded a cinéclub that lasted one performance. Most of this became the stuff of *The 400 Blows* (1959), Truffaut's first feature and international success. At one of the film societies, Truffaut met Bazin; a little later, his articles started hitting the public prints.

At age eighteen, having ended an unhappy love affair and clandestinely sold all of Lachenay's books for rent money, Truffaut recklessly enlisted in the army, expecting to be shipped to Indochina. Lachenay took the skullduggery well, and the army shipped Truffaut to Germany. Not enjoying any of it, except target practice, he was soon going AWOL and doing time in army prisons and hospitals. At the intercession of Bazin and others, he was finally discharged for a "personality disorder."

In 1953, he worked briefly for the Ministry of Agriculture, then joined Bazin at the soon-to-become-renowned *Cahiers du Cinéma*; there and in *Arts,* he published articles and reviews that aroused attention; he also made his first short film. In 1956, he got a job as an assistant to Roberto Rossellini; the Italian director took the paternal place of Bazin during Truffaut's transition from film journalist to filmmaker. Since childhood, Truffaut had been jotting down the title of every film he saw, also the name of the director, especially if the movie was attacked: "I was always for the artist, the misunderstood artist who provokes sneers." Soon he had three

hundred files in alphabetical order, from Marc Allégret to Fred Zinnemann.

He met and, later, married "the very sweet Madeleine Morgenstern," the daughter of a powerful film producer whose products the young critic used to revile. Enabled to form his own film company, named Les Films du Carrosse after Jean Renoir's *The Golden Coach,* one of his adored films, Truffaut started with a charming short, *Les Mistons (The Mischief-Makers)* in 1957; the following year, he began filming *The 400 Blows,* which would make him someone to reckon with. It was also the beginning—one of the beginnings—of *la nouvelle vague,* the "new wave" in filmmaking.

Whose brainchild was the New Wave? The question has been endlessly debated. Truffaut, Chabrol, and Resnais are usually cited; also Godard, though *Breathless* came later. Claims have been made, too, for Jacques Rivette, less plausibly for Alexandre Astruc, and implausibly for Roger Vadim (*And God Created Woman,* 1959). Oddly enough, these last three claims can be found in the writings of Truffaut. He could, however, have mentioned another film (which he liked), *The Lovers,* by Louis Malle, who also was in there pitching.

The fairest way of putting it is that the New Wave was the creation—largely, but not exclusively—of the *Cahiers du Cinéma.* It was the Young Turks of that publication who, first in print and then on screen, advocated and implemented a kind of movie-making whose salient characteristics are a highly personal approach, irreverence in subject and treatment, equal love for the lowly and the exalted (actually, a preference for the former, if by "lowly" we understand all that is excluded by Official Art), reveling in the technical possibilities of film, and immersion in the process of filmmaking not as in mere work, but as in a sort of sacred river: mystic ritual, religious ecstasy, orgiastic revelry—all of those.

Something essential about Truffaut became visible in *The 400 Blows* (a misnomer in English: *faire les quatre cents coups* means raising hell): a sense of play, serious as well as comic—even, so to speak, sad play. He was already applying that guiding principle that he claimed to have discovered in the films of Joshua Logan, who "wills us to laugh during a sad scene and, conversely, to feel saddened during a funny one." In a letter to Maurice Pons, on whose story *Les Mistons* was based, he writes that "it is impossible to create something—a film, a novel, etc.—that does not *absolutely* resemble oneself." So he explains to Pons that the film will "not correspond to your style but even [contradict] it."

Duality, then, is the principle: humor in sadness, melancholy in joy, Truffaut in Pons. In that same autumn of 1957, Truffaut execrates in a letter André Cayatte, who, like René Clément earlier, represented the well-made film, "that rancid hotch-potch with its seasoning of bluff and naïvety." Truffaut was already recommending Barthes's *Mythologies,* a book full of circuitousness and indirection: "polemical" and "negative" article writers could "learn a great deal" from it. But, at the same time, he likes simplicity. He writes Marcel Moussy, his collaborator on the screenplays of *The 400 Blows* and his next, *Shoot the Piano Player* (1960), about a Sunday he spent among men of letters: "They were shifty, scheming, two-faced, flamboyant and boring beyond belief; the atmosphere was much more evil than the world of the cinema where there's less pretense." And already he is dispensing good, simple advice to a young screenwriter: "I sincerely believe that you should completely revise and restructure your script in such a way as to favor a single character with whom we would identify from the beginning to the end of the film, the others appearing only in the background."

But did Truffaut heed his own counsel? In *The 400 Blows,* the gentler René is just as much needed and appreciated as the more bristling Truffaut alter ego, Antoine Doinel. In *Shoot the Piano Player,* the character played by Charles Aznavour is the indubitable protagonist, but is there one in the next film, *Jules et Jim* (1961)? Here, surely, the two men are of equal importance, and Catherine, the woman they share, may be more important yet. But perhaps for Truffaut—and this may be crucial—appearing in the background was, though more fleeting, as vivid as appearing in the foreground.

Nothing about a film is unimportant to Truffaut, least of all the secondary characters. As he puts it in a letter to an American correspondent, "The revolt, to use a very grand word, of *Cahiers du Cinéma* was more moral than aesthetic. What we were arguing for was an *equality* of observation on the part of the artist vis-à-vis his characters instead of a distribution of sympathy and antipathy, which in most cases betrayed the servility of artists with regard to the stars of their films and, on the other hand, their demagoguery with regard to the public."

Of course, there were exceptions among the older filmmakers, too, and the love for them emerges clearly from these letters. I would say that Truffaut's first three films—probably his best—are all in the sign of a favorite filmmaker: *The 400 Blows,* of Jean Vigo; *Shoot the Piano Player,* of Alfred Hitchcock; *Jules et Jim,* of Jean Renoir. But it must be remembered that books mattered to Truffaut about as much as movies. "I love [books] and films equally," he told Charles T. Samuels, "but how I love them!" "If I knew how to write," he observes in a letter of 1968, "I wouldn't be playing the fool behind my big Mitchell 300," the somewhat unwieldy camera Truffaut was then using. And in a letter of 1978, he speaks of his "occasionally excessive respect for books."

This love of books, a key aspect of Truffaut's filmmaking, is

a childhood phenomenon that kept pace with him wherever he went. Thus he replies to Lachenay's inquiry about a good Balzac biography from Koblenz, in the midst of his struggle to get out of the army:

> What a question, for me it's always been all or nothing, especially where Balzac is concerned.
>
> The 2 volumes of the *Vie de Balzac* by André Billy published by Albin Michel (I think) are interesting but insufficient; René Benjamin's *Balzac* is excellent but also, for other reasons, insufficient (in the Nelson collection. . . ); Claude Mauriac's *Aimer Balzac* is absolutely useless.
>
> But there must exist something better for the Balzac 'specialist': Marcel Bouteron, Pierre Descaves, etc. In my opinion, my humble opinion, one should *first* have bought and *read* all of Balzac including the plays, etc. and one should even, before the biographies, have Balzac's *Correspondence* (at least 4 or 5 volumes), the letters to Zulma, Carraud, etc.

Amazing, this, from a nineteen-year-old army deserter who was also a fifteen-year-old school dropout. But equally amazing is the list of authors this autodidact cherished, as it emerges from these letters—to cite only the French authors, in no particular order: Raymond Queneau, Simenon (whom he considered superior to Camus), Bernanos, Drieu la Rochelle, Pierre Klossowski, Genet, Paul Léautaud, and especially Jacques Audiberti—a roster at once eclectic, esoteric, and exquisite. But, as he also writes Lachenay in another letter, "I would sometimes like to be forced to read stupid books, thrillers, adventure stories, etc. I'm not joking, it can really be very instructive." He does, however, discriminate; in 1951, he writes Lachenay, "See if there's Proust's *A la Recherche du temps perdu* (16 volumes). It's a wonderful book and crucial to the future of the novel: Balzac and Proust are the 2 greatest novelists in the French language." And, in a slightly later letter, "You must be blinded by love if you're reading Paul Géraldy. All things considered, I prefer Prévert even though I like him less and less."

How different this true love of books is from Jean-Luc Godard's phony one. Godard, as Truffaut himself tells us, would pick up books off his host's bookshelf at a party, leaf through them, jot down some prestigious-sounding passage, and quote it in his next film, usually in the form of an irrelevant title card exhibitionistically dragged in. But, then, how different are the movies of those two. What major film director, Bergman not excluded, would have gone as far as Truffaut in this 1970 remark to Samuels: "Making *Fahrenheit* is what taught me that dialogue was more important in a film than I had realized. It is, in fact, the most important thing."

But no filmmaker, least of all the always ambivalent Truffaut, can leave it at that. So we find Truffaut writing (in 1966, the year he made *Fahrenheit 451*), in the introduction to *Le Cinéma selon Hitchcock*, "The most fundamental question of all [is] how to express oneself by purely visual means. . . . Whatever is *said* instead of being *shown* is lost upon the viewer." Still, Truffaut kept refining his sense of how to use words on film. In a 1977 letter to Jean Mambrino, a Jesuit and a screenwriter, he explains: "Three abstract nouns in a sentence (if it's heard instead of read) impede the spectator's train of thought, which is why one has to use short sentences." Similarly, Truffaut kept deepening his comprehension of the visual aspect of cinema. In a 1973 piece on Bergman's *Cries and Whispers* (reprinted in a collection of essays and reviews, *The Films in My Life*), Truffaut proffers his highest praise: "There is nothing on the canvas except what Bergman (who's anti-pictorial, like all true filmmakers) wants there." "Antipictorial" seems to mean selectively, controlledly visual, just as the advice to Mambrino means being selectively, judiciously verbal.

In his rather short life (1932-1984), cut off by a brain tumor, Truffaut produced, as the editors of this book remind us, "21 feature films, 3 shorts, 10 books, 10 unrealized projects, 13 prefaces and literally hundreds of articles." That is considerable, and sometimes gave even Truffaut pause. "I've made too many films in the last 5 years," he writes in 1978, "too many and too quickly." Yet in 1961, he wrote Charles Aznavour, "As you know, I work slowly and never rush things." The tempo never really changed; it was one film every one or two years, except for two films in 1969: the unsuccessful *Mississippi Mermaid* and the rather successful *The Wild Child*. But as he was involved in so many more and various activities with every passing year, the pace, if not the output, kept growing more dizzying.

Mermaid and child, those were Truffaut's chief topics—those and Truffaut himself. He liked to put himself into his movies, either by proxy (Jean-Pierre Léaud was the youthful surrogate of choice; Charles Denner, the middle-aged one) or literally, as in *The Wild Child, Day for Night* (*La Nuit américaine* [1973]), and *The Green Room* (1978). The subject was almost always childhood (*The 400 Blows, The Wild Child, Small Change*, i.e., *L'Argent de poche* [1976]) or grand passions of one kind or another involving fanatically devoted or dangerously destructive women, the two types sometimes overlapping.

In these letters, Truffaut does not have much to say about childhood, but the earlier missives, mostly to Lachenay, are wonderful demonstrations of the functioning of a gifted, artistically inclined adolescent and youth in the France of the Forties and early Fifties. It is interesting, in this context, to note the black moods to which the usually ebullient François could fall prey. Thus the eighteen-year-old writes, "There

was a very real chance of my being in no condition to answer your letter, as I tried to kill myself and had 25 razor slashes in my right arm"—this following a wild party given by Truffaut's then girl friend upon failing her baccalaureate exam. In front of such current and future celebrities as Claude Mauriac, Alexandre Astruc, and Maurice Schérer (a.k.a. Eric Rohmer), she dumped on him; typically, he compared the whole thing to Renoir's *The Rules of the Game,* with himself as its hero, Jurien. After he wounded himself, and the girl cold-bloodedly bandaged his arm, he became Frédéric Lemaître in *The Children of Paradise.*

Films and life became entangled and undistinguishable for him: "I fall in love with people through films," he writes in 1965. To the best of my ability to decipher that remark, it means that he fell in love with the female characters he created, then consummated the love by having affairs with the actresses who portrayed those parts. And what ravishing actresses they were: Jeanne Moreau, Françoise Dorléac, her sister, Catherine Deneuve, Isabelle Adjani, Nicole Berger, Julie Christie, Jacqueline Bisset, Alexandra Stewart, Marie-France Pisier, Sabine Haudepin, Delphine Seyrig, Claude Jade, Leslie Caron—to mention only the most striking ones. Some of these actresses—like Fanny Ardant, with whom he lived during his last couple of years, and by whom he had his third daughter—certainly, a few others probably, were his lovers. Indeed, it is fairly clear even from this heavily censored book that what broke up Truffaut's marriage was the closeness to Jeanne Moreau. One or two of these actresses also seem to have hurt Truffaut when, upon finishing shooting, they were gone like a shot. But Truffaut never stopped looking for the perfect relationship. Among the other women with whom he was involved, and who are veiledly mentioned in the letters, we recognize Soraya, the second wife of the Shah of Iran.

Yet he was not a philanderer, a *coureur.* About to shoot *Jules et Jim* in 1960, he describes the film as "a demonstration through joy and grief of the impossibility of any sexual combination outside of the couple." Even in the film that is most outspoken about his womanizing, *The Man Who Loved Women* (1977), the hero, Bertrand Morane, played by the Truffaut alter ego Charles Denner, is not a mere soulless lecher. Reviewing J. P. Mocky's *Les Vierges* in 1965, Truffaut wrote, "This is a man's film, a film about girls as seen by a man who is both obsessed sexually and a puritan, two hardly incompatible conditions." That fits both Morane and Truffaut, neither of which puritans could be without women for long. As one female character explains his conquests to Morane, "You have a special way of asking. It's as if your life depended on it." The love letters of Truffaut, with their special way of asking, will make fascinating reading when and if they're published.

Meanwhile, we do get some glimpses in this correspondence.

Not yet twenty, François writes his pal Robert from the army in Germany, "What is it you find fault with in my love life? I may lack Balzac's genius, but my love life is just as complicated as his, the objects of my affection being either sixteen or forty years old, with a few ambiguous relationships between these 2 ages; young women of good stock and widows; there's nothing else that matters and how heavenly to correspond with them, I could show you a collection of letters like no other!" I dare say, and what a shame that we have to make do with such teasers. In 1979, the forty-six-year-old Truffaut writes to the young director Jacques Doillon: "Worst of all is the rereading of love letters. That's when one notices how one spends one's life setting oneself up to be hurt rather than doing the best for oneself." So there's the commentary, but where's the text?

Two related phenomena strike me as rather less attractive. One is Truffaut's making dates with the very young or newborn daughters of his friends. To Bob Balaban, he writes in 1978: "Tell [your little girl] to write my name on the first page of her dance card." The editors note that he sent telegrams to Samuel Fuller's daughter the day she was born ("Dear Samantha, already I love you") and on her first birthday ("Dear Samantha, your suitor is waiting to take you to dinner when you are old enough"). In February 1983, the fifty-one-year-old Truffaut writes a letter to the just-born grand-daughter of one of his first film editors: "Since I can already foresee the queues forming, I'm asking you without further delay to reserve for me the 1st Wednesday of March 1996. I'll take you to see a film forbidden to under-13s, and then we'll go to have an ice-cream at Angélina's." I am sure some people—including, probably, the families of these little girls—found this sort of thing charming; it strikes me as mildly creepy.

Creepier yet is Truffaut's relationship with Helen Scott, a woman who worked protractedly for the French Film Office in New York, but also held other film-related jobs in New York and Paris. She was also a translator (though not a very good one) who helped Truffaut write his interview book with Hitchcock: Scott translated Truffaut's questions into English and Hitchcock's answers into French. She was a sort of unofficial publicist for Truffaut, and doubtless a good friend. She was intelligent, but I found her tiresome, officious, and both fawning and overbearing. Large, obese, and horse-faced, she was one of the most repellent-looking women I've ever met. Yet Truffaut's letters to her are, at times, something very close to love letters.

What are we to make of this? If it is merely epistolary flirtatiousness, Gallic *courtoisie*, Truffaldian charm (Truffaut on Truffaut: "I may be a whore, but I'm the coquettish, crafty, subtle type who keeps his hat and shoes on"), it is a rather unattractive leading on of a no doubt susceptible woman—possibly also for personal gain, in exchange for slavish services. But if these things are the literal truth ("I send you a passionate kiss, since, between us, passion is compulsory," "I kiss your foot," "After having been closeted with me for 4 tender and violent weeks [while interviewing Hitchcock]," "My lovely, soft Scottie," etc.), I find it more than a little queasy-making.

Where, then, you may ask, is the "niceness" of Truffaut with which I began? There is a leitmotiv of sweetness, charm, decency, and good humor that runs through this book, very spiritedly, though not always grammatically, translated by Gilbert Adair. It comes out clearly in the nineteen-year-old's letter to Lachenay: "The humanist is the one who loves the individual and not society." It's in the young army jailbird who assesses Daudet's *Lettres de mon moulin,* which he has just reread, as "a mixture of glibness and sometimes vulgarity yet there's talent there." It comes out in the ability to laugh off often very severe bouts of depression: "I contemplate suicide with an extraordinary serenity—I will kill myself out of non-chalance, just letting myself go, the way I let myself go in the cinema with the great satisfaction of knowing that one could rouse oneself if 'one wished,' but that one might just as well not." There is a bit of ham and sham in this from the twenty-year-old, yet his woes at that time were real enough.

To Jean Mambrino, in 1955, he writes that he is unformed and uneducated, but has "the good fortune to be blessed with a slight sense of and great love for the cinema." After finishing *The 400 Blows,* he wants to give up, stay home, play with his daughter, read more and more, and take tap-dancing lessons to stop his fidgets. He doesn't mind typing with just one finger, because "that means I type harder and faster in accordance with the well-known law of compensation which . . . makes one-armed men better in bed." "If friends like [my films], it all seems worth while." In 1960, he explains why he won't write film criticism now that he is a filmmaker: "A number of old directors are unemployed because of the 'New Wave' and it would be tasteless for a lucky young devil . . ." (This is a recurrent theme.) He has compassion for stars: "Stars suffer because they're constantly being harassed; when they're no longer harassed, it's even worse." He recognizes that the only thing that saves *Jules et Jim* is its melancholy, which is its morality. He keeps turning down lucrative offers to film literary masterpieces from Proust to Kafka because he recognizes that film can only betray them.

His favorite contemporary painter is Balthus; he modestly perceives the book on Hitchcock as an opportunity to educate himself. He cries at Godard's *Vivre sa Vie*; goes back to see it with beloved Jeanne Moreau, and they "blub 3 or 4 times." He deplores the contempt for their actors, and indeed their fictional characters, that affects even his favorite directors—Hitchcock, Renoir, Hawks, Rossellini—when they reach fifty-five. He tells how, as a child, he always dreaded Christmas, because he hated his family—then softens this to "was bored by them." In 1964, he writes a lovely letter to Henri-Georges Clouzot, whom, along with other older directors, he attacked in his youthful reviews; gradually, he makes peace with several others, though never, I am sorry to say, with that "butcher" René Clément. He recognizes, as many directors don't, that "people are more important than celluloid." He loves Rossellini so much that he does his utmost to vindicate him, even when he sees the con man in him.

Honorably, he turns down an award for good citizenship (1967). Though he is not especially political (a refreshing thing in a Frenchman), he is co-leader in a quasi-political action to restore Henri Langlois to the Cinémathèque française, from which he has been fired by Malraux; later on, he is not afraid to distribute anti-Algerian War leaflets with Sartre and de Beauvoir. (Godard is.) He writes enthusiastic letters to directors whose films he likes, takes time to read and carefully criticize manuscripts sent by strangers, makes sensible rules for himself never to be on a film jury, never to reply to newspaper attacks, never to take legal action. "I don't have an 'auteur' complex," he writes in 1971, referring to the foolish "auteur theory" he helped spawn as a youth, and he does not minimize the importance of the screenwriter. He refuses to sign a manifesto that is "woolly, vague and insipid and bristling with too many capital letters." In 1973, he writes a most considerate letter to an actor whose big scene ended up on the cutting-room floor.

Truffaut is sensible about screen billing: "We all have equal billing in the cemetery." In 1978, he recognizes his chief problem, the need "to use every girl he meets as a means of settling accounts with his mother." In 1982, he threatens to resign from the Society of Film Directors if they don't stop bad-mouthing some of his colleagues. And, in the very last letter of this collection (to Annette Insdorf, January 16, 1984) he jokes about the brain tumor for which he has been operated on and which was to fell him nine months later: "Film criticism was *20 years ahead* of conventional medicine, since, when my 2nd film, *Tirez sur le Pianiste,* came out, it declared that such a film could only have been made by someone whose brain wasn't functioning normally!"

This is only an almost random sampling. But I must mention also what Truffaut called the *politique des copains* (not to be confused with the silly *politique des auteurs,* which arbitrarily exalted some directors and dismissed others), whereby Truffaut, like his colleagues on *Cahiers,* only perhaps more so, plugged in every conceivable way such filmmaker friends as Rohmer, Rivette, Godard, Chabrol, Resnais, Malle, and the rest. I find endearing his very French inability, or refusal, to learn a foreign language, in this case English, which would have been most advantageous to him. I recall having

lunch with him once when, talking in French, he told me that it was a mistake to have done that book on Hitchcock; he should have done it on Oaks. We were sitting in the Oak Room of the Plaza, and it took me a moment to realize that he meant Howard Hawks. In a letter here, after reviewing the time, money, and effort he had spent on learning English, he comments, "There is in me a refusal to learn as powerful as my wish to know."

But the essence of the man emerges best, perhaps, from what may be considered the centerpiece of the book: the reprinted letter from Godard (May 1973) and Truffaut's answer. Having just seen *Day for Night,* Godard begins by calling his former friend (they had become estranged) what "no one else will . . . a liar." A liar because Ferrand, the film director in that movie—played by Truffaut himself and exhibiting many autobiographical traits—"is the only one who does not screw." This despite the press coverage of Truffaut and Jackie Bisset on the town together. The implication is that Truffaut was dishonest about a lot of things concerning filmmaking (and life); then, brazenly, Godard concludes by asking for a hefty sum to help subsidize *his* film, which will tell the truth. He concludes, "If you want to talk it over, fine."

There is, to be sure, truth in Godard's charge, but Truffaut's answer, which never really answers it, is nonetheless sublime. It begins: "So you won't be obliged to read this unpleasant letter right to the end, I'm starting with the essential point: I will not co-produce your film." What follows is a meticulously itemized list of Godard's human deficiencies and wrongdoings, as well as a statement on his artistic decline. I happen to agree with all Truffaut says—and the evidence he marshals is staggering—but more important than specifics is the human credo that emerges and from which I quote:

> The notion that all men are equal is theoretical with you . . . you have never succeeded in loving anyone or in helping anyone, other than by shoving a few banknotes at them . . . . Between your interest in the masses and your own narcissism there's no room for anything or anyone else . . . . Those who called you a genius, no matter what you did, all belonged to that famous trendy Left that runs the gamut from Susan Sontag to Bertolucci via Richard Roud . . . . I've always had the impression that real militants are like 'cleaning women, doing a thankless, daily but necessary job. But you, you're the Ursula Andress of militancy, you make a brief appearance, just enough time for the cameras to flash, you make two or three duly startling remarks and then you disappear again, trailing clouds of self-serving mystery.

And he, too, concludes with an offer to talk it over, and also—very Truffaut—an apt quotation from Bernanos. What is especially remarkable, though, is that, shortly afterward, in a letter to a journalist, Truffaut calls Godard's *Breathless* a masterpiece.

When it came to humanity—not excluding, needless to say, warts—Truffaut was hard to beat. Read, for example, the tribute of the great cinematographer Nestor Almendros, in his book *A Man With a Camera,* which begins by recalling the excellent, Renoir-like atmosphere of happy filmmaking that Truffaut created on the set, and stresses his willingness to take suggestions from everyone, down to the makeup people and grips. Although Truffaut writes that he is "not a good poetry reader," he will have to allow me to summarize his achievement with a verse and a half from Yves Bonnefoy's poem "Art de la poésie": "On a réconcilié la fièvre. On a dit au coeur/D'être le coeur."

How will history evaluate Truffaut? A strong reaction against him has already set in, and most of his later films are, indeed, indefensible. It may be worth quoting a 1972 interview I conducted with Ingmar Bergman for my book on him:

*Simon*: What about the early Truffaut? Did you like those first ones?

*Bergman*: Very much. Very, very much.

*S*: What happened to this man?

*B*: He wants to make money; it's a very human desire. He wants a comfortable life . . . and he wants people to see his pictures.

*S*: Well, don't you think his early films were seen by people?

*B*: But perhaps not by enough, and he didn't make enough money, and he likes the comfortable life of the modern filmmaker.

*S*: But the trouble is his new films are not going to make much money. [This was before *Day for Night* and *The Last Metro* (1981).]

*B*: Then he made a mistake. Because if you lose both the money and your dignity, it must be a mistake.

It seems to me that *The 400 Blows,* the first half of *Jules et Jim,* and, above all, *Shoot the Piano Player* will survive comfortably. Not far behind will be *Stolen Kisses* (1968), *The Story of Adèle H.* (1975), and parts of some other films, with, I hope, genuine affection for that much underrated (even by Truffaut himself) charmer, *Such a Gorgeous Kid Like Me* (1972). Also for the shorts *Les Mistons* and *Antoine et Colette* (1962). That, I believe, is about as much as most

major filmmakers can claim, and quite enough. The special quality of it is best expressed in Truffaut's 1980 letter to Jean-Claude Grumberg: "When humor can be made to alternate with melancholy, one has a success, but when the *same* things are funny and melancholic at the same time, it's just wonderful."

## Daniel Towner (essay date 1990)

SOURCE: "Antoine Doinel in the Zoetrope," in *Literature/ Film Quarterly,* Vol. 18, No. 4, 1990, pp. 230-35.

[*In the following essay, Towner argues that Truffaut is a revisionist and that his later films reintroduce characters, scenes, and images from his earlier films.*]

It should surprise no one that Francois Truffaut would base one of his later films (*The Green Room,* 1978) on the writings of Henry James. There are a number of aspects about their works that bear comparison, and even if the filmmaker as a youth might have been ignorant of the American novelist's work, Truffaut's later discovery of James must have been a revelation. After all, like James, Truffaut was among the first practitioners of a new national art form to have a clear historical sense on which to draw. (In fact, T.S. Eliot's criticism of James, that he had not so much a sense of the past as "a sense of the sense," could be applied as well to Truffaut). Just as James came to terms with the preceding generation of American novelists (taken seriously by neither American nor European readers) by writing a book on Hawthorne at the beginning of his career, so Truffaut wrote prolifically about film before he became a filmmaker himself. Both men, too, attempted to elevate the question of nationality, both of themselves and of their art, to an aesthetic question.

A most striking parallel, however, is the fact that late in their careers, both James and Truffaut began to *revise* the work of their youth. The effect of James's revisions and introductions in the New York Edition (1907-1917) of his works was to draw together and make more articulate themes and preoccupations present but not always initially clear, and, further, to make the "seeing again" of the past a primary artistic concern. Truffaut, too, tended in later films more and more to add variations on old images, to repeat names and even props in such a way as to make us return to the earlier work and see it as a consciously-crafted whole.

This is not to say that Truffaut was himself always aware of all the implications of his early films. Take, for instance, the sequence accompanying the titles of *The 400 Blows.* Here we see, without any obvious relevance to the film itself, the Eiffel Tower, seen only from a distance, circled, approached but never arrived at, by the camera. Some things must have occurred to Truffaut: this is, of course, a national symbol, one whose origin coincided almost exactly with that of another French invention: cinema. The perception of the Tower, here, is, as well, cinematic: the camera calls attention to itself by being jostled about as it is driven by, and, since it never attains its object, it remains essentially a manifestation of *observation,* separate from the thing viewed.

This "commentary" on the nature of cinematic perception is seen in another image in the same film—an image whose implications become clear only in its development in a later Doinel film. In *The 400 Blows,* Antoine, while playing hooky from school, rides a carnival ride, a revolving cylinder whose centrifugal force makes him stick to the side. It is a magical moment, offhand like the best "trivial" yet poetic sequences in the films of Jean Renoir. The connection between this sequence and the title sequence may not have been obvious to Truffaut in 1959. But by 1979, as Truffaut revised, it had obviously become clear. When Truffaut used this scene as a flashback in *Love on the Run,* he used it as a comment on the nature of film art. After Antoine grows up, seeks love (*Antoine and Colette,* 1962), finds it (*Stolen Kisses,* 1968), loses it (*Bed and Board,* 1970), and finds it again (*Love on the Run*), we see him in his embrace with Sabine—the camera shifts back and forth, and this shot is intercut with the shots of young Antoine spinning in the cylinder, as if viewing adult life from the perspective of childhood. Also, since the sequence encompasses the totality of Truffaut's cinematic life to that point, it comments on the cinema's power both to record and to reconstruct life. The image suggests, too, another aspect of the photographic image spinning in a cylinder. This, after all, is (as Annette Insdorf points out) very much like the zoetrope, a precursor of the device of moving picture. Doinel's history, and the personal history of the man who created him, is here identified with the history of the device which contains his whole life. That Truffaut was conscious of the significance of this image in 1959 we may doubt. (But perhaps Truffaut's reading of Insdorf's books, which appeared in 1978 and for which Truffaut wrote an appreciative blurb, enabled him to use the image as a more explicit metaphor in 1979.) In any case, the meaning of the images, merely suggestive in the early films, is here complete: Antoine as the subject of the film is both in the zoetrope, and from the perspective of the present, his story is a historical artifact which nevertheless provides a vantage point from which to interpret present events.

In *The Man Who Loved Women,* there is a moment which, tonally and thematically, expresses this major concern of Truffaut's late films. Bertrand, the main character, passing by the presses which are printing his memoirs, stops and reads a passage of his work, picked up at random. We hear his voice and see the event described: he passes a girl in a red dress and comforts her, saying, "I wouldn't cry if I had a

pretty red dress like that." He asks the typesetter if he may make a change. He crosses out "red" and writes in "blue." As he makes the change, we see the same event, but this time the girl wears a blue dress.

In this film, as in other late films by Truffaut—particularly *Day for Night* and *Love on the Run*—we see a curious insistence on the filmmaker's part to make us first *see* and then to *revise* the images before us. Often *what* we see (such as the color of the girl's dress) appears insignificant and the change gratuitous. Revision itself becomes the subject—images are placed in new contexts and made the expressions of something new.

In *Day for Night,* traditional boundaries between director and character (the main character is a fictitious film director named Ferrand, played by Truffaut), film and real life, artist and audience, actor and character, are crossed, thus giving expression to a film aesthetic already present in Truffaut's work at least since *The Wild Child.* The demands of the lives of cast and crew intrude on the making of the film (an uninspired romance called *Meet Pamela*), and, when a star dies, the director says in voice over,

> What I had always feared had happened . . . a production halted by death. The era of studio movies died with Alexander. Films will be shot in the streets, without stars . . . or scenarios. There will be no more films like *Meet Pamela.*

It is a curious statement, first because we forget that the "real" events of the film are in fact no less contrived for the camera than those in *Meet Pamela.* Also, Truffaut's prediction about the future of the cinema is not borne out even by his own work: *Day for Night* was immediately followed by the thoroughly conventional *The Story of Adele H.* Also, the description of the style of films of the future might as easily be applied to earlier films which influenced Truffaut, like *Zero de Conduite* and *Toni.*

In *Love on the Run,* Truffaut continues deliberately to blur the distinctions between character, actor, and director, but he makes his statement cinematically, without direct statement in voice-over. This turn in his work, it seems to me, is the logical ethos of a man who espouses the *politique des auteurs.* It is true that there is a certain circularity in some versions of this idea. Truffaut once explained in an interview a major tenet of the *auteur* philosophy:

> There are not good and bad films: there are simply good and bad directors. It might happen that a bad director could make a film which gives the illusion of being good because he had the excellent fortune of having a good scenario and fine actors. Nevertheless, this "good" film would have no value in the

eyes of a critic because it was just a coincidence of circumstances. . . . What is interesting is the career of a good director in that it reflects his thought from his beginning to his more mature phase. Each one of the films marks one phase in his thoughts, and it is of no importance that any particular picture is successful or not, or a good film or not.

Certainly this is a critical can of worms. After all, how do we know the good director from the bad without first establishing an aesthetic principle, judging each film, and ranking them within the director's canon? It is nonsense to say that the quality of the director precedes the quality of his films, since he can be known only by his work.

> In *Love on the Run,* Truffaut continues deliberately to blur the distinctions between character, actor, and director, but he makes his statement cinematically, without direct statement in voice-over.
>
> —*Daniel Towner*

But what happens when the critic turns film director and makes the critical tenet—that the interaction of the director with his artistic past is the real subject of his films—a principle of composition? The application of this principle, it could be argued, has been the case throughout Truffaut's career as a director: he has never made a secret of his identification with Antoine Doinel. Recounting an incident when a stranger, having seen an excerpt of *Stolen Kisses* on television, mistook Truffaut for Jean-Pierre Leaud, Truffaut writes,

> This incident . . . illustrates fairly well the ambiguity (as well as the ubiquity) of that imaginary personage, Antoine Doinel, who happens to be the synthesis of two real-life people, Jean-Pierre Leaud and myself.

In *Love on the Run,* the biographical ambiguity of the film character has come to the thematic fore. Truffaut here ingeniously forces us to consider the growth of the artist simultaneously with and as a result of his relationship with his characters. In *Love on the Run,* it is possible, in fact necessary, for even a strictly textual critic to consider the autobiographical element of the Dionel films, at least insofar as the film is part of the conscious aesthetic biography of its author.

It is fitting that Truffaut would choose a Doinel film as the medium for a statement about the relationship of an artist to his material. Doinel has reappeared throughout Truffaut's

career, growing—or, more properly, aging, and failing to grow—as Truffaut moves through his career. It has been charged that *Love on the Run* is a weak rehash of earlier Doinel material, relying on lengthy flashbacks. In fact, in this last Doinel film, Truffaut, like the hero of *The Man Who Loved Women,* revises the work of his youth, using, it is true, much footage from the earlier films, but often in a new context. The attentive viewer will notice that Truffaut uses footage from non-Doinel films as well, establishing a link, necessary to the understanding of *Love on the Run,* between them and the more overtly autobiographical Doinel cycle, and incorporating into the "text" of the film the "cinematic memory" central to the *politique.*

In the latter film such echoes come constantly. Truffaut uses footage from all the Doinel films here, but also from *Day for Night* and *The Man Who Loved Women.* Many of the details are meaningful only in Truffaut's re-use of them as a medium for conveying the sense of wholeness in his work. The demands he places upon his audience redeems his work from the arrogance of obsession and establishes a relationship with them. A catalog of the visual echoes in Truffaut's later films might begin with the apparently trivial (such as the off-hand re-use of a vase—the same vase which the fictional director in *Day for Night* selects to use in his fictional film; or the zoom shot of an antenna in *Day for Night* which recalls the credit sequence of *Fahrenheit 451.* The catalog ends, however, with some of Truffaut's most enduring and resonant visual preoccupations: the tender fascination of male characters for women who wear glasses, seen also in *Jules and Jim* and *The Man Who Loved Women*; the revelation of the relationships of characters by showing them arrayed in the windows of their houses, as in *Jules and Jim* and *Day for Night* (where we are shown the artificiality of the set where such a scene is filmed). There are many other echoes, so many that the echo becomes the technic of the film. The character of Sabine, the woman who seems to resolve, finally, Antoine's problems with women, bears the name of Jules's and Catherine's daughter. Likewise, Liliane (Dani) retains the name of the character she played in the non-Doinel *Day for Night,* a film dedicated to Lillian Gish; indeed, she seems to be the same character, having played opposite Jean-Pierre Leaud in both films. Truffaut in fact reshot scenes with Dani from *Day for Night* for *Love on the Run* in order to replace Jacqueline Bisset with Claude Jade, and the name "Alphonse" (the actor in *Meet Pamela,* played by Leaud) with "Antoine." "Alphonse," incidentally, is the name of Antoine's and Christine's son.) These echoes have the tone of the director's public cherishing of private delights, and of the delight of being able to make movies out of them.

The story of *Love on the Run* is melodramatic, full of chance encounters and banal intrigue. On the surface it resembles *Meet Pamela.* Thus its story is simple to summarize. It concerns Antoine's further difficulties with the responsibilities of mature love. After having failed in his in marriage to Christine, he begins again with Sabine, whom he obviously loves, though he is incapable of expressing his love to her. Always in a hurry because of his absent-mindedness, Antoine must change his plans about meeting with Sabine later in the day; he has forgotten that this is the day of his divorce from Christine. Just after the divorce, he accidentally encounters Colette, his crush from *Love at Twenty,* who is just reading his autobiographical novel, *Love and Other Difficulties.* He recounts to her the story of his circuitous path toward his meeting and winning of Sabine, whom Colette later mistakenly identifies as the wife of the man she herself loves. (In fact, Sabine and Colette's lover are brother and sister.) She finds out the truth, however, and, at the end of the film, we see both couples at a tentative reconciliation. Antoine explains to Sabine the extremely romantic story of his search for her, and they both express the desire to go on.

The plot, with its twists, surprises, and hackneyed, improbable coincidences comments on the small world of the film. There really *can* be no more *Meet Pamelas.* Yet the backwardness of the plot throws light upon the images which recur from the other films, suggesting that the plot is in fact a medium for the use of them, rather than the other way around. Truffaut's embracing of the unlikely, pedestrian devices typical of the romantic movie are a compromise, similar to the one that the filmmaker must make to the boundaries of the screen. The film image is artificial, but its very smallness makes the lives of the people on the screen and beyond the screen more easily known.

That Doinel is the author of a book with a title similar to the title of the film identifies him with Truffaut, of course, the wielder of the *camera-stylo*; it also recalls the hero of *The Man Who Loved Women,* who writes a book called *The Man Who Loved Women.* As they are all authors, they all revise their work. In one interesting sequence, as Antoine recounts the story of his search for Sabine, we see him *in the flashback,* looking at the camera, and narrating the story. We have already seen this shot in an earlier version, but without Antoine. As Antoine tells, Truffaut revises. Antoine the character here steps forward as Leaud the actor, calling attention to the artifice of the film. So we have a multi-level convergence, and a complicated inter-relationship among the three.

Antoine reveals his love for Sabine as they face a mirror together, a position reminiscent of the scene where he first fell in love with her—at the movies. The "movie" they watch here, however, is themselves: they see themselves and each other simultaneously. The image is a commentary on the relationship of film as a medium by which we know ourselves and each other. We also recognize the hand of the director here, too, as he asserts himself in this visual simile; he is drawn into the frame. We are part of the scene as well,

since we are in the same position—watching a reflection of ourselves in a rectangle of light.

But Truffaut's history does not remain a merely personal one. His films are full of allusions to others, so many, in fact, that I am sure that all his cinematic "quotations" will never be known. To get a flavor of this, though, we might look at some references to a particularly rich source of influence, Jean Vigo.

The most obvious thing to say is that *The 400 Blows* tries to recapture the tone of *Zero de Conduite.* But Truffaut pays other homages to Vigo, often in small ways, as in the brief shot of the room Antoine occupies at his friend Rene's house, overrun by cats like the barge in *L'Atalante.* His use of the actor Jean Daste, who portrayed the sympathetic teacher of *Zero de Conduite,* as an example of conscience in *The Wild Child* and *The Man Who Loved Women* must have been a conscious attempt to make a link between Truffaut's films and Vigo's. There is, too, the loving way the camera lingers in *Day for Night* on the sign indicating the "Rue Jean Vigo." (Could Truffaut have been thinking that, for English-speaking audiences, the sign is, appropriately, an imperative sentence?) Certainly Truffaut could be tracing a similar history of his own films from *The 400 Blows* to *Bed and Board* and *Love on the Run* (and responding to the alleged decline of his own career after the first three films) when he writes of Vigo's films:

> I believe that *L'Atalante* is often underestimated as being concerned with a small subject of *Zero de Conduite.* In reality, *L'Atalante* deals with a major theme, and one that has seldom been treated in films, the beginnings of a young couple's life together, their difficulty in adapting to each other, the early euphoria of coupling. . . . then the first wounds, rebellion, flight, reconciliation, and finally acceptance. *L'Atalante* doesn't treat any less a subject than *Zero de Conduite.*

Perhaps the most efficient statement of Truffaut's concern with the shifting perspective of personal, cinematic, and national history comes during the title sequence of *Stolen Kisses.* The camera starts with a close-up of the barred doors of the Cinemateque Francaise, closed at the beginning of the political upheaval in France in 1968. There is a note superimposed: "*Stolen Kisses* is dedicated to the Cinemateque Francaise of Henri Langlois." The wording is very precise: the film is *not* dedicated to Langlois, though he is certainly a symbol of film history, but to the historical institution that Langlois founded. The camera pulls back, and there is a cut to the Eiffel Tower, recalling the beginning of *The 400 Blows*; the camera pans to the building where Antoine Doinel is confined in a military prison. In this short sequence, Truffaut has managed to link cinematic history with national/political history, and by moving from the place where films are "held prisoner" to Antoine's place of imprisonment, to place the events of his own films in the context of film history.

Jean-Luc Godard once wrote, "To say that Renoir is the most intelligent of filmmakers comes down to saying that he is French to the tip of his toes." We cannot, I think, dismiss the remark as one of mere nationalistic fervor. (Who would be less likely than Godard to espouse such a mundane idea as simple patriotism?) Certainly Godard wants to remind us that the history of French film is the history of *all* film. Truffaut, in celebrating the gallant, if impossible, attempt to embody and revise the whole of national, personal, and cinematic history in his films, remembers.

## Elain DalMolin (essay date 1994)

SOURCE: "A Voice in the Dark: Feminine Figuration in Truffaut's *Jules and Jim*," in *Literature/Film Quarterly*, Vol. 22, No. 4, 1994.

[*In the following essay, DalMolin discusses the role of the female voice in* Jules and Jim.]

In the very beginning of *Jules and Jim,* while the screen is still black, a woman's voice is heard. No musical background, no other artificial sounds accompany this voice so crisp and clear that it sounds like an earnest statement purposely isolated to underscore the intensity of a vocal feminine presence from the start. "Tu m'as dit: je t'aime. Je t'ai dit: attends. J'allais dire: prends-moi. Tu m'as dit: va-t-en." ("You said to me: I love you. I said to you: wait. I was going to say: take me. You said to me: go away.") The voice is deep and sensual—two qualities defining the voice of Jeanne Moreau, the woman behind the voice and the actress in *Jules and Jim.* It mixes childish and mature tones in the same breath; it speaks of love, frustration, and separation. The present study represents first an uncovering of the filmic status of this voice chanting in the dark, and second a questioning of the effects of the voice on the spectator expecting visual, not aural, pleasure. Whose unexpected voice do we hear coming from the darkness of the screen?

Plot provides us with an immediate answer to this question. This voice is the disembodied voice of Catherine, the main female character in Truffaut's 1962 movie *Jules and Jim,* in which two young men, Jules and Jim, fall victim to their dream of idealism represented by the sublime statue of a woman whom they come across by accident during a slide show. The beautiful statue on the slide triggers their desire to search for the actual woman incarnating the statue (Catherine). When they meet Catherine, they know that she is their "statufied" desire come true. However, Catherine's

complex nature leaves her out of psychological reach, and despite her coming into Jules's and Jim's human world, she remains an unattainable object of desire throughout the film. Similarly, her disembodied voice remains an unattainable manifestation of her, as if it were speaking from inside a dream, displaced from the ideal body it represents while enunciating metonymically its feminine desire, adrift between love and rejection: "I love you . . . wait . . . take me . . . go away." As an impossible representation of desire, Catherine raises the question of feminine figuration in *Jules and Jim,* a question prompted by the mysterious female voice opening the movie.

The voice in the dark prefacing the visual experience that is about to begin dramatizes the distinction between the vocal and the specular, a distinction thoroughly investigated by Kaja Silverman in her acclaimed 1988 book *The Acoustic Mirror: The Female Voice in Psychoanalysis and Cinema.* My first task here is to summarize Silverman's argument on the female voice and particularly on the maternal voice in order to understand the dichotomous nature of movies like *Jules and Jim,* in which the division between the vocal and the visual is made clear from the start. It is in light of Silverman's theoretical observations on the different roles of the maternal voice in cinema that we shall uncover the performing presence of the maternal figure invested in the voice prefacing Truffaut's movie *Jules and Jim.*

For the purpose of defining as accurately as possible the female subject represented in cinema, Silverman uses Guy Rosolato's phrase "the acoustic mirror," which indicates the double function of the voice for any subject that simultaneously receives and produces sounds, internalizing the voice of identification while also externalizing it as an object of projection. Seen/heard through the "acoustic mirror," the voice "violates the bodily limits upon which classic subjectivity depends." The bodily limits evoked by Silverman are determined by modes of identification built on the specular order alone. In psychoanalysis, the primacy of the specular over any other modes of perception coincides with the critical oedipal moment when the infant identifies its own body, for the first time separated from the mother's body. According to French psychoanalyst Jacques Lacan, this first coming into subjectivity, into a preamble to subjectivity, occurs in the early life of the infant (for this activity, Lacan indicates the arbitrary age between the sixth and the eighteenth month). For the infant's first meeting with its subject, Lacan proffers a "symbolic" object, a mirror in which the infant first catches sight of its full body image and realizes its selfhood in relation to the other. Lacan's mirror is less an actual mirror than a metaphor for the mother's body, where "mental" separation of bodies first takes place. Past the mirror stage, the child continues to enhance the contours of its own identity, thus becoming capable of operating individually and concurrently into a language "restoring its function as subject". The child acquires its individual image in relation to the bodies it sees evolving around it. These "other" bodies act as mirrors that send back images of differences and similarities to the subject who, subsequently, assumes its identity and the limitations of its own body first in language and then in social situations mediated by cultural practices morally and sexually restricted by the Oedipus complex. Rosolato's concept of the "acoustic mirror" adapts the optical relation that the subject has with the mirror in psychoanalytical theory as if the mirror were reflecting sounds rather than images. The subject constitutes its self as it first differentiates sounds through the "acoustic mirror." Rosolato claims that the process of identification starts from birth and that the child, born with reduced visual powers, first distinguishes sounds —especially the mother's voice— and incorporates them as if they were its own sounds. Rosolato associates the mechanism of emission and reception of the voice with "the images of entry and departure relative to the body." In Rosolato's theory, the voice of the mother creates the vocal subject in similar ways that the *imago* in Lacan's theory of the mirror stage creates the specular subject. Rosolato gives the speaking mother the status of a vocal mirror in which the child recognizes the mother's voice as its own voice. Thus, according to Rosolato, subjectivity is not solely dependent on the image of the mother; but rather, her voice has already set into place the structures of individuation. In the "acoustic mirror" the mother is first perceived as a speaking subject before being perceived as a subject of speech. She is a speaking voice before being an image/body spoken about; as the "acoustic mirror" she becomes the subject's voice providing a vocal model of identification.

Silverman examines the two paradoxical functions of the "acoustic mirror" that she reads as a sonorous envelope that initially provides pleasure and later must be rejected. In the early life of the infant, the voice of the mother is perceived as a swaddling envelope of sounds protecting it. Once the infant becomes an individual subject caught into the cultural structures in place, the mother's voice represents maternal "abjection," in which the subject "hears all the repudiated elements of its infantile babble" that it must reject. The central problem raised by Silverman questions the constant shifting of the subject's position vis-à-vis the "acoustic mirror." Is the infant inside or outside the sonorous envelope created by the maternal voice? Is the mother inside or outside her own vocal envelope? Is the mother's voice a voice of pleasure or a voice of fear? Silverman provides us with an array of critical answers for such complex questions.

She first invokes Michel Chion's theory of the "uterine night," a sort of nightmare within which the child is trapped by the maternal voice. In the uterine night, the mother is outside producing the sounds that form the confining walls of a dark prison. Chion's views on the traumatic implications of the

maternal voice on the formation of the cinematic subject lie in sharp contrast to Rosolato's theory on the cinematic voice perceived as a "protective blanket," an oral surrounding of pleasure. Rosolato indicates that child and mother live in an undifferentiated state of vocal plenitude. According to him, they are both situated inside the circle of sounds created by the mother's voice.

In light of the different critical approaches to voice in cinema provided by Chion and Rosolato, we are able to shed some light on the odd beginning of *Jules and Jim,* a beginning in which there are no images to be seen, just a female voice to be heard. This voice seems to cradle the spectator in the dark as it naïvely narrates/sings a simple, repetitious riddle: "Tu m'as dit: je t'aime. Je t'ai dit: attends. J'allais dire: prends-moi. Tu m'as dit: va-t-en." In resembling the simplicity of a nursery rhyme, this riddle bestows maternal qualities upon the voice. Silverman's question about the position of the mother and the child in relation to the sonorous envelope created by the voice is fully dramatized in this preface of *Jules and Jim.* In a single instant, Silverman's distinctive critical positions on the role of voice as maternal pleasure or maternal fear conflate. We shall try to restore both positions and to see how they determine the double presence of pleasure and fear within the same vocalic representation of the mother.

On the one hand, the voice in the dark in the beginning of *Jules and Jim* dramatizes Chion's "uterine night," and, as such, it speaks from outside the vocal darkness it creates. Catherine's riddle lures its listeners into the darkness of her femininity, and the dark frames accompanying the voice serve as a metaphor for her "threatening" dark womb. The spectators, sitting in the dark movie theater and riveting their eyes to the screen they expect to produce images, are thrown into total confusion by the dark frames that pull them into the "void" in which they become the infant-subject trapped by the maternal voice. In the first few seconds of *Jules and Jim,* the spectators experience a moment of anxiety as they are forced to become listeners against their own will and desire to see. In place of the expected visual pleasure—an anticipated pleasure for which they have paid their dues by buying a ticket—the spectators find themselves trapped in the interiority of the vocal "darkness."

On the other hand, Rosolato's theory of first auditive bliss suggests a different scenario for the spectators thrown into total darkness; the spectators lose all visual sense of subjectivity and return to the undivided world of pre-symbolic plenitude and bliss where the only "other" object is the maternal voice enveloping the subject in its blanket of pleasure. In Rosolato's terms, the spectators listening to the maternal voice at the beginning of *Jules and Jim* introject the voice and make it their own voice. As through an acoustic mirror, phonic utterances detach themselves from their original maternal voice to fill the subject with a sonorous and rhythmical identity.

This moment of vocal identification with Catherine's voice precedes the visual bonding between the spectators and the images of the film. Whether nightmare (in Chion's thesis) or bliss (in Rosolato's thesis), the maternal voice prefacing Truffaut's *Jules and Jim* reenacts a primal scene of subjectivity, a vocal fantasy for blinded spectators.

What happens to Catherine's voice once the visual mechanism of the movies is under way? Her maternal voice, which once protected and cradled the child/spectator with the simplicity of its rhythms and sounds, becomes the voice of a woman expressing sexual desire. Even as the voice in the dark sings its mysterious riddle, Catherine's sexuality can already be differentiated in terms of what she says as opposed to how she says it. In other words, her sexuality depends on the meaning of the words rather than on the musicality supporting the words. Indeed, the female voice that asserts "I love you; wait; take me; go away" utters words of sexual significance depicting in simplistic terms a scene of frustrated love. In this scene, an unidentified lover declares his love ("Je t'aime") to a woman who does not feel ready to respond immediately to such passion. She asks her lover to wait ("attends"). When she feels that the moment has come for them to consummate their passion she offers her body to her lover ("prends-moi"), but the latter tired of waiting casts her off ("va-t-en"). The sexual connotation of these four verbal injunctions leaves behind the maternal resonances of Catherine's rhythmical voice. Understood for what it says, the voice in the dark becomes the voice of sexual desire, a seductive voice speaking a lover's discourse.

The first auditive instant provided by the riddling voice at the beginning of *Jules and Jim* mixes the cradling sounds of motherhood with the riddling language of sexuality. The mother behind the voice in the dark is also a sexual being seducing the blinded audience into its feminine darkness.

We begin to wonder if the feminine voice singing in the dark belongs to a loving mother or to a seductive temptress. Much of the ambiguous nature of the feminine figure is based on the conflict we have just traced between voice and language, sounds and words, rhythms and meanings; and these conflictual terms delineate in turn a conflictual feminine figure, maternal in essence, but divided in nature between platonic love and sexual love. In *La Jeune née*, Hélène Cixous views Voice with a capital "V" as the legacy of motherhood resisting symbolic codification. The voice of the mother is a powerful stream of sounds that cannot be cut off by the symbolic order, the paternal order of language. According to Cixous, the maternal voice stands outside the "law" just as Catherine's voice prefacing *Jules and Jim* stands outside the actual limits of the film, before the credits and the first images of the film. Cixous's views on the way in which the "Symbolic" interrupts the respiratory function of the voice lends itself to the odd beginning of *Jules and Jim* when the female voice in the dark is interrupted by the written credits and the images appearing on the screen, two symbolic occurrences marking the official beginning of the movie. The voice itself survives beyond this interruption, it impregnates the visual order, and resonates throughout the course of the movie.

Beyond its vocal introduction, the film itself provides some answers to the ambiguous nature of the feminine figure. The nature of the female voice prefacing *Jules and Jim* owes much of its ambiguity to the fact that it does not accompany a body or an image. The disembodied maternal voice Silverman evokes in *The Acoustic Mirror* is always a voice-over, a voice separated from its original body but initiating a relation of signification with the images appearing on the screen as it speaks. The voice in the dark in *Jules and Jim* is a voice-over nothing, a voice for voice's sake. As the movie progresses, the voice becomes associated with the visual image of Catherine. However, even when the voice has claimed Catherine's body as its originator, the dichotomy between music and language, between maternal rhythms and sexual signifiers, does not dissolve into the visual order of the movie.

Catherine's singing voice sounds again during the movie when she performs in front of her three lovers a song titled "Le Tourbillon de la vie," "The Swirl of Life." Catherine's song is written by Albert, one of her three lovers; the voice is hers, the lyrics are his. We may view the singing as an emanation from her maternal self and the language of the song as an emanation from the masculine/paternal Other embodied in the three male figures who delineate Catherine's love life. Indeed, either directly or indirectly, the three men listening to her have established a relationship of paternity with her. Jules is the real father of their little girl, Sabine; Jim is the short-lived would-be father of Catherine's miscarried child; and Albert is the "adoptive" father ready to marry Catherine and, in his own words, become Sabine's stepfather. Thus, the division between maternal voice and paternal language manifests itself more clearly as Catherine sings "Le Tourbillon de la vie." The song has a simple and repetitious melody, it has "a catchy tune" eliciting a desire to hum along. The pleasure of singing along is somehow reminiscent of the aural pleasure in early infancy during which the infant incorporates the mother's voice as if it were its own. The melody of the song creates "the acoustic mirror" in which sounds are reflected upon the subject able to receive and produce the song at the same time. The lyrics, however, retell a familiar love scenario in which a man meets a woman, a singer whose voice coaxed him to love her: "Elle chantait avec une voix qui, sitôt, m'enjola" ("She sang with a voice that immediately beguiled me"; translation mine). He loses her to the swirl of time, but, later in his life, finds her again in a café where she sings with her "voix fatale"—her "fatal voice." He gets drunk while listening to her wheedling voice—"Je me suis saoulé en l'écoutant"—and finally wakes up in her arms under her passionate embrace. The fantasy leading the powerless male into the arms of the *femme fatale* is initiated by the bewitching voice of the woman-singer. She is a siren enchanting him with her voice of pleasure. However, in the myth of the sirens, pleasure rapidly recedes, and the sailors are eventually destroyed by the ensnaring song of the nymphs. Their seductive song represents the destruction of male subjectivity. "Le Tourbillon de la vie" has the intoxicating quality of the siren's song, for it describes a chaotic love story for which the woman is responsible. Such chaos also marks the composition of the song. Indeed, the long ending of the song repeats *ad nauseam* the two lovers' separating and meeting over and over again, thus creating a vertiginous and dizzying effect justifying the title of the song: "The Swirl of Life."

The narrator in the song, the "I" speaking the dizzying words of his love affair, is male. There is a complete identification between Albert, the writer of the song, and the male narrator in his song. Albert projects in his song the powerful and seductive effect of Catherine's voice on all men listening to her. In fact, Catherine's voice enacts the vocal seduction already signified by the lyrics of the song. She is the female voice singing a male song for a male audience. She represents the voice, and Albert (also Jules and Jim) represents the language confused by the power of her voice.

The separation of voice and language retroactively bestows meaning upon the first "vocal scene" of the movie. The female voice singing in the dark becomes separated from the content of the riddle. As a melodic voice it falls under the maternal category, and as a spoken language it delineates the sexual content imposed on its maternal musicality by the fathers of Catherine's born and unborn children. The analysis of Catherine's performance of "Le Tourbillon de la vie" dissipates the ambiguity behind the voice opening the movie, because in the final analysis, it casts each component of the act of singing to its particular role: to the mother the voice, and to the father the language.

Thus, the maternal voice emerges from our analysis of *Jules and Jim* as a feminine detail separated from the corpus of images and language constituting the elements of representation most accounted for in film criticism. Situated outside images and language, the maternal voice belongs to a psychoanalytical category outside the Imaginary and the Symbolic, a category Lacan calls the "Real." Lacan defines the "Real" as the missed encounter between subject and language, which translates into a terrifying unknown territory standing beyond all representations. The fear generated by Lacan's "Real" may account for Chion's negative views in

his theory of the "uterine night." The inside of the womb belongs to the biological reality of maternal interiority, and therefore it is not accessible to the subject of language. Outside its metaphoric representation, the maternal womb cannot successfully be conceived of by the subject. It is the maternal body that the subject must reject in order to function linguistically and culturally. A voice capable of recreating the uterine conditions of the pre-linguistic environment surrounding the infant would also re-create the horror standing beyond all possible representations of the mother's body. The voice that brings the subject closer to the maternal womb also destroys the subject of language. Lacan's "Real" stands outside representation like Truffaut's maternal voice stands outside the actual film limits, in the unsettling darkness preceding the film. In *Jules and Jim,* the initial voice catches the spectator unprepared to receive its logic of blindness and pure sound.

The spectator may well confront the initial voice with fear as he is reminded of Chion's "uterine night," the paradigm for the threatening female interiority that the male subject must reject in order to function in his cultural environment. However, he also may let himself be wrapped up inside the pleasurable sonorous envelope of the female voice suggested by Rosolato, thus giving full power to his fantasy of being led back to a lost state of union with the mother. Jules and Jim are Truffaut's creation of male subjectivity fighting the maternal force deployed by Catherine's voice and finding refuge in the visual pleasure provided by filmic representations of her body. As a way to negate the power of the voice singing in the dark, Jules and Jim set up a serious search for the body belonging to the feminine voice heard at the beginning of the movie. As their search progresses, the unidentified woman's voice becomes a figure embodied by Catherine. However, throughout the movie, Catherine will always remain the feminine and maternal force that can never be captured; she will escape the logic of Jules and Jim's world, and at very best, she will give Jules and Jim the frustrated love life prescribed by the lyrics of her opening riddle.

As the movie ends at Catherine's and Jim's funeral, Jules feels almost relieved by her tragic disappearance. He is not afraid to lose Catherine anymore because, as the voice-over declares, "c'était fait" ("it was done"). Her body had been cremated, her image had finally disappeared, she had returned to her initial condition of a presence without a representation, of a voice in the dark. Catherine's maternal presence continues to live beyond the death of her body, and the voice-over accompanying the final images of the movie reveals the undying voice of motherhood manifesting itself through the character of Sabine, Catherine's daughter. The voice-over tells us that Jules feels relieved from the nauseating vertigo that Catherine created in his life; it also tells us about his faith in a better future thanks to Sabine: "Ils 'Catherine et Jim' ne laissaient rien d'eux. Lui, Jules, avait sa fille.

Catherine avait-elle aimé la lutte pour la lutte? Non, mais elle en avait étourdi Jules jusqu'à la nausée" ("They 'Catherine and Jim' left nothing of each other. Jules had his daughter. Did Catherine like struggling for struggling's sake? No, but Jules was disoriented and sickened through her struggle"; translation mine). Jules believes that the nausea that ripped through his disquieted self while Catherine was alive is finally over when Catherine dies; however, he is literally blinded by the voice (-over) reminding him of Sabine's presence. Sabine, the undeniable daughter of Catherine, continues to represent the presence of Catherine's maternal power. In the melancholy darkness filling Jules's mind after Catherine's death, the incorporated voice of motherhood invested in the final voice-over offers to Jules the undying figure of female oral/aural presence represented by Sabine echoing Catherine's voice of mother hood. Sabine offers a filmic version to Cixous's unbreakable chain of maternal sounds. Beyond representation and beyond life itself echoes the ever-lilting voice of the mother.

# FURTHER READING

## Criticism

Curry, Dan, and Peter Lehman. "Interviews with Nestor Almendros." *Wide Angle* 7, Nos. 1-2 (1985): 118-25.
    Interview with Nestor Almendros, focusing on his work with Truffaut.

Durovicova, Natasa. "Biograph as Biography: François Truffaut's *The Wild Child*." *Wide Angle* 7, Nos. 1-2 (1985): 126-35.
    Considers issues of history and autobiography in *The Wild Child*.

Gillain, Anne. "The Little Robber Boy as Master Narrator." *Wide Angle* 7, Nos. 1-2 (1985): 108-17.
    Argues that the key to understanding Truffaut's work is in analyzing his life experiences.

Henderson, Brian. "Bazin Defended against His Devotees." *Film Quarterly* XXXII, No. 4 (Summer 1979): 26-37.
    Considers the work of film critic André Bazin and Truffaut's views on him.

Insdorf, Annette. "Maurice Jaubert and François Truffaut: Musical Continuities from *L'Atalante*." *Yale French Studies*, No. 60 (1980): 204-18.
    Considers the work of music composer Maurice Jaubert in Truffaut's films, particularly *L'Histoire D'Adele H.*

Julian, Robert. "Truffaut's Notes." *Partisan Review* LVII, No. 3 (1990): 407-13.
    Considers what Truffaut's letters, published posthumously as *Correspondance*, reveal about his thoughts on film making.

Klein, Michael. "The Literary Sophistication of François Truffaut." *Film Comment* 3, No. 3 (Summer, 1965): 24-9.
    Considers dislocation, irony, and symbolism in *Shoot the Piano Player* and *Jim and Jules*.

Kline, Michael B. and Nancy C. Mellerski. "Structures of Ambiguity in Truffaut's *Le Dernier Métro*." *The French Review* 62, No. 1 (October 1988): 88-98.
    Argues that Truffaut combines a series of conflicting themes and images in *Le Dernier Métro*.

Kline, T. Jefferson. "Anxious Affinities: Text as Screen in Truffaut's *Jules et Jim*." *L'Esprit Créateur* XXIX, No. 1 (Spring 1989): 61-71.
    Applies methods of intertextual analysis to Truffaut's *Jules et Jim*.

McBride, Joseph. "The Private World of *Fahrenheit 451*." In *Favorite Movies: Critics' Choice*, edited by Philip Nobile, pp. 44-52. Macmillan Publishing, 1973.
    Describes Truffaut's adaptation of *Fahrenheit 451* as the "story of an ordinary guy ... who becomes great through force of circumstancees and through his own moral and intellectual honesty."

Murphy, Kathleen. "La Belle Dame Sans Merci." *Film Comment* 28, No. 6 (November-December, 1992): 28-30.
    Defends *Jules et Jim* against its critical reception.

Nelson, Roy Jay. "The Rotor: Elements of Paradigmatic Structure in Truffaut's *The 400 Blows*." *Wide Angle* 7, Nos. 1-2 (1985): 136-43.
    Centers on the "Rotor sequence," a segment in *The 400 Blows*, which, Nelson argues, acts as a paradigm for Truffaut's interpretation of adolescence.

Shatnoff, Judith. "François Truffaut—The Anarchist Imagination." *Film Quarterly* XVI, No. 3 (Spring, 1963): 3-11.
    Argues that despite Truffaunt's unorthodox storytelling and cinematography, he has created brilliant films.

Vincendeau, Ginette. "Against the Grain." *Sight and Sound* 3, No. 9 (September 1993): 34.
    Reviews *The Early Film Criticism of François Truffaut*, which, Vincendeau argues, publishes difficult to find writings by Truffaut but fails to challenge existing interpretations.

□ Contemporary
Literary Criticism

Indexes

Literary Criticism Series
Cumulative Author Index
Cumulative Topic Index
Cumulative Nationality Index
Title Index, Volume 101

# How to Use This Index

## The main references

### list all author entries in the following Gale Literary Criticism series:

*BLC* = *Black Literature Criticism*
*CLC* = *Contemporary Literary Criticism*
*CLR* = *Children's Literature Review*
*CMLC* = *Classical and Medieval Literature Criticism*
*DA* = *DISCovering Authors*
*DAB* = *DISCovering Authors: British*
*DAC* = *DISCovering Authors: Canadian*
*DAM* = *DISCovering Authors Modules*
  *DRAM* = *dramatists;* *MST* = *most-studied
  authors;* *MULT* = *multicultural authors;* *NOV* =
  *novelists;* *POET* = *poets;* *POP* = *popular/genre
  writers;* *DC* = *Drama Criticism*
*HLC* = *Hispanic Literature Criticism*
*LC* = *Literature Criticism from 1400 to 1800*
*NCLC* = *Nineteenth-Century Literature Criticism*
*PC* = *Poetry Criticism*
*SSC* = *Short Story Criticism*
*TCLC* = *Twentieth-Century Literary Criticism*
*WLC* = *World Literature Criticism, 1500 to the Present*

## The cross-references

### list all author entries in the following Gale biographical and literary sources:

*AAYA* = *Authors & Artists for Young Adults*
*AITN* = *Authors in the News*
*BEST* = *Bestsellers*
*BW* = *Black Writers*
*CA* = *Contemporary Authors*
*CAAS* = *Contemporary Authors Autobiography
Series*
*CABS* = *Contemporary Authors Bibliographical
Series*
*CANR* = *Contemporary Authors New Revision
Series*
*CAP* = *Contemporary Authors Permanent Series*
*CDALB* = *Concise Dictionary of American Literary
Biography*
*CDBLB* = *Concise Dictionary of British Literary
Biography*

*DLB* = *Dictionary of Literary Biography*
*DLBD* = *Dictionary of Literary Biography
Documentary Series*
*DLBY* = *Dictionary of Literary Biography
Yearbook*
*HW* = *Hispanic Writers*
*JRDA* = *Junior DISCovering Authors*
*MAICYA* = *Major Authors and Illustrators for
Children and Young Adults*
*MTCW* = *Major 20th-Century Writers*
*NNAL* = *Native North American Literature*
*SAAS* = *Something about the Author Autobiography
Series*
*SATA* = *Something about the Author*
*YABC* = *Yesterday's Authors of Books for Children*

# Literary Criticism Series
# Cumulative Author Index

See also CA 152

**Appelfeld, Aharon** 1932- ......... **CLC 23, 47**
See also CA 112; 133

**Apple, Max (Isaac)** 1941-........... **CLC 9, 33**
See also CA 81-84; CANR 19, 54; DLB 130

**Appleman, Philip (Dean)** 1926-..... **CLC 51**
See also CA 13-16R; CAAS 18; CANR 6, 29, 56

**Appleton, Lawrence**
See Lovecraft, H(oward) P(hillips)

**Apteryx**
See Eliot, T(homas) S(tearns)

**Apuleius, (Lucius Madaurensis)** 125(?)-175(?)
**CMLC 1**

**Aquin, Hubert** 1929-1977 .............. **CLC 15**
See also CA 105; DLB 53

**Aragon, Louis** 1897-1982   **CLC 3, 22; DAM NOV, POET**
See also CA 69-72; 108; CANR 28; DLB 72; MTCW

**Arany, Janos** 1817-1882 .............. **NCLC 34**

**Arbuthnot, John** 1667-1735 .............. **LC 1**
See also DLB 101

**Archer, Herbert Winslow**
See Mencken, H(enry) L(ouis)

**Archer, Jeffrey (Howard)** 1940- .. **CLC 28; DAM POP**
See also AAYA 16; BEST 89:3; CA 77-80; CANR 22, 52; INT CANR-22

**Archer, Jules** 1915-........................ **CLC 12**
See also CA 9-12R; CANR 6; SAAS 5; SATA 4, 85

**Archer, Lee**
See Ellison, Harlan (Jay)

**Arden, John** 1930- .... **CLC 6, 13, 15; DAM DRAM**
See also CA 13-16R; CAAS 4; CANR 31; DLB 13; MTCW

**Arenas, Reinaldo** 1943-1990  **CLC 41; DAM MULT; HLC**
See also CA 124; 128; 133; DLB 145; HW

**Arendt, Hannah** 1906-1975 ..... **CLC 66, 98**
See also CA 17-20R; 61-64; CANR 26; MTCW

**Aretino, Pietro** 1492-1556 ................ **LC 12**

**Arghezi, Tudor** ................................. **CLC 80**
See also Theodorescu, Ion N.

**Arguedas, Jose Maria** 1911-1969  **CLC 10, 18**
See also CA 89-92; DLB 113; HW

**Argueta, Manlio** 1936-.................. **CLC 31**
See also CA 131; DLB 145; HW

**Ariosto, Ludovico** 1474-1533 ............. **LC 6**

**Aristides**
See Epstein, Joseph

**Aristophanes** 450B.C.-385B.C.... **CMLC 4; DA; DAB; DAC; DAM DRAM, MST; DC 2**
See also DLB 176; YABC

**Arlt, Roberto (Godofredo Christophersen)** 1900-1942  **TCLC 29; DAM MULT; HLC**
See also CA 123; 131; HW

**Armah, Ayi Kwei** 1939- .   **CLC 5, 33; BLC; DAM MULT, POET**
See also BW 1; CA 61-64; CANR 21; DLB 117; MTCW

**Armatrading, Joan** 1950- .............. **CLC 17**
See also CA 114

**Arnette, Robert**
See Silverberg, Robert

**Arnim, Achim von (Ludwig Joachim von Arnim)** 1781-1831 ................ **NCLC 5**
See also DLB 90

**Arnim, Bettina von** 1785-1859 ... **NCLC 38**
See also DLB 90

**Arnold, Matthew** 1822-1888 .   **NCLC 6, 29; DA; DAB; DAC; DAM MST, POET; PC 5; WLC**
See also CDBLB 1832-1890; DLB 32, 57

**Arnold, Thomas** 1795-1842 ......... **NCLC 18**
See also DLB 55

**Arnow, Harriette (Louisa) Simpson** 1908-1986
**CLC 2, 7, 18**
See also CA 9-12R; 118; CANR 14; DLB 6; MTCW; SATA 42; SATA-Obit 47

**Arp, Hans**
See Arp, Jean

**Arp, Jean** 1887-1966 ...................... **CLC 5**
See also CA 81-84; 25-28R; CANR 42

**Arrabal**
See Arrabal, Fernando

**Arrabal, Fernando** 1932-.  **CLC 2, 9, 18, 58**
See also CA 9-12R; CANR 15

**Arrick, Fran** ...................................... **CLC 30**
See also Gaberman, Judie Angell

**Artaud, Antonin (Marie Joseph)** 1896-1948
**TCLC 3, 36; DAM DRAM**
See also CA 104; 149

**Arthur, Ruth M(abel)** 1905-1979 .. **CLC 12**
See also CA 9-12R; 85-88; CANR 4; SATA 7, 26

**Artsybashev, Mikhail (Petrovich)** 1878-1927
**TCLC 31**

**Arundel, Honor (Morfydd)** 1919-1973   **CLC 17**
See also CA 21-22; 41-44R; CAP 2; CLR 35; SATA 4; SATA-Obit 24

**Arzner, Dorothy** 1897-1979 .......... **CLC 98**

**Asch, Sholem** 1880-1957 ................ **TCLC 3**
See also CA 105

**Ash, Shalom**
See Asch, Sholem

**Ashbery, John (Lawrence)** 1927-  **CLC 2, 3, 4, 6, 9, 13, 15, 25, 41, 77; DAM POET**
See also CA 5-8R; CANR 9, 37; DLB 5, 165; DLBY 81; INT CANR-9; MTCW

**Ashdown, Clifford**
See Freeman, R(ichard) Austin

**Ashe, Gordon**
See Creasey, John

**Ashton-Warner, Sylvia (Constance)** 1908-1984
**CLC 19**
See also CA 69-72; 112; CANR 29; MTCW

**Asimov, Isaac** 1920-1992  **CLC 1, 3, 9, 19, 26, 76, 92; DAM POP**
See also AAYA 13; BEST 90:2; CA 1-4R; 137; CANR 2, 19, 36; CLR 12; DLB 8; DLBY 92; INT CANR-19; JRDA; MAICYA; MTCW; SATA 1, 26, 74

**Assis, Joaquim Maria Machado de**
See Machado de Assis, Joaquim Maria

**Astley, Thea (Beatrice May)** 1925-   **CLC 41**
See also CA 65-68; CANR 11, 43

**Aston, James**
See White, T(erence) H(anbury)

**Asturias, Miguel Angel** 1899-1974  **CLC 3, 8, 13; DAM MULT, NOV; HLC**
See also CA 25-28; 49-52; CANR 32; CAP 2; DLB 113; HW; MTCW

**Atares, Carlos Saura**
See Saura (Atares), Carlos

**Atheling, William**
See Pound, Ezra (Weston Loomis)

**Atheling, William, Jr.**
See Blish, James (Benjamin)

**Atherton, Gertrude (Franklin Horn)** 1857-1948
**TCLC 2**
See also CA 104; 155; DLB 9, 78

**Atherton, Lucius**
See Masters, Edgar Lee

**Atkins, Jack**
See Harris, Mark

**Atkinson, Kate** ................................. **CLC 99**

**Attaway, William (Alexander)** 1911-1986
**CLC 92; BLC; DAM MULT**
See also BW 2; CA 143; DLB 76

**Atticus**
See Fleming, Ian (Lancaster)

**Atwood, Margaret (Eleanor)** 1939-   **CLC 2, 3, 4, 8, 13, 15, 25, 44, 84; DA; DAB; DAC; DAM MST, NOV, POET; PC 8; SSC 2; WLC**
See also AAYA 12; BEST 89:2; CA 49-52; CANR 3, 24, 33; DLB 53; INT CANR-24; MTCW; SATA 50

**Aubigny, Pierre d'**
See Mencken, H(enry) L(ouis)

**Aubin, Penelope** 1685-1731(?)............ **LC 9**
See also DLB 39

**Auchincloss, Louis (Stanton)** 1917-  **CLC 4, 6, 9, 18, 45; DAM NOV; SSC 22**
See also CA 1-4R; CANR 6, 29, 55; DLB 2; DLBY 80; INT CANR-29; MTCW

**Auden, W(ystan) H(ugh)** 1907-1973  **CLC 1, 2, 3, 4, 6, 9, 11, 14, 43; DA; DAB; DAC; DAM DRAM, MST, POET; PC 1; WLC**
See also AAYA 18; CA 9-12R; 45-48; CANR 5; CDBLB 1914-1945; DLB 10, 20; MTCW

**Audiberti, Jacques** 1900-1965  **CLC 38; DAM DRAM**
See also CA 25-28R

**Audubon, John James** 1785-1851  **NCLC 47**

**Auel, Jean M(arie)** 1936-....  **CLC 31; DAM POP**
See also AAYA 7; BEST 90:4; CA 103; CANR 21; INT CANR-21; SATA 91

**Auerbach, Erich** 1892-1957......... **TCLC 43**
See also CA 118; 155

**Augier, Emile** 1820-1889............. **NCLC 31**

**August, John**
See De Voto, Bernard (Augustine)

**Augustine, St.** 354-430 ....... **CMLC 6; DAB**

**Aurelius**
See Bourne, Randolph S(illiman)

**Aurobindo, Sri** 1872-1950 ........... **TCLC 63**

**Austen, Jane** 1775-1817  **NCLC 1, 13, 19, 33, 51; DA; DAB; DAC; DAM MST, NOV; WLC**
See also AAYA 19; CDBLB 1789-1832; DLB 116

**Auster, Paul** 1947- ........................ **CLC 47**
See also CA 69-72; CANR 23, 52

**Austin, Frank**
See Faust, Frederick (Schiller)

**Austin, Mary (Hunter)** 1868-1934  **TCLC 25**
See also CA 109; DLB 9, 78

**Autran Dourado, Waldomiro**
See Dourado, (Waldomiro Freitas) Autran

**Averroes** 1126-1198 ...................... **CMLC 7**
See also DLB 115

**Avicenna** 980-1037...................... **CMLC 16**
See also DLB 115

**Avison, Margaret** 1918-  **CLC 2, 4, 97; DAC; DAM POET**
See also CA 17-20R; DLB 53; MTCW

**Axton, David**
See Koontz, Dean R(ay)

**Ayckbourn, Alan** 1939-  **CLC 5, 8, 18, 33, 74; DAB; DAM DRAM**
See also CA 21-24R; CANR 31; DLB 13; MTCW

**Author Index**

See Moorcock, Michael (John)
**Barrol, Grady**
  See Bograd, Larry
**Barry, Mike**
  See Malzberg, Barry N(athaniel)
**Barry, Philip** 1896-1949 ............... **TCLC 11**
  See also CA 109; DLB 7
**Bart, Andre Schwarz**
  See Schwarz-Bart, Andre
**Barth, John (Simmons)** 1930- **CLC 1, 2, 3, 5, 7, 9, 10, 14, 27, 51, 89; DAM NOV; SSC 10**
  See also AITN 1, 2; CA 1-4R; CABS 1; CANR 5, 23, 49; DLB 2; MTCW
**Barthelme, Donald** 1931-1989 **CLC 1, 2, 3, 5, 6, 8, 13, 23, 46, 59; DAM NOV; SSC 2**
  See also CA 21-24R; 129; CANR 20, 58; DLB 2; DLBY 80, 89; MTCW; SATA 7; SATA-Obit 62
**Barthelme, Frederick** 1943- .......... **CLC 36**
  See also CA 114; 122; DLBY 85; INT 122
**Barthes, Roland (Gerard)** 1915-1980 . **CLC 24, 83**
  See also CA 130; 97-100; MTCW
**Barzun, Jacques (Martin)** 1907- ... **CLC 51**
  See also CA 61-64; CANR 22
**Bashevis, Isaac**
  See Singer, Isaac Bashevis
**Bashkirtseff, Marie** 1859-1884 ... **NCLC 27**
**Basho**
  See Matsuo Basho
**Bass, Kingsley B., Jr.**
  See Bullins, Ed
**Bass, Rick** 1958- ............................. **CLC 79**
  See also CA 126; CANR 53
**Bassani, Giorgio** 1916- ...................... **CLC 9**
  See also CA 65-68; CANR 33; DLB 128, 177; MTCW
**Bastos, Augusto (Antonio) Roa**
  See Roa Bastos, Augusto (Antonio)
**Bataille, Georges** 1897-1962 .......... **CLC 29**
  See also CA 101; 89-92
**Bates, H(erbert) E(rnest)** 1905-1974 .. **CLC 46; DAB; DAM POP; SSC 10**
  See also CA 93-96; 45-48; CANR 34; DLB 162; MTCW
**Bauchart**
  See Camus, Albert
**Baudelaire, Charles** 1821-1867 **NCLC 6, 29, 55; DA; DAB; DAC; DAM MST, POET; PC 1; SSC 18; WLC**
**Baudrillard, Jean** 1929- ................. **CLC 60**
**Baum, L(yman) Frank** 1856-1919 **TCLC 7**
  See also CA 108; 133; CLR 15; DLB 22; JRDA; MAICYA; MTCW; SATA 18
**Baum, Louis F.**
  See Baum, L(yman) Frank
**Baumbach, Jonathan** 1933- ....... **CLC 6, 23**
  See also CA 13-16R; CAAS 5; CANR 12; DLBY 80; INT CANR-12; MTCW
**Bausch, Richard (Carl)** 1945- ....... **CLC 51**
  See also CA 101; CAAS 14; CANR 43; DLB 130
**Baxter, Charles** 1947- ... **CLC 45, 78; DAM POP**
  See also CA 57-60; CANR 40; DLB 130
**Baxter, George Owen**
  See Faust, Frederick (Schiller)
**Baxter, James K(eir)** 1926-1972 .... **CLC 14**
  See also CA 77-80
**Baxter, John**
  See Hunt, E(verette) Howard, (Jr.)
**Bayer, Sylvia**
  See Glassco, John

**Baynton, Barbara** 1857-1929 ...... **TCLC 57**
**Beagle, Peter S(oyer)** 1939- ............. **CLC 7**
  See also CA 9-12R; CANR 4, 51; DLBY 80; INT CANR-4; SATA 60
**Bean, Normal**
  See Burroughs, Edgar Rice
**Beard, Charles A(ustin)** 1874-1948 **TCLC 15**
  See also CA 115; DLB 17; SATA 18
**Beardsley, Aubrey** 1872-1898 ....... **NCLC 6**
**Beattie, Ann** 1947- .. **CLC 8, 13, 18, 40, 63; DAM NOV, POP; SSC 11**
  See also BEST 90:2; CA 81-84; CANR 53; DLBY 82; MTCW
**Beattie, James** 1735-1803 ............ **NCLC 25**
  See also DLB 109
**Beauchamp, Kathleen Mansfield** 1888-1923
  See Mansfield, Katherine
  See also CA 104; 134; DA; DAC; DAM MST
**Beaumarchais, Pierre-Augustin Caron de** 1732-1799 ............................... **DC 4**
  See also DAM DRAM
**Beaumont, Francis** 1584(?)-1616 **LC 33; DC 6**
  See also CDBLB Before 1660; DLB 58, 121
**Beauvoir, Simone (Lucie Ernestine Marie Bertrand) de** 1908-1986 **CLC 1, 2, 4, 8, 14, 31, 44, 50, 71; DA; DAB; DAC; DAM MST, NOV; WLC**
  See also CA 9-12R; 118; CANR 28; DLB 72; DLBY 86; MTCW
**Becker, Carl (Lotus)** 1873-1945 .. **TCLC 63**
  See also CA 157; DLB 17
**Becker, Jurek** 1937-1997 ............ **CLC 7, 19**
  See also CA 85-88; 157; DLB 75
**Becker, Walter** 1950- ...................... **CLC 26**
**Beckett, Samuel (Barclay)** 1906-1989 **CLC 1, 2, 3, 4, 6, 9, 10, 11, 14, 18, 29, 57, 59, 83; DA; DAB; DAC; DAM DRAM, MST, NOV; SSC 16; WLC**
  See also CA 5-8R; 130; CANR 33; CDBLB 1945-1960; DLB 13, 15; DLBY 90; MTCW
**Beckford, William** 1760-1844 ...... **NCLC 16**
  See also DLB 39
**Beckman, Gunnel** 1910- ................. **CLC 26**
  See also CA 33-36R; CANR 15; CLR 25; MAICYA; SAAS 9; SATA 6
**Becque, Henri** 1837-1899 ............... **NCLC 3**
**Beddoes, Thomas Lovell** 1803-1849 **NCLC 3**
  See also DLB 96
**Bede** c. 673-735 ........................... **CMLC 20**
  See also DLB 146
**Bedford, Donald F.**
  See Fearing, Kenneth (Flexner)
**Beecher, Catharine Esther** 1800-1878 **NCLC 30**
  See also DLB 1
**Beecher, John** 1904-1980 ................. **CLC 6**
  See also AITN 1; CA 5-8R; 105; CANR 8
**Beer, Johann** 1655-1700 ...................... **LC 5**
  See also DLB 168
**Beer, Patricia** 1924- ........................ **CLC 58**
  See also CA 61-64; CANR 13, 46; DLB 40
**Beerbohm, Max**
  See Beerbohm, (Henry) Max(imilian)
**Beerbohm, (Henry) Max(imilian)** 1872-1956 **TCLC 1, 24**
  See also CA 104; 154; DLB 34, 100
**Beer-Hofmann, Richard** 1866-1945 **TCLC 60**
  See also DLB 81
**Begiebing, Robert J(ohn)** 1946- .... **CLC 70**
  See also CA 122; CANR 40
**Behan, Brendan** 1923-1964 **CLC 1, 8, 11, 15,**

**79; DAM DRAM**
  See also CA 73-76; CANR 33; CDBLB 1945-1960; DLB 13; MTCW
**Behn, Aphra** 1640(?)-1689 ... **LC 1, 30; DA; DAB; DAC; DAM DRAM, MST, NOV, POET; DC 4; PC 13; WLC**
  See also DLB 39, 80, 131
**Behrman, S(amuel) N(athaniel)** 1893-1973 **CLC 40**
  See also CA 13-16; 45-48; CAP 1; DLB 7, 44
**Belasco, David** 1853-1931 ............. **TCLC 3**
  See also CA 104; DLB 7
**Belcheva, Elisaveta** 1893- ............. **CLC 10**
  See also Bagryana, Elisaveta
**Beldone, Phil "Cheech"**
  See Ellison, Harlan (Jay)
**Beleno**
  See Azuela, Mariano
**Belinski, Vissarion Grigoryevich** 1811-1848 **NCLC 5**
**Belitt, Ben** 1911- ............................. **CLC 22**
  See also CA 13-16R; CAAS 4; CANR 7; DLB 5
**Bell, Gertrude** 1868-1926 ............ **TCLC 67**
  See also DLB 174
**Bell, James Madison** 1826-1902 **TCLC 43; BLC; DAM MULT**
  See also BW 1; CA 122; 124; DLB 50
**Bell, Madison Smartt** 1957-........... **CLC 41**
  See also CA 111; CANR 28, 54
**Bell, Marvin (Hartley)** 1937-.... **CLC 8, 31; DAM POET**
  See also CA 21-24R; CAAS 14; DLB 5; MTCW
**Bell, W. L. D.**
  See Mencken, H(enry) L(ouis)
**Bellamy, Atwood C.**
  See Mencken, H(enry) L(ouis)
**Bellamy, Edward** 1850-1898 ......... **NCLC 4**
  See also DLB 12
**Bellin, Edward J.**
  See Kuttner, Henry
**Belloc, (Joseph) Hilaire (Pierre Sebastien Rene Swanton)** 1870-1953 **TCLC 7, 18; DAM POET**
  See also CA 106; 152; DLB 19, 100, 141, 174; 1
**Belloc, Joseph Peter Rene Hilaire**
  See Belloc, (Joseph) Hilaire (Pierre Sebastien Rene Swanton)
**Belloc, Joseph Pierre Hilaire**
  See Belloc, (Joseph) Hilaire (Pierre Sebastien Rene Swanton)
**Belloc, M. A.**
  See Lowndes, Marie Adelaide (Belloc)
**Bellow, Saul** 1915- **CLC 1, 2, 3, 6, 8, 10, 13, 15, 25, 33, 34, 63, 79; DA; DAB; DAC; DAM MST, NOV, POP; SSC 14; WLC**
  See also AITN 2; BEST 89:3; CA 5-8R; CABS 1; CANR 29, 53; CDALB 1941-1968; DLB 2, 28; DLBD 3; DLBY 82; MTCW
**Belser, Reimond Karel Maria de** 1929-
  See Ruyslinck, Ward
  See also CA 152
**Bely, Andrey** ........................ **TCLC 7; PC 11**
  See also Bugayev, Boris Nikolayevich
**Benary, Margot**
  See Benary-Isbert, Margot
**Benary-Isbert, Margot** 1889-1979 **CLC 12**
  See also CA 5-8R; 89-92; CANR 4; CLR 12; MAICYA; SATA 2; SATA-Obit 21
**Benavente (y Martinez), Jacinto** 1866-1954 **TCLC 3; DAM DRAM, MULT**
  See also CA 106; 131; HW; MTCW

**Bjornson, Bjornstjerne (Martinius)** 1832-1910
   **TCLC 7, 37**
   See also CA 104
**Black, Robert**
   See Holdstock, Robert P.
**Blackburn, Paul** 1926-1971 ....... **CLC 9, 43**
   See also CA 81-84; 33-36R; CANR 34; DLB
   16; DLBY 81
**Black Elk** 1863-1950 **TCLC 33; DAM MULT**
   See also CA 144; NNAL
**Black Hobart**
   See Sanders, (James) Ed(ward)
**Blacklin, Malcolm**
   See Chambers, Aidan
**Blackmore, R(ichard) D(oddridge)** 1825-1900
   **TCLC 27**
   See also CA 120; DLB 18
**Blackmur, R(ichard) P(almer)** 1904-1965
   **CLC 2, 24**
   See also CA 11-12; 25-28R; CAP 1; DLB 63
**Black Tarantula**
   See Acker, Kathy
**Blackwood, Algernon (Henry)** 1869-1951
   **TCLC 5**
   See also CA 105; 150; DLB 153, 156, 178
**Blackwood, Caroline** 1931-1996    **CLC 6, 9,
   100**
   See also CA 85-88; 151; CANR 32; DLB 14;
   MTCW
**Blade, Alexander**
   See Hamilton, Edmond; Silverberg, Robert
**Blaga, Lucian** 1895-1961 ............... **CLC 75**
**Blair, Eric (Arthur)** 1903-1950
   See Orwell, George
   See also CA 104; 132; DA; DAB; DAC; DAM
   MST, NOV; MTCW; SATA 29
**Blais, Marie-Claire** 1939- **CLC 2, 4, 6, 13, 22;
   DAC; DAM MST**
   See also CA 21-24R; CAAS 4; CANR 38; DLB
   53; MTCW
**Blaise, Clark** 1940- ......................... **CLC 29**
   See also AITN 2; CA 53-56; CAAS 3; CANR
   5; DLB 53
**Blake, Nicholas**
   See Day Lewis, C(ecil)
   See also DLB 77
**Blake, William** 1757-1827    **NCLC 13, 37, 57;
   DA; DAB; DAC; DAM MST, POET; PC
   12; WLC**
   See also CDBLB 1789-1832; DLB 93, 163;
   MAICYA; SATA 30
**Blake, William J(ames)** 1894-1969 .. **PC 12**
   See also CA 5-8R; 25-28R
**Blasco Ibanez, Vicente** 1867-1928    **TCLC 12;
   DAM NOV**
   See also CA 110; 131; HW; MTCW
**Blatty, William Peter** 1928- ..    **CLC 2; DAM
   POP**
   See also CA 5-8R; CANR 9
**Bleeck, Oliver**
   See Thomas, Ross (Elmore)
**Blessing, Lee** 1949- ......................... **CLC 54**
**Blish, James (Benjamin)** 1921-1975    **CLC 14**
   See also CA 1-4R; 57-60; CANR 3; DLB 8;
   MTCW; SATA 66
**Bliss, Reginald**
   See Wells, H(erbert) G(eorge)
**Blixen, Karen (Christentze Dinesen)** 1885-1962
   See Dinesen, Isak
   See also CA 25-28; CANR 22, 50; CAP 2;
   MTCW; SATA 44
**Bloch, Robert (Albert)** 1917-1994    **CLC 33**
   See also CA 5-8R; 146; CAAS 20; CANR 5;

DLB 44; INT CANR-5; SATA 12; SATA-Obit
82
**Blok, Alexander (Alexandrovich)** 1880-1921
   **TCLC 5**
   See also CA 104
**Blom, Jan**
   See Breytenbach, Breyten
**Bloom, Harold** 1930- ...................... **CLC 24**
   See also CA 13-16R; CANR 39; DLB 67
**Bloomfield, Aurelius**
   See Bourne, Randolph S(illiman)
**Blount, Roy (Alton), Jr.** 1941- ....... **CLC 38**
   See also CA 53-56; CANR 10, 28; INT CANR-
   28; MTCW
**Bloy, Leon** 1846-1917 ................... **TCLC 22**
   See also CA 121; DLB 123
**Blume, Judy (Sussman)** 1938-    **CLC 12, 30;
   DAM NOV, POP**
   See also AAYA 3; CA 29-32R; CANR 13, 37;
   CLR 2, 15; DLB 52; JRDA; MAICYA;
   MTCW; SATA 2, 31, 79
**Blunden, Edmund (Charles)** 1896-1974    **CLC
   2, 56**
   See also CA 17-18; 45-48; CANR 54; CAP 2;
   DLB 20, 100, 155; MTCW
**Bly, Robert (Elwood)** 1926-    **CLC 1, 2, 5, 10,
   15, 38; DAM POET**
   See also CA 5-8R; CANR 41; DLB 5; MTCW
**Boas, Franz** 1858-1942 ................ **TCLC 56**
   See also CA 115
**Bobette**
   See Simenon, Georges (Jacques Christian)
**Boccaccio, Giovanni** 1313-1375    **CMLC 13;
   SSC 10**
**Bochco, Steven** 1943- ...................... **CLC 35**
   See also AAYA 11; CA 124; 138
**Bodenheim, Maxwell** 1892-1954 .    **TCLC 44**
   See also CA 110; DLB 9, 45
**Bodker, Cecil** 1927- ......................... **CLC 21**
   See also CA 73-76; CANR 13, 44; CLR 23;
   MAICYA; SATA 14
**Boell, Heinrich (Theodor)** 1917-1985    **CLC 2,
   3, 6, 9, 11, 15, 27, 32, 72; DA; DAB; DAC;
   DAM MST, NOV; SSC 23; WLC**
   See also CA 21-24R; 116; CANR 24; DLB 69;
   DLBY 85; MTCW
**Boerne, Alfred**
   See Doeblin, Alfred
**Boethius** 480(?)-524(?) ............... **CMLC 15**
   See also DLB 115
**Bogan, Louise** 1897-1970    **CLC 4, 39, 46, 93;
   DAM POET; PC 12**
   See also CA 73-76; 25-28R; CANR 33; DLB
   45, 169; MTCW
**Bogarde, Dirk** ................................. **CLC 19**
   See also Van Den Bogarde, Derek Jules Gaspard
   Ulric Niven
   See also DLB 14
**Bogosian, Eric** 1953- ...................... **CLC 45**
   See also CA 138
**Bograd, Larry** 1953- ...................... **CLC 35**
   See also CA 93-96; CANR 57; SAAS 21; SATA
   33, 89
**Boiardo, Matteo Maria** 1441-1494 ....    **LC 6**
**Boileau-Despreaux, Nicolas** 1636-1711    **LC 3**
**Bojer, Johan** 1872-1959 .............. **TCLC 64**
**Boland, Eavan (Aisling)** 1944-    **CLC 40, 67;
   DAM POET**
   See also CA 143; DLB 40
**Bolt, Lee**
   See Faust, Frederick (Schiller)
**Bolt, Robert (Oxton)** 1924-1995 ..    **CLC 14;
   DAM DRAM**

See also CA 17-20R; 147; CANR 35; DLB 13;
MTCW
**Bombet, Louis-Alexandre-Cesar**
   See Stendhal
**Bomkauf**
   See Kaufman, Bob (Garnell)
**Bonaventura** ................................. **NCLC 35**
   See also DLB 90
**Bond, Edward** 1934-    **CLC 4, 6, 13, 23; DAM
   DRAM**
   See also CA 25-28R; CANR 38; DLB 13;
   MTCW
**Bonham, Frank** 1914-1989 ............ **CLC 12**
   See also AAYA 1; CA 9-12R; CANR 4, 36;
   JRDA; MAICYA; SAAS 3; SATA 1, 49;
   SATA-Obit 62
**Bonnefoy, Yves** 1923-    **CLC 9, 15, 58; DAM
   MST, POET**
   See also CA 85-88; CANR 33; MTCW
**Bontemps, Arna(ud Wendell)** 1902-1973
   **CLC 1, 18; BLC; DAM MULT, NOV,
   POET**
   See also BW 1; CA 1-4R; 41-44R; CANR 4,
   35; CLR 6; DLB 48, 51; JRDA; MAICYA;
   MTCW; SATA 2, 44; SATA-Obit 24
**Booth, Martin** 1944- ...................... **CLC 13**
   See also CA 93-96; CAAS 2
**Booth, Philip** 1925- ......................... **CLC 23**
   See also CA 5-8R; CANR 5; DLBY 82
**Booth, Wayne C(layson)** 1921- ...... **CLC 24**
   See also CA 1-4R; CAAS 5; CANR 3, 43; DLB
   67
**Borchert, Wolfgang** 1921-1947 ..... **TCLC 5**
   See also CA 104; DLB 69, 124
**Borel, Petrus** 1809-1859 ............. **NCLC 41**
**Borges, Jorge Luis** 1899-1986    **CLC 1, 2, 3, 4,
   6, 8, 9, 10, 13, 19, 44, 48, 83; DA; DAB;
   DAC; DAM MST, MULT; HLC; SSC 4;
   WLC**
   See also AAYA 19; CA 21-24R; CANR 19, 33;
   DLB 113; DLBY 86; HW; MTCW
**Borowski, Tadeusz** 1922-1951 ....... **TCLC 9**
   See also CA 106; 154
**Borrow, George (Henry)** 1803-1881    **NCLC 9**
   See also DLB 21, 55, 166
**Bosman, Herman Charles** 1905-1951    **TCLC
   49**
**Bosschere, Jean de** 1878(?)-1953    **TCLC 19**
   See also CA 115
**Boswell, James** 1740-1795    **LC 4; DA; DAB;
   DAC; DAM MST; WLC**
   See also CDBLB 1660-1789; DLB 104, 142
**Bottoms, David** 1949- ...................... **CLC 53**
   See also CA 105; CANR 22; DLB 120; DLBY
   83
**Boucicault, Dion** 1820-1890 ....... **NCLC 41**
**Boucolon, Maryse** 1937(?)-
   See Conde, Maryse
   See also CA 110; CANR 30, 53
**Bourget, Paul (Charles Joseph)** 1852-1935
   **TCLC 12**
   See also CA 107; DLB 123
**Bourjaily, Vance (Nye)** 1922- ....    **CLC 8, 62**
   See also CA 1-4R; CAAS 1; CANR 2; DLB 2,
   143
**Bourne, Randolph S(illiman)** 1886-1918
   **TCLC 16**
   See also CA 117; 155; DLB 63
**Bova, Ben(jamin William)** 1932- ..    **CLC 45**
   See also AAYA 16; CA 5-8R; CAAS 18; CANR
   11, 56; CLR 3; DLBY 81; INT CANR-11;
   MAICYA; MTCW; SATA 6, 68
**Bowen, Elizabeth (Dorothea Cole)** 1899-1973

**Brooke-Rose, Christine** 1926(?)- ...   **CLC 40**
   See also CA 13-16R; CANR 58; DLB 14
**Brookner, Anita** 1928-  **CLC 32, 34, 51; DAB;**
   **DAM POP**
   See also CA 114; 120; CANR 37, 56; DLBY
   87; MTCW
**Brooks, Cleanth** 1906-1994 .....   **CLC 24, 86**
   See also CA 17-20R; 145; CANR 33, 35; DLB
   63; DLBY 94; INT CANR-35; MTCW
**Brooks, George**
   See Baum, L(yman) Frank
**Brooks, Gwendolyn** 1917-  **CLC 1, 2, 4, 5, 15,**
   **49; BLC; DA; DAC; DAM MST, MULT,**
   **POET; PC 7; WLC**
   See also AAYA 20; AITN 1; BW 2; CA 1-4R;
   CANR 1, 27, 52; CDALB 1941-1968; CLR
   27; DLB 5, 76, 165; MTCW; SATA 6
**Brooks, Mel** ...................................   **CLC 12**
   See Kaminsky, Melvin
   See also AAYA 13; DLB 26
**Brooks, Peter** 1938- ........................   **CLC 34**
   See also CA 45-48; CANR 1
**Brooks, Van Wyck** 1886-1963 .......   **CLC 29**
   See also CA 1-4R; CANR 6; DLB 45, 63, 103
**Brophy, Brigid (Antonia)** 1929-1995  **CLC 6,**
   **11, 29**
   See also CA 5-8R; 149; CAAS 4; CANR 25,
   53; DLB 14; MTCW
**Brosman, Catharine Savage** 1934- .   **CLC 9**
   See also CA 61-64; CANR 21, 46
**Brother Antoninus**
   See Everson, William (Oliver)
**Broughton, T(homas) Alan** 1936- .   **CLC 19**
   See also CA 45-48; CANR 2, 23, 48
**Broumas, Olga** 1949- ...............   **CLC 10, 73**
   See also CA 85-88; CANR 20
**Brown, Alan** 1951- ........................   **CLC 99**
**Brown, Charles Brockden** 1771-1810  **NCLC**
   **22**
   See also CDALB 1640-1865; DLB 37, 59, 73
**Brown, Christy** 1932-1981 .............   **CLC 63**
   See also CA 105; 104; DLB 14
**Brown, Claude** 1937-   **CLC 30; BLC; DAM**
   **MULT**
   See also AAYA 7; BW 1; CA 73-76
**Brown, Dee (Alexander)** 1908-   **CLC 18, 47;**
   **DAM POP**
   See also CA 13-16R; CAAS 6; CANR 11, 45;
   DLBY 80; MTCW; SATA 5
**Brown, George**
   See Wertmueller, Lina
**Brown, George Douglas** 1869-1902  **TCLC 28**
**Brown, George Mackay** 1921-1996   **CLC 5,**
   **48, 100**
   See also CA 21-24R; 151; CAAS 6; CANR 12,
   37; DLB 14, 27, 139; MTCW; SATA 35
**Brown, (William) Larry** 1951- ......   **CLC 73**
   See also CA 130; 134; INT 133
**Brown, Moses**
   See Barrett, William (Christopher)
**Brown, Rita Mae** 1944- .....   **CLC 18, 43, 79;**
   **DAM NOV, POP**
   See also CA 45-48; CANR 2, 11, 35; INT
   CANR-11; MTCW
**Brown, Roderick (Langmere) Haig-**
   See Haig-Brown, Roderick (Langmere)
**Brown, Rosellen** 1939- ..................   **CLC 32**
   See also CA 77-80; CAAS 10; CANR 14, 44
**Brown, Sterling Allen** 1901-1989  **CLC 1, 23,**
   **59; BLC; DAM MULT, POET**
   See also BW 1; CA 85-88; 127; CANR 26; DLB
   48, 51, 63; MTCW
**Brown, Will**

   See Ainsworth, William Harrison
**Brown, William Wells** 1813-1884   **NCLC 2;**
   **BLC; DAM MULT; DC 1**
   See also DLB 3, 50
**Browne, (Clyde) Jackson** 1948(?)-   **CLC 21**
   See also CA 120
**Browning, Elizabeth Barrett** 1806-1861
   **NCLC 1, 16, 61; DA; DAB; DAC; DAM**
   **MST, POET; PC 6; WLC**
   See also CDBLB 1832-1890; DLB 32
**Browning, Robert** 1812-1889  **NCLC 19; DA;**
   **DAB; DAC; DAM MST, POET; PC 2**
   See also CDBLB 1832-1890; DLB 32, 163;
   YABC; 1
**Browning, Tod** 1882-1962 .............   **CLC 16**
   See also CA 141; 117
**Brownson, Orestes (Augustus)** 1803-1876
   **NCLC 50**
**Bruccoli, Matthew J(oseph)** 1931-   **CLC 34**
   See also CA 9-12R; CANR 7; DLB 103
**Bruce, Lenny** ...................................   **CLC 21**
   See also Schneider, Leonard Alfred
**Bruin, John**
   See Brutus, Dennis
**Brulard, Henri**
   See Stendhal
**Brulls, Christian**
   See Simenon, Georges (Jacques Christian)
**Brunner, John (Kilian Houston)** 1934-1995
   **CLC 8, 10; DAM POP**
   See also CA 1-4R; 149; CAAS 8; CANR 2, 37;
   MTCW
**Bruno, Giordano** 1548-1600 .............   **LC 27**
**Brutus, Dennis** 1924-   **CLC 43; BLC; DAM**
   **MULT, POET**
   See also BW 2; CA 49-52; CAAS 14; CANR 2,
   27, 42; DLB 117
**Bryan, C(ourtlandt) D(ixon) B(arnes)** 1936-
   **CLC 29**
   See also CA 73-76; CANR 13; INT CANR-13
**Bryan, Michael**
   See Moore, Brian
**Bryant, William Cullen** 1794-1878  **NCLC 6,**
   **46; DA; DAB; DAC; DAM MST, POET**
   See also CDALB 1640-1865; DLB 3, 43, 59
**Bryusov, Valery Yakovlevich** 1873-1924
   **TCLC 10**
   See also CA 107; 155
**Buchan, John** 1875-1940 .   **TCLC 41; DAB;**
   **DAM POP**
   See also CA 108; 145; DLB 34, 70, 156; 2
**Buchanan, George** 1506-1582 ...........   **LC 4**
**Buchheim, Lothar-Guenther** 1918-   **CLC 6**
   See also CA 85-88
**Buchner, (Karl) Georg** 1813-1837  **NCLC 26**
**Buchwald, Art(hur)** 1925- .............   **CLC 33**
   See also AITN 1; CA 5-8R; CANR 21; MTCW;
   SATA 10
**Buck, Pearl S(ydenstricker)** 1892-1973  **CLC**
   **7, 11, 18; DA; DAB; DAC; DAM MST,**
   **NOV**
   See also AITN 1; CA 1-4R; 41-44R; CANR 1,
   34; DLB 9, 102; MTCW; SATA 1, 25
**Buckler, Ernest** 1908-1984 .   **CLC 13; DAC;**
   **DAM MST**
   See also CA 11-12; 114; CAP 1; DLB 68; SATA
   47
**Buckley, Vincent (Thomas)** 1925-1988  **CLC**
   **57**
   See also CA 101
**Buckley, William F(rank), Jr.** 1925-   **CLC 7,**
   **18, 37; DAM POP**
   See also AITN 1; CA 1-4R; CANR 1, 24, 53;

   DLB 137; DLBY 80; INT CANR-24; MTCW
**Buechner, (Carl) Frederick** 1926-   **CLC 2, 4,**
   **6, 9; DAM NOV**
   See also CA 13-16R; CANR 11, 39; DLBY 80;
   INT CANR-11; MTCW
**Buell, John (Edward)** 1927- ..........   **CLC 10**
   See also CA 1-4R; DLB 53
**Buero Vallejo, Antonio** 1916- ..   **CLC 15, 46**
   See also CA 106; CANR 24, 49; HW; MTCW
**Bufalino, Gesualdo** 1920(?)- ..........   **CLC 74**
**Bugayev, Boris Nikolayevich** 1880-1934
   See Bely, Andrey
   See also CA 104
**Bukowski, Charles** 1920-1994   **CLC 2, 5, 9,**
   **41, 82; DAM NOV, POET; PC 18**
   See also CA 17-20R; 144; CANR 40; DLB 5,
   130, 169; MTCW
**Bulgakov, Mikhail (Afanas'evich)** 1891-1940
   **TCLC 2, 16; DAM DRAM, NOV; SSC**
   **18**
   See also CA 105; 152
**Bulgya, Alexander Alexandrovich** 1901-1956
   **TCLC 53**
   See also Fadeyev, Alexander
   See also CA 117
**Bullins, Ed** 1935-   **CLC 1, 5, 7; BLC; DAM**
   **DRAM, MULT; DC 6**
   See also BW 2; CA 49-52; CAAS 16; CANR
   24, 46; DLB 7, 38; MTCW
**Bulwer-Lytton, Edward (George Earle Lytton)**
   1803-1873 .........................   **NCLC 1, 45**
   See also DLB 21
**Bunin, Ivan Alexeyevich** 1870-1953   **TCLC**
   **6; SSC 5**
   See also CA 104
**Bunting, Basil** 1900-1985 ..   **CLC 10, 39, 47;**
   **DAM POET**
   See also CA 53-56; 115; CANR 7; DLB 20
**Bunuel, Luis** 1900-1983   **CLC 16, 80; DAM**
   **MULT; HLC**
   See also CA 101; 110; CANR 32; HW
**Bunyan, John** 1628-1688   **LC 4; DA; DAB;**
   **DAC; DAM MST; WLC**
   See also CDBLB 1660-1789; DLB 39
**Burckhardt, Jacob (Christoph)** 1818-1897
   **NCLC 49**
**Burford, Eleanor**
   See Hibbert, Eleanor Alice Burford
**Burgess, Anthony**  **CLC 1, 2, 4, 5, 8, 10, 13, 15,**
   **22, 40, 62, 81, 94; DAB**
   See also Wilson, John (Anthony) Burgess
   See also AITN 1; CDBLB 1960 to Present; DLB
   14
**Burke, Edmund** 1729(?)-1797   **LC 7, 36; DA;**
   **DAB; DAC; DAM MST; WLC**
   See also DLB 104
**Burke, Kenneth (Duva)** 1897-1993   **CLC 2,**
   **24**
   See also CA 5-8R; 143; CANR 39; DLB 45,
   63; MTCW
**Burke, Leda**
   See Garnett, David
**Burke, Ralph**
   See Silverberg, Robert
**Burke, Thomas** 1886-1945 ..........   **TCLC 63**
   See also CA 113; 155
**Burney, Fanny** 1752-1840 .....   **NCLC 12, 54**
   See also DLB 39
**Burns, Robert** 1759-1796 ...................   **PC 6**
   See also CDBLB 1789-1832; DA; DAB; DAC;
   DAM MST, POET; DLB 109; WLC
**Burns, Tex**
   See L'Amour, Louis (Dearborn)

See also CA 13-16R; CANR 15

**Carlsen, Chris**
  See Holdstock, Robert P.

**Carlson, Ron(ald F.)** 1947- ........... **CLC 54**
  See also CA 105; CANR 27

**Carlyle, Thomas** 1795-1881    **NCLC 22; DA; DAB; DAC; DAM MST**
  See also CDBLB 1789-1832; DLB 55; 144

**Carman, (William) Bliss** 1861-1929 **TCLC 7; DAC**
  See also CA 104; 152; DLB 92

**Carnegie, Dale** 1888-1955 ........... **TCLC 53**

**Carossa, Hans** 1878-1956 ........... **TCLC 48**
  See also DLB 66

**Carpenter, Don(ald Richard)** 1931-1995
    **CLC 41**
  See also CA 45-48; 149; CANR 1

**Carpentier (y Valmont), Alejo** 1904-1980
    **CLC 8, 11, 38; DAM MULT; HLC**
  See also CA 65-68; 97-100; CANR 11; DLB 113; HW

**Carr, Caleb** 1955(?)- ........................ **CLC 86**
  See also CA 147

**Carr, Emily** 1871-1945 ................. **TCLC 32**
  See also DLB 68

**Carr, John Dickson** 1906-1977 ........ **CLC 3**
  See also CA 49-52; 69-72; CANR 3, 33; MTCW

**Carr, Philippa**
  See Hibbert, Eleanor Alice Burford

**Carr, Virginia Spencer** 1929- ........ **CLC 34**
  See also CA 61-64; DLB 111

**Carrere, Emmanuel** 1957- ............ **CLC 89**

**Carrier, Roch** 1937-  **CLC 13, 78; DAC; DAM MST**
  See also CA 130; DLB 53

**Carroll, James P.** 1943(?)- ............ **CLC 38**
  See also CA 81-84

**Carroll, Jim** 1951- ........................ **CLC 35**
  See also AAYA 17; CA 45-48; CANR 42

**Carroll, Lewis** ...  **NCLC 2, 53; PC 18; WLC**
  See also Dodgson, Charles Lutwidge
  See also CDBLB 1832-1890; CLR 2, 18; DLB 18, 163, 178; JRDA

**Carroll, Paul Vincent** 1900-1968 .. **CLC 10**
  See also CA 9-12R; 25-28R; DLB 10

**Carruth, Hayden** 1921-  **CLC 4, 7, 10, 18, 84; PC 10**
  See also CA 9-12R; CANR 4, 38; DLB 5, 165; INT CANR-4; MTCW; SATA 47

**Carson, Rachel Louise** 1907-1964    **CLC 71; DAM POP**
  See also CA 77-80; CANR 35; MTCW; SATA 23

**Carter, Angela (Olive)** 1940-1992  **CLC 5, 41, 76; SSC 13**
  See also CA 53-56; 136; CANR 12, 36; DLB 14; MTCW; SATA 66; SATA-Obit 70

**Carter, Nick**
  See Smith, Martin Cruz

**Carver, Raymond** 1938-1988  **CLC 22, 36, 53, 55; DAM NOV; SSC 8**
  See also CA 33-36R; 126; CANR 17, 34; DLB 130; DLBY 84, 88; MTCW

**Cary, Elizabeth, Lady Falkland** 1585-1639
    **LC 30**

**Cary, (Arthur) Joyce (Lunel)** 1888-1957
    **TCLC 1, 29**
  See also CA 104; CDBLB 1914-1945; DLB 15, 100

**Casanova de Seingalt, Giovanni Jacopo** 1725-1798 ........................... **LC 13**

**Casares, Adolfo Bioy**
  See Bioy Casares, Adolfo

**Casely-Hayford, J(oseph) E(phraim)** 1866-1930
    **TCLC 24; BLC; DAM MULT**
  See also BW 2; CA 123; 152

**Casey, John (Dudley)** 1939- ........... **CLC 59**
  See also BEST 90:2; CA 69-72; CANR 23

**Casey, Michael** 1947- ...................... **CLC 2**
  See also CA 65-68; DLB 5

**Casey, Patrick**
  See Thurman, Wallace (Henry)

**Casey, Warren (Peter)** 1935-1988 . **CLC 12**
  See also CA 101; 127; INT 101

**Casona, Alejandro** ......................... **CLC 49**
  See also Alvarez, Alejandro Rodriguez

**Cassavetes, John** 1929-1989 .......... **CLC 20**
  See also CA 85-88; 127

**Cassian, Nina** 1924- ........................ **PC 17**

**Cassill, R(onald) V(erlin)** 1919-  **CLC 4, 23**
  See also CA 9-12R; CAAS 1; CANR 7, 45; DLB 6

**Cassirer, Ernst** 1874-1945 ........... **TCLC 61**
  See also CA 157

**Cassity, (Allen) Turner** 1929- ....  **CLC 6, 42**
  See also CA 17-20R; CAAS 8; CANR 11; DLB 105

**Castaneda, Carlos** 1931(?)- ........... **CLC 12**
  See also CA 25-28R; CANR 32; HW; MTCW

**Castedo, Elena** 1937- ...................... **CLC 65**
  See also CA 132

**Castedo-Ellerman, Elena**
  See Castedo, Elena

**Castellanos, Rosario** 1925-1974 ...  **CLC 66; DAM MULT; HLC**
  See also CA 131; 53-56; CANR 58; DLB 113; HW

**Castelvetro, Lodovico** 1505-1571 ....  **LC 12**

**Castiglione, Baldassare** 1478-1529 ..  **LC 12**

**Castle, Robert**
  See Hamilton, Edmond

**Castro, Guillen de** 1569-1631 ...........  **LC 19**

**Castro, Rosalia de** 1837-1885  **NCLC 3; DAM MULT**

**Cather, Willa**
  See Cather, Willa Sibert

**Cather, Willa Sibert** 1873-1947    **TCLC 1, 11, 31; DA; DAB; DAC; DAM MST, NOV; SSC 2; WLC**
  See also CA 104; 128; CDALB 1865-1917; DLB 9, 54, 78; DLBD 1; MTCW; SATA 30

**Cato, Marcus Porcius** 234B.C.-149B.C.
    **CMLC 21**

**Catton, (Charles) Bruce** 1899-1978  **CLC 35**
  See also AITN 1; CA 5-8R; 81-84; CANR 7; DLB 17; SATA 2; SATA-Obit 24

**Catullus** c. 84B.C.-c. 54B.C. ........  **CMLC 18**

**Cauldwell, Frank**
  See King, Francis (Henry)

**Caunitz, William J.** 1933-1996 ......  **CLC 34**
  See also BEST 89:3; CA 125; 130; 152; INT 130

**Causley, Charles (Stanley)** 1917- ....  **CLC 7**
  See also CA 9-12R; CANR 5, 35; CLR 30; DLB 27; MTCW; SATA 3, 66

**Caute, David** 1936- ....  **CLC 29; DAM NOV**
  See also CA 1-4R; CAAS 4; CANR 1, 33; DLB 14

**Cavafy, C(onstantine) P(eter)** 1863-1933
    **TCLC 2, 7; DAM POET**
  See also Kavafis, Konstantinos Petrou
  See also CA 148

**Cavallo, Evelyn**
  See Spark, Muriel (Sarah)

**Cavanna, Betty** ................................ **CLC 12**
  See also Harrison, Elizabeth Cavanna

See also JRDA; MAICYA; SAAS 4; SATA 1, 30

**Cavendish, Margaret Lucas** 1623-1673    **LC 30**
  See also DLB 131

**Caxton, William** 1421(?)-1491(?) ..... **LC 17**
  See also DLB 170

**Cayrol, Jean** 1911- ........................ **CLC 11**
  See also CA 89-92; DLB 83

**Cela, Camilo Jose** 1916-  **CLC 4, 13, 59; DAM MULT; HLC**
  See also BEST 90:2; CA 21-24R; CAAS 10; CANR 21, 32; DLBY 89; HW; MTCW

**Celan, Paul** ........  **CLC 10, 19, 53, 82; PC 10**
  See also Antschel, Paul

**Celine, Louis-Ferdinand**  **CLC 1, 3, 4, 7, 9, 15, 47**
  See also Destouches, Louis-Ferdinand
  See also DLB 72

**Cellini, Benvenuto** 1500-1571 ...........  **LC 7**

**Cendrars, Blaise** .............................. **CLC 18**
  See also Sauser-Hall, Frederic

**Cernuda (y Bidon), Luis** 1902-1963  **CLC 54; DAM POET**
  See also CA 131; 89-92; DLB 134; HW

**Cervantes (Saavedra), Miguel de** 1547-1616
    **LC 6, 23; DA; DAB; DAC; DAM MST, NOV; SSC 12; WLC**

**Cesaire, Aime (Fernand)** 1913-  **CLC 19, 32; BLC; DAM MULT, POET**
  See also BW 2; CA 65-68; CANR 24, 43; MTCW

**Chabon, Michael** 1963- ................. **CLC 55**
  See also CA 139; CANR 57

**Chabrol, Claude** 1930- .................. **CLC 16**
  See also CA 110

**Challans, Mary** 1905-1983
  See Renault, Mary
  See also CA 81-84; 111; SATA 23; SATA-Obit 36

**Challis, George**
  See Faust, Frederick (Schiller)

**Chambers, Aidan** 1934- ................. **CLC 35**
  See also CA 25-28R; CANR 12, 31, 58; JRDA; MAICYA; SAAS 12; SATA 1, 69

**Chambers, James** 1948-
  See Cliff, Jimmy
  See also CA 124

**Chambers, Jessie**
  See Lawrence, D(avid) H(erbert Richards)

**Chambers, Robert W.** 1865-1933   **TCLC 41**

**Chandler, Raymond (Thornton)** 1888-1959
    **TCLC 1, 7; SSC 23**
  See also CA 104; 129; CDALB 1929-1941; DLBD 6; MTCW

**Chang, Jung** 1952- ........................ **CLC 71**
  See also CA 142

**Channing, William Ellery** 1780-1842   **NCLC 17**
  See also DLB 1, 59

**Chaplin, Charles Spencer** 1889-1977 .   **CLC 16**
  See also Chaplin, Charlie
  See also CA 81-84; 73-76

**Chaplin, Charlie**
  See Chaplin, Charles Spencer
  See also DLB 44

**Chapman, George** 1559(?)-1634 .....    **LC 22; DAM DRAM**
  See also DLB 62, 121

**Chapman, Graham** 1941-1989 ......  **CLC 21**
  See also Monty Python

See also CA 93-96; DLB 53

**Cook, Robin** 1940- ..... **CLC 14; DAM POP**
See also BEST 90:2; CA 108; 111; CANR 41; INT 111

**Cook, Roy**
See Silverberg, Robert

**Cooke, Elizabeth** 1948- ................. **CLC 55**
See also CA 129

**Cooke, John Esten** 1830-1886 ....... **NCLC 5**
See also DLB 3

**Cooke, John Estes**
See Baum, L(yman) Frank

**Cooke, M. E.**
See Creasey, John

**Cooke, Margaret**
See Creasey, John

**Cook-Lynn, Elizabeth** 1930- **CLC 93; DAM MULT**
See also CA 133; DLB 175; NNAL

**Cooney, Ray** ..................................... **CLC 62**

**Cooper, Douglas** 1960- ................. **CLC 86**

**Cooper, Henry St. John**
See Creasey, John

**Cooper, J(oan) California** .... **CLC 56; DAM MULT**
See also AAYA 12; BW 1; CA 125; CANR 55

**Cooper, James Fenimore** 1789-1851 **NCLC 1, 27, 54**
See also CDALB 1640-1865; DLB 3; SATA 19

**Coover, Robert (Lowell)** 1932- **CLC 3, 7, 15, 32, 46, 87; DAM NOV; SSC 15**
See also CA 45-48; CANR 3, 37, 58; DLB 2; DLBY 81; MTCW

**Copeland, Stewart (Armstrong)** 1952- **CLC 26**

**Coppard, A(lfred) E(dgar)** 1878-1957 **TCLC 5; SSC 21**
See also CA 114; DLB 162; 1

**Coppee, Francois** 1842-1908 ....... **TCLC 25**

**Coppola, Francis Ford** 1939- ........ **CLC 16**
See also CA 77-80; CANR 40; DLB 44

**Corbiere, Tristan** 1845-1875 ...... **NCLC 43**

**Corcoran, Barbara** 1911- ............. **CLC 17**
See also AAYA 14; CA 21-24R; CAAS 2; CANR 11, 28, 48; DLB 52; JRDA; SAAS 20; SATA 3, 77

**Cordelier, Maurice**
See Giraudoux, (Hippolyte) Jean

**Corelli, Marie** 1855-1924 ............. **TCLC 51**
See also Mackay, Mary
See also DLB 34, 156

**Corman, Cid** ..................................... **CLC 9**
See also Corman, Sidney
See also CAAS 2; DLB 5

**Corman, Sidney** 1924-
See Corman, Cid
See also CA 85-88; CANR 44; DAM POET

**Cormier, Robert (Edmund)** 1925- **CLC 12, 30; DA; DAB; DAC; DAM MST, NOV**
See also AAYA 3, 19; CA 1-4R; CANR 5, 23; CDALB 1968-1988; CLR 12; DLB 52; INT CANR-23; JRDA; MAICYA; MTCW; SATA 10, 45, 83

**Corn, Alfred (DeWitt III)** 1943- ... **CLC 33**
See also CA 104; CAAS 25; CANR 44; DLB 120; DLBY 80

**Corneille, Pierre** 1606-1684 . **LC 28; DAB; DAM MST**

**Cornwell, David (John Moore)** 1931- **CLC 9, 15; DAM POP**
See also le Carre, John
See also CA 5-8R; CANR 13, 33; MTCW

**Corso, (Nunzio) Gregory** 1930- **CLC 1, 11**

See also CA 5-8R; CANR 41; DLB 5, 16; MTCW

**Cortazar, Julio** 1914-1984 **CLC 2, 3, 5, 10, 13, 15, 33, 34, 92; DAM MULT, NOV; HLC; SSC 7**
See also CA 21-24R; CANR 12, 32; DLB 113; HW; MTCW

**CORTES, HERNAN** 1484-1547 ....... **LC 31**

**Corwin, Cecil**
See Kornbluth, C(yril) M.

**Cosic, Dobrica** 1921- ..................... **CLC 14**
See also CA 122; 138

**Costain, Thomas B(ertram)** 1885-1965 **CLC 30**
See also CA 5-8R; 25-28R; DLB 9

**Costantini, Humberto** 1924(?)-1987 **CLC 49**
See also CA 131; 122; HW

**Costello, Elvis** 1955- ..................... **CLC 21**

**Cotes, Cecil V.**
See Duncan, Sara Jeannette

**Cotter, Joseph Seamon Sr.** 1861-1949 **TCLC 28; BLC; DAM MULT**
See also BW 1; CA 124; DLB 50

**Couch, Arthur Thomas Quiller**
See Quiller-Couch, Arthur Thomas

**Coulton, James**
See Hansen, Joseph

**Couperus, Louis (Marie Anne)** 1863-1923 **TCLC 15**
See also CA 115

**Coupland, Douglas** 1961- .. **CLC 85; DAC; DAM POP**
See also CA 142; CANR 57

**Court, Wesli**
See Turco, Lewis (Putnam)

**Courtenay, Bryce** 1933- ................. **CLC 59**
See also CA 138

**Courtney, Robert**
See Ellison, Harlan (Jay)

**Cousteau, Jacques-Yves** 1910- ...... **CLC 30**
See also CA 65-68; CANR 15; MTCW; SATA 38

**Coward, Noel (Peirce)** 1899-1973 **CLC 1, 9, 29, 51; DAM DRAM**
See also AITN 1; CA 17-18; 41-44R; CANR 35; CAP 2; CDBLB 1914-1945; DLB 10; MTCW

**Cowley, Malcolm** 1898-1989 ......... **CLC 39**
See also CA 5-8R; 128; CANR 3, 55; DLB 4, 48; DLBY 81, 89; MTCW

**Cowper, William** 1731-1800 **NCLC 8; DAM POET**
See also DLB 104, 109

**Cox, William Trevor** 1928- . **CLC 9, 14, 71; DAM NOV**
See also Trevor, William
See also CA 9-12R; CANR 4, 37, 55; DLB 14; INT CANR-37; MTCW

**Coyne, P. J.**
See Masters, Hilary

**Cozzens, James Gould** 1903-1978 **CLC 1, 4, 11, 92**
See also CA 9-12R; 81-84; CANR 19; CDALB 1941-1968; DLB 9; DLBD 2; DLBY 84; MTCW

**Crabbe, George** 1754-1832 .......... **NCLC 26**
See also DLB 93

**Craddock, Charles Egbert**
See Murfree, Mary Noailles

**Craig, A. A.**
See Anderson, Poul (William)

**Craik, Dinah Maria (Mulock)** 1826-1887
**NCLC 38**

See also DLB 35, 163; MAICYA; SATA 34

**Cram, Ralph Adams** 1863-1942 .. **TCLC 45**

**Crane, (Harold) Hart** 1899-1932 **TCLC 2, 5; DA; DAB; DAC; DAM MST, POET; PC 3; WLC**
See also CA 104; 127; CDALB 1917-1929; DLB 4, 48; MTCW

**Crane, R(onald) S(almon)** 1886-1967. **CLC 27**
See also CA 85-88; DLB 63

**Crane, Stephen (Townley)** 1871-1900 **TCLC 11, 17, 32; DA; DAB; DAC; DAM MST, NOV, POET; SSC 7; WLC**
See also AAYA 21; CA 109; 140; CDALB 1865-1917; DLB 12, 54, 78; 2

**Crase, Douglas** 1944- ..................... **CLC 58**
See also CA 106

**Crashaw, Richard** 1612(?)-1649 ...... **LC 24**
See also DLB 126

**Craven, Margaret** 1901-1980 **CLC 17; DAC**
See also CA 103

**Crawford, F(rancis) Marion** 1854-1909
**TCLC 10**
See also CA 107; DLB 71

**Crawford, Isabella Valancy** 1850-1887
**NCLC 12**
See also DLB 92

**Crayon, Geoffrey**
See Irving, Washington

**Creasey, John** 1908-1973 ................ **CLC 11**
See also CA 5-8R; 41-44R; CANR 8; DLB 77; MTCW

**Crebillon, Claude Prosper Jolyot de (fils)** 1707-1777 ......................................... **LC 28**

**Credo**
See Creasey, John

**Creeley, Robert (White)** 1926- **CLC 1, 2, 4, 8, 11, 15, 36, 78; DAM POET**
See also CA 1-4R; CAAS 10; CANR 23, 43; DLB 5, 16, 169; MTCW

**Crews, Harry (Eugene)** 1935- **CLC 6, 23, 49**
See also AITN 1; CA 25-28R; CANR 20, 57; DLB 6, 143; MTCW

**Crichton, (John) Michael** 1942- . **CLC 2, 6, 54, 90; DAM NOV, POP**
See also AAYA 10; AITN 2; CA 25-28R; CANR 13, 40, 54; DLBY 81; INT CANR-13; JRDA; MTCW; SATA 9, 88

**Crispin, Edmund** ............................. **CLC 22**
See also Montgomery, (Robert) Bruce
See also DLB 87

**Cristofer, Michael** 1945(?)-. **CLC 28; DAM DRAM**
See also CA 110; 152; DLB 7

**Croce, Benedetto** 1866-1952 ........ **TCLC 37**
See also CA 120; 155

**Crockett, David** 1786-1836 ............ **NCLC 8**
See also DLB 3, 11

**Crockett, Davy**
See Crockett, David

**Crofts, Freeman Wills** 1879-1957 **TCLC 55**
See also CA 115; DLB 77

**Croker, John Wilson** 1780-1857. **NCLC 10**
See also DLB 110

**Crommelynck, Fernand** 1885-1970 **CLC 75**
See also CA 89-92

**Cronin, A(rchibald) J(oseph)** 1896-1981
**CLC 32**
See also CA 1-4R; 102; CANR 5; SATA 47; SATA-Obit 25

**Cross, Amanda**
See Heilbrun, Carolyn G(old)

**Crothers, Rachel** 1878(?)-1958 ... **TCLC 19**

See also CA 113; DLB 7

**Croves, Hal**
See Traven, B.

**Crow Dog, Mary (Ellen)** (?)- ......... **CLC 93**
See also Brave Bird, Mary
See also CA 154

**Crowfield, Christopher**
See Stowe, Harriet (Elizabeth) Beecher

**Crowley, Aleister** ........................... **TCLC 7**
See also Crowley, Edward Alexander

**Crowley, Edward Alexander** 1875-1947
See Crowley, Aleister
See also CA 104

**Crowley, John** 1942- ...................... **CLC 57**
See also CA 61-64; CANR 43; DLBY 82; SATA
65

**Crud**
See Crumb, R(obert)

**Crumarums**
See Crumb, R(obert)

**Crumb, R(obert)** 1943- .................. **CLC 17**
See also CA 106

**Crumbum**
See Crumb, R(obert)

**Crumski**
See Crumb, R(obert)

**Crum the Bum**
See Crumb, R(obert)

**Crunk**
See Crumb, R(obert)

**Crustt**
See Crumb, R(obert)

**Cryer, Gretchen (Kiger)** 1935- ...... **CLC 21**
See also CA 114; 123

**Csath, Geza** 1887-1919 ............... **TCLC 13**
See also CA 111

**Cudlip, David** 1933- ...................... **CLC 34**

**Cullen, Countee** 1903-1946 ... **TCLC 4, 37;**
**BLC; DA; DAC; DAM MST, MULT,**
**POET**
See also BW 1; CA 108; 124; CDALB 1917-
1929; DLB 4, 48, 51; MTCW; SATA 18;
YABC

**Cum, R.**
See Crumb, R(obert)

**Cummings, Bruce F(rederick)** 1889-1919
See Barbellion, W. N. P.
See also CA 123

**Cummings, E(dward) E(stlin)** 1894-1962
**CLC 1, 3, 8, 12, 15, 68; DA; DAB; DAC;**
**DAM MST, POET; PC 5; WLC 2**
See also CA 73-76; CANR 31; CDALB 1929-
1941; DLB 4, 48; MTCW

**Cunha, Euclides (Rodrigues Pimenta) da** 1866-
1909 ...................................... **TCLC 24**
See also CA 123

**Cunningham, E. V.**
See Fast, Howard (Melvin)

**Cunningham, J(ames) V(incent)** 1911-1985
**CLC 3, 31**
See also CA 1-4R; 115; CANR 1; DLB 5

**Cunningham, Julia (Woolfolk)** 1916-. **CLC**
**12**
See also CA 9-12R; CANR 4, 19, 36; JRDA;
MAICYA; SAAS 2; SATA 1, 26

**Cunningham, Michael** 1952- ......... **CLC 34**
See also CA 136

**Cunninghame Graham, R(obert) B(ontine)**
1852-1936 .............................. **TCLC 19**
See also Graham, R(obert) B(ontine)
Cunninghame
See also CA 119; DLB 98

**Currie, Ellen** 19(?)- ....................... **CLC 44**

**Curtin, Philip**
See Lowndes, Marie Adelaide (Belloc)

**Curtis, Price**
See Ellison, Harlan (Jay)

**Cutrate, Joe**
See Spiegelman, Art

**Czaczkes, Shmuel Yosef**
See Agnon, S(hmuel) Y(osef Halevi)

**Dabrowska, Maria (Szumska)** 1889-1965
**CLC 15**
See also CA 106

**Dabydeen, David** 1955- .................. **CLC 34**
See also BW 1; CA 125; CANR 56

**Dacey, Philip** 1939- ........................ **CLC 51**
See also CA 37-40R; CAAS 17; CANR 14, 32;
DLB 105

**Dagerman, Stig (Halvard)** 1923-1954 **TCLC
17**
See also CA 117; 155

**Dahl, Roald** 1916-1990.... **CLC 1, 6, 18, 79;**
**DAB; DAC; DAM MST, NOV, POP**
See also AAYA 15; CA 1-4R; 133; CANR 6,
32, 37; CLR 1, 7, 41; DLB 139; JRDA;
MAICYA; MTCW; SATA 1, 26, 73; SATA-
Obit 65

**Dahlberg, Edward** 1900-1977 **CLC 1, 7, 14**
See also CA 9-12R; 69-72; CANR 31; DLB 48;
MTCW

**Dale, Colin** .................................... **TCLC 18**
See also Lawrence, T(homas) E(dward)

**Dale, George E.**
See Asimov, Isaac

**Daly, Elizabeth** 1878-1967 ............... **CLC 52**
See also CA 23-24; 25-28R; CAP 2

**Daly, Maureen** 1921- ...................... **CLC 17**
See also AAYA 5; CANR 37; JRDA; MAICYA;
SAAS 1; SATA 2

**Damas, Leon-Gontran** 1912-1978. **CLC 84**
See also BW 1; CA 125; 73-76

**Dana, Richard Henry Sr.** 1787-1879 **NCLC
53**

**Daniel, Samuel** 1562(?)-1619 ........... **LC 24**
See also DLB 62

**Daniels, Brett**
See Adler, Renata

**Dannay, Frederic** 1905-1982 **CLC 11; DAM
POP**
See also Queen, Ellery
See also CA 1-4R; 107; CANR 1, 39; DLB 137;
MTCW

**D'Annunzio, Gabriele** 1863-1938 **TCLC 6,
40**
See also CA 104; 155

**Danois, N. le**
See Gourmont, Remy (-Marie-Charles) de

**d'Antibes, Germain**
See Simenon, Georges (Jacques Christian)

**Danticat, Edwidge** 1969- .............. **CLC 94**
See also CA 152

**Danvers, Dennis** 1947- ................... **CLC 70**

**Danziger, Paula** 1944- ................... **CLC 21**
See also AAYA 4; CA 112; 115; CANR 37; CLR
20; JRDA; MAICYA; SATA 36, 63; SATA-
Brief 30

**Da Ponte, Lorenzo** 1749-1838 ..... **NCLC 50**

**Dario, Ruben** 1867-1916 .... **TCLC 4; DAM
MULT; HLC; PC 15**
See also CA 131; HW; MTCW

**Darley, George** 1795-1846 ............. **NCLC 2**
See also DLB 96

**Darwin, Charles** 1809-1882 ......... **NCLC 57**
See also DLB 57, 166

**Daryush, Elizabeth** 1887-1977 .. **CLC 6, 19**

See also CA 49-52; CANR 3; DLB 20

**Dashwood, Edmee Elizabeth Monica de la Pas-
ture** 1890-1943
See Delafield, E. M.
See also CA 119; 154

**Daudet, (Louis Marie) Alphonse** 1840-1897
**NCLC 1**
See also DLB 123

**Daumal, Rene** 1908-1944 ............. **TCLC 14**
See also CA 114

**Davenport, Guy (Mattison, Jr.)** 1927- **CLC
6, 14, 38; SSC 16**
See also CA 33-36R; CANR 23; DLB 130

**Davidson, Avram** 1923-
See Queen, Ellery
See also CA 101; CANR 26; DLB 8

**Davidson, Donald (Grady)** 1893-1968 **CLC
2, 13, 19**
See also CA 5-8R; 25-28R; CANR 4; DLB 45

**Davidson, Hugh**
See Hamilton, Edmond

**Davidson, John** 1857-1909 .......... **TCLC 24**
See also CA 118; DLB 19

**Davidson, Sara** 1943- ...................... **CLC 9**
See also CA 81-84; CANR 44

**Davie, Donald (Alfred)** 1922-1995 **CLC 5, 8,
10, 31**
See also CA 1-4R; 149; CAAS 3; CANR 1, 44;
DLB 27; MTCW

**Davies, Ray(mond Douglas)** 1944- **CLC 21**
See also CA 116; 146

**Davies, Rhys** 1903-1978 ................. **CLC 23**
See also CA 9-12R; 81-84; CANR 4; DLB 139

**Davies, (William) Robertson** 1913-1995
**CLC 2, 7, 13, 25, 42, 75, 91; DA; DAB;**
**DAC; DAM MST, NOV, POP; WLC**
See also BEST 89:2; CA 33-36R; 150; CANR
17, 42; DLB 68; INT CANR-17; MTCW

**Davies, W(illiam) H(enry)** 1871-1940 **TCLC
5**
See also CA 104; DLB 19, 174

**Davies, Walter C.**
See Kornbluth, C(yril) M.

**Davis, Angela (Yvonne)** 1944- **CLC 77; DAM
MULT**
See also BW 2; CA 57-60; CANR 10

**Davis, B. Lynch**
See Bioy Casares, Adolfo; Borges, Jorge Luis

**Davis, Gordon**
See Hunt, E(verette) Howard, (Jr.)

**Davis, Harold Lenoir** 1896-1960 .. **CLC 49**
See also CA 89-92; DLB 9

**Davis, Rebecca (Blaine) Harding** 1831-1910
**TCLC 6**
See also CA 104; DLB 74

**Davis, Richard Harding** 1864-1916. **TCLC
24**
See also CA 114; DLB 12, 23, 78, 79; DLBD
13

**Davison, Frank Dalby** 1893-1970. **CLC 15**
See also CA 116

**Davison, Lawrence H.**
See Lawrence, D(avid) H(erbert Richards)

**Davison, Peter (Hubert)** 1928- ...... **CLC 28**
See also CA 9-12R; CAAS 4; CANR 3, 43; DLB
5

**Davys, Mary** 1674-1732 ..................... **LC 1**
See also DLB 39

**Dawson, Fielding** 1930- ................. **CLC 6**
See also CA 85-88; DLB 130

**Dawson, Peter**
See Faust, Frederick (Schiller)

**Day, Clarence (Shepard, Jr.)** 1874-1935

See Ellison, Harlan (Jay)
**Edson, Russell** ........................ **CLC 13**
See also CA 33-36R
**Edwards, Bronwen Elizabeth**
See Rose, Wendy
**Edwards, G(erald) B(asil)** 1899-1976 . **CLC 25**
See also CA 110
**Edwards, Gus** 1939- ....................... **CLC 43**
See also CA 108; INT 108
**Edwards, Jonathan** 1703-1758 .. **LC 7; DA; DAC; DAM MST**
See also DLB 24
**Efron, Marina Ivanovna Tsvetaeva**
See Tsvetaeva (Efron), Marina (Ivanovna)
**Ehle, John (Marsden, Jr.)** 1925- ... **CLC 27**
See also CA 9-12R
**Ehrenbourg, Ilya (Grigoryevich)**
See Ehrenburg, Ilya (Grigoryevich)
**Ehrenburg, Ilya (Grigoryevich)** 1891-1967 **CLC 18, 34, 62**
See also CA 102; 25-28R
**Ehrenburg, Ilyo (Grigoryevich)**
See Ehrenburg, Ilya (Grigoryevich)
**Eich, Guenter** 1907-1972 ................ **CLC 15**
See also CA 111; 93-96; DLB 69, 124
**Eichendorff, Joseph Freiherr von** 1788-1857 **NCLC 8**
See also DLB 90
**Eigner, Larry** ....................... **CLC 9**
See also Eigner, Laurence (Joel)
See also CAAS 23; DLB 5
**Eigner, Laurence (Joel)** 1927-1996
See Eigner, Larry
See also CA 9-12R; 151; CANR 6
**Einstein, Albert** 1879-1955 .......... **TCLC 65**
See also CA 121; 133; MTCW
**Eiseley, Loren Corey** 1907-1977 ..... **CLC 7**
See also AAYA 5; CA 1-4R; 73-76; CANR 6
**Eisenstadt, Jill** 1963- ...................... **CLC 50**
See also CA 140
**Eisenstein, Sergei (Mikhailovich)** 1898-1948 **TCLC 57**
See also CA 114; 149
**Eisner, Simon**
See Kornbluth, C(yril) M.
**Ekeloef, (Bengt) Gunnar** 1907-1968 **CLC 27; DAM POET**
See also CA 123; 25-28R
**Ekelof, (Bengt) Gunnar**
See Ekeloef, (Bengt) Gunnar
**Ekwensi, C. O. D.**
See Ekwensi, Cyprian (Odiatu Duaka)
**Ekwensi, Cyprian (Odiatu Duaka)** 1921- **CLC 4; BLC; DAM MULT**
See also BW 2; CA 29-32R; CANR 18, 42; DLB 117; MTCW; SATA 66
**Elaine** ........................ **TCLC 18**
See also Leverson, Ada
**El Crummo**
See Crumb, R(obert)
**Elia**
See Lamb, Charles
**Eliade, Mircea** 1907-1986 ............. **CLC 19**
See also CA 65-68; 119; CANR 30; MTCW
**Eliot, A. D.**
See Jewett, (Theodora) Sarah Orne
**Eliot, Alice**
See Jewett, (Theodora) Sarah Orne
**Eliot, Dan**
See Silverberg, Robert
**Eliot, George** 1819-1880 **NCLC 4, 13, 23, 41, 49; DA; DAB; DAC; DAM MST, NOV;**

WLC
See also CDBLB 1832-1890; DLB 21, 35, 55
**Eliot, John** 1604-1690 ........................ **LC 5**
See also DLB 24
**Eliot, T(homas) S(tearns)** 1888-1965 **CLC 1, 2, 3, 6, 9, 10, 13, 15, 24, 34, 41, 55, 57; DA; DAB; DAC; DAM DRAM, MST, POET; PC 5; WLC 2**
See also CA 5-8R; 25-28R; CANR 41; CDALB 1929-1941; DLB 7, 10, 45, 63; DLBY 88; MTCW
**Elizabeth** 1866-1941 ..................... **TCLC 41**
**Elkin, Stanley L(awrence)** 1930-1995 **CLC 4, 6, 9, 14, 27, 51, 91; DAM NOV, POP; SSC 12**
See also CA 9-12R; 148; CANR 8, 46; DLB 2, 28; DLBY 80; INT CANR-8; MTCW
**Elledge, Scott** ................................. **CLC 34**
**Elliot, Don**
See Silverberg, Robert
**Elliott, Don**
See Silverberg, Robert
**Elliott, George P(aul)** 1918-1980 .... **CLC 2**
See also CA 1-4R; 97-100; CANR 2
**Elliott, Janice** 1931- ......................... **CLC 47**
See also CA 13-16R; CANR 8, 29; DLB 14
**Elliott, Sumner Locke** 1917-1991 . **CLC 38**
See also CA 5-8R; 134; CANR 2, 21
**Elliott, William**
See Bradbury, Ray (Douglas)
**Ellis, A. E.** ............................... **CLC 7**
**Ellis, Alice Thomas** ......................... **CLC 40**
See also Haycraft, Anna
**Ellis, Bret Easton** 1964- **CLC 39, 71; DAM POP**
See also AAYA 2; CA 118; 123; CANR 51; INT 123
**Ellis, (Henry) Havelock** 1859-1939 **TCLC 14**
See also CA 109
**Ellis, Landon**
See Ellison, Harlan (Jay)
**Ellis, Trey** 1962- ................................ **CLC 55**
See also CA 146
**Ellison, Harlan (Jay)** 1934- **CLC 1, 13, 42; DAM POP; SSC 14**
See also CA 5-8R; CANR 5, 46; DLB 8; INT CANR-5; MTCW
**Ellison, Ralph (Waldo)** 1914-1994 **CLC 1, 3, 11, 54, 86; BLC; DA; DAB; DAC; DAM MST, MULT, NOV; SSC 26; WLC**
See also AAYA 19; BW 1; CA 9-12R; 145; CANR 24, 53; CDALB 1941-1968; DLB 2, 76; DLBY 94; MTCW
**Ellmann, Lucy (Elizabeth)** 1956- .. **CLC 61**
See also CA 128
**Ellmann, Richard (David)** 1918-1987 **CLC 50**
See also BEST 89:2; CA 1-4R; 122; CANR 2, 28; DLB 103; DLBY 87; MTCW
**Elman, Richard** 1934- ..................... **CLC 19**
See also CA 17-20R; CAAS 3; CANR 47
**Elron**
See Hubbard, L(afayette) Ron(ald)
**Eluard, Paul** ............................... **TCLC 7, 41**
See also Grindel, Eugene
**Elyot, Sir Thomas** 1490(?)-1546 ...... **LC 11**
**Elytis, Odysseus** 1911-1996 **CLC 15, 49, 100; DAM POET**
See also CA 102; 151; MTCW
**Emecheta, (Florence Onye) Buchi** 1944- **CLC 14, 48; BLC; DAM MULT**
See also BW 2; CA 81-84; CANR 27; DLB 117; MTCW; SATA 66

**Emerson, Ralph Waldo** 1803-1882 **NCLC 1, 38; DA; DAB; DAC; DAM MST, POET; PC 18; WLC**
See also CDALB 1640-1865; DLB 1, 59, 73
**Eminescu, Mihail** 1850-1889 ...... **NCLC 33**
**Empson, William** 1906-1984 **CLC 3, 8, 19, 33, 34**
See also CA 17-20R; 112; CANR 31; DLB 20; MTCW
**Enchi Fumiko (Ueda)** 1905-1986 .. **CLC 31**
See also CA 129; 121
**Ende, Michael (Andreas Helmuth)** 1929-1995 **CLC 31**
See also CA 118; 124; 149; CANR 36; CLR 14; DLB 75; MAICYA; SATA 61; SATA-Brief 42; SATA-Obit 86
**Endo, Shusaku** 1923-1996 **CLC 7, 14, 19, 54, 99; DAM NOV**
See also CA 29-32R; 153; CANR 21, 54; MTCW
**Engel, Marian** 1933-1985 ............. **CLC 36**
See also CA 25-28R; CANR 12; DLB 53; INT CANR-12
**Engelhardt, Frederick**
See Hubbard, L(afayette) Ron(ald)
**Enright, D(ennis) J(oseph)** 1920- **CLC 4, 8, 31**
See also CA 1-4R; CANR 1, 42; DLB 27; SATA 25
**Enzensberger, Hans Magnus** 1929- **CLC 43**
See also CA 116; 119
**Ephron, Nora** 1941- ....................... **CLC 17, 31**
See also AITN 2; CA 65-68; CANR 12, 39
**Epicurus** 341B.C.-270B.C. .......... **CMLC 21**
See also DLB 176
**Epsilon**
See Betjeman, John
**Epstein, Daniel Mark** 1948- ........... **CLC 7**
See also CA 49-52; CANR 2, 53
**Epstein, Jacob** 1956- ...................... **CLC 19**
See also CA 114
**Epstein, Joseph** 1937- ..................... **CLC 39**
See also CA 112; 119; CANR 50
**Epstein, Leslie** 1938- ..................... **CLC 27**
See also CA 73-76; CAAS 12; CANR 23
**Equiano, Olaudah** 1745(?)-1797 ..... **LC 16; BLC; DAM MULT**
See also DLB 37, 50
**Erasmus, Desiderius** 1469(?)-1536 .. **LC 16**
**Erdman, Paul E(mil)** 1932- .......... **CLC 25**
See also AITN 1; CA 61-64; CANR 13, 43
**Erdrich, Louise** 1954- .. **CLC 39, 54; DAM MULT, NOV, POP**
See also AAYA 10; BEST 89:1; CA 114; CANR 41; DLB 152, 175; MTCW; NNAL; SATA 94
**Erenburg, Ilya (Grigoryevich)**
See Ehrenburg, Ilya (Grigoryevich)
**Erickson, Stephen Michael** 1950-
See Erickson, Steve
See also CA 129
**Erickson, Steve** ................................. **CLC 64**
See also Erickson, Stephen Michael
**Ericson, Walter**
See Fast, Howard (Melvin)
**Eriksson, Buntel**
See Bergman, (Ernst) Ingmar
**Ernaux, Annie** 1940- ..................... **CLC 88**
See also CA 147
**Eschenbach, Wolfram von**
See Wolfram von Eschenbach
**Eseki, Bruno**
See Mphahlele, Ezekiel

See also CA 97-100; CANR 25

**Field, Eugene** 1850-1895 ............... **NCLC 3**
See also DLB 23, 42, 140; DLBD 13; MAICYA; SATA 16

**Field, Gans T.**
See Wellman, Manly Wade

**Field, Michael** .............................. **TCLC 43**

**Field, Peter**
See Hobson, Laura Z(ametkin)

**Fielding, Henry** 1707-1754 **LC 1; DA; DAB; DAC; DAM MST, NOV; WLC**
See also CDBLB 1660-1789; DLB 39, 84, 101

**Fielding, Sarah** 1710-1768 ................. **LC 1**
See also DLB 39

**Fierstein, Harvey (Forbes)** 1954-. **CLC 33; DAM DRAM, POP**
See also CA 123; 129

**Figes, Eva** 1932- ................................ **CLC 31**
See also CA 53-56; CANR 4, 44; DLB 14

**Finch, Robert (Duer Claydon)** 1900- **CLC 18**
See also CA 57-60; CANR 9, 24, 49; DLB 88

**Findley, Timothy** 1930- **CLC 27; DAC; DAM MST**
See also CA 25-28R; CANR 12, 42; DLB 53

**Fink, William**
See Mencken, H(enry) L(ouis)

**Firbank, Louis** 1942-
See Reed, Lou
See also CA 117

**Firbank, (Arthur Annesley) Ronald** 1886-1926 **TCLC 1**
See also CA 104; DLB 36

**Fisher, M(ary) F(rances) K(ennedy)** 1908-1992 **CLC 76, 87**
See also CA 77-80; 138; CANR 44

**Fisher, Roy** 1930- ............................. **CLC 25**
See also CA 81-84; CAAS 10; CANR 16; DLB 40

**Fisher, Rudolph** 1897-1934 **TCLC 11; BLC; DAM MULT; SSC 25**
See also BW 1; CA 107; 124; DLB 51, 102

**Fisher, Vardis (Alvero)** 1895-1968 .. **CLC 7**
See also CA 5-8R; 25-28R; DLB 9

**Fiske, Tarleton**
See Bloch, Robert (Albert)

**Fitch, Clarke**
See Sinclair, Upton (Beall)

**Fitch, John IV**
See Cormier, Robert (Edmund)

**Fitzgerald, Captain Hugh**
See Baum, L(yman) Frank

**FitzGerald, Edward** 1809-1883 .... **NCLC 9**
See also DLB 32

**Fitzgerald, F(rancis) Scott (Key)** 1896-1940 **TCLC 1, 6, 14, 28, 55; DA; DAB; DAC; DAM MST, NOV; SSC 6; WLC**
See also AITN 1; CA 110; 123; CDALB 1917-1929; DLB 4, 9, 86; DLBD 1; DLBY 81, 96; MTCW

**Fitzgerald, Penelope** 1916- **CLC 19, 51, 61**
See also CA 85-88; CAAS 10; CANR 56; DLB 14

**Fitzgerald, Robert (Stuart)** 1910-1985 **CLC 39**
See also CA 1-4R; 114; CANR 1; DLBY 80

**FitzGerald, Robert D(avid)** 1902-1987 **CLC 19**
See also CA 17-20R

**Fitzgerald, Zelda (Sayre)** 1900-1948 **TCLC 52**
See also CA 117; 126; DLBY 84

**Flanagan, Thomas (James Bonner)** 1923- **CLC 25, 52**

See also CA 108; CANR 55; DLBY 80; INT 108; MTCW

**Flaubert, Gustave** 1821-1880 **NCLC 2, 10, 19; DA; DAB; DAC; DAM MST, NOV; SSC 11; WLC**
See also DLB 119

**Flecker, Herman Elroy**
See Flecker, (Herman) James Elroy

**Flecker, (Herman) James Elroy** 1884-1915 **TCLC 43**
See also CA 109; 150; DLB 10, 19

**Fleming, Ian (Lancaster)** 1908-1964 **CLC 3, 30; DAM POP**
See also CA 5-8R; CDBLB 1945-1960; DLB 87; MTCW; SATA 9

**Fleming, Thomas (James)** 1927- ... **CLC 37**
See also CA 5-8R; CANR 10; INT CANR-10; SATA 8

**Fletcher, John** 1579-1625 ....... **LC 33; DC 6**
See also CDBLB Before 1660; DLB 58

**Fletcher, John Gould** 1886-1950 . **TCLC 35**
See also CA 107; DLB 4, 45

**Fleur, Paul**
See Pohl, Frederik

**Flooglebuckle, Al**
See Spiegelman, Art

**Flying Officer X**
See Bates, H(erbert) E(rnest)

**Fo, Dario** 1926- ...... **CLC 32; DAM DRAM**
See also CA 116; 128; MTCW

**Fogarty, Jonathan Titulescu Esq.**
See Farrell, James T(homas)

**Folke, Will**
See Bloch, Robert (Albert)

**Follett, Ken(neth Martin)** 1949- .. **CLC 18; DAM NOV, POP**
See also AAYA 6; BEST 89:4; CA 81-84; CANR 13, 33, 54; DLB 87; DLBY 81; INT CANR-33; MTCW

**Fontane, Theodor** 1819-1898 ...... **NCLC 26**
See also DLB 129

**Foote, Horton** 1916- ..... **CLC 51, 91; DAM DRAM**
See also CA 73-76; CANR 34, 51; DLB 26; INT CANR-34

**Foote, Shelby** 1916- .. **CLC 75; DAM NOV, POP**
See also CA 5-8R; CANR 3, 45; DLB 2, 17

**Forbes, Esther** 1891-1967 ............. **CLC 12**
See also AAYA 17; CA 13-14; 25-28R; CAP 1; CLR 27; DLB 22; JRDA; MAICYA; SATA 2

**Forche, Carolyn (Louise)** 1950- **CLC 25, 83, 86; DAM POET; PC 10**
See also CA 109; 117; CANR 50; DLB 5; INT 117

**Ford, Elbur**
See Hibbert, Eleanor Alice Burford

**Ford, Ford Madox** 1873-1939 **TCLC 1, 15, 39, 57; DAM NOV**
See also CA 104; 132; CDBLB 1914-1945; DLB 162; MTCW

**Ford, John** 1895-1973 ................... **CLC 16**
See also CA 45-48

**Ford, Richard** ................................... **CLC 99**

**Ford, Richard** 1944- ....................... **CLC 46**
See also CA 69-72; CANR 11, 47

**Ford, Webster**
See Masters, Edgar Lee

**Foreman, Richard** 1937- ................ **CLC 50**
See also CA 65-68; CANR 32

**Forester, C(ecil) S(cott)** 1899-1966 **CLC 35**
See also CA 73-76; 25-28R; SATA 13

**Forez**

See Mauriac, Francois (Charles)

**Forman, James Douglas** 1932- ...... **CLC 21**
See also AAYA 17; CA 9-12R; CANR 4, 19, 42; JRDA; MAICYA; SATA 8, 70

**Fornes, Maria Irene** 1930-...... **CLC 39, 61**
See also CA 25-28R; CANR 28; DLB 7; HW; INT CANR-28; MTCW

**Forrest, Leon** 1937- ......................... **CLC 4**
See also BW 2; CA 89-92; CAAS 7; CANR 25, 52; DLB 33

**Forster, E(dward) M(organ)** 1879-1970 **CLC 1, 2, 3, 4, 9, 10, 13, 15, 22, 45, 77; DA; DAB; DAC; DAM MST, NOV; WLC**
See also AAYA 2; CA 13-14; 25-28R; CANR 45; CAP 1; CDBLB 1914-1945; DLB 34, 98, 162, 178; DLBD 10; MTCW; SATA 57

**Forster, John** 1812-1876 .............. **NCLC 11**
See also DLB 144

**Forsyth, Frederick** 1938- **CLC 2, 5, 36; DAM NOV, POP**
See also BEST 89:4; CA 85-88; CANR 38; DLB 87; MTCW

**Forten, Charlotte L.** ........... **TCLC 16; BLC**
See also Grimke, Charlotte L(ottie) Forten
See also DLB 50

**Foscolo, Ugo** 1778-1827 ................. **NCLC 8**

**Fosse, Bob** .......................................... **CLC 20**
See also Fosse, Robert Louis

**Fosse, Robert Louis** 1927-1987
See Fosse, Bob
See also CA 110; 123

**Foster, Stephen Collins** 1826-1864 **NCLC 26**

**Foucault, Michel** 1926-1984 **CLC 31, 34, 69**
See also CA 105; 113; CANR 34; MTCW

**Fouque, Friedrich (Heinrich Karl) de la Motte** 1777-1843 ............................... **NCLC 2**
See also DLB 90

**Fourier, Charles** 1772-1837 ........ **NCLC 51**

**Fournier, Henri Alban** 1886-1914
See Alain-Fournier
See also CA 104

**Fournier, Pierre** 1916- ................... **CLC 11**
See also Gascar, Pierre
See also CA 89-92; CANR 16, 40

**Fowles, John** 1926- **CLC 1, 2, 3, 4, 6, 9, 10, 15, 33, 87; DAB; DAC; DAM MST**
See also CA 5-8R; CANR 25; CDBLB 1960 to Present; DLB 14, 139; MTCW; SATA 22

**Fox, Paula** 1923- .......................... **CLC 2, 8**
See also AAYA 3; CA 73-76; CANR 20, 36; CLR 1, 44; DLB 52; JRDA; MAICYA; MTCW; SATA 17, 60

**Fox, William Price (Jr.)** 1926- ....... **CLC 22**
See also CA 17-20R; CAAS 19; CANR 11; DLB 2; DLBY 81

**Foxe, John** 1516(?)-1587 ................... **LC 14**

**Frame, Janet** 1924-. **CLC 2, 3, 6, 22, 66, 96**
See also Clutha, Janet Paterson Frame

**France, Anatole** ............................. **TCLC 9**
See also Thibault, Jacques Anatole Francois
See also DLB 123

**Francis, Claude** 19(?)- ................... **CLC 50**

**Francis, Dick** 1920- .. **CLC 2, 22, 42; DAM POP**
See also AAYA 5, 21; BEST 89:3; CA 5-8R; CANR 9, 42; CDBLB 1960 to Present; DLB 87; INT CANR-9; MTCW

**Francis, Robert (Churchill)** 1901-1987 **CLC 15**
See also CA 1-4R; 123; CANR 1

**Frank, Anne(lies Marie)** 1929-1945 **TCLC 17; DA; DAB; DAC; DAM MST; WLC**
See also AAYA 12; CA 113; 133; MTCW; SATA

CDALB 1941-1968; DLB 5, 16, 169; MTCW

**Ginzburg, Natalia** 1916-1991 **CLC 5, 11, 54, 70**
See also CA 85-88; 135; CANR 33; DLB 177; MTCW

**Giono, Jean** 1895-1970 .............. **CLC 4, 11**
See also CA 45-48; 29-32R; CANR 2, 35; DLB 72; MTCW

**Giovanni, Nikki** 1943- **CLC 2, 4, 19, 64; BLC; DA; DAB; DAC; DAM MST, MULT, POET**
See also AITN 1; BW 2; CA 29-32R; CAAS 6; CANR 18, 41; CLR 6; DLB 5, 41; INT CANR-18; MAICYA; MTCW; SATA 24; YABC

**Giovene, Andrea** 1904- .................... **CLC 7**
See also CA 85-88

**Gippius, Zinaida (Nikolayevna)** 1869-1945
See Hippius, Zinaida
See also CA 106

**Giraudoux, (Hippolyte) Jean** 1882-1944 **TCLC 2, 7; DAM DRAM**
See also CA 104; DLB 65

**Gironella, Jose Maria** 1917-........... **CLC 11**
See also CA 101

**Gissing, George (Robert)** 1857-1903 **TCLC 3, 24, 47**
See also CA 105; DLB 18, 135

**Giurlani, Aldo**
See Palazzeschi, Aldo

**Gladkov, Fyodor (Vasilyevich)** 1883-1958 **TCLC 27**

**Glanville, Brian (Lester)** 1931- ....... **CLC 6**
See also CA 5-8R; CAAS 9; CANR 3; DLB 15, 139; SATA 42

**Glasgow, Ellen (Anderson Gholson)** 1873(?)-1945 ...................................... **TCLC 2, 7**
See also CA 104; DLB 9, 12

**Glaspell, Susan** 1882(?)-1948 ...... **TCLC 55**
See also CA 110; 154; DLB 7, 9, 78; 2

**Glassco, John** 1909-1981 ................. **CLC 9**
See also CA 13-16R; 102; CANR 15; DLB 68

**Glasscock, Amnesia**
See Steinbeck, John (Ernst)

**Glasser, Ronald J.** 1940(?)-........... **CLC 37**

**Glassman, Joyce**
See Johnson, Joyce

**Glendinning, Victoria** 1937-......... **CLC 50**
See also CA 120; 127; DLB 155

**Glissant, Edouard** 1928- **CLC 10, 68; DAM MULT**
See also CA 153

**Gloag, Julian** 1930-....................... **CLC 40**
See also AITN 1; CA 65-68; CANR 10

**Glowacki, Aleksander**
See Prus, Boleslaw

**Gluck, Louise (Elisabeth)** 1943- **CLC 7, 22, 44, 81; DAM POET; PC 16**
See also CA 33-36R; CANR 40; DLB 5

**Gobineau, Joseph Arthur (Comte) de** 1816-1882 ...................................... **NCLC 17**
See also DLB 123

**Godard, Jean-Luc** 1930-................ **CLC 20**
See also CA 93-96

**Godden, (Margaret) Rumer** 1907- **CLC 53**
See also AAYA 6; CA 5-8R; CANR 4, 27, 36, 55; CLR 20; DLB 161; MAICYA; SAAS 12; SATA 3, 36

**Godoy Alcayaga, Lucila** 1889-1957
See Mistral, Gabriela
See also BW 2; CA 104; 131; DAM MULT; HW; MTCW

**Godwin, Gail (Kathleen)** 1937- **CLC 5, 8, 22, 31, 69; DAM POP**
See also CA 29-32R; CANR 15, 43; DLB 6; INT CANR-15; MTCW

**Godwin, William** 1756-1836 ........ **NCLC 14**
See also CDBLB 1789-1832; DLB 39, 104, 142, 158, 163

**Goebbels, Josef**
See Goebbels, (Paul) Joseph

**Goebbels, (Paul) Joseph** 1897-1945 . **TCLC 68**
See also CA 115; 148

**Goebbels, Joseph Paul**
See Goebbels, (Paul) Joseph

**Goethe, Johann Wolfgang von** 1749-1832 **NCLC 4, 22, 34; DA; DAB; DAC; DAM DRAM, MST, POET; PC 5; WLC 3**
See also DLB 94

**Gogarty, Oliver St. John** 1878-1957 **TCLC 15**
See also CA 109; 150; DLB 15, 19

**Gogol, Nikolai (Vasilyevich)** 1809-1852 **NCLC 5, 15, 31; DA; DAB; DAC; DAM DRAM, MST, DC 1; SSC 4; WLC**

**Goines, Donald** 1937(?)-1974 **CLC 80; BLC; DAM MULT, POP**
See also AITN 1; BW 1; CA 124; 114; DLB 33

**Gold, Herbert** 1924-......... **CLC 4, 7, 14, 42**
See also CA 9-12R; CANR 17, 45; DLB 2; DLBY 81

**Goldbarth, Albert** 1948- ............ **CLC 5, 38**
See also CA 53-56; CANR 6, 40; DLB 120

**Goldberg, Anatol** 1910-1982 ......... **CLC 34**
See also CA 131; 117

**Goldemberg, Isaac** 1945-.............. **CLC 52**
See also CA 69-72; CAAS 12; CANR 11, 32; HW

**Golding, William (Gerald)** 1911-1993 **CLC 1, 2, 3, 8, 10, 17, 27, 58, 81; DA; DAB; DAC; DAM MST, NOV; WLC**
See also AAYA 5; CA 5-8R; 141; CANR 13, 33, 54; CDBLB 1945-1960; DLB 15, 100; MTCW

**Goldman, Emma** 1869-1940 ........ **TCLC 13**
See also CA 110; 150

**Goldman, Francisco** 1955- ............ **CLC 76**

**Goldman, William (W.)** 1931- ... **CLC 1, 48**
See also CA 9-12R; CANR 29; DLB 44

**Goldmann, Lucien** 1913-1970 ....... **CLC 24**
See also CA 25-28; CAP 2

**Goldoni, Carlo** 1707-1793 ...... **LC 4; DAM DRAM**

**Goldsberry, Steven** 1949- ............. **CLC 34**
See also CA 131

**Goldsmith, Oliver** 1728-1774 .... **LC 2; DA; DAB; DAC; DAM DRAM, MST, NOV, POET; WLC**
See also CDBLB 1660-1789; DLB 39, 89, 104, 109, 142; SATA 26

**Goldsmith, Peter**
See Priestley, J(ohn) B(oynton)

**Gombrowicz, Witold** 1904-1969 **CLC 4, 7, 11, 49; DAM DRAM**
See also CA 19-20; 25-28R; CAP 2

**Gomez de la Serna, Ramon** 1888-1963 **CLC 9**
See also CA 153; 116; HW

**Goncharov, Ivan Alexandrovich** 1812-1891 **NCLC 1**

**Goncourt, Edmond (Louis Antoine Huot) de** 1822-1896................................ **NCLC 7**
See also DLB 123

**Goncourt, Jules (Alfred Huot) de** 1830-1870 **NCLC 7**

See also DLB 123

**Gontier, Fernande** 19(?)- .............. **CLC 50**

**Goodman, Paul** 1911-1972 ... **CLC 1, 2, 4, 7**
See also CA 19-20; 37-40R; CANR 34; CAP 2; DLB 130; MTCW

**Gordimer, Nadine** 1923- **CLC 3, 5, 7, 10, 18, 33, 51, 70; DA; DAB; DAC; DAM MST, NOV; SSC 17**
See also CA 5-8R; CANR 3, 28, 56; INT CANR-28; MTCW; YABC

**Gordon, Adam Lindsay** 1833-1870 **NCLC 21**

**Gordon, Caroline** 1895-1981 **CLC 6, 13, 29, 83; SSC 15**
See also CA 11-12; 103; CANR 36; CAP 1; DLB 4, 9, 102; DLBY 81; MTCW

**Gordon, Charles William** 1860-1937
See Connor, Ralph
See also CA 109

**Gordon, Mary (Catherine)** 1949- **CLC 13, 22**
See also CA 102; CANR 44; DLB 6; DLBY 81; INT 102; MTCW

**Gordon, Sol** 1923- ......................... **CLC 26**
See also CA 53-56; CANR 4; SATA 11

**Gordone, Charles** 1925-1995 **CLC 1, 4; DAM DRAM**
See also BW 1; CA 93-96; 150; CANR 55; DLB 7; INT 93-96; MTCW

**Gorenko, Anna Andreevna**
See Akhmatova, Anna

**Gorky, Maxim** ........... **TCLC 8; DAB; WLC**
See also Peshkov, Alexei Maximovich

**Goryan, Sirak**
See Saroyan, William

**Gosse, Edmund (William)** 1849-1928 **TCLC 28**
See also CA 117; DLB 57, 144

**Gotlieb, Phyllis Fay (Bloom)** 1926- **CLC 18**
See also CA 13-16R; CANR 7; DLB 88

**Gottesman, S. D.**
See Kornbluth, C(yril) M.; Pohl, Frederik

**Gottfried von Strassburg** fl. c. 1210- **CMLC 10**
See also DLB 138

**Gould, Lois** .................................... **CLC 4, 10**
See also CA 77-80; CANR 29; MTCW

**Gourmont, Remy (-Marie-Charles) de** 1858-1915 ...................................... **TCLC 17**
See also CA 109; 150

**Govier, Katherine** 1948- .............. **CLC 51**
See also CA 101; CANR 18, 40

**Goyen, (Charles) William** 1915-1983 **CLC 5, 8, 14, 40**
See also AITN 2; CA 5-8R; 110; CANR 6; DLB 2; DLBY 83; INT CANR-6

**Goytisolo, Juan** 1931- **CLC 5, 10, 23; DAM MULT; HLC**
See also CA 85-88; CANR 32; HW; MTCW

**Gozzano, Guido** 1883-1916 ............. **PC 10**
See also CA 154; DLB 114

**Gozzi, (Conte) Carlo** 1720-1806 **NCLC 23**

**Grabbe, Christian Dietrich** 1801-1836 **NCLC 2**
See also DLB 133

**Grace, Patricia** 1937- .................... **CLC 56**

**Gracian y Morales, Baltasar** 1601-1658 **LC 15**

**Gracq, Julien** ............................ **CLC 11, 48**
See also Poirier, Louis
See also DLB 83

**Grade, Chaim** 1910-1982............. **CLC 10**
See also CA 93-96; 107

**Graduate of Oxford, A**
See Ruskin, John

See also BW 2; CA 25-28R; 114; CANR 22;
DLB 2, 76, 143; MTCW
**Hinde, Thomas** ............................ **CLC 6, 11**
See also Chitty, Thomas Willes
**Hindin, Nathan**
See Bloch, Robert (Albert)
**Hine, (William) Daryl** 1936- .......... **CLC 15**
See also CA 1-4R; CAAS 15; CANR 1, 20; DLB
60
**Hinkson, Katharine Tynan**
See Tynan, Katharine
**Hinton, S(usan) E(loise)** 1950- **CLC 30; DA;
DAB; DAC; DAM MST, NOV**
See also AAYA 2; CA 81-84; CANR 32; CLR
3, 23; JRDA; MAICYA; MTCW; SATA 19,
58
**Hippius, Zinaida** ............................. **TCLC 9**
See also Gippius, Zinaida (Nikolayevna)
**Hiraoka, Kimitake** 1925-1970
See Mishima, Yukio
See also CA 97-100; 29-32R; DAM DRAM;
MTCW
**Hirsch, E(ric) D(onald), Jr.** 1928-. **CLC 79**
See also CA 25-28R; CANR 27, 51; DLB 67;
INT CANR-27; MTCW
**Hirsch, Edward** 1950- ................. **CLC 31, 50**
See also CA 104; CANR 20, 42; DLB 120
**Hitchcock, Alfred (Joseph)** 1899-1980 **CLC
16**
See also CA 97-100; SATA 27; SATA-Obit 24
**Hitler, Adolf** 1889-1945 ............... **TCLC 53**
See also CA 117; 147
**Hoagland, Edward** 1932-............... **CLC 28**
See also CA 1-4R; CANR 2, 31, 57; DLB 6;
SATA 51
**Hoban, Russell (Conwell)** 1925- **CLC 7, 25;
DAM NOV**
See also CA 5-8R; CANR 23, 37; CLR 3; DLB
52; MAICYA; MTCW; SATA 1, 40, 78
**Hobbes, Thomas** 1588-1679 ............. **LC 36**
See also DLB 151
**Hobbs, Perry**
See Blackmur, R(ichard) P(almer)
**Hobson, Laura Z(ametkin)** 1900-1986 **CLC
7, 25**
See also CA 17-20R; 118; CANR 55; DLB 28;
SATA 52
**Hochhuth, Rolf** 1931- **CLC 4, 11, 18; DAM
DRAM**
See also CA 5-8R; CANR 33; DLB 124; MTCW
**Hochman, Sandra** 1936- ............. **CLC 3, 8**
See also CA 5-8R; DLB 5
**Hochwaelder, Fritz** 1911-1986 ..... **CLC 36;
DAM DRAM**
See also CA 29-32R; 120; CANR 42; MTCW
**Hochwalder, Fritz**
See Hochwaelder, Fritz
**Hocking, Mary (Eunice)** 1921-...... **CLC 13**
See also CA 101; CANR 18, 40
**Hodgins, Jack** 1938- ...................... **CLC 23**
See also CA 93-96; DLB 60
**Hodgson, William Hope** 1877(?)-1918 **TCLC
13**
See also CA 111; DLB 70, 153, 156, 178
**Hoeg, Peter** 1957- .......................... **CLC 95**
See also CA 151
**Hoffman, Alice** 1952- **CLC 51; DAM NOV**
See also CA 77-80; CANR 34; MTCW
**Hoffman, Daniel (Gerard)** 1923- **CLC 6, 13,
23**
See also CA 1-4R; CANR 4; DLB 5
**Hoffman, Stanley** 1944- .................. **CLC 5**
See also CA 77-80

**Hoffman, William M(oses)** 1939-.. **CLC 40**
See also CA 57-60; CANR 11
**Hoffmann, E(rnst) T(heodor) A(madeus)** 1776-
1822 .......................... **NCLC 2; SSC 13**
See also DLB 90; SATA 27
**Hofmann, Gert** 1931- ..................... **CLC 54**
See also CA 128
**Hofmannsthal, Hugo von** 1874-1929 **TCLC
11; DAM DRAM; DC 4**
See also CA 106; 153; DLB 81, 118
**Hogan, Linda** 1947- **CLC 73; DAM MULT**
See also CA 120; CANR 45; DLB 175; NNAL
**Hogarth, Charles**
See Creasey, John
**Hogarth, Emmett**
See Polonsky, Abraham (Lincoln)
**Hogg, James** 1770-1835 ................. **NCLC 4**
See also DLB 93, 116, 159
**Holbach, Paul Henri Thiry Baron** 1723-1789
**LC 14**
**Holberg, Ludvig** 1684-1754 ................ **LC 6**
**Holden, Ursula** 1921- ..................... **CLC 18**
See also CA 101; CAAS 8; CANR 22
**Holderlin, (Johann Christian) Friedrich** 1770-
1843 ............................ **NCLC 16; PC 4**
**Holdstock, Robert**
See Holdstock, Robert P.
**Holdstock, Robert P.** 1948- ............ **CLC 39**
See also CA 131
**Holland, Isabelle** 1920- .................. **CLC 21**
See also AAYA 11; CA 21-24R; CANR 10, 25,
47; JRDA; MAICYA; SATA 8, 70
**Holland, Marcus**
See Caldwell, (Janet Miriam) Taylor (Holland)
**Hollander, John** 1929-........ **CLC 2, 5, 8, 14**
See also CA 1-4R; CANR 1, 52; DLB 5; SATA
13
**Hollander, Paul**
See Silverberg, Robert
**Holleran, Andrew** 1943(?)-............ **CLC 38**
See also CA 144
**Hollinghurst, Alan** 1954- ......... **CLC 55, 91**
See also CA 114
**Hollis, Jim**
See Summers, Hollis (Spurgeon, Jr.)
**Holly, Buddy** 1936-1959 .............. **TCLC 65**
**Holmes, John**
See Souster, (Holmes) Raymond
**Holmes, John Clellon** 1926-1988 .. **CLC 56**
See also CA 9-12R; 125; CANR 4; DLB 16
**Holmes, Oliver Wendell** 1809-1894 **NCLC 14**
See also CDALB 1640-1865; DLB 1; SATA 34
**Holmes, Raymond**
See Souster, (Holmes) Raymond
**Holt, Victoria**
See Hibbert, Eleanor Alice Burford
**Holub, Miroslav** 1923- .................... **CLC 4**
See also CA 21-24R; CANR 10
**Homer** c. 8th cent. B.C.- **CMLC 1, 16; DA;
DAB; DAC; DAM MST, POET**
See also DLB 176; YABC
**Honig, Edwin** 1919-........................ **CLC 33**
See also CA 5-8R; CAAS 8; CANR 4, 45; DLB
5
**Hood, Hugh (John Blagdon)** 1928- **CLC 15,
28**
See also CA 49-52; CAAS 17; CANR 1, 33;
DLB 53
**Hood, Thomas** 1799-1845 ............ **NCLC 16**
See also DLB 96
**Hooker, (Peter) Jeremy** 1941- ....... **CLC 43**
See also CA 77-80; CANR 22; DLB 40
**hooks, bell** ........................................ **CLC 94**

See also Watkins, Gloria
**Hope, A(lec) D(erwent)** 1907- ... **CLC 3, 51**
See also CA 21-24R; CANR 33; MTCW
**Hope, Brian**
See Creasey, John
**Hope, Christopher (David Tully)** 1944- **CLC
52**
See also CA 106; CANR 47; SATA 62
**Hopkins, Gerard Manley** 1844-1889 **NCLC
17; DA; DAB; DAC; DAM MST, POET;
PC 15; WLC**
See also CDBLB 1890-1914; DLB 35, 57
**Hopkins, John (Richard)** 1931-....... **CLC 4**
See also CA 85-88
**Hopkins, Pauline Elizabeth** 1859-1930
**TCLC 28; BLC; DAM MULT**
See also BW 2; CA 141; DLB 50
**Hopkinson, Francis** 1737-1791 ........ **LC 25**
See also DLB 31
**Hopley-Woolrich, Cornell George** 1903-1968
See Woolrich, Cornell
See also CA 13-14; CANR 58; CAP 1
**Horatio**
See Proust, (Valentin-Louis-George-Eugene-)
Marcel
**Horgan, Paul (George Vincent O'Shaughnessy)**
1903-1995 ....... **CLC 9, 53; DAM NOV**
See also CA 13-16R; 147; CANR 9, 35; DLB
102; DLBY 85; INT CANR-9; MTCW;
SATA 13; SATA-Obit 84
**Horn, Peter**
See Kuttner, Henry
**Hornem, Horace Esq.**
See Byron, George Gordon (Noel)
**Horney, Karen (Clementine Theodore
Danielsen)** 1885-1952 .......... **TCLC 71**
See also CA 114
**Hornung, E(rnest) W(illiam)** 1866-1921
**TCLC 59**
See also CA 108; DLB 70
**Horovitz, Israel (Arthur)** 1939- ... **CLC 56;
DAM DRAM**
See also CA 33-36R; CANR 46; DLB 7
**Horvath, Odon von**
See Horvath, Oedoen von
See also DLB 85, 124
**Horvath, Oedoen von** 1901-1938 **TCLC 45**
See also Horvath, Odon von
See also CA 118
**Horwitz, Julius** 1920-1986............. **CLC 14**
See also CA 9-12R; 119; CANR 12
**Hospital, Janette Turner** 1942- ..... **CLC 42**
See also CA 108; CANR 48
**Hostos, E. M. de**
See Hostos (y Bonilla), Eugenio Maria de
**Hostos, Eugenio M. de**
See Hostos (y Bonilla), Eugenio Maria de
**Hostos, Eugenio Maria**
See Hostos (y Bonilla), Eugenio Maria de
**Hostos (y Bonilla), Eugenio Maria de** 1839-
1903 ...................................... **TCLC 24**
See also CA 123; 131; HW
**Houdini**
See Lovecraft, H(oward) P(hillips)
**Hougan, Carolyn** 1943-.................... **CLC 34**
See also CA 139
**Household, Geoffrey (Edward West)** 1900-1988
**CLC 11**
See also CA 77-80; 126; CANR 58; DLB 87;
SATA 14; SATA-Obit 59
**Housman, A(lfred) E(dward)** 1859-1936
**TCLC 1, 10; DA; DAB; DAC; DAM
MST, POET; PC 2**

See Stewart, J(ohn) I(nnes) M(ackintosh)

**Ionesco, Eugene** 1909-1994 **CLC 1, 4, 6, 9, 11, 15, 41, 86; DA; DAB; DAC; DAM DRAM, MST; WLC**
See also CA 9-12R; 144; CANR 55; MTCW; SATA 7; SATA-Obit 79

**Iqbal, Muhammad** 1873-1938 ..... **TCLC 28**

**Ireland, Patrick**
See O'Doherty, Brian

**Iron, Ralph**
See Schreiner, Olive (Emilie Albertina)

**Irving, John (Winslow)** 1942- **CLC 13, 23, 38; DAM NOV, POP**
See also AAYA 8; BEST 89:3; CA 25-28R; CANR 28; DLB 6; DLBY 82; MTCW

**Irving, Washington** 1783-1859 **NCLC 2, 19; DA; DAB; DAM MST; SSC 2; WLC**
See also CDALB 1640-1865; DLB 3, 11, 30, 59, 73, 74; 2

**Irwin, P. K.**
See Page, P(atricia) K(athleen)

**Isaacs, Susan** 1943-..... **CLC 32; DAM POP**
See also BEST 89:1; CA 89-92; CANR 20, 41; INT CANR-20; MTCW

**Isherwood, Christopher (William Bradshaw)** 1904-1986. **CLC 1, 9, 11, 14, 44; DAM DRAM, NOV**
See also CA 13-16R; 117; CANR 35; DLB 15; DLBY 86; MTCW

**Ishiguro, Kazuo** 1954- **CLC 27, 56, 59; DAM NOV**
See also BEST 90:2; CA 120; CANR 49; MTCW

**Ishikawa, Hakuhin**
See Ishikawa, Takuboku

**Ishikawa, Takuboku** 1886(?)-1912 **TCLC 15; DAM POET; PC 10**
See also CA 113; 153

**Iskander, Fazil** 1929-..... **CLC 47**
See also CA 102

**Isler, Alan (David)** 1934-............. **CLC 91**
See also CA 156

**Ivan IV** 1530-1584 ..................... **LC 17**

**Ivanov, Vyacheslav Ivanovich** 1866-1949 **TCLC 33**
See also CA 122

**Ivask, Ivar Vidrik** 1927-1992 ........ **CLC 14**
See also CA 37-40R; 139; CANR 24

**Ives, Morgan**
See Bradley, Marion Zimmer

**J. R. S.**
See Gogarty, Oliver St. John

**Jabran, Kahlil**
See Gibran, Kahlil

**Jabran, Khalil**
See Gibran, Kahlil

**Jackson, Daniel**
See Wingrove, David (John)

**Jackson, Jesse** 1908-1983 ............... **CLC 12**
See also BW 1; CA 25-28R; 109; CANR 27; CLR 28; MAICYA; SATA 2, 29; SATA-Obit 48

**Jackson, Laura (Riding)** 1901-1991
See Riding, Laura
See also CA 65-68; 135; CANR 28; DLB 48

**Jackson, Sam**
See Trumbo, Dalton

**Jackson, Sara**
See Wingrove, David (John)

**Jackson, Shirley** 1919-1965 **CLC 11, 60, 87; DA; DAC; DAM MST; SSC 9; WLC**
See also AAYA 9; CA 1-4R; 25-28R; CANR 4, 52; CDALB 1941-1968; DLB 6; SATA 2

**Jacob, (Cyprien-)Max** 1876-1944 . **TCLC 6**
See also CA 104

**Jacobs, Jim** 1942- ........................... **CLC 12**
See also CA 97-100; INT 97-100

**Jacobs, W(illiam) W(ymark)** 1863-1943 **TCLC 22**
See also CA 121; DLB 135

**Jacobsen, Jens Peter** 1847-1885 .. **NCLC 34**

**Jacobsen, Josephine** 1908-............. **CLC 48**
See also CA 33-36R; CAAS 18; CANR 23, 48

**Jacobson, Dan** 1929- .................. **CLC 4, 14**
See also CA 1-4R; CANR 2, 25; DLB 14; MTCW

**Jacqueline**
See Carpentier (y Valmont), Alejo

**Jagger, Mick** 1944- ........................ **CLC 17**

**Jakes, John (William)** 1932- **CLC 29; DAM NOV, POP**
See also BEST 89:4; CA 57-60; CANR 10, 43; DLBY 83; INT CANR-10; MTCW; SATA 62

**James, Andrew**
See Kirkup, James

**James, C(yril) L(ionel) R(obert)** 1901-1989 **CLC 33**
See also BW 2; CA 117; 125; 128; DLB 125; MTCW

**James, Daniel (Lewis)** 1911-1988
See Santiago, Danny
See also CA 125

**James, Dynely**
See Mayne, William (James Carter)

**James, Henry Sr.** 1811-1882 ........ **NCLC 53**

**James, Henry** 1843-1916 **TCLC 2, 11, 24, 40, 47, 64; DA; DAB; DAC; DAM MST, NOV; SSC 8; WLC**
See also CA 104; 132; CDALB 1865-1917; DLB 12, 71, 74; DLBD 13; MTCW

**James, M. R.**
See James, Montague (Rhodes)
See also DLB 156

**James, Montague (Rhodes)** 1862-1936 **TCLC 6; SSC 16**
See also CA 104

**James, P. D. ................................ CLC 18, 46**
See also White, Phyllis Dorothy James
See also BEST 90:2; CDBLB 1960 to Present; DLB 87

**James, Philip**
See Moorcock, Michael (John)

**James, William** 1842-1910 ..... **TCLC 15, 32**
See also CA 109

**James I** 1394-1437 ............................ **LC 20**

**Jameson, Anna** 1794-1860 ........... **NCLC 43**
See also DLB 99, 166

**Jami, Nur al-Din 'Abd al-Rahman** 1414-1492 **LC 9**

**Jandl, Ernst** 1925- .......................... **CLC 34**

**Janowitz, Tama** 1957- **CLC 43; DAM POP**
See also CA 106; CANR 52

**Japrisot, Sebastien** 1931-............... **CLC 90**

**Jarrell, Randall** 1914-1965 **CLC 1, 2, 6, 9, 13, 49; DAM POET**
See also CA 5-8R; 25-28R; CABS 2; CANR 6, 34; CDALB 1941-1968; CLR 6; DLB 48, 52; MAICYA; MTCW; SATA 7

**Jarry, Alfred** 1873-1907 **TCLC 2, 14; DAM DRAM; SSC 20**
See also CA 104; 153

**Jarvis, E. K.**
See Bloch, Robert (Albert); Ellison, Harlan (Jay); Silverberg, Robert

**Jeake, Samuel, Jr.**
See Aiken, Conrad (Potter)

**Jean Paul** 1763-1825 ..................... **NCLC 7**

**Jefferies, (John) Richard** 1848-1887 **NCLC 47**
See also DLB 98, 141; SATA 16

**Jeffers, (John) Robinson** 1887-1962 **CLC 2, 3, 11, 15, 54; DA; DAC; DAM MST, POET; PC 17; WLC**
See also CA 85-88; CANR 35; CDALB 1917-1929; DLB 45; MTCW

**Jefferson, Janet**
See Mencken, H(enry) L(ouis)

**Jefferson, Thomas** 1743-1826 ..... **NCLC 11**
See also CDALB 1640-1865; DLB 31

**Jeffrey, Francis** 1773-1850 ......... **NCLC 33**
See also DLB 107

**Jelakowitch, Ivan**
See Heijermans, Herman

**Jellicoe, (Patricia) Ann** 1927-........ **CLC 27**
See also CA 85-88; DLB 13

**Jen, Gish ...................................... CLC 70**
See also Jen, Lillian

**Jen, Lillian** 1956(?)-
See Jen, Gish
See also CA 135

**Jenkins, (John) Robin** 1912- ......... **CLC 52**
See also CA 1-4R; CANR 1; DLB 14

**Jennings, Elizabeth (Joan)** 1926- **CLC 5, 14**
See also CA 61-64; CAAS 5; CANR 8, 39; DLB 27; MTCW; SATA 66

**Jennings, Waylon** 1937-................. **CLC 21**

**Jensen, Johannes V.** 1873-1950 ... **TCLC 41**

**Jensen, Laura (Linnea)** 1948- ....... **CLC 37**
See also CA 103

**Jerome, Jerome K(lapka)** 1859-1927 **TCLC 23**
See also CA 119; DLB 10, 34, 135

**Jerrold, Douglas William** 1803-1857 **NCLC 2**
See also DLB 158, 159

**Jewett, (Theodora) Sarah Orne** 1849-1909 **TCLC 1, 22; SSC 6**
See also CA 108; 127; DLB 12, 74; SATA 15

**Jewsbury, Geraldine (Endsor)** 1812-1880 **NCLC 22**
See also DLB 21

**Jhabvala, Ruth Prawer** 1927- **CLC 4, 8, 29, 94; DAB; DAM NOV**
See also CA 1-4R; CANR 2, 29, 51; DLB 139; INT CANR-29; MTCW

**Jibran, Kahlil**
See Gibran, Kahlil

**Jibran, Khalil**
See Gibran, Kahlil

**Jiles, Paulette** 1943- ................. **CLC 13, 58**
See also CA 101

**Jimenez (Mantecon), Juan Ramon** 1881-1958 **TCLC 4; DAM MULT, POET; HLC; PC 7**
See also CA 104; 131; DLB 134; HW; MTCW

**Jimenez, Ramon**
See Jimenez (Mantecon), Juan Ramon

**Jimenez Mantecon, Juan**
See Jimenez (Mantecon), Juan Ramon

**Joel, Billy ......................................... CLC 26**
See also Joel, William Martin

**Joel, William Martin** 1949-
See Joel, Billy
See also CA 108

**John of the Cross, St.** 1542-1591 ..... **LC 18**

**Johnson, B(ryan) S(tanley William)** 1933-1973 **CLC 6, 9**
See also CA 9-12R; 53-56; CANR 9; DLB 14, 40

**Krylov, Ivan Andreevich** 1768(?)-1844
**NCLC 1**
See also DLB 150
**Kubin, Alfred (Leopold Isidor)** 1877-1959
**TCLC 23**
See also CA 112; 149; DLB 81
**Kubrick, Stanley** 1928- ................. **CLC 16**
See also CA 81-84; CANR 33; DLB 26
**Kumin, Maxine (Winokur)** 1925- **CLC 5, 13, 28; DAM POET; PC 15**
See also AITN 2; CA 1-4R; CAAS 8; CANR 1, 21; DLB 5; MTCW; SATA 12
**Kundera, Milan** 1929- **CLC 4, 9, 19, 32, 68; DAM NOV; SSC 24**
See also AAYA 2; CA 85-88; CANR 19, 52; MTCW
**Kunene, Mazisi (Raymond)** 1930- **CLC 85**
See also BW 1; CA 125; DLB 117
**Kunitz, Stanley (Jasspon)** 1905- **CLC 6, 11, 14**
See also CA 41-44R; CANR 26, 57; DLB 48; INT CANR-26; MTCW
**Kunze, Reiner** 1933- ...................... **CLC 10**
See also CA 93-96; DLB 75
**Kuprin, Aleksandr Ivanovich** 1870-1938
**TCLC 5**
See also CA 104
**Kureishi, Hanif** 1954(?)- ................ **CLC 64**
See also CA 139
**Kurosawa, Akira** 1910- ....... **CLC 16; DAM MULT**
See also AAYA 11; CA 101; CANR 46
**Kushner, Tony** 1957(?)- ....... **CLC 81; DAM DRAM**
See also CA 144
**Kuttner, Henry** 1915-1958 .......... **TCLC 10**
See also Vance, Jack
See also CA 107; 157; DLB 8
**Kuzma, Greg** 1944- .......................... **CLC 7**
See also CA 33-36R
**Kuzmin, Mikhail** 1872(?)-1936 ... **TCLC 40**
**Kyd, Thomas** 1558-1594 ....... **LC 22; DAM DRAM; DC 3**
See also DLB 62
**Kyprianos, Iossif**
See Samarakis, Antonis
**La Bruyere, Jean de** 1645-1696 ....... **LC 17**
**Lacan, Jacques (Marie Emile)** 1901-1981
**CLC 75**
See also CA 121; 104
**Laclos, Pierre Ambroise Francois Choderlos de** 1741-1803 ................................ **NCLC 4**
**Lacolere, Francois**
See Aragon, Louis
**La Colere, Francois**
See Aragon, Louis
**La Deshabilleuse**
See Simenon, Georges (Jacques Christian)
**Lady Gregory**
See Gregory, Isabella Augusta (Persse)
**Lady of Quality, A**
See Bagnold, Enid
**La Fayette, Marie (Madelaine Pioche de la Vergne Comtes** 1634-1693 ......... **LC 2**
**Lafayette, Rene**
See Hubbard, L(afayette) Ron(ald)
**Laforgue, Jules** 1860-1887 **NCLC 5, 53; PC 14; SSC 20**
**Lagerkvist, Paer (Fabian)** 1891-1974 **CLC 7, 10, 13, 54; DAM DRAM, NOV**
See also Lagerkvist, Par
See also CA 85-88; 49-52; MTCW
**Lagerkvist, Par** ................................ **SSC 12**

See also Lagerkvist, Paer (Fabian)
**Lagerloef, Selma (Ottiliana Lovisa)** 1858-1940
**TCLC 4, 36**
See also Lagerlof, Selma (Ottiliana Lovisa)
See also CA 108; SATA 15
**Lagerlof, Selma (Ottiliana Lovisa)**
See Lagerloef, Selma (Ottiliana Lovisa)
See also CLR 7; SATA 15
**La Guma, (Justin) Alex(ander)** 1925-1985
**CLC 19; DAM NOV**
See also BW 1; CA 49-52; 118; CANR 25; DLB 117; MTCW
**Laidlaw, A. K.**
See Grieve, C(hristopher) M(urray)
**Lainez, Manuel Mujica**
See Mujica Lainez, Manuel
See also HW
**Laing, R(onald) D(avid)** 1927-1989 **CLC 95**
See also CA 107; 129; CANR 34; MTCW
**Lamartine, Alphonse (Marie Louis Prat) de** 1790-1869 **NCLC 11; DAM POET; PC 16**
**Lamb, Charles** 1775-1834 .. **NCLC 10; DA; DAB; DAC; DAM MST; WLC**
See also CDBLB 1789-1832; DLB 93, 107, 163; SATA 17
**Lamb, Lady Caroline** 1785-1828 **NCLC 38**
See also DLB 116
**Lamming, George (William)** 1927- **CLC 2, 4, 66; BLC; DAM MULT**
See also BW 2; CA 85-88; CANR 26; DLB 125; MTCW
**L'Amour, Louis (Dearborn)** 1908-1988 **CLC 25, 55; DAM NOV, POP**
See also AAYA 16; AITN 2; BEST 89:2; CA 1-4R; 125; CANR 3, 25, 40; DLBY 80; MTCW
**Lampedusa, Giuseppe (Tomasi) di** 1896-1957
**TCLC 13**
See also Tomasi di Lampedusa, Giuseppe
See also DLB 177
**Lampman, Archibald** 1861-1899 **NCLC 25**
See also DLB 92
**Lancaster, Bruce** 1896-1963 .......... **CLC 36**
See also CA 9-10; CAP 1; SATA 9
**Lanchester, John** ............................. **CLC 99**
**Landau, Mark Alexandrovich**
See Aldanov, Mark (Alexandrovich)
**Landau-Aldanov, Mark Alexandrovich**
See Aldanov, Mark (Alexandrovich)
**Landis, Jerry**
See Simon, Paul (Frederick)
**Landis, John** 1950- ......................... **CLC 26**
See also CA 112; 122
**Landolfi, Tommaso** 1908-1979 **CLC 11, 49**
See also CA 127; 117; DLB 177
**Landon, Letitia Elizabeth** 1802-1838 **NCLC 15**
See also DLB 96
**Landor, Walter Savage** 1775-1864 **NCLC 14**
See also DLB 93, 107
**Landwirth, Heinz** 1927-
See Lind, Jakov
See also CA 9-12R; CANR 7
**Lane, Patrick** 1939- . **CLC 25; DAM POET**
See also CA 97-100; CANR 54; DLB 53; INT 97-100
**Lang, Andrew** 1844-1912 ............ **TCLC 16**
See also CA 114; 137; DLB 98, 141; MAICYA; SATA 16
**Lang, Fritz** 1890-1976 ................... **CLC 20**
See also CA 77-80; 69-72; CANR 30
**Lange, John**
See Crichton, (John) Michael
**Langer, Elinor** 1939- ..................... **CLC 34**

See also CA 121
**Langland, William** 1330(?)-1400(?)    **LC 19; DA; DAB; DAC; DAM MST, POET**
See also DLB 146
**Langstaff, Launcelot**
See Irving, Washington
**Lanier, Sidney** 1842-1881 .. **NCLC 6; DAM POET**
See also DLB 64; DLBD 13; MAICYA; SATA 18
**Lanyer, Aemilia** 1569-1645 ......... **LC 10, 30**
See also DLB 121
**Lao Tzu** ........................................... **CMLC 7**
**Lapine, James (Elliot)** 1949- ......... **CLC 39**
See also CA 123; 130; CANR 54; INT 130
**Larbaud, Valery (Nicolas)** 1881-1957 **TCLC 9**
See also CA 106; 152
**Lardner, Ring**
See Lardner, Ring(gold) W(ilmer)
**Lardner, Ring W., Jr.**
See Lardner, Ring(gold) W(ilmer)
**Lardner, Ring(gold) W(ilmer)** 1885-1933
**TCLC 2, 14**
See also CA 104; 131; CDALB 1917-1929; DLB 11, 25, 86; MTCW
**Laredo, Betty**
See Codrescu, Andrei
**Larkin, Maia**
See Wojciechowska, Maia (Teresa)
**Larkin, Philip (Arthur)** 1922-1985 **CLC 3, 5, 8, 9, 13, 18, 33, 39, 64; DAB; DAM MST, POET**
See also CA 5-8R; 117; CANR 24; CDBLB 1960 to Present; DLB 27; MTCW
**Larra (y Sanchez de Castro), Mariano Jose de** 1809-1837 ............................ **NCLC 17**
**Larsen, Eric** 1941- ......................... **CLC 55**
See also CA 132
**Larsen, Nella** 1891-1964 .... **CLC 37; BLC; DAM MULT**
See also BW 1; CA 125; DLB 51
**Larson, Charles R(aymond)** 1938- **CLC 31**
See also CA 53-56; CANR 4
**Larson, Jonathan** 1961(?)-1996 .... **CLC 99**
**Las Casas, Bartolome de** 1474-1566 **LC 31**
**Lasker-Schueler, Else** 1869-1945 **TCLC 57**
See also DLB 66, 124
**Latham, Jean Lee** 1902- ............... **CLC 12**
See also AITN 1; CA 5-8R; CANR 7; MAICYA; SATA 2, 68
**Latham, Mavis**
See Clark, Mavis Thorpe
**Lathen, Emma** ..................................... **CLC 2**
See also Hennissart, Martha; Latsis, Mary J(ane)
**Lathrop, Francis**
See Leiber, Fritz (Reuter, Jr.)
**Latsis, Mary J(ane)**
See Lathen, Emma
See also CA 85-88
**Lattimore, Richmond (Alexander)** 1906-1984
**CLC 3**
See also CA 1-4R; 112; CANR 1
**Laughlin, James** 1914- .................. **CLC 49**
See also CA 21-24R; CAAS 22; CANR 9, 47; DLB 48; DLBY 96
**Laurence, (Jean) Margaret (Wemyss)** 1926-1987 **CLC 3, 6, 13, 50, 62; DAC; DAM MST; SSC 7**
See also CA 5-8R; 121; CANR 33; DLB 53; MTCW; SATA-Obit 50
**Laurent, Antoine** 1952- .................. **CLC 50**
**Lauscher, Hermann**

**Macdonald, Ross** ..... **CLC 1, 2, 3, 14, 34, 41**
See also Millar, Kenneth
See also DLBD 6
**MacDougal, John**
See Blish, James (Benjamin)
**MacEwen, Gwendolyn (Margaret) 1941-1987**
**CLC 13, 55**
See also CA 9-12R; 124; CANR 7, 22; DLB
53; SATA 50; SATA-Obit 55
**Macha, Karel Hynek 1810-1846** **NCLC 46**
**Machado (y Ruiz), Antonio 1875-1939**
**TCLC 3**
See also CA 104; DLB 108
**Machado de Assis, Joaquim Maria 1839-1908**
**TCLC 10; BLC; SSC 24**
See also CA 107; 153
**Machen, Arthur** ................ **TCLC 4; SSC 20**
See also Jones, Arthur Llewellyn
See also DLB 36, 156, 178
**Machiavelli, Niccolo 1469-1527** .. **LC 8, 36;**
**DA; DAB; DAC; DAM MST**
See also YABC
**MacInnes, Colin 1914-1976** ....... **CLC 4, 23**
See also CA 69-72; 65-68; CANR 21; DLB 14;
MTCW
**MacInnes, Helen (Clark) 1907-1985 CLC 27,**
**39; DAM POP**
See also CA 1-4R; 117; CANR 1, 28, 58; DLB
87; MTCW; SATA 22; SATA-Obit 44
**Mackay, Mary 1855-1924**
See Corelli, Marie
See also CA 118
**Mackenzie, Compton (Edward Montague)**
**1883-1972** .................................. **CLC 18**
See also CA 21-22; 37-40R; CAP 2; DLB 34,
100
**Mackenzie, Henry 1745-1831** ..... **NCLC 41**
See also DLB 39
**Mackintosh, Elizabeth 1896(?)-1952**
See Tey, Josephine
See also CA 110
**MacLaren, James**
See Grieve, C(hristopher) M(urray)
**Mac Laverty, Bernard 1942-** ......... **CLC 31**
See also CA 116; 118; CANR 43; INT 118
**MacLean, Alistair (Stuart) 1922-1987** **CLC**
**3, 13, 50, 63; DAM POP**
See also CA 57-60; 121; CANR 28; MTCW;
SATA 23; SATA-Obit 50
**Maclean, Norman (Fitzroy) 1902-1990 CLC**
**78; DAM POP; SSC 13**
See also CA 102; 132; CANR 49
**MacLeish, Archibald 1892-1982** **CLC 3, 8,**
**14, 68; DAM POET**
See also CA 9-12R; 106; CANR 33; DLB 4, 7,
45; DLBY 82; MTCW
**MacLennan, (John) Hugh 1907-1990 CLC 2,**
**14, 92; DAC; DAM MST**
See also CA 5-8R; 142; CANR 33; DLB 68;
MTCW
**MacLeod, Alistair 1936-** .... **CLC 56; DAC;**
**DAM MST**
See also CA 123; DLB 60
**MacNeice, (Frederick) Louis 1907-1963**
**CLC 1, 4, 10, 53; DAB; DAM POET**
See also CA 85-88; DLB 10, 20; MTCW
**MacNeill, Dand**
See Fraser, George MacDonald
**Macpherson, James 1736-1796** ........ **LC 29**
See also DLB 109
**Macpherson, (Jean) Jay 1931-** ...... **CLC 14**
See also CA 5-8R; DLB 53
**MacShane, Frank 1927-** ................ **CLC 39**

See also CA 9-12R; CANR 3, 33; DLB 111
**Macumber, Mari**
See Sandoz, Mari(e Susette)
**Madach, Imre 1823-1864** ............. **NCLC 19**
**Madden, (Jerry) David 1933-** .... **CLC 5, 15**
See also CA 1-4R; CAAS 3; CANR 4, 45; DLB
6; MTCW
**Maddern, Al(an)**
See Ellison, Harlan (Jay)
**Madhubuti, Haki R. 1942-** **CLC 6, 73; BLC;**
**DAM MULT, POET; PC 5**
See Lee, Don L.
See also BW 2; CA 73-76; CANR 24, 51; DLB
5, 41; DLBD 8
**Maepenn, Hugh**
See Kuttner, Henry
**Maepenn, K. H.**
See Kuttner, Henry
**Maeterlinck, Maurice 1862-1949** **TCLC 3;**
**DAM DRAM**
See also CA 104; 136; SATA 66
**Maginn, William 1794-1842** .......... **NCLC 8**
See also DLB 110, 159
**Mahapatra, Jayanta 1928-** . **CLC 33; DAM**
**MULT**
See also CA 73-76; CAAS 9; CANR 15, 33
**Mahfouz, Naguib (Abdel Aziz Al-Sabilgi)**
**1911(?)-**
See Mahfuz, Najib
See also BEST 89:2; CA 128; CANR 55; DAM
NOV; MTCW
**Mahfuz, Najib** ............................ **CLC 52, 55**
See also Mahfouz, Naguib (Abdel Aziz Al-
Sabilgi)
See also DLBY 88
**Mahon, Derek 1941-** ....................... **CLC 27**
See also CA 113; 128; DLB 40
**Mailer, Norman 1923-** **CLC 1, 2, 3, 4, 5, 8, 11,**
**14, 28, 39, 74; DA; DAB; DAC; DAM MST,**
**NOV, POP**
See also AITN 2; CA 9-12R; CABS 1; CANR
28; CDALB 1968-1988; DLB 2, 16, 28;
DLBD 3; DLBY 80, 83; MTCW
**Maillet, Antonine 1929-** ...... **CLC 54; DAC**
See also CA 115; 120; CANR 46; DLB 60; INT
120
**Mais, Roger 1905-1955** ................. **TCLC 8**
See also BW 1; CA 105; 124; DLB 125; MTCW
**Maistre, Joseph de 1753-1821** ..... **NCLC 37**
**Maitland, Frederic 1850-1906** .... **TCLC 65**
**Maitland, Sara (Louise) 1950-** ...... **CLC 49**
See also CA 69-72; CANR 13
**Major, Clarence 1936-** **CLC 3, 19, 48; BLC;**
**DAM MULT**
See also BW 2; CA 21-24R; CAAS 6; CANR
13, 25, 53; DLB 33
**Major, Kevin (Gerald) 1949-** **CLC 26; DAC**
See also AAYA 16; CA 97-100; CANR 21, 38;
CLR 11; DLB 60; INT CANR-21; JRDA;
MAICYA; SATA 32, 82
**Maki, James**
See Ozu, Yasujiro
**Malabaila, Damiano**
See Levi, Primo
**Malamud, Bernard 1914-1986 CLC 1, 2, 3, 5,**
**8, 9, 11, 18, 27, 44, 78, 85; DA; DAB; DAC;**
**DAM MST, NOV, POP; SSC 15; WLC**
See also AAYA 16; CA 5-8R; 118; CABS 1;
CANR 28; CDALB 1941-1968; DLB 2, 28,
152; DLBY 80, 86; MTCW
**Malaparte, Curzio 1898-1957** ..... **TCLC 52**
**Malcolm, Dan**
See Silverberg, Robert

**Malcolm X** ............................... **CLC 82; BLC**
See also Little, Malcolm
See also YABC
**Malherbe, Francois de 1555-1628** ..... **LC 5**
**Mallarme, Stephane 1842-1898 NCLC 4, 41;**
**DAM POET; PC 4**
**Mallet-Joris, Francoise 1930-** ........ **CLC 11**
See also CA 65-68; CANR 17; DLB 83
**Malley, Ern**
See McAuley, James Phillip
**Mallowan, Agatha Christie**
See Christie, Agatha (Mary Clarissa)
**Maloff, Saul 1922-** ........................... **CLC 5**
See also CA 33-36R
**Malone, Louis**
See MacNeice, (Frederick) Louis
**Malone, Michael (Christopher) 1942-** **CLC**
**43**
See also CA 77-80; CANR 14, 32, 57
**Malory, (Sir) Thomas 1410(?)-1471(?)** . **LC**
**11; DA; DAB; DAC; DAM MST**
See also CDBLB Before 1660; DLB 146; SATA
59; SATA-Brief 33; YABC
**Malouf, (George Joseph) David 1934-** **CLC**
**28, 86**
See also CA 124; CANR 50
**Malraux, (Georges-)Andre 1901-1976** **CLC**
**1, 4, 9, 13, 15, 57; DAM NOV**
See also CA 21-22; 69-72; CANR 34, 58; CAP
2; DLB 72; MTCW
**Malzberg, Barry N(athaniel) 1939-** **CLC 7**
See also CA 61-64; CAAS 4; CANR 16; DLB
8
**Mamet, David (Alan) 1947-** **CLC 9, 15, 34,**
**46, 91; DAM DRAM; DC 4**
See also AAYA 3; CA 81-84; CABS 3; CANR
15, 41; DLB 7; MTCW
**Mamoulian, Rouben (Zachary) 1897-1987**
**CLC 16**
See also CA 25-28R; 124
**Mandelstam, Osip (Emilievich) 1891(?)-1938(?)**
**TCLC 2, 6; PC 14**
See also CA 104; 150
**Mander, (Mary) Jane 1877-1949 TCLC 31**
**Mandeville, John fl. 1350-** .......... **CMLC 19**
See also DLB 146
**Mandiargues, Andre Pieyre de** ...... **CLC 41**
See Pieyre de Mandiargues, Andre
See also DLB 83
**Mandrake, Ethel Belle**
See Thurman, Wallace (Henry)
**Mangan, James Clarence 1803-1849** **NCLC**
**27**
**Maniere, J.-E.**
See Giraudoux, (Hippolyte) Jean
**Manley, (Mary) Delariviere 1672(?)-1724**
**LC 1**
See also DLB 39, 80
**Mann, Abel**
See Creasey, John
**Mann, Emily 1952-** ............................. **DC 7**
See also CA 130; CANR 55
**Mann, (Luiz) Heinrich 1871-1950 TCLC 9**
See also CA 106; DLB 66
**Mann, (Paul) Thomas 1875-1955 TCLC 2, 8,**
**14, 21, 35, 44, 60; DA; DAB; DAC; DAM**
**MST, NOV; SSC 5; WLC**
See also CA 104; 128; DLB 66; MTCW
**Mannheim, Karl 1893-1947** ........ **TCLC 65**
**Manning, David**
See Faust, Frederick (Schiller)
**Manning, Frederic 1887(?)-1935 TCLC 25**
See also CA 124

See Maugham, W(illiam) Somerset
**Maugham, W(illiam) Somerset** 1874-1965
   **CLC 1, 11, 15, 67, 93; DA; DAB; DAC;**
   **DAM DRAM, MST, NOV; SSC 8; WLC**
   See also CA 5-8R; 25-28R; CANR 40; CDBLB
   1914-1945; DLB 10, 36, 77, 100, 162;
   MTCW; SATA 54
**Maugham, William Somerset**
   See Maugham, W(illiam) Somerset
**Maupassant, (Henri Rene Albert) Guy de** 1850-
   1893 **NCLC 1, 42; DA; DAB; DAC; DAM**
   **MST; SSC 1; WLC**
   See also DLB 123
**Maupin, Armistead** 1944- ... **CLC 95; DAM**
   **POP**
   See also CA 125; 130; CANR 58; INT 130
**Maurhut, Richard**
   See Traven, B.
**Mauriac, Claude** 1914-1996 ............ **CLC 9**
   See also CA 89-92; 152; DLB 83
**Mauriac, Francois (Charles)** 1885-1970
   **CLC 4, 9, 56; SSC 24**
   See also CA 25-28; CAP 2; DLB 65; MTCW
**Mavor, Osborne Henry** 1888-1951
   See Bridie, James
   See also CA 104
**Maxwell, William (Keepers, Jr.)** 1908- **CLC**
   **19**
   See also CA 93-96; CANR 54; DLBY 80; INT
   93-96
**May, Elaine** 1932- ........................... **CLC 16**
   See also CA 124; 142; DLB 44
**Mayakovski, Vladimir (Vladimirovich)** 1893-
   1930 ............................... **TCLC 4, 18**
   See also CA 104
**Mayhew, Henry** 1812-1887 ........ **NCLC 31**
   See also DLB 18, 55
**Mayle, Peter** 1939(?)- ..................... **CLC 89**
   See also CA 139
**Maynard, Joyce** 1953- ................. **CLC 23**
   See also CA 111; 129
**Mayne, William (James Carter)** 1928- **CLC**
   **12**
   See also AAYA 20; CA 9-12R; CANR 37; CLR
   25; JRDA; MAICYA; SAAS 11; SATA 6, 68
**Mayo, Jim**
   See L'Amour, Louis (Dearborn)
**Maysles, Albert** 1926- ..................... **CLC 16**
   See also CA 29-32R
**Maysles, David** 1932- ..................... **CLC 16**
**Mazer, Norma Fox** 1931- .............. **CLC 26**
   See also AAYA 5; CA 69-72; CANR 12, 32;
   CLR 23; JRDA; MAICYA; SAAS 1; SATA
   24, 67
**Mazzini, Guiseppe** 1805-1872 .... **NCLC 34**
**McAuley, James Phillip** 1917-1976 **CLC 45**
   See also CA 97-100
**McBain, Ed**
   See Hunter, Evan
**McBrien, William Augustine** 1930- **CLC 44**
   See also CA 107
**McCaffrey, Anne (Inez)** 1926- ...... **CLC 17;**
   **DAM NOV, POP**
   See also AAYA 6; AITN 2; BEST 89:2; CA 25-
   28R; CANR 15, 35, 55; DLB 8; JRDA;
   MAICYA; MTCW; SAAS 11; SATA 8, 70
**McCall, Nathan** 1955(?)- .............. **CLC 86**
   See also CA 146
**McCann, Arthur**
   See Campbell, John W(ood, Jr.)
**McCann, Edson**
   See Pohl, Frederik
**McCarthy, Charles, Jr.** 1933-

See McCarthy, Cormac
   See also CANR 42; DAM POP
**McCarthy, Cormac** 1933-  **CLC 4, 57, 59, 101**
   See also McCarthy, Charles, Jr.
   See also DLB 6, 143
**McCarthy, Mary (Therese)** 1912-1989 **CLC**
   **1, 3, 5, 14, 24, 39, 59; SSC 24**
   See also CA 5-8R; 129; CANR 16, 50; DLB 2;
   DLBY 81; INT CANR-16; MTCW
**McCartney, (James) Paul** 1942- **CLC 12, 35**
   See also CA 146
**McCauley, Stephen (D.)** 1955- ...... **CLC 50**
   See also CA 141
**McClure, Michael (Thomas)** 1932- **CLC 6,**
   **10**
   See also CA 21-24R; CANR 17, 46; DLB 16
**McCorkle, Jill (Collins)** 1958- ....... **CLC 51**
   See also CA 121; DLBY 87
**McCourt, James** 1941- .................... **CLC 5**
   See also CA 57-60
**McCoy, Horace (Stanley)** 1897-1955 **TCLC**
   **28**
   See also CA 108; 155; DLB 9
**McCrae, John** 1872-1918 ............. **TCLC 12**
   See also CA 109; DLB 92
**McCreigh, James**
   See Pohl, Frederik
**McCullers, (Lula) Carson (Smith)** 1917-1967
   **CLC 1, 4, 10, 12, 48, 100; DA; DAB;**
   **DAC; DAM MST, NOV; SSC 9, 24; WLC**
   See also AAYA 21; CA 5-8R; 25-28R; CABS
   1, 3; CANR 18; CDALB 1941-1968; DLB
   2, 7, 173; MTCW; SATA 27
**McCulloch, John Tyler**
   See Burroughs, Edgar Rice
**McCullough, Colleen** 1938(?)- ..... **CLC 27;**
   **DAM NOV, POP**
   See also CA 81-84; CANR 17, 46; MTCW
**McDermott, Alice** 1953- ................. **CLC 90**
   See also CA 109; CANR 40
**McElroy, Joseph** 1930- ............. **CLC 5, 47**
   See also CA 17-20R
**McEwan, Ian (Russell)** 1948- . **CLC 13, 66;**
   **DAM NOV**
   See also BEST 90:4; CA 61-64; CANR 14, 41;
   DLB 14; MTCW
**McFadden, David** 1940- ................. **CLC 48**
   See also CA 104; DLB 60; INT 104
**McFarland, Dennis** 1950- ............... **CLC 65**
**McGahern, John** 1934- **CLC 5, 9, 48; SSC 17**
   See also CA 17-20R; CANR 29; DLB 14;
   MTCW
**McGinley, Patrick (Anthony)** 1937- **CLC 41**
   See also CA 120; 127; CANR 56; INT 127
**McGinley, Phyllis** 1905-1978 ......... **CLC 14**
   See also CA 9-12R; 77-80; CANR 19; DLB 11,
   48; SATA 2, 44; SATA-Obit 24
**McGinniss, Joe** 1942- ..................... **CLC 32**
   See also AITN 2; BEST 89:2; CA 25-28R;
   CANR 26; INT CANR-26
**McGivern, Maureen Daly**
   See Daly, Maureen
**McGrath, Patrick** 1950- ................. **CLC 55**
   See also CA 136
**McGrath, Thomas (Matthew)** 1916-1990
   **CLC 28, 59; DAM POET**
   See also CA 9-12R; 132; CANR 6, 33; MTCW;
   SATA 41; SATA-Obit 66
**McGuane, Thomas (Francis III)** 1939- **CLC**
   **3, 7, 18, 45**
   See also AITN 2; CA 49-52; CANR 5, 24, 49;
   DLB 2; DLBY 80; INT CANR-24; MTCW
**McGuckian, Medbh** 1950- .. **CLC 48; DAM**

**POET**
   See also CA 143; DLB 40
**McHale, Tom** 1942(?)-1982 ......... **CLC 3, 5**
   See also AITN 1; CA 77-80; 106
**McIlvanney, William** 1936- ........... **CLC 42**
   See also CA 25-28R; DLB 14
**McIlwraith, Maureen Mollie Hunter**
   See Hunter, Mollie
   See also SATA 2
**McInerney, Jay** 1955-  **CLC 34; DAM POP**
   See also AAYA 18; CA 116; 123; CANR 45;
   INT 123
**McIntyre, Vonda N(eel)** 1948- ....... **CLC 18**
   See also CA 81-84; CANR 17, 34; MTCW
**McKay, Claude**  **TCLC 7, 41; BLC; DAB; PC**
   **2**
   See also McKay, Festus Claudius
   See also DLB 4, 45, 51, 117
**McKay, Festus Claudius** 1889-1948
   See McKay, Claude
   See also BW 1; CA 104; 124; DA; DAC; DAM
   MST, MULT, NOV, POET; MTCW; WLC
**McKuen, Rod** 1933- ..................... **CLC 1, 3**
   See also AITN 1; CA 41-44R; CANR 40
**McLoughlin, R. B.**
   See Mencken, H(enry) L(ouis)
**McLuhan, (Herbert) Marshall** 1911-1980
   **CLC 37, 83**
   See also CA 9-12R; 102; CANR 12, 34; DLB
   88; INT CANR-12; MTCW
**McMillan, Terry (L.)** 1951- .... **CLC 50, 61;**
   **DAM MULT, NOV, POP**
   See also AAYA 21; BW 2; CA 140
**McMurtry, Larry (Jeff)** 1936-  **CLC 2, 3, 7,**
   **11, 27, 44; DAM NOV, POP**
   See also AAYA 15; AITN 2; BEST 89:2; CA 5-
   8R; CANR 19, 43; CDALB 1968-1988; DLB
   2, 143; DLBY 80, 87; MTCW
**McNally, T. M.** 1961- ..................... **CLC 82**
**McNally, Terrence** 1939-  **CLC 4, 7, 41, 91;**
   **DAM DRAM**
   See also CA 45-48; CANR 2, 56; DLB 7
**McNamer, Deirdre** 1950- ............... **CLC 70**
**McNeile, Herman Cyril** 1888-1937
   See Sapper
   See also DLB 77
**McNickle, (William) D'Arcy** 1904-1977
   **CLC 89; DAM MULT**
   See also CA 9-12R; 85-88; CANR 5, 45; DLB
   175; NNAL; SATA-Obit 22
**McPhee, John (Angus)** 1931- ........ **CLC 36**
   See also BEST 90:1; CA 65-68; CANR 20, 46;
   MTCW
**McPherson, James Alan** 1943-  **CLC 19, 77**
   See also BW 1; CA 25-28R; CAAS 17; CANR
   24; DLB 38; MTCW
**McPherson, William (Alexander)** 1933-
   **CLC 34**
   See also CA 69-72; CANR 28; INT CANR-28
**Mead, Margaret** 1901-1978 ........... **CLC 37**
   See also AITN 1; CA 1-4R; 81-84; CANR 4;
   MTCW; SATA-Obit 20
**Meaker, Marijane (Agnes)** 1927-
   See Kerr, M. E.
   See also CA 107; CANR 37; INT 107; JRDA;
   MAICYA; MTCW; SATA 20, 61
**Medoff, Mark (Howard)** 1940-  **CLC 6, 23;**
   **DAM DRAM**
   See also AITN 1; CA 53-56; CANR 5; DLB 7;
   INT CANR-5
**Medvedev, P. N.**
   See Bakhtin, Mikhail Mikhailovich
**Meged, Aharon**

14
See also O'Connor, Frank
See also CA 93-96
**Oe, Kenzaburo** 1935- **CLC 10, 36, 86; DAM NOV; SSC 20**
See also CA 97-100; CANR 36, 50; DLBY 94; MTCW
**O'Faolain, Julia** 1932- ......... **CLC 6, 19, 47**
See also CA 81-84; CAAS 2; CANR 12; DLB 14; MTCW
**O'Faolain, Sean** 1900-1991 **CLC 1, 7, 14, 32, 70; SSC 13**
See also CA 61-64; 134; CANR 12; DLB 15, 162; MTCW
**O'Flaherty, Liam** 1896-1984 **CLC 5, 34; SSC 6**
See also CA 101; 113; CANR 35; DLB 36, 162; DLBY 84; MTCW
**Ogilvy, Gavin**
See Barrie, J(ames) M(atthew)
**O'Grady, Standish (James)** 1846-1928 **TCLC 5**
See also CA 104; 157
**O'Grady, Timothy** 1951- .............. **CLC 59**
See also CA 138
**O'Hara, Frank** 1926-1966 **CLC 2, 5, 13, 78; DAM POET**
See also CA 9-12R; 25-28R; CANR 33; DLB 5, 16; MTCW
**O'Hara, John (Henry)** 1905-1970 **CLC 1, 2, 3, 6, 11, 42; DAM NOV; SSC 15**
See also CA 5-8R; 25-28R; CANR 31; CDALB 1929-1941; DLB 9, 86; DLBD 2; MTCW
**O Hehir, Diana** 1922- .................... **CLC 41**
See also CA 93-96
**Okigbo, Christopher (Ifenayichukwu)** 1932-1967 **CLC 25, 84; BLC; DAM MULT, POET; PC 7**
See also BW 1; CA 77-80; DLB 125; MTCW
**Okri, Ben** 1959-.............................. **CLC 87**
See also BW 2; CA 130; 138; DLB 157; INT 138
**Olds, Sharon** 1942- . **CLC 32, 39, 85; DAM POET**
See also CA 101; CANR 18, 41; DLB 120
**Oldstyle, Jonathan**
See Irving, Washington
**Olesha, Yuri (Karlovich)** 1899-1960 **CLC 8**
See also CA 85-88
**Oliphant, Laurence** 1829(?)-1888 **NCLC 47**
See also DLB 18, 166
**Oliphant, Margaret (Oliphant Wilson)** 1828-1897 .................. **NCLC 11, 61; SSC 25**
See also DLB 18, 159
**Oliver, Mary** 1935- ............. **CLC 19, 34, 98**
See also CA 21-24R; CANR 9, 43; DLB 5
**Olivier, Laurence (Kerr)** 1907-1989 **CLC 20**
See also CA 111; 150; 129
**Olsen, Tillie** 1913- .. **CLC 4, 13; DA; DAB; DAC; DAM MST; SSC 11**
See also CA 1-4R; CANR 1, 43; DLB 28; DLBY 80; MTCW
**Olson, Charles (John)** 1910-1970 **CLC 1, 2, 5, 6, 9, 11, 29; DAM POET**
See also CA 13-16; 25-28R; CABS 2; CANR 35; CAP 1; DLB 5, 16; MTCW
**Olson, Toby** 1937-......................... **CLC 28**
See also CA 65-68; CANR 9, 31
**Olyesha, Yuri**
See Olesha, Yuri (Karlovich)
**Ondaatje, (Philip) Michael** 1943- **CLC 14, 29, 51, 76; DAB; DAC; DAM MST**
See also CA 77-80; CANR 42; DLB 60

**Oneal, Elizabeth** 1934-
See Oneal, Zibby
See also CA 106; CANR 28; MAICYA; SATA 30, 82
**Oneal, Zibby** ..................................... **CLC 30**
See also Oneal, Elizabeth
See also AAYA 5; CLR 13; JRDA
**O'Neill, Eugene (Gladstone)** 1888-1953 **TCLC 1, 6, 27, 49; DA; DAB; DAC; DAM DRAM, MST; WLC**
See also AITN 1; CA 110; 132; CDALB 1929-1941; DLB 7; MTCW
**Onetti, Juan Carlos** 1909-1994 **CLC 7, 10; DAM MULT, NOV; SSC 23**
See also CA 85-88; 145; CANR 32; DLB 113; HW; MTCW
**O Nuallain, Brian** 1911-1966
See O'Brien, Flann
See also CA 21-22; 25-28R; CAP 2
**Oppen, George** 1908-1984 ... **CLC 7, 13, 34**
See also CA 13-16R; 113; CANR 8; DLB 5, 165
**Oppenheim, E(dward) Phillips** 1866-1946 **TCLC 45**
See also CA 111; DLB 70
**Origen** c. 185-c. 254 .................... **CMLC 19**
**Orlovitz, Gil** 1918-1973 ................. **CLC 22**
See also CA 77-80; 45-48; DLB 2, 5
**Orris**
See Ingelow, Jean
**Ortega y Gasset, Jose** 1883-1955 **TCLC 9; DAM MULT; HLC**
See also CA 106; 130; HW; MTCW
**Ortese, Anna Maria** 1914- ............. **CLC 89**
See also DLB 177
**Ortiz, Simon J(oseph)** 1941- **CLC 45; DAM MULT, POET; PC 17**
See also CA 134; DLB 120, 175; NNAL
**Orton, Joe** .................... **CLC 4, 13, 43; DC 3**
See also Orton, John Kingsley
See also CDBLB 1960 to Present; DLB 13
**Orton, John Kingsley** 1933-1967
See Orton, Joe
See also CA 85-88; CANR 35; DAM DRAM; MTCW
**Orwell, George** **TCLC 2, 6, 15, 31, 51; DAB; WLC**
See also Blair, Eric (Arthur)
See also CDBLB 1945-1960; DLB 15, 98
**Osborne, David**
See Silverberg, Robert
**Osborne, George**
See Silverberg, Robert
**Osborne, John (James)** 1929-1994 **CLC 1, 2, 5, 11, 45; DA; DAB; DAC; DAM DRAM, MST; WLC**
See also CA 13-16R; 147; CANR 21, 56; CDBLB 1945-1960; DLB 13; MTCW
**Osborne, Lawrence** 1958-.............. **CLC 50**
**Oshima, Nagisa** 1932- .................... **CLC 20**
See also CA 116; 121
**Oskison, John Milton** 1874-1947 **TCLC 35; DAM MULT**
See also CA 144; DLB 175; NNAL
**Ossoli, Sarah Margaret (Fuller marchesa d')** 1810-1850
See Fuller, Margaret
See also SATA 25
**Ostrovsky, Alexander** 1823-1886 **NCLC 30, 57**
**Otero, Blas de** 1916-1979 ............... **CLC 11**
See also CA 89-92; DLB 134
**Otto, Whitney** 1955- ...................... **CLC 70**

See also CA 140
**Ouida** ............................................... **TCLC 43**
See also De La Ramee, (Marie) Louise
See also DLB 18, 156
**Ousmane, Sembene** 1923- .... **CLC 66; BLC**
See also BW 1; CA 117; 125; MTCW
**Ovid** 43B.C.-18(?) **CMLC 7; DAM POET; PC 2**
**Owen, Hugh**
See Faust, Frederick (Schiller)
**Owen, Wilfred (Edward Salter)** 1893-1918 **TCLC 5, 27; DA; DAB; DAC; DAM MST, POET; WLC**
See also CA 104; 141; CDBLB 1914-1945; DLB 20
**Owens, Rochelle** 1936- ..................... **CLC 8**
See also CA 17-20R; CAAS 2; CANR 39
**Oz, Amos** 1939- ... **CLC 5, 8, 11, 27, 33, 54; DAM NOV**
See also CA 53-56; CANR 27, 47; MTCW
**Ozick, Cynthia** 1928- **CLC 3, 7, 28, 62; DAM NOV, POP; SSC 15**
See also BEST 90:1; CA 17-20R; CANR 23, 58; DLB 28, 152; DLBY 82; INT CANR-23; MTCW
**Ozu, Yasujiro** 1903-1963 ............... **CLC 16**
See also CA 112
**Pacheco, C.**
See Pessoa, Fernando (Antonio Nogueira)
**Pa Chin** ............................................. **CLC 18**
See also Li Fei-kan
**Pack, Robert** 1929- ......................... **CLC 13**
See also CA 1-4R; CANR 3, 44; DLB 5
**Padgett, Lewis**
See Kuttner, Henry
**Padilla (Lorenzo), Heberto** 1932- . **CLC 38**
See also AITN 1; CA 123; 131; HW
**Page, Jimmy** 1944- ......................... **CLC 12**
**Page, Louise** 1955-......................... **CLC 40**
See also CA 140
**Page, P(atricia) K(athleen)** 1916- **CLC 7, 18; DAC; DAM MST; PC 12**
See also CA 53-56; CANR 4, 22; DLB 68; MTCW
**Page, Thomas Nelson** 1853-1922 ... **SSC 23**
See also CA 118; DLB 12, 78; DLBD 13
**Paget, Violet** 1856-1935
See Lee, Vernon
See also CA 104
**Paget-Lowe, Henry**
See Lovecraft, H(oward) P(hillips)
**Paglia, Camille (Anna)** 1947- ........ **CLC 68**
See also CA 140
**Paige, Richard**
See Koontz, Dean R(ay)
**Pakenham, Antonia**
See Fraser, (Lady) Antonia (Pakenham)
**Palamas, Kostes** 1859-1943 .......... **TCLC 5**
See also CA 105
**Palazzeschi, Aldo** 1885-1974 .......... **CLC 11**
See also CA 89-92; 53-56; DLB 114
**Paley, Grace** 1922- **CLC 4, 6, 37; DAM POP; SSC 8**
See also CA 25-28R; CANR 13, 46; DLB 28; INT CANR-13; MTCW
**Palin, Michael (Edward)** 1943-..... **CLC 21**
See also Monty Python
See also CA 107; CANR 35; SATA 67
**Palliser, Charles** 1947- .................. **CLC 65**
See also CA 136
**Palma, Ricardo** 1833-1919 .......... **TCLC 29**
**Pancake, Breece Dexter** 1952-1979
See Pancake, Breece D'J

**Porter, Peter (Neville Frederick)** 1929- **CLC 5, 13, 33**
See also CA 85-88; DLB 40

**Porter, William Sydney** 1862-1910
See Henry, O.
See also CA 104; 131; CDALB 1865-1917; DA; DAB; DAC; DAM MST; DLB 12, 78, 79; MTCW; 2

**Portillo (y Pacheco), Jose Lopez**
See Lopez Portillo (y Pacheco), Jose

**Post, Melville Davisson** 1869-1930 **TCLC 39**
See also CA 110

**Potok, Chaim** 1929- **CLC 2, 7, 14, 26; DAM NOV**
See also AAYA 15; AITN 1, 2; CA 17-20R; CANR 19, 35; DLB 28, 152; INT CANR-19; MTCW; SATA 33

**Potter, Beatrice**
See Webb, (Martha) Beatrice (Potter)
See also MAICYA

**Potter, Dennis (Christopher George)** 1935-1994 **CLC 58, 86**
See also CA 107; 145; CANR 33; MTCW

**Pound, Ezra (Weston Loomis)** 1885-1972 **CLC 1, 2, 3, 4, 5, 7, 10, 13, 18, 34, 48, 50; DA; DAB; DAC; DAM MST, POET; PC 4; WLC**
See also CA 5-8R; 37-40R; CANR 40; CDALB 1917-1929; DLB 4, 45, 63; MTCW

**Povod, Reinaldo** 1959-1994 .......... **CLC 44**
See also CA 136; 146

**Powell, Adam Clayton, Jr.** 1908-1972 **CLC 89; BLC; DAM MULT**
See also BW 1; CA 102; 33-36R

**Powell, Anthony (Dymoke)** 1905- **CLC 1, 3, 7, 9, 10, 31**
See also CA 1-4R; CANR 1, 32; CDBLB 1945-1960; DLB 15; MTCW

**Powell, Dawn** 1897-1965 ................ **CLC 66**
See also CA 5-8R

**Powell, Padgett** 1952- ..................... **CLC 34**
See also CA 126

**Power, Susan** ................................. **CLC 91**

**Powers, J(ames) F(arl)** 1917- **CLC 1, 4, 8, 57; SSC 4**
See also CA 1-4R; CANR 2; DLB 130; MTCW

**Powers, John J(ames)** 1945-
See Powers, John R.
See also CA 69-72

**Powers, John R.** ............................. **CLC 66**
See also Powers, John J(ames)

**Powers, Richard (S.)** 1957- ............ **CLC 93**
See also CA 148

**Pownall, David** 1938- ..................... **CLC 10**
See also CA 89-92; CAAS 18; CANR 49; DLB 14

**Powys, John Cowper** 1872-1963 **CLC 7, 9, 15, 46**
See also CA 85-88; DLB 15; MTCW

**Powys, T(heodore) F(rancis)** 1875-1953 **TCLC 9**
See also CA 106; DLB 36, 162

**Prager, Emily** 1952- ....................... **CLC 56**

**Pratt, E(dwin) J(ohn)** 1883(?)-1964 **CLC 19; DAC; DAM POET**
See also CA 141; 93-96; DLB 92

**Premchand** ..................................... **TCLC 21**
See also Srivastava, Dhanpat Rai

**Preussler, Otfried** 1923- .................. **CLC 17**
See also CA 77-80; SATA 24

**Prevert, Jacques (Henri Marie)** 1900-1977 **CLC 15**
See also CA 77-80; 69-72; CANR 29; MTCW;

SATA-Obit 30

**Prevost, Abbe (Antoine Francois)** 1697-1763 **LC 1**

**Price, (Edward) Reynolds** 1933- **CLC 3, 6, 13, 43, 50, 63; DAM NOV; SSC 22**
See also CA 1-4R; CANR 1, 37, 57; DLB 2; INT CANR-37

**Price, Richard** 1949- .................. **CLC 6, 12**
See also CA 49-52; CANR 3; DLBY 81

**Prichard, Katharine Susannah** 1883-1969 **CLC 46**
See also CA 11-12; CANR 33; CAP 1; MTCW; SATA 66

**Priestley, J(ohn) B(oynton)** 1894-1984 **CLC 2, 5, 9, 34; DAM DRAM, NOV**
See also CA 9-12R; 113; CANR 33; CDBLB 1914-1945; DLB 10, 34, 77, 100, 139; DLBY 84; MTCW

**Prince** 1958(?)- ............................... **CLC 35**

**Prince, F(rank) T(empleton)** 1912- **CLC 22**
See also CA 101; CANR 43; DLB 20

**Prince Kropotkin**
See Kropotkin, Peter (Alekseevich)

**Prior, Matthew** 1664-1721 ................. **LC 4**
See also DLB 95

**Pritchard, William H(arrison)** 1932- **CLC 34**
See also CA 65-68; CANR 23; DLB 111

**Pritchett, V(ictor) S(awdon)** 1900-1997 **CLC 5, 13, 15, 41; DAM NOV; SSC 14**
See also CA 61-64; 157; CANR 31; DLB 15, 139; MTCW

**Private 19022**
See Manning, Frederic

**Probst, Mark** 1925- ....................... **CLC 59**
See also CA 130

**Prokosch, Frederic** 1908-1989 .. **CLC 4, 48**
See also CA 73-76; 128; DLB 48

**Prophet, The**
See Dreiser, Theodore (Herman Albert)

**Prose, Francine** 1947- .................... **CLC 45**
See also CA 109; 112; CANR 46

**Proudhon**
See Cunha, Euclides (Rodrigues Pimenta) da

**Proulx, E. Annie** 1935- ................... **CLC 81**

**Proust, (Valentin-Louis-George-Eugene-) Marcel** 1871-1922 **TCLC 7, 13, 33; DA; DAB; DAC; DAM MST, NOV; WLC**
See also CA 104; 120; DLB 65; MTCW

**Prowler, Harley**
See Masters, Edgar Lee

**Prus, Boleslaw** 1845-1912 ............ **TCLC 48**

**Pryor, Richard (Franklin Lenox Thomas)** 1940- **CLC 26**
See also CA 122

**Przybyszewski, Stanislaw** 1868-1927 **TCLC 36**
See also DLB 66

**Pteleon**
See Grieve, C(hristopher) M(urray)
See also DAM POET

**Puckett, Lute**
See Masters, Edgar Lee

**Puig, Manuel** 1932-1990 **CLC 3, 5, 10, 28, 65; DAM MULT; HLC**
See also CA 45-48; CANR 2, 32; DLB 113; HW; MTCW

**Purdy, Al(fred Wellington)** 1918- **CLC 3, 6, 14, 50; DAC; DAM MST, POET**
See also CA 81-84; CAAS 17; CANR 42; DLB 88

**Purdy, James (Amos)** 1923- **CLC 2, 4, 10, 28, 52**
See also CA 33-36R; CAAS 1; CANR 19, 51;

DLB 2; INT CANR-19; MTCW

**Pure, Simon**
See Swinnerton, Frank Arthur

**Pushkin, Alexander (Sergeyevich)** 1799-1837 **NCLC 3, 27; DA; DAB; DAC; DAM DRAM, MST, POET; PC 10; WLC**
See also SATA 61

**P'u Sung-ling** 1640-1715 .................... **LC 3**

**Putnam, Arthur Lee**
See Alger, Horatio, Jr.

**Puzo, Mario** 1920- .. **CLC 1, 2, 6, 36; DAM NOV, POP**
See also CA 65-68; CANR 4, 42; DLB 6; MTCW

**Pygge, Edward**
See Barnes, Julian (Patrick)

**Pym, Barbara (Mary Crampton)** 1913-1980 **CLC 13, 19, 37**
See also CA 13-14; 97-100; CANR 13, 34; CAP 1; DLB 14; DLBY 87; MTCW

**Pynchon, Thomas (Ruggles, Jr.)** 1937- **CLC 2, 3, 6, 9, 11, 18, 33, 62, 72; DA; DAB; DAC; DAM MST, NOV, POP; SSC 14; WLC**
See also BEST 90:2; CA 17-20R; CANR 22, 46; DLB 2, 173; MTCW

**Pythagoras** c. 570B.C.-c. 500B.C. **CMLC 22**
See also DLB 176

**Qian Zhongshu**
See Ch'ien Chung-shu

**Qroll**
See Dagerman, Stig (Halvard)

**Quarrington, Paul (Lewis)** 1953- .. **CLC 65**
See also CA 129

**Quasimodo, Salvatore** 1901-1968 . **CLC 10**
See also CA 13-16; 25-28R; CAP 1; DLB 114; MTCW

**Quay, Stephen** 1947- ..................... **CLC 95**

**Quay, The Brothers**
See Quay, Stephen; Quay, Timothy

**Quay, Timothy** 1947- ..................... **CLC 95**

**Queen, Ellery** ............................... **CLC 3, 11**
See also Dannay, Frederic; Davidson, Avram; Lee, Manfred B(ennington); Marlowe, Stephen; Sturgeon, Theodore (Hamilton); Vance, John Holbrook

**Queen, Ellery, Jr.**
See Dannay, Frederic; Lee, Manfred B(ennington)

**Queneau, Raymond** 1903-1976 **CLC 2, 5, 10, 42**
See also CA 77-80; 69-72; CANR 32; DLB 72; MTCW

**Quevedo, Francisco de** 1580-1645 ... **LC 23**

**Quiller-Couch, Arthur Thomas** 1863-1944 **TCLC 53**
See also CA 118; DLB 135, 153

**Quin, Ann (Marie)** 1936-1973 ......... **CLC 6**
See also CA 9-12R; 45-48; DLB 14

**Quinn, Martin**
See Smith, Martin Cruz

**Quinn, Peter** 1947- ........................ **CLC 91**

**Quinn, Simon**
See Smith, Martin Cruz

**Quiroga, Horacio (Sylvestre)** 1878-1937 **TCLC 20; DAM MULT; HLC**
See also CA 117; 131; HW; MTCW

**Quoirez, Francoise** 1935- ................. **CLC 9**
See also Sagan, Francoise
See also CA 49-52; CANR 6, 39; MTCW

**Raabe, Wilhelm** 1831-1910 .......... **TCLC 45**
See also DLB 129

**Rabe, David (William)** 1940- **CLC 4, 8, 33;**

Author Index

See also CA 17-20R; CANR 31, 54

**Sagan, Carl (Edward)** 1934-1996 .    **CLC 30**
See also AAYA 2; CA 25-28R; 155; CANR 11, 36; MTCW; SATA 58; SATA-Obit 94

**Sagan, Francoise** ............    **CLC 3, 6, 9, 17, 36**
See Quoirez, Francoise
See also DLB 83

**Sahgal, Nayantara (Pandit)** 1927-    **CLC 41**
See also CA 9-12R; CANR 11

**Saint, H(arry) F.** 1941- ...................    **CLC 50**
See also CA 127

**St. Aubin de Teran, Lisa** 1953-
See Teran, Lisa St. Aubin de
See also CA 118; 126; INT 126

**Sainte-Beuve, Charles Augustin** 1804-1869
    **NCLC 5**

**Saint-Exupery, Antoine (Jean Baptiste Marie Roger) de** 1900-1944 **TCLC 2, 56; DAM NOV; WLC**
See also CA 108; 132; CLR 10; DLB 72; MAICYA; MTCW; SATA 20

**St. John, David**
See Hunt, E(verette) Howard, (Jr.)

**Saint-John Perse**
See Leger, (Marie-Rene Auguste) Alexis Saint-Leger

**Saintsbury, George (Edward Bateman)** 1845-1933 ......................    **TCLC 31**
See also DLB 57, 149

**Sait Faik** ...........................    **TCLC 23**
See also Abasiyanik, Sait Faik

**Saki** .........................    **TCLC 3; SSC 12**
See also Munro, H(ector) H(ugh)

**Sala, George Augustus** .................    **NCLC 46**

**Salama, Hannu** 1936- ................    **CLC 18**

**Salamanca, J(ack) R(ichard)** 1922-    **CLC 4, 15**
See also CA 25-28R

**Sale, J. Kirkpatrick**
See Sale, Kirkpatrick

**Sale, Kirkpatrick** 1937- .................    **CLC 68**
See also CA 13-16R; CANR 10

**Salinas, Luis Omar** 1937- ...    **CLC 90; DAM MULT; HLC**
See also CA 131; DLB 82; HW

**Salinas (y Serrano), Pedro** 1891(?)-1951
    **TCLC 17**
See also CA 117; DLB 134

**Salinger, J(erome) D(avid)** 1919- **CLC 1, 3, 8, 12, 55, 56; DA; DAB; DAC; DAM MST, NOV, POP; SSC 2; WLC**
See also AAYA 2; CA 5-8R; CANR 39; CDALB 1941-1968; CLR 18; DLB 2, 102, 173; MAICYA; MTCW; SATA 67

**Salisbury, John**
See Caute, David

**Salter, James** 1925- ...............    **CLC 7, 52, 59**
See also CA 73-76; DLB 130

**Saltus, Edgar (Everton)** 1855-1921 **TCLC 8**
See also CA 105

**Saltykov, Mikhail Evgrafovich** 1826-1889
    **NCLC 16**

**Samarakis, Antonis** 1919- ................    **CLC 5**
See also CA 25-28R; CAAS 16; CANR 36

**Sanchez, Florencio** 1875-1910 .....    **TCLC 37**
See also CA 153; HW

**Sanchez, Luis Rafael** 1936- ..........    **CLC 23**
See also CA 128; DLB 145; HW

**Sanchez, Sonia** 1934- ..    **CLC 5; BLC; DAM MULT; PC 9**
See also BW 2; CA 33-36R; CANR 24, 49; CLR 18; DLB 41; DLBD 8; MAICYA; MTCW; SATA 22

**Sand, George** 1804-1876 ..    **NCLC 2, 42, 57; DA; DAB; DAC; DAM MST, NOV; WLC**
See also DLB 119

**Sandburg, Carl (August)** 1878-1967 **CLC 1, 4, 10, 15, 35; DA; DAB; DAC; DAM MST, POET; PC 2; WLC**
See also CA 5-8R; 25-28R; CANR 35; CDALB 1865-1917; DLB 17, 54; MAICYA; MTCW; SATA 8

**Sandburg, Charles**
See Sandburg, Carl (August)

**Sandburg, Charles A.**
See Sandburg, Carl (August)

**Sanders, (James) Ed(ward)** 1939-    **CLC 53**
See also CA 13-16R; CAAS 21; CANR 13, 44; DLB 16

**Sanders, Lawrence** 1920- ...    **CLC 41; DAM POP**
See also BEST 89:4; CA 81-84; CANR 33; MTCW

**Sanders, Noah**
See Blount, Roy (Alton), Jr.

**Sanders, Winston P.**
See Anderson, Poul (William)

**Sandoz, Mari(e Susette)** 1896-1966 **CLC 28**
See also CA 1-4R; 25-28R; CANR 17; DLB 9; MTCW; SATA 5

**Saner, Reg(inald Anthony)** 1931- ...    **CLC 9**
See also CA 65-68

**Sannazaro, Jacopo** 1456(?)-1530 .......    **LC 8**

**Sansom, William** 1912-1976 **CLC 2, 6; DAM NOV; SSC 21**
See also CA 5-8R; 65-68; CANR 42; DLB 139; MTCW

**Santayana, George** 1863-1952 ....    **TCLC 40**
See also CA 115; DLB 54, 71; DLBD 13

**Santiago, Danny** .............................    **CLC 33**
See also James, Daniel (Lewis)
See also DLB 122

**Santmyer, Helen Hoover** 1895-1986 **CLC 33**
See also CA 1-4R; 118; CANR 15, 33; DLBY 84; MTCW

**Santos, Bienvenido N(uqui)** 1911-1996 **CLC 22; DAM MULT**
See also CA 101; 151; CANR 19, 46

**Sapper** ...........................    **TCLC 44**
See also McNeile, Herman Cyril

**Sapphire** 1950- ...........................    **CLC 99**

**Sappho** fl. 6th cent. B.C.- ...    **CMLC 3; DAM POET; PC 5**
See also DLB 176

**Sarduy, Severo** 1937-1993 .........    **CLC 6, 97**
See also CA 89-92; 142; CANR 58; DLB 113; HW

**Sargeson, Frank** 1903-1982 ...........    **CLC 31**
See also CA 25-28R; 106; CANR 38

**Sarmiento, Felix Ruben Garcia**
See Dario, Ruben

**Saroyan, William** 1908-1981    **CLC 1, 8, 10, 29, 34, 56; DA; DAB; DAC; DAM DRAM, MST, NOV; SSC 21; WLC**
See also CA 5-8R; 103; CANR 30; DLB 7, 9, 86; DLBY 81; MTCW; SATA 23; SATA-Obit 24

**Sarraute, Nathalie** 1900-  **CLC 1, 2, 4, 8, 10, 31, 80**
See also CA 9-12R; CANR 23; DLB 83; MTCW

**Sarton, (Eleanor) May** 1912-1995 **CLC 4, 14, 49, 91; DAM POET**
See also CA 1-4R; 149; CANR 1, 34, 55; DLB 48; DLBY 81; INT CANR-34; MTCW; SATA 36; SATA-Obit 86

**Sartre, Jean-Paul** 1905-1980    **CLC 1, 4, 7, 9, 13, 18, 24, 44, 50, 52; DA; DAB; DAC; DAM DRAM, MST, NOV; DC 3; WLC**
See also CA 9-12R; 97-100; CANR 21; DLB 72; MTCW

**Sassoon, Siegfried (Lorraine)** 1886-1967
    **CLC 36; DAB; DAM MST, NOV, POET; PC 12**
See also CA 104; 25-28R; CANR 36; DLB 20; MTCW

**Satterfield, Charles**
See Pohl, Frederik

**Saul, John (W. III)** 1942- ....    **CLC 46; DAM NOV, POP**
See also AAYA 10; BEST 90:4; CA 81-84; CANR 16, 40

**Saunders, Caleb**
See Heinlein, Robert A(nson)

**Saura (Atares), Carlos** 1932- ........    **CLC 20**
See also CA 114; 131; HW

**Sauser-Hall, Frederic** 1887-1961 ..    **CLC 18**
See also Cendrars, Blaise
See also CA 102; 93-96; CANR 36; MTCW

**Saussure, Ferdinand de** 1857-1913 **TCLC 49**

**Savage, Catharine**
See Brosman, Catharine Savage

**Savage, Thomas** 1915- .................    **CLC 40**
See also CA 126; 132; CAAS 15; INT 132

**Savan, Glenn** 19(?)- ....................    **CLC 50**

**Sayers, Dorothy L(eigh)** 1893-1957 **TCLC 2, 15; DAM POP**
See also CA 104; 119; CDBLB 1914-1945; DLB 10, 36, 77, 100; MTCW

**Sayers, Valerie** 1952- ....................    **CLC 50**
See also CA 134

**Sayles, John (Thomas)** 1950-  **CLC 7, 10, 14**
See also CA 57-60; CANR 41; DLB 44

**Scammell, Michael** 1935- ...............    **CLC 34**
See also CA 156

**Scannell, Vernon** 1922- .................    **CLC 49**
See also CA 5-8R; CANR 8, 24, 57; DLB 27; SATA 59

**Scarlett, Susan**
See Streatfeild, (Mary) Noel

**Schaeffer, Susan Fromberg** 1941-  **CLC 6, 11, 22**
See also CA 49-52; CANR 18; DLB 28; MTCW; SATA 22

**Schary, Jill**
See Robinson, Jill

**Schell, Jonathan** 1943- ...................    **CLC 35**
See also CA 73-76; CANR 12

**Schelling, Friedrich Wilhelm Joseph von** 1775-1854 ......................    **NCLC 30**
See also DLB 90

**Schendel, Arthur van** 1874-1946   **TCLC 56**

**Scherer, Jean-Marie Maurice** 1920-
See Rohmer, Eric
See also CA 110

**Schevill, James (Erwin)** 1920- .........    **CLC 7**
See also CA 5-8R; CAAS 12

**Schiller, Friedrich** 1759-1805 ....    **NCLC 39; DAM DRAM**
See also DLB 94

**Schisgal, Murray (Joseph)** 1926- ....    **CLC 6**
See also CA 21-24R; CANR 48

**Schlee, Ann** 1934- ..........................    **CLC 35**
See also CA 101; CANR 29; SATA 44; SATA-Brief 36

**Schlegel, August Wilhelm von** 1767-1845
    **NCLC 15**
See also DLB 94

**Schlegel, Friedrich** 1772-1829 ....    **NCLC 45**
See also DLB 90

See West, Nathanael

**Weir, Peter (Lindsay)** 1944- ......... **CLC 20**
See also CA 113; 123

**Weiss, Peter (Ulrich)** 1916-1982    **CLC 3, 15, 51; DAM DRAM**
See also CA 45-48; 106; CANR 3; DLB 69, 124

**Weiss, Theodore (Russell)** 1916-  **CLC 3, 8, 14**
See also CA 9-12R; CAAS 2; CANR 46; DLB 5

**Welch, (Maurice) Denton** 1915-1948    **TCLC 22**
See also CA 121; 148

**Welch, James** 1940- ..  **CLC 6, 14, 52; DAM MULT, POP**
See also CA 85-88; CANR 42; DLB 175; NNAL

**Weldon, Fay** 1933-  **CLC 6, 9, 11, 19, 36, 59; DAM POP**
See also CA 21-24R; CANR 16, 46; CDBLB 1960 to Present; DLB 14; INT CANR-16; MTCW

**Wellek, Rene** 1903-1995 ................. **CLC 28**
See also CA 5-8R; 150; CAAS 7; CANR 8; DLB 63; INT CANR-8

**Weller, Michael** 1942- ............. **CLC 10, 53**
See also CA 85-88

**Weller, Paul** 1958- ........................ **CLC 26**

**Wellershoff, Dieter** 1925- ............... **CLC 46**
See also CA 89-92; CANR 16, 37

**Welles, (George) Orson** 1915-1985    **CLC 20, 80**
See also CA 93-96; 117

**Wellman, Mac** 1945- ...................... **CLC 65**

**Wellman, Manly Wade** 1903-1986    **CLC 49**
See also CA 1-4R; 118; CANR 6, 16, 44; SATA 6; SATA-Obit 47

**Wells, Carolyn** 1869(?)-1942 ....... **TCLC 35**
See also CA 113; DLB 11

**Wells, H(erbert) G(eorge)** 1866-1946    **TCLC 6, 12, 19; DA; DAB; DAC; DAM MST, NOV; SSC 6; WLC**
See also AAYA 18; CA 110; 121; CDBLB 1914-1945; DLB 34, 70, 156, 178; MTCW; SATA 20

**Wells, Rosemary** 1943- ................... **CLC 12**
See also AAYA 13; CA 85-88; CANR 48; CLR 16; MAICYA; SAAS 1; SATA 18, 69

**Welty, Eudora** 1909-  **CLC 1, 2, 5, 14, 22, 33; DA; DAB; DAC; DAM MST, NOV; SSC 1; WLC**
See also CA 9-12R; CABS 1; CANR 32; CDALB 1941-1968; DLB 2, 102, 143; DLBD 12; DLBY 87; MTCW

**Wen I-to** 1899-1946 ...................... **TCLC 28**

**Wentworth, Robert**
See Hamilton, Edmond

**Werfel, Franz (V.)** 1890-1945 ........ **TCLC 8**
See also CA 104; DLB 81, 124

**Wergeland, Henrik Arnold** 1808-1845    **NCLC 5**

**Wersba, Barbara** 1932- ................. **CLC 30**
See also AAYA 2; CA 29-32R; CANR 16, 38; CLR 3; DLB 52; JRDA; MAICYA; SAAS 2; SATA 1, 58

**Wertmueller, Lina** 1928- ............... **CLC 16**
See also CA 97-100; CANR 39

**Wescott, Glenway** 1901-1987 ........ **CLC 13**
See also CA 13-16R; 121; CANR 23; DLB 4, 9, 102

**Wesker, Arnold** 1932- .  **CLC 3, 5, 42; DAB; DAM DRAM**
See also CA 1-4R; CAAS 7; CANR 1, 33; CDBLB 1960 to Present; DLB 13; MTCW

**Wesley, Richard (Errol)** 1945- ........ **CLC 7**

See also BW 1; CA 57-60; CANR 27; DLB 38

**Wessel, Johan Herman** 1742-1785 ..... **LC 7**

**West, Anthony (Panther)** 1914-1987  **CLC 50**
See also CA 45-48; 124; CANR 3, 19; DLB 15

**West, C. P.**
See Wodehouse, P(elham) G(renville)

**West, (Mary) Jessamyn** 1902-1984    **CLC 7, 17**
See also CA 9-12R; 112; CANR 27; DLB 6; DLBY 84; MTCW; SATA-Obit 37

**West, Morris L(anglo)** 1916- .....  **CLC 6, 33**
See also CA 5-8R; CANR 24, 49; MTCW

**West, Nathanael** 1903-1940  **TCLC 1, 14, 44; SSC 16**
See also CA 104; 125; CDALB 1929-1941; DLB 4, 9, 28; MTCW

**West, Owen**
See Koontz, Dean R(ay)

**West, Paul** 1930- ................... **CLC 7, 14, 96**
See also CA 13-16R; CAAS 7; CANR 22, 53; DLB 14; INT CANR-22

**West, Rebecca** 1892-1983    **CLC 7, 9, 31, 50**
See also CA 5-8R; 109; CANR 19; DLB 36; DLBY 83; MTCW

**Westall, Robert (Atkinson)** 1929-1993    **CLC 17**
See also AAYA 12; CA 69-72; 141; CANR 18; CLR 13; JRDA; MAICYA; SAAS 2; SATA 23, 69; SATA-Obit 75

**Westlake, Donald E(dwin)** 1933- **CLC 7, 33; DAM POP**
See also CA 17-20R; CAAS 13; CANR 16, 44; INT CANR-16

**Westmacott, Mary**
See Christie, Agatha (Mary Clarissa)

**Weston, Allen**
See Norton, Andre

**Wetcheek, J. L.**
See Feuchtwanger, Lion

**Wetering, Janwillem van de**
See van de Wetering, Janwillem

**Wetherell, Elizabeth**
See Warner, Susan (Bogert)

**Whale, James** 1889-1957 ............. **TCLC 63**

**Whalen, Philip** 1923- ................. **CLC 6, 29**
See also CA 9-12R; CANR 5, 39; DLB 16

**Wharton, Edith (Newbold Jones)** 1862-1937    **TCLC 3, 9, 27, 53; DA; DAB; DAC; DAM MST, NOV; SSC 6; WLC**
See also CA 104; 132; CDALB 1865-1917; DLB 4, 9, 12, 78; DLBD 13; MTCW

**Wharton, James**
See Mencken, H(enry) L(ouis)

**Wharton, William (a pseudonym)**  **CLC 18, 37**
See also CA 93-96; DLBY 80; INT 93-96

**Wheatley (Peters), Phillis** 1754(?)-1784    **LC 3; BLC; DA; DAC; DAM MST, MULT, POET; PC 3; WLC**
See also CDALB 1640-1865; DLB 31, 50

**Wheelock, John Hall** 1886-1978 ... **CLC 14**
See also CA 13-16R; 77-80; CANR 14; DLB 45

**White, E(lwyn) B(rooks)** 1899-1985  **CLC 10, 34, 39; DAM POP**
See also AITN 2; CA 13-16R; 116; CANR 16, 37; CLR 1, 21; DLB 11, 22; MAICYA; MTCW; SATA 2, 29; SATA-Obit 44

**White, Edmund (Valentine III)** 1940-    **CLC 27; DAM POP**
See also AAYA 7; CA 45-48; CANR 3, 19, 36; MTCW

**White, Patrick (Victor Martindale)** 1912-1990    **CLC 3, 4, 5, 7, 9, 18, 65, 69**

See also CA 81-84; 132; CANR 43; MTCW

**White, Phyllis Dorothy James** 1920-
See James, P. D.
See also CA 21-24R; CANR 17, 43; DAM POP; MTCW

**White, T(erence) H(anbury)** 1906-1964    **CLC 30**
See also CA 73-76; CANR 37; DLB 160; JRDA; MAICYA; SATA 12

**White, Terence de Vere** 1912-1994    **CLC 49**
See also CA 49-52; 145; CANR 3

**White, Walter F(rancis)** 1893-1955  **TCLC 15**
See White, Walter
See also BW 1; CA 115; 124; DLB 51

**White, William Hale** 1831-1913
See Rutherford, Mark
See also CA 121

**Whitehead, E(dward) A(nthony)** 1933-  **CLC 5**
See also CA 65-68; CANR 58

**Whitemore, Hugh (John)** 1936- .... **CLC 37**
See also CA 132; INT 132

**Whitman, Sarah Helen (Power)** 1803-1878    **NCLC 19**
See also DLB 1

**Whitman, Walt(er)** 1819-1892  **NCLC 4, 31; DA; DAB; DAC; DAM MST, POET; PC 3; WLC**
See also CDALB 1640-1865; DLB 3, 64; SATA 20

**Whitney, Phyllis A(yame)** 1903- ..  **CLC 42; DAM POP**
See also AITN 2; BEST 90:3; CA 1-4R; CANR 3, 25, 38; JRDA; MAICYA; SATA 1, 30

**Whittemore, (Edward) Reed (Jr.)** 1919-  **CLC 4**
See also CA 9-12R; CAAS 8; CANR 4; DLB 5

**Whittier, John Greenleaf** 1807-1892    **NCLC 8, 59**
See also DLB 1

**Whittlebot, Hernia**
See Coward, Noel (Peirce)

**Wicker, Thomas Grey** 1926-
See Wicker, Tom
See also CA 65-68; CANR 21, 46

**Wicker, Tom** ....................................... **CLC 7**
See also Wicker, Thomas Grey

**Wideman, John Edgar** 1941-  **CLC 5, 34, 36, 67; BLC; DAM MULT**
See also BW 2; CA 85-88; CANR 14, 42; DLB 33, 143

**Wiebe, Rudy (Henry)** 1934-    **CLC 6, 11, 14; DAC; DAM MST**
See also CA 37-40R; CANR 42; DLB 60

**Wieland, Christoph Martin** 1733-1813    **NCLC 17**
See also DLB 97

**Wiene, Robert** 1881-1938 ........... **TCLC 56**

**Wieners, John** 1934- ........................ **CLC 7**
See also CA 13-16R; DLB 16

**Wiesel, Elie(zer)** 1928-  **CLC 3, 5, 11, 37; DA; DAB; DAC; DAM MST, NOV**
See also AAYA 7; AITN 1; CA 5-8R; CAAS 4; CANR 8, 40; DLB 83; DLBY 87; INT CANR-8; MTCW; SATA 56; YABC

**Wiggins, Marianne** 1947- ............. **CLC 57**
See also BEST 89:3; CA 130

**Wight, James Alfred** 1916-
See Herriot, James
See also CA 77-80; SATA 55; SATA-Brief 44

**Wilbur, Richard (Purdy)** 1921-  **CLC 3, 6, 9, 14, 53; DA; DAB; DAC; DAM MST, POET**
See also CA 1-4R; CABS 2; CANR 2, 29; DLB

# Literary Criticism Series
# Cumulative Topic Index

This index lists all topic entries in Gale's *Classical and Medieval Literature Criticism, Contemporary Literary Criticism, Literature Criticism from 1400 to 1800, Nineteenth-Century Literature Criticism,* and *Twentieth-Century Literary Criticism.*

**Age of Johnson** LC 15: 1-87
Johnson's London, 3-15
aesthetics of neoclassicism, 15-36
"age of prose and reason," 36-45
clubmen and bluestockings, 45-56
printing technology, 56-62
periodicals: "a map of busy life," 62-74
transition, 74-86

**AIDS in Literature** CLC 81: 365-416

**Alcohol and Literature** TCLC 70: 1-58
overview, 2-8
fiction, 8-48
poetry and drama, 48-58

**American Abolitionism** NCLC 44: 1-73
overviews, 2-26
abolitionist ideals, 26-46
the literature of abolitionism, 46-72

**American Black Humor Fiction** TCLC 54: 1-85
characteristics of black humor, 2-13
origins and development, 13-38
black humor distinguished from related literary trends, 38-60
black humor and society, 60-75
black humor reconsidered, 75-83

**American Civil War in Literature** NCLC 32: 1-109
overviews, 2-20
regional perspectives, 20-54
fiction popular during the war, 54-79
the historical novel, 79-108

**American Frontier in Literature** NCLC 28: 1-103
definitions, 2-12
development, 12-17

nonfiction writing about the frontier, 17-30
frontier fiction, 30-45
frontier protagonists, 45-66
portrayals of Native Americans, 66-86
feminist readings, 86-98
twentieth-century reaction against frontier literature, 98-100

**American Humor Writing** NCLC 52: 1-59
overviews, 2-12
the Old Southwest, 12-42
broader impacts, 42-5
women humorists, 45-58

**American Popular Song, Golden Age of** TCLC 42: 1-49
background and major figures, 2-34
the lyrics of popular songs, 34-47

**American Proletarian Literature** TCLC 54: 86-175
overviews, 87-95
American proletarian literature and the American Communist Party, 95-111
ideology and literary merit, 111-7
novels, 117-36
Gastonia, 136-48
drama, 148-54
journalism, 154-9
proletarian literature in the United States, 159-74

**American Romanticism** NCLC 44: 74-138
overviews, 74-84
sociopolitical influences, 84-104
Romanticism and the American frontier, 104-15
thematic concerns, 115-37

**American Western Literature** TCLC 46: 1-100

definition and development of American Western literature, 2-7
characteristics of the Western novel, 8-23
Westerns as history and fiction, 23-34
critical reception of American Western literature, 34-41
the Western hero, 41-73
women in Western fiction, 73-91
later Western fiction, 91-9

**Art and Literature** TCLC 54: 176-248
overviews, 176-93
definitions, 193-219
influence of visual arts on literature, 219-31
spatial form in literature, 231-47

**Arthurian Literature** CMLC 10: 1-127
historical context and literary beginnings, 2-27
development of the legend through Malory, 27-64
development of the legend from Malory to the Victorian Age, 65-81
themes and motifs, 81-95
principal characters, 95-125

**Arthurian Revival** NCLC 36: 1-77
overviews, 2-12
Tennyson and his influence, 12-43
other leading figures, 43-73
the Arthurian legend in the visual arts, 73-6

**Australian Literature** TCLC 50: 1-94
origins and development, 2-21
characteristics of Australian literature, 21-33
historical and critical perspectives, 33-41
poetry, 41-58
fiction, 58-76

Topic Index

Topic Index

Topic Index

**Topic Index**

# Contemporary Literary Criticism
## Cumulative Nationality Index

Nationality Index

Nationality Index

Nationality Index

**Nationality Index**

# *CLC-101* Title Index

**Title Index**

ISBN 0-7876-1191-3

90000